PRENTICE HALL

THE AMERICAN NATION

Beginnings Through 1877

James West Davidson
Author

IN ASSOCIATION WITH
American Heritage®

Prentice
Hall

Dr. Michael B. Stoff
Senior Consultant

Dr. Herman J. Viola
Senior Consultant

Upper Saddle River, New Jersey
Glenview, Illinois
Needham, Massachusetts

Collections of the Fort Ticonderoga Museum

ISBN 0-13-058848-2

2 3 4 5 6 7 8 9 10   05 04 03 02

Author

James West Davidson who earned his Ph.D. at Yale University, is coauthor of *After the Fact: The Art of Historical Detection* and *Nation of Nations: A Narrative History of the American Republic.* Dr. Davidson has taught at both the college and high school levels. He has also consulted on curriculum design for American history courses. Dr. Davidson is an avid canoeist and hiker. His published works on these subjects include *Great Heart,* the true story of a 1903 canoe trip in the Canadian wilderness.

Senior Consultant

Dr. Michael B. Stoff received his Ph.D. in history from Yale University. He currently teaches at the University of Texas at Austin, where he also directs the graduate program in history. He is the author of *Oil, War, and American Security: The Search for a National Policy on Foreign Oil, 1941-1947,* coauthor of *Nation of Nations: A Narrative History of the American Republic,* and co-editor of *The Manhattan Project: A Documentary Introduction to the Atomic Age.* Dr. Stoff has won numerous grants, fellowships, and teaching awards.

Dr. Herman J. Viola, curator emeritus with the Smithsonian Institution, is a distinguished historian and author. Dr. Viola received his Ph.D. in American history from Indiana University. He founded the scholarly journal *Prologue* at the National Archives. Dr. Viola also served as director of the National Anthropological Archives at the Smithsonian Institution. A nationally recognized authority on American Indians, the history of the American West, and the Civil War, Dr. Viola is the author of many historical works for both adults and young readers.

AmericanHeritage® **American Heritage** magazine was founded in 1954, and it quickly rose to the position it occupies today: the country's preeminent magazine of history and culture. Dedicated to presenting the past in entertaining narratives underpinned by scrupulous scholarship, *American Heritage* today goes to more than 300,000 subscribers and counts the country's very best writers and historians among its contributors.

Program Reviewers

Academic Consultants

David Beaulieu, Ph.D.
Professor, School of Education
University of Wisconsin–Milwaukee
Milwaukee, Wisconsin

William R. Childs, Ph.D.
Associate Professor of History
Ohio State University
Columbus, Ohio

Theodore DeLaney, Ph.D.
Associate Professor of History
Washington & Lee University
Lexington, Virginia

Emma Lapsansky, Ph.D.
Professor of History and
  Curator of Special Collections
Haverford College
Haverford, Pennsylvania

William A. McClenaghan
Professor of Political Science
Oregon State University
Corvallis, Oregon

Timothy R. Mahoney, Ph.D.
Professor of History
University of Nebraska–Lincoln
Lincoln, Nebraska

Ralph Mann, Ph.D.
Associate Professor of History
University of Colorado
Boulder, Colorado

Teacher Reviewers

Joanne Alexander
Reading Supervisor
Manassas City Public Schools
Manassas, Virginia

Chris Beech
Social Studies Teacher
Lamar Junior High School
Rosenberg, Texas

Bob Borjes
Social Studies Teacher
Hal Peterson Middle School
Kerrville, Texas

Phyllis Bridges
Social Studies Teacher
Chaffin Middle School
Ft. Smith, Arkansas

Clement Brown
Social Studies Teacher
Madison Junior High School
Naperville, Illinois

Susan Buha
Social Studies Teacher
Hobart Middle School
Hobart, Indiana

Marilyn Bunner
Social Studies Teacher
Decatur Middle School
Indianapolis, Indiana

Steve Bullick
Supervisor of Social Studies
Mt. Lebanon School District
Mt. Lebanon, Pennsylvania

Ronald Concklin
Social Studies Teacher
Will Rogers Middle School
Fair Oaks, California

Sandra Lee Eades, Ph.D.
Social Studies Content Leader
Ridgely Middle School
Lutherville, Maryland

Nancy Foss
Social Studies Teacher
Glenn Hills Middle School
Augusta, Georgia

Mike Harter
Social Studies Teacher
Austin Middle School
Amarillo, Texas

Beverly Hooper
Social Studies Teacher
Dartmouth Middle School
San Jose, California

Patricia Mymbs
Social Studies Teacher
Edward H. Cary Middle School
Dallas, Texas

Denis O'Rourke
Social Studies Teacher
Hommocks Middle School
Larchmont, New York

David Peterson
Social Studies Teacher
Fairmont Junior High School
Boise, Idaho

Lauri Rule
Social Studies Teacher
Shackleford Junior High School
Arlington, Texas

Dana Sanders
Social Studies Teacher
Knox County Public Schools
Edina, Missouri

W. David Scott
Social Studies Teacher
Havenview Middle School
Memphis, Tennessee

Bill Speer
Social Studies Teacher
Albright Middle School
Houston, Texas

Donna Wenger
Social Studies Teacher
Wilson Middle School
Plano, Texas

Pamela West
Social Studies Teacher
Greshman Middle School
Birmingham, Alabama

Reading Specialist

Bonnie Armbruster, Ph.D.
Professor of Education
University of Illinois at Urbana-Champaign
Champaign, Illinois

Curriculum and Assessment Specialist

Jan Moberley
Dallas, Texas

Accuracy Panel

Esther Ratner
Greyherne Information Services
Lynn D. Hoover, The Hoover Associates
Jane B. Malcolm, Professional Research Services
Alice Radosh, Ph.D., Academy of Educational
  Development
Lorrain Rosenberg, Baldwin School District, New York
  (Ret.)
Cathy S. Zazueta, California State University, Los
  Angeles

Program Advisors

Pat Easterbrook
Social Studies Consultant
Cary, North Carolina

Michal Howden
Social Studies Consultant
Zionsville, Indiana

Kathy Lewis
Social Studies Consultant
Fort Worth, Texas

Rick Moulden
Social Studies Consultant
Federal Way, Washington

Joe Wieczorek
Social Studies Consultant
Baltimore, Maryland

Contents

Hopi kachina doll

Building the Massachusetts Bay colony

Ratifying the Constitution

Drum from the American Revolution

The Jefferson Memorial, Washington, D.C.

UNIT 3 THE EARLY REPUBLIC 274

1840 model of frontier log cabin

On the Oregon Trail

The 54th Massachusetts Regiment in battle, 1863

UNIT 5 DIVISION AND REUNION 456

Special Features

Master skills you will use all your life.

Reference Section

Connecting With...

See how history has fascinating links with other subjects.

Connecting With... **Geography**

Connecting With... **Economics**

Connecting With... **Culture**

Connecting With... **Science and Technology**

Connecting With... **Government and Citizenship**

Working for the Patriot cause

Special Features

(continued)

Special Features/Primary Sources

Primary Sources

Relive history through eyewitness accounts, literature, and documents.

Primary Sources and Literature

In-text Primary Sources

(continued)

Primary Sources

(continued)

Maps

Chapter Maps

(continued)

Growth of the United States to 1853

(Ceded by Britain, 1818)

BRITISH TERRITORY

L. Superior

OREGON COUNTRY
(Agreement with
Britain, 1846)

L. Michigan   L. Huron   L. Ontario

L. Erie

LOUISIANA PURCHASE
(Purchased from France, 1803)

THE UNITED STATES, 1783

ORIGINAL 13 STATES

N
W   E
S

Albers Equal-Area Projection
0   200   400 Miles
0   200   400 Kilometers

40°N

MEXICAN CESSION
(Treaty of Guadalupe-Hidalgo,
1848)

ATLANTIC
OCEAN

30°N

TEXAS ANNEXATION
(Annexed by Congress, 1845)

GADSDEN
PURCHASE
(Purchased from
Mexico, 1853)

PACIFIC
OCEAN

(Annexed, 1810)   (Annexed, 1812)   FLORIDA
(Ceded by Spain,
1819)

MEXICO

Gulf of Mexico

120°W   110°W   100°W   90°W   80°W   70°W

Key
Present-day
state boundaries

Maps/Political Cartoons

The Horse "America" Throwing His Master

Charts and Graphs

Charts and Graphs

(continued)

The Tariff of 1816

How a Protective Tariff Works

Cloth made in United States
Cost = $6.00

British cloth in United States
Cost = $5.00
  + $1.25 Tariff

Final
Cost = $6.25

Cloth made in Britain
Cost = $5.00

Effects of a Protective Tariff, 1810–1840

Source: *Historical Statistics of the United States*

Charts and Graphs

Cause and Effect

Graphic Organizers

France Enters the War

France and Britain in conflict for many years

→ Conflict between France and Britain increases after the French and Indian War

→ Americans appeal to France for support during the Revolutionary War

→ France gives American rebels money and supplies but stays neutral

→ Americans defeat British at Saratoga

→ Victory at Saratoga proves to France that Americans can win

→ France gives military and naval support to American forces

Use This Book for Success

You can use this book as a tool to master American history. Spend a few minutes becoming familiar with the way the book is set up, and see how you can unlock the secrets of American history.

Read for Content Mastery

Before You Read The sections in this book begin with Reading Focus questions. These questions point out important ideas in the section. They give you a purpose for reading. Another helpful aid is the Taking Notes exercise at the beginning of each section. It will help you take notes as you read.

As You Read This book also helps you while you are reading. From time to time, you will see a question or thinking activity beside a paragraph in the text. If you are reading about the Civil War, it might ask you to predict which side will win. If you are reading about a wagon train heading west, it might ask you to list what you already know about transportation in the 1800s. By stopping to really think as you read, you will gain a better understanding of the text.

After You Read The questions in the Section Assessment will help you understand what you have read. Use these questions to assess your understanding. Then, show what you know by completing the activity. When you do activities, you continue to learn.

2 No Easy Victory

Reading Focus
- What strategies did each side adopt to win the war?
- How did early encounters dispel hopes for a quick end to the war?
- What victories did the Confederates achieve?
- What victories did the Union achieve?

Key Terms
Battle of Bull Run
Virginia
Monitor
Battle of Antietam
Battle of Fredericksburg
Battle of Chancellorsville
Battle of Shiloh

Taking Notes
As you read, prepare an outline of the section. Use roman numerals to indicate major headings, capital letters for subheadings, and numbers for supporting details. The sample below will help you get started.

> I. Strategies for Victory
>   A. Union plans
>   1.
>   2.
>   3.
>   B. Confederate plans
>   1.
>   2.
> II. Early Encounters

Main Idea Despite hopes for a quick victory, both northerners and southerners soon learned that they were in for a long, difficult struggle.

Setting the Scene At first, the armies of the North and the South marched proudly off to war. Each side expected a quick and painless victory. The reality of war soon shattered this expectation. Over and over, soldiers wrote home describing the awful face of battle:

> 66 I never saw so many broken down and exhausted men in all my life. I was sick as a horse, and as wet with blood and sweat as I could be. . . . Our tongues were parched and cracked for water, and our faces blackened with powder and smoke. 99
> —quoted by Shelby Foote in *The Civil War: A Narrative*

It soon became clear that there would be no quick end to the struggle. Both sides began to dig in for a long, difficult war.

Bullet caught in shoulder plate
Predict What effect would improved weapons have upon the war?

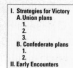

Section 2 Assessment

Recall
1. **Identify** Explain the significance of (a) Stonewall Jackson, (b) Battle of Bull Run, (c) George McClellan, (d) *Virginia*, (e) *Monitor*, (f) Battle of Antietam, (g) Battle of Fredericksburg, (h) Battle of Chancellorsville, (i) Ulysses S. Grant, (j) Battle of Shiloh.

Comprehension
2. Describe (a) the North's three-part plan for defeating the South, (b) the South's plan to defeat the North.
3. What did both sides learn from the Battle of Bull Run?

4. Why was the Confederate victory at Fredericksburg critical?
5. How did Union victories at New Orleans and Memphis affect the South?

Critical Thinking and Writing
6. **Exploring the Main Idea** Review the Main Idea statement at the beginning of this section. Make a list of five events and their results during the first two years of the war.
7. **Analyzing Ideas** Analyze the meaning of this statement: "The South could win the war by not losing, but the North could win only by winning."

ACTIVITY
Take It to the NET
Connecting to Today
Both the Union and Confederate navies developed ironclad ships during the Civil War. Use the Internet to research technological advances in modern naval vessels. Prepare an oral class presentation including pictures. Visit *The American Nation* section of www.phschool.com for help in completing the activity.

494 ★ Chapter 17 *The Civil War*

Develop Your Skills

Each chapter has a Skills for Life feature. Use these features to learn and practice social studies skills. These skills will help you be successful in understanding American history. Complete the Skills Assessment at the end of every chapter to apply the skills that you have learned.

Use the Internet to Explore

At the click of a mouse, the Internet offers you access to a wealth of American history resources. Use the Take It to the NET activities to research and learn more about key concepts in American history. The Virtual Field Trips in the American Heritage® History Happened Here feature let you go online to explore historic sites.

Prepare for Tests

This book helps you prepare for tests. Start by answering the questions at the end of every section and chapter. Go to www.phschool.com at the end of each chapter to take the practice Chapter Self-Test. Then, use the Test Preparation pages at the end of the unit to check yourself further.

Skills for Life

What are the keys to social studies success?

In every social studies course you will ever take, you will need to know how to use the following 20 core skills. Building these skills year by year will make you a stronger student.

Read through this list of skills and their definitions. Which ones do you know well? Which ones do you need to strengthen? Beside each definition, the page where you can find help in developing that skill is listed.

Skill	Definition	Example
GEOGRAPHIC LITERACY		
1. Using the Cartographer's Tools	The ability to use the • compass rose to find directions and relative location. • scale to estimate distance. • latitude and longitude grid to determine exact location. • key, or legend, to understand map symbols and colors.	p. 10
2. Using Special Purpose Maps	The ability to analyze and interpret maps of • natural features, such as elevation and climate. • features made by people, such as land use, roads, countries, population density, and battles.	p. 390
VISUAL ANALYZING		
3. Analyzing Graphic Data	The ability to read and interpret numeric information represented in • bar graphs. • line graphs. • circle graphs.	p. 258
4. Analyzing Images	The ability to identify and interpret symbols, tone, and message in • paintings and drawings. • photos. • posters and political cartoons.	p. 511
CRITICAL THINKING AND READING		
5. Identifying Main Ideas/ Summarizing	Identifying the main idea is the ability to distinguish the general idea of a passage from its supporting details. Summarizing is the ability to combine main ideas into an overview.	p. 61
6. Sequencing	The ability to organize items in order according to time, size, or priority.	p. 73
7. Identifying Cause and Effect/ Making Predictions	Identifying cause and effect is the ability to understand how an action or event leads to a result. Making predictions is the ability to use cause-and-effect understanding to determine the likely outcome of subsequent events or actions.	p. 161

Skill	Definition	Example
8. Drawing Inferences and Conclusions	Drawing inferences is the ability to determine the necessary consequences of an assumption: if this is true, that must be true. Drawing conclusions is the ability to analyze several inferences to make a reasoned judgment.	p. 295
9. Making Valid Generalizations	The ability to apply conclusions from specific circumstances to larger circumstances while maintaining accuracy.	p. 427
10. Distinguishing Fact and Opinion	The ability to separate those statements that can be proven to be true from those that reflect a personal viewpoint.	p. 369
11. Comparing and Contrasting	The ability to identify how different ideas, objects, historical figures, or situations are alike and/or different.	p. 347
12. Analyzing Primary Sources	The ability to evaluate a firsthand account for accuracy, tone, viewpoint, and frame of reference.	p. 219
13. Recognizing Bias and Propaganda	The ability to identify a stated or unstated viewpoint or slant that is designed to promote one set of beliefs over another.	p. 477
14. Identifying Frame of Reference and Point of View	The ability to identify an opinion expressed in writing or visual art and to understand the influences that shaped the writer's or artist's position.	p. 172
15. Decision making	The ability to state a question clearly, identify and evaluate possible choices, and select the option that seems to produce the best outcome.	p. 443
16. Problem solving	The ability to state a problem clearly, identify possible solutions, determine the likely outcome of each, select an option, and then evaluate its effectiveness.	p. 520
COMMUNICATIONS		
17. Using Reliable Information	The ability to locate and apply information for a variety of purposes that has been evaluated for its accuracy, age, authority, and bias.	p. 428
18. Transferring Information From One Medium to Another	The ability to translate numerical or visual information into text and to translate written information into graphs, tables, or diagrams.	p. 567
19. Synthesizing Information	The ability to analyze and combine information from several sources to draw conclusions and/or to create a new presentation of information.	p. 315
20. Supporting a Position	The ability to present evidence or reasoning that defends a given opinion or statement.	p. 72

Success in social studies comes from doing three things well—reading, testing, and writing. The following pages present strategies to help you read for meaning, understand test questions, and write well for social studies.

Reading for Meaning

Do you have trouble remembering what you read? Here are some tips from experts that will improve your ability to recall and understand what you read:

▶ Before You Read

Preview the text to identify important information.
Like watching the coming attractions at a movie theater, previewing the text helps you know what to expect. Study the questions and strategies below to learn how to preview what you read.

Ask yourself these questions:	Use these strategies to find the answers:
• What is the text about?	Read the headings, subheadings, and captions. Study the photos, maps, tables, or graphs.
• What do I already know about the topic?	Read the questions at the end of the text to see if you can answer any of them.
• What is the purpose of the text?	Turn the headings into *who, what, when, where, why,* or *how* questions. This will help you decide if the text compares things, tells a chain of events, or explains causes and effects.

▶ As You Read

Organize information in a way that helps you see meaningful connections or relationships.

Taking notes as you read will improve your understanding. Use graphic organizers like the ones below to record the information you read. Study these descriptions and examples to learn how to create each type of organizer.

Sequencing

A **flowchart** helps you see how one event led to another. It can also display the steps in a process.

Use a flowchart if the text—
- tells about a chain of events.
- explains a method of doing something.

TIP▶ List the events or steps in order.

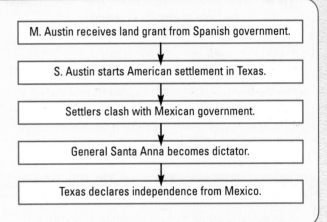

M. Austin receives land grant from Spanish government.

↓

S. Austin starts American settlement in Texas.

↓

Settlers clash with Mexican government.

↓

General Santa Anna becomes dictator.

↓

Texas declares independence from Mexico.

Comparing and Contrasting

A **Venn diagram** displays similarities and differences.

Use a Venn diagram if the text—
- compares and contrasts two individuals, groups, places, things, or events.

TIP▶ Label the outside section of each circle and list differences.
Label the shared section and list similarities.

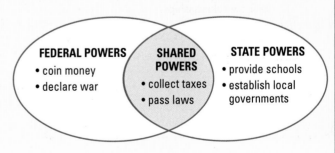

FEDERAL POWERS
- coin money
- declare war

SHARED POWERS
- collect taxes
- pass laws

STATE POWERS
- provide schools
- establish local governments

▶ **As You Read** *(continued)*

Categorizing Information

A **table** organizes information in categories.

Use a table if the text—
- lists similar facts about several places or things.
- presents characteristics of different groups.

TIP▶ Write an appropriate heading for each column in the table to identify its category.

COLONY	FOUNDED	LEADERS
Massachusetts	1620	William Bradford John Winthrop
New Hampshire	1623	John Wentworth
Connecticut	1636	Thomas Hooker
Rhode Island	1636	Roger Williams

Identifying Main Ideas and Details

A **concept web** helps you understand relation-ships among ideas.

Use a concept web if the text—
- provides examples to support a main idea.
- links several ideas to a main topic.

TIP▶ Write the main idea in the largest circle.
Write details in smaller circles and draw lines to show relationships.

Organizing Information

An **outline** provides an overview, or a kind of blueprint for reading.

Use an outline to organize ideas—
- according to their importance.
- according to the order in which they are presented.

TIP▶ Use roman numerals for main ideas, capital letters for secondary ideas, arabic numerals for supporting details.

> **I. Differences Between the North and the South**
>   **A.** Views on slavery
>   **1.** Northern abolitionists
>   **2.** Southern slave owners
>   **B.** Economies
>   **1.** Northern manufacturing
>   **2.** Southern agriculture

Identifying Cause and Effect

A **cause-and-effect** chart shows the relationship between what happened (effect) and the reason why it happened (cause).

Use a cause-and-effect chart if the text—
- lists one or more causes for an event.
- lists one or more results of an event.

TIP▶ Label causes and effects. Draw arrows to indicate how ideas are related.

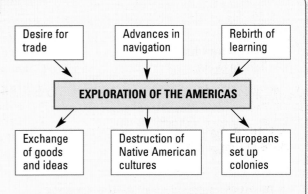

▶ After You Read

Test yourself to find out what you learned from reading the text.

Go back to the questions you asked yourself before you read the text. You should be able to give more complete answers to these questions:
- What is the text about?
- What is the purpose of the text?

You should also be able to make connections between the new information you learned from the text and what you already knew about the topic.

Study your graphic organizer. Use this information as the *answers*. Make up a meaningful *question* about each piece of information.

Taking Tests

Do you panic at the thought of taking a standardized test? Here are some tips that most test developers recommend to help you achieve good scores.

▶ Multiple-Choice Questions

Read each part of a multiple-choice question to make sure you understand what is being asked.

Many tests are made up of multiple-choice questions. Some multiple-choice items are **direct questions.** They are complete sentences followed by possible answers, called distractors.

Direct Question	What did early settlers build on New England's rugged coastline?
The **distractors** list the possible answers.	**A** factories **B** port cities **C** farms **D** office parks
TIP▶ Try each distractor as an answer to your question. Rule out the ones that don't work.	You can rule out A and D because factories and office parks did not exist at the time. You can rule out C because a rugged coastline was not a good place to build farms.

Other multiple-choice questions are **incomplete sentences** that you are to finish. They are followed by possible answers.

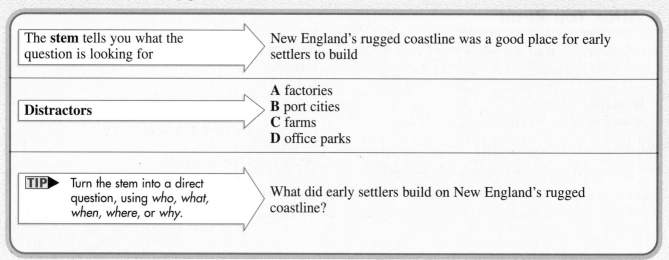

The **stem** tells you what the question is looking for	New England's rugged coastline was a good place for early settlers to build
Distractors	**A** factories **B** port cities **C** farms **D** office parks
TIP▶ Turn the stem into a direct question, using *who, what, when, where,* or *why.*	What did early settlers build on New England's rugged coastline?

▶ What's Being Tested?

Identify the type of question you are being asked.

Social studies tests often ask questions that involve reading comprehension. Other questions may require you to gather or interpret information from a map, graph, or chart. The following strategies will help you answer different kinds of questions.

Reading Comprehension Questions

What to do:	How to do it:
1. Determine the content and organization of the selection.	Read the **title.** Skim the selection. Look for key words that indicate time, cause-and-effect, or comparison.
2. Analyze the questions. Do they ask you to *recall facts?*	Look for **key words** in the stem: <u>According to</u> the selection . . . The selection <u>states</u> that . . .
Do they ask you to *make judgments?*	The <u>main idea</u> of the selection is. . . The author <u>would likely</u> agree that. . .
3. Read the selection.	Read quickly. Keep the questions in mind.
4. Answer the questions.	Try out each distractor and choose the best answer. Refer back to the selection if necessary.

Example:

The Dust Bowl During the 1930s, an area of the southern Great Plains became known as the "Dust Bowl." Climate and farming methods combined to cause one of the worst environmental disasters in United States history. As a result of a severe drought, the soil was dry. When farmers plowed the land, they removed the prairie grasses that held the soil in place. When strong winds swept the region, the soil was easily eroded and carried hundreds of miles away. A series of destructive duststorms brought economic ruin to farmers.

What caused the soil to become dry?
A strong winds
B plowing
C drought
D high temperatures

TIP▶ The key words <u>as a result</u> tell why the soil was dry.

(The correct answer is C.)

Student Success Handbook

▶ What's Being Tested? (continued)

Map Questions

What to do:	**How to do it:**
1. Determine what kind of information is presented on the map.	Read the map **title.** It will indicate the purpose of the map. Study the **map key.** It will explain the symbols used on the map. Look at the **scale.** It will help you calculate distance between places on the map.
2. Read the question. Determine which component on the map will help you find the answer.	Look for **key words** in the stem. About <u>how far</u> . . . [use the scale] <u>What crops</u> were grown in . . . [use the map key]
3. Look at the map and answer the question in your own words.	Do not read the distractors yet.
4. Choose the best answer.	Decide which distractor agrees with the answer you determined from the map.

Example

Which of the southern colonies produced ship supplies, tobacco, rice, and indigo?

A New Jersey
B North Carolina
C Virginia
D South Carolina

TIP▶ Read the labels and the key to understand the map.

(The correct answer is B.)

Graph Questions

What to do:

1. Determine the purpose of the graph.

2. Determine what information on the graph will help you find the answer.

3. Choose the best answer.

How to do it:

Read the graph **title.** It indicates what the graph represents.

Read the **labels** on the graph or on the key. They tell the units of measurement used by the graph.

Decide which distractor agrees with the answer you determined from the graph.

Example

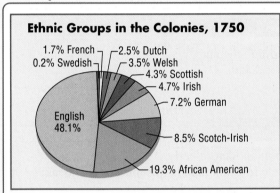

A **circle graph** shows the relationship of parts to the whole in terms of percentages.

After the English, the next largest ethnic group in the colonies was
A French   C German
B Irish   D African American

TIP ▶ Compare the percentages listed in the labels.
(The correct answer is D.)

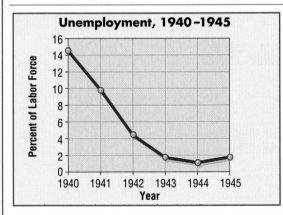

A **line graph** shows a pattern or change over time by the direction of the line.

Between 1940 and 1943, unemployment
A decreased a little   C stayed about the same
B decreased greatly   D increased a little

TIP ▶ Compare the vertical distance between the two points on the line graph.
(The correct answer is B.)

A **bar graph** compares differences in quantity by showing bars of different lengths.

Between 1850 and 1860, school enrollment increased by about
A 1 million   C 3 million
B 2 million   D 4 million

TIP ▶ Compare the heights of the bars to find the difference.
(The correct answer is B.)

Writing for Social Studies

When you face a writing assignment, do you think, "How will I ever get through this?" Here are some tips to guide you through any writing project from start to finish.

▶ The Writing Process

Follow each step of the writing process to communicate effectively.

Step 1. Prewrite

- Establish the purpose.
- Define the topic.
- Determine the audience.
- Gather details.

Step 2. Draft

- Organize information logically in an outline or graphic organizer.
- Write an introduction, body, and conclusion.
- State main ideas clearly.
- Include relevant details to support your ideas.

Step 3. Revise

- Edit for clarity of ideas and elaboration.

Step 4. Proofread

- Correct any errors in spelling, grammar, and punctuation.

Step 5. Publish and Present

- Copy text neatly by hand, typewriter, or word processor.
- Illustrate as needed.
- Create a cover if appropriate.

▶ Types of Writing for Social Studies

Identify the purpose for your writing.

Each type of writing assignment has a specific purpose, and each purpose needs a different plan for development. The following descriptions and examples will help you identify the three purposes for social studies writing. The lists of steps will help you plan your writing.

Writing to Inform

Purpose: to present facts or ideas

Example

During the 1960s, research indicated the dangers of the insecticide DDT. It killed insects but also had long-term effects. When birds and fish ate poisoned insects, DDT built up in their fatty tissue. The poison also showed up in human beings who ate birds and fish contaminated by DDT.

TIP ▶ Look for these **key terms** in the assignment: explain, describe, report, narrate

How to get started:
- Determine the topic you will write about.
- Write a topic sentence that tells the main idea.
- List all the ideas you can think of that are related to the topic.
- Arrange the ideas in logical order.

Writing to Persuade

Purpose: to influence someone

Example

Teaching computer skills in the classroom uses time that could be spent teaching students how to think for themselves or how to interact with others. Students who can reason well, express themselves clearly, and get along with other people will be better prepared for life than those who can use a computer.

TIP ▶ Look for these **key terms** in the assignment: convince, argue, request

How to get started:
- Make sure you understand the problem or issue clearly.
- Determine your position.
- List evidence to support your arguments.
- Predict opposing views.
- List evidence you can use to overcome the opposing arguments.

Writing to Provide Historical Interpretation

Purpose: to present the perspective of someone in a different era

Example

The crossing took a week, but the steamship voyage was hard. We were cramped in steerage with hundreds of others. At last we saw the huge statue of the lady with the torch. In the reception center, my mother held my hand while the doctor examined me. Then, my father showed our papers to the official, and we collected our bags. I was scared as we headed off to find a home in our new country.

TIP ▶ Look for these **key terms** in the assignment: go back in time, create, suppose that, if you were

How to get started:
- Study the events or issues of the time period you will write about.
- Consider how these events or issues might have affected different people at the time.
- Choose a person whose views you would like to present.
- Identify the thoughts and feelings this person might have experienced.

Student Success Handbook

► Research for Writing

Follow each step of the writing process to communicate effectively.

After you have identified the purpose for your writing, you may need to do research. The following steps will help you plan, gather, organize, and present information.

Step 1. Ask Questions

Ask yourself questions to help guide your research.	What do I already know about the topic? What do I want to find out about the topic?

Step 2. Acquire Information

Locate and use appropriate sources of information about the topic.	Library Internet search Interviews
Take notes.	Follow accepted format for listing sources.

Step 3. Analyze Information

Evaluate the information you find.	Is it relevant to the topic? Is it up to date? Is it accurate? Is the writer an authority on the topic? Is there any bias?

Step 4. Use Information

Answer your research questions with the information you have found. (You may find that you need to do more research.)	Do I have all the information I need?
Organize your information into the main points you want to make. Identify supporting details.	Arrange ideas in outline form or in a graphic organizer.

Step 5. Communicate What You've Learned

	Purpose	Presentation
Review the purpose for your writing and choose an appropriate way to present the information.	inform	formal paper, documentary, multimedia
	persuade	essay, letter to the editor, speech
	interpret	journal, newspaper account, drama
Draft and revise your writing, then evaluate it.	Use a rubric for self-evaluation.	

▶ Evaluating Your Writing

Use the following rubric to help you evaluate your writing.

	Excellent	Good	Acceptable	Unacceptable
Purpose	Achieves purpose—to inform, persuade, or provide historical interpretation—very well	Informs, persuades, or provides historical interpretation reasonably well	Reader cannot easily tell if the purpose is to inform, persuade, or provide historical interpretation	Lacks purpose
Organization	Develops ideas in a very clear and logical way	Presents ideas in a reasonably well-organized way	Reader has difficulty following the organization	Lacks organization
Elaboration	Explains all ideas with facts and details	Explains most ideas with facts and details	Includes some supporting facts and details	Lacks supporting details
Use of Language	Uses excellent vocabulary and sentence structure with no errors in spelling, grammar, or punctuation	Uses good vocabulary and sentence structure with very few errors in spelling, grammar, or punctuation	Includes some errors in grammar, punctuation, and spelling	Includes many errors in grammar, punctuation, and spelling

Unit 1

Roots of American History

An Untouched Landscape
Grand Canyon by William Robinson
Leigh captures the natural beauty of
the American continent.

"*For this is what America is all about. It is the uncrossed desert and the unclimbed ridge. It is the star that is not reached and the harvest sleeping in the unplowed ground.*"

—Lyndon B. Johnson, President of the United States (1965)

CHAPTER

1

Geography, History, and the Social Sciences

PREHISTORY–PRESENT

1 Thinking Geographically
2 Lands and Climates of the United States
3 The Tools of History
4 Economics and Other Social Sciences

Early encounter between Europeans and Native Americans

Settlers clearing the land

AMERICAN EVENTS

1500s
The first global age begins with the meeting between Europeans and Native Americans.

1600s
England sets up colonies in North America.

1700s
Thirteen English colonies separate from Great Britain and form the United States of America.

Prehistory 1500 · · · 1600 · · · 1700

WORLD EVENTS

▲ **1500s**
Europeans explore the Americas.

▲ **1600s**
European nations struggle for control of North America.

Physical Features of the United States

The United States is divided into different physical regions.

Elevations Key

- Above 10,000 feet (3,000 meters)
- 7,000–10,000 feet (2,000–3,000 meters)
- 3,000–7,000 feet (1,000–2,000 meters)
- 700–3,000 feet (200–1,000 meters)
- 0–700 feet (0–200 meters)
- Below sea level

Worker in an early textile mill

Citizens register to vote

1800s
The growth of industry leads to economic and social changes in the United States.

1900s
The United States extends voting rights to all citizens 18 years and older.

1700 · · · 1800 · · · 1900 · **Present**

1800s ▲
Millions of immigrants move to the United States.

1 Thinking Geographically

BEFORE YOU READ

Reading Focus

- How do the five themes of geography help define the connections between geography and history?
- How did geography influence population trends in United States history?
- How are maps made and used?

Key Terms

geography

latitude

longitude

natural resources

irrigation

cartographer

map projection

thematic map

Taking Notes

Copy the chart below. As you read, fill in the chart with information about the five themes of geography. Add boxes for the remaining themes.

LOCATION	PLACE
• Exact Location: longitude and latitude	• •

Main Idea Geography helps us to understand the way people have lived in different places throughout history.

AS YOU READ
A map by Samuel de Champlain

Draw Inferences How did making the map help Champlain and the Native Americans communicate?

Setting the Scene In a tiny Native American fishing village, a small group gathered around a man who began to draw in the sand. They watched closely as Samuel de Champlain, a French explorer, drew a sweeping line on the ground. The line represented the coastline where they stood. The local chief drew additional lines. A young man added piles of rocks to represent the village and nearby settlements. When they were done, they had an informal map of the local area.

Champlain and the Native Americans he met on Cape Ann in Massachusetts in the 1600s did not speak the same language. Yet, they both understood the basic language of geography.

Five Themes of Geography

Geography is the study of people, their environments, and their resources. Geographers ask how the natural environment affects the way we live and how we, in turn, affect the environment.

Geography is closely linked to history. Both historians and geographers want to understand how the natural environment affects people and events. To help show these connections, geographers have developed five themes: location, place, interaction between people and their environment, movement, and regions.

Location Often, the most basic question we ask about an event is, "Where did it happen?" The answer to this question involves the geographic theme of location. There are two types of location: exact and relative.

To describe the exact location of a place, geographers use a grid of numbered lines on a map or globe. Lines of latitude measure distance north and south from the Equator. The Equator is an imaginary line that lies at 0° (degrees) latitude. It divides the Earth into two halves, called hemispheres. Lines of longitude measure distance

The Five Themes of Geography

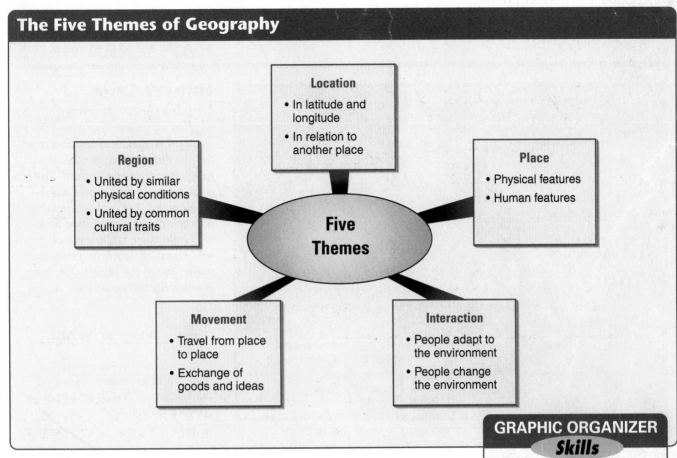

Location
- In latitude and longitude
- In relation to another place

Region
- United by similar physical conditions
- United by common cultural traits

Place
- Physical features
- Human features

Five Themes

Movement
- Travel from place to place
- Exchange of goods and ideas

Interaction
- People adapt to the environment
- People change the environment

east and west from the Prime Meridian, which runs through Greenwich (GREHN ihch), England. For example, the city of San Antonio, Texas, is located at 29 degrees (°) north latitude and 99 degrees (°) west longitude. This location is written as 29°N/99°W. In the same way, New York City is located at 41°N/74°W.

Sometimes, you will find it more useful to know relative location, or the location of a place in relation to some other place. For example, San Antonio is about 125 miles from the Mexican border. New York City is located where the Hudson River empties into the Atlantic Ocean. Relative location can help explain why people settled in certain areas or why battles took place at certain places.

Place Geographers use the theme of place to describe an area's physical and human features. Physical features include climate, soil, vegetation, animal life, and bodies of water. One of the most important aspects of a place is its natural resources, materials that humans can take from the environment to survive and satisfy their needs. For example, a mountain range may contain reserves of coal or iron, while a nearby river or ocean may supply fish.

People help shape the character of a place through their ideas and actions. The human features of a place include the kinds of houses people build, their means of transportation, their ways of earning a living, their languages, and their religions.

Interaction Interaction between people and their environment is a third theme of geography. Throughout history, people have adapted

GRAPHIC ORGANIZER
Skills

Geographers have developed five themes to help us understand the connections between people and the natural environment, and between geography and history.

1. **Comprehension** What are two ways to describe the location of a place?

2. **Critical Thinking Applying Information** Which geographic theme would be most concerned with trade among nations?

Hoover Dam

Hoover Dam

Considered one of the greatest engineering projects ever, the building of the Hoover Dam demonstrates the successful interaction between people and their environment. The presence of the dam makes it possible for people to live in an area that is largely desert. Surrounding farmland is irrigated, and there is a ready supply of water and electric power. Today, the Hoover Dam is a national historic landmark.

Take It to the NET

Virtual Field Trip For an interactive look at the Hoover Dam, visit *The American Nation* section of **www.phschool.com**.

to and changed their natural surroundings. Ancient American hunters learned to plant seeds and grow food crops. This adaptation meant they no longer had to move from place to place in search of food. Later, Native Americans in the Southwest developed methods of irrigation, or bringing water to dry lands. By digging ditches that channeled water from the Salt and Gila rivers, they turned arid, unproductive desert into farmland.

Today, advanced technology allows people to change their environment in even more dramatic ways. People have wiped out pests that destroyed crops and found ways to take oil from the ocean floor.

Movement A fourth geographic theme involves the movement of people, goods, and ideas. Movement occurs because people and resources are scattered unevenly around the globe. To get what they need or want, people travel from place to place. As they meet other people, they exchange ideas and technology as well as goods.

History provides many examples of movement. Early hunters populated the Americas as they followed herds of large animals. Much later, people from all over the world moved to the United States in search of opportunity or liberty. They brought customs and beliefs that have helped shape American life.

Regions A region has certain unifying characteristics. It may be defined by its physical characteristics, such as its climates or landforms. For example, the Great Plains is a region with fairly level land, hot summers, cold winters, and little rainfall. In the 1930s, when parts of the plains were hit by drought, the region was called the "Dust Bowl." The Pacific Coast region is known for rugged mountains, dense forests, and scenic ocean shores.

A region's characteristics may also be human and cultural. San Francisco's Chinatown is a region where Chinese Americans have preserved their language and culture. Bourbon Street in the city of New Orleans is associated with jazz.

Case Study: Population Trends and the Five Themes

As you study events and trends in history, you will often need to think geographically. For practice, let us see how population trends throughout the history of the United States relate to the five themes of geography.

When the United States won its independence in 1783, it was made up of 13 states located on the Atlantic coast (*region, exact location*). The majority of the population lived along the coast or near rivers (*relative location*), where water transportation was easy (*movement*). The Appalachian Mountains and other geographic features limited westward movement (*region, movement*). In 1790, the nation's center of population was located in Maryland.

The Nation Expands The United States added vast new territories in the early 1800s, eventually stretching to the Pacific Ocean (*movement, exact location*). As the nation expanded, its rapidly growing population shifted westward (*movement*). Settlers dug canals, built roads and railroads, and cut down forests to clear farmland and build log cabins (*interaction, place*).

A New Trend The westward trend continued in the late 1800s. As white settlers displaced Native Americans, the human and cultural characteristics of the West changed (*place*). By 1900, the center of population had shifted to Indiana.

In the mid-1900s, a new population trend began to emerge. Many people began to move from the Northeast to the Sunbelt, a region stretching from Florida across Texas to California (*region, movement*). Many people were attracted by the area's mild climate (*place*). In 1960, only 2 of the 10 largest American cities were located in the South or West (*region*). By 2000, six of them were: Houston, Dallas, San Antonio, Los Angeles, San Diego, and Phoenix. Furthermore, the center of the nation's population had shifted again, both southward and westward, to Missouri.

Maps and Globes

The most common tools used to understand geography are maps and globes. A map is a drawing of the surface of the Earth or part of the Earth. A globe is a sphere with a map of the Earth printed on it.

Maps and globes have different uses. Because a globe is about the same shape as the Earth, it can accurately show sizes and shapes of landforms. However, compared to a map, a globe is awkward to use. In addition, a map can show more detail than a globe and allows

AS YOU READ **Use Prior Knowledge** Before you read this subsection, think about what you already know about maps and globes. Then, read to find out new information.

Mercator Projection

Robinson Projection

GEOGRAPHY
Skills

Map projections make it possible for mapmakers to show a round world on a flat map.

1. **Location** On the map, locate **(a)** North America, **(b)** Africa, **(c)** Asia.

2. **Place** What differences appear in the two projections of North America?

3. **Critical Thinking Comparing** On the Mercator map, which areas are most distorted?

you to see all of the Earth's surface at one time. Still, a flat map has the disadvantage that it distorts some parts of the Earth.

Map Projections Mapmakers, or cartographers, have developed dozens of ways of drawing the Earth on a flat surface. These methods are known as map projections. Each map projection has benefits and drawbacks. Some show the sizes of landmasses correctly but distort their shape. Others give continents their true shape but distort their sizes.

For hundreds of years, the most widely used map projection was the Mercator projection. It was developed in 1569 by the Flemish cartographer Gerardus Mercator. The Mercator projection was valuable because it gave sailors an accurate picture of ocean distances and the shapes of landmasses. Mercator boasted:

❝ If you wish to sail from one port to another, here is a chart, and a straight line on it, and if you follow this line carefully you will certainly arrive at your destination. ❞
—Gerardus Mercator, "To the Readers of This Chart, Greeting!"

However, the Mercator projection distorts size, especially for places that are far from the Equator. For example, on a Mercator map, Greenland appears as big as all of South America, even though South America is more than eight times larger!

Today, many geographers use the Robinson projection. It shows the correct sizes and shapes of landmasses for most parts of the world. The Robinson projection also gives a fairly accurate view of the relationship between landmasses and bodies of water. There are many other types of map projections as well. On each map in this book, you will see a label identifying the type of projection used.

Types of Maps As you study American history, you will use various types of maps. Each one has a special purpose. Physical maps show mountain ranges, bodies of water, and other physical features. Political maps show features that are determined by people. These include the boundaries of countries and states, as well as the location of capitals and other cities. You will see examples of these types of maps in the Geographic Atlas in the Reference Section of this book.

You will also use a wide variety of thematic maps, or maps that deal with specific topics, that can help you understand the connections between geography and history. Population maps show the number of people who live in a particular area. Economic maps show how people make a living. Battle maps show the locations of major battles and the routes of advancing and retreating armies. Other thematic maps may provide information on natural resources, rainfall, vegetation, elections, or the religious or ethnic makeup of a place.

Making Accurate Maps The oldest surviving map in the world today was created by an ancient cartographer somewhere around 2300 B.C. Ever since, geographers have worked to make maps more accurate.

Today, cartographers create maps with the help of computers and satellites. This new technology provides incredibly complete information about the most remote corners of the Earth. As a result, today's mapmakers create maps that are more accurate than anyone had previously thought possible.

★ ★ ★ **Section 1 Assessment** ★ ★ ★ ★

Recall

1. **Define** **(a)** geography, **(b)** latitude, **(c)** longitude, **(d)** natural resources, **(e)** irrigation, **(f)** cartographer, **(g)** map projection, **(h)** thematic map.

Comprehension

2. Briefly describe the five themes of geography.
3. List three population trends in the history of the United States. Give the theme, or themes, of geography illustrated by each.
4. Why does a globe show the Earth more accurately than a flat map?

Critical Thinking and Writing

5. **Exploring the Main Idea** Review the Main Idea statement at the beginning of this section. Name two ways that geography affects life in the community or state where you live. Write your findings in a paragraph.
6. **Synthesizing Information** Study the picture of the Hoover Dam on page 6. How does the dam illustrate the geographic theme of interaction?

ACTIVITY

Take It to the NET
Connecting to Today
Use the Internet to research the satellite mapping program started in 1972. Choose a site where you can find images of the Earth taken by satellites. Select a picture. Print it out. In a paragraph, describe the picture. Explain how it would be useful to a cartographer. Visit *The American Nation* section of **www.phschool.com** for help in completing the activity.

Early maps were crude but useful pictures drawn on animal skins, clay tablets, and cloth. Today, maps are even more important tools in providing information about places on Earth. Learning how to read and interpret a map is also helpful in understanding how geography affects history.

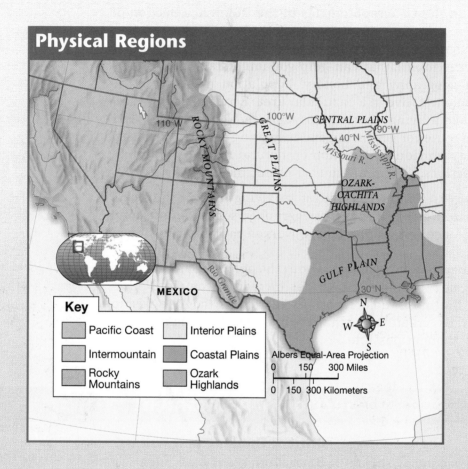

Physical Regions

Key

- Pacific Coast
- Intermountain
- Rocky Mountains
- Interior Plains
- Coastal Plains
- Ozark Highlands

Albers Equal-Area Projection
0   150   300 Miles
0   150 300 Kilometers

Learn the Skill *To review basic map-reading skills, use the following steps:*

1. **Read the title.** The title summarizes the basic information included on a map.

2. **Refer to the map key.** The key identifies what the different symbols on the map mean.

3. **Find the scales of distance.** Maps are miniature pictures of places on Earth, so they are drawn to scale. To determine actual distance, you need to know how many inches represent miles or kilometers.

4. **Use the compass rose.** The arrows on this symbol indicate directions on a map.

5. **Check for a locator map.** A locator map helps you see where on Earth a place is located.

Practice the Skill *Answer the following questions about the map above:*

1. What is the purpose of this map?

2. **(a)** What does the color tan represent on this map? **(b)** Through which physical regions does the Missouri River flow?

3. How many miles does one-half inch represent?

4. **(a)** What country is south of the United States? **(b)** In what direction are the Great Plains from the Mississippi River?

5. **(a)** What parts of the United States are not shown on the large map? **(b)** How do you know?

Apply the Skill *See the Chapter Review and Assessment.*

2 Lands and Climates of the United States

Reading Focus

- What are the main physical regions of the United States?
- How do rivers and lakes affect American life?
- How do climates vary across the United States?

Key Terms

isthmus

elevation

erosion

tributary

weather

climate

precipitation

altitude

Taking Notes

Copy the cause-and-effect chart. As you read, fill in additional factors that explain the causes and effects of climate.

CAUSES
I. Distance from Equator
2.
3.

CLIMATE

EFFECTS
I. Hot and wet
2.
3.

Main Idea The United States is a nation of diverse landforms and climates.

Setting the Scene The view took her breath away. Katharine Lee Bates, a teacher from the East, had journeyed westward to Colorado in 1893. Standing atop the towering Pikes Peak, looking across the "sea-like expanse" below, Bates was moved to write a tribute to her land. Her poem was later set to music:

> 66 O beautiful for spacious skies,
> For amber waves of grain,
> For purple mountain majesties
> Above the fruited plain!
> America America!
> God shed His grace on thee
> And crown thy good with brotherhood
> From sea to shining sea! 99
>
> —Katharine Lee Bates, "America the Beautiful"

Besides plains and mountains, the United States is also a land of arid deserts and frozen tundras, quiet forests and crashing seas. This wide variety of climates and landforms has had a powerful impact on American life and history.

Physical Regions of the United States

North America is the world's third largest continent. It is surrounded on three sides by oceans: the Atlantic Ocean to the east, the Pacific Ocean to the west, and the icy Arctic Ocean to the north. To the south, an **isthmus** (IHS muhs), or narrow strip of land, links North America to South America.

The United States is one of the largest countries in the world. Its physical regions offer great contrasts. In some regions, the land is fertile. Other regions have natural resources such as coal and oil.

AS YOU READ **Pikes Peak**

Visualize Think about a magnificent view you have seen. Describe it in a short paragraph.

Physical Regions of the United States

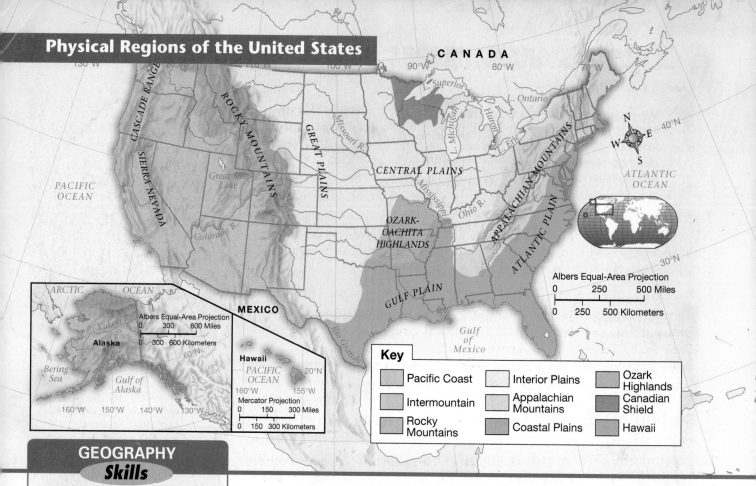

Key

▨ Pacific Coast	▨ Interior Plains	▨ Ozark Highlands
▨ Intermountain	▨ Appalachian Mountains	▨ Canadian Shield
▨ Rocky Mountains	▨ Coastal Plains	▨ Hawaii

GEOGRAPHY *Skills*

Geographers divide the United States into different physical regions.

1. **Location** On the map, locate **(a)** Sierra Nevada, **(b)** Great Lakes, **(c)** Atlantic Plain, **(d)** Mississippi River, **(e)** Rocky Mountains

2. **Region** Through what three physical regions does the Mississippi River flow?

3. **Critical Thinking**
   Comparing Compare the Pacific Coast and the Rocky Mountain regions. Why do you think more people live on the Pacific Coast than in the Rocky Mountains?

Primary Sources

See Pare Loretz, "The River" on page 572 in the Reference Section.

Geographers divide the United States into different physical regions marked by contrasting landforms and physical features.*

Pacific Coast The westernmost region of North America is the Pacific Coast. It includes high mountain ranges that stretch from Alaska to Mexico. In the United States, some of these western ranges are near the Pacific Ocean. The Cascades and the Sierra Nevada stand a bit farther inland. Important cities of the Pacific Coast region include Seattle, Portland, San Francisco, San Diego, and Los Angeles.

A notable feature of the Pacific Coast region is the San Andreas Fault. This 600-mile fracture in the Earth's crust runs through California from northwest to southeast. Movement of the Earth's crust along this fault can cause earthquakes. For example, powerful quakes shook San Francisco in 1906 and Los Angeles in 1994, causing significant damage and loss of life.

Intermountain Region East of the Pacific Coast mountain ranges lies the Intermountain Region. This region is marked by mountain peaks, high plateaus, deep canyons, and dry, sandy deserts. The Grand Canyon, more than a mile deep, cuts through the Intermountain Region. Another prominent physical feature is the Great Salt Lake of Utah, the nation's largest saltwater lake.

---

*To review definitions of major landforms and other geographic terms, refer to the Glossary of Geographic Terms at the end of this section.

The rugged terrain limits where people can live in the Intermountain Region. Among the few major cities located there are Phoenix and Salt Lake City.

Rocky Mountains The Rocky Mountains stretch from Alaska through Canada into the western United States. They include the Bitterroot Range in Idaho and Montana, the Big Horn Mountains in Wyoming, and the Sangre de Cristo Mountains in Colorado and New Mexico. In Mexico, the Rockies become the Sierra Madre (MAH dray), or "mother range."

The Rockies include some of the highest peaks in North America—some with an *elevation,* or height above sea level, of more than 14,000 feet. Throughout history, visitors like Katharine Lee Bates have marveled at the beauty and grandeur of the Rocky Mountains. Today, Denver is a major city of the Rocky Mountain Region.

Interior Plains Between the Rockies in the West and the Appalachian Mountains in the East is a large lowland area called the Interior Plains. The dry western part of the region is called the Great Plains. The eastern part is called the Central Plains.

Scientists believe that a great inland sea once covered the Interior Plains. Today, some parts are rich in resources such as coal and petroleum. Other parts offer fertile soil for farming and grasslands for raising cattle. Major cities of the Interior Plains include Dallas, St. Louis, Chicago, Cincinnati, Detroit, and Indianapolis.

Ozark Highlands The Ozark Highlands extend across southern Missouri and Northern Arkansas and into eastern Kansas. Thick with forests, the region includes mountains that rise more than 2,000 feet. The highest are the Boston Mountains in Arkansas. Important industries in the region include forestry, agriculture, and mining.

Appalachian Mountains The Appalachian Mountains run along the eastern part of North America. They stretch from Canada in the North to Georgia and Mississippi in the South. The Appalachians have different names in different places. For example, the Green Mountains, Alleghenies, and Great Smoky Mountains are all part of the Appalachians.

The Appalachians are lower and less rugged than the Rockies. The highest peak is Mt. Mitchell in North Carolina, with an elevation of 6,684 feet. Today, hearty hikers enjoy the challenge of walking the Appalachian Trail from Georgia to Maine.

Canadian Shield The Canadian Shield is a lowland area that lies mostly in eastern Canada. The southern part extends into Michigan, Wisconsin, and Minnesota. This region was once an area of high mountains. Centuries of *erosion,* or gradual wearing away, reduced the area to low hills and plains. The Canadian Shield is rich in minerals.

Coastal Plains The easternmost region of North America is called the Coastal Plains, a fairly flat, lowland area. This was the first region settled by Europeans who crossed the Atlantic Ocean. It is made up of two subregions, the Atlantic Plain and the Gulf Plain.

The Atlantic Plain lies between the Atlantic Ocean and the foothills of the Appalachians. The Atlantic Plain is narrow in the North, where major cities such as Boston, New York, and Philadelphia are located. It broadens in the South to include all of Florida.

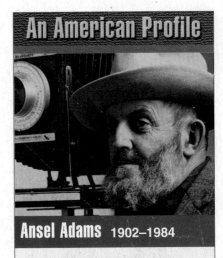

An American Profile

Ansel Adams 1902–1984

Ansel Adams was a landscape photographer known for his dramatic images of the American West. Adams's photographs (one of which appears on page 14) have inspired millions of people to seek out the wilderness and preserve it.

In 1980, President Jimmy Carter awarded Adams the Medal of Freedom, which is presented to citizens for outstanding achievement in culture, world peace, or public service. "It is through [Adams's] foresight and fortitude," noted Carter, "that so much of America has been saved for future Americans."

How did Adams's art have a political effect?

Regional Contrasts

The miles of hot, dry sand covering this desert (left) are contrasted against the snow-capped mountains and winding river (right) in the photograph taken by Ansel Adams. **Applying Information** *How have people adapted to desert and mountainous conditions?*

The Gulf Plain lies along the Gulf of Mexico. This region is economically important because of its large deposits of petroleum. New Orleans and Houston are major cities of the Gulf Plain.

Hawaiian Islands The Hawaiian Islands lie far out in the Pacific, about 2,400 miles west of California. Much of Hawaii has a wet tropical climate and dense tropical rain forest vegetation. The region includes eight large islands and many smaller ones.

The islands are actually the visible tops of volcanoes that erupted through the floor of the Pacific many centuries ago. Mauna Loa (man uh LOH uh), on the island of Hawaii, is an active volcano that rises 13,680 feet above sea level.

American Rivers and Lakes

Great rivers crisscross North America, linking many of the different physical regions. Many of these rivers begin in the mountains. They collect runoff water from rains and melting snows and carry it to the oceans.

The Mississippi-Missouri River System The Mississippi and Missouri rivers make up the longest and most important river system in the United States. The system carries water thousands of miles through the Interior Plains to the Gulf of Mexico.

AS YOU READ **Ask Questions** Before you read, write two or three questions that you would expect to find answered in this section. Then, read to see whether your questions are answered.

In addition to the two main branches, the Mississippi-Missouri river system includes many tributaries. A **tributary** is a stream or smaller river that flows into a larger one. Among the most important tributaries are the Ohio, Tennessee, Arkansas, and Platte rivers. These and other rivers provide water for the rich farmlands of the Interior Plains. The Mississippi River also serves as a means of transportation. Today, as in the past, barges carry freight up and down the river.

Other Rivers The United States includes dozens of other rivers, both large and small. The Colorado River begins in the Rocky Mountains and flows for about 1,450 miles through Colorado, Utah, Arizona, and Nevada. It forms the border between California and Arizona as it winds toward the Gulf of California.

Smaller rivers have also been important in American history. The Hudson River, for example, forms part of the border between New York and New Jersey. Only 306 miles long, it provided a vital link between New York City and the rich farmlands of upstate New York. In the 1960s, efforts to clean up pollution of the Hudson River helped launch the modern environmental movement.

Rivers form political boundaries between the United States and its neighbors. To the south, the Rio Grande forms part of the border between Texas and Mexico. To the north, the St. Lawrence River separates the Northeast from Canada.

The Great Lakes The Great Lakes also form part of the border between the United States and Canada. These five lakes—Superior, Michigan, Huron, Erie, and Ontario—form the largest body of fresh water in the world. Today, artificial waterways connect the Great Lakes to the St. Lawrence and Mississippi rivers. As a result, goods can be shipped from the Central Plains eastward to the Atlantic Ocean and southward to the Gulf of Mexico.

Climate and Weather

The condition of the Earth's atmosphere at a given time and place is its **weather.** The weather in one region can influence the weather in another area. It also affects the jobs we do, the leisure activities we enjoy, and the kinds of homes we build. In history, weather has determined the outcome of battles and even destroyed civilizations.

The average weather of a place over a period of 20 to 30 years is known as **climate.** Two main features that help define an area's climate are temperature and **precipitation** (pree sihp uh TAY shuhn), or water that falls in the form of rain, sleet, hail, or snow. A region may be hot and dry, cold and rainy, or any other combination.

Several factors influence climate. Perhaps the most important is distance from the Equator. Lands near the Equator are usually hot and wet all year. Closer to the North and South poles, temperatures are colder. **Altitude,** or height of the land above sea level, also affects climate. In general, highlands are cooler than lowlands. Other factors that affect climate include ocean currents, wind currents, and location of landforms such as inland mountains, large desert areas, lakes, or forests.

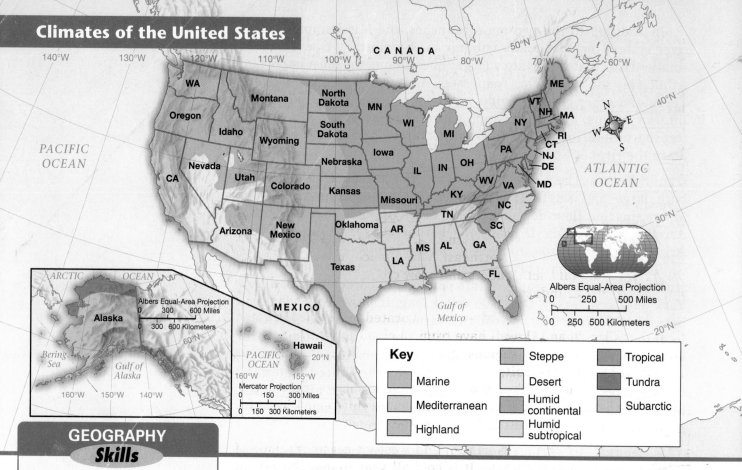

Climates of the United States

Key

Marine	Steppe	Tropical
Mediterranean	Desert	Tundra
Highland	Humid continental	Subarctic
	Humid subtropical	

GEOGRAPHY Skills

The United States is a land of many climates.

1. **Location** On the map, locate **(a)** an area with a Mediterranean climate **(b)** an area with a desert climate.

2. **Place** What states have three or more different climates?

3. **Critical Thinking**
   Applying Information
   (a) Identify a state or a part of a state where water is probably scarce. **(b)** Why is water in such short supply there?

Climates of the United States

The United States has 10 major climates. Today, as in the past, these climates strongly influence the nation's population patterns and economic activities.

Marine The strip of land from southern Alaska to northern California is sometimes called the Pacific Northwest. This region has a mild, moist marine climate, with warm summers and cool winters. The Pacific Northwest has many forests, making it a center of the lumber industry.

Mediterranean Much of California has a Mediterranean climate. Winters are mild and wet. Summers are hot and dry. Because of dry conditions, farmers and fruit growers must often irrigate the land. This region produces almost all of the nation's almonds, walnuts, olives, apricots, dates, and figs.

Highland In the Cascades, Sierra Nevada, and Rocky Mountains, a highland climate brings cooler temperatures. Conditions in a highland climate vary according to altitude. For example, Mount Rainier in the state of Washington, at over 14,000 feet above sea level, is snowcapped all year. The highland climate attracts vacationers eager to ski in the winter and escape the heat during the summer.

Desert and Steppe Much of the southwestern United States has a desert climate, with hot days and cold nights. This dry region stretches as far east as the Rockies. The deserts of New Mexico, Nevada,

Arizona, and southeastern California get almost no rainfall. In many places, people irrigate the land so that they can grow crops.

East of the Rockies, the Great Plains have a steppe climate with limited rainfall, hot summers, and cold winters. In the 1800s, settlers brought cattle and built a prosperous beef industry in the region.

Humid Continental The Central Plains and the northeastern United States have a humid continental climate. This climate has more precipitation than the steppe. The seasons are marked by mild summers and cold winters. Tall prairie grasses once covered the Central Plains. Today, American farmers raise much of the world's food in this region.

At one time, the humid continental climate supported forests that covered much of the Northeast. While much of this forestland was cleared to build settlements and grow crops, the region still has a thriving lumber industry.

Tropical and Humid Subtropical Located near the Equator, Southern Florida and Hawaii have tropical climates. The hot, humid conditions make these regions good for growing such crops as pineapples and citrus fruits.

The southeastern United States has a humid subtropical climate. Warm temperatures and regular rainfall make this region ideal for growing crops such as cotton, soybeans, and peanuts.

Tundra and Subarctic Northern and western coastal regions of Alaska have a tundra climate. It is cold all year round. The rest of Alaska, as well as northern Canada, has a subarctic climate with long, cold winters and short summers.

Relatively few people live in these harsh climates. Farming is limited to a small fertile valley in southern Alaska. However, the dense forests that cover almost one third of Alaska are ideal for logging and production of paper pulp.

Section 2 Assessment

Recall

1. **Define** (a) isthmus, (b) elevation, (c) erosion, (d) tributary, (e) weather, (f) climate, (g) precipitation, (h) altitude.

Comprehension

2. Name the eight physical regions of the United States and describe one feature of each region.
3. How do rivers and lakes benefit the economy of the United States?
4. Describe the climate of the region in which you live.

Critical Thinking and Writing

5. **Exploring the Main Idea** List the physical regions and climates of the United States. Then, choose the three regions and climates where you would most like to live. Explain your choices.
6. **Linking Past and Present** (a) How do you think the role of rivers and lakes has changed over the course of the nation's history? (b) What are the most important roles of rivers and lakes today?

ACTIVITY

Create a Chart Using information from the map on page 16, find the climate of your state. Prepare a chart showing how the climate affects your lifestyle. Consider how you dress, the food you eat, and where you live.

Glossary of Geographic Terms

The list below includes important geographic terms and their definitions. Sometimes, the definition of a term includes an example in parentheses. An asterisk (*) indicates that the term is illustrated on page 19.

altitude height above sea level

*archipelago chain of islands (Hawaiian Islands)

basin low-lying land area that is surrounded by land of higher elevation; land that is drained by a river system (Great Basin)

*bay part of a body of water that is partly enclosed by land (San Francisco Bay)

canal waterway made by people that is used to drain or irrigate land or to connect two bodies of water (Erie Canal)

*canyon deep, narrow valley with high, steep sides (Grand Canyon)

*cape narrow point of land that extends into a body of water (Cape Cod)

climate pattern of weather in a particular place over a period of 20 to 30 years

*coast land that borders the sea (Pacific Coast)

coastal plain lowland area lying along the ocean (Gulf Plain)

continent any of seven large landmasses on the Earth's surface (Africa, Antarctica, Asia, Australia, Europe, North America, South America)

continental divide mountain ridge that separates river systems flowing toward opposite sides of a continent

*delta land formed by soil that is deposited at the mouth of a river (Mississippi Delta)

desert area that has little or no moisture or vegetation (Painted Desert)

directional arrow arrow on a map that always points north

downstream in the direction of a river's flow; toward a river's mouth

elevation the height above sea level

fall line place where rivers drop from a plateau or foothills to a coastal plain, usually marked by many waterfalls

foothills low hills at the base of a mountain range

*gulf arm of an ocean or sea that is partly enclosed by land, usually larger than a bay (Gulf of Mexico)

hemisphere half of the Earth (Western Hemisphere)

*hill area of raised land that is lower and more rounded than a mountain (San Juan Hill)

*island land area that is surrounded by water (Puerto Rico)

*isthmus narrow strip of land joining two large areas or joining a peninsula to a mainland (Isthmus of Panama)

*lake body of water surrounded entirely by land (Lake Superior)

latitude the distance in degrees north and south from the Equator

longitude the distance in degrees east or west from the Prime Meridian

marsh lowland with moist soils and tall grasses

*mountain high, steep, rugged land that rises sharply above the surrounding land (Mount McKinley)

mountain range chain of connected mountains (Allegheny Mountains)

mouth of a river place where a river or stream empties into a larger body of water

ocean any of the five largest bodies of salt water on the Earth's surface (Arctic Ocean, Atlantic Ocean, Indian Ocean, Pacific Ocean, and Antarctic Ocean)

*peninsula piece of land that is surrounded by water on three sides (Delmarva Peninsula)

piedmont rolling land along the base of a mountain range

*plain broad area of fairly level land that is generally close to sea level

*plateau large area of high, flat, or gently rolling land

prairie large area of natural grassland with few or no trees or hills

*river large stream of water that empties into an ocean or a lake or another river (Pecos River)

*sea large body of salt water that is smaller than an ocean (Caribbean Sea)

sea level average level of the ocean's surface from which the height of land or depth of the ocean is measured

*source of a river place where a river begins

steppe flat, treeless land with limited moisture

strait narrow channel that connects two larger bodies of water (Straits of Florida)

*tributary stream or small river that flows into a larger river or stream

upstream in the direction that is against a river's flow; toward a river's source

valley land that lies between hills or mountains (Shenandoah Valley)

*volcano cone-shaped mountain formed by an outpouring of lava—hot, liquid rock—from a crack in the Earth's surface (Mount St. Helens or Mauna Loa)

weather condition of the Earth's atmosphere at any given time and place

3 The Tools of History

Reading Focus

- How do historians evaluate and interpret historical evidence?
- How do archaeologists add to our knowledge of history?
- What can we learn about history by understanding chronology and eras?

Key Terms

primary source

secondary source

authenticity

bias

artifact

archaeology

culture

chronology

Taking Notes

As you read, prepare an outline of this section. Use roman numerals to indicate major headings, capital letters for subheadings, and numbers for the supporting details. The sample at right will help you get started.

> I. Using Historical Evidence
>   A. Primary and secondary sources
>   1. Official documents
>   2. Eyewitness accounts
>   B. Evaluating evidence
>   1.
>   2.
>   3.
>   C. Interpreting evidence
>   1.
>   2.
> II. Archaeologists Uncover the Past

Main Idea Historians have developed many tools to study and interpret history.

Setting the Scene "It has been coming on for a long time," warned David McCullough, "like a creeping disease." McCullough was not talking about a flu epidemic or an outbreak of measles. Instead, he was alarmed that young Americans did not know enough about their nation's past.

> **66** Everything we have, all our great institutions, hospitals, universities, libraries, this city, our laws, our music, art, poetry, our freedoms, everything is because somebody went before us and did the hard work. . . . Indifference to history isn't just ignorant, it's rude. It's a form of ingratitude. **99**
>
> —David McCullough, *Why History?*

David McCullough

AS YOU READ **Find Main Ideas** Why does McCullough think history is important?

Historians like David McCullough have devoted their lives to making sure we do not forget our shared past and values. They have developed a wide variety of methods to accomplish this goal.

Using Historical Evidence

Studying the lives of people in different times and places is the work of the historian. The most basic tool for this work is historical evidence. Historians collect the evidence, then use it to interpret events.

Primary and Secondary Sources Historians look first for primary sources. A primary source is firsthand information about people or events. Primary sources include official documents such as laws or court decisions, public speeches, eyewitness accounts such as diaries and letters, and autobiographies. Primary sources may also include visual evidence such as a news photograph or a videotape. A special type of primary source is oral—or spoken—history, which may be based on interviews with people of today recalling the past.

Historians also make use of secondary sources. A secondary source is an account provided after the fact by people who did not directly witness or participate in the event. Secondary sources are usually based on primary sources. This textbook is an example of a secondary source. Encyclopedias, biographies, or books and articles written by historians are also secondary sources.

Evaluating Evidence When dealing with a primary source, the first job of a historian may be to determine whether it is authentic. Authenticity refers to whether or not the source is actually what it seems to be. For example, in 1928, a magazine published a series of newly discovered letters that were said to have been written by a young Abraham Lincoln. After careful detective work, historian Paul Angle concluded that the letters were clever forgeries. Angle described some of the questions historians ask when deciding if a source is authentic:

> 66 Is the paper of the proper age, and is the ink that of the period in which the documents are supposed to have been written? . . . Does [the handwriting] resemble that of letters and papers of undoubted genuineness? . . . Do specific incidents mentioned in the challenged documents check with [provable] historical fact? 99
>
> —Paul M. Angle, "The Minor Collection: A Criticism"

AS YOU READ **Visualize** Form a mental image of a historian as a detective. List some tools historians use to evaluate evidence.

After showing that a source is authentic, historians must determine whether it is reliable. Reliability refers to whether or not the source gives an accurate account of the events being described. Was the person describing the event really an eyewitness or just passing on stories told by other people? How accurate was the witness's memory? Do the records of a meeting between two officials report their exact words? What was left out, and why? Such questions help a historian determine reliability.

In evaluating reliability, historians must always be on the lookout for bias. Bias is a leaning toward or against a certain person, group, or idea. Cultural background, personal experiences, economic status, and political beliefs may all contribute to bias. An account of a battle given by a soldier on one side may differ widely from an account of the same battle given by a soldier on the other side. A description of a political candidate may be affected by whether the writer is for or against that candidate. In this book, you will find lessons on how to look for signs of bias in order to determine the reliability of sources.

Interpreting Evidence In addition to evaluating sources, historians interpret what the sources mean. Often, the historian's goal is to determine the causes of a certain development or event, such as a war or an economic collapse. By explaining why things happened in the past, the historian can help us understand what is going on today and what may happen tomorrow.

Still, different historians may interpret the same evidence in different ways. Although historians try to be objective, they may be influenced by their own biases. Interpretations of events also change over time, influenced by current events, new ideas, and new sources.

Primary Source

Preserving Historical Evidence

Historian Robin Winks tells how even the simplest documents can provide important evidence of the past:
"Precisely because the historian must turn to all possible witnesses, he is the most bookish of men. For him, no printed statement is without its interest. For him, the destruction of old cookbooks, gazetteers, road maps, Sears Roebuck catalogues, children's books, railway timetables, or drafts of printed manuscripts, is the loss of potential evidence. Does one wish to know how the mail-order business was operated or how a Nebraska farmer might have dressed in 1930? Look to those catalogues."

—Robin Winks,
The Historian as Detective

Analyzing Primary Sources
What can the historian learn from the items that Winks mentions?

Beware the Archaeologist
This cartoon appeared in the British humor magazine *Punch* in 1971. At that time, many amateur archaeologists were traveling to England to search for ancient artifacts.

1. **Comprehension** What kind of work are the three people in the cartoon doing?

2. **Understanding Main Ideas** **(a)** What has Sam pieced together? **(b)** Why is he eager to show it?

3. **Critical Thinking Identifying Points of View** How do you think the cartoonist feels about amateur archaeologists? Explain.

"Good effort, Sam, but it was a water jug!"

Archaeologists Uncover the Past

Most of the evidence that historians use to study American history is in written form. However, when examining the distant past, historians must often rely on artifacts (AHRT uh faktz), or objects made by humans. Artifacts include items such as stone tools, weapons, baskets, and carvings.

The Science of Archaeology Artifacts are the building blocks of archaeology (ahr kee AHL uh jee). Archaeology is the study of evidence left by early people in order to find out about their way of life.

As ancient cultures disappear, their remains are buried by centuries of sand, dirt, and water. Later people then build new settlements in the same spot, burying the artifacts even deeper. In places like the desert Southwest, archaeologists dig into the earth. They carefully preserve, photograph, and label the artifacts they find. Each new find can provide valuable information about the past.

In laboratories, experts analyze the finds. By testing the level of carbon in a piece of pottery or bone, they can date it to within a few hundred years. They might study kernels of ancient corn through a microscope to find out about the climate in which it grew. They might compare clay pots from different areas to find out about the people who made them.

Studying Ancient Cultures From artifacts and other evidence, archaeologists form theories about the cultures of ancient peoples. A culture is the way of life that a people has developed. It includes their homes, clothing, economy, arts, and government. It also includes the customs, ideas, beliefs, and skills that they pass on from generation to generation.

By studying artifacts, archaeologists can determine approximately when the objects were made. They can also form theories about the people who made them. Modern technology, such as computers, helps the archaeologist study artifacts. A finely carved arrowhead suggests that a people knew how to make weapons and hunt. Woven plant fibers suggest that they were skilled basket makers.

In the Americas, archaeologists often focus on the cultures that existed before the arrival of Europeans. Their work has given us valuable insight into the lives of the first Americans, as you will see. Still, some Native Americans have objected to the disturbance of ancient burial grounds or other sites. In recent years, archaeologists have grown more aware of the need to respect Native American landmarks and traditions.

Chronology and Historical Eras

Perhaps you feel that the study of history is a collection of dates, names, and facts. Actually, it is much more than that. It is a story that has many parts.

Learn From the Past When you study history, you learn how the past is linked to the present. As you begin to study the past, you will find that it is like unraveling a fascinating mystery. There is always

Viewing History

Finding Artifacts
Members of an archaeological team in Boston searched for and found artifacts from colonial Boston. The teapot and glass bottle were found at the site.
Analyzing Information *What might these items tell archaeologists about the people who used them?*

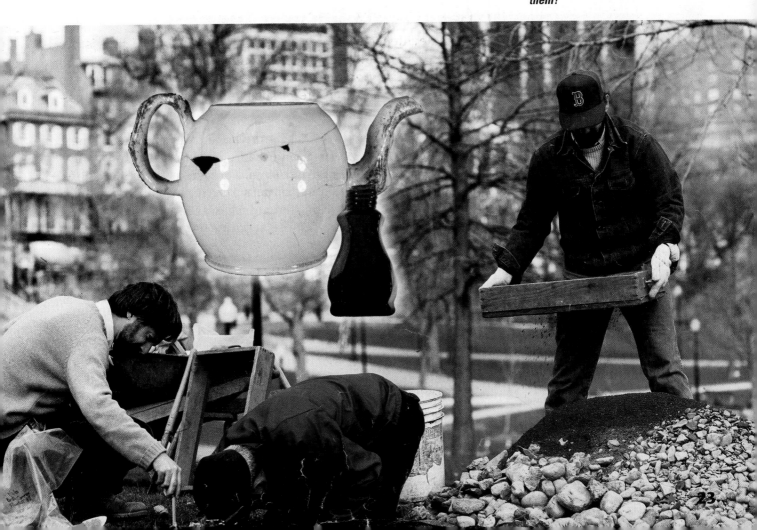

Eras in American History

First Americans, or Pre-Columbian	Before 1492	Diverse cultures developed in North America and South America.
Era of Exploration	1492–1600s	Europeans explored and settled in the Americas, resulting in the decline or destruction of a number of Native American cultures.
Colonial Era	1607–1775	The thirteen English colonies were settled in North America. The era ended with the start of the American Revolution.
Revolutionary Era	1763 – 1781	Following a war for independence from Great Britain, the United States became a nation. Some historians mark the end of this era as 1789, when the Constitution went into effect.
Early Republic	1789 – 1828	The new United States government, with George Washington as its first President, took shape. The country began to expand, and its economy began to develop.
Jacksonian Era or the Age of Jackson	1828 – 1840	Andrew Jackson's inauguration symbolized a new era in which the interests of the people were addressed. Democratic rights were extended to more Americans.
Era of Expansion	1840s – 1853	The United States expanded from the Atlantic to the Pacific Ocean, adding many new territories.
Civil War Era	1850s – 1877	Disputes about the growth of slavery, as well as other conflicts, led to the Civil War between the North and South. The era ended with Reconstruction, when the North and South reunited as one nation.
Progressive Era	1898 – 1917	Reformers sought to improve society. They were successful in passing laws for regulating business, limiting child labor, and protecting natural resources.
The Great Depression	1929 – 1941	After the boom of the 1920s, a severe economic crisis affected all Americans. Millions lost jobs as factories closed down.
Post–World War II	1945 – Present	As we get closer to the present day, it becomes more difficult to divide American history neatly. The years after World War II, however, are variously known as the Cold War Era, the Civil Rights Era, the Vietnam Era, the Atomic Age, and the Space Age.

CHART Skills

American history can be divided into several eras, or major periods of time.

1. **Comprehension** During which era did the United States begin to establish a new government?

2. **Critical Thinking Applying Information** Why is it useful to organize history into eras?

more to know. Often by studying how people solved problems in the past, we can apply these insights to solving today's problems.

History is the story of the men and women we honor as heroes. These exceptional men and women dared to believe they could change the world—and they did. Some were great leaders such as George Washington. Still others, such as Harriet Tubman, Abraham Lincoln, Dr. Martin Luther King, Jr., and Charles Lindbergh, changed people's view of the world.

Learn About People History is also the story of ordinary people who do the everyday things that shape the character of our country. It is also the story of how people lived, where they traveled, and how they felt about their lives. Ordinary people work hard, raise families, and fight wars. In addition, ordinary people also settled the frontier, built cities, and participated in protest marches.

Furthermore, there is much that historians can learn from what we consider everyday items. Children's toys and games may give clues about a culture. The clothes people wear, the music they listen to, and even the kind of work people do can give clues to historians.

On the practical side, studying history provides you with useful skills. As you begin to analyze events, you will learn how to research topics, recognize different points of view, make connections, and understand causes and effects.

Absolute Chronology The study of history starts with chronology (kruh NAHL uh gee), the sequence of events over time. Just as geography answers the question *where*, chronology answers the question *when*.

There are two types of chronology: absolute and relative. Absolute chronology refers to the exact time an event took place. Depending on the information available, absolute chronology may be expressed in terms of centuries, years, days, or even hours. For example, according to eyewitnesses, President Abraham Lincoln died of an assassin's bullet on April 15, 1865, at 7:22 A.M.

Relative Chronology The time when an event took place in relation to other events is called relative chronology. For example, in 1773, Britain imposed a tea tax on its American colonies. Later that year, protesters in Boston raided British ships and dumped chests of tea into the harbor. Within three months, the British passed new laws to punish Boston. The phrases "later that year" and "within three months" show the relative chronology of the three events.

Relative chronology helps us understand connections between different events. Still, the fact that one event came before another one does not necessarily mean that the first event caused the second. For example, suppose your neighbor washes his car and an hour later there is a thunderstorm. Did washing the car cause it to rain? In January 1837, Martin Van Buren became President. Two months later the nation faced a terrible economic crisis. Did Van Buren's becoming President cause the crisis? Only careful study can help you decide if and how the two events are linked.

Section 3 Assessment

Recall

1. **Define** (a) primary source, (b) secondary source, (c) authenticity, (d) bias, (e) artifact, (f) archaeology, (g) culture, (h) chronology.

Comprehension

2. What steps must a historian take to evaluate historical evidence?
3. How do archaeologists learn about the past?
4. Why do historians divide history into eras?

Critical Thinking and Writing

5. **Exploring the Main Idea** Review the Main Idea statement at the beginning of this section. List five sources that a historian might use to write a history of your life. Then, evaluate them for authenticity, reliability, and bias.
6. **Solving Problems** How can archaeologists continue to study ancient remains without infringing on the rights of Native Americans?

ACTIVITY

Take It to the NET

Exploring Primary Sources Choose one of the eras of American history listed on page 24. Then, use the Internet to find a primary source from that era. Write a short summary of the source. Then, analyze it for authenticity, reliability, and bias. Visit *The American Nation* section of **www.phschool.com** for help in completing this activity.

4 Economics and Other Social Sciences

Reading Focus

- What basic questions do economists ask about society?
- What are the benefits of free enterprise?
- How can the social sciences support the study of history?

Key Terms

economics
consumer
cash economy
free enterprise
social sciences
political science
civics
anthropology
sociology
psychology

Taking Notes

Copy the concept web below. As you read, fill in the blank ovals with information about the study of economics. Add as many ovals as you need.

Main Idea The study of history is closely linked to economics and other social sciences.

Stacks of coins
Draw Inferences Why do you think our economy is called a cash economy?

Setting the Scene

If you were growing up in an Iroquois village 300 years ago, you would have depended on the local forests and rivers for all your needs. Americans living on the frontier in the 1800s also relied on what they could raise or hunt themselves. A lucky family might expand its supply of goods by growing a few pounds of cotton. They would then trade the cloth they wove from the cotton for a pig or a calf.

Today, Americans take for granted their ability to consume an almost limitless supply of goods from all over the world. With a short trip to the local shopping mall, we buy shoes from Italy or shirts from Hong Kong. Shopping on the Internet can bring leather backpacks and wool sweaters from Australia or stone carvings and colorful beadwork from Kenya.

People in every society have wants and needs. At the same time, every society—no matter how rich—has limited resources. In this section, we will examine the ways that different societies manage their limited resources to meet their wants and needs.

Three Economic Questions

The study of how people manage their limited resources to satisfy their wants and needs is called economics. Every society must answer three basic economic questions: (1) What goods and services should we produce? (2) How should we produce them? (3) For whom should we produce them? The answers to these questions define every society's economic system.

What Goods and Services Should We Produce? A society's first economic task is to fulfill people's basic needs—food, shelter, and clothing. After that, the society must make choices about how to use the rest of its limited resources. Should it focus on producing consumer goods, such as cars and washing machines? Should it use its resources for education? Should it concentrate on heavy industry such as construction or trucking?

Decisions about what to produce vary according to the time and culture. Developing nations are less concerned about producing private automobiles. They are more concerned with building industries that will provide jobs and improve their quality of life. In the United States, on the other hand, we see cars as a necessity of life. Special situations also affect decision making. During World War II, for example, the United States government limited the manufacture of items such as cars and washing machines in favor of tanks and fighter planes.

How Should We Produce Goods and Services? Even when people agree on what to produce, they must choose how to produce it and how much of it to produce. Technology plays a major role in these decisions. For example, in the past, each family grew enough fruits, grains, and vegetables to meet its needs. Or small, family-run farms grew crops for the local community. With the invention of new farm machinery, agriculture changed. Today in the United States, most of the food we eat is grown on giant mechanized farms run by large corporations.

Advances in technology also changed manufacturing. At one time, most manufactured items were produced by hand in homes or small workshops. Then, the Industrial Revolution introduced new methods and machines that allowed large factories to mass-produce great quantities of manufactured goods. Today, computers and robot technology have once more revolutionized manufacturing.

For Whom Should We Produce Goods and Services? We are all consumers, or users of goods and services. However, just as resources are limited, supplies of goods and services are limited. What goods and services should be available to what consumers? How do consumers pay for what they want and need?

In past societies, consumers and producers were often the same people. They consumed the goods they produced themselves. Today, we live in a cash economy, that is, an economy where we exchange

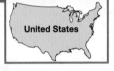

Glossary of Economic Terms

barter	the direct exchange of one set of goods or services for another
budget	a plan for spending and saving
capital	any human-made resource that is used to create other goods or services
command economy	an economy in which one organization decides what goods are produced and how much stores will charge for these goods
credit	any form of deferred payment
entrepreneur	ambitious leader who combines land, labor, and capital to create and market new goods or services
export	a good that is sent to another country for sale
free enterprise	an economic system characterized by private or corporate ownership of capital goods; investments that are determined by private decision rather than by state control
free market	an economic system in which individuals rather than the government make most of the decisions about economic activities
import	a good that is brought in from another country for sale
labor	the effort that people devote to a task for which they are paid
private property	something owned by an individual; especially land or buildings
profit	the amount of money a company has once it has sold its products
scarcity	limited quantities of resources to meet unlimited wants
supply and demand	a feature of the capitalist economy; when supplies of goods or services are plentiful, prices drop; when supplies are scarce, prices rise
surplus	situation in which quantity supplied is greater than quantity demanded; also known as excess supply

CHART
Skills

This glossary gives the meaning of some basic economic terms.

1. **Comprehension** Which term refers to an economic system where ownership of goods can be private or corporate?

2. **Critical Thinking Making Decisions** Why might an entrepreneur be better off in a free-market economy than in a command economy?

Primary Sources

See Alexis de Tocqueville, "Democracy in America" on page 573 in the Reference Section.

money for goods and services. Your income and wealth determine the goods and services you can consume. How to supply basic needs to people who cannot afford to buy them is a difficult issue for governments, charities, religious communities, and individuals.

The American Free Enterprise System

The economy of the United States is based on an economic principle known as free enterprise. In a free enterprise system, the government plays a limited role in the economy. Businesses are owned by private citizens. Owners decide what products to make, how much to produce, where to sell products, and what prices to charge. Furthermore, competition is encouraged. Competition gives businesses an incentive, or reason, for working harder. Companies compete for consumers by making the best product at the lowest price.

The free enterprise system began early in the United States. After the War for Independence, Americans were free to engage in any economic activity without government interference. The Framers of the Constitution believed that the prosperity of the nation depended on a free-market economy. Provisions for private property and competition, for example, are included in the Constitution.

Until the late 1800s, the United States government did relatively little to control the economy. Since then, government has gradually taken on a more active role. Many Americans argue that government regulations are needed to end abuses or ensure against economic collapse. Others claim that government interference keeps the free enterprise system from working efficiently.

Despite such disagreements, Americans have long recognized free enterprise as one of the nation's greatest strengths.

The "know-how" of individual American traders, inventors, and investors helped create vast personal fortunes, as well as prosperity for the nation. Today, many nations around the world look to the American free enterprise system as a model.

The free enterprise system also allows consumers freedom to make economic choices. Through their buying decisions, consumers can tell businesses what to make, how much, and at what price. In this respect, the economic system is much like a democracy. People are allowed to express their preferences.

Other Social Sciences

Economics, history, and geography are considered social sciences because they relate to human society and social behavior. Other social sciences include political science, civics, anthropology, sociology, and psychology.

AS YOU READ **Draw Inferences** As you read, ask yourself why each of the social sciences is important to the study of American history.

Political Science and Civics The study of government is called political science. Political scientists look at the ideas behind different forms of government, how these governments are organized, and how they work. Like economics, political science raises many basic questions. Who should have the most power in a government? How are decisions made? How do governments change?

Before 1776, Americans lived as subjects of a foreign king, to whom they owed loyalty and obedience. After throwing off that form of government, they built what Abraham Lincoln called a "government of the people, by the people, for the people." As citizens, Americans owe loyalty to the nation and have a say in their government. The basic principles and organization of American government are contained in the Constitution of the United States. You will learn more about the Constitution in later chapters.

Civics An important branch of political science is civics, the study of the rights and responsibilities of citizens. In 1776, the Declaration of Independence stated the idea that every person had basic rights that could not be taken away:

66 We hold these truths to be self-evident, that all men are created equal; that they are endowed by their Creator with certain inalienable rights; that among these are life, liberty, and the pursuit of happiness. 99
—Declaration of Independence

Throughout the nation's history, Americans have worked to expand and protect the rights of individuals. The addition of the Bill of Rights to the Constitution ensures individual rights to all

Americans. These rights include freedom of speech, which means the newspapers, books, and magazines you read can print the news. Your rights to worship as you please and to assemble freely are also guaranteed. Americans have also recognized their responsibility to serve the nation in many ways, including obeying its laws, voting, and serving in the military.

Anthropology, Sociology, and Psychology The study of how people and cultures develop is called *anthropology* (an thruh PAHL uh gee). Anthropologists look at the ways people thought and behaved at different times and places. For example, an anthropologist might examine how the first Americans spread across North and South America and the different ways of life they developed. One branch of anthropology is archaeology, as discussed in Section 3.

Sociology is the study of how people behave in groups. Looking at a particular society, a sociologist might ask: Is this society divided into different social classes? How are families organized? How do the roles of men and women differ? What values and beliefs do people share? Even a single nation, such as the United States, contains many different social groups. For example, a sociologist may be interested in how life in a small farming community in upstate New York differs from life in a big-city neighborhood in New York, Los Angeles, or Houston. A sociologist might even study how different student groups in a middle school relate to one another.

Psychology is the study of how people think and behave. Psychology is linked to history because history is the study of human beings. For example, a person writing a biography of a well-known figure might look to psychology to understand why that person acted in a certain way. Psychology can also help us evaluate primary sources by helping us understand people's views and biases.

Section 4 Assessment

Recall

1. **Define** (a) economics, (b) consumer, (c) cash economy, (d) free enterprise, (e) social sciences, (f) political science, (g) civics, (h) anthropology, (i) sociology, (j) psychology.

Comprehension

2. What three basic economic questions must every society answer?

3. Explain why the free enterprise system was developed in the new nation.

4. Choose two of the social sciences discussed in this section. Describe how they support the study of history.

Critical Thinking and Writing

5. **Exploring the Main Idea** Review the Main Idea statement at the beginning of this section. Then, write three questions that you might ask about the development of the economy of the United States from independence to today.

6. **Identifying Alternatives** Why would a developing nation answer the three basic economic questions differently than a country like the United States?

ACTIVITY

Creating a Comic Strip Create a comic strip for Free Enterprise Publishers showing the steps an ambitious young American would take to start and run a new business. Be sure to include a panel showing how our hero would respond to competition from other businesses.

American Entrepreneurs

American history is filled with stories of successful entrepreneurs. Their success makes it easy to see why the United States is often called the "land of opportunity."

Walt Disney

Walt Disney owed his success to a mouse. In 1928, he introduced Mickey Mouse in the animated cartoon "Steamboat Willie." Mickey's worldwide popularity helped Disney build a business empire that came to include a movie studio and huge theme parks in Florida and California.

Madame C. J. Walker

Madame C. J. Walker's money-making idea was to market hair-care products for African Americans. Starting in 1905, she created her own formulas and sold them door-to-door. Five years later, she was running a factory that provided employment for some 3,000 people. By the time of her death in 1919, Walker was one of the first American women to have become a millionaire through her own efforts.

Junior Achievement

Since 1919, Junior Achievement has worked "to educate and inspire young people to value free enterprise, business, and economics." Junior Achievement volunteers run programs in schools across the country, including a competition in which students have an opportunity to experience running an actual business.

ACTIVITY

With a partner, write a plan for a new business. Describe the goods or services you plan to market, explain who your customers would be, and list what you would need to get started.

CREATING A CHAPTER SUMMARY

On a sheet of paper, copy the concept web below. As you read, fill in the blank ovals with information about the different social sciences that affect the study of history. Add as many ovals as you need to complete the chart. Some information has been filled in to help you get started.

HISTORY

Economics

Archaeology

iTEXT For additional review and enrichment activities, see the interactive version of *The American Nation,* available on the Web and on CD-ROM.

Take It to the NET

Chapter Self-Test For practice test questions for Chapter 1, visit *The American Nation* section of **www.phschool.com**.

Building Vocabulary

Review the chapter vocabulary words listed below. Then, use the words and their definitions to create a matching quiz. Exchange quizzes with another student. Check each other's answers when you are finished.

1. geography
2. cartographer
3. climate
4. precipitation
5. altitude
6. primary source
7. artifact
8. chronology
9. cash economy
10. free enterprise

Reviewing Key Facts

11. What are the different uses for maps and globes? (Section 1)
12. Describe three physical regions of the United States. (Section 2)
13. Name three kinds of evidence that archaeologists study. (Section 3)
14. How does the American free enterprise system work? (Section 4)

Critical Thinking and Writing

15. Connecting to Geography: **Movement** How does the movement of people, goods, and ideas shape a society?
16. Evaluating Information Which would be more reliable: a map of North America from the 1500s or a map of North America from the 1900s? Explain your answer.
17. Synthesizing Information Look at the picture of Pikes Peak on page 11. **(a)** Describe the physical region in which Pikes Peak is located. **(b)** Describe the climate of that region.
18. Applying Information Imagine that you are an archaeologist living 1,000 years from now. What conclusions about our society might you draw from the following artifacts: **(a)** coins and dollar bills, **(b)** automobile, **(c)** fast food containers, **(d)** TV set, **(e)** cell phone?
19. Making Decisions Review the discussion on page 28 about the proper role of government in the economy. Do you agree with the Americans who argue for a smaller or a larger government role? Explain your answer.

Analyzing Primary Sources

In 1845, Lansford W. Hastings wrote a guide for people traveling to the West. In it, he made the following statements about the West:

66 The time is not distant, when those wild forests, trackless plains, untrodden valleys . . . will present one grand scene of continuous improvements . . . when those vast forests shall have disappeared before the hardy pioneer; those extensive plains shall abound with innumerable herds of domestic animals; those fertile valleys shall groan under the weight of their abundant products. **99**

—Lansford W. Hastings, from *The Emigrants' Guide to Oregon and California*

20. According to Hastings, what did the West look like before 1845?
21. What changes did Hastings predict once the people settled the West?
22. How do you think he felt about the changes he predicted? Explain.

Reviewing Map Skills

Eastern Physical Regions

23. What region is northwest of the Appalachian mountains?
    A Ozark Highlands
    B Atlantic Plain
    C Gulf Plain
    D Central Plains
24. Which is the smallest region? Describe its location.

ACTIVITIES

Connecting With . . . Geography

Using the Five Themes Use the five themes of geography to describe the neighborhood, community, or state in which you live. Develop your description by writing one or two sentences for each of the five themes.

Consider the following questions:
1. Where is the place located?
2. How do people interact with the environment?
3. How do people and ideas move between places?

Take It to the NET

Connecting to Today

Creating a Chart Some scientists are worried that human activities such as driving cars and operating factories are causing a dangerous rise in the Earth's temperatures. Other scientists do not agree with this global-warming theory. They point out that the Earth has gone through warm and cold cycles in the past. Use the Internet to find out about the global-warming debate. Create a chart showing the arguments on both sides and the evidence used to support them. For help in starting this activity, visit *The American Nation* section of **www.phschool.com**.

Evaluating Internet Sites

Reviewing Eras in American History Select one of the historical eras listed on page 24. Use the Internet to research the major events of that era. Then, create a timeline of the era. For help in starting this activity, visit *The American Nation* section of **www.phschool.com**.

Before the First Global Age

PREHISTORY—1600

1 The First Civilizations of the Americas
2 Native American Cultures
3 Trade Networks of Africa and Asia
4 Tradition and Change in Europe

A Spanish map from the 1300s showing Mansa Musa seated on his throne

30,000 to 10,000 years ago

The first people arrive in the Americas.

Early 1300s

The African kingdom of Mali is at its most powerful. Its king, Mansa Musa, makes a famous pilgrimage to Mecca, Islam's holiest city.

Late 1300s

The Renaissance begins in southern Europe.

Prehistory   1300   1400

The World Around 1500

In 1500, the world was on the brink of major changes.

Key Empires Around 1500

- Aztec empire
- Incan empire
- Holy Roman Empire
- Songhai
- Russia
- Ottoman empire
- Safavid empire
- Mughal India
- Ming China

ATLANTIC OCEAN
PACIFIC OCEAN
INDIAN OCEAN

Tenochtitlán
Cuzco
Paris
Rome
Augsburg
Moscow
Constantinople
Tabriz
Baghdad
Cairo
Gao
Delhi
Gaur
Vijayanagar
Goa
Beijing
Nanjing
Hangzhou
Guangzhou

Robinson Projection
0   1500   3000 Miles
0   1500 3000 Kilometers

Gutenberg's printing press

A detail from *The Great City of Tenochtitlán*, by Diego Rivera

Mid 1400s
Europe's first books are printed on presses, such as this one built by Johannes Gutenberg.

Late 1400s
Tenochtitlán, capital city of the Aztecs, becomes one of the world's largest cities. The emperor (center) is worshipped and feared.

1591
Songhai empire falls to invaders from Morocco.

1400   1500   1600

1 The First Civilizations of the Americas

Reading Focus

- How did people first reach the Americas?
- What were the Olmec, Mayan, Aztec, and Incan civilizations like?
- How did early cultures develop in North America?

Key Terms

glacier

surplus

causeway

quipu

terrace

culture

adobe

pueblo

Mound Builders

Taking Notes

Copy this incomplete Venn diagram. As you read, write key facts about the Aztecs and the Incas in the appropriate sections. Write common achievements in the overlapping section.

AZTECS
-
-
-

• Ruled large empires

INCAS
-
-
-

Main Idea In several parts of the Americas, the development of farming enabled some groups of people to build complex civilizations.

Ancient Indian spear points

Visualize Think about the weapons Native Americans used and the animals they hunted. Why did Native American hunters work together when they hunted?

Setting the Scene The hunters crept slowly forward. Ahead, a herd of bison grazed near a swamp. At a signal, the hunters leaped up, shouting loudly. The startled herd stampeded into the swamp. As the bison struggled in the deep mud, the hunters hurled their spears.

Scenes much like this took place on North America's Great Plains more than 10,000 years ago. Hunters tracking herds of bison were among the first people to reach the Americas. Over time, their descendants spread out across two continents.

Reaching the Americas

Like other early people around the world, the first Americans left no written records to tell us where they came from or when they arrived. However, scientists have found evidence to suggest that the first people reached the Americas sometime during the last ice age.

According to geologists, the Earth has gone through several ice ages. The last ice age occurred between 100,000 and 10,000 years ago. During that time, thick sheets of ice, called **glaciers,** covered almost one third of the Earth. In North America, glaciers stretched across Canada and reached as far south as present-day Kentucky.

Crossing the Land Bridge Glaciers locked up water from the oceans, causing sea levels to fall and uncovering land that had been under water. In the far north, a land bridge joined Siberia in northeastern Asia to Alaska in North America.

Most scientists think that bands of hunters reached North America across this land bridge. These hunters tracked herds of grazing animals. Other scientists disagree. They think that the first Americans crossed the icy arctic waters by boat, reaching North America by sea. Another theory claims that people could have reached the Americas from

Europe, Africa, or islands in the South Pacific.

Once these early hunters reached the Americas, they had to keep moving in search of food. Slowly, over thousands of years, they spread across North America, Central America, and South America. The lands they settled varied widely. Native Americans settled on mountain plateaus, dry deserts, fertile plains, lush woodlands and thick rain forests. In these very different environments, Native American groups developed many different customs and languages.

Adapting to New Conditions About 12,000 years ago, the last ice age ended. As temperatures rose, the glaciers melted. The land bridge between Siberia and Alaska disappeared under the Bering Strait.

About the same time, some types of large animals died out. This forced hunting bands to adapt to new conditions. Smaller animals, wild berries, nuts, grains, and fish became a larger part of their diets.

About 5,000 years ago, people in Central America learned to grow crops such as corn, beans, and squash. Farming brought great changes to those who practiced it. Farmers no longer had to keep moving to find food. Instead, they stayed in one place and began to build permanent villages. As farming methods improved, people produced more food, which in turn allowed the population to grow.

Olmec Civilization

Farming was a key advance. In time, some farming communities in Central America grew enough surplus, or extra, food to support large populations, and the first cities emerged.

Cities marked the rise of the first civilization in the Americas. A civilization is a society that has certain basic features. Among these are cities, a well-organized government, different social classes, a complex religion, and some method of record keeping.

The earliest known civilization in the Americas was that of the Olmecs in Central America. The Olmecs lived in the lowlands along the Gulf of Mexico, about 3,500 years ago. Scientists have found huge stone heads carved by the Olmecs. Some were ten feet tall and weighed several tons. Smaller figures showed creatures that were part human and part animal.

Olmec farmers supplied nearby cities with food. There, powerful leaders built stone temples. The Olmecs left few written records, but

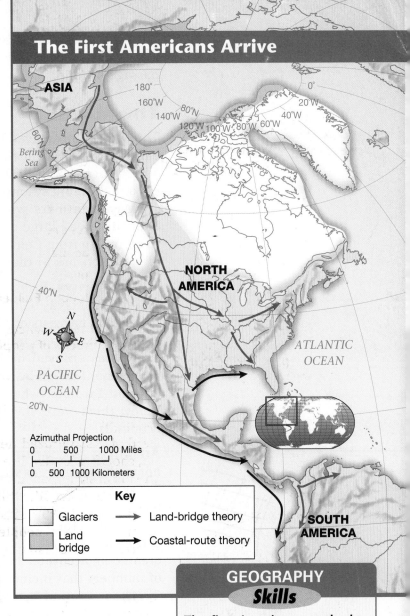

The First Americans Arrive

ASIA

NORTH AMERICA

PACIFIC OCEAN

ATLANTIC OCEAN

SOUTH AMERICA

Azimuthal Projection

0   500   1000 Miles

0   500 1000 Kilometers

Key

Glaciers → Land-bridge theory

Land bridge → Coastal-route theory

GEOGRAPHY
Skills

The first Americans reached North America from Asia. Over thousands of years, these hunters populated two huge continents.

1. **Location** On the map, locate: **(a)** Asia, **(b)** Bering Sea, **(c)** North America, **(d)** South America.

2. **Movement** According to the land-bridge theory, in which direction did early hunters travel once they reached North America?

3. **Critical Thinking Drawing Conclusions** Why do you think many of the first Americans continued to travel south after reaching North America?

they did make many advances. They studied the stars and developed a calendar so they could predict the change of seasons and mark the passage of time.

The Mayas

The Olmecs influenced many later peoples, including the Mayas. The early Mayas lived in the rain forests of what are today Guatemala and Mexico. About 3,000 years ago, they began clearing the rain forest and draining swamps to create farmland.

Mayan farmers were able to produce great harvests of corn, enough to feed large cities. As Mayan population grew, cities began to spring up from Central America to southern Mexico. Trade flowed along a network of roads that linked inland cities and the coast.

Social Classes Priests held great power in Mayan society. Only priests, the Mayas believed, could perform the ceremonies needed to bring good harvests or victory in battle. Priests conducted these ceremonies in temples built on top of huge stone pyramids.

Nobles enjoyed high status, too. They served as warriors and government officials. Near the bottom of Mayan society were laborers and farmers, who grew corn, squash, and many other crops. Below them were slaves, most of whom were prisoners of war or criminals.

Advances in Learning Mayan priests had to know exactly when to honor the many gods who were thought to control the natural world. Every day, priests anxiously studied the sun, moon, and stars. They learned much about the movement of these bodies.

Based on their observations, priests made impressive advances in astronomy and mathematics. They learned to predict eclipses and created an accurate, 365-day calendar. They also developed a system of numbers that included the concept of zero.

Then, around A.D. 900, the Mayas abandoned their cities. Historians are not sure why. Perhaps they did so because of warfare, a drought—or both. The rain forests swallowed up the great Mayan temples and palaces. Although Mayan cities decayed, the Mayan people survived. Today, more than 2 million people in Guatemala and southern Mexico speak Mayan languages.

The Aztecs

Long after the Mayan cities were abandoned, a new civilization rose far to the north. Its builders were the Aztecs. The early Aztecs were nomads, people who moved from place to place in search of food. In the 1300s, the Aztecs settled around Lake Texcoco (tay SKOH koh) in central Mexico. From there, they built a powerful empire.

Tenochtitlán On an island in the middle of the lake, the Aztecs built their capital, Tenochtitlán (tay noch tee TLAHN). They constructed a system of causeways, or raised roads made of packed earth. The causeways linked the capital to the mainland.

The Aztecs learned to farm the shallow swamps of Lake Texcoco. In some places, they dug canals, using the mud they removed to fill

AS YOU READ **Monitor Your Reading** As you read about the Mayas, the Aztecs, and the Incas, check to see if you understand how their accomplishments were similar and how they were different.

in parts of the lake. In other places, they attached reed mats to the lake bottom with long stakes. Then, they piled mud onto the mats to create farmland. Aztec farmers harvested several crops a year on these *chinampas,* or floating gardens.

With riches from trade and conquest, Tenochtitlán prospered. Its markets offered a wide variety of goods. "There are daily more than 60,000 people bartering and selling," wrote a Spanish visitor in the 1500s.

Religion Like the Mayas, Aztec priests studied the heavens and developed complex calendars. Such calendars gave them the ability to tell their people when to plant or harvest. Priests also performed rituals designed to please the many Aztec gods.

The Aztecs paid special attention to the sun god. They believed that each day the sun battled its way across the heavens. They compared the sun's battle to their own, calling themselves "warriors of the sun." They believed that the sun required human sacrifices in order to rise each day. The Aztecs therefore sacrificed thousands of captives each year to please this powerful god.

A Powerful Empire By 1500, the Aztecs ruled a huge empire. It stretched from the Gulf of Mexico to the Pacific Ocean and included millions of people. The Aztecs took great pride in their empire and their capital. "Who could conquer Tenochtitlán?" boasted an Aztec poet. "Who could shake the foundation of heaven?"

The Aztec world was far from peaceful, however. Heavy taxes and the sacrifice of huge numbers of prisoners of war sparked many revolts. Across the empire, people conquered by the Aztecs were eager for revenge. As you will read in Chapter 3, enemies of the Aztecs would help outsiders from distant lands destroy the Aztec empire.

The Incas

Far to the south of the Aztecs, the Incas built one of the largest empires in the Americas. By 1500, their empire stretched for almost 2,500 miles along the west coast of South America.

The center of the Incan empire was the magnificent capital at Cuzco (KOO skoh), located high in the Andes. Cuzco was a holy city to the Incas. All nobles in the empire tried to visit it at least once in their lifetimes. The city had massive palaces and temples made of stone and decorated with gold ornaments. At the center was the

Aztec Society

Emperor
Chosen by nobles and priests to lead in war

Priests
Performed rituals, gave advice, and ran schools

Nobles
Served as officials, judges, and governors

Warriors
Could become nobles by killing or capturing enemies

Merchants
Often acted as spies for the empire

Artisans
Passed skills on to their children

Farmers
Made up most of the population

Slaves
Were mostly captives or criminals

GRAPHIC ORGANIZER
Skills

Like many other ancient civilizations, Aztec society was strictly divided into social classes.

1. **Comprehension**
   (a) Who occupied the highest position in Aztec society? **(b)** Which classes of people were equal to one another?

2. **Critical Thinking**
   Analyzing Information How does this graphic organizer suggest the importance of warfare in Aztec society? Give two examples.

palace of the emperor, who was known as the Sapa Inca. The emperor was regarded as a god who was descended from the sun god.

From Cuzco, the emperor ruled more than 10 million people. They lived in varied environments, from coastal deserts to lowland jungles to the highlands of the Andes.

The Incan empire was very well organized. The emperor kept well informed about affairs in all parts of his empire. He sent high officials out to act as governors of his domain. The governors made sure that every person worked at least part of the time on projects for the state.

To unite their empire, the Incas maintained a system of roads that covered more than 10,000 miles. Builders carved roads in rock cliffs and stretched rope bridges across deep gorges. Teams of runners quickly spread royal orders across the empire using these roads.

The runners carried with them a device known as a **quipu** (KEE poo). This was a cord or string with knots that stood for quantities. The quantities might be bags of grain, numbers of soldiers, or other amounts. The quipu was also used by government officials to keep records.

The Incas were skilled engineers. They built massive stone temples and forts. With only human labor, ropes, and wooden rollers, they moved stones weighing up to 200 tons. They used all their engineering skills to farm the dry, rugged mountain lands. They became experts at creating **terraces,** or wide steps of land, out of the steep mountainsides. Sturdy stone walls kept rain from washing away the soil.

Early Cultures of North America

Scholars have found evidence of Mayan and Aztec ideas among some groups of people farther north. Traders and migrating people carried foods, goods, arts, and beliefs from Central America and Mexico to the early peoples of North America. This flow of products and ideas helped lead to the development of many distinct cultures in North America. A **culture** is the entire way of life of a people. It includes their homes, clothing, economy, arts, and government.

People of the Southwest At least 3,000 years ago, knowledge of farming spread northward. Gradually, farming societies emerged in what is today the American Southwest. They included the Hohokams (hoh HOH kahmz) and Anasazis (ah nuh SAH zeez).

The Hohokams lived in present-day southern Arizona. About 2,000 years ago, they dug networks of irrigation ditches so they could farm the desert land. The ditches carried water from the Salt and Gila rivers to fields, where farmers produced corn, squash, and beans.

The Anasazis lived in the Four Corners region, where Colorado, Utah, New Mexico, and Arizona meet. Like the Hohokams, the Anasazis irrigated the desert in order to farm. They also created a network of roads to link dozens of towns. Traders traveled these roads, carrying cotton, sandals, and blankets woven from turkey feathers.

Anasazi Houses The Anasazis built large houses with walls of stone and adobe, or sun-dried brick. When the Spanish later saw these houses in the early 1500s, they called them pueblos (PWEHB lohz), the Spanish word for "village." (They also called the descendants of the Anasazis the Pueblos.)

About 1,000 years ago, some Anasazi villages faced attacks from warlike neighbors. To escape that threat, they built new homes along steep cliffs. Toeholds cut into the rock let people climb the cliff walls. Farmers planted their crops on land above the cliffs.

Mound Builders To the east, other farming cultures flourished in North America. Among them were the Mound Builders, various cultures that built large earth mounds beginning about 3,000 years ago. Thousands of these mounds dot the landscape from the Appalachian Mountains to the Mississippi Valley and from Wisconsin to Florida.

The first mounds were used for burials. Later mounds were used for religious ceremonies. They were similar in function to the pyramid temples of the Mayas.

The best-known groups of Mound Builders were the Hopewells and the Mississippians. Between A.D. 700 and 1500, the Mississippians built a large city at Cahokia (kah HOH kee ah) in present-day Illinois. As many as 30,000 people may have lived there at one time.

Viewing History

Cliff Dwellings The cliff dwellings of Mesa Verde are examples of the homes of Native Americans in the canyons and cliffs of southwest Colorado. **Drawing Inferences** *Do you think the inhabitants of these dwellings were a peaceful or a warlike people? Explain.*

AFTER YOU READ

Section 1 Assessment

Recall

1. **Identify** Explain the significance of (a) Olmecs, (b) Mayas, (c) Aztecs, (d) Incas, (e) quipu, (f) Mound Builders.
2. **Define** (a) glacier, (b) surplus, (c) causeway, (d) terrace, (e) culture, (f) adobe, (g) pueblo.

Comprehension

3. In the opinion of most scientists, how did the first people reach the Americas?
4. Describe one achievement of each of the following early civilizations in the Americas: (a) Mayan, (b) Aztec, (c) Incan.

5. How did early people adapt to the desert Southwest?

Critical Thinking and Writing

6. **Exploring the Main Idea** Review the Main Idea statement at the beginning of this section. Then, write a paragraph explaining how farming was necessary for the first American civilizations to emerge.
7. **Applying Information** Review the subsection entitled "Early Cultures of North America." Then, make a list showing how the information in this subsection supports the idea that geography affects history.

ACTIVITY

Take It to the NET
Connecting to Today
Mexico City was built on the site of ancient Tenochtitlán. Use the Internet to find out how archaeologists discovered evidence of Aztec life in modern Mexico City. Write a paragraph describing how their findings help Mexicans understand their past. Visit *The American Nation* section of **www.phschool.com** for help in completing the activity.

2 Native American Cultures

Reading Focus

- How did people live in different culture areas of North America?
- How did climate and resources affect Native American cultures?
- What beliefs did different Native American groups share?
- What was life like among the Iroquois?

Key Terms

culture area

tribe

pit house

potlatch

kachina

clan

League of the Iroquois

sachem

Taking Notes

Copy the table below. As you read the section, fill in the ways that each Native American culture adapted to the climate and resources in its area.

CULTURE	CLIMATE/RESOURCES	HOW ADAPTED
• Arctic • Great Basin • Northwest • Southeast • Eastern Woodlands	• Harsh, limited	• Hunted small animals

Main Idea Native American cultures in North America varied greatly due in part to differences in climate and resources.

AS YOU READ

Cheyenne shield made of buffalo hide

Draw Inferences How would the Cheyenne who owned this shield have felt about Columbus?

Setting the Scene When Christopher Columbus reached the Americas in 1492, he thought he had landed in the East Indies—islands off the coast of Asia. So, he called the people he met "Indios," or "Indians." Other Europeans picked up the term. Even after Europeans realized Columbus's error, they continued to call the people of the Americas Indians.

The term Indian is misleading for another, more important, reason. Native Americans do not belong to a single group. In 1492, as now, Native Americans included many different people with many distinct cultures. In North America alone, there were hundreds of Native American languages spoken. Native American cultures, too, varied greatly, much like the cultures of the people of Europe. In the years that followed Columbus's arrival, Europeans would have difficulty understanding this complexity.

Culture Areas of North America

The map on page 44 shows the major culture areas of North America, north of Mexico, around A.D. 1450. A culture area is a region in which people share a similar way of life.

Each culture area was home to many different tribes. A tribe is a community of people who share common customs, language, and rituals. Members of a tribe saw themselves as a distinct people who shared a common origin. Tribal leaders often made decisions for the group.

Hunting, Gathering, and Fishing Native Americans developed a variety of ways to meet their basic needs for food, clothing, and shelter. In some culture areas, tribes hunted animals and gathered the nuts and fruits that grew in the wild. Other tribes depended on the sea for food. They made boats out of animal skins or carved canoes out of trees. From their boats and canoes, they speared fish or hunted marine animals such as seals, walrus, and whales.

Farming Other tribes lived mostly by farming, planting corn, beans, and squash. Native American tribes farmed in many parts of North America, from California in the West to the Eastern Woodlands. Over time, farmers improved their crops. For example, more than 5,000 years ago, wild corn was tiny, about the size of a human finger. Indian farmers developed dozens of varieties of corn including ones with larger ears.

Trade Indian tribes traded with one another for goods not found within their own region. Trade networks linked people across large distances. Goods sometimes traveled more than 1,000 miles from where they were made.

In the Northwest, traders met near the Dalles on the Columbia River. Local Indians caught and dried salmon, which they exchanged for goods and produce from other places. Other traders brought shells, fish oil, and whalebone from the Pacific Coast. People from the Great Basin traded black obsidian, a hard stone that was used to make knives. Traders from the Great Plains brought skins and dried buffalo meat.

Climate, Resources, and Culture

Climate and natural resources helped shape Native American cultures in different regions. Climate and natural resources influenced the crops people grew and the animals they hunted. Climate also affected people's needs for clothing and shelter. Resources provided the materials for their clothing and shelter.

Climate and resources affected tribal organization. Where climates were harsh and resources limited, people struggled to find enough food and shelter. In such regions, people were often nomadic. They lived in small hunting bands. Each band included a number of families. In regions with more favorable climates and plentiful resources, people tended to live in larger groups and stay in one place for longer periods.

Cultures of the Far North and Plateau Regions Frozen seas and icy, treeless plains made up the world of the Inuits, who lived in the Arctic region. The Inuits used all the limited resources of their environment. In the short summer season, they collected driftwood along the ocean shore, using it for tools and shelters. For most of the year, the Inuits lived in **pit houses,** houses dug into the ground and covered with wood and skins. Lamps filled with seal oil kept their homes warm even in the bitter cold. Women made warm clothing out of furs and waterproof boots out of sealskins.

Geography and History

Living With Arctic Cold

The Inuit had to rely on the resources of the icy Arctic environment to survive. They built igloos and insulated them with seal skins and sod. They also used caribou and seal fur to make warm clothing. Because caribou hair is hollow, it traps air and offers good insulation against the cold. So, in the fall and winter, the Inuit wore caribou parkas.

Inuit parkas had two layers. The soft inner layer had the fur facing in. A heavier outer layer had fur on the outside. This design was comfortable and protected the wearer from the cold.

In the spring and summer, the coastal Inuit fished or hunted from boats. Because seal fur repels water, the Inuit wore sealskin during the spring and summer.

 How might Inuit culture have been different in a warmer climate?

Native American Culture Areas of North America, About 1450

ARCTIC OCEAN

KUTCHINS

INUITS

INUITS

Arctic Circle

Hudson Bay   INUITS

60°N

TLINGITS

BELLA COOLAS

KWAKIUTLS

CREES

MONTAGNAIS

40°N

NEZ PERCÉS   BLACKFEET   MANDANS   DAKOTAS   OJIBWAS   ALGONQUINS   HURONS

COOS   CROWS

SHOSHONES   CHEYENNES   IROQUOIS   PEQUOTS

POMOS   ARAPAHOS   MIAMIS   LENI-LENAPES

PACIFIC OCEAN

NAVAJOS   OSAGES   SHAWNEES

PUEBLOS

HOHOKAMS   HOPIS   CHEROKEES

COMANCHES   NATCHEZ

APACHES

Gulf of Mexico

ATLANTIC OCEAN

Tropic of Cancer

Azimuthal Projection

0   500   1000 Miles

0   500   1000 Kilometers

140°W   120°W   100°W   80°W   60°W   40°W

20°N

Caribbean Sea

Key

- Arctic/Subarctic
- Northwest Coast
- California/Great Basin/Plateau
- Southwest
- Great Plains
- Eastern Woodlands
- Southeast

GEOGRAPHY Skills

Native Americans spread out to populate North America. In the process, they developed many different cultures. Within these culture areas, tribes shared similar ways of life.

1. **Location** On the map, locate **(a)** Northwest Coast culture area, **(b)** Eastern Woodlands culture area, **(c)** Great Plains culture area.

2. **Place (a)** Name two tribes in the Southwest culture area. **(b)** With which culture area are the Cherokees associated?

3. **Critical Thinking Analyzing Information** In which culture areas could Native Americans probably not depend on the sea for food? Explain.

The Plateau region has a cold and dry environment. Surprisingly, however, numbers of hardy plants and animals thrive in the region.

Among the people of the Plateau region were the Utes (YOOTZ) and Shoshones (shoh SHOH neez). They collected pine nuts and dug for roots in the dry soil. They also hunted mountain sheep and rabbits. The Native Americans of the region had few possessions beyond digging sticks, baskets, and tools and weapons needed for hunting.

Cultures of the Northwest Elsewhere in North America the climate was kinder, which helped more complex cultures emerge. The people of the Northwest Coast enjoyed milder temperatures and abundant food supplies. They gathered rich harvests of fish from the sea. From nearby forests, they cut down tall cedar trees and split the trunks into planks for houses and canoes.

With plenty of food, the people of the Pacific Northwest stayed in one place. They built permanent villages and prospered from trade with nearby groups.

Within a village, a family gained status according to how much it owned. Families sometimes competed with one another. To improve its standing, a family might hold a potlatch, or ceremonial dinner, to show off its wealth. The potlatch could last for many days. The family invited many guests and gave everyone gifts. The more goods a family gave away, the more respect it earned. However, people who received gifts at a potlatch were then expected to hold their own potlatches and give gifts.

Native American Culture Groups of North America

ARCTIC/SUBARCTIC

Crees, Inuits, Kutchins, Montagnais
Lived as nomadic hunters and food gatherers in cold climate; honored ocean, weather, and animal spirits

CALIFORNIA/GREAT BASIN/PLATEAU

Nez Percés, Pomos, Shoshones
Lived as hunters and gatherers in small family groups; ate mainly fish, berries, acorns

SOUTHWEST

Apaches, Hohokams, Hopis, Navajos, Pueblos
Lived in villages in homes made of adobe; built irrigation systems to grow corn and other crops; honored earth, sky, and water spirits

SOUTHEAST

Cherokees, Natchez
Grew corn, squash, beans, and other crops; held yearly Green Corn Ceremony to mark end of year and celebrate harvest

GREAT PLAINS

Arapahos, Blackfeet, Cheyennes, Comanches, Crows, Dakotas, Mandans, Osages
Lived in tepees; animals hunted by men; crops grown by women; relied on buffalo to meet basic needs of food, shelter, and clothing

EASTERN WOODLANDS

Algonquins, Ojibwas, Hurons, Iroquois, Leni-Lenapes, Miamis, Pequots, Shawnees
Lived in farming villages, but also hunted for food; long houses shared by several families; women shared social and political power

NORTHWEST COAST

Bella Coolas, Coos, Kwakiutls, Tlingits
Lived in villages; benefited from rich natural resources in forests, rivers, and ocean; held potlatches, or ceremonial dinners, where host families gave gifts to guests to show wealth and gain status

Cultures of the Southeast Many tribes inhabited the southeastern region of North America. Among them were the Natchez (NACH ihz). They benefited from the region's warm, moist climate. They hunted, fished, and farmed along the fertile coast of the Gulf of Mexico.

The Natchez calendar divided the year into 13 months. Each month was named after a food or an animal that the Natchez harvested or hunted. Their months included Strawberry, Little Corn, Mulberry, Deer, Turkey, and Bear.

The ruler of the Natchez was known as the Great Sun and was worshipped as a god. The Great Sun's feet never touched the ground. Either he was carried on a litter or he walked on mats. Below the Great Sun were members of his family, called Little Suns. Next came Nobles, then Honored People, and finally Stinkards, or commoners, who made up the majority of the people.

Marriage laws ensured that membership in each class kept changing. By law, Nobles had to marry Stinkards. Even the Great Sun chose a Stinkard as a wife. In this way, no one family could hold the position of Great Sun forever. In time, even descendants of a Great Sun became Stinkards.

Shared Beliefs

The many Native American groups had a wide variety of beliefs. Yet, they shared some basic ideas.

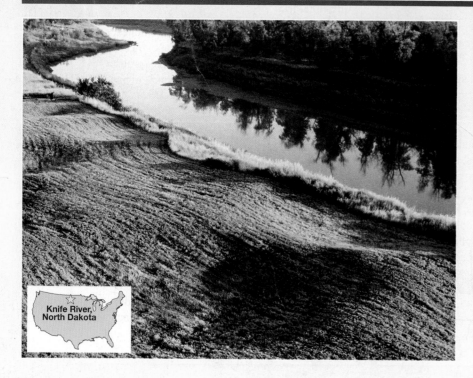

Knife River, North Dakota

Knife River Indian Villages National Historic Site

For thousands of years, Native American groups were drawn to the Knife River in North Dakota by the herds of buffalo that came to the river to drink. Once the area was dotted with the Indians' earthlodges. Time and weather have destroyed the earthlodges. However, visitors can still see depressions where lodges were located.

 Take It to the NET

Virtual Field Trip For an interactive look at Knife River Indian Villages, visit *The American Nation* section of **www.phschool.com**.

Respect for Nature Central to Native American beliefs was a deep respect for the earth. People felt a close bond to plants, animals, and the forces of nature.

Whether hunting, fishing, farming, or gathering wild plants, Native Americans had a great respect for the natural world. Their prayers and ceremonies were designed to maintain a balance between people and the forces of nature. They believed that they must adapt their ways to the natural world in order to survive and prosper.

Native Americans believed that the world was full of powerful, unseen forces and spirits. They honored those spirits, which were thought to act and feel like humans.

In the Pacific Northwest, many tribes relied on fishing. One such group was the Kwakiutls (kwah kee OOT lz). Each year when they caught their first fish of the season, they chanted this prayer:

AS YOU READ **Draw Inferences** As you read this poem, consider how it reflects a respect for the natural world.

> 66 We have come to meet alive, Swimmer,
> do not feel wrong about what I have done to you,
> friend Swimmer,
> for that is the reason why you came,
> that I may spear you,
> that I may eat you,
> Supernatural One, you, Long-Life-Giver, you Swimmer.
> Now protect us, me and my wife. 99

—Kwakiutl Prayer of Thanks

Special Ceremonies In farming areas, tribes held special ceremonies to ensure good rainfall. At midsummer, Pueblo villages in the

Cooking down the sap over heated rocks

Thickened syrup turns into taffy when poured on fresh snow

Collecting the sap from maple trees in early spring

Southwest rang with cries of: "The *kachinas* are coming!" **Kachinas** were spirits, who were represented by masked Native American dancers. The Pueblos believed that the kachinas had the power to bring good harvests.

At Pueblo festivals, the kachinas danced. Religious leaders prayed to the spirits and gave them gifts. Only if the spirits were treated well would they return each year with rain for the Pueblos' crops.

In the Southeast, many tribes held a Green Corn Ceremony when the corn ripened in the fall. The ceremony lasted for several days. It marked the end of the old year and the beginning of a new one. On the last day, a sacred fire was lighted. Dancers circled the flames, and the people enjoyed a great feast. Women then used coals from the sacred fire to make new fires in their own houses.

The Iroquois Confederacy

Among the many Native American groups in the Eastern Woodlands were the Iroquois (IHR uh kwoi) people. They lived mostly in present-day New York State.

The Iroquois called themselves "The People of the Long House." They took great pride in their sturdy dwellings, called long houses. A typical long house was about 150 feet long and 20 feet wide. Twelve or more families lived in a long house.

Viewing History

Iroquois Women at Work

Iroquois homeland

In several Native American cultures, including the Iroquois, women were responsible for growing and gathering food. Here, Iroquois women collect sap to make maple sugar. **Applying Information** *How does making maple taffy require both cold and heat?*

Women had a special place in Iroquoian society. They owned all the household property and were in charge of planting and harvesting. When a man married, he moved in with his wife's family.

Women also had political power. They chose clan leaders. A clan was a group of two or more related families. If a clan leader did not do his job well, the women could remove him from his position.

The Iroquois included five nations that spoke similar languages: the Mohawk, Seneca, Onondaga (ahn uhn DAW guh), Oneida (oh NI duh), and Cayuga (kay YOO guh). Each nation had its own ruling council. Until the late 1500s, the five nations were frequently at war.

Then, around 1570, the five Iroquois nations formed an alliance to end the fighting. According to legend, a religious leader named Dekanawida (deh kan ah WEE dah) inspired Hiawatha (hi ah WAH thah) to organize the alliance. It became known as the League of the Iroquois.

A council of 50 specially chosen tribal leaders, called sachems, met once a year. The council made decisions for the League. Here, too, women had a political role because they chose the sachems and watched over their actions.

Looking Ahead

Scholars do not know exactly how many people lived north of Mexico in 1500. Their figures range from about 1 million to 10 million. Many experts put the figure at about 2.5 million.

Across North America, hundreds of tribes followed their own ways of life. Trade and warfare brought some tribes into contact with one another. Yet, those contacts were limited. By the late 1400s, however, events were taking place on far-off continents that would forever change all of the Native American cultures.

Primary Sources

See "The Constitution of the Iroquois" on page 574 of the Reference Section.

AFTER YOU READ

Section 2 Assessment

Recall

1. **Identify** Explain the significance of (a) Natchez, (b) League of the Iroquois.
2. **Define** (a) culture area, (b) tribe, (c) pit house, (d) potlatch, (e) kachina, (f) clan, (g) sachem.

Comprehension

3. List three ways Native Americans in different culture areas met their needs for food, clothing, and shelter.
4. Give three examples of how climate and resources affected Native American cultures.
5. Describe one belief that Native Americans shared.

6. How did women play an important role in Iroquois culture?

Critical Thinking and Writing

7. **Exploring the Main Idea** Review the Main Idea statement at the beginning of this section. Choose the culture area that you think offered the most favorable conditions for people. Then, make a list of at least three reasons for your choice.
8. **Formulating Questions** Study the map and chart on pages 44–45. Then, pose a question that links the two graphics. Exchange questions with a classmate and answer his or her question.

ACTIVITY

Design a Magazine Cover Design a cover for a special issue of a magazine on the variety of Native American cultures. Include a cover illustration as well as the titles of three or four articles that will appear in the magazine.

Native American Dwellings

Native Americans developed a wide variety of dwellings to suit their different environments. Shown here are a pueblo from the Southwest, a tepee from the Great Plains, and a long house from the Eastern Woodlands.

Pueblo

The walls are made of sandstone blocks plastered with adobe.

Kivas are rooms used for religious ceremonies.

Winter cooking room

Roofs are used as a center for work and socializing.

Sleeping room

Storage room

Drainspouts and splash blocks keep moisture away from roofs and walls.

Tepee

Lodge poles

Smoke flaps

Buffalo sinew

Buffalo hide

Inner lining

This entrance almost always faced the rising sun in the east.

Wooden stakes

Long House

Storage shelves

The stockade provided protection from enemies.

Each fire was shared by two families on either side of the center aisle.

Sleeping benches

The support divided the long house into separate rooms.

Elm bark walls

ACTIVITY

You have been assigned to create a poster promoting an exhibit on different styles of Native American dwellings. Use the information in this chapter to create an original poster that will make people want to attend the exhibit.

3 Trade Networks of Africa and Asia

Reading Focus

- Why did trade flourish in the Muslim world?
- What trading states rose in Africa and what was life like for people in many African cultures?
- How did China's overseas trade expand in the early 1400s?

Key Terms

first global age
Islam
Quran
Silk Road
caravan
city-state
Swahili
savanna
extended family
kinship

Taking Notes

As you read, prepare an outline of this section. Use roman numerals to indicate the major headings of the section, capital letters for the subheadings, and numbers for the supporting details. The outline has been started for you.

> I. The Muslim World
>   A. Rise and spread of Islam
>   1.
>   2.
>   B. Trade routes
>   1.
>   2.
>   C. Silk Road
> II. African Trading States and Cultures
>   A. City-states of East Africa
>   1.
>   2.
>   B. Trading kingdoms of West Africa

Main Idea Busy trade networks linked peoples across large areas of Africa and Asia long before Europeans reached the Americas.

Ancient caravans across the desert

Ask Questions Based on this picture and the description at right, write one question you would ask Ibn Battuta when he returned home from his travels.

Setting the Scene

Ibn Battuta was just 21 years old in 1325 when he set off to see the world. During the next 30 years, he would cover more than 73,000 miles. Ibn Battuta visited lands from Spain and North Africa to the Middle East, India, and China. When he finally returned home for good, he wrote proudly of his travels:

> 66 I have indeed—praise be to God—attained my desire in this world, which was to travel through the earth, and I have attained in this respect what no other person has attained to my knowledge. 99
>
> —Ibn Battuta, *Rhila (Book of Travels)*, 1355

Ibn Battuta was a scholar from North Africa who wanted to learn all he could about the many lands and the different peoples of the Muslim world. In the 1300s, that world reached from lands along the Atlantic Ocean to the borders of China.

Travelers like Ibn Battuta, as well as trade goods, moved along the land and sea routes that linked the peoples of Africa, the Middle East, and Asia. The amount of long-distance trade and travel increased dramatically in the 1400s. For the first time, far-off parts of the world began to be linked. For this reason, this period marks the beginning of what historians call the **first global age.**

The Muslim World

Arab merchants played a large role in this growing trade. Arabia's location in the Middle East made it a major crossroads of the world. It stood at the center of trade routes that linked the Mediterranean world in the west with Asia in the east and Africa in the south.

Rise and Spread of Islam The growth of trade was also linked to the growth of a new religion. In the early 600s, a new religion, **Islam,**

Trade Routes of Asia and Africa

GEOGRAPHY
Skills

Before the 1500s, Asian and African cultures had established important trade routes. This enabled the movement of goods and ideas between civilizations that had had few outside contacts.

1. **Location** On the map locate (a) the Silk Road, (b) Xianyang, (c) Baghdad.

2. **Place** Through what Asian desert did the trade route from Xianyang to Baghdad pass?

3. **Critical Thinking Drawing Conclusions** Why might large cities have developed on the eastern and western ends of the Silk Road but not in the middle?

emerged in Arabia. Its founder was the prophet Muhammad. The central teaching of Islam was belief in one God. (The Arabic word for God is *Allah*.) Followers of Islam, called Muslims, believed that the **Quran** (ku RAHN), the sacred book of Islam, contained the exact word of God as revealed to Muhammad.

Muhammad won many followers among the Arabs. After his death in 632, Islam spread rapidly. Devout followers carried Islam across North Africa and into Spain. Islam spread eastward, too, from Persia to India and beyond.

Islam expanded through trade and conquest. Many people in conquered lands chose to convert to the successful new religion. Elsewhere, Muslim merchants carried the new faith to people living along the trade routes of Asia and Africa.

Islam united Muslims from many lands. Muslims had a basic duty to make a pilgrimage, or journey, to the holy city of Mecca at least once in their lives. Every year, people from across the Muslim world traveled to Mecca. Muslims from North Africa, Persia, Afghanistan, India, Spain, and West Africa crowded Mecca's dusty streets. They prayed in Arabic, the language of Islam.

Trade Routes Muslim merchants traded across a vast area. They sailed to ports around the Indian Ocean. Their ships used large, triangular sails that allowed captains to use the wind even if it changed direction.

Muslim sailors had expert knowledge of wind and weather conditions of the Indian Ocean. As a result, merchants in ports around

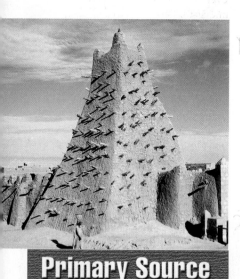

AS YOU READ **Visualize** Form a mental image of a Muslim caravan crossing the desert 2,000 years ago.

Silk Road Some Muslim traders traveled the overland routes that crossed the grasslands, mountains, and deserts of Central Asia and linked China and the Middle East. These routes had become known as the Silk Road because prized Chinese silks had been carried westward along them for more than 2,000 years.

Travel on the Silk Road was dangerous. Desert storms, hunger, and bandits were a constant threat. Traders formed caravans, or groups of people who traveled together for safety. Despite the dangers, trade along the Silk Road prospered.

By the 1400s, trade goods flowed across a huge area. Muslim merchants sold fine porcelains from China, cloth from India, ivory and gold from East Africa, and spices from Southeast Asia.

African Trading States and Cultures

Trade routes played a large role in Africa, too. Long-distance trade routes crossed the vast Sahara, the desert linking West Africa and North Africa.

A peaceful afternoon in a West African village might be pierced by sounds of a horn. Children would shout, "Batafo! Batafo!" Traders! Soon, a long line of porters and camels arrived. Villagers watched as the tired travelers unloaded sacks of salt or dried fish. Gold, fabrics, jewelry, and slaves were also part of the caravan.

City-States of East Africa Trade had long flowed up and down the coast of East Africa. Small villages that had good natural harbors grew into busy trading centers.

Gold from Zimbabwe (zihm BAH bweh), a powerful inland state, was carried to coastal cities such as Kilwa and Sofala. From there, ships carried the gold, and prized goods such as hardwoods and ivory, across the Indian Ocean to India and China.

Wealth from trade helped local East African rulers build strong city-states. A city-state is a large town that has its own government and controls the surrounding countryside.

Many rulers of these city-states became Muslims. In time, Muslim culture influenced East African traditions. The blend of cultures led to the rise of a new language, Swahili, which blended Arabic words and local African languages.

Trading Kingdoms of West Africa A region of grasslands, called the savanna, covers much of West Africa. Several rich trading kingdoms emerged there. Among the best known were Mali and Songhai (SAWNG hi). The city of Timbuktu was the major trading center for both kingdoms.

The kingdom of Mali rose in about A.D. 1200 and flourished for about 200 years. Like the rulers of East Africa's city-states, many rulers in West African kingdoms adopted the religion of Islam.

Mali's most famous ruler, Mansa Musa, was a Muslim. In 1324, the emperor made a pilgrimage to Mecca. On the way, he and his caravan stopped in Cairo, Egypt. His wealth in gold amazed the Egyptians. In time, stories of Mansa Musa's immense wealth reached Europe. A

Primary Source

Timbuktu

Hasan al-Wazan, also known as Leo Africanus, described Timbuktu in 1526:

"The inhabitants are very rich. . . . The royal court is magnificent and very well organized. . . . There are in Timbuktu numerous judges, teachers, and priests, all properly appointed by the king. He greatly honors learning. Many handwritten books . . . are also sold. There is more profit from this commerce than from all other merchandise."

—Hasan al-Wazan, from *The Description of Africa,* 1526

Analyzing Primary Sources
What were some signs of prosperity in Timbuktu?

Spanish map from that time shows Mansa Musa on his throne, holding a golden object. The mapmaker wrote these words nearby:

> **❝** So abundant is the gold in his country that this lord is the richest and most noble king in all the land. **❞**
>
> —Catalan Atlas, 1375

In the 1400s, Songhai emerged as the most powerful kingdom in West Africa. Muslim emperors extended Songhai's power and made Timbuktu into a thriving city.

Village and Family Life Ways of life varied greatly across the huge continent of Africa. While powerful trading states flourished in some regions, most people lived outside these kingdoms. Many lived in small villages. They made a living by herding, fishing, or farming.

Family relationships were important in African cultures. Although family patterns varied across Africa, many people lived within an extended family. In an **extended family,** several generations live in one household. An extended family usually included grandparents, parents, children, and sometimes aunts, uncles, and cousins. The grandparents, or elders, received special respect for their wisdom and knowledge.

Ties of **kinship,** or sharing a common ancestor, linked families. People related by kinship owed loyalty to one another. Kinship ties encouraged a strong sense of community and cooperation.

Religious beliefs varied widely across Africa. Yet, African beliefs reflected some common threads. Links among family members lasted even after a person died. In their rituals and ceremonies, Africans honored the spirits of their ancestors as well as the forces of nature. Powerful spirits, they believed, could harm or could help the living.

Chinese Voyages of Trade and Exploration

Africa had many different cultures and kingdoms. By contrast, in China, power was centered on the emperor. Although most Chinese rulers allowed trade, they were often suspicious of outsiders. After all, they thought, outsiders did not speak Chinese or follow Chinese ways.

The Great Treasure Fleet The young emperor who came to power in 1402 was eager for trade. He ordered a huge fleet to be built and named Zheng He (DZUNG HEH) to command it. Zheng He's fleet numbered more than 300 ships. It

Historic Journeys Between 1405 and 1433, the Chinese admiral Zheng He (bottom left) led a fleet of large ships like this one on journeys of exploration to Southeast Asia, India, and Arabia. By the time of Zheng He's death, Chinese influence had spread across a wide region. **Drawing Inferences** *What do you think it would take to maintain Chinese influence in these areas of Southeast Asia, India, and Arabia after Zheng He's death?*

carried about 28,000 sailors and tons of trade goods. The largest ships were more than 400 feet long. Each had nine tall masts that held giant square red sails.

Between 1405 and 1433, Zheng He made seven long voyages. His fleet traded at ports in Southeast Asia, India, and Arabia. Chinese ships then sailed on to Mogadishu in East Africa. At every port, Chinese traders carried on a brisk business. They expanded Chinese trade and influence across a wide region.

The Voyages End The great fleet returned home with exotic goods and animals, such as giraffes, that the Chinese had never seen. Soon after Zheng He's death in 1435, China's overseas voyages abruptly ended. A new emperor decided that China had nothing to learn from the outside world. He outlawed foreign travel, and the great fleet was left to rot in coastal ports.

What Might Have Been Historians sometimes discuss what might have happened if events had taken a slightly different course. One question historians ponder is what if Zheng He had led his fleet around the southern tip of Africa or across the Pacific?

Chinese ships could certainly have made such long voyages. They were much larger than the ships commanded by Christopher Columbus in 1492. When Columbus sailed westward across the Atlantic Ocean, he had three tiny ships. They carried only 90 sailors, compared to the approximately 28,000 on Zheng He's ships.

If Zheng He had crossed the Pacific Ocean and reached the Americas, American history might have turned out very different. Instead, China stopped its voyages and closed its doors to trade. Within a few years, however, several small European nations began to hunt for new trade routes to Asia. Their eagerness for trade led to daring voyages across the Atlantic Ocean.

Section 3 Assessment

Recall

1. **Identify** Explain the significance of **(a)** Ibn Battuta, **(b)** first global age, **(c)** Islam, **(d)** Quran, **(e)** Silk Road, **(f)** Swahili, **(g)** Timbuktu, **(h)** Zheng He.
2. **Define (a)** caravan, **(b)** city-state, **(c)** savanna, **(d)** extended family, **(e)** kinship.

Comprehension

3. How did trade and religion link people in the Muslim world?
4. What were some common values that linked the people of many different African cultures?
5. How did China's emperor encourage overseas trade in the early 1400s?

Critical Thinking and Writing

6. **Exploring the Main Idea** Review the Main Idea statement at the beginning of this section. Then, write a paragraph describing networks linking Africa and Asia in 1400. Explain how these networks helped the movement of goods, people, and ideas.
7. **Solving Problems** Suppose a European ruler wanted to profit from trade with Asia. The routes through the Mediterranean and across Asia were already controlled by others, however. How might the ruler try to get a foothold in the Asian trade?

ACTIVITY

Take It to the NET
Connecting to Today
Use the Internet to find out more about either Ibn Battuta or the Chinese admiral Zheng He. With the information you find, prepare a script for a TV news report. Visit *The American Nation* section of **www.phschool.com** for help in completing the activity.

4 Tradition and Change in Europe

Reading Focus

- What Jewish and Christian traditions influenced European civilization?
- How did ancient Greek and Roman traditions affect later Europeans?
- How did the Crusades and the growth of trade change Europe in the Middle Ages?
- How was the Renaissance a time of expanding horizons?

Key Terms

salvation
missionary
direct democracy
republic
feudalism
manor
Crusades
astrolabe
Renaissance

Taking Notes

Copy the concept web below. Add as many ovals as you need. As you read, fill in each blank oval with important facts about the traditions that shaped European civilization. Two ovals have been completed to help you get started.

Ancient Greek democracy

EUROPEAN TRADITIONS

Jewish tradition of obeying God's law

Main Idea European civilization, which was shaped by many ancient traditions, emerged from a long period of isolation during the 1400s.

Setting the Scene

The sturdy ship dipped in and out of the rolling waves of the Atlantic Ocean. Above, stars dotted the night sky.

At the first hint of dawn, a cabin boy checked the hourglass, which was used to keep track of time. It took 30 minutes for sand to run from the top half of the glass into the bottom. So every half-hour, the boy had to turn the glass. Afterward, he prayed aloud:

> **66** Blessed be the light of day and the Holy Cross, we say; and the Lord of Truth and the Holy Trinity. Blessed be the immortal soul and the Lord who keeps it whole. **99**
>
> —Eugenio de Salazar, 1573

The boy's prayer was a tradition on European sailing ships. In the 1400s, bold Europeans set out to explore the world. They brought with them their traditions that, over time, would affect people in many lands.

AS YOU READ Sailing the high seas

Draw Inferences How did attitudes toward the unknown affect exploration of the high seas?

Jewish and Christian Traditions

European civilization emerged slowly during the long period from about A.D. 500 to 1400. As in other societies, religious beliefs played an important role in European life. They provided moral guidance and helped people understand their place in the world. European beliefs were shaped by two religions of the ancient Middle East, Judaism and Christianity.

Judaism and the Importance of Laws Judaism refers to the religious beliefs of the Israelites, who lived more than 3,000 years ago. (Later, the Israelites became known as Jews.) Jews believe in one God and feel a sacred duty to obey God's rules.

The history and laws of the ancient Jews were recorded in the Torah. The Jews credited Moses with bringing God's laws to them. Those laws included the Ten Commandments, a set of religious and moral rules.

The Jews believed that every Jew must obey the Ten Commandments and other religious laws. No one was above God's laws, even the most powerful ruler. That view differed from most religions of that time, which regarded rulers as gods. More than 2,000 years ago, many Jews left their homeland. This scattering of people sent Jews to different parts of the world. Wherever they settled, Jews maintained their identity as a people by obeying their religion's laws and traditions.

Christianity and the Teachings of Jesus About 2,000 years ago, a Jew named Jesus lived in a province of the Roman empire. Jesus believed in the Ten Commandments and other Jewish traditions. He preached about God's goodness and mercy. Some followers began to call him the Messiah, a savior chosen by God.

The Gospels, which recount the life of Jesus, tell how crowds flocked to hear Jesus teach and perform miracles. Local officials, however, saw Jesus as a political threat. They had him arrested, tried, and crucified—a Roman form of execution.

The life and teachings of Jesus inspired a new religion, Christianity. The new faith included many Jewish traditions, such as belief in one God and the Ten Commandments, along with the teachings of Jesus. Like Jewish teachers, Jesus emphasized love, mercy, and forgiveness.

Jesus taught that anyone, rich or poor, could achieve salvation, or everlasting life. That belief, which meant that everyone was equal in the eyes of God, appealed to many people. As Christianity spread across the Roman empire, officials sometimes persecuted Christians. However, the persecutions did not slow the growth of the religion. Eventually, around A.D. 391, Christianity became the official religion of the empire.

By then, Christians had organized a strong church with its own government and officials. The church sent out missionaries, people who spread Christian teachings across Europe. Slowly, missionaries brought many non-Christian peoples of Europe into the new faith.

Greek and Roman Traditions

Two ancient civilizations shaped European traditions over the centuries. They were the civilizations that grew up in ancient Greece and Rome.

Greek Ideas About Government Around 500 B.C., Greece entered a golden age. Greek artists created fine marble statues and designed elegant temples. Poets and playwrights created works that are still read today.

Greek thinkers, such as Socrates and Aristotle, valued human reason. Using reason, they said, individuals could understand the natural world. Other Greek thinkers made important contributions to science and mathematics. They developed the study of geometry and pioneered the idea that all matter is made up of small moving atoms. Greek doctors tried to diagnose and treat diseases using scientific methods. Greek thinkers debated many issues, including the best kind of government. Greek ideas about government would have a great impact on later European thinking.

Unlike in the large empires of the ancient world, the Greeks lived in small city-states. At first, a monarch ruled each city-state. Slowly, some city-states developed other kinds of government. In some, a king ruled. In others, a few wealthy people controlled the government. Ancient Athens, for example, first created direct democracy. **Direct democracy** is a form of government in which ordinary citizens have the power to govern.

Athenians were proud of their government. They believed that people could think and act for themselves. All citizens could attend the assembly and make laws for the city. Athenian democracy was very limited, however. Only free men whose parents had been born in Athens were citizens. Most people in Athens were not citizens. This included all women and slaves and men who came to Athens from other city-states.

Roman Government and Law As the Greeks entered their golden age, a few small villages in Italy were growing into the city of Rome. From a small city-state, Rome would one day become a huge empire. In the process, it absorbed ideas from many other peoples, including the Greeks. It also created its own traditions, especially in the fields of law and government.

In 509 B.C., the Romans overthrew their king and set up a republic. A **republic** is a system of government in which citizens choose representatives to govern them. In the Roman Republic, a senate and assembly made the laws.

As Rome expanded, the republic faced a series of crises that caused military leaders to seize power. Among them was Julius Caesar, who named himself dictator for life. After Caesar's murder, his nephew, Octavian, declared himself emperor in 27 B.C. He received the title Caesar Augustus.

The Roman empire lasted for almost 500 years. Rome spread its language, Latin, and ideas about law across a wide area. In Roman tradition, everyone was equal before the law. Accused people were considered innocent until proven guilty. Rome also set up rules about the use of evidence in court. Roman legal traditions would later influence Europe.

Decline of Rome The Roman empire declined slowly. Invaders attacked and overran many regions. Trade and travel slowed. In place of the Roman empire, Europe was splintered into many small, warring kingdoms.

During this time, the achievements of Greece and Rome were largely forgotten. A few Christian monasteries preserved ancient manuscripts. Others survived in the Islamic world. Much later, as you will read, Europeans would rediscover these ancient texts. Then, Greek and Roman traditions would, in turn, come to play a key role in American history.

AS YOU READ **Ask Questions**
Rephrase the subheadings in this section as questions. As you read, look for answers to these questions.

Viewing History

Roman Senators

In the Roman Republic, forms of government were established to take power away from the few and give it to the many. The bas-relief below shows two Roman senators. **Summarizing** *Based on the information on Roman government, write two sentences explaining how the Romans established traditions of government that would influence later societies.*

The Middle Ages

The period from about A.D. 500 to about 1400 is known as the Middle Ages. During the early Middle Ages, invasion and war were common. Without Roman armies, people had to find other means of defending themselves.

Feudalism A new kind of government evolved during the Middle Ages. Kings and queens divided their lands among warrior nobles. In return, nobles promised to fight for the ruler when asked. This system of rule by lords who ruled their lands but owed loyalty and military service to a monarch is called feudalism (FYOOD 'l ihz uhm).

At the top of feudal society stood the king and the most powerful lords. Next came the lesser nobles. Most people in feudal society were peasants who farmed the lord's lands and could not leave the land without the lord's permission.

Daily Life Feudal life revolved around the manor, which included the lord's castle and the lands around it. Manor lands might include several villages.

Each manor was self-sufficient. That is, people made almost everything they needed. Life for peasants was hard. They struggled to produce enough food just to survive.

The most powerful force was the Roman Catholic Church. It ruled more than religious life. The Church owned large amounts of land and was the source of education. The clergy were often the only people who could read and write. Because of their efforts, much of the learning from the ancient world was preserved.

By about A.D. 900, life began to change. Peasants used new methods of farming to produce more food. Warfare declined and trade began to grow. Slowly, people began to look beyond their isolated villages.

The Crusades The pace of change increased between 1100 and 1300 in part because of the Crusades. The Crusades were a series of wars fought by Christians to control the Holy Land. The Holy Land included Jerusalem and the other places where Jesus had lived and taught. Muslims had controlled this region for centuries.

During the Crusades, tens of thousands of Christians journeyed to the Middle East. Fighting between Christians and Muslims continued for almost 200 years. Christians won some victories. But in the end, they failed to win control of the Holy Land.

Growth of Trade The Crusades had important effects on Europe, however. Crusaders traveled beyond their villages

Viewing History

Peasants and Lords
In the Middle Ages, it was the peasants' duty to farm the lord's lands. The lord in his magnificent castle had the duty of protecting the peasants. **Making Predictions** *Based on this painting from France in the early 1400s, and the information on the Middle Ages, what problems do you think could arise between peasant and lord?*

France

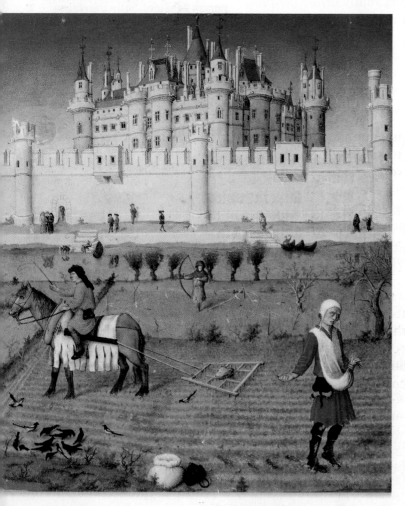

and came into contact with other civilizations. In the Middle East, they tasted new foods, such as rice, oranges, dates, and new spices. They saw beautiful silks and woven rugs.

Europe had traded with the Middle East for many years before the Crusades. However, returning Crusaders demanded more of the Asian foods, spices, silks, and rugs. Italian merchants realized that people would pay high prices for such goods. They outfitted ships and increased trade with the Muslim world.

New Tools for Navigation Trade brought new knowledge. From the Muslim world, Europeans acquired sailing skills and the magnetic compass. Muslims had earlier adopted the magnetic compass from the Chinese. The special needle of the compass always pointed north, which helped ships stay on course.

Another useful instrument was the astrolabe (AS troh layb), which helped sailors determine their latitude while at sea. These new instruments let Europeans sail far out to sea, beyond sight of land. By 1500, Portugal had taken the lead in this new overseas travel.

The Renaissance Expands Horizons

Increased trade and travel made Europeans eager to learn more about the wider world. Scholars looked in monastery libraries for manuscripts of ancient Greek and Roman works. Some traveled to the Muslim world, where many ancient works had been preserved.

As scholars studied ancient learning, they began to make their own discoveries. They produced new books on art, medicine, astronomy, and chemistry. This great burst of learning was called the Renaissance (REHN uh sahns), a French word meaning rebirth. It lasted from the late 1300s until the 1600s.

A new invention, the printing press, helped to spread Renaissance learning. A German printer named Johannes Gutenberg (GOOT uhn berg) is credited with this invention in the 1430s. Before then, books were scarce and costly because each was copied by hand. With the printing press, large numbers of books could be produced quickly and at a low cost. Soon more people began to read, and learning spread more quickly.

The Search for New Trade Routes During the Renaissance, trade brought new prosperity. European rulers began to increase their power. In England and France, kings and queens tried to bring powerful feudal lords under their control. In Spain and Portugal,

Portuguese Routes of Exploration

Key
- - -> Dias, 1487–1488
——> Da Gama, 1497–1499

Robinson Projection

0   1000   2000 Miles

0   1000   2000 Kilometers

GEOGRAPHY Skills

New technologies and new skills allowed Portuguese sailors to make historic voyages along the coast of Africa and across the Indian Ocean to India.

1. **Location** On the map locate (a) Portugal, (b) Cape of Good Hope, (c) Indian Ocean.

2. **Movement** Describe the route taken by Da Gama.

3. **Critical Thinking Drawing Inferences** Why do you think the Cape of Good Hope was an important landmark to sailors?

Primary Sources

See William Fichet, "The Printing Press: 'New Makers of Books'" on page 575 of the Reference Section.

West Africa

The ivory carving above was done by an African artisan in the 1500s. **Drawing Inferences** *How do you think Africans perceived the Portuguese?*

Christian monarchs drove out Muslim rulers, who had governed there for centuries.

Rulers in England, France, Spain, and Portugal were eager to increase their wealth. They saw the great profits that could be made through trade. However, Muslim and Italian merchants controlled the trade routes across the Mediterranean Sea. So, Western Europe's leaders began hunting for other routes to Asia.

European rulers also looked to Africa as a source of riches. Tales of Mansa Musa's wealth had created a stir in Europe, but no one knew the source of African gold.

Portuguese Voyages Portugal was an early leader in the search for a new trade route to Asia and for the source of African gold. In the early 1400s, Prince Henry, known as Henry the Navigator, encouraged sea captains to sail south along the coast of West Africa. Realizing that Portugal needed better navigators to accomplish the task, he set up an informal school to teach sailors techniques of navigation and the art of shipbuilding.

Under Henry's guidance, the Portuguese designed a new type of ship, the caravel (KAR uh vehl). With triangular sails and a steering rudder, caravels could be sailed into the wind. Portuguese caravels stopped at many places along the coast of West Africa. They traded cloth, silver, textiles, and grain for gold, ivory, and slaves.

Slowly, Portuguese explorers ventured farther south, hoping to find a sea route around Africa to the rich spice trade of Asia. In 1488, Bartolomeu Dias reached the southern tip of Africa.

Nine years later, in 1497, Vasco da Gama rounded the Cape of Good Hope at the southern tip of Africa. He then sailed up the coast of East Africa and across the Indian Ocean to India. The Portuguese pushed on to the East Indies, the islands of Southeast Asia and the source of valuable spices.

AFTER YOU READ

Section 4 Assessment

Recall

1. Identify Explain the significance of **(a)** Crusades, **(b)** Renaissance, **(c)** Johannes Gutenberg, **(d)** Prince Henry.

2. Define (a) salvation, **(b)** missionary, **(c)** direct democracy, **(d)** republic, **(e)** feudalism, **(f)** manor, **(g)** astrolabe.

Comprehension

3. Describe one tradition from Judaism and Christianity that influenced later Europeans.

4. What were three ideas that Europeans learned from ancient Greece and Rome?

5. How did the Crusades help bring changes to Europe?

6. Why did Renaissance rulers in Western Europe want to find new routes to Asia?

Critical Thinking and Writing

7. Exploring the Main Idea Review the Main Idea statement at the beginning of this section. Then, identify reasons for the European exploration of North America.

8. Drawing Conclusions Write an editorial explaining whether you think the Crusades were a success or a failure.

ACTIVITY

Writing a Diary You are a sailor on Vasco da Gama's voyage of 1497. With a partner, write two different diary entries that express your hopes and fears about the voyage.

History books are bursting with information. Although you can't remember every fact, you can learn to identify the main ideas and note the details that explain and support them. The passage below describes the growth of trade between Europe and other regions of the world. After you have read the passage, use "Learn the Skill" below to help you identify the main idea.

Toward the end of the Middle Ages, European nations developed an interest in trading with Asia. Several factors contributed to this interest. Perhaps the most important of these was the huge profit that European nations could gain through such trade. Rulers of countries including Spain, France, England, and Portugal quickly saw that increased prosperity from trade could be turned into increased power for them.

Trade with Asia promised several other benefits as well. The shimmering silks and colorful rugs of Asia pleased and intrigued Europeans. So, too, did foreign foods such as oranges, rice, and dates. Exotic spices such as ginger and pepper not only improved food but also helped to preserve it. Still other reasons that Europeans sought trade were a new awareness of the rest of the world and a curiosity to learn more about it.

Learn the Skill *To identify main ideas and supporting details, use the following steps:*

1. **Find the main idea.** The main idea is what the passage is about. Often, the main idea is stated in the first sentence of a paragraph. However, it can occur in other parts of a paragraph as well.

2. **Restate the main idea.** To be sure you understand what a paragraph is about, restate the main idea in your own words.

3. **Look for details.** These include facts, reasons, explanations, examples, and descriptions that tell more about the main idea.

4. **Make connections.** Note how the details support and expand the main idea.

Practice the Skill *Answer the following questions about the paragraphs above:*

1. What is the main idea sentence in each of the two paragraphs?

2. Restate the main idea in each paragraph in your own words.

3. Identify a detail that supports the main idea in the first paragraph.

4. **(a)** How do the details in the first paragraph help explain the main idea of that paragraph? **(b)** How do the details in the second paragraph expand the main idea of that paragraph?

Apply the Skill *See the Chapter Review and Assessment.*

Review and Assessment

CREATING A CHAPTER SUMMARY

On a sheet of paper, make a table like this one to describe the world in 1500. For each area of the world, include the key events or developments that were taking place there. Some information has been filled in to help you get started.

THE AMERICAS	ASIA	AFRICA	EUROPE
Aztec empire prospers	Chinese civilization already 3,000 years old		

For additional review and enrichment activities, see the interactive version of *The American Nation,* available on the Web and on CD-ROM.

Take It to the NET

Chapter Self-Test For practice test questions for Chapter 2, visit *The American Nation* section of **www.phschool.com**.

Building Vocabulary

Write sentences, using the chapter vocabulary words listed below, leaving blanks where the vocabulary words would go. Exchange your sentences with another student and fill in the blanks in each other's sentences.

1. glacier
2. surplus
3. culture area
4. pit house
5. sachem
6. city-state
7. extended family
8. direct democracy
9. republic
10. feudalism

Reviewing Key Facts

11. What civilizations emerged in present-day Mexico? (Section 1)
12. Name two Native American cultures that developed in North America and explain how each adapted to its environment. (Section 2)
13. What role did trade play in the Muslim world? (Section 3)
14. How did trade affect East Africa and West Africa before the 1500s? (Section 3)

15. How did the Renaissance open new horizons for Europeans? (Section 4)

Critical Thinking and Writing

16. **Comparing** Make a list comparing the methods used by the Aztecs to farm swampy Lake Texcoco to those used by the Anasazi to farm the desert Southwest.
17. **Contrasting** **(a)** Make a list of differences between the cultures of the Great Basin and those of the Southeast. **(b)** Write a paragraph explaining how those differences were related to the climate and resources of each region.
18. **Connecting to Geography: Movement** The movement of people, goods, and ideas is another key link between geography and history. **(a)** Describe the trade networks that had grown up across Africa and Asia by the 1400s. **(b)** Give one example of how trade led to the exchange of ideas.
19. **Synthesizing Information** Write a paragraph describing how the Renaissance led Europeans to explore unfamiliar lands.

Analyzing Primary Sources

Not all primary sources consist of words. A painting can also be a primary source. For example, the painting below contains some valuable information about how the Aztecs lived. Study it, and then answer the questions below.

20. The seated person is the emperor. What is the other person doing?
21. What kinds of gifts can you see in the picture?
22. What do you think is the attitude of the person at right?
23. What title would you give to this painting? Explain why you chose this title.

Finding Main Ideas and Supporting Details

Read the passage below, which comes from a high school American history textbook. Then, answer the questions that follow.

❝ No matter how Native Americans adapted to their environment, they generally looked to the family to fulfill many of their social needs. Their families provided them with many of the services we expect today, from governments, churches, and private organizations. Such services included medical care, child care, settlement of disputes, and education. ❞

—Andrew Cayton,
America: Pathways to the Present, 1998

24. Which statement best reflects the main idea of the selection?
    A Families provide medical care.
    B Families support people.
    C Indian families were not important.
    D Families provided for many social needs of Native Americans.
25. What details does the author use to support the main point of the selection?

ACTIVITIES

Connecting With . . . Science and Technology

Identifying Causes and Effects By the 1400s, Europeans were beginning to use new instruments and knowledge about navigation. Several new technologies are discussed in the chapter. Write a news bulletin for two new technologies, describing how each one helped Europeans undertake voyages of exploration.

 ## Take It to the NET

Connecting to Today

Use the Internet to find out more about a Native American tribe that still lives in its traditional culture area. Create a fact sheet describing its location, leadership, traditions, and goals for the future. For help in starting this activity, visit *The American Nation* section of **www.phschool.com**.

Evaluating Internet Sites

Reviewing Sites About the First American Civilizations Use the Internet to find at least two sites with visual materials about the Mayas, Aztecs, or Incas. Write a review of these sites. In it, describe the kind of information they gave, the quality and quantity of visuals, and their usefulness in learning about the civilization. Include the addresses of the sites. For help in starting this activity, visit *The American Nation* section of **www.phschool.com**.

The Mother of Nations

Joseph Bruchac

Introduction Joseph Bruchac is a scholar of Native American culture and an author, poet, novelist, and storyteller. He has written more than 50 books and has won a Lifetime Achievement Award of the Native Writers' Circle of the Americas. Bruchac grew up and still lives in the foothills of the Adirondack Mountains in New York State. His story "The Mother of Nations" deals with the founding of the Iroquois Confederation.

Vocabulary Before you read the selection, find the meanings of these words in a dictionary: **longhouse, descendent, stockaded, exhort.**

Joseph Bruchac

Long ago there was a woman whose longhouse stood to the west at Oniagara. Her people, whom she led, were those known as the Cultivators, the Hadiyent-togeo-no and they were cousins to the Ongwe-oweh.

It was said that this woman was the direct descendent of the first woman born on the Earth. Her name was Jigonsahseh, the Lynx. Her longhouse stood by the warriors' path which ran from east to west. Though she was unable to stop the continual war which tore apart the nations in those days, still her words were respected. She always fed those who passed by her door and she was called by many "The Great Mother."

When The Peacemaker, who brought the great message from the Master of Life, set out into the world he went first to the land of the Cultivators. He crossed Sganya-dai-yo, the Great Beautiful Lake, in his canoe made of white stone. He saw that there were no cornfields planted because of the continual warfare. The towns were stockaded and filled with people who were hungry and quarrelling.

The Peacemaker went to the house of Jigonsahseh. She welcomed him and placed food before him. When he had finished eating she spoke. "You have come to bring a message," she said. "My mind is open to it. I wish to hear."

Then The Peacemaker spoke. He told her he was acting as the messenger of the Master of Life. He said that his message was to bring justice, peace, and good laws for the people. The wars between the Ongweoweh, the True Human Beings, would cease.

"This message is good," said Jigonsahseh. "What form shall it take among the People?"

Then The Peacemaker explained. "It will take the form of the Longhouse. There will be many fires within the Longhouse, many families. But all will live together under the guidance of a wise Clan Mother. The five nations of the Ongwe-oweh will become of one mind and be known as the People of the Longhouse. Together they will seek the way of Peace which would be open to all the nations.

"My hands are open to this message. I reach out and grasp it," said Jigonsahseh.

Then it was decided that, since a woman was the first to accept this new way, from that day on the women would possess the titles and give them to the men who would speak for their nations in the Longhouse. These women would name from their clans the men who would serve the people. The Clan Mothers would give them the horns of office and if they did not do their jobs well the women could take back their titles.

Iroquois flag showing the five-nation symbol

From that day on, the longhouse of Jigonsahseh would be known as the Peace House. All would now call her the Yegowaneh, "The Mother of Nations." In the land of her people there would be no war. The Cultivators would now be known as the Attiwendaronk, "The Neutral Nation."

So it came to be that in the land of the Yegowaneh, the Mother of Nations, there was no war. Her name was passed down from mother to eldest daughter. When it was necessary for the People of the Longhouse to deal with other nations who had not joined the League of Peace or when there were disputes between nations, the War Captains would always pass first through her land and deliver Peace Belts to the Yegowaneh.

She would give them food, as had been the custom of all those who carried the name of Jigonsahseh and were descended from the first woman born on Earth. Then the Mother of Nations would exhort them to seek peace and accept war only as a last resort. So it is said among the People of the Longhouse that the path of war runs through the House of Peace.

Analyzing Literature

1. Why was The Peacemaker troubled when he visited the land of the Cultivators?
   - **A** They were not worshipping him in the proper ways.
   - **B** They were not planting crops because they were fighting among themselves.
   - **C** They had gone off to war in far-off lands, leaving their families behind.
   - **D** They spent too much time hunting and trapping and not enough raising crops.

2. How did the long house symbolize the Iroquois?
   - **A** Many families lived under one roof in the long house, just as the tribes lived together in unity in the world.
   - **B** The long house was made of strong wood, just as the people were strong.
   - **C** Women built the long house, just as women held titles of power.
   - **D** People shared the long house, just as they shared land with the woodland animals.

3. **Critical Thinking and Writing** **Comparing** List three ways the information in this story supports the information about the Iroquois in Section 2 of Chapter 2.

Exploration and Colonization

1492–1675

1 **An Era of Exploration**
2 **Spain Builds an Empire**
3 **Colonizing North America**
4 **Building the Jamestown Colony**
5 **Seeking Religious Freedom**

Christopher
Columbus

Fort of Castillo de San Marcos at St. Augustine

**AMERICAN
EVENTS**

1492

Seeking a westward
route from Europe to
Asia, Christopher
Columbus reaches
the Caribbean. His
voyage marks the
start of regular con-
tact between Europe
and the Americas.

1519

Spanish warrior
Hernando Cortés
begins conquest of
the Aztec empire.

1565

Spain builds a fort at
St. Augustine. Today,
St. Augustine, Florida,
is the oldest city in
the United States.

1475 ★ 1525 ★ 1575

**WORLD
EVENTS**

1500s ▲
Atlantic slave
trade begins.

▲ **1517**
Protestant Reformation
begins in Europe.

European Voyages of Exploration, 1487–1522

In the late 1400s, European explorers began to sail and chart the oceans of the world.

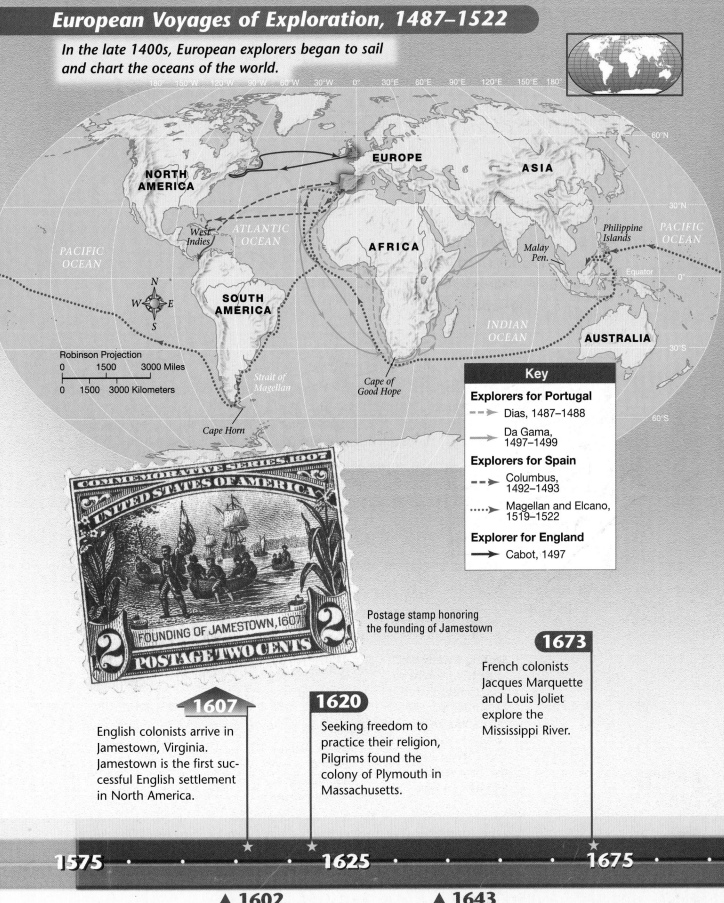

NORTH AMERICA

EUROPE

ASIA

West Indies

ATLANTIC OCEAN

AFRICA

PACIFIC OCEAN

Philippine Islands

Malay Pen.

PACIFIC OCEAN

SOUTH AMERICA

INDIAN OCEAN

AUSTRALIA

Equator

Robinson Projection

0   1500   3000 Miles

0   1500   3000 Kilometers

Strait of Magellan

Cape of Good Hope

Cape Horn

Key

Explorers for Portugal

- - - ► Dias, 1487–1488

——► Da Gama, 1497–1499

Explorers for Spain

- - - ► Columbus, 1492–1493

·····► Magellan and Elcano, 1519–1522

Explorer for England

——► Cabot, 1497

Postage stamp honoring the founding of Jamestown

1607

English colonists arrive in Jamestown, Virginia. Jamestown is the first successful English settlement in North America.

1620

Seeking freedom to practice their religion, Pilgrims found the colony of Plymouth in Massachusetts.

1673

French colonists Jacques Marquette and Louis Joliet explore the Mississippi River.

1575 · · · · · 1625 · · · · 1675 · · ·

▲ **1602**
Dutch East India Company is formed to trade in Asia.

▲ **1643**
Louis XIV becomes king of France.

1 An Era of Exploration

Reading Focus

- Why did the voyage of Christopher Columbus have a more lasting impact than earlier voyages?
- How did Spanish explorers find a route across the Pacific Ocean?
- How did exploration set off a global exchange of goods and ideas?

Key Terms

colony

turning point

circumnavigate

Columbian Exchange

Taking Notes

Copy the chart below. As you read, complete the chart to show some of the effects of the journey of Christopher Columbus. Add as many boxes as you need.

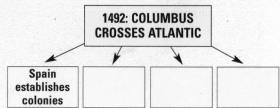

1492: COLUMBUS CROSSES ATLANTIC

→ Spain establishes colonies

Main Idea Despite some earlier contacts, Europeans began to explore the Americas fully only after Columbus reached the West Indies in 1492.

Viking warriors

Draw Inferences Based on this story, what impact do you think the Viking settlement had on future events?

Setting the Scene

A band of seafarers sailed across the Atlantic to settle at a place they called Vinland. To their surprise, a multitude of kayaks came paddling by one morning—"so many that the bay looked as though it was sown with charcoal." One settler recalled:

> **66** As soon as [the two peoples] met they began trading together. Most of all, these people wanted to buy red cloth, in return for which they had furs to offer and gray [seal] skins. **99**
>
> —*Saga of Erik the Red*

Trading continued until a large bull that the seafarers had brought with them "ran out of the forest bellowing loudly." The natives, who had never seen such an animal, ran to their kayaks and paddled away.

This meeting took place about 1,000 years ago. It was one of the earliest encounters between Native Americans and Europeans. The people in kayaks were Inuits. The settlers were Vikings, seafaring people from Scandinavia in Northern Europe.

The Vikings abandoned the settlement after only a few years. Nearly 500 years later, an expedition from Spain sailed into the Caribbean Sea. This time, the arrival of Europeans launched an era of exploration that dramatically affected both the Americas and Europe.

Early Voyages to the Americas

Many stories exist about early people from Europe or Asia sailing to the Americas. Yet, real evidence has been hard to find. Most experts agree that such voyages were rare, if they occurred at all.

The Vikings left behind the most detailed record of their voyages. In 1001, Viking sailors led by Leif Ericson reached the northern tip of North America. Today, many archaeologists believe that the Viking settlement of Vinland was located in present-day Newfoundland. The Vikings did not stay in Vinland long and no one is sure why they left. However, Viking stories describe fierce battles with Skraelings, the Viking name for the Inuits.

Some historians suggest that Asians continued to cross the Bering Sea into North America after the last ice age ended. Others believe that ancient seafarers from Polynesia may have traveled to the Americas using their knowledge of the stars and winds. Modern Polynesians have sailed canoes thousands of miles in this way. Still others claim that fishing boats from China and Japan blew off course and landed on the western coast of South America.

Perhaps such voyages occurred. If so, they were long forgotten. The peoples of Asia and Europe had no knowledge of the Americas and their remarkable civilizations.

Columbus Reaches the Americas

As you read, Portuguese sailors pioneered new routes around Africa toward Asia in the late 1400s. Spain, too, wanted a share of the Asian spice trade. King Ferdinand and Queen Isabella agreed to finance a voyage of exploration by Christopher Columbus. Columbus, an Italian sea captain, planned to reach the East Indies by sailing west across the Atlantic.

The Atlantic Crossing In August 1492, Columbus set out with three ships and a crew of about 90 sailors. As captain, he commanded the largest vessel, the *Santa María*. The other ships were the *Niña* and the *Pinta*.

After a brief stop at the Canary Islands, the little fleet continued west into unknown seas. Fair winds sped them along, but a month passed without the sight of land. Some sailors began to grumble. They had never been away from land for so long. Still, Columbus sailed on.

On October 7, sailors saw flocks of birds flying southwest. Columbus changed course to follow the birds. A few days later, crew members spotted tree branches and flowers floating in the water. At 2 A.M. on October 12, the lookout on the *Pinta* spotted white cliffs shining in the moonlight. *"Tierra! Tierra!"* he shouted. "Land! Land!"

At dawn, Columbus rowed ashore and planted the banner of Spain on the beach. He was convinced that he had reached the East Indies in Asia. In fact, he had reached islands off the coasts of North America and South America in the Caribbean Sea. These islands later became known as the West Indies.

For three months, Columbus explored the West Indies. To his delight, he found signs of gold on the islands. Eager to report his success, he returned to Spain.

Spain Authorizes Colonies In Spain, Columbus presented Queen Isabella and King

Viewing History

The *Santa María*

Columbus's route, 1492

Columbus's report on his first voyage included this picture of the *Santa María*. Improved navigational equipment, such as the astrolabe (inset), enabled Columbus to cross the Atlantic. **Evaluating Information** *The artist who made this drawing never saw the Santa María. Would you consider it a reliable piece of historical evidence? Why or why not?*

Oceanica Classis

Columbus Meets the Tainos

In his journals, Christopher Columbus recorded his first meeting with the Tainos:
"All whom I saw were young, not above thirty years of age, well made, with fine shapes and faces; their hair short, and coarse like that of a horse's tail, combed toward the forehead. . . . It appears to me that the people are ingenious, and would be good servants and I am of opinion that they would very readily become Christians, as they appear to have no religion. They very quickly learn such words as are spoken to them. If it please our Lord, I intend at my return to carry home six of them to your Highnesses, that they may learn our language."

—Christopher Columbus, *Journal*

Analyzing Primary Sources
How would you describe Columbus's attitude toward the Tainos?

Ferdinand with gifts of pink pearls and brilliantly colored parrots. The royal couple listened intently as Columbus described many things that Europeans had never seen before: tobacco, pineapples, and hammocks used for sleeping. Columbus also described the "Indians" he had met, the Tainos (TI nohz). The Tainos, he promised, could easily be converted to Christianity and could also be used as slaves.

The Spanish monarchs were impressed. They gave Columbus the title Admiral of the Ocean Sea. They also agreed to finance future voyages.

Columbus made three more voyages across the Atlantic. In 1493, he founded the first Spanish colony in the Americas, on an island he called Hispaniola (present-day Haiti and the Dominican Republic). A colony is a group of people who settle in a distant land but are still ruled by the government of their native land. Columbus also explored present-day Cuba and Jamaica and sailed along the coasts of Central America and northern South America. He claimed all these lands for Spain.

Columbus proved to be a better explorer than a governor. During his third expedition, settlers at Hispaniola complained of his harsh rule. Queen Isabella appointed an investigator, who sent Columbus back to Spain in chains. In the end, the queen pardoned Columbus, but he never regained the honors he had won earlier. He died in 1506, still convinced that he had reached Asia.

A Lasting Impact

Columbus has long been honored as the bold sea captain who "discovered America." Today, we recognize that Native Americans had "discovered" and settled these lands long before 1492. Still, in at least one sense, Columbus deserves the honors history has given him. Europeans knew nothing of the Americas until Columbus told them about this "new world." His daring voyages marked the beginning of lasting contact among the peoples of Europe, Africa, and the Americas.

For a great many Native Americans, contact had tragic results. Columbus and those who followed were convinced that European culture was superior to that of the Indians. The Spanish claimed Taino lands and forced Tainos to work in gold mines, on ranches, or in Spanish households. Many Tainos died from harsh conditions or European diseases. Within 100 years of Columbus's arrival, the Taino population was virtually wiped out.

For better or worse, the voyages of Columbus signaled a turning point for the Americas. A turning point is a moment in history that marks a decisive change. Curious Europeans saw the new lands as a place where they could settle, trade, and grow rich.

The Spanish Cross the Pacific

After Columbus, the Spanish explored and settled other Caribbean islands. By 1511, they had conquered Puerto Rico, Jamaica, and Cuba. They also explored the eastern coasts of North America and South America in search of a western route to Asia.

In 1513, Vasco Núñez de Balboa (bal BOH uh) plunged into the jungles of the Isthmus of Panama. Native Americans had told him that a large body of water lay to the west. With a party of Spanish soldiers and Indians, Balboa reached the Pacific Ocean after about 25 days. He stood in the crashing surf and claimed the ocean for Spain.

The Spanish had no idea how wide the Pacific was until a sea captain named Ferdinand Magellan (muh JEHL uhn) sailed across it. The expedition—made up of five ships and about 250 crew members—left Spain in 1519. Fifteen months later, it rounded the stormy southern tip of South America and entered the Pacific Ocean. Crossing the Pacific, the sailors ran out of food. One sailor recalled:

66 We remained 3 months and 20 days without taking in provisions or other refreshments and ate only old biscuit reduced to powder, full of grubs and stinking from the dirt which rats had made on it. We drank water that was yellow and stinking. 99
—Antoñio Pigafetta, *The Diary of Antoñio Pigafetta*

Magellan himself was killed in a battle with the local people of the Philippine Islands off the coast of Asia.

In 1522, only one ship and 18 sailors returned to Spain. They were the first people to **circumnavigate,** or sail completely around, the world. In doing so, they had found an all-water western route to Asia. Their voyage made Europeans aware of the true size of the Earth.

A Global Cultural Exchange

The encounter between the peoples of the Eastern and Western hemispheres sparked a global exchange of goods and ideas. Because it started with the voyages of Columbus, this transfer is known as the **Columbian Exchange.** The Columbian Exchange covered a wide range of areas, including food, medicine, government, technology, the arts, and language.

The exchange went in both directions. Europeans learned much from Native Americans. At the same time, Europeans contributed in many ways to the culture of the Americas.

European Influences Europeans introduced domestic animals such as chickens from Europe and Africa. European pigs, cattle, and horses often escaped into the wild and multiplied rapidly. As horses spread through North America, Indians learned to ride them and used them to carry heavy loads.

Plants from Europe and Africa changed the way Native Americans lived. The first bananas came from the Canary Islands. By

The Columbian Exchange

From the Americas to Europe, Africa, and Asia

maize
potato
sweet potato
beans
peanut
squash
pumpkin
peppers
pineapple
tomato
cocoa

From Europe, Africa, and Asia to the Americas

wheat
sugar
banana
rice
grape (wine)
olive oil
dandelion
horse
pig
cow
goat
chicken
smallpox
typhus

CHART Skills

The four voyages of Christopher Columbus set off a worldwide exchange of goods and ideas.

1. **Comprehension**
   (a) Identify two kinds of livestock that Europeans brought to the Americas.
   (b) Identify two food crops that Europeans carried from the Americas.

2. **Critical Thinking Identifying Causes and Effects** What elements shown here led to a decline in Native American population?

Economics $

1520, one Spaniard reported that banana trees had spread "so greatly that it is marvelous to see the great abundance of them." Oranges, lemons, and figs were also new to the Americas. In North America, explorers also brought such plants as bluegrass, the daisy, and the dandelion. These plants spread quickly in American soil.

Tragically, Europeans also brought new diseases, such as smallpox and influenza. Native Americans had no resistance to these diseases. Historians estimate that within 75 years, diseases from Europe had killed almost 90 percent of the people in the Caribbean islands and in Mexico.

 Use Prior Knowledge Before you read the section "Native American Influences," think about what you already know about Native American influences on the rest of the world. Then, read to verify your existing knowledge and add new information.

Native American Influences For their part, Native Americans introduced Europeans to new customs and ideas. After 1492, elements of Native American ways of life gradually spread around the world.

Native Americans introduced Europeans to valuable food crops such as corn, potatoes, beans, tomatoes, manioc, squash, peanuts, pineapples, and blueberries. Today, almost half the world's food crops come from plants that were first grown in the Americas.

Europeans carried the new foods with them as they sailed around the world. Everywhere, people's diets changed and populations increased. In South Asia, people used American hot peppers and chilis to spice stews. Chinese peasants began growing sweet potatoes. Italians made sauces from tomatoes. People in West Africa grew manioc and maize.

European settlers often adopted Native American skills. In the North, Indians showed Europeans how to use snowshoes and trap beavers and other fur-bearing animals. European explorers learned how to paddle Indian canoes. Some leaders studied Native American political structures. Benjamin Franklin admired the League of the Iroquois and urged colonists to unite in a similar way.

Section 1 Assessment

Recall

1. **Identify** Explain the significance of **(a)** Leif Ericson, **(b)** Ferdinand and Isabella, **(c)** Christopher Columbus, **(d)** Vasco Núñez de Balboa, **(e)** Ferdinand Magellan, **(f)** Columbian Exchange.
2. **Define** **(a)** colony, **(b)** turning point, **(c)** circumnavigate.

Comprehension

3. Describe two effects of Columbus's voyage.
4. What route did Magellan's expedition take?
5. **(a)** Identify two European influences on the Americas.

(b) Identify two Native American influences on the rest of the world.

Critical Thinking and Writing

6. **Exploring the Main Idea** Review the Main Idea statement at the beginning of this section. Then, write a paragraph explaining why historians consider Columbus to be more important than Leif Ericson.
7. **Supporting a Point of View** Today, Columbus Day is a national holiday. Yet, some Americans oppose the celebration. List one reason to support each point of view.

ACTIVITY

 Take It to the NET
Connecting to Today
Use the Internet to find examples of English words that were borrowed from Native American languages. Create fact cards for three of these words, describing what language the word came from, what it originally meant, and what it means today. Visit *The American Nation* section of **www.phschool.com** for help in completing the activity.

When learning about past events, such as Columbus's voyage, you must first understand sequence. In what order did various events take place? How was one event related to another? To start this lesson, read the excerpt and study the timetable below.

The following excerpts are from the log that Columbus kept on his first voyage:

Sunday, 9 September 1492 This day we completely lost sight of land, and many men sighed and wept for fear they would not see it again for a long time. I comforted them with great promises of lands and riches.

Saturday, 15 September 1492 I sailed to the west day and night for 81 miles, or more. Early this morning I saw a marvelous meteorite fall into the sea 12 to 15 miles away to the SW. This was taken by some people as a bad omen . . .

Sunday, 7 October 1492 This morning we saw what appeared to be land to the west . . . the *Niña* . . . ran ahead and fired a cannon and ran up a flag on her mast to indicate that land had been sighted. Joy turned to dismay as the day progressed, for by evening we had found no land . . .

Thursday, 11 October 1492 Then, at two hours after midnight, the *Pinta* fired a cannon, my prearranged signal for the sighting of land.

1492: First Voyage of Columbus

Date	Event
August 3	Sets sail from Palos
August 9	Stops for repairs in Canary Islands
September 6	Sets sail from Canary Islands
September 15	Sees a meteorite
September 24	Writes of trouble with crew
October 7	Alters course to follow birds
October 12	Goes ashore

Learn the Skill *To sequence information, use the following steps:*

1. **Identify the order in which events happen.** Applying absolute and relative chronology gives you a clearer picture of events.

2. **Identify time-order words.** Words such as first, next, and last give helpful time signals. Pay attention to other words such as later, now, then, while, this evening, before, and after.

3. **Figure out time intervals.** Understand how much time takes place between events.

4. **Make connections.** Ask: Are the events related? How does one event lead to the next?

Practice the Skill *Use the log entries and timetable to answer the following questions:*

1. **(a)** On what date did Columbus first set sail? **(b)** On what date did Columbus leave the Canary Islands? **(c)** Did Columbus see a meteorite before or after he changed course?

2. Identify two time words or phrases that Columbus used in his log.

3. **(a)** How much time passed between the false sighting of land and the true one? **(b)** About how much time did Columbus spend in the Canary Islands?

4. **(a)** On September 24, Columbus wrote of trouble with the crew. What earlier event might have contributed to this? **(b)** How might the events of October 7 and October 11 be related?

Apply the Skill *See the Chapter Review and Assessment.*

2 Spain Builds an Empire

BEFORE YOU READ

Reading Focus

- How did conquistadors defeat two Indian empires?
- What areas did the Spanish explore?
- How did Spain settle and organize its colonies?
- What was life like for Native Americans under Spanish rule?

Key Terms

conquistador
pueblo
presidio
mission
peninsulare
creole
mestizo
encomienda
plantation

Taking Notes

Copy the concept web below. As you read, fill in the blank ovals with important facts about Spain's American empire. Add as many ovals as you need.

Main Idea Spain's conquest, exploration, and colonization of the Americas brought wealth to some and tragedy to others.

AS YOU READ
Spanish coin found in Florida

Ask Questions Write two questions you would ask Bernal Díaz del Castillo about his goals and his experience in the Americas.

Setting the Scene

"What a troublesome thing it is to discover new lands. The risks we took, it is hardly possible to exaggerate." Thus spoke Bernal Díaz del Castillo, one of the many Spanish **conquistadors** (kahn KWIS tuh dorz), or conquerors, who marched into the Américas in the 1500s. When asked why they traveled to the Americas, Díaz responded, "We came here to serve God and the king and also to get rich."

In their search for glory and gold, the conquistadors made Spain one of the richest nations in Europe. Spanish colonists followed the conquistadors and created a vast new empire in the Americas.

Spanish Conquistadors

The rulers of Spain gave conquistadors permission to establish settlements in the Americas. In return, conquistadors agreed to give Spain one fifth of any gold or treasure they captured.

Like other conquistadors, Hernando Cortés was eager to win riches and glory. He had heard rumors of a fabulously wealthy Native American empire in Mexico. With only about 600 soldiers and 16 horses, Cortés set sail for Mexico in 1519 in search of gold.

Conquest of the Aztecs Moctezuma (mokt uh ZOO muh), the Aztec emperor who ruled over much of Mexico, heard disturbing reports of a large house floating on the sea. It was filled with white men with long, thick beards. Aztec sacred writings predicted that a powerful white-skinned god would come from the east to rule the Aztecs. As the strangers neared Tenochtitlán, the Aztec capital, Moctezuma decided to welcome them as his guests.

Cortés took advantage of Moctezuma's invitation. Shrewdly, Cortés had already begun to win the support of other Indians who resented Aztec rule. One of his trusted advisors was an Indian

This Aztec drawing depicts a meeting between Spanish conquistadors (left) and Aztecs (right). Not all encounters between the two sides were as peaceful as this one. **Analyzing Information** *What elements shown here might have seemed unfamiliar to the Aztecs? To the Spanish?*

woman the Spanish called Doña Marina. She gave Cortés valuable information about the Aztecs and acted as a translator and negotiator.

On November 8, 1519, Cortés marched into Tenochtitlán. Thousands upon thousands of Aztecs turned out to see the astonishing newcomers riding horses. Díaz recalled:

> ❝ Who could count the multitude of men, women and children which had come out on the roofs, in their boats on the canals, or in the streets, to see us? ❞
>
> —Bernal Díaz del Castillo, *True History of the Conquest of New Spain*

At first, Cortés was friendly to Moctezuma. Soon, however, he made the emperor a prisoner in his own city. Tensions mounted in Tenochtitlán over the next half year.

Finally, the Aztecs drove out the Spanish. Their victory, however, was brief. Aided by people whom the Aztecs had conquered, Cortés recaptured the city. In the end, the Spanish killed Moctezuma and destroyed Tenochtitlán. The Aztec empire had fallen.

Conquest of the Incas Another bold conquistador, Francisco Pizarro (pee SAR oh), set his sights on the Incan empire. Pizarro sailed down the Pacific coast of South America with fewer than 200 Spanish soldiers. In 1532, he captured the Incan emperor Atahualpa (ah tuh WAHL puh) and later executed him. Without the leadership of Atahualpa, Incan resistance collapsed. By 1535, Pizarro controlled much of the Incan empire.

Reasons for Spanish Victories How were the Spanish able to conquer two great empires with only a handful of soldiers? First, the Spanish had superior military equipment. They were protected by steel armor and had guns. The Aztecs and Incas relied on clubs, bows and arrows, and spears. Also, the Native Americans had never seen horses. They were frightened by mounted Spanish soldiers.

In addition, the Native Americans did not fight as hard as they might have. The Aztecs hesitated to attack at first because they thought the Spanish might be gods. The Incas were weak from fighting among themselves over control of their government.

Finally, many Indians died from European diseases, such as chickenpox, measles, and influenza. Some historians believe that disease alone would have ensured Spanish victory over the Indians.

Exploring the Spanish Borderlands

The Spanish search for treasure reached beyond the lands of the Aztecs and Incas. Moving north, conquistadors explored the area known as the Spanish borderlands. The borderlands spanned the present-day United States from Florida to California.

Juan Ponce de León (PAWN suh day LAY awn) traveled through parts of Florida in 1513, looking for a legendary fountain of youth. Indians claimed that anyone who bathed in its magical water would remain young forever. Ponce de León found no such fountain.

An Ill-Fated Journey Another explorer, Pánfilo Narváez (nar vah EHS), led an expedition that ended in disaster. In 1528, a storm struck his fleet in the Gulf of Mexico. Narváez and many others were lost at sea. The rest landed on an island near present-day Texas. Indians captured the few survivors and held them prisoner. Álvar Núñez Cabeza de Vaca assumed leadership of the small group.

Cabeza de Vaca, an enslaved African named Estevanico, and two others finally escaped their captors in 1533. The four walked across the plains of Texas, searching for a Spanish settlement. Finally, in 1536, they reached a town in Mexico. They had traveled by foot more than 1,000 miles through the Southwest.

GEOGRAPHY Skills

In the 1500s, the Spanish explored and settled North American lands from Florida to California.

1. **Location** On the maps, locate **(a)** Ponce de León's route, **(b)** De Soto's route, **(c)** St. Augustine, **(d)** San Antonio, **(e)** Santa Fe, **(f)** San Francisco.

2. **Movement** Which Spanish explorers crossed the Rio Grande?

3. **Critical Thinking Linking Past and Present** Compare these maps to a map of the modern United States. Identify three states in which you would expect Spanish influence to be strong.

Spanish Explorers/Spanish Settlements

Key
← Ponce de León, 1513   ← De Soto, 1539–1542
← Narváez/Cabeza de Vaca/Estevanico, 1528–1536   ← Coronado, 1540–1547
Azimuthal Projection
0   400   800 Miles
0 400 800 Kilometers

Key
‡ Missions, 1565–1776   Present-day borders are shown.
• Other settlements, 1565–1776
Azimuthal Projection
0   400   800 Miles
0 400 800 Kilometers

De Soto and Coronado From 1539 to 1542, Hernando De Soto explored Florida and other parts of the Southeast. In his search for gold, he reached the Mississippi River. De Soto died along the riverbank, without finding the riches he sought.

The conquistador Francisco Coronado (koh roh NAH doh) heard legends about "seven cities of gold." In 1540, he led an expedition into the southwestern borderlands. He traveled to present-day Arizona and New Mexico. Some of his party went as far as the Grand Canyon. Still, the Zuñi villages he visited had no golden streets.

The Spanish expeditions into the borderlands met with little success. Faced with strong Indian resistance in the north, Spain focused instead on bringing order to its empire in the south.

Settling New Spain

At first, Spain let the conquistadors govern the lands they conquered. When the conquistadors proved to be poor rulers, the Spanish king took away their authority. He then set up a strong system of government to rule his growing empire. In 1535, he divided his American lands into New Spain and Peru. The borderlands were part of New Spain. The king put a viceroy in charge of each region to rule in his name.

A code called the Laws of the Indies stated how the colonies should be organized and ruled. The code provided for three kinds of settlements in New Spain: pueblos, presidios (prih SIHD ee ohz), and missions. Some large communities included all three.

Pueblos and Presidios The pueblos, or towns, were centers of farming and trade. In the middle of the town was a plaza, or public square. Here, townspeople and farmers came to do business or worship at the church. Shops and homes lined the four sides of the plaza.

The Spanish took control of Indian pueblos and built new towns as well. In 1598, Juan de Oñate (oh NYAH tay) founded the colony of New Mexico among the adobe villages of the Pueblo Indians. He used brutal force to conquer the Native Americans of the region. Don Pedro de Paralta later founded Santa Fe as the Spanish capital of New Mexico.

Presidios were forts where soldiers lived. Inside the high, thick walls were shops, stables, and storehouses for food. Soldiers protected the farmers who settled nearby. The first presidio in the borderlands was built in 1565 at St. Augustine, Florida.

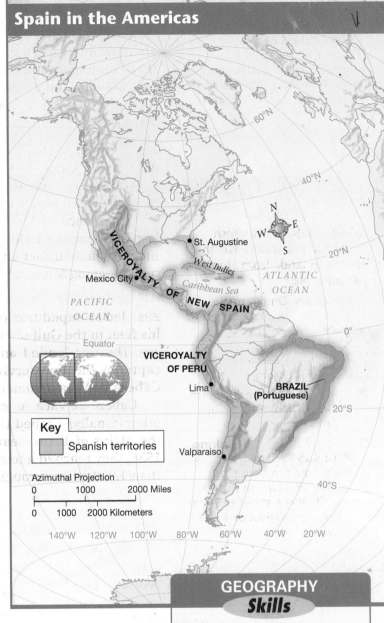

Spain in the Americas

GEOGRAPHY
Skills

In 1535, the king of Spain divided his American colonies into New Spain and Peru.

1. **Location** On the map, locate **(a)** New Spain, **(b)** Peru, **(c)** West Indies, **(d)** Mexico City.

2. **Region** **(a)** Which viceroyalty included Florida? **(b)** What other European power colonized part of South America?

3. **Critical Thinking Drawing Conclusions** Why was control of the Caribbean Sea important to Spain?

Find Main Ideas Use the vocabulary words *pueblo, presidio,* and *mission* to write a main idea statement about the settlement of New Spain.

Missions Like other Europeans in the Americas, the Spanish believed they had a duty to convert Indians to Christianity. They set up **missions,** religious settlements run by Catholic priests and friars. They often forced Indians to live and work on the missions.

Missionaries gradually spread across the Spanish borderlands. The first mission in Texas was founded in 1659 at El Paso. In 1691, Father Eusebio Francisco Kino (KEE noh) crossed into present-day Arizona. He eventually set up 24 missions in the area. By the late 1700s, a string of missions also dotted the California coast from San Diego to San Francisco.

Society in New Spain

The Laws of the Indies also set up a strict social system. People in Spanish colonies were divided into four social classes: peninsulares (puh NIHN suh LAH rayz), creoles (KREE ohlz), mestizos (mehs TEE zohz), and Indians.

Four Social Classes At the top of the social scale were the **peninsulares.** Born in Spain, peninsulares held the highest jobs in government and the Church. They also owned large tracts of land as well as rich gold and silver mines.

Below the peninsulares were the **creoles,** people born in the Americas to Spanish parents. Many creoles were wealthy and well educated. They owned farms and ranches, taught at universities, and practiced law. However, they could not hold the jobs that were reserved for peninsulares.

Below the creoles were people of mixed Spanish and Indian background, known as **mestizos.** Mestizos worked on farms and ranches owned by peninsulares and creoles. In the cities, they worked as carpenters, shoemakers, tailors, and bakers.

The lowest class in the colonies was the Indians. The Spanish treated them as a conquered people. Under New Spain's strict social system, Indians were kept in poverty for hundreds of years.

A Blend of Cultures A new way of life took shape in New Spain that blended Spanish and Indian ways. Spanish settlers brought their own culture to the colonies. They introduced their language, laws, religion, and learning. In 1551, the Spanish founded the University of Mexico.

Native Americans also influenced the culture of New Spain. As you have read, colonists adopted Indian foods and items of Indian clothing, such as the poncho and moccasins. Indian workers used materials they knew well, such as adobe bricks, to build fine libraries, theaters, and churches. Sometimes, Indian artists decorated church walls with paintings of local traditions.

Harsh Life for Native Americans

Spanish colonists needed workers for their ranches, farms, and mines. To help them, the Spanish government gave settlers encomiendas (ehn koh mee EHN dahz), land grants that included the right to demand labor or taxes from Native Americans.

Primary Sources

See Bartolomé de Las Casas, "The Conquest of the Indies," on page 576 of the Reference Section.

Atlantic Slave Trade

NORTH AMERICA FRENCH TERRITORY

MEXICO

WEST INDIES

ATLANTIC OCEAN

40°N

20°N

PACIFIC OCEAN

Equator

SOUTH AMERICA

Robinson Projection

0   1000   2000 Miles

0   1000 2000 Kilometers

BRAZIL

100°W   80°W   60°W   40°W   20°W

20°S

40°S

ASIA

EUROPE

AFRICA

SENEGAMBIA

ASANTE GOLD COAST

KONGO

ANGOLA

N W E S

0°   20°E

Destinations of Enslaved Africans, 1500–1870

15%

37%

41%

4.5%

2.5%

Source: Albert M. Craig, *World Civilizations*

Key

- Spanish America
- Non-Spanish Caribbean islands
- British America
- Portuguese Brazil
- Europe and Asia
- → Slave-trade route

Hard Labor Mines in Mexico, Peru, and other parts of the Americas made Spain rich. Treasure ships laden with thousands of tons of gold and silver sailed regularly across the Atlantic.

The Spanish forced Native Americans to work in the gold and silver mines. In flickering light, Indians hacked out rich ores in narrow, dark tunnels. Many died when tunnels caved in.

These harsh conditions led one priest, Bartolomé de Las Casas (day lahs KAH sahs), to seek reform. Traveling through New Spain, Las Casas witnessed firsthand the deaths of Indians due to hunger, disease, and mistreatment. What he saw horrified him:

❝ The Indians were totally deprived of their freedom. . . . Even beasts enjoy more freedom when they are allowed to graze in the field. ❞

—Bartolomé de Las Casas, *Tears of the Indians*

Las Casas journeyed to Spain and asked the king to protect the Indians. In the 1540s, the royal government did pass laws prohibiting the enslavement of Native Americans. The laws also allowed Indians to own cattle and grow crops. However, few officials in New Spain enforced the new laws.

The Atlantic Slave Trade Begins The death toll among Native Americans continued to rise. Faced with a severe shortage of workers, Spanish colonists looked across the Atlantic Ocean for a new source of labor.

GEOGRAPHY Skills

Destinations of Enslaved Africans

The Atlantic slave trade began with Spain's efforts to supply labor for its American empire.

1. **Comprehension** Which two regions of the Americas received the largest number of enslaved Africans?

2. **Critical Thinking Drawing Conclusions** Why do you think the growth of the slave trade had relatively little effect on eastern Africa?

Still seeking to protect Native Americans, Bartolomé de Las Casas made a suggestion that had a lasting, tragic impact. His idea was that Africans be brought as slaves to replace Indian laborers. Las Casas argued that Africans would not catch European diseases and die from them like Native Americans did. He also claimed that Africans would suffer less because they were used to doing hard farm work in their homelands.

By the time he died in 1566, Las Casas had come to regret his suggestion to use African labor. He saw that African slaves suffered as much as the Indians. By that time, however, it was too late to undo the damage. Slavery had already become a key part of the colonial economy.

The Slave Trade Spreads   Demand for African labor grew rapidly, not only in New Spain, but elsewhere in the Americas. Enslaved Africans were especially valued on sugar plantations on Caribbean islands and in the Portuguese colony of Brazil. A **plantation** is a large estate farmed by many workers. Sugar could not be grown on small estates because it required too much land and labor. African slaves often worked all through the night cutting sugar, which was then sold in Europe for a large profit.

Some scholars today estimate that more than 10 million enslaved Africans were transported to the Americas between the 1500s and the 1800s. (See the map and chart on page 79.) The vast majority came from West Africa.

Most of the Africans were sent to Brazil or the Caribbean. However, a total of more than 500,000 enslaved Africans would eventually arrive in the British colonies of North America. (You will read more about the effects of the Atlantic slave trade on the Americas and Africa in the next chapter.)

AS YOU READ   **Visualize** Form a mental image of what Las Casas must have seen that caused him to regret his suggestion to use African slave labor.

 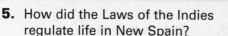

AFTER YOU READ

Section 2 Assessment

Recall

1. **Identify** Explain the significance of **(a)** Hernando Cortés, **(b)** Moctezuma, **(c)** Francisco Pizarro, **(d)** Juan Ponce de León, **(e)** Bartolomé de Las Casas.
2. **Define** **(a)** conquistador, **(b)** pueblo, **(c)** presidio, **(d)** mission, **(e)** peninsulare, **(f)** creole, **(g)** mestizo, **(h)** encomienda, **(i)** plantation.

Comprehension

3. Why were the Spanish able to conquer the Americas?
4. What areas of North America did the Spanish explore?

5. How did the Laws of the Indies regulate life in New Spain?
6. **(a)** What was life like for Native Americans under Spanish rule? **(b)** Why did Spain bring Africans to the Americas?

Critical Thinking and Writing

7. **Exploring the Main Idea** Review the Main Idea statement at the beginning of this section. Then, write two generalizations about Spanish rule, from the viewpoints of a peninsulare and of an Indian.
8. **Drawing Inferences** Why do you think Spain reserved the most powerful positions for Spanish-born officials?

ACTIVITY

Writing an Obituary Based on what you have read, write an obituary for one of the figures discussed in this section, such as Hernando Cortés, Estevanico, or Bartolomé de Las Casas. Briefly summarize that person's most notable achievement and express a point of view about him or her.

3 Colonizing North America

Reading Focus

- Why did England, France, and the Netherlands seek a northwest passage to Asia?
- How did the Protestant Reformation affect rivalries among European nations?
- How did rivalry develop between New France and New Netherland?

Key Terms

northwest passage

Protestant Reformation

coureur de bois

missionary

alliance

Taking Notes

Copy this incomplete Venn diagram. As you read, fill in key facts about French and Dutch settlements in North America. Write common characteristics in the overlapping section.

NEW FRANCE
- St. Lawrence River

• Fur trading

NEW NETHERLAND
- Hudson River

Main Idea Following Spain's example, England, France, and the Netherlands set out to establish colonies in North America.

Setting the Scene The court of King Henry VII of England buzzed with excitement in August 1497. Italian sea captain Giovanni Caboto and a crew of English sailors had just returned from a 79-day Atlantic voyage.

Caboto, called John Cabot by the English, cut a swaggering figure on the streets of London. He dressed himself in fine silks and made such a stir that ordinary Londoners "[ran] after him like madmen," reported one observer. Cabot appeared before King Henry to announce that he had reached a "new-found island" in Asia where fish were plentiful.

Cabot was one of many Europeans who explored North America between the 1400s and 1600s. England, France, and the Netherlands all envied Spain's new empire. They wanted American colonies of their own.

AS YOU READ
John Cabot
Use Prior Knowledge
How was Cabot's return to England similar to Columbus's return to Spain?

Search for a Northwest Passage

Throughout the 1500s, European nations continued to look for new ways to reach the riches of Asia. Magellan's route around South America seemed long and difficult. They wanted to discover a shorter northwest passage, or waterway through or around North America.

Although John Cabot was confident he had found such a passage, he was mistaken. His "new-found island" off the Asian coast in fact lay off the coast of North America. Today, Newfoundland is the easternmost province of Canada.

Exploring for France The French sent another Italian captain, Giovanni da Verrazano (vehr rah TSAH noh), in search of a northwest passage. Verrazano journeyed along the North American coast from the Carolinas to Canada. During the 1530s, Jacques Cartier (kar tee YAY), also sailing for the French, traveled more than halfway up the river now known as the St. Lawrence.

Greenland

Iceland

Hudson Bay

Newfoundland

ENGLAND

NETHERLANDS

NORTH AMERICA

Great Lakes

St. Lawrence R.

Quebec

Montreal

New France

FRANCE

SPAIN

Louisiana (Fr.)

English Colonies

Mississippi R.

ATLANTIC OCEAN

60°N

30°N

AFRICA

PACIFIC OCEAN

Robinson Projection

0   500   1000 Miles

0   500   1000 Kilometers

90°W   60°W   30°W   0°

N
W · E
S

SOUTH AMERICA

Key

France
- - → Verrazano, 1524
•••• → Cartier, 1534–1536
- - - → Marquette and Joliet, 1673
——— → La Salle, 1678–1682

England
——→ Cabot, 1497
- -→ Hudson, 1610–1611

Netherlands
——→ Hudson, 1609

GEOGRAPHY Skills

Explorers from England, France, and the Netherlands competed to find a northwest passage to Asia.

1. **Location** On the map, locate (a) New France, (b) Newfoundland, (c) St. Lawrence River, (d) Hudson Bay, (e) Mississippi River.

2. **Movement** Describe the route taken by Henry Hudson when he explored for the Netherlands.

3. **Critical Thinking Making Predictions** Based on this map, why might you expect conflict to develop between the English and French in North America?

Henry Hudson In 1609, the English explorer Henry Hudson sailed for the Dutch. His ship, the *Half Moon*, entered present-day New York harbor. Hudson continued to sail some 150 miles up the river that now bears his name.

The following year, Hudson made a voyage into the far north—this time for the English. After spending a harsh winter in present-day Hudson Bay, his crew rebelled. They set Hudson, his son, and seven loyal sailors adrift in a small boat. The boat and its crew were never seen again.

Failure and Success None of these explorers found a northwest passage to Asia. However, they did map and explore many parts of North America. The rulers of Western Europe began thinking about how to profit from the region's rich resources.

Rivalries Among European Nations

European nations began to compete for riches around the world. Religious differences heightened their rivalry. Until the 1500s, the Roman Catholic Church was the only church in Western Europe. That unity ended when a major religious reform movement sharply divided Christians.

Religious Divisions In 1517, a German monk named Martin Luther publicly challenged many practices of the Catholic Church. Soon after, he split with the Church entirely. Luther believed that the Church had become too worldly. He opposed the power of popes. He also objected to the Catholic teaching that believers could gain eternal life by performing good works. Luther argued that people could be saved only by faith in God.

Because of their protests against the church, Luther's supporters became known as Protestants. The Protestant Reformation, as the new movement was known, divided Europe. Soon, the Protestants themselves split, forming many different churches.

By the late 1500s, religion divided the states of Western Europe. Roman Catholic monarchs ruled Spain and France. A Protestant queen, Elizabeth I, ruled England. In the Netherlands, the Dutch people were mostly Protestant.

Rivalries in the Americas As Europeans settled in the Americas, they brought their religious conflicts with them. Queen Elizabeth encouraged English adventurers to raid Spanish colonies and capture Spanish treasure fleets. Protestant England also competed with Catholic France for lands in North America.

Not all rivalries were religious. Both the Netherlands and England were Protestant. Still, they competed for control of land in North America and for economic markets all over the world.

New France

Samuel de Champlain (sham PLAYN) founded Port Royal, the first permanent French settlement in North America, in 1605. Three years later, he led another group of settlers along the route Cartier had pioneered. On a rocky cliff high above the St. Lawrence River, Champlain built a trading post known as Quebec (kwi BEHK).

Economy of New France Unlike Spain's American empire, New France had little gold or silver. Instead, the French profited from fishing, trapping, and trading.

French colonists who lived and worked in the woods became known as *coureurs de bois* (koo RYOOR duh BWAH), or "runners of the woods." The French brought knives, kettles, cloth, and other items for trade with Native Americans. In return, the Indians gave them beaver skins and other furs that sold for high prices in Europe.

Coureurs de bois established friendly relations with the Native Americans. Unlike the Spanish, the French did not attempt to conquer the Indians. Also, because *coureurs de bois* did not build farms, they did not interfere with Indian

AS YOU READ Draw Inferences As you read, think about how the Protestant Reformation "divided" Europe. Do religious differences still divide nations?

Viewing History

Fur Trapper in New France

Coureurs de bois, like the one shown here, depended on beaver furs for a living. By 1675, trappers and traders in New France were exporting nearly 90,000 pounds of beaver pelts a year. **Applying Information** *Based on what you have read, how does this picture show that* coureurs de bois *made use of Native American technology?*

lands. Indians taught the French trapping and survival skills, such as how to make snowshoes and canoes. Many coureurs married Indian women.

Missionary Work Catholic missionaries often traveled with fur traders. A *missionary* is a person who goes to another land to win converts for a religion. French missionaries worked to teach Native Americans about Christianity. They also drew maps and wrote about the lands they explored.

Life was difficult, especially in winter. One French priest recalled traveling on foot through deep snow:

> 66 If a thaw came, dear Lord, what pain! . . . I was marching on an icy path that broke with every step I took; as the snow softened . . . we often sunk in it up to our . . . waist. 99
>
> —Paul Le Jeune, quoted in *The Jesuits in North America* (Parkman)

Expansion to the Mississippi French trappers followed the St. Lawrence deep into the heart of North America. Led by Indian guides, they reached the Great Lakes. Here, Indians spoke of a mighty river, which they called Mississippi, or "Father of the Waters."

A French missionary, Father Jacques Marquette (mar KEHT), and a fur trader, Louis Joliet (joh lee EHT), set out to reach the Mississippi in 1673. Led by Indian guides, they followed the river for more than 700 miles before turning back. Nine years later, Robert de La Salle completed the journey to the Gulf of Mexico. La Salle named the region Louisiana in honor of the French king, Louis XIV.

To keep Spain and England out of Louisiana, the French built forts in the north along the Great Lakes. Among them was Fort Detroit, built by Antoine Cadillac near Lake Erie. The French also built New Orleans, a fort at the mouth of the river. New Orleans grew into a busy trading center.

French colonists imported thousands of Africans to work as slaves on nearby plantations. Some slaves, however, joined with the Natchez Indians in a revolt against the French. The French put down the Natchez Revolt in 1729. Some slaves who fought on the side of the French received their freedom. In Louisiana, free and enslaved Africans together made up the majority of settlers.

Government of New France New France was governed much like New Spain. The French king controlled the government directly, and people had little freedom. A council appointed by the king made all decisions.

Louis XIV worried that too few French were moving to New France. In the 1660s, therefore, he sent about a thousand farmers to the colony, including many young women. Despite the king's efforts to increase the population, New France grew slowly. Only about 10,000 settlers lived in the colony by 1680. Of those, one third lived on farms along the St. Lawrence. Many more chose to become *coureurs de bois*, living largely free of government control.

New Netherland

Like the French, the Dutch hoped to profit from their discoveries in the Americas. In 1626, Peter Minuit (MIHN yoo wiht) led a group of Dutch settlers to the mouth of the Hudson River. There, he bought Manhattan Island from local Indians. Minuit called his settlement New Amsterdam. Other Dutch colonists settled farther up the Hudson River. The entire colony was known as New Netherland (now known as New York).

From a tiny group of 30 houses, New Amsterdam grew into a busy port. The Dutch welcomed people of many nations and religions to their colony. A Roman Catholic priest who visited New Netherland in 1643 reported:

66 On the island of Manhattan, and in its environs, there may well be four or five hundred men of different sects and nations: the Director General told me that there were men of eighteen different languages; they are scattered here and there on the river, above and below, as the beauty and convenience of the spot has invited each to settle. 99

—Father Isaac Jogues, quoted in *Narratives of New Netherland, 1609–1664* (Jameson)

The Dutch also built trading posts along the Hudson River. The most important one was Fort Orange, today known as Albany. Dutch merchants became known for their good business sense.

The Dutch enlarged New Netherland in 1655 by taking over the colony of New Sweden. The Swedes had established New Sweden along the Delaware River some 15 years earlier.

Rivalry Over Furs Dutch traders sent furs to the Netherlands. The packing list for the first shipment included "the skins of 7,246 beaver, 853 otter, 81 mink, 36 cat lynx, and 34 small rats."

The Dutch and French became rivals in the fur trade. Both sought alliances with Native Americans. An alliance is an agreement between nations to aid and protect one another. The Dutch

Cause *and* Effect

Causes

- Europeans want more goods from Asia
- Muslims gain control of trade between Europe and Asia
- Rulers of European nations seek ways to increase their wealth
- European nations look for a sea route to Asia
- Columbus reaches the Americas

EXPLORATION OF THE AMERICAS

Effects

- Spain builds an empire in the Americas
- English, French, and Dutch set up colonies in North America
- Millions of Native Americans die from "European" diseases
- Slave traders bring enslaved Africans to the Americas
- Foods from the Americas are introduced into Europe

Effects Today

- The United States is a multicultural society
- American foods, such as corn and potatoes, are important to people's diets around the world

GRAPHIC ORGANIZER
Skills

Exploration had a dramatic impact on the Americas, Europe, Africa, and Asia.

1. **Comprehension** Identify two economic causes of European exploration.

2. **Critical Thinking Linking Past and Present** Based on the chart, what cultures may have helped shape American culture today?

made friends with the Iroquois. The Hurons (HYOO rahnz) helped the French. Fighting raged for years among the Europeans and their Native American allies.

Dutch Ways in North America The Dutch brought many of their customs from Europe to New Netherland. They liked to ice-skate, and in winter, the frozen rivers and ponds filled with skaters. Every year on Saint Nicholas's birthday, Dutch children put out their shoes to be filled with all sorts of presents. Later, "Saint Nick" came to be called Santa Claus.

Some Dutch words entered the English language. A Dutch master was a *boss*. The people of New Amsterdam sailed in *yachts*. Dutch children munched on *cookies* and rode through the snow on *sleighs*.

Impact on Native Americans European settlement of North America brought major changes to Native Americans. As in New Spain, European diseases killed thousands of Indians. Rivalry over the fur trade increased Indian warfare as European settlers encouraged their Native American allies to attack one another. The scramble for furs also led to overtrapping. By 1640, trappers had almost wiped out the beavers on Iroquois lands in upstate New York.

The arrival of Europeans affected Native Americans in other ways. Missionaries tried to convert Indians to Christianity. Indians eagerly adopted European trade goods, such as copper kettles and knives. They also bought muskets and gunpowder for hunting and warfare. Alcohol sold by European traders had a harsh effect on Native American life.

The French, Dutch, and English all waged warfare to seize Indian lands. As Indians were forced off their lands, they moved westward onto lands of other Indians. The conflict between Native Americans and Europeans would continue for many years.

Section 3 Assessment

Recall

1. **Identify** Explain the significance of **(a)** John Cabot, **(b)** Jacques Cartier, **(c)** Protestant Reformation, **(d)** Samuel de Champlain, **(e)** Marquette and Joliet, **(f)** Peter Minuit.
2. **Define (a)** northwest passage, **(b)** *coureur de bois,* **(c)** missionary, **(d)** alliance.

Comprehension

3. Why did Europeans seek a northern route to Asia?
4. **(a)** What religious differences divided Europe? **(b)** How did these differences affect the race for American colonies?

5. How did the rivalry between French and Dutch colonists affect Native Americans?

Critical Thinking and Writing

6. **Exploring the Main Idea** Review the Main Idea statement at the beginning of this section. Then, write a paragraph explaining whether you think the French and Dutch achieved their goals.
7. **Making Decisions** Both *coureurs de bois* and missionaries endured great hardships in New France. For each of them, list two reasons they might have decided to come to North America.

4 Building the Jamestown Colony

BEFORE YOU READ

Reading Focus

- What challenges did the first English colonies in North America face?
- How did Virginia begin a tradition of representative government?
- What groups of people made up the new arrivals in Virginia after 1619?

Key Terms

charter
burgess
House of Burgesses
representative government
Magna Carta
Parliament

Taking Notes

As you read, prepare an outline of this section. Use roman numerals to indicate the major headings, capital letters for the subheadings, and numbers for the supporting details. The sample at right will help you get started.

> I. The First English Colony
>   A. England seeks riches
>   B.
> II. Challenge and Survival
>   A. Setting up Jamestown
>   1. King grants charter
>   2.
>   B. Early problems
>   1. Geography
>   2.

Main Idea Founded in 1607, the English colony at Jamestown in Virginia survived hard times and went on to set up a representative government.

Setting the Scene Thomas Gates was full of plans as he sailed from England to help run the Jamestown Colony in Virginia. The colony had been founded three years earlier, in 1607. Since then, nearly 700 English colonists had crossed the Atlantic Ocean to settle in Jamestown.

Gates was hardly prepared for the sight that greeted him. Of the 700 colonists, only 60 remained. They came staggering out to the shore, he reported, "so lean that they looked like [skeletons], crying out, 'We are starved, we are starved.'" Many had resorted to eating turtles, poisonous snakes, or their own horses.

Discouraged, Gates loaded everyone onto his ships and turned to sail for home. By chance, however, a new fleet from England arrived that day, bringing supplies and more settlers. The colony survived. Yet, it would take more than ten years before the English colony in Virginia put down permanent roots.

AS YOU READ Tortoise shell found in Jamestown

Visualize Visualize the scene described in this story. Describe your thoughts and feelings as if you had been Thomas Gates.

The First English Colony

England watched with envy as Spain gained riches from its American colonies. Several ambitious English gentlemen proposed that England settle the Americas as well. With Queen Elizabeth's permission, Sir Walter Raleigh raised money to outfit a colony in North America. In 1585, about 100 men set sail across the Atlantic.

The colonists landed on Roanoke (ROH uh nohk), an island off the coast of present-day North Carolina. Within a year, however, the colonists had run short of food and were quarreling with neighboring Indians. When an English ship stopped in the harbor, the weary settlers sailed home.

In 1587, Raleigh sent John White, one of the original colonists, back to Roanoke with a new group of settlers, including women and children. When supplies ran low, White returned to England, leaving behind 117 colonists. He planned to return in a few months. When he

Viewing History

James-town Rebuilt

Jamestown

This photograph shows a modern reconstruction of what the early settlement in Jamestown looked like. The strong leadership of Captain John Smith (inset) enabled the struggling colony to survive starvation and disease. **Drawing Conclusions** *What sources of information might historians use to accurately re-create a historic site like this one?*

got back to England, however, he found the country was then preparing for war with Spain. It was three years before he was able to sail back to Roanoke.

When White arrived, he found the settlement strangely quiet. Houses stood empty. Vines twined through the windows and pumpkins sprouted from the earthen floors. On a tree, someone had carved the word CROATOAN, the name of a nearby island. No other trace of the colonists remained.

White was eager to investigate, but a storm was blowing up and his crew refused to make the trip. To this day, the fate of the "Lost Colony" remains a mystery.

Challenge and Survival in Jamestown

After the failure of Roanoke, nearly 20 years passed before England again tried to establish a colony in North America. In 1606, the Virginia Company of London received a charter from King James I. A charter is a legal document giving certain rights to a person or company.

The royal charter gave the Virginia Company the right to settle lands between present-day North Carolina and the Potomac River. The charter also guaranteed that colonists of this land, called Virginia, would have the same rights as English citizens.

A Disastrous Start In the spring of 1607, a group of 105 colonists arrived in Virginia. They sailed into Chesapeake Bay and began building homes along the James River. They named their tiny outpost Jamestown after their king.

The colonists soon discovered that Jamestown was located in a swampy area. The water was unhealthy, and mosquitoes spread malaria. Many settlers suffered or died from disease.

Governing the colony also proved difficult. The Virginia Company had chosen a council of 13 men to rule the settlement. Members of the council quarreled with one another and did little to plan for the colony's future. By the summer of 1608, the colony was near failure.

Starvation and Recovery Another major problem the Jamestown colonists faced was starvation. Captain John Smith, a young soldier and explorer, observed that the colonists were not planting enough crops. He complained that people wanted only to "dig gold, wash gold, refine gold, load gold." As they searched in vain for gold, the colony ran out of food.

Smith helped to save the colony. He set up stern rules that forced colonists to work if they wished to eat. He also visited nearby Indian villages. Powhatan (pow uh TAN), the most powerful chief in the area, agreed to supply corn to the English.

Peaceful relations with Native Americans did not last, however. Whenever the Indians refused to supply food, the colonists used force to seize what they needed. Once, Smith aimed a gun at Powhatan's brother until the Indians provided corn to buy his freedom. Such incidents led to frequent and bloody warfare. Peace was restored briefly when the colonist John Rolfe married Pocahontas, daughter of Powhatan.

Even in times of peace, Jamestown did not prosper. Problems arose soon after John Smith returned to England in 1609. As you read, the colony suffered terribly for the next few years. Desperate settlers cooked "dogs, cats, snakes, [and] toadstools" to survive. To keep warm, they broke up houses to burn as firewood.

A Profitable Crop Jamestown's economy finally improved after 1612, when colonists began growing tobacco. Europeans had learned about tobacco from Native Americans.

King James called pipe smoking "a vile custom." Still, the new fad caught on quickly. By 1620, England was importing more than 30,000 pounds of tobacco a year. At last, Virginians had found a way to make their colony succeed.

Representative Government

For a time, the governors sent by the Virginia Company ran the colony like a military outpost. Each morning, a drumbeat summoned settlers to work at assigned tasks. Harsh laws imposed the death penalty even for small offenses, like stealing an ear of corn. Such conditions were unlikely to attract new colonists. As John Smith commented after his return to England, "No Man will go . . . to have less freedom there than here."

Primary Sources

See John Smith, "The General History of Virginia," on page 577 of the Reference Section.

An American Profile

Pocahontas 1596?–1617

As a young woman, Pocahontas, whose name means "playful one," captured the affections of John Rolfe, a Jamestown tobacco planter. They were married in 1614.

In 1616, when she was about twenty years old, Pocahontas accompanied her husband and infant son, Thomas, to England. The English were fascinated by this "Indian princess." She was invited to the court of King James I. A painting shows her dressed as an English noblewoman in velvet and lace. In 1617, as she prepared to return to Virginia, Pocahontas became ill. She died and was buried in England.

Why do you think the English wanted to meet Pocahontas?

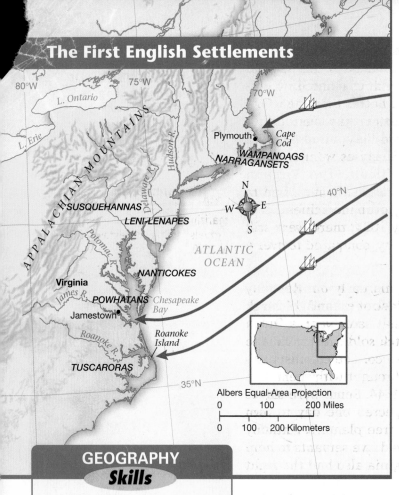

The First English Settlements

80°W   75°W   70°W

L. Ontario
L. Erie
APPALACHIAN MOUNTAINS
Hudson R.
Delaware R.
Plymouth   Cape Cod
WAMPANOAGS
NARRAGANSETS
SUSQUEHANNAS
LENI-LENAPES
Potomac R.
ATLANTIC OCEAN
40°N
NANTICOKES
Virginia
James R.   POWHATANS   Chesapeake Bay
Jamestown
Roanoke R.   Roanoke Island
TUSCARORAS
35°N

N W E S

Albers Equal-Area Projection
0   100   200 Miles
0   100   200 Kilometers

Reforms of 1619 To attract more settlers, the Virginia Company took steps to establish a more stable government. In 1619, it sent a new governor with orders to consult settlers on all important matters. Male settlers were allowed to elect burgesses, or representatives to the government.

The burgesses met in an assembly called the House of Burgesses. Together with the governor and his council, they made laws for the colony. The first session met in the Jamestown church in July and August 1619. In steamy weather, the burgesses sat in the church pews, while the governor and council took their places in the choir stalls.

The House of Burgesses marked the beginning of representative government in the English colonies. In a representative government, voters elect representatives to make laws for them.

English Traditions The idea that people had political rights was deeply rooted in English history. In 1215, English nobles had forced King John to sign the Magna Carta, or Great Charter. This document said that the king could not raise taxes without first consulting a Great Council of nobles and church leaders.

Over time, the rights won by nobles were extended to other people. The Great Council grew into a representative assembly, called Parliament. Parliament was divided into the House of Lords, made up of nobles, and an elected House of Commons. Only a few rich men had the right to vote. Still, the English had established the principle that even monarchs had to obey the law.

Virginia's Representative Tradition At first, free Virginians had even greater rights than citizens in England. They did not have to own property in order to vote. In 1670, however, the colony restricted the vote to free, white, male property owners.

Despite these limits, representative government remained important. The idea took root that settlers should have a say in the affairs of the colony. Colonists came to refer to the Virginia Company's 1619 frame of government as their own "Great Charter."

New Arrivals

During the early years of the Jamestown Colony, only a few women chose to make the journey from England. Nor did enough workers come to raise tobacco and other crops.

Women in Virginia The colony's first women arrived in 1608—a "Mistress Forrest" and her maid, Anne Burras. Few others followed until 1619, when the Virginia Company sent about 100 women to help "make the men more settled." This shipload of women quickly found husbands. The Virginia Company profited from the marriages because it charged each man who found a wife 150 pounds of tobacco.

Women survived the hardships of Virginia better than men. One colonist commented that women "escape better than men, either that their work lies chiefly [inside] or because they are of a colder temper." In fact, men were almost twice as likely as women to die from diseases or other causes.

Still, life for women remained a daily struggle. Women had to make everything from scratch—food, clothing, even medicines. Many died young from hard work or childbirth. By 1624, there were still fewer than 300 women in the Jamestown colony, compared to over a thousand men.

The First Africans Africans came to Virginia early on. Recently discovered records show that at least 15 black men and 17 black women were already living there by 1619. That same year, a Dutch ship arrived with about 20 Africans. The Dutch sold the Africans to Virginians who needed laborers to grow tobacco. The colonists valued the agricultural skills that the Africans brought with them.

About 300 Africans lived in Virginia by 1644. Some were slaves for life. Others worked as servants and expected one day to own their own farms. Some Africans did become free planters. Anthony Johnson owned 250 acres of land and employed five servants to help him work it. For a time, free Africans in Virginia also had the right to vote.

Later in the 1600s, Virginia set up a system of laws allowing white colonists to enslave Africans for life. As slavery expanded, free Africans lost rights. By the early 1700s, free African property owners could not vote.

AS YOU READ **Summarize** Write two or three sentences summarizing the impact of the "new arrivals" to the Jamestown Colony in 1619.

Section 4 Assessment

Recall

1. **Identify** Explain the significance of **(a)** Walter Raleigh, **(b)** John Smith, **(c)** Powhatan, **(d)** House of Burgesses, **(e)** Magna Carta, **(f)** Parliament.
2. **Define** **(a)** charter, **(b)** burgess, **(c)** representative government.

Comprehension

3. **(a)** Describe three problems the Jamestown Colony faced after 1607. **(b)** Why was the colony finally able to survive?
4. What were the origins of representative government in the English colonies?

5. What new arrivals helped the Jamestown Colony thrive?

Critical Thinking and Writing

6. **Exploring the Main Idea** Review the Main Idea statement at the beginning of this section. Then, list what you would consider to be the four most important milestones in the growth of Jamestown.
7. **Linking Past and Present** Name three important features of Jamestown's government. For each item, write a sentence explaining how it is also an element of American representative government today.

ACTIVITY

Creating an Advertisement You are an investor in the Virginia Company. In order to make a profit, you must encourage people to leave England and move to Jamestown. Create an advertisement describing the advantages of living in Virginia. If possible, include an illustration.

The House of Burgesses

The House of Burgesses first met in Jamestown, Virginia, on July 30, 1619. That hot day marks the beginning of representative government in what became the United States.

The first session passed a variety of laws. The burgesses decreed:

- that colonists plant mulberry trees and grape vines.
- that penalties be imposed for drunkenness, idleness, and gambling.
- that colonists attend church twice on Sunday—and that they bring their guns and swords with them.
- that "no injury or oppression be [committed] by the English against the Indians."
- that each town and plantation had to educate a number of Indian children.

The first burgesses wore multiple layers of velvets and silks, like upper-class members of the British Parliament (left). But Jamestown's hot, humid July climate proved deadly. Several burgesses got sick, and one died.

The 22 elected burgesses gathered in the Jamestown church. Parson Buck opened the meeting with a prayer. As each burgess heard his name called, he took his seat before the governor.

ACTIVITY

Choose one of the laws listed above. With a partner, enact a discussion in the House of Burgesses about that law. Explain why you think such a law is necessary for the well-being of the colony.

5 Seeking Religious Freedom

BEFORE YOU READ

Reading Focus

- How did European states control or regulate religion?
- Why did the colonists at Plymouth feel they needed the Mayflower Compact?
- How were the Pilgrims able to survive early hardships?

Key Terms

Pilgrims

established church

persecution

Mayflower Compact

precedent

Thanksgiving

Taking Notes

Copy this flowchart. As you read, fill in the boxes with the major events and developments relating to the founding of the Plymouth Colony. The first and last boxes have been completed to help you get started. Add as many boxes as you need.

England persecutes Separatists
↓
↓
↓
↓
First successful harvest in Plymouth

Main Idea The Pilgrims founded Plymouth Colony in 1620 in order to practice their religion freely.

Setting the Scene The small sailing ship had been tossed by so many storms that leaks had sprung in the ship's hull. After two hard months at sea, the colonists on board were relieved to see the shores of New England. Still, there were no European colonies for hundreds of miles. Worse, it was already November of 1620, much too late for crops to be planted. One of the voyagers, William Bradford, vividly remembered the situation:

> 66 Being thus passed the vast ocean . . . they had now no friends to welcome them nor inns to entertain or refresh their weatherbeaten bodies; no houses or much less towns to repair to . . . And for the season it was winter, and they that know the winters of that country know them to be sharp and violent. 99
>
> —William Bradford, *Of Plymouth Plantation*

Despite many hardships, the newcomers made their new colony succeed. Unlike the Jamestown colonists or the Spanish, they sought neither gold nor silver nor great riches. What they wanted most was to practice their religion freely. Years later, the founders of Plymouth became known to history as the Pilgrims.*

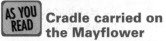

AS YOU READ **Cradle carried on the Mayflower**

Use Prior Knowledge Before reading this section, freewrite a list of things you know about the Pilgrims. After you read, decide whether any items on your list were incorrect.

European States and Religion

It was not easy for people to practice religion freely in Europe during the 1500s. As you have read, after the Protestant Reformation, European Christians were divided into Protestants and Roman Catholics. This division led to fierce religious wars. In France, for example, Protestants and Catholics fought each other for nearly 40

---

*The founders of the Plymouth Colony did not call themselves Pilgrims. However, William Bradford once wrote that they were "pilgrims . . . [who] lifted up their eyes to the heavens, their dearest country." A pilgrim is anyone who makes a long journey for religious reasons.

years. Thousands upon thousands of people were killed because of their religious beliefs.

Most European rulers believed that they could not maintain order unless the state supported a particular religion. The chosen religion was known as the **established church.** In England, for example, the established church was the Anglican church, or Church of England. In the 1530s, Parliament passed laws making the English monarch the head of the Church of England.

In England and other nations, people who did not follow the established religion were often persecuted. **Persecution** is the mistreatment or punishment of certain people because of their beliefs. Sometimes, members of persecuted groups had to worship secretly. If they were discovered, they might be imprisoned or even executed by being burned at the stake.

Separatists Seek Religious Freedom One religious group in England that faced persecution were the people we now call the Pilgrims. At the time, they were known as Separatists. They were called that because, although they were Protestant, they wanted to separate from the Church of England.

The English government bitterly opposed the Separatists. William Bradford remembered what some Separatists suffered:

66 They . . . were hunted and persecuted on every side. . . . For some were taken and clapped up in prison, others had their houses beset and watched night and day . . . and the most were [glad] to flee and leave their houses. 99
—William Bradford, *Of Plymouth Plantation*

In the early 1600s, a group of Separatists left England for Leyden, a city in the Netherlands. The Dutch allowed the newcomers to worship freely. Still, the Pilgrims missed their English way of life. They were also worried that their children were growing up more Dutch than English.

The Pilgrim Colony at Plymouth

A group of Separatists decided to return to England. Along with some other English people who were not Separatists, they won a charter to set up a colony in Virginia. In September 1620, more than 100 men, women, and children set sail aboard a small ship called the *Mayflower.* As you have read, the journey was long and difficult.

At last, in November 1620, the *Mayflower* landed on the cold, bleak shore of Cape Cod, in present-day Massachusetts. The passengers had planned to settle farther south along the Hudson River, but the difficult sea voyage exhausted them. The colonists decided to travel no further. They called their new settlement Plimoth, or Plymouth, because the *Mayflower* had sailed from the port of Plymouth, England.

The Mayflower Compact Before going ashore, the Pilgrims realized that they would not be settling within the boundaries of Virginia. As a result, the terms of their charter would not apply to their new colony. In that case, who would govern them? The question

Primary Source

The Mayflower Compact

On November 11, 1620, the 41 male passengers on the Mayflower *signed a binding agreement for self-government:*

"We, whose names are underwritten. . . . Having undertaken for the Glory of God, and Advancement of the Christian Faith and honor of our King and country, a voyage to plant the first colony in the northern parts of Virginia, do . . . solemnly and mutually in the presence of God, and one of another, covenant and combine ourselves into a civil body politic . . . to enact, constitute, and frame, such just and equal Laws . . . as shall be thought most [fitting] and convenient for the general Good of the Colony; unto which we promise all due submission and obedience."

—Mayflower Compact

Analyzing Primary Sources
Identify two promises the signers of the Mayflower Compact made with regard to laws for their colony.

Viewing History

Signing
the
Mayflower
Compact

Plymouth

Before the *Mayflower* anchored in what is now Provincetown Harbor off Cape Cod, the male passengers signed the Mayflower Compact. This painting depicts the event. **Drawing Inferences** *What does this painting suggest about the women aboard the* Mayflower?

was important because not all colonists on the Mayflower were Pilgrims. Some of these "strangers," as the Pilgrims called them, said they were not bound to obey the Pilgrims, "for none had power to command them."

In response, the Pilgrims joined together to write a framework for governing their colony. On November 11, 1620, the 41 male passengers—both Pilgrims and non-Pilgrims—signed the **Mayflower Compact.** They pledged themselves to unite into a "civil body politic," or government. They agreed to make and abide by laws that insured "the general Good of the Colony." (See the Primary Source on the preceding page.)

The Mayflower Compact established an important tradition. When the Pilgrims found themselves without a government, they banded together themselves to make laws. In time, they set up a government in which adult male colonists elected a governor and council. Thus, like Virginia's Great Charter, the Mayflower Compact strengthened the English tradition of governing through elected representatives.

Tradition of Religious Freedom The Pilgrims were the first of many English settlers who came to North America in order to worship as they pleased. Still, as you will read in the next chapter, that did not mean that religious freedom spread quickly through England's colonies. Many settlers who wished to worship as they

Plymouth

Plimoth Plantation

By 1627, Plymouth was a stable settlement. Using records from that year, historians carefully re-created Plimoth Plantation on the grounds of the old village in Massachusetts. Plimoth is a "living museum," where people in authentic costumes tend crops, make tools, and tell you about their lives. Even the animals at Plimoth are all breeds that were raised by the Pilgrims.

 Take It to the NET

Virtual Field Trip For an interactive look at Plimoth Plantation, visit *The American Nation* section of **www.phschool.com**.

pleased still believed that only their own religious beliefs should be observed. Most of the later English colonies set up their own established churches.

Still, the Pilgrims' desire to worship freely set an important **precedent,** or example for others to follow in the future. Plymouth's leaders announced "that any honest men may live with them, that will carry themselves peaceably and seek the common good." In time, the idea of religious freedom for all would become a cornerstone of American democracy.

Early Hardships

The Pilgrims built their settlement on the site of a Native American village that had been abandoned because of disease. The colonists even found baskets filled with corn that they were able to eat.

First Winter in Plymouth However, the corn was not enough to get the Pilgrims through their first winter. The Pilgrims had failed to bring enough food with them, and it was too late in the season to plant new crops.

The harsh season was also difficult to survive because the Pilgrims had not had enough time to build proper shelters. Most threw together crude houses of sod, or clumps of earth. Some dug themselves into pits in the ground, covered by branches to protect themselves from the weather. Nearly half the settlers perished of disease or starvation.

Among those who died that winter was the colony's first governor. William Bradford was chosen to take his place. Bradford's able leadership helped the colony survive. Reelected many times, he would lead Plymouth for most of the next 36 years.

Despite the great suffering of the "Starving Time," the Pilgrims' religious faith remained strong. They believed that it was God's will for them to remain in Plymouth. "What could now sustain them," wrote Bradford, "but the Spirit of God and His grace?"

Help From Native Americans In the spring, the Pilgrims began to clear land and plant crops. They also received help from neighboring Native Americans. A Pemaquid Indian, Samoset, had learned English from earlier explorers sailing along the coast. He introduced the Pilgrims to Massasoit (MAS uh soit), chief of the local Wampanoag (wahm puh NOH ahg) Indians.

The Wampanoag who helped the Pilgrims most was named Squanto. As a young man, Squanto had been captured by an English expedition led by John Smith. Squanto lived for a time in England, where he learned to speak the language. As a result, he could communicate easily with the Pilgrims.

Squanto brought the Pilgrims seeds of native plants—corn, beans, and pumpkins—and showed them how to plant them. He also taught the settlers how to catch eels from nearby rivers. By treading water, he stirred up eels from the mud at the river bottom and then snatched them up with his hands. The grateful Pilgrims called Squanto "a special instrument sent of God."

In the fall, the Pilgrims had a very good harvest. Because they believed that God had given them this harvest, they set aside a day for giving thanks. In later years, the Pilgrims celebrated after each harvest season with a day of thanksgiving. Americans today celebrate Thanksgiving as a national holiday.

 AS YOU READ **Ask Questions** What questions do you think the Pilgrims might have asked Squanto? What questions do you think Squanto might have asked the Pilgrims?

Section 5 Assessment

Recall
1. **Identify** Explain the significance of **(a)** William Bradford, **(b)** Pilgrims, **(c)** Mayflower Compact, **(d)** Squanto, **(e)** Thanksgiving.
2. **Define** **(a)** established church, **(b)** persecution, **(c)** precedent.

Comprehension
3. Why did many religious groups in Europe face persecution?
4. **(a)** How did the Mayflower Compact resolve a conflict among the Plymouth settlers? **(b)** Why is this document important?
5. How did Native Americans help the Pilgrims survive?

Critical Thinking and Writing
6. **Exploring the Main Idea** Review the Main Idea statement at the beginning of this section. Then, write a letter from one Separatist in England to another explaining why you have decided to sail on the *Mayflower*.
7. **Comparing** Write a list of three ways the founding of Plymouth was different from or similar to the founding of Jamestown.

ACTIVITY

Take It to the NET

Exploring Tradition Freewrite a list of images that you think describe the first Thanksgiving. Then, use the Internet to find accounts of the Pilgrims' harvest celebration in 1621. Explain two things you learned that surprised you. Visit *The American Nation* section of **www.phschool.com** for help in completing the activity.

CREATING A CHAPTER SUMMARY

Copy the table below. Fill in the blank cells with information relating to European exploration and settlement of the Americas. Some cells have been partially filled in to help you get started.

COUNTRY	EXPLORERS	COLONIES	ECONOMIC ACTIVITIES	RELATIONS WITH INDIANS
SPAIN			• Gold and silver mining	
FRANCE				
THE NETHERLANDS	• Henry Hudson			
ENGLAND				

For additional review and enrichment activities, see the inter-active version of *The American Nation*, available on the Web and on CD-ROM.

Take It to the NET

Chapter Self-Test For practice test questions for Chapter 3, visit *The American Nation* section of **www.phschool.com**.

Building Vocabulary

Write sentences, using the chapter vocabulary words listed below, leaving blanks where the vocabulary words would go. Exchange your sentences with another student and fill in the blanks.

1. colony
2. circumnavigate
3. conquistador
4. presidio
5. mission
6. peninsulare
7. northwest passage
8. charter
9. representative government
10. established church

Reviewing Key Facts

11. Identify one reason Spain financed Columbus's voyage in 1492. (Section 1)
12. How were European and Native American cultures blended in New Spain? (Section 2)
13. How did Dutch ways help shape American culture? (Section 3)
14. Describe two English political traditions of the Jamestown Colony. (Section 4)
15. Why did the Pilgrims decide to start a colony? (Section 5)

Critical Thinking and Writing

16. **Linking Past and Present** List three ways today's world might have been different if the Columbian Exchange had not taken place.
17. **Recognizing Points of View** For each of the following, write one sentence explaining how that person might have felt about Bartolomé de Las Casas: **(a)** a Native American working on a plantation in the Caribbean; **(b)** a Spanish plantation owner; **(c)** a slave trader in East Africa; **(d)** an African sent to the Americas as a slave.
18. **Connecting to Geography: Movement** Look at a world map or a map of North America. **(a)** Write a description of a possible northern sea route around the Americas to Asia. **(b)** Based on what you know of this part of the world, why do you think the British, French, or Dutch never found a northwest passage?
19. **Comparing (a)** List one similarity and one difference between Jamestown's "Great Charter" of 1619 and the Mayflower Compact. **(b)** Write a paragraph evaluating the importance of these documents.

Analyzing Primary Sources

Jacques Marquette and Louis Joliet had many encounters with Indians along the Mississippi. Read the following excerpt from Marquette's journal and answer the questions that follow:

> 66 We slept in the chief's cabin, and on the following day we took leave of him, promising to pass again by his village, within four moons. He conducted us to our canoes, with nearly 600 persons who witnessed our embarkation, giving us every possible sign of the joy that our visit had caused them. For my own part, I promised . . . that I would come the following year, and reside with them to instruct them. 99

—Jacques Marquette, quoted in *The Jesuit Relations and Allied Documents* (Thwaites)

20. According to Marquette, how were he and Joliet treated by the Native Americans?
21. What do you think he means when he promises to "instruct" the Indians?
22. Would you consider Marquette's journal a reliable source of information about relations between the French and Native Americans? Why or why not?

Sequencing

Below are some key events relating to the first English colonies. The events are not listed in correct time sequence. Look at the events and answer the questions that follow.

I.	House of Burgesses is formed
II.	Pilgrims leave England
III.	Jamestown Colony is founded
IV.	Mayflower Compact is signed
V.	Roanoke colonists disappear
VI.	Squanto teaches Pilgrims
VII.	Colonists begin to grow tobacco

23. In which set below are the events listed in the correct sequence?
 A VII, IV, II
 B V, I, VI
 C III, VI, IV
 D II, VII, VI
24. Choose two events from the list above. Identify the correct time sequence and explain how the two events are related.

ACTIVITIES

Connecting With . . . Geography

Creating a Thematic Map With the class, create a map of the Era of Exploration and Colonization. Use the information found on the various maps in this chapter. (Your teacher may suggest that you look at additional maps as well.) Draw a large base map of the world. Label important continents, countries, oceans, and rivers. Create a color key for the major European powers discussed in the chapter. Choose who you consider to be the 10 most important explorers and show their routes on the map. Then, color in the areas of the Americas that were colonized by European nations. Use the same color key to show a nation, its explorers, and its colonies.

Take It to the NET

Connecting to Today

Preparing a Tourist Guide Look at the History Happened Here picture in Section 5. Select another of the early European settlements described in this chapter. Use the Internet to discover what you can now see if you visit that location. With a partner, create an illustrated guide for modern tourists. For help in starting this activity, visit *The American Nation* section of **www.phschool.com**.

Exploring Historical Scholarship

Summarizing Use the Internet to find one theory about the disappearance of the colony at Roanoke. In a one-minute talk, summarize the theory and the evidence for it. For help in starting this activity, visit *The American Nation* section of **www.phschool.com**.

The Thirteen English Colonies

1630–1750

1 **The New England Colonies**
2 **The Middle Colonies**
3 **The Southern Colonies**
4 **Roots of Self-Government**
5 **Life in the Colonies**

Puritan settlers building homes

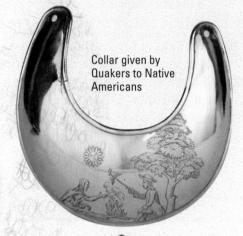

Collar given by Quakers to Native Americans

AMERICAN EVENTS

1630
Puritans from England set up the Massachusetts Bay Colony.

1675
Metacom leads fight against settlers in New England.

1682
William Penn founds the colony of Pennsylvania.

1630 · · · · 1660 · · · 1690

WORLD EVENTS

1660 ▲
English Parliament passes a stronger version of the Navigation Act.

1689 ▲
William and Mary sign the English Bill of Rights.

The Thirteen Colonies

By 1750, the 13 English colonies extended along the eastern coast of North America.

FRENCH TERRITORY

L. Superior

80°W

90°W

L. Huron

L. Michigan

L. Ontario

L. Erie

40°N

FRENCH TERRITORY

100°W

NH

MA

New York

CT

RI

APPALACHIAN MOUNTAINS

Pennsylvania

New Jersey

Delaware

ATLANTIC OCEAN

Virginia

Maryland

North Carolina

South Carolina

Georgia

SPANISH TERRITORY

70°W

30°N

Key

New England Colonies

Middle Colonies

Southern Colonies

Claimed by NH and NY

Albers Equal-Area Projection

0   150   300 Miles

0   150   300 Kilometers

Jonathan Edwards and his famous sermon

SINNERS IN THE HANDS OF AN ANGRY GOD. A SERMON

BY JONATHAN EDWARDS, A.M.

1730s

A religious movement, known as the Great Awakening, sweeps through the colonies.

1700s

Plantations in the Southern Colonies begin to rely heavily on slave labor.

1732

The colony of Georgia becomes a refuge for people jailed for debt.

1690   1720   1750

1700s ▲

The Enlightenment begins.

▲ 1725

British Quakers speak out against slavery.

1 The New England Colonies

BEFORE YOU READ

Reading Focus

- Why did the Puritans decide to leave England?
- What problems in Massachusetts colony caused people to leave?
- Why were the Puritans and Native Americans at war?
- Why were towns and villages important in New England life?

Key Terms

Puritans

General Court

Fundamental Orders of Connecticut

religious tolerance

Sabbath

town meeting

Taking Notes

Copy this chart. As you read, fill in the boxes with the name of each New England Colony, the date it was settled, and why. The first two boxes have been started for you. Add as many boxes as you need.

COLONY	DATE SETTLED	REASONS FOR SETTLEMENT
• Plymouth • Massachusetts Bay	• 1620 • 1630	• •

Main Idea The New England Colonies were founded by political and religious reformers and developed around tightly knit towns and villages.

AS YOU READ

Powdered wig from the 1700s

Find Main Ideas According to Samuel Sewall, why was Hayward's wig a problem?

Setting the Scene
Boston merchant Samuel Sewall frowned as he greeted Mr. Hayward, an acquaintance. Hayward had cut off his long gray hair. In its place, he was wearing a full wig of dark hair that made him look younger! Sewall protested that in the Bible, Jesus had said a person cannot "make one's Hair white or black." Hayward gulped nervously. He claimed that his doctors had advised him to wear the wig.

By the time Sewall recorded this story in 1685, Boston had become the busiest town in the Massachusetts Bay Colony. Most of the colony's founders were no longer living. Yet, Sewall shared their ideals. He looked to the Bible to guide him in matters large and small—even the treatment of one's hair. Sewall wanted his colony to be a "holy commonwealth" that followed the laws of God.

Religion played a large part in the founding of colonies in New England. During the 1630s, thousands of English settlers came to live around Massachusetts Bay, north of Plymouth. Gradually, English settlers built towns and farms throughout the region. These settlements shared a distinctive way of life.

The Puritans Leave England for Massachusetts

The migration to Massachusetts Bay during the 1630s was led by a religious group known as the **Puritans**. Unlike the Pilgrims, the Puritans did not want to separate entirely from the Church of England. Instead, they hoped to reform the church by introducing simpler forms of worship. They wanted to do away with many practices inherited from the Roman Catholic Church, such as organ music, finely decorated houses of worship, and special clothing for priests.

Leaving England During "Evil Times"

The Puritans were a powerful group in England. Although some were small farmers, many were well-educated and successful merchants or landowners.

Charles I, who became king in 1625, disapproved of the Puritans and their ideas. He canceled Puritan business charters and even had a few Puritans jailed.

By 1629, some Puritan leaders were convinced that England had fallen on "evil and declining times." They persuaded royal officials to grant them a charter to form the Massachusetts Bay Company. The company's bold plan was to build a new society based on biblical laws and teachings. John Winthrop, a lawyer and a devout Puritan, believed that the new colony would set an example to the world.

Some settlers joined the Massachusetts colonists for economic rather than religious reasons. In wealthy English families, the oldest son usually inherited his father's estate. With little hope of owning land, younger sons sought opportunity elsewhere. They were attracted to Massachusetts Bay because it offered cheap land or a chance to start a business.

Governing the Colony

In 1629, the Puritans sent a small advance party to North America. John Winthrop and a party of more than 1,000 arrived the following year. Winthrop was chosen first governor of the Massachusetts Bay Colony.

Once ashore, Winthrop set an example for others. Although he was governor, he worked hard to build a home, clear land, and plant crops.

There was discontent among some colonists, though. Under the charter, only stockholders who had invested money in the Massachusetts Bay Company had the right to vote. Most settlers, however, were not stockholders. They resented taxes and laws passed by a government in which they had no say.

Winthrop and other stockholders saw that the colony would run more smoothly if a greater number of settlers could take part. At the same time, Puritan leaders wished to keep non-Puritans out of the government. As a result, they granted the right to vote for governor to all men who were church members. Later, male church members also elected representatives to an assembly called the General Court.

Under the leadership of Winthrop and other Puritans, the Massachusetts Bay Colony prospered. Between 1629 and 1640, some 15,000 men, women, and children journeyed from England to Massachusetts. This movement of people is known as the Great Migration. Many of the newcomers settled in Boston, which grew into the colony's largest town.

The New England Colonies

Key

- 🌾 Grain
- 🐂 Cattle
- 🌲 Lumber
- 🐟 Fish
- 🐋 Whales
- 🎩 Furs
- ⚓ Ships
- ▬ Iron
- 🏺 Rum

St. Lawrence R.

70° W
45° N
75° W

Maine (part of MA)

Falmouth

Area claimed by New York and New Hampshire

New Hampshire
Portsmouth

New York

Newburyport

Salem

Massachusetts
Boston

Connecticut
Plymouth

Pennsylvania
New Haven

Rhode Island
Newport

New Jersey

40° N

ATLANTIC OCEAN

Albers Equal-Area Projection
0   50   100 Miles
0   50 100 Kilometers

GEOGRAPHY Skills

The New England colonies were among the first English settlements in North America. Major economic activities in the region included shipbuilding, fishing, and fur trapping.

1. **Location** On the map, locate: **(a)** Massachusetts, **(b)** Connecticut, **(c)** Rhode Island, **(d)** New Hampshire, **(e)** Boston, **(f)** Plymouth.

2. **Interaction** In which colonies did settlers mine iron ore?

3. **Critical Thinking** **Analyzing Information** How did New England's geography encourage the growth of shipbuilding?

Primary Sources

See "The Fundamental Orders of Connecticut" on page 578 in the Reference Section.

Problems in Massachusetts Bay

The Puritan leaders did not like anyone to question their religious beliefs or the way the colony was governed. Usually, discontented colonists were forced to leave. Some colonists who left Massachusetts founded other colonies in New England.

Thomas Hooker Founds Connecticut In May 1636, a Puritan minister named Thomas Hooker led about 100 settlers out of Massachusetts Bay. Pushing west, they drove their cattle, goats, and pigs along Indian trails that cut through the forests. When they reached the Connecticut River, they built a town, which they called Hartford.

Hooker left Massachusetts Bay because he believed that the governor and other officials had too much power. He wanted to set up a colony in Connecticut with strict limits on government.

The settlers wrote a plan of government called the **Fundamental Orders of Connecticut** in 1639. It created a government much like that of Massachusetts. There were, however, two important differences. First, the Fundamental Orders gave the vote to all men who were property owners, including those who were not church members. Second, the Fundamental Orders limited the governor's power. In this way, the Fundamental Orders expanded the idea of representative government in the English colonies.

Connecticut became a separate colony in 1662, with a new charter granted by the king of England. By then, 15 towns were thriving along the Connecticut River.

Viewing History

Roger Williams in Narragansett Bay
After Williams was cast out of the Massachusetts Bay Colony, he stayed for a time with Native Americans in Narragansett Bay. **Drawing Inferences** *How would you describe Williams's relationship with the Native Americans?*

Roger Williams Settles Rhode Island Another Puritan who challenged the leaders of Massachusetts Bay was Roger Williams. A young minister in the village of Salem, Williams was gentle and good-natured. William Bradford described him as "zealous but very unsettled in judgment." Some Puritan leaders probably agreed with this. Most people, including Governor Winthrop, liked him. Williams's ideas, however, alarmed Puritan leaders.

Williams believed that the Puritan church in Massachusetts had too much power. In Williams's view, the business of church and state should be completely separate since concern with political affairs would corrupt the church. The role of the state, said Williams, was to maintain order and peace. It should not support a particular church. Finally, Williams did not believe that the Puritan leaders had the right to force people to attend religious services.

Williams also believed in religious tolerance. **Religious tolerance** means a willingness to let others practice their own beliefs.

In Puritan Massachusetts, non-Puritans were not allowed to worship freely.

Puritan leaders viewed Williams as a dangerous troublemaker. In 1635, the General Court ordered him to leave Massachusetts. Fearing that the court would send him back to England, Williams fled to Narragansett Bay, where he spent the winter with Indians. In the spring of 1636, the Indians sold him land for a settlement. After a few years, the settlement became the English colony of Rhode Island.

In Rhode Island, Williams put into practice his ideas about tolerance. He allowed complete freedom of religion for all Protestants, Jews, and Catholics.* He did not set up a state church or require settlers to attend church services. He also gave all white men the right to vote. Before long, settlers who disliked the strict Puritan rule of Massachusetts flocked to Providence and other towns in Rhode Island.

Anne Hutchinson Speaks Out

Among those who fled to Rhode Island was Anne Hutchinson. A devout Puritan, Hutchinson regularly attended church services in Boston, where she first lived. After church, she and her friends gathered at her home to discuss the minister's sermon. Often, she seemed to question some of the minister's teachings. Hutchinson was very persuasive, and neighbors flocked to hear her.

Puritan leaders grew angry. They believed that Hutchinson's opinions were full of religious errors. Even worse, they said, a woman did not have the right to explain God's law. In November 1637, Hutchinson was ordered to appear before the Massachusetts General Court.

At her trial, Hutchinson answered the questions put to her by Governor Winthrop and other members of the court. Each time, her answers revealed weaknesses in their arguments. They could not prove that she had broken any Puritan laws or that she had disobeyed any religious teachings.

Then, after two long days of hostile questioning, Hutchinson made a serious mistake. She told the court that God spoke directly to her, "By the voice of His own spirit to my soul." Members of the court were shocked. Puritans believed that God spoke only through the Bible, not directly to individuals. The court ordered her out of the colony.

In 1638, Hutchinson, along with her family and some friends, went to Rhode Island. The Puritan leaders had won their case. For later Americans, however, Hutchinson became an important symbol of the struggle for religious freedom.

Viewing History

Anne Hutchinson

Known in the colony as a "woman of ready wit with a bold spirit," Hutchinson won the respect of Puritan leaders at first. However, they soon saw her as a troublemaker. Here, she defends herself before the General Court.
Making Decisions *Do you think Hutchinson was a "bold spirit"? Explain.*

---

*In 1763, Jewish settlers in Rhode Island built Touro Synagogue, the first Jewish house of worship in North America. It still stands today.

Puritans at War With Native Americans

From Massachusetts Bay, settlers fanned out across New England. Some built trading and fishing villages along the coast north of Boston. In 1680, the king made these coastal settlements into a separate colony called New Hampshire.

The first meetings between English settlers and Native Americans did not foreshadow the conflict that would eventually occur between them. Some colonial leaders such as William Penn and Roger Williams tried to treat Native Americans fairly.

As more colonists settled in New England, they began to take over more Native American lands. By 1670, nearly 45,000 English settlers were living in the towns in New England. As a result, fighting broke out between white settlers and Indian nations of the region.

The largest conflict came in 1675. Metacom, also known by his English name, King Phillip, was chief of the Wampanoag Indians. He watched for years as English towns were built on Wampanoag lands. "I am resolved not to see the day when I have no country," he told an English friend. Metacom's people attacked villages throughout New England. Other Indian groups, from Rhode Island to Maine, soon allied themselves with the Wampanoags. They were determined to drive the English settlers off their land. Metacom and his allies destroyed 12 towns and killed more than 600 European settlers.

After more than a year of fighting, however, Metacom was captured and killed. The English sold his family and about 1,000 other Indians into slavery in the West Indies. Other Indians were forced from their homelands.

The pattern of English expansion followed by war was repeated between colonists and Indians throughout the colonies. It would continue for many years to come.

Life in New England Towns and Villages

Puritans believed that people should worship and tend to local matters as a community. As a result, New England became a land of tightly knit towns and villages.

At the center of each village was the common, an open field where cattle grazed. Nearby stood the meetinghouse, where Puritans worshiped and held town meetings.

Religion and Family The Puritans took their Sabbath, or holy day of rest, very seriously. On Sundays, no one was allowed to play games or visit taverns to joke, talk, and drink. The law required all citizens to attend Sunday church services, which would last all day.

Connecting to Today

Democracy in Action

In New England and some other states, town meetings still occur. Citizens discuss and vote on important issues, such as town laws or how to use the town's money.

Today, new technology is giving a whole new meaning to town meetings. In "electronic town meetings" (ETM), televisions, telephones, or computers link people from distant locations and provide instant voting results. Experts give background talks on an issue. Citizens ask questions, speak their minds, and then vote. The way in which citizens conduct their meetings is different from the way it was in colonial times. However, the citizens' desire to make their voices heard is the same.

What issues might you like to see addressed by a town meeting in your community?

During the 1600s, women sat on one side of the church and men on the other. Blacks and Indians stood in a balcony at the back. Children had separate pews, where an adult watched over them.

Government At town meetings, settlers discussed and voted on many issues. What roads should be built? How much should the schoolmaster be paid? Town meetings gave New Englanders a chance to speak their minds. This early experience encouraged the growth of democratic ideas in New England.

Puritan laws were strict. About 15 crimes carried the death penalty. One crime punishable by death was witchcraft. In 1692, Puritans in Salem Village executed 20 men and women as witches.

Economy New England was a difficult land for colonists. The rocky soil was poor for farming. After a time, however, Native Americans taught English settlers how to grow many crops, such as Indian corn, pumpkins, squash, and beans.

Although the soil was poor, the forests were full of riches. Settlers hunted wild turkey and deer. Settlers also cut down trees and floated them to sawmills near ports such as Boston, Massachusetts, or Portsmouth, New Hampshire. These cities grew into major shipbuilding centers.

Other New Englanders fished for cod and halibut. In the 1600s, people began to hunt whales. Whales supplied oil for lamps and other products. In the 1700s and 1800s, whaling grew into a big business.

Decline of the Puritans During the 1700s, the Puritan tradition declined. Fewer families left England for religious reasons. Ministers had less influence on the way colonies were governed. Nevertheless, the Puritans had stamped New England with their distinctive customs and their dream of a religious society.

Section 1 Assessment

Recall

1. **Identify** Explain the significance of (a) Puritans, (b) John Winthrop, (c) General Court, (d) Thomas Hooker, (e) Fundamental Orders of Connecticut, (f) Roger Williams, (g) Anne Hutchinson, (h) Metacom.
2. **Define** (a) religious tolerance, (b) Sabbath, (c) town meeting.

Comprehension

3. Why did the Puritans settle the Massachusetts Bay Colony?
4. Why did Thomas Hooker leave the colony?
5. Discuss how the settlement affected Native Americans.

6. What was the purpose of the town meeting?

Critical Thinking and Writing

7. **Exploring the Main Idea** Review the Main Idea statement at the beginning of this section. Then, write a paragraph about how religion and politics affected the development of the New England Colonies.

8. **Drawing Conclusions** The way in which the Puritans governed the Massachusetts Bay Colony led to its success. List arguments to support this viewpoint. Then, list arguments that do not support this statement.

ACTIVITY

Writing a Persuasive Letter You have followed Roger Williams to Rhode Island. Write a letter persuading some friends from Massachusetts to join you.

2 The Middle Colonies

Reading Focus

- Why did the colony of New Netherland become the colony of New York?
- Why did New Jersey separate from New York?
- How was Pennsylvania founded?
- What was life like in the Middle Colonies?

Key Terms

patroon
proprietary colony
royal colony
Quakers
Pennsylvania Dutch
cash crop

Taking Notes

Copy the concept web below. As you read, fill in the blank ovals with important facts about the settlement of the Middle Colonies. Add as many ovals as you need.

New Jersey — THE MIDDLE COLONIES — New York

Main Idea The Middle Colonies attracted a wide variety of immigrants who settled on farms and in the cities of Philadelphia and New York.

A chair from colonial Philadelphia

Draw Inferences Why might different styles of furniture have been available in the Middle Colonies?

Setting the Scene A doctor from the colony of Maryland traveled north to Philadelphia in the summer of 1744. Dr. Hamilton kept his eyes open to see how the customs in that city differed from those of Maryland. Merchants opened for business much earlier, he discovered: at five in the morning. For dinner at a tavern, Hamilton sat around a single large table with 24 other diners. Unfortunately, the "great hall [was] well stocked with flies," he complained.

However, what most surprised Hamilton was the variety of people at the table:

> 66 I dined at a tavern with a very mixed company of different nations and religions. There were Scots, English, Dutch, Germans, and Irish. There were Roman Catholics, Church [of England] men, Presbyterians, Quakers, . . . Moravians . . . and one Jew. 99
> —Alexander Hamilton, *Itinerarium*, 1744

By 1700, England had four colonies in the region south of New England. These colonies became known as the Middle Colonies because they were located between New England and the Southern Colonies. As Dr. Hamilton observed, the Middle Colonies had a much greater mix of people than either New England or the Southern Colonies.

New Netherland Becomes New York

As you have read, the Dutch set up the colony of New Netherland along the Hudson River. In the colony's early years, settlers traded with Indians for furs and built the settlement of New Amsterdam into a thriving port. Since beaver skins were very valuable, most people came to the colonies to trade furs.

To encourage farming in New Netherland, Dutch officials granted large parcels of land to a few rich families. A single land grant could stretch for miles. Indeed, one grant was as big as Rhode Island! Owners of these huge estates were called **patroons.** In return for the grant, each patroon promised to settle at least 50 European farm families on the land. Few farmers wanted to work for the patroons, however. Patroons had great power and could charge whatever rents they pleased.

Most settlers lived in the trading center of New Amsterdam. They came from all over Europe. Many were attracted by the chance to practice their religion freely. African slaves were in demand as well. In the early years they made up more than a quarter of the population of the town.

Dutch colonists were mainly Protestants who belonged to the Dutch Reformed Church. Still, they permitted members of other religions—including Roman Catholics, French Protestants, and Jews—to buy land. "People do not seem concerned what religion their neighbor is," wrote a shocked visitor from Virginia. "Indeed, they do not seem to care if he has any religion at all."

By 1664, the rivalry between England and the Netherlands for trade and colonies was at its height. In August of that year, English warships entered New Amsterdam's harbor. Peter Stuyvesant (STI vuh sehnt), the governor of New Netherland, swore to defend the city. However, he had few weapons and little gunpowder. Also, Stuyvesant had made himself so unpopular with his harsh rule and heavy taxes that the colonists refused to help him. In the end, he surrendered without firing a shot.

King Charles II of England then gave New Netherland to his brother, the Duke of York. He renamed the colony New York in the duke's honor.

New Jersey Separates From New York

At the time of the English takeover, New York stretched as far south as the Delaware River. The Duke of York decided that the colony was too big to govern easily. He gave some of the land to friends, Lord Berkeley and Sir George Carteret. They set up a proprietary (proh PRI uh tehr ee) colony, which they called New Jersey, in 1664.

In setting up a **proprietary colony,** the king gave land to one or more people in return for a yearly payment. These proprietors were free to divide the land and rent it to others. They made laws for the colony but had to respect the rights of colonists under English law.

Like New York, New Jersey had fertile farmland and a wealth of other resources that attracted people from many lands. Settlers came from Finland, Ireland, Scotland, Germany, and Sweden. There were also English and Dutch settlers who moved there from the colony of New York. In addition, some New England colonists, hoping to find better farmland, chose to relocate to New Jersey.

In 1702, New Jersey became a **royal colony,** which is a colony under the direct control of the English crown. The colony's charter protected religious freedom and the rights of an assembly that voted on local matters.

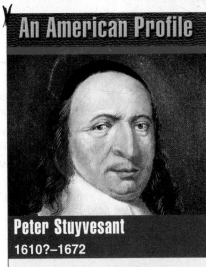

An American Profile

Peter Stuyvesant
1610?–1672

When Peter Stuyvesant arrived in New Amsterdam in 1647, the town was in chaos. "I shall govern you as a father his children," he told the colonists. On his orders, roaming pigs were fenced in. Outdoor toilets were removed from public streets. A new police force patrolled the town after dark. With his big sword, heavy mustache, and silver-tipped wooden leg, Stuyvesant was a commanding sight. Many colonists disliked him. They said he dressed like a one-legged peacock and that he ruled them like the czar of Russia. Even so, Stuyvesant restored law and order in New Amsterdam.

How does your town or county protect the health and safety of its citizens?

The Founding of Pennsylvania

West of New Jersey, William Penn founded the colony of Pennsylvania in 1681. Penn came from a wealthy English family and was a personal friend of King Charles II. At age 22, however, Penn shocked family and friends by joining the **Quakers,** one of the most despised religious groups in England.

The Quakers Like Pilgrims and Puritans, Quakers were Protestant reformers. Their reforms went further than those of other groups, however. Quakers believed that all people—men and women, nobles and commoners—were equal in God's sight. They allowed women to preach in public and refused to bow or remove their hats in the presence of nobles. Quakers spoke out against all war and refused to serve in the army.

To most English people, Quaker beliefs seemed wicked. In both England and New England, Quakers were arrested, fined, or even hanged for their ideas. Penn became convinced that the Quakers must leave England. He turned to the king for help.

Charles II issued a royal charter naming Penn proprietor of a large tract of land in North America. The king named the new colony Pennsylvania, or Penn's woodlands.

A Policy of Fairness Penn thought of his colony as a "holy experiment." He wanted it to be a model of religious freedom, peace, and Christian living. Protestants, Catholics, and Jews went to Pennsylvania to escape persecution. Later, English officials forced Penn to turn away Catholic and Jewish settlers.

Penn's Quaker beliefs led him to speak out for fair treatment of Native Americans. Penn believed that the land in North America belonged to the Indians. He insisted that settlers should pay for the land. Native Americans respected him for this policy. As a result, Pennsylvania colonists enjoyed many years of peace with their Indian neighbors. One settler remarked, "as Penn treated the Indians with extraordinary humanity, they became civil and loving to us."

The Colony Grows Penn sent pamphlets describing his colony all over Europe. Soon, settlers from England, Scotland, Wales, the Netherlands, France, and Germany began to cross the Atlantic Ocean to Pennsylvania.

Among the new arrivals were large numbers of German-speaking Protestants. They became known as **Pennsylvania Dutch** because people could not pronounce the word Deutsch (DOICH), which means German. African slaves were also brought to Pennsylvania. They made up about one-third of all immigrants to the colony between 1730 and 1750. Most stayed in Philadelphia, working as laborers.

Penn carefully planned a capital city along the Delaware River. He named it Philadelphia, a Greek word meaning "brotherly love." Philadelphia grew quickly. By 1710, a visitor wrote that it was "the most noble, large, and well-built city I have seen."

Delaware For a time, Pennsylvania included some lands along the lower Delaware River. The region was known as Pennsylvania's Lower Counties.

Primary Source

A Letter to the Native Americans

Before he would allow people to settle his colony, William Penn insisted on establishing good relations with the Native Americans. He wrote this letter:

"The king of the country where I live hath given me a great province, but I desire to enjoy it with your love and consent, that we may always live together as neighbors and friends, else what would the great God say to us, who hath made us not to devour and destroy one another, but live soberly and kindly together in the world. . . ."

—William Penn, Letter to the Indians, 1681

Analyzing Primary Sources
How does Penn explain his belief about living peacefully with Native Americans?

Settlers in the Lower Counties did not want to send delegates to a distant assembly in Philadelphia. In 1701, Penn allowed them to elect their own assembly. Later, in 1704, the Lower Counties would break away to form the colony of Delaware.

Life in the Middle Colonies

The majority of the people made their living by farming. Farmers found more favorable conditions in the Middle Colonies than in New England. The broad Hudson and Delaware river valleys were rich and fertile. Winters were milder than in New England, and the growing season lasted longer.

A Thriving Economy in the Eastern Counties On such promising land, farmers in the eastern counties of the Middle Colonies cleared their fields. They raised wheat, barley, and rye. These were **cash crops,** or crops that are sold for money at market. In fact, the Middle Colonies exported so much grain that they became known as the Breadbasket Colonies.

Farmers of the Middle Colonies also raised herds of cattle and pigs. Every year, they sent tons of beef, pork, and butter to the ports of New York and Philadelphia. From there, the goods went by ship to New England and the South or to the West Indies, England, and other parts of Europe.

Farms in the Middle Colonies were generally larger than those in New England. Landowners hired workers to help with the planting, harvesting, and other tasks. Enslaved African Americans worked on a few large farms. However, most workers were farmhands who worked alongside the families that owned the land.

Aside from farmers, there were also skilled artisans in the Middle Colonies. Encouraged by William Penn, skilled German craftsworkers set up shop in Pennsylvania. In time, the colony became a center of manufacturing and crafts. One visitor reported that workshops turned out "hardware, clocks, watches, locks, guns, flints, glass, stoneware, nails, [and] paper."

Settlers in the Delaware River valley profited from the region's rich deposits of iron ore. Heating the ore in furnaces, they purified it and then hammered it into nails, tools, and parts for guns.

Middle Colony Homes Because houses tended to be far apart in the Middle Colonies, towns were less important than in New England. Counties, rather than villages, became centers of local government.

The different groups who settled the Middle Colonies had their own favorite ways of building. Swedish settlers introduced log cabins to the Americas. The Dutch used red bricks to build narrow, high-walled

The Middle Colonies

Key
- Grain
- Cattle
- Lumber
- Fish
- Iron
- Rum

Area claimed by New York and New Hampshire

L. Ontario
L. Erie
New York
Albany
New Hampshire
Massachusetts
Connecticut
Rhode Island
Maine (part of MA)
Pennsylvania
Susquehanna R.
Delaware R.
Hudson R.
New York
Perth Amboy
New Jersey
Philadelphia
Wilmington
Baltimore
Maryland
Dover
Delaware
Great Wagon Road
Virginia
ATLANTIC OCEAN

Albers Equal-Area Projection
0   50   100 Miles
0 50 100 Kilometers

75° W
80° W
70° W
45° N
40° N

GEOGRAPHY
Skills

The Middle Colonies were located to the south and west of New England and north of the Southern Colonies.

1. **Location** On the map, locate: **(a)** New York, **(b)** New Jersey, **(c)** Pennsylvania, **(d)** Delaware, **(e)** Hudson River, **(f)** Philadelphia, **(g)** Great Wagon Road.

2. **Movement** Identify two ways settlers could have traveled inland from the Atlantic coast.

3. **Critical Thinking Analyzing Information** Based on the map, why do you think Philadelphia would become a major trading center?

houses. German settlers developed a wood-burning stove that heated a home better than a fireplace, which let blasts of cold air leak down the chimney.

Everyone in a household had a job to do. Households were self-sufficient, which meant that everything needed for survival—food, clothing, and any other items—was made at home. As one farmer said, "Nothing to wear, eat, or drink was purchased, as my farm provided all."

The Backcountry In the 1700s, thousands of German and Scotch-Irish settlers arrived in Philadelphia. From there, they traveled west into the backcountry, the area of land along the eastern slopes of the Appalachian Mountains. Settlers followed an old Iroquois trail that became known as the Great Wagon Road.

Although settlers planned to follow farming methods they had used in Europe, they found the challenge of farming the backcountry more difficult than they had thought it would be. To farm the backcountry, settlers had to clear thick forests. From Indians, settlers learned how to use knots from pine trees as candles to light their homes. They made wooden dishes from logs, gathered honey from hollows in trees, and hunted wild animals for food. German gunsmiths developed a lightweight rifle for use in forests. Sharpshooters boasted that the "Pennsylvania rifle" could hit a rattlesnake between the eyes at 100 yards.

Many of the settlers who arrived in the backcountry moved onto Indian lands. "The Indians . . . are alarmed at the swarm of strangers," one Pennsylvania official reported. "We are afraid of a [fight] between them for the [colonists] are very rough to them." On more than one occasion, disputes between settlers and Indians resulted in violence.

Section 2 Assessment

Recall
1. **Identify** Explain the significance of **(a)** Peter Stuyvesant, **(b)** William Penn, **(c)** Quakers, **(d)** Pennsylvania Dutch.
2. **Define** **(a)** patroon, **(b)** proprietary colony, **(c)** royal colony, **(d)** cash crop.

Comprehension
3. How did New Netherland become New York?
4. Why did New Jersey become a proprietary colony?
5. Why did the Quakers settle Pennsylvania?
6. How did life in the Middle Colonies differ from life in the backcountry?

Critical Thinking and Writing
7. **Exploring the Main Idea** Review the Main Idea statement at the beginning of this section. Then, write a paragraph explaining why settlers were attracted to the Middle Colonies.
8. **Comparing** **(a)** How was Penn's "holy experiment" like the Puritan idea of setting an example for the world? **(b)** How was it different?

ACTIVITY

Take It to the NET
Connecting to Today
Descendants of the Pennsylvania Dutch still live in Pennsylvania today. Use the Internet to find out about the Pennsylvania Dutch. Write a brief report or create a short Powerpoint presentation describing how and where they live. Visit *The American Nation* section of **www.phschool.com** for help in completing the activity.

3 The Southern Colonies

Reading Focus

- Why was Maryland important to Roman Catholics?
- How were the Carolinas and Georgia founded?
- What two ways of life developed in the Southern Colonies?
- Why did the slave trade grow in the 1700s?

Key Terms

Mason-Dixon Line
Act of Toleration
Bacon's Rebellion
indigo
debtor
slave code
racism

Taking Notes

Copy the chart below. As you read, complete the chart to show the causes that led to the founding of the Southern Colonies. Add as many boxes as you need.

Religious freedom → → → → SOUTHERN COLONIES

Main Idea The large tobacco and rice plantations of the Tidewater region contrasted with the settlements of hunters and farmers in the backcountry.

Setting the Scene
In 1763, two English surveyors, Charles Mason and Jeremiah Dixon, began a remarkable journey that lasted nearly four years. Their mission was to survey the 244-mile boundary between Pennsylvania and Maryland.

Mason and Dixon used surveyors' instruments and long chains to map their line. As they went, they carefully laid stone markers on the border between the two colonies. If the line crossed a river, they stretched chains across to measure. If the line went up hills or through swamps, Mason and Dixon followed. More than once, fierce thunderstorms swirled around them:

> 66 The Lightning . . . continued [in] streams or streaks, from the Cloud to the ground all round us; about 5 minutes before the hurricane of wind and Rain; the Cloud from the Western part of the Mountain put on the most Dreadful appearance I ever saw . . . 99
> —Charles Mason *Journal*, August 4, 1766

AS YOU READ Charles Mason and Jeremiah Dixon

Ask Questions After reading the journal passage, what questions would you want to ask Mason and Dixon?

The Mason-Dixon Line was more than just the boundary between Pennsylvania and Maryland. It also divided the Middle Colonies from the Southern Colonies. South of the Mason-Dixon Line, the Southern Colonies developed a way of life different in many ways from that of the other English colonies.

Lord Baltimore's Colony of Maryland

In 1632, Sir George Calvert persuaded King Charles I to grant him land for a colony in the Americas. Calvert had ruined his career in Protestant England by becoming a Roman Catholic. Now, he planned to build a colony where Catholics could practice their religion freely.

He named the colony Maryland in honor of Queen Henrietta Maria, the king's wife.

Calvert died before his colony could get underway. His son Cecil, Lord Baltimore, pushed on with the project.

Settling the Colony In the spring of 1634, about 200 colonists landed along the upper Chesapeake Bay, across from England's first southern colony, Virginia. Maryland was truly a land of plenty. Chesapeake Bay was full of fish, oysters, and crabs. Across the bay, Virginians were already growing tobacco for profit. Maryland's new settlers hoped to do the same.

Remembering the early problems at Jamestown, the newcomers avoided the swampy lowlands. They built their first town, St. Mary's, in a drier location.

As proprietor of the colony, Lord Baltimore appointed a governor and a council of advisers. He gave colonists a role in government by creating an elected assembly. Eager to attract settlers to Maryland, Lord Baltimore made generous land grants to anyone who brought over servants, women, and children.

A few women took advantage of Lord Baltimore's offer of land. Two sisters, Margaret and Mary Brent, arrived in Maryland in 1638 with nine male servants. In time, they set up two plantations of about 1,000 acres each. Later, Margaret Brent helped prevent a rebellion among the governor's soldiers. The Maryland assembly praised her efforts, saying that "the colony's safety at any time [was better] in her hands than in any man's."

Religious Tolerance To make sure Maryland continued to grow, Lord Baltimore welcomed Protestants as well as Catholics to the colony.

Later, Lord Baltimore came to fear that Protestants might try to deprive Catholics of their right to worship freely. In 1649, he asked the assembly to pass an Act of Toleration. The law provided religious freedom for all Christians. As in many colonies, this freedom did not extend to Jews.

Bacon's Rebellion Meanwhile, English settlers continued to arrive in Virginia, attracted by the promise of profits from tobacco. Wealthy planters, however, controlled the best lands near the coast. Newcomers had to push farther inland, onto Indian lands.

As in New England, conflicts over land led to fighting between some white settlers and Indians. After several bloody clashes, settlers called on the governor to take action against Native Americans. The governor refused. He was unwilling to act, in part because he profited from his own fur trade with Indians. Frontier settlers were furious.

Finally, in 1676, Nathaniel Bacon, an ambitious young planter, organized angry men and women on the frontier. He raided Native American villages, regardless of whether the Indians there had been friendly to the colonists or not. Then, he led his followers to Jamestown and burned the capital.

The uprising, known as Bacon's Rebellion, lasted only a short time. When Bacon died suddenly, the revolt fell apart. The governor hanged 23 of Bacon's followers. Still, he could not stop English settlers from moving onto Indian lands along the frontier.

The Carolinas

South of Virginia and Maryland, English colonists settled in a region which they called the Carolinas. In 1663, a group of eight English nobles received a grant of land from King Charles II. Settlement took place in two separate areas, one in the north and the other in the south.

In the northern part of the Carolinas, settlers were mostly poor tobacco farmers who had drifted south from Virginia. They tended to have small farms. Eventually, in 1712, the colony became known as North Carolina.

Farther south, the group of eight English nobles set up a larger colony. The largest settlement, Charles Town, sprang up where the Ashley and Cooper rivers met. Later, Charles Town's name was shortened to Charleston. The colony became known as South Carolina in 1719.

Most early settlers in Charleston were English people who had been living in Barbados, a British colony in the Caribbean. Later, other immigrants arrived, including Germans, Swiss, French Protestants, and Spanish Jews.

Rise of Plantation Slavery Around 1685, a few planters discovered that rice grew well in the swampy lowlands along the coast. However, they were unable to grow rich crops until slaves from rice-growing areas of Africa arrived in the colony. Before long, Carolina rice was a profitable crop traded around the world. Settlers in southern Carolina later learned to raise **indigo,** a plant used to make a valuable blue dye.

Carolina planters needed large numbers of workers to grow rice. At first, they tried to enslave local Indians; however, many Indians died of disease or mistreatment, while others escaped into the forests.

Planters then turned to slaves from Africa. By 1700, most people coming to Charleston were African men and women brought against their will. Soon, African Americans in South Carolina outnumbered European Americans by more than two to one. On the mainland of North America, South Carolina was the only English colony where African Americans made up the majority of the population.

Georgia

The last of England's 13 colonies was carved out of the southern part of South Carolina. James Oglethorpe, a respected English soldier and energetic reformer, founded Georgia in 1732. He wanted the new colony to be a

GEOGRAPHY
Skills

The five Southern Colonies stretched along the Atlantic coast from Maryland to Georgia. Farm products and lumber were important to the economy of the region.

1. **Location** On the map, locate: **(a)** Maryland, **(b)** Virginia, **(c)** North Carolina, **(d)** South Carolina, **(e)** Georgia, **(f)** Chesapeake Bay, **(g)** Charles Town.

2. **Place** Describe the area where cattle herding took place.

3. **Critical Thinking Comparing** Compare this map to the maps on pages 103 and 111. **(a)** What crops were grown only in the Southern Colonies? **(b)** Why do you think such products were not grown farther north?

The Southern Colonies

Key
- Cattle
- Fish
- Grain
- Indigo
- Iron
- Lumber
- Rice
- Rum
- Tobacco

Great Wagon Road
APPALACHIAN MOUNTAINS
Potomac R.
James R.
Roanoke R.
Savannah R.

PA
Philadelphia
NJ
Baltimore
Maryland
DE
St. Mary's
Virginia
Williamsburg
Norfolk
Chesapeake Bay
ATLANTIC OCEAN
North Carolina
Wilmington
South Carolina
Charles Town
Georgia
Savannah

75° W
35° N
80° W

Albers Equal-Area Projection
0   50   100 Miles
0   50 100 Kilometers

place where **debtors,** or people who owed money they could not pay back, could make a fresh start.

Under English law, the government could imprison debtors until they paid what they owed. If they ever got out of jail, debtors often had no money and no place to live. Oglethorpe offered to pay for debtors and other poor people to travel to Georgia. "In America," he said, "there are enough fertile lands to feed all the poor of England."

In 1733, Oglethorpe and 120 colonists built the colony's first settlement at Savannah, above the Savannah River. Oglethorpe set strict rules for the colony. Farms could be no bigger than 500 acres, and slavery was forbidden.

At first, Georgia grew slowly. Later, however, Oglethorpe changed the rules to allow large plantations and slave labor. After that, the colony grew more quickly.

Two Ways of Life

Today, we often think of the colonial South as a land where wealthy planters lived in elegant homes, with large numbers of enslaved African Americans toiling in the fields. In fact, this picture is only partly true. As the Southern Colonies grew, two distinct ways of life emerged—one along the Atlantic coast and another in the back-country.

AS YOU READ **Summarize** Summarize the two ways of life in the colonial South by creating a graphic organizer to take notes.

Tidewater Plantations The Southern Colonies enjoyed warmer weather and a longer growing season than the colonies to the north. Virginia, Maryland, and parts of North Carolina all became major tobacco-growing areas. Settlers in South Carolina and Georgia raised rice and indigo.

Colonists soon found that it was most profitable to raise tobacco and rice on large plantations. As you recall, a plantation is a large estate farmed by many workers. On these southern plantations, anywhere from 20 to 100 slaves did most of the work. Most slaves worked in the fields. Others were skilled workers, such as carpenters, barrel makers, or blacksmiths. Still other slaves worked in the main house as cooks, servants, or housekeepers.

The earliest planters settled along rivers and creeks of the coastal plain. Because the land was washed by ocean tides, the region was known as the Tidewater. The Tidewater's gentle slopes and rivers offered rich farmland for plantations.

Farther inland, planters settled along rivers. Rivers provided an easy way to move goods to market. Planters loaded crops onto ships bound for the West Indies and Europe. On the return trip, the ships carried English manufactured goods and other luxuries for planters and their families.

Most Tidewater plantations had their own docks along the river, and merchant ships picked up crops and delivered goods directly to them. For this reason, few large seaport cities developed in the Southern Colonies.

Only a small percentage of white southerners owned large plantations. Yet, planters set the style of southern living. Life centered around the Great House. There, the planter's family lived in elegant quarters, including a parlor for visitors, a dining room, and guest bedrooms.

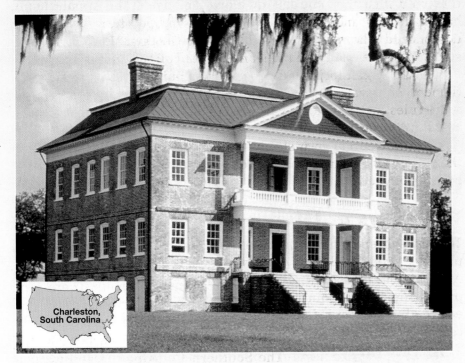

Charleston,
South Carolina

Drayton Hall

By the 1700s, there were plantations in South Carolina that produced cash crops such as rice, tobacco, and indigo. One plantation in Charleston, South Carolina, was Drayton Hall. Completed in 1742, it is one of the oldest surviving plantation houses in the South.

Take It to the NET

Virtual Field Trip For an interactive look at Drayton Hall, visit *The American Nation* section of **www.phschool.com**.

During the growing season, planters decided which fields to plant, what crops to grow, and when to harvest the crops. Planters' wives kept the household running smoothly. They directed house slaves and made sure daily tasks were done, such as milking cows.

Enslaved Africans played a crucial role on many plantations. They used farming skills they had brought from West Africa. With their help, English settlers learned how to grow rice. Africans also knew how to use wild plants unfamiliar to the English. They made water buckets out of gourds, and they used palmetto leaves to make fans, brooms, and baskets.

The Backcountry South West of the Tidewater, life was very different. Here, at the base of the Appalachians, rolling hills and thick forests covered the land. As in the Middle Colonies, this inland area was called the backcountry. Attracted by rich soil, settlers followed the Great Wagon Road into the backcountry of Maryland, Virginia, and the Carolinas.

The backcountry was more democratic than the Tidewater. Settlers there were more likely to treat one another as equals. Men tended smaller fields of tobacco or garden crops such as beans, corn, or peas. They also hunted game. Largely self-sufficient, these farmers provided all the food they needed. Surplus goods were sold at local markets. Women cooked meals and fashioned simple, rugged clothing out of wool or deerskins. Another major difference between the backcountry and the Tidewater was slavery. Few enslaved Africans worked on the smaller farms in the backcountry.

The hardships of backcountry life brought settlers closer together. Families gathered to husk corn or help one another build barns. Spread out along the edge of the Appalachians, these hardy settlers felled trees, grew crops, and changed the face of the land.

Growth of Slavery and the Slave Trade

In the early years, Africans in the English colonies included free people and servants as well as slaves. Indeed, during the 1600s, even Africans who were enslaved enjoyed some freedom. The first enslaved Africans arrived in Virginia in 1619. However, for the next fifty years, since the African population was small, the status of Africans in the colony was not clearly established. Some Africans were enslaved and some became servants. There were instances where enslaved Africans could purchase their freedom. Several Africans during the 1600s, such as Anthony Johnson, became successful property owners. In South Carolina some enslaved Africans worked without supervision as cowboys, herding cattle to market.

By 1700, plantations in the Southern Colonies had come to rely on slave labor. After a time, slaves made up the majority of the population in South Carolina and Georgia. Slaves cleared the land, worked the crops, and tended the livestock. In order to maintain the supply of slaves, southern planters relied on a system of slave trading that stretched halfway across the globe.

Slavery in Africa In Africa, as elsewhere around the world, slavery had been part of the social and economic system since ancient times. Usually, slaves were people who had been captured in war. Slaves were part of a community and were often treated as servants rather than property. In Africa, traders often transported and sold slaves as laborers. Muslim merchants also carried African slaves into Europe and the Middle East.

Over a period of less than 400 years, as the transatlantic slave trade grew, millions of Africans were enslaved. Slave traders from many Western European nations set up posts along the West African coast. They offered guns and other goods in exchange for slaves. As the demand for slaves increased, Africans who lived along the coast made raids into the interior, seeking captives to sell to the Europeans. They marched their captives to the coast. There, the slaves were loaded aboard European ships headed for the Americas.

The Middle Passage In the 1700s, English sailors began referring to the passage of slave ships west across the Atlantic Ocean as the Middle Passage. Below the decks of the slave ships, slaves were crammed tightly together on shelves. One observer noted that they were "chained to each other hand and foot, and stowed so close, that they were not allowed above a foot and a half for each in breadth." The captives were allowed above deck to eat and exercise in the fresh air only once or twice a day."

Many enslaved Africans resisted, but only a few escaped. Some fought for their freedom during the trip. They would stage a mutiny or revolt. The slave traders lived in constant fear of this and were heavily armed. Other slaves resisted by refusing to eat or even jumping overboard to avoid a life of slavery.

Records of slave ships show that about 10 percent of Africans loaded aboard a ship for passage to the Americas died during the voyage. Many died of illnesses that spread rapidly in the filthy, crowded conditions inside a ship's hold. Others died of mistreatment. The Atlantic slave trade would last about 400 years. During that time, it may have caused the deaths of as many as 2 to 3 million Africans.

Limiting Rights As the importance of slavery increased, greater limits were placed on the rights of slaves. Colonists passed laws that set out rules for slaves' behavior and denied slaves their basic rights. These slave codes treated enslaved Africans not as human beings but as property.

Most English colonists did not question the justice of owning slaves. They believed that black Africans were inferior to white Europeans. The belief that one race is superior to another is called racism. Some colonists believed that they were helping slaves by introducing them to Christianity.

A handful of colonists spoke out against the evils of slavery. In 1688, Quakers in Germantown, Pennsylvania, became the first group of colonists to call for an end to slavery.

Section 3 Assessment

Recall

1. **Identify** Explain the significance of (a) Mason-Dixon Line, (b) Lord Baltimore, (c) Act of Toleration, (d) Bacon's Rebellion, (e) James Oglethorpe.
2. **Define** (a) indigo, (b) debtor, (c) slave code, (d) racism.

Comprehension

3. Why did Lord Baltimore set up the colony of Maryland?
4. Why was Georgia called a "haven for debtors"?
5. How was life in the Tidewater different from life in the backcountry South?

6. What role did Africans play in the economy of the Southern Colonies by 1700?

Critical Thinking and Writing

7. **Exploring the Main Idea** Review the Main Idea statement at the beginning of this section. List the reasons why you think tensions might have developed between the backcountry and the Tidewater.
8. **Analyzing Information** Review the discussion of religious tolerance. Did Maryland's Act of Toleration provide true religious tolerance? Write your answer in a paragraph.

ACTIVITY

Creating Flashcards
Do you get confused about the 13 English colonies? Use the text, including the maps and charts, to create 13 flashcards. On one side, write the name of a colony. On the other, write three facts about that colony. You may later use these cards for review.

4 Roots of Self-Government

BEFORE YOU READ

Reading Focus

- Why did England want to regulate colonial trade?
- What were colonial governments like?
- How were the liberties of the colonists limited?

Key Terms

mercantilism
export
import
Navigation Acts
Yankee
triangular trade
legislature
Glorious Revolution
bill of rights
English Bill of Rights

Taking Notes

As you read, prepare an outline of this section. Use roman numerals to indicate the major headings, capital letters for subheadings, and numbers for the supporting details. The sample below will help you get started.

```
I.  England Regulates Trade
    A.
        1.
        2.
II. Trade in Rum and Slaves
    A.
    B.
    C.
III. Colonial Government
```

Main Idea During the late 1600s and 1700s, England regulated colonial trade, while in each colony a governor carried out laws passed by the colony's legislature.

AS YOU READ

Horse-drawn carriage

Predict As cities grew more crowded, what other problems might have developed?

Setting the Scene Young Stephen Lamb hardly had time to look up before it was too late. A horse-drawn cart raced by, and the next instant Stephen was pulled beneath the wheels. One of Boston's newspapers reported the sad news: "A Child of about Five Years old, at the South End of the Town, was run over by a Cart, and died immediately after."

The streets in colonial cities like Boston had become busy—and sometimes dangerous—by the early 1700s. Farmers drove cattle, pigs, and sheep to market along narrow cobblestone streets. New York merchants complained that "Mischievous Mastiffs, Bull Doggs and Other Useless Dogs" chased their cattle and horses. Philadelphia spaced wooden posts along both sides of its main streets. The posts protected pedestrians from the "excessive Galloping, Trotting & Pacing of Horses."

Colonial city streets were becoming hazardous because there was so much activity. By the 1700s, trade flourished all along the Atlantic coast. As trade increased, England began to take a new interest in its colonies.

England Regulates Trade

Like other European nations at the time, England believed that its colonies should benefit the home country. This belief was part of an economic theory known as **mercantilism** (MER kuhn tihl ihz uhm). According to this theory, a nation became strong by keeping strict control over its trade. As one English gentleman put it, "Whosoever commands the trade of the world commands the riches of the world."

Mercantilists thought that a country should export more than it imported. **Exports** are goods sent to markets outside a country. **Imports** are goods brought into a country. If England sold more goods abroad, gold would flow into the home country as payment for those exports.

Beginning in the 1650s, the English Parliament passed a series of Navigation Acts that regulated trade between England and its colonies. The purpose of these laws was to ensure that only England benefited from colonial trade.

Under the new laws, only colonial or English ships could carry goods to and from the colonies. The Navigation Acts also listed certain products, such as tobacco and cotton, that colonial merchants could ship only to England. In this way, Parliament created jobs for English workers who cut and rolled tobacco or spun cotton into cloth.

The Navigation Acts helped the colonies as well as England. For example, the law encouraged colonists to build their own ships. As a result, New England became a prosperous shipbuilding center. Also, because of the acts, colonial merchants did not have to compete with foreign merchants because they were sure of having a market for their goods in England.

Still, many colonists resented the Navigation Acts. In their view, the laws favored English merchants. Colonial merchants often ignored the Navigation Acts or found ways to get around them.

Trade in Rum and Slaves

The colonies produced a wide variety of goods, and merchant ships sailed up and down the Atlantic coast. Merchants from New England dominated colonial trade. They were known as Yankees, a nickname that implied they were clever and hardworking. Yankee traders earned a reputation for profiting from any deal.

Colonial merchants developed many trade routes. One route was known as the triangular trade because the three legs of the route formed a triangle. On the first leg, ships from New England carried fish, lumber, and other goods to the West Indies. There, Yankee traders bought molasses—a dark-brown syrup made from sugar cane—and sugar. The ships then sailed back to New England, where colonists used the molasses and sugar to make rum.

On the second leg of the journey, ships carried rum, guns, gunpowder, cloth, and tools from New England to West Africa. In Africa, Yankee merchants traded these goods for slaves. On the final leg, ships carried enslaved Africans to the West Indies. With the profits from selling the enslaved Africans, traders bought more molasses.

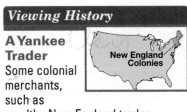

Viewing History

A Yankee Trader
Some colonial merchants, such as wealthy New England trader Moses Marcy, benefited from the Navigation Acts. **Drawing Inferences** *How can you tell that Moses Marcy is successful?*

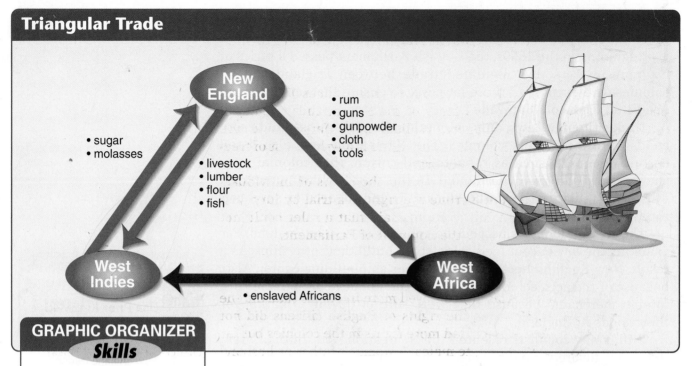

New England

• rum
• guns
• gunpowder
• cloth
• tools

• sugar
• molasses

• livestock
• lumber
• flour
• fish

West Indies

West Africa

• enslaved Africans

GRAPHIC ORGANIZER

Skills

Colonists traded with the West Indies, Africa, and Europe in a route known as the triangular trade.

1. **Comprehension**
   (a) What did American ships bring to Africa?
   (b) Where were enslaved African Americans traded for molasses?

2. **Critical Thinking**
   Making Decisions How did New England benefit from the slave trade?

Economics $

Many New England merchants grew wealthy from the triangular trade. In doing so, they often disobeyed the Navigation Acts. Traders were supposed to buy sugar and molasses only from English colonies in the West Indies. However, the demand for molasses was so high that New Englanders smuggled in cargoes from the Dutch, French, and Spanish West Indies, too. Bribes made customs officials look the other way.

Colonial Government

Although each colony developed its own government, the governments had much in common. A governor directed the colony's affairs and enforced the laws. Most governors were appointed, either by the king or by the colony's proprietor. In Rhode Island and Connecticut, however, colonists elected their own governors.

Elected Assemblies Each colony also had a legislature. A legislature is a group of people who have the power to make laws. In most colonies, the legislature had an upper house and a lower house. The upper house was made up of advisers appointed by the governor.

The lower house was an elected assembly. It approved laws and protected the rights of citizens. Just as important, it had the right to approve any taxes the governor asked for. This "power of the purse," or right to raise or spend money, was an important check on the governor's power. Any governor who ignored the assembly risked losing his salary.

The Right to Vote Each colony had its own rules about who could vote. By the 1720s, however, all the colonies had laws that restricted the right to vote to white Christian men over the age of 21. In some colonies, only Protestants or members of a particular church could vote. All voters had to own property. Colonial leaders believed that only property owners knew what was best for a colony.

A Bill of Rights Colonists took great pride in their elected assemblies. They also valued the rights that the Magna Carta gave them as English subjects.

Colonists won still more rights as a result of the Glorious Revolution of 1688. Parliament removed King James II from the throne and asked William and Mary of the Netherlands to rule. In return for Parliament's support, William and Mary signed the English Bill of Rights in 1689. A bill of rights is a written list of freedoms the government promises to protect.

The English Bill of Rights protected the rights of individuals and gave anyone accused of a crime the right to a trial by jury. Just as important, the English Bill of Rights said that a ruler could not raise taxes or an army without the approval of Parliament.

Limits on Liberties

English colonists in the Americas enjoyed more freedoms than did the English themselves. However, the rights of English citizens did not extend to all colonists. Women had more rights in the colonies but far fewer rights than did free, white males. A woman's father or husband was supposed to protect her. A married woman could not start her own business or sign a contract unless her husband approved it.

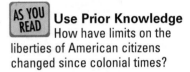

AS YOU READ **Use Prior Knowledge** How have limits on the liberties of American citizens changed since colonial times?

In most colonies, unmarried women and widows had more rights than married women. They could make contracts and sue in court. In Maryland and the Carolinas, women settlers who headed families could buy land on the same terms as men.

Africans and Native Americans in the colonies had almost no rights. While so many colonists enjoyed English liberties, most Africans were bound in slavery. The conflict between liberty and slavery would not be resolved until the 1860s.

AFTER YOU READ

★ Section 4 Assessment ★

Recall

1. **Identify** Explain the significance of (a) Navigation Acts, (b) Yankee, (c) Glorious Revolution, (d) English Bill of Rights.
2. **Define** (a) mercantilism, (b) export, (c) import, (d) triangular trade, (e) legislature, (f) bill of rights.

Comprehension

3. List two ways in which the Navigation Acts benefited (a) England (b) the colonies.
4. How were colonial governments organized?
5. Which colonists had the right to vote?

Critical Thinking and Writing

6. **Exploring the Main Idea** Review the Main Idea statement at the beginning of this section. Then, write a paragraph in which you analyze how colonial legislatures reflected the tradition of self-rule.
7. **Making Predictions** How do you think the Navigation Acts might affect future relations between England and the colonies? Write your answer in a paragraph.

ACTIVITY

Start a Dialogue You are a New England merchant who meets with another colonial merchant. Write a conversation you might have about trade in the colonies. Consider the Navigation Acts and triangular trade.

Summarizing

What were the sources of the English colonists' ideas about self-government? As you read different references to learn about these roots, you'll find it helpful to summarize information.

A document deeply rooted in the English concept of representative government is the Magna Carta signed by King John in 1215. These excerpts are from this important document.

(12) No [tax] may be levied in our kingdom without its general consent, unless it is for the ransom of our person, to make our eldest son a knight, and (once) to marry our eldest daughter. For these purposes only a reasonable [tax] may be levied.

(14) To obtain the general consent of the realm for the assessment of a [tax]—except in the three cases specified above—we will cause the archbishops, bishops, abbots, earls, and greater barons to be summoned individually by letter. To those who hold lands directly of us we will cause a general summons to be issued, through the sheriffs and other officials, to come together on a fixed day (of which at least forty days notice shall be given) and at a fixed place. In all letters of summons, the cause of the summons will be stated. When a summons has been issued, the business appointed for the day shall go forward in accordance with the resolution of those present, even if not all those who were summoned have appeared.

—The Magna Carta, 1215

King John signing the Magna Carta

Learn the Skill *To summarize information, use the following steps:*

1. **Identify the main idea.** The main idea of a passage explains its purpose. Usually, the main idea is presented in the first sentence of the passage.

2. **Look for details.** These include facts, reasons, explanations, examples, and descriptions that expand the main idea.

3. **Restate the main idea.** Put the main idea in your own words.

4. **Choose important details.** Select the most significant details to include in your summary. Remember, a summary should be brief and to the point.

Practice the Skill *Answer the following questions about the passages above:*

1. Which sentence contains the main point of these passages?

2. **(a)** What three exceptions are given? **(b)** Who has to approve the assessment of a tax? **(c)** Identify another detail about approving taxes.

3. Restate the main idea in your own words.

4. Complete your summary by adding two important details to go with your main idea statement.

Apply the Skill *See the Chapter Review and Assessment.*

5 Life in the Colonies

BEFORE YOU READ

Reading Focus

- What class differences existed in colonial society?
- How did the Great Awakening affect the colonies?
- How did the colonists educate their children?
- How were the colonies affected by the spread of new ideas?

Key Terms

gentry
middle class
indentured servant
Gullah
Great Awakening
public school
tutor
apprentice
dame school
Enlightenment
libel

Taking Notes

Copy the cause-and-effect chart at right. As you read, complete the chart to show the effect of different factors in shaping life in the colonies. Add as many entries as you need.

```
       ┌──  CAUSES  ──┐
       ▽
   1. Puritan belief in education
   2.
   3.

   ┌─ LIFE IN THE COLONIES ─┐

       ┌──  EFFECTS  ──┐
       ▽
   1. Public school system in
      New England
   2.
   3.
```

Main Idea During the 1700s, England's 13 colonies became societies with their own ideas and traditions.

Setting the Scene

On a warm May day in the 1750s, a parade made its way down a main street in Newport, Rhode Island. Most of the city's Africans had turned out for a holiday known as Negro Election Day. Dressed in their finest clothes, enslaved and free Africans alike sang and marched. One resident recalled:

> 66 All the various languages of Africa, mixed with broken . . . English, filled the air, accompanied with the music of the fiddle, tambourine, the banjo [and African] drum. 99

—Henry Bull, *Memoir of Rhode Island,* 1837

AS YOU READ
African drum
Draw Inferences Why was it important for Africans in the colonies to have their own celebration?

Similar parades took place throughout New England. Each year, at about the time white New Englanders voted for their colonial government, Africans elected a leader of their community. The winner's job was to settle disputes that arose among black townspeople during the year.

Negro Election Day was a truly American custom, blending traditions from Africa and England. As the American colonies grew in the 1700s, they became more than rough settlements. Gradually, old customs and ideas were being shaped into a new culture that was distinctly American.

Colonial Society

For the most part, colonists enjoyed more social equality than people in England, where a person's opportunities in life were largely determined by birth. Still, class differences existed. Like Europeans, colonial Americans thought it was only natural that some people rank more highly than others. A person's birth and wealth still determined his or her social status.

The Gentry and the Middle Class At the top of society stood the gentry. The gentry included wealthy planters, merchants, ministers, successful lawyers, and royal officials. They could afford to dress in the latest fashions from London.

Below the gentry were the middle class. The middle class included farmers who worked their own land, skilled craftsworkers, and some tradespeople. Nearly three quarters of all white colonists belonged to the middle class. They prospered because land in the colonies was plentiful and easy to buy.

Indentured Servants The lowest social class included hired farmhands, indentured servants, and slaves. Indentured servants signed contracts to work without wages for a period of four to seven years for anyone who would pay their ocean passage to the Americas. When their term of service was completed, indentured servants received "freedom dues": a set of clothes, tools, and 50 acres of land. Because there were so few European women in the colonies, female indentured servants often shortened their terms of service by marrying.

Thousands of men, women, and children came to North America as indentured servants. After completing their terms, some became successful and rose into the middle class.

Women's Work in the Colonies From New Hampshire to Georgia, colonial women performed many of the same tasks. A wife took care of her household, husband, and family. By the kitchen fire, she cooked the family's meals. She milked cows, watched the children, and made clothing.

In the backcountry, wives and husbands often worked side by side in the fields at harvest time. With so much to be done, no one worried whether harvesting was proper "woman's work." One surprised visitor described a backcountry woman's activities: "She will carry a gunn in the woods and kill deer, turkeys &c., shoot down wild cattle, catch and tye hoggs, knock down [cattle] with an ax, and perform the most manfull Exercises as well as most men."

In cities, women sometimes worked outside the home. A young single woman from a poorer family might work for one of the gentry as a maid, a cook, or a nurse. Other women were midwives, who delivered babies. Still others sewed fine hats or dresses to be sold to women who could afford them. Learning such skills often required years of training.

Some women learned trades from their fathers, brothers, or husbands. They worked as butchers, shoemakers, or silversmiths. Quite a few women became printers. A woman might take over her husband's business when he died.

African Cultural Influences By the mid-1700s, the culture of Africans in the colonies varied greatly. On rice plantations in South Carolina, slaves saw few white colonists. As a result, African customs remained strong. For example, parents often chose African names for their children, such as Quosh or Juba or Cuff. In some coastal areas, African Americans spoke a distinctive combination of English and West African languages known as Gullah.

Primary Source

An Indentured Servant

This is a contract Richard Garfford entered into with Thomas Workman. Garfford wanted to become an indentured servant:
"The Condition of this obligation is such that . . . Richard Garfford . . . shall well and truly deliver or cause to be delivered [to] . . . Thomas Workman . . . in Virginia a sound and able man servant between Eighteen and 25 years of age that shall have [four] years to serve at the least, and that [when] the first second or third ship . . . [arrives] in the Port of James Ariver in Virginia from London, that then the bond above [will] be [void] . . ."

—Richard Garfford, 1654

Analyzing Primary Sources
What kind of worker is Thomas Workman looking for?

In Charleston and other South Carolina port towns, many African Americans worked along the docks, making rope or barrels or helping to build ships. Skilled craftsworkers made fine wooden cabinets or silver plates and utensils. Many of their designs reflected African artistic styles. Although most Africans in these towns were enslaved, many opened their own shops or stalls in the market. Some used their earnings to buy their own and their family's freedom.

In Virginia and Maryland, Africans were less isolated from white farmers and planters. Even so, many African customs survived. For instance, mourners took part in a ceremony to speed a dead man's spirit to his home, which they believed was in Africa.

In the Middle Colonies and New England, the African population increased during the 1700s. As you have read, customs like Negro Election Day became a part of colonial life, especially in cities.

The Great Awakening

In the 1730s and 1740s, a religious movement known as the Great Awakening swept through the colonies. Its drama and emotion touched women and men of all backgrounds and classes.

Powerful Preachers A New England preacher, Jonathan Edwards, helped set off the Great Awakening. In powerful sermons, Edwards called on colonists, especially young people, to examine their lives. He preached of the sweetness and beauty of God. At the same time, he warned listeners to heed the Bible's teachings. Otherwise, they would be "sinners in the hands of an angry God," headed for the fiery torments of hell.

In 1739, when an English minister named George Whitefield arrived in the colonies, the movement spread like wildfire. Whitefield drew huge crowds to outdoor meetings. An enthusiastic and energetic preacher, his voice would ring with feeling as he called on sinners to repent. After hearing Whitefield speak, Jonathan Edwards's wife reported, "I have seen upwards of a thousand people hang on his words with breathless silence, broken only by an occasional half-suppressed sob."

Impact of the Great Awakening The Great Awakening aroused bitter debate. People who supported the movement often split away from their old churches to form new ones. Opponents warned that the movement was too emotional. Still, the growth of so many new churches forced colonists to become more tolerant of people with different beliefs.

The Great Awakening contributed in another way to the spread of democratic feelings in the colonies. Many of the new preachers were not as well educated as most ministers. They argued that formal training was less important than a heart filled with the holy spirit. Such teachings encouraged a spirit of independence. Many believers felt more free to challenge authority when their liberties were at stake. People began to think differently about their political rights and their governments. They felt if they could figure out how to worship on their own, then they could govern themselves. Eventually, many of these colonists would challenge British authority.

Viewing History

George Whitefield

The English Colonies

George Whitefield was the most popular preacher of the Great Awakening. Nathan Cole, who attended one of Whitefield's sermons said "[he] appeared almost angelical before thousands of people with a bold, [fearless] countenance."

Synthesizing Information
Why did some American preachers oppose preachers like Whitefield?

Education in the Colonies

Among the colonists, New Englanders were the most concerned about education. Puritans taught that all people had a duty to study the Bible. If colonists did not learn to read, how would they fulfill this duty?

New England In 1642, the Massachusetts assembly passed a law ordering all parents to teach their children "to read and understand the principles of religion." They also required all towns with 50 or more families to hire a schoolteacher. Towns with 100 or more families also had to set up a grammar school to prepare boys for college.

In this way, Massachusetts set up the first public schools, or schools supported by taxes. Public schools allowed both rich and poor children to receive an education.

The first New England schools had only one room for students of all ages. Parents paid the schoolteacher with corn, peas, or other foods. Each child was expected to bring a share of wood to burn in the stove. Students who forgot would find themselves seated in the coldest corner of the room!

Middle and Southern Colonies In the Middle Colonies, churches and individual families set up private schools. Because pupils paid to attend, only wealthy families could afford to educate their children.

In the Southern Colonies, people lived too far from one another to bring children together in one school building. Some planters engaged tutors, or private teachers. The wealthiest planters sent their sons to school in England. As a rule, slaves were denied education of any kind.

Apprenticeships and Dame Schools Boys whose parents wished them to learn a trade or craft served as apprentices (uh PREHN tihs ehz). An apprentice worked for a master to learn a trade or a craft. For example, when a boy reached the age of 12 or 13, his parents might apprentice him to a master glassmaker. The young apprentice lived in the glassmaker's home for six or seven years while learning the craft. The glassmaker gave the boy food and clothing. He was also supposed to teach his apprentice how to read and write and provide him with religious training.

In return, the apprentice worked without pay in the glassmaker's shop and learned the skills he needed to set up his own shop. Boys were apprenticed in many trades, including papermaking and printing, and tanning (making leather).

In New England, most schools accepted only boys. However, some girls attended dame schools, or private schools run by women in their own homes. Other girls, though, usually learned skills from their mothers, who taught them to spin wool, weave, and embroider. A few learned to read and write.

Spread of Ideas

During the 1600s, European scientists began to use reason and logic instead of superstition to understand the world. They developed theories, and then performed experiments to test them. In doing so,

▲ Past

▲ Present

they discovered many of the laws of nature. The English scientist Isaac Newton, for example, explained the law of gravity.

The Enlightenment Spreads European thinkers of the late 1600s and 1700s believed that reason and scientific methods could be applied to the study of society. They tried to discover the natural laws that governed human behavior. Because these thinkers believed in the light of human reason, the movement that they started is known as the Enlightenment. John Locke, an English philosopher, wrote works that were widely read in the colonies. He said people could gain knowledge of the world by observing and by experimenting.

In the 13 colonies, the Enlightenment spread among better educated colonists. They included wealthy merchants, lawyers, ministers, and others who had the leisure to read the latest books from Europe. Urban craftsmen also heard and discussed these ideas.

Benjamin Franklin The best example of the Enlightenment spirit in the 13 colonies was Benjamin Franklin. Franklin was born in 1706, the son of a poor Boston soap and candle maker. Although he had only two years of formal schooling, he used his spare time to study literature, mathematics, and foreign languages.

At age 17, Franklin made his way to Philadelphia. There, he built up a successful printing business. His most popular publication was *Poor Richard's Almanack.* Published yearly, it contained useful information and clever quotes, such as "Early to bed, early to rise, makes a man healthy, wealthy, and wise."

Viewing History

School Days Students in colonial times attended one-room schools. Usually, they studied subjects that would help them in their daily lives. Today, students attend schools that offer many subjects and the latest technology. Sometimes, students study in special classrooms, such as computer rooms like the one shown here.

United States

Applying Information *(a) How has public education changed since colonial times? (b) How is it the same?*

Primary Sources

See Benjamin Franklin, "Autobiography," on page 579 in the Reference Section.

Like other Enlightenment thinkers, Franklin wanted to use reason to improve the world around him. He invented practical devices such as a lightning rod, a smokeless fireplace, and bifocal glasses. As a community leader, Franklin persuaded Philadelphia officials to pave streets, organize a fire company, and set up the first lending library in the Americas. Franklin's inventions and his public service earned him worldwide fame.

Colonial Cities While most colonists lived on farms, towns and cities strongly influenced colonial life. Through the great ports of Philadelphia, New York, Boston, and Charleston, merchants shipped products overseas. Towns and cities also served as the center of a busy trade between the coast and the growing backcountry.

Culture flourished in the cities. By the mid-1700s, many colonial cities had their own theaters. City dwellers found entertainment at singing societies, traveling circuses, carnivals, and horse races.

In 1704, John Campbell founded the *Boston News-Letter,* the first regular weekly newspaper in the English colonies. Within 50 years, each of the colonies, except New Jersey and Delaware, had at least one weekly paper.

 Find Main Ideas Write a sentence explaining the importance of the Zenger trial.

The Trial of John Peter Zenger The growth of colonial newspapers led to a dispute over freedom of the press. John Peter Zenger published the *Weekly Journal* in New York City. In 1734, he was arrested for publishing stories that criticized the governor. Zenger was put on trial for libel—the act of publishing a statement that may unjustly damage a person's reputation. Zenger's lawyer argued that, since the stories were true, his client had not committed libel. The jury agreed and freed Zenger. At the time, the case did not attract a great deal of attention. However, freedom of the press would become recognized as a basic American right.

 AFTER YOU READ

Section 5 Assessment

Recall

1. **Identify** Explain the significance of (a) Gullah, (b) Great Awakening, (c) Jonathan Edwards, (d) George Whitefield, (e) Enlightenment, (f) Benjamin Franklin, (g) John Peter Zenger.
2. **Define** (a) gentry, (b) middle class, (c) indentured servant, (d) public school, (e) tutor, (f) apprentice, (g) dame school, (h) libel.

Comprehension

3. What social classes existed in the colonies?
4. How did the Great Awakening affect religion in the colonies?

5. Why did the Puritans support public education?
6. In what ways did Benjamin Franklin's ideas reflect the ideas of the Enlightenment?

Critical Thinking and Writing

7. **Exploring the Main Idea** Review the Main Idea statement at the beginning of this section. Then, make a list of five statements that support the main idea.
8. **Drawing Inferences** Why do you think there was greater social equality in the colonies than in England?

 ACTIVITY

Take It to the NET
Use the Internet to find out more about the John Peter Zenger trial. Then, prepare a class skit of the trial. Visit *The American Nation* section of **www.phschool.com** for help in completing the activity.

Benjamin Franklin,
Scientist and Inventor

In his day, Benjamin Franklin was a well-known journalist and diplomat. He was also well known for his scientific experiments and inventions.

Benjamin Franklin

Bifocals

After he turned forty, the nearsighted Franklin needed a second pair of glasses for reading. He invented bifocals. Now, he could see objects far away and read—all without changing glasses. Every major optical store still sells bifocals.

Odometer

When he was postmaster, Franklin had to map the mailing routes for surrounding towns. He came up with a simple odometer for his carriage. It counted the number of times the wheels of his wagon rotated on a trip. Today, odometers are used in cars to measure mileage.

Electricity Experiments

Franklin was curious about electricity. In some of his experiments, he used a vacuum pump (shown here). An experiment he tried in 1752 gave him the idea for a lightning rod. Variations of this device protect homes and buildings from lightning to this day.

ACTIVITY

Make a list of at least three inventions that you think would make people's lives easier, healthier, or just more fun. For each of your ideas, explain how you think it might work, whom it would benefit, and if you think it will ever be used.

Review and Assessment

CREATING A CHAPTER SUMMARY

On a sheet of paper, draw a chart like the one below. As you read, fill in the chart with information about the settlement of the 13 colonies, including the political, economic, and social reasons. Add as many boxes as you need to complete the chart.

For additional review and enrichment activities, see the interactive version of *The American Nation,* available on the Web and on CD-ROM.

Colony	Date Founded	Leader	Reason Founded
Massachusetts Plymouth	1620	William Bradford	Religious freedom
Massachusetts Bay	1630	John Winthrop	Religious freedom
New Hampshire	1623	David Thomson	Economic

Take It to the NET

Chapter Self-Test For practice test questions for Chapter 4, visit *The American Nation* section of **www.phschool.com**.

Building Vocabulary

Review the chapter vocabulary words listed below. Then, use the words and their definitions to create a matching quiz. Exchange quizzes with another student. Check each other's answers when you are finished.

1. religious tolerance
2. town meeting
3. royal colony
4. cash crop
5. indigo
6. mercantilism
7. import
8. bill of rights
9. apprentice
10. libel

Reviewing Key Facts

11. What caused conflicts between the New England colonists and the Native Americans? (Section 1)
12. What policies did William Penn follow in the Pennsylvania Colony? (Section 2)
13. What events caused Nathaniel Bacon and his followers to rebel in 1676? (Section 3)
14. How did England's belief in mercantilism affect the colonies? (Section 4)

15. How did cities influence colonial life? (Section 5)

Critical Thinking and Writing

16. **Connecting to Geography: Location** Analyze the way in which location influenced the economy of each colony.
17. **Comparing** Discuss the differences between the Southern plantations and the farms in the Middle and New England Colonies.
18. **Analyzing Information** Explain how each of the following individuals contributed to the growth of self-government: (a) John Winthrop, (b) Thomas Hooker, (c) Lord Baltimore.
19. **Synthesizing Information** Why do you think the colonists were open to the ideas of the Enlightenment?
20. **Linking Past and Present** What rights and freedoms enjoyed by Americans today had their beginnings in colonial times?

Analyzing Primary Sources

In the trial of John Peter Zenger, his lawyer Andrew Hamilton gave a speech to the jury defending Zenger. Read the excerpt, and then answer the questions.

> 66 . . . the question before the court and you gentlemen of the jury, is not of small nor private concern. It is not the cause of the poor printer . . . it may in its consequence affect every freeman that lives under a British Government on the main of America. It is the best cause. It is the cause of liberty; and I make no doubt but your upright conduct, this day, will . . . entitle you to the love and esteem of your fellow citizens. . . . 99

> —Andrew Hamilton, speech before the jury in the Zenger trial, New York, 1735

21. According to Hamilton, what is the issue that is being decided?
22. Whom will the verdict affect?
23. How would the public react to a verdict of innocence?
24. Why do you think the governor of New York tried to prevent freedom of the press?

Summarizing

Read the following passage about river trade in colonial Virginia. Answer the questions.

An early Tye River Scottish tobacco planter, Parson Robert Rose, was one of the first to use the Indian dugout canoe to carry his hogsheads [of tobacco] to the Richmond market, but found them neither large enough nor stable enough to carry much cargo. By the mid 1740s, Parson Rose . . . devised a method of lashing two canoes together with a sawn board platform in between which enabled him to carry up to nine hogshead at a time down the James . . . . Hogsheads could now be transported downriver . . . to the market in Richmond.

> —Dian McNaught, "The Early Virginia River Trade of the 1700s"

25. What is the main idea of this passage?
    A Indian dugout canoes are sturdy.
    B Hogsheads are durable holding devices.
    C Double dugout canoes are best for carrying goods.
    D Parson Rose was a wealthy planter.
26. (a) What details in the passage support the main idea? (b) Write a summary of the paragraph.

ACTIVITIES

Connecting With... Culture

Making a Chart Make a chart that describes the lifestyle in the colonies. Write the names of the colonial regions—New England, Middle Colonies, and Southern Colonies—at the top of the chart. The left column should include: Geography, Economy, Government, Education, Region, Population Density. You may add other categories.

Take It to the NET

Connecting to Today

A Comparison Report Use the Internet to research facts about past and present-day immigration. Compare the challenges faced by immigrants coming to the United States today with those of the English colonists in the 1600s and early 1700s. Work with a partner to complete your report. For help in starting this activity, visit *The American Nation* section of **www.phschool.com**.

Researching Colonial Houses

Reviewing Sites About Colonial House Design Use the Internet to research how houses were built and designed in the English colonies during the 1700s. Find out about one type of house design. Make a diagram or build a model of the house. For help in starting this activity, visit *The American Nation* section of **www.phschool.com**.

TEST PREPARATION

1   Which of the following is not an example of a primary source?

   A   An entry from Christopher Columbus's journal

   B   The cargo list of a colonial slave ship

   C   A modern biography of Benjamin Franklin

   D   The Fundamental Orders of Connecticut

Use the map <u>and</u> your knowledge of social studies to answer the following question.

2   In what sequence were the three English colonies shown on the map settled?

   A   A, B, C

   B   C, B, A

   C   B, A, C

   D   B, C, A

3   The Navigation Acts were linked to which economic system?

   A   Mercantilism

   B   Feudalism

   C   Encomienda system

   D   Free enterprise

4   "Nomadic bands learned to make the most of limited resources." This statement best applies to Native Americans living in which region?

   A   Eastern Woodlands

   B   Arctic

   C   Southeast

   D   Pacific Northwest

Use the quotation <u>and</u> your knowledge of social studies to answer the following question.

> "There has been a great lasting change in this town in many respects. There has been vastly more religion kept up. . . . There has also been an evident change with respect to a charitable spirit to the poor."

5   What event or development is described in this passage?

   A   The founding of Pennsylvania

   B   The signing of the Mayflower Compact

   C   The Enlightenment

   D   The Great Awakening

6 How was the founding of the Virginia House of Burgesses similar to the signing of the Mayflower Compact?

A Both strengthened the English Parliament's control over the colonies.

B Both gave settlers the right to establish colonies.

C Both contributed to the development of representative democracy.

D Both created elected legislatures.

7 Which kind of thematic map would you use to find out how much of your state is made up of farmland?

A A political map

B A climate map

C A land use map

D A population density map

8 Which of the following individuals is best known for helping the spread of new ideas in Europe?

A Prince Henry of Portugal

B Johannes Gutenberg

C Augustus Caesar

D Martin Luther

Use the chart <u>and</u> your knowledge of social studies to answer the following question.

Ethnic Division of Colonial Population, 1775

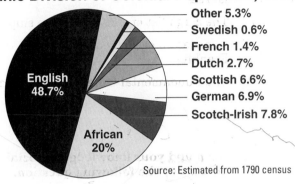

Source: Estimated from 1790 census

9 What valid conclusion about the colonial population can you draw from this pie chart?

A More people in the colonies were of English descent than all other European nationalities combined.

B Slaves made up 20 percent of the colonial population.

C The Dutch population lived entirely in New York.

D One out of every ten colonists was of either German or French background.

Writing Practice

10 (a) What are the major elements of the free enterprise system? **(b)** Describe some of the benefits of free enterprise. Use at least one example from modern life.

11 Trace the development of religious freedom in the 13 colonies. Describe at least three milestones. Then, make two generalizations about the roots of religious freedom.

Revolutionary Turning Point
General George Washington looks determined to win an American victory in Emanuel Leutze's *Washington Crossing the Delaware.*

"If we separate from Britain, what code of laws will be established? How shall we be governed so as to retain our liberties?"

—Abigail Adams, wife of John Adams (1775)

Crisis in the Colonies

1745–1775

1 The French and Indian War
2 Turmoil Over Taxation
3 From Protest to Revolution

British capture Quebec

1759
British forces climb to the Plains of Abraham and capture Quebec, the capital of New France.

1740s
The first migration of settlers across the Appalachian Mountains sets off conflicts with the Indians of the Ohio River Valley.

1754
The Albany Congress proposes to unite the British colonies. However, the proposal is rejected by all the colonies.

AMERICAN EVENTS

1740 · · **1750** · · **1760**

WORLD EVENTS

▲ **1748**
Britain and France fight for control of trade in India.

▲ **1756**
Seven Years' War begins in Europe between France and Britain.

North America in 1753

In the mid-1700s, France and Spain claimed land to the north, south, and west of the 13 British colonies.

Hudson Bay

ATLANTIC OCEAN

NEW FRANCE

13 COLONIES

Missouri R.

LOUISIANA

Ohio R.

PACIFIC OCEAN

Colorado R.

Rio Grande

NEW SPAIN

Mississippi R.

FLORIDA

Gulf of Mexico

West Indies

Key
- Claimed by Britain
- Claimed by Spain
- Claimed by France
- French forts

Azimuthal Projection

| 0 | 250 | 500 Miles |
| 0 | 250 | 500 Kilometers |

Paul Revere's print of the Boston Massacre

Concord's minuteman statue

1770
British troops fire on demonstrators in the Boston Massacre, killing five. Paul Revere's print of the attack provokes anti-British outrage in all the colonies.

1765
Parliament passes the Stamp Act, sparking protests in the American colonies.

1775
Fighting breaks out at Lexington and Concord between British soldiers and colonial minutemen.

1760 · · · 1770 · · · 1780 · ·

▲ **1763**
Treaty of Paris ends French power in North America.

1773 ▲
British Parliament passes the Tea Act.

1 The French and Indian War

Reading Focus

- How did the rivalry of Britain and France lead to war in North America?
- How did lack of unity and mistakes lead to British defeats early in the war?
- What turned the tide of war in Britain's favor?
- How did British troops bring about the fall of New France?

Key Terms

French and Indian War

Albany Plan of Union

Plains of Abraham

Treaty of Paris

Taking Notes

As you read, prepare an outline of this section. Use roman numerals to indicate major headings, capital letters for subheadings, and numbers for supporting details. The sample at right will get you started.

> I. European Rivals in North America
>   A.
>   B.
> II. The French and Indian War Begins
> III. The Albany Congress

Main Idea Britain's victory in the French and Indian War marked the end of the French empire in North America.

George Washington as a young officer

Draw Inferences How do you think Captain Joncaire reacted when Washington warned the French to get out of the Ohio River Valley?

Setting the Scene When Captain Daniel Joncaire sat down to dinner on December 4, 1753, he wasn't expecting company. The weather was cold, rainy, and miserable at the French fort near Lake Erie. To Joncaire's surprise, a tall young stranger strode into the room. He introduced himself as Major George Washington. Washington had traveled several hundred miles from Virginia to deliver a letter to the French.

Joncaire politely invited Washington to dine. As they ate, the captain boasted that France was determined to control the Ohio River Valley. Washington reported:

> 66 He told me, That it was their absolute Design to take possession of the Ohio [River], and by God they would do it. 99
>
> —George Washington, in his journal

Joncaire's remark made Washington pause. The letter he was carrying from Virginia's governor warned the French to get out of the Ohio River Valley! For years, tensions had been building between France and England. At stake was more than control of the Ohio River Valley. The two rivals wanted to drive each other out of North America. In the end, the issue was decided by war. And Washington was the man who struck the first blow.

European Rivals in North America

By the mid-1700s, the major powers of Europe were locked in a worldwide struggle for empire. England, France, Spain, and the Netherlands competed for trade and colonies in far-flung corners of the globe. The English colonies in North America soon became caught up in the contest.

The most serious threat came from France. It claimed a vast area that stretched from the St. Lawrence River west to the Great Lakes and south to the Gulf of Mexico. To protect their land claims, the French built an extensive system of forts. These forts blocked the English colonies from expanding to the west.

Conflict in the Ohio Valley At first, most English settlers were content to remain along the Atlantic coast. By the 1740s, however, traders were crossing the Appalachian Mountains in search of furs. Pushing into the Ohio Valley, they tried to take over the profitable French trade with the Indians.

France was determined to stop the English from expanding westward. The Ohio River was especially important to the French because it provided a vital link between their lands in Canada and their settlements along the Mississippi River.

Native Americans Choose Sides Native Americans had hunted animals and grown crops in the Ohio Valley for centuries. They did not want to give up the land to European settlers, French or English. One Native American protested to an English trader, "You and the French are like the two edges of a pair of shears. And we are the cloth which is to be cut to pieces between them."

Still, the growing conflict between England and France was too dangerous to ignore. Some Native Americans decided that the only way to protect their way of life was to take sides in the struggle.

The French expected the Indians to side with them. Most French in North America were trappers and traders. Generally, they did not destroy Indian hunting grounds by clearing forests for farms. Also, many French trappers married Native American women and adopted their ways. As a result, France had built strong alliances with such Native American groups as the Algonquins and the Hurons.

Many English settlers were farmers. These settlers usually ignored Indian rights by felling trees and clearing land for crops. In the end, though, Britain managed to convince the powerful Iroquois nations to join with them. The British alliance was attractive to the Iroquois because they were old enemies of the Algonquin and the Huron peoples.

An English trader and official, William Johnson, helped gain Iroquois support for England. The Iroquois respected Johnson. He was one of the few English settlers who had an Indian wife, Molly Brant. She was the sister of the Mohawk chief Thayendanegea, known to the English as Joseph Brant. Both Joseph and Molly Brant became valuable allies for the English. The English also won Native American allies in the Ohio Valley by charging lower prices than the French for trade goods.

Viewing History

A Pioneer Home
After clearing the woods, pioneer families built their log cabins and set out to harvest the riches of the land. This romantic view of a pioneer homestead was created more than 100 years after pioneers started crossing the Appalachian Mountains.
Identifying Points of View
Do you think the artist admired the early pioneers? Explain your answer. How does he show his point of view?

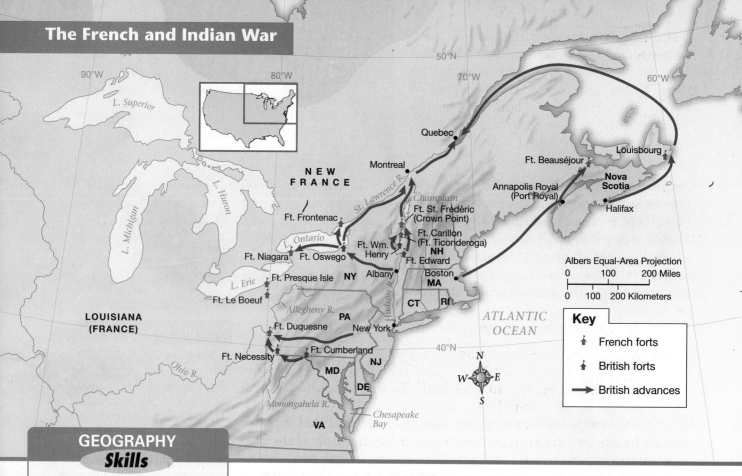

The French and Indian War Begins

Three times between 1689 and 1748, France and Great Britain* fought for power in Europe and North America. Each war ended with an uneasy peace.

In 1754, fighting broke out for a fourth time. English settlers called the conflict the French and Indian War because it pitted them against France and its Native American allies. Once again, the Ohio River Valley was at the center of the dispute. There, the opening shots of the war were fired by soldiers led by George Washington.

A Bold Young Leader Washington was only 22 years old in 1754. He had grown up on a plantation in Virginia, the son of wealthy parents. Gifted at mathematics, he began working as a land surveyor at the age of 15. His job took him to frontier lands in western Virginia.

After Washington returned from his first visit to the French, the governor of Virginia sent him west again. This time Washington's assignment was to build a fort where the Monongahela and Allegheny rivers meet to form the Ohio River.

Washington led 150 men into the Ohio country in April 1754. Along the way, he heard that the French had just completed Fort

---

*In 1707, England and Scotland were officially joined into the United Kingdom of Great Britain. After that date, the terms *Great Britain* and *British* were used to describe the country and its people. However, the terms *England* and *English* were still used throughout much of the 1700s.

Duquesne (doo KAYN) at the very spot where Washington hoped to build his fort.

Conflict at Fort Necessity Determined to carry out his orders, Washington hurried on. Indian allies revealed that French scouts were camped in the woods ahead. Marching quietly through the night, Washington launched a surprise attack and scattered the French.

His success was brief, however. Hearing that the French were about to counterattack, Washington and his men quickly threw up a makeshift stockade. They named it Fort Necessity. A force of 700 French and Indians surrounded the fort. Badly outnumbered, the Virginians surrendered. The French then released Washington, and he returned home.

British officials recognized the significance of Washington's skirmish. "The volley fired by this young Virginian in the forests of America," a British writer noted, "has set the world in flames."

The Albany Congress

While Washington was defending Fort Necessity, delegates from seven colonies gathered in Albany, New York. One purpose of the meeting was to cement the alliance with the Iroquois. Another goal was to plan a united colonial defense.

The delegates in Albany knew that the colonists had to work together to defeat the French. Benjamin Franklin, the delegate from Pennsylvania, proposed the Albany Plan of Union. The plan was an attempt to create "one general government" for the 13 colonies. It called for a Grand Council made up of representatives from each colony. The council would make laws, raise taxes, and set up the defense of the colonies.

The delegates voted to accept the Plan of Union. However, when the plan was submitted to the colonial assemblies, not one approved it. None of the colonies wanted to give up any of its powers to a central council. A disappointed Benjamin Franklin expressed his frustration at the failure of his plan:

66 Everyone cries a union is necessary. But when they come to the manner and form of the union, their weak noodles are perfectly distracted. 99

—Benjamin Franklin, in a letter to Governor William Shirley, 1755

A String of British Defeats

In 1755, General Edward Braddock led British and colonial troops in an attack against Fort Duquesne. Braddock was a stubborn man who had little experience at fighting in the forests of North America. Still, the general boasted that he would sweep the French from the Ohio Valley.

Disaster for Braddock Braddock's men moved slowly and noisily through the forests. Although warned of danger by Washington and by Indian scouts, Braddock pushed ahead.

As the British neared Fort Duquesne, the French and their Indian allies launched a surprise attack. Sharpshooters hid in the

Monitor Your Reading
As you read about Washington and Fort Necessity, think about the meaning of the British writer's comment. Why did he say that Washington had "set the world in flames"?

Primary Source

Battle in the Wilderness

Early in the war, a small force of Native Americans and French routed an army led by Edward Braddock. George Washington later wrote of the defeat:

"The Virginia troops showed a good deal of bravery, and were near all killed. For I believe out of three companies that were there, there are scarce 30 men left alive.... The general [Braddock] was wounded; of which he died three days after. Sir Peter Halket was killed in the field, where died many other brave officers. I luckily escaped without a wound, though I had four bullets through my coat and two horses shot under me."

—George Washington in a letter to his mother, July 18, 1755

Analyzing Primary Sources
How did the battle build Washington's reputation among his fellow colonists?

forest and picked off British soldiers, whose bright red uniforms made easy targets.

Braddock himself had five horses shot out from under him before he fell, fatally wounded. Almost half the British were killed or wounded. Washington, too, was nearly killed.

Further British Setbacks During the next two years, the war continued to go badly for the British. British attacks against several French forts failed. Meanwhile, the French won important victories, capturing Fort Oswego on Lake Ontario and Fort William Henry on Lake George. All these defeats put a serious strain on the alliances with Native Americans who had been counting on the British to protect them from the French.

The Tide of Battle Turns

In 1757, William Pitt became the new head of the British government. Pitt made it his first job to win the war in North America. Once that goal was achieved, he argued, the British would be free to focus on victory in other parts of the world. So Pitt sent Britain's best generals to North America. To encourage the colonists to support the war, he promised large payments for military services and supplies.

Under Pitt's leadership, the tide of battle turned. In 1758, Major General Jeffrey Amherst captured Louisbourg, the most important fort in French Canada. That year, the British also seized Fort Duquesne, which they renamed Fort Pitt after the British leader. The city of Pittsburgh later grew up on the site of Fort Pitt.

The Fall of New France

The British enjoyed even greater success in 1759. By summer, they had pushed the French from Fort Niagara, Crown Point, and Fort Ticonderoga (ty kahn duh ROH guh). Next, Pitt sent General James Wolfe to take Quebec, capital of New France.

Battle for Quebec Quebec was vital to the defense of New France. Without Quebec, the French could not supply their forts farther up the St. Lawrence River. Quebec was well defended, though. The city sat on the edge of the Plains of Abraham, on top of a steep cliff high above the St. Lawrence. An able French general, the Marquis de Montcalm, was prepared to fight off any British attack.

General Wolfe devised a bold plan to capture Quebec. He knew that Montcalm had only a few soldiers guarding the cliff because the French thought that it was too steep to climb. Late at night, Wolfe ordered

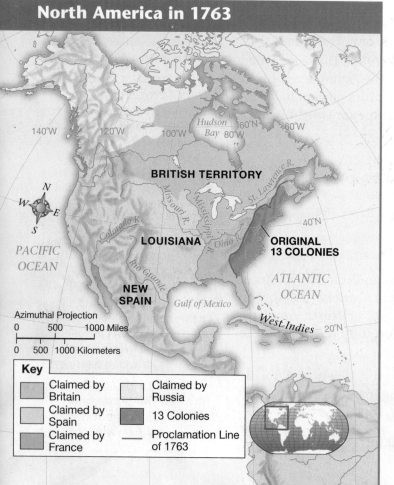

GEOGRAPHY
Skills

The Treaty of Paris ended the French and Indian War and greatly changed the map of North America.

1. **Location** On the map, locate **(a)** the 13 colonies, **(b)** Louisiana, **(c)** New Spain.

2. **Region** Which countries shared control of North America after 1763?

3. **Critical Thinking**
   Comparing Compare this map to the map at the beginning of the chapter. What effect did the Treaty of Paris have on French power in North America?

North America in 1763

British troops to row quietly in small boats to the foot of the cliff. In the dark, the soldiers swarmed ashore, climbed up the cliff, and assembled at the top.

The next morning, Montcalm awakened to a surprise. A force of 4,000 British troops was drawn up and ready for battle on the Plains of Abraham.

Quickly, Montcalm marched his own troops out to join in battle. By the time the fierce fighting was over, both Montcalm and Wolfe lay dead. Moments before Wolfe died, a soldier gave him the news that the British had won. Wolfe is said to have whispered, "Now, God be praised, I will die in peace." On September 18, 1759, Quebec surrendered to the British.

Treaty of Paris The fall of Quebec sealed the fate of New France, though fighting dragged on in Europe for several more years. Finally, in 1763, Britain and France signed the Treaty of Paris, bringing the long conflict to an end.

The Treaty of Paris marked the end of French power in North America. By its terms, Britain gained Canada and all French lands east of the Mississippi River except New Orleans. France was allowed to keep only two islands in the Gulf of St. Lawrence and its prosperous sugar-growing islands in the West Indies. Spain, which had entered the war on the French side in 1762, gave up Florida to Britain. In return, Spain received all French land west of the Mississippi. In addition, Spain gained the vital port city of New Orleans. Spain retained control of its vast empire in Central America and South America.

After years of fighting, peace returned to North America. Yet, in a few short years, a new conflict would break out. This time, the struggle would pit Britain against its own 13 colonies.

Section 1 Assessment

Recall

1. **Identify** Explain the significance of **(a)** George Washington, **(b)** Joseph Brant, **(c)** French and Indian War, **(d)** Benjamin Franklin, **(e)** Albany Plan of Union, **(f)** Edward Braddock, **(g)** William Pitt, **(h)** Plains of Abraham, **(i)** Treaty of Paris.

Comprehension

2. Why did France and Britain go to war in 1754?
3. How did defeat and disunity hurt the early British war effort?
4. What events turned the tide of battle after William Pitt became head of the British government?

5. How did the battle of Quebec lead to the fall of New France to the British?

Critical Thinking and Writing

6. **Exploring the Main Idea** Review the Main Idea statement at the beginning of this section. Write a paragraph explaining how Britain's victory in the French and Indian War made it the most powerful force in North America.
7. **Analyzing Ideas** **(a)** List two ways in which the Albany Plan of Union would have helped the colonies fight the French. **(b)** Why did the colonists reject the Plan of Union?

ACTIVITY

  Take It to the NET

Writing a Skit Use the Internet to find resources describing the strategies of Generals Wolfe and Montcalm at Quebec. Then, prepare a five-minute skit about an imaginary meeting between the two generals. Visit *The American Nation* section of **www.phschool.com** for help in completing the activity.

2 Turmoil Over Taxation

Reading Focus

- How did Britain attempt to ease growing tensions on the American frontier?
- How did the colonists react to new taxes imposed by Parliament?
- Which new colonial leaders emerged as the conflict with Britain escalated?
- What events led to the Boston Massacre?

Key Terms

Pontiac's War
Proclamation of 1763
Stamp Act
petition
boycott
repeal
Townshend Acts
writ of assistance
Boston Massacre
committee of correspondence

Taking Notes

Copy the concept web below. As you read the section, fill in the blank ovals with important facts that led to the conflict between Britain and its American colonies. Add as many ovals as you need.

CONFLICT BETWEEN BRITAIN AND THE COLONIES — The western frontier — Tax on sugar and tea

Main Idea Many colonists opposed Parliament's attempts to tighten control over Britain's North American empire.

A tax stamp
Predict Based on what you already know, how do you think the American colonists would react to higher taxes imposed by the British?

Setting the Scene

The lieutenant governor of Massachusetts, Thomas Hutchinson, was at supper with his children in Boston when an out-of-breath messenger arrived. A mob was coming for Hutchinson, he warned. "I directed my children to fly to a secure place," Hutchinson recalled. Then, he fled to a neighbor's house.

> 66 I had been there but a few minutes before the hellish crew fell upon my house with the Rage of devils and in a moment with axes split down the doors and entered. . . . 99
>
> —Thomas Hutchinson, lieutenant governor of Massachusetts, 1765

The furious mob went to work. It smashed windows and broke down walls. It ripped up Hutchinson's garden and chopped down his trees. The entire house would have been demolished except that daylight came before the job could be finished. "Such ruins were never seen in America," Hutchinson mourned.

How could such a riot take place? Only two years earlier, in 1763, British colonists had celebrated Britain's victory over France. They lit bonfires and set church bells ringing. Now, some of these same people were destroying the homes of royal officials. In truth, the riots of 1765 were only the beginning of a growing dispute with Great Britain.

New Troubles on the Frontier

By 1760, the British and their Indian allies had driven France from the Ohio Valley. Their troubles in the region were not over, however. For many years, fur traders had sent back glowing reports of the land beyond the Appalachian Mountains. With the French gone, British colonists eagerly headed west to claim the lands for themselves.

Clashes With Native Americans Many Native American nations lived in the Ohio Valley. They included the Senecas, Delawares, Shawnees, Ottawas, Miamis, and Hurons. As British settlers moved into the valley, they often clashed with these Native Americans.

In 1762, the British sent Lord Jeffrey Amherst to the frontier to keep order. French traders had always treated Native Americans as friends, holding feasts for them and giving them presents. Amherst refused to do this. Instead, he raised the price of goods traded to Indians. Also, unlike the French, Amherst allowed settlers to build farms and forts on Indian lands.

Angry Native Americans found a leader in Pontiac, an Ottawa chief who had fought on the French side. An English trader remarked that Pontiac "commands more respect amongst these nations than any Indian I ever saw." In April 1763, Pontiac spoke out against the British, calling them "dogs dressed in red, who have come to rob [us] of [our] hunting grounds and drive away the game."

War on the Frontier Soon after, Pontiac led an attack on British troops at Fort Detroit. A number of other Indian nations joined him. In a few short months, they captured most British forts in the Ohio country. British and colonial troops then struck back and regained much of what they had lost.

Pontiac's War, as it came to be called, did not last long. In October 1763, the French told Pontiac that they had signed the Treaty of Paris. Because the treaty marked the end of French power in North America, the Indians could no longer hope for French aid against the British. One by one, the Indian nations stopped fighting and returned home.

Proclamation of 1763

Pontiac's War convinced British officials that they should stop British subjects from settling on the western frontier. To do this, the government issued the **Proclamation of 1763.** The proclamation drew an imaginary line along the crest of the Appalachian Mountains. Colonists were forbidden to settle west of the line. All settlers already west of the line were "to remove themselves" at once.

The proclamation was meant to protect Indians in the western lands. To enforce it, Britain sent 10,000 troops to the colonies. Few troops went to the frontier, however. Most stayed in cities along the Atlantic coast.

The proclamation angered colonists. Some colonies, including New York, Pennsylvania, and Virginia, claimed lands in the west. Also, colonists now had to pay for the additional British troops that had been sent to enforce the proclamation. In the end, many settlers simply ignored the proclamation and moved west anyway.

Crisis on the Frontier

Colonists settle on Indian lands in the west

Pontiac's War breaks out on the frontier

Proclamation of 1763 stops settlement in the west

Sugar and Stamp Acts burden colonists with new taxes

British government decides American colonists should help pay for troops

Stationing British troops in the colonies proves costly

Stormy protests break out in many colonies

One colonist who defied the Proclamation of 1763 was Daniel Boone. In 1767, Boone visited Kentucky, west of the Appalachians. In 1769, he began what became a two-year journey of exploration through Kentucky. He traveled as far as the Falls of the Ohio, the site of the present-day city of Louisville. Later, he led settlers through the Cumberland Gap along an old Indian path. During his travels, Boone fought a number of battles against the Indians and was taken captive for a short period.

Britain Imposes New Taxes

The French and Indian War plunged Britain deeply into debt. As a result, the taxes paid by citizens in Britain rose sharply. The British prime minister, George Grenville, decided that colonists in North America should help share the burden. In a mercantilist system, colonies were expected to serve the colonial power. Grenville reasoned that the colonists would not oppose small tax increases.

Sugar Act In 1764, Grenville asked Parliament to approve the Sugar Act, which put a new tax on molasses. Molasses, you will recall, was a valuable item in the triangular trade.

The Sugar Act replaced an earlier tax, which had been so high that any merchant who paid it would have been driven out of business. As a result, most colonial merchants simply avoided the tax by smuggling molasses into the colonies. Often, they bribed tax collectors to look the other way. The Sugar Act of 1764 lowered the tax. At the same time, the law made it easier for British officials to bring colonial smugglers to trial. Grenville made it clear that he expected the new tax to be paid.

Stamp Act Grenville also persuaded Parliament to pass the Stamp Act of 1765. The act placed new duties on legal documents such as wills, diplomas, and marriage papers. It also taxed newspapers, almanacs, playing cards, and even dice.

All items named in the law had to carry a stamp showing that the tax had been paid. Stamp taxes were used in Britain and other countries to raise money. However, Britain had never required American colonists to pay such a tax.

Protesting the Stamp Act

When British officials tried to enforce the Stamp Act, they met with stormy protests from colonists. Lieutenant Governor Hutchinson in Massachusetts was not the only official to feel the anger of a mob. Some colonists threw rocks at agents trying to collect the unpopular tax. Others tarred and feathered the agents. In addition to riots in Boston, other disturbances broke out in New York City, Newport, and Charleston. In New York City, rioters destroyed the home of a British official who had said he would "cram the stamps down American throats" at the point of his sword.

The fury of the colonists shocked the British. After all, Britain had spent a great deal of money to protect the colonies against the French. The British at home were paying much higher taxes than the colonists. Why, British officials asked, were colonists so angry about the Stamp Act? As one English letter-writer commented,

> 66 Our Colonies must be the biggest Beggars in the World, if such small Duties appear to be intolerable Burdens in their Eyes. 99
>
> —"Pacificus," Maryland *Gazette*, March 20, 1766

"No Taxation Without Representation!" Colonists replied that the Stamp Act taxes were unjust. The taxes, they claimed, went against the principle that there should be no taxation without representation. That principle was rooted in English traditions dating back to the Magna Carta.

Colonists insisted that only they or their elected representatives had the right to pass taxes. Since the colonists did not elect representatives to Parliament, Parliament had no right to tax them. The colonists were willing to pay taxes—but only if the taxes were passed by their own colonial legislatures.

Uniting in Peaceful Protest The Stamp Act crisis united colonists from New Hampshire to Georgia. Critics of the law called for delegates from every colony to meet in New York City. There, a congress would form to consider actions against the hated Stamp Act.

In October 1765, nine colonies sent delegates to what became known as the Stamp Act Congress. The delegates drew up petitions to King George III and to Parliament. A petition is a formal written request to someone in authority, signed by a group of people. In these petitions, the delegates rejected the Stamp Act and asserted that Parliament had no right to tax the colonies. Parliament paid little attention.

Viewing History

Protesting the Stamp Act

Boston

The Stamp Act created a storm of opposition in the colonies. Colonists expressed their opposition to the tax in many ways, including this message on a teapot. **Linking Past and Present** *How do people today display their support or opposition to a political issue?*

Primary Sources

See "The English Bill of Rights" on page 580 of the Reference Section.

The colonists took other steps to change the law. They joined together to boycott British goods. To **boycott** means to refuse to buy certain goods and services. The boycott of British goods took its toll. Trade fell off by 14 percent. British merchants complained that they were facing ruin. So, too, did British workers who made goods for the colonies.

Finally, in 1766, Parliament **repealed,** or canceled, the Stamp Act. At the same time, however, it passed a law asserting that Parliament had the right to raise taxes in "all cases whatsoever."

AS YOU READ **Find Main Ideas** Write two cause-and-effect statements based on the information in this subsection.

The Townshend Acts

In May 1767, Parliament reopened the debate over taxing the colonies. In a fierce exchange, George Grenville, now a member of Parliament, clashed with Charles Townshend, the official in charge of the British treasury. "You are cowards, you are afraid of the Americans, you dare not tax America!" Grenville shouted.

"Fear? Cowards?" Townshend snapped back. "I dare tax America!"

The next month, Parliament passed the **Townshend Acts,** which taxed goods such as glass, paper, paint, lead, and tea. The taxes were low, but colonists still objected. The principle was the same: Parliament did not have the right to tax them without their consent.

Searching Without a Reason The Townshend Acts also set up new ways to collect taxes. Customs officials were sent to American ports with orders to stop smuggling. Using legal documents known as **writs of assistance,** the officers would be allowed to inspect a ship's cargo without giving a reason.

Colonists protested that the writs of assistance violated their rights as British citizens. Under British law, a government official could not search a person's property without a good reason for suspecting that the person had committed a crime. Colonists angrily cited the words of James Otis of Massachusetts. Arguing against a British attempt to impose writs of assistance six years earlier, he had said:

> ❝ Now, one of the most essential branches of English liberty is the freedom of one's house. A man's house is his castle; and while he is quiet, he is as well guarded as a prince in his castle. This writ, if it should be declared legal, would totally destroy this privilege. Customhouse officers may enter our houses when they please . . . break locks, bars, and everything in their way. . . . ❞
>
> —James Otis, February 24, 1761

Colonial Protests Widen Colonists responded swiftly and strongly to the Townshend Acts. From north to south, colonial merchants and planters signed agreements promising to stop importing goods taxed by the Townshend Acts. The colonists hoped that the new boycott would win repeal of the Townshend Acts.

To protest British policies, some angry colonists formed the Sons of Liberty. From Boston to Charleston, Sons of Liberty staged mock hangings of cloth or straw effigies, or likenesses, dressed as British

▲ Past

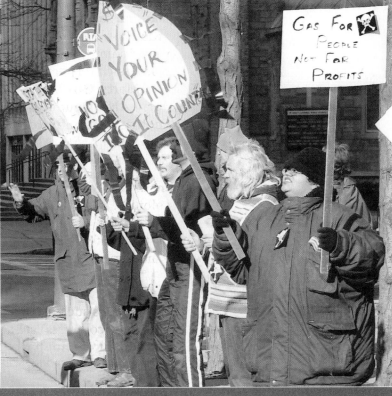

▲ Present

officials. The hangings were meant to show tax collectors what might happen to them if they tried to collect the unpopular taxes.

Some women joined the Daughters of Liberty. They paraded, signed petitions, and organized a boycott of fine British cloth. They urged colonial women to raise more sheep, prepare more wool, and spin and weave their own cloth. A slogan of the Daughters of Liberty declared, "It is better to wear a Homespun coat than to lose our Liberty."

Some Sons and Daughters of Liberty also used other methods to support their cause. They visited merchants and urged them to boycott British imports. A few even threatened people who continued to buy British goods.

New Colonial Leaders

As the struggle over taxes continued, new leaders emerged in all the colonies. Men and women in New England and Virginia were especially active in the colonial cause.

In Massachusetts Samuel Adams of Boston stood firmly against Britain. Sam Adams seemed an unlikely leader. He was a failure in business and a poor public speaker. Often, he wore a red suit and a cheap gray wig for which people poked fun at him. Still, Adams loved politics. He always attended Boston town meetings and Sons of Liberty rallies. Adams's real talent was organizing people. He worked behind the scenes, arranging protests and stirring public support.

Viewing History

Demonstrations Then and Now

Cleveland
Boston

Colonial demonstrations over taxes imposed by the British could get pretty nasty, as when protestors tarred and feathered a tax collector and poured tea down his throat. The recent demonstration at right is more peaceful, but also deals with a controversial issue. **Drawing Inferences** *Why do issues such as taxes and gas prices bring out strong emotions?*

Sam's cousin John was another important Massachusetts leader. John Adams had been a schoolteacher before becoming a skilled lawyer. Adams longed for fame and could often be difficult. Still he was more cautious than his cousin Sam. He weighed evidence carefully before taking any actions. His knowledge of British law earned him much respect.

Mercy Otis Warren also aided the colonial cause. Warren wrote plays that made fun of British officials. The plays were published in newspapers and widely read in the colonies. Warren formed a close friendship with Abigail Adams, the wife of John Adams. The two women used their pens to spur the colonists to action. They also called for greater rights for women in the colonies.

In Virginia Virginia contributed many leaders to the struggle against taxes. In the House of Burgesses, George Washington joined other Virginians to protest the Townshend Acts.

A young lawyer, Patrick Henry, became well known as a vocal critic of British policies. His speeches in the House of Burgesses moved listeners to both tears and anger. Once, Henry attacked Britain with such fury that some listeners cried out, "Treason!" Henry boldly replied, "If this be treason, make the most of it!" Henry's words moved a young listener, Thomas Jefferson. At the time, Jefferson was a 22-year-old law student.

The Boston Massacre

Port cities like Boston and New York were centers of protest. In New York, a dispute arose over the Quartering Act. Under that law, colonists had to provide housing, candles, bedding, and beverages to soldiers stationed in the colonies. When the New York assembly refused to obey the law, Britain dismissed the assembly in 1767.

Britain also sent two regiments to Boston to protect customs officers from local citizens. To many Bostonians, the soldiers were a daily reminder that Britain was trying to bully them into paying unjust taxes. When British soldiers walked along the streets of Boston, they risked insults or even beatings. A serious clash was not long in coming.

A Bloody Night On the night of March 5, 1770, a crowd gathered outside the Boston customs house. Colonists shouted insults at the "lobsterbacks," as they called the red-coated British who guarded the building. Then the Boston crowd began to throw snowballs, oyster shells, and chunks of ice at the soldiers.

The crowd grew larger and rowdier. Suddenly, the soldiers panicked. They fired into the crowd. When the smoke from the musket volley cleared, five people lay dead or dying. Among the first to die were Samuel Maverick, a 17-year-old white youth, and Crispus Attucks, an African American sailor.

Colonists were quick to protest the incident, which they called the Boston Massacre. A Boston silversmith named Paul Revere fanned anti-British feeling with an engraving that showed British soldiers firing on unarmed colonists. Sam Adams wrote letters to other colonists to build outrage about the shooting.

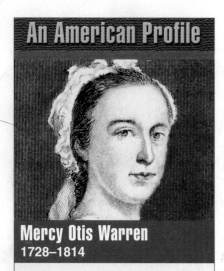

An American Profile

Mercy Otis Warren
1728–1814

Like most young women in the American colonies, Mercy Otis Warren received no formal schooling. She managed to educate herself, however, and like her brother, James Otis, became dedicated to the cause of freedom.

She was infuriated when James Otis was struck on the head by a British officer and suffered permanent brain damage. Warren used her writing skills to stir feelings against the British. In plays like *The Blockheads,* she ridiculed British officials. Her home became a meeting place for colonists who opposed British policies.

How do writers influence public opinion today?

The soldiers were arrested and tried in court. John Adams agreed to defend them, saying that they deserved a fair trial. He wanted to show the world that the colonists believed in justice, even if the British government did not. At the trial, Adams argued that the crowd had provoked the soldiers. His arguments convinced the jury. In the end, the heaviest punishment any soldier received was a branding on the hand.

Samuel Adams later expanded on the idea of a letter-writing campaign by forming a committee of correspondence. Members of the committee regularly wrote letters and pamphlets reporting to other colonies on events in Massachusetts. Within three months, there were 80 committees organized in Massachusetts. Before long, committees of correspondence became a major tool of protest in every colony.

A Temporary Calm By chance, on the very day of the Boston Massacre, a bill was introduced into Parliament to repeal most of the Townshend Acts. British merchants, harmed by the American boycott of British goods, had again pressured Parliament to end the taxes. The Quartering Act was repealed and most of the taxes that had angered the Americans were ended. However, King George III asked Parliament to retain the tax on tea. "There must always be one tax to keep up the right [to tax]," he argued. Parliament agreed.

News of the repeal delighted the colonists. Most people dismissed the remaining tax on tea as unimportant and ended their boycott of British goods. For a few years, calm returned. Yet the basic issue—Britain's power to tax the colonies—remained unsettled. The debate over taxes had forced the colonists to begin thinking more carefully about their political rights.

Section 2 Assessment

Recall

1. Identify Explain the significance of **(a)** Pontiac's War, **(b)** Proclamation of 1763, **(c)** Stamp Act, **(d)** Townshend Acts, **(e)** writ of assistance, **(f)** Boston Massacre, **(g)** committee of correspondence.

2. Define (a) petition, **(b)** boycott, **(c)** repeal.

Comprehension

3. How did Pontiac's War and the Proclamation of 1763 grow out of the migration of colonists?

4. Why did colonists oppose the Stamp Act and the Townshend Acts?

5. Name some of the new leaders who protested British policy.

6. What role did the Townshend Acts play in the events that led to the Boston Massacre?

Critical Thinking and Writing

7. Exploring the Main Idea Review the Main Idea statement at the beginning of this section. Then, write a letter to a newspaper explaining why colonists object to the new taxes.

8. Supporting a Point of View Write a position paper explaining how British policies spurred the growth of representative government during the colonial period.

ACTIVITY

Take It to the NET
Connecting to Today
Use the Internet to find out more about Paul Revere's engraving of the Boston Massacre and other protest art in American history. Visit *The American Nation* section of **www.phschool.com** for help in completing the activity.

The Economic Effects of the Stamp Act

Much of the opposition to the Stamp Act in the colonies focused on whether Americans could be taxed by a parliament in which they were not represented. Yet, the Stamp Act also stirred opposition because of its economic effects.

Fast Facts

1. Britain believed that the tax would cover 20 percent of the cost of keeping an army in North America.
2. Samuel Adams, one of the most outspoken opponents of the Stamp Act, had once been a tax collector.

New Yorkers protest the Stamp Act

Fighting Back

The Stamp Act placed a tax on almost every business record, such as invoices, bills, and receipts. It took effect at a time when economies were slumping following the French and Indian War. Businesses were hurt when the British Army stopped buying food and clothing in the colonies.

Not surprisingly, the opposition to the Stamp Act was led by the very people who were most affected by it—shippers, manufacturers, merchants, lawyers, journalists, and clergy. They faced a major loss of income because they expected other Americans to resist buying stamps.

To protest, many American merchants stopped trading with Britain. This led British business leaders to voice serious opposition to the Stamp Act. As a result, Parliament repealed the Stamp Act in March 1766.

English Exports to the 13 Colonies

Pounds Sterling (in thousands)

2,250 — 2,000 — 1,750 — 1,500

1763   1764   1765   1766   1767
Year

Source: *Historical Statistics of the United States*

English exports fell soon after Americans began the boycott.

ACTIVITY

You are the editor of a London newspaper. Write a one-paragraph editorial either supporting or opposing the Stamp Act. Give reasons for your point of view.

3 From Protest to Revolution

BEFORE YOU READ

Reading Focus

- How did a dispute over tea lead to tension between the colonists and the British government?
- How did Parliament strike back at the people of Boston?
- Why did fighting break out at Lexington and Concord?

Key Terms

Tea Act

Boston Tea Party

Intolerable Acts

Quebec Act

First Continental Congress

militia

minuteman

battles of Lexington and Concord

Taking Notes

Copy this flowchart. As you read, fill in the boxes with some of the major events described in this section that led from the dispute over taxes on tea to fighting at Lexington and Concord. Add as many boxes as you need.

> British East India Company has millions of pounds of unsold tea in its warehouses.
>
> ↓
>
> [ ]
>
> ↓
>
> Fighting breaks out at Lexington and Concord.

Main Idea Crises such as the Boston Tea Party and the Intolerable Acts led to the outbreak of fighting between Britain and the colonies.

Setting the Scene All day, the men collected burnt cork and coal dust. As dusk approached, they began to gather in small groups. In twos and threes, they met in homes across Boston. It was December 16, 1773. Outside, a cold drizzle was falling. Inside, by warm fires, the men were smearing coal dust and cork on their faces. Then, they threw blankets over their shoulders, trying to disguise themselves as Indians.

George Hewes, a shoemaker, waited with some of the others for a signal from a packed town meeting. By the time the signal came, the rain had stopped and night had fallen. As Hewes recalled:

> 66 When I first appeared in the street after being disguised, I fell in with many who were dressed, equipped and painted as I was, and . . . marched in order to the place of our destination. 99
>
> —George Hewes, *Recollections,* 1834

That place was Griffin's Wharf, and the painted "Indians" were after tea. By 1773, the quarrel between Britain and the 13 colonies had erupted again over taxes. Only this time, colonists began to think the unthinkable. Perhaps the time had come to reject British rule and declare independence.

A Dispute Over Tea

Tea was tremendously popular in the colonies. By 1770, at least one million Americans brewed tea twice a day. People "would rather go without their dinners than without a dish of tea," a visitor to the colonies noted.

Parliament Passes the Tea Act Most of the tea was brought to the colonies by the British East India Company. The company bought

Colonial tea jar

AS YOU READ
Monitor Your Reading
What was the goal of the men who disguised themselves as Indians?

tea in southern Asia, shipped it to the colonies, and then sold it to colonial tea merchants. The merchants then sold the tea to the colonists. To make a profit, the merchants sold the tea at a higher price than they had paid for it.

In the 1770s, however, the British East India Company found itself in deep financial trouble. The British Parliament had kept a tax on tea as a symbol of its right to tax the colonies. The tax was a small one, but colonists resented it. Many of them refused to buy British tea. As a result, more than 15 million pounds of tea sat unsold in British warehouses.

Parliament tried to help the British East India Company by passing the Tea Act of 1773. The act let the company bypass the tea merchants and sell directly to colonists. Although colonists would still have to pay the tea tax, they would not have to pay the higher price charged by tea merchants. As a result, the tea itself would cost less than ever before. Parliament hoped this would encourage Americans to buy more British tea.

To the surprise of Parliament, colonists protested the Tea Act. American tea merchants were angry because they had been cut out of the tea trade. They believed that forcing Americans to buy tea through the British East India Company violated the Americans' right to conduct free enterprise.

Even tea drinkers, who would have benefited from the law, scorned the Tea Act. They believed that it was a British trick to make them accept Parliament's right to tax the colonies.

A New Boycott Once again, colonists responded to the new tax with a boycott. A Philadelphia poet, Hannah Griffitts, urged American women to:

> 66 Stand firmly resolved and bid Grenville to see
> That rather than freedom we part with our tea,
> And well as we love the dear drink when a-dry,
> As American patriots our taste we deny. 99
>
> —Hannah Griffitts in Milcah Martha Moore, *Commonplace Book,* 1773

Daughters of Liberty and women like Griffitts led the boycott. They served coffee or made "liberty tea" from raspberry leaves. At some ports, Sons of Liberty enforced the boycott by keeping the British East India Company from unloading cargoes of tea.

Boston Tea Party Three ships loaded with tea reached Boston harbor in late November 1773. The colonial governor of Massachusetts, Thomas Hutchinson, insisted that they unload their cargo as usual.

Sam Adams and the Sons of Liberty had other plans. On the night of December 16, they met in Old South Meetinghouse. They sent a message to the governor, demanding that the ships leave the harbor. When the governor rejected the demand, Adams stood up and declared, "This meeting can do nothing further to save the country."

Adams's words seemed to be a signal. As if on cue, a group of men in Indian disguises burst into the meetinghouse. From the gallery above, voices cried, "Boston harbor a teapot tonight! The Mohawks are come!"

Primary Sources

See "Revolutionary Tea" on page 581 of the Reference Section.

An American Profile

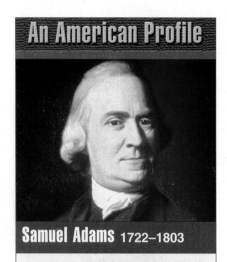

Samuel Adams 1722–1803

Sam Adams was not afraid of a little controversy. For example, when he was a student at Harvard University, Sam read his graduation paper to a large audience that included the governor of Massachusetts. Sam's subject, disobeying the law, deeply disturbed the governor. Sam argued that when a law was morally wrong, a person was entitled to break the law. This belief paved the way for his challenge to British authority.

Why might Sam Adams's graduation paper have disturbed many people in his audience?

The disguised colonists left the meetinghouse and headed for the harbor. Others joined them along the way. Under a nearly full moon, the men boarded the ships, split open the tea chests, and dumped the tea into the harbor. By 10 P.M., the Boston Tea Party, as it was later called, was over. The contents of 342 chests of tea floated in Boston harbor. The next day, John Adams wrote about the event in his diary.

66 This destruction of the tea is so bold, so daring, so firm . . . it must have such important and lasting results that I can't help considering it a turning point in history. 99

—Diary of John Adams, December 17, 1773

Parliament Strikes Back

Colonists had mixed reactions to the Boston Tea Party. Some cheered it as a firm protest against unfair British laws. Others worried that it would encourage lawlessness in the colonies. Even those who condemned the Boston Tea Party, though, were shocked at Britain's harsh response to it.

Punishing Massachusetts The British were outraged by what they saw as Boston's lawless behavior. In 1774, Parliament, encouraged by King George III, acted to punish Massachusetts. Colonists called the four laws they passed the Intolerable Acts because they were so harsh.

Viewing History

Boston Tea Party

Disguised as Indians, some 50 or 60 Bostonians attacked British tea ships. A crowd watched as the colonists dumped tea into Boston harbor. British officials called the Boston Tea Party "the most wanton and unprovoked insult offered to the civil power that is recorded in history." At lower right is a tea chest. **Drawing Conclusions** *Why did the colonists disguise themselves as Indians?*

First, Parliament shut down the port of Boston. No ship could enter or leave the harbor—not even a small boat. The harbor would remain closed until the colonists paid for the tea they had destroyed in the Boston Tea Party and repaid British officials, such as Thomas Hutchinson, for damage to personal property.

Second, Parliament forbade Massachusetts colonists to hold town meetings more than once a year without the governor's permission. In the past, colonists had called town meetings whenever they wished. All juries would now be selected by the king's officials, rather than be elected by citizens.

Third, Parliament allowed customs officers and other officials who might be charged with major crimes to be tried in Britain or Canada instead of in Massachusetts. Colonists protested. They argued that a dishonest official could break the law in the colonies and avoid punishment by being tried before a sympathetic jury.

Fourth, Parliament passed a new Quartering Act. No longer would redcoats camp in tents on Boston Common. Instead, colonists would have to house British soldiers in their homes when no other housing was available.

Quebec Act About the same time, Parliament also passed the Quebec Act. It set up a government for Canada and gave complete religious freedom to French Catholics. The Quebec Act also extended the borders of Quebec to include the landing between the Ohio and Missouri rivers. The act pleased French Canadians. But it angered the American colonists, because some of the colonies claimed ownership of these lands.

Other Colonies Support Boston The committees of correspondence spread news of the Intolerable Acts to other colonies. They warned that the people of Boston faced hunger while their port was closed. People from other colonies responded quickly. Carts rolled into the city with rice from South Carolina, corn from Virginia, and flour from Pennsylvania.

In the Virginia assembly, Thomas Jefferson suggested that a day be set aside to mark the shame of the Intolerable Acts. The royal governor of Virginia rejected the idea. The colonists went ahead anyway. On June 1, 1774, church bells tolled slowly. Merchants closed their shops. Many colonists prayed and fasted all day.

In September 1774, colonial leaders called a meeting in Philadelphia. Delegates from 12 colonies gathered in what became known as the First Continental Congress. Only Georgia did not send delegates.

After much debate, the delegates passed a resolution backing Massachusetts in its struggle. They agreed to boycott all British goods and to stop exporting goods to Britain until the Intolerable Acts were repealed. The delegates also urged each colony to set up and train its own militia (muh LIHSH uh). A militia is an army of citizens who serve as soldiers during an emergency.

Before leaving Philadelphia, the delegates agreed to meet again in May 1775. Little did they suspect that before then, an incident in Massachusetts would change the fate of the colonies forever.

Minute Man National Park

The battles at Lexington and Concord began the long struggle for independence of the 13 American colonies against Britain. Today, Minute Man National Historical Park in Massachusetts preserves the historic sites. Here, present-day Americans re-create the battle at the Concord Bridge.

Take It to the NET

Virtual Field Trip For an interactive look at Minute Man National Historical Park, visit *The American Nation* section of **www.phschool.com**.

Lexington and Concord

In Massachusetts, colonists were already preparing to resist. Newspapers called on citizens to prevent what they called "the Massacre of American Liberty." Volunteers known as minutemen trained regularly. Minutemen got their name because they kept their muskets at hand and were prepared to fight at a minute's notice. In towns near Boston, minutemen collected weapons and gunpowder. Meanwhile, Britain built up its forces. More troops arrived in Boston, bringing the total number of British soldiers in that city to 4,000.

Early in 1775, General Thomas Gage, the British commander, sent scouts to towns near Boston. They reported that minutemen had a large store of arms in Concord, a village about 18 miles from Boston. Gage planned a surprise march to Concord to seize the arms.

Sounding the Alarm On April 18, about 700 British troops quietly left Boston in the darkness. Their goal was to seize the colonial arms. The Sons of Liberty were watching. As soon as the British set out, the Americans hung two lamps from the Old North Church in Boston. This signal meant that the redcoats were crossing the Charles River.

Colonists who were waiting across the Charles River saw the signal. Messengers mounted their horses and galloped through the night toward Concord. One midnight rider was Paul Revere. "The redcoats are coming! The redcoats are coming!" shouted Revere as he passed through each sleepy village along the way.

AS YOU READ

Visualize Use the description in this subsection and the picture above to form a mental image of the battles of Lexington and Concord.

"The Shot Heard Round the World" At daybreak on April 19, the redcoats reached Lexington, a town near Concord. On the village green, some 70 minutemen were waiting, commanded by Captain John Parker. The British ordered the minutemen to go home.

Outnumbered, the colonists began to leave. Suddenly, a shot rang out through the chill morning air. No one knows who fired it. In the brief struggle that followed, eight colonists were killed.

The British pushed on to Concord. Finding no arms in the village, they turned back to Boston. On a bridge outside Concord, they met 300 minutemen. Again, fighting broke out. This time, the British were forced to retreat. As the redcoats withdrew, colonial sharp-shooters took deadly aim at them from the woods and fields. Local women also fired at the British from their windows. By the time they reached Boston, the redcoats had lost 73 men. Another 200 British soldiers were wounded or missing.

News of the battles of Lexington and Concord spread swiftly. To many colonists, the fighting ended all hope of a peaceful settlement. Only war would decide the future of the 13 colonies.

More than 60 years after the battles of Lexington and Concord, a well-known New England writer, Ralph Waldo Emerson, wrote a poem honoring the minutemen. Emerson's "Concord Hymn" created a vivid picture of the clash at Concord. It begins:

> 66 By the rude bridge that arched the flood,
> Their flag to April's breeze unfurled,
> Here once the embattled farmers stood,
> And fired the shot heard round the world. 99
>
> —Ralph Waldo Emerson, "Concord Hymn," 1837

The "embattled farmers" faced six long years of fighting. At war's end, though, the 13 colonies would be a new, independent nation.

Section 3 Assessment

Recall

1. **Identify** Explain the significance of **(a)** Tea Act, **(b)** Samuel Adams, **(c)** Boston Tea Party, **(d)** Intolerable Acts, **(e)** Quebec Act, **(f)** First Continental Congress, **(g)** minuteman, **(h)** Lexington and Concord.
2. **Define** militia.

Comprehension

3. Why did the Tea Act anger many people in the colonies?
4. Describe two of the Intolerable Acts.
5. Explain why fighting broke out at Lexington and Concord in 1775.

Critical Thinking and Writing

6. **Exploring the Main Idea** Review the Main Idea statement at the beginning of this section. Then, draw a flowchart showing the connection between the Boston Tea Party and the fighting at Lexington and Concord.
7. **Analyzing Information** You are a concerned citizen of Boston in 1775. Write a letter to the editor of your newspaper analyzing the political and economic causes of the American Revolution.

ACTIVITY

Composing a Catchy Tune You are a colonist in Boston in 1773. You are so angry at British actions that you are composing a ditty—a catchy tune—to encourage other colonists to boycott British goods. Take any tune you know and write eight lines of lyrics that will support a boycott.

The events that shape history don't just happen. They are related to earlier events. To understand historical events, it is important to recognize their causes. It also is important to recognize the effects of the events—what resulted because the event happened.

Cause and Effect

Causes

- Parliament passes the Townshend Acts
- Parliament repeals the Townshend Acts but later passes a new tax, the Tea Act
- The colonies oppose the tax by boycotting tea
- The British ship tea to Boston harbor

THE BOSTON TEA PARTY

Effects

- Parliament passes the Intolerable Acts to punish Massachusetts
- Other colonies back Massachusetts in its struggle against Britain
- Massachusetts minutemen clash with British soldiers at Lexington and Concord

Learn the Skill *To learn to analyze a cause-and-effect chart, use the following steps:*

1. **Look at the headings.** The headings on the chart indicate which statements are the causes of an event and which statements are the results of it.

2. **Read the causes.** These statements give reasons why a particular event occurred. Some events have one cause. Others have many.

3. **Identify the effects.** These statements tell what happened because of the event. Very important events may have effects in many different areas.

4. **Make connections.** Think about why certain causes led to the event and why the event in turn had the results it did. Remember that an event will be both cause and effect. It may flow out of a previous event while itself creating many results.

Practice the Skill *Answer the following questions about the chart above.*

1. **(a)** What event do the causes on this chart lead to? **(b)** If you could add to the chart, under which heading would you put the outbreak of the French and Indian War?

2. Give two reasons for the Boston Tea Party.

3. Give two effects of the Boston Tea Party.

4. **(a)** Why did the tea shipped to Boston harbor lead to the Boston Tea Party? **(b)** How was the clash at Lexington and Concord a result of the Boston Tea Party?

Apply the Skill *See the Chapter Review and Assessment.*

CREATING A CHAPTER SUMMARY

On a sheet of paper, draw a diagram like this one. Fill in each box with the causes and effects of the events at the top of the table. For each event, include the date. Some information has been filled in to help you get started.

	French and Indian War (1754–1763)	Stamp Act (1765)	Boston Tea Party (1773)
CAUSES	• Britain and France compete for Ohio River Valley. (1750s)		
EFFECTS			

For additional review and enrichment activities, see the interactive version of *The American Nation,* available on the Web and on CD-ROM.

 Take It to the NET

Chapter Self-Test For practice test questions for Chapter 5, see *The American Nation* section of **www.phschool.com**.

Building Vocabulary

Write sentences using the vocabulary words below. Leave blanks where the vocabulary words go. Exchange your sentences with a classmate, and fill in the blanks in each other's sentences.

1. petition
2. boycott
3. repeal
4. militia
5. minuteman
6. French and Indian War
7. Albany Plan of Union
8. Pontiac's War
9. Proclamation of 1763
10. writ of assistance

Reviewing Key Facts

11. What were the main results of the Treaty of Paris of 1763? (Section 1)
12. Why were many Indians of the Ohio Valley angry in 1763? (Section 2)
13. What role did Sam Adams play in aiding the colonial cause? (Section 2)
14. How did British economic policies and mercantilism anger American colonists? (Section 3)
15. How did the Intolerable Acts unite people in the American colonies? (Section 3)

Critical Thinking and Writing

16. **Analyzing Primary Sources** Review the statement made by a Native American to an English trader: "You and the French are like the two edges of a pair of shears. And we are the cloth which is to be cut to pieces between them." **(a)** Write a paragraph explaining what the speaker meant by these words. **(b)** Do you think he believed that Native Americans could hold out against the British and French? Write a paragraph explaining your answer.
17. **Drawing Conclusions** List three ways your life might be different if France, not Britain, had won the French and Indian War.
18. **Ranking** List the events described in Sections 2 and 3. Then, rank them in the order of their importance in bringing about war between the American colonies and Britain. Put the most important event at the top of the list and the least important event at the bottom.
19. **Connecting to Geography: Place** Describe how the geographic setting influenced the way the battles of Lexington and Concord were fought.

Analyzing Primary Sources

Patrick Henry of Virginia was an eloquent critic of British rule. Read this selection from a famous speech and answer the questions that follow:

> 66 . . . The war is inevitable—and let it come! I repeat, sir, let it come. . . . The next gale that sweeps from the north will bring to our ears the clash of resounding arms! Our brethren are already in the field! Why stand we here idle? What is it that gentlemen wish? What would they have? Is life so dear, or peace so sweet, as to be purchased at the price of liberty and slavery? Forbid it, Almighty God! I know not what course others may take; but as for me, give me liberty or give me death. 99
>
> —From a speech by Patrick Henry, March 23, 1775

20. When Henry says, "let it come! I repeat, sir, let it come," to what is he referring?

21. What is "The next gale that sweeps from the north"?

22. Who are the "brethren . . . already in the field"?

23. How do you think Henry's audience responded?

Identifying Causes and Effects

The French and Indian War

Causes
- British colonists settle on lands claimed by France
- France and Britain involved in a worldwide struggle for empire

THE FRENCH AND INDIAN WAR

Effects
- Britain left with a large debt
- Colonists begin settling in Ohio River Valley

24. What was Britain's financial situation after the French and Indian War?
A It was in debt.
B It was extremely prosperous.
C It had so much money it was able to lend some to hard-pressed colonies.
D It had to pay large amounts of money to France.

25. How did the French and Indian War lead to the Proclamation of 1763?

ACTIVITIES

Connecting With . . . Culture

Write a Poem At the end of this chapter, you read a portion of Emerson's "Concord Hymn," which celebrates the minutemen at Concord Bridge. Another famous poem about this period is Henry Wadsworth Longfellow's "Paul Revere's Ride." It begins "Listen, my children, and you shall hear / Of the midnight ride of Paul Revere." Pick another event covered in this chapter and write a short poem about it. The poem should convey a sense of the emotions of the time. It need not be longer than eight lines.

Take It to the NET

Connecting to Today

Creating a Poster Taxes are still a leading political issue. Use the Internet to find Web sites concerned with taxing Americans. Create a poster promoting or opposing the point of view of the people who have created the Web site. For help in starting this activity, visit *The American Nation* section of **www.phschool.com**.

Creating a Database

Collecting Information About Colonial Leaders
Use the Internet to research the colonial leaders mentioned in this chapter. Find the following information: date of birth, date of death, home state/colony, major event involved in. Use the computer to list the information on a chart. Then, sort the information by (1) alphabetized last name, (2) date of birth, and (3) home state/colony. For help in starting this activity, visit *The American Nation* section of **www.phschool.com**.

History Through Literature

Johnny Tremain
Esther Forbes

Introduction *Johnny Tremain* is a work of historical fiction, a novel that uses actual people, places, and events to tell a fictional story. The author, Esther Forbes, wrote both real histories and historical fiction. The selection below begins as Boston is facing punishment by Britain for the Boston Tea Party.

Vocabulary Before you read the selection, find the meanings of these words in a dictionary: **paroxysm, indifferent, submission, gesticulating, wharfingers, tethered, flintlocks, impartially, filching, misdemeanor.**

Esther Forbes (1891–1967)

When that bill [for the Tea Party] came . . . , it was so much heavier than anyone expected, Boston was thrown into a paroxysm of anger and despair. There had been many a moderate man who had thought the Tea Party a bit lawless and was now ready to vote payment for the tea. But when these men heard how cruelly the Town was to be punished, they swore it would never be paid for. And those other thirteen colonies. Up to this time many of them had had little interest in Boston's struggles. Now they were united as never before. The punishment united the often jealous, often indifferent, separate colonies, as the Tea Party itself had not.

Sam Adams was so happy his hands shook worse than ever.

For it had been voted in far-off London that the port of Boston should be closed—not one ship might enter, not one ship might leave the port, except only His Majesty's warships and transports, until the tea was paid for. Boston was to be starved into submission.

On that day, that first of June, 1774, Johnny and Rab, like almost all the other citizens, did no work, but wandered from place to place over the town. People were standing in angry knots talking, gesticulating, swearing that yes, they would starve, they would go down to ruin rather than give in now. Even many of the Tories were talking like that, for the punishment fell equally heavily upon the King's most loyal subjects in Boston and the very "Indians" who had tossed the tea overboard. This closing of the port of Boston was indeed tyranny; this was oppression; this was the last straw upon the back of many a moderate man.

The boys strolled the waterfront. Here, on Long Wharf, merchants' counting houses were closed and shuttered, sail lofts deserted, the riggers and porters stood idle. Overnight, hundreds of such, and sailors and ropemakers, wharfingers and dock hands, had been thrown out of work. The great ships of Boston, which had been bringing wealth for over a hundred years, were idle at their berths. No one might come and go. . . .

June was ending and the boys stood about the Common watching the soldiers of the First Brigade camped there under Earl Percy. Row upon row of identical tents, cook fires, tethered horses of officers, camp followers, stacked muskets, the quick, smart pacing of sentries. All was neat and orderly.

Muskets. It was the muskets which interested Rab the most. Already on every village green throughout New England, men and boys were drilling in defiance of the King's orders. They said they were afraid of an attack from the French. These men had no uniforms. They came from the fields and farms in the very clothes they used for plowing. That was all right. But the weapons they brought to their drilling were not. Many had ancient flintlocks, old squirrel guns, handed down for generations. Rab, for instance, all that spring had been going to Lexington once or twice a week to drill with his fellow townsmen. But he could not beg nor buy a decent gun. . . .

Rab, so concerned over a gun as he was, did an uncharacteristic, foolish thing. The two boys were standing close to a stack of muskets. As Rab explained to Johnny their good points, he put out a hand and touched the lock on one.

Without even showing bad temper, almost impartially, a mounted officer sitting on his horse close by [and] chatting with a couple of Boston's Tory girls, swung about and struck Rab a heavy blow on the side of his head with the flat of his sword. Then he went on flirting with the girls as though nothing had happened. Rab never knew what hit him. . . .

A gray, older man, a medical officer, approached, called for water, sponged Rab's face for him, and said he was coming to. Johnny was not to worry.

"What was he doing?"

"Just looking at a gun."

"Touching it?"

"Well. . . yes."

British soldiers entering Boston

"And only got hit over the head? He got off easy. Filching a soldier's arms is a serious misdemeanor. Wonder Lieutenant Bragg didn't kill him."

Rab said thickly, "I hadn't thought to filch it! Not a bad idea. Guess I'll. . . guess I'll. . ." He was still groggy from the blow. "If ever I get a chance I'll. . . ."

The medical man only laughed at him.

Analyzing Literature

1. When Johnny and Rab strolled along the waterfront, they found that people were
   A ready to give in to the British.
   B saying they would starve rather than give in to the British.
   C so busy with their jobs they took little notice of British actions.
   D agreeing with the British.

2. How would you describe the attitude of the British medical officer toward Rab and Johnny?
   A Angry
   B Uncaring
   C Sympathetic
   D Nervous

3. **Critical Thinking and Writing** **Drawing Inferences** (a) What do the actions of the British officer, Lieutenant Bragg, suggest about his attitude toward the colonists? (b) In what ways do you think the medical officer agreed with Lieutenant Bragg? In what ways do you think he disagreed with Bragg?

The American Revolution

1775–1783

1 **Fighting Begins in the North**
2 **The Colonies Declare Independence**
3 **Struggles in the Middle States**
4 **Fighting for Liberty on Many Fronts**
5 **Winning the War in the South**

Drum carried at the battle

The Battle of Bunker Hill

AMERICAN EVENTS

1775
In the first major battle of the American Revolution, the colonists face the British at Bunker Hill.

1777
The American victory at the Battle of Saratoga is the turning point of the war. After this victory, the French decide to join the Americans in their fight against the British.

1775 • 1777 • 1779

WORLD EVENTS

1778 ▲
France recognizes American independence.

1779 ▲
Spain enters the war against Britain.

Turning Points in the Revolution

In spite of early defeats in the war, the Americans scored victories that renewed their hopes for winning independence.

BRITISH TERRITORY

Key
- ⚔ American victories
- ⚔ British victories
- ⚑ Forts
- (1777) Date of battle

Albers Equal-Area Projection
0   150   300 Miles
0   150   300 Kilometers

Quebec
Maine (part of MA)
Montreal
St. Lawrence R.
L. Superior
Champlain
Ft. Ticonderoga
Saratoga (1777)
NH
Boston
Albany
Bunker Hill (1775)
Ft. Oswego
Ft. Stanwix
L. Ontario
MA
CT
NY
RI
40°N
L. Huron
L. Michigan
L. Erie
Ft. Detroit
Trenton (1776)
New York
NJ
Princeton (1777)
Mississippi R.
Pennsylvania
Ft. Pitt
Valley Forge
Philadelphia
Ft. Miami
Brandywine (1777)
MD
DE
Wabash R.
Ohio R.
Virginia
Cahokia (1778)
Vincennes (1779)
James R.
Chesapeake Bay
Richmond
Kaskaskia (1778)
Yorktown (1781)
Potomac R.
Delaware R.
Hudson R.
Roanoke R.
Guilford Courthouse (1781)
North Carolina
Camden (1780)
Kings Mt. (1780)
Wilmington
South Carolina
APPALACHIAN MOUNTAINS
Savannah R.
Georgia
Charles Town
ATLANTIC OCEAN
70°W
30°N
Savannah
80°W
90°W
N W E S

Marquis de Lafayette, Major General, American army

1781
The British surrender to the Americans at Yorktown.

Flag of a new nation

1783
Great Britain recognizes American independence in the Treaty of Paris.

1779 · **1781** · **1783** ·

▲ **1780**
Tupac Armaru, a descendant of the Incas, leads a revolt against Spain.

1 Fighting Begins in the North

Reading Focus

- How did Congress struggle between peace and war with Britain?
- What advantages did each side have as it entered the war?
- How did the Continental Army gain control of Boston?

Key Terms

Olive Branch Petition

Green Mountain Boys

Continental Army

Patriot

Loyalist

Battle of Bunker Hill

blockade

mercenary

Taking Notes

Copy the chart. As you read, add facts to show how Americans struggled between keeping peace and waging war.

PEACE	WAR
• Many colonists hope to avoid final break with Britain • •	• Green Mountain Boys capture Fort Ticonderoga • •

Main Idea Even while Congress tried to make peace with Britain, fighting began in New England.

Uniform of a colonial soldier

Predict How do you think most colonists felt when they heard about the battles in Lexington and Concord?

Setting the Scene News of the fighting at Lexington and Concord spread like wildfire. Riders galloped off carrying hurriedly scrawled messages about the battles. The messengers were urged to "ride day and night" and spread the news "without the least delay." Within a few days, between 10,000 and 15,000 militia rushed to Boston. They surrounded the city and the British troops stationed there.

The sudden arrival of rebellious colonists was a clear sign that the quarrel between Britain and its American colonies was about to blaze into war. Still, many colonists hoped for a peaceful solution. Was there no way to heal relations with Britain?

Peace or War?

Just a few weeks after the battles at Lexington and Concord, on May 10, 1775, colonial delegates met at the Second Continental Congress in Philadelphia. Most of the delegates still hoped to avoid a final break with Britain. However, while they were meeting, the fighting spread.

A Peace Petition After much debate, the delegates sent a petition to King George. In the Olive Branch Petition, they declared their loyalty to the king and asked him to repeal the Intolerable Acts.

George III was furious when he heard about the petition. The colonists, he raged, were trying to begin a war "for the purpose of establishing an independent empire!" The king vowed to bring the rebels to justice. He ordered 20,000 more troops to the colonies to crush the revolt.

Congress did not learn of the king's response until months later. But even before the petition was sent, leaders like John and Sam Adams were convinced that war could not be avoided.

Rebels Take Ticonderoga Ethan Allen, a Vermont blacksmith, did not wait for Congress to act. Allen decided to lead a band of Vermonters, known as the Green Mountain Boys, in a surprise attack on Fort Ticonderoga, located at the southern tip of Lake Champlain. (See the map on page 170.) Allen knew that the fort held cannons that the colonists could use.

In early May, the Green Mountain Boys crept quietly through the morning mists to Fort Ticonderoga. They quickly overpowered the guard on duty and entered the fort. Allen rushed to the room where the British commander slept. "Come out, you old rat!" he shouted. The commander demanded to know by whose authority Allen acted. "In the name of the Great Jehovah and the Continental Congress!" Allen replied.

The British commander surrendered Ticonderoga. With the fort, the Green Mountain Boys won a valuable supply of cannons and gunpowder. Allen's success also gave Americans control of a key route into Canada.

Setting Up an Army In the meantime, the Second Continental Congress had to decide what to do about the makeshift army gathering around Boston. In June, delegates took the bold step of setting up the Continental Army. They appointed George Washington of Virginia as commander.

Washington knew that he would be fighting against one of the world's toughest armies. Still, he was willing to do his best. He set off at once to take charge of the forces around Boston.

Viewing History

Rebels Take Fort Ticonderoga In May 1775, Ethan Allen and the Green Mountain Boys made a bold attack on Fort Ticonderoga. In this painting, Allen demands that the British commander surrender the fort. **Applying Information** *Why was Fort Ticonderoga an important prize?*

Advantages of the Opposing Sides

The colonists who favored war against Britain called themselves Patriots. They thought British rule was harsh and unjust. About one third of the colonists were Patriots, one third were Loyalists, and one third did not take sides.

Patriots The Patriots entered the war with many disadvantages. Colonial forces were poorly organized and untrained. They had few cannons, little gunpowder, and no navy. Also, few colonists were willing to enlist in the Continental Army for long terms of service. They preferred to fight near home, as part of a local militia.

Yet, the Patriots also had advantages. Many Patriots owned rifles and were good shots. Their leader, George Washington, developed into a brilliant commander. Furthermore, Patriots were determined to fight to defend their homes and property. Reuben Stebbins of Massachusetts was

The War for Independence Begins

Key
← American forces ← British forces
✳ American victories ✳ British victories

Quebec
70° W
Three Rivers ✳
Arnold
Montgomery
Carleton
Montreal
BRITISH TERRITORY
45° N
St. Lawrence R.
Maine (part of MA)
Valcour Island
Lake Champlain
Crown Point
Kennebec R.
Ft. Ticonderoga
New Hampshire
ATLANTIC OCEAN
Connecticut R.
New York
Newburyport
Lexington
Howe To Halifax
Concord
Hudson R.
Massachusetts
Boston
Connecticut
Rhode Island
N
W E
S
Pennsylvania
New Jersey
Albers Equal-Area Projection
0   50   100 Miles
0   50   100 Kilometers
40° N

GEOGRAPHY Skills

At the beginning of the War for Independence, most of the fighting took place in the northern colonies and in Canada.

1. **Location** On the map, locate **(a)** Lexington, **(b)** Concord, **(c)** Boston, **(d)** Fort Ticonderoga, **(e)** Quebec.

2. **Movement (a)** Describe Arnold's route to Canada. **(b)** Describe Montgomery's route from Crown Point to Quebec.

3. **Critical Thinking Making Decisions** Based on the map, which American commander would have a harder time reaching Quebec? Explain.

typical of many patriotic farmers. When the British approached, he rode off to battle. "We'll see who's going t'own this farm!" he cried.

The British The British were a powerful foe. They had highly trained, experienced troops. Their navy was the best in the world. In addition, many colonists supported the British.

Still, Britain faced problems. Its armies were 3,000 miles from home. News and supplies took months to travel from Britain to North America. Also, British soldiers risked attacks by colonists once they marched out of the cities into the countryside.

Loyalists American colonists who remained loyal to Britain were known as **Loyalists.** They included wealthy merchants and former officials of the royal government. However, some farmers and craftsworkers were also Loyalists. There were more Loyalists in the Middle Colonies and the South than in New England.

Loyalists faced hard times during the war. Patriots tarred and feathered people known to favor the British. Many Loyalists fled to England or Canada. Others found shelter in cities controlled by the British. Those who fled lost their homes, stores, and farms.

The Fight for Boston

During the first year of conflict, much of the fighting centered around Boston. About 6,000 British troops were stationed there. Colonial militia surrounded the city and prevented the British from marching out.

Battle of Bunker Hill Even before Washington reached Boston, the Patriots took action. On June 16, 1775, Colonel William Prescott led 1,200 minutemen up Bunker Hill, across the river from Boston. From there, they could fire on British ships in Boston harbor. Prescott, however, noticed that nearby Breed's Hill was an even better position. He ordered his men to move there.

At sunrise, the British general, William Howe, spotted the Americans. He ferried about 2,400 redcoats across the harbor to attack the rebels' position. As the British approached, the Patriots held their fire.

When the Americans finally fired, the British were forced to retreat. A second British attack was also turned back. On the third try, the British pushed over the top. They took both Bunker Hill and Breed's Hill, but they paid a high price for their victory. More than

1,000 redcoats lay dead or wounded. American losses numbered only about 400.

The Battle of Bunker Hill was the first major battle of the Revolution. It proved that the Americans could fight bravely. It also showed that the British would not be easy to defeat.

The British Leave Boston When Washington reached Boston a few weeks after the Battle of Bunker Hill, he found about 16,000 troops camped in huts and tents at the edge of the city.

General Washington quickly began to turn raw recruits into a trained army. His job was especially difficult because soldiers from different colonies mistrusted one another. "Connecticut wants no Massachusetts men in her corps," he wrote. And "Massachusetts thinks there is no necessity for a Rhode Islander to be introduced into her [ranks]." However, Washington won the loyalty of his troops. They, in turn, learned to take orders and work together.

In January 1776, Washington had a stroke of good fortune. The cannons that the Green Mountain Boys had captured at Fort Ticonderoga arrived in Boston. Soldiers had dragged them across the mountains from Fort Ticonderoga. Washington had the cannons placed on Dorchester Heights, overlooking the harbor.

Once General Howe saw the American cannons in place, he knew that he could not hold Boston. In March 1776, he and his troops sailed from Boston to Halifax, Canada. About 1,000 American Loyalists went with them.

Although the British left New England, they did not give up. King George III ordered a blockade of all colonial ports. A blockade is the shutting of a port to keep people or supplies from moving in or out. The king also used mercenaries, or troops for hire, from Germany to help fight the colonists.

Section 1 Assessment

Recall

1. **Identify** Explain the significance of **(a)** King George III, **(b)** Olive Branch Petition, **(c)** Green Mountain Boys, **(d)** Continental Army, **(e)** George Washington, **(f)** Patriot, **(g)** Loyalist, **(h)** Battle of Bunker Hill.

2. **Define (a)** blockade, **(b)** mercenary.

Comprehension

3. **(a)** What steps did the Continental Congress take to pursue peace with Britain? **(b)** What steps did the Congress take to pursue war with Britain?

4. **(a)** What advantages did the Patriots have as the war began? **(b)** What advantages did the British have?

5. How did Washington force the British to leave Boston?

Critical Thinking and Writing

6. **Exploring the Main Idea** Review the Main Idea statement at the beginning of this section. Then, write a letter to Congress explaining why you think war can or cannot be avoided.

7. **Drawing Inferences** Why did some Loyalists feel they had to go with the British to Canada?

ACTIVITY

Writing a Diary Entry You have George Washington's job at the beginning of the war. Write several diary entries describing the task you face as commander of the Continental Army.

Identifying Points of View

When reading about a historical event, it is important to keep in mind that people wrote about an event from different points of view.

Ann Hulton was a Loyalist who lived with her brother in Boston just before the Revolution. His job was to collect taxes for the British. In this letter, Hulton describes an attack by a mob:

This engraving shows boys laughing at a Loyalist.

66 You will be surprised to hear how we were obliged to take refuge on board the *Romney* man of war lying in Boston Harbor. Mrs. Burch at whose house I was, had frequently been alarmed with the Sons of Liberty surrounding her house with most hideous howlings. . . . She had been exposed since her arrival and threatened with greater violence. She had removed her most valuable [possessions] and held herself in readiness to depart at an hour's notice. The occasion soon happened . . . we soon found that the mobs here are very different from those in Old England . . . these Sons of Violence after attacking houses, breaking windows, beating, stoning and bruising several gentlemen belonging to the Customs, the Collector mortally and burning his boat. . . . All was ended with a speech from one of the leaders, concluding thus, 'We will defend our Liberties and property, by the Strength of our Arm and the Help of our God. . . .' This is a specimen of the Sons of Liberty, of whom no doubt you have heard, and will hear more. . . . 99

—Ann Hulton, in a letter written June 30, 1768

Learn the Skill *Use these steps to identify points of view:*

1. **Identify the source.** If you know the background of the writer, you can evaluate that person's attitude.

2. **Note the frame of reference.** The place, time, and circumstances can make a difference.

3. **Find main ideas.** What is the main point that the writer or speaker is making?

4. **Look for emotionally charged words.** How information is presented affects the point of view.

5. **Identify points of view.** How does the writer or speaker feel?

Practice the Skill *Use the introduction and the letter to answer the following questions:*

1. How do you know Ann Hulton was writing to a Loyalist?

2. **(a)** Where did the event described take place? **(b)** How would you characterize the event?

3. Restate the main point of the letter.

4. Identify three emotionally charged words used in the letter.

5. **(a)** What is the writer's point of view? **(b)** Explain how you can tell.

Apply the Skill *See the Chapter Review and Assessment.*

2 The Colonies Declare Independence

BEFORE YOU READ

Reading Focus

- How did *Common Sense* influence the colonists?
- What steps did Congress take to declare independence?
- What are the main ideas of the Declaration of Independence?

Key Terms

Common Sense
traitor
Declaration of Independence
preamble
natural rights

Taking Notes

Copy the concept web. As you read, fill in the blank ovals with information about the creation and contents of the Declaration of Independence. Add as many ovals as you need.

Thomas Jefferson writes the Declaration

Preamble

Part 1

DECLARATION OF INDEPENDENCE

Main Idea In July 1776, the colonies declared independence from Britain.

Setting the Scene Dr. Benjamin Rush of Philadelphia looked down at the manuscript in his hand. A line referring to King George as "the royal brute of Great Britain" seemed to leap off the page. Apparently, that was only the beginning! Would any printer dare to publish such a document?

Rush had asked his friend Thomas Paine to write an essay urging the colonies to declare independence. By the winter of 1775, the Patriots had been fighting Britain for months. Yet, many colonists were still reluctant to cut their ties with Britain. In a fiery pamphlet, Paine told these colonists that it was time to make the break. He called the pamphlet *Common Sense.*

When *Common Sense* appeared in January 1776, curious readers snatched up copies. In six months, more than 500,000 were sold. "*Common Sense* is working a powerful change in the minds of men," George Washington observed.

Urged on by Paine and other radicals—people who want to make drastic changes in society—the colonists were beginning to think the unthinkable. They were thinking of creating a nation of their own.

AS YOU READ **Thomas Paine**
Draw Inferences Why did Paine call his pamphlet *Common Sense*?

Common Sense

By 1776, many colonists had come to believe that Parliament did not have the right to make laws for the 13 colonies. After all, they argued, the colonists had their own elected legislatures. At the same time, however, most colonists still felt a bond of loyalty to Britain. They especially felt that they owed allegiance to the king.

In *Common Sense,* Thomas Paine set out to change the colonists' attitudes toward Britain and the king. Colonists, he said, did not owe loyalty to George III or any other monarch. The very idea of having kings and queens was wrong, he said.

> **"** In England a King hath little more to do than to make war and give away [jobs]; which in plain terms, is

Primary Sources

See Thomas Paine, "Common Sense," on page 582 in the Reference Section.

Signing the Declaration

Philadelphia

Thomas Jefferson labored many hours perfecting the Declaration of Independence. In this painting, Jefferson and other committee members present the Declaration to the Continental Congress.
Evaluating Information *How does the artist show the significance of the meeting?*

to impoverish the nation. . . . Of more worth is one honest man to society and in the sight of God, than all the crowned ruffians that ever lived. **99**

—Thomas Paine, *Common Sense,* 1776

The colonists did not owe anything to Britain, either, Paine went on. If the British had helped the colonists, they had done so for their own profit. It could only hurt the colonists to remain under British rule. "Everything that is right or reasonable pleads for separation," he concluded. " 'Tis time to part."

Congress Votes for Independence

Common Sense sold many colonists on the idea of independence. It also deeply impressed many members of the Continental Congress. Richard Henry Lee of Virginia wrote to Washington, "I am now convinced . . . of the necessity for separation." In June 1776, Lee arose in Congress to introduce a resolution in favor of independence:

66 *Resolved,* That these United Colonies are and of right ought to be, free and independent States, that they are absolved from all allegiance to the British Crown, and that all political connection between them and the State of Great Britain is, and ought to be, totally dissolved. **99**

—Richard Henry Lee, Resolution at the Second Continental Congress, June 7, 1776

Making the Break The delegates faced a difficult decision. There could be no turning back once they declared independence. If they fell into British hands, they would be hanged as traitors. A traitor is a person who betrays his or her country.

After long debate, the Congress took a fateful step. They appointed a committee to draw up a formal declaration of independence. The committee included John Adams, Benjamin Franklin, Thomas Jefferson, Robert Livingston, and Roger Sherman. Their job was to tell the world why the colonies were breaking away from Britain.

The committee asked Thomas Jefferson to write the document. Jefferson was one of the youngest delegates. He was a quiet man who spoke little at formal meetings. Among friends, however, he liked to sprawl in a chair with his long legs stretched out and talk for hours. His ability to write clearly and gracefully had earned him great respect.

Signing the Document In late June, Jefferson completed the declaration, and it was read to the Congress. On July 2, the Continental Congress voted that the 13 colonies were "free and independent States." After polishing Jefferson's language, the delegates adopted the document on the night of July 4, 1776. They then ordered the Declaration of Independence to be printed.

John Hancock, president of the Continental Congress, signed the Declaration first. He penned his signature boldly, in large, clear letters. "There," he said, "I guess King George will be able to read that."

Copies of the Declaration were distributed throughout the colonies. Patriots greeted the news of independence with joyous—and sometimes rowdy—celebrations. In New York, colonists tore down a statue of King George III. In Boston, the sound of cannons could be heard for hours.

The Declaration of Independence

The Declaration of Independence consists of a preamble, or introduction, followed by three main parts.*

Natural Rights The first section of the Declaration stresses the idea of natural rights, or rights that belong to all people from birth. In bold, ringing words, Jefferson wrote:

> 66 We hold these truths to be self-evident, that all men are created equal; that they are endowed by their Creator with certain unalienable rights; that among these are life, liberty, and the pursuit of happiness. 99

According to the Declaration of Independence, people form governments in order to protect their natural rights and liberties. Governments can exist only if they have the "consent of the governed." If a government fails to protect the rights of its citizens, then it is the people's "right [and] duty, to throw off such government, and to provide new guards for their future security."

---

*The complete Declaration of Independence is printed at the end of this section on pages 177–180.

Primary Source

"Remember the Ladies"

While John Adams served as a delegate in the second Continental Congress, his wife, Abigail, wrote him the following letter:

"I long to hear that you have independence. And . . . in the new Code of Laws which I suppose it will be necessary for you to make I desire you would Remember the Ladies, and be more generous and favourable to them than your ancestors. Do not put such unlimited power into the hands of the Husbands. . . . If particular care and attention is not paid to the Ladies we are determined to foment a Rebellion, and will not hold ourselves bound by any Laws in which we have no voice, or Representation."

—Abigail Adams, letter to John Adams, March 31, 1776

Analyzing Primary Sources
How did Abigail Adams use arguments for independence made by Patriots to promote greater rights for women?

British Wrongs The second part of the Declaration lists the wrongs that led the Americans to break away from Britain. Jefferson condemned King George III for disbanding colonial legislatures and for sending troops to the colonies in peacetime. He complained about limits on trade and about taxes imposed without the consent of the people.

Jefferson listed many other wrongs to show why the colonists had the right to rebel. He also pointed out that the colonies had petitioned the king to correct these injustices. Yet, the injustices remained. A ruler who treated his subjects in this manner, he boldly concluded, is a tyrant and not fit to rule:

> 66 In every state of these oppressions, we have petitioned for redress in the most humble terms; our repeated petitions have been answered only by repeated injury. A prince whose character is thus marked by every act which may define a tyrant is unfit to be the ruler of a free people. 99

Independence The last part of the Declaration announces that the colonies are the United States of America. All political ties with Britain have been cut. As a free and independent nation, the United States has the full power to "levy war, conclude peace, contract alliances, establish commerce, and to do all other acts and things which independent states may of right do."

The signers close the declaration with a solemn pledge:

> 66 And, for the support of this declaration, with a firm reliance on the protection of Divine Providence, we mutually pledge to each other our lives, our fortunes, and our sacred honor. 99

 Summarize Write a paragraph that summarizes the three major parts of the Declaration of Independence.

 Section 2 Assessment

Recall

1. **Identify** Explain the significance of (a) Thomas Paine, (b) *Common Sense,* (c) Richard Henry Lee, (d) Thomas Jefferson, (e) Declaration of Independence.
2. **Define** (a) traitor, (b) preamble, (c) natural rights.

Comprehension

3. What arguments did Thomas Paine use in *Common Sense* to persuade the colonists to declare independence?
4. What actions did Congress take to make the final break with Britain?

5. Describe the main parts of the Declaration of Independence.

Critical Thinking and Writing

6. **Exploring the Main Idea** Review the Main Idea statement at the beginning of this section. Explain the arguments that the colonies used for declaring independence from Britain.
7. **Analyzing Primary Sources** Review the excerpt from Thomas Paine's *Common Sense* that appears on pages 173–174. Explain the meaning of this excerpt in your own words.

ACTIVITY

 Take It to the NET
Connecting to Today
Use the Internet to visit the exhibition of the original Declaration of Independence in Washington, D.C. Prepare a guided tour of the exhibit. Include information about the meaning of the document to Americans today. Visit *The American Nation* section of **www.phschool.com** for help in completing this activity.

The Declaration of Independence

On June 7, 1776, the Continental Congress approved the resolution that "these United Colonies are, and of right ought to be, free and independent States." Congress then appointed a committee to write a declaration of independence. The committee members were John Adams, Benjamin Franklin, Robert Livingston, Roger Sherman, and Thomas Jefferson.

Jefferson actually wrote the Declaration, but he got advice from the others. On July 2, Congress discussed the Declaration and made some changes. On July 4, 1776, it adopted the Declaration of Independence in its final form.

The Declaration is printed in black. The headings have been added to show the parts of the Declaration. They are not part of the original text. Annotations, or explanations, are on the white side of the page. Difficult words are defined.

When in the course of human events it becomes necessary for one people to dissolve the political bands which have connected them with another and to assume, among the powers of the earth, the separate and equal station to which the laws of nature and of nature's God entitle them, a decent respect to the opinions of mankind requires that they should declare the causes which impel them to the separation.

dissolve: break **powers of the earth:** other nations **station:** place **impel:** force

The colonists feel that they must explain to the world the reasons why they are breaking away from England.

The Purpose of Government Is to Protect Basic Rights

We hold these truths to be self-evident, that all men are created equal; that they are endowed by their Creator with certain unalienable rights; that among these are life, liberty, and the pursuit of happiness. That, to secure these rights, governments are instituted among men, deriving their just powers from the consent of the governed; that, whenever any form of government becomes destructive of these ends, it is the right of the people to alter or to abolish it, and to institute a new government, laying its foundation on such principles and organizing its powers in such form, as to them shall seem most likely to effect their safety and happiness. Prudence, indeed, will dictate that governments long established should not be changed for light and transient causes; and, accordingly, all experience hath shown that mankind are more disposed to suffer, while evils are sufferable, than to right themselves by abolishing the forms to which they are accustomed. But when a long train of abuses and usurpations, pursuing invariably the same object, evinces a design to reduce them under absolute despotism, it is their right, it is their duty, to throw off such government and to provide new guards for their future security. Such has been the patient sufferance of these colonies, and such is now the necessity which constrains them to alter their former systems of government. The history of the present King of Great Britain is a history of repeated injuries and usurpations, all having, in direct object, the establishment of an absolute tyranny over these States. To prove this, let facts be submitted to a candid world:

endowed: given **unalienable rights:** so basic that they cannot be taken away **secure:** protect **instituted:** set up **deriving:** getting **alter:** change **effect:** bring about

People set up governments to protect their basic rights. Governments get their power from the consent of the governed. If a government takes away the basic rights of the people, the people have the right to change the government.

prudence: wisdom **transient:** temporary, passing **disposed:** likely

usurpations: taking and using powers that do not belong to a person **invariably:** always **evinces a design to reduce them under absolute despotism:** makes a clear plan to put them under complete and unjust control **sufferance:** endurance

constrains: forces **absolute tyranny:** harsh and unjust government **candid:** free from prejudice

People do not readily change governments. But they are forced to do so when a government becomes tyrannical. King George III has a long record of abusing his power.

Wrongs Done by the King

assent: approval **relinquish:** give up **inestimable:** too great a value to be measured **formidable:** causing fear

This part of the Declaration spells out three sets of wrongs that led the colonists to break with Britain.

The first set of wrongs is the king's unjust use of power. The king refused to approve laws that are needed. He has tried to control the colonial legislatures.

depository: storehouse **fatiguing:** tiring out **compliance:** giving in **dissolved:** broken up **annihilation:** total destruction **convulsions:** disturbances

The king has tried to force colonial legislatures into doing his will by wearing them out. He has dissolved legislatures (such as those of Massachusetts).

endeavored: tried **obstructing:** blocking **naturalization:** process of becoming a citizen **migration:** moving **hither:** here **appropriations:** grants **obstructed the administration of justice:** prevented justice from being done **judiciary powers:** system of law courts **tenure:** term (of office) **erected:** set up **multitude:** large number **swarms:** huge crowds **harass:** cause trouble **render:** make

Among other wrongs, he has refused to let settlers move west to take up new land. He has prevented justice from being done. Also, he has sent large numbers of customs officials to cause problems for the colonists.

jurisdiction: authority **quartering:** housing **mock:** false

The king has joined with others, meaning Parliament, to make laws for the colonies. The Declaration then lists the second set of wrongs—unjust acts of Parliament.

He has refused his assent to laws the most wholesome and necessary for the public good.

He has forbidden his governors to pass laws of immediate and pressing importance, unless suspended in their operation till his assent should be obtained; and, when so suspended, he has utterly neglected to attend to them.

He has refused to pass other laws for the accommodation of the large districts of people, unless those people would relinquish the right of representation in the legislature; a right inestimable to them and formidable to tyrants only.

He has called together legislative bodies at places unusual, uncomfortable, and distant from the depository of their public records, for the sole purpose of fatiguing them into compliance with his measures.

He has dissolved representative houses, repeatedly for opposing, with manly firmness, his invasions on the rights of the people.

He has refused, for a long time after such dissolutions, to cause others to be elected: whereby the legislative powers, incapable of annihilation, have returned to the people at large for their exercise; the state remaining, in the meantime, exposed to all the danger of invasion from without and convulsions within.

He has endeavored to prevent the population of these States; for that purpose, obstructing the laws for naturalization of foreigners, refusing to pass others to encourage their migration hither, and raising the conditions of new appropriations of lands.

He has obstructed the administration of justice by refusing his assent to laws for establishing judiciary powers.

He has made judges dependent on his will alone for the tenure of their offices and the amount and payment of their salaries.

He has erected a multitude of new offices and sent hither swarms of officers to harass our people and eat out their substance.

He has kept among us, in time of peace, standing armies, without the consent of our legislatures.

He has affected to render the military independent of, and superior to, the civil power.

He has combined with others to subject us to a jurisdiction foreign to our Constitution and unacknowledged by our laws, giving his assent to their acts of pretended legislation:

For quartering large bodies of armed troops among us;

For protecting them by a mock trial from punishment for any murders which they should commit on the inhabitants of these States;

For cutting off our trade with all parts of the world;

For imposing taxes on us without our consent;

For depriving us, in many cases, of the benefit of trial by jury;

For transporting us beyond seas to be tried for pretended offences;

For abolishing the free system of English laws in a neighboring province, establishing therein an arbitrary government, and enlarging its boundaries, so as to render it at once an example and fit instrument for introducing the same absolute rule into these colonies;

For taking away our charters, abolishing our most valuable laws, and altering, fundamentally, the powers of our governments;

For suspending our own legislatures and declaring themselves invested with power to legislate for us in all cases whatsoever.

He has abdicated government here by declaring us out of his protection and waging war against us.

He has plundered our seas, ravaged our coasts, burnt our towns, and destroyed the lives of our people.

He is, at this time, transporting large armies of foreign mercenaries to complete the works of death, desolation, and tyranny already begun with circumstances of cruelty and perfidy scarcely paralleled in the most barbarous ages, and totally unworthy the head of a civilized nation.

He has constrained our fellow citizens, taken captive on the high seas, to bear arms against their country, to become the executioners of their friends and brethren, or to fall themselves by their hands.

He has excited domestic insurrections amongst us and has endeavored to bring on the inhabitants of our frontiers, the merciless Indian savages, whose known rule of warfare is an undistinguished destruction of all ages, sexes, and conditions.

In every state of these oppressions, we have petitioned for redress in the most humble terms; our repeated petitions have been answered only by repeated injury. A prince whose character is thus marked by every act which may define a tyrant is unfit to be the ruler of a free people.

Nor have we been wanting in attention to our British brethren. We have warned them, from time to time, of attempts made by their legislature to extend an unwarrantable jurisdiction over us. We have reminded them of the circumstances of our emigration and settlement here. We have appealed to their native justice and magnanimity, and we have conjured them, by the ties of our common kindred, to disavow these usurpations, which would inevitably interrupt our connections and correspondence. They, too, have been deaf to the voice of justice and consanguinity. We must, therefore, acquiesce in the necessity which denounces our separation, and hold them, as we hold the rest of mankind, enemies in war, in peace, friends.

imposing: forcing *depriving:* taking away *transporting us beyond seas:* sending colonists to England for trial *neighboring province:* Quebec *arbitrary government:* unjust rule *fit instrument:* suitable tool *invested with power:* having the power

During the years leading up to 1776, the colonists claimed that Parliament had no right to make laws for them because they were not represented in Parliament. Here, the colonists object to recent laws of Parliament, such as the Quartering Act and the blockade of colonial ports, which cut off their trade. They also object to Parliament's claim that it had the right to tax them without their consent.

abdicated: given up *plundered:* robbed *ravaged:* attacked *mercenaries:* hired soldiers *desolation:* misery *perfidy:* falseness *barbarous:* uncivilized *constrained:* forced *brethren:* brothers *domestic insurrections:* internal revolts

Here, the Declaration lists the third set of wrongs—warlike acts of the king. Instead of listening to the colonists, the king has made war on them. He has hired soldiers to fight in America.

oppressions: harsh rule *petitioned:* asked *redress:* relief *unwarrantable jurisdiction over:* unfair authority *magnanimity:* generosity *conjured:* called upon *common kindred:* relatives *disavow:* turn away from *consanguinity:* blood relationships, kinship *acquiesce:* agree *denounces:* speaks out against

During this time, colonists have repeatedly asked for relief. But their requests have brought only more suffering. They have appealed to the British people but received no help. So they are forced to separate.

Colonies Declare Independence

appealing: calling on **rectitude of our intentions:** moral rightness of our plans **absolved from all allegiance:** freed from loyalty **levy war:** declare war **contract alliances:** make treaties

As the representatives of the United States, they declare that the colonies are free and independent states.

The states need no longer be loyal to the British king. They are an independent nation that can make war and sign treaties.

Relying on help from Divine Providence, the signers of the Declaration promise their lives, money, and honor to fight for independence.

We, therefore, the representatives of the United States of America, in general Congress assembled, appealing to the Supreme Judge of the world for the rectitude of our intentions, do, in the name and by the authority of the good people of these colonies, solemnly publish and declare, that these united colonies are, and of right ought to be, free and independent states: that they are absolved from all allegiance to the British Crown, and that all political connection between them and the state of Great Britain is, and ought to be, totally dissolved; and that, as free and independent states, they have full power to levy war, conclude peace, contract alliances, establish commerce, and to do all other acts and things which independent states may of right do. And, for the support of this declaration, with a firm reliance on the protection of Divine Providence, we mutually pledge to each other our lives, our fortunes, and our sacred honor.

Signers of the Declaration of Independence

John Hancock, President

Charles Thomson, Secretary

New Hampshire
Josiah Bartlett
William Whipple
Matthew Thornton

Massachusetts
Samuel Adams
John Adams
Robert Treat Paine
Elbridge Gerry

Rhode Island
Stephen Hopkins
William Ellery

Connecticut
Roger Sherman
Samuel Huntington
William Williams
Oliver Wolcott

Delaware
Caesar Rodney
George Read
Thomas McKean

New York
William Floyd
Philip Livingston
Francis Lewis
Lewis Morris

New Jersey
Richard Stockton
John Witherspoon
Francis Hopkinson
John Hart
Abraham Clark

Georgia
Button Gwinnett
Lyman Hall
George Walton

Maryland
Samuel Chase
William Paca
Thomas Stone
Charles Carroll

North Carolina
William Hooper
Joseph Hewes
John Penn

Virginia
George Wythe
Richard Henry Lee
Thomas Jefferson
Benjamin Harrison
Thomas Nelson, Jr.
Francis Lightfoot Lee
Carter Braxton

South Carolina
Edward Rutledge
Thomas Heyward, Jr.
Thomas Lynch, Jr.
Arthur Middleton

Pennsylvania
Robert Morris
Benjamin Rush
Benjamin Franklin
John Morton
George Clymer
James Smith
George Taylor
James Wilson
George Ross

3   Struggles in the Middle States

BEFORE YOU READ

Reading Focus

- What battles were fought in New York and New Jersey?
- How did the Battle of Saratoga mark a turning point in the war?
- What hardships did the Continental Army suffer at Valley Forge?

Key Terms

Battle of Long Island

Battle of Trenton

Battle of Saratoga

ally

cavalry

Valley Forge

Taking Notes

Copy the flowchart. As you read, fill in the boxes with the major events of the struggles in the Middle States.

August, 1776 Defeat at Long Island forces Washington to retreat
↓
↓
↓
Winter, 1777–1778 Washington's troops suffer hardships at Valley Forge

Main Idea After a series of Patriot defeats, an American victory at Saratoga marked a major turning point in the Revolution.

Setting the Scene

Setting the Scene   Early one morning in June 1776, Daniel McCurtin glanced out his window at New York harbor. He was amazed to see "something resembling a wood of pine trees trimmed." He watched the forest move across the water. Then, he understood. The trees were the masts of ships!

> 66 I could not believe my eyes . . . the whole bay was full of shipping as ever it could be. I declare that I thought all London was afloat. 99
>
> —George F. Scheer and Hugh F. Rankin, *Rebels and Redcoats*

McCurtin had witnessed the arrival of a large British fleet in New York. Aboard the ships were General Howe and thousands of redcoats. Thus began a new stage in the war. Previously, most of the fighting of the American Revolution had taken place in New England. In mid-1776, the heavy fighting shifted to the Middle States. There, the Continental Army suffered through the worst days of the war.

AS YOU READ   A British redcoat
Use Prior Knowledge
Why was a strong navy an advantage for the British?

The British Take New York

Washington, expecting Howe's attack, had led his forces south from Boston to New York City. His army, however, was no match for the British. Howe had about 34,000 troops and 10,000 sailors. He also had ships to ferry them ashore. Washington had fewer than 20,000 poorly trained troops. Worse, he had no navy.

In August, Howe's army landed on Long Island. In the Battle of Long Island, more than 1,400 Americans were killed, wounded, or captured. The rest retreated to Manhattan. The British pursued. To avoid capture, Washington hurried north.

Throughout the autumn, Washington fought a series of battles with Howe's army. In November, he crossed the Hudson River into

The Revolutionary War, 1776–1777

Albers Equal-Area Projection

Key
- American forces
- American victories
- British forces
- British victories
- Forts

GEOGRAPHY Skills

In 1776 and 1777, the Americans and British battled over a large area. The American victory at Saratoga marked a major turning point in the war.

1. **Location** On the map, locate (a) Long Island, (b) New York City, (c) Trenton, (d) Hudson River, (e) Saratoga, (f) Valley Forge.

2. **Movement** How did the British use sea power to help them capture Philadelphia?

3. **Critical Thinking Applying Information** How did Burgoyne and St. Leger use geography to help move their armies quickly toward Albany?

New Jersey. Chased by the British, the Americans retreated across the Delaware River into Pennsylvania.

During the campaign for New York, Washington needed information about Howe's forces. Nathan Hale, a young Connecticut officer, volunteered to go behind British lines. On his way back with the information, Hale was seized by the British and searched. Hidden in the soles of his shoes was information about British troop movements.

There was no trial. Howe ordered Hale to be hanged the next morning. As Hale walked to the gallows, he is said to have declared: "I only regret that I have but one life to lose for my country."

Washington Turns Retreat Into Victory in New Jersey

Months of hard campaigning took a toll on the Continental Army. In December 1776, Washington described his troops as sick, dirty, and "so thinly clad as to be unfit for service." Every day, soldiers deserted. Washington wrote to his brother: "I am wearied to death. I think the game is pretty near up."

Washington decided on a bold move: a surprise attack on Trenton. On Christmas night, he secretly led his troops across the icy Delaware River. Soldiers shivered as spray from the river froze on their faces. Once ashore, they marched through swirling snow. Some had no shoes. They tied rags around their feet. "Soldiers, keep by your officers," Washington urged.

Early on December 26, the Americans surprised the Hessian troops guarding Trenton and took most of them prisoner. The Hessians were soldiers from Germany. An American summed up the **Battle of Trenton:** "Hessian population of Trenton at 8 A.M.—1,408 men and 39 officers; Hessian population at 9 A.M.—0."

British General Charles Cornwallis set out at once to retake Trenton and to capture Washington. Late on January 2, 1777, he saw the lights of Washington's campfires. "At last we have run down the old fox," he said, "and we will bag him in the morning."

Washington fooled Cornwallis. He left the fires burning and slipped behind British lines to attack a British force that was marching toward Princeton. There, the Continental Army won another victory. From Princeton, Washington moved to Morristown, where the army would spend the winter. The victories at Trenton and Princeton gave the Americans new hope.

A Turning Point in the War

In London, British officials were dismayed by the army's failure to crush the rebels. Early in 1777, General John Burgoyne (buhr GOIN) presented a new plan for victory. If British troops cut off New England from the other colonies, he argued, the war would soon be over.

Burgoyne's Plan Burgoyne wanted three British armies to march on Albany, New York, from different directions. They would crush American forces there. Once they controlled the Hudson River, the British could stop the flow of soldiers and supplies from New England to Washington's army.

Burgoyne's plan called for General Howe to march on Albany from New York City. George III, however, wanted Howe to capture Philadelphia first.

In July 1777, Howe sailed from New York to Chesapeake Bay, where he began his march on Philadelphia. Howe captured Philadelphia, defeating the Americans at the battles of Brandywine and Germantown. But instead of moving toward Albany to meet Burgoyne as planned, he retired to comfortable quarters in Philadelphia for the winter. For his part, Washington retreated to Valley Forge, Pennsylvania.

Meanwhile, British armies under Burgoyne and Barry St. Leger (lay ZHAIR) marched from Canada toward Albany. St. Leger tried to take Fort Stanwix. However, a strong American army, led by Benedict Arnold, drove him back.

Victory at Saratoga Only Burgoyne was left to march on Albany. His army moved slowly because it had many heavy baggage carts to drag through the woods. To slow Burgoyne further, Patriots cut down trees and dammed up streams to block the route.

Despite these obstacles, Burgoyne recaptured Fort Ticonderoga. He then sent troops into Vermont to find food and horses. There, Patriots attacked the redcoats. At the Battle of Bennington, they wounded or captured nearly 1,000 British.

Burgoyne's troubles grew. The Green Mountain Boys hurried into New York to help American forces there. At the village of Saratoga, the Americans surrounded the British. When Burgoyne tried to break free, the Americans beat him back. Realizing that he was trapped, Burgoyne surrendered his entire army to the Americans on October 17, 1777.

The American victory at the Battle of Saratoga was a major turning point in the war. It ended the British threat to New England. It boosted American spirits at a time when Washington's army was suffering defeats. Most important, it convinced France to become an ally of the United States. Nations that are allies work together to achieve a common goal.

Aid From Europe The Continental Congress had long hoped for French aid. In 1776, the Congress had sent Benjamin Franklin to Paris to persuade Louis XVI, the French king, to give the Americans weapons and other badly needed supplies. In addition, the Congress wanted France to declare war on Britain.

AS YOU READ Find Main Ideas Make an outline of the subheadings in *A Turning Point in the War*. Under each subheading, write notes about how the event affected the war.

France Enters the War

France and Britain in conflict for many years → Conflict between France and Britain increases after the French and Indian War → Americans appeal to France for support during the Revolutionary War → France gives American rebels money and supplies but stays neutral → Americans defeat British at Saratoga → Victory at Saratoga proves to France that Americans can win → **France gives military and naval support to American forces**

The French were eager to defeat Britain, but they were also cautious. France was still angry about its defeat at British hands in the French and Indian War. However, Louis XVI did not want to help the Americans openly unless he was sure that they could win.

The American victory at Saratoga convinced France that the United States could stand up to Britain. In February 1778, France became the first nation to sign a treaty with the United States. It recognized the new nation and agreed to provide military aid. Later, the Netherlands and Spain also joined in the war against Britain. France, the Netherlands, and Spain all provided loans to the United States.

Even before European nations agreed to help the United States, individual volunteers had been coming from Europe to join the American cause. Some became leading officers in the American army.

The Marquis de Lafayette (lah fee EHT), a young French noble, brought trained soldiers to help the Patriot cause. Lafayette, who fought at Brandywine, became one of Washington's most trusted friends.

From the German state of Prussia came Friedrich von Steuben (STOO buhn), who helped train Washington's troops to march and drill. Von Steuben had served in the Prussian army, which was considered the best in Europe.

Two Polish officers also joined the Americans. Thaddeus Kosciusko (kahs ee UHS koh), an engineer, helped build forts and other defenses. Casimir Pulaski trained **cavalry,** or troops on horseback.

The Hardships of Valley Forge

The victory at Saratoga and the promise of help from Europe boosted American morale. Even so, Washington's Continental Army had to face hard times as it suffered through the long, cold winter of 1777–1778 at a makeshift camp at Valley Forge.

Conditions at Valley Forge were terrible. Soldiers shivered in damp, drafty huts. Many slept on the frozen ground. Some soldiers stood guard wrapped only in blankets. Others had no shoes, so they wrapped bits of cloth around their feet. As the bitter winter wore on, soldiers suffered from frostbite and disease. An army surgeon from Connecticut wrote about his hardships:

> **"** I am sick—discontented—and out of humor. Poor food—hard lodging—cold weather—fatigue—nasty clothes—nasty cookery . . . a pox on my bad luck! There comes a bowl of beef soup, full of burnt leaves and dirt. . . . Away with it, boys!—I'll live like the chameleon upon air. **"**
>
> —Albigence Waldo, *Diary,* December 14, 1777

As news of the suffering at Valley Forge spread, Patriots from around the nation sent help. Women collected food, medicine, warm clothes, and ammunition for the army. Some women, like Martha Washington, wife of the commander, went to Valley Forge to help the sick and wounded.

The arrival of desperately needed supplies was soon followed by warmer weather. The drills of Baron von Steuben helped the Continentals to march and fight with a new skill. By the spring of 1778, the army at Valley Forge was more hopeful. Washington could not know it at the time, but the Patriots' bleakest hour had passed.

Primary Sources

See Benjamin Rush, "On the Care of the Wounded," on page 583 in the Reference Section.

Section 3 Assessment

Recall

1. **Identify** Explain the significance of **(a)** Battle of Long Island, **(b)** Nathan Hale, **(c)** Battle of Trenton, **(d)** General John Burgoyne, **(e)** Battle of Saratoga, **(f)** Marquis de Lafayette, **(g)** Friedrich von Steuben, **(h)** Thaddeus Kosciusko, **(i)** Valley Forge.
2. **Define (a)** ally, **(b)** cavalry.

Comprehension

3. How did Washington turn retreat into victory in New Jersey?
4. Explain the results of the Battle of Saratoga.

5. How did the Continental Army come through the terrible winter at Valley Forge with new hope?

Critical Thinking and Writing

6. **Exploring the Main Idea** Review the Main Idea statement at the beginning of this section. Then, write a newspaper article celebrating the victory at Saratoga. Why was it a turning point?
7. **Analyzing Information** Why do you think people from other lands, such as Lafayette and Pulaski, were willing to risk their lives to help the American cause?

ACTIVITY

Creating a Dramatic Scene Write a scene in which Benjamin Franklin meets with the French King Louis XVI to convince him to support the Continental Army. Focus on how France and the Continental Army would benefit from such an alliance.

4 Fighting for Liberty on Many Fronts

Reading Focus

- What role did women play in the war?
- What choices did African Americans have?
- How was the war fought on the frontier and at sea?

Taking Notes

Copy the cause chart below. As you read, fill in the chart to show how the cause of fighting for independence united different groups of colonists. Add as many boxes as you need.

Patriots → → → → **COLONISTS JOIN THE FIGHT**

Main Idea During the Revolution, Americans fought for liberty on many fronts and in many ways.

An African American sailor

Predict Why might some African Americans support the Patriot cause?

Setting the Scene Ten years before the Revolution, white colonists in Charleston protested the Stamp Act. "Liberty! Liberty and stamped paper!" they cried as they paraded around the homes of British officials. Shortly after, a group of African Americans held their own parade. To the amazement of white colonists, the marchers chanted the same cry: "Liberty! Liberty!"

Many African Americans believed that the ideal of liberty applied to them just as it did to whites. In Massachusetts, a group of slaves presented petitions to the governor, asking for their freedom. One slave compared the situation of whites and African Americans:

66 You [white colonists] are taxed without your consent, because you are not represented in parliament. I grant that [is] a grievance . . . [But] pray, sir, . . . are not your hearts also hard, when you hold [Africans] in slavery who are entitled to liberty by the law of nature, equal as yourselves? 99

—Letter to a Boston newspaper *The Massachusetts Spy,* February 10, 1774

As the fighting continued, Americans worked for liberty in many ways and on many fronts. Sailors, as well as soldiers, fought in the various battles of the war. Women and African Americans took part too.

Women Take Part in the War

When men went off to fight in the Revolution, women took on added work at home. Some planted and harvested the crops. Others made shoes and wove cloth for blankets and uniforms. One woman, called "Handy Betsy the Blacksmith," was known for making cannons and guns for the army.

Helping the Army Many women joined their husbands at the front. They cared for the wounded, washed clothes, and cooked. Martha Washington joined her husband whenever she could.

Some women achieved lasting fame for their wartime service. Betsy Ross of Philadelphia sewed flags for Washington's army. Legend claims that she made the first American flag of stars and stripes.

A few women even took part in battle. During the Battle of Monmouth in 1778, Mary Ludwig Hays carried water to her husband and other soldiers. The soldiers called her Molly Pitcher. When her husband was wounded, she took his place, loading and firing the cannon.

New Attitudes As women participated in the war, they began to think differently about their rights. Those women who had taken charge of farms or their husbands' businesses became more confident and willing to speak out.

Most men in Congress did not agree that women should be treated equally. Still, the Revolution established important ideals of liberty and equality. In later years, these ideals of the Revolution would encourage women to campaign for equal treatment—and eventually to win it.

African Americans Face Hard Choices

By 1776, more than a half million African Americans lived in the colonies. At first, the Continental Congress refused to let African Americans, whether free or enslaved, join the army. Some members doubted the loyalty of armed African Americans. The British, however, offered freedom to some male slaves who would serve the king. Washington feared that this would greatly increase the ranks of the British army. In response, Washington changed his policy and asked Congress to allow free African Americans to enlist.

Joining the Fight About 5,000 African Americans from all the colonies, except South Carolina, served in the army. Another 2,000 served in the navy which, from the start, allowed African Americans to join. At least nine black minutemen saw action at Lexington and Concord. One of them, Prince Estabrook, was wounded. Two others, Peter Salem and Salem Poor, went on to fight bravely at Bunker Hill.

Some African Americans formed special regiments. Others served in white regiments as drummers, fifers, spies, and guides. Saul Matthews and James Armistead were among those African Americans who served as spies. Whites recognized the courage of their African American comrades. As one eyewitness recalled, "Three times in succession, [African Americans] were attacked . . . by [British troops] and three times did they successfully repel the assault and . . . preserve our army from capture. . . ."

Enslaved African Americans faced difficult choices. If they joined the American army or continued to work on Patriot plantations, the British might capture and sell them. If they tried to flee to the British army to gain freedom, they risked being hanged by angry Patriots.

Hoping for Freedom Yet, many slaves did flee their masters, especially those who lived near the coast, where the British navy patrolled. One British captain reported that "near 500" runaway slaves offered their services to him. Toward the end of the war, several thousand slaves sought freedom by following British troops through the Carolinas.

Black Patriots hoped that the Revolution would bring an end to slavery. After all, the Declaration of Independence proclaimed that "all men are created equal." Some white leaders also hoped the war would end slavery. James Otis wrote that "the colonists are by the law of nature free born, as indeed all men are, white or black." Quakers in particular spoke out strongly against slavery.

By the 1770s, slavery was declining in the North, where a number of free African Americans lived. During the American Revolution, several states moved to make slavery illegal, including Massachusetts, New Hampshire, and Pennsylvania. Other states also began to debate the slavery issue.

The War on the Western Frontier

As the war spread to Indian lands in the West, the Americans and British both tried to win the support of Indian tribes. In the end, the British were more successful. They convinced many Native Americans that a Patriot victory would mean more white settlers crossing the Appalachians and taking Indian lands.

Indian Allies of the British In the South, the British gained the support of the Cherokees, Creeks, Choctaws, and Chickasaws. The British encouraged the Cherokees to attack dozens of settlements on the southern frontier. Only after hard fighting were Patriot militia able to drive the Native Americans into the mountains.

Fighting was equally fierce on the northern frontier. In 1778, Iroquois forces led by the Mohawk leader Joseph Brant joined with Loyalists in raiding settlements in Pennsylvania and New York. The next year, Patriots struck back by destroying dozens of Iroquois villages.

Victory at Vincennes Farther west, in 1778, George Rogers Clark led Virginia frontier fighters against the British in the

GEOGRAPHY Skills

American, British, and Native American forces fought for control of lands in the West.

1. **Location** On the map, locate (a) Kaskaskia, (b) Vincennes, (c) Ohio River, (d) Fort Detroit.

2. **Place** What was the importance of the place where Fort Pitt was built?

3. **Critical Thinking Applying Information** Why did many Native Americans ally themselves with the British?

The War in the West

Key

← American forces ← British forces

✶ American victories ⬆ Forts

Albers Equal-Area Projection

0   100   200 Miles

0   100   200 Kilometers

Ohio Valley. With help from Miami Indians, Clark captured the British forts at Kaskaskia and Cahokia.

Clark then plotted a surprise attack on the British fort at Vincennes. When Clark's small force reached the fort, they spread out through the woods to make their numbers appear greater than they really were. The British commander thought it was useless to fight so many Americans. He surrendered Vincennes in February 1779.

Spanish Aid On the southwestern frontier, Americans received help from New Spain. In the early years of the war, Spain was neutral. However, Bernardo de Gálvez, governor of Spanish Louisiana, favored the Patriots. He secretly supplied medicine, cloth, muskets, and gunpowder to the Americans.

When Spain entered the war against Britain in 1779, Gálvez took a more active role. He seized British forts along the Mississippi River and the Gulf of Mexico. He also drove the British out of West Florida. The city of Galveston, in Texas, is named after this courageous leader.

Fighting at Sea

At sea, the Americans could do little against the powerful British navy. British ships blockaded American ports. From time to time, however, a bold American captain captured a British ship.

The greatest American sea victory took place in September 1779 in Britain's backyard, on the North Sea. After a hard-fought battle, Captain John Paul Jones captured the powerful British warship *Serapis*.

Raids on the high seas and along the frontiers kept many Americans on the alert. However, the war between the Americans and Great Britain would be settled by battles in the South.

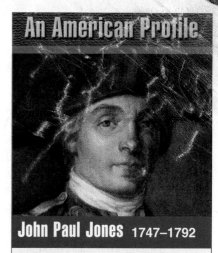

An American Profile

John Paul Jones 1747–1792

John Paul Jones was the first lieutenant commissioned in the Continental Navy. He showed his daring by sailing into British waters to raid enemy merchant ships. On September 23, 1779, Jones, at the helm of *Bonhomme Richard*, attacked the clearly superior British warship *Serapis* in the North Sea. The *Richard* was badly damaged in the first few minutes of battle. With their ship sinking beneath them, Jones and his men fought on. But the *Serapis* was also hurt. At last, the British captain of the *Serapis* lowered his flag and surrendered.

How did John Paul Jones help the Patriot cause?

AFTER YOU READ

Section 4 Assessment

Recall

1. **Identify** Explain the significance of **(a)** Mary Ludwig Hays, **(b)** Peter Salem, **(c)** George Rogers Clark, **(d)** Bernardo de Gálvez, **(e)** John Paul Jones.

Comprehension

2. How did the war change many women's attitudes?
3. **(a)** Why did some slaves escape to the British?
   (b) Why did African American Patriots hope that the Revolution would end slavery?
4. Why was John Paul Jones a hero to Americans?

Critical Thinking and Writing

5. **Exploring the Main Idea** Review the Main Idea statement at the beginning of this section. List three ways in which Americans fought for liberty during the Revolution.
6. **Identifying Causes and Effects** Read the following two statements. Decide which is the cause and which is the effect: **(a)** Many Native Americans sided with the British. **(b)** During the Revolution, settlers continued to push west of the Appalachians. Write a paragraph explaining the importance of the effect on the war.

ACTIVITY

Take It to the NET

Making an Almanac Use the Internet to research women who took part in the Revolution. Among the women you might research are Margaret Corbin and Deborah Sampson. Use what you find to draw up a Who's Who of Women During the Revolution. Visit *The American Nation* section of **www.phschool.com** for help in completing the activity.

Women in the Revolution

Many women patriots of the Revolution performed courageous deeds. They were spies and couriers, and disguised as men, enlisted in the army. Many women, just as courageous, fought for the cause on the home front.

Deborah Sampson When young Robert Shurtleff was wounded, he deliberately concealed his leg wound. But when he came down with yellow fever and was taken to a hospital, the truth was discovered: "He" was really Deborah Sampson, a woman in disguise! Instead of being punished for her deception, Deborah earned respect from her comrades. She received an honorable discharge.

Sybil Ludington Sometimes called the "female Paul Revere," Sybil Ludington was just 16 years old when on a chilly April night in 1777 she mounted her horse, Star, to gallop through the countryside and call the militia to report. The British were attacking, and there was no one to call the men to arms but Sybil.

Other Supporters Women at home worked to keep farms and households running smoothly. They raised money to buy military supplies and sewed soldiers' uniforms. One group of women in Philadelphia sewed 2,200 shirts for Pennsylvania soldiers. Colonial women were proud to support the Patriots' cause in any way.

ACTIVITY

Imagine you are a woman during the Revolutionary War. Write several diary entries telling what you are doing to help the Patriots' cause.

5 Winning the War in the South

BEFORE YOU READ

Reading Focus

- Why did Britain decide to start fighting in the South?
- How did the Americans and French defeat the British at the Battle of Yorktown?
- What were the terms of the Treaty of Paris?
- What factors helped the Americans win the war?

Key Terms

Battle of Cowpens

guerrilla

siege

Battle of Yorktown

Treaty of Paris

ratify

Taking Notes

As you read, prepare an outline of the section. Use roman numerals to indicate major headings, capital letters for subheadings, and numbers for supporting details. The sample at right will help you get started.

> I. Fighting in the South
>   A. Patriots versus Loyalists
>   1. Patriots and Loyalists launch raids
>   2.
>   B. Green and Morgan help turn the tide
>   1.
>   2.
>   C.
> II. Victory at Yorktown
>   A.
>   B.

Main Idea After the British surrendered at Yorktown, Britain recognized the United States as an independent country.

Setting the Scene When he was only 16 years old, Thomas Young set out with about 900 other Patriots to capture Kings Mountain in South Carolina. Although they were barefoot, they moved quickly up the wooded hillside, shouldering their old muskets. They were determined to take the mountain from the Loyalists who were dug in at the top.

Whooping and shouting, Young and his comrades dashed from tree to tree, dodging bullets as they fired back. Suddenly, Thomas heard the frantic cry, "Colonel Williams is shot!"

> **❝** I ran to his assistance for I loved him as a father. . . .
> He revived, and his first words were, 'For God's sake boys, don't give up the hill!'**❞**
>
> —Thomas Young, Memoir, *The Orion*

The Patriots captured Kings Mountain on October 7, 1780. The victory was an important sign. Britain had decided to make the South the key to winning the war. The American victory at Kings Mountain showed that Britain's new strategy might not work.

AS YOU READ Colonial soldiers received badges of honor for acts of bravery **Draw Inferences** Based on the passage, did the Americans at Kings Mountain deserve a medal for bravery?

Fighting in the South

The South became the main battleground of the war in 1778. Sir Henry Clinton, the new British commander-in-chief, knew that many Loyalists lived in the southern backcountry. He hoped that if British troops marched through the South, Loyalists would join them.

At first, Clinton's plan seemed to work. In short order, beginning in December 1778, the British seized Savannah in Georgia and Charleston and Camden in South Carolina. "I have almost ceased to hope," wrote Washington when he learned of the defeats.

Patriots versus Loyalists In the Carolina backcountry, Patriots and Loyalists launched violent raids against one another. Both sides

The War Ends in the South

Key

→ American and French forces

★ American victories

← British forces

✦ British victories

GEOGRAPHY
Skills

The war ended in the South. After a string of defeats, the Americans gradually gained the upper hand. The last major battle was the American victory at Yorktown.

1. **Location** On the map, locate **(a)** Savannah, **(b)** Kings Mountain, **(c)** Guilford Courthouse, **(d)** Chesapeake Bay, **(e)** Yorktown.

2. **Region** Did the British have greater control over coastal or inland regions of the South?

3. **Critical Thinking Drawing Conclusions** Why was it a mistake for Cornwallis to retreat to the Yorktown peninsula?

burned farms, killed civilians, and sometimes even tortured prisoners.

After 1780, attacks by British troops and Loyalist militia became especially cruel. As a result, more settlers began to side with the Patriots. As one Loyalist admitted, "Great Britain has now a hundred enemies, where it had one before."

Greene and Morgan Help Turn the Tide After the victory at Kings Mountain, two able American generals helped turn the tide against the main British army, led by General Charles Cornwallis. They were Nathanael Greene of Rhode Island and Daniel Morgan of Virginia.

General Greene's ability as a military leader was perhaps second only to Washington's. In 1780, Greene took command of the Continental Army in the South. Using his knowledge of local geography, Greene engaged the British only on ground that put them at a disadvantage. General Cornwallis wore out his soldiers trying to catch Greene's army.

In January 1781, General Morgan won an important victory at Cowpens, South Carolina. Morgan used a clever tactic to defeat the British. He divided his soldiers into a front line and a rear line. He ordered the front line to retreat after firing just two volleys. The British, thinking the Americans were retreating, charged forward—straight into the fire of Morgan's second rank. In this way, the Americans won the Battle of Cowpens.

Greene and Morgan combined their armies when they fought Cornwallis at Guilford Courthouse, near present-day Greensboro, North Carolina. The battle was one of the bloodiest of the war. Although the Americans retreated, the British sustained great losses.

Hit and Run Known as the Swamp Fox, Francis Marion of South Carolina added to British frustrations. He led a small band of militia, who often slept by day and traveled by night. His soldiers used guerrilla, or hit-and-run, tactics to harass the British. Marion's band appeared suddenly out of the swamps, attacked quickly, and retreated swiftly back into the swamps.

Victory at Yorktown

Cornwallis abandoned his plan to take the Carolinas. In the spring of 1781, he moved his troops north into Virginia. He planned to conquer Virginia and cut off the Americans' supply routes to the South.

An American Traitor The British had achieved some success in Virginia, even before the arrival of Cornwallis. Benedict Arnold, formerly one of the Americans' best generals, was now leading British troops. Arnold captured and burned the capital city of Richmond. His forces also raided and burned other towns.

Arnold had turned traitor to the American cause in September 1780, while commanding West Point, a key fort in New York. The ambitious general was angry because he felt that he had not received enough credit for his victories. He also needed money. Arnold secretly agreed to turn over West Point to the British. The plot was uncovered by a Patriot patrol, but Arnold escaped to join the British.

Arnold's treason and his raids on towns in Connecticut and Virginia enraged the Patriots. Thomas Jefferson, governor of Virginia, offered a sizable reward for his capture. Washington ordered Arnold to be hanged. However, he was never captured.

Battle at Yorktown Cornwallis hoped to meet with the same kind of success in Virginia that Arnold had achieved. At first, things went well. Cornwallis sent Loyalist troops to attack Charlottesville, where the Virginia legislature was meeting. Governor Thomas Jefferson and other officials had to flee.

American troops under Lafayette fought back by staging raids against the British. Lafayette did not have enough troops to fight a major battle. Still, his strategy kept Cornwallis at bay.

Then, Cornwallis made a mistake. He disregarded an order from Sir Henry Clinton to send part of his army to New York. Instead, he retreated to Yorktown peninsula, a strip of land jutting into Chesapeake Bay. He felt confident that British ships could supply his army from the sea.

Washington saw an opportunity to trap Cornwallis on the Yorktown peninsula. He marched his Continental troops south from New York. With the Americans were French soldiers under the Comte de Rochambeau (roh shahm BOH). The combined army rushed to join Lafayette in Virginia.

Meanwhile, a French fleet under Admiral de Grasse was also heading toward Virginia. Once in Chesapeake Bay, De Grasse's fleet closed the trap. Cornwallis was cut off. He could not get supplies. He could not escape by land or by sea.

The British Surrender By the end of September, more than 16,000 American and French troops laid siege to Cornwallis's army of fewer than 8,000. A siege occurs when an army surrounds and blockades an enemy position in an attempt to capture it. Day after day, American and French artillery pounded the British.

For several weeks, Cornwallis held out. Finally, with casualties mounting and his supplies running low, the general decided that the situation was hopeless. The British had lost the Battle of Yorktown.

On October 19, 1781, the British surrendered their weapons. The French and the Americans lined up in two facing columns. As the defeated redcoats marched between the victorious troops, a British army band played the tune "The World Turned Upside Down."

Geography and History

Britain's Dilemma

Because they controlled the seas, the British could land and establish bases almost anywhere along the American coast. The navigable rivers that flowed inland from the coast provided convenient invasion routes into the interior. To win the war, the British Army had to move away from these coastal bases and rivers. Yet when it did so, it opened its lines of communications and supply to constant attack. British armies nearly always met defeat when they moved away from the areas where they could be supplied by ships from the homeland. These problems, a British colonel noted in 1777, had "absolutely prevented us this whole war from going fifteen miles from a navigable river."

 Why did the British face problems when they moved away from the coast?

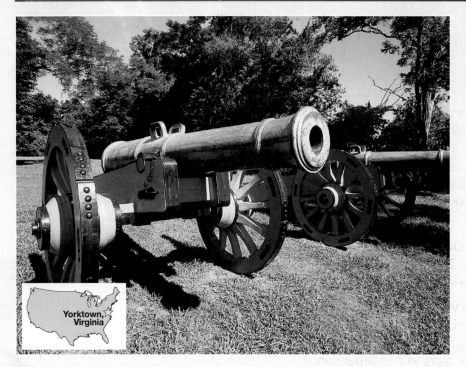

Yorktown, Virginia

Yorktown

October 17, 1781, marked the end of a long battle between the American army and powerful Great Britain. The Yorktown victory led to peace talks, which began in Paris in 1782. The next year, the representatives from the new nation and Great Britain signed the Treaty of Paris. The battle site of Yorktown is part of the Colonial National Historic Park.

Take It to the NET

Virtual Field Trip For an interactive look at Yorktown, visit *The American Nation* section of **www.phschool.com**.

The Peace Treaty

In London, the defeat shocked the British. "It is all over," cried the British prime minister, Lord North. Discouraged, he agreed to peace talks.

The talks began in Paris in 1782. Congress sent Benjamin Franklin and John Adams, along with John Jay of New York and Henry Laurens of South Carolina, to work out a treaty. Because Britain was eager to end the war, the Americans got most of what they wanted.

Under the Treaty of Paris, the British recognized the United States as an independent nation. It extended from the Atlantic Ocean to the Mississippi River. The northern border of the United States stopped at the Great Lakes. The southern border stopped at Florida, which was returned to Spain.

For their part, the Americans agreed to ask the state legislatures to pay Loyalists for property they had lost in the war. In the end, however, most states ignored Loyalist claims.

On April 15, 1783, Congress ratified, or approved, the Treaty of Paris. It was almost eight years to the day since the battles of Lexington and Concord.

Why the Americans Won

Geography played an important role in the American victory. The British had to send soldiers and supplies to a war that was several thousand miles from home. They also had to fight an enemy that was spread over a wide area. For their part, the Americans were familiar with the local geography. They knew the best routes and the best places to fight.

Foreign Help Help from other nations was crucial to the American cause. Spanish forces attacked the British along the Gulf of Mexico and in the Mississippi Valley. French money helped pay for supplies, and French military aid provided vital support to American troops. Without French soldiers and warships, for example, the Americans might not have won the Battle of Yorktown.

Americans' Growing Patriotism The Americans' patriotic spirit and fighting skills were another key to their victory. Despite early setbacks, the Patriots battled on. Gradually, Washington's inexperienced troops learned how to drill, how to march, and how to fight. Perhaps most important was Washington himself. By the end of the war, the general's leadership and military skills were respected by Americans and British alike.

Washington's Farewell In December 1783, General Washington bid farewell to his officers at Fraunces Tavern in New York City. Colonel Benjamin Tallmadge recalled the event:

> 66 Such a scene of sorrow and weeping I had never before witnessed. . . . We were then about to part from the man who had conducted us through a long and bloody war, and under whose conduct the glory and independence of our country had been achieved. 99
>
> —Benjamin Tallmadge, *Memoir*

All along Washington's route home to Virginia, crowds cheered their hero. The new nation faced difficult days ahead. In time, Americans would call on Washington to lead them once again.

Section 5 Assessment

Recall

1. **Identify** Explain the significance of **(a)** Henry Clinton, **(b)** Charles Cornwallis, **(c)** Nathanael Greene, **(d)** Daniel Morgan, **(e)** Battle of Cowpens, **(f)** Francis Marion, **(g)** Benedict Arnold, **(h)** Comte de Rochambeau, **(i)** Battle of Yorktown, **(j)** Treaty of Paris.
2. **Define (a)** guerrilla, **(b)** siege, **(c)** ratify.

Comprehension

3. Why did the South become the main battleground of the war in 1778?
4. Why was Cornwallis forced to surrender at Yorktown?

5. Describe the major points of the Treaty of Paris.
6. Give three reasons why the Americans defeated the British in the Revolution.

Critical Thinking and Writing

7. **Exploring the Main Idea** Review the Main Idea statement at the beginning of this section. Then, create a timeline of the major events at the end of the war, beginning with the Battle of Kings Mountain and ending with the Treaty of Paris.
8. **Making Predictions** Suppose that Britain had won the war. What might have been the effects of a British victory?

ACTIVITY

Writing a Letter You are General Cornwallis. In a letter to George III, describe the events at Yorktown.

Review and Assessment

CREATING A CHAPTER SUMMARY

Copy the chart below. As you read, describe the major documents and events of the American Revolution in the chart. For each item, include a date and one or two important facts. Some information has been filled in to help you get started.

For additional review and enrichment activities, see the interactive version of *The American Nation,* available on the Web and on CD-ROM.

MOVING TOWARD WAR	MAJOR BATTLES			MAKING PEACE
	North	Middle States	South	
Olive Branch Petition		Saratoga, 1777		Treaty of Paris
• King George rejects the Olive Branch Petition • Declaration of Independence • •		• Turning point • •	• • •	

Take It to the NET

Chapter Self-Test For practice test questions for Chapter 6, see *The American Nation* section of **www.phschool.com**.

Building Vocabulary

Use the chapter vocabulary words listed below to create a crossword puzzle. Exchange puzzles with a classmate. Complete the puzzles, and then check each other's answers.

1. blockade
2. mercenary
3. traitor
4. preamble
5. natural rights
6. ally
7. cavalry
8. guerrilla
9. siege
10. ratify

Reviewing Key Facts

11. What did the Battle of Bunker Hill show about each side in the conflict? (Section 1)
12. Describe three ideas contained in the Declaration of Independence. (Section 2)
13. When did France decide to help the Americans? (Section 3)
14. How did African Americans support the Patriot cause? (Section 4)
15. List the terms of the Treaty of Paris. (Section 5)

Critical Thinking and Writing

16. **Analyzing Primary Sources** According to the Declaration of Independence, when do people have a right and duty to rebel against their government?
17. **Identifying Causes and Effects** **(a)** Apply absolute chronology by placing the following events in order: **(1)** British defeat at Yorktown, **(2)** American victory at Saratoga, **(3)** French entry into the war against Britain, **(4)** signing of the Treaty of Paris. **(b)** Explain how each event caused the following event.
18. **Connecting to Geography: Place** How did the Patriots' knowledge of local geography help them to defeat the British?
19. **Synthesizing Information** What were the three biggest mistakes that British political and military leaders made between 1775 and 1783? Explain.
20. **Linking Past and Present** Today, the United States and Britain are close allies. Why do you think the two nations now have such close ties?

Analyzing Primary Sources

Thomas Paine had retreated with Washington's army through New Jersey. Seated by a campfire and using a drum for a desk, he wrote *The Crisis*. Read the following excerpt. Then, answer the questions:

> 66 These are the times that try men's souls. The summer soldier and the sun-shine patriot will, in this crisis, shrink from the service of his country; but he that stands it now deserves the love and thanks of man and woman. Tyranny . . . is not easily conquered; yet we have this consolation with us . . . the harder the conflict, the more glorious the triumph. 99
>
> Thomas Paine, *The Crisis*, 1776

21. What does Paine mean by "the times that try men's souls"?

22. What kind of person do you think Paine is describing by the phrase "sunshine patriot"?

23. What tyranny is Paine speaking of?

24. Why do you think Washington had these lines read aloud to his troops?

Identifying Points of View

THE HORSE AMERICA, *throwing his Master.*

This cartoon was published in 1779. Read the caption. Then, answer the questions.

25. How would you describe the event shown?
  A The colonies are at peace with Britain.
  B The colonies want independence.
  C Britain won the war.
  D The colonies are at war with France.

26. How does the cartoonist feel about the Patriot cause? Explain.

ACTIVITIES

Connecting With . . . Geography

On a large sheet of paper, draw an outline map of the United States. On the map, show the sites of major battles of the American Revolution. Mark each site with a symbol to show who won. For each battle, include a text box giving one or two important facts about it.

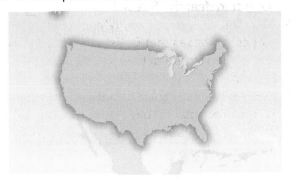

Take It to the NET

Connecting to Today

Conducting an Interview During the Revolution, African Americans fought in special regiments. Use the Internet to research significant contributions of African Americans to the United States military since then. Prepare a short fictional interview with the group or person that you have researched. For help in starting this activity, visit *The American Nation* section of **www.phschool.com**.

Preparing a Docudrama

Researching British Spies Use the Internet to research the activities of British spies during the Revolution. Use the results to prepare a TV docudrama dramatizing the exploits of one of the spies. For help in starting this activity, visit *The American Nation* section of **www.phschool.com**.

Creating a Republic

1776–1790

1 **A Loose Confederation**

2 **The Constitutional Convention**

3 **Ideas Behind the Constitution**

4 **Ratification and the Bill of Rights**

Articles of
Confederation

Surveyors (right) and
surveying compass (left)

 1777

The Continental Congress
approves the Articles of
Confederation. The
Articles create a loose
association of states.

 1785

Congress passes the Land Ordinance of
1785. It sets up a system for surveying
and settling the Northwest Territory
between the Mississippi and Ohio
Rivers.

1781

The Articles of Confederation
take effect.

**AMERICAN
EVENTS**

Presidential Terms:

• **1775** • • • • • **1780** • • • • • **1785**

**WORLD
EVENTS**

▲ **1776**
Adam Smith publishes
The Wealth of Nations.

▲ **1781**
The Emperor of Austria
grants religious toleration.

Ratifying the Constitution

A new, united nation took shape as each of the 13 original states in turn ratified, or approved, the Constitution.

BRITISH TERRITORY

Claimed by Great Britain and the United States

Maine (part of Mass.)

New Hampshire (June 21, 1788)

Massachusetts (Feb. 6, 1788)

Rhode Island (May 29, 1790)

Connecticut (Jan. 9, 1788)

(claimed by NY & NH)

New York (July 26, 1788)

Pennsylvania (Dec. 12, 1787)

New Jersey (Dec. 18, 1787)

Delaware (Dec. 7, 1787)

Maryland (Apr. 28, 1788)

NORTHWEST TERRITORY

SPANISH LOUISIANA

Virginia (June 25, 1788)

North Carolina (Nov. 21, 1789)

South Carolina (May 23, 1788)

Georgia (Jan. 2, 1788)

SPANISH FLORIDA

Chesapeake Bay

L. Superior

L. Michigan

L. Huron

L. Erie

Ontario

St. Lawrence R.

Mississippi R.

Missouri R.

Wabash R.

Ohio R.

ATLANTIC OCEAN

60°W

40°N

30°N

70°W

90°W

80°W

Key

(Dec. 7, 1787)	Date of ratification

Albers Equal-Area Projection

0   150   300 Miles

0   150   300 Kilometers

Writing of the Constitution

Timeline

1787
The Constitutional Convention meets in Philadelphia. The new Constitution creates a stronger central government.

1789
The first election under the new Constitution takes place.

1791
The Bill of Rights is added to the Constitution to protect individual liberties.

George Washington 1789–1797

1785 · · · ★ · · · 1790 · · · ★ · · · 1795 · · · ·

1789 ▲
The French Revolution begins.

1793 ▲
The Emperor of China rejects British trade.

1 A Loose Confederation

BEFORE YOU READ

Reading Focus

- Why did state governments write constitutions?
- What were the weaknesses of the Articles of Confederation?
- What process did the Articles create for admitting new states?
- Why did many Americans call for changes in the Articles?

Key Terms

constitution
bill of rights
execute
Articles of Confederation
cede
currency
Land Ordinance of 1785
Northwest Ordinance
depression
Shays' Rebellion

Taking Notes

As you read, prepare an outline of this section. Use roman numerals to indicate the major headings, capital letters for the subheadings, and numbers for the supporting details. The sample at right will help you get started.

> I. The States Write Constitutions
> A. Type of government
>   1. Legislature
>   2.
> B.
> II. The Articles of Confederation
> A. Limited power
>   1.
>   2.
> B.

Main Idea The Articles of Confederation created a weak central government and a loose alliance of independent states.

AS YOU READ
Thomas Jefferson
Find Main Ideas In your own words, restate the main idea of this Setting the Scene story.

Setting the Scene In 1775, Thomas Jefferson rode 300 miles from Virginia to attend the Continental Congress in Philadelphia. The roads were so poorly marked that Jefferson got lost twice. The only way he could get back on the path was to hire guides.

The ties uniting the 13 states often seemed as hard to find as the roads linking them. The Declaration of Independence had created a new nation. But the former colonies had little experience working together. Many Americans wondered if they could create a central government that would unite the states effectively.

The States Write Constitutions

In forming a government, most states wrote constitutions. A **constitution** is a document that sets out the laws, principles, organization, and processes of a government. States wrote constitutions for two reasons. First, a written constitution would spell out the rights of all citizens. Second, it would limit the power of government.

Virginia's constitution included a **bill of rights,** or list of freedoms that the government promises to protect. Virginia's bill of rights guaranteed trial by jury, freedom of religion, and freedom of the press. Several other states followed Virginia's lead. For example, the Massachusetts state constitution guaranteed people:

> 66 . . . the right of enjoying and defending their lives and liberties; that of acquiring, possessing, and protecting property; in [short], that of seeking and obtaining their safety and happiness. 99
>
> —Massachusetts Constitution of 1780

The new state governments were somewhat similar to the colonial governments in structure. The states divided power between an executive and a legislature. The legislature was elected by the voters to pass laws. Every state but Pennsylvania had a governor to **execute,** or carry out, the laws.

Under the state constitutions, more people had the right to vote than in colonial times. To vote, a citizen had to be white, male, and over age 21. He had to own a certain amount of property or pay a certain amount of taxes. For a time, some women in New Jersey could vote. In a few states, free African American men who owned property could vote.

The Articles of Confederation

As citizens formed state governments, the Continental Congress was drafting a plan for the nation as a whole. Delegates believed that the colonies needed to be united by a national government in order to win independence.

It was hard to write a constitution that all states would approve. They were reluctant to give up power to a central government. Few Americans saw themselves as citizens of one nation. Instead, they felt loyal to their own states. Also, people feared replacing the "tyranny" of British rule with another strong government.

After much debate, the Continental Congress approved the first American constitution in 1777. The Articles of Confederation created a very loose alliance of 13 independent states.

Limited Powers Under the Articles of Confederation, the states sent delegates to Congress. Each state had one vote. Congress could declare war, appoint military officers, and coin money. It was also responsible for foreign affairs.

Still, compared to the states, Congress had very limited powers. Congress could pass laws, but nine states had to approve a law before it could go into effect. Congress could not regulate trade between states or between states and foreign countries. Nor did it have the power to tax. To raise money, Congress had to ask the states for it or borrow it. No state could be forced to contribute funds.

The Articles included no president to execute laws. It was up to the states to enforce the laws passed by Congress. There was also no system of courts to settle conflicts between states.

Dispute Over Western Lands A dispute arose even before the Articles of Confederation went into effect. Maryland refused to ratify

Claims to Western Lands

Key

Original 13 states

Areas claimed

(1784) Date ceded to the United States

GEOGRAPHY
Skills

By 1783, several states claimed land west of the Appalachians.

1. **Location** On the map, locate western lands claimed by **(a)** Virginia, **(b)** New York, **(c)** Massachusetts, **(d)** Spain.

2. **Region** Which states had no western land claims?

3. **Critical Thinking Making Predictions** Based on this map, how might western land claims threaten national unity?

the Articles unless Virginia and other states **ceded,** or gave up, their claims to lands west of the Appalachian Mountains. Like other small states, Maryland feared that "landed" states would become too powerful.

One by one, the states agreed to cede their western claims to Congress. Finally, only Virginia held out. However, Thomas Jefferson and other leading Virginians recognized the great need to form a central government. They persuaded state lawmakers to give up Virginia's claims in the West.

With its demands met, Maryland ratified the Articles of Confederation in 1781. The new American government could at last go into effect.

Weaknesses of the Confederation

By 1783, the United States had won its independence. Yet, the end of the American Revolution did not solve the confederation's troubles. Americans had reason to doubt whether "these United States" could survive.

Conflicts Between States Disputes continued to arise among states. For example, both New Hampshire and New York claimed Vermont. The Articles did not give the central government power to resolve such conflicts. Noah Webster, a teacher from New England, saw the problem clearly:

66 So long as any individual state has power to defeat the measures of the other twelve, our pretended union is but a name, and our confederation, a cobweb. 99

—Noah Webster, *Sketches of American Policy*

Money Problems After the Revolution, the United States owed millions of dollars to individuals and foreign nations. Without the power to tax, Congress had no way to repay these debts. It asked the states for money, but the states often refused.

During the Revolution, the Continental Congress had solved the problem of raising funds by printing paper **currency,** or money. However, the Continental dollar had little value because it was not backed by gold or silver.* Before long, Americans began to describe any useless thing as "not worth a Continental."

As Continental dollars became nearly worthless, states printed their own currency. This caused confusion. How much was a North Carolina dollar worth? Was a Virginia dollar as valuable as a Maryland dollar? Most states refused to accept the money of others. As a result, trade became very difficult.

Other Nations Take Advantage Foreign countries took advantage of the confederation's weakness. Ignoring the Treaty of Paris, Britain refused to withdraw its troops from the Ohio Valley. Spain

---

*In a stable economy, currency has value because the government keeps reserves of gold or silver. Coins and paper money represent a portion of this reserve. Today, the United States government keeps its gold reserves in underground vaults at Fort Knox, Kentucky.

Northwest Territory

Section

1 mile

Half Section
320 Acres

1 mile

Quarter
Section
160 Acres

Township

6	5	4	3	2	1
7	8	9	10	11	12
18	17	16*	15	14	13
19	20	21	22	23	24
30	29	28	27	26	25
31	32	33	34	35	36

6 miles

6 miles

* Income reserved to support schools

closed its port in New Orleans to American shipping. This was a serious blow to western farmers, who depended on the port to ship their products to the East.

Admitting New States

Despite its troubles, Congress did pass important laws about how to govern the Northwest Territory. These lands lay north of the Ohio River and east of the Mississippi. The laws established how territories would be governed and how they could become states.

The **Land Ordinance of 1785** set up a system for settling the Northwest Territory. The law called for the territory to be surveyed and divided into townships. Each township would then be further divided into 36 sections of 1 square mile each. Congress planned to sell sections to settlers for $640 apiece. One section in every township was set aside to support public schools.

In 1787, Congress passed the **Northwest Ordinance.** It set up a government for the Northwest Territory, guaranteed basic rights to settlers, and outlawed slavery there. It also provided for the vast region to be divided into separate territories in the future.

The Northwest Ordinance provided a way to admit new states to the nation. Once a territory had a population of 60,000 free settlers, it could ask Congress to be admitted as a new state. Each new state would be "on an equal footing with the original states in all respects whatsoever." In time, the states of Ohio, Indiana, Illinois, Michigan, and Wisconsin were created from the Northwest Territory.

GEOGRAPHY
Skills

Under the Articles of Confederation, Congress set up a system for settling and governing the Northwest Territory.

1. **Location** On the map, locate **(a)** Ohio, **(b)** Michigan, **(c)** Indiana, **(d)** Illinois, **(e)** Wisconsin.

2. **Place** What was the size of a township? A section?

3. **Critical Thinking Synthesizing Information** Did Indiana have public education when it became a state in 1816? Explain.

A Call for Change

The Northwest Ordinance was the finest achievement of the national government under the Articles. Still, the government was unable to solve its economic problems. After the Revolution, the nation suffered an economic depression. A depression is a period when business activity slows, prices and wages fall, and unemployment rises.

Farmers Revolt The depression hit farmers hard. The war had created a high demand for farm products. Farmers borrowed money for land, seed, animals, and tools. However, when the Revolution ended, demand for farm goods went down. As prices fell, many farmers could not repay their loans.

In Massachusetts, matters worsened when the state raised taxes. The courts seized the farms of those who could not pay their taxes or loans. Angry farmers felt they were being treated unfairly.

Daniel Shays, a Massachusetts farmer who had fought at Bunker Hill and Saratoga, organized an uprising in 1786. More than 1,000 farmers took part in Shays' Rebellion. They attacked courthouses and prevented the state from seizing farms. Finally, the Massachusetts legislature sent the militia to drive them off.

Monitor Your Reading
Check to see whether you understand George Washington's warning. Why was there a "call for change"?

A Convention Is Called Many Americans saw Shays' Rebellion as a sign that the Articles of Confederation did not work. Warned George Washington, "I predict the worst consequences from a half-starved, limping government, always moving upon crutches and tottering at every step."

To avert a crisis, leaders from several states called for a convention to revise the Articles of Confederation. They met in Philadelphia in May 1787. In the end, however, this convention would create an entirely new framework of government.

Section 1 Assessment

Recall

1. **Identify** Explain the significance of (a) Articles of Confederation, (b) Land Ordinance of 1785, (c) Northwest Ordinance, (d) Shays' Rebellion.
2. **Define** (a) constitution, (b) bill of rights, (c) execute, (d) cede, (e) currency, (f) depression.

Comprehension

3. What kind of governments did state constitutions create?
4. Describe two weaknesses of the Articles of Confederation.
5. Explain the process by which a territory became a state.

6. How did many Americans react to Shays' Rebellion?

Critical Thinking and Writing

7. **Exploring the Main Idea** Review the Main Idea statement at the beginning of this section. Then, list two arguments in favor of creating a stronger central government.
8. **Solving Problems** Choose one of the problems the nation faced in 1787. Then, write a letter to a delegate to the upcoming Philadelphia Convention. Suggest one idea to solve that problem.

Settling the Western Frontier

Migration into the Northwest Territory was slow at first. Clarksville, the first American town to be set up in the territory, had only 40 settlers in 1793. In time, more and more Americans endured hardship and danger to make the journey west.

Why did people go west? Reports like this one certainly attracted eager and adventurous Americans:

> 66 The toils of agriculture will here be rewarded with a greater variety of valuable productions, than in any part of America. The advantages of almost every climate are here blended together; every considerable commodity that is [grown] in any part of the United States is here produced in the greatest plenty and perfection. The high and dry lands are of a deep, rich soil—producing, in abundance, wheat, rye, Indian corn, buck wheat, oats, barley, flax. . . . 99
> —Manasseh Cutler, *The First Map and Description of Ohio,* 1787

After 1780, pioneers from the east floated down the Ohio River in large, flat-bottomed rafts such as these. Settlers sweated and strained as they propelled the boats with long barge poles. Down river, families dismantled the rafts, using the planks to build wilderness homes.

All settlers did their part to clear land and build homes in the thick forest. Families then outfitted their log cabins with the necessities they had brought on their raft—from rifles and seed to pots and the family Bible.

ACTIVITY

Based on the pictures and reading here, write a letter from a settler in the Northwest Territory to a friend back east. Explain how you feel about living on the frontier and what you hope the future will bring.

2 The Constitutional Convention

Reading Focus

- Who were the leading delegates to the Constitutional Convention?
- What were the main differences between the two rival plans for the new Constitution?
- What compromises did the delegates have to reach before the Constitution could be signed?

Key Terms

Constitutional Convention
Virginia Plan
legislative branch
executive branch
judicial branch
New Jersey Plan
compromise
Great Compromise
Three-Fifths Compromise

Taking Notes

Copy the table below. As you read, complete the table with information about rival plans proposed at the Constitutional Convention. Add as many rows as you need to finish the table.

VIRGINIA PLAN	NEW JERSEY PLAN	GREAT COMPROMISE
•	• Proposed by Paterson	• Proposed by Sherman
• Favored large states	•	•
•	•	•
•	•	•

Main Idea Delegates to the Constitutional Convention of 1787 had to compromise on key issues in order to complete a new constitution.

The Liberty Bell at the State House

Ask Questions Write two questions that Susannah Dillwyn might have asked the delegates to the convention.

Setting the Scene

An air of mystery hung over the State House in Philadelphia. All through the hot summer of 1787, the nation's great leaders passed in and out of the doors. Guards allowed only the delegates to enter. The windows remained closed, to keep passersby from overhearing any debates.

Like other Philadelphians, Susannah Dillwyn was curious and excited. She wrote to her father, "There is now sitting in this city a grand convention, who are to form some new system of government or mend the old one."

What would the convention decide? Rumors buzzed. Wrote Dillwyn, "They say it depends entirely upon their pleasure whether we shall in the future have a congress." For almost four months, Americans waited to learn the fate of their infant republic.

The Delegates to the Convention

The Constitutional Convention opened on May 25, 1787. Its goal was to revise the Articles of Confederation. Every state except Rhode Island sent representatives.

An Amazing Assembly The convention's 55 delegates were a remarkable group. Eight of them had signed the Declaration of Independence, including the oldest, Benjamin Franklin. At age 81, Franklin was wise in the ways of government and human nature. George Washington was a representative from Virginia. Washington was so well respected that the delegates at once elected him president of the Convention.

Still, most of the delegates represented a new generation of American leaders. Nearly half were young men in their thirties, including Alexander Hamilton of New York. During the Revolution,

Independence Hall

To many, the birthplace of the United States is the old Pennsylvania State House in Philadelphia, known today as Independence Hall. Here, independence was declared, the Articles of Confederation were approved, and the Constitution was debated and signed. Enter the chamber today and you can almost see patriots like Washington, Madison, Franklin, and Hamilton forging a new nation.

Take It to the NET

Virtual Field Trip For an interactive look at Independence Hall, visit *The American Nation* section of **www.phschool.com**.

Hamilton had served for a time as Washington's private secretary. Hamilton despised the Articles of Confederation. "The nation," he wrote, "is sick and wants powerful remedies." The powerful remedy he prescribed was a strong central government.

AS YOU READ **Use Prior Knowledge** Why did Hamilton believe that the nation was "sick"?

James Madison Perhaps the best-prepared delegate was 36-year-old James Madison of Virginia. For months, he had been reading books on history, politics, and commerce. He arrived in Philadelphia with a case bulging with volumes of research.

Madison was quiet and rather shy. Still, his keen intelligence and his ideas about how to structure a democratic government strongly influenced the other delegates. Today, Madison is often called the "Father of the Constitution."

Secret Debates When the Convention began, the delegates decided to keep their talks secret. They wanted to speak their minds freely and be able to explore issues without pressures from outside.

The closed windows helped keep the debates secret, but they made the room very hot. New Englanders in their woolen suits suffered terribly in the summer heat. Southerners, with clothing more suited to warm temperatures, were less bothered.

Two Rival Plans

Soon after the meeting began, the delegates realized they would have to do more than simply revise the Articles of Confederation. They chose instead to write an entirely new constitution for the nation. They disagreed, however, about what form the new national government should take.

The Virginia Plan Edmund Randolph and James Madison, both from Virginia, proposed a plan for the new government. This Virginia Plan called for a strong national government with three branches. The legislative branch would pass the laws. The executive branch would carry out the laws. The judicial branch, or system of courts, would decide if laws were carried out fairly.

According to the Virginia Plan, the legislature would consist of two houses. Seats would be awarded on the basis of population. Thus, in both houses, larger states would have more representatives than smaller ones. Under the Articles of Confederation, each state, regardless of population, only had one vote in Congress.

The New Jersey Plan Small states opposed the Virginia Plan. They feared that the large states could easily outvote them in Congress. Supporters of the Virginia Plan replied that it was only fair for a state with more people to have more representatives.

After two weeks of debate, William Paterson of New Jersey presented a plan that had the support of the small states. Like the Virginia Plan, the New Jersey Plan called for three branches of government. However, it provided for a legislature that had only one house. Each state, regardless of its population, would have one vote in the legislature.

The Great Compromise

For a while, no agreement could be reached. With tempers flaring, it seemed that the Convention would fall apart without adopting any plan. Finally, Roger Sherman of Connecticut worked out a compromise that he hoped would satisfy both the large and small states. A compromise is a settlement in which each side gives up some of its demands in order to reach an agreement.

Sherman's compromise called for the creation of a two-house legislature. Members of the lower house, known as the House of Representatives, would be elected by popular vote. As the larger states wished, seats in the lower house would be awarded to each state according to its population.

Members of the upper house, called the Senate, would be chosen by state legislatures. Each state, no matter what its size, would have two senators. This part of Sherman's compromise appealed to the smaller states.

On July 16, the delegates narrowly approved Sherman's plan. It became known as the Great Compromise. Each side gave up some demands to achieve unity.

Northern and Southern States Compromise

Just as there were disagreements between large states and small states, there were also disagreements between northern states and southern states. The most serious disagreements concerned the issue of slavery. Would slaves be counted as part of a state's population?

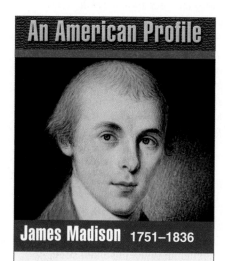

An American Profile

James Madison 1751–1836

Someone once said that James Madison looked "no bigger than a half a piece of soap." If so, looks were deceiving. By the age of 25, Madison was a skilled politician and a learned scholar.

Madison kept a close record of the debates at the Constitutional Convention. He chose a seat directly in front of the president's chair. "I was not absent a single day," he said. Unpublished for more than 50 years, Madison's notebooks are now our main source of information about the birth of the Constitution.

Why do you think Madison did not publish his notebooks immediately?

Would the slave trade continue to bring enslaved Africans into the United States?

The Three-Fifths Compromise Southerners wanted to include slaves in the population count even though they would not let slaves vote. If slaves were counted, southern states would have more representatives in the House of Representatives. Northerners objected. They argued that, since slaves could not vote, they should not be counted when assigning representatives.

Once again, the delegates compromised. They agreed that three fifths of the slaves in any state would be counted. In other words, if a state had 5,000 slaves, 3,000 of them would be included in the state's population count. This agreement became known as the Three-Fifths Compromise.

The Slave Trade There was another disagreement over slavery. By 1787, some northern states had banned the slave trade within their borders. Delegates from these states urged that the slave trade be banned in the entire nation. Southerners warned that such a ban would ruin their economy.

In the end, northern and southern states compromised once more. Northerners agreed that Congress could not outlaw the slave trade for at least 20 years. After that, Congress could regulate the slave trade if it wished. Northerners also agreed that no state could stop a fugitive slave from being returned to an owner who claimed that slave.

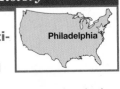

Viewing History

Signing the Constitution This painting by Howard Chandler Christy shows the signing of the Constitution on September 17, 1787. Some of the same men had signed the Declaration of Independence 11 years earlier. **Evaluating Information** *How would you describe the way Washington is portrayed? Why do you think Christy painted him this way?*

Roger Sherman

James Madison

Benjamin Franklin

George Washington

Primary Sources

See James Madison, "Debates in the Federal Convention of 1787," on page 584 of the Reference Section.

Signing the Constitution

As the long, hot summer drew to a close, the weary delegates struggled with one difficult question after another. How many years should the President, head of the executive branch, serve? How should the system of federal courts be organized? Would members of Congress be paid?

Finally, on September 17, 1787, the Constitution was ready to be signed. Its opening lines, or Preamble, expressed the goals of the framers: "We the People of the United States, in order to form a more perfect union . . . "

Gathering for the last time, delegates listened quietly as Benjamin Franklin rose to speak. He pleaded that the document be accepted:

> 66 I doubt . . . whether any other Convention . . . may be able to make a better Constitution. . . . I cannot help expressing a wish, that every member of the Convention who may still have objections to it, would with me, on this occasion, doubt a little of his own infallibility, and . . . put his name to this instrument. 99
>
> —Benjamin Franklin, *Records of the Federal Convention of 1787*

AS YOU READ **Find Main Ideas** Restate Franklin's main idea in your own words.

One by one, delegates came forward to sign the document. All but three of the delegates remaining in Philadelphia did so. Edmund Randolph and George Mason of Virginia, along with Elbridge Gerry of Massachusetts, refused to sign. They feared that the new Constitution gave too much power to the national government.

The Constitution called upon each state to hold a convention to approve or reject the plan for the new government. Once nine states endorsed it, the Constitution would go into effect.

 AFTER YOU READ

 Section 2 Assessment

Recall

1. **Identify** Explain the significance of (a) Constitutional Convention, (b) James Madison, (c) Virginia Plan, (d) New Jersey Plan, (e) Roger Sherman, (f) Great Compromise, (g) Three-Fifths Compromise.
2. **Define** (a) legislative branch, (b) executive branch, (c) judicial branch, (d) compromise.

Comprehension

3. In what way did the delegates to the 1787 Convention represent a new generation of American leaders?

4. (a) Why did small states oppose the Virginia Plan? (b) How was this conflict resolved?
5. What compromises did the North and South reach?

Critical Thinking and Writing

6. **Exploring the Main Idea** Review the Main Idea statement at the beginning of this section. Then, list two or three things you think might have happened if the delegates had been unable to compromise.
7. **Drawing Inferences** Some historians call slavery the "unfinished business" of the 1787 Convention. Write a paragraph explaining why.

 ACTIVITY

Drawing a Political Cartoon Draw a political cartoon analyzing the conflict between the large and small states at the Constitutional Convention. Identify in which state your cartoon might have appeared. Select a viewpoint, either in favor of the larger states, in favor of the smaller states, or in favor of compromise.

3 Ideas Behind the Constitution

Reading Focus

- What did American leaders learn from studying ancient Rome?
- What traditions of freedom did Americans inherit from Great Britain and from their own colonial past?
- How did Enlightenment ideas shape the development of the Constitution?

Key Terms

Founding Fathers

republic

dictatorship

Magna Carta

English Bill of Rights

habeas corpus

separation of powers

Taking Notes

Copy the concept web below. As you read, fill in the blank ovals with ideas that influenced the Constitution. Add as many ovals as you need.

Rome — English Tradition — Magna Carta — THE CONSTITUTION — American Experience — Enlightenment

Main Idea In writing the Constitution, Americans drew on ancient traditions, Enlightenment ideas, and their own experience.

Setting the Scene

Serving as the ambassador to France, Thomas Jefferson did not attend the Constitutional Convention. James Madison, however, kept in touch with his friend in Paris. As Madison prepared for the convention, he asked Jefferson to send whatever books "may throw light" on various governments.

Jefferson sent not five or ten books but hundreds. Some discussed the laws of nations. Others were biographies of important leaders. A French encyclopedia alone came to 37 volumes. In gratitude, Madison shipped Jefferson unusual American plants to show the French. (Jefferson had also asked for a live opossum, but that, alas, Madison could not manage!)

Today, we often refer to Madison, Jefferson, and other leaders who laid the groundwork for the United States as the **Founding Fathers.** These patriots were well aware that their nation was embarking on a bold experiment. Still, they did not have to invent a government from scratch.

ENCYCLOPÉDIE,
OU
DICTIONNAIRE RAISONNÉ
DES SCIENCES,
DES ARTS ET DES MÉTIERS,
PAR UNE SOCIÉTÉ DE GENS DE LETTRES.

TOME PREMIER.

A PARIS,

M. DCC. LI.

AS YOU READ French encyclopedia **Draw Inferences** Why do you think American leaders like Madison sought out European books?

The Lessons of Rome's Republic

Long before the Revolution, John Adams called on Americans to investigate how governments worked:

> ❝ Let us . . . search into the spirit of the British constitution; read the histories of ancient ages; contemplate the great examples of Greece and Rome; [and] set before us the conduct of our own British ancestors. . . . ❞
> —John Adams, *Dissertation on the Canon and Feudal Law*

The delegates to the Constitutional Convention followed this advice. They wanted to create a **republic,** a government in which citizens rule themselves through elected representatives. Few

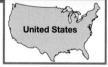
republics in the history of the world had survived very long. In order to create one that would last, American leaders looked first to the ancient examples of Greece and, especially, Rome.

The Roman Example Americans greatly admired the Roman Republic. General Charles Lee, one of George Washington's commanders, commented, "I used to regret not being thrown into the World in the glorious [era] of the Romans."

Independence and public service were virtues that the Founding Fathers saw in the citizens of Rome. Roman citizens were willing to serve in public office, not for money, but because they were devoted to their republic. American colonists admired Rome so much that when they debated politics in the newspapers, they often signed their opinions with Roman names like Cincinnatus or Cicero.

The Roman Warning At the same time, the Founding Fathers saw the collapse of Rome's republic as a warning to the United States. No republic could survive unless its citizens remained independent and devoted to public service. Under the ruler Caesar Augustus, Rome eventually became a dictatorship, a government in which one person or a small group holds complete authority. The leaders of the American Revolution believed that Romans stumbled once they began to value luxury and comfort more than independence.

Historians today admit that the Founding Fathers somewhat exaggerated the virtues of Rome's republic. Yet, the lessons they learned still have force. Republics do not always die because they are invaded from outside. Without educated and dedicated citizens, republics can decay from within.

Britain's Traditions of Freedom

Greece and Rome were not the only examples of democratic government. Despite their quarrel with Great Britain, leaders of the Revolution valued British traditions of freedom.

Magna Carta As you learned in Chapter 3, King John of England signed the Magna Carta in 1215. The Magna Carta contained two basic ideas that helped to shape both British and American government. First, it made it clear that English monarchs themselves had to obey the law. King John agreed not to raise taxes without first consulting the Great Council of nobles and church officials. Eventually, the Great Council grew into the British Parliament.

Just as important, the Magna Carta stated that English nobles had certain rights—rights that were later extended to other classes of people as well. These included rights to private property and the right to trial by jury.

English Bill of Rights In 1689, the English Bill of Rights went further in protecting the rights of citizens. The document said that parliamentary elections should be held regularly. It upheld the right to a trial by jury and allowed citizens to bear arms. It also affirmed the right of habeas corpus, the idea that no person could be held in prison without first being charged with a specific crime.

AS YOU READ **Use Prior Knowledge** List three things that you have already learned about British and colonial democratic traditions.

The American Experience

Americans enjoyed a long tradition of representative government. The Virginia colonists set up the House of Burgesses. Eventually, each British colony elected its own legislature.

A Constitutional Tradition Americans were also used to relying on written documents that clearly identified the powers and limits of government. The Mayflower Compact, written in 1620, was the first document of self-government in North America. Each of the 13 colonies had a written charter granted by the monarch or by Parliament.

The Revolutionary Era The framers of the Constitution also drew on their own experiences. The Founding Fathers bitterly remembered their grievances against the English king. In writing the Constitution, they sought to prevent such abuses.

For example, the Declaration of Independence accused the king of placing military power above civilian authority. The Constitution made the elected President "Commander in Chief of the Army and Navy . . . and of the militia of the several states." The Declaration protested that the king had made judges "dependent on his will alone." The Constitution set up a court system independent of the President and legislature.

The framers were very familiar with the workings of the Second Continental Congress, the Articles of Confederation, and their own state governments. Much that went into the Constitution came either from the Articles or from the state constitutions.

Teachings of the Enlightenment

The Constitution was also based on the ideas of the European Enlightenment. As you read in Chapter 4, Enlightenment thinkers believed that people could improve society through the use of reason. Many of the Constitution's framers had read the works of Enlightenment thinkers.

Locke and Natural Rights The English writer John Locke published *Two Treatises of Government* in 1690. In it, he stated two important ideas. First, Locke declared that all people had natural rights to life, liberty, and property. Second, he suggested that government is an agreement between the ruler and the ruled. The ruler must enforce the laws and protect the people. If a ruler violates the people's natural rights, the people have a right to rebel.

Locke's ideas were popular among Americans. The framers of the Constitution wanted to protect people's natural rights and limit the power of government. They saw the Constitution as a contract between the people and their government.

Montesquieu and the Separation of Powers The French Enlightenment thinker Baron de Montesquieu (MOHN tehs kyoo) influenced American ideas of how a government should be constructed. In his 1748 book *The Spirit of the Laws*, Montesquieu stressed the importance of the rule of law. The powers of government, he said, should be clearly defined and divided up. He suggested that three separate branches be created: the legislative, executive, and judicial. This idea, known as the separation of powers, was designed to keep any person or group from gaining too much power. In the next chapter, you will see how the Constitution established separation of powers in the United States government.

From Out of the Old, the New The Founding Fathers drew on many traditions. In the end, though, the new system of government was not quite like anything that came before it.

When John Adams received the news from Philadelphia, he wrote, "As we say at sea, huzza for the new world and farewell to the old one!" He called the Constitution "the greatest single effort of national deliberation that the world has ever seen."

AFTER YOU READ

Section 3 Assessment

Recall

1. **Identify** Explain the significance of (a) Founding Fathers, (b) Magna Carta, (c) English Bill of Rights, (d) John Locke, (e) Baron de Montesquieu.
2. **Define** (a) republic, (b) dictatorship, (c) habeas corpus, (d) separation of powers.

Comprehension

3. How did the Roman republic provide both an example and a warning to Americans?
4. Identify two ways the Constitution addressed grievances listed in the Declaration of Independence.

5. What ideas did Americans adopt from John Locke?

Critical Thinking and Writing

6. **Exploring the Main Idea** Review the Main Idea statement at the beginning of this section. Then, write a letter from Madison to Jefferson discussing why American leaders looked to the past.
7. **Applying Information** The Magna Carta states, "Neither we nor our [representatives] shall take . . . wood which is not ours, against the will of the owner of that wood." Write a paragraph explaining how this principle applies to the United States.

ACTIVITY

Take It to the NET

Giving a Talk Use the Internet to find quotations from an Enlightenment writer such as Locke, Montesquieu, or Voltaire. Choose one quotation and give a one-minute talk explaining how it relates to American ideals and principles. Visit *The American Nation* section of **www.phschool.com** for help in completing this activity.

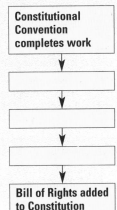

4 Ratification and the Bill of Rights

BEFORE YOU READ

Reading Focus

- What were the key issues in the debate between the Federalists and the Antifederalists?
- How was the Constitution finally ratified?
- How was the Bill of Rights added to the Constitution?

Key Terms

Federalists

Antifederalists

The Federalist Papers

amend

Bill of Rights

Taking Notes

Copy this flowchart. As you read, fill in the boxes with the major events relating to the ratification of the Constitution. The first and last boxes have been completed to help you get started. Add as many boxes as you need.

```
┌────────────────────┐
│ Constitutional     │
│ Convention         │
│ completes work     │
└────────────────────┘
          ↓
┌────────────────────┐
│                    │
└────────────────────┘
          ↓
┌────────────────────┐
│                    │
└────────────────────┘
          ↓
┌────────────────────┐
│                    │
└────────────────────┘
          ↓
┌────────────────────┐
│ Bill of Rights added │
│ to Constitution     │
└────────────────────┘
```

Main Idea After heated debates, the 13 states voted one by one to approve the new Constitution.

Setting the Scene Across the nation, Americans discussed the new Constitution. The Boston *Daily Advertiser* called for citizens to debate the new plan in the pages of its newspaper:

> 66 Come on brother scribblers, 'tis idle to lag!
> The Convention has let the cat out of the bag. 99
> —quoted in *Miracle at Philadelphia* (Bowen)

The Constitutional Convention had done its work. Now, in the fall of 1787, the debates began. Each state had to decide whether or not to ratify the new framework of government.

Federalists Debate Antifederalists

The framers of the Constitution sent the document to Congress, along with a letter from George Washington. Washington warmly approved the document, predicting that the Constitution would "promote the lasting welfare of that country so dear to us all."

The framers had set up a process for the states to approve the new government. At least 9 of the 13 states had to ratify the Constitution before it could go into effect. In 1787 and 1788, voters in each state elected delegates to special state conventions. These delegates would decide whether or not to ratify the Constitution.

The Federalist Position In every state, heated debates took place. Supporters of the Constitution called themselves **Federalists** because they favored a strong federal, or national, government. They called people who opposed the Constitution **Antifederalists.**

Federalists argued that the Articles of Confederation left too much power with the individual states. This imbalance produced a dangerously weak central government. Disputes among the states, Federalists said, made it too difficult for the government to function.

Federalists believed that the Constitution gave the national government the authority it needed to function effectively. At the same

AS YOU READ

Printing press

Use Prior Knowledge

Why did the Boston newspaper writer say, "The Convention has let the cat out of the bag"?

Primary Sources

See Alexander Hamilton, "The Federalist Papers," on page 585 of the Reference Section.

time, they said, the Constitution still protected the rights and powers of the individual states.

Federalists James Madison, Alexander Hamilton, and John Jay wrote a series of essays, known today as *The Federalist Papers.* Their purpose was to explain and defend the Constitution. They used pen names, but most people knew who they were. Today, The *Federalist Papers* remains one of the best discussions of the political theory behind the American system of government.

The Antifederalist Position Antifederalists felt that the Constitution made the national government too strong and left the states too weak. They also thought that the Constitution gave the President too much power. Patrick Henry of Virginia protested:

> 66 This Constitution is said to have beautiful features, but . . . they appear to me horribly frightful. . . . Your President may become king . . . If your American chief be a man of ambition and abilities, how easy is it for him to render himself absolute! 99
>
> —Patrick Henry, Speech to the Virginia Convention, June 1788

Most people expected George Washington to be elected President. Antifederalists admired Washington, but they warned that future Presidents might lack Washington's honor and skill. For this reason, they said, the office should not be too powerful.

Key Issue: Need for a Bill of Rights

The chief objection of Antifederalists was that the Constitution had no bill of rights. Americans, they said, had just fought a revolution to protect their freedoms. A bill of rights was needed to protect such basic liberties as freedom of speech and religion.

One of the strongest supporters of a bill of rights was George Mason of Virginia. In 1776, Mason had written the bill of rights for Virginia's constitution. After the Constitutional Convention refused to include a bill of rights, Mason joined the Antifederalists.

Federalists replied that it was impossible to list all the natural rights of people. Besides, they said, the Constitution protected citizens well enough as it was. Antifederalists responded that unless rights were spelled out, they could be too easily ignored.

The States Vote to Ratify

One by one, the states voted. Delaware led the way, ratifying on December 7, 1787. Pennsylvania and New Jersey soon followed.

New England Approves Massachusetts was the first key battleground. There, the old patriots Sam Adams and John Hancock held back their support. The delay seemed "very ominous," wrote Madison. Finally, Adams and Hancock convinced the state convention to recommend adding a bill of rights to the Constitution.

Still the debate continued. "Some gentlemen say, don't be in a hurry . . . don't take a leap in the dark," a Federalist farmer told his fellow delegates. "I say . . . gather fruit when it is ripe." In February 1788, Massachusetts became the sixth state to ratify.

Connecting to Today

A Coin for Every State

Delaware, the second smallest state in the nation, enjoys one big honor no other state can match. It has the right to call itself "The First State." On December 7, 1787, Delaware became the first state to ratify the Constitution.

Delaware again led the way more than 200 years later. The United States mint began to issue a series of special quarters honoring the 50 states. The "heads" side of each coin carries the familiar image of George Washington. The "tails" side displays a different design for each state, in the order they ratified the Constitution or joined the Union. The Delaware quarter was issued on January 1, 1999. The final coins—honoring Alaska and Hawaii—are scheduled to be released in 2008.

Why do you think many people are eager to collect all 50 state quarters?

In June, New Hampshire joined ranks as the ninth state. The new government could now go into effect. Still, the nation's unity remained in doubt. New York and Virginia, two of the largest states, had not yet ratified the plan. In both states, Federalists and Antifederalists were closely matched.

Last Holdouts In Virginia, Patrick Henry, George Mason, and Governor Edmund Randolph led the opposition. Still a spellbinding speaker, Henry at one point spoke for seven hours. Soft-spoken, James Madison could not match Henry's dramatic style. Yet his arguments in favor of the Constitution were always clear, patient, and to the point.

The tide finally turned when Governor Randolph changed his mind. He gave his support when the Federalists promised to support a bill of rights. Virginia voted to ratify in late June.

In New York, the struggle went on for another month. In July 1788, the state convention voted to ratify. North Carolina followed in November 1789. Only Rhode Island, which had refused to send delegates to the Constitutional Convention, remained. On May 29, 1790, Rhode Island became the last state to ratify.

The Nation Celebrates Throughout the land, Americans celebrated the news that the Constitution was ratified. The city of Philadelphia set its festival for July 4, 1788.

A festive parade filed along Market Street, led by soldiers who had fought in the Revolution. Thousands cheered as six colorfully outfitted horses pulled a blue carriage shaped like an eagle. Thirteen stars and stripes were painted on the front, and the Constitution was raised proudly above it. Benjamin Rush, a Philadelphia doctor and strong supporter of the Constitution, wrote to a friend, "'Tis done. We have become a nation."

Adding a Bill of Rights

Americans voted in the first election under the Constitution in January 1789. As expected, George Washington was elected President, while John Adams was chosen as Vice President.

The first Congress met in New York City, which was chosen as the nation's first capital. Congress quickly turned its attention to adding a bill of rights to the Constitution. As you have read, several states had agreed to ratify the Constitution only on the condition that a bill of rights be added.

Cause and Effect

Causes

- Articles of Confederation creates weak national government
- Trade and money problems arise between states
- Foreign nations take advantage of weak government
- Shays' Rebellion breaks out
- Convention meets to revise Articles of Confederation

THE WRITING OF THE CONSTITUTION

Effects

- New government includes President and two-house legislature
- Power is divided between national and state governments
- Compromises allow slavery to continue
- States debate and ratify Constitution
- Bill of Rights is added

Effects Today

- United States is world's oldest continuing constitutional democracy
- Debate about federal versus state power continues
- Amendments extend rights to more citizens
- New democracies look to the Constitution as a model

GRAPHIC ORGANIZER
Skills

The long-term impact of the Constitutional Convention reached far beyond its original goals.

1. **Comprehension** Why is Shays' Rebellion listed as a cause?

2. **Critical Thinking Linking Past and Present** Why do you think new nations see the United States Constitution as a model?

Civics 🏛

Proposed and Ratified The framers had established a way to amend, or change, the Constitution. They did not want people to make changes lightly, however. Thus, they made the process of amending the Constitution fairly difficult. (You will read more about the amendment process in Chapter 8.)

In 1789, the first Congress proposed a set of twelve amendments, written by James Madison. As required by the Constitution, the amendments then went to the states. By December 1791, three fourths of the states had ratified 10 of the 12 amendments. These 10 amendments became known as the **Bill of Rights.**

The Bill of Rights James Madison insisted that the Bill of Rights does not give Americans any rights. The rights listed, he said, were natural rights that belong to all human beings. The Bill of Rights simply prevents the government from taking these rights away.

Some of the first 10 amendments were intended to prevent the kind of abuses Americans had suffered under English rule. For example, the Declaration of Independence had condemned the king for forcing colonists to quarter troops in their homes and for suspending trial by jury. The Third Amendment forbids the government to quarter troops in citizens' homes without their consent. The Sixth and Seventh Amendments guarantee the right to trial by jury.

Other amendments protected individual freedoms as many states had already done. In 1786, the Virginia Statute of Religious Freedom stated that "No man shall be compelled to frequent or support any religious worship . . . or otherwise suffer, on account of his religious opinions or belief." Religious freedom became the very first right listed in the First Amendment. (You will read more about the freedoms protected by the Bill of Rights in Chapter 8.)

With the Bill of Rights in place, the new framework of government was complete. Over time, the Constitution became a living document that grew and changed along with the nation.

Section 4 Assessment

Recall

1. **Identify** Explain the significance of **(a)** Federalists, **(b)** Antifederalists, **(c)** *The Federalist Papers,* **(d)** George Mason, **(e)** Bill of Rights.
2. **Define** amend.

Comprehension

3. **(a)** Why did Federalists support the Constitution? **(b)** Why did Antifederalists oppose it?
4. Describe the ratification debate in one battleground state.
5. Why did the new government quickly take steps to amend the Constitution?

Critical Thinking and Writing

6. **Exploring the Main Idea** Review the Main Idea statement at the beginning of this section. Then, write a paragraph explaining what you think was the single most important reason in favor of ratifying the Constitution.
7. **Drawing Conclusions** Analyze the views of George Mason and Alexander Hamilton about the Bill of Rights. Explain how the influence of both shaped the Bill of Rights as it now exists.

ACTIVITY

Planning a Celebration You are an official in an American city or village in 1789. With a group of classmates, create a plan for your own celebration of the ratification of the Constitution. Make a list of activities you would include. If you like, you may also design a banner, prepare a short speech, or select music.

Analyzing Primary Sources

Why did the Antifederalists oppose the new Constitution? To gain an accurate understanding of past events, it is often helpful to analyze the words of those who were present when the events took place.

Patrick Henry, a fiery patriot and a firm Antifederalist, spoke against the ratification of the Constitution to the delegates at the Virginia state convention:

Patrick Henry

" You ought to be extremely cautious, watchful, jealous of your liberty; for instead of securing your rights, you may lose them forever. If a wrong step be now made, the republic may be lost forever. If this new government will not come up to the expectation of the people, and they shall be disappointed, their liberty will be lost, and tyranny must and will arise. I repeat it again, and I beg gentlemen to consider that a wrong step made now will plunge us into misery, and our republic will be lost. . . .

And here I would make this inquiry of those worthy characters who composed a part of the late federal Convention. . . . I have the highest veneration for those gentlemen; but, sir, give me leave to demand: What right had they to say, 'We, the people?' My political curiosity, exclusive of my anxious [concern] for the public welfare, leads me to ask: Who authorized them to speak the language of, 'We, the people,' instead of, 'We, the states?' "

—Patrick Henry, Speech at the Virginia Convention, June 1788

Learn the Skill *To analyze a primary source, use the following steps:*

1. **Identify the writer.** Knowing the source of a document helps you evaluate the writer's information and point of view.

2. **Identify the context.** When was the document written? What was its purpose?

3. **Identify the main idea.** What is the main idea of the document?

4. **Look for words that indicate the point of view.** Emotional words can be a clue to the writer's feelings about the subject matter.

5. **Analyze.** What conclusions can you reach about the writer and the information given?

Practice the Skill *Answer the following questions about the document above:*

1. What do you know about Patrick Henry and his political views?

2. What was Henry's purpose in giving the speech?

3. In this excerpt, what are Henry's main objections to the new Constitution?

4. **(a)** What words indicate that Henry has strong feelings about the Constitution? **(b)** Describe his attitude toward the framers.

5. Analyze Henry's view of the relationship of the central government to the states.

Apply the Skill *See the Chapter Review and Assessment.*

CREATING A CHAPTER SUMMARY

Copy the concept web below. Fill in the blank ovals with information about the Articles of Confederation and the Constitution. Add as many ovals as you need.

For additional review and enrich-ment activities, see the interactive version of *The American Nation,* available on the Web and on CD-ROM.

Take It to the NET

Chapter Self-Test For prac-tice test questions for Chapter 7, visit *The American Nation* section of **www.phschool.com.**

Building Vocabulary

Review the meaning of the chapter vocabulary words listed below. Then, write a sentence for each word in which you define the word and describe its relation to the writing of the Constitution.

1. constitution
2. bill of rights
3. depression
4. legislative branch
5. executive branch
6. judicial branch
7. compromise
8. republic
9. habeas corpus
10. separation of powers

Reviewing Key Facts

11. Summarize the strengths and weaknesses of the Articles of Confederation. (Section 1)
12. What kind of legislature did the Constitution create? Why? (Section 2)
13. How did the Constitution build on the earlier experience of Americans? (Section 3)
14. Identify one way Antifederalists influenced the Constitution. (Section 4)

Critical Thinking and Writing

15. **Connecting to Geography: Regions** Review the map Claims to Western Lands in Section 1. **(a)** Describe the region that was considered "the West" in the 1780s. **(b)** Write a paragraph describing what would have happened if Virginia had won all of its land claims.
16. **Analyzing Information** Choose one issue at the Philadelphia Convention of 1787. Describe what each side won and gave up. Was the issue resolved successfully? Explain.
17. **Applying Information** Review the opening lines of the Declaration of Independence in Chapter 6. Copy two sentences or phrases that reflect the ideas of John Locke. Explain how they show that Locke influenced Jefferson.
18. **Supporting a Point of View** When the Constitution was ratified, Benjamin Rush com-mented, "We have become a nation." List three reasons to support Rush's comment. Explain in what way the United States was not a "nation" before the Constitution.

Analyzing Primary Sources

The cartoon below appeared in an American newspaper in 1788. Look at the cartoon and answer the questions that follow:

United we stand—Divided we fall!

19. **(a)** What do the pillars represent? **(b)** Which pillar is first? Ninth?
20. What event is the subject of this cartoon?
21. Based on your reading, why is the ninth pillar important?
22. **(a)** Describe the action going on at the far right. **(b)** Which pillars are missing and why?
23. Do you think the cartoonist favored the Federalists or the Antifederalists? Give reasons for your answer.

Analyzing a Primary Source

In this letter, George Washington discusses the weaknesses of the early government. Read the excerpt and answer the questions that follow:

> 66 I am told that even respectable characters speak of a monarchical form of government without horror. . . . What a triumph for the advocates of [tyranny] to find that we are incapable of governing ourselves, and that systems founded on the basis of equal liberty are merely ideal and [false]! Would to God that wise measures be taken in time to avert the consequences. 99
>
> —George Washington, Letter to John Jay, August 1, 1786

24. Washington is disturbed because
   A the Constitution has no bill of rights.
   B the Articles of Confederation have no executive.
   C some Americans want a monarchy.
   D a government based on equal liberty can never succeed.
25. How does this letter help explain why Washington agreed to serve as president of the Constitutional Convention?

ACTIVITIES

Connecting With . . . Government and Citizenship

Making a Chart With a partner, review the Declaration of Independence printed in Chapter 6. Identify the list of grievances against the king of England. Then, skim the Constitution and Bill of Rights, which appear at the end of this chapter. Make a chart showing how specific grievances in the Declaration were addressed in the Constitution. Include at least five grievances.

 ## Take It to the NET

Connecting to Today

Exploring American Symbols In 1782, Congress declared the bald eagle to be an official symbol of the new nation. Use the Internet to find out more about another familiar American symbol. Prepare a three-minute report on the meaning of that symbol. For help in starting this activity, visit *The American Nation* section of **www.phschool.com**.

Creating a Database

With the class, create an information bank on the delegates to the Constitutional Convention. Use the Internet to find information about one delegate. Prepare a fact sheet showing his background, the state he represented, and his position on a key issue. Combine your fact sheet with those of the rest of the class. For help in starting this activity, visit *The American Nation* section of **www.phschool.com**.

The Constitution at a Glance

Original Constitution

Preamble

Article

1   The Legislative Branch
2   The Executive Branch
3   The Judicial Branch
4   Relations Among the States
5   Amending the Constitution
6   National Supremacy
7   Ratification

Amendments

Bill of Rights

1   Freedoms of Religion, Speech, Press, Assembly, and Petition
2   Right to Bear Arms
3   Lodging Troops in Private Homes
4   Search and Seizure
5   Rights of the Accused
6   Right to Speedy Trial by Jury
7   Jury Trial in Civil Cases
8   Bail and Punishment
9   Powers Reserved to the People
10   Powers Reserved to the States

Additional Amendments

11   Suits Against States
12   Election of President and Vice-President
13   Abolition of Slavery
14   Rights of Citizens
15   Voting Rights
16   The Income Tax
17   Direct Election of Senators
18   Prohibition of Alcoholic Beverages
19   Women's Suffrage
20   Presidential Terms, Sessions of Congress
21   Repeal of Prohibition
22   Limit on Number of President's Terms
23   Presidential Electors for District of Columbia
24   Abolition of Poll Tax in National Elections
25   Presidential Succession and Disability
26   Voting Age
27   Congressional Pay Increases

The Constitution of the United States of America

The Constitution is printed in black. The titles of articles, sections, and clauses are not part of the original document. They have been added here to help you find information in the Constitution. Some words or lines are crossed out because they have been changed by amendments or no longer apply. Annotations, or explanations, are on the tan side of the page. Difficult words are defined.

Preamble

We the people of the United States, in order to form a more perfect Union, establish justice, insure domestic tranquillity, provide for the common defense, promote the general welfare, and secure the blessings of liberty to ourselves and our posterity, do ordain and establish this Constitution for the United States of America.

The Preamble describes the purpose of the government set up by the Constitution. Americans expect their government to defend justice and liberty and provide peace and safety from foreign enemies.

Article 1. The Legislative Branch

Section 1. A Two-House Legislature

All legislative powers herein granted shall be vested in a Congress of the United States, which shall consist of a Senate and House of Representatives.

The Constitution gives Congress the power to make laws. Congress is divided into the Senate and the House of Representatives.

Section 2. House of Representatives

1. **Election of Members**   The House of Representatives shall be composed of members chosen every second year by the people of the several states, and the electors in each state shall have the qualifications requisite for electors of the most numerous branch of the state legislature.

2. **Qualifications**   No person shall be a Representative who shall not have attained to the age of twenty-five years, and been seven years a citizen of the United States, and who shall not, when elected, be an inhabitant of that state in which he shall be chosen.

3. **Determining Representation**   Representatives and direct taxes shall be apportioned among the several states which may be included within this Union, according to their respective numbers which shall be determined by adding to the whole number of free persons, including those bound to service for a term of years, and excluding Indians not taxed, three fifths of all other persons. The actual enumeration shall be made within three years after the first meeting of the Congress of the United States, and within every subsequent term of ten years, in such manner as they shall by law direct. The number of Representatives shall not exceed one for every 30,000, but each state shall have at least one Representative; and until such enumeration shall be made, the state of New Hampshire shall be entitled to choose three; Massachusetts, eight; Rhode Island and Providence Plantations, one; Connecticut, five; New York, six; New Jersey, four; Pennsylvania, eight; Delaware, one; Maryland, six; Virginia, ten; North Carolina, five; South Carolina, five; and Georgia, three.

Clause 1   *Electors* refers to voters. Members of the House of Representatives are elected every two years. Any citizen allowed to vote for members of the larger house of the state legislature can also vote for members of the House.

Clause 2   A member of the House of Representatives must be at least 25 years old, an American citizen for 7 years, and a resident of the state he or she represents.

Clause 3   The number of representatives each state elects is based on its population. An *enumeration,* or census, must be taken every 10 years to determine population. Today, the number of representatives in the House is fixed at 435.
This is the famous Three-Fifths Compromise worked out at the Constitutional Convention. *Persons bound to service* meant indentured servants. *All other persons* meant slaves. All free people in a state were counted. However, only three fifths of the slaves were included in the population count. This three-fifths clause became meaningless when slaves were freed in 1865 by the Thirteenth Amendment.

Clause 4 *Executive authority* means the governor of a state. If a member of the House leaves office before his or her term ends, the governor must call a special election to fill the seat.

Clause 5 The House elects a speaker. Today, the speaker is usually chosen by the party that has a majority in the House. Also, only the House has the power to *impeach,* or accuse, a federal official of wrongdoing.

Clause 1 Each state has two senators, who serve for six-year terms. The Seventeenth Amendment changed the way senators were elected.

Clause 2 Every two years, one third of the senators run for reelection. Thus, the makeup of the Senate is never totally changed by any one election. The Seventeenth Amendment changed the way that *vacancies,* or empty seats, are filled. Today, the governor of a state must choose a senator to fill a vacancy that occurs between elections.

Clause 3 A senator must be at least 30 years old, an American citizen for 9 years, and a resident of the state he or she represents.

Clause 4 The Vice President presides over Senate meetings, but he or she can vote only to break a tie.

Clause 5 *Pro tempore* means "temporary." The Senate chooses a member to serve as president *pro tempore* when the Vice President is absent.

Clause 6 The Senate acts as a jury if the House impeaches a federal official. The Chief Justice of the Supreme Court presides if the President is on trial. Two thirds of all senators present must vote for *conviction,* or a finding of guilty. No President has ever been convicted, though the House impeached President Andrew Johnson in 1868 and President Bill Clinton in 1998. In 1974, President Richard Nixon resigned before he could be impeached.

Clause 7 If an official is found guilty by the Senate, he or she can be removed from office and barred from holding federal office in the future. These are the only punishments the Senate can impose. However, the convicted official can still be tried in a criminal court.

4. **Filling Vacancies** When vacancies happen in the representation from any state, the executive authority thereof shall issue writs of election to fill such vacancies.

5. **Selection of Officers; Power of Impeachment** The House of Representatives shall choose their Speaker and other officers; and shall have the sole power of impeachment.

Section 3. The Senate

1. **Selection of Members** The Senate of the United States shall be composed of two Senators from each state chosen by the legislature thereof, for six years, and each Senator shall have one vote.

2. **Alternating Terms; Filling Vacancies** Immediately after they shall be assembled in consequence of the first election, they shall be divided as equally as may be into three classes. The seats of the Senators of the first class shall be vacated at the expiration of the second year, of the second class at the expiration of the fourth year, and of the third class at the expiration of the sixth year, so that one-third may be chosen every second year; and if vacancies happen by resignation, or otherwise, during the recess of the legislature of any state, the executive thereof may make temporary appointments until the next meeting of the legislature, which shall then fill such vacancies.

3. **Qualifications** No person shall be a Senator who shall not have attained to the age of thirty years, and been nine years a citizen of the United States, and who shall not, when elected, be an inhabitant of that state for which he shall be chosen.

4. **President of the Senate** The Vice-President of the United States shall be president of the Senate, but shall have no vote, unless they be equally divided.

5. **Election of Senate Officers** The Senate shall choose their other officers, and also a president *pro tempore,* in the absence of the Vice-President, or when he shall exercise the office of the President of the United States.

6. **Impeachment Trials** The Senate shall have the sole power to try all impeachments. When sitting for that purpose, they shall be on oath or affirmation. When the President of the United States is tried, the Chief Justice shall preside; and no person shall be convicted without the concurrence of two-thirds of the members present.

7. **Penalties Upon Conviction** Judgment in cases of impeachment shall not extend further than to removal from office, and disqualification to hold and enjoy any office of honor, trust, or profit under the United States; but the party convicted shall nevertheless be liable and subject to indictment, trial, judgment, and punishment, according to law.

Section 4. Elections and Meetings

1. **Election of Congress** The times, places, and manner of holding elections for Senators and Representatives shall be prescribed in each state by the legislature thereof; but the Congress may at any time by law make or alter such regulations, except as to the places of choosing Senators.

2. **Annual Sessions** The Congress shall assemble at least once in every year, ~~and such meeting shall be on the first Monday in December, unless they shall by law appoint a different day.~~

Section 5. Rules for the Conduct of Business

1. **Organization** Each house shall be the judge of the elections, returns, and qualifications of its own members, and a majority of each shall constitute a quorum to do business; but a smaller number may adjourn from day to day, and may be authorized to compel the attendance of absent members, in such manner, and under such penalties, as each house may provide.

2. **Procedures** Each house may determine the rules of its proceedings, punish its members for disorderly behavior, and with the concurrence of two-thirds, expel a member.

3. **A Written Record** Each house shall keep a journal of its proceedings, and from time to time publish the same, excepting such parts as may in their judgment require secrecy; and the yeas and nays of the members of either house on any question shall, at the desire of one-fifth of those present, be entered on the journal.

4. **Rules for Adjournment** Neither house, during the session of Congress, shall, without the consent of the other, adjourn for more than three days, nor to any other place than that in which the two houses shall be sitting.

Section 6. Privileges and Restrictions

1. **Salaries and Immunities** The Senators and Representatives shall receive a compensation for their services, to be ascertained by law and paid out of the Treasury of the United States. They shall in all cases, except treason, felony, and breach of the peace, be privileged from arrest during their attendance at the session of their respective houses, and in going to and returning from the same; and for any speech or debate in either house, they shall not be questioned in any other place.

2. **Restrictions on Other Employment** No Senator or Representative shall, during the time for which he was elected, be appointed to any civil office under the authority of the United States, which shall have been created, or the emoluments whereof shall have been increased, during such time; and no person holding any office under the United States shall be a member of either house during his continuance in office.

Clause 1 Each state legislature can decide when and how congressional elections take place, but Congress can overrule these decisions. In 1842, Congress required each state to set up congressional districts with one representative elected from each district. In 1872, Congress decided that congressional elections must be held in every state on the same date in even-numbered years.

Clause 2 Congress must meet at least once a year. The Twentieth Amendment moved the opening date of Congress to January 3.

Clause 1 Each house decides whether a member has the qualifications for office set by the Constitution. A *quorum* is the smallest number of members who must be present for business to be conducted. Each house can set its own rules about absent members.

Clause 2 Each house can make rules for the conduct of members. It can only expel a member by a two-thirds vote.

Clause 3 Each house keeps a record of its meetings. *The Congressional Record* is published every day with excerpts from speeches made in each house. It also records the votes of each member.

Clause 4 Neither house can *adjourn,* or stop meeting, for more than three days unless the other house approves. Both houses of Congress must meet in the same city.

Clause 1 *Compensation* means "salary." Congress decides the salary for its members. While Congress is in session, a member is free from arrest in civil cases and cannot be sued for anything he or she says on the floor of Congress. This allows for freedom of debate. However, a member can be arrested for a criminal offense.

Clause 2 *Emolument* also means "salary." A member of Congress cannot hold another federal office during his or her term. A former member of Congress cannot hold an office created while he or she was in Congress. An official in another branch of government cannot serve at the same time in Congress. This strengthens the separation of powers.

Clause 1 *Revenue* is money raised by the government through taxes. Tax bills must be introduced in the House. The Senate, however, can make changes in tax bills. This clause protects the principle that people can be taxed only with their consent.

Clause 2 A *bill*, or proposed law, that is passed by a majority of the House and Senate is sent to the President. If the President signs the bill, it becomes law.

A bill can also become law without the President's signature. The President can refuse to act on a bill. If Congress is in session at the time, the bill becomes law 10 days after the President receives it.

The President can *veto*, or reject, a bill by sending it back to the house where it was introduced. Or if the President refuses to act on a bill and Congress adjourns within 10 days, then the bill dies. This way of killing a bill without taking action is called the *pocket veto.*

Congress can override the President's veto if each house of Congress passes the bill again by a two-thirds vote. This clause is an important part of the system of checks and balances.

1. **Tax Bills** All bills for raising revenue shall originate in the House of Representatives; but the Senate may propose or concur with amendments as on other bills.

2. **How a Bill Becomes a Law** Every bill which shall have passed the House of Representatives and the Senate shall, before it become a law, be presented to the President of the United States; if he approve, he shall sign it, but if not, he shall return it, with his objections, to that house in which it shall have originated, who shall enter the objections at large on their journal, and proceed to reconsider it. If after such reconsideration two-thirds of that house shall agree to pass the bill, it shall be sent, together with the objections, to the other house, by which it shall likewise be reconsidered, and, if approved by two-thirds of that house, it shall become a law. But in all such cases the votes of both houses shall be determined by yeas and nays, and the names of the persons voting for and against the bill shall be entered on the journal of each house respectively. If any bill shall not be returned by the President within ten days (Sundays excepted) after it shall have been presented to him, the same bill shall be a law, in like manner as if he had signed it, unless the Congress by their adjournment prevent its return, in which case it shall not be a law.

How a Bill Becomes a Law

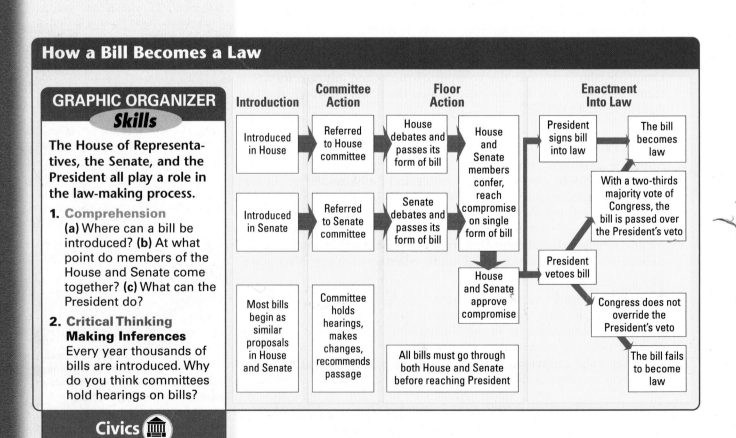

GRAPHIC ORGANIZER
Skills

The House of Representatives, the Senate, and the President all play a role in the law-making process.

1. **Comprehension**
   (a) Where can a bill be introduced? (b) At what point do members of the House and Senate come together? (c) What can the President do?

2. **Critical Thinking**
   Making Inferences
   Every year thousands of bills are introduced. Why do you think committees hold hearings on bills?

Civics

226 ★ Constitution

3. **Resolutions Passed by Congress** Every order, resolution, or vote to which the concurrence of the Senate and House of Representatives may be necessary (except on a question of adjournment) shall be presented to the President of the United States; and before the same shall take effect, shall be approved by him, or being disapproved by him, shall be repassed by two-thirds of the Senate and House of Representatives, according to the rules and limitations prescribed in the case of a bill.

Clause 3 Congress can pass resolutions or orders that have the same force as laws. Any such resolution or order must be signed by the President (except on questions of adjournment). This clause prevents Congress from bypassing the President simply by calling a bill by another name.

Section 8. Powers Delegated to Congress

The Congress shall have the power

1. **Taxes** To lay and collect taxes, duties, imposts, and excises, to pay the debts and provide for the common defense and general welfare of the United States; but all duties, imposts, and excises shall be uniform throughout the United States;

Clause 1 *Duties* are tariffs. *Imposts* are taxes in general. *Excises* are taxes on the production or sale of certain goods. Congress has the power to tax and spend tax money. Taxes must be the same in all parts of the country.

2. **Borrowing** To borrow money on the credit of the United States;

Clause 2 Congress can borrow money for the United States. The government often borrows money by selling *bonds,* or certificates that promise to pay the holder a certain sum of money on a certain date.

3. **Commerce** To regulate commerce with foreign nations, and among the several states, and with the Indian tribes;

Clause 3 Only Congress has the power to regulate foreign and *interstate trade,* or trade between states. Disagreement over interstate trade was a major problem with the Articles of Confederation.

4. **Naturalization; Bankruptcy** To establish a uniform rule of naturalization, and uniform laws on the subject of bankruptcies throughout the United States;

Clause 4 *Naturalization* is the process whereby a foreigner becomes a citizen. *Bankruptcy* is the condition in which a person or business cannot pay its debts. Congress has the power to pass laws on these two issues. The laws must be the same in all parts of the country.

5. **Coins; Weights; Measures** To coin money, regulate the value thereof, and of foreign coin, and fix the standard of weights and measures;

Clause 5 Congress has the power to coin money and set its value. Congress has set up the National Bureau of Standards to regulate weights and measures.

6. **Counterfeiting** To provide for the punishment of counterfeiting the securities and current coin of the United States;

Clause 6 *Counterfeiting* is the making of imitation money. *Securities* are bonds. Congress can make laws to punish counterfeiters.

7. **Post Offices** To establish post offices and post roads;

Clause 7 Congress has the power to set up and control the delivery of mail.

8. **Copyrights; Patents** To promote the progress of science and useful arts by securing for limited times to authors and inventors the exclusive right to their respective writings and discoveries;

Clause 8 Congress may pass copyright and patent laws. A *copyright* protects an author. A *patent* makes an inventor the sole owner of his or her work for a limited time.

9. **Federal Courts** To constitute tribunals inferior to the Supreme Court;

Clause 9 Congress has the power to set up *inferior,* or lower, federal courts under the Supreme Court.

10. **Piracy** To define and punish piracies and felonies committed on the high seas and offenses against the law of nations;

Clause 10 Congress can punish *piracy,* or the robbing of ships at sea.

Clause 11 Only Congress can declare war. Declarations of war are granted at the request of the President. *Letters of marque and reprisal* were documents allowing merchant ships to arm themselves. They are no longer issued.

11. **Declarations of War**   To declare war, ~~grant letters of marque and reprisal,~~ and make rules concerning captures on land and water;

Clauses 12, 13, 14 These clauses place the army and navy under the control of Congress. Congress decides on the size of, and the amount of money to spend on, the armed forces. It also has the power to write rules governing the armed forces.

12. **Army**   To raise and support armies, but no appropriation of money to that use shall be for a longer term than two years;

13. **Navy**   To provide and maintain a navy;

14. **Rules for the Military**   To make rules for the government and regulation of the land and naval forces;

Clauses 15, 16 The *militia* is a body of citizen soldiers. Congress can call up the militia to put down rebellions or fight foreign invaders. Each state has its own militia, today called the National Guard. Normally, the militia is under the command of a state's governor. However, it can be placed under the command of the President.

15. **Militia**   To provide for calling forth the militia to execute the laws of the Union, suppress insurrections, and repel invasions;

16. **Rules for the Militia**   To provide for organizing, arming, and disciplining the militia, and for governing such part of them as may be employed in the service of the United States, reserving to the states, respectively, the appointment of the officers, and the authority of training the militia according to the discipline prescribed by Congress;

Clause 17 Congress controls the district around the national capital. In 1790, Congress made Washington, D.C., the nation's capital. In 1973, it gave residents of the District the right to elect local officials.

17. **National Capital**   To exercise exclusive legislation in all cases whatsoever, over such district (not exceeding ten miles square) as may, by cession of particular states, and the acceptance of Congress, become the seat of government of the United States, and to exercise like authority over all places purchased by the consent of the legislature of the state in which the same shall be, for the erection of forts, magazines, arsenals, dock-yards, and other needful buildings;—and

Clause 18 Clauses 1–17 list the powers delegated to Congress. The framers added Clause 18 so that Congress could make laws as needed to carry out the first 17 clauses. Clause 18 is sometimes called the elastic clause because it lets Congress stretch the meaning of its power.

18. **Necessary Laws**   To make all laws which shall be necessary and proper for carrying into execution the foregoing powers, and all other powers vested by this Constitution in the government of the United States, or in any department or officer thereof.

Section 9. Powers Denied to the Federal Government

Clause 1 *Such persons* refers to slaves. This clause resulted from a compromise between the supporters and the opponents of the slave trade. In 1808, as soon as Congress was permitted to abolish the slave trade, it did so. The import tax was never imposed.

1. **The Slave Trade**   ~~The migration or importation of such persons as any of the states now existing shall think proper to admit shall not be prohibited by the Congress prior to the year 1808; but a tax or duty may be imposed on such importation, not exceeding $10 for each person.~~

Clause 2 A *writ of habeas corpus* is a court order requiring government officials to bring a prisoner to court and explain why he or she is being held. A writ of habeas corpus protects people from unlawful imprisonment. This right cannot be suspended except in times of rebellion or invasion.

2. **Writ of Habeas Corpus**   The privilege of the writ of habeas corpus shall not be suspended, unless when in cases of rebellion or invasion the public safety may require it.

3. **Bills of Attainder and *Ex Post Facto* Laws** No bill of attainder or *ex post facto* law shall be passed.

4. **Apportionment of Direct Taxes** ~~No capitation or other direct tax shall be laid, unless in proportion to the census or enumeration herein before directed to be taken.~~

5. **Taxes on Exports** No tax or duty shall be laid on articles exported from any state.

6. **Special Preference for Trade** No preference shall be given any regulation of commerce or revenue to the ports of one state over those of another; nor shall vessels bound to, or from, one state, be obliged to enter, clear, or pay duties in another.

7. **Spending** No money shall be drawn from the Treasury, but in consequence of appropriations made by law; and a regular statement and account of the receipts and expenditures of all public money shall be published from time to time.

8. **Creation of Titles of Nobility** No title of nobility shall be granted by the United States; and no person holding any office of profit or trust under them, shall, without the consent of the Congress, accept of any present, emolument, office, or title, of any kind whatever, from any king, prince, or foreign state.

Section 10. Powers Denied to the States

1. **Unconditional Prohibitions** No state shall enter into any treaty, alliance, or confederation; grant letters of marque and reprisal; coin money; emit bills of credit; make anything but gold and silver coin a tender in payment of debts; pass any bill of attainder, *ex post facto* law, or law impairing the obligation of contracts, or grant any title of nobility.

2. **Powers Conditionally Denied** No state shall, without the consent of the Congress, lay any imposts or duties on imports or exports, except what may be absolutely necessary for executing its inspection laws; and the net produce of all duties and imposts, laid by any state on imports or exports, shall be for the use of the Treasury of the United States; and all such laws shall be subject to the revision and control of the Congress.

3. **Other Denied Powers** No state shall, without the consent of Congress, lay any duty of tonnage, keep troops, or ships of war in time of peace, enter into any agreement or compact with another state, or with a foreign power, or engage in war, unless actually invaded, or in such imminent danger as will not admit of delay.

Clause 3 A ***bill of attainder*** is a law declaring that a person is guilty of a particular crime. An ***ex post facto law*** punishes an act which was not illegal when it was committed. Congress cannot pass such laws.

Clause 4 A ***capitation tax*** is a tax placed directly on each person. ***Direct taxes*** are taxes on people or on land. They can be passed only if they are divided among the states according to population. The Sixteenth Amendment allowed Congress to tax income without regard to the population of the states.

Clause 5 This clause forbids Congress to tax exports. Southerners insisted on this clause because their economy depended on exports.

Clause 6 Congress cannot make laws that favor one state over another in commerce. Also, states cannot place tariffs on interstate trade.

Clause 7 The federal government cannot spend money unless Congress ***appropriates*** it, or passes a law allowing it. The government must publish a statement showing how it spends public funds.

Clause 8 The government cannot award titles of nobility, such as Duke or Duchess. Americans cannot accept titles of nobility from foreign governments without the consent of Congress.

Clause 1 The writers of the Constitution did not want the states to act like separate nations. So, they prohibited states from making treaties or coining money. Some powers denied to the federal government are also denied to the states. For example, states cannot pass *ex post facto laws*.

Clauses 2, 3 Powers listed here are forbidden to the states, but Congress can lift these prohibitions by passing laws that give these powers to the states.
Clause 2 forbids states from taxing imports and exports without the consent of Congress. States may charge inspection fees on goods entering the states. Any profit from these fees must be turned over to the United States Treasury.
Clause 3 forbids states from keeping an army or navy without the consent of Congress. States cannot make treaties or declare war unless an enemy invades or is about to invade.

Article 2. The Executive Branch

Section 1. President and Vice-President

Clause 1 The President is responsible for *executing,* or carrying out, laws passed by Congress.

1. **Chief Executive**   The executive power shall be vested in a President of the United States of America. He shall hold his office during the term of four years, and together with the Vice-President, chosen for the same term, be elected as follows:

2. **Selection of Electors**   Each state shall appoint, in such manner as the legislature thereof may direct, a number of electors, equal to the whole number of Senators and Representatives to which the state may be entitled in the Congress; but no Senator or Representative, or person holding an office or trust or profit under the United States, shall be appointed an elector.

Clauses 2, 3 Some writers of the Constitution were afraid to allow the people to elect the President directly. Therefore, the Constitutional Convention set up the electoral college. Clause 2 directs each state to choose electors, or delegates to the electoral college, to vote for President. A state's electoral vote is equal to the combined number of senators and representatives. Each state may decide how to choose its electors. Members of Congress and federal officeholders may not serve as electors. This much of the original electoral college system is still in effect.

Clause 3 called upon each elector to vote for two candidates. The candidate who received a majority of the electoral votes would become President. The runner-up would become Vice President. If no candidate won a majority, the House would choose the President. The Senate would choose the Vice President.

The election of 1800 showed a problem with the original electoral college system. Thomas Jefferson was the Republican candidate for President, and Aaron Burr was the Republican candidate for Vice President. In the electoral college, the vote ended in a tie. The election was finally decided in the House, where Jefferson was chosen President. The Twelfth Amendment changed the electoral college system so that this could not happen again.

3. **Electoral College Procedures**   The electors shall meet in their respective states, and vote by ballot for two persons, of whom one at least shall not be an inhabitant of the same state with themselves. And they shall make a list of all the persons voted for, and of the number of votes for each; which list they shall sign and certify, and transmit sealed to the seat of the government of the United States, directed to the president of the Senate. The president of the Senate shall, in the presence of the Senate and House of Representatives, open all the certificates, and the votes shall then be counted. The person having the greatest number of votes shall be President, if such number be a majority of the whole number of electors appointed; and if there be more than one who have such majority, and have an equal number of votes, then the House of Representatives shall immediately choose by ballot one of them for President; and if no person have a majority, then from the five highest on the list the said House shall in like manner choose the President. But in choosing the President the votes shall be taken by states, the representation from each state having one vote. A quorum for this purpose shall consist of a member or members from two thirds of the states, and a majority of all the states shall be necessary to a choice. In every case, after the choice of the President, the person having the greatest number of votes of the electors shall be the Vice President. But if there should remain two or more who have equal votes, the Senate shall choose from them by ballot the Vice President.

Clause 4 By a law passed in 1792, electors are chosen on the Tuesday after the first Monday of November every four years. Electors from each state meet to vote in December.

Today, voters in each state choose **slates**, or groups, of electors who are pledged to a candidate for President. The candidate for President who wins the popular vote in each state wins that state's electoral vote.

4. **Time of Elections**   The Congress may determine the time of choosing the electors, and the day on which they shall give their votes; which day shall be the same throughout the United States.

5. **Qualifications for President** No person except a natural-born citizen ~~or a citizen of the United States, at the time of the adoption of this Constitution,~~ shall be eligible to the office of the President; neither shall any person be eligible to that office who shall not have attained to the age of thirty-five years, and been fourteen years a resident within the United States.

6. **Presidential Succession** In case of the removal of the President from office, or of his death, resignation, or inability to discharge the powers and duties of the said office, the same shall devolve on the Vice-President, and the Congress may by law provide for the case of removal, death, resignation, or inability, both of the President and Vice-President, declaring what officer shall then act as President, and such officer shall act accordingly, until the disability be removed, or a President shall be elected.

7. **Salary** The President shall, at stated times, receive for his services, a compensation, which shall neither be increased nor diminished during the period for which he shall have been elected, and he shall not receive within that period any other emolument from the United States, or any of them.

8. **Oath of Office** Before he enter on the execution of his office, he shall take the following oath or affirmation:—"I do solemnly swear (or affirm) that I will faithfully execute the office of President of the United States, and will to the best of my ability, preserve, protect, and defend the Constitution of the United States."

Section 2. Powers of the President

1. **Commander in Chief of the Armed Forces** The President shall be Commander in Chief of the Army and Navy of the United States, and of the militia of the several states, when called into the actual service of the United States; he may require the opinion, in writing, of the principal officer in each of the executive departments, upon any subject relating to the duties of their respective offices, and he shall have power to grant reprieves and pardons for offenses against the United States, except in cases of impeachment.

Clause 5 The President must be a citizen of the United States from birth, at least 35 years old, and a resident of the country for 14 years. The first seven Presidents of the United States were born under British rule, but they were allowed to hold office because they were citizens at the time the Constitution was adopted.

Clause 6 The powers of the President pass to the Vice President if the President leaves office or cannot discharge his or her duties. The wording of this clause caused confusion the first time a President died in office. When President William Henry Harrison died, it was uncertain whether Vice President John Tyler should remain Vice President and act as President or whether he should be sworn in as President. Tyler persuaded a federal judge to swear him in. So he set the precedent that the Vice President assumes the office of President when it becomes vacant. The Twenty-fifth Amendment clarified this clause.

Clause 7 The President is paid a salary. It cannot be raised or lowered during his or her term of office. The President is not allowed to hold any other federal or state position while in office. Today, the President's salary is $200,000 a year.

Clause 8 Before taking office, the President must promise to protect and defend the Constitution. Usually, the Chief Justice of the Supreme Court gives the oath of office to the President.

Clause 1 The President is head of the armed forces and the state militias when they are called into national service. So, the military is under *civilian*, or nonmilitary, control.

The President can get advice from the heads of executive departments. In most cases, the President has the power to grant a reprieve or pardon. A *reprieve* suspends punishment ordered by law. A *pardon* prevents prosecution for a crime or overrides the judgment of a court.

Clause 2 The President has the power to make treaties with other nations. Under the system of checks and balances, all treaties must be approved by two thirds of the Senate. Today, the President also makes agreements with foreign governments. These executive agreements do not need Senate approval.

The President has the power to appoint ambassadors to foreign countries and to appoint other high officials. The Senate must *confirm*, or approve, these appointments.

Clause 3 If the Senate is in *recess*, or not meeting, the President may fill vacant government posts by making temporary appointments.

The President must give Congress a report on the condition of the nation every year. This report is now called the State of the Union Address. Since 1913, the President has given this speech in person each January.

The President can call a special session of Congress and can adjourn Congress if necessary. The President has the power to receive, or recognize, foreign ambassadors.

The President must carry out the laws. Today, many government agencies oversee the execution of laws.

Civil officers include federal judges and members of the Cabinet. *High crimes* are major crimes. *Misdemeanors* are lesser crimes. The President, Vice President, and others can be forced out of office if impeached and found guilty of certain crimes.

Judicial power is the right of the courts to decide legal cases. The Constitution creates the Supreme Court but lets Congress decide the size of the Supreme Court. Congress has the power to set up inferior, or lower, courts. The Judiciary Act of 1789 set up district and circuit courts, or courts of appeal. Today, there are 94 district courts and 13 courts of appeal. All federal judges serve for life.

2. Making Treaties and Nominations He shall have power, by and with the advice and consent of the Senate, to make treaties, provided two-thirds of the Senators present concur; and he shall nominate, and by and with the advice and consent of the Senate, shall appoint ambassadors, other public ministers and consuls, judges of the Supreme Court, and all other officers of the United States, whose appointments are not herein otherwise provided for, and which shall be established by law; but the Congress may by law vest the appointment of such inferior officers, as they think proper, in the President alone, in the courts of law, or in the heads of departments.

3. Temporary Appointments The President shall have power to fill up all vacancies that may happen during the recess of the Senate, by granting commissions which shall expire at the end of their next session.

Section 3. Duties

He shall from time to time give to the Congress information of the state of the Union, and recommend to their consideration such measures as he shall judge necessary and expedient; he may, on extraordinary occasions, convene both houses, or either of them, and in case of disagreement between them, with respect to the time of adjournment, he may adjourn them to such time as he shall think proper; he shall receive ambassadors and other public ministers; he shall take care that the laws be faithfully executed, and shall commission all the officers of the United States.

Section 4. Impeachment and Removal From Office

The President, Vice-President, and all civil officers of the United States, shall be removed from office on impeachment for, and conviction of, treason, bribery, or other high crimes or misdemeanors.

Article 3. The Judicial Branch

Section 1. Federal Courts

The judicial power of the United States shall be vested in one Supreme Court, and in such inferior courts as the Congress may from time to time ordain and establish. The judges, both of the Supreme and inferior courts, shall hold their offices during good behavior, and shall, at stated times, receive for their services a compensation, which shall not be diminished during their continuance in office.

Separation of Powers

Legislative Branch (Congress)	Executive Branch (President)	Judicial Branch (Supreme Court and Other Federal Courts)
Passes Laws	**Carries Out Laws**	**Interprets Laws**
• Can override President's veto	• Proposes laws	• Can declare laws unconstitutional
• Approves treaties and presidential appointments	• Can veto laws	• Can declare executive actions unconstitutional
• Can impeach and remove President and other high officials	• Negotiates foreign treaties	
• Creates lower federal courts	• Serves as commander in chief of the armed forces	
• Appropriates money	• Appoints federal judges, ambassadors, and other high officials	
• Prints and coins money	• Can grant pardons to federal offenders	
• Raises and supports the armed forces		
• Can declare war		
• Regulates foreign and interstate trade		

GRAPHIC ORGANIZER
Skills

The Constitution set up three branches of government. Each branch has its own powers.

1. **Comprehension**
   (a) Who heads the executive branch? **(b)** What is the role of the legislative branch?

2. **Critical Thinking**
   Analyzing Information
   Based on this chart, what is the relationship between the judicial branch and the legislative branch?

Civics 🏛

Section 2. Jurisdiction of Federal Courts

1. **Scope of Judicial Power**   The judicial power shall extend to all cases, in law and equity, arising under this Constitution, the laws of the United States, and treaties made or which shall be made, under their authority; to all cases affecting ambassadors, other public ministers and consuls; to all cases of admiralty and maritime jurisdiction; to controversies to which the United States shall be a party; to controversies between two or more states; ~~between a state and citizens of another state;~~ between citizens of the same state claiming lands under grants of different states, and between a state or the citizens thereof, and foreign states, citizens, or subjects.

2. **The Supreme Court**   In all cases affecting ambassadors, other public ministers and consuls, and those in which a state shall be a party, the Supreme Court shall have original jurisdiction. In all the other cases before mentioned, the Supreme Court shall have appellate jurisdiction, both as to law and fact, with such exceptions, and under such regulations as the Congress shall make.

Clause 1 *Jurisdiction* refers to the right of a court to hear a case. Federal courts have jurisdiction over cases that involve the Constitution, federal laws, treaties, foreign ambassadors and diplomats, naval and maritime laws, disagreements between states or between citizens from different states, and disputes between a state or citizen and a foreign state or citizen.

In *Marbury* v. *Madison,* the Supreme Court established the right to judge whether or not a law is constitutional.

Clause 2 *Original jurisdiction* means the power of a court to hear a case where it first arises. The Supreme Court has original jurisdiction over only a few cases, such as those involving foreign diplomats. More often, the Supreme Court acts as an appellate court. An *appellate court* does not decide guilt. It decides whether the lower court trial was properly conducted and reviews the lower court's decision.

Clause 3 This clause guarantees the right to a jury trial for anyone accused of a federal crime. The only exceptions are impeachment cases. The trial must be held in the state where the crime was committed.

3. **Trial by Jury** The trial of all crimes, except in cases of impeachment, shall be by jury; and such trial shall be held in the state where the said crimes shall have been committed; but when not committed within any state, the trial shall be at such place or places as the Congress may by law have directed.

Section 3. Treason

Clause 1 Treason is clearly defined. An *overt act* is an actual action. A person cannot be convicted of treason for what he or she thinks. A person can be convicted of treason only if he or she confesses or two witnesses testify to it.

1. **Definition** Treason against the United States shall consist only in levying war against them, or in adhering to their enemies, giving them aid and comfort. No person shall be convicted of treason unless on the testimony of two witnesses to the same overt act, or on confession in open court.

Clause 2 Congress has the power to set the punishment for traitors. Congress may not punish the children of convicted traitors by taking away their civil rights or property.

2. **Punishment** The Congress shall have power to declare the punishment of treason, but no attainder of treason shall work corruption of blood or forfeiture except during the life of the person attainted.

Article 4. Relations Among the States

Section 1. Official Records and Acts

Each state must recognize the official acts and records of any other state. For example, each state must recognize marriage certificates issued by another state. Congress can pass laws to ensure this.

Full faith and credit shall be given in each state to the public acts, records, and judicial proceedings of every other state. And the Congress may by general laws prescribe the manner in which such acts, records, and proceedings shall be proved, and the effect thereof.

Section 2. Privileges of Citizens

Clause 1 All states must treat citizens of another state in the same way it treats its own citizens. However, the courts have allowed states to give residents certain privileges, such as lower tuition rates.

1. **Privileges** The citizens of each state shall be entitled to all privileges and immunities of citizens in the several states.

Clause 2 *Extradition* means the act of returning a suspected criminal or escaped prisoner to a state where he or she is wanted. State governors must return a suspect. However, the Supreme Court has ruled that governors cannot be forced to do so if they feel that justice will not be done.

2. **Extradition** A person charged in any state with treason, felony, or other crime, who shall flee from justice, and be found in another state, shall on demand of the executive authority of the state from which he fled, be delivered up, to be removed to the state having jurisdiction of the crime.

Clause 3 *Persons held to service or labor* refers to slaves or indentured servants. This clause required states to return runaway slaves to their owners. The Thirteenth Amendment replaces this clause.

3. **Return of Fugitive Slaves** ~~No person held to service or labor in one state, under the laws thereof, escaping into another, shall in consequence of any law or regulation therein, be discharged from such service or labor, but shall be delivered up on claim of the party to whom such service or labor may be due.~~

Section 3. New States and Territories

Clause 1 Congress has the power to admit new states to the Union. Existing states cannot be split up or joined together to form new states unless both Congress and the state legislatures approve. New states are equal to all other states.

1. **New States** New states may be admitted by the Congress into this Union; but no new state shall be formed or erected within the jurisdiction of any other state; nor any state be formed by the junction of two of more states, or parts of states, without the consent of the legislatures of the states concerned as well as of the Congress.

Clause 2 Congress can make rules for managing and governing land owned by the United States. This includes territories not organized into states, such as Puerto Rico, and federal lands within a state.

2. **Federal Lands** The Congress shall have power to dispose of and make all needful rules and regulations respecting the territory or other property belonging to the United States; and nothing in this Constitution shall be so construed as to prejudice any claims of the United States, or of any particular state.

The Federal System

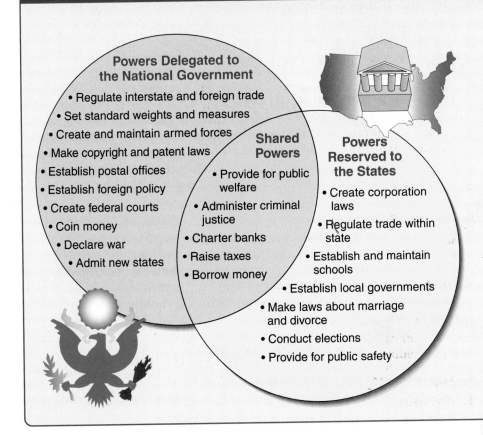

Powers Delegated to the National Government
- Regulate interstate and foreign trade
- Set standard weights and measures
- Create and maintain armed forces
- Make copyright and patent laws
- Establish postal offices
- Establish foreign policy
- Create federal courts
- Coin money
- Declare war
- Admit new states

Shared Powers
- Provide for public welfare
- Administer criminal justice
- Charter banks
- Raise taxes
- Borrow money

Powers Reserved to the States
- Create corporation laws
- Regulate trade within state
- Establish and maintain schools
- Establish local governments
- Make laws about marriage and divorce
- Conduct elections
- Provide for public safety

GRAPHIC ORGANIZER
Skills

Federalism is the distribution of power between the national government and the state governments.

1. **Comprehension**
   (a) Name two powers reserved to the states.
   (b) Name two powers shared by the national and state governments.

2. **Critical Thinking**
   Applying Information
   Why do you think the power to create and maintain the armed forces was delegated to the national government?

Civics

Section 4. Guarantees to the States

The United States shall guarantee to every state in this Union a republican form of government, and shall protect each of them against invasion; and on application of the legislature, or of the executive (when the legislature cannot be convened) against domestic violence.

In a *republic*, voters choose representatives to govern them. The federal government must protect the states from foreign invasion and from *domestic*, or internal, disorder if asked to do so by a state.

Article 5. Amending the Constitution

The Congress, whenever two-thirds of both houses shall deem it necessary, shall propose amendments to this Constitution, or, on the application of the legislatures of two-thirds of the several states, shall call a convention for proposing amendments, which, in either case, shall be valid to all intents and purposes, as part of this Constitution, when ratified by the legislatures of three-fourths of the several states, or by conventions in three-fourths thereof, as the one or the other mode of ratification may be proposed by the Congress; provided that no amendments which may be made prior to the year 1808 shall in any manner affect the first and fourth clauses in the Ninth Section of the First Article; and that no state, without its consent, shall be deprived of its equal suffrage in the Senate.

The Constitution can be *amended*, or changed, if necessary. An amendment can be proposed by (1) a two-thirds vote of both houses of Congress or (2) a national convention called by Congress at the request of two thirds of the state legislatures. (This second method has never been used.) An amendment must be *ratified*, or approved, by (1) three fourths of the state legislatures or (2) special conventions in three fourths of the states. Congress decides which method will be used.

Article 6. National Supremacy

Section 1. Prior Public Debts

The United States government promised to pay all debts and honor all agreements made under the Articles of Confederation.

All debts contracted and engagements entered into, before the adoption of this Constitution, shall be as valid against the United States under this Constitution, as under the Confederation.

Section 2. Supreme Law of the Land

The Constitution, federal laws, and treaties that the Senate has ratified are the supreme, or highest, law of the land. Thus, they outweigh state laws. A state judge must overturn a state law that conflicts with the Constitution or with a federal law.

This Constitution, and the laws of the United States which shall be made in pursuance thereof, and all treaties made, or which shall be made, under the authority of the United States, shall be the supreme law of the land; and the judges in every state shall be bound thereby, anything in the constitution or laws of any state to the contrary notwithstanding.

Section 3. Oaths of Office

State and federal officeholders take an oath, or solemn promise, to support the Constitution. However, this clause forbids the use of religious tests for officeholders. During the colonial period, every colony except Rhode Island required a religious test for officeholders.

The Senators and Representatives before mentioned, and the members of the several state legislatures, and all executive and judicial officers, both of the United States and of the several states, shall be bound by oath or affirmation, to support this Constitution; but no religious test shall ever be required as a qualification to any office or public trust under the United States.

Article 7. Ratification

During 1787 and 1788, states held special conventions. By October 1788, the required nine states had ratified the Constitution.

The ratification of the conventions of nine states shall be sufficient for the establishment of the Constitution between the states so ratifying the same.

Done in convention, by the unanimous consent of the states present, the seventeenth day of September, in the year of our Lord one thousand seven hundred and eighty-seven, and of the independence of the United States of America the twelfth. In Witness whereof, we have hereunto subscribed our names.

Attest: William Jackson
Secretary

George Washington
President and deputy from Virginia

New Hampshire
John Langdon
Nicholas Gilman

Massachussetts
Nathaniel Gorham
Rufus King

Connecticut
William Samuel
  Johnson
Roger Sherman

New York
Alexander Hamilton

New Jersey
William Livingston
David Brearley
William Paterson
Jonathan Dayton

Pennsylvania
Benjamin Franklin
Thomas Mifflin
Robert Morris
George Clymer
Thomas FitzSimons
Jared Ingersoll
James Wilson
Gouverneur Morris

Delaware
George Read
Gunning Bedford, Jr.
John Dickinson
Richard Bassett
Jacob Broom

Maryland
James McHenry
Dan of St. Thomas
  Jennifer
Daniel Carroll

Virginia
John Blair
James Madison, Jr.

North Carolina
William Blount
Richard Dobbs Spaight
Hugh Williamson

South Carolina
John Rutledge
Charles Cotesworth
  Pinckney
Charles Pinckney
Pierce Butler

Georgia
William Few
Abraham Baldwin

Amendments to the Constitution

Amendment 1

Freedoms of Religion, Speech, Press, Assembly, and Petition

Congress shall make no law respecting an establishment of religion, or prohibiting the free exercise thereof; or abridging the freedom of speech, or of the press; or the right of the people peaceably to assemble, and to petition the government for a redress of grievances.

Congress cannot set up an established, or official, church or religion for the nation. During the colonial period, most colonies had established churches. However, the authors of the First Amendment wanted to keep government and religion separate.

Congress may not *abridge*, or limit, the freedom to speak and write freely. The government may not censor, or review, books and newspapers before they are printed. This amendment also protects the right to assemble, or hold public meetings. *Petition* means "ask." *Redress* means "to correct." *Grievances* are wrongs. The people have the right to ask the government for wrongs to be corrected.

Amendment 2

Right to Bear Arms

A well-regulated militia, being necessary to the security of a free state, the right of the people to keep and bear arms shall not be infringed.

Each state has the right to maintain a *militia*, an armed force for its own protection. Today, the militia is the National Guard. The national government and the states can and do regulate the private ownership and use of firearms.

Amendment 3

Lodging Troops in Private Homes

No soldier shall, in time of peace, be quartered in any house, without the consent of the owner; nor in time of war, but in a manner to be prescribed by law.

During the colonial period, the British quartered, or housed, soldiers in private homes without the permission of the owners. This amendment limits the government's right to use private homes to house soldiers.

Amendment 4

Search and Seizure

The right of the people to be secure in their persons, houses, papers, and effects, against unreasonable searches and seizures, shall not be violated; and no warrants shall issue but upon probable cause, supported by oath or affirmation, and particularly describing the place to be searched, and the persons or things to be seized.

This amendment protects Americans from unreasonable searches and seizures. Search and seizure are permitted only if a judge has issued a *warrant*, or written court order. A warrant is issued only if there is probable cause. This means an officer must show that it is probable, or likely, that the search will produce evidence of a crime. A search warrant must name the exact place to be searched and the things to be seized. In some cases, courts have ruled that searches can take place without a warrant. For example, police may search a person who is under arrest. However, evidence found during an unlawful search cannot be used in a trial.

This amendment protects the rights of the accused. *Capital crimes* are those that can be punished with death. *Infamous crimes* are those that can be punished with prison or loss of rights. The federal government must obtain an *indictment,* or formal accusation, from a *grand jury* to prosecute anyone for such crimes. A grand jury is a panel of between 12 and 23 citizens who decide if the government has enough evidence to justify a trial. This procedure prevents prosecution with little or no evidence of guilt. (Soldiers and the militia in wartime are not covered by this rule.)

Double jeopardy is forbidden. This means that a person cannot be tried twice for the same crime—unless a court sets aside a conviction because of a legal error. A person on trial cannot be forced to testify, or give evidence, against himself or herself. A person accused of a crime is entitled to *due process of law,* or a fair hearing or trial. Finally, the government cannot seize private property for public use without paying the owner a fair price for it.

In criminal cases, the jury must be *impartial,* or not favor either side. The accused is guaranteed the right to a trial by jury. The trial must be speedy. If the government purposely postpones the trial so that it becomes hard for the person to get a fair hearing, the charge may be dismissed. The accused must be told the charges against him or her and be allowed to question prosecution witnesses. Witnesses who can help the accused can be ordered to appear in court.

The accused must be allowed a lawyer. Since 1942, the federal government has been required to provide a lawyer if the accused cannot afford one. In 1963, the Supreme Court decided that states must also provide lawyers for a defendant too poor to pay for one.

Common law refers to rules of law established by judges in past cases. This amendment guarantees the right to a jury trial in lawsuits where the sum of money at stake is more than $20. An appeals court cannot change a verdict because it disagrees with the decision of the jury. It can set aside a verdict only if legal errors made the trial unfair.

Bail is money the accused leaves with the court as a pledge to appear for trial. If the accused does not appear for trial, the court keeps the money. *Excessive* means too high. This amendment forbids courts to set unreasonably high bail. The amount of bail usually depends on the seriousness of the charge and whether the accused is likely to appear for the trial. The amendment also forbids cruel and unusual punishments such as mental and physical abuse.

Amendment 5

Rights of the Accused

No person shall be held to answer for a capital, or otherwise infamous, crime, unless on a presentment or indictment of a grand jury, except in cases arising in the land or naval forces, or in the militia, when in actual service in time of war or public danger; nor shall any person be subject for the same offense to be twice put in jeopardy of life and limb; nor shall be compelled, in any criminal case, to be a witness against himself; nor be deprived of life, liberty, or property, without due process of law; nor shall private property be taken for public use, without just compensation.

Amendment 6

Right to Speedy Trial by Jury

In all criminal prosecutions, the accused shall enjoy the right to a speedy and public trial, by an impartial jury of the state and district wherein the crime shall have been committed, which district shall have been previously ascertained by law, and to be informed of the nature and cause of the accusation; to be confronted with the witnesses against him; to have compulsory process for obtaining witnesses in his favor, and to have the assistance of counsel for his defense.

Amendment 7

Jury Trial in Civil Cases

In suits at common law, where the value in controversy shall exceed $20, the right of trial by jury shall be preserved, and no fact tried by a jury shall be otherwise re-examined in any court of the United States than according to the rules of the common law.

Amendment 8

Bail and Punishment

Excessive bail shall not be required, nor excessive fines imposed, nor cruel and unusual punishments inflicted.

Amendment 9

Powers Reserved to the People

The enumeration in the Constitution, of certain rights, shall not be construed to deny or disparage others retained by the people.

People have rights not listed in the Constitution. This amendment was added because some people feared that the Bill of Rights would be used to limit rights to those actually listed.

Amendment 10

Powers Reserved to the States

The powers not delegated to the United States by the Constitution, nor prohibited by it to the states, are reserved to the states respectively, or to the people.

This amendment limits the power of the federal government. Powers that are not given to the federal government belong to the states. The powers reserved to the states are not listed in the Constitution.

Amendment 11

Suits Against States

Passed by Congress on March 4, 1794. Ratified on January 23, 1795.

The judicial power of the United States shall not be construed to extend to any suit in law or equity, commenced or prosecuted against one of the United States, by citizens of another state, or by citizens or subjects of any foreign state.

This amendment changed part of Article 3, Section 2, Clause 1. As a result, a private citizen from one state cannot sue the government of another state in federal court. However, a citizen can sue a state government in a state court.

Amendment 12

Election of President and Vice-President

Passed by Congress on December 9, 1803. Ratified on June 15, 1804.

The electors shall meet in their respective states, and vote by ballot for President and Vice-President, one of whom, at least, shall not be an inhabitant of the same state with themselves; they shall name in their ballots the person voted for as President, and in distinct ballots the person voted for as Vice-President, and they shall make distinct lists of all persons voted for as President, and of all persons voted for as Vice-President, and of the number of votes for each, which lists they shall sign and certify, and transmit, sealed, to the seat of government of the United States, directed to the President of the Senate; the President of the Senate shall, in the presence of the Senate and House of Representatives, open all the certificates and the votes shall then be counted; the person having the greatest number of votes for President shall be the President, if such number be a majority of the whole number of electors appointed; and if no person have such majority, then from the persons having the highest numbers not exceeding three on the list of those voted for as President, the House of Representatives shall choose immediately, by ballot, the President. But in choosing the President, the votes shall be taken by the states, the representation from each state having one vote; a quorum for this purpose shall consist of a member or members from two-thirds of the states, and a majority of all the states shall be necessary to a choice. And if the House of Representatives shall not choose a President whenever the right of choice shall devolve upon them, before the fourth day of March next following, then the Vice-President shall act as President, as in the case of the death or other constitutional disability of the President. The person having the greatest number of votes as Vice-President, shall be the Vice-President, if such number be a majority of the whole

This amendment changed the way the electoral college voted. Before the amendment was adopted, each elector simply voted for two people. The candidate with the most votes became President. The runner-up became Vice President. In the election of 1800, however, a tie vote resulted between Thomas Jefferson and Aaron Burr.

In such a case, the Constitution required the House of Representatives to elect the President. Federalists had a majority in the House. They tried to keep Jefferson out of office by voting for Burr. It took 35 ballots in the House before Jefferson was elected President.

To keep this from happening again, the Twelfth Amendment was passed and ratified in time for the election of 1804.

This amendment provides that each elector choose one candidate for President and one candidate for Vice President. If no candidate for President receives a majority of electoral votes, the House of Representatives chooses the President. If no candidate for Vice President receives a majority, the Senate elects the Vice President. The Vice President must be a person who is eligible to be President.

This system is still in use today. However, it is possible for a candidate to win the popular vote and lose in the electoral college. This happened in 1876 and again in 2000.

Senators who had already been elected by the state legislatures were not affected by this amendment.

This amendment, known as **Prohibition,** banned the making, selling, or transporting of alcoholic beverages in the United States. Later, the Twenty-first Amendment **repealed,** or canceled, this amendment.

Both the states and the federal government had the power to pass laws to enforce this amendment.

This amendment had to be approved within seven years. The Eighteenth Amendment was the first amendment to include a time limit for ratification.

Neither the federal government nor state governments can deny the right to vote on account of sex. Thus, women won **suffrage,** or the right to vote. Before 1920, some states had allowed women to vote in state elections.

Congress can pass laws to carry out this amendment.

The date for the President and Vice President to take office is January 20. Members of Congress begin their terms of office on January 3. Before this amendment was adopted, these terms of office began on March 4.

Congress must meet at least once a year. The new session of Congress begins on January 3. Before this amendment, members of Congress who had been defeated in November continued to hold office until the following March. Such members were known as **lame ducks.**

By Section 3, if the President-elect dies before taking office, the Vice President–elect becomes President. If no President has been chosen by January 20 or if the elected candidate fails to qualify for office, the Vice President–elect acts as President, but only until a qualified President is chosen.

Section 3. Exception ~~This amendment shall not be so construed as to affect the election or term of any Senator chosen before it becomes valid as part of the Constitution.~~

⇀Amendment 18 ↲

Prohibition of Alcoholic Beverages

Passed by Congress on December 18, 1917. Ratified on January 16, 1919.

Section 1. Ban on Alcohol ~~After one year from the ratification of this article the manufacture, sale, or transportation of intoxicating liquors within, the importation thereof into, or the exportation thereof from, the United States and all territory subject to the jurisdiction thereof for beverage purposes is hereby prohibited.~~

Section 2. Enforcement ~~The Congress and the several states shall have concurrent power to enforce this article by appropriate legislation.~~

Section 3. Method of Ratification ~~This article shall be inoperative unless it shall have been ratified as an amendment to the Constitution by the legislatures of the several states, as provided in the Constitution, within seven years from the date of the submission hereof to the states by the Congress.~~

⇀Amendment 19 ↲

Women's Suffrage

Passed by Congress on June 4, 1919. Ratified on August 18, 1920.

Section 1. The Right to Vote The right of citizens of the United States to vote shall not be denied or abridged by the United States or by any state on account of sex.

Section 2. Enforcement Congress shall have power to enforce this article by appropriate legislation.

⇀Amendment 20 ↲

Presidential Terms; Sessions of Congress

Passed by Congress on March 2, 1932. Ratified on January 23, 1933.

Section 1. Beginning of Term The terms of the President and Vice-President shall end at noon on the 20th day of January, and the terms of Senators and Representatives at noon on the 3rd day of January, of the years in which such terms would have ended if this article had not been ratified; and the terms of their successors shall then begin.

Section 2. Congressional Sessions The Congress shall assemble at least once in every year, and such meeting shall begin at noon on the 3rd day of January, unless they shall by law appoint a different day.

Section 3. Presidential Succession If at the time fixed for the beginning of the term of the President, the President-elect shall have died, the Vice-President-elect shall become President. If a President shall not have been chosen before the time fixed for the beginning of his term, or if the President-elect shall have failed to qualify, then the Vice-President-elect shall act as President until a President shall have qualified; and the Congress may by law provide for the case wherein neither a President-elect nor a Vice-President-elect shall have qualified, declaring who shall then act as President, or the manner in which one who is to act shall be selected, and such person shall act accordingly until a President or Vice-President shall have qualified.

Finally, Congress can choose a person to act as President if neither the President-elect nor Vice President-elect is qualified to take office.

Section 4. Elections Decided by Congress The Congress may by law provide for the case of the death of any of the persons from whom the House of Representatives may choose a President whenever the right of choice shall have devolved upon them, and for the case of the death of any of the persons from whom the Senate may choose a Vice-President whenever the right of choice shall have devolved upon them.

Congress can pass laws in cases where a presidential candidate dies while an election is being decided in the House. Congress has similar power in cases where a candidate for Vice President dies while an election is being decided in the Senate.

Section 5. Date of Effect ~~Sections 1 and 2 shall take effect on the 15th day of October following the ratification of this article.~~

Section 5 sets the date for the amendment to become effective.

Section 6. Ratification Period ~~This article shall be inoperative unless it shall have been ratified as an amendment to the Constitution by the legislatures of three-fourths of the several states within seven years from the date of its submission.~~

Section 6 sets a time limit for ratification.

Amendment 21

Repeal of Prohibition

Passed by Congress on February 20, 1933. Ratified on December 5, 1933.

Section 1. Repeal of National Prohibition The eighteenth article of amendment to the Constitution of the United States is hereby repealed.

The Eighteenth Amendment is repealed, making it legal to make and sell alcoholic beverages. Prohibition ended December 5, 1933.

Section 2. State Laws The transportation or importation into any state, territory, or possession of the United States for delivery or use therein of intoxicating liquors, in violation of the laws thereof, is hereby prohibited.

Each state was free to ban the making and selling of alcoholic drink within its borders. This section makes bringing liquor into a "dry" state a federal offense.

Section 3. Ratification Period ~~This article shall be inoperative unless it shall have been ratified as an amendment to the Constitution by conventions in the several states, as provided in the Constitution, within seven years from the date of the submission hereof to the states by the Congress.~~

Special state conventions were called to ratify this amendment. This is the only time an amendment was ratified by state conventions rather than state legislatures.

Amendment 22

Limit on Number of President's Terms

Passed by Congress on March 12, 1947. Ratified on March 1, 1951.

Section 1. Two-Term Limit No person shall be elected to the office of the President more than twice, and no person who has held the office of President, or acted as President, for more than two years of a term to which some other person was elected President shall be elected to the office of the President more than once. ~~But this Article shall not apply to any person holding the office of President when this Article was proposed by the Congress, and shall not prevent any person who may be holding the office of President, or acting as President, during the term within which this Article becomes operative from holding the office of President or acting as President during the remainder of such term.~~

Before Franklin Roosevelt became President, no President served more than two terms in office. Roosevelt broke with this custom and was elected to four terms. This amendment provides that no President may serve more than two terms. A President who has already served more than half of someone else's term can serve only one more full term. However, the amendment did not apply to Harry Truman, who had become President after Franklin Roosevelt's death in 1945.

A seven-year time limit is set for ratification.

Section 2. Ratification Period ~~This Article shall be inoperative unless it shall have been ratified as an amendment to the Constitution by the legislatures of three-fourths of the several states within seven years from the date of its submission to the states by the Congress.~~

Amendment 23

Presidential Electors for District of Columbia

Passed by Congress on June 16, 1960. Ratified on April 3, 1961.

Section 1. Determining the Number of Electors The District constituting the seat of Government of the United States shall appoint in such manner as the Congress may direct: A number of electors of President and Vice-President equal to the whole number of Senators and Representatives in Congress to which the District would be entitled if it were a State, but in no event more than the least populous State; they shall be in addition to those appointed by the States, but they shall be considered, for the purposes of the election of President and Vice-President, to be electors appointed by a State; and they shall meet in the District and perform such duties as provided by the twelfth article of amendment.

This amendment gives residents of Washington, D.C., the right to vote in presidential elections. Until this amendment was adopted, people living in Washington, D.C., could not vote for President because the Constitution had made no provision for choosing electors from the nation's capital. Washington, D.C., has three electoral votes.

Congress can pass laws to carry out this amendment.

Section 2. Enforcement The Congress shall have power to enforce this article by appropriate legislation.

Amendment 24

Abolition of Poll Tax in National Elections

Passed by Congress on August 27, 1962. Ratified on January 23, 1964.

Section 1. Poll Tax Banned The right of citizens of the United States to vote in any primary or other election for President or Vice-President, for electors for President or Vice-President, or for Senator or Representative in Congress, shall not be denied or abridged by the United States or any state by reason of failure to pay any poll tax or other tax.

A *poll tax* is a tax on voters. This amendment bans poll taxes in national elections. Some states used poll taxes to keep blacks from voting. In 1966, the Supreme Court struck down poll taxes in state elections, also.

Congress can pass laws to carry out this amendment.

Section 2. Enforcement The Congress shall have the power to enforce this article by appropriate legislation.

Amendment 25

Presidential Succession and Disability

Passed by Congress on July 6, 1965. Ratified on February 11, 1967.

Section 1. President's Death or Resignation In case of the removal of the President from office or his death or resignation, the Vice-President shall become President.

If the President dies or resigns, the Vice President becomes President. This section clarifies Article 2, Section 1, Clause 6.

When a Vice President takes over the office of President, he or she appoints a Vice President who must be approved by a majority vote of both houses of Congress. This section was first applied after Vice President Spiro Agnew resigned in 1973. President Richard Nixon appointed Gerald Ford as Vice President.

Section 2. Vacancies in Vice-Presidency Whenever there is a vacancy in the office of the Vice-President, the President shall nominate a Vice-President who shall take the office upon confirmation by a majority vote of both houses of Congress.

Section 3. Disability of the President Whenever the President transmits to the President *pro tempore* of the Senate and the Speaker of the House of Representatives his written declaration that he is unable to discharge the powers and duties of his office, and until he transmits to them a written declaration to the contrary, such powers and duties shall be discharged by the Vice-President as Acting President.

Section 4. Whenever the Vice-President and a majority of either the principal officers of the executive departments or of such other body as Congress may by law provide, transmit to the President *pro tempore* of the Senate and the Speaker of the House of Representatives their written declaration that the President is unable to discharge the powers and duties of his office, the Vice-President shall immediately assume the powers and duties of the office as Acting President.

Thereafter, when the President transmits to the President *pro tempore* of the Senate and the Speaker of the House of Representatives his written declaration that no inability exists, he shall resume the powers and duties of his office unless the Vice-President and a majority of either the principal officers of the executive department or of such other body as Congress may by law provide, transmit within four days to the President *as* of the Senate and the Speaker of the House of Representatives their written declaration that the President is unable to discharge the powers and duties of his office. Thereupon Congress shall decide the issue, assembling within 48 hours for that purpose if not in session. If the Congress, within 21 days after receipt of the latter written declaration, or, if Congress is not in session, within 21 days after Congress is required to assemble, determines by two-thirds vote of both houses that the President is unable to discharge the powers and duties of his office, the Vice-President shall continue to discharge the same as Acting President; otherwise, the President shall assume the powers and duties of his office.

If the President declares in writing that he or she is unable to perform the duties of office, the Vice President serves as Acting President until the President recovers.

Two Presidents, Woodrow Wilson and Dwight Eisenhower, have fallen gravely ill while in office. The Constitution contained no provision for this kind of emergency.
 Section 3 provided that the President can inform Congress that he or she is too sick to perform the duties of office. However, if the President is unconscious or refuses to admit to a disabling illness, Section 4 provides that the Vice President and Cabinet may declare the President disabled. The Vice President becomes Acting President until the President can return to the duties of office. In case of a disagreement between the President and the Vice President and Cabinet over the President's ability to perform the duties of office, Congress must decide the issue. A two-thirds vote of both houses is needed to decide that the President is disabled or unable to fulfill the duties of office.

Amendment 26

Voting Age

Passed by Congress on March 23, 1971. Ratified on July 1, 1971.

Section 1. Lowering of Voting Age The right of citizens of the United States, who are 18 years of age or older, to vote shall not be denied or abridged by the United States or any state on account of age.

Section 2. Enforcement The Congress shall have the power to enforce this article by appropriate legislation.

In 1970, Congress passed a law allowing 18-year-olds to vote. However, the Supreme Court decided that Congress could not set a minimum age for state elections. So this amendment was passed and ratified.

Congress can pass laws to carry out this amendment.

Amendment 27

Congressional Pay Increases

Proposed by Congress on September 25, 1789. Ratified on May 7, 1992.

No law varying the compensation for the services of the Senators and Representatives shall take effect, until an election of Representatives shall have intervened.

If members of Congress vote themselves a pay increase, it cannot go into effect until after the next congressional election.

Government, Citizenship, and the Constitution

1787–PRESENT

1 **Goals and Principles of the Constitution**
2 **How the Federal Government Works**
3 **Changing the Constitution**
4 **State and Local Governments**
5 **Rights and Responsibilities of Citizenship**

Constitution of the
United States

African American man
voting for the first time

1787

The Constitution is
written. It will serve
as the framework of
the United States
government up to
the present.

1830

In most states,
white men over
21 can vote.

1870

As a result of the
Fifteenth Amendment,
African American men
win the vote.

**AMERICAN
EVENTS**

1780 ★   ★ 1840   ★ 1900

**WORLD
EVENTS**

▲ **1791**
French constitution sets
up a limited monarchy.

▲ **1821**
Mexico wins independence
from Spain.

1893 ▲
New Zealand extends
the vote to women.

The Electoral College

To become President, a candidate must win the majority of electoral votes.

Washington (11)
Montana (3)
North Dakota (3)
Minnesota (10)
CANADA
Maine (4)
VT (3)
NH (4)
Oregon (7)
Idaho (4)
Wyoming (3)
South Dakota (3)
Wisconsin (10)
Michigan (17)
New York (31)
MA (12)
RI (4)
CT (7)
Nevada (5)
Utah (5)
Colorado (9)
Nebraska (5)
Iowa (7)
Illinois (21)
Indiana (11)
Ohio (20)
Pennsylvania (21)
NJ (15)
Delaware (3)
Washington, D.C. (3)
California (55)
Kansas (6)
Missouri (11)
Kentucky (8)
WV (5)
Virginia (13)
Maryland (10)
Arizona (10)
New Mexico (5)
Oklahoma (7)
Arkansas (6)
Tennessee (11)
North Carolina (15)
South Carolina (8)
PACIFIC OCEAN
Texas (34)
MS (6)
Alabama (9)
Georgia (15)
ATLANTIC OCEAN
MEXICO
Louisiana (9)
Florida (27)

Alaska (3)
Albers Equal-Area Projection
0   300   600 Miles
0   300   600 Kilometers
CANADA

Hawaii (4)
PACIFIC OCEAN
Mercator Projection
0   150   300 Miles
0   150   300 Kilometers

Albers Equal-Area Projection
0   250   500 Miles
0   250   500 Kilometers

Key

(25) Indicates number of electoral votes for the state

Women's suffrage banner

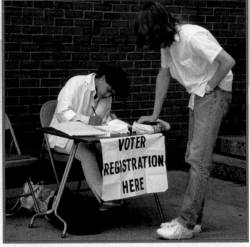

Voter registration drive

1920
The Nineteenth Amendment guarantees the right to vote to women.

1951
The Twenty-second Amendment limits the President to two terms.

1971
The Twenty-sixth Amendment extends the right to vote to Americans 18–21 years of age.

1900 · · · ★ · · · **1960** · · · ★ · · · **PRESENT** · · ·

1947 ▲
Japan adopts a democratic constitution.

1994 ▲
South Africa holds free multiracial elections.

1 Goals and Principles of the Constitution

Reading Focus

• How does the Preamble define the basic goals of the Constitution?

• What framework of government is established by the articles of the Constitution?

• What are the seven basic principles of American government?

Key Terms

Preamble

domestic tranquillity

civilian

general welfare

liberty

Articles

popular sovereignty

limited government

checks and balances

federalism

Taking Notes

Copy the concept web below. As you read, add ovals and fill them in with goals and principles of the Constitution.

Main Idea The goals and principles of the Constitution have guided the United States for more than 200 years.

Use Prior Knowledge Identify two branches of the federal government mentioned at right.

Setting the Scene

On Election Day, 2000, some 100 million Americans went to the polls to elect a new President. But they woke up the next morning to learn that the election was not over. Across the nation, the vote was split almost down the middle. Neither the Democratic candidate, Albert Gore, nor the Republican candidate, George W. Bush, had the 270 electoral votes needed to become President. The result would depend on the vote in Florida—a race that was too close to call!

For 36 days, Americans watched and argued as the candidates battled for Florida's 25 electoral votes. Teams of lawyers, local election officials, state legislators, and state and federal judges all became involved in the battle. At last, a ruling by the Supreme Court of the United States allowed Bush to claim victory. Gore offered his opponent best wishes for a successful presidency.

The election of 2000 raised some troubling issues. In the end, though, the election showed the strength of our constitutional system. The electoral battle was fierce but not violent. The candidates fought bitterly to win, but they fought in the courts, not in the streets. As in the past, in a time of crisis Americans relied on the system established by their Constitution.

The Preamble Sets Goals

The Constitution is divided into three main parts: the Preamble, or opening statement, the Articles, and the Amendments. The Preamble defines six goals:

“ We the people of the United States, in order to form a more perfect Union, establish justice, insure domestic tranquillity, provide for the common defense, promote the general welfare, and secure the blessings of liberty to

ourselves and our posterity, do ordain and establish this
Constitution for the United States of America. **"**

—Preamble to the Constitution

To Form a More Perfect Union When the Constitution was written, the states saw themselves almost as separate nations. The framers wanted to work together as a unified nation. Fortunately for us, they achieved this goal. Think of what it would be like if you had to exchange your money every time you visited another state!

To Establish Justice The framers knew the nation needed a uniform system to settle legal disputes. Today, the American justice system requires that the law be applied fairly to every American, regardless of race, religion, gender, or country of origin.

To Insure Domestic Tranquillity Under the Constitution, the national government has the power to insure domestic tranquillity, or peace and order at home. Have you seen reports of the National Guard providing assistance in a disaster area? By such actions, the government works to insure domestic tranquillity.

To Provide for the Common Defense Every country has a duty to protect its citizens against foreign attack. The framers of the Constitution gave the national government the power to raise armies and navies. At the same time, they placed the military under civilian, or nonmilitary, control.

To Promote the General Welfare The Constitution set out to give the national government the means to promote the general welfare, or the well-being of all its citizens. For example, today the National Institutes of Health leads the fight against many diseases.

To Secure the Blessings of Liberty During the Revolution, the colonists fought and died for liberty, or freedom. It is no surprise that the framers made liberty a major goal of the Constitution. Over the years, amendments to the Constitution have extended the "blessings of liberty" to more and more Americans.

Articles and Amendments

The main body of the Constitution is a short document, divided into seven sections called Articles. Together, they establish the framework for our government.

The Articles The first three Articles describe the three branches of the national government: legislative, executive, and judicial. Article I establishes the powers of and limits on Congress. Articles II and III do the same for the President and the courts.

Article IV deals with relations between the states. It requires states to honor one another's laws and legal decisions. It also sets out a system for admitting new states. Article V provides a process to amend the Constitution.

Article VI states that the Constitution is the "supreme law of the land." This means that states may not make laws that violate the Constitution. If a state law conflicts with a federal law, the federal

Viewing History

Working to Fulfill the Constitution

United States

Every day, hundreds of Americans like these work to fulfill the goals set out in the Constitution. **Applying Information** *Which of the goals set out in the Preamble is associated with each of the people shown here?*

System of Checks and Balances

Executive Branch
(President carries out laws)

Checks on the Legislative Branch
- Can propose laws
- Can veto laws
- Can call special sessions of Congress
- Makes appointments
- Negotiates foreign treaties

Checks on the Judicial Branch
- Appoints federal judges
- Can grant pardons to federal offenders

Legislative Branch
(Congress makes laws)

Checks on the Executive Branch
- Can override President's veto
- Confirms executive appointments
- Ratifies treaties
- Can declare war
- Appropriates money
- Can impeach and remove President

Checks on the Judicial Branch
- Creates lower federal courts
- Can impeach and remove judges
- Can propose amendments to overrule judicial decisions
- Approves appointments of federal judges

Judicial Branch
(Supreme Court interprets laws)

Check on the Executive Branch
- Can declare executive actions unconstitutional

Check on the Legislative Branch
- Can declare acts of Congress unconstitutional

CHART Skills

Through checks and balances, each branch of the government limits the power of the other two.

1. **Comprehension** Identify two ways in which the President can check Congress.

2. **Critical Thinking Ranking** What do you think is the most important check Congress has on the President? Explain.

Civics

 Monitor Your Reading Check to see whether you understand how the ideas of popular sovereignty and limited government differ from monarchy.

law prevails. The final article, Article VII, sets up a procedure for the states to ratify the Constitution.

Amendments In more than 200 years, only 27 formal changes have been made to the Constitution. The first ten amendments, known as the Bill of Rights, were added in 1791. In Section 3, you will read how other amendments have changed the working of the government or extended rights to more Americans.

Seven Basic Principles

The Constitution rests on seven basic principles. They are popular sovereignty, limited government, separation of powers, federalism, checks and balances, republicanism, and individual rights.

Popular Sovereignty The framers of the Constitution lived at a time when monarchs claimed that their power came from God. The Preamble, with its talk of "We the people," reflects a revolutionary new idea: that a government gets its authority from the people. This principle, known as popular sovereignty, states that the people have the right to alter or abolish their government.

Limited Government The colonists had lived under the harsh rule of a king. To avoid such tyranny in their new government, the framers made limited government a principle of the Constitution. In a limited government, the government has only the powers that the Constitution gives it. Just as important, everyone from you to the President must obey the law.

Separation of Powers To further limit government power, the framers provided for separation of powers. The Constitution divides the government into three branches. Congress, or the legislative branch, makes the laws. The executive branch, headed by the President, carries out the laws. The judicial branch, composed of the courts, explains and interprets the laws.

Checks and Balances A system of checks and balances safeguards against abuse of power. Each branch of government has the power to check, or limit, the actions of the other two. (You will read more about checks and balances in Section Two.)

Federalism The Constitution also establishes the principle of federalism, or division of power between the federal government and the states. Among the powers the Constitution gives the federal government are the power to coin money, declare war, and regulate trade between the states. States regulate trade within their own borders, make rules for state elections, and establish schools. Some powers are shared between the federal government and the states. (See the chart on page 235.) Powers not clearly given to the federal government belong to the states.

Republicanism The Constitution provides for a republican form of government. Instead of taking part directly in government, citizens elect representatives to carry out their will. Once in office, representatives vote according to their own judgment. However, they must remain open to the opinions of the people they represent. For that reason, members of Congress maintain offices in their home districts, and often Web sites as well.

Individual Rights The Constitution protects individual rights, such as freedom of speech, freedom of religion, and the right to trial by jury. You will read more about the rights protected by the Constitution later in this chapter.

Primary Source

Limits on Individual Rights

Although the Constitution protects individual rights, these rights are not unlimited. Here, Oliver Wendell Holmes, Jr., a justice of the Supreme Court, talks about the limits on free speech:

"The character of every act depends upon the circumstances in which it is done. The most [strict] protection of free speech would not protect a man in falsely shouting fire in a theatre and causing a panic. . . . The question in every case is whether the words used are used in such circumstances and are of such a nature as to create a clear and present danger that they will bring about the [real] evils that Congress has a right to prevent."

—Oliver Wendell Holmes, Jr., *Schenck* v. *United States,* 1919

Analyzing Primary Sources
What do you think Holmes meant by "a clear and present danger"?

Section 1 Assessment

Recall

1. **Identify** Explain the significance of **(a)** Preamble, **(b)** Articles.
2. **Define (a)** domestic tranquility, **(b)** civilian, **(c)** general welfare, **(d)** liberty, **(e)** popular sovereignty, **(f)** limited government, **(g)** checks and balances, **(h)** federalism.

Comprehension

3. Identify the six goals of the Constitution.
4. What system is established in Articles I, II, and III?

5. List the seven basic principles behind the Constitution.

Critical Thinking and Writing

6. **Exploring the Main Idea** Review the Main Idea statement at the beginning of this section. Then, choose three principles of the Constitution. Analyze the meaning of each, and list two ways in which you can see that principle at work today.
7. **Ranking** Which of the goals set out in the Preamble do you think is most important? Write a paragraph explaining why.

ACTIVITY

Designing a Poster
With a partner, design a poster as part of a display celebrating the Constitution. The poster should highlight one of the six goals or seven principles described in this section. Use a combination of words and pictures to create your poster.

2 How the Federal Government Works

BEFORE YOU READ

Reading Focus

- What are the powers of the legislative branch?
- What roles does the President fill as head of the executive branch?
- How is the judicial branch organized?
- How can each branch of the government check the powers of the other two?

Key Terms

House of Representatives
Senate
bill
electoral college
Supreme Court
appeal
unconstitutional
veto
override
impeach

Taking Notes

Copy the table below. As you read, complete the table with information about the three branches of the federal government.

LEGISLATIVE	EXECUTIVE	JUDICIAL
• Congress • Makes laws	• President •	• •

Main Idea The United States government is divided into three branches with separate roles and responsibilities.

AS YOU READ **Great Seal of the United States**

Draw Inferences Why do you think so many people want to watch the State of the Union Address?

Setting the Scene Tonight, the vast chamber of the House of Representatives is packed to capacity. Applause begins as the President of the United States enters the room and steps to the podium. Behind the President sit the Vice President and the Speaker of the House. In the audience are many of the most powerful people in the nation—members of Congress, justices of the Supreme Court, Cabinet secretaries. At home, millions of Americans tune in on their television sets to watch the event. The State of the Union Address is about to begin.

In delivering this speech each January, the President fulfills a duty spelled out in the Constitution: "He shall from time to time give to the Congress information of the state of the Union, and recommend to their consideration such measures as he shall judge necessary and expedient." The State of the Union Address also gives Americans a rare chance to see leaders of the legislative, executive, and judicial branches in one place at one time. Our government depends on these three branches working together.

The Legislative Branch

The first and longest article of the Constitution deals with the legislative, or lawmaking, branch. Article I sets up the Congress to make the nation's laws. Congress is made up of two bodies: the House of Representatives and the Senate.

House of Representatives The larger of the two bodies is the House of Representatives, which currently has 435 members. Representation in the House is based on population, with larger states having more representatives than smaller states. Every state has at least one representative.

Federal Officeholders

Office	Number	Term	Selection	Requirements
Representative	At least 1 per state; based on population	2 years	Elected by voters of congressional district	Age 25 or over Citizen for 7 years Resident of state in which elected
Senator	2 per state	6 years	Original Constitution—elected by state legislature Amendment 17—elected by voters	Age 30 or over Citizen for 9 years Resident of state in which elected
President and Vice President	1	4 years	Elected by electoral college	Age 35 or over Natural-born citizen Resident of United States for 14 years
Supreme Court Justice	9	Life	Appointed by President Approved by Senate	No requirements in Constitution

CHART
Skills

The Constitution details the length of term, method of selection, and requirements for officeholders in the three branches of government.

1. **Comprehension**
(a) At what age can you be elected to the Senate? The House of Representatives? (b) How long may a Supreme Court Justice remain in office?

2. **Critical Thinking**
Drawing Inferences
Why are the requirements for President and Vice President the same?

Civics

Representatives are elected by the people of their district for two-year terms. As a result, the entire House is up for election every other year. Representatives may run for reelection as many times as they want.

The leader of the House is called the Speaker. The Speaker of the House is one of the most powerful people in the federal government. The Speaker regulates debates and controls the agenda. If the President dies or leaves office, the Speaker of the House is next in line after the Vice President to become President.

The Senate Unlike the House, the Senate is based on equal representation, with two senators for each state. Senators are elected to six-year terms. Their terms overlap, however, so that one third of the members come up for election every two years. This way, there is always a majority of experienced senators.

Not all of the Founding Fathers trusted the judgment of the common people. As a result, they called for senators to be chosen by state legislatures. Over the years, the nation slowly became more democratic. The Seventeenth Amendment, ratified in 1913, provided that senators be directly elected by the people, like members of the House.

The Vice President of the United States is president of the Senate. The Vice President presides over the Senate and casts a vote when there is a tie. The Vice President cannot, however, take part in Senate debates. When the Vice President is absent, the president pro tempore, or temporary president, presides.

Powers of Congress The most important power of Congress is the power to make the nation's laws. All laws start as proposals called bills. A new bill may be introduced in either the House or the Senate. However, an appropriations bill, which is a bill designed to raise money for the government, must be introduced in the House. After a bill is introduced, it is debated. If both houses vote to approve the bill, it is then sent to the President, who must sign it before it becomes a law. (See the chart on page 226 to see the steps a bill must follow in order to become a law.)

The Constitution gives Congress many other powers besides law-making. Article I, Section 8, lists most of the powers of Congress. They include the power to levy, or collect, taxes and to borrow money. Congress also has the power to coin money, to establish post offices, to fix standard weights and measures, and to declare war.

The Elastic Clause Not all the powers of Congress are specifically listed. Article I, Section 8, Clause 18, states that Congress can "make all laws which shall be necessary and proper" for carrying out its specific duties. This clause is known as the elastic clause because it enables Congress to stretch its powers to deal with the changing needs of the nation.

Americans have long debated the true meaning of the elastic clause. What did the framers mean by the words *necessary* and *proper*? For example, early leaders debated whether the elastic clause gave Congress the right to set up a national bank, even though the Constitution does not specifically give Congress that power. Today, some Americans still worry that Congress might use the clause to abuse its powers.

Committees The first Congress, meeting from 1789 to 1791, considered a total of 31 new bills. Today, more than 10,000 bills are introduced in Congress each year. Clearly, it would be impossible for every member of Congress to give each new bill careful study. To deal with this problem, Congress relies on committees.

Both the House and the Senate have permanent, or standing, committees. Each committee deals with a specific topic, such as agriculture, banking, business, defense, education, science, or transportation. Members who have served in Congress the longest are usually appointed to the most important committees.

Congress may sometimes create joint committees made up of both Senate and House members. One of the most important kinds of joint committees is the conference committee. Its task is to settle differences between House and Senate versions of the same bill.

The Executive Branch

Article II of the Constitution sets up an executive branch to carry out the laws and run the affairs of the national government. The President is the head of the executive branch. Other members include the Vice President, the Cabinet, and the many departments and agencies that help them in their work.

Roles of the President You are probably more familiar with the President than with any other government leader. You see him on television climbing in and out of airplanes, greeting foreign leaders, or making speeches. Yet, many Americans do not know exactly what the President does.

AS YOU READ **Monitor Your Reading** The framers of the Constitution left a great deal of flexibility in many aspects of American government. As you read this page, look for two examples of constitutional flexibility.

The White House

No building is more a symbol of the United States than the White House, official home of the President. Originally called the "Presidential Palace," it got its white coat of paint after being burned during the War of 1812. Here, Presidents meet with leaders of Congress and host grand dinners for foreign leaders. The front lawn is also the site of an annual Easter egg roll for local children!

Take It to the NET

Virtual Field Trip For an interactive look at the White House, visit *The American Nation* section of **www.phschool.com**.

The framers thought that Congress would be the most important branch of government. Thus, while the Constitution is very specific about the role of the legislature, it offers fewer details about the powers of the President. Beginning with George Washington, Presidents have often taken those actions they thought necessary to carry out the job. In this way, they have shaped the job of President to meet the nation's changing needs.

The President is our highest elected official and, along with the Vice President, the only one who represents all Americans. As head of the executive branch, the President has the duty to carry out the nation's laws. The President directs foreign policy and has the power to make treaties with other nations and to appoint ambassadors.

The President is Commander in Chief of the armed forces. (Only Congress, however, has the power to declare war.) As the nation's chief legislator, the President suggests new laws and works for their passage. The President can grant pardons and call special sessions of Congress. The President is also the living symbol of the nation. Presidents welcome foreign leaders, make speeches to commemorate national holidays, and give medals to national heroes.

Electing the President The President is elected for a four-year term. As a result of the Twenty-second Amendment, adopted in 1951, no President may be elected to more than two complete terms.

The framers set up a complex system for electing the President, known as the electoral college. When Americans vote for President, they do not vote directly for the candidate of their choice. Rather, they

AS YOU READ **Draw Inferences** Why do you think the framers of the Constitution set a specific term of office for the President?

Federal Court System

United States Supreme Court

- Nation's highest court
- Reviews the decisions of lower courts
- Decides cases involving United States Constitution and federal laws

State Route

State Supreme Court
- Highest state court
- Hears appeals of appellate court cases

Appellate Court
- Hears appeals of trial court cases

Trial Court
- Handles civil and criminal cases
- Juries render verdicts based on evidence
- Judges enforce rules of procedure

Federal Route

Court of Appeals
- Hears appeals of cases originating in United States District Courts
- Can review decisions by federal administrative agencies

District Court
- Federal trial court
- Handles civil and criminal cases
- Juries render verdicts based on evidence
- Judges ensure fair trial

CHART *Skills*

Cases may come before the Supreme Court either through federal courts or through state courts.

1. **Comprehension** Describe the steps by which a case might travel from a state trial court to the Supreme Court.

2. **Critical Thinking Drawing Conclusions** Why do you think relatively few cases come before the Supreme Court?

Civics 🏛

vote for a group of electors who are pledged to the candidate. The number of a state's electors depends on the number of its Senators and Representatives. No state has fewer than three electors.

A few weeks after Election Day, the electors meet in each state to cast their votes for President. In most states, the candidate with the majority of the popular vote receives all that state's electoral votes. The candidate who receives a majority of the electoral votes nationwide becomes President.

Because of the "winner-take-all" nature of the electoral college, a candidate can lose the popular vote nationwide but still be elected President. This has happened four times. Today, some people favor replacing the electoral college with a system that directly elects the President by popular vote. Others oppose any change, pointing out that the system has served the nation well for over 200 years.

The Judicial Branch

The Constitution establishes a **Supreme Court** and authorizes Congress to establish any other courts that are needed. Under the Judiciary Act of 1789, Congress set up the system of federal courts that is still in place today.

Lower Courts Most federal cases begin in district courts. Evidence is presented during trials, and a jury or a judge decides the facts of the case. A party that disagrees with the decision of the judge or jury may **appeal** it, that is, ask that the decision be reviewed by a higher court. The next level of courts is the appellate court, or court of appeal. Appellate court judges review decisions of district courts to decide whether the lower court judges interpreted and applied the law correctly.

Supreme Court At the top of the American judicial system is the Supreme Court. The Court is made up of a Chief Justice and eight Associate Justices. The President appoints the justices, but Congress must approve the appointments. Justices serve for life.

The main job of the Supreme Court is to serve as the nation's final court of appeals. It hears cases that have been tried and appealed in lower courts. Because its decisions are final, the Supreme Court is called "the court of last resort."

The Supreme Court hears and decides fewer than 100 cases each year. Most of the cases are appeals from lower courts that involve federal laws. After hearing oral arguments, the justices vote. Decisions rest on a majority vote of at least five justices.

The greatest power of the Supreme Court is the power to decide what the Constitution means. In the words of Chief Justice Charles Evans Hughes, "The Constitution is what the judges say it is." Early on, the Court asserted the right to declare whether acts of the President or laws passed by Congress are **unconstitutional,** that is, not allowed under the Constitution.

Checks and Balances

The framers hoped that the separation of powers among three branches would prevent the rise of an all-powerful leader who would rob the people of their liberty. But how could the framers prevent one of the branches from abusing its power? To answer this problem, they set up a system of checks and balances.

The system of checks and balances allows each of the three branches of government to check, or limit, the power of the other two. The President, for example, can check the actions of Congress by **vetoing,** or rejecting, bills that Congress has passed. Congress can check the President by **overriding,** or overruling, the veto. Congress must also approve presidential appointments and ratify treaties made by the President. The Supreme Court can check both the President and Congress by declaring laws unconstitutional.

Congress's most extreme check on the President is its power to remove the President from office. To do this, the House of Representatives must **impeach,** or bring charges of serious wrongdoing against, the President. The Senate then conducts a trial. If two thirds of the senators vote to convict, the President must leave office. Throughout our history, only two Presidents—Andrew Johnson and Bill Clinton—have been impeached by the House. Neither was convicted by the Senate.

Section 2 Assessment

Recall

1. **Identify** Explain the significance of **(a)** House of Representatives, **(b)** Senate, **(c)** electoral college, **(d)** Supreme Court.
2. **Define** **(a)** bill, **(b)** appeal, **(c)** unconstitutional, **(d)** veto, **(e)** override, **(f)** impeach.

Comprehension

3. What is the most important power given to Congress?
4. Describe two powers or roles of the President.
5. What is the main job of the Supreme Court?
6. **(a)** Describe one way the President can check the power of Congress. **(b)** Describe one way Congress can check the power of the President.

Critical Thinking and Writing

7. **Exploring the Main Idea** Review the Main Idea statement at the beginning of this section. Then, write a paragraph summarizing the reasons that the Constitution separated the government into branches.
8. **Supporting a Point of View** Write a letter to the editor of your local newspaper explaining whether or not you think the electoral college should be retained.

ACTIVITY

Take It to the NET

Reviewing a Web Site Use the Internet to find the Web site of your own Senator or Representative. Write a review of the Web site describing the kind of information that is available and how useful it is. Visit *The American Nation* section of **www.phschool.com** for help in completing the activity.

Interpreting Bar and Line Graphs

Graphs are visual presentations of data organized so that you can see information at a glance. Two types of graphs that show changes over time are bar graphs and line graphs.

A bar graph shows statistics in the form of bars at regular time intervals.

A line graph shows statistics as connected points. The line that connects the points shows a pattern over time.

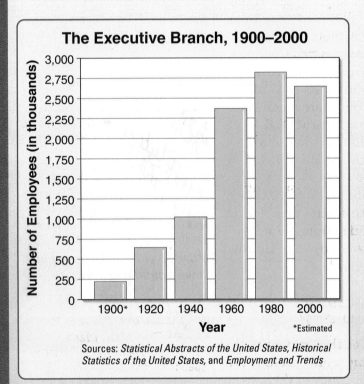

The Executive Branch, 1900–2000

Number of Employees (in thousands)

Year

*Estimated

Sources: *Statistical Abstracts of the United States, Historical Statistics of the United States,* and *Employment and Trends*

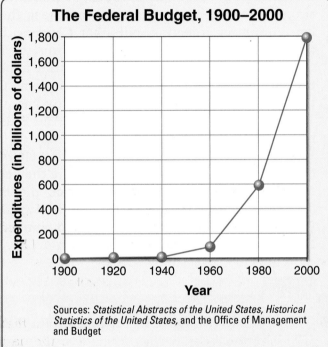

The Federal Budget, 1900–2000

Expenditures (in billions of dollars)

Year

Sources: *Statistical Abstracts of the United States, Historical Statistics of the United States,* and the Office of Management and Budget

Learn the Skill *To review how to read line and bar graphs, use the following steps:*

1. **Read the title.** The title identifies the basic information shown on a graph.

2. **Read the graph labels.** Both the horizontal axis and the vertical axis of a graph have labels that give more specific information about the data. When you read a graph, check the intervals between the dates or other statistics.

3. **Read the statistics on the graph.** Find the points where the horizontal axis meets the vertical axis.

4. **Interpret the statistics.** Draw conclusions or make predictions about the data given on the graph.

Practice the Skill *Use the graphs above to answer the following questions:*

1. **(a)** What is the subject of the bar graph? **(b)** What does the line graph show?

2. **(a)** What years do both graphs show? **(b)** Which graph shows the number of employees?

3. **(a)** In what year were there about one million employees in the executive branch? **(b)** What was the federal budget in 1960? **(c)** During what years did the budget increase the most?

4. Make one generalization about the federal government based on these two graphs.

Apply the Skill *See the Chapter Review and Assessment.*

3 Changing the Constitution

Reading Focus

- How can the Constitution be amended?
- What rights does the Bill of Rights protect?
- How did later amendments expand democratic rights?

Key Terms

First Amendment

Second Amendment

incriminate

civil

Civil War Amendments

Nineteenth Amendment

Twenty-sixth Amendment

Taking Notes

Copy this chart. As you read, fill in the boxes with information about constitutional amendments discussed in this section. The first box has been completed to help you get started. Add as many boxes as you need.

FIRST AMENDMENT
- Part of Bill of Rights
- Freedom of speech, religion, press

↓

↓

↓

↓

Main Idea The amendment process has made the Constitution a living document that reflects changing times.

Setting the Scene

"My faith in the Constitution is whole, it is complete, it is total." The speaker was Barbara Jordan, the first African American elected to Congress from Texas. In her rich voice, Jordan reminded her listeners of the first words of the Constitution:

> ❝ When that document was completed, on the seventeenth of September in 1787, I was not included in that *We, the people.* . . . But through the process of amendment, interpretation, and court decision I have finally been included in *We, the people.* ❞
>
> —Barbara Jordan, testimony before the House Judiciary Committee,
> July 25, 1974

AS YOU READ **Barbara Jordan**
Find Main Ideas
Restate the main idea of Jordan's speech in your own words.

Jordan lived in a different world from that of the framers of the Constitution. They did not know *how* the nation would change. But they knew it *would* change and that the Constitution would have to change with it. The formal amendment process that they designed has helped make the Constitution a living document.

The Amendment Process

The framers did not want to make it too easy for Americans to change the Constitution. As a result, they created a complex amendment process. (See the chart on the next page.) The process may take months, or even years, to complete.

Article V outlines two ways to propose an amendment. An amendment may be proposed by two thirds of both the House and the Senate, or by a national convention called by Congress at the request of two thirds of the state legislatures. The second method has never been used.

An amendment may also be ratified in one of two ways. An amendment may be approved by the legislatures of three fourths of

Methods of Amending the Constitution

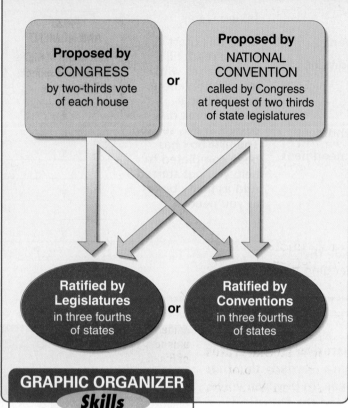

Proposed by CONGRESS by two-thirds vote of each house

or

Proposed by NATIONAL CONVENTION called by Congress at request of two thirds of state legislatures

Ratified by Legislatures in three fourths of states

or

Ratified by Conventions in three fourths of states

GRAPHIC ORGANIZER *Skills*

The amendment process requires two steps: proposal and ratification.

1. **Comprehension** **(a)** Can an amendment proposed by Congress be ratified by state conventions? **(b)** Can an amendment proposed by a national convention be ratified by state legislatures?

2. **Critical Thinking Evaluating Information** Which method of proposing an amendment seems more difficult? Explain.

Civics

---

the states. Every amendment but the Twenty-first was ratified using this method. In the second method, an amendment may be approved by special conventions in three fourths of the states.

The Bill of Rights

As one of its first acts, the new Congress drafted a series of amendments in 1789 and sent them to the states for approval. In 1791, the Bill of Rights, the first ten amendments, became part of the Constitution.

Protecting Individual Liberties The First Amendment safeguards basic individual liberties. It protects freedom of religion, speech, and the press. It also guarantees people the right to assemble peacefully and to petition the government to change its policies.

Because of the First Amendment, you cannot be arrested for criticizing a government official. You can attend the house of worship of your choice or none at all. You can read newspapers that do not represent the views of an official party. Still, there are limits on the First Amendment. For example, a newspaper cannot knowingly publish lies about someone.

Protecting Against Abuse of Power The next three amendments reflect the colonists' experiences under British rule. (See Chapter 5.) The Second Amendment states, "A well-regulated militia being necessary to the security of a free state, the right of the people to keep and bear arms shall not be infringed." The Third Amendment says that Congress may not force citizens to put up troops in their homes. The Fourth Amendment protects Americans from unlawful searches of home or property.

Since early times, Americans have debated the exact meaning of the Second Amendment. Some experts believe that it guarantees individuals a basic right to bear arms. Others argue that it simply guarantees the individual states the right to maintain a militia. Gun control is one of the most complex and controversial constitutional issues facing Americans today.

Protecting Rights of the Accused The Fifth through Eighth amendments deal with the rights of people accused of crimes. The Fifth Amendment states that people cannot be forced to incriminate, or give evidence against, themselves. The Sixth Amendment guarantees the right to a speedy and public trial by an impartial, or fair, jury. It also states that people accused of crimes have the right to know the charges against them, as well as the right to confront the person making the charges.

The Seventh Amendment provides for juries for civil, or non-criminal, trials. The Eighth Amendment forbids judges from ordering excessive bail or fines or "cruel and unusual punishments."

Amendments Nine and Ten Some Americans had opposed adding a Bill of Rights. They argued that, if specific rights were listed in the Constitution, Americans might lose other rights that were not listed. The Ninth Amendment solved that problem. It makes clear that a citizen's rights are not limited to those listed in the Constitution.

The Tenth Amendment reaffirmed the framers' plan to create a limited federal government. It states that all powers not given to the national government or denied to the states are reserved for the states or for the people.

Later Amendments

Since the addition of the Bill of Rights, the Constitution has been amended only 17 times. Many later amendments reflect changing attitudes about equality and the expansion of democracy.

The Thirteenth, Fourteenth, and Fifteenth amendments are known as the Civil War Amendments. The Thirteenth Amendment abolished slavery. The Fourteenth Amendment guaranteed citizenship to former slaves. The Fifteenth Amendment declared that states may not deny the vote to any citizen on the basis of "race, color, or previous condition of servitude." This guaranteed African American men the right to vote.

Other amendments further expanded voting rights. The Nineteenth Amendment, ratified in 1920, gave women the right to vote. Women achieved this victory after more than 70 years of struggle. In 1971, changing attitudes toward the rights and responsibilities of young people gave birth to the Twenty-sixth Amendment. It lowered the minimum voting age from 21 to 18.

AS YOU READ **Summarize** Write a few sentences summarizing some of the changes made by amendments passed after the Bill of Rights.

AFTER YOU READ

Section 3 Assessment

Recall
1. **Identify** Explain the significance of **(a)** First Amendment, **(b)** Second Amendment, **(c)** Civil War Amendments, **(d)** Nineteenth Amendment, **(e)** Twenty-sixth Amendment.
2. **Define** **(a)** incriminate, **(b)** civil.

Comprehension
3. How can an amendment to the Constitution be ratified?
4. Summarize the rights protected by the Bill of Rights.

5. How did later amendments reflect changing ideas about equality?

Critical Thinking and Writing
6. **Exploring the Main Idea** Review the Main Idea statement at the beginning of this section. Then, write a sentence giving your own definition of the term "living document."
7. **Drawing Conclusions** Why do you think the Bill of Rights carefully spells out the rights of people accused of crimes?

ACTIVITY

Prepare a Dialogue With a partner, act out a scene between two students. One of you is an American. The other has fled from a country that does not protect freedom of speech, the press, or religion. Discuss the importance of these freedoms to Americans.

4 State and Local Governments

BEFORE YOU READ

Reading Focus

- How are state constitutions similar to and different from the national Constitution?
- What services do state governments provide?
- How do local governments affect our daily lives?

Key Terms

constitutional initiative

infrastructure

local government

Taking Notes

Copy this incomplete Venn diagram. As you read, write key services provided by state and local governments. Include shared services in the overlapping section.

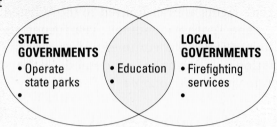

STATE GOVERNMENTS
- Operate state parks
-

• Education
•

LOCAL GOVERNMENTS
- Firefighting services
-

Main Idea State and local governments often play a more direct role in our daily lives than does the federal government.

AS YOU READ **Visitors to the Bronx Zoo**

Draw Inferences Why were the zoo program and the others described here handled by state and local governments rather than by the federal government?

Primary Sources

See "Three State Constitutions" on page 586 of the Reference Section.

Setting the Scene In the Bronx, New York, more families wanted to enjoy the area's most popular attraction: the Bronx Zoo, the largest zoo in the United States. A state senator introduced a law allowing local families free admission to the zoo one day a week.

In Oxnard, California, the Police Commissioner learned that 20 percent of all 9-1-1 emergency calls—many of them false alarms—were being made by children. To solve the problem, he got together with state education officials to create "9-1-1 for Kids." This program educates young children on what to do in a real emergency.

In Bexar County, Texas, parents needed help getting their children to school. Local officials banded together to start a program called SchoolPool. It identifies parents who live near one another and provides information about driving duties. Besides helping busy parents, the program reduced the number of cars on local roads.

When we hear the word *government,* most of us think first of the national government in Washington, D.C. Yet, day to day, state and local governments often have a more direct impact on our lives.

State Constitutions

The Constitution divides power between the federal government and the states. The federal government deals with national issues. The states have the power to meet more local needs.

A Frame of Government Each of the 50 states has a constitution that sets forth the principles and framework of its government. Although constitutions vary from state to state, they must all conform to the Constitution of the United States. If a conflict arises, the national Constitution—the "supreme law of the land"—prevails.

Most state constitutions resemble the national Constitution in form. They start with a preamble stating their goals and include a bill of rights guaranteeing individual liberties. State constitutions tend to be longer and more detailed than the national Constitution. Many include provisions on finance, education, and other matters.

State constitutions set up a government with three branches. The powers of the legislative, executive, and judicial branches on the state level are similar to those of the national government.

Changing Constitutions State constitutions can be changed in several ways. In the most common method, amendments are proposed by the state legislature and approved by the people in an election.

In almost one half of the states, citizens can act directly to change the constitution. In a process known as the constitutional initiative, sponsors of an amendment gather signatures on a petition. When the required number of signatures is attained, the petition goes to the legislature or to the voters for approval.

Finally, a state can rewrite its constitution. With the approval of the legislature or the people, the state may call a constitutional convention. The new constitution is then submitted to the people.

States Provide Services

State governments provide a wide range of services. They maintain law and order, enforce criminal law, protect property, and regulate business. They also supervise public education, provide public health and welfare programs, build and maintain highways, operate state parks and forests, and regulate use of state-owned land.

The states, not the federal government, have the main responsibility for public education in the United States. Most students attend schools paid for and overseen by the state. The state sets general standards for schools and establishes a recommended course of study. It also sets requirements for promotion and graduation.

Each state must build and maintain its own infrastructure, or system of roads, bridges, and tunnels. State departments or agencies manage more than 3,000 state parks and recreation areas. To help maintain high standards, state governments license the professionals who serve you, such as doctors, lawyers, and teachers. When you are old enough to drive, the state will test you and, if you pass, give you a license. State police keep highways safe and protect us against criminal acts.

Local Governments

The Constitution defines the powers of the federal and state governments. But it does not mention local government, that is, government on the county, parish, city, town, village, or district level. Local governments are created

Viewing History

Firefighter in Action

Maintaining fire departments is one of the responsibilities of local governments. Some communities hire professional firefighters. Others rely on highly trained volunteers. **Drawing Conclusions** *In addition to training, what other costs would be necessary for a community to support a fire department?*

TEST PREPARATION

Use the table **and** your knowledge of social studies to answer the following question.

Ratification of the Constitution

STATE	DATE	VOTE
Delaware	Dec. 7, 1787	30–9
Pennsylvania	Dec. 12, 1787	46–23
New Jersey	Dec. 18, 1787	38–0
Georgia	Jan. 2, 1788	26–0
Connecticut	Jan. 9, 1788	128–40
Massachusetts	Feb. 6, 1788	187–168
Maryland	Apr. 28, 1788	63–11
South Carolina	May 23, 1788	149–73
New Hampshire	June 21, 1788	57–47
Virginia	June 25, 1788	89–79
New York	July 26, 1788	30–27
North Carolina	Nov. 21, 1789	194–77
Rhode Island	May 29, 1790	34–32

1 Which conclusion about the ratification of the Constitution is supported by this table?

A Antifederalist influence was strong in Georgia.

B Federalists faced little opposition in New England.

C Antifederalist influence was stronger in New York than in New Jersey.

D The Constitution could go into effect by June 1, 1788.

2 Which statement best summarizes the main idea of Thomas Paine's *Common Sense*?

A The colonists must make one last effort to reconcile with the king.

B The best strategy for winning the war would be for Americans to seek help from France.

C At this time, Washington and the army need the full support of all Patriots.

D Separation from England is the most logical course for the American colonies.

3 How did the French and Indian War lead to the American Revolution?

A The British king encouraged colonists to settle on lands won from France.

B The British government taxed the colonists to help pay for the war.

C The French encouraged American colonists to seek independence from Britain.

D After the war, more British troops were permanently stationed in the colonies.

4 Which is not a power of Congress under the Constitution?

A Declaring war

B Ratifying constitutional amendments

C Removing a President from office

D Regulating foreign trade

Use the quotation **and** your knowledge of social studies to answer the following question.

Constitution of the United States, Article I, Section 1

"The House of Representatives shall be composed of members chosen every second year by the people of the several states. . . ."

---

5 Which principle of the Constitution is primarily reflected in the passage above?

A Republicanism

B Federalism

C Checks and balances

D Individual rights

6 In which of the following pairs was the first event an immediate cause of the second?

   A Intolerable Acts; Boston Tea Party

   B Battle of Saratoga; French aid to colonies

   C Declaration of Independence; Battle of Lexington

   D Stamp Act; Shays' Rebellion

Use the map <u>and</u> your knowledge of social studies to answer the following question.

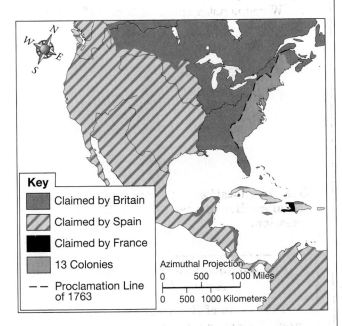

Key

- Claimed by Britain
- Claimed by Spain
- Claimed by France
- 13 Colonies
- – – Proclamation Line of 1763

Azimuthal Projection

0   500   1000 Miles

0   500 1000 Kilometers

7 How would a map showing the same area 10 years earlier have looked different?

   A The original 13 colonies would have taken up a larger area.

   B British land claims would have taken up a larger area.

   C French land claims would have taken up a larger area.

   D The map would have looked about the same.

8 Which of these grievances against England listed in the Declaration of Independence was later addressed in the Bill of Rights?

   A "... imposing taxes on us without our consent"

   B "... depriving us, in many cases, of the benefit of trial by jury"

   C "... cutting off our trade with all parts of the world"

   D "... suspending our own legislatures"

9 The dispute between large states and small states at the Constitutional Convention largely concerned what subject?

   A Legislative branch of government

   B Executive branch of government

   C Judicial branch of government

   D Checks and balances among the three branches of government

Writing Practice

10 Compare the advantages and disadvantages of the Americans and the British during the American Revolution. Then, explain why the United States won the war.

11 Choose one of the following principles of the Constitution: republicanism, checks and balances, federalism, separation of powers, popular sovereignty, or individual rights. Explain its meaning, why the framers valued that principle, and how it affects American government and society.

Unit 3

The Early Republic

Life on the Canals
The building of canals like the one shown in *Junction of the Erie and Northern (Champlain) Canals* by John Hill helped spur economic growth during the early 1800s.

"We have learned to love our country . . . because the sweat of our fathers' brows has subdued its soil . . . because it embraces our fathers and mothers."

—John Thornton Kirkland, Boston minister (1798)

Launching the New Government

1789–1800

1 Washington Takes Office
2 Creating a Foreign Policy
3 Political Parties Emerge
4 The Second President

Map of the new capital city

Washington's inaugural flag, 1789

Benjamin Banneker

1789

George Washington is inaugurated as the first President of the United States.

1791

Benjamin Banneker helps lay out the District of Columbia, the nation's new capital.

1793

Washington issues the Neutrality Proclamation to prevent the United States from being dragged into a European war.

AMERICAN EVENTS

Presidential Terms: George Washington 1789–1797

1788   **1791**   **1794**

WORLD EVENTS

▲ **1789**
The French Revolution begins.

1793 ▲
French radicals execute the king and queen of France.

Where Americans Lived, 1800

In the early years of the United States, most Americans lived along the eastern coastal plain.

BRITISH TERRITORY

Claimed by Great Britain and the United States

Maine (part of MA)

L. Superior
L. Michigan
L. Huron
L. Ontario
L. Erie

Mississippi R.
Missouri R.

VT
NH
MA
CT
RI

New York

Indiana Territory

Territory NW of the Ohio River

Pennsylvania

NJ
MD
DE

SPANISH LOUISIANA

Ohio R.

Virginia

Kentucky

Tennessee

North Carolina

South Carolina

ATLANTIC OCEAN

Territory claimed by Georgia until 1802

Georgia

Mississippi Territory

SPANISH FLORIDA

Key

Number of persons per square mile

- 90 or more
- 45–89
- 18–44
- 6–17
- 2–5
- Fewer than 2

Albers Equal-Area Projection

0   150   300 Miles
0   150   300 Kilometers

N
W   E
S

Washington reviewing troops during the Whiskey Rebellion

1794
Firm action by Washington puts down the Whiskey Rebellion on the frontier.

1796
Washington's Farewell Address lays out basic principles of American foreign policy.

1798
Congress passes the Alien and Sedition acts, which restrict entry of foreigners into the United States and limit freedom of speech.

John Adams   1797-1801

1794 · **1797** · **1800** ·

1796 ▲
Emperor Qianlong ends his 60-year reign in China by resigning from office.

1799 ▲
Napoleon Bonaparte seizes power in France.

1 Washington Takes Office

Reading Focus

- What steps did Washington take to make the new government work?
- What was Hamilton's plan to reduce the nation's debt and build the economy?
- What were the causes and results of the Whiskey Rebellion?

Key Terms

inauguration
precedent
Cabinet
Judiciary Act
national debt
bond
speculator
Bank of the United States
tariff
Whiskey Rebellion

Taking Notes

As you read, prepare an outline of this section. Use roman numerals to indicate the major headings, capital letters for the subheadings, and numbers for the supporting details. The sample at right will help you get started.

> I. Washington's First Steps
>   A. The first Cabinet
>   B.
> II. Reducing the Nation's Debt
>   A. Hamilton's plan
>   1.
>   2.
>   B.
>   C.
> III. Plans to Build the Economy
> IV.

Main Idea As the nation's first President, George Washington faced many challenges, including how to organize the new government and build a strong economy.

AS YOU READ

Washington's first inaugural

Use Prior Knowledge The first inauguration was a simple affair. How do you think Washington's desire for simplicity grew out of the experiences of Americans over the previous 30 years?

Setting the Scene

When the new Congress met in 1789, it debated a curious question. How should people address the President? Some members of Congress favored the simple title "President Washington." Others urged a more dignified title, such as "His Highness the President of the United States and Protector of the Rights of the Same."

Washington soon let Congress know that he preferred "President of the United States." By choosing that simple title, he rejected the grandeur and power linked to European monarchs. With that decision, as with many others, Washington set an example for later Presidents.

Washington's First Steps

George Washington was inaugurated in New York City on April 30, 1789. A presidential inauguration is the ceremony in which the President officially takes the oath of office. A witness reported that the new President looked "grave, almost to sadness." Washington, no doubt, felt a great burden. He knew that Americans were looking to him to make the new government work.

As the first President, Washington was setting an example for future generations. Although the Constitution provided a framework for the new government, it did not explain how the President should govern from day to day. "There is scarcely any part of my conduct," he said, "which may not hereafter be drawn into precedent." A precedent (PREHS uh dehnt) is an act or a decision that sets an example for others to follow.

Washington set an important precedent at the end of his second term. In 1796, he decided not to run for a third term. Not until 1940 did any President seek a third term.

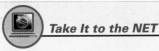

Mount Vernon, Virginia

Mount Vernon

Mount Vernon was George Washington's home for more than 45 years. He had a deep affection for the place. "I can truly say I had rather be at home at Mount Vernon with a friend or two about me than to be attended at the seat of the government by the officers of State and the representatives of every power in Europe." Today, more than a million people a year visit the estate.

Take It to the NET

Virtual Field Trip For an interactive look at Mount Vernon, visit *The American Nation* section of **www.phschool.com**.

The First Cabinet The Constitution said little about how the executive branch should be organized. It was clear, however, that the President needed talented people to help him carry out his duties.

In 1789, the first Congress created five executive departments. They were the departments of State, Treasury, and War and the offices of Attorney General and Postmaster General. The heads of these departments made up the President's Cabinet. Members of the Cabinet gave Washington advice and were responsible for directing their departments.

Washington set a precedent by choosing well-known leaders to serve in his Cabinet. The two most influential were the Secretary of State, Thomas Jefferson, and the Secretary of the Treasury, Alexander Hamilton.

The Federal Court System The Constitution called for a Supreme Court. Congress, however, had to set up the federal court system. In 1789, Congress passed the Judiciary Act. It called for the Supreme Court to consist of one Chief Justice and five Associate Justices.* Washington named John Jay the first Chief Justice of the United States.

The Judiciary Act also set up a system of district courts and circuit courts across the nation. Decisions made in these lower courts could be appealed to the Supreme Court, the highest court in the land.

---

*Today, the Supreme Court has a Chief Justice and eight Associate Justices.

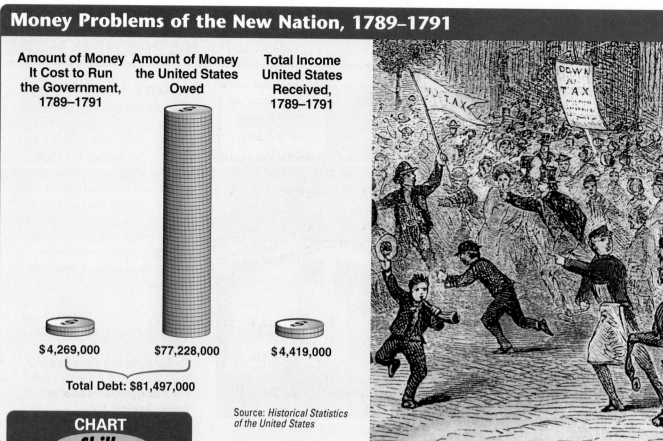

Money Problems of the New Nation, 1789–1791

Amount of Money It Cost to Run the Government, 1789–1791
$4,269,000

Amount of Money the United States Owed
$77,228,000

Total Debt: $81,497,000

Total Income United States Received, 1789–1791
$4,419,000

Source: *Historical Statistics of the United States*

CHART
Skills

The U.S. government had far greater expenses than income and desperately needed money. The solution: Congress raised taxes, which led to a rebellion on the frontier (right).

1. **Comprehension**
   (a) What was the government's total income between 1789 and 1791?
   (b) What were its total expenses during that period?

2. **Critical Thinking**
   Applying Information Does the chart provide information suggesting the government should raise or lower taxes? Explain.

Economics $

Reducing the Nation's Debt

As Secretary of the Treasury, Alexander Hamilton faced many problems. Among the most pressing was the large national debt. The national debt is the total amount of money that a government owes to others.

During the Revolution, both the national government and individual states had desperately needed money. They had borrowed heavily from foreign countries and ordinary citizens to pay soldiers and buy supplies. Then, as now, governments borrowed money by issuing bonds. A bond is a certificate that promises to repay the money loaned, plus interest, on a certain date. For example, if a person pays $100 for a bond, the government agrees to pay back $100 plus interest by a certain time.

Hamilton's Plan Hamilton called for the government to repay both federal and state debts. He wanted the government to buy up all the bonds issued by both the national and state governments before 1789. He then planned to issue new bonds to pay off the old debts. As the economy improved, the government would then be able to pay off the new bonds. Many people, including bankers and investors, welcomed Hamilton's plan. Others attacked it.

Debating Hamilton's Plan James Madison led the opposition. Madison argued that Hamilton's plan would reward speculators. A speculator is someone who invests in a risky venture in the hope of making a large profit.

During the Revolution, the government had issued bonds to soldiers and citizens who supplied goods. Many of these bondholders needed cash to survive. So, they sold their bonds to speculators. Speculators bought bonds worth one dollar for only 10 or 15 cents. If the government paid off the old bonds in full, speculators stood to make fortunes. Madison thought that speculators did not deserve to make such profits.

Hamilton replied that the United States must repay its debts in full. Otherwise, he said, it risked losing the trust of investors in the future. The support of investors, he argued, was crucial to building the new nation's economy. After much debate, Congress approved full repayment of the national debt.

As a southerner, James Madison also led the fight against the other part of Hamilton's plan, the repaying of state debts. By 1789, most southern states had paid off their debts from the Revolution. They thought that other states should do the same. As a result, they bitterly opposed Hamilton's plan.

Hamilton's Compromise In the end, Hamilton proposed a compromise. Many southerners wanted the nation's capital to be located in the South. Hamilton offered to support that goal if southerners agreed to his plan to repay state debts.

Madison and others accepted the compromise. In July 1790, Congress voted to repay state debts and to build a new capital city. The new capital would not be part of any state. Instead, it would be built on land along the Potomac River between Virginia and Maryland. Congress called the area the District of Columbia. Today, it is known as Washington, D.C. Plans called for the new capital to be ready by 1800. Meanwhile, the nation's capital was moved from New York to Philadelphia.

Plans to Build the Economy

Hamilton's next challenge was to strengthen the faltering national economy. His economic plan was designed to help both agriculture and industry.

Hamilton called on Congress to set up a national bank. In 1791, Congress created the Bank of the United States. The government deposited money from taxes in the Bank. In turn, the Bank issued paper money to pay the government's bills and to make loans to farmers and businesses. Through these loans, the Bank encouraged economic growth.

To help American manufacturers, Hamilton asked Congress to pass a tariff, or tax, on foreign goods brought into the country. He wanted a high tariff, to make imported goods more expensive than American-made goods. A tariff meant to protect local industry from foreign competition is called a protective tariff.

In the North, where there were more and more factories, many people supported Hamilton's plan. Southern farmers, however, bought many imported goods. They opposed a protective tariff that would make imports more expensive.

In the end, Congress did pass a tariff, but it was much lower than the protective tariff Hamilton wanted.

The Whiskey Rebellion

To raise money for the Treasury, Congress approved a tax on all liquor made and sold in the United States. Hamilton wanted this tax to raise money for the Treasury. Instead, the new tax sparked a rebellion that tested the strength of the new government.

A Hated Tax Like many Americans, backcountry farmers grew corn. However, corn was bulky and hard to haul over rough roads. Instead, farmers converted their corn into whiskey. Barrels of whiskey could be shipped more easily to markets in the East.

Backcountry farmers hated the tax on whiskey. Many refused to pay it. They compared it to the taxes Britain had forced on the colonies.

In 1794, when officials in western Pennsylvania tried to collect the tax, farmers rebelled. Thousands marched in protest through the streets of Pittsburgh. They sang Revolutionary songs and tarred and feathered the tax collectors.

A Show of Strength Washington responded quickly. He called up the militia and dispatched them to Pennsylvania. When the rebels heard that thousands of troops were marching against them, they fled back to their farms. Hamilton wanted the leaders of the rebellion executed, but Washington disagreed and pardoned them. He believed that the government had shown its strength to all. Now, it was time to show mercy.

The Whiskey Rebellion tested the will of the new government. Washington's quick response proved to Americans that their new government would act firmly in times of crisis. The President also showed those who disagreed with the government that violence would not be tolerated.

Section 1 Assessment

Recall

1. **Identify** Explain the significance of **(a)** Judiciary Act, **(b)** Bank of the United States, **(c)** Whiskey Rebellion.
2. **Define** **(a)** inauguration, **(b)** precedent, **(c)** Cabinet, **(d)** national debt, **(e)** bond, **(f)** speculator, **(g)** tariff.

Comprehension

3. Describe two steps that George Washington took as President to organize the new government.
4. What were three features of Alexander Hamilton's plan to lower the national debt and strengthen the economy?

5. How did the Whiskey Rebellion reveal George Washington's concern with national security?

Critical Thinking and Writing

6. **Exploring the Main Idea** Review the Main Idea statement at the beginning of this section. Then, write five statements of fact that support the main idea.
7. **Supporting a Point of View** Hamilton and Madison disagreed about paying off bonds issued during the Revolution. Suppose that you had to defend one side. Write a statement explaining which side you support in that debate and why.

ACTIVITY

Take It to the NET
Connecting to Today
Use the Internet to find the names of the current Cabinet departments and the person who runs each today. Make a chart listing each department and its head. Then, summarize its main functions. Visit *The American Nation* section of **www.phschool.com** for help in completing the activity.

EARLY AMERICAN *Folk Art*

Early American folk artists were rarely trained in art. They were usually house painters, carpenters, cabinetmakers, blacksmiths, sailors, farmers, and homemakers. They believed that what they were creating would be used, not left to sit in museums.

Whirligigs, or wind toys, were made as outdoor decorations, usually carved of wood. The wind caused the arms of a whirligig, such as those of this swordsman from the 1800s, to turn.

This 1730 painting of a child named Susanna Truax was created by an unknown artist who painted it on a mattress cover.

Shipping was an important industry in the new nation, and ship carvers created figureheads and other parts of a ship. This figurehead was carved in the early 1800s, probably for a small ship.

Early Americans used much imagination in creating weather vanes. This "trumpeting angel" weather vane was made of sheet iron around 1800.

ACTIVITY

Design your own piece of folk art. Think of an object that you see or use every day—a storage chest, a pencil sharpener, a tablecloth, or some other object. Then, sketch a design for it that expresses some emotion or patriotic feeling.

2 Creating a Foreign Policy

Reading Focus

- How was American opinion divided over the French Revolution?
- Why did Washington want the nation to remain neutral in foreign affairs?
- Why was it difficult for the United States to remain neutral?

Key Terms

French Revolution

foreign policy

neutral

Neutrality Proclamation

Jay's Treaty

Farewell Address

Taking Notes

Copy the concept web below. As you read, fill in each blank oval with events and developments that affected President Washington's foreign policy. Add as many ovals as you need.

French Revolution — Old treaty with France — WASHINGTON'S FOREIGN POLICY — Neutrality Proclamation

Main Idea As the French Revolution and wars raged in Europe, President Washington steered a neutral course in foreign affairs.

The guillotine: death machine of the French Revolution

Use Prior Knowledge How did the level of violence against ordinary citizens of the French Revolution compare with what happened to ordinary citizens during the American Revolution?

Setting the Scene Late in 1789, French ships arrived in American ports with startling news. On July 14, an angry mob in Paris, France, had destroyed the Bastille (bahs TEEL), an ancient fort that was used as a prison. The attack on the Bastille was an early event in the French Revolution. Before long, the revolution would topple the monarch and lead to the execution of thousands of ordinary French citizens.

The French Revolution broke out a few years after Americans had won their independence. Like Americans, the French fought for liberty and equality. As the French Revolution grew more violent, however, it deepened political divisions within the United States.

Responses to the French Revolution

The French had many reasons to rebel against their king, Louis XVI. The peasants and the middle class paid heavy taxes, while nobles paid none. Reformers wanted a constitution to limit the king's power and protect basic rights, as the American Constitution did.

American Support At first, most Americans supported the French Revolution. They knew what it meant to struggle for liberty. Then, too, France had been their first ally. Also, many Americans admired the Marquis de Lafayette, a leading French reformer, who had fought with them in the American Revolution.

In 1793, however, the French Revolution turned more and more violent. Radical reformers gained power. They beheaded the king and later the queen. During the Reign of Terror, tens of thousands of ordinary French citizens were executed.

Violence Stirs Division The violence in France divided Americans. Some, like Thomas Jefferson, continued to support the French. He condemned the executions of the king and queen. Still, he felt that the French had the right to use violence to win freedom.

Alexander Hamilton, John Adams, and others strongly disagreed. One could no more create democracy through widespread violence, claimed Adams, "than a snowball can exist in the streets of Philadelphia under a burning sun."

The United States Remains Neutral

The French Revolution frightened most European rulers and nobles. They wanted to prevent revolutionary ideas from spreading to their lands. Europe was soon plunged into a string of wars that lasted on and off for more than 20 years.

A Difficult Decision Faced with war in Europe, President Washington had to decide on a foreign policy. Foreign policy refers to the actions that a nation takes in relation to other nations. During the American Revolution, the United States and France had signed a treaty that made the two countries allies. Now, France wanted to use American ports to supply its ships and launch attacks on British ships. Washington worried that the United States could not honor its treaty with France and still remain neutral in the European conflict. Neutral means not taking sides in a conflict.

Divisions in the Cabinet The issue of the treaty deepened the divisions within Washington's Cabinet. Hamilton pointed out that the United States had signed the treaty with Louis XVI. With the king dead, he argued, the treaty was no longer valid. Jefferson, a supporter of France, urged strict acceptance of the treaty.

After much debate, Washington issued the Neutrality Proclamation in April 1793. It stated that the United States would not support either side in the war. Further, it forbade Americans from aiding either Britain or France.

The Neutrality Proclamation was a defeat for Jefferson. This and other defeats eventually led Jefferson to leave the Cabinet.

Viewing History

On the March

At the start of the French Revolution, famine gripped Paris. Thousands of angry women marched on the palace of the king shouting "Bread, Bread." **Drawing Conclusions** *Why might women such as these expect Americans to support their revolution?*

Struggling to Remain Neutral

Declaring neutrality was easier than enforcing it. Americans wanted to trade with both Britain and France. However, those warring nations seized American cargoes headed for each other's ports.

Jay's Treaty In 1793, the British captured more than 250 American ships trading in the French West Indies. Some Americans called for war. Washington, however, knew that the United States was too weak to fight. He sent Chief Justice John Jay to Britain for talks.

Jay negotiated an agreement that called for Britain to pay damages for the seized American ships. Britain also agreed to give up the forts it still held in the West. Meanwhile, Americans had to pay debts long owed to British merchants.

Jay's Treaty sparked loud protests because it did nothing to protect the rights of neutral American ships. After furious debate, the Senate finally approved the treaty in 1795.

Washington Retires Before retiring in 1796, George Washington published his Farewell Address. In it, he advised Americans against becoming involved in European affairs:

Primary Sources

See George Washington, "Farewell Address," on page 588 of the Reference Section.

> 66 Tis our true policy to steer clear of permanent Alliances, with any portion of the foreign World. . . . The great rule of conduct for us, in regard to foreign nations is . . . to have with them as little political connection as possible. 99
>
> —George Washington, Farewell Address, 1796

Washington did not oppose foreign trade, but he did reject alliances that could drag the country into war. His advice guided American foreign policy for many years.

Section 2 Assessment

Recall

1. **Identify** Explain the significance of (a) French Revolution, (b) Neutrality Proclamation, (c) Jay's Treaty, (d) Farewell Address.
2. **Define** (a) foreign policy, (b) neutral.

Comprehension

3. Why did the French Revolution divide Americans?
4. Describe two actions that Washington took to avoid war.
5. What problems did the United States have remaining neutral when France and Britain went to war?

Critical Thinking and Writing

6. **Finding the Main Idea** Review the Main Idea statement at the beginning of this section. Then, list two threats to American neutrality during the 1790s. Explain how Washington responded to each.
7. **Identifying Points of View** Writing about the French Revolution, Thomas Jefferson said that he was willing to see "half the earth devastated" in order to win the "liberty of the whole." (a) Restate Jefferson's main idea in your own words. (b) What does this idea tell you about Jefferson's values?

ACTIVITY

Giving an Introduction
President Washington has decided to give his Farewell Address in your school auditorium. You have been asked to introduce him. Prepare a two-minute introduction, mentioning what you consider to be Washington's greatest achievements.

3 Political Parties Emerge

BEFORE YOU READ

Reading Focus

- Why did many Americans distrust the idea of political parties?
- How did the views of Hamilton and Jefferson differ?
- Why did political parties develop?
- How did the election of 1796 increase political tensions?

Key Terms

faction

unconstitutional

Democratic Republican

Federalist

Taking Notes

Copy the table below. As you read, fill in each column with the views of Hamilton and Jefferson. Add as many rows as you need.

HAMILTON'S VIEWS	JEFFERSON'S VIEWS
• Admired British economy; favored manufacturing, trade, cities	•
•	• Wanted to keep federal government small
•	•

Main Idea During the 1790s, two political parties were formed: the Federalists and the Republicans.

Setting the Scene When George Washington took office in 1789, the United States had no political parties. In fact, most American leaders disliked even the idea of parties. "If I could not go to heaven but with a party," said Thomas Jefferson, "I would not go at all."

Early on, though, political disagreements divided Americans. "Men who have been [friends] all their lives," noted Jefferson, "cross streets to avoid meeting, and turn their heads another way, lest they should be obliged to touch their hats." Before Washington left office in 1797, two rival political parties had emerged to compete for power.

AS YOU READ
E pluribus unum
Find Main Ideas Did the development of political parties go against the motto of the new nation, *E pluribus unum* ("Out of many, one")?

A Distrust of Political Parties

Americans had reason to distrust political parties. They had seen how **factions,** or opposing groups within parties, worked in Britain. There, members of factions often plotted to win government favors and bribes. Many were more interested in personal gain than in the public good.

Americans also saw political parties as a threat to national unity. They agreed with George Washington, who warned Americans that parties would lead to "jealousies and false alarms."

Despite the President's warning, factions grew up around two members of his Cabinet, Alexander Hamilton and Thomas Jefferson. The two men differed in background, looks, and personality as well as in politics. Born in the West Indies, Hamilton had worked his way up from poverty. He dressed in fine clothes and spoke forcefully. Energetic, brilliant, and restless, Hamilton enjoyed political debate.

Jefferson was tall and lanky. Although he was a wealthy Virginia planter, he dressed and spoke informally. One senator recalled:

66 His clothes seem too small for him. He sits in a lounging manner, on one hip commonly, and with one of his shoulders elevated much above the other. His face has a sunny aspect. His whole figure has a loose, shackling air. . . . [His conversation] was loose and rambling; and yet he scattered information wherever he went. 99

—The Diary of William Maclay and Other Notes on Senate Debates

Differing Views

Hamilton and Jefferson disagreed on many issues. Their quarrels were rooted in their different views about what was best for the new nation.

Manufacturing or Farming The two leaders differed on economic policy. Hamilton wanted the United States to model itself on Britain. The government, he thought, should encourage manufacturing and trade. He also favored the growth of cities and the merchant class.

Jefferson thought that farmers, rather than merchants, were the backbone of the new nation. "Cultivators of the earth," he wrote, "are the most valuable citizens." He feared that a manufacturing economy would corrupt the United States by concentrating power in the hands of a small group of wealthy Americans.

Federal or State Power Hamilton and Jefferson also disagreed about the power of the federal government. Hamilton wanted the federal government to have greater power than state governments. A strong federal government, he argued, was needed to increase commerce. It would also be able to restrain mob violence like that of the Whiskey Rebellion.

In contrast, Jefferson wanted as small a federal government as possible, in order to protect individual freedom. He feared that a strong federal government might take over powers that the Constitution gave to the states.

Strict or Loose Interpretation of the Constitution Jefferson and Hamilton also clashed over the Bank of the United States. Jefferson worried that a national bank would give too much power to wealthy investors who would help run it and to the government.

Jefferson opposed the law setting up the bank. He claimed that it was **unconstitutional,** or not permitted by the Constitution. Nowhere did the Constitution give Congress the power to create a Bank, he argued. For Jefferson, any power not specifically given to the federal government belonged to the states.

Hamilton did not agree with Jefferson's strict interpretation of the Constitution. He preferred a looser interpretation. The Constitution gave Congress the power to make all laws "necessary and proper" to carry out its duties. Hamilton argued that the Bank was necessary for the government to collect taxes and pay its bills.

Federalists vs. Republicans

FEDERALISTS	REPUBLICANS
1 Were led by Alexander Hamilton	1 Were led by Thomas Jefferson
2 Believed wealthy and well educated should lead nation	2 Believed people should have political power
3 Favored strong central government	3 Favored strong state governments
4 Emphasized manufacturing, shipping, and trade	4 Emphasized agriculture
5 Favored loose interpretation of Constitution	5 Favored strict interpretation of Constitution
6 Were pro-British	6 Were pro-French
7 Favored national bank	7 Opposed national bank
8 Favored protective tariff	8 Opposed protective tariff

VS.

GRAPHIC ORGANIZER
Skills

By the late 1790s, there were two political parties in the United States: the Federalist party and the Republican party.

1. **Comprehension** Describe two ways in which the Republicans and the Federalists differed on economic issues.

2. **Critical Thinking Analyzing Primary Sources** "The average person is far too ignorant to make wise political decisions." Do you think a Republican or a Federalist would be more likely to agree with this statement? Explain your answer.

Civics

Britain or France Finally, the two leaders disagreed over foreign policy. Hamilton wanted close ties with Britain, a major trading partner. Jefferson favored France, the first ally of the United States.

Development of Political Parties

At first, Hamilton and Jefferson clashed in private. Then, as Congress began to pass many of Hamilton's programs, Jefferson and James Madison decided to organize supporters of their views.

The two men moved cautiously at first. In 1791, they went to New York, telling people that they wanted to study its wildlife. In fact, Jefferson was interested in nature. Their main goal, though, was to meet with leading New York politicians like Governor George Clinton and Aaron Burr, a fierce critic of Hamilton. Jefferson asked them to help defeat Hamilton's program by convincing New Yorkers to vote for Jefferson's supporters.

Republicans and Federalists Soon, leaders in other states were organizing to support either Hamilton or Jefferson. Jefferson's supporters called themselves Democratic Republicans, often shortened to Republicans.* This group included small farmers, artisans, and some wealthy planters.

Hamilton and his supporters were called Federalists because they wanted a strong federal government. Federalists drew support mainly from merchants and manufacturers in such cities as Boston and New York. They also had the backing of some southern planters.

Newspapers Take Sides In the late 1700s, the number of American newspapers more than doubled. This growth met a

AS YOU READ **Monitor Your Reading** As you read, check to see if you understand the major differences between the Republicans and the Federalists.

---

*Jefferson's Republican party was not the same as today's Republican party. In fact, his party later grew into the Democratic party.

demand for information. A European visitor was surprised that so many Americans could read. "The common people . . . all read and write, and understand arithmetic," he reported, and "almost every little town now furnishes a circulating library."

As party rivalry grew, newspapers took sides. In the *Gazette of the United States,* publisher John Fenno backed Hamilton and the Federalists. Jefferson's friend Philip Freneau (frih NOH) started a rival paper, the *National Gazette,* which supported Republicans.

Newspapers had great influence on public opinion. In stinging language, they raged against political opponents. Often, articles mixed rumor and opinion with facts. Emotional attacks and counter-attacks fanned the flames of party rivalry.

Election of 1796

Political parties played a large role in the election of George Washington's successor. In 1796, Republicans backed Thomas Jefferson for President and Aaron Burr for Vice President. Federalists supported John Adams for President and Thomas Pinckney for Vice President.

The election had an unexpected outcome. Under the Constitution, the person with the most electoral votes became President. The candidate with the next highest total was made Vice President. John Adams, a Federalist, won office as President. The leader of the Republicans, Thomas Jefferson, came in second and became Vice President.

Having the President and Vice President from opposing parties further increased political tensions. John Adams took office in March 1797 as the nation's second President. Events soon deepened the distrust between him and Jefferson.

Section 3 Assessment

Recall

1. **Identify** Explain the significance of **(a)** Democratic Republican, **(b)** Federalist.
2. **Define (a)** faction, **(b)** unconstitutional.

Comprehension

3. What reasons did Americans have to distrust political parties?
4. List two issues on which Thomas Jefferson and Alexander Hamilton disagreed and describe their points of view.
5. Explain why political parties emerged in the 1790s.
6. What role did political parties play in the election of 1796?

Critical Thinking and Writing

7. **Exploring the Main Idea** Review the Main Idea statement at the beginning of this section. Then, write a letter to the editor supporting either the Republicans or the Federalists in the election of 1796.
8. **Supporting a Point of View** Whose political ideas do you favor, Jefferson's or Hamilton's? Explain your answer.

ACTIVITY

Writing Newspaper Headlines You are the publisher of either the *Gazette of the United States* or the *National Gazette.* Write three headlines about the election of 1796. Be sure that your headlines express the point of view of your newspaper.

4 The Second President

BEFORE YOU READ

Reading Focus

- How did John Adams handle the conflict with France?
- Why did the Federalist party split?
- How did the Alien and Sedition acts raise the issue of the rights of states?
- What role did Congress play in the election of 1800?

Key Terms

XYZ Affair
frigate
Alien and Sedition acts
sedition
nullify
Kentucky and Virginia resolutions
states' rights

Taking Notes

As you read, complete this table describing the major events of John Adams's presidency. Add as many rows as needed to complete the table.

CONFLICT WITH FRANCE	ALIEN AND SEDITION ACTS	ELECTION OF 1800
• French seize U.S. ships	•	•

Main Idea As President, John Adams pursued policies that made the Federalists increasingly unpopular.

Setting the Scene John Adams was very different from George Washington. Washington was tall and dignified. Adams was short and a bit pudgy. Washington spoke little and chose his words carefully. Adams was outspoken. He said what he believed, and he held strong beliefs. Jefferson recalled how Adams sometimes became so angry during an argument that he ended up "dashing and trampling his wig on the floor."

Despite his temper, Adams was an honest and able leader. As President, he tried to act in the best interests of the nation, even when he knew his actions could hurt him politically. More than once, Adams stood up to public opinion or the leaders of his party.

Conflict With France

No sooner had Adams taken office than he faced a crisis with France. The French objected to Jay's Treaty because they felt that it favored Britain. In 1797, French ships began to seize American ships in the West Indies, as the British had done.

Once again, Americans called for war, this time against France. To avoid war, Adams sent diplomats to Paris to discuss the rights of neutral nations.

The French foreign minister, Charles Maurice de Talleyrand, did not deal directly with the Americans. Instead, he sent three agents to offer the Americans a deal. Before Talleyrand would even begin talks, the agents said, he wanted $250,000 for himself and a $10 million loan to France. "Not a sixpence!" replied one of the Americans angrily.

The diplomats informed Adams about the offer. He then told Congress. Adams did not reveal the names of the French agents, referring to them only as X, Y, and Z.

AS YOU READ **Adams as President**
Predict Based on the description of Adams at left, do you think he will have more or less trouble than Washington did in dealing with his opponents?

Many Americans were outraged when they heard about the XYZ Affair in 1798. They took up the slogan, "Millions for defense, but not one cent for tribute!" They were willing to spend money to defend their country, but they would not pay a bribe to another nation.

The XYZ Affair ignited war fever in the United States. Despite strong pressure, Adams refused to ask Congress to declare war on France. Like Washington, he wanted to keep the country out of European affairs. However, he could not ignore French attacks on American ships, so he strengthened the navy by building **frigates,** fast-sailing ships with many guns. That move helped convince France to stop attacking American ships.

The Federalist Party Splits

Led by Hamilton, many Federalists criticized Adams. They hoped a war would weaken the Republicans, who supported France. War would also force the nation to build its military forces. A strong military would increase federal power, a key Federalist goal.

Although Adams was a Federalist, he resisted Hamilton's pressure for war. Their disagreement created a split in the Federalist party.

Over Hamilton's opposition, Adams again sent diplomats to France. When they arrived, they found an ambitious young army officer, Napoleon Bonaparte, in charge. Napoleon was planning for war against several European powers. Thus, he had no time for a war with the United States. He signed an agreement to stop seizing American ships.

Like Washington, Adams kept the nation out of war. His success, however, cost him the support of many Federalists and weakened the party for the election of 1800.

Primary Sources

See Thomas Jefferson, "A Letter to John Adams, 1796," on page 589 of the Reference Section.

Alien and Sedition Acts

In 1798, during the crisis with France, Federalists pushed several laws through Congress. These laws were known as the **Alien and Sedition acts.**

Under the Alien Act, the President could expel any alien, or foreigner, thought to be dangerous to the country. Another law made it harder for immigrants to become citizens. Before 1798, white immigrants could become citizens after living in the United States for five years. The new law made immigrants wait 14 years. The Federalists passed this act because many recent immigrants supported Jefferson and the Republicans. The act would keep these immigrants from voting for years.

Republicans grew even angrier when Congress passed the Sedition Act. **Sedition** means stirring up rebellion against a government. Under this law, citizens could be fined or jailed if they criticized the government or its officials. In fact, several Republican newspaper editors, and even members of Congress, were fined and jailed for expressing their opinions.

Republicans protested that the Sedition Act violated the Constitution. The First Amendment, they argued, protected freedom of speech and of the press. Jefferson warned that the new laws threatened American liberties:

> 66 They have brought into the lower house a sedition bill, which . . . undertakes to make printing certain matters criminal . . . Indeed this bill & the alien bill both are so [against] the Constitution as to show they mean to pay no respect to it. 99
>
> —*The Writings of Thomas Jefferson,* 1798

The Rights of States

Vice President Jefferson bitterly opposed the Alien and Sedition acts. He could not ask the courts for help because the Federalists controlled them. So, he urged the states to take strong action against the acts. He argued that the states had the right to **nullify,** or cancel, a law passed by the federal government. In this way, states could resist the power of the federal government.

With help from Jefferson and Madison, Kentucky and Virginia passed resolutions in 1798 and 1799. The **Kentucky and Virginia resolutions** claimed that each state "has an equal right to judge for itself" whether a law is constitutional. If a state decides a law is unconstitutional, said the resolutions, it has the power to nullify that law within its borders.

The Kentucky and Virginia resolutions raised the issue of **states' rights.** Did the federal government have only those powers that were listed in the Constitution? If so, the states possessed all other powers—for example, the power to declare a federal law unconstitutional? Within a few years, the Alien and Sedition acts were changed or dropped. Still, the issue of a state's right to nullify federal laws would come up again.

Primary Source

The Virginia Resolution

The Virginia Resolution was a protest against the Alien and Sedition acts passed by Congress: "[Virginia protests] against the . . . alarming infractions of the Constitution, . . . the first of which exercises a power no where delegated to the federal government, . . . and the other of which acts, exercises in like manner, a power which . . . [violates] that right of freely examining public characters and measures, and of free communication among the people . . . which has ever been justly deemed, the only [effective] guardian of every other right."

Analyzing Primary Sources
What right is "the only [effective] guardian of every other right"?

Election of 1800

By 1800, the war cry against France was fading. As the election neared, Republicans focused on two issues. First, they attacked the Federalists for raising taxes to prepare for war. Second, they opposed the unpopular Alien and Sedition acts.

Republicans backed Thomas Jefferson for President and Aaron Burr for Vice President. Despite the bitter split in the Federalist party, John Adams was again named its candidate.

Deadlock In the race for the presidency, Republicans won the popular vote. However, when the electoral college voted, Jefferson and Burr each received 73 votes. At the time, the electoral college did not vote separately for President and Vice President. Each Republican elector cast one vote for Jefferson and one vote for Burr.

Under the Constitution, if no candidate wins the electoral vote, the House of Representatives decides the election. Only after four days and 36 votes was the tie finally broken. The House chose Jefferson as President. Burr became Vice President.

Soon after, Congress passed the Twelfth Amendment. It required electors to vote separately for President and Vice President. The states ratified the amendment in 1804.

The election of 1800 set an important precedent. From then until today, power has passed peacefully from one party to another.

The Federalist Era Ends After 1800, the Federalist party slowly declined. Federalists won fewer seats in Congress. In 1804, the party was greatly weakened after its leader, Alexander Hamilton, was killed in a duel with Aaron Burr. Despite its early decline, the Federalist party did help shape the new nation. Even Republican Presidents kept most of Hamilton's economic programs.

 AS YOU READ **Draw Inferences** As you read, make an inference about the relations between Jefferson and Burr after the election.

 AFTER YOU READ ★ ★ **Section 4 Assessment** ★ ★ ★

Recall

1. **Identify** Explain the significance of (a) XYZ Affair, (b) Alien and Sedition acts, (c) Kentucky and Virginia resolutions.
2. **Define** (a) frigate, (b) sedition, (c) nullify, (d) states' rights.

Comprehension

3. How did President Adams deal with the French seizure of American ships?
4. Why did Adams lose the support of many Federalists?
5. Why did Thomas Jefferson and the Republicans oppose the Alien and Sedition acts?

6. Why did Congress have to settle the election of 1800?

Critical Thinking and Writing

7. **Finding the Main Idea** Review the Main Idea statement at the beginning of this section. Then, write a paragraph explaining why the Federalists lost popular support during Adams's presidency.
8. **Applying Information** How did the Kentucky and Virginia resolutions reflect Jefferson's view of government?

 ACTIVITY

Take It to the NET

Creating a Timeline Use the Internet to discover the many ways in which John Adams served his country. Use the information you find to make a timeline of Adams's life. Visit *The American Nation* section of **www.phschool.com** for help in completing the activity.

Drawing Inferences

As you study history, you are constantly interpreting what you read. Sometimes, you make *inferences*. This involves adding what you already know to ideas that are implied but not directly stated in the text. By making inferences, you can more fully understand what you read and can analyze different points of view.

Read this passage comparing John Adams with George Washington:

George Washington and John Adams were a study in contrasts. Washington was tall and dignified, and because he was a general, his officers addressed him as "Excellency." Adams was short and a bit pudgy. His rivals referred to him as "His Rotundity."

Washington spoke little and chose his words carefully, but John Adams could never do the same. He said what he believed, and he held strong beliefs. At times, his anger led him to trample his wig on the floor. Still, Adams was an honest and able leader who always tried to act in the nation's best interests.

Learn the Skill *To make inferences, use the following steps:*

1. **Identify main ideas.** What is the main point being made in the passage?

2. **Note stated facts and opinions.** What information is directly stated?

3. **Identify unstated ideas.** What ideas or information are suggested but not directly stated in the passage?

4. **Add what you know.** What details can you fill in from your own knowledge or experience to make inferences about the text?

5. **Identify the point of view.** Based on the inferences you made, what does the writer or speaker feel or believe about this topic?

Practice the Skill *Answer the following questions about the passage above:*

1. (a) How did his officers address Washington?
   (b) What did the rivals of Adams call him?

2. (a) Find a sentence that directly states a fact.
   (b) Find a sentence that directly states an opinion.

3. What does the passage suggest about how Adams was viewed by others?

4. How could always speaking one's mind create problems for a President?

5. What does the writer infer about Adams's leadership qualities?

Apply the Skill *See the Chapter Review and Assessment.*

Review and Assessment

CREATING A CHAPTER SUMMARY

On a sheet of paper, draw a chart like this one. Show the leading figures and challenges facing the first two Presidents of the United States as they launched the new government. Some information has been filled in to help you get started.

THE FIRST TWO PRESIDENTS

Leading Political Figures	Economic Issues	Foreign Policy Issues	Other Challenges
• Alexander Hamilton	•	• British seize U.S. ships	• Whiskey Rebellion
•	•	•	•
•	•	•	•

For additional review and enrichment activities, see the interactive version of *The American Nation*, available on the Web and on CD-ROM.

Take It to the NET

Chapter Self-Test For practice test questions for Chapter 9, visit *The American Nation* section of **www.phschool.com**.

Building Vocabulary

Use the chapter vocabulary words listed below to create a crossword puzzle. Exchange puzzles with a classmate. Complete the puzzles, and then check each other's answers.

1. inauguration
2. precedent
3. bond
4. tariff
5. foreign policy
6. faction
7. unconstitutional
8. frigate
9. sedition
10. nullify

Reviewing Key Facts

11. Describe how the Judiciary Act provided the framework for the nation's court system. (Section 1)
12. What advice did George Washington give in his Farewell Address? (Section 2)
13. Name three differences between the Federalists and the Republicans. (Section 3)
14. How did President Adams avoid war? (Section 4)
15. How was the Sedition Act used to silence Republicans? (Section 4)

Critical Thinking and Writing

16. **Connecting to Geography: Location**
(a) Describe the relative location of the United States in regard to Europe. (b) How did location help the United States "steer clear of permanent alliances" with European nations for many years? (c) How did location make the possession of a strong navy important to the United States?
17. **Summarizing** Summarize arguments for and against protective tariffs and a national banking system.
18. **Ranking** (a) List the disagreements that divided Jefferson and Hamilton. (b) In your opinion, which of these disagreements was the most serious? Explain.
19. **Analyzing Information** Write a paragraph explaining how the Twelfth Amendment helped prevent deadlocks like the one that took place in the election of 1800.

George Washington was the focus of attention when he arrived in New York in 1789 for his first inauguration.

20. Locate Washington. What is he doing?
21. What is the mood of the people greeting Washington?
22. How does the artist focus attention on Washington?
23. Why are inaugurations such important events in our history?

APPLYING YOUR SKILLS
Drawing Inferences

Read this passage from your textbook, and then answer the questions below:

> When George Washington took office in 1789, the United States had no political parties. . . . Early on, though, political disagreements divided Americans. "Men who have been [friends] all their lives," noted Jefferson, "cross streets to avoid meeting, and turn their heads another way, lest they should be obliged to touch their hats." Before Washington left office in 1797, two rival political parties had emerged. . . .

24. The author does not say why the men avoid meeting, but a reader can infer that
  A the men have quarreled over finances.
  B religion is starting to divide the nation.
  C old wounds from the American Revolution are still open.
  D the men support different political parties.
25. If the men were forced to meet, what do you think they would talk about? Explain your reasoning.

ACTIVITIES

Connecting With . . .
Government and Citizenship

Creating a Line Graph While John Adams was President, the United States strengthened its navy by training more sailors. The chart below shows the change in the number of people serving in the navy. **(a)** Use the data to describe what happened to the United States Navy between 1798 and 1801. **(b)** Use the figures below to create a line graph.

YEAR	NUMBER OF PEOPLE
1798	1,856
1799	2,200
1800	5,400
1801	2,700

Source: *Historical Statistics of the United States*

 Take It to the NET

Connecting to Today

Making a Database Use the Internet to find information about the Federal Reserve Bank. Then, make a database that includes the main functions of the Federal Reserve Bank and the location of the 12 regional reserve banks. For help in starting this activity, visit *The American Nation* section of **www.phschool.com**.

Evaluating Internet Sites

Reviewing Sites About George Washington Use the Internet to find sites devoted to Washington's presidency. Write a review comparing two of these sites. For help in starting this activity, visit *The American Nation* section of **www.phschool.com**.

The Age of Jefferson

1801–1816

1 **A Republican Takes Office**

2 **The Louisiana Purchase**

3 **New Threats From Overseas**

4 **The Road to War**

5 **The War of 1812**

Thomas Jefferson

Lewis and Clark with Native American translator Sacagawea

1801

Thomas Jefferson becomes President. Jefferson seeks to reduce the power of the federal government.

1803

The United States purchases Louisiana from France. The next year, Jefferson sends Lewis and Clark to explore the Louisiana Purchase.

1807

The Embargo Act halts American overseas trade.

AMERICAN EVENTS

Presidential Terms:

Thomas Jefferson 1801–1809

1800   **1804**   **1808**

WORLD EVENTS

1804 ▲
Haiti declares independence from France.

▲ 1805
British and French navies clash at the Battle of Trafalgar.

The Louisiana Purchase, 1803

President Thomas Jefferson bought the territory of Louisiana from France, doubling the size of the United States.

BRITISH TERRITORY

PACIFIC OCEAN

Columbia R.

OREGON COUNTRY
(claimed by Great Britain, Russia, Spain, and the United States)

(claimed by Great Britain and the United States)

Claimed by Great Britain and the United States

L. Superior

St. Lawrence R.

Montana (1889)

North Dakota (1889)

Minnesota (1858)

Huron

ROCKY MOUNTAINS

Snake R.

Wyoming (1890)

South Dakota (1889)

Missouri R.

L. Michigan

L. Ontario

L. Erie

40°N

Key

United States 1803

Louisiana Purchase

Present-day boundaries

(1889) Date when state was admitted to U.S.

Great Salt Lake

Colorado R.

Colorado (1876)

▲ Pikes Peak

Nebraska (1867)

Kansas (1861)

Iowa (1846)

St. Louis

Missouri (1821)

Ohio R.

ATLANTIC OCEAN

Albers Equal-Area Projection

0   200   400 Miles

0   200   400 Kilometers

Santa Fe

SPANISH TERRITORY

New Mexico (1912)

Oklahoma (1907)

Arkansas (1836)

30°N

110°W

Texas (1845)

100°W

Rio Grande

Natchitoches

San Antonio

LA (1812)

New Orleans

SPANISH FLORIDA

Gulf of Mexico

90°W

80°W

The White House in flames

1811
American troops face Native American forces in Indiana at the Battle of Tippecanoe.

1812
The War of 1812 begins as Congress declares war on Britain.

1814
British troops set fire to much of Washington, D.C. The war ends later that year.

James Madison   1809–1817

1808 ★   1812 ★   1816 ★

1810 ▲
Mexico declares independence from Spain.

1815 ▲
Napoleon is defeated at the Battle of Waterloo.

1 A Republican Takes Office

BEFORE YOU READ

Reading Focus

- How did Jefferson's presidency reflect a democratic style?
- What actions did Jefferson take to reduce the power of the federal government?
- How did Chief Justice John Marshall strengthen the Supreme Court?

Key Terms

democratic

laissez faire

free market

Marbury v. *Madison*

judicial review

Taking Notes

Copy this incomplete Venn diagram. As you read, fill in key facts about Thomas Jefferson and John Marshall. Write common characteristics in the overlapping section.

THOMAS JEFFERSON
- Republican
-

JOHN MARSHALL
- Federalist
-

Main Idea As President, Thomas Jefferson sought to set a democratic tone and to reduce the role of the federal government.

AS YOU READ
Banner celebrating Jefferson's inauguration **Use Prior Knowledge** How did Jefferson's election in 1800 mark a change in the nation?

Setting the Scene The morning Thomas Jefferson became President of the United States, he ate breakfast at Conrad and McMunn's, the boardinghouse where he was staying. Washington, D.C., the nation's capital, was so new that the Capitol Building was still unfinished. Even so, Congress assembled there on March 4, 1801, to witness Jefferson's inauguration.

Jefferson wanted his inauguration to be simple, not showy. Rather than riding in a carriage to the Capitol, he walked. The new President gave a speech at the ceremony, but in a voice so low, hardly anyone could hear him. Then, he walked back to Conrad and McMunn's for a quiet dinner. When he entered, only one of his fellow diners even bothered to stand and offer Jefferson a chair.

Jefferson deliberately made his inauguration a low-key affair. Although he came from a wealthy family, he believed that the nation's strength came from ordinary people, such as farmers. As President, he rejected most Federalist ideas and turned the nation in a new direction.

Jefferson's Democratic Style

Jefferson was determined to make the government more democratic. Democratic means ensuring that all people have the same rights. Years before, in a letter to James Madison, he stressed that each citizen should play a part in a democracy:

> 66 Educate and inform the whole mass of the people. Enable them to see that it is their interest to preserve peace and order, and they will preserve them. . . . They are the only [ones to rely on] for the preservation of our liberty. 99

—Thomas Jefferson, letter to James Madison, 1787

Jefferson's personal style matched his democratic beliefs. The new President preferred quiet dinners to the formal parties that George Washington and John Adams had given. He wore casual clothes and greeted people by shaking hands instead of bowing. With his informal manner, Jefferson showed that the President was an ordinary citizen.

Some Federalists were worried about Jefferson's democratic beliefs. They knew that he supported the French Revolution and they feared that he might bring revolutionary change to the United States. They were also afraid that he might punish Federalists who had used the Alien and Sedition acts to jail Republicans.

In his inaugural address, Jefferson tried to calm Federalists' fears. He promised that, although the Republicans were in the majority, he would not treat the Federalists harshly. "The minority possess their equal rights, which equal laws must protect," he told the nation. He called for an end to the political disputes of the past few years. "We are all Republicans, we are all Federalists," the President concluded.

A Smaller Role for the Federal Government

Jefferson had no plan to punish Federalists. He did, however, want to change their policies. In his view, the Federalists had made the national government too large and too powerful.

New Economic Policies One way Jefferson wanted to lessen government power was by reducing the federal budget. Such budget cuts would also keep the federal debt low. His Secretary of the Treasury, Albert Gallatin (GAHL uh tin), helped him achieve this goal. A financial wizard, Gallatin reduced government spending through careful management.

Jefferson believed in an economic idea known as **laissez faire** (lehs ay FAYR), a French term meaning "let alone." The idea of laissez faire was promoted by the Scottish economist Adam Smith. In his book *The Wealth of Nations*, Smith argued in favor of a **free market** where goods and services are exchanged with little regulation. Free competition, Smith said, would benefit everyone, not just the wealthy.

Laissez faire economists believed that government should play as small a role as possible in economic affairs. Laissez faire was very different from the Federalist idea of government. Alexander Hamilton, you recall, wanted government to promote trade and manufacturing.

Goals and Policies of Jefferson

Policies
- Tries to cut federal budget and reduce federal debt
- Promotes laissez-faire policies in economic affairs
- Decreases the size of government departments
- Reduces the size of the army and navy
- Asks Congress to repeal the whiskey tax

Reduce size of government

GOAL

Reconcile party differences

Policies
- Retains the Bank of the United States
- Continues to pay off state debts using federal moneys
- Allows many Federalists to keep their government jobs

GRAPHIC ORGANIZER
Skills

Jefferson set the nation in a new direction, but kept some existing policies.

1. **Comprehension** Identify two ways Jefferson continued Federalist policies.

2. **Critical Thinking Linking Past and Present** Which of the goals and policies shown here might still be issues today? Why?

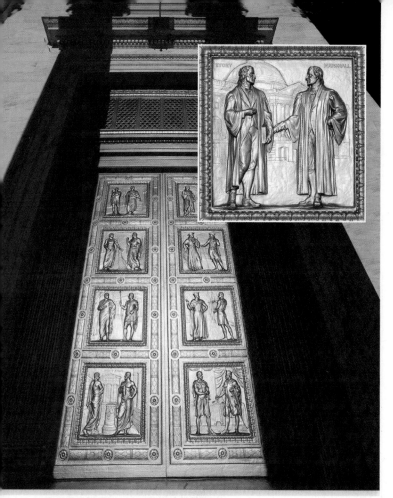

A Less Active Government Jefferson believed that the government should protect the rights of its citizens. Beyond that, he wanted the federal government to take a less active role in governing the nation. He decreased the size of government departments and cut the federal budget. With the approval of Congress, he reduced the size of the army and navy. He also asked Congress to repeal the unpopular whiskey tax.

The Sedition Act expired the day before Jefferson took office. Jefferson hated the law, and he pardoned those who were in jail because of it. He also asked Congress to restore the law allowing foreign-born people to become citizens after only a five-year waiting period.

Federalist Policies Remain Jefferson did not discard all Federalist programs. On the advice of Albert Gallatin, he kept the Bank of the United States. The federal government also continued to pay off state debts, which it had taken over while Washington was President. In addition, Jefferson let many Federalists keep their government jobs.

Strengthening the Supreme Court

The election of 1800 gave Republicans control of Congress. Federalists, however, remained powerful in the courts.

Several months passed between Jefferson's election and his inauguration. In that time, Federalists in the old Congress passed a law increasing the number of federal judges. President Adams then appointed Federalists to fill these new judicial positions.

One of the judges that Adams appointed was John Marshall, the Chief Justice of the Supreme Court. Like Jefferson, Marshall was a rich Virginia planter with a brilliant mind. Unlike Jefferson, however, Marshall was a staunch Federalist. He wanted to make the federal government stronger.

The framers of the Constitution expected the courts to balance the powers of the President and Congress. However, John Marshall found the courts to be much weaker than the other branches of government. In his view, it was not clear what powers the federal courts had.

Marbury v. Madison In 1803, Marshall decided a case that increased the power of the Supreme Court. The case involved William Marbury, one of the judges appointed by Adams. Adams made the appointment on his last night as President. The Republicans refused to accept this "midnight judge." They accused Federalists of using unfair tactics to keep control of the courts. Jefferson ordered Secretary of State James Madison not to deliver the official papers confirming Marbury's appointment.

Viewing History

Chief Justice John Marshall

Washington, D.C.

Today, these 20-foot-tall bronze doors lead into the Supreme Court chambers. The carved panels stand for important moments in legal history—including John Marshall delivering the decision in *Marbury* v. *Madison* (inset). **Applying Information** *Why do you think the sculptor included* **Marbury v. Madison** *as an important moment?*

Primary Sources

See John Marshall, "Marbury v. Madison," on page 590 of the Reference Section.

Marbury sued Madison. According to the Judiciary Act of 1789, only the Supreme Court could decide a case that was brought against a federal official. Therefore, the case of *Marbury* v. *Madison* was tried before the Supreme Court.

An Important Precedent The Supreme Court ruled against Marbury. Chief Justice Marshall wrote the decision, stating that the Judiciary Act was unconstitutional. The Constitution, Marshall argued, did not give the Supreme Court the right to decide cases brought against federal officials. Therefore, Congress could not give the Court that power simply by passing the Judiciary Act.

The Supreme Court's decision in *Marbury* v. *Madison* set an important precedent. It gave the Supreme Court the power to decide whether laws passed by Congress were constitutional and to reject laws that it considered to be unconstitutional. This power of the Court is called **judicial review.**

Jefferson was displeased with the decision. True, Marshall had ruled against Marbury, the Federalist judge. But Marshall's decision gave more power to the Supreme Court, where Federalists were still strong. Jefferson also argued that the decision upset the balance of power among the three branches of government:

> 66 The opinion which gives to the judges the right to decide what laws are constitutional and what not, not only for themselves . . . but for the Legislature and Executive also . . . would make the Judiciary a [tyrannical] branch. 99
>
> —Thomas Jefferson, letter to Abigail Adams, 1804

In the end, the President and Congress accepted the right of the Court to overturn laws. Today, judicial review remains one of the most important powers of the Supreme Court.

Connecting to Today

The Supreme Court

Under the strong hand of John Marshall, the Supreme Court increased its power. Today, as in Marshall's time, the justices base their decisions on the Constitution, as well as on past decisions. They may overturn a law because it violates the Constitution. They may reverse decisions by lower courts that did not apply the Constitution correctly.

Today, the Court faces questions that Marshall could not have imagined. How does freedom of speech apply to the Internet? Can members of a school athletic team be required to submit to random drug tests? Can a state government release information contained in a driver's license? Such decisions reach into the lives of every American.

Why do Supreme Court decisions have a wider effect than decisions by state courts?

Section 1 Assessment

Recall

1. **Identify** Explain the significance of **(a)** Albert Gallatin, **(b)** John Marshall, **(c)** *Marbury* v. *Madison.*

2. **Define** **(a)** democratic, **(b)** laissez faire, **(c)** free market, **(d)** judicial review.

Comprehension

3. **(a)** How did Jefferson's actions as President reflect his democratic beliefs? **(b)** Why did his beliefs worry Federalists?

4. Describe three steps that Jefferson took to reduce the power of the federal government.

5. What important precedent did John Marshall set in the case of *Marbury* v. *Madison*?

Critical Thinking and Writing

6. **Exploring the Main Idea** Review the Main Idea statement at the beginning of this section. Then, write an outline for a speech Jefferson might have given to explain his goals.

7. **Supporting a Point of View** Write a paragraph explaining whether or not you think judicial review upsets the balance of power in the government.

ACTIVITY

Take It to the NET

Connecting to Today

Use the Internet to find out about a current law that affects the goods Americans buy. Summarize the law, and explain what a laissez faire economist would think of it. Visit *The American Nation* section of **www.phschool.com** for help in completing the activity.

2 The Louisiana Purchase

Reading Focus

- Why was control of the Mississippi River important to the United States?
- How did the United States purchase Louisiana?
- What were the results of the explorations of Lewis and Clark and of Zebulon Pike?

Key Terms

Pinckney Treaty

Louisiana Purchase

expedition

continental divide

Taking Notes

Copy this flowchart. As you read, fill in the boxes with events that led up to the Lewis and Clark expedition. Two boxes have been completed to help you get started. Add as many boxes as you need.

Western farmers rely on Mississippi River
↓
↓
↓
Lewis and Clark explore Louisiana Purchase

Main Idea In 1803, the United States purchased the territory of Louisiana from France, doubling the size of the nation.

William Clark's journal

Draw Inferences Based on this story, do you think Americans knew very much about their new territory?

Setting the Scene In Jefferson's day, riders of the "post" usually traveled on horseback, carrying mail in saddlebags. But the parcels arriving at the White House this particular day must have required a whole cart. Jefferson eagerly opened package after package, to find a remarkable assortment of goods.

The smaller items included more than a hundred plants, a tin box full of insects, and mineral specimens. Skeletons of pronghorned antelope and the horns of a mountain ram took up more room. There was even live cargo—a prairie dog and a magpie!

Almost two years earlier, the United States had purchased from France vast lands west of the Mississippi River. Jefferson then sent Meriwether Lewis and William Clark to explore the territory. The President carefully examined their reports and packages, and later read their detailed journals. All this evidence confirmed Jefferson's belief that the new lands were a valuable addition to the nation.

Control of the Mississippi

By 1800, almost one million Americans lived between the Appalachian Mountains and the Mississippi River. Most were farmers. With few roads west of the Appalachians, western farmers relied on the Mississippi to ship their wheat and corn. First, they sent their produce down the river to the city of New Orleans. From there, ocean-going ships carried the produce to ports along the Atlantic coast.

Spain, which controlled New Orleans, sometimes threatened to close the port to Americans. In 1795, President Washington sent Thomas Pinckney to find a way to keep the vital port open. In the **Pinckney Treaty**, Spain agreed to let Americans ship their goods down the Mississippi and store them in New Orleans.

For a time, Americans shipped their goods through New Orleans peacefully. In 1800, however, Spain signed a treaty giving Louisiana back to France. President Jefferson was alarmed. He knew that the

French ruler, Napoleon Bonaparte, had already set out to conquer Europe. Would he now try to build an empire in North America?

Jefferson had reason to worry. Napoleon wanted to grow food in Louisiana and ship it to French islands in the West Indies. However, events in Haiti, a French colony in the Caribbean, soon ruined Napoleon's plan. Inspired by the French Revolution, enslaved Africans in Haiti decided to fight for their liberty. Toussaint L'Ouverture (too SAN loo vehr TYOOR) led the revolt. By 1801, Toussaint and his followers had nearly forced the French out of Haiti.

Napoleon sent troops to retake Haiti. Although the French captured Toussaint, they did not regain control of the island. In 1804, Haitians declared their independence.

The United States Buys Louisiana

Meanwhile, Jefferson decided to try to buy New Orleans. He wanted to be sure that American farmers would always be able to ship their goods through the port. The President sent Robert Livingston and James Monroe to buy New Orleans and West Florida from Napoleon. Jefferson said they could offer as much as $10 million.

A Surprise Offer Livingston and Monroe negotiated with Talleyrand, the French foreign minister. At first, Talleyrand showed little interest in their offer. However, losing Haiti caused Napoleon to give up his plan for an empire in the Americas. He also needed money to pay for his costly wars in Europe. Suddenly, Talleyrand asked Livingston if the United States wanted to buy all of Louisiana, not just New Orleans.

The question surprised Livingston. He offered $4 million. "Too low," replied Talleyrand. "Reflect and see me tomorrow."

Livingston and Monroe carefully debated the matter. They had no authority to buy all of Louisiana. However, they knew that Jefferson wanted control of the Mississippi. They agreed to pay the French $15 million for Louisiana. "This is the noblest work of our whole lives," declared Livingston when he signed the treaty. "From this day the United States take their place among the powers of the first rank."

Was the Purchase Constitutional? Jefferson hailed the news from France. Still, he was not sure whether the President had the power to purchase Louisiana. He had always insisted that the federal government had only those powers spelled out in the Constitution. The document said nothing about a President having the power to buy land.

Viewing History

Celebrating the Louisiana Purchase

New Orleans

This painting depicts a ceremony held in New Orleans on December 20, 1803. The French flag has been lowered and the American flag is being raised. **Evaluating Information** *What would you need to know to decide if this painting is accurate?*

Exploring the West, 1804–1807

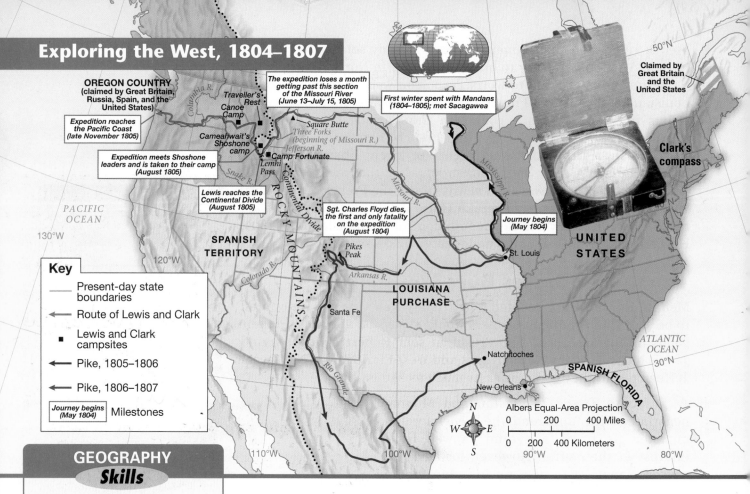

OREGON COUNTRY
(claimed by Great Britain, Russia, Spain, and the United States)

Traveller's Rest Canoe Camp

Columbia R.

The expedition loses a month getting past this section of the Missouri River (June 13–July 15, 1805)

First winter spent with Mandans (1804–1805); met Sacagawea

Claimed by Great Britain and the United States

50°N

Expedition reaches the Pacific Coast (late November 1805)

Cameahwait's Shoshone camp

Camp Fortunate

Square Butte
Three Forks (beginning of Missouri R.)
Jefferson R.

Clark's compass

Expedition meets Shoshone leaders and is taken to their camp (August 1805)

Snake R.

Lemhi Pass

Missouri R.

Mississippi R.

PACIFIC OCEAN

130°W

Lewis reaches the Continental Divide (August 1805)

ROCKY MOUNTAINS

Continental Divide

Sgt. Charles Floyd dies, the first and only fatality on the expedition (August 1804)

Journey begins (May 1804)

St. Louis

UNITED STATES

120°W

SPANISH TERRITORY

Colorado R.

Pikes Peak

Arkansas R.

LOUISIANA PURCHASE

ATLANTIC OCEAN

30°N

Key

—— Present-day state boundaries

← Route of Lewis and Clark

▪ Lewis and Clark campsites

← Pike, 1805–1806

← Pike, 1806–1807

Journey begins (May 1804) Milestones

Santa Fe

Rio Grande

Natchitoches

SPANISH FLORIDA

New Orleans

N W E S

Albers Equal-Area Projection
0   200   400 Miles
0 200 400 Kilometers

110°W   100°W   90°W   80°W

GEOGRAPHY Skills

The explorations of Lewis and Clark and of Zebulon Pike helped Americans learn more about the West.

1. **Location** On the map, locate **(a)** Louisiana Purchase, **(b)** Mississippi River, **(c)** St. Louis, **(d)** Rocky Mountains, **(e)** Pikes Peak.

2. **Movement** Along which rivers did Lewis and Clark travel in order to reach the Pacific Ocean?

3. **Critical Thinking Making Predictions** Based on this map, how might westward expansion lead to conflict with other nations?

In the end, Jefferson decided that he did have the authority to buy Louisiana. The Constitution, he reasoned, allowed the President to make treaties. At his request, the Senate approved the treaty, and the Louisiana Purchase went into effect. In 1803, the United States took control of the vast lands west of the Mississippi. With one stroke, the size of the nation had doubled.

Planning an Expedition Few Americans knew anything about the Louisiana territory. In 1803, Congress provided money for a team of explorers to study the new lands. Jefferson chose Meriwether Lewis, his private secretary, to head the **expedition,** or long voyage of exploration. Lewis asked William Clark to go with him.

Jefferson asked Lewis and Clark to map a route to the Pacific Ocean. He also told them to study the geography of the territory, including:

> ❝ . . . climate as characterized by the thermometer, by the proportion of rainy, cloudy, and clear days, by lightning, hail, snow, ice . . . the dates at which particular plants put forth or lose their flower, or leaf, times of appearance of particular birds, reptiles or insects. ❞
>
> —Thomas Jefferson, letter to Meriwether Lewis, 1803

Jefferson also instructed Lewis and Clark to learn about the Indian nations who lived in the Louisiana Purchase. These Native Americans carried on a busy trade with English, French, and Spanish merchants. Jefferson hoped that the Indians might trade with American merchants instead. Therefore, he urged Lewis and Clark to tell the Indians of "our wish to be neighborly, friendly, and useful to them."

The Lewis and Clark Expedition

Dozens of adventurous young men eagerly competed to join the expedition. Lewis and Clark judged volunteers on the basis of their character, strength, hunting skills, and ability to survive in the wilderness. In the end, about 50 men made up the "Corps of Discovery." The party also included York, an enslaved African American who had been Clark's companion since boyhood.

In May 1804, Lewis and Clark started up the Missouri River from St. Louis. At first, the expedition's boats made slow progress against the Missouri's swift current. One night, the current tore away the riverbank where they were camping. The party had to scramble into the boats to avoid being swept downstream.

Across the Plains Lewis and Clark marveled at the broad, grassy plains that stretched "as far as the eye can reach." Everywhere, they saw "immense herds of buffalo, deer, elk, and antelope."

As they traveled across the plains, the expedition met people of various Indian nations. Lewis and Clark had brought many gifts for Native Americans. They carried "peace medals" stamped with the United States seal. They also brought mirrors, beads, knives, blankets, and thousands of sewing needles and fishhooks.

During the first winter, Lewis and Clark stayed with the Mandans in present-day North Dakota. The explorers planned to continue up the Missouri in the spring. However, they worried about how they would cross the steep Rocky Mountains.

Also staying with the Mandans was an Indian woman named Sacagawea (sahk uh guh WEE uh). Sacagawea belonged to the Shoshone (shoh SHOH nee) people, who lived in the Rockies. She and her French Canadian husband agreed to accompany Lewis and Clark as translators.

Over the Rockies In early spring, the party set out. In the foothills of the Rockies, the landscape and wildlife changed. Bighorn sheep ran along the high hills. The thorns of prickly pear cactus jabbed the explorers' moccasins. Once, a grizzly bear chased Lewis while he was exploring alone.

Finally, Lewis and Clark met some Shoshones. One of them was Sacagawea's brother, whom she had not seen for many years. Upon seeing her own people, wrote Clark, she began to "dance and show every mark of the most extravagant joy." The Shoshones supplied the expedition with food and horses. They also advised Lewis and Clark about the best route to take over the Rockies.

In the Rocky Mountains, Lewis and Clark crossed the Continental Divide. A **continental divide** is a mountain ridge that separates river systems flowing toward opposite sides of a continent. In North America, some rivers flow east from the Rockies into the Mississippi, which drains into the Gulf of Mexico. Other rivers flow west from the Rockies and empty into the Pacific Ocean.

An American Profile

Sacagawea 1790?–1812?

Sacagawea proved invaluable to the Lewis and Clark expedition. Because she knew about the healing qualities of plants and herbs, the expedition relied on her for medical help. The presence of Sacagawea and her baby showed Indians in the area that the party was friendly. As Clark noted, "a woman with a party of men is a token of peace." She helped win the needed gift of horses from her people, the Shoshone. After the journey was completed, Clark wrote that she "deserved a greater reward . . . than we had in our power to give her."

Why would the presence of a woman and baby be seen as a sign of peace?

AS YOU READ **Predict** What do you think might be some of the effects of the Lewis and Clark expedition?

To the Pacific After building canoes, Lewis and Clark's party floated toward the Columbia River into the Pacific Northwest. Finally, on November 7, 1805, Clark wrote in his journal, "Great joy in camp. We are in view of the ocean, this great Pacific Ocean which we have been so long anxious to see." Lewis and Clark had reached their goal.

The return trip to St. Louis took another year. In 1806, Americans celebrated the return of Lewis and Clark. The explorers brought back much useful information about the Louisiana Purchase.

Pike Explores the West

Before Lewis and Clark returned, another explorer set out from St. Louis. From 1805 to 1807, Zebulon Pike explored the upper Mississippi River, the Arkansas River, and parts of present-day Colorado and New Mexico. In November 1806, Pike viewed a mountain peak rising above the Colorado plains. Today, this mountain is known as Pikes Peak.

AS YOU READ **Draw Inferences** Why do you think the Spanish arrested Pike and took his maps and journals?

Continuing southward, Pike entered into Spanish territory. Spanish troops soon arrested Pike and his men and took them into Mexico. The Americans were later escorted through Texas back into the United States. The Spanish took Pike's maps and journals, but he was able to hide one map in the barrel of his gun. His report on the expedition greatly expanded Americans' knowledge about the Southwest.

The journeys of Pike and Lewis and Clark excited Americans. However, settlers did not move into the rugged western lands for a number of years. As you will read, they first settled the region closest to the Mississippi River. Soon, the territory around New Orleans had a large enough population of American citizens for the settlers to apply for statehood. In 1812, this territory entered the Union as the state of Louisiana.

 AFTER YOU READ

Section 2 Assessment

Recall

1. **Identify** Explain the significance of **(a)** Pinckney Treaty, **(b)** Napoleon Bonaparte, **(c)** Toussaint L'Ouverture, **(d)** Louisiana Purchase, **(e)** Lewis and Clark, **(f)** Sacagawea, **(g)** Zebulon Pike.
2. **Define** **(a)** expedition, **(b)** continental divide.

Comprehension

3. Why did Jefferson seek to control the Mississippi River?
4. Why did the French offer to sell Louisiana to the United States?

5. Identify two goals and one result of the Lewis and Clark expedition.

Critical Thinking and Writing

6. **Exploring the Main Idea** Review the Main Idea statement at the beginning of this section. Then, list three ways in which the United States might be different today if Jefferson had not bought Louisiana in 1803.
7. **Making Decisions** If you had been a Shoshone or Mandan leader, would you have decided to help Lewis and Clark? Explain your reasons.

ACTIVITY

Writing a Journal You are a member of Lewis and Clark's "Corps of Discovery." Write three journal entries describing what you feel as you explore the territory and meet the Native Americans who live there.

AMERICAN WILDLIFE

In their trek though the West, Lewis and Clark saw a world unfamiliar to Americans who lived on the Atlantic coast. An impressed Lewis wrote: "What a field for a botanist and a naturalist." Their notes and samples informed American scientists of 122 animals and 178 plants they had not known about before.

The only animals named for the explorers are this woodpecker (left) named for Lewis and this nutcracker (right) named for Clark.

At the expedition's winter quarters on the Pacific coast, Indians caught a 2-foot, 8-inch long coho salmon. Lewis sketched and described the fish in his journal.

In Nebraska, Lewis first saw these "barking squirrels." Another member of the expedition gave them the name they have today— prairie dogs.

Native Americans had warned the explorers about the fierce grizzly bear. Lewis wrote that the explorers were "anxious to meet them." After being chased up a tree by a grizzly, Lewis wrote "I find the curiosity of our party is pretty well satisfied with respect to this animal."

ACTIVITY

With the class or in a small group, brainstorm a list of the wildlife native to your area. Choose one animal from the list. Prepare an entry for a visitor's guide describing that animal and how it reflects the local geography.

3 New Threats From Overseas

BEFORE YOU READ

Reading Focus

- What were the benefits and risks of overseas trade?
- How did the British and French violate the neutrality of American ships?
- Why did Jefferson decide to impose an embargo?

Key Terms

tribute

impressment

embargo

Embargo Act

smuggling

Nonintercourse Act

Taking Notes

As you read, prepare an outline of this section. Use roman numerals to indicate the major headings, capital letters for the subheadings, and numbers for the supporting details. The sample at right will help you get started.

```
I. Trading Around the World
   A. Yankee traders
      1. China trade
      2.
   B.
      1.
      2.
II. American Neutrality Is
    Violated
   A.
   B.
```

Main Idea As Great Britain went to war against France, both sides ignored the claim of the United States that American ships were neutral.

AS YOU READ British seize American sailors

Predict How do you think the United States will respond to reports of American sailors being forced to serve on British ships?

Setting the Scene It was along the coast of India that Jacob Nagle saw his chance to escape. An American sailor, Nagle had been forced to work on a British ship. He and three shipmates jumped into a small boat and rowed away as fast as they could.

The surf and wind made it difficult to reach shore before dark. Finally, Nagle and his mates rowed to another ship instead. Unfortunately, officers from their own ship were lying in wait. "Not suspecting, we asked for some water," Nagle later recalled:

> 66 The captain said if we would come up, he would give us some [drink]. . . . As soon as we got on the quarter deck they all surrounded us and the second mate clapped a pistol to my breast. 'If you move an inch, I will blow your brains out.' 99
>
> —Jacob Nagle, *The Nagle Journal: A Diary of the Life of Jacob Nagle, Sailor, From the Year 1775 to 1841*

In the early 1800s, the British navy forced thousands of American sailors to serve on their ships. This was only one of many dangers that Americans faced as their sea trade began to thrive.

Trading Around the World

After the Revolution, American overseas trade grew rapidly. Ships sailed from New England on voyages that sometimes lasted three years.

Yankee Traders Wherever they went, Yankee captains kept a sharp lookout for new goods and new markets. Clever traders sawed winter ice from New England ponds into blocks, packed it in sawdust, and carried it to India. There, they traded the ice for silk and spices. In 1784, the *Empress of China* became the first American ship to trade with China. New England merchants quickly built up a profitable China trade.

More than 10 years before Lewis and Clark, Yankee merchants sailed up the Pacific coast of North America. So many traders from Boston visited the Pacific Northwest that Indians there called every white man "Boston." Traders bought furs from Native Americans and sold them for large profits in China.

Conflict With the Barbary States Traders ran great risks, especially in the Mediterranean Sea. Pirates from the Barbary States, the nations along the coast of North Africa, attacked passing vessels. To protect American ships, the United States paid a yearly tribute, or bribe, to rulers of Barbary States such as Tripoli.

In 1801, Tripoli increased its demands. When Jefferson refused to pay, Tripoli declared war on the United States. Jefferson then ordered the navy to blockade the port of Tripoli.

During the blockade, the American ship *Philadelphia* ran aground near Tripoli. Pirates boarded the ship and hauled the crew off to prison. The pirates planned to use the *Philadelphia* to attack other ships. To prevent this, American naval officer Stephen Decatur and his crew quietly sailed into Tripoli harbor by night. They then set the captured American ship on fire.

In the meantime, American marines landed on the coast of North Africa. They marched 500 miles to launch a surprise attack on Tripoli. In 1805, the ruler of Tripoli signed a treaty promising not to interfere with American ships.

American Neutrality Is Violated

American ships faced another problem. Britain and France went to war again in 1803. At first, Americans profited from the conflict. British and French ships were too busy fighting to engage in trade. American merchants eagerly traded with both sides. As profits increased, Americans hurried to build new ships.

Neither Britain nor France wanted the United States to sell supplies to its enemy. As in the 1790s, they ignored American claims of neutrality. Napoleon seized American ships bound for England. At the same time, the British stopped Yankee traders on their way to France. Between 1805 and 1807, hundreds of American ships were captured.

Needing more sailors, the British navy stepped up impressment, the practice of forcing people into service. In Britain, impressment gangs raided English villages and took young men to serve in the navy. On the seas, British ships stopped American vessels, seizing any British sailors serving on American ships. Many American-born sailors were also impressed. Furious Americans clamored for war.

Viewing History

Trading in China Chinese tea and fine dishes, or china, fetched high prices in the United States. Still, China permitted foreigners to trade in just a few ports, such as Canton (below). **Drawing Conclusions** *How would you describe the china shown here? Why do you think Americans were willing to pay high prices for such goods?*

Jefferson Tries an Embargo

Jefferson knew that the small American fleet was no match for the powerful British navy. Like Washington and Adams, he sought to avoid war.

A Total Ban Jefferson hoped that an American **embargo,** or ban on trade, would hurt France and Britain by cutting off needed supplies. "Our trade is the most powerful weapon we can use in our defense," one Republican newspaper wrote. In 1807, Jefferson persuaded Congress to impose a total embargo on foreign trade.

The **Embargo Act** did hurt Britain and France. But it hurt Americans even more. Supplies of imports such as sugar, tea, and molasses were cut off. Exports dropped by more than $80 million in one year. Docks in the South were piled high with cotton and tobacco. The Embargo Act hurt New England merchants most of all.

Merchants protested loudly against the embargo. Some turned to **smuggling,** importing or exporting goods in violation of trade laws. Jefferson began using the navy and federal troops to enforce the embargo. On the border between New York and Canada, some smugglers engaged in skirmishes with federal troops.

A Limited Ban In 1809, Jefferson admitted that the Embargo Act had failed. Congress replaced it with the milder **Nonintercourse Act.** It allowed Americans to carry on trade with all nations except Britain and France.

The embargo was the most unpopular measure of Jefferson's presidency. Still, Republicans remained strong. Following President Washington's precedent, Jefferson refused to run for a third term. Republican James Madison easily won the 1808 presidential election. Madison hoped that Britain and France would soon agree to respect American neutrality.

> **AS YOU READ**
>
> **Summarize** Write two or three sentences explaining the purpose of the Embargo Act and its effects on Britain, France, and the United States.

AFTER YOU READ

Section 3 Assessment

Recall

1. **Identify** Explain the significance of **(a)** *Empress of China,* **(b)** Stephen Decatur, **(c)** Embargo Act, **(d)** Nonintercourse Act.
2. **Define** **(a)** tribute, **(b)** impressment, **(c)** embargo, **(d)** smuggling.

Comprehension

3. How did increased overseas trade lead to conflict with the Barbary States?
4. Why did Britain and France begin to seize American ships after 1803?

5. **(a)** What was the goal of the Embargo Act? **(b)** Why did it fail?

Critical Thinking and Writing

6. **Exploring the Main Idea** Review the Main Idea statement at the beginning of this section. Then, list as many ways as you can think of that a war between two foreign powers can affect a neutral nation.
7. **Making Predictions** Write a paragraph explaining what you think President Madison might do if Britain and France continue to violate American neutrality.

ACTIVITY

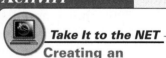 **Take It to the NET**

Creating an Advertisement Use the Internet to find out what goods were traded in China in the early 1800s. Create an advertisement offering American goods to Chinese merchants or Chinese goods to Americans. Visit *The American Nation* section of **www.phschool.com** for help in completing the activity.

Synthesizing Information

How did Jefferson's attempt to maintain American neutrality affect the nation's economy? As you learn about history, you will often use evidence from many types of sources. To get the most from these sources, you need to synthesize—that is, put different pieces of information together to form conclusions. To start this lesson, read the excerpt below and study the graph to the right.

A New Englander sent a letter to President Jefferson about the Embargo Act. It began with these words:

> **"**You Infernal Villain:
>
> How much longer are you going to keep this [cursed] Embargo on to starve us poor people? . . . One of my children has already starved to death of which I [am] ashamed and declared that it died of apoplexy. . . . I am a Federalist.**"**
>
> —quoted in *A Diplomatic History of the American People* (Bailey)

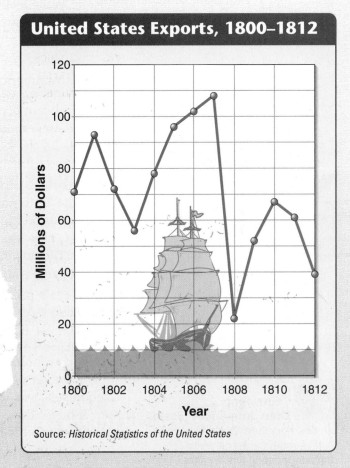

United States Exports, 1800–1812

Source: *Historical Statistics of the United States*

Learn the Skill *To synthesize information, use the following steps:*

1. **Identify the sources.** Knowing the background of a writer or the source of a graph helps you evaluate the information.
2. **Identify key facts and ideas.** What are the main points being made?
3. **Analyze the evidence.** Examine and compare the different kinds of evidence—graphs, pictures, text, primary sources—you are using.
4. **Draw conclusions.** Use the different pieces of evidence to form conclusions.

Practice the Skill *Use the letter, the graph, and what you have read in Section 3 to answer the following questions:*

1. **(a)** Who wrote the letter? **(b)** How did the writer feel about the embargo? **(c)** What is the source of the graph information?
2. **(a)** Restate the main point of the letter. **(b)** Describe the changes in the value of exports shown on the graph.
3. **(a)** Based on your reading, why did American exports fall sharply in 1807? **(b)** How does the graph explain the letter writer's point of view?
4. Based on the evidence, draw one conclusion about American trade in the early 1800s.

Apply the Skill *See the Chapter Review and Assessment.*

4 The Road to War

Reading Focus

- Why did conflicts between white settlers and Native Americans increase during the early 1800s?
- What was the goal of Tecumseh's Native American confederation?
- Why did the War Hawks push for war against Britain?

Key Terms

Treaty of Greenville

confederation

Battle of Tippecanoe

War Hawks

nationalism

Taking Notes

Copy the chart below. As you read, complete the chart by filling in some of the causes that led Congress to declare war. Add as many boxes as you need.

British impressment of American sailors			

↓ ↓ ↓ ↓

CONGRESS DECLARES WAR

🏴 **Main Idea** Conflicts with Native Americans in the West and with the British at sea led to the War of 1812.

Tecumseh
Draw Inferences Based on this story, how well do you think Native Americans and white settlers understood one another?

Setting the Scene

August 1810: William Henry Harrison, governor of the Indiana Territory, was ready to welcome an Indian delegation. Under a canopy, government officials sat and waited.

At last, the leader of the Indian delegation approached. His name was Tecumseh (tih KUHM suh). Behind him stood 30 members of the Shawnee nation.

"Your father requests you to sit by his side," Harrison's assistant told Tecumseh. He meant Harrison was a chief, a "white father."

Scornfully, Tecumseh pointed to the sky. "My father! The Great Spirit is my father! The earth is my mother. . . . Houses are made for white men to hold councils in. Indians hold theirs in open air." He and his men sat down where they were.

Tecumseh was determined to push back white settlers from Indian lands. Soon, the United States was fighting on two fronts—against Tecumseh's Indian allies and against Great Britain.

Conflict With Native Americans

About 900,000 white settlers moved west of the Appalachians between 1790 and 1810. Native Americans resented these newcomers, who built farms on Indian lands and hunted the animals Indians needed for food. The settlers ignored treaties that the United States had signed with Indian nations of the region.

Fighting often broke out between the Native Americans and settlers. Isolated acts of violence led to larger acts of revenge. As both sides killed innocent people, warfare spread. In Ohio, Little Turtle of the Miamis and Blue Jacket of the Shawnees organized Indian resistance in 1791. Armed with British muskets and gunpowder, the Indians drove white settlers from the area.

President Washington sent General Anthony Wayne into Ohio in 1794. Native American forces gathered at a place called Fallen Timbers. They thought that Wayne would have trouble fighting there because fallen trees covered the land. But Wayne's well-trained army pushed through the tangle of logs and defeated the Indians.

In 1795, leaders of the Miamis and other Indian nations signed the Treaty of Greenville. They gave up land that would later become part of Ohio. In return, they received $20,000 and the promise of more money if they kept the peace.

Tecumseh's Confederation

Ohio joined the Union in 1803. By then, white settlers were pushing beyond Ohio into the Indiana Territory. Angry Native Americans vowed to keep settlers from taking more Indian land. They included two Shawnee leaders: Tecumseh and his brother Tenskwatawa (tehn SKWAH tuh wuh), a religious leader also called the Prophet.

Unity and Old Ways The Prophet and Tecumseh taught that white customs corrupted the Indian way of life. They said that many Indians depended on white trade goods, such as muskets, cloth, cooking pots, and whiskey. They believed that by returning to the old ways, Indians could gain the power to resist white invaders.

In 1808, the Prophet built a village for his followers along Tippecanoe Creek in Indiana Territory. Indians from lands as far away as Missouri, Iowa, and Minnesota traveled to Prophetstown to hear his message.

Tecumseh worked to organize Indian nations into a confederation, or league. He called for unity against settlers:

❝ The whites have driven us from the great salt water, forced us over the mountains. . . . The way, the only way, to check and stop this evil is for all red men to unite in claiming a common equal right in the land. ❞
—Tecumseh, quoted in *Tecumseh: Vision of Glory* (Tucker)

Tecumseh impressed white leaders. Governor William Henry Harrison grudgingly admitted, "He is one of those uncommon geniuses which spring up occasionally to produce revolutions and overturn the established order of things."

Showdown at Tippecanoe Rivalries among Native American nations kept Tecumseh from uniting all Indians east of the Mississippi River. Still, white settlers were alarmed at his success.

In 1811, Harrison marched 1,000 soldiers against Prophetstown on the Tippecanoe Creek. The Prophet was in charge because

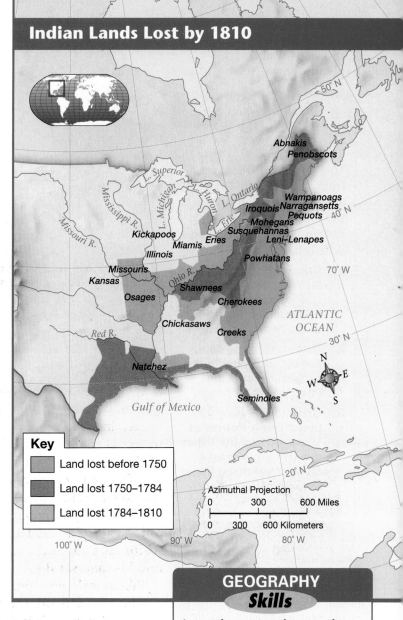

Indian Lands Lost by 1810

Key
- Land lost before 1750
- Land lost 1750–1784
- Land lost 1784–1810

Azimuthal Projection

0   300   600 Miles

0   300   600 Kilometers

GEOGRAPHY Skills

As settlers moved west, they settled on Native American lands.

1. **Location** On the map, locate the original lands of the **(a)** Iroquois, **(b)** Miamis, **(c)** Shawnees.

2. **Regions** When did Indian nations west of the Ohio River begin to lose land?

3. **Critical Thinking Drawing Inferences** Why do you think many of the lands lost by Indians were located along rivers?

POLITICAL CARTOON
Skills

The Embargo Continues
This famous political cartoon appeared in 1811, after Congress renewed the embargo against Britain. (The ship is flying a British flag.)

1. **Comprehension**
(a) What is Ograbme spelled backward?
(b) Describe the actions of the two speakers.

2. **Understanding Main Ideas** According to the cartoon, what is the effect of the embargo?

3. **Critical Thinking Identifying Points of View** Do you think that this cartoonist was in favor of enforcing the embargo? Explain.

Economics $

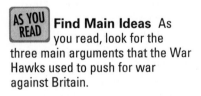
Find Main Ideas As you read, look for the three main arguments that the War Hawks used to push for war against Britain.

Tecumseh was away trying to organize Indians in the South. The Prophet led a surprise night attack on Harrison's troops. Both sides suffered heavy losses in the Battle of Tippecanoe. In the end, Harrison's troops defeated the Prophet's forces and destroyed Prophetstown. Whites celebrated the battle as a major victory. Still, Tecumseh and his followers continued to resist white settlement.

A Push Toward War

Fighting with Native Americans hurt relations between the United States and Britain. The British were supplying guns and ammunition to the Native Americans on the frontier. They also encouraged Indians to attack United States settlements.

Meanwhile, the continuing ban on trade with Britain and France was due to expire. Congress then authorized President Madison to make a tantalizing offer. If either the British or French stopped seizing American ships, the United States would halt trade with the other nation. Napoleon quickly announced that France would respect American neutrality. As promised, the United States continued trade with France, but stopped all shipments to Britain.

The War Hawks While Madison did not want war, other Americans were not as cautious. Except in New England, where many merchants wanted to restore trade with Britain, anti-British feeling ran strong. Members of Congress from the South and the West called for war. They were known as War Hawks.

War Hawks were stirred by a strong sense of nationalism, or devotion to one's country. War Hawks felt that Britain was treating the United States as if it were still a British colony. They were willing to fight a war to defend American rights.

The most outspoken War Hawk was Henry Clay of Kentucky. Clay wanted to punish Britain for seizing American ships. He also hoped to conquer Canada. "The militia of Kentucky are alone [able] to place Montreal and Upper Canada at your feet," Clay boasted to Congress.

War Hawks saw other advantages of war with Britain. If Americans went to war with Britain, War Hawks said, the United States could seize Florida from Britain's ally, Spain. They also pointed out that Britain was arming Native Americans on the frontier and encouraging them to attack settlers. The War Hawks felt that winning a war against Britain would bring lasting safety to settlers on the frontier.

Congress Declares War The United States and Britain drifted closer to war. The British continued to board American ships and impress American seamen. To cut off American trade with France, British warships blockaded some American ports. In May 1811, near New York Harbor, a brief battle broke out between an American frigate and a British warship. The Americans crippled the British ship and left 32 British sailors dead or wounded.

The War Hawks urged Congress to prepare for war. Others in Congress disagreed. John Randolph of Virginia warned that the people of the United States would "not submit to be taxed for this war of conquest and dominion." Representatives of New England were especially concerned. They feared that the British navy would attack New England seaports.

At last, President Madison gave in to war fever. In June 1812, he asked Congress to declare war on Britain. The House and Senate both voted in favor of war. Americans would soon learn, though, that declaring war was easier than winning.

Section 4 Assessment

Recall
1. **Identify** Explain the significance of **(a)** Treaty of Greenville, **(b)** Tecumseh, **(c)** the Prophet, **(d)** William Henry Harrison, **(e)** Battle of Tippecanoe, **(f)** War Hawks, **(g)** Henry Clay.
2. **Define** **(a)** confederation, **(b)** nationalism.

Comprehension
3. Why did war break out between Indians and white settlers in Ohio?
4. Why did Tecumseh want to unite Indian nations?
5. Identify three reasons why the War Hawks wanted Congress to declare war on Britain.

Critical Thinking and Writing
6. **Exploring the Main Idea** Review the Main Idea statement at the beginning of this section. Then, write a paragraph explaining how the Battle of Tippecanoe helped to pave the way for the coming war between Britain and the United States.
7. **Supporting a Point of View** Write an outline for a speech Tecumseh or the Prophet might have given to persuade Native Americans to join his league. Include at least two different reasons.

ACTIVITY

Drawing a Political Cartoon Draw a political cartoon that might have appeared in a War Hawk newspaper in 1812. Your cartoon should express one of the reasons that you favor a declaration of war against Britain. Use human figures to represent the United States and Britain.

5 The War of 1812

BEFORE YOU READ

Reading Focus

- How was the United States unprepared early in the war?
- What successes did Americans have in the West?
- How did the final battles of the war progress?
- Why did New Englanders protest against the war?

Key Terms

Battle of Lake Erie

Battle of New Orleans

Hartford Convention

Treaty of Ghent

Taking Notes

Copy the concept web below. As you read, fill in blank ovals with important facts about the War of 1812. Add as many ovals as you need.

Main Idea Although neither Great Britain nor the United States won the War of 1812, Americans proved that their republic would remain independent.

AS YOU READ
Soldier's uniform of 1812

Draw Inferences Do you think an American soldier would have agreed with the attitude expressed in the poem at right?

Setting the Scene

Many Americans welcomed the news of war with Britain. In some cities, they fired cannons and guns and danced in the streets. A Republican newspaper published this poem:

> 66 Since war is the word, let us strain every nerve
> To save our America, her glory increase;
> So shoulder your firelock, your country preserve,
> For the hotter the war, boys, the quicker the peace. 99
>
> —War poem, quoted in *The Oxford History of the American People* (Morison)

Other Americans were less enthusiastic. New Englanders, especially, talked scornfully of "Mr. Madison's War." In fact, before the war ended, some New Englanders would threaten to leave the Union.

Early Days of the War

The American declaration of war took the British by surprise. They were locked in a bitter struggle with Napoleon and could not spare troops to fight the United States. As the war began, however, the United States faced difficulties of its own.

Unprepared for War The United States was not ready for war. Because Jefferson had reduced spending on defense, the navy had only 16 ships to meet the huge British fleet. The army was small and ill equipped, and many of the officers knew little about warfare. "The state of the Army," said a member of Congress, "is enough to make any man who has the smallest love of country wish to get rid of it."

Since there were few regular troops, the government relied on volunteers. Congress voted to give them a bounty of cash and land. The money was equal to about a year's salary for most workers. Attracted by the high pay and the chance to own their own farms, young men eagerly enlisted. They were poorly trained, however, with little experience in battle. Many deserted after a few months.

USS *Constitution*

The USS Constitution *is affectionately known as "Old Ironsides." During the War of 1812, British cannonballs bounced off her thick wooden hull. Later, a public outcry saved the old ship from being scrapped. Today, if you visit Boston, you can step aboard the restored "Old Ironsides." In the nearby museum, you can relive naval history by hoisting a sail or firing a cannon.*

Take It to the NET

Virtual Field Trip For an interactive look at the *Constitution*, visit *The American Nation* section of **www.phschool.com**.

Fighting at Sea The British navy blockaded American ports to stop American trade. Though unable to break the blockade, several American sea captains won stunning victories.

One famous battle took place early in the war, in August 1812. As he was sailing near Newfoundland, Isaac Hull, captain of the USS *Constitution,* spotted the British ship HMS *Guerrière* (gai ree AIR). For nearly an hour, the two ships jockeyed for position. At last, the guns of the *Constitution* roared into action. They tore holes in the sides of the *Guerrière* and shot off both masts. Stunned, the British captain had no choice but to surrender.

American sea captains won other victories at sea. These victories cheered Americans but did little to win the war.

War in the West

One goal of the War Hawks was to conquer Canada. They were convinced that Canadians would welcome the chance to throw off British rule and join the United States.

Invasion of Canada General William Hull moved American troops into Canada from Detroit. The Canadians had only a few untrained troops to ward off the invasion. However, they were led by a clever British general, Isaac Brock.

Brock paraded his soldiers in red coats to make it appear that experienced British troops were helping the Canadians. He also led Americans to think that a large number of Indians were fighting

AS YOU READ **Ask Questions** Write one question relating to each subheading under the heading "War in the West." As you read, look for the answers to your questions.

At age 14, Oliver Hazard Perry joined the United States Navy. He spent the rest of his life there.

At the Battle of Lake Erie, Perry's ship, the USS *Lawrence,* drew most of the British fire in the early hours of the battle. When the *Lawrence* could no longer fight, Perry took down his ship's flag. He then rowed a mile—while under fire—to reach another American ship. Raising his flag again, he fought on to victory.

Perry was hailed across the country as a hero. Today, the U.S. Naval Academy treasures his battle flag from Lake Erie.

Why did Americans consider Perry a hero?

Primary Sources

See "Francis Scott Key: The Star-Spangled Banner" on page 591 of the Reference Section.

alongside the Canadians. Brock's scare tactics worked. Hull retreated from Canada. Other attempts to invade Canada also failed.

Battle of Lake Erie In 1813, the Americans set out to win control of Lake Erie. Captain Oliver Hazard Perry had no fleet, so he designed and built his own ships. In September 1813, he sailed his tiny fleet against the British.

During the Battle of Lake Erie, the British battered Perry's own ship and left it helpless. Perry rowed over to another American ship and continued to fight. Finally, the Americans won the battle. Captain Perry wrote his message of victory on the back of an envelope: "We have met the enemy and they are ours."

Native American Losses After losing control of Lake Erie, the British and their ally Tecumseh retreated from Detroit into Canada. General William Henry Harrison, veteran of Tippecanoe, pursued them. The Americans won a decisive victory at the Battle of the Thames. Tecumseh died in the fighting. Without Tecumseh's leadership, the Indian confederation soon fell apart.

Still, the Creeks continued their fight against the settlers in the South. Andrew Jackson, a Tennessee officer, took command of American troops in the Creek War. In 1814, with the help of the Cherokees, Jackson won a crushing victory at the Battle of Horseshoe Bend. The leader of the Creeks walked alone into Jackson's camp to surrender. "Your people have destroyed my nation," he said.

Final Battles

In 1814, Britain and its allies defeated France. With the war in Europe over, Britain could send more troops and ships against the United States.

The British Burn Washington In August 1814, British ships sailed into Chesapeake Bay and landed an invasion force about 30 miles from Washington, D.C. American troops met the British at Bladensburg, Maryland. As President Madison watched, the battle-hardened British quickly scattered the untrained Americans. The British met little further resistance on their march to the capital.

In the White House, First Lady Dolley Madison waited for her husband to return. Hastily, she scrawled a note to her sister:

66 Will you believe it, my sister? We have had a battle or skirmish near Bladensburg and here I am still within sound of the cannon! Mr. Madison comes not. May God protect us. Two messengers covered with dust come bid me fly. But here I mean to wait for him. 99

—Dolley Madison, *Memoirs and Letters of Dolley Madison*

Soon after, British troops marched into the capital. Dolley Madison gathered up important papers of the President and a portrait of George Washington. Then, she fled south. She was not there to see the British set fire to the White House and other buildings.

From Washington, the British marched north toward the city of Baltimore. The key to Baltimore's defense was Fort McHenry. From

The War of 1812

Key

→ American forces
✶ American victories
→ British forces
✶ British victories

L. Superior

Indiana Territory

Illinois Territory

Ft. Mackinac

BRITISH TERRITORY

Claimed by Great Britain and the United States

St. Lawrence R.

Sorel
Montreal
Lake Champlain
Plattsburgh

Maine (part of MA)

VT   NH

Action in the South

90° W   85° W

35° N

Mississippi R.

Huntsville

Mississippi Territory

Horseshoe Bend
Ft. Jackson

LA

Mobile   Pensacola

New Orleans   Ft. Bowyer

Gulf of Mexico

0   200 Miles

0   200 Kilometers

L. Michigan

L. Huron

Michigan Territory

Detroit

Frenchtown

Lundy's Lane

L. Ontario

Chippewa

The Thames

L. Erie

Put-in-Bay   Erie

Indiana Territory

Ohio

Pennsylvania

New York

Hartford
CT

MA

RI

Hudson R.

45°N

40°N

ATLANTIC OCEAN

British blockade

Kentucky

Tennessee

Potomac R.

Ohio R.

Washington, D.C.

Virginia

North Carolina

Baltimore

NJ

DE
MD

Chesapeake Bay

Albers Equal-Area Projection
0   100   200 Miles
0   100   200 Kilometers

35°N

the evening of September 13 until dawn on September 14, British rockets bombarded the harbor.

When the early morning fog lifted, the "broad stripes and bright stars" of the American flag still waved over Fort McHenry. The British withdrew. Francis Scott Key, a young American lawyer who witnessed the battle, wrote a poem about it. Soon, "The Star-Spangled Banner" was published and set to music. Today, it is the national anthem of the United States.

Battle of New Orleans In late 1814, the British prepared to attack New Orleans. From there, they hoped to sail up the Mississippi. However, Andrew Jackson was waiting. Jackson had turned his frontier fighters into a strong army. He took Pensacola in Spanish Florida to keep the British from using it as a base. He then marched through Mobile and set up camp in New Orleans.

Jackson's force included thousands of frontiersmen and Choctaw Indians. The Choctaws were longtime rivals of the northern Indian nations who had been allied with the British. Many of Jackson's troops were expert riflemen. Citizens of New Orleans also joined the army to defend their city from the British. Among the volunteers were hundreds of African Americans.

The American soldiers dug trenches to defend themselves. On January 8, 1815, the British attacked. Again and again, British soldiers marched toward the American trenches. More than 2,000 British fell under the deadly fire of American sharpshooters and, especially, American cannons. Only seven Americans died.

GEOGRAPHY Skills

The War of 1812 was fought along several fronts.

1. **Location** On the map, locate the following: **(a)** Lake Erie, **(b)** Horseshoe Bend, **(c)** Baltimore, **(d)** New Orleans.

2. **Movement** Describe the American route from Huntsville to New Orleans.

3. **Critical Thinking Drawing Conclusions** Based on the map, do you think the British blockade had a serious impact on Americans? Explain.

Viewing History

Battle of New Orleans

New Orleans

The Battle of New Orleans was the single bloodiest engagement of the War of 1812. Here, Americans under the command of Andrew Jackson fire at advancing British soldiers.

Analyzing Information *How does this painting show the varied makeup of Jackson's troops?*

Americans cheered the victory at the Battle of New Orleans. Overnight, Andrew Jackson became a national hero. His fame did not dim even when Americans learned that the battle had taken place two weeks after the war ended. The United States and Britain had already signed a treaty in Europe.

African Americans in the War The Battle of New Orleans was not the only place where black and white soldiers fought side by side. Throughout the War of 1812, African Americans joined in defending the nation against the British.

Following the British attacks on Washington and Baltimore, African American volunteers helped defend Philadelphia against a possible British attack. Bishop Richard Allen and the Reverend Absalom Jones recruited more than 2,000 men to help build Philadelphia's fortifications. The state of New York organized two regiments of black volunteers to serve in the army.

African Americans also served with distinction in the United States Navy. They helped win the Battle of Lake Erie as well as other naval battles. Commander Nathaniel Shaler praised one particular black sailor who was killed in battle:

> **❝** He fell near me, and several times requested to be thrown overboard, saying he was only in the way of others. When America has such [sailors], she has little to fear from the tyrants of the ocean. **❞**
>
> —Nathaniel Shaler, letter to his agent, January 1, 1813

Protest and Peace

In the early 1800s, news took weeks to cross the Atlantic Ocean. By late 1814, Americans knew that peace talks had begun, but they did not know if they would succeed or how long they would last. As Jackson was preparing to fight the British at New Orleans, New Englanders were meeting to protest "Mr. Madison's War."

New Englanders Protest The British blockade had hurt New England's sea trade. Also, many New Englanders feared that the United States might win land in Florida and Canada. If new states were carved out of these lands, the South and the West would become more influential than New England.

Delegates from around New England met in Hartford, Connecticut, in December 1814. Most were Federalists. They disliked the Republican President and the war. The delegates to the Hartford Convention threatened to leave the Union if the war continued.

Then, while the delegates debated what to do, news of the peace treaty arrived. The Hartford Convention ended quickly. With the war over, the protest was meaningless. In the end, the threat of secession further weakened the dying Federalist party.

"Nothing Was Settled" A peace treaty was signed in the city of Ghent, Belgium, on December 24, 1814. John Quincy Adams, one of the American delegates, summed up the Treaty of Ghent in one sentence: "Nothing was adjusted, nothing was settled."

Britain and the United States agreed to restore prewar conditions. The treaty said nothing about impressment or neutrality. These issues had faded due to the end of the wars in Europe. Other issues were settled later. In 1818, for example, the two nations settled a dispute over the border between Canada and the United States.

Looking back, some Americans felt that the War of 1812 had been a mistake. Others argued that Europe would now treat the young republic with more respect. The victories of heroes like Oliver Hazard Perry, William Henry Harrison, and Andrew Jackson gave Americans new pride in their country. As one Republican leader remarked, "The people are now more American. They feel and act more as a nation."

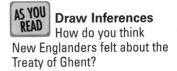 **Draw Inferences** How do you think New Englanders felt about the Treaty of Ghent?

 AFTER YOU READ

Section 5 Assessment

Recall

1. Identify Explain the significance of **(a)** Oliver Hazard Perry, **(b)** Battle of Lake Erie, **(c)** Andrew Jackson, **(d)** Dolley Madison, **(e)** Battle of New Orleans, **(f)** Hartford Convention, **(g)** Treaty of Ghent.

Comprehension

2. What military problems did the United States face at the start of the war?

3. How did the death of Tecumseh affect the war in the West?

4. How did Andrew Jackson achieve victory in the Battle of New Orleans?

5. Why did New Englanders threaten to leave the Union?

Critical Thinking and Writing

6. Exploring the Main Idea Review the Main Idea statement at the beginning of this section. Then, list two reasons supporting and two reasons opposing John Quincy Adams's statement, "Nothing was adjusted, nothing was settled."

7. Drawing Conclusions Both William Henry Harrison and Andrew Jackson later became President. Write a paragraph explaining why war heroes often make attractive political candidates.

ACTIVITY

Writing a Song Like Francis Scott Key, you are a witness to one of the major conflicts of the War of 1812. With a partner, write a song or poem describing your feelings about the events going on around you.

CREATING A CHAPTER SUMMARY

Copy the concept web below. Fill in the blank ovals with important developments that shaped the United States during the Age of Jefferson. Add as many ovals as you need.

- AGE OF JEFFERSON
  - Government
    - Marbury v. Madison
  - Economics
    - Jefferson supports laissez faire
  - National growth
  - Foreign affairs

iTEXT

For additional review and enrichment activities, see the interactive version of *The American Nation,* available on the Web and on CD-ROM.

Take It to the NET

Chapter Self-Test For practice test questions for Chapter 10, visit *The American Nation* section of **www.phschool.com**.

Building Vocabulary

Review the chapter vocabulary words listed below. Then, use the words and their definitions to create a matching quiz. Exchange quizzes with another student. Check each other's answers.

1. democratic
2. laissez faire
3. free market
4. judicial review
5. expedition
6. continental divide
7. impressment
8. embargo
9. confederation
10. nationalism

Reviewing Key Facts

11. Describe two ways that Jefferson reversed Federalist policies. (Section 1)
12. Why did Jefferson decide that the Louisiana Purchase was constitutional? (Section 2)
13. How did Americans react to the British practice of impressment? (Section 3)
14. What were the results of the battles of Fallen Timbers and Tippecanoe? (Section 4)
15. What role did African American soldiers play in the War of 1812? (Section 5)

Critical Thinking and Writing

16. **Applying Information** In 1787, Jefferson stated, "The policy of the American government is to leave their citizens free, neither restraining nor aiding them in their pursuits." **(a)** Restate Jefferson's main point in your own words. **(b)** List two ways in which Jefferson's economic policies reflected this idea.
17. **Connecting to Geography: Place** Jefferson had Lewis and Clark take detailed notes about the Louisiana Purchase. Make a list of at least five geographic features, such as climate or plant life. For each item on your list, write a sentence explaining why information about this feature might be important for future settlers.
18. **Linking Past and Present** Suppose that a law like the Embargo Act of 1807 were passed today. List five ways a ban on foreign trade might affect the nation and your own life.
19. **Ranking** List the reasons the War Hawks wanted to go to war with Britain. Circle the reason you think is most valid, and underline the reason you think is least valid. Write a sentence explaining your ranking.

Analyzing Primary Sources

In 1812, a New York newspaper printed an editorial in favor of war with Britain. Nicholas Smyth of Boston wrote this reply. Read the excerpt and answer the questions that follow:

> 66 We hear from the halls of Congress the cry 'On to Canada!' It is the fur dealer and the land speculator who want war, but it is we of New England who will pay the price. If war comes, it is our seaports that will be blockaded; it is our cities that will be destroyed. The War Hawks of Tennessee and Kentucky are safe. I doubt if the English navy can reach them. 99

—Nicholas Smyth, Records of the House Foreign Affairs Committee

20. According to Smyth, who is in favor of conquering Canada?
21. Why does Smyth say that New England will "pay the price" of the war?
22. Summarize Smyth's attitude toward the "War Hawks of Tennessee and Kentucky."
23. Do you think that Smyth would be likely to support the Hartford Convention? Explain.

Synthesizing Information

War of 1812 Vote in House of Representatives

REGIONS	FOR WAR	AGAINST WAR
New England	12	20
Middle States	21	18
The South	37	11
The West	9	0
Total	79	49

Source: Thomas A. Bailey, *A Diplomatic History of the American People*

This table shows the war vote in the House of Representatives in 1812. Look at the table and compare it to the letter at left.

24. Based on the table, which is a true statement?
   A New England was largely in favor of war.
   B The West was largely in favor of war.
   C The war had overwhelming support.
   D Regional differences played no role.
25. How did the vote in Congress reflect the concerns expressed in Smyth's letter?

ACTIVITIES

Connecting With . . . Government and Citizenship

Giving a Talk Give a one-minute talk based on one of the following quotations from Thomas Jefferson. Explain what Jefferson meant and how that idea still applies today.

- "The minority possess their equal rights, which equal laws must protect."
- "No government can continue good, but under the control of the people."
- "Whenever the people are well-informed, they can be trusted with their own government."
- "There is a debt of service due from every man to his country."
- "The true foundation of republican government is the equal right of every citizen in his person and property."

Take It to the NET

Connecting to Today
Preparing a Report Use the Internet to find out about one of the Indian nations shown on the map in Section 4. Prepare a report showing where they live today and how they maintain their traditions. For help in starting this activity, visit *The American Nation* section of **www.phschool.com**.

Evaluating Internet Sites
Reviewing Sites About Lewis and Clark Use the Internet to find sites relating to the Lewis and Clark expedition. Write a review comparing two of these sites in terms of source, type of information, visuals, primary sources, interactivity, and reliability. For help in starting this activity, visit *The American Nation* section of **www.phschool.com**.

The Nation Grows and Prospers

1790–1825

1 **The Industrial Revolution**
2 **Americans Move Westward**
3 **Unity and Division**
4 **New Nations in the Americas**

Slater's Mill

One of Fulton's early steamboats

1793

Samuel Slater builds a textile mill in Pawtucket, Rhode Island. It is the first successful textile mill in the United States.

1790s

The Lancaster Road improves travel between Philadelphia and central Pennsylvania.

Early 1800s

Development of the steam-powered boat creates a new age of steamboat travel on the major rivers of the United States.

AMERICAN EVENTS

| | George Washington | | Thomas Jefferson 1801–1809 | James Madison |
| Presidential Terms: | 1789–1797 | John Adams 1797–1801 | | 1809–1817 |

1790 ★ ★ **1800** ★ **1810**

WORLD EVENTS

▲ **1791**
Enslaved plantation workers in Haiti revolt against their French masters.

▲ **1802**
Britain passes a law limiting child labor.

Early Roads West

In the early 1800s, new roads linked the East to settlements in the West.

Key

Main roads

Albers Equal-Area Projection

0   200   400 Miles

0   200   400 Kilometers

BRITISH TERRITORY

80° W

100° W

Michigan Territory

Illinois

Indiana

Missouri

Vandalia

Louisville

KY

Cumberland Gap

Nashville

Tennessee

Arkansas Territory

Mississippi

Alabama

Georgia

Louisiana

L. Ontario

Buffalo

L. Erie

Cleveland

Ohio

Columbus

Pittsburgh

Wheeling

Boonesborough

Wilderness Rd.

Nashville Road

National Road

Ohio R.

APPALACHIAN MTS.

Cumberland

Great Valley Rd.

Virginia

Richmond

North Carolina

Raleigh

South Carolina

Charleston

Savannah

St. Augustine

Florida Territory

Mohawk Tpk.

Catskill Tpk.

Seneca Road

Hudson R.

Lancaster Turnpike

Pennsylvania Rd.

PA

NJ

New York

Philadelphia

Lancaster

Baltimore

DE

MD

Washington, D.C.

Coastal Post Rd.

Maine

Claimed by Great Britain and the United States

Portland

VT

NH

Albany

MA

Boston

Providence

RI

CT

Boston Post Road

New York

40° N

30° N

90° W

Gulf of Mexico

ATLANTIC OCEAN

Rio Grande

Missouri R.

Mississippi R.

N E S W

Flag of the United States, 1818

LOWELL OFFERING

November, 1845.

"Is Saul also among the prophets?"

A REPOSITORY OF ORIGINAL ARTICLES, WRITTEN BY "FACTORY GIRL."

LOWELL: MISSES CURTIS & FARLEY.
BOSTON: JORDAN & WILEY, 121
Washington street.
1845.

The *Lowell Offering*

1817

With the admission of Mississippi to the Union, the United States comprises 20 states.

1818

The National Road provides an alternative to travel over rocky, muddy older roads.

1830s

Young women workers in the Lowell textile mills publish their own literary journal.

James Madison 1809–1817

James Monroe 1817–1825

John Quincy Adams 1825–1829

Andrew Jackson 1829–1837

1810

1820

1830

▲ **1810**

Father Miguel Hidalgo leads revolt against Spanish rule in Mexico.

▲ **1821**

Mexico wins independence from Spain.

1 The Industrial Revolution

BEFORE YOU READ

Reading Focus

- What was the Industrial Revolution, and how did it take hold in the United States?
- Why was Lowell, Massachusetts, called a model factory town?
- What was daily life like in early factories?
- What impact did the Industrial Revolution have on American cities?

Key Terms

Industrial Revolution
spinning jenny
capital
capitalist
factory system
interchangeable parts
Lowell girl
urbanization

Taking Notes

Copy this flowchart. As you read the section, fill in the boxes with some of the major events described in it that led to the Industrial Revolution in the United States. Add as many boxes as you need to finish the flowchart.

```
┌─────────────────────┐
│ The Industrial      │
│ Revolution begins in│
│ Britain             │
└─────────────────────┘
         │
         ▼
┌─────────────────────┐
│ Crosses Atlantic to │
│ the United States   │
└─────────────────────┘
         │
         ▼
┌─────────────────────┐
│                     │
└─────────────────────┘
         │
         ▼
┌─────────────────────┐
│                     │
└─────────────────────┘
```

Main Idea During the first half of the 1800s, the Industrial Revolution caused dramatic changes in the way Americans worked and lived.

AS YOU READ

Lucy Larcom

Ask Questions Write one question that you might ask Lucy Larcom about her youthful years spent working in the Lowell spinning mills.

Setting the Scene At dawn, the factory bell woke 11-year-old Lucy Larcom. Rising quickly, she ate her breakfast and hurried to her job at a spinning mill in Lowell, Massachusetts. Years later, Larcom described her workplace:

> 66 The buzzing and hissing and whizzing of pulleys and rollers and spindles and flyers around me often grew tiresome. . . . I could look across the room and see girls moving backward and forward among the spinning frames, sometimes stooping, sometimes reaching up their arms, as their work required. 99
>
> —Lucy Larcom, *Among Lowell Mill-Girls: A Reminiscence*, 1881

In the early 1800s, busy factories and whirring machinery had become part of a revolution that was reaching the United States. Unlike the American Revolution, this one had no battles or fixed dates. The new revolution—the Industrial Revolution—was a long, slow process that completely changed the way in which goods were produced.

The Industrial Revolution Begins

Before the 1800s, most Americans were farmers and most goods were produced by hand. As a result of the Industrial Revolution, this situation slowly changed. Machines replaced hand tools. New sources of power, such as steam, replaced human and animal power. While most Americans continued to farm for a living, the economy began a gradual shift toward manufacturing.

New Technology The Industrial Revolution started in Britain in the mid-1700s. British inventors developed new machines that transformed the textile industry.

Viewing History

Changing Landscape The Industrial Revolution changed the face of the nation. In this painting, the artist shows an early factory among the church spires and green fields of a New England town. **Identifying Points of View** *What do you think is the point of view of the artist toward the changing face of the village? Explain.*

New England

Since the Middle Ages, workers had used spinning wheels to make thread. A spinning wheel, however, could spin only one thread at a time. In 1764, James Hargreaves developed the spinning jenny, a machine that could spin several threads at once. Other inventions speeded up the process of weaving thread into cloth. In the 1780s, Edmund Cartwright built a loom powered by water. It allowed a worker to produce a great deal more cloth in a day than was possible before.

The Factory System New inventions led to a new system of producing goods. Before the Industrial Revolution, most spinning and weaving took place in the home. Large machines however, had to be housed in large mills near rivers. Water flowing downstream or over a waterfall turned a wheel that produced the power to run the machines.

To set up and operate a spinning mill required large amounts of capital, or money. Capitalists supplied this money. A capitalist is a person who invests in a business in order to make a profit. Capitalists built factories and hired workers to run the machines.

The new factory system brought workers and machinery together in one place to produce goods. Factory workers earned daily or weekly wages. They had to work a set number of hours each day.

A Revolution Crosses the Atlantic

Britain wanted to keep its new technology secret. It did not want rival nations to copy the new machines. Therefore, the British Parliament passed a law forbidding anyone to take plans of the new machinery out of the country.

Slater Breaks the Law Samuel Slater soon proved that this law could not be enforced. Slater was a skilled mechanic in a British textile mill. When he heard that Americans were offering large rewards for plans of British factories, he decided to leave Britain. In 1789,

Slater boarded a ship bound for New York City. He knew that British officials searched the baggage of passengers sailing to the United States. To avoid getting caught, he memorized the design of the machines in the mill.

The First American Mill Slater soon visited Moses Brown, a Quaker capitalist who had a mill in Pawtucket, Rhode Island. The mill was not doing well because its machinery constantly broke down. Slater set to work on improving the machinery. By 1793, in Pawtucket, he built what became the first successful textile mill in the United States that was powered by water. Slater's wife, Hannah Slater, contributed to the success of the mill. She discovered how to make thread stronger so that it would not snap on the spindles.

Slater's factory was a huge success. Before long, other American manufacturers began using his ideas.

Interchangeable Parts American manufacturers benefited from the pioneering work of American inventor Eli Whitney. Earlier, skilled workers made goods by hand. For example, gunsmiths spent days making the barrel, stock, and trigger for a single musket. Because the parts were handmade, each musket differed a bit from every other musket. If a part broke, a gunsmith had to make a new part to fit that particular gun.

Whitney wanted to speed up the making of guns by having machines manufacture each part. All machine-made parts would be alike—for example, one trigger would be identical to another. Interchangeable parts would save time and money.

Because the government bought many guns, Whitney went to Washington, D.C., to try to sell his idea. At first, officials laughed at his plan. Carefully, Whitney sorted parts for 10 muskets into separate piles. He then asked an official to choose one part from each pile. In minutes, the first musket was assembled. Whitney repeated the process until 10 muskets were complete.

The idea of interchangeable parts spread rapidly. Inventors designed machines to produce interchangeable parts for clocks, locks, and many other goods. With such machines, small workshops grew into factories.

Lowell, Massachusetts: A Model Factory Town

The War of 1812 provided a boost to American industries. The British blockade cut Americans off from their supply of foreign goods. As a result, they had to produce more goods themselves.

The Lowell Mills During the war, Francis Cabot Lowell, a Boston merchant, found a way to improve on British textile mills. In Britain, one factory spun thread and a second factory wove it into cloth. Why not, Lowell wondered, combine spinning and weaving under one roof? The new mill that he built in Waltham, Massachusetts, had all the machines needed to turn raw cotton into finished cloth.

After Lowell's death, his partners took on a more ambitious project. They built an entire factory town and named it after him. In

Viewing History

Inside a Textile Mill

Lowell, Massachusetts

Work in the textile mills in the early 1800s was hard. Workers faced long hours on their feet amid the noisy machines. Yet, the mills were generally clean and orderly.

Analyzing Primary Sources
What clues does the picture give to conditions in this mill?

1821, Lowell, Massachusetts, was a village of five farm families. By 1836, it boasted more than 10,000 people. Visitors to Lowell described it as a model community composed of "small wooden houses, painted white, with green blinds, very neat, very snug, very nicely carpeted."

"Lowell Girls" To work in their new mills, the company hired young women from nearby farms. The Lowell girls, as they came to be called, usually worked for a few years in the mills before returning home to marry. Most sent their wages home to their families.

At first, parents hesitated to let their daughters work in the mills. To reassure parents, the company built boardinghouses. The company also made rules to protect the young women.

Although factory work was often tedious and hard, many women valued the economic freedom they got from working in the mills. One worker wrote her sister Sarah back on a farm in New Hampshire:

> 66 Since I have wrote you, another pay day has come around. I earned 14 dollars and a half . . . I like it well as ever and Sarah don't I feel independent of everyone! 99
> — from *Lowell Offering: Writings by New England Mill Women*

Daily Life During the Industrial Revolution

In Lowell and elsewhere, mill owners hired mostly women and children. They did this because they could pay women and children half of what they would have had to pay men.

▲ **Past**

▲ **Present**

Child Labor Boys and girls as young as seven worked in factories. Small children were especially useful in textile mills because they could squeeze around the large machines to change spindles.

Today, most Americans look upon child labor as cruel. Yet in the 1800s, farm children also worked hard. Most people did not see much difference between children working in a factory or on a farm. Often, a child's wages were needed to help support the family.

Long Hours Working hours in the mills were long—12 hours a day, 6 days a week. True, farmers also put in long hours. However, farmers worked shorter hours in winter. Mill workers, in contrast, worked nearly the same hours all year round.

In the early 1800s, conditions in American mills were generally much better than in most factories in Europe. As industries grew, however, competition increased and employers took less interest in the welfare of their workers. In later chapters, you will read how working conditions grew worse.

Changes in Home Life The Industrial Revolution had a great impact on home life. As the factory system spread, more family members left the home to earn a living.

These changes affected ideas about the role of women. In poorer families, women often had to go out to work. In wealthier families, husbands supported the family while wives stayed at home. For many husbands, having a wife who stayed at home became a sign of success.

Growing Cities

In 1800, the vast majority of Americans lived in rural areas. During the Industrial Revolution, many people left farms to work in factories. Older cities expanded rapidly, while new cities sprang up around factories. This movement of the population from farms to cities is called **urbanization.**

Urbanization was a steady but gradual process. In 1800, only 6 percent of the nation's population lived in urban areas. By 1850, the number had risen to 15 percent. Not until 1920 did more Americans live in cities than on farms.

By today's standards, these early cities were small. A person could walk from one end of any American city to the other in as little as 30 minutes. Buildings were only a few stories tall. As the factory system spread, the nation's cities grew.

Hazards Growing cities had many problems. Dirt and gravel streets turned into mudholes when it rained. Cities had no sewers, and people threw garbage into the streets. A visitor to New York reported that "The streets are filthy, and the stranger is not a little surprised to meet the hogs walking about in them, for the purpose of devouring the vegetables and trash thrown into the gutter."

Under these conditions, disease spread easily. Epidemics of influenza and cholera (KAHL er uh) raged through cities, killing hundreds.

Attractions Cities had attractions, too. Theaters, museums, and circuses created an air of excitement. In cities, people could shop in fine stores that sold the latest fashions from Europe. Some offered modern "ready-to-wear" clothing. While most women continued to sew their own clothes, many enjoyed visiting hat shops, china shops, shoe stores, and "fancy-goods" stores.

AS YOU READ

Summarize Write two or three sentences summarizing the major results of urbanization in the early 1800s.

Section 1 Assessment

AFTER YOU READ

Recall

1. **Identify** Explain the significance of **(a)** Industrial Revolution, **(b)** Samuel Slater, **(c)** Eli Whitney, **(d)** Lowell girl.
2. **Define** **(a)** spinning jenny, **(b)** capital, **(c)** capitalist, **(d)** factory system, **(e)** interchangeable parts, **(f)** urbanization.

Comprehension

3. How did the Industrial Revolution begin in the United States?
4. What was unusual about the factory town of Lowell, Massachusetts?
5. What were conditions like for workers during the early Industrial Revolution?

6. Describe three ways in which American cities were changed by the early Industrial Revolution.

Critical Thinking and Writing

7. **Exploring the Main Idea** Review the Main Idea statement at the beginning of the section. Then, list three examples of changes in the way Americans lived and worked that were a result of the Industrial Revolution.
8. **Drawing Conclusions** Make a list of the reasons why both inventors and capitalists were needed to bring about the Industrial Revolution.

ACTIVITY

 Take It to the NET
Use the Internet to learn more about life for the "Lowell girls" of the early 1800s. Then, suppose that you are a worker at the mill, and compose a diary entry describing a typical day. Visit *The American Nation* section of **www.phschool.com** for help in completing the activity.

How a Textile Mill Worked

New technology, like that used by Samuel Slater's mill, helped spark the Industrial Revolution. The diagram shows how rapidly moving water turned a water wheel. The wheel produced the power to run the machines.

Samuel Slater

1 Wagons bring raw cotton to the mill to be spun into thread.

2 Fast-moving water causes the water wheel to turn.

3 The turning water wheel powers the mill's main shaft.

4 The main shaft drives pulleys, which turn belts that drive the mill machinery.

5 Carding machines comb the raw cotton fiber.

6 Drawing machines pull the combed cotton fibers into ropelike strands.

7 Spinning frames twist combed and drawn cotton strands into thread and wind them onto a bobbin.

8 Wagons carry spun thread to weavers, who use it to make cloth.

ACTIVITY

Make a drawing of the mill's water wheel and main mill shaft. Show how water power is transmitted through the water wheel to the mill's main shaft.

2 Americans Move Westward

Reading Focus

- How did settlers travel west in the early 1800s?
- What steps did Americans take to improve their roads?
- How did steamboats and canals improve transportation for Americans?

Key Terms

flatboat

turnpike

Lancaster Turnpike

corduroy road

National Road

Clermont

Erie Canal

Taking Notes

As you read, complete this table listing important developments in transportation in the United States at the beginning of the 1800s. Add as many rows as you need.

TRAVELING WEST	IMPROVING ROAD TRANSPORTATION	NEW STEAMBOATS AND CANALS
• Roads to the West • Travel by flatboat	•	•

Main Idea Improvements in transportation in the first half of the 1800s helped make it easier to move people and goods in the expanding nation.

Setting the Scene The stagecoach was bogged down in the spring mud, its big wheels sunk up to the axles. The passengers stood by the side of the road while the stage driver urged his horses to pull the coach out of the mud. Suddenly, one traveler spotted a beautiful fur cap lying in the middle of a huge mudhole just ahead. He had to have that cap!

The traveler stepped through the mud until at last he snatched up the hat. To his surprise, he saw a man's head *underneath*—a man buried in the mud! "Come help pull this fellow out!" called the traveler to his friends. The man in the mud shook his head. "Just leave me alone, stranger," he said. "I have a good horse under me, and have just found bottom."

Americans during the 1830s loved to tell this tall tale. The story was so popular because travel in the United States was often difficult. As the young nation grew, Americans saw an urgent need to improve transportation, both on water and over land.

AS YOU READ **A necessary stop** **Draw Inferences** What details in the story and painting suggest that travelers often had a rough ride?

Traveling West

Settlers had been moving steadily westward since the 1600s. In the early 1800s, the stream of pioneers turned into a flood. By 1820, so many people had moved west that the population in some of the original 13 states had actually declined!

Western Routes Settlers took a number of routes west. One well-traveled path was the Great Wagon Road across Pennsylvania. It dated back to colonial days. Some settlers then continued south and west along the trail opened by Daniel Boone before the Revolution. Known as the Wilderness Road, it led through the Cumberland Gap into Kentucky.

Other settlers pushed west to Pittsburgh. There, they loaded their animals and wagons onto **flatboats** and journeyed down the Ohio River into Indiana, Kentucky, and Illinois. Flatboats were well

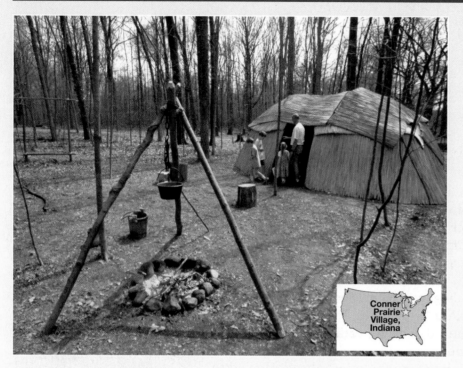

Conner Prairie Village

Conner Prairie is a center for entertainment and education focusing on the lives and times of western settlers in the early 1800s. It consists of five historic areas, including the re-created 1836 village of Prairietown. Another site is the Lenape (luh-NAH-pay) Indian Camp and McKinnen's Trading Post, shown here. The historic areas are set on a 210-acre woodland site.

 Take It to the NET

Virtual Field Trip For an interactive look at Conner Prairie Village, visit *The American Nation* section of **www.phschool.com**.

suited to the shallow waters of the Ohio. Even when carrying heavy cargoes, these barges rode high in the water.

Pioneers from Georgia and South Carolina followed other trails west to Alabama, Mississippi, and Louisiana. Enslaved African Americans helped to carve plantations in the rich, fertile soil of these territories.

People from New England, New York, and Pennsylvania pushed into the Northwest Territory. Some settlers traveled west from Albany, New York, along the Mohawk River and across the Appalachians. Many then sailed across Lake Erie into Ohio.

New States Before long, some western territories had populations large enough to apply for statehood. Between 1792 and 1819, eight states joined the Union: Kentucky (1792), Tennessee (1796), Ohio (1803), Louisiana (1812), Indiana (1816), Mississippi (1817), Illinois (1818), and Alabama (1819).

AS YOU READ **Ask Questions** As you read the next two sections, turn each blue heading into a question. Then, read to find the answers to these questions.

Improvements to Roads

Settlers faced difficult journeys to the West. Many roads were narrow trails, barely wide enough for a single wagon. Trails often plunged through muddy swamps. Tree stumps stuck up through the road and often broke the wagon axles of careless travelers. The nation badly needed better roads.

Turnpikes and Corduroy Roads In the United States, as in Europe, private companies built gravel and stone roads. To pay for these roads, the companies collected tolls from travelers. At various points along the road, a pike, or pole, blocked the road. After a wagon driver had paid a toll, the pike keeper turned the pole aside to let the wagon pass. As a result, these toll roads were called **turnpikes.**

Probably the best road in the United States was the **Lancaster Turnpike.** Built in the 1790s by a private company, the road linked Philadelphia and Lancaster, Pennsylvania. Because the road was set on a bed of gravel, water drained off quickly. For a smooth ride, the road was topped with flat stones.

Other roads were more primitive. In swampy areas, roads were made of logs. These roads were known as **corduroy roads** because the lines of logs looked like corduroy cloth. Corduroy roads kept wagons from sinking into the mud, but they made for a very noisy and bumpy ride.

The National Road Some states set aside money to improve roads or build new ones. In 1806, for the first time, Congress approved funds for a national road-building project. The National Road was to run from Cumberland, Maryland, to Wheeling, in western Virginia.

Work on the National Road began in 1811. Because of the War of 1812, it was not completed until 1818. Later, the road was extended into Illinois. As each new section of road was built, settlers eagerly used it to drive their wagons west.

Steam Transport

Whenever possible, travelers and freight haulers used river transportation. Floating downstream on a flatboat was both faster and more comfortable than bumping along rutted roads. It also cost less.

Yet, river travel had its own problems. Moving upstream was difficult. People used paddles or long poles to push boats against the current. Sometimes, they hauled boats from the shore with ropes. Both methods were slow. A boat could travel downstream from Pittsburgh to New Orleans in about six weeks. However, the return trip upstream took at least 17 weeks!

Fitch and Fulton A new invention, the steam engine, opened a new era in river travel. In 1787, John Fitch showed members of the Constitutional Convention how a steam engine could power a boat. He then opened a ferry service on the Delaware River. However, few people used the ferry, and Fitch went out of business.

Inventor Robert Fulton may have seen Fitch's steamboat in Philadelphia. In 1807, Fulton launched his own steamboat, the *Clermont,* on the Hudson River. On its first run, the *Clermont* carried passengers from New York City to Albany and back. The 300-mile trip took just 62 hours—a record at the time.

The Age of Steamboats Fulton's success ushered in the age of steamboats. Soon, steamboats were ferrying passengers up and down the Atlantic coast. More important, steamboats revolutionized travel in the West. Besides carrying people, steamboats on the Mississippi, Ohio, and Missouri rivers gave farmers and merchants a cheap means of moving goods.

Primary Sources

See Mark Twain, "Life on the Mississippi," on page 592 of the Reference section.

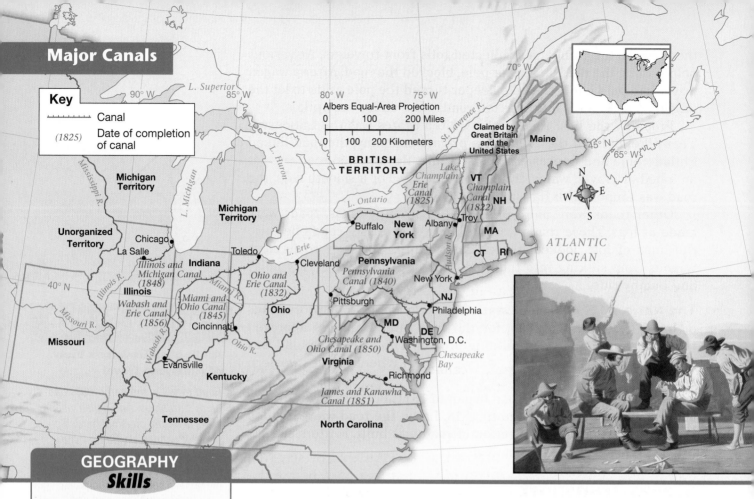

Major Canals

Key

——|—— Canal

(1825) Date of completion of canal

Albers Equal-Area Projection

0   100   200 Miles

0   100   200 Kilometers

BRITISH TERRITORY

Michigan Territory

Unorganized Territory

Michigan Territory

Chicago
La Salle
Illinois and Michigan Canal (1848)
Illinois
Wabash and Erie Canal (1856)
Indiana
Toledo
Cleveland
Ohio and Erie Canal (1832)
Miami and Ohio Canal (1845)
Cincinnati
Ohio
Evansville
Kentucky
Tennessee

Missouri

L. Superior
L. Michigan
L. Huron
L. Ontario
L. Erie

Buffalo
New York
Albany
Troy
Lake Champlain Erie Canal (1825)
VT
Champlain Canal (1822)
NH
MA
CT   RI
Maine
Claimed by Great Britain and the United States

ATLANTIC OCEAN

Pennsylvania
Pennsylvania Canal (1840)
Pittsburgh
New York
NJ
Philadelphia
MD
DE   Washington, D.C.
Chesapeake and Ohio Canal (1850)
Virginia
Richmond
James and Kanawha Canal (1851)
Chesapeake Bay
North Carolina

GEOGRAPHY Skills

The success of the Erie Canal, completed in 1825, set off an age of canal building. The painting by George Caleb Bingham shows boatsmen relaxing after a long workday.

1. **Location** On the map, locate **(a)** New York City, **(b)** Troy, **(c)** Buffalo, **(d)** Lake Erie, **(e)** Erie Canal.

2. **Movement** What two bodies of water were linked by the Illinois and Michigan Canal?

3. **Critical Thinking Applying Information** Use the map to trace an all-water route from Evansville, Indiana, to New York City.

Because western rivers were shallow, Henry Shreve designed a flat-bottomed steamboat. It could carry heavy loads without getting stuck on sandbars.

Still, steamboat travel could be dangerous. Sparks from smokestacks could cause fires. As steamboat captains raced each other along the river, high-pressure boilers sometimes exploded. Between 1811 and 1851, 44 steamboats collided, 166 burned, and more than 200 exploded.

The Canal Boom

Steamboats and better roads brought many improvements. But they did not help western farmers get their goods directly to markets in the East. To meet this need, Americans dug canals. A canal is an artificial channel filled with water that allows boats to cross a stretch of land.

The earliest American canals were no more than a few miles long. Some provided routes around waterfalls on a river. Other canals linked rivers to nearby lakes. By the early 1800s, however, Americans were building longer canals.

Building the Erie Canal Some New Yorkers had a bold idea. They wanted to build a canal linking the Great Lakes with the Mohawk and Hudson rivers. The Erie Canal would let western farmers ship their goods to the port of New York. It would also bring business to towns along the route.

To many people, the idea of such a canal seemed far-fetched. When Thomas Jefferson heard of the plan, he exclaimed:

66 Why, sir, you talk of making a canal 350 miles through the wilderness—it is little short of madness to think of it at this day! 99

—Thomas Jefferson to Joshua Forman of New York, 1809

New York's governor DeWitt Clinton ignored such criticism. He persuaded state lawmakers to provide money for the Erie Canal. Scoffers referred to the project as "Clinton's Ditch."

Work on the Erie Canal began in 1817. At first, thousands of workers dug the waterway by hand. To speed up progress, inventors developed new equipment. One machine, a stump-puller, could pull out nearly 40 tree stumps a day. In two places, the canal had to cross over rivers. Workers built stone bridges to carry the canal over the rivers.

An Instant Success By 1825, the immense job was finished. On opening day of the Erie Canal, a cannon fired a volley in Buffalo, New York. When the sound got to the next town along the route, that town, too, fired a cannon. Town after town fired cannons—all the way to New York City. The thunderous salute took 80 minutes to complete.

The Erie Canal was an instant success. The cost of shipping goods dropped to about one tenth of what it had been before the canal was built. The canal also helped to make New York City a center of commerce.

The success of the Erie Canal led other states to build canals. These canals created vital economic links between western farms and eastern cities.

Section 2 Assessment

Recall
1. **Identify** Explain the significance of **(a)** Lancaster Turnpike, **(b)** National Road, **(c)** John Fitch, **(d)** Robert Fulton, **(e)** *Clermont,* **(f)** Henry Shreve, **(g)** DeWitt Clinton, **(h)** Erie Canal.
2. **Define** **(a)** flatboat, **(b)** turnpike, **(c)** corduroy road.

Comprehension
3. What routes did settlers use to reach the West in the early 1800s?
4. Describe two ways in which road transportation improved in the early 1800s.

5. What role did the steamboat play in the growing nation?

Critical Thinking and Writing
6. **Exploring the Main Idea** Review the Main Idea statement at the beginning of this section. Then, write an imaginary diary entry of a trip along the National Road that explains how the road has made travel easier.
7. **Identifying Alternatives** Examine the maps in this chapter. Then, describe two ways a farmer might have shipped a cargo of grain from Cleveland, Ohio, to New York City. Explain the advantages of each route.

ACTIVITY

Writing a Newspaper Story Review the chapter's description of opening day on the Erie Canal. Write a newspaper story reporting on that first day. Write a newspaper-style headline and a lead sentence that covers the *who, what, when, where,* and *why* of the event.

3 Unity and Division

BEFORE YOU READ

Reading Focus

- What role did sectionalism play in the nation during the Era of Good Feelings?
- How did Congress help American industry after the War of 1812?
- What was Henry Clay's American System?
- How did the Supreme Court give more power to the federal government?

Key Terms

Era of Good Feelings

sectionalism

American System

internal improvements

McCulloch v. *Maryland*

Gibbons v. *Ogden*

interstate commerce

Taking Notes

As you read, prepare an outline of this section. Use roman numerals to indicate the major headings of this section, capital letters for the subheadings, and numbers for the supporting details. The sample at right will help you get started.

> I. An Era of Good Feelings
> II. Three Sectional Leaders
>   A. Calhoun of the South
>   1.
>   2.
>   B. Webster of the North
>   1.
>   2.
>   C.
>   1.
>   2.
> III. Helping American Businesses Grow

Main Idea Despite some tensions between different sections, the nation enjoyed an "era of good feelings" after the War of 1812.

AS YOU READ The Fourth of July in 1819

Use Prior Knowledge Name some of the reasons why Americans were especially proud of their country after 1815.

Setting the Scene

In Charleston, a cook named Abigail Jones put her advertisement in the newspaper early. Turtle meat would be available for sale on July 4 only. When Americans celebrated the Fourth of July in the early 1800s, turtle soup was one of the two most popular holiday foods.

What was the other? For a hot summer holiday like the Fourth, Americans loved the rare treat of ice cream. In Boston, a Mr. Shindles advertised "iced creams, of the best quality" in four flavors. At Vauxhall Gardens in Charleston, sellers warned people to come early, before all the ice cream was eaten.

After the War of 1812, Fourth of July celebrations became more popular than ever. Americans were proud of their country. They were especially proud that the nation was growing rapidly. Improved transportation allowed the opening of new lands to settlers. New industries were appearing. In Congress, a new generation of political leaders sought to direct this expansion.

An Era of Good Feelings

In 1816, the Republican candidate for President, James Monroe, easily defeated the Federalist, Senator Rufus King of New York. The election showed how seriously the Federalist party had declined in popularity. Many Federalists had joined the Republican party and voted for Monroe.

Monroe was the last Revolutionary War officer to become President. He was almost 60 years old when he took office, and he still followed the fashions of the late 1700s. He wore a powdered wig at a time when young men were wearing their hair loose. While other Americans wore long trousers, he still wore breeches and long stockings.

Americans were fond of his old-fashioned ways. In 1817, he made a goodwill tour of the country. In Boston, crowds cheered Monroe enthusiastically. Boston newspapers expressed surprise at this warm welcome for a Republican from Virginia. After all, Boston had long been a Federalist stronghold.

Monroe hoped to create a new sense of national unity. One newspaper wrote that the United States was entering an **"era of good feelings."** By the time Monroe ran for a second term in 1820, no candidate opposed him. The Federalist party had disappeared.

Three Sectional Leaders

While conflict between political parties declined, disputes between different sections of the nation sharpened. In Congress, three ambitious young men took center stage. All three would play key roles in Congress for more than 30 years, as well as serving in other offices. Each represented a different section of the country.

Calhoun of the South John C. Calhoun spoke for the South. He had grown up on a frontier farm in South Carolina. Calhoun's immense energy and striking features earned him the nickname "young Hercules." He was slim and handsome, with deep-set eyes and a high forehead. His way of speaking was so intense that it sometimes made people uncomfortable to be in his presence.

Calhoun had supported the War of 1812. Like many southerners, he was a firm defender of slavery. In general, he opposed policies that would strengthen the power of the federal government.

Webster of the North Daniel Webster of New Hampshire was perhaps the most skillful public speaker of his time. With eyes flashing and shoulders thrown back, Webster was an impressive sight when he stood up to speak in Congress. An observer described him as a "great cannon loaded to the lips."

Like many New Englanders, Webster had opposed the War of 1812. He even refused to vote for taxes to pay for the war effort. After the war, he wanted the federal government to take a larger role in building the nation's economy. Unlike Calhoun, Webster thought that slavery was evil.

Clay of the West Henry Clay spoke for the West. You have already met Clay as a leader of the War Hawks, who pushed for war against Britain in 1812.

Clay was born in Virginia but moved to Kentucky when he was 20. As a young lawyer, he was once fined for brawling with an opponent. Usually, however, he charmed both friends and rivals. Supporters called him "Gallant Harry of the West." Like Webster, Clay strongly favored a more active role for the central government in promoting the country's growth.

Helping American Businesses Grow

After the War of 1812, leaders like Calhoun, Webster, and Clay had to deal with serious economic issues. Despite the nation's great physical growth and the soaring spirits of its people, the United States

An American Profile

Henry Clay 1777–1852

During his long service to his country, Henry Clay was a firm defender of the Union. Clay helped to guide his country through some of its most difficult crises. Three times he helped resolve bitter disputes that threatened to tear the nation apart.

One office that eluded him was the presidency. He was defeated three times in efforts to become President. Yet, he was proud that he had held to his principles. Once, when asked if he was bitter about his failure to become President, he responded: "No. I had rather be right than be President."

Name two qualities that Clay demonstrated during his career in public service.

AS YOU READ **Monitor Your Reading** Check to see if you understand the relationship between the money supply and the Bank of the United States.

economy faced severe problems. This was due in part to the lack of a national bank.

The charter that had set up the Bank of the United States ran out in 1811. Without the Bank to lend money and regulate the nation's money supply, the economy suffered. State banks made loans and issued money. However, they often put too much money into circulation. With so much money available to spend, prices rose rapidly.

In the nation's early years, Republicans like Jefferson and Madison had opposed a national bank. By 1816, however, many Republicans believed that a bank was needed. They supported a law to charter the second Bank of the United States. By lending money and restoring order to the nation's money supply, the Bank helped American businesses grow.

Protection From Foreign Competition Another economic problem facing the nation was foreign competition, especially from Britain. In the early 1800s, the Embargo Act and then the War of 1812 kept most British goods out of the United States. In response, ambitious American business leaders like Francis Cabot Lowell established their own mills and factories. As a result, American industry grew quickly until 1815.

A Flood of British Goods With the end of the War of 1812, British goods again poured into the United States. Because the British had a head start in industrializing, they could make and sell goods more cheaply than Americans could. Most British factory buildings and machines were older and had already been paid for. In contrast, Americans still had to pay for their new factory buildings.

Sometimes, British manufacturers sold cloth in the United States for less than it cost to make. British manufacturers hoped to put American rivals out of business. Then, the British planned to raise prices.

Congress Passes a Protective Tariff The British plan caused dozens of New England businesses to fail. Angry owners asked Congress to place a protective tariff on all goods imported from Europe. As you have read, the purpose of a protective tariff is to protect a country's industries from foreign competition.

Viewing History

Cheapened Money

Massachusetts
Washington, D.C.

Without a national bank, the states began issuing money, like this one-dollar bank note issued by the state of Massachusetts. With so much money being issued, the value of the money declined. **Analyzing Primary Sources** *What do the illustrations on the money show about the changing nature of work at the time?*

In what ways w
their country al
need to compar
similarities and
often helpful in

The Beginn

- Economy: `
  and new fa
- Spokesper
- Favored Ta
  because it
  from sellin
  a lower pric
  American g

Learn the Skill
tion, use the follo

1. **Read the title**
   subject and te
   contrasted.

2. **Identify simila**
   being compar

3. **Identify differ**
   ences are give

4. **Analyze the i**
   lems might th

The Tariff of 1816

How a Protective Tariff Works

Cloth made in United States
Cost = $6.00

British cloth in United States
Cost = $5.00
  + $1.25 Tariff
Final
Cost = $6.25

Cloth made in Britain
Cost = $5.00

Effects of a Protective Tariff, 1810–1840

Source: *Historical Statistics of the United States*

Congress responded by passing the Tariff of 1816. It greatly raised tariffs on imports. This increase made imported goods far more expensive than similar American-made goods. Higher tariffs led to angry protests from southerners. Southerners had built few factories. As a result, they did not benefit from the tariff. Also, southerners bought many British goods. The new tariff drove up the price of British-made goods. Southerners complained that the tariff made northern manufacturers rich at the expense of the South.

Clay's American System

The bitter dispute over tariffs reflected the growth of sectionalism. Sectionalism is loyalty to one's state or section rather than to the nation as a whole. Americans identified themselves as southerners, northerners, or westerners. In Congress, representatives from different sections often clashed.

Henry Clay wanted to promote economic growth for all sections. His program, known as the American System, called for high tariffs on imports, which would help northern factories. With wealth from industry, Clay believed, northerners would have the money to buy farm products from the West and the South. High tariffs would also reduce American dependence on foreign goods.

Clay also urged Congress to use money from tariffs to build roads, bridges, and canals. A better transportation system, he believed, would make it easier and cheaper for farmers in the West and the South to ship goods to city markets.

McCulloch v. Mary...
(1819)

In McCulloch v. Maryla...
Chief Justice John Ma...
that no state has the ri...
trol any federal organiz...
its borders. Here is a p...
explaining his reasonir...

"The American people...
declared their Constitu...
laws . . . to be supreme...
principle would transfe...
supremacy, in fact, to t...
the States may tax one...
employed by the goverr...
execution of its powers...
tax any and every other...
They may tax the mail;...
tax the mint; they may t...
process. . . . This was n...
by the American people...
not [want] to make their...
ment dependent on the...

Analyzing Primary
What does Marshal...
may happen if the s...
tax federal banks?

AFTER YOU READ

Recall

1. **Identify** Expla...
   cance of (a) Era...
   Feelings, (b) An...
   (c) *McCulloch* v...
   (d) *Gibbons* v. (...

2. **Define** (a) sec...
   (b) internal imp...
   (c) interstate co...

Comprehension

3. How did Calhou...
   Clay each repres...
   of his own secti...

4. How did protect...
   American indus...
   War of 1812?

5. Why did southe...
   Clay's American...

4 New Nations in the Americas

BEFORE YOU READ

Reading Focus

- How did the Latin American nations win independence and become republics?
- How did the United States gain Florida from Spain?
- What was the purpose of the Monroe Doctrine?

Key Terms

creole
Republic of Great Colombia
United Provinces of Central America
Negro Fort
Adams-Onís Treaty
Monroe Doctrine
intervention

Taking Notes

As you read, complete the following chart to show some of the events that led to the Monroe Doctrine. Add as many boxes as you need.

Mexico wins independence from Spain → MONROE DOCTRINE

Main Idea The United States issued the Monroe Doctrine to discourage Europe from meddling in the affairs of the newly independent nations of Latin America.

Setting the Scene

On a quiet Sunday in September 1810, the church bell rang in the Mexican village of Dolores. In the square, Indians gathered around the village priest, Miguel Hidalgo (mee GEHL ee DAHL goh).

Hidalgo issued a bold call for Indians to join the struggle to make Mexico independent. No one knows the exact words Hidalgo used, but these are the words that have been passed down:

> 66 My children. . . . Will you be free? Will you recover the lands stolen 300 years ago from your forefathers by the hated Spaniards? We must act at once! 99
>
> —Father Miguel Hidalgo y Costilla, "Cry of Dolores" speech, September 16, 1810

AS YOU READ **Father Hidalgo speaks**
Find Main Ideas What do the sculpture and the story tell about Father Hidalgo's character?

Thousands of Mexicans rallied to Father Hidalgo's call for freedom.

Like Mexico, other Spanish colonies were reacting to the call for freedom from Spain. In most parts of Latin America,* people in the early 1800s fought wars for independence. As new nations emerged, President Monroe formed a bold new foreign policy. His goal was to keep Europeans from using the fighting as an excuse to create new colonies in the Americas.

Revolution in Latin America

By 1810, many people in Spain's American colonies were eager for independence. They had many reasons to be unhappy. Most people, even wealthy creoles, had little or no say in government. In Latin America, the term **creole** described people born to Spanish parents there. They demanded a role in government. Opposition to Spain was also growing among Indians. Harsh rules kept Indians forever in

---

* Latin America refers to the Western Hemisphere region in which Latin-based languages, such as Spanish, French, and Portuguese, are spoken. It includes Mexico, Central America, South America, and the West Indies.

debt. All over Latin America, people were eager to be free of the Spanish.

Mexican Independence As you have read, Miguel Hidalgo sounded the call for Mexican independence in 1810. Rebel forces won control of several provinces before Father Hidalgo was captured. In 1811, he was executed.

Another priest, José Morelos (hoh ZAY moh RAY lohs), took up the fight. Because he called for a program to give land to peasants, wealthy creoles opposed him. Before long, Morelos, too, was captured and killed by the Spanish.

Slowly, creoles began to join the revolutionary movement. In 1821, revolutionary forces led by creoles won control of Mexico. A few years later, Mexico became a republic with its own constitution.

The Liberator In South America, too, a series of revolutions freed colonies from Spanish rule. The best-known revolutionary leader was Simón Bolívar (see MOHN boh LEE vahr). He became known as The Liberator for his role in the Latin American wars of independence.

Bolívar came from a wealthy creole family in Venezuela. As a young man, he took up the cause of Venezuelan independence. Bolívar promised, "I will never allow my hands to be idle, nor my soul to rest until I have broken the shackles which chain us to Spain."

Bolívar rose to become a leader of the rebel forces. In a bold move, he led an army from Venezuela over the high Andes Mountains into Colombia. There, Bolívar took the Spanish forces by surprise and defeated them in 1819.

Soon after, Bolívar became president of the independent **Republic of Great Colombia.** It included the present-day nations of Venezuela, Colombia, Ecuador, and Panama.

Other New Nations Other independent nations emerged in Latin America. José de San Martín (san mahr TEEN) led Argentina to freedom in 1816. He then helped the people of Chile, Peru, and Ecuador win independence.

In 1821, the peoples of Central America declared independence from Spain. Two years later, they formed the **United Provinces of Central America.** It included the present-day nations of Nicaragua, Costa Rica, El Salvador, Honduras, and Guatemala. By 1825, Spain had lost all its colonies in Latin America except Puerto Rico and Cuba.

The Portuguese colony of Brazil won independence peacefully. When Brazilian revolutionaries demanded independence, Prince Pedro, son of the Portuguese king, joined their cause. He became emperor of the new independent nation of Brazil.

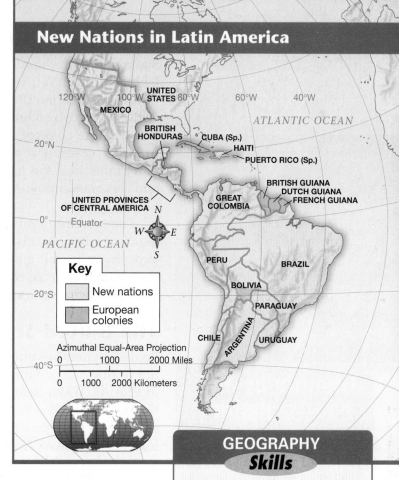

New Nations in Latin America

Key
New nations
European colonies

Azimuthal Equal-Area Projection
0   1000   2000 Miles
0   1000   2000 Kilometers

GEOGRAPHY Skills

Wars of independence led to the creation of many new countries in Latin America.

1. **Location** On the map, locate **(a)** Mexico, **(b)** Great Colombia, **(c)** United Provinces of Central America, **(d)** Brazil, **(e)** Argentina, **(f)** Chile, **(g)** Bolivia.

2. **Region** What parts of Latin America remained European colonies?

3. **Critical Thinking Applying Information** Use the world map in the Reference Section to identify the modern nations that were eventually carved out of Great Colombia.

The New Republics

Spain's former colonies modeled their constitutions on that of the United States. Yet, their experience after independence was very different from that of their neighbor to the north. Unlike the people of the 13 British colonies, the peoples of Latin America did not unite into a single country. In part, geography made unity difficult. Latin America covered a much larger area than the English colonies. Mountains like the high, rugged Andes acted as barriers to travel and communication. Also, the Spanish colonies were spread out over a huge area.

The new republics had a hard time setting up stable governments. Under Spanish rule, the colonists had gained little or no experience in self-government. Powerful leaders took advantage of the turmoil to seize control. As a result, the new nations were often unable to achieve democratic rule.

The United States Gains Florida

Spain lost another one of its colonies, Florida—not to independence, but to the United States. Many Americans wanted to gain possession of Florida. White southerners were especially worried about disturbances across the border. Creek and Seminole Indians in Florida sometimes raided settlements in Georgia. Also, Florida was a refuge for many enslaved African Americans.

"Black Seminoles" Since the 1700s, Spanish officials had protected slaves who had fled from plantations in Georgia and South Carolina. Seminole Indians allowed African Americans to live near their villages. In return, these "black Seminoles" gave the Indians a share of the crops they raised. The black Seminoles adopted many Indian customs.

One settlement on the Apalachicola River known as the Negro Fort contained about 1,000 African Americans. General Andrew Jackson demanded that Spain demolish the Negro Fort. (See Geography and History feature on this page.) When the Spanish governor refused, the United States invaded Florida and destroyed the fort.

Spain Gives Up Florida In 1818, Jackson again headed to Florida with a force of more than 3,000 soldiers. Spain protested but did little else. It was busy fighting rebels in Latin America and could not risk war with the United States.

In the end, Spain agreed to peace talks. Secretary of State John Quincy Adams worked out a treaty with Spain. In it, Spain agreed to give Florida to the United States in exchange for $5 million. The Adams-Onís (oh NEES) Treaty took effect in 1821.

The Monroe Doctrine

Americans cheered as Latin American nations won independence. The actions of European powers, however, worried Secretary Adams and President Monroe. In 1815, Prussia, France, Russia, and Austria formed an alliance aimed at crushing any revolution that sprang up

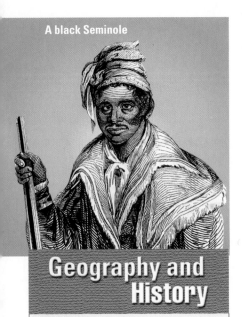

A black Seminole

Geography and History

The Negro Fort

The Negro Fort was built along the Apalachicola River, in the Spanish territory of Florida, about 60 miles from Georgia. At its height, some 1,000 African Americans farmed along the river. They worried Georgia planters, who feared they would encourage slaves to revolt.

The fort sat on a hill surrounded on three sides by forests and swamps. The weak side lay along the river. In early skirmishes against the Americans, the defenders beat their land forces. Then, the Americans launched an all-out attack by land and river. Gunboats bombarding the fort hit the room where gunpowder was stored. The explosion destroyed the fort, killing most of the inhabitants. The survivors were returned to slavery.

How might the defenders of the Negro Fort have inspired enslaved African Americans in the United States?

6 Which of the following actions would President Monroe have viewed as a violation of the Monroe Doctrine?

A Spain invades Portugal.

B Spain retakes Mexico.

C Spain refuses to sell Florida.

D Simón Bolívar declares himself king of Venezuela.

Use the graph <u>and</u> your knowledge of social studies to answer the following question.

Population Growth and Distribution, 1800–1830

Source: *Historical Statistics of the United States*

7 Which generalization about the period from 1800–1830 is supported by the graph?

A The West had a larger population than the South.

B The population of the South declined.

C The West grew at a faster rate than the North.

D All three regions grew at an equal rate.

8 Which group would have been most likely to support the aims of the War Hawks?

A New England merchants

B Settlers on the western frontier

C Members of Tecumseh's federation

D Delegates to the Hartford Convention

9 Which of the following is the best example of the impact of geography on the Industrial Revolution?

A The location of the first American textile mill

B The invention of interchangeable parts

C The use of child labor

D The combination of spinning and weaving in a single factory

Writing Practice

10 "The first five Presidents provided models of bold leadership and creative thinking." Using at least two different Presidents, give three examples that support this statement.

11 Trace the development of American foreign policy from Washington to Monroe. Choose what you think were the three most important policies or events involving foreign nations. Describe the key issues and the course followed by the President. Then, make two generalizations about foreign policy in this period.

Unit 4
An Era of Expansion

The Nation Grows
In Oscar E. Berninghaus's *Westward Ho!*, a long line of wagons carries settlers west.

"Our population is rolling toward the shores of the Pacific. . . . It will soon . . . reach the Rocky Mountains and be ready to pour into the Oregon territory."

—John C. Calhoun, South Carolina Senator (1843)

The Jacksonian Era

1824–1840

1 **A New Era in Politics**
2 **Jackson in the White House**
3 **A New Crisis**

Discussing politics

Cherokees on the Trail of Tears

1820s

A growing spirit of equality spreads through the nation. As President, Andrew Jackson supports the interests of the common people.

1830

Congress passes the Indian Removal Act, which forces Native Americans to move west of the Mississippi.

AMERICAN EVENTS

Presidential Terms: John Quincy Adams 1825–1829   Andrew Jackson 1829–1837

1824   **1828**   **1832**

WORLD EVENTS
▲ **1824**
Simón Bolívar becomes dictator of Peru.

▲ **1829**
The Swiss adopt universal male suffrage.

The Election of 1824

Andrew Jackson received the most popular votes in the 1824 election but not a majority of the electoral votes. The election was decided in the House of Representatives.

Key

- Andrew Jackson
- John Quincy Adams
- William Crawford
- Henry Clay

States with more than one color divided their electoral votes among two or more candidates

Albers Equal-Area Projection

0   200   400 Miles

0   200   400 Kilometers

Claimed by Great Britain and the United States

BRITISH TERRITORY

Michigan Territory

Unorganized Territory

MEXICO

Arkansas Territory

Missouri

Illinois Indiana

Ohio

Kentucky

Tennessee

MS Alabama

Louisiana

Georgia

South Carolina

North Carolina

Virginia

Pennsylvania

New York

Maine

VT NH

MA

CT

RI

New Jersey

Delaware

Maryland

Florida Territory

ATLANTIC OCEAN

Gulf of Mexico

L. Superior

L. Michigan

L. Huron

L. Ontario

L. Erie

40°N

70°W

30°N

90°W   80°W

N S E W

The Bank of the United States

Nicholas Biddle, President of the Bank of the United States

1832

President Jackson vetoes the bill to renew the charter of the Bank of the United States.

1836

The second Seminole War begins.

Martin Van Buren 1837–1841

1832   •   •   •   1836   •   •   •   1840   •   •

▲ 1832

The Reform Act doubles the number of eligible voters in Britain.

▲ 1837

Canadian colonists revolt and demand democratic reform.

1 A New Era in Politics

BEFORE YOU READ

Reading Focus

- How did the growing spirit of equality change voting rights in the 1820s?
- Why was there a dispute over the election of 1824?
- Why was John Quincy Adams an unpopular President?
- What new political parties developed?

Key Terms

suffrage

majority

Whigs

Democrats

caucus

nominating convention

Taking Notes

Copy the chart below. As you read, complete the chart to show some of the developments that cause changes in political parties in the 1820s. Add as many boxes as you need.

Main Idea As President, Andrew Jackson became the symbol for the new democratic spirit that brought political and social changes to the nation.

AS YOU READ

Statue of Andrew Jackson

Summarize Write one or two sentences describing how people in Ohio felt about Jackson.

Setting the Scene Harry Ward, a New England teacher, made a visit to Cincinnati, Ohio, during the 1824 presidential election campaign. Writing to a friend, he described how Ohioans felt about Andrew Jackson, who was running for President. Jackson's supporters, he observed were "Strange! Wild! Infatuated! All for Jackson!"

On election day, more people voted for Andrew Jackson than for any of the other candidates. Oddly enough, Jackson did not become President that year.

Growing Spirit of Equality

The spirit of democracy, which was changing the political system, affected American ideas about social classes. Most Americans did not feel that the rich deserved special respect.

Wealthy European visitors to the United States were surprised that American servants expected to be treated as equals. Others were amazed that butlers and maids refused to be summoned with bells, as in Europe.

Alexis de Tocqueville A visitor from France, Alexis de Tocqueville (TOHK veel) became especially well known for his observations on American Democracy. He arrived in the United States in 1831. The French government had sent him to study the American prison system. For several months, Tocqueville toured much of the United States. However, he observed much more than prisons. He observed a society that was becoming more and more democratic.

After his return to France, Tocqueville recorded his experiences and observations in a book titled *Democracy in America*. In it, he admired the American democratic spirit and its goals of equality and freedom. He found the results of the "revolution taking place" in America while "still far from coming to an end" were "already incomparably greater than anything which has taken place in the world before."

More Voters During the 1820s, more people gained **suffrage,** or the right to vote. Others, however, were denied full participation in the growing democracy.

The United States was growing rapidly. New states were joining the Union, and there were many citizens eager to participate in elections. Some of the first states to give voting privileges to white males without property were in the West. In these states, any white man over age 21 could vote.

Reformers in the East worked to expand suffrage. By the 1830s, most eastern states dropped the requirement that voters own land. In this way, many craftsworkers and shopkeepers won the right to vote.

Throughout the country, growing numbers of Americans exercised their right to vote. Before 1828, the turnout of eligible voters was never more than 27 percent. That low percentage rose to nearly 58 percent in the election of 1828. By 1840, voter turnout was nearly 80 percent.

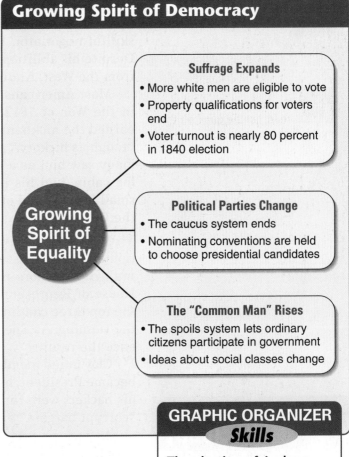

Growing Spirit of Democracy

Growing Spirit of Equality

Suffrage Expands
• More white men are eligible to vote
• Property qualifications for voters end
• Voter turnout is nearly 80 percent in 1840 election

Political Parties Change
• The caucus system ends
• Nominating conventions are held to choose presidential candidates

The "Common Man" Rises
• The spoils system lets ordinary citizens participate in government
• Ideas about social classes change

GRAPHIC ORGANIZER
Skills

The election of Andrew Jackson in 1828 marked a change in ideas about democracy.

1. Comprehension How were candidates chosen for office?

2. Critical Thinking Supporting a Point of View Do you think the growing spirit of democracy helped Jackson in the 1828 election? Explain.

Civics

Limits on Suffrage Despite the nation's growing democratic spirit, a great many Americans did not have the right to vote. They included women, Native Americans, and a vast majority of African Americans. Slaves had no political rights at all.

As more white men were winning suffrage, free African Americans were losing it. In the early years of the nation, most northern states had allowed free African American men to vote. In the 1820s, many of these states took away that right. By 1830, only a few New England states permitted African American men to vote on equal terms with white men. In New York, African American men had to own property in order to vote. White men did not.

The Disputed Election of 1824

There were four candidates for President in 1824. All four were members of the old Republican party. However, each had support in different parts of the country. John Quincy Adams was strong in New England. Henry Clay and Andrew Jackson had support in the West. William Crawford was favored in the South. However, he became too ill to campaign.

The Candidates John Quincy Adams of Massachusetts was the son of Abigail and John Adams, the second President. A graduate of Harvard University, the younger Adams had served as Secretary of State and helped end the War of 1812. People admired Adams for his intelligence and high morals. Adams, however, was uncomfortable campaigning among the common people. In fact, to most people he seemed hard and cold.

A Kentuckian, Henry Clay was a shrewd politician who became Speaker of the House of Representatives. In Congress, Clay was a skillful negotiator. He worked out several important compromises. Despite his abilities, Clay was less popular than the other candidate from the West, Andrew Jackson.

Most Americans knew Andrew Jackson for his military victories in the War of 1812. He was the "Hero of New Orleans." He also earned the nickname "Old Hickory" after a soldier said that he was "tough as hickory." Although he was a landowner and a slave owner, many saw him as a man of the people. Jackson had been born in a log cabin, and his parents were poor farmers. He was admired by small farmers and others who felt left out of the growing economy in the United States.

The "Corrupt Bargain" No clear winner emerged from the election of 1824. Jackson won the popular vote, but no candidate won a majority, or more than half, of the electoral votes. As a result, the House of Representatives had to choose the President from among the top three candidates. Because he finished fourth, Clay was out of the running. As Speaker of the House, though, he was able to influence the results.

Clay urged members of the House to vote for Adams. After Adams became President, he named Clay his Secretary of State. Jackson and his backers were furious. They accused Adams and Clay of making a "corrupt bargain" and stealing the election from Jackson.

As Jackson was riding home to Tennessee, he met an old friend. "Well, General," said the friend, "we did all we could for you here, but the rascals at Washington cheated you out of it."

"Indeed, my old friend," replied Jackson, "there was cheating and corruption and bribery, too."

The charges were not true, however. The election was decided as the Constitution stated. Still, the anger of Jackson and his supporters seriously hampered President Adams's efforts to unify the nation.

An Unpopular President

Adams knew that the election had angered many Americans. To "bring the whole people together," he pushed for a program of economic growth through internal improvements. His plan backfired, however, and opposition to him grew.

Promoting Economic Growth Similar to Alexander Hamilton and Henry Clay, Adams thought that the federal government should promote economic growth. He called for the government to pay for new roads and canals. These internal improvements would help farmers to transport goods to market.

Adams also favored projects to promote the arts and the sciences. He suggested building a national university and an observatory from which astronomers could study the stars.

Most Americans objected to spending money on such programs. They feared that the federal government would become too powerful. Congress approved money for a national road and some canals but turned down most of Adams's other programs.

Connecting to Today

Promoting Science

John Quincy Adams failed to win popular support for his plan to promote the arts and sciences. Today, however, the federal government funds art programs and scientific research. Here are two of the science projects the government supports:

Robofly Scientists developed a pair of robotic wings that helped them learn how insects such as flies and bees can hover and perform amazing flying maneuvers.

What ancient people ate Scientists have found stone tools that are about 2.5 million years old. Now, they are searching for fossil animal bones that show tool cut marks. Such marks would prove that ancient ancestors used these tools to cut meat.

Why do you think some people still oppose such programs?

A Bitter Campaign In 1828, Adams faced an uphill battle for reelection. This time, Andrew Jackson was Adams's only opponent.

The campaign was a bitter contest. The focus was not on issues, but on the candidates' personalities. Jackson supporters, however, renewed charges that Adams made a "corrupt bargain" after the 1824 election. But they also attacked Adams as an aristocrat, or member of the upper class. Adams supporters replied with similar attacks. They called Jackson a dangerous "military chieftain." If Jackson became President, they warned, he could become a dictator like Napoleon Bonaparte of France.

Jackson won the election easily. His supporters cheered the outcome as a victory for common people. For the first time, the politics of the common people were important. By common people, they meant farmers in the West and South and city workers in the East.

Jacksonian Democracy Andrew Jackson's inauguration in 1829 reflected the growing spirit of democracy. The spread of political power to more people was part of what became known as Jacksonian democracy.

Jackson was also the first westerner to occupy the White House. His election represented the beginning of a shift of political power to the West.

As Jackson traveled to Washington to be inaugurated, large crowds cheered him along the way. For the first time, thousands of ordinary people flooded the capital to watch the President take the oath of office. After Jackson was sworn in, the crowd followed the new President to a reception at the White House. One onlooker described the scene with amazement:

> 66 Country men, farmers, gentlemen, mounted and dismounted, boys, women and children, black and white. Carriages, wagons, and carts all pursuing [Jackson] to the President's house. 99
>
> —Margaret Bayard Smith, *The First Forty Years of Washington Society*

The crowds were so huge, the observer continued, that the President was "almost suffocated and torn to pieces by the people in their eagerness to shake hands."

Jackson's critics said the scene showed that "King Mob" was ruling the nation. Amos Kendall, a loyal Jackson supporter, viewed the inauguration celebration in a more positive way: "It was a proud day for the people. General Jackson is their own President."

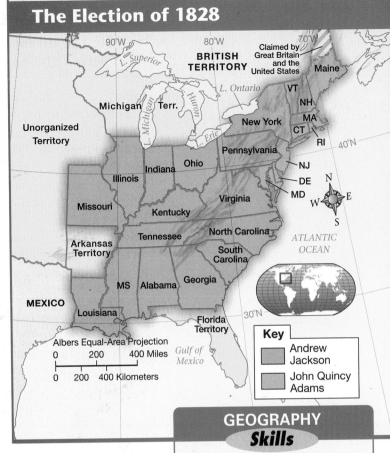

The Election of 1828

Key
Andrew Jackson
John Quincy Adams

GEOGRAPHY Skills

In the election of 1828, Andrew Jackson defeated John Quincy Adams. Unlike in the election of 1824, Jackson was a decisive winner in 1828.

1. **Location** On the map, locate **(a)** Massachusetts, **(b)** Kentucky, **(c)** Tennessee.

2. **Place** In which section of the country did Adams have the most support?

3. **Critical Thinking Applying Information** Which of the two candidates would probably have won Florida and Arkansas if they had been states in 1828? Explain.

Primary Sources

See Mrs. Samuel Harrison Smith, "The Inauguration of Andrew Jackson," on page 594 of the Reference Section.

New Political Parties

By 1820, the disappearance of the Federalist party temporarily ended party differences. In the 1830s, however, new political parties took shape. These parties grew out of the conflict between John Quincy Adams and Andrew Jackson.

People who supported Adams and his programs for national growth called themselves National Republicans. In 1834, they became known as **Whigs.** Whigs wanted the federal government to spur the economy. Those who supported the Whigs included eastern business people, some southern planters, and many former Federalists. Jackson and his supporters called themselves **Democrats.** Today's Democratic party traces its roots to Andrew Jackson's time. Democrats included frontier farmers, as well as workers in eastern cities.

New Ways to Choose Candidates The two new political parties developed more democratic ways to choose candidates for President. In the past, powerful members of each party held a **caucus,** or private meeting. There, they chose their candidate. Critics called the caucus system undemocratic because only a few powerful people were able to take part in it.

In the 1830s, each party began to hold a **nominating convention,** where delegates from all the states chose the party's candidate for President. Party leaders might still dominate a particular convention, but the people could now have some influence in the nominating process. Also, state nominating conventions encouraged citizen participation in elections. Once citizens learned about the events of the convention, they would work for their party's choices. Today, the major political parties still hold conventions.

Section 1 Assessment

Recall

1. **Identify** Explain the significance of
   (a) Alexis de Tocqueville,
   (b) John Quincy Adams,
   (c) Whigs, (d) Democrats.
2. **Define** (a) suffrage,
   (b) majority, (c) caucus,
   (d) nominating convention.

Comprehension

3. How did political parties reflect the growing spirit of equality?
4. Why did Andrew Jackson feel that the election of 1824 was unfair?
5. What programs did Adams propose that made him unpopular?

Critical Thinking and Writing

6. **Exploring the Main Idea** Review the Main Idea statement at the beginning of this section. Then, write a paragraph explaining how a Jackson supporter might respond to this question: "Does a man become wiser, stronger, or more virtuous and patriotic because he has a fine house?"
7. **Supporting a Point of View** Write a paragraph in which you agree or disagree with John Quincy Adams's position that government should spend money to support the arts and sciences. Explain your answer.

ACTIVITY

Writing a Dialogue
Write a dialogue in which John Quincy Adams and Andrew Jackson discuss the election of 1824.

2 Jackson in the White House

BEFORE YOU READ

Reading Focus

- What qualities helped Andrew Jackson succeed?
- What was the spoils system?
- Why did President Jackson fight the Bank of the United States?

Key Terms

spoils system

"kitchen cabinet"

Taking Notes

Copy this flowchart. As you read, fill in the boxes with the events that led to the closing of the Bank of the United States in 1836. The first and last boxes have been completed for you. Add as many boxes as you need.

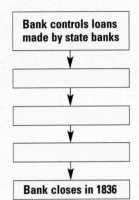

Bank controls loans made by state banks

↓

↓

↓

↓

Bank closes in 1836

Main Idea President Jackson showed the strength of his will in his fight with the Bank of the United States.

Setting the Scene During the 1828 election campaign, many stories about Andrew Jackson spread. One recalled his days as a judge in Tennessee. A frontiersman named Russell Bean was supposed to appear before Jackson's court, but he refused to come inside. Jackson came roaring out of the courthouse. "Surrender, you infernal villain," he shouted, "or I'll blow you through." Bean looked into Jackson's blazing eyes and quietly surrendered. The iron will that made Russell Bean surrender also made Jackson a powerful President.

AS YOU READ
Andrew Jackson confronts Russell Bean

Draw Inferences What does this story tell you about Jackson and Bean?

Andrew Jackson

Like many who admired him, Jackson was born in a log cabin on the frontier. His parents had left Ireland to settle in the Carolinas. Both died before Jackson was 15. Young Andrew had to grow up quickly.

A Self-made Man Although he was lean, he was a strong fighter. A friend who wrestled with him recalled, "I could throw him three times out of four, but he would never stay throwed."

Always determined, Jackson showed his toughness at 13 when he joined the Patriots during the American Revolution. He was captured by the British. When a British officer ordered the young prisoner to clean his boots, Jackson refused. The officer took a sword and slashed the boy's hand and face. The memory of that attack stayed with Jackson for the rest of his life.

After the Revolution, Jackson studied law in North Carolina. Later, he moved to Tennessee and set up a successful law practice. He became very wealthy by buying and selling land in Georgia and Alabama. While still in his twenties, he was elected to Congress.

Jackson won national fame for his achievements during the War of 1812. He led American forces to a major victory over the British at the Battle of New Orleans. He also defeated the Creek Indians and forced them to give up vast amounts of land in Georgia and Alabama.

A Man of Many Qualities Andrew Jackson was a complex person. He had led a violent and adventurous life. He was quick to lose his temper, and he dealt with his enemies harshly. When he became President, his opponents sarcastically called him "King Andrew." Jackson intended to be a strong president by expanding the powers of the presidency.

At the same time, Jackson's supporters admired his ability to inspire and lead others. They considered him a man of his word and a champion of the common people.

To the Creek Indians, however, Jackson was an enemy who showed no mercy. After defeating them in battle during the War of 1812, Jackson threatened to kill their leaders if they did not give up lands guaranteed them by earlier treaties. As a result, the Creeks had no affection for Jackson. Their name for him was "Sharp Knife."

The Spoils System

In 1828, President Jackson knew that Americans wanted change. "The people expected reform," he said. "This was the cry from Maine to Louisiana."

Reward for Victory After taking office, Jackson fired many government employees. He replaced them with his own supporters. Most other Presidents had done the same, but Jackson did it on a larger scale. He dismissed more than 200 previous presidential appointees.

Critics accused Jackson of rewarding Democrats who had helped elect him instead of choosing qualified men. Jackson replied that he was serving democracy by letting more citizens take part in government. According to Jackson, this would prevent a small group of wealthy men from controlling the government. He felt that ordinary Americans could fill government jobs. "The duties of all public officers are . . . so plain and simple that men of intelligence may readily qualify themselves for their performance," he said.

A Jackson supporter explained the system another way. "To the victor belong the spoils," he declared. Spoils are profits or benefits. From then on, the practice of rewarding supporters with government jobs became known as the spoils system.

The "Kitchen Cabinet" Jackson rewarded a number of his supporters with Cabinet jobs. However, few of them were qualified for the positions. Only Secretary of State Martin Van Buren was truly qualified for his position.

As a result, Jackson seldom met with his official Cabinet. Instead, he relied on a group of unofficial advisers. They included Democratic leaders and newspaper editors. These men had a good sense of the nation's mood. Because Jackson met with them in the White House kitchen, the group became known as the "kitchen cabinet."

AS YOU READ **Find Main Ideas** After you read this section, make sure you understand the issues involved in the Bank dispute.

The Bank War

President Jackson waged war on the Bank of the United States. Like many westerners, he thought that it was too powerful.

POLITICAL CARTOON
Skills

Andrew Jackson Battles the Bank of the United States In this cartoon, President Jackson battles the Bank of the United States and its branches (represented by the multiple heads).

1. **Comprehension** Read the cane Jackson is holding. What does it say?

2. **Understanding Main Ideas** How does Jackson fight the bank?

3. **Critical Thinking Identifying Bias** How do you think the cartoonist felt about the Bank of the United States?

Civics

Mr. Biddle's Bank The Bank of the United States had been a subject of dispute since its early days. The Bank had great power because it controlled loans made by state banks. When the Bank's directors thought that state banks were making too many loans, they limited the amount these banks could lend. The cutbacks angered farmers and merchants who borrowed money to buy land or finance new businesses.

President Jackson and other leading Democrats saw the Bank as undemocratic. Although Congress created the Bank, it was run by private bankers. Jackson condemned these men as agents of "special privilege" who grew rich with public funds. He especially disliked Nicholas Biddle, president of the Bank since 1823.

Biddle came from a wealthy Philadelphia family. He was well qualified to run the bank, but he was also arrogant and vain. Jackson felt that Biddle used the Bank to benefit only the rich. He also resented Biddle's influence over certain members of Congress.

The War Begins Biddle and other Whigs worried that the President might try to destroy the Bank. Two Whig senators, Henry Clay and Daniel Webster, thought of a way to save the Bank and defeat Jackson at the same time.

The Bank's charter was not due for renewal by Congress until 1836. However, Clay and Webster wanted to make the Bank an issue in the 1832 election. They persuaded Biddle to apply for renewal early.

The Whigs believed that most Americans supported the Bank of the United States. If Jackson vetoed the bill to renew the charter, they felt sure that he would anger voters and lose the election. Clay pushed the charter renewal bill through Congress in 1832. Jackson was sick in bed when he heard that Congress had renewed the Bank's charter. "The Bank . . . is trying to kill me," Jackson fumed, "but I will kill it!"

Jackson's Veto In an angry message to Congress, Jackson vetoed the Bank bill. He gave two reasons for his veto. First, he declared the Bank unconstitutional, even though the Supreme Court had ruled in the Bank's favor. Jackson believed that only states, not the federal government, had the right to charter banks. Second, Jackson felt that the Bank helped aristocrats at the expense of the common people. He warned:

> 66 When the laws undertake . . . to make the rich richer and the potent more powerful, the humble members of the society—the farmers, mechanics, and laborers— who have neither the time nor the means of [getting] like favors for themselves . . . have a right to complain of the injustice of their government. 99
>
> —Andrew Jackson, Veto Message, July 10, 1832

As planned, the Whigs made the Bank a major issue in the election of 1832. They chose Henry Clay as their candidate to run against Andrew Jackson. The counted votes showed that Jackson had won a stunning election victory. The common people had surprised the Whigs by supporting Jackson and rejecting the Bank of the United States.

The Bank Closes Without a new charter, the Bank would have to close in 1836. Jackson refused to wait. He ordered Secretary of the Treasury Roger Taney to stop putting government money in the Bank. Instead, Taney deposited federal money in state banks. They became known as pet banks because Taney and his friends controlled many of them. The loss of federal money crippled the Bank of the United States. Its closing in 1836 contributed to an economic crisis.

Section 2 Assessment

Recall

1. **Identify** Explain the significance of **(a)** "King Andrew," **(b)** Nicholas Biddle.
2. **Define** **(a)** spoils system, **(b)** "kitchen cabinet."

Comprehension

3. Why was Andrew Jackson called a self-made man?
4. Explain the impact of Andrew Jackson's election on the spoils system.
5. Why did Jackson veto the bill to extend the charter of the Bank of the United States?

Critical Thinking and Writing

6. **Exploring the Main Idea** Review the Main Idea statement at the beginning of this section. Then, analyze the characteristics that made Andrew Jackson a strong leader.
7. **Evaluating Information** Why might one argue that Jackson was not serving democracy with the spoils system? Write your answer in a paragraph.

ACTIVITY

Take It to the NET
Connecting to Today
In the 1800s, the Bank of the United States loaned money to banks and individuals. Today, the Federal Reserve Bank is the central bank of the United States. Use the Internet to find out how the Federal Reserve system works. Then, list four facts about it. Visit *The American Nation* section of **www.phschool.com** for help in completing the activity.

To understand history, it is important to be able to distinguish facts from opinions. A fact is something that can be proved or observed. An opinion is a judgment that reflects someone's feelings or beliefs. An opinion is not necessarily true.

In the following letter, Andrew Jackson writes about his political supporters:

> ❝ The most disagreeable duty I have to perform is the removals and appointments to office. It appears that all who possess office do so as a result of political reward. Thousands who are pressing for office do it upon the ground that they are starving, and say that their families will perish unless they can be relieved by receiving some political office.
>
> These hungry office-seekers, as well as those who are now in office, are dangerous contestants for the public purse. When it is so easy for men seeking these offices to get good recommendations, it requires the greatest skill and judgement to pick men of honesty and integrity.
>
> We have, as you shall see from the newspapers, begun to reform. We are trying to remove those with no ability from office and expose to view the corruption of some of the office-holders appointed by the previous administration. ❞
>
> —Andrew Jackson

Learn the Skill *To distinguish fact from opinion, use the following steps:*

1. **Identify the facts.** What information could be proved or observed in some way?

2. **Distinguish facts from opinions.** Look for phrases such as "I think," "I believe," or "I feel" and for emotion-packed words, which may signal opinions.

3. **Note how facts and opinions are mixed.** A combination of facts and opinions in a statement can be a clue to the writer's point of view. Are opinions supported by facts?

4. **Identify points of view.** How does the writer feel about this topic?

Practice the Skill *Use the letter to answer the following questions:*

1. **(a)** Identify one fact in this letter. **(b)** Explain how the fact could be proved.

2. **(a)** Identify two opinions in this letter. **(b)** Identify three emotion-packed words used by Jackson.

3. Reread the first sentence. **(a)** What part is fact? **(b)** What part is opinion?

4. How would you describe Jackson's point of view?

Apply the Skill *See the Chapter Review and Assessment.*

3 A New Crisis

Reading Focus

- How did the tariff crisis lead to the Nullification Act?
- Why were Native Americans forced off their land?
- What economic problems did Martin Van Buren face?
- How did the Whigs and the Democrats campaign in 1840?

Key Terms

states' rights
Tariff of Abominations
nullification
Nullification Act
Indian Removal Act
Trail of Tears
Seminole War
depression
mudslinging

Taking Notes

Copy the concept web below. As you read, fill in the blank ovals with events that were influenced by the struggle over states' rights. Add as many ovals as you need.

STATES' RIGHTS · Tariffs

Main Idea The states' rights issue led President Jackson to insist that a state cannot defy federal law, but Jackson defied federal law by removing Native Americans from their homes.

John C. Calhoun

Andrew Jackson

AS YOU READ **Find main ideas** Explain Jackson's and Calhoun's views on states' rights.

Setting the Scene They had once been friends and allies. They were still the President and Vice President of the United States. Now, however, Andrew Jackson and John C. Calhoun were about to become fierce opponents. The issue that led them to quarrel was states' rights, or the right of states to limit the power of the federal government.

In 1830, the two men attended a dinner on the anniversary of Thomas Jefferson's birthday. Several guests made toasts in favor of states' rights. The room fell silent as the President rose. Old Hickory raised his glass, looked straight at the Vice President, and said "Our Federal Union—it must be preserved." Calhoun returned Jackson's stare. "The Union!" he returned, his glass trembling in his hand. "Next to our liberty, most dear."

During Andrew Jackson's presidency, the debate over states' rights affected two important issues. One was the tariff question. The second was the rights of Native Americans to lands they had been guaranteed in treaties.

A Crisis Over Tariffs

In 1828, Congress passed the highest tariff in the history of the nation. Southerners called it the Tariff of Abominations. An abomination is something that is hated.

Just like earlier tariffs, the new law, which was passed before Andrew Jackson's first term, protected manufacturers from foreign competition. Most manufacturers lived in the North. Southern planters, however, were hurt by the tariff. They sold their cotton in Europe and bought European goods in return. The high tariff meant that southerners had to pay more for these imports. Many people thought the tariff was unconstitutional.

Calhoun Versus Webster A leader in the South's fight against the tariff was Vice President John C. Calhoun. Calhoun claimed that a state had the right to nullify, or cancel, a federal law that it considered to be unconstitutional. This idea is called **nullification.** Calhoun supported states' rights. He argued that the states had final authority because they had created the national government.

Daniel Webster disagreed. He made a speech in 1830 before the Senate attacking the idea of nullification. The Constitution, he said, united the American people, not just the states. If states had the right to nullify federal laws, the nation would fall apart. Because Calhoun strongly disagreed with Jackson, he resigned from the office of Vice President. He was then elected as a senator from South Carolina. The debate over states' rights would continue for years.

The Nullification Crisis Anger against the tariff increased in the South. Congress passed a new tariff in 1832 that lowered the rate slightly. South Carolina was not satisfied. It passed the **Nullification Act,** declaring the new tariff illegal. It also threatened to secede, or withdraw, from the Union if challenged. Jackson was furious. He knew that nullification could lead to civil war.

Publicly, the President supported a lower compromise tariff proposed by Henry Clay. Jackson also asked Congress to pass the Force Bill. It allowed him to use the army, if necessary, to enforce the tariff.

Faced with Jackson's firm stand, no other state chose to support South Carolina. Calhoun supported the compromise tariff that Clay had proposed. South Carolina repealed the Nullification Act, and the Nullification Crisis passed. However, tensions between the North and South would increase in the years ahead.

Tragedy for Native Americans

Jackson took a firm stand on another key issue. It affected the fate of Native Americans. Since the early colonial era, white settlers had forced Native Americans off their land. Indian leaders like Pontiac and Tecumseh had failed to stop the invasion of white settlers.

Indian Nations in the Southeast The Creek, Choctaw, Chickasaw, Cherokee, and Seminole nations lived in the Southeast. Many hoped to live in peace with their white neighbors. Their fertile land, however, was ideal for growing cotton. Settlers wanted the land for themselves.

Like earlier Presidents, Jackson sided with the white settlers. At his urging, the government set aside lands beyond the Mississippi River and then persuaded or forced Indians to move there. Jackson believed that this policy would provide land for white settlers as well as protect Native Americans from destruction.

Few Indians wanted to move. Some tribes, like the Cherokee nation, had adapted customs in order to preserve their way of life. They created a legal system and government that blended European and Cherokee traditions.

In 1821, Sequoyah (sih KWOY uh) created a written alphabet for his people. Using Sequoyah's letters, Cherokee children learned to read and write. The Cherokees also published a newspaper.

Primary Sources

See Daniel Webster, "The Second Reply to Hayne," on page 595 of the Reference Section.

An American Profile

Sequoyah 1775?–1843

To the Cherokee Sequoyah, written words were power. He knew that white people collected and passed on knowledge with writing. Sequoyah wanted the same for his own people. In 1809 he began developing a writing system for the Cherokees. In his system, each symbol represented a syllable of the spoken Cherokee language.

Sequoyah's system was easy to learn, and it caught on quickly. Cherokees were soon writing and publishing books and newspapers in their own language and teaching the writing system in their schools.

Why do you think Sequoyah believed a writing system could help keep his people independent?

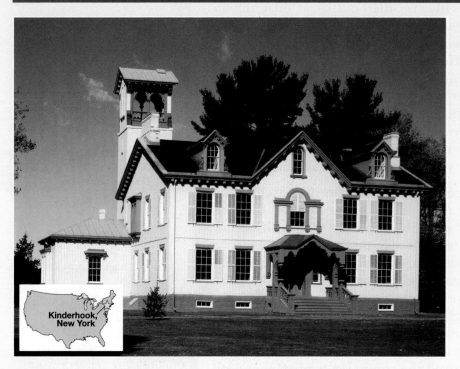

Kinderhook, New York

Martin Van Buren Historic Site

While serving as President in 1839, Van Buren purchased the estate that would become his retirement home. Located near his birthplace, Kinderhook, the estate was named Lindenwald. During his stay there, the estate grew to 226 acres and became a profitable farm. Much of the estate remains as it was during Van Buren's lifetime.

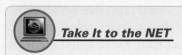
Take It to the NET

Virtual Field Trip For an interactive look at the Van Buren Historic Site, visit *The American Nation* section of **www.phschool.com**.

A Legal Battle Georgia claimed the right to make laws for the Cherokee nation in 1828. The Cherokees went to court to defend their rights. They pointed to treaties with the federal government that protected their rights and property. The Cherokee case reached the Supreme Court. In the 1832 case of *Worcester* v. *Georgia*, Chief Justice John Marshall declared Georgia's action unconstitutional and stated that Native Americans were protected by the United States Constitution.

However, President Jackson refused to enforce the Court's decision. In the Nullification Crisis, Jackson defended the power of the federal government. In the Cherokee case, he backed states' rights. He said that the federal government could not stop Georgia from extending its authority over Cherokee lands.

Forced to Leave Jackson supporters in Congress pushed through the Indian Removal Act in 1830. It forced many Native Americans to move west of the Mississippi. Whites did not mind turning land over to Indians that they thought was a vast desert. In 1838, the United States Army drove more than 15,000 Cherokees westward. The Cherokees trekked hundreds of miles over a period of several months. Thousands perished during the march, mostly children and the elderly. The Cherokees' long, sorrowful journey west became known as the Trail of Tears.

The Seminoles Resist In Florida, the Seminole Indians resisted removal. Led by Chief Osceola (ahs ee oh luh), they began fighting the United States Army in 1817. This conflict, known as the first Seminole War, ended in 1818. The second Seminole War lasted from 1835 to 1842. It was the costliest war waged by the government to gain Indian lands.

In the end, after a third war ending in 1858, the Seminoles were defeated. The government forced the Seminole leaders and most of their people to leave Florida.

Martin Van Buren and Hard Times

Andrew Jackson left office after two terms. Americans then elected Martin Van Buren President. Van Buren had served as Vice President during Jackson's second term.

Although Martin Van Buren did not have the popular appeal of Andrew Jackson, he was also a self-made man. As a politician he was clever and intelligent. As President, however, Van Buren needed more than sharp political instincts.

The Panic of 1837 Two months after taking office, Van Buren faced the worst economic crisis the nation had known. It was called the Panic of 1837. The panic had several causes. During the 1830s, the government sold millions of acres of public land in the West. Farmers bought some land, but speculators bought even more, hoping to earn huge profits. To pay for the land, speculators borrowed money from state banks. After the Bank of the United States closed, the state banks could lend money without limit. To meet the demand for loans, state banks printed more and more paper money. Often, the paper money was not backed by gold or silver.

Before leaving office, Jackson was alarmed at the wild speculation in land. To slow it down, he ordered that anyone buying public land had to pay for it with gold or silver. Speculators and others rushed to state banks to exchange their paper money for gold and silver. Many banks did not have enough gold and silver and were forced to close.

Economic Depression The panic worsened when cotton prices went down because of a surplus. Cotton planters often borrowed money, which they repaid when they sold their crop. Low cotton prices meant that planters could not repay their loans. As a result, more banks failed.

The nation plunged into a deep economic depression, a period when business declines and many people lose their jobs. The depression lasted three years. In the worst days, 90 percent of the nation's factories were closed. Thousands of people were out of work. In some cities, hungry crowds broke into warehouses and stole food.

Many Americans blamed President Van Buren and his policies for the economic depression. Van Buren believed in laissez faire—the idea that government should play as small a role as possible in the nation's economic affairs. His limited actions did little to help the economy. He tried to set up a more stable banking system. He also cut back on government expenses. Still, the depression wore on and criticism of Van Buren increased.

Primary Source

Van Buren Opposes Handouts

Van Buren had scarcely taken office before he was faced with the depression of 1837. His critics blamed his administration for the failing economy, calling it "Van Ruin's Depression." In the following excerpt, Van Buren defends his plan for helping the economy:
"The framers of our excellent Constitution, and the people who approved it . . . acted at a time on a sounder principle. They judged that the less government interferes with private interests, the better for the general prosperity. It is not [the government's] purpose to make men rich, or to repair . . . losses not [received] in the public service."
—President Martin Van Buren, Letter to Congress, 1837

Analyzing Primary Sources
According to Van Buren, what is the relationship between citizens and the federal government?

AS YOU READ **Summarize** As you read, list the reasons why Harrison was chosen by the Whigs as a candidate.

Campaigns of 1840

Although Van Buren lost support, the Democrats chose him to run for reelection in 1840. The Whigs chose William Henry Harrison of Ohio. Harrison was known as the hero of the Battle of Tippecanoe. To run for Vice President, the Whigs chose John Tyler.

To appeal to voters, the Whigs focused on Harrison's war record. "Tippecanoe and Tyler too" became their campaign slogan. The Whigs created an image for Harrison as a "man of the people." They presented him as a humble farmer and boasted that he had been born in a log cabin. Harrison was actually a wealthy, educated man who, at the time of the campaign, lived in a large mansion.

A New Sort of Politics The campaigns of 1840 reflected a new sort of politics. Harrison traveled across the land, making speeches and greeting voters. Both parties competed for votes with rallies, banquets, and entertainment.

In their campaigns, both Whigs and Democrats engaged in mudslinging, or the use of insults to attack an opponent's reputation. They used name-calling, half-truths, and lies to win votes.

Whigs in the White House Harrison won the election of 1840. The Whigs' program included creating a new Bank of the United States, improving roads and canals, and demanding a high tariff.

However, Whig hopes were dashed when, soon after taking office, President Harrison died of pneumonia. John Tyler became President.

President Tyler failed to live up to Whig expectations. A former Democrat, he opposed some Whig plans for developing the economy. When the Whigs in Congress passed a bill to recharter the Bank of the United States, Tyler vetoed it. In response, most of Tyler's Cabinet resigned. The Whigs threw Tyler out of their party.

★ AFTER YOU READ ★ ★ Section 3 Assessment ★ ★ ★ ★

Recall

1. **Identify** Explain the significance of (a) Tariff of Abominations, (b) Nullification Act, (c) Indian Removal Act, (d) Trail of Tears, (e) Seminole War.
2. **Define** (a) states' rights, (b) nullification, (c) depression, (d) mudslinging.

Comprehension

3. Why did South Carolina pass the Nullification Act?
4. How did the Indian Removal Act affect Native Americans?
5. What hardships did citizens face during the Panic of 1837?

6. Describe some of the campaign tactics Democrats and Whigs used in the election of 1840.

Critical Thinking and Writing

7. **Exploring the Main Idea** Review the Main Idea statement at the beginning of this section. Then, answer the following question in a paragraph. Why do you think Andrew Jackson supported states' rights in the case of the Native Americans but not in the Nullification Crisis?
8. **Solving Problems** What do you think President Van Buren could have done to ease the economic crisis in 1837?

ACTIVITY

Take It to the NET
The Banana Wars Tariffs are still part of domestic and international trade. Use the Internet to find out about the recent banana wars between the United States and Europe. Prepare a brief oral report about the dispute. Visit *The American Nation* section of **www.phschool.com** for help in completing the activity.

The LOG CABIN Campaign

William Henry Harrison

In *The Log Cabin Minstrel,* William Henry Harrison is portrayed as a poor farmer who "lives at his cabin, enjoying crackers, hard cider and cheese," while President Van Buren "drank up the milk of the Treasury Cow."

Harrison Song

Tune: "Yankee Doodle"
When our frontiers were drench'd in tears,
Their cabins sack'd and gory,
He struck the blow, chastis'd the foe,
And conquer'd peace with glory.

Then join the throng and swell the song,
Extend the circle wider;
and let us on for HARRISON,
"Log Cabin and Hard Cider."

With HARRISON, our country's one,
No treachery can divide her,
The thing is done with "HARRISON,
Log Cabin and Hard Cider."

Come farmers all, attend the call,
'Tis working like a charmer,
Hitch on the team, and start for him,
For he's a *brother farmer.*

His cabin's fit, and snug and neat,
And full and free his larder,
And though his cider may be hard,
The times are vastly harder.

The South and West will stand the test,
In spite of every spoiler,
And we'll engage to seal the pledge
For HARRISON and TYLER.

—from *The Log Cabin Minstrel,* 1840

Fast Facts
- *The Log Cabin Minstrel* or *Tippecanoe Songster* was compiled in 1840 by the Roxbury, Massachusetts, Democratic Whig Association, and sold for 12 cents per copy.
- More people voted in 1840 than in any previous presidential election.

ACTIVITY
Prepare for a class discussion about the way in which political campaigns are conducted today. How can this affect voter turnout and the results of an election?

CHAPTER 12 Review and Assessment

CREATING A CHAPTER SUMMARY

Copy the flowchart below. As you read, fill in the boxes with information that describes events that occurred during the Jacksonian Era. Some information is filled in to help you get started.

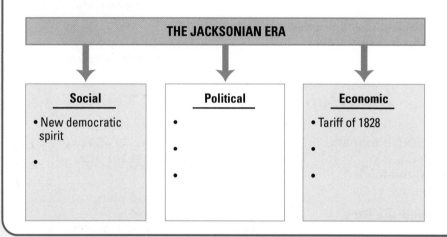

THE JACKSONIAN ERA

Social
- New democratic spirit
-

Political
-
-
-

Economic
- Tariff of 1828
-
-

For additional review and enrichment activities, see the interactive version of *The American Nation,* available on the Web and on CD-ROM.

Take It to the NET

Chapter Self-Test For practice test questions for Chapter 12, visit *The American Nation* section of **www.phschool.com**.

Building Vocabulary

Use the chapter vocabulary words listed below to create a crossword puzzle. Exchange puzzles with a classmate. Complete the puzzles, and then check each other's answers.

1. suffrage
2. Whigs
3. caucus
4. spoils system
5. "kitchen cabinet"
6. states' rights
7. nullification
8. Indian Removal Act
9. depression
10. mudslinging

Reviewing Key Facts

11. How was a winner selected in the election of 1824? Explain. [Section 1]
12. What role did each of the following play in the struggle over the Bank of the United States? **(a)** Nicholas Biddle **(b)** Henry Clay **(c)** Andrew Jackson [Section 2]
13. What were the causes of the Panic of 1837? [Section 3]

Critical Thinking and Writing

14. **Supporting a Point of View** Andrew Jackson said "The President is the direct representative of the people." During his time in office, did Jackson's actions uphold his statement? Write a paragraph in which you agree or disagree.
15. **Analyzing Information** The new voter group in the 1820s consisted of white men who did not own property. Consider the elections of 1828 and 1840. **(a)** How did Jackson appeal to this group in 1828? **(b)** How did the campaign of 1840 appeal to this group?
16. **Connecting to Geography: Regions** Analyze how the different economic interests of the North and the South influenced their views on the tariff of 1828.
17. **Evaluating Information** Do election campaigns today resemble the election campaign of 1840? Why or why not?

Analyzing Primary Sources

Davy Crockett, the frontiersman from Tennessee, served as a member of the Tennessee State legislature from 1821 to 1825. In the following excerpt, he offers advice to those seeking public office. Read the excerpt and answer the questions that follow:

66 Get up on all occasions, and sometimes on no occasion at all, and make long-winded speeches, though composed of nothing else than wind. Talk of your devotion to your country, your modesty . . . or on any such fanciful subject. Rail against taxes of all kinds, officeholders, and bad harvest weather. . . . To be sure, you run the risk of being considered . . . an empty barrel. But never mind that; you will find enough of the same [company] to keep you in favor. 99

—Davy Crockett, *Advice to Politicians,* 1833

18. What is one suggestion Crockett gives to a person seeking office?
19. What topics is the public interested in?
20. What opinion might some people have after listening to a politician?
21. How is humor used?

Distinguishing Facts From Opinions

This is an 1828 election poster that praises Jackson's conduct during the election of 1824. Read the poster. Then, answer the following questions:

22. One fact stated on the poster is
   A Jackson is a man of the people.
   B An election should be derived from the people.
   C Jackson was a hero of two wars.
   D Jackson supports electoral law.
23. What point of view do Jackson's supporters want the public to have?

ACTIVITIES

Connecting With . . .
Government and Citizenship

Researching a Campaign Symbol The use of a donkey as the official campaign symbol for the Democratic party began during Andrew Jackson's campaign for election in 1828. Use the Internet to research the history of this campaign symbol and symbols of other political parties. Present the information you find in an illustrated chart.

Take It to the NET

Connecting to Today
Supporting a Point of View States' rights remains an issue today. Use the Internet to research the decisions in the cases of *Garcia* v. *San Antonio Metropolitan Transit Authority* and *United States* v. *Locke*. How did these cases affect states' rights? Do you agree or disagree with the decision? Be prepared to defend your position. For help in starting this activity, visit *The American Nation* section of **www.phschool.com**.

An Illustrated Report
Researching de Tocqueville Use the Internet to find out more about Alexis de Tocqueville and his visit to the United States in 1831. Choose an event he wrote about. Describe how it reflected American life at that time. Add illustrations to your report. For help in starting this activity, visit *The American Nation* section of **www.phschool.com**.

Westward Expansion

1820–1860

1 Oregon Country
2 The Republic of Texas
3 California and the Southwest
4 The Mexican War
5 Americans Rush West

Mountain man
Jim Beckwourth

Defending the Alamo

1820s

The era of the mountain men is at its height. Mountain men such as Jim Beckwourth open trails through the Rockies into Oregon and California.

1830

Joseph Smith founds the Mormon Church in Fayette, New York.

1836

Texans defend the Alamo during the Texas War of Independence.

AMERICAN EVENTS

Presidential Terms: James Monroe 1817–1825

John Quincy Adams
1825–1829

Andrew Jackson 1829–1837

Martin Van Buren
1837–1841

1820 · · · · · **1830** · · · · · **1840**

WORLD EVENTS

▲ **1821**
Mexico wins independence from Spain.

▲ **1830**
Mexico bars any additional emigration from the United States to Texas.

Growth of the United States to 1853

By 1848, the United States stretched all the way from the Atlantic Ocean to the Pacific Ocean.

BRITISH TERRITORY

(Ceded by Britain, 1818)

OREGON COUNTRY
(Agreement with Britain, 1846)

L. Superior

L. Michigan
L. Huron
L. Ontario
L. Erie

LOUISIANA PURCHASE
(Purchased from France, 1803)

THE UNITED STATES, 1783

40°N

MEXICAN CESSION
(Treaty of Guadalupe-Hidalgo, 1848)

O R I G I N A L   1 3   S T A T E S

ATLANTIC OCEAN

30°N

Albers Equal-Area Projection
0   200   400 Miles
0   200   400 Kilometers

TEXAS ANNEXATION
(Annexed by Congress, 1845)

PACIFIC OCEAN

GADSDEN PURCHASE
(Purchased from Mexico, 1853)

(Annexed, 1812)
(Annexed, 1810)

FLORIDA
(Ceded by Spain, 1819)

Key
——— Present-day state boundaries

M E X I C O

Gulf of Mexico

120°W   10°W   100°W   90°W   80°W   70°W

Pioneer gravesite along the Oregon Trail

UNKNOWN PIONEER

Digging for gold in California

1843
Thousands of people begin traveling the Oregon Trail to find new homes in the West.

1849
The gold rush attracts thousands to California.

1853
The Gadsden Purchase makes it possible to build a transcontinental railroad to the Pacific through the southwestern region of the United States.

William Henry Harrison 1841   John Tyler 1841–1845   James K. Polk 1845–1849   Zachary Taylor 1849–1850   Millard Fillmore 1850–1853   Franklin Pierce 1853–1857   James Buchanan 1857–1861

1840   •   •   •   •   **1850**   •   •   •   •   **1860**   •   •

1846 ▲
The United States fights Mexico during the Mexican War.

1855 ▲
Benito Juárez and other reformers seize power in Mexico.

1 Oregon Country

BEFORE YOU READ

Reading Focus

- Why were settlers and trappers attracted to Oregon and the Far West?
- How did mountain men help explore lands in the Far West?
- What role did missionaries play in the settlement of Oregon?
- What hardships did settlers face on wagon trains to the West?

Key Terms

Oregon Country

mountain man

rugged individualist

rendezvous

Oregon Trail

Taking Notes

As you read, prepare an outline of this section. Use roman numerals to indicate the major headings, capital letters for the subheadings, and numbers for the supporting details. The sample at right will help you get started.

I. The Lure of Oregon
  A. Land and climate
    1.
    2.
  B. Competing claims
    1.
    2.
II. Fur Trappers in the Far West
  A. Lives filled with danger
    1.
    2.
  B.

Main Idea By the 1840s, thousands of pioneers were following in the footsteps of fur traders and missionaries to settle in Oregon Country.

AS YOU READ

Traveling the trail

Visualize Picture what it must have been like to be a young person traveling the Oregon Trail.

Setting the Scene Young John Johnson and Jane Jones fell in love as their families were moving west by wagon train. John's parents did not like the match, so they left the wagon train. John and Jane, though, secretly promised to leave letters for each other on the buffalo skulls that dotted the trail. They signed their letters "Laurie." For the next month, Jane later told John "not a day passed . . . but what I have found a letter signed by Laurie so I knew just where you were and was sure we would overtake you."

The Johnson and Jones families were among thousands of people who traveled to Oregon in the mid-1800s. In 1820, Oregon had seemed a distant and dangerous place. Yet, by the early 1850s, large numbers of pioneers were heading across the Great Plains to the Far West. Their presence would support the claims of the United States to Oregon and put the nation into conflict with Great Britain.

The Lure of Oregon

By the 1820s, white settlers had occupied much of the land between the Appalachians and the Mississippi River. Families in search of good farmland kept moving farther west. Few, however, settled on the Great Plains between the Mississippi and the Rockies. The plains were considered too dry to support settlement. Instead, settlers headed to lands in the Far West.

Americans first heard about the area known as Oregon Country in the early 1800s. Oregon Country was a huge region west of the Rocky Mountains. Today, it includes Oregon, Washington, Idaho, and parts of Wyoming, Montana, and western Canada.

Land and Climate The geography of Oregon Country is varied. Along the Pacific coast, the soil is fertile. Temperatures are mild all year round, and rainfall is plentiful. Early white settlers found fine farmland in the valley of the Willamette River and the lowlands around Puget Sound.

Farther inland, dense forests covered the coastal mountain range. Beavers and other fur-bearing animals roamed these forests and the Rocky Mountains to the east. For this reason, fur trappers were the first whites to head into Oregon Country.

Not all of Oregon Country attracted Americans. Between the coastal mountains and the Rockies is a barren and dry plateau. This region was home to neither fur trappers nor farmers.

Competing Claims In the early 1800s, four countries claimed Oregon. They were the United States, Great Britain, Spain, and Russia. Of course, Native American groups had lived there for centuries. However, the United States and European nations gave little thought to Indian rights.

In 1818, the United States and Britain agreed to occupy Oregon jointly. Citizens of each nation would have equal rights in Oregon. Spain and Russia had few settlers there, so they withdrew their claims to Oregon Country.

Fur Trappers in the Far West

At first, only a handful of Europeans or Americans traveled to Oregon Country. Most were fur traders. Since furs could be sold for huge profits in China, merchants from New England stopped along the Oregon coast before crossing the Pacific. In fact, so many Yankee traders visited Oregon to buy furs that, in some areas, the Indian name for a white man was "Boston."

Only a few hardy trappers actually settled in Oregon. These adventurous men hiked through the region's vast forests, trapping animals and living off the land. They were known as **mountain men.**

Mountain men were admired as **rugged individualists,** people who follow their own independent course in life. Even their colorful appearance set them apart from ordinary society. Their shirts and trousers were made of animal hides and decorated with porcupine quills. Their hair reached to their shoulders. Pistols and tomahawks hung from their belts.

Lives Filled With Danger Mountain men could make fine profits selling their furs. They led dangerous lives, however. The long, cold winters demanded special survival skills. In the forests, mountain men had to watch out for bears, wildcats, or other animals that might attack.

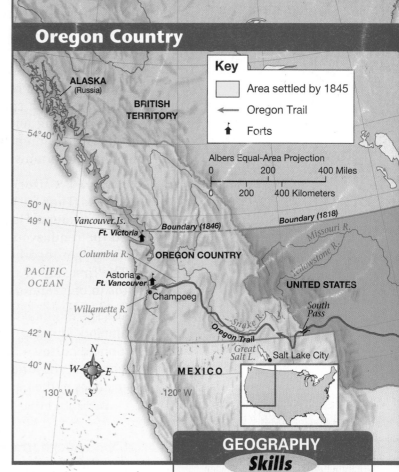

Oregon Country

Key

Area settled by 1845

Oregon Trail

Forts

Albers Equal-Area Projection

0 — 200 — 400 Miles

0 — 200 — 400 Kilometers

GEOGRAPHY
Skills

Oregon Country was the first area in the far west to draw settlers from the United States.

1. **Location** On the map, locate **(a)** Oregon Country, **(b)** British territory, **(c)** Willamette River, **(d)** South Pass.

2. **Region** What line of latitude marked the northern boundary of Oregon Country after 1846?

3. **Critical Thinking Drawing Inferences** Why do you think the Oregon Trail often followed the course of a river?

In winter, food was scarce. Faced with starvation, a hungry trapper would eat almost anything. "I have held my hands in an anthill until they were covered with ants, then greedily licked them off," one mountain man recalled.

Trappers often spent winters in Native American villages. They learned trapping and hunting skills from Indians. Some mountain men married Indian women who helped the newcomers survive in the harsh mountains.

Trading Furs During the fall and spring, mountain men tended their traps. Then in July, they tramped out of the wilderness to meet with fur traders. They headed to a place chosen the year before, called the rendezvous (RAHN day voo). **Rendezvous** is a French word meaning "get-together."

The first day of the rendezvous was a time for entertainment. A visitor to one rendezvous captured the excitement:

> 66 [The mountain men] engaged in contests of skill at running, jumping, wrestling, shooting with the rifle, and running horses. . . . They sang, they laughed, they whooped; they tried to out-brag and out-lie each other in stories of their adventures. 99
>
> —Washington Irving, *The Adventures of Captain Bonneville, U.S.A., in the Rocky Mountains and the Far West,* 1837

Soon enough, trappers and traders settled down to bargain. As long as beaver hats were in demand in the East and in Europe, mountain men got a good price for their furs.

By the late 1830s, however, the fur trade was dying. Trappers had killed too many beavers, and the animals had become scarce. Also, beaver hats went out of style. Even so, the mountain men found new uses for their skills. Some began to lead settlers across rugged mountain trails into Oregon.

Exploring New Lands

In their search for furs, mountain men explored many parts of the West. They followed Indian trails through passes in the Rocky Mountains. Later, they showed these trails to settlers heading west.

Jedediah Smith led settlers across the Rockies through South Pass, in present-day Wyoming. Manuel Lisa, a Latino fur trader, led a trip up the Missouri River in 1807. He founded Fort Manuel, the first outpost on the upper Missouri.

James Beckwourth, an African American, traveled west from Virginia to escape slavery. He was accepted as a chief by the Crow Indians. As a guide, Beckwourth discovered a mountain pass through the Sierra Nevadas that later became a major route to California.

Missionaries in Oregon

The first white Americans to settle permanently in Oregon Country were missionaries. Among them were Marcus and Narcissa Whitman. The couple married in 1836 and set out for Oregon, where they planned to convert local Native Americans to Christianity.

An American Profile

Narcissa Whitman
1808–1847

Marcus and Narcissa Whitman arrived in Oregon after a seven-month journey. In Oregon, Narcissa's life proved harsh and lonely. Marcus was often away for weeks, working among the Indians. Narcissa desperately missed her family back East. Sending or receiving letters, however, was difficult. Often she had to wait a whole year for letters to arrive from home.

Soon after reaching Oregon, Narcissa gave birth to a baby girl. Tragically, her daughter drowned at the age of two.

Why do you think Narcissa did not just give up and return home?

The Whitmans built their mission near the Columbia River and began to work with Cayuse (KI oos) Indians, setting up a mission school and a clinic. Soon, other missionaries and settlers joined them.

Missionaries like the Whitmans helped stir up interest in Oregon Country. Eager to have others join them, the missionaries sent back glowing reports about the land. People throughout the nation read these reports. By 1840, more and more Americans were making the long and difficult journey to Oregon.

As settlers spread onto Cayuse lands, conflicts arose. Worse, the newcomers carried diseases that often killed the Indians.

In 1847, tragedy struck. A measles outbreak among the settlers spread to the Cayuses. Many Cayuse children died. Blaming the settlers, a band of angry Indians attacked the mission, killing the Whitmans and 12 others.

Wagon Trains West

Despite the killings, other pioneers boldly set out for Oregon. They were attracted by tales of wheat that grew taller than a man and turnips five feet around. Stories like these touched off a race to get to Oregon. Americans called it "Oregon fever."

As Oregon fever spread, pioneers clogged the trails west. Beginning in 1843, wagon trains left every spring for Oregon. They followed a route called the Oregon Trail.

Families planning to go west met at Independence, Missouri, in the early spring. By mid-April, the prairie outside Independence was packed with people and wagons. Somehow, the pioneers formed themselves into wagon trains. Each group elected leaders to make decisions along the way.

The Oregon-bound pioneers hurried to leave Independence in May. Timing was important. Travelers had to reach Oregon by early October before the snow fell in the mountains. This meant that pioneers had to cover 2,000 miles in five months. In the 1840s, traveling 15 miles a day was considered making good time!

Life on the Trail On the trail, families woke at dawn to a bugle blast. Everyone had a job to do. Girls helped their mothers prepare food. Men and boys harnessed the horses and oxen. By 6 A.M., the cry of "Wagons Ho!" rang across the plains.

The wagon train stopped for a brief noonday meal. Then, it returned to the trail until 6 or 7 P.M. At night, wagons drew up into a circle to keep the cattle from wandering.

Viewing History

On the Trail

People and wagon trains crowded the trails to the West in the 1840s. Here, families struggle to drive their animals just a few miles farther before darkness. At the bottom of the picture is a trunk that one woman used to get her precious china to the West. **Making Generalizations** *Based on these pictures, make a generalization about the character of the people who journeyed along the Oregon Trail.*

Most pioneer families started the journey with a large amount of gear. As they crossed rivers and scaled mountains, they discarded belongings to lighten their wagons.

The trail west held many dangers. During the spring, travelers risked drowning as they floated their wagons across rain-swollen rivers. In summer, they faced blistering heat on the treeless plains. Early snows could block passes through the mountains. Getting the heavy wagons past these obstacles was hard work.

The biggest threat was sickness. Cholera and other diseases could wipe out whole wagon trains. Because the travelers lived so close together, diseases spread quickly.

Trading With Native Americans As they moved toward the Rockies, pioneers often saw Indians. Many Native Americans traded with the wagon trains. Hungry pioneers were grateful for the food that the Indians sold in return for clothing and tools. A traveler noted:

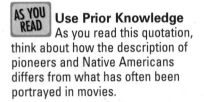

Use Prior Knowledge As you read this quotation, think about how the description of pioneers and Native Americans differs from what has often been portrayed in movies.

66 Whenever we camp near any Indian village, we are no sooner stopped than a whole crowd may be seen coming galloping into our camp. The [women] do all the swapping. 99

—John S. Unruh, quoted in *The Plains Across: The Overland Emigrants and the Trans-Mississippi West, 1840–1860*

Oregon at Last! Despite the many hardships, more than 50,000 people reached Oregon between 1840 and 1860. Their wagon wheels cut so deeply into the plains that the ruts can still be seen today.

By the 1840s, Americans outnumbered the British in Oregon. As you have read, the two nations had agreed to occupy Oregon jointly. Now, many Americans wanted Oregon for the United States alone.

Section 1 Assessment

AFTER YOU READ

Recall

1. **Identify** Explain the significance of (a) Oregon Country, (b) James Beckwourth, (c) Oregon Trail.
2. **Define** (a) mountain man, (b) rugged individualist, (c) rendezvous.

Comprehension

3. Why were trappers and settlers attracted to Oregon Country?
4. How did mountain men contribute to the settlement of the Far West?
5. How did missionaries like the Whitmans attract other people to settle in Oregon?

6. Describe two difficulties that settlers faced on the Oregon Trail.

Critical Thinking and Writing

7. **Exploring the Main Idea** Review the Main Idea statement at the beginning of this section. Then, write a letter that a missionary might have sent East encouraging people to settle in the Oregon Country.
8. **Linking Past and Present** (a) What qualities helped the settlers survive the Oregon Trail? (b) Do you think such qualities are still important today? Write a paragraph explaining your answers.

ACTIVITY

Take It to the NET

Writing a Diary Use the Internet to find out more about the life of the mountain men. Then, use the information to write two or three diary entries describing the way of life of an imaginary mountain man. Visit *The American Nation* section of **www.phschool.com** for help in completing the activity.

2 The Republic of Texas

BEFORE YOU READ

Reading Focus

- Why did American settlers in Texas come into conflict with Mexico?
- How did the siege of the Alamo become a rallying cry for Texans?
- How did Texas become an independent nation?
- What challenges did the Lone Star Republic face?

Key Terms

dictator
Tejano
Alamo
siege
Battle of San Jacinto
Lone Star Republic
annex

Taking Notes

As you read, complete the following chart to show some of the causes that led Texans to declare independence from Mexico.

First Americans settle in Texas → TEXANS DECLARE INDEPENDENCE

Main Idea In 1835, American settlers in Texas revolted against Mexican rule and in 1836, set up the independent republic of Texas.

Setting the Scene News of fighting in Texas spread to the United States in late 1835. People heard how Americans in Texas were rebelling against Mexico. "I was at Chicago, Illinois, practicing medicine," recalled Joseph Barnard, a young doctor, "when the news of the Texan revolt from Mexico reached our ears." The news inspired him. The Texans, he wrote, "were in arms for a cause that I had always been taught to consider sacred, . . . Republican principles and popular institutions. They had entered into the contest with spirit and were carrying it on with vigor."

Along with hundreds of other Americans, Dr. Barnard made his way to Texas. There, he fought alongside other American settlers eager to win independence.

Americans in Mexican Texas

In the early 1800s, American farmers, especially from the South, looked eagerly at the vast region called Texas. At the time, Texas was part of the Spanish colony of Mexico.

At first, Spain refused to let Americans settle in Texas. Then in 1821, Spain gave Moses Austin a land grant there. Although Austin died before he could set up a colony, his son, Stephen, took over the project.

Before Stephen Austin could establish his colony, Mexico won independence from Spain. Austin went to Mexico City to make sure that the new government supported the land grant. The new leaders agreed to let Austin bring settlers to Texas. Mexico wanted settlers to develop the land and control Indian attacks. At the time, only about 4,000 Mexicans lived in Texas.

Austin gathered about 300 families to move to Texas. Starting in 1821, they began settling the colony. Many settlers came from the cotton country of the Southeast. Some built large cotton plantations and brought in slaves to work the land.

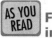

AS YOU READ Fighting for independence

Predict Based on what you have read, in Setting the Scene what issues do you think would lead American settlers in Texas to declare independence from Mexico?

Independence for Texas

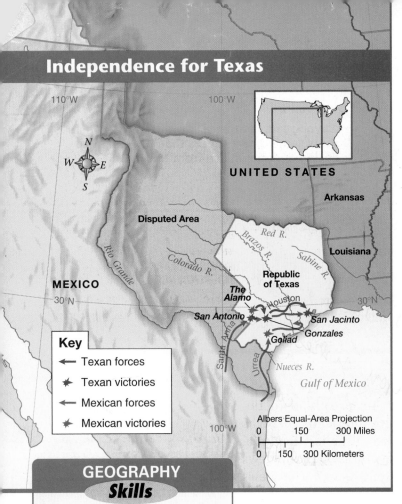

GEOGRAPHY Skills

After a brief but bloody war, Texas gained its independence from Mexico.

1. **Location** On the map, locate **(a)** Rio Grande, **(b)** Nueces River, **(c)** Gonzales, **(d)** San Antonio, **(e)** the Alamo, **(f)** Goliad, **(g)** San Jacinto.

2. **Movement** **(a)** Where did Santa Anna's army first fight the Texans? **(b)** Describe the movement of Mexican and Texan forces after the Alamo.

3. **Critical Thinking Comparing** Refer to the political map of the United States in the Reference Section. How do the boundaries of the Republic of Texas compare with the boundaries of Texas today?

As Austin's colony grew and succeeded, Mexico gave land grants to other people. Some were from Mexico, but the largest number came from the United States. By 1830, about 20,000 Americans had moved to Texas.

Conflict With Mexico

In return for land, Austin and the original American settlers agreed to become Mexican citizens and to worship in the Roman Catholic Church. Later American settlers, however, felt no loyalty to Mexico. They spoke little or no Spanish. Most were Protestant. These and other differences led to conflict between the settlers and the Mexican government.

Mexico Fears Losing Texas In 1830, Mexico barred any more Americans from settling in Texas. Mexico feared that the Americans would try to make Texas a part of the United States. It had good reason to fear this possibility. The United States had already tried twice to buy Texas.

To assert its authority, Mexico began to enforce laws that had long been ignored. One was the law requiring Texans to promise to worship in the Catholic Church. Another law banned slavery in Texas. American settlers resented these laws. Their anger grew when Mexico sent troops to enforce its will.

In 1833, General Antonio López de Santa Anna gained power in Mexico. Two years later, he threw out the Mexican constitution and became a dictator. A **dictator** is a ruler with absolute power and authority. Rumors spread that Santa Anna intended to drive the Americans out of Texas.

Texans Take Action With Santa Anna in power, Americans in Texas felt that the time had come for action. They had the support of many Tejanos (teh HAH nohs), people of Mexican descent born in in Texas. Tejanos did not necessarily want independence from Mexico. They did, however, want to be rid of the dictator, Santa Anna.

In October 1835, Texans in the town of Gonzales (gahn ZAH lehs) clashed with Mexican troops. They forced the troops to withdraw. Inspired by that victory, Stephen Austin vowed to "see Texas forever free from Mexican domination." Two months later, Texans occupied the city of San Antonio. Determined to stamp out the rebellion, Santa Anna marched north with a large army.

While Santa Anna was on the move, a group of Texans declared independence for the Republic of Texas on March 2, 1836. Sam Houston was given command of the army. Volunteers from the United States and from other nations, along with African Americans and Tejanos, joined the fight for Texan independence.

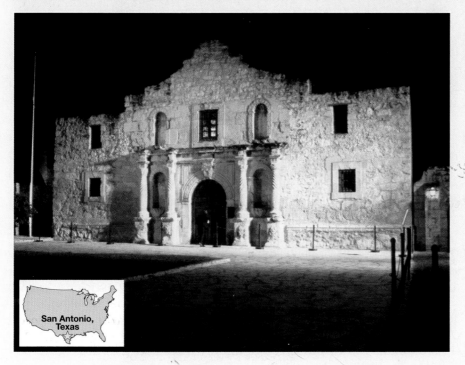

San Antonio, Texas

The Alamo

Each year, millions of tourists visit the Alamo in San Antonio, Texas. Few of them realize just how close the building came to collapsing into ruin. After 1836, the Alamo was used as a warehouse and a general store. Since 1905, however, the Alamo has been managed by the Daughters of the Republic of Texas. Three buildings house exhibits on Texas's struggle for independence.

Take It to the NET

Virtual Field Trip For an interactive look at the Alamo, visit *The American Nation* section of **www.phschool.com**.

Siege at the Alamo

By the time Santa Anna reached San Antonio, the Texans had taken up positions in an old Spanish mission called the Alamo. There they waited for the Mexican attack.

Against Great Odds The Texans were poorly equipped. Their supplies of ammunition, food, water, and medicine were low. Only about 150 Texans faced a force of 6,000 Mexican troops!

Inside the mission, young William B. Travis was in command. Among the volunteers at the Alamo were the famous frontiersmen Jim Bowie and Davy Crockett. Several Tejano families, two Texan women, and two young male slaves were also there.

"Victory or Death!" On February 23, 1836, Mexican troops began the siege of the Alamo. In a siege, enemy forces try to capture a city or fort, often by surrounding and bombarding it. The Texan defenders bravely held out as cannon pounded the walls. Still, Travis knew that without help, the defenders were doomed. He sent a messenger through the Mexican lines with a letter addressed "to the People of Texas and all the Americans in the World":

> **❝** *I shall never surrender or retreat.*
>
> I call on you in the name of Liberty, of patriotism, and of everything dear to the American character to come to our aid with all [speed]. . . . *Victory or Death!* **❞**
>
> —William B. Travis, Letter, February 24, 1836

Santa Anna

Sam Houston

Viewing History

Winning Texas Independence

San Jacinto, Texas

Sam Houston was wounded in the leg during the Battle of San Jacinto. Despite tremendous pain and a boot full of blood, Houston fought on to victory. This painting shows Houston accepting the surrender of the Mexican commander Santa Anna. The flag is that of the Lone Star Republic. **Drawing Conclusions** *Why was San Jacinto a turning point in Texas history?*

Travis also sent scouts to find more volunteers and food. About 40 men managed to slip through enemy lines and join the fighters in the Alamo. Still, no large force arrived.

For 12 days, the Mexican bombardment continued. At dawn on March 6, Mexican cannons shattered the mission walls. Santa Anna now launched an all-out attack. Thousands of Mexican soldiers poured over the broken walls, shouting "Viva Santa Anna!" Attackers and defenders battled in hand-to-hand combat. In the end, about 180 Texans and almost 1,500 Mexicans lay dead. Most of the handful of Texan survivors were executed.

Texan Independence

The fall of the Alamo ignited cries for revenge. Texan fury grew a few weeks later, when Mexican troops killed several hundred soldiers fighting for the Texan cause after they had surrendered at Goliad. News of these events inspired new volunteers to join the Texan forces. Many came from the United States. Houston worked hard to turn the volunteers into an effective army. The Texans were eager to attack, but Houston held them back until the time was right.

Houston soon found the chance to attack Santa Anna. Scouts reported that the Mexican general and his army were camped near the San Jacinto (juh SIN toh) River. On the afternoon of April 21, 1836, the Texans caught their enemies by surprise. With cries of "Remember the Alamo!" and "Remember Goliad!" Texans charged into battle.

The **Battle of San Jacinto** lasted only 18 minutes. Although the Texans were outnumbered, they killed 630 Mexicans and captured 700 more. The next day, they captured Santa Anna, forcing him to sign a treaty granting Texas independence.

The Lone Star Republic

 Find Main Ideas As you read, look for the problems that seem likely to face the new Republic of Texas.

In battle, Texans had carried a flag with a single white star. After winning independence, they nicknamed their nation the **Lone Star Republic.** They wrote a constitution using the United States Constitution as a model. In September 1836, voters elected Sam Houston president of the Republic of Texas.

The new country faced several serious problems. First, the government of Mexico refused to accept the treaty that Santa Anna had signed. For Mexicans, Texas was still a part of their country. Second, Texas was nearly bankrupt. Third, Comanches and other Indian groups threatened to attack small Texan communities. Most Texans thought that the best way to solve their problems was to become part of the United States.

In the United States, people were divided about whether to **annex,** or add on, Texas. The arguments reflected sectional divisions in the country. White southerners generally favored the idea. Many northerners opposed it. At issue was slavery.

By the 1830s, antislavery feeling was growing in the North. Because many Texans owned slaves, northerners feared that Texas would join the Union as a slave-owning state. In addition, President Andrew Jackson worried that annexing Texas would lead to war with Mexico. As a result, Congress refused to annex Texas.

For the next nine years, leaders of the Lone Star Republic worked to attract new settlers. The new Texas government encouraged immigration by offering settlers free land. During the Panic of 1837, thousands of Americans moved to Texas. Settlers also arrived from Germany and Switzerland. They helped the new nation grow and prosper. By the 1840s, about 140,000 people lived in Texas, including many African Americans and some Mexicans.

 Section 2 Assessment

Recall

1. **Identify** Explain the significance of **(a)** Stephen Austin, **(b)** Antonio López de Santa Anna, **(c)** Tejano, **(d)** Sam Houston, **(e)** Alamo, **(f)** William B. Travis, **(g)** Battle of San Jacinto, **(h)** Lone Star Republic.
2. **Define** **(a)** dictator, **(b)** siege, **(c)** annex.

Comprehension

3. Describe two causes of the conflict between American settlers and Mexico.
4. How did the fighting at the Alamo inspire Texans to win their independence?
5. Why did Texas not join the United States after San Jacinto?
6. Explain two problems that Texans tried to solve after winning independence.

Critical Thinking and Writing

7. **Exploring the Main Idea** Review the Main Idea statement at the beginning of this section. Then, write at least five headlines to mark events described in this section.
8. **Supporting a Point of View** As a Texan in 1838, you must vote to support or to oppose Texas's annexation by the United States. Write a position paper stating your opinion.

ACTIVITY

 Take It to the NET
Connecting to Today
Use the Internet to find out what programs are underway today to preserve the Alamo. Then, write a paragraph that describes these efforts. Visit *The American Nation* section of **www.phschool.com** for help in completing the activity.

Maps can help to make clear much of the information that historians collect. For example, a distribution map shows how people or things are spread over an area. A distribution map is a kind of thematic map—a map that presents certain themes. The theme of this map is settlement patterns in the newly formed Republic of Texas.

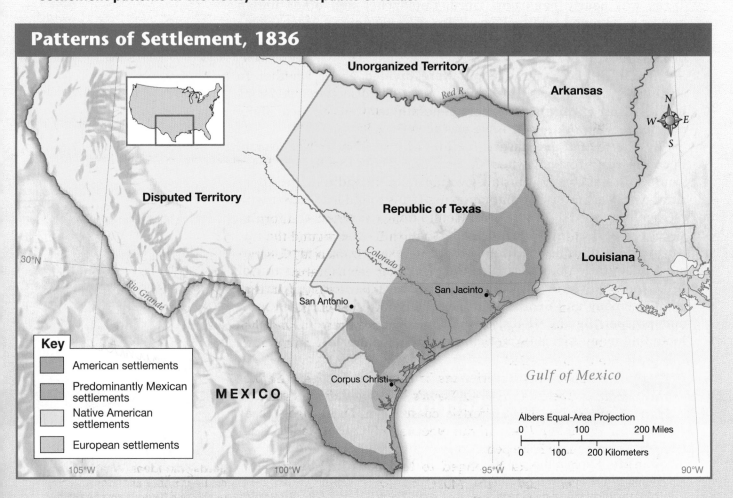

Patterns of Settlement, 1836

Unorganized Territory

Red R.

Arkansas

Disputed Territory

Republic of Texas

Colorado R.

San Jacinto

San Antonio

Louisiana

30°N

Rio Grande

Key

- American settlements
- Predominantly Mexican settlements
- Native American settlements
- European settlements

MEXICO

Corpus Christi

Gulf of Mexico

Albers Equal-Area Projection

0   100   200 Miles

0   100   200 Kilometers

105°W   100°W   95°W   90°W

Learn the Skill *To determine patterns and distribution on a map, use the following steps:*

1. **Read the title.** A map title provides a summary of the information shown on the map. In the case of a distribution map, the title should provide information about where people or things are located.

2. **Study the map key.** The key, or legend, tells what the different symbols on the map represent.

3. **Determine patterns.** Note which groups dominate in different areas.

4. **Analyze the information.** Put together what the map shows and what you already know about the subject to draw conclusions or make predictions.

Practice the Skill *Answer the following questions based on the map above:*

1. What is the title of the map?

2. **(a)** What color indicates Native American settlements on the map? **(b)** How are American settlements shown?

3. **(a)** Where were the Mexican settlements? **(b)** What was the smallest settlement in terms of area in 1836?

4. Analyze the reasons why people settled in Texas where they did by 1836.

Apply the Skill *See the Chapter Review and Assessment.*

3 California and the Southwest

BEFORE YOU READ

Reading Focus

- Why did Americans take an interest in the New Mexico Territory?
- What was life like for Native Americans on California's missions and ranches?
- Why did many Americans support the idea of westward expansion?

Key Terms

New Mexico Territory

Santa Fe Trail

self-sufficient

vaquero

Manifest Destiny

Taking Notes

Copy this incomplete Venn diagram. As you read, write key facts about the Southwest and California in the 1840s in the appropriate sections. Write common characteristics in the overlapping section.

SOUTHWEST
- Includes all or parts of Arizona, New Mexico, Nevada, Utah, Colorado
- Santa Fe is capital
-
-

• Settled by the Spanish
•

CALIFORNIA
- Region of contrasts in land, climate, and rainfall
-
-

Main Idea As Americans learned more about California and the Southwest in the 1840s, many came to think that the United States should expand its borders to the Pacific Ocean.

Setting the Scene Richard Henry Dana reached California after 150 days at sea. His ship had sailed from Boston around the tip of South America. One "fine Saturday afternoon," Dana and his crew sailed into Monterey Bay. "Everything was as green as nature could make it—the grass, the leaves, and all; the birds were singing in the woods and great numbers of wild fowl were flying over our heads. . . . The Mexican flag was flying from the little square Presidio, and the drums and trumpets of the soldiers . . . sounded over the water and gave great life to the scene."

Dana wrote about his experiences in the book *Two Years Before the Mast,* which appeared in 1840. Dana's book contains a detailed description of life on the California coast. In it, Dana gives close attention to the daily lives of the peoples of California: Latino, Native American, and European.

At the time, California belonged to Mexico. With the help of books like *Two Years Before the Mast,* however, many Americans began to think that the United States should take control of all the lands between the Atlantic and Pacific oceans.

 Life in Old California

Find Main Ideas What impact did Dana's book and scenes such as this one have on people in the United States?

New Mexico Territory

In the early 1840s, Mexico ruled not only California but all of the Southwest. The Southwest included most of present-day Arizona and New Mexico, all of Nevada and Utah, and parts of Colorado. This huge region was called New Mexico Territory.

Much of the Southwest is hot and dry with deserts and mountains. In some areas, thick grasses grow. Before the Spanish arrived, the Zuñi (ZOON yee) and other Indians farmed using irrigation. Other Native Americans, such as the Apaches, lived mainly by hunting.

The Spanish explorer Juan de Oñate (ohn YAH tay) claimed the region for Spain in 1598. In the early 1600s, the Spanish built Santa Fe and made it the capital of the territory. In time, Santa Fe grew into a busy trading town.

Spain, however, would not let Americans settle in Santa Fe or anywhere else in New Mexico. Only after Mexico became independent in 1821 were Americans welcome there. William Becknell, a merchant and adventurer, was the first American to head for Santa Fe. In 1821, he led some traders from Franklin, Missouri, across the plains to the New Mexico town. Other Americans soon followed Becknell's route. It became known as the Santa Fe Trail.

California's Missions and Ranches

California, too, was ruled first by Spain and then by Mexico. Spanish explorers had reached California in 1542, long before the English settled in Jamestown. Spanish and Native American cultures shaped life in California.

A String of Missions As you have read, Spanish soldiers and missionaries built the first European settlements in California. In 1769, Captain Gaspar de Portolá led an expedition up the Pacific coast. With him was Father Junípero Serra (hoo NEE peh roh SEHR rah). Father Serra built his first mission at San Diego. Later he and other missionaries set up a string of 21 missions along the California coast.

Each mission included a church and the surrounding land. Each became self-sufficient, producing enough for its own needs. Spanish soldiers built forts near the missions. The missions supplied meat, grain, and other foods to the forts.

California Missions and Ranches Before the Spanish arrived, California Indians lived in small, scattered groups. As a result, they had little success resisting the Spanish soldiers who forced them to work on mission lands.

Native Americans herded sheep and cattle and raised crops for the missions. In return, they lived at the missions and learned about the Roman Catholic faith. Many missionaries were dedicated to converting the Indians to Christianity. However, mission life was hard. Thousands of Native Americans died from overwork and diseases.

In the 1820s, newly independent Mexico decided that California's economy was growing too slowly. Hoping to speed up growth, the government took land from the missions and gave it to wealthy individuals. These people set up huge cattle ranches in California.

Native Americans did most of the work on the ranches, tending cattle and other animals. A new culture developed on the ranches—the culture of the vaqueros. Vaqueros were the Indian and Mexican cowhands who worked on the ranches. They were excellent riders and ropers, and their traditions strongly influenced later cowhands.

Support for Expansion

In the mid-1840s, only about 700 people from the United States lived in California. Every year, however, more Americans began moving west. On several occasions, the United States government offered to

---

AS YOU READ **Ask Questions** Before you read this section, turn the subheadings into questions. Then, read to find the answers to your questions.

Primary Source

A Vaquero Roundup

Many of our traditions of cattle herding began with the vaqueros, Latino ranch hands in the Southwest and California. In this selection, a rancher describes some of the skills of the vaqueros:

"It was my good fortune to be taken on [a roundup]. . . . Even on the ground covered with grass, a huge cloud of dust envelops everything, and nothing is heard but the thundering bank ahead. This is kept up for two or three hours, when the horsemen managed to get into the center of the flying herd. When the dust finally cleared, here and there over the plains could be seen colts and young mares, their forelegs tied to prevent them from escaping, which the vaqueros had lassoed . . ."

—Ygnacio Pedro Villegas,
Roundup, 1895

Analyzing Primary Sources
What is Villegas's (vee YAY gahs) attitude toward the vaqueros?

buy California from Mexico. Some officials were eager to gain control of the ports at San Francisco and San Diego.

The Idea of Manifest Destiny There was another reason for wanting to purchase California. Many Americans saw their nation and its democratic government as the best in the world. They believed that Americans had the right and the duty to spread their culture across the continent all the way to the Pacific Ocean.

In the 1840s, a newspaper in New York called this belief **Manifest Destiny**. Manifest means clear or obvious. Destiny means something that is sure to happen. Americans who believed in Manifest Destiny thought that expansion would also open new opportunities for the United States economy.

Manifest Destiny had a negative side. Many white Americans believed that they were superior to Native Americans and Mexicans. They used this belief to justify taking lands belonging to people whom they considered inferior.

Election of 1844 Manifest Destiny played a role in the election of 1844. The Whigs nominated Henry Clay for President. Clay was a well-known national leader. The Democrats chose a little-known candidate, James K. Polk.

Voters soon labeled Polk the candidate who favored expansion. Polk wanted to add Texas and Oregon to the United States. Clay, on the other hand, opposed the annexation of Texas.

The Democrats made Oregon a campaign issue. Britain and the United States held Oregon jointly. Polk demanded the whole region as far north as latitude 54°40'N. "Fifty-four forty or fight!" became the Democrats' campaign cry. On election day, Americans showed their support for expansion by choosing James Polk President.

An American Profile

James K. Polk 1795–1849

It is easy to forget just how hard life could be 200 years ago. Consider this: As a teenager, James Polk suffered from severe stomach pains. A doctor discovered gallstones and recommended surgery. Anesthesia was unknown at the time. In 1812, when he was 17, Polk was strapped to a table and operated on while he was awake.

James Polk was a very determined person. Although he had little formal education, he mastered Latin and Greek, graduated with honors from the University of North Carolina, and became a lawyer.

What qualities did Polk show in early life that might serve him well as President?

Section 3 Assessment

Recall
1. **Identify** Explain the significance of **(a)** New Mexico Territory, **(b)** William Becknell, **(c)** Santa Fe Trail, **(d)** Junípero Serra, **(e)** Manifest Destiny, **(f)** James K. Polk.
2. **Define** **(a)** self-sufficient, **(b)** vaquero.

Comprehension
3. Why were Americans attracted to the New Mexico Territory?
4. How did mission and ranch life affect Native Americans in California?
5. Why did many Americans feel strongly about expansion to the Pacific Ocean?

Critical Thinking and Writing
6. **Exploring the Main Idea** Review the Main Idea statement at the beginning of this section. Then, write a newspaper editorial that might have appeared in the 1840s for or against expansion.
7. **Supporting a Point of View** You are a supporter of one of the major candidates for President in the election of 1844. Write a paragraph stating whether you support Polk or Clay. Give reasons to support your choice.

ACTIVITY

Drawing a Political Cartoon Draw a political cartoon about Manifest Destiny from the point of view of the people of the Southwest.

4 The Mexican War

BEFORE YOU READ

Reading Focus

- How did the United States gain Oregon and Texas?
- What were the causes and results of the United States war with Mexico?
- What new lands did the United States acquire as a result of the Mexican War?
- How did a mix of cultures shape California and the Southwest?

Key Terms

Bear Flag Republic

Chapultepec

Treaty of Guadalupe-Hidalgo

cede

Mexican Cession

Gadsden Purchase

Taking Notes

As you read, complete the following chart to show some of the causes and effects of the Mexican War.

CAUSES

1. United States annexes Texas
2.
3.

MEXICAN WAR

EFFECTS

1. Treaty of Guadalupe-Hidalgo
2. United States acquires vast new lands
3.
4.

Main Idea As a result of the Mexican War, the United States expanded its borders to the Pacific Ocean.

AS YOU READ Wartime spirit
Use Prior Knowledge
Based on your knowledge of Manifest Destiny, what goals do you think American soldiers wanted to achieve at the beginning of the Mexican War?

Setting the Scene
American troops marched off to war with Mexico in 1846. Many of them proudly sang new words to the popular tune "Yankee Doodle": "They attacked our men upon our land, / And crossed our river too, sir. / Now show them all with sword in hand / What yankee boys can do, sir."

The bloody Mexican War would last 20 months. When it ended, the United States had expanded its borders to the Pacific Ocean. In the end, the war helped the United States achieve its dream of Manifest Destiny.

War Clouds Over Oregon and Texas

James K. Polk took office in March 1845 on a wave of support for expansion. Acting on his campaign promise, Polk took steps to gain control of Oregon. That move brought close the possibility of war with Britain.

Dividing Oregon Polk did not really want to fight Britain. Instead, in 1846, he agreed to a compromise. Oregon was divided at latitude 49°N. Britain got the lands north of the line, and the United States got the lands south of the line.

The United States named its lands the Oregon Territory. Later, the states of Oregon (1859), Washington (1889), and Idaho (1890) were carved out of the Oregon Territory.

Annexing Texas Texas proved a more difficult problem. As you have read, the United States at first had refused to annex Texas. Then, in 1844, Texan president Sam Houston signed a treaty of annexation with the United States. However, the Senate again refused to ratify the treaty. Senators feared that annexing Texas would cause a war with Mexico.

Sam Houston would not give up. To pressure the United States to annex Texas, he pretended that Texas might ally itself with Britain. The trick worked. Americans did not want Britain to gain a foothold in Texas. In 1845, Congress passed a joint resolution admitting Texas to the Union.

The United States and Mexico Clash

The annexation of Texas outraged Mexicans. They had never accepted Texan independence. They also worried that Americans might encourage rebellions in California and New Mexico as they had in Texas.

At the same time, Americans resented Mexico. They were annoyed when Mexico rejected President Polk's offer of $30 million to buy California and New Mexico. Many Americans felt that Mexico stood in the way of Manifest Destiny.

War Begins A border dispute finally sparked war. Both the United States and Mexico claimed control over the land between the Rio Grande and the Nueces (noo AY says) River. In January 1846, Polk ordered General Zachary Taylor to set up posts in the disputed area. (See the map above.) Polk knew that the move might lead to war. In April 1846, Mexican troops crossed the Rio Grande and clashed with the Americans. Soldiers on both sides were killed.

When Polk heard about the fighting, he asked Congress to declare war. "Mexico," he said, "has passed the boundary of the United States, has invaded our territory, and shed American blood upon American soil." At Polk's urging, Congress declared war on Mexico.

Americans Respond Americans were divided over the war. Many people in the South and West were eager to fight, hoping to win new lands. Some northerners, however, opposed the war. They saw it as a southern plot to add slave states to the Union. The writer Henry David Thoreau refused to pay taxes because he thought the war was unjust. For this, Thoreau was arrested and imprisoned. Still, the war was generally popular. When the army called for volunteers, thousands of young recruits flocked to the cause. A large number came from the South and West.

Fighting in Mexico

During the Mexican War, the United States attacked on several fronts at once. President Polk hoped this strategy would win a quick victory. General Taylor crossed the Rio Grande into northern Mexico.

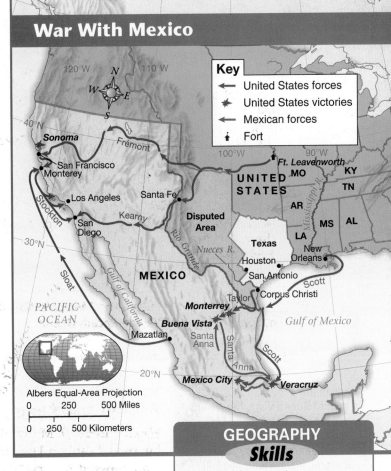

War With Mexico

Key
← United States forces
✱ United States victories
← Mexican forces
⚑ Fort

GEOGRAPHY
Skills

Fighting along a disputed border between Texas and Mexico triggered the Mexican War.

1. **Location** On the map, locate **(a)** Rio Grande, **(b)** Nueces River, **(c)** Buena Vista, **(d)** Veracruz, **(e)** Mexico City.

2. **Movement** Describe the movements of each of the following American commanders: **(a)** Winfield Scott, **(b)** Stephen Kearny, **(c)** John C. Frémont.

3. **Critical Thinking Drawing Inferences** Based on the map, was sea power important to the United States in the Mexican War? Explain.

Viewing History

Battle at Buena Vista

Buena Vista

Early in the Battle of Buena Vista, the Americans faced a determined Mexican attack. An American officer cried out to General Zachary Taylor: "General, we are whipped." "I know it," replied Taylor. "But the volunteers don't know it. Let them alone. We'll see what they do." The Americans drove the Mexicans back and won the battle. In this picture, Taylor, at center, gives instructions to his artillery.
Drawing Inferences *Do you think Taylor really believed that his forces were "whipped"?*

In February 1847, he met Mexican General Santa Anna at the Battle of Buena Vista. The Americans were outnumbered more than two to one but were better armed and led. After fierce fighting, they forced Santa Anna to retreat.

Meanwhile, a second army under General Winfield Scott landed at Mexico's port of Veracruz. After a long battle, the Americans took the city. Scott then headed toward Mexico City, the capital.

Revolt in California A third army, led by General Stephen Kearny, captured Santa Fe without firing a shot. Kearny hurried on to San Diego. After several battles, he won control of southern California early in 1847.

Even before hearing of the war, Americans in northern California had begun a revolt against Mexican rule. The rebels declared California an independent republic on June 14, 1846. They nicknamed their new nation the Bear Flag Republic.

Led by a young American officer, John C. Frémont (FREE mont), rebel forces then drove the Mexican troops out of northern California. Frémont later joined forces with United States troops.

The Final Battle By 1847, the United States controlled all of New Mexico and California. General Scott, meanwhile, had reached Mexico City. There, his forces faced fierce resistance.

Young Mexican soldiers made a heroic stand at Chapultepec (chah POOL tuh pehk), a fort just outside the capital. Today, Mexicans honor those young soldiers as heroes.

Peace Brings New Lands

AS YOU READ **Monitor Your Reading** As you read, make sure that you understand what new lands the United States gained after the Mexican War.

With Mexico City in American hands, the Mexican government moved to make peace. In 1848, it signed the Treaty of Guadalupe-Hidalgo (gwah duh LOOP ay ih DAHL goh). Mexico had to cede, or give up, all of California and New Mexico to the United States. These lands were called the Mexican Cession. In return, the United States paid Mexico $15 million and agreed to respect the rights of Spanish-speaking people in the Mexican Cession.

A few years later in 1853, the United States paid Mexico $10 million for a strip of land in present-day Arizona and New Mexico. The Americans needed the land to complete a railroad. The land was called the Gadsden Purchase. With the Gadsden Purchase, many Americans felt that their dream of Manifest Destiny had been fulfilled.

A Mix of Cultures

After 1848, English-speaking settlers flocked to the Southwest. They brought their own culture, including ideas about democracy. Still, the newcomers had much to learn from earlier residents. Mexican Americans taught them how to mine silver and irrigate crops. Many Spanish and Native American words—such as stampede, buffalo, tortilla, soda, and tornado—were added to the English language.

The newcomers often treated Mexican Americans and Native Americans poorly. Earlier residents tried hard to protect their traditions and rights. However, when Mexican Americans went to court to defend their property, they often lost their cases. Mariano Vallejo (vah YAY hoh), whose family had settled in California long before the Mexican War wrote that American settlers "took advantage of laws which they understood, but which were new to the Spaniards."

In the Southwest, however, Americans kept some Mexican laws. One law said that a husband and wife owned property jointly. In the rest of the United States, married women could not own property. Another Mexican law prevented landowners from cutting off water to their neighbors. This law was especially important in the desert Southwest, where water was scarce.

Viewing History

The Bear Flag As a symbol of their freedom, the California rebels raised this "Bear Flag." It remains California's state flag today. **Analyzing Primary Sources** *(a) Why do you think the flag makers put a single star on the flag? (b) Why do you suppose they chose a grizzly bear as their main symbol?*

Section 4 Assessment

Recall

1. **Identify** Explain the significance of (a) Zachary Taylor, (b) Winfield Scott, (c) Stephen Kearny, (d) Bear Flag Republic, (e) John C. Frémont, (f) Chapultepec, (g) Treaty of Guadalupe-Hidalgo, (h) Mexican Cession, (i) Gadsden Purchase.
2. **Define** cede.

Comprehension

3. Describe how the United States gained (a) Oregon, (b) Texas.
4. Describe two causes of the Mexican War.
5. What new lands were added to the United States as a result of the Mexican War?

6. Name three groups whose cultures influenced California and the Southwest, and describe some of their influences.

Critical Thinking and Writing

7. **Exploring the Main Idea** Review the Main Idea statement at the beginning of this section. Then, write a paragraph or two summarizing how the Mexican War helped the United States expand.
8. **Identifying Alternatives** Do you think the United States could have avoided going to war with Mexico in 1846? Explain.

ACTIVITY

Conduct a Panel Discussion With your classmates, choose the following parts: a citizen of Mexico; an American settler living in Texas; a Tejano or Tejana living in Texas; an American living in California; or President Polk. Hold a panel discussion about whether the United States should go to war with Mexico.

5 Americans Rush West

Reading Focus
- Why did the Mormons move west to settle in Utah?
- How did the gold rush affect life in California?
- Why did California develop such a diverse population?

Key Terms
Mormons
Nauvoo
refuge
Sutter's Mill
forty-niner
vigilante
lynch

Taking Notes

As you read, complete the following chart to show some of the effects of the gold rush on California.

GOLD RUSH

Flood of settlers	Law-and-order issues	Changes in government	
•	•	•	
•	•	•	

Main Idea In the late 1840s, thousands of Americans headed west, including the Mormons who went to Utah and the forty-niners who headed to California.

AS YOU READ Entering the new land

Ask Questions Make up two questions you would ask new arrivals from China if you had the chance to greet them as they entered the United States.

Setting the Scene

In 1848, exciting news reached the people of Toishan in southern China. Mountains of gold had been discovered across the Pacific Ocean, in a place called California. The gold was there just for the digging!

At the time, strict laws forbade Chinese citizens from leaving the country. Anyone caught leaving could be beheaded. Still, tens of thousands of Chinese risked their lives to sail across the Pacific to California. There, they joined the flood of people arriving from Europe, South America, and other parts of the United States. All were eager to find gold.

Gold was not the only attraction of the West. By 1848, California, New Mexico Territory, Oregon Country, and Texas had all been added to the United States. Pioneers set out hoping to make new lives. There, they put their hopes and dreams into building homes and working to make a living.

Mormons Settle in Utah

The largest group of settlers to move into the Mexican Cession were the **Mormons**. Mormons belonged to the Church of Jesus Christ of Latter-Day Saints. The church was founded by Joseph Smith in 1830. Smith, a farmer in upstate New York, attracted many followers to his faith.

Troubles With Neighbors Smith was an energetic, popular man. His teachings, however, angered many non-Mormons. For example, Mormons at first believed that property should be owned in common. Smith also said that a man could have more than one wife. Angry neighbors forced the Mormons to leave New York.

The Mormons moved west to Ohio. There, too, they faced opposition. From Ohio, they went to Missouri and then to Illinois. In the 1840s, the Mormons built a community called **Nauvoo** on the banks of the Mississippi River in Illinois. Once again, the Mormons and their neighbors clashed. In 1844, an angry mob killed Joseph Smith. The Mormons then chose Brigham Young as their new leader.

Young realized that the Mormons needed to find a refuge, a place where they would be safe from persecution. He had read about a valley between the Rocky Mountains and the Great Salt Lake in Utah. Young hoped that this isolated valley might make a good home for the Mormons.

A Difficult Journey To move 15,000 men, women, and children from Illinois to Utah was an awesome challenge. Relying on religious faith and careful planning, Brigham Young achieved his goal. In 1847, Young led an advance party into the valley of the Great Salt Lake. Later, waves of Mormon families followed. For several years, Mormon wagon trains struggled across the plains and over the Rockies to Utah. When they ran short of wagons or their oxen died, the families made the long trip pulling their gear in handcarts.

Life in the Desert In Utah, the Mormons had to learn how to survive in the desert climate. Harsh as the environment was, Young was convinced that Utah was Zion, or the promised land for the Mormons:

> 66 We will raise our wheat, build our houses, fence our farms, plant our vineyards and orchards, and produce everything that will make our bodies comfortable and happy and in this manner we intend to build up Zion on the earth. 99
>
> —Brigham Young, "Building Up and Adornment of Zion by the Saints," February 23, 1862

To meet these goals, Young planned an irrigation system to bring water to farms. He also drew up plans for a large city, called Salt Lake City, to be built in the desert.

The Mormon settlements in Utah grew quickly. Like other white settlers, however, Mormons took over Native American land, usually paying nothing for it.

Congress recognized Brigham Young as governor of the Utah Territory in 1850. Later, as non-Mormons began moving into the area, trouble broke out. In time, though, peace was restored, and Utah became a state in 1896.

California Gold Rush

While the Mormons were making the long trek to Utah, thousands of other Americans were racing even farther west to California. The great attraction there was gold.

Cause *and* Effect

Causes

- Oregon has fertile land
- Texas is ideal for raising cattle and growing cotton
- Many Americans believe in Manifest Destiny
- Mormons seek a safe home
- Gold is discovered in California

WESTWARD MOVEMENT

Effects

- Texas wins war for independence
- United States annexes Texas
- Britain and United States divide Oregon
- United States defeats Mexico in war
- Cotton Kingdom spreads

Effects Today

- United States stretches from sea to sea
- California and Texas are the most populous states
- Mexican American culture enriches the United States

GRAPHIC ORGANIZER
Skills

Westward movement increased at a tremendous rate in the mid-1800s.

1. **Comprehension** List two attractions that drew Americans to the West.

2. **Critical Thinking Drawing Conclusions** According to this chart, was Manifest Destiny successful? Explain.

AS YOU READ **Predict** Skim the subheadings in this section. Then, predict how the gold rush would affect the population in the West. Read to learn new information about population change in the West.

Trails to the West

Albers Equal-Area Projection

0   200   400 Miles

0   200   400 Kilometers

Key

← Trails to the West

↑ Forts

GEOGRAPHY Skills

In the 1800s, Americans followed a number of different trails to the West. Mountain passes allowed settlers to cross the Rockies and Sierra Nevada.

1. **Location** On the map, locate **(a)** Santa Fe, **(b)** Santa Fe Trail, **(c)** Sierra Nevada, **(d)** Rocky Mountains, **(e)** San Diego, **(f)** San Francisco, **(g)** Salt Lake City.

2. **Movement** Which trails ended in cities in California?

3. **Critical Thinking Applying Information (a)** What would be the best route for a pioneer family to take from Independence, Missouri, to Sutter's Fort, California? **(b)** What mountains would they have to cross? **(c)** In which community might they seek shelter along the way?

Sutter's Mill In 1848, John Sutter was having a sawmill built on the American River, north of Sacramento, California. Sutter had hired James Marshall to supervise the job. Early on January 24, Marshall set out to inspect a ditch his crew was digging. He later recalled the events of that day:

> 66 It was a clear, cold morning; I shall never forget that morning. As I was taking my usual walk, . . . my eye was caught with the glimpse of something shining in the bottom of the ditch. There was about a foot of water running then. I reached my hand down and picked it up; it made my heart thump, for I was certain it was gold. 99
>
> —James Marshall, quoted in *Hutchings' Illustrated California Magazine*, 1857–1858

At first, Sutter tried to keep the news a secret. His efforts failed. Within a few days, news reached San Francisco that gold had been found at **Sutter's Mill.** Carpenters threw down their saws. Bakers left bread in their ovens. Schools emptied as teachers and students joined the rush to the gold fields.

From San Francisco, the news spread across the United States and to the rest of the world. Thousands of Americans caught "gold fever." People from Europe, China, Australia, and South America joined in the great gold rush. More than 80,000 people made the long journey to California in 1849. They became known as **forty-niners.**

Working the Gold Fields At first, gold was easy to find near the surface of the Earth. Miners could dig it out with knives. Later on, miners found a better way to get the gold out of riverbeds. They loaded sand and gravel from the riverbed into a washing pan. Then, they held the pan under water, gently swirling it. The water washed away the gravel, leaving the heavier gold in the pan. This process was known as "panning for gold."

Very few miners actually struck it rich. Many went broke trying to make their fortunes in the gold fields. Still, although many miners left the gold fields, they stayed in California. In time, they found jobs or took up farming.

Women joined the gold rush, too. Some staked claims and mined for gold. Others took advantage of economic opportunities in the mining camps. Women ran boardinghouses, took in laundry, sewed for the miners, and opened bakeries.

A New State The gold rush brought big changes to California. Almost overnight, San Francisco grew from a sleepy town to a bustling city as newcomers poured in from all over the world. In the gold fields, towns sprang up just as quickly.

Greed led some forty-niners into crime. Murders and robberies plagued many mining camps. As the crime wave grew, miners and even some city-dwellers formed vigilance committees. Vigilantes (vihj uh LAN teez), or self-appointed law enforcers, dealt out punishment even though they had no legal right to do so. Sometimes, a person accused of a crime was lynched—hanged without a legal trial.

Californians soon realized that they needed a strong government to stop such lawlessness. In 1849, they drafted a state constitution. They then asked to be admitted to the Union. Their request caused an uproar in the United States. Many people wanted to know whether the new state would allow slavery. As you will read, after a heated debate, California was admitted to the Union in 1850 as a free state.

A Diverse Population

The gold rush changed California in many ways. It brought diverse groups of people to the West. Most of the newcomers were white Americans. However, California's mining camps included runaway slaves from the South, Native Americans, and New Englanders. There were also people from Hawaii, China, Peru, Chile, France, Germany, Italy, Ireland, and Australia.

Mexican Americans and Indians Before the gold rush, California's population included large numbers of Mexicans. Due to the efforts of people such as José Carrillo (cah REE yoh), much of their culture was preserved. Carillo came from an old California family. In part through his efforts, the state's first constitution was written in both Spanish and English. Despite such efforts, many Mexican Americans faced serious hardships. During the 1850s and 1860s, many lost land that their families had owned for generations.

Native Americans fared even worse. Many were driven off the lands where they lived. Without any means to earn a living, large

Primary Sources

See Bret Harte, "The Luck of Roaring Camp," on page 597 of the Reference Section.

Connecting to Today

California's Water Wars

Pioneer settlers in California sometimes fought over water rights. Although tempers have cooled since then, control of water still creates conflict in California.

Today, farmers, city dwellers, and environmentalists compete for the state's limited water resources. Farmers use 80 percent of the state's water to grow crops and support the economy. Cities want more water to supply a growing population. Environmental groups want to cut water usage to preserve rivers and wetlands and the plants and animals that depend on them.

These three groups have to compete to achieve their goals. In the long run, however, they will have to work together if California is to make the best use of its limited water resources.

Describe one thing people in California can do to solve the state's water problems.

numbers died of starvation or diseases brought by the newcomers. Still others were murdered.

In 1850, about 100,000 Indians lived in California. By the 1870s, the state's Indian population had dropped to 17,000.

Chinese Americans Attracted by the tales of a "mountain of gold," thousands of Chinese sailed across the Pacific to California. At first, the Chinese were welcomed because California needed workers. When the Chinese staked claims in the gold fields, however, white miners often drove them off.

Chinese Americans and, later, other immigrants from Asia, faced prejudice in California. Despite the harsh treatment, many Chinese Americans stayed in California. They helped the state to grow. They drained swamplands and dug irrigation systems to turn dry land into fertile farmland. They also helped build the railroads that linked California with other parts of the country.

African Americans Free blacks, too, joined the gold rush in California, hoping to strike it rich. Some became well-off. In fact, by the 1850s, California had the richest African American population of any state. Yet, African Americans faced discrimination and were denied certain rights. For example, under California law, African Americans and other minorities were denied the right to testify against whites in court. After a long struggle, African Americans won this right in 1863.

In spite of these problems, California continued to grow and prosper. Settlers from other states and immigrants from all over the world kept arriving. With their diverse backgrounds, the newcomers added to California's unique culture. By 1860, the state's population was about 300,000.

Section 5 Assessment

Recall
1. **Identify** Explain the significance of **(a)** Mormons, **(b)** Joseph Smith, **(c)** Nauvoo, **(d)** Brigham Young, **(e)** Sutter's Mill.
2. **Define** **(a)** refuge, **(b)** forty-niner, **(c)** vigilante, **(d)** lynch.

Comprehension
3. Why did Brigham Young decide to lead the Mormons to Utah?
4. Describe two effects of the gold rush on California.
5. How did California's population become so diverse?

Critical Thinking and Writing
6. **Exploring the Main Idea** Review the Main Idea statement at the beginning of this section. Then, write at least two paragraphs describing how settlers in California and Utah modified their environment.
7. **Linking Past and Present** California is still a diverse land. In the 1990s, almost 30 percent of immigrants to the United States settled in California. Most came from Asia. **(a)** Why do you think California still attracts many immigrants? **(b)** Why might many Asian immigrants settle in California?

ACTIVITY

Take It to the NET

Visualizing the Gold Rush Use the Internet to learn more about the California gold rush. Look for photos and paintings. Then, describe life in: **(a)** the gold fields, **(b)** a gold-rush city. Visit *The American Nation* section at **www.phschool.com** for help in completing the activity.

Women and the California Gold Rush

Women as well as men had the vision and willpower to make a profit in the mining towns of the California gold rush. One enterprising woman was Luzena Stanley Wilson, who in 1849 arrived at the gold mines near Sacramento with her husband and two sons. At first, the Wilsons built and ran a hotel in Sacramento, but lost it in a flood. Then, the family moved to Nevada City, where Luzena started a new business.

Miners' tools

Working a claim

"I determined to set up [another] hotel. So I bought two boards from a precious pile belonging to a man who was building the second wooden house in town. With my own hands I chopped stakes, drove them into the ground, and set up my table. I bought provisions at a neighboring store, and when my husband came back at night he found, mid the weird light of the pine torches, twenty miners eating at my table. Each man as he rose put a dollar in my hand and said I might count him as a permanent customer. I called my hotel 'El Dorado.'

"From the first day it was well patronized, and I shortly after took my husband into partnership."

ACTIVITY

Luzena Wilson wanted to run her own business. What were the advantages of running her own business? Divide a piece of paper into two columns, "Advantages" and "Disadvantages." List four items in each column.

Review and Assessment

CREATING A CHAPTER SUMMARY

Copy this table onto a sheet of paper. Then, review the westward expansion of the United States by placing the important facts in the chapter in the correct categories. Part of the table has been filled in to help you get started.

WESTWARD EXPANSION, 1820–1860

REGION	ATTRACTIONS	ORIGINAL OCCUPANTS	WHEN/HOW ACQUIRED BY UNITED STATES
Oregon	Fur-bearing animals; fertile soil	Native Americans	
Texas			Annexed in 1845
Southwest			

For additional review and enrichment activities, see the interactive version of *The American Nation,* available on the Web and on CD-ROM.

Take It to the NET

Chapter Self-Test For practice test questions for Chapter 13, visit *The American Nation* section of **www.phschool.com**.

Building Vocabulary

Review the chapter vocabulary words listed below. Then, use the words and their definitions to create a matching quiz. Exchange quizzes with another student. Check each other's answers when you are finished.

1. mountain man
2. rendezvous
3. dictator
4. siege
5. annex
6. cede
7. forty-niner
8. vigilante

Reviewing Key Facts

9. Describe the life of the mountain men in Oregon Country. (Section 1)
10. How did Texans force Santa Anna to grant Texas independence? (Section 2)
11. Why was the idea of Manifest Destiny important to many Americans? (Section 3)
12. How did the Treaty of Guadalupe-Hidalgo affect the United States? (Section 4)
13. Why did California try to become a state in 1849? (Section 5)

Critical Thinking and Writing

14. **Analyzing Information** Analyze the relationship between Manifest Destiny and the westward growth of the United States.
15. **Understanding Causes and Effects** Write a paragraph explaining one result of the battle of San Jacinto.
16. **Drawing Conclusions** Explain how the fall of the Alamo was both a defeat and a victory for Texas.
17. **Sequencing** Apply absolute chronology by sequencing the following events in their correct chronological order: Mexican War; annexation of Texas; founding of the Lone Star Republic; Battle of San Jacinto; Treaty of Guadalupe-Hidalgo.
18. **Connecting to Geography: Regions** Use the map at the beginning of this chapter that shows the growth of the United States to 1853. **(a)** List three of today's states that were added to the United States between 1820 and 1860. **(b)** How did westward expansion change the borders of the United States?

In the 1840s, American clipper ships broke every speed record. One clipper sped from New York to Hong Kong in 81 days, flying past older ships that took five months to reach China. The speed of the clippers helped the United States win a large share of the world's sea trade in the 1840s and 1850s.

The golden age of the clipper ship was brief. In the 1850s, Britain launched the first oceangoing iron steamships. These sturdy vessels carried more cargo and traveled even faster than clippers.

The Northern Economy Expands

By the 1830s, factories began to use steam power instead of water power. Machines that were driven by steam were powerful and cheap to run. Also, factories that used steam power could be built almost anywhere, not just along the banks of swift-flowing rivers. As a result, American industry expanded rapidly.

AS YOU READ **Find Main Ideas** As you read, look for the causes of the expansion of the northern economy.

At the same time, new machines made it possible to produce more goods at a lower cost. These more affordable goods attracted eager buyers. Families no longer had to make clothing and other goods in their homes. Instead, they could buy factory-made products.

Railroads allowed factory owners to transport large amounts of raw materials and finished goods cheaply and quickly. Also, as railroads stretched across the nation, they linked distant towns with cities and factories. These towns became new markets for factory goods.

The growth of railroads also affected northern farming. Railroads brought cheap grain and other foods from the West to New England. New England farmers could not compete with this new source of cheap foods. Many left their farms to find new jobs as factory workers, store clerks, and sailors.

 AFTER YOU READ

Section 1 Assessment

Recall

1. **Identify** Explain the significance of (a) Elias Howe, (b) John Deere, (c) Cyrus McCormick, (d) Samuel F. B. Morse, (e) John Griffiths.
2. **Define** (a) telegraph, (b) locomotive, (c) clipper ship.

Comprehension

3. What new inventions made work easier for farmers?
4. Why was safety a major concern with the first railroads?
5. How did steam power and railroads change the northern economy?

Critical Thinking and Writing

6. **Exploring the Main Idea** Review the Main Idea statement at the beginning of this section. Then, write a paragraph about how the new inventions affected the rapid growth of factories in the North.
7. **Understanding Cause and Effect** How do you think life might have changed in a small Ohio town after a railroad linked it to New York City in 1840?

ACTIVITY

Creating an Advertisement It is the mid-1800s. Create an advertisement poster urging people to buy or use one of the inventions of the period. Use both words and pictures to make your advertisement persuasive.

The Telegraph

Like the Internet today, the telegraph had a revolutionary effect on communication. Before the telegraph, messages were hand carried. With the telegraph, people could communicate across great distances almost instantly.

The telegraph used electricity that traveled along wires. Operators sent messages by using a device to transmit short and long bursts of electricity with spaces in between. These bursts translated letters into the dots and dashes of the Morse code. At the receiving end, a telegraph operator translated the dots and dashes of Morse code back into letters.

In 1861, transcontinental telegraph lines were erected along the route of the Pony Express. The Pony Express had operated between St. Joseph, Missouri, and Sacramento, California. Riding relays of fast horses, Pony Express riders could deliver a letter from point to point in ten days or less. Once the telegraph lines were completed, the Pony Express was no longer needed.

ACTIVITY

Working with a partner, create your own Morse code. Then, use it to write a brief message from one to the other.

2 Life in the North

Reading Focus

- How were conditions in factories in the 1840s worse than those in the 1820s?
- What did factory workers hope to accomplish by joining together?
- Who were the new immigrants in the mid-1800s?
- How were free African Americans treated in the North?

Key Terms

artisan

trade union

strike

famine

nativist

Know-Nothing party

discrimination

Taking Notes

As you read, prepare an outline of this section. Use roman numerals to indicate the major headings of this section, capital letters for the subheadings, and numbers for the supporting details. The sample at right will help you get started.

> I. Factory Conditions Become Worse
> A. A change in values
>   1. Factory workers feel differently about their jobs
>   2.
> B. Families in factories
>   1.
>   2.
> C. Hazards at work
>   1.
>   2.

Main Idea Industry in the North changed with the arrival of new immigrants and the efforts of factory workers to improve their working conditions.

Setting the Scene Alzina Parsons never forgot her thirteenth birthday. The day began as usual, with work in the local spinning mill. Suddenly, Alzina cried out. She had caught her hand in the spinning machine, badly mangling her fingers. The foreman summoned the factory doctor. He cut off one of the injured fingers and sent the girl back to work.

Twenty years earlier, such an incident probably would not have occurred. Factory work was hard, but mill owners treated workers like human beings. By the 1840s, however, there was an oversupply of workers. Many factory owners now treated workers like machines.

Factory workers Find Main Idea How had factories changed by the 1840s?

Factory Conditions Become Worse

Factories of the 1840s and 1850s were very different from the mills of the early 1800s. The factories were larger, and they used steam-powered machines. Laborers worked longer hours for lower wages. Usually, workers lived in dark, dingy houses in the shadow of the factory.

A Change in Values The emphasis on mass production changed the way workers felt about their jobs. Before the growth of factories, skilled workers, or artisans, were proud of the goods they made. The factory owner, however, was more interested in how much could be produced than in how well it was made. Workers could not be creative. Furthermore, unlike the artisan who could have his own business, the factory worker was not likely to rise to a management position.

Families in Factories As the need for workers increased, entire families labored in factories. In some cases, a family agreed to work for one year. If even one family member broke the contract, the entire family might be fired.

The factory day began when a whistle sounded at 4 A.M. The entire family—father, mother, and children—headed off to work. Many factories, at that time, employed young children. The workday did not end until 7:30 P.M., when a final whistle sent the workers home.

Hazards at Work Factory workers faced discomfort and danger. Few factories had windows or heating systems. In summer, the heat and humidity inside the factory were stifling. In winter, the extreme cold contributed to frequent sickness.

Factory machines had no safety devices, and accidents were common. There were no laws regulating factory conditions, and injured workers often lost their jobs.

Workers Join Together

Poor working conditions and low wages led workers to organize. The first workers to organize were artisans.

Trade Unions and Strikes In the 1820s and 1830s, artisans in each trade united to form **trade unions.** The unions called for a shorter workday, higher wages, and better working conditions. Sometimes, unions went on strike to gain their demands. In a **strike,** union workers refuse to do their jobs.

At the time, strikes were illegal in many parts of the United States. Strikers faced fines or jail sentences. Employers often fired strike leaders.

Progress for Artisans Slowly, however, workers made progress. In 1840, President Van Buren approved a ten-hour workday for government employees. Workers celebrated another victory in 1842 when a Massachusetts court declared that they had the right to strike.

Artisans won better pay because factory owners needed their skills. Unskilled workers, however, were unable to bargain for better wages since their jobs required little or no training. Because these workers were easy to replace, employers did not listen to their demands.

Women Workers Organize The success of trade unions encouraged other workers to organize. Workers in New England textile mills were especially eager to protest cuts in wages and unfair work rules. Many of these workers were women.

Women workers faced special problems. First, they had always earned less money than men did. Second, most union leaders did not want women in their ranks. Like many people at the time, they believed that women should not work outside the home. In fact, the goal of many unions was to raise men's wages so that their wives could leave their factory jobs.

Despite these problems, women workers organized. They staged several strikes at Lowell, Massachusetts, in the 1830s. In the 1840s, Sarah Bagley organized the Lowell Female Labor Reform Association. The group petitioned the state legislature for a ten-hour workday.

Primary Sources

See "Factory Rules From the Handbook to Lowell" on page 598 of the Reference Section.

A New Wave of Immigrants

By the late 1840s, many factory workers in the North were immigrants. An immigrant is a person who enters a new country in order to settle there. In the 1840s and 1850s, about 4 million immigrants arrived in the United States. Among them were immigrants from Great Britain who came to the United States to earn higher wages. There was a greater demand for skilled machinists, carpenters, and miners.

From Ireland and Germany In the 1840s, a disease destroyed the potato crop in Ireland, which was the main food of the poor people. Other crops, such as wheat and oats, were not affected. At the time, Ireland was under British rule and most Irish crops were exported to Great Britain. When a large part of the potato crop was lost to disease, British landowners continued to ship the wheat and oats to England. There was little left for the Irish to eat. This situation caused a **famine,** or severe food shortage. Thousands of people died of starvation. Nearly as many died from disease. Between 1845 and 1860, over 1.5 million Irish fled to the United States.

Meanwhile, many Germans were also arriving in the United States. Harsh weather conditions from 1829 to 1830 resulted in severe food shortages. By 1832, more than 10,000 Germans were coming to the United States in a single year. In 1848, revolutions had broken out in several parts of Germany. The rebels fought for democratic reforms. When the revolts failed, thousands had to flee. Many other German immigrants came simply to make a better life for themselves. Between 1848 and 1860, nearly one million Germans arrived in the United States.

Enriching the Nation Immigrants supplied much of the labor that helped the nation's economy grow. Although most of the Irish immigrants had been farmers, few had money to buy farmland. Many settled in the northern cities where low-paying factory jobs were available. Other Irish workers helped build many new canals and railroads. Irish women often worked as servants in private homes.

Immigrants from Germany often had enough money to move west and buy good farmland. Others were artisans and merchants. Towns of the Midwest such as St. Louis, Milwaukee, and Cincinnati had German grocers, butchers, and bakers.

A small minority of the immigrants from Germany were Jewish. German Jews began immigrating to the United States in the 1820s. By the early 1860s, there were about 150 communities in the United States with large Jewish populations.

Sources of Immigration, 1820–1860

- English immigrants
- Irish immigrants
- German immigrants

Number of Immigrants (in thousands)

Year: 1820, 1830, 1840, 1850, 1860

Source: *Historical Statistics of the United States*

CHART Skills

Throughout the 1800s, immigrants from Great Britain, Ireland, and Germany came to the United States. From 1840 to 1850, the numbers increased as more immigrants wanted to escape the political and economic difficulties in Europe.

1. **Comprehension**
   (a) About how many more Irish immigrants arrived in 1850 than did in 1860?
   (b) In 1860, how many more German immigrants than Irish immigrants arrived?

2. **Critical Thinking**
   Synthesizing Information Why do you think fewer immigrants came from Great Britain than from Ireland and Germany during the 1800s?

Civics

Portsmouth Black Heritage Trail

The first known African to arrive in Portsmouth, New Hampshire, landed in 1645 at a wharf (shown here) near what is now Prescott Park. For the next 350 years, African Americans, both enslaved and free, would be part of this seacoast town. Visitors can tour the communities where Portsmouth's African American population lived, worked, and served their town and state.

Portsmouth, New Hampshire

Take It to the NET

Virtual Field Trip For an interactive look at the Black Heritage Trail, visit *The American Nation* section of **www.phschool.com**.

A Reaction Against Immigrants Not everyone welcomed the flood of immigrants. One group of Americans, called nativists, wanted to preserve the country for native-born, white citizens. Using the slogan "Americans must rule America," they called for laws to limit immigration. They also wanted to keep immigrants from voting until they had lived in the United States for 21 years. At the time, newcomers could vote after only 5 years in the country.

Some nativists protested that newcomers "stole" jobs from native-born Americans because they worked for lower pay. Furthermore, when workers went out on strike, factory owners often hired immigrant workers to replace them. Many distrusted the different language, customs, and dress of the immigrants. Others blamed immigrants for the rise in crime in the growing cities. Still others mistrusted Irish newcomers because many of them were Catholics. Until the 1840s, the majority of immigrants from Europe had been Protestants.

By the 1850s, hostility to immigrants was so strong that nativists formed a new political party. Members of the party were anti-Catholic and anti-immigrant. Many meetings and rituals of the party were kept secret. It was called the Know-Nothing party because members answered, "I know nothing," when asked about the party. The message of the party did gain supporters. In 1856, the Know-Nothing candidate for President won 21 percent of the popular vote. Soon after, however, the party died out. Still, many Americans continued to blame the nation's problems on immigrants.

African Americans in the North

During the nation's early years, slavery was legal in the North. By the early 1800s, however, all the northern states had outlawed slavery. As a result, thousands of free African Americans lived in the North.

Denied Equal Rights Free African Americans in the North faced discrimination. Discrimination is a policy or an attitude that denies equal rights to certain groups of people. As one writer pointed out, African Americans were denied "the ballot-box, the jury box, the halls of the legislature, the army, the public lands, the school, and the church."

Even skilled African Americans had trouble finding good jobs. One black carpenter was turned away by every furniture maker in Cincinnati. At last, a shop owner hired him. However, when he entered the shop, the other carpenters dropped their tools. Either he must leave or they would, they declared. Similar experiences occurred throughout the North. In addition, African Americans faced competition from immigrants who settled in northern cities.

Some Success Despite such obstacles, some African Americans achieved notable success in business. William Whipper grew wealthy as the owner of a lumberyard in Pennsylvania. He devoted much of his time and money to help bring an end to slavery. Henry Boyd operated a profitable furniture company in Cincinnati.

African Americans made strides in other areas as well. Henry Blair invented a corn planter and a cottonseed planter. In 1845, Macon Allen became the first African American licensed to practice law in the United States. After graduating from Bowdoin College in Maine, John Russwurm became one of the editors of *Freedom's Journal,* the first African American newspaper.

Section 2 Assessment

Recall

1. **Identify** Explain the significance of **(a)** Sarah Bagley, **(b)** Know-Nothing party, **(c)** William Whipper, **(d)** Henry Boyd, **(e)** Macon Allen, **(f)** John Russwurm.
2. **Define** **(a)** artisan, **(b)** trade union, **(c)** strike, **(d)** famine, **(e)** nativist, **(f)** discrimination.

Comprehension

3. Describe factory conditions in the 1840s.
4. How did factory workers improve working conditions?
5. Why did German and Irish immigrants come to the United States in the mid-1800s?
6. **(a)** How did discrimination affect free African Americans in the North? **(b)** What successes did they have?

Critical Thinking

7. **Exploring the Main Idea** Review the Main Idea statement at the beginning of this section. Then, prepare a cause-and-effect chart about the effects of immigration on the United States from 1820 to 1860. The first entry in the "Causes" box can be "Famine in Ireland."
8. **Making Inferences** How would a nativist define a "real" American?

ACTIVITY

Delivering a Speech
You are a worker in a northern factory. Prepare a speech urging other workers to strike. Deliver your finished speech to the class.

3 Cotton Kingdom in the South

Reading Focus

- How did the cotton gin improve cotton production in the South?
- How did the South become an agricultural economy?
- In what ways was the South dependent on the North?

Taking Notes

Copy the concept web below. As you read, fill in the blank ovals with important facts about the southern economy in the 1800s. Add as many ovals as you need.

Main Idea Cotton was the leading crop in the agricultural economy of the South.

AS YOU READ

A cotton plant
Summarize How did the cotton crop affect life in the South?

Setting the Scene An Englishman, Basil Hall, traveled through much of the South aboard a riverboat in 1827. He complained that the southerners he met were interested in only one thing—cotton:

> ❝ All day and almost all night long, the captain, pilot, crew and passengers were talking of nothing else; and sometimes our ears were so wearied with the sound of cotton! cotton! cotton! that we gladly hailed fresh . . . company in hopes of some change—but alas! . . . 'What's cotton at?' was the first eager inquiry. ❞
> —Basil Hall, *Travels in North America in the Years 1827 and 1828*

Cotton became even more important to the South in the years after Hall's visit. It was so profitable, southerners did not even feel a need to invest in factories. Even though southerners grew other crops, cotton remained the region's leading export. Cotton plantations—and the slave system on which they depended—shaped the way of life in the South.

Cotton Gin, Cotton Boom

The Industrial Revolution greatly increased the demand for southern cotton. Textile mills in the North and in Britain needed more and more cotton to make cloth. At first, southern planters could not meet the demand. They could grow plenty of cotton because the South's soil and climate were ideal. However, removing the seeds from the cotton by hand was a slow process. Planters needed a better way to clean cotton.

Eli Whitney's Invention Eli Whitney, a young Connecticut schoolteacher, was traveling to Georgia in 1793. He was going to be a tutor on a plantation. At that time, there were few public schools in the South. When Whitney learned of the planters' problem, he decided to build a machine to clean cotton.

In only 10 days, Whitney came up with a model. His cotton engine, or gin, had two rollers with thin wire teeth. When cotton was swept between the rollers, the teeth separated the seeds from the fibers.

The simple cotton gin had an enormous effect on the southern economy. A single worker using a gin could do the work of 50 people cleaning cotton by hand. Because of the gin, planters could now grow cotton at a huge profit.

Cotton Kingdom and Slavery The cotton gin led to a boom in cotton production. In 1792, planters grew only 6,000 bales of cotton a year. By 1850, the figure was over 2 million bales.

Planters soon learned that soil wore out if planted with cotton year after year. They needed new land to cultivate. After the War of 1812, cotton planters began to move west.

By the 1850s, there were cotton plantations extending in a wide band from South Carolina through Alabama and Mississippi to Texas. This area of the South became known as the Cotton Kingdom.

Tragically, as the Cotton Kingdom spread, so did slavery. Even though cotton could now be cleaned by machine, it still had to be planted and picked by hand. The result was a cruel cycle in which the work of slaves brought profits to planters, who then used the profits to buy more land and more slaves, which brought even greater profits.

An Agricultural Economy

Cotton was the South's most profitable cash crop. However, the best conditions for growing cotton could be found mostly in the southernmost portion of the region. In other areas of the South, rice, sugar cane, and tobacco were major crops. In addition, southerners raised much of the nation's livestock.

Rice was an important crop along the coasts of South Carolina and Georgia. Sugar cane was important in Louisiana and Texas. Growing rice and sugar cane required expensive irrigation and drainage systems. Cane growers also needed costly machinery to grind their harvest. Small-scale farmers could not afford such expensive equipment, however. As a result, the plantation system dominated sugar and rice production just as it did cotton production.

Tobacco had been an export of the South since 1619, and it continued to be planted in Virginia, North Carolina, and Kentucky. However, in the early 1800s, the large tobacco plantations of colonial days had given way to small tobacco farms. On these farms, a few field hands tended five or six acres of tobacco.

In addition to the major cash crops of cotton, rice, sugar, and tobacco, the South also led the nation in livestock production. Southern livestock owners profited from hogs, oxen, horses, mules, and beef cattle. Over 90 percent of the nation's mules and over 60 percent of its hogs were raised in the South. Much of this livestock was raised in areas that were unsuitable for growing crops, such as the pine woods of North Carolina. Kentucky developed a rural economy that included the breeding of horses.

Primary Source

The Cotton Gin

Thomas Jefferson was secretary of state and inspector of patents in 1793. He received a request for a patent from a schoolteacher named Eli Whitney. Interested in learning more about it, Jefferson asked Whitney the following questions:

"Has the machine been thoroughly tried in the ginning of cotton, or is it as yet but a machine in theory? What quantity of cotton has it cleaned on an average of several days, worked by hand, and by how many hands? . . . Favorable answers to these questions would induce me to engage one of them to be forwarded to Richmond for me."

—Thomas Jefferson, from "That With This Ginn," 1793

Analyzing Primary Sources
Why do you think Jefferson was interested in the cotton gin?

Cotton Production and Slavery

Cotton Production

Source: *Historical Statistics of the United States*

Growth of Slavery

Source: *Historical Statistics of the United States*

GRAPH
Skills

As cotton production increased in the South, so did the number of enslaved African Americans.

1. **Comprehension**
   (a) How many more bales of cotton were produced in 1850 than in 1820? **(b)** In which decade did the number of slaves increase the most?

2. **Critical Thinking**
   Making Predictions In what way do you think ending slavery would affect the southern economy?

Economics $

Limited Industry Most of the industry in the South remained small and existed only to meet the needs of a farming society. Agricultural tools such as cotton gins, planters, and plows were manufactured. Factories also made goods such as ironware, hoes, and materials made of hemp, which were used to make bags for holding bales of cotton. Cheap cotton cloth was made for use in slaves' clothing. Some southerners wanted to encourage the growth of industry in the South. William Gregg, for example, modeled his cotton mill in South Carolina on the mills in Lowell, Massachusetts. Gregg built houses and gardens for his workers and schools for their children.

The South also developed a few other successful industries. In Richmond, Virginia, for example, the Tredegar Iron Works turned out railroad equipment, machinery, tools, and cannons. Flour milling was another important southern industry.

Even so, the South lagged behind the North in manufacturing. Rich planters preferred to invest their money in land and slaves rather than in factories.

Slavery also reduced the need for southern industry. In the North, most people had enough money to buy factory goods. In the South, however, millions of slaves could not buy anything. As a result, the demand for manufactured goods in the South was not as great as it was in the North.

Southern Cities Although the South was mainly rural, there were some cities. The major ones were New Orleans, Louisiana; Charleston, South Carolina; and Richmond, Virginia. These cities had the same problems as northern cities, including poor housing and poor sanitation.

Fewer than 8 percent of white southerners lived in towns of more than 4,000 people. However, many free African Americans lived in towns and cities.

Economically Dependent

With little industry of its own, the South came to depend more and more on the North and on Europe. Southern planters often borrowed money from northern banks in order to expand their plantations. They also purchased much of their furniture, farm tools, and machines from northern or European factories.

Many southerners resented this situation. One southerner described a burial to show how the South depended on the North for many goods in the 1850s:

 Monitor Your Reading As you read this quote, make sure you understand how the writer's description shows the South's dependence on the North.

66 The grave was dug through solid marble, but the marble headstone came from Vermont. It was in a pine wilderness but the pine coffin came from Cincinnati. An iron mountain overshadowed it but the coffin nails and the screws and the shovel came from Pittsburgh. . . . A hickory grove grew nearby, but the pick and shovel handles came from New York. . . . That country, so rich in underdeveloped resources, furnished nothing for the funeral except the corpse and the hole in the ground. 99

—Henry Grady, Speech to the Bay Street Club, Boston, 1889

Still, most southerners were proud of the booming cotton industry in their region. As long as cotton remained king, southerners believed, they could look to the future with confidence.

 Section 3 Assessment

Recall

1. **Identify** Explain the significance of **(a)** Eli Whitney, **(b)** Cotton Kingdom, **(c)** William Gregg.

Comprehension

2. How did the cotton gin lead to the spread of slavery?
3. Explain the importance of cotton as a cash crop in the southern economy.
4. Why was there limited growth of industry in the South?

Critical Thinking and Writing

5. **Exploring the Main Idea** Review the Main Idea statement at the beginning of this section. Then, list the positive and negative effects of cotton production on life in the South.
6. **Drawing Conclusions** Although most southerners owned no slaves, many defended slavery. Why do you think this was so?

ACTIVITY

 Take It to the NET **Connecting to Today** Today, cotton is still widely used in fabrics. Use the Internet to find out more about cotton. Write a brief report with interesting cotton facts. Visit *The American Nation* section of **www.phschool.com** for help in completing the activity.

4 Life in the South

BEFORE YOU READ

Reading Focus

- Which groups of white southerners made up southern society?
- How were free African Americans treated?
- What laws restricted the freedom of African Americans?
- How did African Americans resist slavery?

Key Terms

"cottonocracy"

slave codes

extended family

Taking Notes

Copy this table. As you read, complete the table with information about the white southerners and the African American southerners. The first entry is done for you.

WHITE SOUTHERNERS	AFRICAN AMERICAN SOUTHERNERS
• Rich southern planter • Owned slaves •	• •

🏴 **Main Idea** Most white southerners were not plantation owners; however, the plantation system and slavery were at the center of southern life.

AS YOU READ

Katie Darling

Ask Questions Based on this passage, what questions would you ask Katie Darling about her life?

Setting the Scene

In 1937, at the age of 88, Katie Darling recalled her life growing up as an enslaved person in East Texas:

> 66 Miss Stella, my young mistress, got all our ages down in a Bible, that is how I knows I was born in 1849. . . . Mammy died in slavery, and Pappy run away. . . . By the time I was big enough to tote a cow pail they put me to milking. Master had over a hundred head of cows and most of the time me and Violet, another house girl, did all the milking. We was up before five. By five we better be in that cow pen. We better milk all of them cows too or they'd bull-whip us. 99

—Katie Darling, Interview, August 2, 1937

With her brothers and sisters, Darling worked from dawn to dusk and often on Sundays. She was only one of millions of African Americans throughout the South who suffered the anguish of slavery.

White Southerners

The Old South is often pictured as a land of vast plantations worked by hundreds of slaves. Such grand estates did exist in the South. However, most white southerners were not rich planters. In fact, most whites owned no slaves at all.

The "Cottonocracy" A planter was someone who owned at least 20 slaves. In 1860, only one white southerner in 30 belonged to a planter family. An even smaller number—less than 1 percent—owned 50 or more slaves. These wealthy families were called the "cottonocracy" because they made huge amounts of money from cotton. Though few in number, their views and way of life dominated the South.

The richest planters built elegant homes and filled them with expensive furniture from Europe. They entertained lavishly. They tried to dress and behave like European nobility.

Because of their wealth and influence, many planters became political leaders. They devoted many hours to local, state, and national politics. Planters hired overseers to run day-to-day affairs on their plantations and to manage the work of slaves.

Small Farmers About 75 percent of southern whites were small farmers. These "plain folk" owned the land they farmed. They might also own one or two slaves. Unlike planters, plain folk worked with their slaves in the fields.

Among small farmers, helping each other was an important duty. "People who lived miles apart counted themselves as neighbors," wrote a farmer in Mississippi. "And in case of sorrow or sickness, there was no limit to the service neighbors provided."

Poor Whites Lower on the social ladder was a small group of poor whites. They did not own the land they farmed. Instead, they rented it, often paying the owner with part of their crop. Many barely made a living.

Poor whites often lived in the hilly, wooded areas of the South. They planted crops such as corn, potatoes, and other vegetables. They also herded cattle and pigs. Poor whites had hard lives, but they enjoyed rights that were denied to all African Americans, enslaved or free.

African American Southerners

Both free and enslaved African Americans lived in the South. Although free under the law, free African Americans faced harsh discrimination. Enslaved African Americans had no rights at all.

Free African Americans Most free African Americans were descendants of slaves freed during and after the American Revolution. Others had bought their freedom. In 1860, over 200,000 free blacks lived in the South. Most lived in Maryland and Delaware, where slavery was in decline. Others lived in cities such as New Orleans, Richmond, and Charleston.

Slave owners did not like free African Americans living in the South. They feared that free African Americans set a bad example, encouraging slaves to rebel. Also, slave owners justified slavery by claiming that African Americans could not take care of themselves. Free African American workers proved this idea wrong.

To discourage free African Americans, southern states passed laws that made life even harder for them. Free African Americans were not allowed to vote or travel. In some southern states, they either had to move out of the state or allow themselves to be enslaved.

Despite these limits, free African Americans were able to make a life for themselves. Some even made valuable contributions to southern life. For example, Norbert Rillieux (RIHL yoo) invented a machine that revolutionized the way sugar was refined. Another inventor, Henry Blair, patented a seed planter.

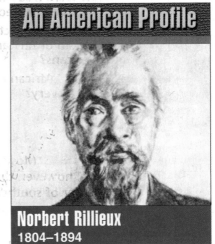

An American Profile

Norbert Rillieux
1804–1894

In the early 1800s, sugar was refined by boiling sugar cane in huge vats. Moving the hot liquid between vats was dangerous.

Norbert Rillieux invented a machine that cooked the sugar in closed vats under low air pressure. Since pipes moved the liquid from one vat to another, there was no danger to workers. Rillieux's machine made better sugar, too. The method quickly spread across Louisiana and to Mexico and Cuba. Factories today use essentially the same technique. Rillieux also invented a machine that improved the processing of sugar from sugar beets.

Was Rillieux's method less or more costly to operate than the old technique? Why?

Primary Sources

See "Life and Times of Frederick Douglass" on page 599 of the Reference Section.

Enslaved African Americans By 1860, enslaved African Americans made up one third of the South's population. Most worked as field hands on cotton plantations. Both men and women cleared new land and planted and harvested crops. Children helped by pulling weeds, collecting wood, and carrying water to the field hands. By the time they were teenagers, they worked between 12 and 14 hours a day.

On large plantations, some African Americans became skilled workers, such as carpenters and blacksmiths. A few worked in cities and lived almost as if they were free. Their earnings, however, belonged to their owners.

Life Without Freedom

The life of enslaved African Americans was determined by strict laws and the practices of individual slave owners. Conditions varied from plantation to plantation. Some owners made sure their slaves had clean cabins, decent food, and warm clothes. Other planters spent as little as possible on their slaves.

Slave Codes Southern states passed laws known as slave codes to keep slaves from either running away or rebelling. Under the codes, enslaved African Americans were forbidden to gather in groups of more than three. They could not leave their owner's land without a written pass. They were not allowed to own guns.

Viewing History

Two Ways of Life

Wealthy southern planters lived in large, beautiful homes with many slaves and acres of fertile land. More typical of the South during the 1800s was the small farmer who lived in a modest home and worked hard to make a living. Most white farmers did not have slaves. **Synthesizing Information** *Why do you think rich planters thought of themselves as aristocrats?*

424

Slave codes also made it a crime for slaves to learn how to read and write. Owners hoped that this law would make it hard for African Americans to escape slavery. They reasoned that uneducated runaway slaves would not be able to use maps or read train schedules. They would not be able to find their way north.

Some laws were meant to protect slaves, but only from the worst forms of abuse. However, enslaved African Americans did not have the right to testify in court. As a result, they were not able to bring charges against owners who abused them.

Enslaved African Americans had only one real protection against mistreatment. Owners looked on their slaves as valuable property. Most slave owners wanted to keep this human property healthy and productive.

Hard Work Even the kindest owners insisted that their slaves work long, hard days. Slaves worked from "can see to can't see," or from dawn to dusk, up to 16 hours a day. Frederick Douglass, who escaped slavery, recalled his life under one harsh master:

66 We were worked in all weathers. It was never too hot or too cold; it could never rain, blow, hail, or snow too hard for us to work in the field. Work, work, work. . . . The longest days were too short for him and the shortest nights too long for him. 99

—Frederick Douglass, *Narrative of the Life of Frederick Douglass, An American Slave*

Family Life It was hard for enslaved African Americans to keep their families together. Southern laws did not recognize slave marriages or slave families. As a result, owners could sell a husband and wife to different buyers. Children were often taken from their parents and sold.

On large plantations, many enslaved families did manage to stay together. For those African Americans, the family was a source of strength, pride, and love. Grandparents, parents, children, aunts, uncles, and cousins formed a close-knit group. This idea of an extended family had its roots in Africa.

Enslaved African Americans preserved other traditions as well. Parents taught their children traditional African stories and songs. They used folk tales to pass on African history and moral beliefs.

Religion Offers Hope By the 1800s, many enslaved African Americans were devout Christians. Planters often allowed white ministers to preach to their slaves. African Americans also had their own preachers and beliefs.

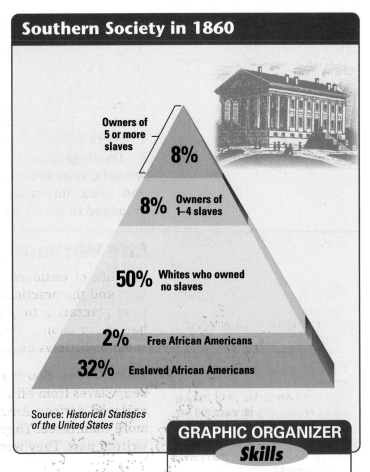

Southern Society in 1860

Owners of 5 or more slaves **8%**

8% Owners of 1–4 slaves

50% Whites who owned no slaves

2% Free African Americans

32% Enslaved African Americans

Source: *Historical Statistics of the United States*

GRAPHIC ORGANIZER

Skills

This social pyramid represents the structure of southern society in 1860. At the top are wealthy and powerful planters. At the bottom are millions of enslaved African Americans.

1. **Comprehension** Which group in southern society was most numerous?

2. **Critical Thinking Analyzing Information** How did the social structure of the South reflect the importance of slavery?

Economics $

Religion helped African Americans cope with the harshness of slave life. Bible stories about how the ancient Hebrews had escaped from slavery inspired a new type of religious song called a spiritual. As they worked in the fields, slaves would often sing about a coming day of freedom.

Resistance Against Slavery

Enslaved African Americans struck back against the system that denied them both freedom and wages. Some broke tools, destroyed crops, and stole food.

Many enslaved African Americans tried to escape to the North. Because the journey was long and dangerous, very few made it to freedom. Every county had slave patrols and sheriffs ready to question an unknown black person.

A few African Americans used violence to resist the brutal slave system. Denmark Vesey, a free African American, planned a revolt in 1822. Vesey was betrayed before the revolt began. He and 35 other people were executed.

In 1831, an African American preacher named Nat Turner led a major revolt. An enslaved worker on a plantation in Southampton County, Virginia, Turner believed his mission was to take revenge on plantation owners. Turner led his followers through Virginia, killing more than 57 whites. For nearly two months terrified whites hunted the countryside looking for Turner. They killed many innocent African Americans before catching and hanging him.

Nat Turner's revolt increased southern fears of an uprising of enslaved African Americans. Revolts were rare, however. Since whites were cautious and well armed, a revolt by African Americans had almost no chance of success.

Section 4 Assessment

Recall

1. **Identify** Explain the significance of **(a)** Norbert Rillieux, **(b)** Henry Blair, **(c)** Denmark Vesey, **(d)** Nat Turner.
2. **Define (a)** "cottonocracy," **(b)** slave codes, **(c)** extended family.

Comprehension

3. Describe the way of life of each of the following groups in the South: **(a)** rich planters, **(b)** small farmers, **(c)** poor whites.
4. How did laws restrict the freedom of both free and enslaved African Americans?

5. In what ways did enslaved African Americans struggle against slavery?

Critical Thinking and Writing

6. **Exploring the Main Idea** Review the Main Idea statement at the beginning of this section. Then, write a paragraph discussing the importance of plantations in the southern economy.
7. **Synthesizing Information** Few southerners were planters. Why do you think this small group was able to dominate the political and social life of the South?

ACTIVITY

Take It to the NET

Learning More About Spirituals During slavery, African American spirituals were passed on by word of mouth. Use the Internet to learn the words to a spiritual sung during the 1800s. Explain what the words mean. Visit *The American Nation* section of **www.phschool.com** for help in completing the activity.

Making Generalizations

You can extend your understanding of how new technology affected American life by making generalizations. Making generalizations means taking a number of examples and facts and arriving at a general statement.

This passage tells about the daguerreotype, an image printed on a chemically treated copper plate, and developed by a Frenchman named Louis Daguerre in 1839:

In 1847, two Americans began a collaboration that would advance science on several fronts. The men were John A. Whipple, a photographer, and William Cranch Bond, an astronomer who headed the Harvard College Observatory. Whipple had already developed a technique for making paper prints from the daguerreotype images. Bond had just acquired the world's largest telescope. The collaborators' goal was to photograph the sky through the telescope. Although their first attempts were unsuccessful, Whipple and Bond finally produced the first astronomical daguerreotype—an image of the star Vega. This was soon followed by pictures of the moon. Bond and Whipple then toured Europe to great acclaim, distributing copies of the exciting new images to observatories on the continent.

The chart shows how to organize facts to make a generalization based on the passage.

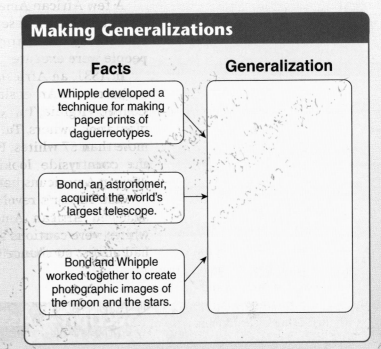

Learn the Skill *To make generalizations, use the following steps:*

1. **Identify the main idea and details.** What information is being given?

2. **Compile a list of relevant facts.** You may find that not every fact given is necessary for a generalization.

3. **Find a common element.** Look for a single feature that is true of all the facts you have listed.

4. **Make a generalization.** Make a general statement based on the facts. Accurate generalizations often include words such as *many, most, often, usually, some, few,* and *sometimes.* Faulty generalizations may include words such as *all, none, always, never,* or *every.*

Practice the Skill *Answer the following questions about the passage and chart:*

1. What is the subject of the passage?

2. **(a)** Identify a fact that is not relevant to those listed on the chart. **(b)** Identify a relevant fact that fits with those given on the chart.

3. How are the facts on the chart related?

4. Write a generalization based on the facts. Use a clue word.

Apply the Skill *See the Chapter Review and Assessment.*

CREATING A CHAPTER SUMMARY

Copy the table below. As you read, fill in the boxes with information about the economy and society of the North and the South. Add as many boxes as you need.

LIFE IN THE NORTH	LIFE IN THE SOUTH
• Industrial economy	• Agricultural economy

For additional review and enrichment activities, see the interactive version of *The American Nation,* available on the Web and on CD-ROM.

Take It to the NET

Chapter Self-Test For practice test questions for Chapter 14, visit *The American Nation* section of **www.phschool.com**.

Building Vocabulary

Write sentences using the chapter vocabulary words listed below, leaving blanks where the vocabulary words would go. Exchange your sentences with another student and fill in the blanks in each other's sentences.

1. telegraph
2. locomotive
3. clipper ship
4. trade union
5. strike
6. nativist
7. discrimination
8. "cottonocracy"
9. slave codes
10. extended family

Reviewing Key Facts

11. Describe three inventions that caused the North's economy to expand. (Section 1)
12. Give two reasons for Irish and German immigration to the United States in the 1840s and 1850s. (Section 2)
13. Explain how the cotton gin changed life in the South. (Section 3)
14. Discuss the difference between the planter and the small farmer. (Section 4)

Critical Thinking and Writing

15. **Comparing** Compare two inventions that you think had the greatest impact on American life during the mid-1800s. Explain your answer.
16. **Evaluating Information** Why is transportation important to economic progress?
17. **Analyzing Information** How did the political, social, and economic situation of free African Americans and enslaved African Americans differ?
18. **Connecting to Geography: Regions** Make a comparison chart that shows how economic differences affected life in the North and in the South.

Analyzing Primary Sources

Frederick Law Olmstead, who often wrote about social issues, gives his view on poor white women working in the South. Read the excerpt. Then, answer the questions that follow:

> 66 Poor white girls never hired themselves out to do servants' work, but they would come and help another white woman with her sewing or quilting, and take wages for it. . . . That their condition is not as unfortunate by any means as that of Negroes, however, is most obvious, since among them, people may sometimes elevate themselves to positions and habits of usefulness and respectability. 99
>
> —Frederick Law Olmsted,
> *A Journey in the Seaboard Slave States,* 1856

19. According to Olmstead, how do poor white girls find work?
20. What is Olmstead's conclusion about the condition of poor working girls?
21. Why do you think poor white girls would refuse to be hired as servants?

Making Generalizations

Read the following passage about steamboats. Then, answer the questions that follow:

> 66 The western steamboat carried both freight and passengers; but it won its greatest fame as a way to travel. The most luxurious boats, called 'floating palaces,' offered accommodations far beyond the experience of the average American. Steamboats also provided the cheapest form of inland transportation before the Civil War.
>
> Despite the discomforts of swarming mosquitoes, heat from the boilers, and noisy engines at all hours of the night, observers agreed that journeying by steamboat was far more pleasant than taking a stagecoach, the principal alternative in the West before 1850. 99
>
> —Davidson, et al., *Nation of Nations*

22. What is the main idea of the passage?
   A Steamboat travel was costly.
   B Steamboats are the best way to travel.
   C Steamboats carried freight and people.
   D Steamboat travel was comfortable.
23. Make a generalization based on the passage.

ACTIVITIES

Connecting With . . . Culture

Understanding the Nation in the 1800s Read the following quotations. Determine which person or event is being referred to. Then, write a brief paragraph describing how each person or event affected American society.

"Not one of them having the courage to lead off, I . . . became impatient and started on ahead, saying with childish bravado, 'I don't care what you do, I am going to strike, whether anyone else does or not'; and I marched out, and was followed by the others."

"The roads, the canals, and the mails play [an important] part in the prosperity of the Union. . . ."

"I thank God I am not property now, but am regarded as a man like yourself. . . ."

Take It to the NET

Connecting to Today

Creating a Comparison Chart In the 1800s, there were strong economic differences between the North and the South. Use the Internet to find out about the economies of these regions today. Make a chart in which you compare their economies. For help in starting this activity, visit *The American Nation* section of **www.phschool.com**.

Becoming a Citizen

A Citizenship Pamphlet Immigrants in the mid-1800s had to live in the United States for five years before gaining voting privileges. Use the Internet to find out how immigrants can become citizens today. Present the information in a pamphlet. For help in starting this activity, visit *The American Nation* section of **www.phschool.com**.

Incidents in the Life of a Slave Girl

Harriet A. Jacobs

Harriet Jacobs

Introduction **Born in Edenton, North Carolina, in the early 1800s, Harriet Jacobs did not realize she was a slave until she was six years old. When Jacobs was 11, her mistress died and she was sent to a new master, Dr. James Norcom. Jacobs found her new situation at the Norcom household unbearable. In 1835, she escaped from Norcom and went into hiding in her hometown. For seven years, she hid in the cramped space of an attic in her grandmother's house. The following selection describes her life in the attic.**

Vocabulary Before you read the selection, find the meanings of these words in a dictionary: **benumb, delirious, stupefy, kindle.**

I suffered much more during the second winter than I did during the first. My limbs were benumbed by inaction, and the cold filled them with cramp. I had a very painful sensation of coldness in my head; even my face and tongue stiffened, and I lost the power of speech. Of course it was impossible, under the circumstances, to summon any physician. My brother William came and did all he could for me. Uncle Philip also watched tenderly over me; and poor grandmother crept up and down to inquire whether there were any signs of returning life. I was restored to full consciousness by the dashing of cold water on my face, and found myself leaning against my brother's arm, while he bent over me with streaming eyes. He afterwards told me he thought I was dying, for I had been in an unconscious state for sixteen hours. I next became delirious, and was in great danger of betraying myself and my friends. To prevent this, they stupefied me with drugs. I remained in bed for six weeks, weary in body and sick at heart. How to get medical advice was the question. William finally went to a Thompsonian doctor, and described himself as having all my pains and aches. He returned with herbs, roots, and ointment. He was especially charged to rub on the ointment by a fire, but how could a fire be made in my little den? Charcoal in a furnace was tried, but there was no outlet for the gas, and it nearly cost my life. Afterwards coals, already kindled, were brought up in an iron pan, and placed on bricks. I was so weak, and it was so long since I had enjoyed the warmth of a fire, that those few coals actually made me weep. I think the medicines did me some good; but my recovery was very slow. Dark thoughts passed through my mind as I lay there day after day. I tried to be thankful for my little cell, dismal as it was, and even to love it, as part of the price I had paid for the redemption of my children. Sometimes I thought God was a compassionate Father, who would forgive my sins for the sake of my sufferings. At other times, it seemed to me there was no justice or mercy in the divine government. I asked why the curse of slavery was permitted to exist, and why I had been so persecuted and wronged from youth upward. These things took the shape of mystery, which is to this day not so clear to my soul as I trust it will be hereafter.

In the midst of my illness, grandmother broke down under the weight of anxiety and

This house was a "station" where runaway slaves could hide.

toil. The idea of losing her, who had always been my best friend and a mother to my children, was the sorest trial I had yet had. O, how earnestly I prayed that she might recover! How hard it seemed, that I could not tend upon her, who had so long and so tenderly watched over me!

One day the screams of a child nerved me with strength to crawl to my peeping-hole, and I saw my son covered with blood. A fierce dog, usually chained, had seized and bitten him. A doctor was sent for, and I heard the groans and screams of my child while the wounds were being sewed up. O, what torture to a mother's heart, to listen to this and be unable to go to him!

But childhood is like a day in spring, alternately shower and sunshine. Before long Benny was bright and lively, threatening the destruction of the dog; and great was his delight when the doctor told him the next day that the dog had bitten another boy and been shot. Benny recovered from his wounds; but it was long before he could walk.

Analyzing Literature

1. What hardships did Harriet endure the second winter in the attic?
   A She was always hungry and lonely.
   B Her body was stiff from cold and she could not talk.
   C The attic was too warm and she could not communicate with anyone.
   D She was not able to let anyone know that she was ill.

2. How did Harriet's brother help her?
   A He helped her send messages to the doctor.
   B He sealed the cracks in the walls of the attic.
   C He managed to bring her ointments.
   D He brought her children to the attic.

3. Critical Thinking **Drawing Inferences** What inner conflicts does Harriet experience?

Reform and a New American Culture

1820–1860

1 **The Reforming Spirit**
2 **Opposing Slavery**
3 **A Call for Women's Rights**
4 **American Art and Literature**

Religious revival meeting

William Lloyd Garrison and his antislavery vow

AMERICAN EVENTS

Early 1800s
The Second Great Awakening sweeps the nation. At outdoor revival meetings, converts promise to reform their lives.

1831
William Lloyd Garrison begins publishing his antislavery newspaper, *The Liberator*.

1837
Horace Mann pushes for education reform in Massachusetts.

Presidential Terms: James Monroe 1817–1825 | John Quincy Adams 1825–1829 | Andrew Jackson 1829–1837 | Martin Van Buren 1837–1841

1820 ····· **1830** ····· **1840**

▲ **1822**
Liberia is founded in western Africa.

1837 ▲
First kindergarten opens in Germany.

The Underground Railroad

Some reformers helped enslaved African Americans escape to the North or Canada by a route known as the Underground Railroad.

BRITISH TERRITORY

Unorganized Territory
Minnesota
Maine
Nebraska Territory
Wisconsin
Michigan
VT
NH
New York
MA
CT RI
Milton
Iowa
Davenport
Des Moines
Illinois
Indiana
Ohio
Pennsylvania
New York
NJ
Washington, D.C.
MD DE
Utah Territory
Kansas Territory
St. Louis
Indianapolis
Virginia
Richmond
New Mexico Territory
Missouri
Kentucky
North Carolina
Indian Territory
Arkansas
Tennessee
South Carolina
ATLANTIC OCEAN
MS
Georgia
Charleston
Alabama
Savannah
Texas
Louisiana
New Orleans
Florida
MEXICO
Gulf of Mexico

L. Superior
L. Michigan
L. Huron
L. Ontario
Erie

50°N
60°W
40°N
70°W
30°N
80°W
90°W
100°W
110°W

Albers Equal-Area Projection
0   200   400 Miles
0   200   400 Kilometers

Key
→ Railroad routes
▢ Free states
▢ Slave states
▢ Territories

Monument to women's rights leaders.

Illustration from *Moby-Dick*

1841
Dorothea Dix begins a crusade to improve treatment of the mentally ill.

1848
The first convention on women's rights meets in Seneca Falls, New York.

1851
Herman Melville publishes *Moby-Dick*. The novel tells of a sea captain's mad pursuit of a white whale.

William Henry Harrison 1841

John Tyler 1841–1845

James K. Polk 1845–1849

Zachary Taylor 1849–1850

Millard Fillmore 1850–1853

Franklin Pierce 1853–1857   James Buchanan 1857–1861

1840   **1850**   **1860**

▲ **1840**
World Antislavery Convention opens in London.

1859 ▲
Charles Dickens publishes *A Tale of Two Cities*.

1 The Reforming Spirit

BEFORE YOU READ

Reading Focus

- How did political and religious ideals provide inspiration for reform?
- Why did Dorothea Dix seek to reform the treatment of prisoners and the mentally ill?
- What were the goals of the temperance movement?
- How did reformers improve American education?

Key Terms

social reform
predestination
Second Great Awakening
revival
debtor
temperance movement

Taking Notes

Copy the chart below. As you read this section, complete the chart to show some of the effects of the reforming spirit of the 1800s. Add as many boxes as you need.

THE REFORMING IMPULSE

Dorothea Dix fights for mentally ill and prisoners

Main Idea Between 1820 and 1860, a wide variety of reform movements sprang up to improve conditions in the United States.

AS YOU READ
Caves at Newgate prison

Visualize Picture Newgate when it was used to house prisoners. Describe what you see.

Setting the Scene

Two reporters entered the small, ordinary-looking brick hut. Opening a trapdoor in the floor, they peered down the dark shaft of an abandoned copper mine. Nervously, they climbed 50 feet down an old wooden ladder until they reached the bottom:

> 66 Lighting the candles . . . I led the way down a series of stone steps. . . . The roof was very low, and the candle gave so little light, that I was compelled to feel my way forward with my walking-stick. . . . [I] groped forward twenty or thirty feet into the caverns . . . where the prisoners used to sleep. 99
>
> —quoted in Phelps, *Newgate of Connecticut*

Years earlier, these cramped caves had served as Connecticut's state prison, Newgate. It was shut down in 1827.

In the mid-1800s, some Americans began to condemn the way prisoners were treated. Prison reform was just one of many movements that sprang up to cure the nation's ills.

The Reforming Impulse

The impulse toward social reform had both political and religious roots. Social reform is an organized attempt to improve what is unjust or imperfect in society.

Political Ideals As you have read, during the Jackson era, politics was becoming more democratic. More people could vote and take part in government than ever before.

Still, some critics said American society was not democratic enough. They pointed to the promise of liberty and equality expressed in the Declaration of Independence. A true democracy, they argued, would not allow slavery. Others asked why women had fewer rights than men. By changing such injustices, reformers hoped to move the nation closer to its political ideals.

The Second Great Awakening During the colonial era, many American Protestants believed in predestination. According to this idea, God decided in advance which people would attain salvation after death. This belief led many people to worry that they could do nothing to be saved.

In the early 1800s, a dynamic religious movement known as the Second Great Awakening swept the nation. Its leaders stressed free will rather than predestination. They taught that individuals could choose to save their souls by their own actions.

To stir religious feelings, preachers held revivals, huge outdoor meetings. Revivals might last for days and attract thousands of people. A witness recalled the excitement of a revival at Cane Ridge, Kentucky:

> **❝** The vast sea of human beings seemed to be agitated as if by storm. I counted seven ministers all preaching at once. . . . Some of the people were singing, others praying, some crying for mercy. **❞**
>
> —James B. Finley, *Autobiography*

One leader of the Second Great Awakening was a minister named Charles Grandison Finney. A powerful speaker, Finney taught that individual salvation was the first step toward "the complete reformation of the whole world." Such teachings inspired new efforts to improve society.

Hospital and Prison Reform

One of the most vigorous social reformers was Dorothea Dix, a Boston schoolteacher. She turned her attention to what one minister called the "outsiders" in society: criminals and the mentally ill.

Reforms for the Mentally Ill In 1841, Dix visited a jail for women near Boston. She was outraged to discover that some of the prisoners were not criminals, but mentally ill. Dix demanded to know why these women were locked in small, dark, unheated cells. The jailer replied that "lunatics" did not feel the cold.

During the next 18 months, Dix visited every jail, poorhouse, and hospital in Massachusetts. Her shocking reports helped persuade state legislators to fund a new mental hospital:

> **❝** I proceed, gentlemen, briefly to call your attention to the present state of Insane Persons confined . . . in cages, closets, cellars, stalls, pens! Chained, naked, beaten with rods, and lashed into obedience. **❞**
>
> —Dorothea Dix, "Memorial to the State Legislators of Massachusetts"

Dix went on to inspect jails as far away as Louisiana and Illinois. Her reports persuaded most legislatures to treat the mentally ill as patients, not criminals.

Roots of Reform

The Reform Movement

Political Origins
- The ideals of liberty and equality in the Declaration of Independence inspire people to try to improve society
- During Jackson era, more people can vote than ever before
- Critics say slavery and other injustices violate democratic ideals

Religious Influences
- Second Great Awakening stresses free will rather than predestination
- Revivals encourage people to reform their lives
- Finney teaches that individual salvation is the first step to the reform of a society

GRAPHIC ORGANIZER
Skills

Both political and religious ideas inspired Americans to work for reform.

1. **Comprehension** Identify one political change in the country that encouraged reform.

2. **Critical Thinking Identifying Causes and Effects** Why might a belief in free will inspire a spirit of reform?

Civics

▲ Past

▲ Present

Viewing History

Reforming Fashions

United States

In the 1800s, tightly laced dresses that crushed women's rib cages often caused them to faint. Journalist Amelia Bloomer promoted a new fashion: loose-fitting trousers. Many Americans objected to these "bloomers" (left). Today, Amelia Bloomer would be pleased to see that women wear comfortable clothes every day.

Linking Past and Present
Do changing fashions ever cause controversy today? Give examples.

A Long Struggle The Seneca Falls Convention marked the start of an organized campaign for equal rights, or the women's rights movement. Other leaders took up the struggle. Susan B. Anthony built a close working partnership with Elizabeth Cady Stanton. While Stanton usually had to stay at home with her seven children, Anthony was free to travel across the country. Anthony was a tireless speaker. Even when audiences heckled her and threw eggs, she always finished her speech.

In the years after 1848, women worked for change in many areas. They won additional legal rights in some states. For example, New York passed laws allowing married women to keep their own property and wages. Still, many men and women opposed the women's rights movement. The struggle for equal rights would last many years.

New Opportunities in Education

The women at Seneca Falls believed that education was a key to equality. Elizabeth Cady Stanton said:

66 The girl must be allowed to romp and play, climb, skate, and swim. Her clothing must be more like those of the boy—strong, loose-fitting garments, thick boots. . . . She must be taught to look forward to a life of self-dependence and, like the boy, prepare herself for some [profitable] trade profession. 99
—Elizabeth Cady Stanton, Letter, 1851

Such an idea was startling in the early 1800s. Women from poor families had little hope of learning even to read. Middle-class girls who went to school learned dancing and drawing rather than science or mathematics. After all, people argued, women were expected to care for their families. Why did they need an education?

AS YOU READ **Monitor Your Reading** Check to see whether you understand how educational opportunities were limited in the early 1800s.

Schools for Women Reformers worked to improve education for women. Emma Willard opened a high school for girls in Troy, New York. Here, young women studied "men's" subjects, such as mathematics and physics.

Mary Lyon opened Mount Holyoke Female Seminary in Massachusetts in 1837. She did not call the school a college because many people thought it was wrong for women to attend college. In fact, however, Mount Holyoke was the first women's college in the United States.

New Careers At about this time, a few men's colleges began to admit women. As their education improved, women found jobs teaching, especially in grade schools.

A few women entered fields such as medicine. Elizabeth Blackwell attended medical school at Geneva College in New York. To the surprise of school officials, she graduated first in her class. Women had provided medical care since colonial times, but Blackwell was the first woman in the United States to earn a medical degree. She later helped found the nation's first medical school for women.

Women made their mark in other fields as well. Maria Mitchell was a noted astronomer. Sarah Josepha Hale edited *Godey's Lady's Book*, an influential magazine for women. Antoinette Blackwell became the first American woman ordained a minister. She also campaigned for abolitionism, temperance, and women's right to vote.

Section 3 Assessment

Recall
1. **Identify** Explain the significance of (a) Sojourner Truth, (b) Elizabeth Cady Stanton, (c) Seneca Falls Convention, (d) Emma Willard, (e) Elizabeth Blackwell.
2. **Define** women's rights movement.

Comprehension
3. What legal rights did women lack in the early 1800s?
4. (a) Why did Mott and Stanton organize a women's rights convention? (b) Describe two resolutions passed by the convention.

5. How did reformers change education for women?

Critical Thinking and Writing
6. **Exploring the Main Idea** Review the Main Idea statement at the beginning of this section. Then, write a sentence summarizing the link between the abolitionist and women's rights movements.
7. **Making Predictions** How do you think the growth of educational opportunities in the mid-1800s would affect the future of the women's rights movement later in the century? Write a paragraph explaining the reasons for your prediction.

ACTIVITY

Designing a Banner With a partner, design a banner to be displayed at the Seneca Falls Convention. Make a clever and attractive design that expresses the feelings of early women's rights crusaders. Include a brief slogan.

4 American Art and Literature

BEFORE YOU READ

Reading Focus

- How did American painters develop their own style?
- What themes did American poets, novelists, and storytellers explore?
- Why was the "inner light" important to Emerson and Thoreau?

Key Terms

Hudson River School

transcendentalist

individualism

civil disobedience

Taking Notes

Copy the concept web below. As you read, fill in the blank ovals with information about American art and literature. Add as many ovals as you need.

Main Idea In the mid-1800s, American writers and artists began to create a new vision that reflected the continuity and change of American life.

AS YOU READ

Painter's easel and equipment

Draw Inferences What standard is Smith using to judge American literature and art?

Setting the Scene In 1820, a Scottish minister named Sydney Smith deplored what he saw as a lack of culture in the United States:

> 66 In the four quarters of the globe, who reads an American book? Or goes to an American play? Or looks at an American picture or statue? What does the world yet owe to Americans? 99
>
> —Sydney Smith, *The Edinburgh Review*

Even as Smith wrote these words, American artists and writers were breaking free of European traditions to create a unique American vision. At the same time, their work expressed universal themes—such as the love of nature or the desire for liberty—that appealed to audiences far beyond the United States.

American Painters

Before 1800, most American painters studied in Europe. Benjamin West of Philadelphia was appointed historical painter to King George III. Many American painters journeyed to London to study with West. Two of them, Charles Willson Peale and Gilbert Stuart, later painted famous portraits of George Washington.

By the mid-1800s, American artists began to develop their own style. The first group to do so became known as the **Hudson River School.** Artists such as Thomas Cole and Asher B. Durand painted vivid landscapes of New York's Hudson River region. African American artist Robert S. Duncanson reflected the style of the Hudson River School.

Other artists painted scenes of hard-working country people. George Caleb Bingham of Missouri created a timeless picture of frontier life along the rivers that feed the great Mississippi. George Catlin and Alfred Jacob Miller traveled to the Far West to record the daily life of Indians on the Great Plains and in the Rockies.

The Poetry of Democracy

Henry Wadsworth Longfellow was the favorite poet of Americans in the mid-1800s. Longfellow based many poems on events from the past. "Paul Revere's Ride" honored the Revolutionary War hero. "The Song of Hiawatha" idealized Native American life.

Other poets spoke out on social issues. John Greenleaf Whittier, a Quaker from Massachusetts, and Frances Watkins Harper, an African American woman from Maryland, used their pens to make readers aware of the evils of slavery.

Walt Whitman published only one book of poems, *Leaves of Grass.* However, he added to it over a period of 27 years. Whitman had great faith in the common people. His poetry celebrated democracy. He wrote proudly of being part of a "nation of many nations":

> 66 At home on the hills of Vermont or in the
>   woods of Maine, or the Texan ranch,
> Comrade of Californians, comrade of free
>   North-Westerners. . . .
> Of every hue and caste am I, of every rank
>   and religion. 99
>
> —Walt Whitman, *Song of Myself*

Only seven of Emily Dickinson's more than 1,700 poems were published in her lifetime. A shy woman who rarely left her home, Dickinson called her poetry "my letter to the world / That never wrote to me." Today, she is recognized as one of the nation's greatest poets.

Novels and Stories

Like painters, early American writers also depended on Europe for their ideas and inspiration. In the 1820s, however, a new crop of writers began to write stories with American themes.

Two Early Writers One of the most popular American writers was Washington Irving, a New Yorker. Irving first became known for *The Sketch Book,* a collection of tales published in 1820. Two of his best-loved tales are "Rip Van Winkle" and "The Legend of Sleepy Hollow."

The exciting novels of James Fenimore Cooper were also set in the American past. In *The Deerslayer* and *The Last of the Mohicans,* Cooper created Natty Bumppo, a heroic model of a strong, solitary frontiersman. The novels gave an idealized view of relations between whites and Native Americans on the frontier.

Viewing History

Hudson River School
Hudson River

In his 1849 painting *Kindred Spirits,* Asher B. Durand depicts the grandeur of New York's Catskill Mountains. The two men shown are nature poet William Cullen Bryant and Durand's fellow painter Thomas Cole.
Analyzing Information *What kinds of emotions might a painting like this stir?*

Primary Sources

See Herman Melville, "Moby-Dick," on page 601 of the Reference Section.

The stories of Cooper and Irving gave Americans a sense of the richness of their past. Their appeal went beyond the United States, however. Washington Irving was the first American writer to enjoy fame in Europe.

Later Writers In 1851, Herman Melville published *Moby-Dick*. The novel tells the story of Ahab, the crazed captain of a whaling ship. Ahab vows revenge on the white whale that years earlier bit off his leg. *Moby-Dick* had only limited success when it was first published. Today, however, critics rank it among the finest American novels.

Nathaniel Hawthorne often drew on the history of New England in his novels and short stories. In *The Scarlet Letter*, published in 1850, Hawthorne explored Puritan notions of sin and salvation. The novel shows how a young man is consumed by guilt when he tries to hide his wrongdoing from the world.

Edgar Allan Poe became famous for his many tales of horror. His short story "The Tell-Tale Heart" is about a murderer, driven mad by guilt, who imagines he can hear his victim's heartbeat. Poe is also known as the "father of the detective story" for his mystery stories, such as "The Murders in the Rue Morgue."

William Wells Brown was the first African American to earn his living as a writer. He published *Clotel*, a novel about slave life, in 1853. Brown also wrote a play inspired by his own experiences as a fugitive slave and a conductor on the Underground Railroad. His lectures and readings drew large audiences in Europe as well as throughout the North.

Women Writers Many best-selling novels of the period were written by women. Some novels told about young women who gained wealth and happiness through honesty and self-sacrifice. Others showed the hardships faced by widows and orphans.

Few of these novels are read today. However, writers like Catherine Sedgwick and Fanny Fern earned far more than Hawthorne or Melville. Hawthorne complained about the success of a "mob of scribbling women."

The "Inner Light"

In New England, a small but influential group of writers and thinkers emerged. They called themselves transcendentalists because they believed that the most important truths in life transcended, or went beyond, human reason. Transcendentalists valued the spark of deeply felt emotions more than reason. They believed that each individual should live up to the divine possibilities within. This belief influenced many transcendentalists to support social reform.

Viewing History

Sleepy Hollow

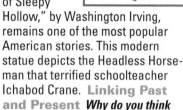

"The Legend of Sleepy Hollow," by Washington Irving, remains one of the most popular American stories. This modern statue depicts the Headless Horseman that terrified schoolteacher Ichabod Crane. **Linking Past and Present** *Why do you think this story is so popular?*

Emerson The leading transcendentalist was Ralph Waldo Emerson. Emerson was the most popular essayist and lecturer of his day. Audiences flocked to hear him talk on subjects such as self-reliance and character. Emerson believed that the human spirit was reflected in nature. Civilization might provide material wealth, he said, but nature exhibited higher values that came from God.

In his essays and lectures, Emerson stressed individualism, or the importance of each individual. Each person, Emerson said, has an "inner light." He urged people to use this inner light to guide their lives and improve society. "Trust thyself," he wrote. "Every heart vibrates to that iron string."

Thoreau Henry David Thoreau (thuh ROW), Emerson's friend and neighbor, believed that the growth of industry and the rise of cities were ruining the nation. He urged people to live as simply and as close to nature as possible. In *Walden*, his best-known work, Thoreau describes spending a year alone in a cabin on Walden Pond in Massachusetts.

Like Emerson, Thoreau believed that each individual must decide what is right or wrong. "If a man does not keep pace with his companions," he wrote, in *Walden*, "perhaps it is because he hears a different drummer. Let him step to the music he hears."

Thoreau's "different drummer" told him that slavery was wrong. He argued in favor of civil disobedience, the idea that people have a right to disobey unjust laws if their consciences demand it. He once went to jail for refusing to pay taxes to support the Mexican War, which he felt promoted slavery. Thoreau's writings on civil disobedience and nonviolence later influenced Mohandas Gandhi and Martin Luther King, Jr.

Primary Source

Civil Disobedience

In his famous essay "Civil Disobedience," Henry David Thoreau discussed his refusal to pay taxes to support the Mexican War:
"I have paid no poll tax for six years. I was put into a jail once on this account, for one night; and, as I stood considering the walls of solid stone, two or three feet thick, the door of wood and iron, a foot thick, and the iron grating which strained the light, I could not help being struck with the foolishness of that institution which treated me as if I were mere flesh and blood and bones, to be locked up. . . . I was not born to be forced. I will breathe after my own fashion. Let us see who is the strongest."

—Henry David Thoreau,
"Civil Disobedience"

Analyzing Primary Sources
How does this passage show Thoreau's belief in the individual conscience?

Section 4 Assessment

Recall
1. **Identify** Explain the significance of **(a)** Hudson River School, **(b)** Emily Dickinson, **(c)** Washington Irving, **(d)** Herman Melville, **(e)** William Wells Brown, **(f)** Ralph Waldo Emerson, **(g)** Henry David Thoreau.
2. **Define** **(a)** transcendentalist, **(b)** individualism, **(c)** civil disobedience.

Comprehension
3. How did American painting change in the mid-1800s?
4. Describe the themes explored by two of the following: **(a)** Henry Wadsworth Longfellow, **(b)** Walt Whitman,

(c) James Fenimore Cooper, **(d)** Nathaniel Hawthorne.
5. Identify the reasons for and the impact of Thoreau's idea of civil disobedience.

Critical Thinking and Writing
6. **Exploring the Main Idea** Review the Main Idea statement at the beginning of this section. Then, analyze how the work of one writer reflected continuity or change in American life.
7. **Drawing Conclusions** List two themes expressed by American writers. For each one, give reasons why it was also meaningful to audiences outside the United States.

ACTIVITY

Take It to the NET
Writing a Museum Guide Use the Internet to find other examples of American painting from 1800–1865. Choose one work, and write a description that might appear in a museum guide. Include the title, artist, and date, as well as a description of the subject matter. Visit *The American Nation* section of **www.phschool.com** for help in completing the activity.

CREATING A CHAPTER SUMMARY

Copy the table below. Fill in the blank spaces with goals and accomplishments of key American reformers. Add as many rows as you need to complete the table.

AMERICAN REFORMERS

GOAL	REFORMER	IMPACT
• Religious revival	• Charles Grandison Finney	• Encouraged spirit of reform
•	• Dorothea Dix	•
•	• Temperance movement	•
•	• Elizabeth Cady Stanton	•
•	•	•
•	•	•

i TEXT

For additional review and enrichment activities, see the interactive version of *The American Nation,* available on the Web and on CD-ROM.

Take It to the NET

Chapter Self-Test For practice test questions for Chapter 15, visit *The American Nation* section of **www.phschool.com**.

Building Vocabulary

Use the chapter vocabulary words listed below to create a crossword puzzle. Exchange puzzles with a classmate. Complete the puzzles, and then check each other's answers.

1. social reform
2. predestination
3. revival
4. debtor
5. temperance movement
6. abolitionist
7. Underground Railroad
8. women's rights movement
9. individualism
10. civil disobedience

Reviewing Key Facts

11. What were the effects of the Second Great Awakening? (Section 1)
12. How did public education improve in the early 1800s? (Section 1)
13. Describe two methods that abolitionists used to achieve their goals. (Section 2)
14. What ideas were contained in the Seneca Falls Declaration of Sentiments? (Section 3)
15. Identify two writers who explored the American past in their work. (Section 4)

Critical Thinking and Writing

16. **Drawing Inferences** In his *Appeal to the Colored Citizens of the World,* David Walker wrote that "all men are created equal; that they are endowed by their Creator with certain inalienable rights." **(a)** From which document did Walker borrow this idea? **(b)** Write a paragraph explaining why he included this phrase.
17. **Comparing** Compare the abolitionist movement and the women's rights movement in terms of causes and impact.
18. **Connecting to Geography: Place** Look at the painting from the Hudson River School in Section 4. Write down five adjectives that describe the geographic setting of the painting. Then, list five places or types of landform found in the United States that you think would attract landscape painters.
19. **Synthesizing Information** Write a paragraph explaining how the Second Great Awakening, the educational reform movement, and the work of Emerson and Thoreau all stressed the importance of the individual.

Analyzing Primary Sources

At an 1852 abolitionist meeting in Rochester, New York, Frederick Douglass denounced the continuing slave trade in the United States:

> ❝ Fellow citizens, this murderous traffic is, today, in active operation in this boasted republic. In the solitude of my spirit, I see clouds of dust raised on the highways of the South; I see the bleeding footsteps; I hear the doleful [sad] wail of fettered humanity on the way to the slave markets where victims are to be sold like horse, sheep, and swine. . . . My soul sickens at the sight. ❞

—Frederick Douglass,
"What, to the Slave, Is the Fourth of July?"

20. What scene is Douglass describing?
21. **(a)** What emotions is Douglass trying to stir up? **(b)** How does he use words and images to achieve this goal? Give examples.
22. What point is Douglass making by using the phrase "boasted republic"?
23. How did Douglass's background increase the validity of his views on slavery?

Making Decisions

ARGUMENTS FOR	ARGUMENTS AGAINST
A. Men, women, and children live in poor conditions	**C.** Cost of building new prisons is too high
B. Eighth Amendment prohibits "cruel and unusual" punishment	**D.** Tax money should be used to benefit law-abiding citizens

You are a state legislator trying to decide whether to use state money to build new prisons. Copy the table above. Add any arguments for or against. Then, answer the following questions:

24. Argument B is most closely linked to
   A Second Great Awakening
   B Declaration of Independence
   C Bill of Rights
   D Economics
25. Would you have voted in favor of funding new prisons? Explain your decision.

ACTIVITIES

Connecting With . . . Culture

Writing a Song With a group of students, write a marching song that might have been used at one of the following events: a temperance rally, an abolitionist meeting, a march for women's rights. Use a familiar tune, or write your own. Write words. Include a refrain, or repeated phrase, that emphasizes the main goal of the song. Gather musical instruments, and perform the song in class.

Take It to the NET

Connecting to Today

Giving a Report Today, Gallaudet University in Washington, D.C., is the nation's leading college for the deaf. Use the Internet to find out more about the school. Report to the class on the history of the school, its goals, and the courses and programs it offers. For help in starting this activity, visit *The American Nation* section of **www.phschool.com**.

Researching

Preparing a Biographical Sketch Use the Internet to find information on one of the following women: Antoinette Blackwell, Sara Josepha Hale, Emily Blackwell, Elizabeth Blackwell, Amelia Bloomer, Myra Bradwell, Margaret Fuller, Mary Ann Cary, Maria Mitchell, or Lucy Stone. Write a brief sketch explaining her contribution to women's rights. Include a timeline of major events in her life. For help in starting this activity, visit *The American Nation* section of **www.phschool.com**.

TEST PREPARATION

1 "Individual reform is the first step toward social reform." This statement represents a key idea of what reform movement?

  A The Second Great Awakening

  B The temperance movement

  C The abolitionist movement

  D The women's rights movement

Use the quotation <u>and</u> your knowledge of social studies to answer the following question.

> **Daniel Webster, Reply to Robert Hayne, 1830** (adapted)
>
> "While the people choose to maintain the Constitution as it is, while they are satisfied with it, and refuse to change it, who has given, or who can give, to the state legislatures a right to alter it?"

2 What idea or policy is the subject of Webster's speech?

  A Nullification

  B Manifest Destiny

  C Federalism

  D Civil disobedience

3 What was one result of the rise of the Cotton Kingdom?

  A Slavery began to decline.

  B The South developed an industrial economy.

  C Eli Whitney invented the cotton gin.

  D Large planters gained political influence.

Use the map <u>and</u> your knowledge of social studies to answer the following question.

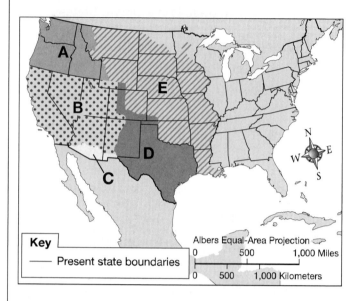

Key
—— Present state boundaries

Albers Equal-Area Projection
0   500   1,000 Miles
0   500   1,000 Kilometers

4 Which two areas shown on this map did the United States acquire by the same method?

  A A and B

  B C and E

  C B and D

  D C and D

5 How were the works of James Fenimore Cooper similar to those of Henry Wadsworth Longfellow?

  A Both were best known for their poetry.

  B Both used their pens to oppose slavery.

  C Both explored historical subjects in their work.

  D Both were transcendentalists.

6 Which statement is true of both Texas and California?

   A It was admitted to the Union as a slave state.

   B American settlers there rebelled against Mexican rule.

   C It became part of the United States as a result of the Mexican War.

   D Its annexation was an important issue in the election of 1844.

Use the graph <u>and</u> your knowledge of social studies to answer the following question.

School Enrollment, 1840–1870

Source: *American Education: The National Experience, 1783–1876,* by Lawrence A. Cemin

7 The trend shown on this graph is most closely related to what development?

   A The expansion of voting rights

   B Increased immigration from Ireland

   C The abolitionist movement

   D The rise of the Hudson River School

8 Which slogan best reflects the main beliefs of the Know-Nothing party?

   A "Fifty-four forty or fight!"

   B "America for Americans!"

   C "To the victor go the spoils!"

   D "Stamp out demon rum!"

9 Which was one result of Andrew Jackson's Native American policy?

   A The Seminole nation was completely destroyed.

   B The United States annexed Florida and Texas.

   C Few Native Americans remained east of the Mississippi.

   D War broke out between the United States Army and the Cherokees.

Writing Practice

10 Describe and evaluate one political, one social, and one economic effect of westward expansion.

11 Analyze the impact of transportation systems on the nation. Choose at least two advances in transportation and explain how each one affected the growth, development, or urbanization of the United States.

Unit 5

Division and Reunion

The Soldiers of the Civil War
In *A Rainy Day in Camp* by Winslow Homer, Civil War soldiers find time to gather around a campfire.

"Union! I can more easily conceive of the Lion and Lambs lying down together, than of a union of the North and South."

—Sarah Chase, Massachusetts teacher in the South (1866)

Slavery Divides the Nation

1820–1861

1 **Slavery in the Territories**
2 **The Compromise of 1850**
3 **The Crisis Deepens**
4 **The Republican Party Emerges**
5 **A Nation Divides**

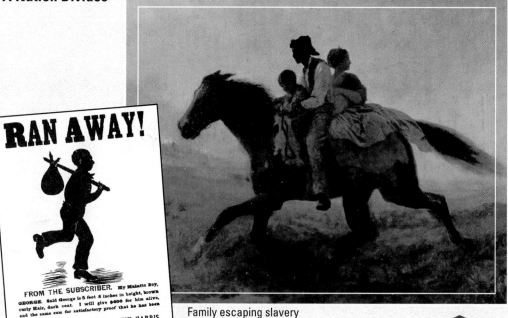

Family escaping slavery

RAN AWAY!

FROM THE SUBSCRIBER. My Mulatto Boy,
GEORGE. Said George is 5 feet 8 inches in height, brown
curly Hair, dark coat. I will give $400 for him alive,
and the same sum for satisfactory proof that he has been
killed.
Vide ANTHONY & ELLIS MAMMOTH
"UNCLE TOM'S CABIN."   WM. HARRIS.

Fugitive slave poster

1850

Congress passes the Compromise of 1850.
One new law requires all Americans to help
recapture fugitive slaves.

1820

The Missouri
Compromise
maintains the bal-
ance of free and
slave states in the
Union.

John Quincy Adams	1825–1829
Andrew Jackson	1829–1837
Martin Van Buren	1837–1841
William Henry Harrison	1841

1848

The Free-Soil party is
formed to oppose
the extension of
slavery in the West.

AMERICAN EVENTS

Presidential Terms: James Monroe 1817–1825   John Tyler 1841–1845   James K. Polk 1845–1849   Zachary Taylor 1849–1850

1820   **1845**   **1850**

▲ **1833**
Slavery is abolished in
the British Empire.

1850 ▲
Civil war breaks
out in China.

Slave and Free States, 1850

As new states entered the Union, the balance between slave and free states became harder to maintain.

BRITISH TERRITORY

Oregon Territory

Minnesota Territory

Unorganized Territory

Utah Territory

California (1850)

New Mexico Territory

WI (1848)

Iowa (1846)

MI (1837)

Illinois (1818)

IN (1816)

Ohio (1803)

Missouri (1821)

KY (1792)

Indian Territory

Arkansas (1836)

TN (1796)

MS (1817)

AL (1819)

LA (1812)

Texas (1845)

Virginia (1788)

NC (1789)

SC (1788)

Georgia (1788)

FL (1845)

ME (1820)

VT (1791)

NH (1788)

NY (1788)

MA (1788)

RI (1790)

CT (1788)

PA (1787)

NJ (1787)

DE (1787)

MD (1788)

Washington, D.C. (slave trade banned)

MEXICO

PACIFIC OCEAN

ATLANTIC OCEAN

Gulf of Mexico

Albers Equal-Area Projection

0   200   400 Miles

0   200   400 Kilometers

Key

- Free states
- Slave states
- Territories
- **1787** Date of entry into Union

Stephen Douglas

Flag from Fort Sumter

1854

Senator Stephen Douglas proposes the Kansas-Nebraska Act, allowing new territories to decide whether or not to permit slavery.

1857

In *Dred Scott* v. *Sandford,* the Supreme Court rules that Congress cannot ban slavery in any territory.

1861

The Confederate States of America is formed. Confederate troops later fire on Fort Sumter, South Carolina, where this flag flew. The bombardment marks the beginning of the Civil War.

Millard Fillmore 1850–1853

Franklin Pierce 1853–1857

James Buchanan 1857–1861

Abraham Lincoln 1861–1865

1850 • **1855** • **1860** •

1854 ▲
Slavery is abolished in Venezuela.

1861 ▲
Czar Alexander II frees all Russian serfs.

1 Slavery in the Territories

Reading Focus

- What was the purpose of the Missouri Compromise?
- Why did conflict arise over the issue of slavery in the western territories?
- Why was the Free-Soil party founded?

Key Terms

Missouri Compromise

Wilmot Proviso

popular sovereignty

Free-Soil party

Taking Notes

Copy the concept web below. Include three or four blank ovals. As you read, fill in each blank oval with important facts about slavery in the territories. Some ovals have been completed to help you get started.

Disagreements over Missouri entering Union

SLAVERY IN THE TERRITORIES

Free-Soil party opposes extension of slavery

Main Idea The Missouri Compromise attempted to settle the issue of whether slavery should be allowed in the western territories.

Jefferson at 78
Use Prior Knowledge
Why would the failure of the Union be especially painful for Jefferson?

Setting the Scene When he reached his seventies, Thomas Jefferson vowed "never to write, talk, or even think of politics." Still, in 1820 at the age of 77, he broke this vow. Jefferson voiced alarm at the fierce debate going on in Congress:

> 66 This momentous question, like a fire bell in the night, awakened and filled me with terror. I considered it at once as the [funeral bells] of the Union. . . . We have the wolf by the ears, and we can neither hold him, nor safely let him go. 99
>
> —Thomas Jefferson, Letter to John Holmes, April 22, 1820

Jefferson knew the "wolf," or the issue of slavery, could tear the North and South apart. As settlers moved west, Congress faced an agonizing decision. Should it ban slavery in the territories and later admit them to the Union as free states? Or should it permit slavery in the territories and later admit them as slave states? This was the critical question that filled Jefferson with terror in the night.

The Missouri Compromise

There were 11 free states and 11 slave states in 1819. That year, Congress considered Missouri's application to join the Union as a slave state. Immediately, a crisis erupted. Missouri's admission would give the South a majority in the Senate. Determined not to lose power, northerners opposed letting Missouri enter as a slave state.

The argument lasted many months. Finally, Senator Henry Clay made a proposal. During the long debate, Maine had also applied for statehood. Clay suggested admitting Missouri as a slave state and Maine as a free state. His plan, called the Missouri Compromise, kept the number of slave and free states equal.

As part of the Missouri Compromise, Congress drew an imaginary line across the southern border of Missouri at latitude 36°30′ N.

Slavery was permitted in the part of the Louisiana Purchase south of that line. It was banned north of the Missouri Compromise line. The only exception to this was Missouri itself.

Slavery in the West

The Missouri Compromise applied only to the Louisiana Purchase. In 1848, the Mexican War added vast western lands to the United States. Once again, the question of slavery in the territories arose.

Wilmot Proviso Many northerners feared that the South would extend slavery into the West. David Wilmot, a member of Congress from Pennsylvania, called for a law to ban slavery in any territories won from Mexico. Southern leaders angrily opposed this **Wilmot Proviso.** They said that Congress had no right to ban slavery in the West.

The House passed the Wilmot Proviso in 1846, but the Senate defeated it. As a result, Americans continued to argue about slavery in the West even while their army fought in Mexico.

Opposing Views As the debate heated up, people found it hard not to take sides. Abolitionists wanted slavery banned throughout the country. They insisted that slavery was morally wrong.

Southern slaveholders thought that slavery should be allowed in any territory. They also demanded that slaves who escaped to the North be returned to them. Even white southerners who did not own slaves generally agreed with these ideas.

Between these two extreme views were more moderate positions. Some moderates argued that the Missouri Compromise line should be extended across the Mexican Cession to the Pacific. Any new state north of the line would be a free state. Any new state south of the line could

Viewing History

A Family for Sale

As Americans debated the issue of slavery, slave auctions continued in the South. The family members on the auction block here might never see each other again.
Drawing Inferences *What do the poster (above) and the painting (left) suggest about the attitude of slaveholders toward slaves?*

allow slavery. Other moderates supported the idea of popular sovereignty, or the right of people to create their government. Under popular sovereignty, voters in a new territory would decide for themselves whether or not to allow slavery.

The Free-Soil Party

The debate over slavery led to the birth of a new political party. By 1848, many northern Democrats and Whigs opposed the spread of slavery. However, the leaders of both parties refused to take a stand. They did not want to lose any southern votes. Some also feared that the slavery issue would split the nation.

In 1848, antislavery members of both parties met in Buffalo, New York. There, they founded the Free-Soil party. The main goal of the Free-Soil party was to keep slavery out of the western territories. Only a few Free-Soilers were abolitionists who wanted to end slavery in the South.

In the 1848 presidential campaign, Free-Soilers named former President Martin Van Buren as their candidate. Democrats chose Lewis Cass of Michigan. The Whigs selected Zachary Taylor, a hero of the Mexican War.

For the first time, slavery was an important election issue. Van Buren called for a ban on slavery in the Mexican Cession. Cass supported popular sovereignty. Taylor did not speak on the issue. However, because he was a slave owner from Louisiana, many southern voters assumed that he supported slavery.

Zachary Taylor won the election. Still, Van Buren took 10 percent of the popular vote, and 13 other Free-Soil candidates won seats in Congress. The success of the new Free-Soil party showed that slavery had become a national issue.

 Predict What does the success of the Free-Soil party suggest about the future of the slavery issue?

Section 1 Assessment

Recall

1. **Identify** Explain the significance of **(a)** Missouri Compromise, **(b)** Wilmot Proviso, **(c)** Free-Soil party, **(d)** Zachary Taylor.
2. **Define** popular sovereignty.

Comprehension

3. What was the Missouri Compromise?
4. Describe three conflicting views on slavery in the West.
5. Why did voters leave the Whig and Democratic parties to join the Free-Soil party in 1848?

Critical Thinking and Writing

6. **Exploring the Main Idea** Review the Main Idea statement at the beginning of this section. Then, write a paragraph explaining whether the Missouri Compromise settled the issue of slavery in the western territories.
7. **Drawing Conclusions** The goals of the Free-Soil party pleased some northerners but not others. Write a paragraph explaining why some northerners were pleased and others displeased by the Free-Soil party.

ACTIVITY

Drawing a Political Cartoon With a partner, plan and sketch a political cartoon about the issue of slavery in the western territories. Assume one of the opposing viewpoints described in this section: southern slaveholder, abolitionist, supporter of extending the Missouri Compromise line across the country, or supporter of popular sovereignty. Then, create a cartoon that represents your point of view.

2 The Compromise of 1850

BEFORE YOU READ

Reading Focus

- Why did the slavery debate erupt again in 1850?
- What was the impact of the Compromise of 1850?
- How did *Uncle Tom's Cabin* affect attitudes toward slavery?

Key Terms

secede

fugitive

civil war

Compromise of 1850

Fugitive Slave Act

Uncle Tom's Cabin

Taking Notes

As you read, complete the chart at right to show some of the causes and effects of the Compromise of 1850.

CAUSES

I. California seeks statehood
2.
3.

COMPROMISE OF 1850

EFFECTS

I. North reacts to Fugitive Slave Act
2.
3.

Main Idea The Compromise of 1850, which was supposed to save the Union, only inflamed tensions.

Setting the Scene Tempers in Congress had reached the boiling point. California had applied to be admitted to the Union as a free state in 1850. Senator Thomas Hart Benton of Missouri supported California's request. He denounced Senator Henry Foote of Mississippi for opposing California's admission.

In response, Senator Foote rose angrily, picked up a pistol, and aimed it at Benton. As other senators watched in horror, Benton turned toward Foote and roared, "Let him fire. Stand out of the way and let the assassin fire!"

No blood was shed in the Senate that day. However, even as Congress tried to reach a new compromise, many Americans began to fear that a peaceful solution to the slavery issue was impossible.

The Slavery Debate Erupts Again

For a time after the Missouri Compromise, both slave and free states entered the Union peacefully. However, when California requested admission to the Union as a free state in 1850, the balance of power in the Senate was once again threatened.

California's Impact In 1849, there were 15 slave states and 15 free states in the nation. If California entered the union as a free state, the balance of power would be broken. Furthermore, it seemed quite possible that Oregon, Utah, and New Mexico might also join the Union as free states.

Many southerners feared that the South would be hopelessly outvoted in the Senate. Some even suggested that southern states might want to **secede,** or remove themselves, from the United States. Northern congressmen, meanwhile, argued that California should enter the Union as a free state because most of the territory lay north of the Missouri Compromise line.

It was clear that the nation faced a crisis. Many in Congress looked to Senator Henry Clay for a solution.

AS YOU READ
Violence threatens in the Senate

Ask Questions Write one question you would have asked Senator Benton and one question you would have asked Senator Foote if you had been on the floor of the Senate on the day of the conflict.

Balance of Free and Slave States

Free States	Slave States
California (1850)	
Wisconsin (1848)	Texas (1845)
Iowa (1846)	Florida (1845)
Michigan (1837)	Arkansas (1836)
Maine (1820)	Missouri (1821)
Illinois (1818)	Alabama (1819)
Indiana (1816)	Mississippi (1817)
Ohio (1803)	Louisiana (1812)
Vermont (1791)	Tennessee (1796)
Rhode Island	Kentucky (1792)
New York	Virginia
New Hampshire	North Carolina
Massachusetts	South Carolina
Connecticut	Maryland
New Jersey	Georgia
Pennsylvania	Delaware

Original 13 states

John C. Calhoun

Daniel Webster

Henry Clay

Viewing History

Crisis in the Senate

California
Washington, D.C.

The admission of California to the Union threatened to upset the delicate balance of slave and free states. The issue led to the final showdown in Congress for Henry Clay, Daniel Webster, and John C. Calhoun. **Analyzing Primary Sources** *Why do you think the gallery was filled with spectators to hear this debate?*

AS YOU READ **Find Main Ideas** What were the main differences between the views of Henry Clay and those of John C. Calhoun?

Clay vs. Calhoun Clay had won the nickname "the Great Compromiser" for working out the Missouri Compromise. Now, nearly 30 years later, the 73-year-old Clay was frail and ill. Still, he pleaded for the North and South to reach an agreement. If they failed to do so, Clay warned, the nation could break apart.

Senator John C. Calhoun of South Carolina replied to Clay. Calhoun was dying of tuberculosis and could not speak loudly enough to address the Senate. He stared defiantly at his northern foes while Senator James Mason of Virginia read his speech.

Calhoun refused to compromise. He insisted that slavery be allowed in the western territories. In addition, Calhoun demanded that fugitive, or runaway, slaves be returned to their owners. He wanted northerners to admit that southern slaveholders had the right to reclaim their "property."

If the North rejected the South's demands, Calhoun told the Senate, "let the states . . . agree to part in peace. If you are unwilling that we should part in peace, tell us so, and we shall know what to do." Everyone knew what Calhoun meant. If an agreement could not be reached, the South would use force to leave the Union.

Webster Calls for Unity Daniel Webster of Massachusetts spoke next. He supported Clay's plea to save the Union. Webster stated his position clearly:

> 66 I speak today not as a Massachusetts man, nor as a northern man, but as an American. . . . I speak today for the preservation of the Union. . . . There can be no such thing as a peaceable secession. 99
> —Daniel Webster, Speech in the U.S. Senate, July 17, 1850

Webster feared that the states could not separate without starting a bloody civil war. A **civil war** is a war between people of the same country.

Like many northerners, Webster viewed slavery as evil. The breakup of the United States, however, he believed was worse. To save the Union, Webster was willing to compromise. He would support southern demands that northerners be forced to return fugitive slaves.

Compromise of 1850

In 1850, as the debate raged, Calhoun died. His last words reportedly were "The South! The poor South! God knows what will become of her now!" President Taylor also died in 1850. The new President was Millard Fillmore. Unlike Taylor, he supported Clay's compromise plan.

The Compromise Passes Henry Clay gave more than 70 speeches in favor of a compromise. At last, however, he became too sick to continue. Stephen Douglas, of Illinois, took up the fight for him and guided Clay's plan, the Compromise of 1850, through Congress.

The Compromise of 1850 had five parts. First, it allowed California to enter the Union as a free state. Second, it divided the rest of the Mexican Cession into the territories of New Mexico and Utah. Voters in each would decide the slavery question according to popular sovereignty. Third, it ended the slave trade in Washington, D.C., the nation's capital. Congress, however, declared that it had no power to ban the slave trade between slave states. Fourth, it included a strict fugitive slave law. Fifth, it settled a border dispute between Texas and New Mexico.

Fugitive Slave Act The Fugitive Slave Act of 1850 required all citizens to help catch runaway slaves. People who let fugitives escape could be fined $1,000 and jailed. The new law also set up special courts to handle the cases of runaways. Suspects were not allowed a jury trial. Judges received $10 for sending an accused runaway to the South but only $5 for setting someone free. Lured by the extra money, some judges sent African Americans to the South whether or not they were runaways.

Reaction The Fugitive Slave Act enraged antislavery northerners. By forcing them to catch runaways, the law made northerners feel as if they were part of the slave system. In several northern cities, crowds tried to rescue fugitive slaves from their captors.

Despite the compromise, tensions remained high because neither side got everything that it wanted. The new Fugitive Slave Act was especially hard for northerners to accept. Each time the act was

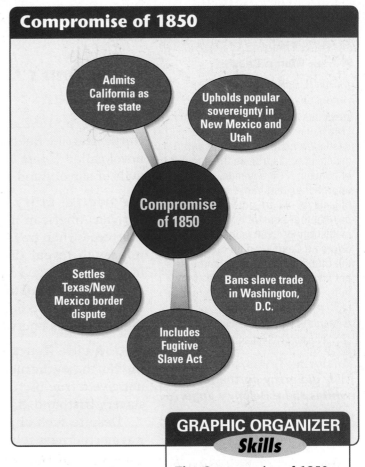

Compromise of 1850

- Admits California as free state
- Upholds popular sovereignty in New Mexico and Utah
- Compromise of 1850
- Settles Texas/New Mexico border dispute
- Includes Fugitive Slave Act
- Bans slave trade in Washington, D.C.

GRAPHIC ORGANIZER
Skills

The Compromise of 1850 was a desperate attempt to save the Union.

1. **Comprehension** Which parts of the Compromise would have been favored by the South?

2. **Critical Thinking Identifying Points of View** Would an abolitionist approve of the Compromise of 1850? Why or why not?

Civics

Primary Sources

See Levi Coffin, "A Slave Escapes," on page 602 of the Reference Section.

enforced, it convinced more northerners that slavery was immoral and evil.

Uncle Tom's Cabin: An Antislavery Bestseller

An event in 1852 added to the growing antislavery mood of the North. Harriet Beecher Stowe, a New England woman, published a novel called *Uncle Tom's Cabin.* Stowe wrote the novel to show the evils of slavery and the injustice of the Fugitive Slave Act.

A Powerful Story Stowe told the story of Uncle Tom, an enslaved African American noted for his kindness and piety. Tom's world is shattered when he is bought by the brutal Simon Legree. When Tom refuses to reveal the whereabouts of two runaways, Legree whips him to death.

Uncle Tom's Cabin had wide appeal among northern readers. The first printing sold out in just two days. Eventually, the book sold millions of copies and was translated into dozens of languages.

Nationwide Reaction Although *Uncle Tom's Cabin* was popular in the North, southerners objected to the book. They claimed that it did not give a true picture of slave life. Indeed, Stowe had seen little of slavery firsthand.

Despite such objections, *Uncle Tom's Cabin* helped to change the way northerners felt about slavery. No longer could they ignore slavery as a political problem for Congress to settle. More and more northerners now saw slavery as a moral problem facing every American. For this reason, *Uncle Tom's Cabin* was one of the most important books in American history.

Primary Source

A Free Man's Castle

Martin R. Delany, an African American newspaper editor, responds to the Fugitive Slave Act: "My house is my castle; in that castle are none but my wife and my children, as free as the angels of heaven. . . . If any man approaches that house in search of a slave—I care not who he may be, whether constable or sheriff, magistrate or even judge of the Supreme Court . . . if he crosses the threshold of my door, and I do not lay him a lifeless corpse at my feet, I hope the grave may refuse my body a resting place."

—Martin R. Delany, speech given in Pittsburgh, September 30, 1850

Analyzing Primary Sources
Why did many northern whites share Delany's anger?

Section 2 Assessment

Recall

1. **Identify** Explain the significance of (a) Stephen Douglas, (b) Compromise of 1850, (c) Fugitive Slave Act, (d) Harriet Beecher Stowe, (e) *Uncle Tom's Cabin.*
2. **Define** (a) secede, (b) fugitive, (c) civil war.

Comprehension

3. How did the issue of admitting California to the Union in 1850 again raise the debate over slavery?
4. How did Americans respond to the Compromise of 1850?
5. What was the impact of *Uncle Tom's Cabin?*

Critical Thinking and Writing

6. **Exploring the Main Idea** Review the Main Idea statement at the beginning of this section. Then, write a letter to a newspaper editor explaining whether you think the Compromise of 1850 was a success or a failure. Give reasons for your answer.
7. **Summarizing** For each of the following leaders, write one sentence summarizing his attitude toward the need for a compromise in 1850: (a) Calhoun, (b) Webster, (c) Clay.

ACTIVITY

Making a Decision You are a northerner during the 1850s. There is a knock at your door. It's a fugitive slave! Will you help the runaway, or will you turn the person in to the authorities? Write a brief statement explaining the reasons for your decision.

Uncle Tom's Cabin

Harriet Beecher Stowe saw the horrors of slavery while living in Cincinnati. Across the Ohio River was Kentucky, a slave state. Her hatred of slavery led her to write *Uncle Tom's Cabin.* The novel had an impact that lasted long after slavery ended.

Harriet Beecher Stowe

Uncle Tom Defies Simon Legree

"Well, Tom!" said Legree, walking up and seizing him grimly by the collar of his coat, and speaking through his teeth, in a paroxysm of determined rage, "do you know I've made up my mind to KILL you?"

"It's very likely, Mas'r," said Tom, calmly.

"I have," said Legree, with grim terrible calmness, "done—just—that—thing, Tom, unless you tell me what you know about these yer gals!"

Tom stood silent.

"D'ye hear?" said Legree, stamping with a roar like that of an incensed lion. "Speak!"

"I han't got nothing to tell, Mas'r," said Tom with a slow, firm deliberate utterance.

"Do you dare to tell me, ye old black Christian, ye don't know?"…

"I know, Mas'r; but I can't tell anything. I can die!"

— Harriet Beecher Stowe,
Uncle Tom's Cabin, Chapter 40

Fast Facts

- The character of Tom was inspired by Josiah Henson, a Methodist preacher who had escaped slavery.
- Some southerners wrote "anti-Tom" novels to defend slavery.
- The first movie of *Uncle Tom's Cabin* was made in 1903.

In this poster for a stage version of *Uncle Tom's Cabin,* the fugitive slave Eliza flees across an icy river.

Simon Legree and Uncle Tom

ACTIVITY

You are hosting a dinner honoring Harriet Beecher Stowe. Prepare a brief speech introducing Stowe. Explain how her book reflects divisions in the United States.

3 The Crisis Deepens

Reading Focus

- What was the goal of the Kansas-Nebraska Act?
- Why did violence erupt in Kansas and in the Senate?
- What impact did the Dred Scott case have on the nation?

Key Terms

Kansas-Nebraska Act

Border Ruffians

guerrilla warfare

lawsuit

Dred Scott v. *Sandford*

Taking Notes

As you read, complete the following chart to show some of the causes that directly led the United States to become a more divided nation.

Main Idea In the 1850s, violence in Kansas and the Dred Scott decision inflamed tensions over slavery.

Setting the Scene Americans had hoped that the Compromise of 1850 would end the debate over slavery in the West. Before long, though, proslavery and antislavery forces were battling for control of the territory of Kansas. An observer described election day in one Kansas district in 1855:

> 66 On the morning of the election, before the polls were opened, some 300 or 400 Missourians and others were collected in the yard . . . where the election was to be held, armed with bowie-knives, revolvers, and clubs. They said they came to vote, and whip the . . . Yankees, and would vote without being sworn. Some said they came to have a fight, and wanted one. 99
>
> —Report of the Congressional Committee, July 1, 1856

Hearing of events in Kansas, Abraham Lincoln, then a young lawyer in Illinois, predicted that "the contest will come to blows, and bloodshed." Once again, the issue of slavery in the territories divided the nation.

Kansas-Nebraska Act

The Compromise of 1850 dealt mainly with lands that were part of the Mexican Cession. It did not resolve the issue of slavery in lands that had been part of the Louisiana Purchase. In January 1854, Senator Stephen Douglas introduced a bill to set up a government for the Nebraska Territory. This territory stretched from Texas north to Canada, and from Missouri west to the Rockies.

Douglas knew that white southerners did not want to add another free state to the Union. He proposed that the Nebraska Territory be divided into two territories, Kansas and Nebraska. The settlers living in each territory would then be able to decide the issue of slavery by popular sovereignty. Douglas's bill was known as the Kansas-Nebraska Act.

AS YOU READ An election in Kansas

Ask Questions Based on this picture and the description at right, write one question you would ask these Kansas voters.

Support for the Act The Kansas-Nebraska Act seemed fair to many people. After all, the Compromise of 1850 had applied popular sovereignty in New Mexico and Utah. Southern leaders especially supported the Kansas-Nebraska Act. They were sure that slave owners from neighboring Missouri would move with their slaves across the border into Kansas. In time, they hoped, Kansas would become a slave state.

President Franklin Pierce, a Democrat elected in 1852, also supported the bill. With the President's help, Douglas pushed the Kansas-Nebraska Act through Congress. He did not realize it at the time, but he had lit a fire under a powder keg.

Northern Outrage Many northerners were unhappy with the new law. The Missouri Compromise had already banned slavery in Kansas and Nebraska, they insisted. In effect, the Kansas-Nebraska Act would repeal the Missouri Compromise.

The northern reaction to the Kansas-Nebraska Act was swift and angry. Opponents of slavery called the act a "criminal betrayal of precious rights." Slavery could now spread to areas that had been free for more than 30 years. Some northerners protested by openly challenging the Fugitive Slave Act.

The Crisis Turns Violent

Kansas now became a testing ground for popular sovereignty. Stephen Douglas hoped that settlers would decide the slavery issue peacefully on election day. Instead, proslavery and antislavery forces sent settlers to Kansas to fight for control of the territory.

GEOGRAPHY Skills

The issue of whether to allow slavery in the territories created tension between the North and the South.

1. **Location** On the map, locate **(a)** Missouri Compromise Line, **(b)** Kansas Territory, **(c)** Nebraska Territory.

2. **Region** **(a)** Which territories were open to slavery after 1854? **(b)** Which territories were closed to slavery?

3. **Critical Thinking** **Making Predictions** How would the balance of power in the Senate change if western territories became slave states?

Slavery After the Kansas-Nebraska Act

Key
- Free states and territories
- Slave states and territories
- Open to slavery by popular vote, Compromise of 1850
- Open to slavery by popular vote, Kansas-Nebraska Act, 1854

Albers Equal-Area Projection

0   200   400 Miles

0   200   400 Kilometers

Most of the new arrivals were farmers from neighboring states. Their main interest in moving to Kansas was to acquire cheap land. Few of these settlers owned slaves. At the same time, abolitionists brought in more than 1,000 settlers from New England.

Proslavery settlers moved into Kansas as well. They wanted to make sure that antislavery forces did not overrun the territory. Proslavery bands from Missouri often rode across the border. These **Border Ruffians,** as they were called, battled the antislavery forces in Kansas.

Two Governments In 1855, Kansas held elections to choose law-makers. Hundreds of Border Ruffians crossed into Kansas and voted illegally. They helped to elect a proslavery legislature.

The new legislature quickly passed laws to support slavery. One law said that people could be put to death for helping slaves escape. Another made speaking out against slavery a crime punishable by two years of hard labor.

Antislavery settlers refused to accept these laws. They elected their own governor and legislature. With two rival governments, Kansas was in chaos. Armed gangs roamed the territory looking for trouble.

"Bleeding Kansas" A band of proslavery men raided the town of Lawrence, an antislavery stronghold, in 1856. The attackers destroyed homes and smashed the press of a Free-Soil newspaper.

John Brown, an abolitionist, decided to strike back. Brown had moved to Kansas to help make it a free state. He claimed that God had sent him to punish supporters of slavery.

Brown rode with his four sons and two other men to the town of Pottawatomie (paht uh WAHT uh mee) Creek. In the middle of the night, they dragged five proslavery settlers from their beds and murdered them.

The killings at Pottawatomie Creek led to even more violence. Both sides fought fiercely and engaged in **guerrilla warfare,** or the use of hit-and-run tactics. By late 1856, more than 200 people had been killed. Newspapers started calling the territory "Bleeding Kansas."

Violence in the Senate

Even before John Brown's attack, the battle over Kansas had spilled into the Senate. Charles Sumner of Massachusetts was the leading abolitionist senator. In one speech, the sharp-tongued Sumner denounced the proslavery legislature of Kansas. He then viciously criticized his southern foes, singling out Andrew Butler, an elderly senator from South Carolina.

Butler was not in the Senate on the day Sumner spoke. A few days later, however, Butler's nephew, Congressman Preston Brooks, marched into the Senate chamber. Using a heavy cane, Brooks beat Sumner until he fell down, bloody and unconscious, to the floor. Sumner did not fully recover from the beating for three years.

Many southerners felt that Sumner got what he deserved for his verbal abuse of another senator. Hundreds of people sent canes to

Connecting to Today

Stopping the Violence

Today, you would not be likely to see a physical fight on the floor of the Senate. However, violence remains a disturbing problem in our society. We all know of cases when angry words had tragic results.

Many schools have launched antiviolence campaigns. Students use the Internet, posters, essays, and school activities to call attention to the problem. Some schools also use "peer mediation" programs to find peaceful solutions to conflicts. Volunteers train to act as negotiators between other students. The mediator listens to both sides and tries to get them to reach an agreement. In schools, as in the world, communication can be the key to ending violence.

List two things young people can do to keep a dispute from becoming violent.

Brooks to show their support. To northerners, however, the brutal act was more evidence that slavery led to violence.

The Dred Scott Case

With Congress in an uproar, many Americans looked to the Supreme Court to settle the slavery issue and restore peace. In 1857, the Court ruled on a case that involved an enslaved person named Dred Scott. Instead of bringing harmony, however, the Court's decision further divided the North and the South.

Dred Scott had been enslaved for many years in Missouri. Later, he moved with his owner to Illinois and then to the Wisconsin Territory, where slavery was not allowed. After they returned to Missouri, Scott's owner died. Antislavery lawyers helped Scott to file a lawsuit, a legal case brought to settle a dispute between people or groups. Scott's lawyers argued that, because Scott had lived in a free territory, he had become a free man.

The Supreme Court's Decision In time, the case reached the Supreme Court as *Dred Scott v. Sandford.* The Court's decision shocked and dismayed Americans who opposed slavery. First, the Court ruled that Scott could not file a lawsuit because, as an enslaved person, he was not a citizen. Also, the Court's written decision clearly stated that slaves were considered to be property.

The Court's ruling did not stop there. Instead, the Justices went on to make a sweeping decision about the larger issue of slavery in

Viewing History

Bleeding Kansas

In 1856, the slavery issue sparked bloodshed in Kansas. Here, Border Ruffians attack antislavery settlers. Abolitionists like John Brown also committed acts of violence. **Identifying Bias** *What details in the picture suggest that the artist favored the antislavery settlers?*

Primary Sources

See "Dred Scott v. Sandford" on page 603 of the Reference Section.

the territories. According to the Court, Congress did not have the power to outlaw slavery in any territory. The Court's ruling meant that the Missouri Compromise was unconstitutional.

AS YOU READ Use Prior Knowledge Why did the Dred Scott decision make the Missouri Compromise unconstitutional?

The Nation Reacts White southerners rejoiced at *Dred Scott* v. *Sandford*. It meant that slavery was legal in all the territories. This was just what white southerners had been demanding for years.

African Americans responded angrily to the Dred Scott decision. In the North, many held public meetings to condemn the ruling. At one meeting in Philadelphia, a speaker hoped that the ruling would lead more whites to "join with us in our efforts to recover the long lost boon of freedom."

White northerners were also shocked by the ruling. Many had hoped that slavery would eventually die out if it were restricted to the South. Now, however, slavery could spread throughout the West. Even northerners who disliked abolitionists felt that the ruling in *Dred Scott* v. *Sandford* was wrong. A newspaper in Cincinnati declared, "We are now one great . . . slaveholding community."

Abolitionist Frederick Douglass also spoke out against *Dred Scott* v. *Sandford*: "This infamous decision," he declared, "maintains that slaves . . . are property in the same sense that horses, sheep, and swine are property . . . that [people] of African descent are not and cannot be citizens of the United States." He told his listeners:

> 66 All I ask of the American people is that they live up to the Constitution, adopt its principles, [take in] its spirit, and enforce its provisions. When this is done . . . liberty . . . will become the inheritance of all the inhabitants of this highly favored country. 99
>
> —Frederick Douglass, *Collected Speeches,* 1857

AFTER YOU READ

Section 3 Assessment

Recall
1. **Identify** Explain the significance of (a) Kansas-Nebraska Act, (b) Franklin Pierce, (c) Border Ruffians, (d) Charles Sumner, (e) *Dred Scott* v. *Sandford.*
2. **Define** (a) guerrilla warfare, (b) lawsuit.

Comprehension
3. Why did Stephen Douglas propose the Kansas-Nebraska Act?
4. How did the Kansas-Nebraska Act lead to violence?
5. How did white southerners, African Americans, and white northerners react to the Dred Scott decision?

Critical Thinking and Writing
6. **Exploring the Main Idea** Review the Main Idea statement at the beginning of this section. Then, make a list of five statements from this section that support the main idea.
7. **Analyzing Primary Sources** After the Kansas-Nebraska Act was passed, Stephen Douglas stated: "The struggle for freedom was forever banished from the halls of Congress to the western plains." Rewrite Douglas's statement in your own words. Then, explain why you agree or disagree with it.

ACTIVITY

Take It to the NET
Connecting to Today
Use the Internet to find out more about a recent Supreme Court decision involving the rights of workers, minorities, or students. Write a brief summary describing both sides of the issue and what the court decided. Visit *The American Nation* section of **www.phschool.com** for help in completing the activity.

4 The Republican Party Emerges

BEFORE YOU READ

Reading Focus

- Why did the Republican party come into being in the mid-1850s?
- What events lay behind the rapid emergence of Abraham Lincoln as a Republican leader?
- How did Americans react to John Brown's raid on Harpers Ferry?

Key Terms

Republican party
arsenal
treason
martyr

Taking Notes

As you read, complete this table listing the conflicting views of Abraham Lincoln and Stephen Douglas. Add as many rows as needed to finish the table.

LINCOLN'S VIEWS	DOUGLAS'S VIEWS
• Slavery was morally wrong	•
•	• Western territories should decide slavery issue by popular sovereignty
•	•

Main Idea Abraham Lincoln emerged as a leader of the new Republican party, which was dedicated to halting the spread of slavery.

Setting the Scene The tall lawyer stood before a political convention in Springfield, Illinois. People in the packed hall listened carefully as he addressed the number one issue of the day—slavery:

> 66 A house divided against itself cannot stand. I believe this government cannot endure permanently half slave and half free. I do not expect the Union to be dissolved—I do not expect the house to fall—but I do expect it will cease to be divided. It will become all one thing, or all the other. 99
>
> —Abraham Lincoln, Speech, June 16, 1858

Few people outside of Illinois had heard of Abraham Lincoln. Yet, his speech became famous. Many northerners were soon repeating his prediction about the "house divided." Lincoln and the new party he represented—the Republican party—moved to the forefront of the debate over slavery.

AS YOU READ **Figure of Abraham Lincoln**

Use Prior Knowledge
Freewrite a list of 3–5 things that you already know about Abraham Lincoln.

The Republican Party

By the mid-1850s, people who opposed slavery in the territories sought a new political voice. Neither Whigs nor Democrats, they argued, would take a strong stand against slavery. "We have submitted to slavery long enough," an Ohio Democrat declared.

A group of Free-Soilers, northern Democrats, and antislavery Whigs gathered in Michigan in 1854. There they formed the Republican party. Its main goal was to keep slavery out of the western territories. A few Republicans were abolitionists. They hoped to end slavery in the South as well. Most Republicans, however, wanted only to stop the spread of slavery.

The new party grew quickly. By 1856, it was ready to challenge the older parties for power. Republicans selected John C. Frémont to run for President. Frémont was a frontiersman who had fought for

POLITICAL CARTOON
Skills

The Election of 1856 In this 1856 cartoon, Millard Fillmore steps in between John C. Frémont (left) and James Buchanan (right).

1. **Comprehension** What accusations do Frémont and Buchanan make against one another?

2. **Finding the Main Idea** How does the cartoonist show that the slavery issue stirred strong feelings?

3. **Critical Thinking Identifying Points of View** Which candidate do you think the cartoonist favored? Explain.

Civics

California's independence. He had little political experience, but he opposed the spread of slavery.

Frémont's main opponent was Democrat James Buchanan of Pennsylvania. Many Democrats saw Buchanan as a "northern man with southern principles." They hoped that he would attract voters in both the North and the South. Former President Millard Fillmore also ran as the candidate of the American, or "Know-Nothing," party. A strong supporter of the Union, Fillmore feared that a Republican victory would split the nation apart.

Buchanan won the election with support from a large majority of southerners and many northerners. Still, the Republicans made a strong showing in the election. Without the support of a single southern state, Frémont won one third of the popular vote. Southerners worried that their influence in the national government was fading.

Abe Lincoln of Illinois

The next test for the Republican party came in 1858 in Illinois. Abraham Lincoln, a Republican, challenged Democrat Stephen Douglas for his seat in the Senate. Because most Americans expected Douglas to run for President in 1860, the race captured the attention of the whole nation.

From the Backwoods of Kentucky Abraham Lincoln was born on the Kentucky frontier. Like many frontier people, his parents moved often to find better land. The family lived in Indiana and later in Illinois. As a child, Lincoln spent only a year in school. Still, he taught himself to read, poring over his books by firelight.

 Predict What might happen to the nation if the Republican party wins a presidential election?

After Lincoln left home, he opened a store in Illinois. There, he studied law on his own and launched a career in politics. He served eight years in the state legislature and one term in Congress. Bitterly opposed to the Kansas-Nebraska Act, he decided to run for the Senate in 1858.

When the race began, Lincoln was not a national figure. Still, people in Illinois knew him well and liked him. To them, he was "just folks"—someone who enjoyed picnics, wrestling contests, and all their favorite pastimes. His honesty, wit, and plain-spoken manner made him a good speaker.

Lincoln-Douglas Debates During the Senate campaign, Lincoln challenged Douglas to a series of debates. Douglas was not eager to accept, but he did. During the campaign, the two debated seven times. Slavery was the important issue.

Douglas wanted to settle the slavery question by popular sovereignty. He personally disliked slavery, but stated that he did not care whether people in the territories voted "down or up" for it.

Lincoln, like nearly all whites of his day, did not believe in "perfect equality" between blacks and whites. He did, however, believe that slavery was wrong:

> 66 There is no reason in the world why the negro is not entitled to all the natural rights [listed] in the Declaration of Independence, the right to life, liberty, and the pursuit of happiness. . . . In the right to eat the bread, without the leave of anybody else, which his own hand earns, he is my equal and the equal of Judge Douglas, and the equal of every living man. 99
>
> —Abraham Lincoln, Speech at Ottawa, Illinois, August 21, 1858

Since slavery was a "moral, social, and political wrong," said Lincoln, Douglas and other Americans should not treat it as an unimportant question to be voted "down or up." Lincoln was totally opposed to slavery in the territories. Still, he was not an abolitionist. He had no wish to interfere with slavery in the states where it already existed.

A Leader Emerges Week after week, both men spoke nearly every day to large crowds. Newspapers reprinted their campaign speeches. The more northerners read Lincoln's words, the more they thought about the injustice of slavery.

In the end, Douglas won the election by a slim margin. Still, Lincoln was a winner, too. He was now known throughout the country. Two years later, the two rivals would again meet face to face—both seeking the office of President.

John Brown's Raid

In the meantime, more bloodshed inflamed divisions between the North and the South. In 1859, the radical abolitionist John Brown carried his antislavery campaign from Kansas to the East. He led a group of followers, including five African Americans, to the town of Harpers Ferry, Virginia.

Primary Source

Douglas Debates Lincoln

In his first debate with Lincoln, Stephen Douglas defended the principle of popular sovereignty: "We have settled the slavery question as far as we are concerned; we have prohibited it in Illinois forever, . . . but when we settled it for ourselves, we exhausted all our power over that subject. We must leave each and every other state to decide for itself the same question. . . . Now, my friends, if we will only act conscientiously and rigidly upon this great principle of popular sovereignty, we will continue at peace, one with another."

—Stephen Douglas, Speech at Ottawa, Illinois, August 21, 1858

Analyzing Primary Sources
How might an abolitionist respond to Douglas?

There, Brown planned to raid a federal **arsenal,** or gun warehouse. He thought that enslaved African Americans would flock to him at the arsenal. He would then give them weapons and lead them in a revolt.

Sentenced to Death Brown quickly gained control of the arsenal. No slave uprising took place, however. Instead, troops under the command of Robert E. Lee killed ten raiders and captured Brown.

Most people, in both the North and the South, thought that Brown's plan to lead a slave revolt was insane. After all, there were few enslaved African Americans in Harpers Ferry. Furthermore, after seizing the arsenal, Brown did nothing further to encourage a slave revolt. At his trial, however, Brown seemed perfectly sane. He sat quietly as the court found him guilty of murder and **treason,** or actions against one's country. Before hearing his sentence, he gave a moving defense of his actions. He showed no emotion as he was sentenced to death.

Hero or Villain? Because he conducted himself with such dignity during his trial, John Brown became a hero to many northerners. Some considered him a **martyr** because he was willing to give up his life for his beliefs. On the morning he was hanged, church bells rang solemnly throughout the North. In years to come, New Englanders would sing a popular song with the chorus: "John Brown's body lies a mold'ring in the grave, but his soul is marching on."

To white southerners, the northern response to John Brown's death was outrageous. People were singing the praises of a man who had tried to lead a slave revolt! Many southerners became convinced that the North wanted to destroy slavery—and the South along with it. The nation was poised for a violent clash.

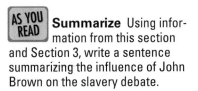
AS YOU READ

Summarize Using information from this section and Section 3, write a sentence summarizing the influence of John Brown on the slavery debate.

AFTER YOU READ

Section 4 Assessment

Recall

1. **Identify** Explain the significance of **(a)** Republican party, **(b)** John C. Frémont, **(c)** James Buchanan, **(d)** Abraham Lincoln, **(e)** Harpers Ferry.
2. **Define** **(a)** arsenal, **(b)** treason, **(c)** martyr.

Comprehension

3. What issue led to the founding of the Republican party?
4. How did Abraham Lincoln emerge as a Republican leader?
5. How did northerners and southerners respond to John Brown's raid?

Critical Thinking and Writing

6. **Exploring the Main Idea** Review the Main Idea statement at the beginning of this section. Then, write a paragraph explaining how the views of the Republican party differed from the views of earlier parties.
7. **Supporting a Point of View** Lincoln said the nation could not "endure permanently half slave and half free." Do you agree that slavery was too important an issue to allow differences among the states? Write a paragraph explaining the reasons for your opinion.

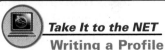
ACTIVITY

Take It to the NET
Writing a Profile
Use the Internet to find out more about the Lincoln-Douglas debates. Use the information to prepare a profile of either Douglas or Lincoln for a TV news report on the debates. Visit *The American Nation* section of **www.phschool.com** for help in completing the activity.

Identifying Bias

Was John Brown a hero or a villain? That depends on your point of view. To evaluate historical evidence correctly, you must be able to identify *bias*, strong beliefs that prejudice someone's point of view.

A North Carolina newspaper ran this editorial after the execution of John Brown:

The Execution of Brown

66 We give to-day full accounts of the scenes attending the execution of the traitor, murderer, and thief, John Brown. He died, as he lived, a hardened criminal. [When] his wretched confederates shall have paid the penalty of their crimes, we hope that their allies and sympathizers at the North will realize the fact that the South has the power to protect her soil and property, and will exercise it in spite of all the measures which can be leveled at her by the abolitionists and their [supporters]. 99

—Raleigh, North Carolina, *Register*, December 9, 1859

In this abolitionist painting, John Brown pauses on his way to his execution to kiss an enslaved woman's baby.

Learn the Skill *To identify bias, use the following steps:*

1. **Identify the sources.** Knowing a person's background helps you evaluate that person's attitudes.
2. **Identify main ideas.** What is the main point that is being made?
3. **Distinguish facts from opinions.** Remember, facts are statements that can be proven, while opinions are someone's beliefs.
4. **Look for emotion-packed words or images.** How information is presented is an important clue to the point of view.
5. **Identify bias.** How do the writer's or artist's feelings and beliefs affect his or her presentation?

Practice the Skill *Answer the following questions about the editorial and picture above:*

1. Where was the newspaper published?
2. What are the points of view of the editorial and the painting?
3. (a) Which statements made by the writer can be proven as facts? (b) Which are opinions?
4. (a) Evaluate the language the writer uses to describe John Brown. (b) What emotions do the images in the painting create?
5. (a) What bias does the editorial show? (b) What bias does the painting show?

Apply the Skill *See the Chapter Review and Assessment.*

5 A Nation Divides

BEFORE YOU READ

Reading Focus

- How did the election of 1860 reflect sectional divisions?
- How did the South react to the election results?
- How did the Civil War begin in 1861?

Taking Notes

As you read, prepare an outline of this section. Use roman numerals to indicate the major headings, capital letters for the subheadings, and numbers for the supporting details. The sample at right will help you get started.

```
I.  The Election of 1860
    A. Candidates and political
       parties
       1.
       2.
       3.
       4.
    B. Results of the election
       1.
       2.
II. The South Reacts
    A. Secession
       1.
       2.
    B. The Confederacy
```

Main Idea The election of Abraham Lincoln as President in 1860 led a number of southern states to secede from the Union.

AS YOU READ
Lincoln campaign badge

Use Prior Knowledge Why would some people view Lincoln's nomination as a step toward civil war?

Setting the Scene Thousands of people swarmed into Chicago, Illinois, for the 1860 Republican national convention. They filled all of the city's 42 hotels. When beds ran out, people slept on billiard tables. All were there to find out one thing: Who would win the Republican nomination for President—William Seward of New York or Abraham Lincoln of Illinois?

On the third day of the convention, a delegate rushed to the roof of the hall. There, a man stood waiting next to a cannon. "Fire the salute," ordered the delegate. "Old Abe is nominated!" Amid the celebration, though, a delegate from Kentucky struck a somber note. "Gentlemen, we are on the brink of a great civil war."

The Election of 1860

The Democrats held their convention in Charleston, South Carolina. Southerners wanted the party to support slavery in the territories. However, northern Democrats refused to do so. In the end, the party split in two. Northern Democrats chose Stephen Douglas to run for President. Southern Democrats picked John Breckinridge of Kentucky.

Some Americans tried to heal the split between the North and the South by forming a new party. The Constitutional Union party chose John Bell of Tennessee to run for President. Bell was a moderate who wanted to keep the Union together. He got support only in a few southern states that were still seeking a compromise.

Douglas was sure that Lincoln would win. However, he believed that Democrats "must try to save the Union." He urged southerners to stay with the Union, no matter who was elected.

When the votes were counted, Lincoln had carried the North and won the election. Southern votes did not affect the outcome at all. Lincoln's name was not even on the ballot in 10 southern states. Northerners outnumbered southerners and outvoted them.

The South Reacts

Lincoln's election brought a strong reaction in the South. A South Carolina woman described how the news was received:

> 66 The excitement was very great. Everybody was talking at the same time. One . . . more moved than the others, stood up saying . . . 'No more vain regrets—sad forebodings are useless. The stake is life or death—.' 99
>
> —Mary Boykin Chesnut, *A Diary From Dixie*, 1860

To many southerners, Lincoln's election meant that the South no longer had a voice in national government. They believed that the President and Congress were now set against their interests—especially slavery. Even before the election, South Carolina's governor had written to other southern governors. If Lincoln won, he wrote, it would be their duty to leave the Union.

Secession Senator John Crittenden of Kentucky made a last effort to save the Union. In December 1860, he introduced a bill to extend the Missouri Compromise line to the Pacific. Crittenden also proposed an "unamendable" amendment to the Constitution that would guarantee forever the right to hold slaves in states south of the compromise line.

The compromise bill received little support. Slavery in the West was no longer the issue. Many southerners believed that the North had put an abolitionist in the White House. They felt that secession was their only choice. Most Republicans also were unwilling to surrender what they had won in the national election.

GEOGRAPHY Skills

Abraham Lincoln won the election of 1860 with less than 40 percent of the popular vote.

1. **Location** On the map, locate (a) Kentucky, (b) Illinois, (c) South Carolina.

2. **Region** (a) Which political party did the northern states support? (b) Which party did most southern states support?

3. **Critical Thinking Drawing Conclusions** Did the results of the popular vote weaken or strengthen Lincoln's chances of effectively leading the nation? Explain.

Election of 1860

Key
- Lincoln, Republican
- Douglas, Northern Democrat
- Bell, Constitutional Union
- Breckinridge, Southern Democrat

PERCENTAGE ELECTORAL VOTE
4% | 13% | 59% | 24%

PERCENTAGE POPULAR VOTE
12.6% | 39.8% | 18.1% | 29.5%

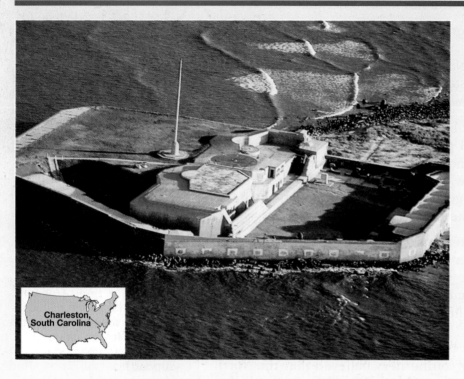

Fort Sumter

The Civil War began in 1861 when Confederate forces bombarded and captured Fort Sumter in Charleston Harbor, South Carolina. Later in the war, Union gunships reduced Sumter to rubble. The fort was rebuilt, and it remained part of the seacoast defenses until 1947. Today, Fort Sumter is a national monument. Tour boats to the fort leave regularly from downtown Charleston.

Charleston, South Carolina

 Take It to the NET

Virtual Field Trip For an interactive look at Fort Sumter, visit *The American Nation* section of **www.phschool.com**.

On December 20, 1860, South Carolina became the first state to secede. By late February, 1861, Alabama, Florida, Georgia, Louisiana, Mississippi, and Texas had also seceded.

The Confederacy Most southerners believed that they had every right to secede. After all, the Declaration of Independence said that "it is the right of the people to alter or to abolish" a government that denies the rights of its citizens. Lincoln, they believed, would deny white southerners the right to own slaves.

At a convention in Montgomery, Alabama, the seven states formed a new nation, the Confederate States of America. Jefferson Davis of Mississippi became the first president of the Confederacy.

The Civil War Begins

When Lincoln took the oath of office on March 4, 1861, he faced a dangerous situation. In his inaugural address, Lincoln warned that "no state . . . can lawfully get out of the Union." Still, he pledged that there would be no war unless the South started it:

AS YOU READ **Draw Inferences** What did Lincoln mean by the statement "In your hands, . . . is the momentous issue of civil war"?

66 In YOUR hands, my dissatisfied fellow-countrymen, and not in MINE, is the momentous issue of civil war. . . . We are not enemies, but friends. We must not be enemies. Though passion may have strained, it must not break our bonds of affection. 99

— Abraham Lincoln, First Inaugural Address

Lincoln's Difficult Decision Jefferson Davis, however, had already ordered Confederate forces to begin seizing federal forts in the South. President Lincoln faced a difficult decision. Should he let the Confederates take over federal property? If he did, he would seem to be admitting that states had the right to leave the Union. On the other hand, if he sent troops to hold the forts, he might start a civil war. He might also lose the support of the eight slave states that had not seceded from the Union.

In April, the Confederacy forced Lincoln to make up his mind. By then, Confederate troops controlled nearly all forts, post offices, and other federal buildings in the South. The Union held only three forts off the Florida coast and Fort Sumter in South Carolina. Fort Sumter was important to the Confederacy because it guarded Charleston Harbor.

Bombardment of Fort Sumter President Lincoln learned that food supplies at Fort Sumter were running low. He notified the governor of South Carolina that he was going to ship food to the fort. Lincoln promised not to send troops or weapons.

The Confederates, however, felt that they could not leave the fort in Union hands. On April 11, 1861, they demanded that Fort Sumter surrender. Major Robert Anderson, the Union commander, refused to give in until he had run out of food or was ordered to surrender by the United States government. Confederate guns then opened fire. The Union troops quickly ran out of ammunition. On April 13, Anderson surrendered the fort.

When Confederate troops shelled Fort Sumter, people in Charleston gathered on their rooftops to watch. To many, it was like a fireworks show. No one knew that the fireworks marked the start of a civil war that would last four terrible years.

An American Profile

Jefferson Davis
1808–1889

After service in the Mexican War, Jefferson Davis became a United States Senator from Mississippi. Here, he championed states' rights. Then, as secretary of war, he influenced President Pierce to sign the Kansas-Nebraska Act. But Davis opposed splitting the Union. As tensions grew between the South and the North, he urged southern states not to secede.

They disregarded his advice. When Mississippi left the Union in 1861, Davis left the Senate and became president of the Confederacy.

Why do you think Jefferson Davis opposed secession?

Section 5 Assessment

Recall
1. **Identify** Explain the significance of **(a)** John Breckinridge, **(b)** John Bell, **(c)** John Crittenden, **(d)** Jefferson Davis.

Comprehension
2. How did the four candidates for President in 1860 reflect the nation's sectional differences?
3. Why did many southerners support secession after Lincoln won the presidency in 1860?
4. What happened at Fort Sumter in 1861 to begin the Civil War?

Critical Thinking and Writing
5. **Exploring the Main Idea** Review the Main idea statement at the beginning of this section. Then, write a newspaper editorial about Lincoln's election that might have appeared in a southern newspaper in November 1860.
6. **Solving Problems** Write an outline for a compromise plan that tries to save the Union in 1861. Your plan should offer advantages to both the North and the South.

ACTIVITY

Planning a Political Campaign You are a political campaign manager in 1860. Write a campaign slogan for each of the four candidates in the presidential election of 1860. Or, choose one of the candidates and design a campaign poster for that candidate.

CHAPTER 16 Review and Assessment

CREATING A CHAPTER SUMMARY

On a sheet of paper, draw a flow-chart like this one. Include 6–8 boxes. Fill in each box with a key event or development in the growing conflict between the North and the South. For each event, include the date as well as one important result of the event. Some information has been filled in to help you get started.

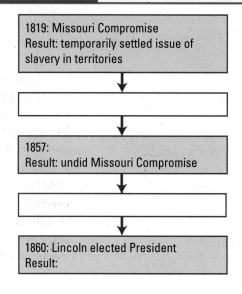

1819: Missouri Compromise
Result: temporarily settled issue of slavery in territories

1857:
Result: undid Missouri Compromise

1860: Lincoln elected President
Result:

For additional review and enrichment activities, see the interactive version of *The American Nation,* available on the Web and on CD-ROM.

 Take It to the NET

Chapter Self-Test For practice test questions for Chapter 16, visit *The American Nation* section of **www.phschool.com**.

Building Vocabulary

Review the chapter vocabulary words listed below. Then, use the words and their definitions to create a matching quiz. Exchange quizzes with another student. Check each other's answers when you are finished.

1. popular sovereignty
2. fugitive
3. civil war
4. guerrilla warfare
5. lawsuit
6. arsenal
7. treason
8. martyr
9. Missouri Compromise
10. Kansas-Nebraska Act

Reviewing Key Facts

11. Describe three positions on slavery held by Americans in the 1840s. (Section 1)
12. What were the five parts of the Compromise of 1850? (Section 2)
13. How did Kansas gain the nickname "Bleeding Kansas"? (Section 3)
14. What groups combined to form the Republican party? (Section 4)
15. Why did South Carolina secede from the Union? (Section 5)

Critical Thinking and Writing

16. **Connecting to Geography: Regions** Study the map of the election of 1860 in Section 5. **(a)** From which regions did Lincoln draw his support? **(b)** Which candidate was most popular in the upper south? **(c)** Does the map show from what regions Douglas drew most of his support? Why or why not?
17. **Supporting a Point of View** Many northerners condemned Daniel Webster for supporting the Fugitive Slave Act. Write two brief statements summarizing one argument for and one argument against Webster's position.
18. **Identifying Causes and Effects (a)** List two causes for the split in the Democratic party in the 1860 election. **(b)** List two effects of the election.
19. **Identifying Alternatives (a)** Write a paragraph suggesting one alternative to secession that the slave states could have chosen in 1860–1861. **(b)** Why do you think they chose secession?

This drawing appeared in northern newspapers in 1856. Look at the drawing and answer the questions that follow.

20. How is Sumner defending himself in the drawing?
21. What is the attitude of the other senators?
22. Which side does the artist support? Explain your answer.
23. What does the artist's view of the incident tell you about the mood of the country in 1856?

The election of 1860 outraged white southerners. They were especially upset that a President had been elected without any southern electoral votes. According to an Augusta, Georgia, newspaper editor, the Republican party:

66 stands forth today, hideous, revolting, loathsome, a menace not only to the Union of these states, but to Society, to Liberty, and to Law. It has drawn to it the corrupt, the vile, and [immoral], the [wasteful], the lawless. . . . It is a fiend, the type of lawless Democracy, a law unto itself, its only Lord King Numbers, its decrees but the will of a wild mob. 99

—Augusta, Georgia, *Chronicle*, November 1860, quoted in "Michael Holt, the Political Crisis of the 1850s"

24. Which of the following titles best reflects the viewpoint of the editorial writer?
    A A Tribute to the Republicans
    B A Loathsome Menace
    C Separation of Powers
    D Dangers of the Party System
25. What does this editorial tell you about the state of relations between the North and the South in November 1860?

ACTIVITIES

Connecting With . . . Economics

Transferring Information to Charts By 1861, the North had 65 percent of the farmland, 71 percent of the railroad track, 85 percent of the factories, 92 percent of the industrial workers, and 63 percent of the population of the United States. Use this information to create a series of pie charts comparing the resources of the North and the South. One pie chart has already been completed. After making the charts, use them to make two generalizations about the economic situation of the Confederate States.

35%
65%

■ Farmland in North
▨ Farmland in South

Take It to the NET

Connecting to Today
Creating a Fact Sheet Like the Free-Soil party, new political parties often form in response to specific issues. Use the Internet to find out about a current "third party." Create a fact sheet describing the third party. For help in starting this activity, visit *The American Nation* section of **www.phschool.com**.

Researching a Biography
Ranking Lincoln Web Sites Use the Internet to find sites relating to Abraham Lincoln. Write a report listing the resources you found on these sites that make them valuable for a Lincoln biography. List five sites, and rank them in order of usefulness. For help in starting this activity, visit *The American Nation* section of **www.phschool.com**.

The Civil War

1861–1865

The Battle of Bull Run

1861

The first major battle of the war takes place at Bull Run on July 21.

1862

Union gunboats capture New Orleans and Memphis.

1863

The Battle of Gettysburg ends the Confederate drive into the North.

AMERICAN EVENTS

Presidential Terms: Abraham Lincoln 1861-1865

1861   1862   1863

WORLD EVENTS   ▲ **1861**
The Russian czar frees the serfs.

▲ **1862**
Great Britain refuses to recognize the Confederacy.

Choosing Sides

By February 1861, eight slave states were still in the Union. These states would have to decide whether to remain in the Union or join the Confederacy.

BRITISH TERRITORY

Washington

Oregon Territory

Nevada Territory

Utah Territory

California

New Mexico Territory

Dakota Territory

Nebraska Territory

Colorado Territory

Kansas

Indian Territory

Texas

Minnesota

Wisconsin

Michigan

Iowa

Illinois

Missouri

AR

MS

LA

IN

Ohio

Kentucky

Tennessee

AL

Georgia

Maine

VT

NH

MA

CT

RI

New York

PA

NJ

MD

DE

*WV

Virginia

NC

SC

FL

ATLANTIC OCEAN

MEXICO

Gulf of Mexico

Rio Grande

Mississippi R.

Ohio R.

L. Superior

L. Michigan

L. Huron

L. Ontario

L. Erie

50° N

40° N

30° N

20° N

120° W

110° W

100° W

90° W

80° W

70° W

Key

- Union states
- Confederate states
- Border states that stayed in the Union
- States that joined the Confederacy after April 1861
- Territories
- Confederate States of America

* West Virginia separated from Virginia in 1861 and was admitted to the Union in 1863.

Albers Equal-Area Projection

0   300   600 Miles

0   300   600 Kilometers

ABRAHAM LINCOLN

Emancipation Proclamation

The Emancipation Proclamation

The surrender at Appomattox Court House

1863

Abraham Lincoln issues the Emancipation Proclamation.

1864

General Grant becomes commander of the Union Army.

1865

General Lee surrenders at Appomattox Court House.

| 1863 | 1864 | 1865 |

▲ **1863**
The first Red Cross societies are established in Europe.

▲ **1864**
Archduke Maximilian of Austria becomes emperor of Mexico.

1 The Conflict Takes Shape

BEFORE YOU READ

Reading Focus

- What issues divided the nation when the war began?
- What were the primary strengths and weaknesses of the North and the South at the beginning of the war?
- Who were the leaders of each side in the war?

Key Terms

border state

martial law

Taking Notes

Copy the table below. As you read the section, fill in the table with the strengths of the North and the South at the start of the war and their reasons for fighting. Add as many entries as you need.

NORTH	SOUTH
Strengths	**Strengths**
•	•
•	•
Reasons for fighting	**Reasons for fighting**
•	•
•	•

Main Idea Although both sides believed that their cause was just, the North had important advantages at the start of the war.

AS YOU READ
A poster calling for volunteers

Draw Inferences Why would volunteers be eager to enlist?

Setting the Scene President Abraham Lincoln called for 75,000 volunteers to serve as soldiers in a campaign against the South. The term of enlistment was only 90 days—most northerners believed that the war would be over quickly. In the words of one confident Union supporter, "We shall crush out this rebellion as an elephant would trample on a mouse."

Southerners were just as convinced that a Confederate victory would be quick. A Confederate in North Carolina predicted, "Just throw three or four [bomb]shells among those blue-bellied Yankees and they'll scatter like sheep."

With flags held high, both northerners and southerners marched off to war. Most felt certain that a single, gallant battle would bring a quick end to the conflict. Few suspected that the Civil War would last four terrible years. By the time the fighting was over, every part of American society would be affected by the Civil War.

A Nation Divided

When the war began, each side was convinced that its cause was just. Southerners believed that they had the right to leave the Union. In fact, they called the conflict the War for Southern Independence. Southerners wanted independence so that they could keep their traditional way of life—including the institution of slavery.

Northerners, meanwhile, believed that they had to fight to save the Union. At the outset of the war, abolishing slavery was not an official goal of the North. In fact, many northerners, guided by feelings of racism, approved of slavery. Racism is the belief that one race is by nature superior to another.

In April 1861, eight slave states were still in the Union. As the war began, they had to make the difficult decision of which side to join. Their decision would greatly affect the outcome of the war. These states had more than half of the South's population and food crops. In addition, many of the South's factories were in these states.

Four of these states—Virginia,* North Carolina, Tennessee, and Arkansas—quickly joined the Confederacy. However, after some wavering between the North and South, the four border states—Kentucky, Missouri, Maryland, and Delaware—decided to remain in the Union. Maryland was especially critical to the Union cause since it bordered the nation's capital at Washington, D.C.

Still, there were some citizens of the border states who supported the South. In April 1861, pro-Confederate mobs attacked Union troops in Baltimore, Maryland. In response, President Lincoln declared martial law, or rule by the army instead of the elected government. Many people who sided with the South were arrested.

Strengths and Weaknesses

Both sides in the conflict had strengths and weaknesses as the war began. The South had the strong advantage of fighting a defensive war. "We seek no conquest," said Confederate President Jefferson Davis. "All we ask is to be let alone." If the North did not move its forces into the South, the Confederacy would remain a separate country.

The South White southerners believed that they were fighting a war for independence, similar to the American Revolution. Defending their homeland and their way of life gave them a strong reason to fight. "Our men must prevail in combat," one Confederate said, "or they will lose their property, country, freedom—in short, everything."

Confederate soldiers also enjoyed an advantage because they knew the southern countryside better. Friendly civilians often guided soldiers along obscure roads that did not appear on maps. Much of the South was wooded, too. Confederate forces used the woods for cover as they defended themselves against invading Union troops.

The South, however, had serious economic weaknesses. It had few factories to produce weapons and other vital supplies. It also had few railroads to move troops and supplies. The railroads that it did have often did not connect to one another. Tracks simply ran between two points and then stopped.

*In western Virginia, where there were few slave owners, many people supported the Union. When Virginia seceded, westerners formed their own government. West Virginia became a state of the Union in 1863.

Resources of the North and South, 1861

Total Population — 29% / 71%

Factory Production — 9% / 91%

Railroad Mileage — 29% / 71%

Farmland — 25% / 75%

Cotton Production — 4% / 96%

Northern resources
Southern resources

Source: *The Times Atlas of World History*

CHART Skills

As the Civil War began, the North had a number of economic advantages over the South.

1. **Comprehension (a)** How much farmland did each side have? **(b)** What percentage of the nation's factories did the South have?

2. **Critical Thinking Making Predictions (a)** Which side had more railroad track? **(b)** How would this affect the war?

Economics $

The South also had political problems. The Confederate constitution favored states' rights and limited the authority of the central government. As a result, the Confederate government often found it difficult to get things done. On one occasion, for example, the governor of Georgia insisted that only Georgian officers should command Georgian troops.

Finally, the South had a small population. Only about 9 million people lived in the Confederacy, compared with 22 million in the Union. More than one third of the southern population were enslaved African Americans. As a result, the South did not have enough people to serve as soldiers and to support the war effort.

The North The North had almost four times as many free citizens as the South. Thus, it had a large source of volunteers. It also had many people to grow food and to work in factories making supplies.

Industry was the North's greatest resource. Before the war, northern factories produced more than 90 percent of the nation's manufactured goods. Once the war began, these factories quickly began making guns, bullets, cannons, boots, uniforms, and other supplies for the Union army. In addition, the North had more than 70 percent of the nation's rail lines, which it used to transport both troops and supplies.

The North benefited from a strong navy and a large fleet of trading ships. With few warships and only a small merchant fleet, the South was unable to compete with the North at sea.

Despite these advantages, the North faced a difficult military challenge. To bring the South back into the Union, northern soldiers had to conquer a huge area. Instead of defending their homes, they were invading unfamiliar land. As Union armies marched into the South, their lines of supply would be much longer than those of the Confederates and thus more open to attack.

The War's Leaders

Leadership was a crucial factor in the Civil War. President Jefferson Davis of the Confederacy, President Abraham Lincoln of the Union, and military leaders on both sides played key roles in determining the war's outcome.

President Jefferson Davis Many people thought that Davis was a stronger leader than Lincoln. Davis's experience prepared him for the position. However, he did not want it. As one observer stated:

66 Mr. Davis's military instincts still predominate, and his eager wish was to have joined the army instead of being elected President. 99

—Arthur James Freemantle, from *The Freemantle Diary*

Davis had attended the United States Military Academy at West Point. He had served as an officer in the Mexican War. Later, he served as Secretary of War under President Franklin Pierce. Furthermore, Davis was widely respected for his honesty and courage.

Davis, however, did not like to turn over to others the details of military planning. As a result, he spent much time worrying about small matters and arguing with his advisers.

President Abraham Lincoln At first, some northerners had doubts about Abraham Lincoln's ability to lead. He did not have much experience in national politics or military matters. However, Lincoln proved to be a patient but strong leader and a fine war planner.

Day by day, Lincoln gained the respect of those around him. Many liked his sense of humor. They noted that Lincoln even accepted criticism with a smile. When Secretary of War Edwin Stanton called Lincoln a fool, Lincoln commented, "Did Stanton say I was a fool? Then I must be one, for Stanton is generally right and he always says what he means."

Military Leaders As the war began, army officers in the South had to decide whether to stay in the Union army and fight against their home states, or join the Confederate forces.

Robert E. Lee of Virginia faced this dilemma when Lincoln asked him to command the Union army. He explains in a letter to a friend:

> 66 If Virginia stands by the old Union, so will I. But if she secedes . . . , then I will still follow my native State with my sword and, if need be, with my life. 99
>
> —Robert E. Lee, quoted in Carl Sandburg, *Abraham Lincoln*

Virginia did secede and Lee refused Lincoln's offer. Later, Lee became commander of the Confederate army.

Many of the army's best officers served the Confederacy. As a result, President Lincoln had trouble finding generals to match those of the South.

An American Profile

Robert E. Lee 1807–1870

Robert E. Lee came from a distinguished Virginia family. After graduating with honors from West Point, he served in the Army Corps of Engineers. During the Mexican War, his superior officer described him as "the very best soldier I ever saw in the field." Despite that, Lee hated the horror of war.

When the Civil War broke out, Lee was torn between the Union and his home state of Virginia. In the end, he chose Virginia. "I have not been able to make up my mind to raise my hand against my relatives, my children, my home," he said.

Why did Lee choose to side with the Confederacy?

AFTER YOU READ

Section 1 Assessment

Recall

1. **Identify** Explain the significance of **(a)** Abraham Lincoln, **(b)** Jefferson Davis, **(c)** Robert E. Lee.
2. **Define (a)** border state, **(b)** martial law.

Comprehension

3. What were the goals of each side as the war began?
4. Describe two advantages that the North had over the South at the start of the Civil War.
5. Describe one strength and one weakness of **(a)** President Abraham Lincoln, **(b)** President Jefferson Davis.

Critical Thinking and Writing

6. **Exploring the Main Idea** Review the Main Idea statement at the beginning of this section. Then, list five statements from the section that support the main idea.
7. **Making Decisions** Imagine that you are an army officer from the South at the beginning of the war. Would you side with the Union or with the Confederacy? Give at least two reasons for your decision.

ACTIVITY

Analyzing a Chart
Study the chart on page 487. Then, use the information on the chart to write a report analyzing the strengths and weaknesses of each side at the start of the Civil War. Based on your analysis, which side do you think will win the war? Explain.

2 No Easy Victory

BEFORE YOU READ

Reading Focus

- What strategies did each side adopt to win the war?
- How did early encounters dispel hopes for a quick end to the war?
- What victories did the Confederates achieve?
- What victories did the Union achieve?

Key Terms

Battle of Bull Run

Virginia

Monitor

Battle of Antietam

Battle of Fredericksburg

Battle of Chancellorsville

Battle of Shiloh

Taking Notes

As you read, prepare an outline of the section. Use roman numerals to indicate major headings, capital letters for subheadings, and numbers for supporting details. The sample below will help you get started.

> I. Strategies for Victory
>   A. Union plans
>   1.
>   2.
>   3.
>   B. Confederate plans
>   1.
>   2.
> II. Early Encounters

Main Idea Despite hopes for a quick victory, both northerners and southerners soon learned that they were in for a long, difficult struggle.

AS YOU READ **Bullet caught in a shoulder plate**

Predict What effect would improved weapons have on the war?

Setting the Scene

At first, the armies of the North and the South marched proudly off to war. Each side expected a quick and painless victory. The reality of war soon shattered this expectation. Over and over, soldiers wrote home describing the awful face of battle:

> 66 I never saw so many broken down and exhausted men in all my life. I was sick as a horse, and as wet with blood and sweat as I could be. . . . Our tongues were parched and cracked for water, and our faces blackened with powder and smoke. 99
>
> —quoted by Shelby Foote in *The Civil War: A Narrative*

It soon became clear that there would be no quick end to the struggle. Both sides began to dig in for a long, difficult war.

Strategies for Victory

The North and South had different strategies for victory. The Union planned an aggressive campaign against the South. The South, meanwhile, planned to hold tight until the North lost the will to fight.

Union Plans First, the Union planned to use its navy to blockade southern ports. This would cut off the South's supply of manufactured goods from Europe.

In the East, Union generals aimed to seize Richmond, Virginia, the Confederate capital. They thought that they might end the war quickly by capturing the Confederate government.

In the West, the Union planned to seize control of the Mississippi River. This would prevent the South from using the river to supply its troops. It would also separate Arkansas, Texas, and Louisiana from the rest of the Confederacy.

Confederate Plans The South's strategy was simpler: The Confederate army would fight a defensive war until northerners tired of fighting. If the war became unpopular in the North, President Lincoln would have to stop the war and recognize the South's independence.

The Confederacy counted on European money and supplies to help fight the war. Southern cotton was important to the textile mills of England and other countries. Southerners were confident that Europeans would recognize the Confederacy as an independent nation and continue to buy southern cotton for their factories.

Early Encounters

"Forward to Richmond! Forward to Richmond!" Every day for more than a month, the influential *New York Tribune* blazed this war cry across its front page. At last, responding to popular pressure, President Lincoln ordered an attack.

Battle of Bull Run On July 21, 1861, Union troops set out from Washington, D.C., for Richmond, about 100 miles away. Hundreds of Washingtonians, in a festive mood, rode out along with them to watch the battle.

The Union troops had not gone far when they met up with Confederate soldiers. A battle quickly followed. It took place near a small Virginia stream known as Bull Run.

At first, Union forces succeeded in breaking up Confederate battle lines. "The war is over!" yelled some soldiers from Massachusetts. But General Thomas Jackson rallied the Virginia troops on a nearby hill. "Look!" cried a Confederate officer to his men, "There is Jackson standing like a stone wall! Rally behind the Virginians!" From that day on, the general was known as "Stonewall" Jackson.

In the end, it was the Union troops who panicked and ran. "Off they went," reported one observer, "across fields, toward the woods, anywhere, everywhere, to escape." For most of the soldiers, the retreat did not stop until they reached Washington, D.C.

The Battle of Bull Run showed both the Union and the Confederacy that their soldiers needed training. It also showed that the war would be long and bloody.

Caution, Delay, and Retreat After the shocking disaster at Bull Run, President Lincoln appointed General George McClellan as commander of the Union army of the East, known as the Army of the Potomac. McClellan, a superb organizer, transformed inexperienced recruits into an army of trained soldiers prepared for battle.

GEOGRAPHY Skills

Early in the war, Union armies were unsuccessful in their attempts to capture Richmond, the Confederate capital.

1. **Location** On the map, locate **(a)** Washington, D.C., **(b)** Richmond, **(c)** Bull Run, **(d)** Chancellorsville.

2. **Movement** Describe the route that General McClellan took when he tried to capture Richmond in 1862.

3. **Critical Thinking Making Decisions** Do you think that the Confederacy made a wise decision in locating its capital at Richmond? Explain.

The Civil War in the East

Pennsylvania
Gettysburg
Lee 1863
Meade 1863
Potomac R.
Harpers Ferry
Antietam
McClellan 1862
Maryland
Washington, D.C.
West Virginia
Chesapeake Bay
Bull Run
Fredericksburg
Shenandoah R.
Chancellorsville
Lee 1862
Richmond
James R.
Seven Days
York R.
McClellan 1862
Virginia
Monitor versus Merrimac (no victor)
NJ
DE

Albers Equal-Area Projection
0   50   100 Miles
0   50   100 Kilometers

Key
← Union troops
← Confederate troops
★ Union victories
★ Confederate victories

McClellan, however, was very cautious. He delayed leading his troops into battle. Newspapers reported "all quiet along the Potomac" so often that the phrase became a national joke. Finally, President Lincoln lost patience. "If General McClellan does not want to use the army," the President snapped, "I would like to borrow it."

At last, in March 1862, McClellan and most of his troops left Washington and sailed down the Potomac River. After landing south of Richmond, McClellan began inching slowly toward the Confederate capital.

Learning of the Union approach, General Robert E. Lee launched a series of counterattacks. At the same time, Lee sent General Stonewall Jackson north to threaten Washington. As a result, Lincoln was prevented from sending the rest of the Union army to help McClellan. Cautious as usual, McClellan abandoned the attack and retreated.

AS YOU READ Draw Inferences Before you read this section, think about why the Union wanted to blockade southern ports. Then, read to find the reason.

Naval Action Early in the war, Union ships blockaded southern ports. At first, some small, fast ships slipped through the blockade. These "blockade runners" brought everything from matches to guns to the Confederacy.

In time, however, the blockade became more effective. Trade through southern ports dropped by more than 90 percent. The South desperately needed a way to break the Union blockade. One method it tried was the ironclad ship.

Confederates took over an abandoned Union warship, the USS *Merrimack.* They covered it with iron plates and renamed it the *Virginia.* On its first day out in March 1862, the *Virginia* destroyed two Union ships and drove three more aground. Union cannonballs bounced harmlessly off the *Virginia's* metal skin.

The Union countered with its own ironclad, the *Monitor.* The two ships clashed in the waters off Hampton Roads, Virginia. Despite an exhausting battle, neither vessel seriously damaged the other, and both withdrew. Two months later Confederates had to sink the *Virginia* when the Union captured Norfolk. The Union eventually built more than 50 ironclads.

Ironclad ships changed naval warfare. However, the South was never again able to mount a serious attack against the Union navy. The Union blockade held throughout the war.

Antietam In September 1862, General Lee took the offensive and marched his troops north into Maryland. He believed that a southern victory on northern soil would be a great blow to northern morale.

Luck was against Lee, however. At an abandoned Confederate campsite, a Union officer found a copy of Lee's battle plan. It was wrapped around three cigars, left behind by a careless general. General McClellan was overjoyed to have the information. "If I cannot whip 'Bobbie Lee,' I will be willing to go home," he boasted.

However, McClellan was slow to act. Finally, after a few days, he attacked Lee's main force at Antietam (an TEE tuhm) on September 17. In the day-long battle that followed, more than 23,000 Union and Confederate soldiers were killed or wounded.

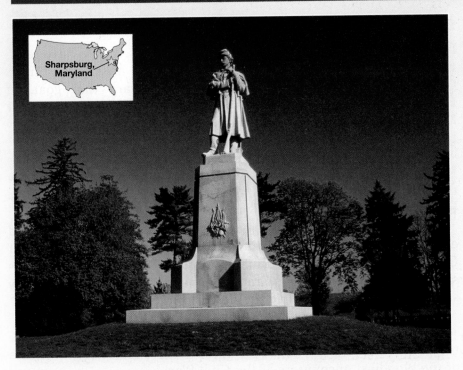

Antietam National Battlefield

On September 17, 1862, Union and Confederate troops faced one another at Antietam Creek near Sharpsburg, Maryland.

Today, 103 monuments at Antietam honor those who fought there. Most of the monuments were built by Civil War veterans. The barrels of 500 cannons, which were used in the Civil War, are on the battlefield. These mark the location of artillery during the battle.

 Take It to the NET

Virtual Field Trip For an interactive look at the Antietam battle site, visit *The American Nation* section of **www.phschool.com**.

On the night of September 18, Lee ordered his troops to slip back into Virginia. The Confederates breathed a sigh of relief when they saw that McClellan was not pursuing them.

Neither side was a clear winner at the Battle of Antietam. The North was able to claim victory, though, because Lee had ordered his forces to withdraw. As a result, northern morale increased. Still, President Lincoln was keenly disappointed. General McClellan had failed to follow up his victory by pursuing the Confederates. In November, Lincoln appointed General Ambrose Burnside to replace McClellan as commander of the Army of the Potomac.

Confederate Victories in the East

Two stunning victories for the Confederacy came in late 1862 and 1863. In December 1862, Union forces set out once again toward Richmond.

Meeting Burnside's army outside Fredericksburg, Virginia, Lee's forces dug into the crest of a hill. There, in a strong defensive position, Confederate guns mowed down wave after wave of charging Union troops. The Battle of Fredericksburg was one of the Union's worst defeats. (See page 495.)

Half a year later, in May 1863, Lee, aided by Stonewall Jackson, again outmaneuvered Union forces. The Battle of Chancellorsville took place on thickly wooded ground near Chancellorsville, Virginia. Lee and Jackson defeated the Union troops in three days. Victory came at a high price for the South, however. During the battle, nervous

Ulysses S. Grant 1822–1885

General Ulysses S. Grant's troops had the Confederates surrounded at Fort Donelson. Confederate General Simon Bolivar Buckner wanted to discuss terms of surrender.

Grant's response was to the point: "No terms except an unconditional and immediate surrender can be accepted." Buckner immediately surrendered the fort. Grant's victory caused great celebration in the North. It also earned him the nickname "Unconditional Surrender" Grant.

What characteristics did Grant reveal by his actions at Fort Donelson?

Confederate sentries fired at what they thought was an approaching Union soldier. The "Union soldier" was General Stonewall Jackson. Several days later, Jackson died as a result of his injuries.

Union Victories in the West

In the West, Union forces met with better success. As you have read, the Union strategy was to seize control of the Mississippi River. General Ulysses S. Grant began moving toward that goal. In February 1862, Grant attacked and captured Fort Henry and Fort Donelson in Tennessee. These Confederate forts guarded two important tributaries of the Mississippi.

Grant now pushed south to Shiloh, a village on the Tennessee River. There, on April 6, he was surprised by Confederate forces. By the end of the day, the Confederates had driven the Union troops back toward the river.

Grant now showed the toughness and determination that would enable him to win many battles in the future. That night, one of Grant's soldiers approached him. The officer thought Union forces should retreat. But, seeing Grant's stubborn face, the officer only said, "Well, Grant, we've had the devil's own day, haven't we?"

"Yes," Grant replied. "Lick 'em tomorrow, though."

And they did. With the aid of reinforcements, Grant beat back the Confederates and won the Battle of Shiloh. It was, however, one of the bloodiest encounters of the Civil War.

While Grant was fighting at Shiloh, the Union navy moved to gain control of the Mississippi River. In April 1862, Union gunboats captured New Orleans. Other ships seized Memphis, Tennessee. By capturing these two cities, the Union controlled both ends of the Mississippi. The South could no longer use the river as a supply line.

AFTER YOU READ

Section 2 Assessment

Recall

1. **Identify** Explain the significance of **(a)** Stonewall Jackson, **(b)** Battle of Bull Run, **(c)** George McClellan, **(d)** *Virginia,* **(e)** *Monitor,* **(f)** Battle of Antietam, **(g)** Battle of Fredericksburg, **(h)** Battle of Chancellorsville, **(i)** Ulysses S. Grant, **(j)** Battle of Shiloh.

Comprehension

2. **Describe (a)** the North's three-part plan for defeating the South, **(b)** the South's plan to defeat the North.
3. What did both sides learn from the Battle of Bull Run?

4. Why was the Confederate victory at Fredericksburg critical?
5. How did Union victories at New Orleans and Memphis affect the South?

Critical Thinking and Writing

6. **Exploring the Main Idea** Review the Main Idea statement at the beginning of this section. Make a list of five events and their results during the first two years of the war.
7. **Analyzing Ideas** Analyze the meaning of this statement: "The South could win the war by not losing, but the North could win only by winning."

The Battle of Fredericksburg

Fredericksburg, Virginia, was located between Washington, D.C., and Richmond, the Confederate capital. Taking Fredericksburg was a step toward capturing Richmond.

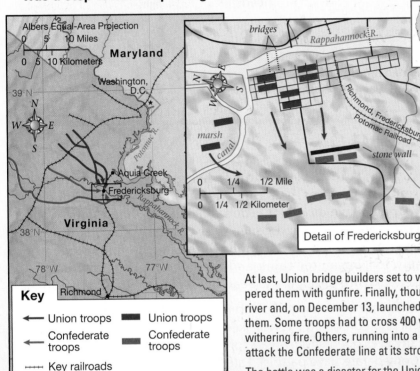

Detail of Fredericksburg

Key
- ← Union troops
- ← Confederate troops
- ┼┼┼ Key railroads
- ▬ Union troops
- ▬ Confederate troops

In the fall of 1862, General Ambrose Burnside began moving his Union army toward Fredericksburg. They were stopped by the Rappahannock River. While the Union troops waited for engineers to bridge the river, General Robert E. Lee's Confederate forces occupied the city and the high ground behind it. They took up a strong position, overlooking a large, open field.

At last, Union bridge builders set to work, but Confederate snipers peppered them with gunfire. Finally, though, the Union army got across the river and, on December 13, launched an attack. The terrain was against them. Some troops had to cross 400 yards of open ground in the face of withering fire. Others, running into a canal and a marsh, were forced to attack the Confederate line at its strongest point—the top of a hill.

The battle was a disaster for the Union army. For hours, soldiers marched up the hill only to be mowed down by gunfire. Finally, Burnside halted the attack. His army had lost 13,000 men, compared with only 5,000 for Lee's.

ACTIVITY

You are a correspondent for a northern or southern newspaper, and you saw the Battle of Fredericksburg. Write a description of the battle that explains how geography affected the outcome.

3 A Promise of Freedom

Reading Focus

- What was Lincoln's primary goal in the war?
- What were the effects of the Emancipation Proclamation?
- How did African Americans contribute to the war effort both in the Union army and behind Confederate lines?

Key Terms

emancipate

Emancipation Proclamation

54th Massachusetts Regiment

Fort Wagner

Taking Notes

Copy the chart. As you read, complete the chart to show the causes and effects of the Emancipation Proclamation. Add as many entries as you need.

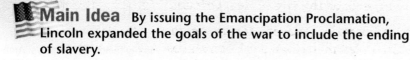

```
┌─────── CAUSES ───────┐
1.
2. Lincoln wanted to weaken
   the Confederacy's ability to
   fight

┌─── EMANCIPATION ───┐
│    PROCLAMATION    │

┌─── EFFECTS ───┐

1. Union fighting to end slavery
2.
```

Main Idea By issuing the Emancipation Proclamation, Lincoln expanded the goals of the war to include the ending of slavery.

African American soldier

Draw Inferences Why were the Union lines a symbol of freedom to the enslaved African Americans?

Setting the Scene

John Finnely heard the news first thing in the morning: Ten slaves had run off the night before. Finnely, a twelve-year-old slave on a plantation in Alabama, had a pretty good idea where the escapees had gone. Most certainly, they had headed for Union troops camped a few miles to the north—and freedom.

Finnely, too, began to "think and think 'bout gittin' freedom." At last, with a mixture of hope and fear, he decided to make the break:

> 66 I makes up my mind to go and I leaves with a chunk of meat and cornbread . . . half skeert to death. I sure have my eyes open and my ears forward, watchin' for the [Confederate slave patrols]. I step off the road in the night, at the sight of anything, and in the day I take to the woods. 99
>
> —John Finnely, quoted in *Remembering Slavery*

At first, the Civil War was not a war against slavery. But as thousands of slaves like John Finnely rushed into the arms of Union troops with the hope of freedom, some northerners began to rethink the aims of the war.

Lincoln's Goal

The Civil War began as a war to restore the Union, not to end slavery. President Lincoln made this point clear in a letter that was widely distributed:

> 66 If I could save the Union without freeing any slave, I would do it; and if I could save it by freeing all the slaves, I would do it; and if I could do it by freeing some and leaving others alone, I would also do that. 99
>
> —Abraham Lincoln, August 22, 1862, quoted in Carl Sandburg, *Abraham Lincoln*

Lincoln had a reason for handling the slavery issue cautiously. As you have read, four slave states remained in the Union. The President did not want to do anything that might cause these states to shift their loyalty to the Confederacy. The resources of the border states might allow the South to turn the tide of the war.

The Emancipation Proclamation

By mid-1862, Lincoln came to believe that he could save the Union only by broadening the goals of the war. He decided to emancipate, or free, enslaved African Americans living in the Confederacy. In the four loyal slave states, however, slaves would not be freed. Nor would slaves be freed in Confederate lands that had already been captured by the Union, such as the city of New Orleans.

Motives and Timing Lincoln had practical reasons for his emancipation plan. At the start of the Civil War, more than 3 million slaves labored for the Confederacy. They helped grow the food that fed Confederate soldiers. They also worked in iron and lead mines that were vital to the South's war effort. Some served as nurses and cooks for the army. Lincoln knew that emancipation would weaken the Confederacy's ability to carry on the war.

However, Lincoln did not want to anger slave owners in the Union. Also, he knew that many northerners opposed freedom for enslaved African Americans. Lincoln hoped to introduce the idea of emancipation slowly, by limiting it to territory controlled by the Confederacy.

The President had another motive. As you read in Chapter 16, Lincoln believed that slavery was wrong. When he felt that he could act to free slaves without threatening the Union, he did so.

Lincoln was concerned about the timing of his announcement. The war was not going well for the Union. He did not want Americans to think he was freeing slaves as a desperate effort to save a losing cause. He waited for a victory to announce his plan.

On September 22, 1862, following the Union victory at Antietam, Lincoln issued a preliminary proclamation. He issued the formal Emancipation Proclamation on January 1, 1863.

Impact of the Proclamation Because the rebelling states were not under Union control, no slaves actually gained their freedom on January 1, 1863. Still, the Emancipation Proclamation changed the purpose of the war. Now, Union troops were fighting to end slavery as well as to save the Union.

The opponents of slavery greeted the proclamation with joy. In Boston, African American abolitionist Frederick Douglass witnessed one of the many emotional celebrations that took place:

> 66 The effect of this announcement was startling . . . and the scene was wild and grand. . . . My old friend Rue, a Negro preacher, . . . expressed the heartfelt emotion of the hour, when he led all voices in the anthem, 'Sound the loud timbrel o'er Egypt's dark sea, Jehovah hath triumphed, his people are free!' 99
> —Frederick Douglass, *Life and Times of Frederick Douglass*

Primary Source

The Emancipation Proclamation

On January 1, 1863, President Lincoln issued the Emancipation Proclamation. The document declared the following:
"On the 1st day of January, in the year of our Lord 1863, all persons held as slaves within any state or . . . part of a state [whose] people . . . shall then be in rebellion against the United States, shall be then, thenceforward, and forever free."

Analyzing Primary Sources
Were all enslaved African Americans freed? Explain.

AS YOU READ **Visualize** Form a mental picture of how slaves would have reacted to hearing about the Emancipation Proclamation.

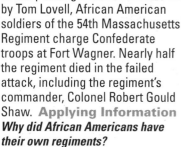

Viewing History

Assault on Fort Wagner

In this painting by Tom Lovell, African American soldiers of the 54th Massachusetts Regiment charge Confederate troops at Fort Wagner. Nearly half the regiment died in the failed attack, including the regiment's commander, Colonel Robert Gould Shaw. **Applying Information** *Why did African Americans have their own regiments?*

In the South, Lincoln's proclamation was seen as a "fiend's act" that destroyed expensive property. The proclamation won the sympathy of Europeans, especially workers. As a result, it became less likely that Britain or any other European country would come to the aid of the South.

African American Contributions

When the war began, thousands of free blacks volunteered to fight for the Union. At first, federal law forbade African Americans to serve as soldiers. When Congress repealed that law in 1862, however, both free African Americans and escaped slaves enlisted in the Union army.

In the Union Army The army assigned African American volunteers to all-black units, commanded by white officers. At first, the black troops served only as laborers. They performed noncombat duties such as building roads and guarding supplies. Black troops received only half the pay of white soldiers.

African American soldiers protested against this policy of discrimination that denied them the same treatment as other soldiers. Gradually, conditions changed. By 1863, African American troops were fighting in major battles against the Confederates. In 1864, the United States War Department announced that all soldiers would receive equal pay. By the end of the war, about 200,000 African Americans had fought for the Union. Nearly 40,000 lost their lives.

Acts of Bravery One of the most famous African American units in the Union army was the **54th Massachusetts Regiment.** The 54th accepted African Americans from all across the North. Frederick Douglass helped recruit troops for the regiment, and two of his sons served in it.

On July 18, 1863, the 54th Massachusetts Regiment led an attack on **Fort Wagner** near Charleston, South Carolina. Under heavy fire, troops fought their way into the fort before being forced to withdraw. In the desperate fighting, almost half the regiment was killed.

The courage of the 54th Massachusetts and other regiments helped to win respect for African American soldiers. Sergeant William Carney of the 54th Massachusetts was the first of 16 African American soldiers to win the Medal of Honor in the Civil War. Such soldiers had "proved themselves among the bravest of the brave," Secretary of War Edwin Stanton told Lincoln.

Behind Confederate Lines Despite the Emancipation Proclamation, African Americans still worked in the South as slaves on plantations. However, many slaves slowed down their work or refused to work at all. In this way, they hoped to weaken the South's war effort. They knew that when victorious Union troops arrived in their area, they would be free.

Thousands of enslaved African Americans took direct action to free themselves. Whenever a Union army appeared, slaves from all over the area would flee their former masters. They crossed the Union lines to freedom. By the end of the war, about one fourth of the South's enslaved population had escaped to freedom.

Section 3 Assessment

Recall

1. **Identify** Explain the significance of **(a)** Emancipation Proclamation, **(b)** 54th Massachusetts Regiment, **(c)** Fort Wagner.
2. **Define** emancipate.

Comprehension

3. Why was President Lincoln cautious about making the abolition of slavery a goal of the war?
4. How did the Emancipation Proclamation affect the status of enslaved African Americans?
5. How did enslaved African Americans help to hurt the Confederate war effort?

Critical Thinking and Writing

6. **Exploring the Main Idea** Review the Main Idea statement at the beginning of this section. Write a newspaper article explaining why Lincoln issued the Emancipation Proclamation.
7. **Analyzing Primary Sources** In 1861, Frederick Douglass said, "This is no time to fight with one hand when both hands are needed. This is no time to fight with only your white hand, and allow your black hand to remain tied!" **(a)** What did Douglass mean by this statement? **(b)** Did the United States Congress agree with Douglass? Explain.

ACTIVITY

Writing a Poem A monument is being built to honor the courageous African American soldiers of the Civil War. Write a poem to be inscribed on the monument, mentioning some of the facts you learned in this section.

4 Hardships of War

BEFORE YOU READ

Reading Focus

- What was life like for Confederate and Union soldiers?
- What problems did each side face at home?
- How did the war affect the economy of the North and the South?
- What role did women play in the war?

Key Terms

Copperhead

draft

habeas corpus

income tax

inflation

profiteer

Taking Notes

Copy this incomplete Venn diagram. As you read, fill in key facts about conditions in the North and South during the Civil War. Write common characteristics in the overlapping section.

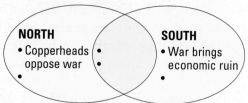

NORTH
- Copperheads oppose war
- •

SOUTH
- War brings economic ruin

Main Idea The demands of the war hurt civilians as well as soldiers on both sides, but the problems were worse in the Confederate States.

AS YOU READ

Homecoming
Summarize Why did the war cause more damage in the South?

Primary Sources

See Stephen Crane, "The Red Badge of Courage," on page 604 of the Reference Section.

Setting the Scene

John Jones knew that he was not alone in the hardships he experienced. All he had to do was look around in the Confederate capital of Richmond. Some of the city's residents, he noted, looked "like vagabonds . . . gaunt and pale with hunger." As for his own family:

> **❝** My daughter's cat is staggering today, for want of animal food. Sometimes I fancy I stagger myself. We do not average two ounces of meat daily; and some do not get any for several days together. **❞**
>
> —John B. Jones, *A Rebel War Clerk's Diary*

The Civil War caused hardships not only for soldiers but for people at home as well. Southerners were especially hard hit, because most of the fighting took place in the South. But for both North and South, the war affected every area of life.

The Hard Life of Soldiers

On both sides, most soldiers were under the age of 21. War, however, quickly turned gentle boys into tough men. Soldiers drilled and marched for long hours. They slept on the ground even in rain and snow. In combat, boys of 18 learned to stand firm as cannon blasts shook the earth and bullets whizzed past their ears.

As the death toll rose, the age restrictions for soldiers were relaxed. The South drafted boys as young as 17 and men as old as 50.

New technology added to the horror of war. Cone-shaped bullets made rifles twice as accurate. Improved cannons hurled exploding shells several miles. The new weapons had deadly results. In most battles, one fourth or more of the soldiers were killed or wounded.

Sick and wounded soldiers faced other horrors. Medical care on the battlefield was crude. Surgeons routinely amputated injured arms and legs. At the time, doctors did not know how germs cause infection and disease. As a result, minor wounds often became infected. In addition, poor sanitary conditions in the army camps allowed diseases to spread rapidly. Diseases such as pneumonia and malaria killed more men than guns or cannons did.

On both sides, prisoners of war faced horrifying conditions. At Andersonville, a prison camp in Georgia, many Union prisoners died of disease or starvation.

The difficult life of soldiers led many to desert. One out of every seven Union soldiers and one out of every nine Confederate soldiers deserted.

Opposition to War in the North

Some northerners opposed using force to keep the South in the Union. Supporters of the war called these people Copperheads, after the poisonous snake. Other northerners supported the war but opposed the way Lincoln was conducting it.

The Draft Law As the war dragged on, public support dwindled. When the war began, the North offered men money to enlist. However, some men abused the system. They would sign up, collect the money, and then desert. Soon, however, there was a shortage of volunteers to serve in the Union army.

Viewing History

Battlefield Medicine
Improved weapons during the Civil War made the injuries suffered by soldiers worse. Soldiers hit with the Minié ball suffered severe bone damage. Shown at left are the tools used by surgeons to amputate the limb. Unlike today, surgeons at that time worked without gloves, antiseptic, or masks. Now, there are better ways to care for wounds and, as shown at right, improved surgical procedures. **Drawing Conclusions** *How has technology been an advantage and a disadvantage in war?*

LINKING PAST AND PRESENT

▲ **Past**

▲ **Present**

Congress passed a **draft** law in 1863. It required all able-bodied males between the ages of 20 and 45 to serve in the military if they were called. Under the law, a man could avoid the draft by paying the government $300 or by hiring someone to serve in his place. This angered many people, who began to see the Civil War as "a rich man's war and a poor man's fight."

Riots in the Cities Opposition to the draft law led to riots in several northern cities. The law had gone into effect soon after Lincoln issued the Emancipation Proclamation. Some white northerners, especially recent immigrants in the cities, believed that they were being forced to fight to end slavery. They also worried that they would have to compete with free African Americans for jobs.

The worst riot took place in New York City during July 1863. For four days, white workers attacked free blacks. Rioters also attacked rich New Yorkers who had paid to avoid serving in the army. At least 74 people were killed during the riot.

President Lincoln moved to stop the riots and other "disloyal practices." Several times, he suspended **habeas corpus** (HAY bee uhs KOR puhs), the right to be charged or have a hearing before being jailed. Lincoln argued that the Constitution allowed him to deny people their rights "when in the cases of rebellion or invasion, the public safety may require it." The President also said that those arrested could be tried under the stricter rules of a military court. Eventually, nearly 14,000 people were arrested. However, most were never charged with a specific crime or brought to trial.

Problems in the South

President Davis, meanwhile, struggled to create a strong federal government for the Confederacy. Many southerners firmly believed in states' rights. They resisted paying taxes to a central government. At one point, Georgia even threatened to secede from the Confederacy!

Like the North, the South was forced to pass a draft law to fill its army. However, men who owned or supervised more than 20 slaves did not have to serve. Southern farmers who had few or no slaves resented this law.

Near the end of the war, the South no longer had enough white men to fill the ranks. Robert E. Lee urged that enslaved African Americans be allowed to serve as soldiers. Desperate, the Confederate congress finally agreed. The war ended, however, before any enslaved people put on Confederate uniforms.

AS YOU READ **Summarize** Write two or three sentences summarizing how the Civil War affected the northern economy.

The Northern Economy

The Civil War cost far more than any previous war. The Union had to use several strategies to raise money. In some ways, however, war helped the North's economy.

Taxation and Inflation To pay for the war, Congress established the nation's first **income tax,** or tax on people's earnings, in 1861. A new agency, the Internal Revenue Bureau, oversaw the collection process. The Union also issued bonds worth millions of dollars. Still, taxes and bonds did not raise enough money. To get the funds it needed, the North printed more than $400 million in paper money.

As the money supply increased, each dollar was worth less. In response, businesses charged more for their goods. The North was experiencing inflation, a rise in prices and a decrease in the value of money. During the war, prices for goods nearly doubled in the North.

Economic Benefits The war helped the North's economy in several ways. Since many farmers went off to fight, there was a greater need for machines to plant and harvest crops. The purchase of reapers rose to nearly 165,000 during the war. As a result, farm production actually went up during the war.

The wartime demand for clothing, shoes, guns, and other goods helped many northern industries. Some manufacturers made fortunes by profiteering. Profiteers charged excessive prices for goods that the government desperately needed for the war.

The Southern Economy

For the South, war brought economic ruin. The South had to struggle with the cost of the war, the loss of the cotton trade, and severe shortages brought on by the Union blockade.

The Economy Suffers To raise money, the Confederacy imposed an income tax and a tax-in-kind. The tax-in-kind required farmers to turn over one tenth of their crops to the government. The government took crops because it knew that southern farmers had little money.

Like the North, the South printed paper money. It printed so much that wild inflation set in. By 1865, one Confederate dollar was worth only two cents in gold. Prices were especially high in Richmond, where a barrel of flour was $275 in early 1864, potatoes were $25 a bushel, and butter was $15 a pound.

The war did serious damage to the cotton trade, the South's main source of income. Early in the war, President Davis halted cotton shipments to Britain. He hoped to force Britain to side with the South in return for renewed shipments of cotton. The tactic backfired. Britain simply bought more cotton from Egypt and India. Davis succeeded only in cutting the South's income.

Effects of the Blockade The Union blockade created severe shortages in the South. Confederate armies sometimes had to wait weeks for supplies of food and clothing. With few factories of its own, the South bought many of its weapons in Europe. However, the

Cause and Effect

Causes
- Issue of slavery in the territories divides the North and South
- Abolitionists want slavery to end
- South fears it will lose power in the national government
- Southern states secede after Lincoln's election
- Confederates bombard Fort Sumter

THE CIVIL WAR

Effects
- Lincoln issues the Emancipation Proclamation
- Northern economy booms
- South loses its cotton trade with Britain
- Total war destroys the South's economy
- Hundreds of thousands of Americans killed

Effects Today
- Disagreements over states' rights persist
- African Americans have equal protection under the Constitution
- Millions of Americans visit Civil War battlefields each year

GRAPHIC ORGANIZER
Skills

The Civil War was a major turning point in the history of the United States.

1. **Comprehension** How did the war affect the northern and southern economies?

2. **Critical Thinking Identifying Causes and Effects** Describe another cause or effect that could be added to this chart.

blockade cut off most deliveries from across the Atlantic. To acquire goods, the government began building and running factories. Private manufacturers were offered contracts and draft exemptions for their workers if they started making war goods.

For civilians, the blockade brought food shortages. The production of food became critical to the economy. Many plantations switched from growing cotton to raising grain and livestock, or animals raised for food. In some states, cotton production was limited.

Women in the War

Women of both the North and the South played vital roles during the war. As men left for the battlefields, women took jobs in industry and on farms.

Women's aid societies helped supply the troops with food, bedding, clothing, and medicine. Throughout the North, women held fairs and other fundraising events to pay for supplies.

Nursing the Wounded Women on both sides worked as nurses. At first, doctors were unwilling to permit even trained nurses to work in military hospitals. When wounded men began to swamp army hospitals, however, this attitude soon changed. In fact, women performed so well that nursing became an accepted occupation for women after the war.

Dorothea Dix, famous for her work reforming prisons and mental hospitals, and Clara Barton, who later founded the American Red Cross, both became nurses for the Union army. Sojourner Truth, the African American antislavery leader, worked in Union hospitals and in camps for freed slaves. In the South, Sally Tompkins set up a hospital in Richmond, Virginia.

Section 4 Assessment

Recall

1. **Identify** Explain the significance of **(a)** Copperhead, **(b)** Dorothea Dix, **(c)** Clara Barton, **(d)** Sojourner Truth, **(e)** Sally Tompkins.
2. **Define** **(a)** draft, **(b)** habeas corpus, **(c)** income tax, **(d)** inflation, **(e)** profiteer.

Comprehension

3. Describe three hardships faced by soldiers during the Civil War.
4. **(a)** Why did some northerners oppose the war? **(b)** How did the blockade affect the southern economy?

5. Describe three ways in which women contributed to the war effort.

Critical Thinking and Writing

6. **Exploring the Main Idea** Review the Main Idea statement at the beginning of this section. Then, write a diary entry describing conditions in the South during the later days of the Civil War.
7. **Linking Past and Present** **(a)** What advances in technology made Civil War battles deadly? **(b)** In what ways would war today be even more deadly?

ACTIVITY

Take It to the NET
Writing a Report
Use the Internet to find out more about Civil War medicine. Among the topics you might research are nurses, surgeons, field hospitals, battle wounds, and disease. Then, use what you find to write a report about battlefield medicine during the Civil War. Visit *The American Nation* section of **www.phschool.com** for help in completing the activity.

5 The War Ends

BEFORE YOU READ

Reading Focus

- Why were the Union victories at Vicksburg and Gettysburg important?
- What plan did Grant have for ending the war with the South?
- After his reelection, what hopes did Lincoln have for the Union?
- Why was the Civil War a major turning point in American history?

Key Terms

siege

Battle of Gettysburg

Pickett's Charge

Gettysburg Address

total war

Appomattox Court House

Taking Notes

Copy the flowchart. As you read the section, fill in the boxes with information about the conclusion of the war. Add as many boxes and bullets as you need.

Vicksburg
• Grant makes many attempts to capture
• Grant has brilliant plan
•

↓

Gettysburg
•
•

↓

↓

Main Idea Under the leadership of General Ulysses S. Grant, Union armies used their resources and manpower to defeat the Confederacy.

Setting the Scene

To General Ulysses S. Grant, every problem had a solution. For example, he needed telegraph lines to coordinate the march of his Union troops into the South. So, he had them strung as his troops advanced. Some of Grant's operators even learned to receive messages without a telegraph station. Touching the ends of the bare wires to their tongues, these resourceful men picked up the faint spark of the Morse Code signals.

In 1864, President Lincoln had appointed Ulysses S. Grant commander in chief of the Union army. "The art of war is simple," Grant said. "Find out where your enemy is, get at him as soon as you can and strike him as hard as you can, and keep moving on." It seemed the President had finally found the general who could lead the Union to victory.

The Fall of Vicksburg

As you have read, Confederate armies won major battles at Fredericksburg in December 1862 and at Chancellorsville in May 1863. These were gloomy days for the North. Then, in July 1863, the tide of war turned against the South as Union forces won major victories in both the East and the West.

In the West, Union triumph came along the Mississippi River. The Union, which had captured New Orleans and Memphis, already controlled both ends of the Mississippi River. Still, the Confederates held Vicksburg, Mississippi. Vicksburg sat on a cliff high above the river.

Early in 1863, Grant's forces tried again and again to seize Vicksburg. The Confederates held out bravely. At last, Grant devised a brilliant plan. Marching his troops inland, he launched a surprise attack on Jackson, Mississippi. Then, he turned west and attacked Vicksburg from the rear. (See the map on page 507.)

AS YOU READ **Civil War soldier on a telegraph pole**

Summarize How was the telegraph used in the war?

For more than six weeks, Grant's forces lay siege to Vicksburg. A **siege** is a military encirclement of an enemy position and blockading or bombarding it in order to force it to surrender. Finally, on July 4, 1863, the Confederates surrendered Vicksburg.

On July 9, Union forces also captured Port Hudson, Louisiana. The entire Mississippi was now under Union control. The Confederacy was split into two parts. Texas, Arkansas, and Louisiana were cut off from the rest of the Confederate states.

Union Victory at Gettysburg

Meanwhile, in the East, after his victory at Chancellorsville, General Lee moved his army north into Pennsylvania. He hoped to take the Yankees by surprise. If he succeeded in Pennsylvania, Lee planned to swing south and capture Washington, D.C.

On June 30, 1863, a Union force under General George C. Meade met part of Lee's army at the small town of Gettysburg, Pennsylvania. Both sides quickly sent in reinforcements. The three-day **Battle of Gettysburg** that followed was one of the most important battles of the Civil War.

On the first day of battle, July 1, the Confederates drove the Union forces out of Gettysburg. The Yankees, however, took up strong positions on Cemetery Ridge, overlooking the town.

The next day, Lee ordered an attack on both ends of the Union line. Southern troops fought hard, but the Union army was well prepared for Lee's offensive. At the end of a day of savage fighting, Lee's forces had suffered heavy casualties but failed to dislodge the Union army from its strong position.

Pickett's Charge Despite his losses, Lee decided to attack again. He wanted to "create a panic and virtually destroy the [Union] army." On July 3, he ordered General George Pickett to lead 15,000 men in a daring charge against the center of the Union line. To reach their target, Pickett's men would have to march 1,000 yards across open ground and climb up a steep slope within clear view of the enemy.

This last attack led by Pickett is known as **Pickett's Charge.** Pickett gave the order to charge. As the men rushed forward, Union guns opened fire. Row after row of soldiers fell to the ground, dead. The battle noise, one soldier recalled, was "strange and terrible, a sound that came from thousands of human throats . . . like a vast mournful roar."

Pickett's Charge failed. The steady barrage of bullets and shells kept all but a few Confederate soldiers from reaching the Union lines. The next day, a Union officer trying to ride over the battlefield could not because "the dead and wounded lay too thick to guide a horse through them."

As the survivors limped back, Lee rode among them. "It's all my fault," he admitted humbly. Lee had no choice but to retreat. After they were defeated at Gettysburg, the Confederates would never invade the North again.

Geography and History

The Vicksburg Campaign

Set on high bluffs overlooking the Mississippi River, Vicksburg was a major strategic target during the Civil War. If Union forces captured Vicksburg, they would control the river and split the Confederacy into two parts. "Vicksburg is the key!" said President Lincoln.

The swamps, rivers, and bluffs around Vicksburg made a direct attack almost impossible. At the same time, Confederate artillery, perched high above the Mississippi, could easily blast Union ships attempting to sail past the city.

In the end, General Grant determined that the only way to subdue Vicksburg was to lay siege to the city. After 48 days of being cut off from all supplies and of constant hammering by cannon fire, the Confederates finally surrendered.

Analyze the effect of geography on the Battle of Vicksburg.

Union Advances in the South

General Meade was proud of the victory. Lincoln, however, was disappointed. He felt that the Union army had once again allowed the Confederate troops to get away.

The Union victories at Vicksburg and Gettysburg marked the turning point of the Civil War. It seemed just a matter of time before the Confederacy would fall. However, the South was still determined to fight. The war would last another two years.

The Gettysburg Address

The Battle of Gettysburg left more than 50,000 dead or wounded. On November 19, 1863, there was a ceremony to dedicate a cemetery to the memory of those soldiers who died in the battle. President Lincoln attended the ceremony. He delivered a speech now known as the Gettysburg Address. Lincoln said that the Civil War was a test of whether or not a democratic nation could survive. He reminded Americans that their nation was founded on the belief that "all men are created equal." Lincoln told the audience:

> 66 We here highly resolve that these dead shall not have died in vain—that this nation, under God, shall have a new birth of freedom—and that government of the people, by the people, for the people, shall not perish from the earth. 99

—Abraham Lincoln, Gettysburg Address, November 19, 1863

GEOGRAPHY Skills

As the Civil War dragged on, Union armies advanced deeper and deeper into the South. General Sherman marched his troops through Georgia and the Carolinas.

1. **Location** On the map, locate **(a)** Vicksburg, **(b)** Atlanta, **(c)** Savannah.

2. **Place** What three Confederate states were cut off from the rest of the Confederacy after Union forces gained control of the Mississippi River?

3. **Critical Thinking Applying Information** Based on the map, why would the South suffer more damage than the North—no matter who won the war?

Primary Sources

See Abraham Lincoln, "The Gettysburg Address," on page 605 of the Reference Section.

Lincoln's entire speech was only ten sentences long and took about three minutes to deliver, but it is honored as a profound statement of American ideals.

Grant's Plan for Total War

Since the beginning of the war, Lincoln had searched for a general who could lead the Union to victory. More and more, he thought of Ulysses S. Grant. After capturing Vicksburg, Grant continued to win battles in the West. In 1864, Lincoln appointed him commander of the Union forces.

Some questioned the choice, but President Lincoln felt that "Unconditional Surrender" Grant was the general who would end the war in the Union's favor. "I can't spare this man," Lincoln said. "He fights."

Grant had a plan for ending the war. He wanted to destroy the South's ability to fight. To achieve this, Grant ordered his generals to wage total war against the South. He wanted the Union army to destroy food, equipment, and anything else they found that might be useful to the enemy. In the past, war had been restricted to soldiers. Total war, however, did not make any distinctions. Civilians in the South suffered the same hardships as the army.

AS YOU READ **Find Main Ideas** As you read, look for specific examples of Grant's strategy for waging total war.

Sheridan in the Shenandoah To set his plan in motion, Grant sent General Philip Sheridan and his cavalry into the rich farmland of Virginia's Shenandoah Valley. He instructed Sheridan:

> ❝ Leave nothing to invite the enemy to return. Destroy whatever cannot be consumed. Let the valley be left so that crows flying over it will have to carry their rations along with them. ❞
> —Ulysses S. Grant, quoted in Bruce Catton, *Grant Takes Command*

Sheridan obeyed. In the summer and fall of 1864, he marched through the valley, destroying farms and livestock. During the campaign, Sheridan's troops burned 2,000 barns filled with grain. There was nothing left for Lee's troops or for southern civilians.

Sherman's March to the Sea Grant also ordered General William Tecumseh Sherman to capture Atlanta, Georgia, and then march to the Atlantic coast. Like Sheridan, Sherman had orders to destroy everything useful to the South.

Sherman's troops captured Atlanta in September 1864. They began their campaign by turning the people of Atlanta out of their homes and burning a large part of the city. Then, Sherman began his "march to the sea."

As they marched through Georgia, Sherman's troops ripped up railroad tracks, built bonfires from the ties, then heated and twisted the rails. They killed livestock and tore up fields. They burned barns, homes, bridges, and factories.

Lincoln Is Reelected

Lincoln ran for reelection in 1864. At first, his defeat seemed, in his own words, "exceedingly probable." Before the capture of Atlanta,

Union chances for victory looked bleak. Lincoln knew that many northerners were unhappy with his handling of the war. He thought that this might cost him the election.

The Democrats nominated General George McClellan to oppose Lincoln. They adopted a resolution demanding the immediate "cessation of hostilities" against the South. Although he had commanded the Union army, McClellan was willing to compromise with the Confederacy. If peace could be achieved, he was ready to restore slavery.

Then, in September, Sherman took Atlanta, and the North rallied around Lincoln. Sheridan's smashing victories in the Shenandoah Valley in October further increased Lincoln's popular support. In the election in November, the vote was close, but Lincoln remained President.

In his second Inaugural Address, Lincoln looked forward to the coming of peace:

66 With malice toward none, with charity for all . . . let us strive . . . to bind up the nation's wounds . . . to do all which may achieve a just and a lasting peace among ourselves and with all nations. 99

—Abraham Lincoln, Second Inaugural Address

The Civil War Ends

Grant had begun a drive to capture Richmond in May 1864. Throughout the spring and summer, he and Lee fought a series of costly battles.

Northerners read with horror that 60,000 men were killed or wounded in a single month at the battles of the Wilderness, Spotsylvania, and Cold Harbor. Still, Grant pressed on. He knew that the Union could replace men and supplies. The South could not.

Lee dug in at Petersburg, near Richmond. Here, Grant kept Lee under siege for nine months. At last, with a fresh supply of troops, Grant took Petersburg on April 2, 1865. The same day, Richmond fell.

Lee and his army withdrew to a small Virginia town called **Appomattox Court House.** There, a week later, they were trapped by Union troops. Lee knew that his men would be slaughtered if he kept fighting. On April 9, 1865, Lee surrendered.

At Appomattox Court House, Grant offered generous terms of surrender to the defeated Confederate army. Soldiers were required to turn over their rifles, but officers were allowed to keep their pistols. Soldiers who had horses could keep them. Grant knew that southerners would need the animals for spring plowing. Finally, ordered Grant, "each officer and man will be allowed to return to his home, not to be disturbed by the United States authorities."

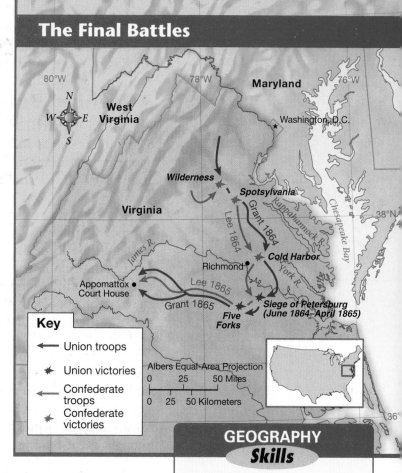

The Final Battles

Key

← Union troops

✴ Union victories

← Confederate troops

✴ Confederate victories

Albers Equal-Area Projection
0   25   50 Miles
0   25   50 Kilometers

GEOGRAPHY Skills

The final battles of the Civil War pitted Grant against Lee in Virginia. Finally, on April 9, 1865, Lee surrendered at Appomattox Court House.

1. **Location** On the map, locate **(a)** Richmond, **(b)** Petersburg, **(c)** Appomattox Court House.

2. **Place** Where did Grant lay siege to Lee's forces for nine months?

3. **Critical Thinking Applying Information** Which battle took place first: Cold Harbor or Spotsylvania? Explain.

As the Confederates surrendered, Union soldiers began to cheer. Grant ordered them to be silent. "The war is over," he said. "The rebels are our countrymen again."

A Turning Point in American History

The toll of the Civil War was immense. More than 360,000 Union soldiers and 250,000 Confederate soldiers lost their lives. No war has ever resulted in more American deaths. In dollars, the war's cost was about 20 billion. That was more than 11 times the entire amount spent by the federal government between 1789 and 1861!

The Civil War was a major turning point in American history. The balance of power was changed. The Democratic party lost its influence and the Republicans were in a commanding position. No longer would Americans speak of the nation as a confederation of states. Before the war, Americans referred to "*these* United States." After, they began speaking of "*the* United States." The idea that each state might secede, if it chose, was dead. As a result, the power of the federal government grew.

The war also put an end to slavery in the United States. For years, Americans had debated whether slavery could exist in a nation dedicated to the ideals of liberty and equality. By the war's end, millions of African Americans had gained their freedom. Millions more Americans, both North and South, began to think about what it meant to be free and equal.

To be sure, a long and difficult struggle for equality lay ahead. Yet, Lincoln's words at Gettysburg were prophetic: "We here highly resolve . . . that this nation, under God, shall have a new birth of freedom." From out of a cruel, bitter, often heart-rending war, the United States did indeed emerge a stronger, freer nation.

Section 5 Assessment

Recall

1. **Identify** Explain the significance of **(a)** Battle of Vicksburg, **(b)** Battle of Gettysburg, **(c)** Pickett's Charge, **(d)** Gettysburg Address, **(e)** Ulysses S. Grant, **(f)** William Tecumseh Sherman, **(g)** Appomattox Court House.
2. **Define** **(a)** siege, **(b)** total war.

Comprehension

3. Which Union victories were a turning point?
4. What was Grant's plan for ending the war?
5. What ideals did Lincoln express in the Gettysburg Address and his Second Inaugural Address?

6. How did the Civil War change the United States?

Critical Thinking and Writing

7. **Exploring the Main Idea** Review the Main Idea statement at the beginning of this section. Then, make a list of the major events of the years 1863–1865 of the Civil War. Indicate the importance of each.
8. **Supporting a Point of View** Some people believe that Grant's decision to wage total war on the South was wrong because it caused great suffering among civilians. Do you agree or disagree? Explain.

ACTIVITY

Writing a Speech
Suppose that you are President of the United States at the end of the Civil War. Write a speech summarizing the important events of the war and explaining what you believe the Union victory accomplished.

Analyzing Photographs

When the Civil War began, photography was just beginning. Pioneer photographers shouldered their bulky cameras and followed armies into battle. The result was the first detailed photographic record of a war.

These Civil War photographs, like all photographs, are valuable primary source documents. Just as with other primary sources, however, we must learn to evaluate them for accuracy and bias.

In this photograph, a family gathers at a Union Army camp in 1862.

Learn the Skill *To analyze a photograph, use the following steps:*

1. **Identify the subject.** What does the photograph show?

2. **Look for details.** What evidence does the photograph include about people, daily life, the weather, events, or the environment?

3. **Analyze the photographer's intent.** Why did the photographer take this picture? How did the photographer feel about the subject?

4. **Draw conclusions.** What can you learn from this photograph? How does it add to your understanding of history?

Practice the Skill *Answer the following questions about the photograph above:*

1. **(a)** Who are the people in the photograph? **(b)** Where are they?

2. **(a)** What tools, utensils, and furniture do you see? **(b)** Where are the people living? **(c)** What other details do you see?

3. **(a)** Why do you think the photographer took this picture? **(b)** How do you think the photographer felt about families and war?

4. What did you learn from this photograph?

Apply the Skill *See the Chapter Review and Assessment.*

CREATING A CHAPTER SUMMARY

Copy the timeline below. As you read, add information about the events and issues of the Civil War. Add as many entries as you need.

BATTLE OF BULL RUN
North and South realize war will be long and hard

1861   1862   1865

iTEXT

For additional review and enrichment activities, see the interactive version of *The American Nation,* available on the Web and on CD-ROM.

Take It to the NET

Chapter Self-Test For practice test questions for Chapter 17, visit *The American Nation* section of **www.phschool.com**.

Building Vocabulary

Review the meaning of the vocabulary words listed below. Then, write a sentence for each word in which you define the word and describe its relationship to the Civil War.

1. border state
2. martial law
3. emancipate
4. draft
5. habeas corpus
6. inflation
7. profiteer
8. total war

Reviewing Key Facts

9. Why did each side go to war? (Section 1)
10. Why was President Lincoln unhappy with General McClellan? (Section 2)
11. (a) What did the Emancipation Proclamation provide? (b) How did it change the nature of the war? (Section 3)
12. (a) Why did some northerners object to the draft law? (b) What was the response to the draft law in the South? (Section 4)
13. How did the Union wage total war on the South in 1864 and 1865? (Section 5)

Critical Thinking and Writing

14. **Making Generalizations** Make a generalization about the strengths and weaknesses of the North and South at the start of the war. List three facts to support your generalization.
15. **Summarizing** Write one or two sentences summarizing Lincoln's attitudes toward slavery and the war.
16. **Making Comparisons** How did the North's General Grant and the South's General Lee compare as military leaders?
17. **Connecting to Geography: Movement** Describe the effects of the Union blockade of southern ports.
18. **Synthesizing Information** Review the excerpt from Lincoln's Second Inaugural Address on page 509. How did Grant's treatment of the defeated Confederate army at Appomattox Court House reflect the ideas in the Inaugural Address?

Analyzing Primary Sources

The Union blockade caused great difficulty for southern families. Dr. Paul Barringer recalls how his family managed. Read the excerpt, then answer the questions that follow:

> 66 Almost at once we began to feel the pinch of war. White sugar disappeared immediately; not only were there no more lumps for gun-shy horses, but there was no sugar for the table. There was, however, an unlimited quantity of sorghum syrup, and around the barrels of sorghum, a thick crust of brown sugar often formed. This was carefully scraped off to be served with coffee and berries, the fluid product going to the slaves. 99
>
> —Dr. Paul B. Barringer, *The Natural Bent: The Memories of Dr. Paul Barringer*

19. According to Barringer, how soon were southerners affected by the blockade?
20. How was sugar used?
21. What substitute was used for sugar?
22. How did southerners meet the challenges posed by the blockade?

Analyzing Photographs

Mathew Brady took this picture of Abraham Lincoln and his son, Tad, in 1864. Look at the picture. Then, answer the questions that follow.

23. What details are emphasized in the photograph?
   A Lincoln's position in the chair.
   B His son's lack of interest in the book.
   C The concentration of Lincoln and his son.
   D Tad's hand resting on his father's chair.
24. What can you learn about Lincoln from this photograph?

ACTIVITIES

Connecting With . . . Economics

Making a Chart You are the graphic illustrator for an economics magazine. Create a flowchart to illustrate how the high cost of the Civil War led to inflation.

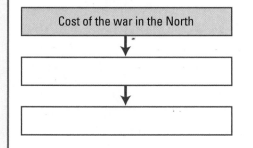

Cost of the war in the North

Take It to the NET

Connecting to Today

Planning a TV Documentary The Civil War ended slavery for African Americans. Use the Internet to find out how African Americans fight for equality today. Choose a leader in the civil rights movement. Use what you learn to write an outline for a TV documentary on the person of your choice. For help in starting this activity, visit *The American Nation* section of **www.phschool.com**.

Researching Civil War Photos

Creating a Photo Essay Photographers like Mathew Brady took thousands of pictures documenting the Civil War. Use the Internet to find photographs taken of the war. Then, download selected pictures to create a photo essay of the war. Write a caption for each photograph that you include. For help in starting this activity, visit *The American Nation* section of **www.phschool.com**.

Reconstruction and the Changing South

1863–1896

1 **Early Steps to Reunion**
2 **Radical Reconstruction**
3 **The South Under Reconstruction**
4 **The End of Reconstruction**

Reward poster (left) and chair in which Lincoln was shot (right)

Thaddeus Stevens

AMERICAN EVENTS

1863
President Abraham Lincoln proposes a mild Reconstruction plan for readmitting southern states after the Civil War.

1865
Lincoln is assassinated five days after the war ends. As the nation mourns, the issue of readmitting southern states remains unresolved.

1867
Radical Reconstruction begins. Republican leaders in Congress like Thaddeus Stevens call for harsh measures against the South.

Presidential Terms:	Abraham Lincoln 1861-1865	Andrew Johnson 1865–1869	Ulysses S. Grant 1869-1877

1860 1865 1870

WORLD EVENTS

1867 ▲
The Dominion of Canada is formed.

1870 ▲
Italy becomes a unified nation.

The South After the Civil War

One by one, southern states rejoined the Union after the Civil War.

Key

Former Confederate states

(1868) Date of readmission to the Union

Albers Equal-Area Projection

0   200   400 Miles
0   200   400 Kilometers

Virginia (1870)
North Carolina (1868)
Tennessee (1866)
SC (1868)
Arkansas (1868)
MS (1870)
Alabama (1868)
Georgia (1870)
LA (1868)
Texas (1870)
FL (1868)

ATLANTIC OCEAN
Gulf of Mexico
MEXICO
CUBA (Sp.)

Hayes campaign poster

1870

Voting during Reconstruction

The Fifteenth Amendment is ratified. It forbids states to deny citizens the right to vote because of race.

1876

Rutherford B. Hayes runs against Samuel Tilden in a disputed election. In time, Hayes becomes President and ends Reconstruction.

James A. Garfield	1881
Chester A. Arthur	1881–1885
Grover Cleveland	1885–1889
Benjamin Harrison	1889–1893
Grover Cleveland	1893–1897
William McKinley	1897–1901

Rutherford B. Hayes 1877–1881

1896

In *Plessy* v. *Ferguson*, the Supreme Court rules that it is legal for a state to create separate facilities for blacks and whites.

1870   **1875**   **1900**

1873 ▲
Slave markets are abolished in Zanzibar.

▲ **1876**
Porfirio Díaz becomes the leader of Mexico.

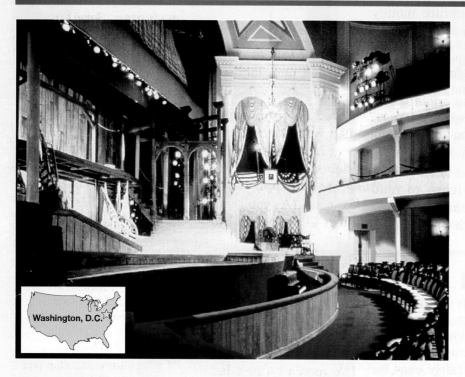

Ford's Theatre

On April 14, 1865, John Wilkes Booth crept into Abraham Lincoln's box at Ford's Theatre. As the President watched the comedy Our American Cousin, *Booth shot him. Today, park rangers at the restored theatre recount the story of the tragic assassination. You can visit a museum devoted to Lincoln's death—and even attend a play.*

Washington, D.C.

Take It to the NET

Virtual Field Trip For an interactive look at Ford's Theatre, visit *The American Nation* section of **www.phschool.com**.

AS YOU READ **Find Main Ideas** As you read, identify the major goals and accomplishments of the Freedmen's Bureau.

One of the bureau's most important tasks was to set up schools for freedmen. Most of the teachers were volunteers, often women, from the North. Grandparents and grandchildren sat side by side in the classroom. Charlotte Forten, an African American volunteer from Philadelphia, wrote:

> **❝** It is wonderful how a people who have been so long crushed to the earth . . . can have so great a desire for knowledge, and such a capacity for attaining it. **❞**
>
> —Charlotte Forten, article in the *Atlantic Monthly*

The Freedmen's Bureau laid the foundation for the South's public school system. It also created colleges for African Americans, including Howard, Morehouse, and Fisk. Many of the graduates of these schools became teachers themselves. By the 1870s, African Americans were teaching in grade schools throughout the South.

Lincoln Is Assassinated

President Lincoln hoped to persuade Congress to accept his Reconstruction plan. However, he never got the chance.

On April 14, 1865, just five days after Lee's surrender, the President attended a play at Ford's Theatre in Washington, D.C. A popular actor from the South, John Wilkes Booth, crept into the President's box and shot Lincoln in the head. Lincoln died the next morning. Booth was later caught and killed in a barn outside the city.

The nation was plunged into grief. Millions who had been celebrating the war's end now mourned Lincoln's death. "Now he belongs to the ages," commented Secretary of War Edwin Stanton.

The New President

Vice President Andrew Johnson was now President. Johnson had represented Tennessee in Congress. When his state seceded, Johnson had remained loyal to the Union.

Johnson's Plan Republicans in Congress believed Johnson would support a strict Reconstruction plan. But his plan was much milder than expected. It called for a majority of voters in each southern state to pledge loyalty to the United States. Each state also had to ratify the Thirteenth Amendment, which Congress had approved in January 1865. It banned slavery throughout the nation. (As you read, the Emancipation Proclamation did not free slaves in states loyal to the Union.)

Congress Rebels The southern states quickly met Johnson's conditions. As a result, the President approved their new state governments in late 1865. Voters in the South then elected representatives to Congress. Many of those elected had held office in the Confederacy. For example, Alexander Stephens, the former vice president of the Confederacy, was elected senator from Georgia.

Republicans in Congress were outraged. The men who had led the South out of the Union were being elected to the House and Senate. Also, no southern state allowed African Americans to vote.

When the new Congress met, Republicans refused to let southern representatives take their seats. Instead, they set up a Joint Committee on Reconstruction to form a new plan for the South. The stage was set for a showdown between Congress and the President.

Section 1 Assessment

Recall

1. **Identify** Explain the significance of **(a)** Reconstruction, **(b)** Ten Percent Plan, **(c)** Wade-Davis Bill, **(d)** Freedmen's Bureau, **(e)** John Wilkes Booth, **(f)** Andrew Johnson, **(g)** Thirteenth Amendment.
2. **Define (a)** freedmen, **(b)** amnesty.

Comprehension

3. Describe two problems faced by the South after the Civil War.
4. What early Reconstruction measure did Lincoln and Congress agree upon?

5. Why did Republicans in Congress oppose Johnson's Reconstruction plan?

Critical Thinking and Writing

6. **Exploring the Main Idea** Review the Main Idea statement at the beginning of this section. Then, write a letter to President Lincoln supporting or opposing his Reconstruction plan.
7. **Drawing Inferences** One teacher said that freedmen "will starve themselves in order to send their children to school." Write a paragraph explaining why you think education meant so much to the freedmen.

ACTIVITY

Take It to the NET **Conducting an Interview** Use the Internet to find out more about the assassination of Lincoln. With a partner, act out an interview between a reporter and a witness to the event. Visit *The American Nation* section of **www.phschool.com** for help in completing the activity.

Learning how to solve problems is an important skill for both citizens and government leaders. Just as the solutions to problems of the past affect the present, the solutions you choose today will have consequences in the future.

African American writer W.E.B. DuBois described some of the problems faced by the Freedmen's Bureau:

66Here, at a stroke of the pen, was erected a government of millions of men,—and not ordinary men, either, but black men [weakened] by a peculiarly complete system of slavery, centuries old; and now, suddenly, violently, they come into a new birthright, at a time of war and passion, in the midst of the stricken, embittered population of their former masters. Any man might well have hesitated to assume charge of such a work, with vast responsibilities, indefinite powers, and limited resources . . . for Congress had appropriated no money for salaries and expenses.99

—W.E.B. DuBois, "The Freedmen's Bureau"

As it set up new schools throughout the South, the Freedmen's Bureau faced the problem of finding enough teachers for so many eager new students.

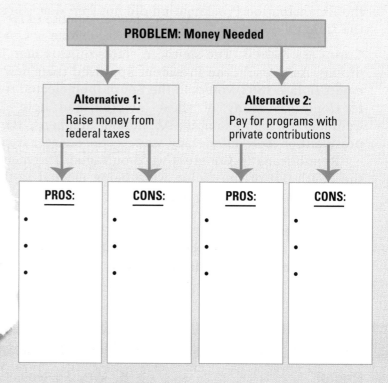

PROBLEM: Money Needed

Alternative 1: Raise money from federal taxes

Alternative 2: Pay for programs with private contributions

PROS:
CONS:
PROS:
CONS:

Learn the Skill *To learn problem-solving skills, use the following steps:*

1. **Identify the problem.** State the problem you want to solve as simply and completely as possible.

2. **List possible solutions.** There is usually more than one way to solve a problem. Identify your alternatives.

3. **Review the alternatives.** What resources would be needed to implement the solution? What would the consequences be?

4. **Choose a course of action.** Decide how you will resolve the problem.

Practice the Skill *Use the information above to answer the following questions:*

1. According to DuBois what was one problem that the Freedmen's Bureau faced?

2. **(a)** What two alternatives are shown on the chart? **(b)** Can you think of a third alternative? Explain.

3. **(a)** What might be some of the pros and cons of Alternative 1? **(b)** What might be some of the pros and cons of Alternative 2?

4. What solution to the problem would you have favored? Why?

Apply the Skill *See the Chapter Review and Assessment.*

2 Radical Reconstruction

BEFORE YOU READ

Reading Focus

- How did Congress react to the passage of black codes in the South?
- How did Radical Republicans gain power in Congress?
- Why was President Johnson impeached?

Key Terms

black codes

Radical Republican

Fourteenth Amendment

Radical Reconstruction

Reconstruction Act

impeach

Fifteenth Amendment

Taking Notes

Copy the chart below. As you read, complete the chart to show some of the effects of the rise of Radical Republicans in Congress. Add as many boxes as you need.

RISE OF RADICAL REPUBLICANS

Congress passes Fourteenth Amendment

Main Idea Angered by the South's response to President Johnson's Reconstruction program, Republicans in Congress put in place a harsher plan.

Setting the Scene

In New Orleans, Confederate flags were being sold in the streets. In Mississippi, the governor refused to fly the American flag over the state capitol. Many southerners were singing, "I'm a good old rebel, that's what I am / And I don't want no pardon for anything I done." Hearing such reports in 1866, Republicans decided to take harsh measures against the South.

Black Codes Anger Congress

After the war, most southern states promptly ratified the Thirteenth Amendment. However, southern legislatures also passed **black codes,** laws that severely limited the rights of freedmen.

Rights and Restrictions The black codes did grant some rights. For example, African Americans could marry legally and own some kinds of property. Still, the codes were clearly meant to keep freedmen from gaining political or economic power.

Black codes forbade freedmen to vote, own guns, or serve on juries. In some states, African Americans were permitted to work only as servants or farm laborers. In others, they had to sign contracts for a year's work. Those without contracts could be arrested and sentenced to work on a plantation.

Congress Reacts Republicans charged that Johnson's lenient Reconstruction plan had encouraged southern legislatures to pass the black codes. Republicans were also outraged by reports of violence against freedmen. In 1866, angry whites burned homes, churches, and schoolhouses in a black section of Memphis, Tennessee. More than 40 African Americans were killed. Similar riots broke out in New Orleans when freedmen met to support the right to vote.

A report by the Joint Committee on Reconstruction accused the South of trying to "preserve slavery . . . as long as possible." When

AS YOU READ **Confederate flag**
Draw Inferences What do these incidents suggest about the mood of many southerners at this time?

Rival Plans for Reconstruction

Plan	Ten Percent Plan	Wade-Davis Bill	Johnson Plan	Reconstruction Act
Proposed by	President Abraham Lincoln (1863)	Republicans in Congress (1864)	President Andrew Johnson (1865)	Radical Republicans (1867)
Conditions for Former Confederate States to Rejoin Union	• 10 percent of voters must swear loyalty to Union • Must abolish slavery	• Majority of white men must swear loyalty • Former Confederate volunteers cannot vote or hold office	• Majority of white men must swear loyalty • Must ratify Thirteenth Amendment • Former Confederate officials may vote and hold office	• Must disband state governments • Must write new constitutions • Must ratify Fourteenth Amendment • African American men must be allowed to vote

GRAPHIC ORGANIZER
Skills

In the early years of Reconstruction, federal leaders debated several plans for readmitting southern states to the Union.

1. **Comprehension**
   (a) Identify one similarity between the Wade-Davis Bill and President Johnson's plan. **(b)** Identify one difference.

2. **Critical Thinking**
   Evaluating Information Which of the plans shown here seems to be the harshest toward the South? Explain.

Civics

President Johnson ignored the report, members of Congress called Radical Republicans vowed to take control of Reconstruction.

Rise of the Radicals

The Radicals were led by Thaddeus Stevens of Pennsylvania in the House and Charles Sumner of Massachusetts in the Senate. Radical Republicans had two main goals. First, they wanted to break the power of wealthy planters who had long ruled the South. Second, they wanted to ensure that freedmen received the right to vote.

Republican Control Radicals needed the support of moderate Republicans, the largest group in Congress. Moderates and Radicals disagreed on many issues, but they shared a strong political motive. Most southerners were Democrats. With southerners barred from Congress, Republicans could control both houses.

To combat the black codes, Congress passed the Civil Rights Act in April 1866. It gave citizenship to African Americans. When Johnson vetoed the bill, Congress overrode the veto.

Fourteenth Amendment Republicans feared that the Supreme Court might use its power of judicial review to declare the Civil Rights Act unconstitutional. In the Dred Scott decision of 1857, the Court had ruled that African Americans were not citizens. To avoid a similar ruling, Republicans proposed the Fourteenth Amendment. It defined citizens as "all persons born or naturalized in the United States." (The amendment did not apply to most Native Americans.) It guaranteed citizens "equal protection of the laws" and forbade states to "deprive any person of life, liberty, or property without due process of law." Thus, states could not legally discriminate against a citizen on unreasonable grounds, such as race.

Under the Fourteenth Amendment, any state that denied any male citizen age 21 or older the right to vote would have its representation in Congress reduced. Republicans believed that freedmen would be able to defend their rights if they could vote.

Republicans hoped the amendment would secure basic political rights for African Americans in the South. That goal would take a century to achieve. In the 1950s, the Fourteenth Amendment became a powerful tool in the struggle for citizenship rights.

Radicals in Power

President Johnson encouraged former Confederate states to reject the Fourteenth Amendment. He also decided to make the amendment an issue in the 1866 congressional elections.

Election of 1866 Across the North, Johnson urged voters to reject the Radicals. When a heckler yelled for Johnson to hang Jefferson Davis, Johnson shouted, "Why not hang Thad Stevens?" Many northerners criticized the President for losing his temper.

In July, white mobs in New Orleans killed 34 African Americans. The violence convinced many northerners that stronger measures were needed. In the end, the elections were a disaster for Johnson. Republicans won majorities in both houses of Congress.

The Radical Program In 1867, Republicans in Congress prepared to take charge of Reconstruction. With huge majorities in both houses, Congress could easily override a veto. The period that followed is often called **Radical Reconstruction.**

Congress passed the first **Reconstruction Act** in March 1867. It threw out the state governments that had refused to ratify the Fourteenth Amendment—all the former Confederate states except Tennessee. The act also divided the South into five military districts. Army commanders were given broad powers to enforce Reconstruction. Many southerners bitterly resented the imposition of military rule.

To rejoin the Union, former Confederate states had to write new constitutions and ratify the Fourteenth Amendment. The Reconstruction Act also required that southern states allow African Americans to vote.

With the new constitutions in place, reconstructed states held elections to set up new state governments. Former Confederate officials were barred from voting. Many other white southerners stayed away from the polls in protest. Protected by the army, freedmen proudly exercised their new right to vote. As a result, Republicans gained control of all of the new southern state governments.

Impeachment and a New President

Congress passed other Reconstruction acts over Johnson's veto. As President, Johnson had a duty to execute the new laws. However, Johnson did what he could to limit their effect. He fired several military commanders who supported Radical Reconstruction. Republicans in Congress decided to remove Johnson from office.

Trial On February 24, 1868, the House of Representatives voted to impeach, or bring formal charges against, Johnson. According to the Constitution, the House may impeach a President for "treason,

AS YOU READ Summarize Explain why the Fourteenth Amendment was a powerful tool in the struggle for citizenship rights.

Primary Source

The Impeachment of Andrew Johnson

At the impeachment trial of President Johnson, Senator James Grimes of Iowa voted against conviction. Here, he explains why:
"Nor can I suffer my judgment of the law governing this case to be influenced by political considerations. I cannot agree to destroy the harmonious working of the Constitution for the sake of getting rid of an unacceptable President. Whatever may be my opinion of [Johnson], I cannot consent to trifle with the high office he holds. I can do nothing which, by implication, may be [seen as] an approval of impeachment as a part of future political machinery."

—James Grimes, quoted in *Trial of Andrew Johnson* (Poore)

Analyzing Primary Sources

Write a sentence summarizing the main reason that Grimes voted against the removal of President Johnson.

bribery, or other high crimes and misdemeanors." The President is removed from office if found guilty by two thirds of the Senate.

During Johnson's trial, it became clear that he was not guilty of high crimes and misdemeanors. Even Charles Sumner, Johnson's bitter foe, admitted that the charges were "political in character."

Despite intense pressure, seven Republican senators refused to vote for conviction. The Constitution, they said, did not allow Congress to remove a President just because they disagreed with him. In the end, the vote was 35 to 19—one vote shy of the two thirds needed to convict.

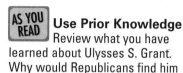

Use Prior Knowledge Review what you have learned about Ulysses S. Grant. Why would Republicans find him an attractive candidate?

A New President Johnson served out the few remaining months of his term. In 1868, Republicans nominated the Union's greatest war hero, Ulysses S. Grant, for President.

By election day, most southern states had rejoined the Union. As Congress demanded, the southern governments allowed African American men to vote. About 500,000 blacks voted—nearly all of them for Grant. He easily won the election.

Fifteenth Amendment In 1869, Congress proposed the Fifteenth Amendment. It forbade any state to deny any citizen the right to vote because of "race, color, or previous condition of servitude."

Republicans had moral and political reasons for supporting the Fifteenth Amendment. They remembered the great sacrifices made by African American soldiers in the Civil War. They also felt it was wrong to let African Americans vote in the South but not in the North. In addition, Republicans knew that if African Americans could vote in the North, they would help Republicans win elections there.

The Fifteenth Amendment was ratified in 1870. At last, all African American men over age 21 had the right to vote.

Section 2 Assessment

Recall
1. **Identify** Explain the significance of (a) Radical Republicans, (b) Thaddeus Stevens, (c) Charles Sumner, (d) Fourteenth Amendment, (e) Radical Reconstruction, (f) Reconstruction Act, (g) Fifteenth Amendment.
2. **Define** (a) black codes, (b) impeach.

Comprehension
3. Why did the black codes anger Republicans in Congress?
4. How did Radical Republicans win control of Congress?

5. Why did Congress impeach President Johnson?

Critical Thinking and Writing
6. **Exploring the Main Idea** Review the Main Idea statement at the beginning of this section. Then, write two sentences evaluating the Reconstruction Act— one from Andrew Johnson's viewpoint, the other from a Radical Republican's viewpoint.
7. **Supporting a Point of View** Write a note from one member of Congress to another explaining why you think the Fourteenth or Fifteenth Amendment is necessary.

ACTIVITY

Drawing a Political Cartoon Draw a political cartoon that might have appeared during the congressional elections of 1866. Your cartoon should express a point of view about the conflict between Radical Republicans and the President over control of Reconstruction.

The Power of the Fourteenth Amendment

The Fourteenth Amendment was originally intended to grant citizenship to former slaves and to ensure their rights. As society changed, the Court's interpretation of the Fourteenth Amendment changed as well.

> " ...No State shall make or enforce any law which shall abridge the privileges or immunities of citizens of the United States; nor shall any State deprive any person of life, liberty, or property, without due process of law; nor deny to any person within its jurisdiction the equal protection of the laws. "
>
> —Fourteenth Amendment

1905

Lochner v. *New York*

The Supreme Court strikes down a law regulating working hours. The Court rules that **equal protection** means that employers have the right to make contracts with workers freely. This ruling is later reversed.

1954

Brown v. *Board of Education of Topeka*

The Supreme Court rules that having separate schools for white and black students discriminates against African Americans and is a violation of **equal protection.** The ruling ends school segregation and becomes a landmark in the fight for equal rights.

1963

Gideon v. *Wainwright*

The Supreme Court rules that **due process** means that all people accused of a crime have the right to an attorney. If a person cannot afford an attorney, the state must provide one for her or him.

1971

Reed v. *Reed*

The Supreme Court strikes down an Idaho law giving men automatic preference over women in certain situations. The Court rules that **equal protection** means that men and women must be treated equally before the law.

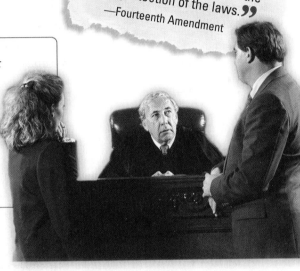

ACTIVITY

The Fourteenth Amendment has affected every citizen's life in some way. List two ways in which your life has been or might be affected by the Fourteenth Amendment.

3 The South Under Reconstruction

Reading Focus

- What groups of people made up the new forces in southern politics?
- How did southern Conservatives resist Reconstruction?
- What challenges did Reconstruction governments face?
- How did many southerners become locked into a cycle of poverty?

Key Terms

scalawag

carpetbagger

Conservatives

Ku Klux Klan

sharecropper

Taking Notes

As you read, prepare an outline of this section. Use roman numerals to indicate the major headings, capital letters for the sub-headings, and numbers for the supporting details. The sample at right will help you get started.

> I. New Forces in Southern Politics
>   A. White southern Republicans
>   1. Opposed secession
>   2.
>   B. Northerners
>   1.
>   2.
>   C.
> II. Conservatives Resist
>   A.
>   B.

Main Idea Reconstruction governments tried to rebuild the South despite sometimes fierce opposition.

Meeting of a southern legislature
Visualize Picture the scene as freedmen crowded in to watch the debate. How would you describe the mood?

Setting the Scene White superintendents in Virginia's tobacco factories were puzzled. Suddenly, many of their black workers were absent from their jobs. White households experienced the same problem. With their servants missing, they were forced "to cook their own dinners or content themselves with a cold lunch."

What was going on? In 1867, as southern states began writing new constitutions, African American delegates took an active part. On days when important issues were debated, freedmen from all around flocked to watch. In Alabama, a political convention of freedmen declared, "We claim exactly the same rights, privileges and immunities as are enjoyed by white men."

Before the Civil War, a small group of rich planters had dominated southern politics. During Reconstruction, however, new groups tried to reshape southern politics.

New Forces in Southern Politics

The state governments created during Radical Reconstruction were different from any governments the South had known before. The old leaders had lost much of their influence. Three groups stepped in to replace them.

White Southern Republicans Some white southerners supported the new Republican governments. Many were businesspeople who had opposed secession in 1860. They wanted to forget the war and get on with rebuilding the South.

Many whites in the South felt that any southerner who helped the Republicans was a traitor. They called the white southern Republicans **scalawags,** a word used for small, scruffy horses.

Northerners Northerners who came to the South after the war were another important force. White southerners accused the new arrivals of hoping to get rich from the South's misery. Southerners claimed that these northerners were in such a hurry they had time only to fling a few clothes into cheap suitcases, or carpetbags. As a result, they became known as **carpetbaggers.**

In fact, northerners went south for various reasons. A few did hope to profit as the South was being rebuilt. Many more, however, were Union soldiers who had grown to love the South's rich land. Others, both white and black, were teachers, ministers, and reformers who sincerely wanted to help the freedmen.

African Americans African Americans were the third major new group in southern politics. Before the war, they had no voice in southern government. During Reconstruction, they not only voted in large numbers, but they also ran for and were elected to public office in the South. African Americans became sheriffs, mayors, and legislators in the new state and local governments. Sixteen African Americans were elected to Congress between 1869 and 1880.

Two African Americans, both representing Mississippi, served in the Senate. Hiram Revels, a clergyman and teacher, became the nation's first black senator in 1870. He completed the unfinished term of former Confederate president Jefferson Davis. In 1874, Blanche K. Bruce became the first African American to serve a full term in the Senate.

Freedmen had less political influence than many whites claimed, however. Only in South Carolina did African Americans win a majority in one house of the state legislature. No state elected a black governor.

Conservatives Resist

Most white southerners who had held power before the Civil War resisted Reconstruction. These **Conservatives** resented the changes imposed by Congress and enforced by the military. They wanted the South to change as little as possible. Conservatives were willing to let African Americans vote and hold a few offices. Still, they were determined that real power would remain in the hands of whites.

A few wealthy planters tried to force African Americans back onto plantations. Many small farmers and laborers wanted the government to take action against freedmen, who now competed with them for land and power.

Most of these white southerners were Democrats. They declared war on anyone who cooperated with the Republicans. "This is a white man's country," declared one southern senator, "and white men must govern it."

Spreading Terror Some white southerners formed secret societies to help them regain power. The most dangerous was the **Ku Klux Klan,** or KKK. The Klan worked to keep African Americans and white Republicans out of office.

Dressed in white robes and hoods to hide their identities, Klansmen rode at night to the homes of African American voters, shouting threats and burning wooden crosses. When threats did not work, the Klan turned to violence. Klan members murdered hundreds of African Americans and their white allies.

An American Profile

Hiram Revels 1822–1901

Hiram Revels was born to free parents in North Carolina. Yet, he had to learn to read in secret because the law banned education for free blacks as well as slaves. Moving north, he became a minister and educator with the African Methodist Episcopal Church. He recalled, "I was imprisoned in Missouri in 1854, for preaching the gospel to Negroes, though I was never subjected to violence." During the Civil War, he helped recruit the first two black regiments in Maryland. This life of service paved the way for Revels to become the first African American in the Senate.

How might his previous experience have prepared Hiram Revels for service in the Senate?

POLITICAL CARTOON
Skills

The Ku Klux Klan
The KKK used terror and violence to keep African Americans from voting. Northern cartoonist Thomas Nast attacked the Klan and other secret societies in this cartoon.

1. **Comprehension** Identify two Klan activities shown in this cartoon.

2. **Understanding Main Ideas** How does Nast show the impact of the Ku Klux Klan and similar groups on African Americans?

3. **Critical Thinking Identifying a Point of View** What details in this cartoon show Nast's view of the Ku Klux Klan?

Congress Responds Many moderate southerners condemned the violence of the Klan. Yet, they could do little to stop the Klan's reign of terror. Freedmen turned to the federal government for help. In Kentucky, African American voters wrote to Congress:

> 66 We believe you are not familiar with the Ku Klux Klan's riding nightly over the country spreading terror wherever they go by robbing, whipping, and killing our people without provocation. 99
>
> — Records of the U.S. Senate, April 11, 1871

In 1870, Congress made it a crime to use force to keep people from voting. Although Klan activities decreased, the threat of violence remained. Some African Americans continued to vote and hold office, but others were frightened away from the ballot box.

The Challenge of Rebuilding

Despite political problems, Reconstruction governments tried to rebuild the South. They built public schools for both black and white children. Many states gave women the right to own property. In addition, Reconstruction governments rebuilt railroads, telegraph lines, bridges, and roads. Between 1865 and 1879, the South put down 7,000 miles of railroad track.

Rebuilding cost money. Before the war, southerners paid low taxes. Reconstruction governments raised taxes sharply. This created discontent among many southern whites.

Southerners were further angered by widespread corruption in the Reconstruction governments. One state legislature, for example, voted $1,000 to cover a member's bet on a horse race. Other items billed to the state included hams, perfume, and a coffin.

Corruption was not limited to the South. After the Civil War, dishonesty plagued northern governments, as well. Most southern officeholders, however, served their states honestly.

A Cycle of Poverty

In the first months after the war, freedmen left the plantations on which they had lived and worked. They found few opportunities, however.

AS YOU READ **Draw Inferences** What does the phrase "cycle of poverty" suggest to you?

"Nothing but Freedom" Some Radical Republicans talked about giving each freedman "40 acres and a mule." Thaddeus Stevens suggested breaking up big plantations and distributing the land. Most Americans opposed the plan, however. In the end, former slaves received—in the words of a freedman—"nothing but freedom."

Through hard work or good luck, some freedmen were able to become landowners. Most, however, had little choice but to return to where they had lived in slavery. At the same time, some large planters found themselves with land but nobody to work it.

Sharecropping During Reconstruction, many freedmen and poor whites went to work on the large plantations. These sharecroppers rented and farmed a plot of land. Planters provided seed, fertilizer, and tools in return for a share of the crop at harvest time. To many freedmen, sharecropping offered a measure of independence. Many hoped to own their own land one day.

In fact, most sharecroppers and small landowners became locked in a cycle of poverty. Each spring, they received supplies on credit. In the fall, they had to repay what they had borrowed. If the harvest did not cover what they owed, they sank deeper into debt. Many farmers lost their land and became sharecroppers themselves.

Section 3 Assessment

Recall

1. **Identify** Explain the significance of **(a)** Hiram Revels, **(b)** Blanche K. Bruce, **(c)** Conservatives, **(d)** Ku Klux Klan.
2. **Define (a)** scalawag, **(b)** carpetbagger, **(c)** sharecropper.

Comprehension

3. What role did freedmen play in Reconstruction governments?
4. What was the goal of groups like the Ku Klux Klan?
5. Describe two economic problems faced by Reconstruction governments in the South.

6. Why did many farmers become sharecroppers?

Critical Thinking and Writing

7. **Exploring the Main Idea** Review the Main Idea statement at the beginning of this section. Then, list two accomplishments of Reconstruction governments. Evaluate the impact of each on the South.
8. **Making Decisions** If you had been an African American during Reconstruction, would you have tried to vote despite threats? Write a paragraph explaining your reasons.

ACTIVITY

Writing a Welcoming Speech You are a Republican member of Congress in 1870. You have been asked to write a brief speech welcoming one of the first African Americans elected to the House of Representatives. Your speech should highlight the importance of this occasion.

4 The End of Reconstruction

Reading Focus

- What events led to the end of Reconstruction?
- How were the rights of African Americans restricted in the South after Reconstruction?
- What industries flourished in the "New South"?

Key Terms

poll tax

literacy test

grandfather clause

segregation

Jim Crow laws

Plessy v. *Ferguson*

"New South"

Taking Notes

Copy the concept web below. As you read, fill in the blank ovals with information about the aftermath of Reconstruction. Add as many ovals as you need.

New South

AFTERMATH OF RECONSTRUCTION

Reconstruction ends

African Americans lose rights

Main Idea When the North lost interest in protecting the goals of Reconstruction, the era came to an end.

Frederick Douglass
Use Prior Knowledge
What have you already learned about Frederick Douglass?

Setting the Scene
Americans flocked to the great Centennial Exposition held in Philadelphia in 1876. Fairgoers gazed at the latest wonders of modern industry—the elevator, a giant steam engine, and the telephone ("Of what use is such an invention?" asked the New York *Tribune*).

At the opening ceremony, Frederick Douglass was invited to sit on the platform. But when the famed abolitionist tried to take his place, a policeman barred the way. The officer could not believe that a black man belonged on stage. Finally, a United States Senator persuaded the policeman to let Douglass pass.

By 1876, Americans were looking ahead to a bright future. Eager to put the past behind them, many northerners lost interest in Reconstruction. For African Americans in the South, the end of Reconstruction meant a slow erosion of their hard-won rights.

The End of Reconstruction

By the 1870s, Radical Republicans were losing power. Many northerners grew weary of trying to reform the South. It was time to let southerners run their own governments, they said—even if it meant that African Americans in the South might lose their rights.

Radicals in Decline Disclosure of widespread corruption also hurt Republicans. President Grant had appointed many friends to government offices. Some used their position to steal large sums of money from the government. Grant won reelection in 1872, but many northerners lost faith in Republicans and their policies.

Congress passed the Amnesty Act in 1872. It restored the right to vote to nearly all white southerners. They voted solidly Democratic. At the same time, threats of violence kept many African Americans from voting. By 1876, only three southern states—South Carolina, Florida, and Tennessee—remained under Republican control.

Election of 1876 The end of Reconstruction came with the election of 1876. The Democrats nominated Samuel Tilden, governor of New York, for President. The Republicans chose Ohio governor Rutherford B. Hayes. Both candidates vowed to fight corruption.

Tilden won the popular vote. However, he had only 184 electoral votes, one short of the number needed to win. The outcome of the election hung on 20 disputed votes. All but one came from the three southern states still controlled by Republicans.

As inauguration day drew near, the nation still had no one to swear in as President. Congress set up a special commission to settle the crisis. The commission, made up mostly of Republicans, decided to give all the disputed electoral votes to Hayes.

Southern Democrats could have fought the decision. Hayes, however, had privately agreed to end Reconstruction. Once in office, he removed all remaining federal troops from Louisiana, South Carolina, and Florida. Reconstruction was over.

Impact of Reconstruction Reconstruction had a deep and lasting impact on southern politics. White southerners had bitter memories of Radical Republican policies and military rule. For the next hundred years, the South remained a stronghold of the Democratic party. At the same time, black southerners steadily lost most of their political rights.

Restricted Rights

As Conservatives tightened their grip on southern governments, states found new ways to keep African Americans from exercising their rights. Many of these laws restricted the right to vote.

GEOGRAPHY
Skills

The 1876 presidential election hinged on the disputed votes of three southern states. Although Samuel Tilden won the popular vote, Rutherford B. Hayes was declared the winner of the election.

1. **Location** On the map, locate **(a)** Florida, **(b)** Louisiana, **(c)** South Carolina.

2. **Regions** Which candidate carried the southern states where the vote was not disputed?

3. **Critical Thinking Drawing Inferences** Based on this map, do you think the Civil War ended sectionalism in the United States? Explain.

Election of 1876

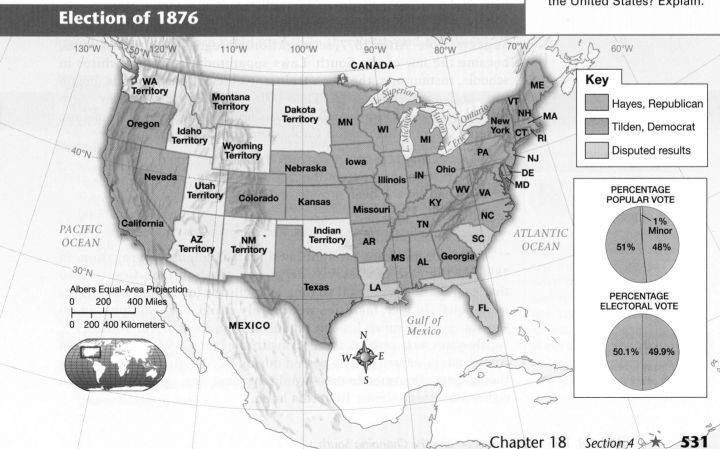

Key
- Hayes, Republican
- Tilden, Democrat
- Disputed results

PERCENTAGE POPULAR VOTE
1% Minor
51% 48%

PERCENTAGE ELECTORAL VOTE
50.1% 49.9%

TEST PREPARATION

Use the map <u>and</u> your knowledge of social studies to answer the following question.

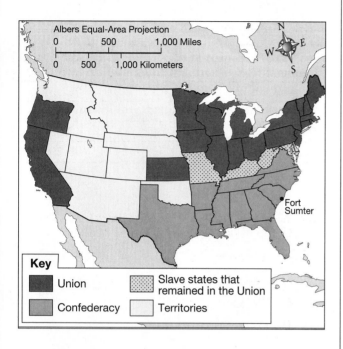

Albers Equal-Area Projection

0   500   1,000 Miles

0   500   1,000 Kilometers

Fort Sumter

Key

Union

Confederacy

Slave states that remained in the Union

Territories

1   Which conclusion can you draw from this map?

   A   More people lived in the Union than in the Confederacy.

   B   The Confederacy occupied most of the Atlantic Coast.

   C   Most of the fighting in the Civil War took place in the South.

   D   All slave states seceded from the Union.

2   Which of the following was not a goal of Radical Reconstruction?

   A   Break the power of southern planters

   B   Guarantee the vote to freedmen

   C   End slavery

   D   Strengthen Republican control of Congress

3   In which of the following pairs was the first event a cause of the second?

   A   Fort Sumter is fired upon; South Carolina secedes

   B   California applies for statehood; Compromise of 1850 passed

   C   Fighting erupts in Kansas; Kansas-Nebraska Act passed

   D   John Brown leads raid on Harpers Ferry; Republican party is formed

4   What was one major effect of the Emancipation Proclamation?

   A   It immediately freed slaves in the North.

   B   It immediately freed slaves in the South.

   C   It allowed African Americans to enlist in the Union army.

   D   It increased support for the Union cause in Europe.

5   With which of these statements would both Abraham Lincoln and Stephen Douglas have agreed?

   A   "The Kansas-Nebraska Act will help save the Union."

   B   "The Union must be preserved."

   C   "The people of each state have the right to decide whether to allow slavery."

   D   "The nation cannot survive half-slave, half-free."

Use the statements below __and__ your knowledge of social studies to answer the following question.

- "All persons formerly held as slaves shall have the right to own, sell, purchase, and inherit property."

- "No one other than white men shall be permitted to serve on juries, hold office, or vote in any election."

---

6 Where would you be most likely to find *both* of the above statements?

A The Wade-Davis Bill

B The Reconstruction Act

C One of the black codes

D The Supreme Court decision in *Plessy* v. *Ferguson*

7 Which of the following individuals would have been most likely to agree with the Dred Scott decision?

A Harriet Beecher Stowe

B Frederick Douglass

C John C. Calhoun

D John Brown

8 Which of the following explained which people were considered to be American citizens?

A Thirteenth Amendment

B Fourteenth Amendment

C Fifteenth Amendment

D Gettysburg Address

Use the table __and__ your knowledge of social studies to answer the following question.

Casualties of Selected Civil War Battles

Battle Site	Union Casualties	Confederate Casualties
Gettysburg	23,053	28,063
Antietam	12,410	10,316
Shiloh	13,047	10,694
Fredericksburg	12,653	5,309

Source: *The Civil War,* Time-Life Books

9 Which battle had the largest percentage of Union casualties?

A Antietam

B Gettysburg

C Shiloh

D Fredericksburg

Writing Practice

10 "Slavery was the chief cause of the Civil War." Agree or disagree with this statement. Give reasons for your answer.

11 Describe one social, one political, and one economic effect of the Civil War on the South. Explain which effect you think had the greatest impact.

Epilogue: The United States Since 1865

1865–PRESENT

1 **Entering Modern Times**
2 **A New Role for the Nation**
3 **The Great Depression and World War II**
4 **The Cold War and the Civil Rights Era**
5 **Into the Future**

Completion of the transcontinental railroad

World War I recruiting poster

AMERICAN EVENTS

1869
The nation's first railroad stretching from coast to coast is completed. The transcontinental railroad contributes to the growth of the West.

1901
Progressive reformer Theodore Roosevelt becomes President.

1917
Three years after World War I begins in Europe, the United States enters the war.

1929
The Great Depression begins.

1865 ⋅ ⋅ ★ ⋅ ⋅ ⋅ ⋅ ⋅ ⋅ ★ 1900 ⋅ ⋅ ★ ⋅ ⋅ ★ 1935

 WORLD EVENTS

▲ **1870s**
The Age of Imperialism begins.

1917 ▲
The Russian Revolution brings Communists to power in Russia.

The United States Since 1865

Between 1867 and 1959, a total of 14 new states entered the Union.

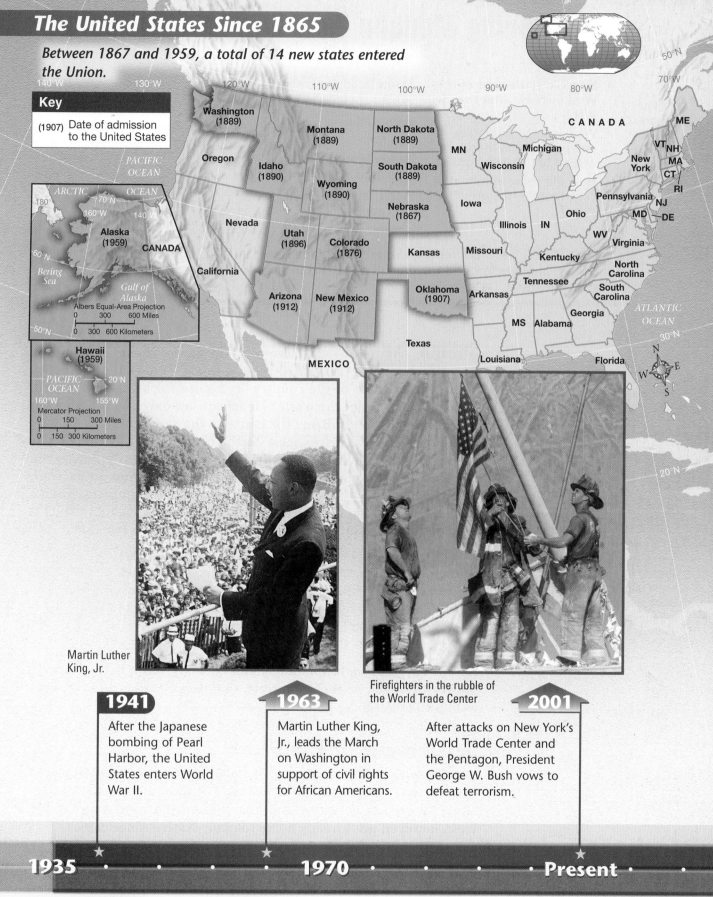

Key

(1907) Date of admission to the United States

Washington (1889)
Montana (1889)
North Dakota (1889)
MN
Michigan
CANADA
ME
VT
NH
New York
MA
CT
RI

Oregon
Idaho (1890)
Wyoming (1890)
South Dakota (1889)
Wisconsin
Pennsylvania
NJ
DE

Nevada
Utah (1896)
Colorado (1876)
Nebraska (1867)
Iowa
Illinois
IN
Ohio
WV
Virginia
MD

California
Arizona (1912)
New Mexico (1912)
Kansas
Missouri
Kentucky
North Carolina

ARCTIC OCEAN
Alaska (1959)
CANADA
Bering Sea
Gulf of Alaska

Albers Equal-Area Projection
0   300   600 Miles
0   300   600 Kilometers

Hawaii (1959)
PACIFIC OCEAN
Mercator Projection
0   150   300 Miles
0   150   300 Kilometers

Oklahoma (1907)
Arkansas
Tennessee
South Carolina
Georgia
MS   Alabama
ATLANTIC OCEAN

PACIFIC OCEAN

Texas
Louisiana
Florida

MEXICO

Martin Luther King, Jr.

Firefighters in the rubble of the World Trade Center

1941
After the Japanese bombing of Pearl Harbor, the United States enters World War II.

1963
Martin Luther King, Jr., leads the March on Washington in support of civil rights for African Americans.

2001
After attacks on New York's World Trade Center and the Pentagon, President George W. Bush vows to defeat terrorism.

1935 · · · **1970** · · · **Present** ·

▲ **1939**
World War II begins in Europe.

▲ **1954**
Vietnam throws off French rule.

1991 ▲
The collapse of the Soviet Union ends the Cold War.

1 Entering Modern Times

Reading Focus

- How did settlement of the West increase after the Civil War?
- What new technologies and business methods helped big business grow?
- How did rising immigration contribute to the growth of cities?

Key Terms

Homestead Act

transcontinental railroad

corporation

capital

Bessemer process

monopoly

American Federation of Labor

urbanization

Taking Notes

Complete the concept web below. As you read the section, fill in the blank ovals with information about changes after the Civil War. Add as many ovals as you need.

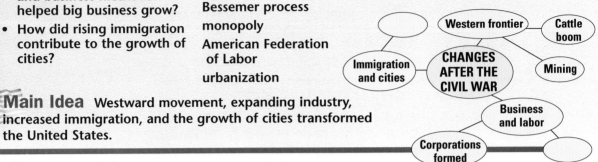

Main Idea Westward movement, expanding industry, increased immigration, and the growth of cities transformed the United States.

Texas longhorn

Use Prior Knowledge

Before you read the Setting the Scene story, list three facts you already know about cowboys and cattle ranching in the American West. How does the story compare to your list?

Setting the Scene "Here was all these cheap long-horned steers over-running Texas," recalled cowboy "Teddy Blue" Abbott. "Here was the rest of the country crying out for beef—and no railroads in Texas to get them out." Ranchers saw only one way to meet the nation's demands: Bring the cattle to the rail centers.

The long cattle drives gave birth to one of the most popular American heroes—the cowboy. In spite of his romantic image, the cowboy's life was rough and dangerous. He spent months on the trail, facing roaring rivers, grass fires, and the threat of stampede. When a cowboy got to town after a long drive, his first thoughts were of a good meal, a haircut, and showy new clothes. Abbott recalled:

> 66 I had a new white Stetson hat that I paid ten dollars for and new pants that cost twelve dollars, and a good shirt and fancy boots. They had colored tops, red and blue, with a half-moon and star on them. . . . I thought I was dressed right for the first time in my life. 99
>
> —"Teddy Blue" Abbott, quoted in *The West* (Burns)

The cattle boom lasted only about 20 years, but it helped change the West forever. At the same time, the nation's cities and factories were also undergoing great changes.

Settlement of the West

Since the Louisiana Purchase of 1803, the nation had expanded steadily westward. After the Civil War, westward movement sped up. Many Americans hoped to find new lives in the wide prairies. The West, however, was already home to many Native Americans.

Moving West The mining boom that began with the California gold rush continued. Valuable strikes of silver or gold brought prospectors to Nevada, the Dakotas, even as far as Alaska. Some mining "boomtowns" grew into permanent settlements. Parts of the West organized as territories, which later became new states.

Cattle ranching became a "boom" industry in the 1870s. For years, herds of longhorns had roamed the open range in Texas and the Southwest. Now, a growing population needed more meat. Ranchers hired cowhands to herd the cattle from grazing lands to railroad lines in the north. Ranching soon spread throughout the Great Plains.

The federal government encouraged settlers. The Homestead Act of 1862 gave land to anyone who would farm it for five years. Eager for land, families from the East endured hardships and harsh weather. African Americans also moved West, looking for freedom they did not have in the South. Farmers plowed grassland with efficient new steel plows. They also built fences, leading to clashes with ranchers.

Railroads carried supplies and settlers to the West. To encourage railroad building, the government granted land and money. In 1869, two railroad companies completed the nation's first transcontinental railroad. Now it was possible for settlers to travel by train all the way from the Atlantic coast to the Pacific.

Indians Lose Their Land Westward movement spelled disaster for Native Americans in the West. The many Indian nations there had rich, varied cultures. While some Indians farmed, many more depended on the huge herds of bison, or buffalo, that roamed the Great Plains. The buffalo supplied meat for food and skins for clothing, warm rugs, and tepees.

As miners and settlers moved onto Native American lands, they broke treaties that the government had made with the Indians. Soldiers and hunters wiped out the huge buffalo herds. Native

GEOGRAPHY *Skills*

Mining, railroad building, and cattle ranching all played a major role in changing the West.

1. **Location** On the map, locate **(a)** Comstock Lode, **(b)** Central Pacific Railroad, **(c)** Chisholm Trail.

2. **Movement** Describe the route of the Goodnight-Loving Trail.

3. **Critical Thinking Drawing Conclusions** Why do you think most railroad lines in the West were built to run east–west rather than north–south?

The Changing West

Key

┈┈┈ Railroads

━━ Cattle trails

✕ Mining centers

Americans tried to resist the loss of their land and their way of life. Leaders such as Sitting Bull and Crazy Horse of the Lakota Sioux and Geronimo of the Apaches led their people in wars against government troops. In the end, however, the federal government gradually forced western Indians onto reservations.

Business and Labor

American business and industry boomed after the Civil War. New technology fueled this rapid growth. Inventions such as refrigeration and the telephone changed both business and daily life. Thomas Edison and his workers invented products that shaped today's world—not only the first practical light bulb but also the electric power plant, the phonograph, and motion pictures. Late in the 1800s, inventors in the United States and Europe built the first automobiles.

Growth of Big Business The railroad industry dominated the American economy. A network of rail lines crossed the country. Powerful "railroad barons" such as Cornelius Vanderbilt bought up smaller lines and built great railroad empires. Some railroad owners abused their power by fixing prices and bribing public officials. Nonetheless, the railroads created jobs and spurred the growth of industry.

To expand, businesses organized as corporations. A **corporation** is a business owned by investors. The company sells shares of stock in exchange for **capital,** or money to invest in future growth. If the business prospers, the value of the stock grows. Investors in corporations faced fewer risks than owners of private businesses. If a private business goes bankrupt, the owners must pay all the debts. By law, stockholders cannot be held responsible for the debts of a corporation.

In the 1850s, scientists developed the **Bessemer process,** a method of making stronger steel at lower cost. The steel industry expanded quickly, creating great fortunes. Andrew Carnegie gained control of all aspects of the American steel industry, from iron mines to steel mills to shipping lines. Carnegie believed that the wealthy had a duty to society. He gave millions of dollars to charities and to public projects such as libraries.

Banks invested heavily in corporations, which allowed bankers to control company policies. Banker J. P. Morgan bought up railroads and steel companies, including Carnegie's. He formed U.S. Steel, the first billion-dollar American business. Other fortunes were based on a new resource, oil. John D. Rockefeller, starting with a single oil refinery, built the highly successful Standard Oil Company. Rockefeller organized his business interests to control the stock of rival companies. Standard Oil thus became a **monopoly,** or a single company that controls or dominates an entire industry.

Critics charged that these business practices reduced competition, hurting smaller companies and consumers. Others defended giant corporations, however. They pointed out that giant corporations brought lower production costs, lower prices, higher wages, and a better way of life. By 1900, Americans enjoyed the highest standard of living in the world.

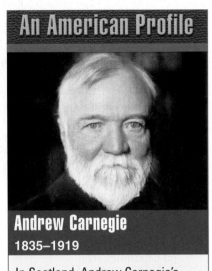

An American Profile

Andrew Carnegie
1835–1919

In Scotland, Andrew Carnegie's father wove linen on a hand loom. His mother cobbled shoes. But, new technology was driving such artisans into poverty. Even after immigrating to the United States, the family continued to plunge deeper into debt.

Young Andrew decided to work *with* technology rather than against it. First, he got a job in a cotton mill. He became a telegram messenger at age 14, then a telegraph operator for the Pennsylvania Railroad. By age 23, Carnegie was superintendent of the railroad's western division. Yet, his greatest success—as the American Steel King—lay ahead.

What qualities do you think helped Carnegie succeed?

AS YOU READ **Summarize** Write two to three sentences explaining why Americans were able to enjoy a high standard of living by 1900.

Rise of Organized Labor

Rise of Organized Labor Factory conditions could be harsh and dangerous. Workers, including young children, labored long hours in crowded sweatshops for low pay. Unsafe conditions were common. In 1911, a deadly fire broke out in the Triangle Shirtwaist Factory in New York City. Nearly 150 workers, mostly young immigrant women, died because the owners had locked the doors.

Workers began to organize for better conditions, shorter hours, and an end to child labor. In 1886, the American Federation of Labor (AFL) brought together trade unions, which represented skilled workers. Some unions used strikes to gain better pay. In the beginning, public officials and the courts generally sided with factory owners. Still, union membership grew steadily.

Immigration and the Growth of Cities

In the late 1800s, millions of immigrants streamed into the United States. Many were fleeing poverty at home. They hoped for factory jobs or farmland. A large number of Jews and Armenian Christians arrived, driven from their homelands by religious persecution.

The New Immigrants Before the Civil War, most immigrants came from northern and western Europe. In the late 1800s, this pattern changed. More people came from southern or eastern Europe—Italy, Poland, Russia, and other countries. A growing number of Asians, mainly Chinese, landed on the West Coast. By the 1890s, most Europeans came through the immigration station at Ellis Island in New York Harbor. Their first sight of the American "promised land" was the Statue of Liberty, with these words inscribed on its base:

> 66 Give me your tired, your poor,
> Your huddled masses yearning to breathe free,
> The wretched refuse of your teeming shore.
> Send these, the homeless, tempest-tossed to me:
> I lift my lamp beside the golden door. 99
>
> —Emma Lazarus, "The New Colossus"

Viewing History

Immigrants in a New Land Above are just some of the millions of European immigrants who first entered the United States at Ellis Island. Inspectors wrote down each immigrant's name and country of origin. **Drawing Conclusions** *Based on your reading and this picture, how do you think these immigrants felt as they arrived in the United States?*

Primary Sources

See Jacob Riis, "How the Other Half Lives," on page 608 of the Reference Section.

Language, religion, and culture set newcomers apart from their neighbors. People of one ethnic group clustered together in city neighborhoods. While older immigrants kept traditional ways, their children hurried to learn English and become citizens.

Many Americans opposed the flood of immigrants. These nativists said that the newcomers competed with Americans for jobs and would never fit into American culture. On the West Coast, anti-Chinese feelings were especially strong. An 1882 federal law barred most Chinese immigrants. Other laws set limits on immigration.

Growing Cities Immigration fueled the rapid growth of cities. The United States was once mainly a rural nation. That changed as people flocked to the cities for jobs in factories, stores, and offices. This process of population shifting from farms to cities is called urbanization. African American migrants from the South formed thriving communities in northern cities such as Chicago and Detroit.

Cities themselves changed with the building of skyscrapers and great public parks. Streetcar lines linked cities and suburbs. In 1897, the nation's first subway line opened in Boston. Cities offered a wide variety of attractions, from music halls and museums to sports.

City life was very different for rich and poor. The poor often lived in small, dark, crowded tenement apartments. In these unhealthy conditions, diseases like tuberculosis spread easily. Middle-class families, on the other hand, lived in comfortable houses. The very wealthy built mansions far from the crowds.

Reformers worked to improve the terrible conditions in the slums. They fought for better city services, such as safe water and clean streets. In Chicago, Jane Addams led the settlement house movement, which offered education and other services. Religious groups such as the Salvation Army also aided the poor.

AFTER YOU READ

Section 1 Assessment

Recall

1. **Identify** Explain the significance of (a) Homestead Act, (b) Thomas Edison, (c) Bessemer process, (d) Andrew Carnegie, (e) American Federation of Labor, (f) Jane Addams.
2. **Define** (a) transcontinental railroad, (b) corporation, (c) capital, (d) monopoly, (e) urbanization.

Comprehension

3. What groups of people contributed to the settlement of the West?
4. (a) How did the growth of big business benefit the nation? (b) Why did some people argue against monopolies?

5. Why did immigrants come to the United States?

Critical Thinking and Writing

6. **Exploring the Main Idea** Review the Main Idea statement at the beginning of this section. Then, list three ways in which modern American life might be different if one of the changes described in this section had not taken place.
7. **Making a Decision** If you were an investor in the late 1800s, would you buy stock or put your money into a privately owned business? Write a letter to another investor explaining your decision.

ACTIVITY

Take It to the NET
Connecting to Today
Choose five American cities, including one in your home state. Then, use the Internet to find out about population growth in those cities. Create a database of tables or graphs showing the population of each city in 1850, 1900, 1950, and 2000. Visit *The American Nation* section of **www.phschool.com** for help in completing the activity.

2 A New Role for the Nation

BEFORE YOU READ

Reading Focus

- What changes did Progressive reformers support?
- How did the United States assume a greater role in world affairs?
- What were the causes and results of World War I?

Key Terms

Progressives
muckraker
civil service
Nineteenth Amendment
isolationism
imperialism
Spanish-American War
Roosevelt Corollary
World War I

Taking Notes

As you read, prepare an outline of this section. Use roman numerals to indicate the major headings, capital letters for the subheadings, and numbers for the supporting details. The sample below will help you get started.

> I. The Progressive Era
>   A. Progressive reformers
>   1. Muckrakers
>   2. Political reforms
>   3.
>   B. Presidents back reform
>   1.
>   2.
> II. Becoming a World Power
>   A.
>   B.

Main Idea As the government began to take on a larger role in people's lives, the nation also became more involved in world affairs.

Setting the Scene Theodore Roosevelt was no ordinary politician. He had been a cattle rancher in North Dakota and head of the New York City police department. He had led the Rough Riders, a volunteer cavalry unit in a war with Spain.

With his dynamic personality, "Teddy" became a popular hero—and he used his popularity to push for an ambitious program of reforms. In an election speech, he promised:

> 66 The principles for which we stand are the principles of fair play and a square deal for every man and every woman in the United States. 99
>
> —Theodore Roosevelt, Address to the Boys' Progressive League, July 3, 1913

Under the leadership of Roosevelt and his successors, the federal government began to take on a new, larger role in people's lives. At the same time, the United States itself took on a new role as a growing world power.

The Progressive Era

In the decades following the Civil War, industrial growth helped create a period of prosperity known as the "Gilded Age." Still, American society had many problems. In the Progressive Era, from 1898 to 1917, reformers worked to reduce the power of big business, improve social conditions, and clean up political corruption.

Progressive Reformers The Progressives were men and women who wanted to improve society, though they had different targets. Crusading journalists known as muckrakers reported on slum conditions and unsafe meatpacking plants. Other Progressives backed political reforms such as primary elections. In 1913, Progressives won passage of two constitutional amendments. The Sixteenth

AS YOU READ **Theodore Roosevelt** **Visualize** Read the story at left and look at the picture above. Describe what you see when you picture Teddy Roosevelt giving his Square Deal speech.

POLITICAL CARTOON
Skills

Women Win the Vote
The Nineteenth Amendment, giving women the right to vote, was ratified in 1920. This cartoon by Rollin Kirby appeared that year.

1. **Comprehension** **(a)** What does the ladder represent? **(b)** What is the woman standing on?

2. **Understanding Main Ideas** **(a)** Based on this cartoon, was the woman's climb easy or difficult? **(b)** What is her mood?

3. **Critical Thinking Identifying Points of View** Based on this cartoon, do you think Rollin Kirby favored the Nineteenth Amendment? Support your answer.

Civics

AS YOU READ **Find Main Ideas** List some ways in which American Presidents backed reforms in the early 1900s.

Amendment gave Congress the power to impose an income tax. The Seventeenth Amendment called for senators to be elected directly by the people, rather than by state legislatures.

Reformers also attacked corruption in government. As you have read, under the spoils system, most government jobs went to loyal party workers. One early reform set up a civil service system that awarded federal jobs on the basis of examination scores, not political influence. Reformers also tried to limit the power of big business. In 1890, Congress passed the Sherman Antitrust Act. Its goal was to limit business monopolies that hurt competition. However, the act proved ineffective at first.

During the Progressive Era, the long campaign for women's suffrage gained strength. In the late 1800s, women gained the right to vote in four western states: Wyoming, Utah, Colorado, and Idaho. As more women entered the work force after 1900, leaders like Carrie Chapman Catt stepped up the campaign. At last, in 1920, the Nineteenth Amendment to the Constitution guaranteed women's right to vote.

Presidents Back Reform In 1901, Theodore Roosevelt became President after the assassination of William McKinley. As President, Roosevelt pushed through a series of Progressive reforms. He enforced the Sherman Antitrust Act against what he saw as unfair monopolies, and he supported organized labor. He also backed laws to conserve natural resources and to make food products and medicines safer.

Roosevelt's successors, William Howard Taft and Woodrow Wilson, also supported reforms. Wilson supported laws to encourage business competition. At Wilson's urging, Congress also passed laws to regulate the banking system.

Seeking Equality Minority groups gained little from Progressive reforms. Since the end of Reconstruction, African Americans had lost many political rights. They faced prejudice and segregation in schools, housing, and jobs. Two leaders offered different answers. Booker T. Washington advised African Americans to accept segregation, at least for the time being. He urged them to concentrate on education, economic self-improvement, and gradual progress.

Educator and writer W.E.B. DuBois disagreed. DuBois believed instead that African Americans should work actively against discrimination. DuBois joined with white reformers to found the National Association for the Advancement of Colored People (NAACP) to work for equal rights for African Americans.

Becoming a World Power

In his Farewell Address, George Washington had advised Americans to "steer clear of permanent alliances." Later Presidents continued this policy of isolationism, or limited involvement in the world's affairs. But, as American trade expanded in the late 1800s, so did American interest in the rest of the world.

By the 1870s, many European nations had launched the Age of Imperialism. Imperialism is the policy of powerful countries seeking to control the political and economic affairs of weaker countries or regions. European powers took over most of Africa and parts of Asia.

Some American politicians believed that the United States should expand overseas, too. Albert Beveridge of Indiana argued:

> 66 Today we are raising more than we can consume. Today we are making more than we can use. Today our industrial society is congested; there are more workers than there is work. . . . Therefore we must find new markets for our produce, new occupations for our capital, new work for our labor. 99

—Albert Beveridge, quoted in *Modern Eloquence* (Reed)

Expansion in the Pacific Once Americans reached the Pacific coast, they looked toward trade and territory around the Pacific Ocean. In the 1850s, the United States Navy forced Japan to open its ports to trade with the West. In 1867, the United States purchased the resource-rich Alaska territory from Russia.

Cause and Effect

Causes

- Western frontier closes
- Businesses seek raw materials and new markets
- European nations compete for resources and markets

OVERSEAS EXPANSION

Effects

- United States develops strong navy
- Open Door Policy protects trade with China
- United States governs lands in Caribbean and Pacific
- United States builds Panama Canal
- United States sends troops to Latin American nations to protect its interests

Effects Today

- United States is global superpower
- Alaska and Hawaii are 49th and 50th states
- Puerto Rico, American Samoa, Guam, and U.S. Virgin Islands remain United States territories
- United States has close economic ties with Latin America and Pacific Rim

GRAPHIC ORGANIZER
Skills

In the late 1800s, the United States gradually became more involved in foreign affairs.

1. **Comprehension** Which of the effects listed here involved Latin America?

2. **Critical Thinking Ranking** Which of the Effects Today listed here do you think is the most important? Explain.

Expansion in the Pacific rested on naval power. The United States acquired the islands of Midway and Samoa, where ships bound for Asia could refuel. The next large acquisition was the island chain of Hawaii. Starting in the mid-1800s, Americans had set up large sugar plantations in Hawaii. In 1893, with the help of United States Marines, the planters overthrew the last Hawaiian queen, Liliuokalani (lih lee oo oh kah LAH nee). The United States soon annexed the islands.

In mainland Asia, the United States competed with European nations for influence in China. The United States supported an "Open Door Policy" that guaranteed access to Chinese ports and trade.

Relations With Latin America Backers of expansion now looked closer to home. In nearby Cuba, people were rebelling against rule by Spain. Sensational newspaper stories made many Americans want to help the rebels. In 1898, after the American battleship *Maine* blew up in Havana harbor, the United States declared war on Spain. American forces won a quick victory in the Spanish-American War. The peace settlement gave Americans their first taste of overseas empire. The United States gained Cuba, Puerto Rico, Guam, and the Philippines. Cubans were given self-rule, though under American control.

Teddy Roosevelt favored American expansion. One of his goals was to build a canal across the narrow Isthmus of Panama. It would let ships sail between the Atlantic and Pacific oceans without going around South America. Taking advantage of a local rebellion, Roosevelt got land for the canal. Despite tropical diseases and engineering challenges, the Panama Canal was completed by 1914.

Roosevelt took another step in establishing an American role in Latin America. As you have read, the Monroe Doctrine of 1823 established the idea that the United States would oppose European interference in Latin America. Roosevelt expanded the Monroe Doctrine. He stated that the United States had the right to intervene in Latin American affairs. This policy became known as the Roosevelt Corollary. In the following decade, Presidents sent troops to protect United States interests in Haiti, the Dominican Republic, and other Caribbean countries.

World War I

In 1914, long-standing tensions in Europe erupted into the largest war the world had yet seen. Imperialism was one cause—major nations were competing for territory. Within those empires, various nationalist groups wanted independence. To maintain power, nations built up their armed forces. They also made alliances with one another, promising support if their allies were attacked.

In June 1914, a Serbian nationalist killed the heir to the Austro-Hungarian throne. Austria-Hungary blamed the Serbian government and declared war. Russia stepped in to protect Serbia. The alliance system drew one country after another into war. The war pitted the Central Powers—Germany; Austria-Hungary; and the Ottoman, or Turkish, Empire—against the Allied Powers of France, Britain, and Russia. In time, more than 20 countries were involved. Across Europe, millions of soldiers fought in long, deadly offensives. People called it the Great War, although we now call it World War I.

Geography and History

Building the Panama Canal

For American engineers and workers, building a canal across Panama was a gigantic undertaking.

- The canal extends 50.72 miles from the Atlantic Ocean to the Pacific Ocean.
- Workers removed 262 million cubic yards of earth and rock in constructing the canal.
- Some 56,600 workers used hand shovels, pickaxes, dynamite, and giant steam shovels to cut through jungles, hills, and swamps.
- The greatest obstacle to construction was disease: Work could begin only after scientists wiped out the mosquitoes that spread yellow fever.
- The canal saved 7,873 miles of travel for a ship bound from New York to California.

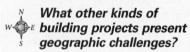

What other kinds of building projects present geographic challenges?

The United States Enters the War President Woodrow Wilson tried to keep the United States neutral. Most Americans viewed the war as a European problem. Soon, though, American opinion shifted. President Wilson angrily denounced German submarine attacks on ships crossing the Atlantic Ocean.

Finally, in April 1917, Wilson asked Congress to declare war on Germany. "The world must be made safe for democracy," he declared.

Americans quickly prepared for war. The government built and trained an army. Industries mobilized to produce weapons and supplies. Other programs boosted food production. On the home front, people bought Liberty Bonds to help pay for the war effort. Many women went to work to fill important jobs. To encourage unity, the government made it a crime to criticize United States involvement in the war.

Results of World War I By the time the United States joined the war, things looked bad for the Allies. Russia had withdrawn from the war after a revolution overthrew the czar's government. American troops landed in France to reinforce British and French armies. By June 1918, the Germans were in retreat. The war ended in November.

The costs of the war were staggering. More than 8 million people had died of wounds or disease, and millions more were wounded. Much of Europe was in ruins.

President Wilson tried to shape the peace settlement. His "Fourteen Points" plan proposed an end to alliances. It outlined a League of Nations that would settle international disputes. However, the final peace treaty left out many of Wilson's ideas. Instead, the Treaty of Versailles imposed harsh terms on Germany.

In the United States, Congress rejected membership in the League of Nations. Many politicians wanted a return to isolationism.

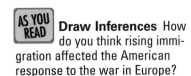 **Draw Inferences** How do you think rising immigration affected the American response to the war in Europe?

 Section 2 Assessment

Recall

1. **Identify** Explain the significance of **(a)** Theodore Roosevelt, **(b)** Progressives, **(c)** Nineteenth Amendment, **(d)** Woodrow Wilson, **(e)** Booker T. Washington, **(f)** W.E.B. DuBois, **(g)** Spanish-American War, **(h)** Roosevelt Corollary, **(i)** World War I.
2. **Define** **(a)** muckraker, **(b)** civil service, **(c)** isolationism, **(d)** imperialism.

Comprehension

3. Describe three Progressive reforms.
4. What new territories did the United States gain?

5. Why did the United States enter World War I?

Critical Thinking and Writing

6. **Exploring the Main Idea** Review the Main Idea statement at the beginning of this section. Then, write two pairs of sentences about events described in this section. Label the first sentence in each pair "BEFORE" and the second sentence in each pair "AFTER."
7. **Drawing Conclusions** Write a paragraph explaining why reformers thought a competitive civil service examination might help solve the problem of government corruption.

ACTIVITY

Drawing a Political Cartoon Reread the statement by Albert Beveridge in this section. Then, draw a political cartoon that might have appeared in an American newspaper at the time. Your cartoon should either support or disagree with Beveridge's point of view.

Honoring Our Veterans

World War I ended on November 11, 1918. Today, we celebrate that date as Veterans Day, a holiday to honor all of those who served in the armed forces in war or peace.

> ❝*Veterans deserve to know that we as a people honor their service. Please honor their sacrifice. Pay tribute each day to their irreplaceable gift to our nation. And take a moment to thank tomorrow's veterans. It's never too early to let them know how deeply we recognize their passionate commitment to keep America safe.*❞
> —2000 Veterans Day Speech, Army Public Affairs Division

The first "unknown soldier" was one of four American dead taken from the French battlefields of World War I. He was honored at Arlington National Cemetery in 1921. Since then, unknowns from World War II, the Korean War, and the Vietnam War have been buried in the "Tomb of the Unknowns." Here, a Marine solemnly stands guard at the tomb.

The Veterans of Foreign Wars (VFW) was begun in 1899 by veterans of the Spanish-American War. Its membership now numbers more than 2 million. This nonprofit organization offers support to veterans. It also sponsors community projects, such as an annual essay contest for seventh, eighth, and ninth graders. Here, VFW members salute a passing parade.

ACTIVITY

With a group of classmates, plan a Veterans Day ceremony. Prepare the opening paragraph of a speech. (If you like, you may choose to focus on a specific veteran you know.) Design a banner or poster, and suggest a list of special activities for your community.

3 The Great Depression and World War II

BEFORE YOU READ

Reading Focus

- How did the Great Depression begin?
- How did the New Deal affect American life?
- What were the causes of World War II?

Key Terms

jazz
margin buying
Great Depression
New Deal
Social Security
deficit spending
totalitarian state
Holocaust
World War II
D-Day

Taking Notes

Copy this flowchart. As you read, fill in the boxes with information about the events discussed in this section. One box has been partly filled in to help you get started.

```
1920s
• Postwar decade
• Business expansion
• Jazz Age
•
    ↓
    
    ↓
```

Main Idea In the 1930s and 1940s, Americans endured the nation's greatest economic crisis and the largest war the world had ever seen.

Setting the Scene Long before World War I, Americans had begun to fall in love with the automobile. A popular song from 1905 showed that the car was already part of American culture:

> 66Come away with me, Lucille,
> In my merry Oldsmobile.
> Down the road of life we'll fly,
> Automo-bubbling you and I.99
>
> —Vincent Bryan, "In My Merry Oldsmobile"

By the 1920s, the automobile was an indispensable part of American life. Mass production made cars more affordable. Car ownership ended the isolation of rural families. Gas stations, motels, and roadside restaurants sprang up.

The car boom was just one sign of the prosperous economy and optimistic spirit of the 1920s. However, Americans would soon be plunged into two crises that threatened their entire way of life.

From Prosperity to Depression

The 1920s began as a hopeful, prosperous time. President Calvin Coolidge declared, "The chief business of the American people is business." The postwar economy grew quickly.

The Prosperous Twenties The auto industry was important in the booming economy. Factories turned out new consumer goods such as radios, vacuum cleaners, and refrigerators. Many people also invested in the stock market for the first time. Stock prices rose steadily.

Women could now vote. More women also joined the work force. Young women known as flappers shocked older Americans with their short skirts and reckless behavior.

AS YOU READ **1925 automobile**
Predict List two other effects you think automobiles might have on American life.

Jazz was an original American musical style that blended West African rhythms, European harmonies, and African American work songs and spirituals. It became so popular that the 1920s are often called the "Jazz Age."

The Crash Some of the prosperity was built on shaky ground. Farmers, miners, and factory workers faced hard times. The soaring stock market encouraged a practice called **margin buying.** Investors would buy stock for a small down payment, borrowing the rest from their brokers, and then sell for a profit when the price of the stock rose. Margin buying worked as long as prices kept rising.

Then, the economy began to slow. Because fewer people could afford to buy goods, factories laid off workers or closed. Worried investors began to sell their stocks. As prices fell, brokers demanded full payment for stocks bought on margin. Many investors had to sell at a loss. On October 29, 1929, the stock market crashed.

The economy plunged into the worst economic slump in American history, the **Great Depression,** which deepened through the early 1930s. Banks closed, wiping out people's savings. Unemployment soared. Hungry people lined up at soup kitchens.

President Herbert Hoover tried to restore confidence in the economy by predicting better times ahead. However, like most Presidents since the time of Jefferson, he did not believe that the government should become directly involved in the economy. In the end, Hoover did take steps to fight the Great Depression with public works programs. Still, people blamed him for the hard times.

The New Deal

In 1932, Americans elected a new President, Franklin Delano Roosevelt. FDR promised to take action against hard times. "I pledge myself to a new deal for the American people," he said.

FDR's Program Roosevelt instituted a series of bold new programs called the **New Deal.** The New Deal had three main goals: relief for the unemployed, plans for recovery, and reforms to prevent another severe depression. The WPA (Works Progress Administration), for example, built schools and public buildings and gave work to artists and writers. The Tennessee Valley Authority (TVA) built dams to supply electric power and control floods in parts of the South. The Federal Deposit Insurance Corporation (FDIC) protected the funds people deposited in their bank accounts.

Unlike most other industrial nations, the United States had no insurance for retired workers. In 1935, the **Social Security** system began. It provided benefits for retired or disabled people.

Impact of the New Deal The New Deal did not end the Great Depression. Still, some New Deal programs did place the nation's banks on a firmer footing, protect farmers, and provide work for millions of people.

The New Deal changed people's relationship with the federal government. Government grew bigger, with more influence on everyday life. Many people came to believe that government had a

Unemployment, 1929–1941

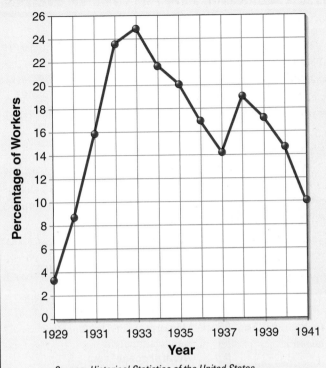

Percentage of Workers vs. Year

Source: *Historical Statistics of the United States*

responsibility to help all its citizens. Supporters of the New Deal argued that social programs had helped people keep their faith in democracy during the crisis.

Some critics argued that the New Deal went too far. They were alarmed that, in order to support massive programs, the government was spending more money than it was taking in. This practice is known as deficit spending. Critics also argued that the growing size and power of the federal government threatened traditional American freedoms. Former President Herbert Hoover warned:

> 66 Either we shall have a society based upon ordered liberty and the initiative of the individual, or we shall have a planned society that means dictation no matter what you call it or who does it. There is no half-way ground. 99
>
> —Herbert Hoover, speech to the Republican National Convention, 1936

The debate about the size of the federal government that began during the New Deal continues to this day.

World War II

Americans and Europeans hoped to avoid another war as destructive as World War I. During the depression, Americans returned to isolationism, focusing on troubles at home. World events soon made neutrality impossible, however.

GRAPH Skills

The Great Depression threw millions of Americans out of work. Bread lines (right) were common in every major American city.

1. **Comprehension** In which year was unemployment at its worst?

2. **Critical Thinking Making Generalizations** Based on this graph (left), make two generalizations about the changing rate of unemployment.

Economics $

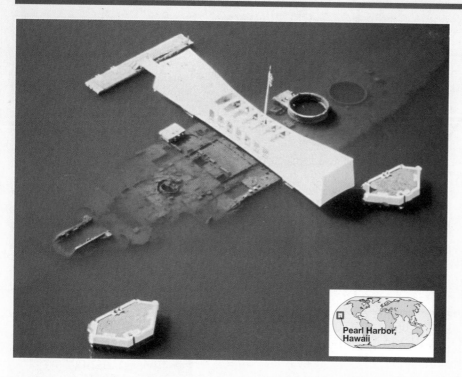

USS *Arizona* Memorial

On December 7, 1941, Japanese planes bombed the United States fleet anchored at Pearl Harbor, Hawaii. The battleship *Arizona* sank with more than 1,100 sailors aboard. Today, you can view the sunken hull of the *Arizona*. At the "remembrance exhibit," you can pay tribute to the first Americans to die in World War II.

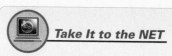

Take It to the NET

Virtual Field Trip For an interactive look at the USS *Arizona* Memorial, visit *The American Nation* section of **www.phschool.com**.

The Rise of Dictators In the 1920s and 1930s, totalitarian governments gained power in many nations. A totalitarian state is one in which a single party controls the government and every aspect of people's lives. In the Soviet Union, Joseph Stalin built a powerful communist dictatorship. Military leaders in Japan began to build an empire in East Asia.

In Italy, Benito Mussolini and his Fascist party played on extreme nationalist feelings. In Germany, Adolf Hitler blamed Germany's losses in the war on Jews and others. His National Socialist, or Nazi, party was brutal and militaristic. During the war years, Hitler and his officers carried out his systematic plan to destroy European Jews. In what is now called the Holocaust, more than 6 million Jews, as well as millions of others, died or were killed in concentration camps.

The War Begins Hitler's armies began to invade neighboring countries one by one. At first, Britain and France gave in to Hitler's demands in order to avoid war. However, when Hitler invaded Poland in 1939, they declared war. World War II pitted the Axis powers—Germany, Italy, and Japan—against the Allies. The Allies included Britain, France, China, the Soviet Union, and many others.

Hitler's armies quickly overran most of Europe. Soon Britain stood alone. In Asia, the Japanese carried out a program of aggression despite American protests.

At first, the United States tried to remain neutral. As the war continued, President Roosevelt pushed programs to send economic

AS YOU READ **Use Prior Knowledge** How was the response of Americans to the start of World War II similar to the response of Americans to the start of World War I?

aid to the Allies. Then, on December 7, 1941, Japan launched a surprise attack on the American Pacific fleet at Pearl Harbor, in Hawaii. The next day, the United States entered the war on the Allied side.

The Home Front The nation mobilized for war quickly. Factories converted to war production. To conserve supplies for the military, the government rationed meat, gasoline, sugar, clothing, and other goods. Millions of women went to work in defense jobs. People from every part of the country and every ethnic group worked for victory.

War fears led to tragedy for many Japanese Americans. Saying that they might be disloyal, the government moved about 110,000 Japanese Americans on the West Coast into relocation camps. They lost homes and businesses. Years later, Congress agreed to pay Japanese American citizens who had lost their homes and farms.

The Allied Victory In 1942, the Allies faced losses everywhere. German forces held most of Europe and were besieging the Soviet Union. Japan occupied islands in the Pacific.

Several Allied victories marked turning points in the war. The United States Navy turned back the Japanese at Midway Island. The Russians withstood the German siege of Stalingrad, and the British drove back the Germans in North Africa. In 1943, the Allies invaded Italy, as Mussolini's government collapsed. The major invasion of Western Europe came on **D-Day,** June 6, 1944. Allied troops landed on the coast of Normandy, France, and pressed eastward toward Germany.

Roosevelt died in April 1945, but Allied advances went on. In May, Hitler committed suicide and Germany surrendered. FDR's successor, Harry Truman, decided to use a powerful new weapon, the atomic bomb, against Japan. The bombing of Hiroshima and Nagasaki in August 1945 brought about Japan's surrender.

Section 3 Assessment

Recall
1. **Identify** Explain the significance of **(a)** Great Depression, **(b)** Herbert Hoover, **(c)** Franklin D. Roosevelt, **(d)** New Deal, **(e)** Social Security, **(f)** Adolf Hitler, **(g)** Holocaust, **(h)** World War II, **(i)** D-Day.
2. **Define (a)** jazz, **(b)** margin buying, **(c)** deficit spending, **(d)** totalitarian state.

Comprehension
3. What were the causes of the Great Depression?
4. Describe the three goals of the New Deal.

5. **(a)** How did World War II begin in Europe? **(b)** Why did the United States enter the war?

Critical Thinking and Writing
6. **Exploring the Main Idea** Review the Main Idea statement at the beginning of this section. Then, write a paragraph explaining whether you think a depression or a war is a greater threat to a nation.
7. **Supporting a Point of View (a)** Summarize one argument for and one argument against the New Deal. **(b)** Write a letter to FDR telling him why you do or do not support his goals.

ACTIVITY

Take It to the NET
Making a Map Use the Internet to find out about the D-Day landing. Then, make a map showing the movement of Allied forces. Visit *The American Nation* section of **www.phschool.com** for help in completing the activity.

4 The Cold War and the Civil Rights Era

BEFORE YOU READ

Reading Focus

- What were the causes of the Cold War?
- What successes did the civil rights movement achieve?
- How did the Vietnam War affect the United States?

Key Terms

Cold War
Marshall Plan
Korean War
Cuban missile crisis
civil rights movement
Brown v. *Board of Education*
Vietnam War

Taking Notes

Copy the concept web below. As you read, fill in the blank ovals with information about the aftermath of World War II. Add as many ovals as you need.

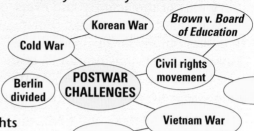

Main Idea After World War II, Americans faced the challenges of the Cold War abroad and the civil rights movement at home.

AS YOU READ American and Soviet flags
Find Main Ideas What is the main idea of Churchill's speech about the Soviet Union?

Setting the Scene British statesman Winston Churchill had warned early on of the Nazi menace. Now, in March 1946, Churchill came to Fulton, Missouri, to speak of a new threat to peace. The Soviet Union, he said, had seized control of most of Eastern Europe:

> 66 From Stettin in the Baltic to Trieste in the Adriatic, an iron curtain has descended across the Continent. . . . All these famous cities and the populations around them lie in what I must call the Soviet sphere. 99
>
> —Winston Churchill, "The Sinews of Peace"

In the audience, President Harry Truman nodded in agreement. Under Truman's leadership, the United States began a long commitment to stop Soviet aggression and the spread of communism.

The Cold War Begins

The United States, Britain, and the Soviet Union were allies in World War II. Still, the two democracies distrusted the Soviet communist dictatorship. Stalin and other Soviet leaders had boasted that they would spread their revolutionary ideas throughout the world.

At the end of the war, the Allies divided Germany into occupation zones. They also divided the city of Berlin, deep inside the Soviet zone. In addition, Soviet troops stayed in Eastern Europe. Stalin set up communist governments in nations such as Poland and Czechoslovakia. In response, President Truman resolved to contain Soviet expansion. He sent aid to anticommunist groups in other countries.

For the next 46 years, the United States and the Soviet Union clashed in a conflict known as the Cold War. The two superpowers did not face each other directly in battle. Instead, they competed for influence around the world. As both nations spent billions on defense and weapons, an arms race sped up. People on both sides worried about the outbreak of a nuclear war.

Postwar Crises In 1947, Secretary of State George C. Marshall proposed a plan to rebuild Europe. With some $12 billion of **Marshall Plan** help, Western Europe began to recover. Stalin, however, kept Eastern Europe from taking American aid.

In 1948, the Western powers united their zones of Germany. In response, the Soviets blockaded supplies coming into West Berlin. Truman's answer was the Berlin Airlift. For nearly a year, American planes dropped tons of food and supplies in West Berlin. Stalin lifted the blockade, but Berlin remained a trouble spot. In 1961, East Germany built a wall dividing East and West Berlin.

The Korean War After World War II, communism gained a foothold in Asia. Communists led by Mao Zedong took control of China in 1949. On the Korean peninsula, a Soviet-backed government ruled the North, above the 38th parallel. The United States backed a non-communist government in South Korea.

In June 1950, North Korean troops invaded the South. Truman asked for a United Nations force to stop them. Most of the UN forces were American. The **Korean War** dragged on until a truce was negotiated in 1953; however, Korea remained divided.

Cold War Fears Many Americans worried that Communists were working inside the United States. Truman ordered loyalty checks for government workers, and Congress carried on investigations.

In 1950, Wisconsin Senator Joseph McCarthy made dramatic charges about Communists in government, in schools, and even in the army. Although he was able to supply little real evidence, many people lost their jobs.

GEOGRAPHY Skills

During the Cold War, the United States and the Soviet Union competed for influence around the world. In many hot spots, the rivalry sparked armed conflict.

1. **Location** On the map, locate **(a)** Soviet Union, **(b)** Germany, **(c)** Korea, **(d)** Cuba, **(e)** Vietnam.

2. **Regions** What continent was most evenly divided into American and Soviet spheres of influence?

3. **Critical Thinking Drawing Conclusions** Why would Americans be concerned about Soviet influence in Cuba?

The Cold War

Key
- Warsaw Pact countries
- NATO countries
- ★ Cold War hot spots

Robinson Projection

Working for Civil Rights

The South

In the early 1960s, black and white protesters rode together on buses throughout the South. Many of these "freedom riders" were from the North. They risked assault and arrest in their struggle for civil rights. **Drawing Inferences** *Why do you think these freedom riders held hands as they sang?*

Primary Sources

See Martin Luther King, Jr., "I Have a Dream," on page 609 of the Reference Section.

Cuba In 1959, the communist threat came closer to home. Fidel Castro led a revolution in Cuba, taking over businesses and private property. Thousands of Cubans fled to the United States as exiles. The Soviet Union sent Castro economic aid.

In October 1962, the Soviets attempted to ship weapons to Castro. President John F. Kennedy then announced that American ships would stop any Soviet ships taking missiles to Cuba. After a tense few days, the Soviet ships turned back. The **Cuban missile crisis** was one of the hottest moments of the Cold War.

The Civil Rights Movement

After World War II, African Americans increased their fight for equal rights. This effort became known as the **civil rights movement.**

The Movement Begins As you read, in 1896 the Supreme Court ruled in *Plessy* v. *Ferguson* that states could legally segregete blacks and whites. Segregation became the law in southern states.

The NAACP sued to end segregation. In *Brown* v. *Board of Education* (1954), the Supreme Court overturned *Plessy* v. *Ferguson,* declaring that "separate educational facilities are inherently unequal." The court ordered schools everywhere to integrate. Despite some protests, the federal government enforced the order.

In 1955, African American Rosa Parks was arrested in Montgomery, Alabama, when she refused to give up her seat on a bus to a white man. In response, African Americans organized a boycott of the city's segregated bus system. During the boycott, Martin Luther King, Jr., emerged as a compelling national leader. A Baptist minister, King urged the use of nonviolent protests against unjust laws. His ideas about civil disobedience were strongly influenced by the writings of Henry David Thoreau. (See Chapter 15.)

The 1960s The civil rights movement grew in the 1960s. The movement drew young people, both black and white. Most protests were peaceful but were often met with violence. Homes and churches were bombed. Civil rights workers were killed or injured. Still, the movement grew. In August 1963, more than 200,000 Americans marched on Washington, D.C., to ask for laws to end discrimination.

President Kennedy supported civil rights policies. After Kennedy was assassinated in November 1963, Lyndon Johnson carried on this program. A Texan who had been a Senate leader, Johnson was skilled at getting laws passed. Congress passed a Civil Rights Act, a Voting Rights Act, and a constitutional amendment against poll taxes.

Despite new civil rights laws, many thought that change was coming too slowly. Leaders such as Malcolm X called upon African Americans to take more aggressive action. In April 1968, Martin Luther King, Jr., was shot and killed in Memphis, Tennessee.

The Movement Widens The civil rights movement inspired other groups. Mexican American leader César Chávez organized migrant workers to form the United Farm Workers. Through a national boycott of grapes, the union won better working conditions.

The women's rights movement also grew. Women often earned less money than men for doing the same jobs. Many professional schools gave preference to male applicants. Congress passed several laws to protect women's rights. The Civil Rights Act of 1964 outlawed discrimination in hiring based on gender as well as race.

The Vietnam War

Early in the 1960s, the American fight against communism led the nation into a painful era. Involvement in Vietnam, a former French colony in Southeast Asia, began slowly.

American Involvement In 1954, Vietnam was divided into a communist North and a noncommunist South. The United States backed the South. Many peasants in South Vietnam, however, joined the pro-communist Vietcong guerrillas.

Gradually, Presidents Kennedy and Johnson sent more and more military aid to South Vietnam. The Vietnam War turned into the longest war in American history. Between 1961 and 1973, more than 58,000 American troops lost their lives. There were few clear-cut victories as Americans fought unseen guerrillas in the jungle.

Impact at Home Americans were bitterly divided over the Vietnam War. Some "hawks" wanted an all-out victory over the communist North. "Doves," however, believed that the United States should not be in Vietnam at all. Antiwar protests were widespread, especially among college students.

Many blamed President Johnson for the worsening war, and he did not run again in 1968. Antiwar protests and violence disrupted the political conventions. The next President, Richard Nixon, promised to end the war. However, as the fighting continued, protests at home increased. Finally, in 1974, the last American troops left Vietnam. The following year, North Vietnam defeated South Vietnam.

Primary Source

A Marine in Vietnam

Michael DeLaney, an American marine stationed in Vietnam, wrote home to his parents in 1968:
"It is bad here, but I don't want you to worry. For the past two days, we went without water and food. Then a chopper came in and we got a couple of meals and about a glass of water for two days. We don't wash or shave. I've got a full beard and no change of clothes. I sleep on the ground, and we get some of our water from the bamboo plants, and eat the roots. We try to catch rainwater and the dew with our ponchos. We get bombarded every day, and at night we get sniper fire. I'm fine and I watch everything I do, so don't worry."

—Michael DeLaney, quoted in *Khe Sanh: Siege in the Clouds* (Hammel)

Analyzing Primary Sources
Why do you think DeLaney urged his parents not to worry about him?

Section 4 Assessment

Recall
1. **Identify** Explain the significance of (a) Cold War, (b) Marshall Plan, (c) Korean War, (d) Joseph McCarthy, (e) Cuban missile crisis, (f) *Brown* v. *Board of Education*, (g) Martin Luther King, Jr., (h) Lyndon Johnson, (i) César Chávez, (j) Vietnam War.
2. **Define** civil rights movement.

Comprehension
3. How did the Cold War begin?
4. Describe two gains made by the civil rights movement.

5. How did the Vietnam War divide Americans?

Critical Thinking and Writing
6. **Exploring the Main Idea** Review the Main Idea statement at the beginning of this section. Then, list two facts that support the following statement: Both the Cold War and the civil rights movement were related to a belief in American democracy.
7. **Contrasting** List two ways that American attitudes toward World War II differed from attitudes toward the Vietnam War.

ACTIVITY
Interviewing Write a list of 5–7 questions about the civil rights movement or the Vietnam War. Then, interview three older relatives or acquaintances who lived through those times. Keep a written or electronic record of their responses, and share them with the class.

5 Into the Future

BEFORE YOU READ

Reading Focus

- Why did a conservative movement take shape?
- How did the Cold War end?
- How did terrorist attacks in 2001 affect Americans?
- What changes and challenges have Americans faced in recent times?

Key Terms

Watergate affair

Reaganomics

détente

free market economy

Persian Gulf War

terrorism

North American Free Trade Agreement

environmentalist

Taking Notes

As you read, prepare an outline of this section. Use roman numerals to indicate the major headings, capital letters for the subheadings, and numbers for the supporting details. The sample at right will help you get started.

> I. The Conservative Movement
> A. Politics of the 1970s
>   1. Watergate
>   2.
> B. The Reagan Revolution
>   1. Conservative goals
>   2.
> C.
> II. New Directions in Foreign Policy
> A.
> B.

🇺🇸 Main Idea In the late 1900s, the United States took new directions politically, economically, and in world affairs.

AS YOU READ **Reagan campaign button**

Draw Inferences Read Reagan's words at right. How does the campaign button above convey a similar message?

Setting the Scene

Beset by economic woes and overseas crises, voters in 1980 turned to Ronald Reagan. A former movie actor and California governor, Reagan won people over with his genial smile, relaxed style, and open patriotism. One of his main targets was the growth of the federal government. He said:

> 66Government is not the solution to our problem, government is the problem. . . . It is not my intention to do away with government. It is, rather, to make it work—work with us, not over us; to stand by our side, not ride on our back.99
>
> —Ronald Reagan, First Inaugural Address, 1981

As President, Reagan united a new generation of conservatives. The "Reagan Revolution" brought enormous changes in how government worked.

The Conservative Movement

Federal government programs expanded in the 1960s and 1970s. Some laws created equal opportunities for women and minorities. Others helped the poor or protected consumers, workers, and the environment. Such programs did not always succeed. To pay for them, the government increased taxes. Businesses complained that regulation cost too much. A reaction against "big government" began.

Politics of the 1970s The unpopular Vietnam War helped bring Richard Nixon, a Republican, to office in 1969. In response to economic problems—rising prices, slow growth, and high unemployment—Nixon cut back spending. Then, political scandal rocked his administration. In 1972, burglars connected with Nixon's reelection campaign broke into Democratic headquarters in the Watergate office building. A congressional investigation showed that Nixon and his advisers had taken steps to cover up the Watergate affair. Faced with the threat of impeachment, Nixon stepped down in August 1974—the first President to resign from office.

Economic problems continued to plague Nixon's successors, Gerald Ford and Jimmy Carter. Under Carter, inflation reached 10 percent a year or more. With prices rising, many families had trouble paying for food, clothing, and shelter. In 1979, a foreign policy crisis further eroded Carter's popularity. Revolutionaries in Iran took over the American embassy and held Americans hostage for over a year. In 1980, discouraged voters turned to Ronald Reagan's upbeat message and promise of change.

The Reagan Revolution The conservatives who elected Reagan had various goals. All wanted a smaller federal government and less government regulation. Some conservatives focused on morality and a return to traditional family values. Many belonged to evangelical Christian churches.

As President, Reagan cut taxes, slowed down spending on social programs, and eliminated many regulations on business. This economic policy became known as Reaganomics. At the same time, he increased military spending to put pressure on the Soviet Union. After Reagan served two terms, his Vice President, George H.W. Bush, was elected in 1988. He continued many of Reagan's policies.

New Directions In 1992, former Arkansas governor Bill Clinton defeated Bush. A Democrat, Clinton was often at odds with the Republican Congress. He vetoed attempts to cut social programs and environmental laws. Clinton and Congress did work together to balance the federal budget.

A strong and growing economy helped keep Clinton's popularity high. Still, conservatives distrusted him. An investigation of Clinton's financial dealings turned up evidence of his improper relationship with a White House intern, which he at first denied. For only the second time in history, the House of Representatives voted to impeach a President, charging him with lying under oath. In February 1999, the Senate acquitted Clinton.

In 2000, Clinton's Vice President, Albert Gore, ran against Texas Governor George W. Bush, a son of the former President. Bush ran on a platform of "compassionate conservatism" and promised a large tax cut. Gore pointed to his political experience and the strong economy. Gore won the popular vote by a narrow margin. The electoral vote, however, remained in doubt as Gore contested Bush's victory in Florida. After the Supreme Court stopped further recounts, Gore conceded. George W. Bush became President in 2001.

Election of 2000

Percentage National Popular Vote

48.39% 47.88% 3.73% Other

Percentage Florida Popular Vote

48.85% 48.84% 2.31% Other

■ Gore, Democrat
■ Bush, Republican

CANDIDATE	TOTAL NATIONAL VOTE	TOTAL FLORIDA VOTE
Gore	50,996,039	2,912,253
Bush	50,456,141	2,912,790
Other	3,928,486	138,037

Source: Federal Election Commission

GRAPH *Skills*

The presidential election of 2000 was the most disputed race since 1876.

1. **Comprehension** What was the difference in the popular vote between Bush and Gore?

2. **Critical Thinking Drawing Conclusions** What role did candidates of other parties play in the election?

Civics

New Directions in Foreign Policy

From the late 1940s on, the Cold War dominated foreign policy. Then, communist rule began to crumble all over Europe. By the mid-1990s, communism was no longer a major threat. New kinds of conflicts erupted in trouble spots all over the world.

The Cold War Ends The Cold War began to thaw in the Nixon administration. A strong anticommunist, Nixon established ties with Communist China and visited the Soviet Union. The policy of **détente,** or relaxation of tensions, continued under Ford and Carter. A Soviet invasion of Afghanistan in 1980 ended détente. President Reagan took a hard line, calling the Soviet Union an "evil empire." Tensions once again increased.

In 1985, a new Soviet leader set great changes in motion. Mikhail Gorbachev relaxed controls on free speech and political opposition. Starting in 1989, communist governments in Eastern Europe began to collapse. The Berlin Wall was torn down, and Germany was reunited under a democratic government.

Finally, in 1991, the Soviet Union itself broke apart. The United States tried to help Russia and the other republics build democracy. It also helped the former communist states develop a **free market economy,** in which individuals rather than the government made decisions about what to produce and sell.

New World Conflicts When the communist government of Yugoslavia fell, old ethnic and religious hatreds flared up in the Balkans. In 1991, the republics of Croatia and Bosnia split off from Yugoslavia. Millions of people were displaced as Serbs, Croats, and Bosnians fought one another. War again erupted in 1998, between Serbs and Albanians in Kosovo. NATO forces intervened, and American soldiers joined European troops as peacekeepers.

The Middle East was another hot spot. One source of trouble was hostility between the Jewish state of Israel and its Arab neighbors. Another was ongoing violence between Israelis and Palestinians within Israel. Presidents Carter and Clinton worked to bring peace. Still, by 2002, violence between Israelis and Palestinians was again on the rise.

American support for Israel angered many Arabs. In 1973, oil-producing Arab countries cut off oil shipments, causing shortages and high prices. Concern about the supply of oil also led to the brief **Persian Gulf War** in 1991. Saddam Hussein, the dictator of Iraq, invaded neighboring oil-rich Kuwait. President Bush organized a UN coalition led by the United States. After six weeks, Iraqi troops withdrew from Kuwait. Still, Hussein remained in power.

The Fight Against Terrorism

After the 1960s, terrorist bombings, kidnappings, and hijackings became more common in Europe, the Middle East, and elsewhere. **Terrorism** is the deliberate use of random acts of violence, often against civilians, in order to achieve a political goal.

Americans and Terrorism In the Middle East, a number of radical Muslim groups sponsored terrorism. These extremists opposed

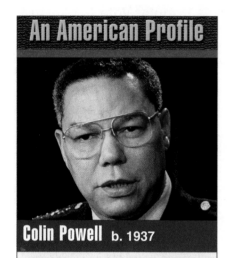

An American Profile

Colin Powell b. 1937

As Chairman of the Joint Chiefs of Staff, General Colin Powell helped direct American strategy in the Persian Gulf War. It was just one of many victories in his life.

Powell was the son of garment workers in New York City's Harlem. Every child in his family was expected to work for a college education. After college, Powell joined the army, earning a Purple Heart in Vietnam. Later in life, he helped found an organization that encouraged Americans to volunteer for pubic service. In 2001, he was named Secretary of State.

What qualities do you think made Colin Powell a strong leader?

American policies in the Middle East and western influence on their culture. As a result, Americans overseas sometimes became targets of terrorism. In 1988, a bomb exploded on an American airliner over Scotland, killing 270 people. Later, bombings hit two United States embassies in Africa and a navy ship off the coast of Yemen.

Terrorism also became a threat within the United States itself. In 1993, a bomb rocked the World Trade Center in New York City. Six Arab men were later convicted of the crime. Not all acts of terror were linked to the Middle East, however. In 1995, two Americans who resented the government exploded a bomb that destroyed a federal office building in Oklahoma City, killing 168 people.

Attacks on the United States On September 11, 2001, terrorists seized control of four American passenger airplanes. The hijackers crashed two of the planes into the Twin Towers of the World Trade Center, the tallest buildings in New York City. As onlookers watched in horror, the two skyscrapers burned, then collapsed. A third hijacked airliner crashed into American military headquarters at the Pentagon near Washington, D.C. The fourth airplane crashed in Pennsylvania after courageous passengers attacked the hijackers.

More than 3,000 people were killed in the terrorist attacks. In New York, the victims included many heroic police and firefighters trying to save people from the burning towers.

Americans Respond American citizens were quick to respond to the tragedy. Millions lined up to give blood, aided in rescue efforts, or donated money and supplies to help the victims and rescuers. Across the nation, people displayed American flags to show their unity.

President George W. Bush voiced the nation's outrage. The attacks, he said, were "acts of war." He committed the nation to an all-out campaign against terrorism and asked other nations to stand with the United States. At the same time, he cautioned Americans not to take their rage out on innocent Arab Americans and Muslims. "No one should be singled out for unfair treatment or unkind words because of their ethnic background or religious faith," Bush said.

Early on, the government blamed the attacks on a network of terrorists led by Osama bin Laden, a wealthy Saudi hiding in Afghanistan. American forces attacked military targets and terrorist training camps in Afghanistan. The Afghan dictatorship soon fell. As the search for bin Laden continued, President Bush vowed to wipe out terrorism everywhere. "Americans should not expect one battle," he said, "but a lengthy campaign unlike any other we have ever seen." As they waited, Americans went on with their lives in a new spirit of unity and patriotism.

Changes and Challenges

The nation faced other challenges and changes. Trade and technology made the world smaller and more interdependent.

A Global Economy Foreign trade became important in the economies of most countries. The United States now competes for trade with European and Asian nations that have strong economies. Some people want to use tariffs to protect American companies and

Take It to the NET

Go to **United We Stand** for updated articles and lessons to guide your classroom discussions of September 11 and beyond. www.phschool.com/social_studies/special_report/index.html

AS YOU READ **Summarize** Summarize two of the challenges that the world faces today.

jobs. Others, however, favor free trade. In 1993, Congress approved the North American Free Trade Agreement (NAFTA). It reduced trade barriers among the United States, Canada, and Mexico.

New Technology The first computers were built after World War II. By the 1980s, smaller and faster computers had become a fixture in homes and offices around the world. The Internet brought people and nations closer together. The possibilities of these technologies seem endless.

Space exploration sparked other new technologies. The United States began its space program in the 1950s as part of its rivalry with the Soviet Union. In 1969, two American astronauts became the first people to walk on the moon. The launching of the first reusable space shuttle in 1981 opened up possibilities for further discovery.

The Environment Environmental issues affect the entire world. Since the 1970s, environmentalists have worked to reduce pollution, protect resources, and improve the quality of air and water. Energy use and climate change remain serious issues. Burning fossil fuels—coal, oil, and natural gas—sends carbon dioxide into the atmosphere. Other human-made chemicals were blamed for damaging the ozone layer of the atmosphere. The ozone layer blocks out harmful radiation from the sun.

New Immigration Patterns The face of the United States has also changed. After the fall of the Soviet Union, many Russians and other former Soviet citizens moved to the United States. Conflicts like those in Asia and the Balkans created many refugees, who sought safety here. Today, most new immigrants come from Latin America, the Caribbean, and Asia. By 2000, Latinos had become the largest ethnic minority in the United States.

Section 5 Assessment

Recall
1. **Identify** Explain the significance of **(a)** Ronald Reagan, **(b)** Watergate affair, **(c)** Reaganomics, **(d)** Bill Clinton, **(e)** George W. Bush, **(f)** Persian Gulf War, **(g)** North American Free Trade Agreement.
2. **Define** **(a)** détente, **(b)** free market economy, **(c)** terrorism, **(d)** environmentalist.

Comprehension
3. Why did conservatives object to "big government"?
4. What event marked the end of the Cold War?

5. How did Americans respond to terrorist attacks in September 2001?
6. How did the American economy change?

Critical Thinking and Writing
7. **Exploring the Main Idea** Review the Main Idea statement at the beginning of this section. Then, list what you see as the three biggest changes described in this section.
8. **Drawing Conclusions** List four ways in which your life would be different today if computers had not been invented.

ACTIVITY

Writing a Speech You have been asked to write a speech welcoming new immigrants from Russia after the breakup of the Soviet Union. Describe the benefits that they will find in the United States and what will be expected of them as citizens.

566 ★ Epilogue *The United States Since 1865*

Transferring Information

Historical information comes in many forms. Sometimes, it is helpful to organize information so that you can compare it with other data.

The data below relate to sources of immigration in 1900. These data have been used to create the pie chart below.

Asia	4 percent
Americas	1.2 percent
Europe	94.7 percent
Africa	less than 1 percent
Other	less than 1 percent

The paragraph below describes modern immigration trends.

Immigration patterns have changed. In 1998, the largest percentage (45.2) came from the Americas. Another sizable percentage (33.2) were people from Asia. Africans now made up 6.2 percent, while Europeans accounted for 13.7 percent. About 1.7 percent of immigrants came from other places.

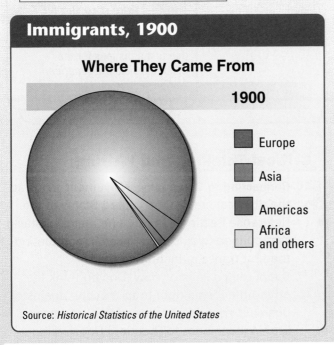

Immigrants, 1900
Where They Came From
1900
- Europe
- Asia
- Americas
- Africa and others

Source: *Historical Statistics of the United States*

Where They Came From, 1998

Learn the Skill *To learn how to transfer information, use the following steps:*

1. **Identify the raw data.** As you read a selection, note the facts given. If many statistics are included, think about how you might organize them so that they are easier to see and use.

2. **List the data.** Compile a list of the facts that you might use. Organize the percentages from greatest to least.

3. **Transfer the data.** To make a pie chart, divide a circle into parts that add up to 100 percent. Color each part to represent the percentage you want to include. Label the chart.

4. **Draw conclusions based on the data.** What can you learn by looking at the data in this form?

Practice the Skill *Use the information above to answer the following questions:*

1. (a) What kind of data does the paragraph provide? (b) What percentage of immigrants to the United States in 1998 were from Europe? From Asia?

2. (a) Order the data in the paragraph in order of percentage. (b) Where did the largest group of immigrants come from in 1998?

3. Copy the blank pie chart, and fit the data from the paragraph into it. Use the same color code as in the completed pie chart.

4. Describe how immigration patterns changed between 1900 and 1998.

Apply the Skill *See the Chapter Review and Assessment.*

Review and Assessment

CREATING A CHAPTER SUMMARY

Copy the timeline below. Add at least one key event or development for each 25-year period since the Civil War began. Some entries have been included to help you get started.

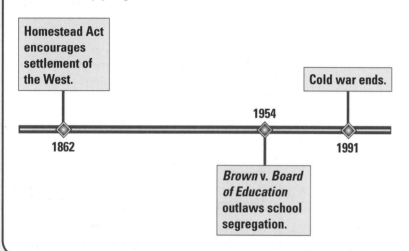

Homestead Act encourages settlement of the West.

Cold war ends.

1954

1862

1991

Brown v. *Board of Education* outlaws school segregation.

i-TEXT For additional review and enrichment activities, see the interactive version of *The American Nation,* available on the Web and on CD-ROM.

Take It to the NET

Chapter Self-Test For practice test questions for the Epilogue, visit *The American Nation* section of **www.phschool.com**.

Building Vocabulary

Write sentences using the chapter vocabulary words listed below, leaving blanks where the vocabulary words would go. Exchange your sentences with another student, and fill in the blanks in each other's sentences.

1. corporation
2. monopoly
3. muckraker
4. isolationism
5. imperialism
6. deficit spending
7. civil rights movement
8. détente
9. free market economy
10. terrorism

Reviewing Key Facts

11. How did city life change in the late 1800s? (Section 1)
12. How did the views of Booker T. Washington and W.E.B. DuBois differ? (Section 2)
13. Describe two effects of the Great Depression. (Section 3)
14. What were the causes of the Korean War? (Section 4)
15. Describe the outcome of the 2000 presidential election. (Section 5)

Critical Thinking and Writing

16. **Connecting to Geography: Movement** Look at the physical map of the United States in the Reference Section. Identify one major obstacle that builders would have faced in completing the first transcontinental railroad.
17. **Supporting a Point of View** Do you think the government was right to take action against business monopolies during the Progressive Era? Write a letter to Theodore Roosevelt giving reasons for your opinion.
18. **Contrasting** List three ways in which totalitarian states, such as those of the Soviet Union or Nazi Germany, differ from a democratic government like that of the United States.
19. **Drawing Inferences** List three personal qualities that a civil rights worker in the 1950s and 1960s would have needed to succeed.
20. **Drawing Conclusions** Events such as the bombing of Pearl Harbor in 1941 or the terrorist attacks in 2001 often stir Americans to a renewed sense of unity and patriotism. Write a paragraph explaining why you think this is so.

Analyzing Primary Sources

Mary Antin, a Russian Jewish immigrant, came to the United States in 1890. Here, she speaks of the opportunities in her new home:

❝Education was free. That subject my father had written about repeatedly, as comprising his chief hope for us children, the essence of American opportunity, the treasure that no thief could touch, not even misfortune or poverty. It was the one thing that he was able to promise us when he sent for us; surer, safer than bread or shelter. . . . No application made, no questions asked, no examinations, rulings, exclusions; no machinations, no fees. The doors stood open for every one of us.❞

—Mary Antin, *The Promised Land*

21. Summarize the main idea of this passage.
22. How do Antin and her father value wealth in comparison with education?
23. **(a)** Why do you think immigrants valued education so highly? **(b)** Do you think Americans value education in the same way today? Why or why not?

Transferring Information

The chart below gives raw data about United States exports in 1999. Examine the data, and answer the questions that follow.

United States Exports by Region

REGION	PERCENTAGE OF U.S. EXPORTS
Europe	24.7
NAFTA (Canada and Mexico)	36.4
Other Latin American Countries	8.0
Asia	27.4
Australia and Oceania	2.1
Africa	1.4

Source: U.S. Office of Trade and Economic Analysis

24. What percentage of United States exports went to Canada and Latin America in 1999?
    A 36.4 percent
    B 8 percent
    C 44.4 percent
    D Cannot tell from the data given
25. Copy the blank pie chart shown here. Use the data given in the table to create a pie chart.

ACTIVITIES

Connecting With . . . Culture

Designing a Poster The motto of the United States is *E pluribus unum,* a Latin phrase that means "Out of many, one." Design a poster about how people of various ethnic, racial, religious, and national groups have contributed to our national identity. Include three different examples chosen from this chapter or from earlier chapters in the textbook.

Take It to the NET

Connecting to Today

Creating a Plaque Thomas Edison was one of many Americans whose inventions shaped our world today. Use the Internet to find out about another American inventor who lived in the period from 1865 to 1920. Prepare a plaque that would appear in a Technology Hall of Fame describing that inventor's major contributions. For help in starting this activity, visit *The American Nation* section of **www.phschool.com**.

Evaluating the Validity of Internet Sites

Reviewing Sites About World War II Use the Internet to find sites relating to World War II. Write a review evaluating one site in terms of source, type of information, visuals, overall usefulness, and reliability. Then, explain whether you consider that site a valid source of information. For help in starting this activity, visit *The American Nation* section of **www.phschool.com**.

Reference Section

Washington Crossing the Delaware
by Emanuel Gottlieb Leutze

Primary Sources and Literature

The River

Pare Lorentz

In 1937, filmmaker Pare Lorentz told the history of the Mississippi River in his film *The River*. As the film begins, the audience hears the prologue, or introductory words.

Vocabulary Before you read the selection, find the meanings of these words in a dictionary: **glacier, rill, rivulet.**

Main Idea The prologue describes the journey of the Mississippi as it progresses from small tributaries to a wide river emptying into the Gulf of Mexico.

From as far West as Idaho,
　Down from the glacier peaks of the Rockies—
From as far East as New York,
　　Down from the turkey ridges of the Alleghenies
Down from Minnesota, twenty-five hundred miles,
　　The Mississippi River runs to the Gulf.
Carrying every drop of water, that flows down two-thirds of the continent,
Carrying every brook and rill, rivulet and creek,
Carrying all the rivers that run down two-thirds of the continent
The Mississippi runs to the Gulf of Mexico.
Down the Yellowstone, the Milk, the White and Cheyenne;
The Cannonball, the Musselshell, the James and the Sioux;
Down the Judith, the Grand, the Osage, and the Platte,
The Skunk, the Salt, the Black, and Minnesota;
Down the Rock, the Illinois, and the Kankakee . . .
Down the Arkansas fifteen hundred miles from the Great Divide;
Down the Red, a thousand miles from Texas;
Down the great Valley, twenty-five hundred miles from Minnesota,
　Carrying every rivulet and brook, creek and rill,
Carrying all the rivers that run down two-thirds of the continent—
The Mississippi runs to the Gulf.

A winding river

Analyzing Literature

1. Into what body of water does the Mississippi River empty?
A　The Wabash
B　The Ohio
C　The Gulf of Mexico
D　The Missouri

2. Three states mentioned in the prologue include:
A　Idaho, New York, and Texas
B　Missouri, Ohio, and New York
C　Arkansas, Colorado, and Idaho
D　New Mexico, New York, and Texas

3. Critical Thinking and Writing Analyzing Ideas Based on the prologue, what kind of story do you think the movie will tell about the Mississippi River?

Historical Document

Democracy in America
Alexis de Tocqueville

Alexis de Tocqueville came to the United States in 1831 to study the prison system. However, during the nine months he spent there, he observed and studied much more. In a series of notebooks, he recorded his impressions of the people he met and what he saw. Eventually, this collection became *Democracy in America*. The following is an excerpt from one of the entries.

Vocabulary Before you read the selection, find the meanings of these words in a dictionary: **compatriots, sedentary, zeal.**

Main Idea Tocqueville praises Americans' commitment to education and working hard.

Of all the countries in the world, America is that in which the spread of ideas and of human industry is most continual and most rapid. There is not an American but knows the resources of all the parts of the vast land that he inhabits; all the able men in the Union know each other by reputation, many of them personally. I have often been struck by astonishment to find how far that is the case. I can say that it has never happened to me to speak to an American about one of his compatriots without finding that he was up-to-date in knowing both how he was now placed and the story of his life.

I know that this intense industrial and intellectual movement is particularly encouraged by education, by the sort of government America enjoys, and by the altogether special situation in which the Americans find themselves. In America populations are not at all sedentary, . . . almost all of them are real industrial entrepreneurs who feel the need for means of communication with a liveliness and use them with a zeal which one could never expect from the routine and lazy spirit of our peasants. The effect of a road or a canal is therefore more noticeable and above all more immediate in America than it would be in France.

Alexis de Tocqueville

Analyzing Primary Sources

1. According to Tocqueville, how has the rapid spread of ideas affected Americans?
   A It shows that Americans communicate too often.
   B Most Americans are well informed.
   C People living in the countryside are not up-to-date.
   D Most Americans are not well educated.

2. How would Tocqueville define an American entrepreneur?
   A A person who works very hard
   B An educated person who welcomes new opportunities
   C A person who is sedentary
   D An educated government worker

3. **Critical Thinking and Writing** **Drawing Inferences** Why does Tocqueville feel that the effect of canals and roads is "more noticeable" and "immediate" in the United States than in France?

Historical Document

The Constitution of the Iroquois

The Iroquois constitution helped put an end to destructive fighting among the five Iroquois nations. It gave each of the Five Nations full control over its own affairs, but it set up two Grand Councils to deal with all matters that affected the Iroquois in general—for example, peace or war. Here are excerpts from the Iroquois constitution.

Vocabulary Before you read the selection, find the meanings of these words in a dictionary: **confederate, defection, manifest, upbraid, heeded, divest, titleship, vested, mentors.**

Main Idea The constitution of the Iroquois confederation provides a blueprint for the people to live together in peace.

. . . All the business of the Five Nations Confederate Council shall be conducted by the two combined bodies of Confederate Lords. . . . If any Confederate Lord neglects or refuses to attend the Confederate Council, the other Lords of the Nation of which he is a member shall require their War Chief to request the female sponsors of the Lord so guilty of defection to demand his attendance of the Council. If he refuses, the women holding the title shall immediately select another candidate for the title. If at any time it shall be manifest that a Confederate Lord has not in mind the welfare of the people, . . . the men or women of the Confederacy . . . shall come to the council and upbraid the erring Lord through his War Chief. If the complaint of the people through the War Chief is not heeded the first time it shall be uttered again and then if no attention is given a third complaint and warning shall be given. If the Lord is [defiant], the matter shall go to the council of the War Chiefs. The War Chiefs shall then divest the erring Lord of his title by order of the women in whom the titleship is vested. . . . The Lords of the Confederacy of the Five Nations shall be mentors of the people for all time. . . . Their hearts shall be full of peace and good will and their minds filled with a yearning for the welfare of the people of the Confederacy.

Flag of the Iroquois Nation

Analyzing Primary Sources

1. Matters of concern to all Iroquois will be considered by

    A the lords of the Mohawk and Cayuga nations

    B a Grand Council made up of all Iroquois

    C two Grand Councils made up of important lords

    D any Iroquois elected in free elections

2. If a member of the grand council does not obey the rules, he

    A cannot attend any more meetings

    B will be exiled to a neighboring group

    C can be criticized by the men and women of the League

    D will be allowed to finish his term on the council

3. Critical Thinking Analyzing Information How did the constitution ensure that the concerns of the people were addressed?

Historical Document

The Printing Press: "New Makers of Books"

William Fichet

Printing was probably the most important new technology developed during the Renaissance. The invention of the printing press helped spread learning throughout Europe. No one had a more important role in this new technology than a German printer named Johannes Gutenberg (GOO tun berg). Gutenberg's press used type in which each letter of the alphabet was on a separate piece of metal. The following selection comes from a letter written by William Fichet (fee SHAY), the man who brought Gutenberg's invention to Paris.

Vocabulary Before you read the selection, find the meanings of these words in a dictionary: **devised, Muses, mortals, transcribed, posterity.**

Main Idea Fichet praises Gutenberg's contribution to humankind.

Great light has been thrown by the breed of new makers of books, whom, within our memory, Germany has broadcast into every quarter. For they say that there, not far from the city of Mainz, there appeared a certain John whose surname was Gutenberg, who first of all men, devised the art of printing, whereby books are made, not by a reed, as did the ancients, nor with a quill pen, as do we, but with metal letters, and that swiftly, neatly, beautifully. Surely this man is worthy to be loaded with divine honors by all the Muses, all the arts, all the tongues of those who delight in books, and is all the more to be preferred to gods and goddesses in that he has put the means of choice within reach of letters themselves and of mortals devoted to culture. . . .

But that great Gutenberg has discovered things far more pleasing and more divine, in carving out letters in such fashion that whatever can be said or thought can by them be written down at once and transcribed and committed to the memory of posterity.

An early printing press

Analyzing Primary Sources

1. According to Fichet, how were books made by "the ancients"?

  A Using styluses

  B Using reeds

  C Using quills

  D Using pens

2. Which of these statements describes Fichet's opinion of Gutenberg?

  A Gutenberg lived near Mainz, Germany.

  B Until now, Europeans wrote books by using quill pens.

  C Gutenberg is worthy of divine honors.

  D Thanks to Gutenberg, ideas can be preserved for the future.

3. Critical Thinking and Writing **Making Predictions** List three ways in which the invention of the printing press will change life in Europe.

Historical Document

A Brief Account of the Devastation of the Indies

Bartolomé de Las Casas

In 1542, Bartolomé de Las Casas returned to Spain to report on Spanish treatment of Native Americans. Although some historians think Las Casas exaggerated some of the facts, no one disputes that his account had a powerful impact.

Vocabulary Before you read the selection, find the meanings of these words in a dictionary: **guileless, duplicity, embroilments, rancors, complaisant, malady, ravening.**

Main Idea Las Casas argues that the greed and cruelty of the Spanish conquerors had a deadly effect on Caribbean Indians.

And of all the infinite universe of humanity, [the Indians] are the most guileless, the most devoid of wickedness and duplicity, the most obedient and faithful to their native masters and to the Spanish Christians whom they serve. They are by nature the most humble, patient, and peaceable, holding no grudges, free from embroilments, neither excitable nor quarrelsome. These people are the most devoid of rancors, hatreds, or desire for vengeance of any people in the world. And because they are so weak and complaisant, they are less able to endure heavy labor and soon die of no matter what malady. . . .

Yet into this sheepfold, into this land of meek outcasts there came some Spaniards who immediately behaved like ravening wild beasts, wolves, tigers, or lions that had been starved for many days. And Spaniards behaved no other way during the past forty years, down to the present time, for they are still acting like ravening beasts, killing, terrorizing, afflicting, torturing, and destroying the native peoples, doing all this with the strangest and most varied methods of cruelty, never seen or heard of before, and to such a degree that this Island of Hispaniola once so populous (having a population that I estimated to be more than three million), has now a population of barely two hundred persons.

A Spanish coin

Analyzing Primary Sources

1. Las Casas is mainly interested in presenting the Indians as

A faithful workers

B innocent victims

C proud warriors

D good Christians

2. Which word best describes the attitude of Las Casas toward the Spanish?

A Admiring

B Forgiving

C Angry

D Afraid

3. Critical Thinking and Writing Evaluating Information (a) What effect did Las Casas hope his report would have? (b) List three ways in which he uses words to stir strong emotions.

The General History of Virginia

John Smith

In 1624, John Smith published *The General History of Virginia*, one of our main sources of information about the founding of Jamestown. Here, Smith describes what happened after the ship that brought the colonists in 1607 returned to England.

Vocabulary Before you read the selection, find the meanings of these words in a dictionary: **pilfer, sassafras, palisades, provision.**

Main Idea The Jamestown colony suffered from exhaustion, a lack of food, and poor leadership.

While the ships stayed, our allowance was somewhat bettered by a daily proportion of biscuits, which the sailors would pilfer to sell, give, or exchange with us for money, sassafras, furs. . . . But when they departed, there remained neither tavern, [nor] beer, [nor] house, nor place of relief, but the [community cooking pot]. . . . and that was half a pint of wheat, and as much barley boiled with water for a man a day, and this having fried some twenty-six weeks in the ship's hold, contained as many worms as grains . . .

With this lodging and diet, our extreme toil in bearing and planning palisades so strained and bruised us, and our continual labor in the extremity of the heat had so weakened us, as were cause sufficient to have made us as miserable in our native country, or any other place in the world.

From May to September, those that escaped lived upon sturgeon, and sea crabs. Fifty in this time we buried. . . .

But now was all our provision spent, the sturgeon gone, all helps abandoned, each hour expecting the fury of the savages; when God, the Patron of all good endeavors in that desperate extremity so changed the hearts of the savages that they brought such plenty of their fruits and provision as no man wanted.

John Smith

Analyzing an Eyewitness Account

1. How did the colonists survive before the ships left?
   - **A** They hunted and fished.
   - **B** They ate crab and sturgeon.
   - **C** The sailors shared or sold food.
   - **D** They had extra provisions.

2. Who supplied the food that finally saved the colonists from starvation?
   - **A** Sailors
   - **B** Native Americans
   - **C** The Spanish
   - **D** John Smith

3. **Critical Thinking and Writing Evaluating Information** Smith wrote this history more than 15 years after the events described here. Would you consider it a reliable account of the early years of Jamestown? Why or why not?

Historical Document

Fundamental Orders of Connecticut

As the first written plan of government in 1639, the Fundamental Orders of Connecticut provided for a representative form of government with a governor, a legislative assembly, and courts. Three of the orders are given below.

Vocabulary Before you read the selection, find the meanings of these words in a dictionary: **Freemen, deputies, Jurisdiction, levied.**

Main Idea The Fundamental Orders of Connecticut provide for each town to be represented in the General Court.

It is Ordered . . . that Windsor, Hartford, and Wethersfield shall have power . . . to send four of their Freemen as their deputies to every General Court; and Whatsoever other Town shall be . . . added to this Jurisdiction, they shall send so many deputies as the Court shall judge meet, a reasonable proportion to the number of Freemen that are in the said Towns being to be attended therein; which deputies shall have the power of the whole Town to give their votes and allowance to all such laws and orders as may be for the public good . . .

It is Ordered, sentenced, and decreed, that the deputies thus chosen shall have power and liberty to appoint a time and a place of meeting together before any General Court, to advise and consult of . . . things as may concern the good of the public . . .

It is Ordered . . . that when any General Court upon the occasions of the Commonwealth have agreed upon any sum, or sums of money to be levied upon the several Towns within this Jurisdiction, that a committee be chosen to set out and appoint what shall be the proportion of every town to pay of the said levy . . .

Colonists settle in Connecticut

Analyzing Primary Sources

1. In what way was the system of government in Connecticut similar to our system today?

  A Each town has a say in decisions through its representatives.

  B Each town government makes its own laws.

  C Only Freemen may be in the government.

  D Every town pays the same amount of taxes to the colonial government.

2. How will the amount of taxes to be collected from each town be decided?

  A The town representative will decide the sum.

  B The General Court will choose an amount that all towns will pay.

  C A chosen committee will decide the sum.

  D The towns will vote.

3. Critical Thinking and Writing Evaluating Information Do you think the Freemen from each town represented all the people? Explain.

Eyewitness Account

Autobiography

Benjamin Franklin

At 17, Benjamin Franklin left his home in Boston to seek his fortune in Philadelphia. After several years, he owned his own printing shop and had gained a reputation as a hard worker and a successful businessman. Always eager to improve his city, Franklin introduced several new ideas in Philadelphia, including that of a lending library.

Vocabulary Before you read the selection, find the meanings of these words in a dictionary: **render, commencing, manifested, utility.**

Main Idea Benjamin Franklin decides to start a public lending library in Philadelphia.

At the time I establish'd myself in Pennsylvania, there was not a good bookseller's shop in any of the colonies to the southward of Boston. In New York and [Philadelphia] the printers were indeed stationers; they sold only paper, etc., almanacs, ballads, and a few common schoolbooks. Those who lov'd reading [had to] send for their books from England; the members of the [club] had each a few. We . . . hired a room to hold our club in. I propos'd that we should all of us bring our books to that room, where they would not only be ready to consult in our conferences, but become a common benefit, each of us being at liberty to borrow such as he wish'd to read at home. This was . . . done, and for some time contented us.

Finding the advantage of this little collection, I propos'd to render the benefit from books more common by commencing a public subscription library. I drew a sketch of the plan and rules that would be necessary . . . each subscriber engag'd to pay a certain sum down for the first purchase of books, and an annual contribution for increasing them. . . . The library was opened one day in the week for lending to the subscribers. . . . The institution soon manifested its utility, [and] was imitated by other towns, and in other provinces. . . . Reading became fashionable. . . .

Benjamin Franklin

Analyzing an Eyewitness Account

1. Why did Franklin feel a place to buy books was necessary?
   A Printers sold books only in Boston.
   B Books arrived in the colonies monthly.
   C Most colonial cities were without bookshops.
   D Colonists had to buy books from France.

2. How was the first library run?
   A Subscribers paid for each book.
   B Subscribers contributed money and then borrowed books free of charge.
   C Subscribers could borrow five books.
   D Anyone could borrow books.

3. **Critical Thinking and Writing** **Synthesizing Information** Benjamin Franklin believed in the ideas of the Enlightenment. How did his founding of the public library advance those ideas?

Historical Document

The English Bill of Rights

When Americans wrote their Bill of Rights, they were inspired by the English Bill of Rights of 1689. This was a list of rights that the English government guaranteed to citizens. It ensured that Parliament, not the monarchy, was the most important branch of government.

Vocabulary Before you read the selections, find the meanings of these words in a dictionary: **regal, consent, levying, petition, proceedings, excessive, inflicted, redress, amending.**

Main Idea The English Bill of Rights of 1689 limited the power of the monarchy.

And thereupon the said lords . . . asserting their ancient rights and liberties, declare:

That the . . . power of suspending of laws, or the execution of laws, by regal authority, without consent of parliament, is illegal.

That levying money for or to the use of the crown, . . . without grant of parliament, . . . is illegal.

That it is the right of the subjects to petition the King, and all commitments and prosecutions for such petitioning are illegal.

That the raising or keeping a standing army within the kingdom in a time of peace, unless it be with consent of parliament, is against the law.

That election of members of parliament ought to be free.

That the freedom of speech, and debates or proceedings in parliament, ought not to be . . . questioned in any court or place out of parliament.

That excessive bail ought not to be required, nor excessive fines imposed; nor cruel and unusual punishments inflicted.

And that for redress of all grievances, and for the amending, strengthening and preserving of the laws, parliaments ought to be held frequently.

Colonial protest

Analyzing Primary Sources

1. According to the English Bill of Rights, the power to levy money

　A belongs entirely to the monarchy

　B requires the approval of Parliament

　C belongs entirely to Parliament

　D belongs entirely to English towns and villages

2. What does the English Bill of Rights say about the rights of the people?

　A They can refuse to pay taxes.

　B They can petition the king without fear of persecution.

　C They can join the army.

　D They can be elected to Parliament.

Critical Thinking **Analyzing Information** List four ways in which the English Bill of Rights makes Parliament stronger than the monarch.

"Revolutionary Tea"

The Tea Act of 1773 placed a new tax on tea sold in the colonies. The song "Revolutionary Tea," written by an anonymous colonist, reveals how many colonists felt about the Tea Act and about their relationship with far-off Britain.

Vocabulary Before you read the selection, find the meanings of these words in a dictionary: **pence, conveyed, quoth, steeped.**

Main Idea A colonial song pokes fun at Britain, comparing it to a rich, old woman who forces her daughter to pay a tax.

There was an old lady lived over the sea.
And she was an Island Queen;
Her daughter lived off in a new country,
With an ocean of water between.
The old lady's pockets were full of gold,
But never contented was she,
So she called on her daughter to pay her a tax
Of three pence a pound on her tea,
Of three pence a pound on her tea. . . .

The tea was conveyed to the daughter's door,
All down by the ocean's side;
And the bouncing girl poured out every pound
In the dark and boiling tide.
And then she called out to the Island Queen,
"Oh, mother, dear mother," quoth she,
"Your tea you may have when 'tis steeped enough,
But never a tax from me.
But never a tax from me."

A colonial teapot

Analyzing Literature

1. What is the main point of "Revolutionary Tea"?
   A The colonists will remain loyal to Britain.
   B The British and the American colonists both love tea.
   C Colonists resent the tax on tea.
   D The American colonists are like disobedient children.

2. The "old lady" represents
   A Massachusetts
   B colonial tea merchants
   C Britain
   D redcoats in Boston

3. **Critical Thinking** **Identifying Points of View** Which point of view does the song represent, the British or the American? Give two examples from the song to support your answer.

Historical Document

Common Sense

Thomas Paine

At the request of Benjamin Franklin, Englishman Thomas Paine came to America in 1776 to help support the cause of independence. Soon after his arrival, Paine published a 47-page pamphlet, *Common Sense*. It played a key role in persuading the colonists to revolt against Great Britain.

Vocabulary Before you read the selection, find the meanings of these words in a dictionary: **advocate, reconciliation, derived, ineffectual, disdain, vanity, obstinancy.**

Main Idea Thomas Paine urges the colonists to break away from Great Britain.

Thomas Paine

I challenge the warmest advocate for reconciliation, to show, a single advantage that this continent can reap, by being connected with Great Britain. I repeat the challenge, not a single advantage is derived. Our corn will fetch its price in any market in Europe, and our imported goods must be paid for, buy them where we will. . . .

Every quiet method for peace hath been ineffectual. Our prayers have been rejected with disdain; and only tended to convince us, that nothing flatters vanity, or confirms obstinancy in Kings more than repeated petitioning and nothing hath contributed more than that very measure to make the Kings of Europe absolute. . . . Wherefore since nothing but blows will do . . . let us come to a final separation. . . .

As to government matters, it is not in the powers of Britain to do this continent justice: The business of it will soon be too weighty, and intricate, to be managed with any tolerable degree of convenience, by a power, so distant from us, and so very ignorant of us; for if they cannot conquer us, they cannot govern us. To be always running three or four thousand miles with a tale or a petition, waiting four or five months for an answer, which when obtained requires five or six more to explain it in, will in a few years be looked upon as folly and childishness. There was a time when it was proper, and there is a proper time for it to cease.

Analyzing Primary Sources

1. According to Paine, how has Great Britain responded to the colonies' attempts at peace?

  A Their petitions are carefully considered.

  B Their petitions are useless.

  C The King is ready to listen to colonial complaints.

  D Great Britain wants war.

2. What is one argument Paine gives for becoming independent of Great Britain?

  A There are too many laws to follow.

  B The distance between the two places makes it difficult to govern effectively.

  C The colonies have economic difficulties.

  D The colonists have to fight Britain's wars.

3. Critical Thinking and Writing Analyzing Information How might Paine's appeal persuade colonists to separate from Great Britain?

Historical Document

On the Care of the Wounded
Benjamin Rush

Dr. Benjamin Rush became Surgeon General of the Continental Army in April 1777. After inspecting the hospitals where the wounded soldiers were treated, Rush complained about the horrible conditions in a letter to General Washington.

Vocabulary Before you read the selection, find the meanings of these words in a dictionary: **redress, calamity, prolonged, contracted, perish, mortality.**

Main Idea Dr. Rush describes how the conditions at the hospitals are often an obstacle to recovery.

I have delayed troubling Your Excellency with the state of our hospitals in hopes you would hear it from the director general, whose business it is to correspond with Your Excellency upon this subject. . . . I beg leave therefore at last to look up to you, and through you to the Congress, as the only powers that can redress our grievances or do us justice.

I need not inform Your Excellency that we have now upward of 5,000 sick in our hospitals. This number would cease to be alarming if our hospitals could afford such accommodations to the poor fellows as would ensure them a speedy recovery. But this is far from being the case. There cannot be a greater calamity for a sick man than to come into our hospital at this season of the year. Old disorders are prolonged, and new ones contracted among us. This last is so much the case that I am safe when I assert that a great majority of those who die under our hands perish with diseases caught in our hospitals. When I consider the present army under Your Excellency's command as the last hope of America, I am more alarmed and distressed at these facts than I have words to express. I can see nothing to prevent the same mortality this winter among our troops that prevailed last year. Every day deprives us 4 or 5 patients out of 500 in a hospital under my care in this place. The same complaints are heard from every quarter. The surgeons have been blamed for these things, but without reason.

Benjamin Rush

Analyzing Primary Sources

1. According to Dr. Rush, why are the soldiers not recovering sooner?
   A Their injuries are too difficult to care for.
   B There are too many soldiers to treat.
   C They catch diseases during their stay in the hospital.
   D The food is poor.

2. What does Rush predict will happen if conditions in the hospitals do not improve?
   A More soldiers will die in the coming winter.
   B Soldiers will desert the army.
   C There will not be enough surgeons.
   D Rush will be forced to leave his position.

3. **Critical Thinking and Writing** **Drawing Inferences** Why does Rush call the army the "last hope of America"?

Eyewitness Account

Debates in the Federal Convention of 1787
James Madison

James Madison took detailed notes of all the debates at the Constitutional Convention of 1787. Here, he describes the final day of the convention.

Vocabulary Before you read the selection, find the meanings of these words in a dictionary: **notwithstanding, venerable, vicissitudes.**

Main Idea Although some delegates refuse to sign the Constitution, the majority agree to put aside their objections and approve the document.

Mr. Randolph [of Virginia] then rose and . . . apologized for his refusing to sign the constitution, notwithstanding the vast majority and venerable names that would give sanction to its wisdom and its worth. He said, however, that he did not mean by this refusal to decide that he should oppose the Constitution [in public]. He meant only to keep himself free to be governed by his duty as it should be prescribed by his future judgment. . . .

Mr. Gouverneur Morris [PA] said that he too had objections, but, considering the present plan as the best that was to be attained, he should take it with all its faults. The majority had determined in its favor, and by that determination he should abide. . . .

The members then proceeded to sign the [document].

While the last members were signing it, Dr. Franklin, looking toward the President's chair, at the back of which a rising sun happened to be painted, observed to a few members near him that painters had found it difficult to distinguish in their art a rising from a setting sun. "I have," said he, "often, and often in the course of the session, and the vicissitudes of my hopes and fears as to its [result], looked at that behind the President without being able to tell whether it was rising or setting. But now at length I have the happiness to know that it is a rising and not a setting sun."

The Liberty Bell

Analyzing an Eyewitness Account

1. How would you describe Randolph's attitude toward the Constitution?

  A He approved of it.

  B He had objections but agreed to sign it.

  C He refused to sign it.

  D He swore to oppose it.

2. How would you describe Morris's attitude toward the Constitution?

  A He approved of it.

  B He had objections but agreed to sign it.

  C He refused to sign it.

  D He swore to oppose it.

3. Critical Thinking and Writing Drawing Inferences (a) Restate the main idea of Franklin's story about the sun. **(b)** Why do you think he felt this way?

Historical Document

The Federalist Papers

Alexander Hamilton

The Federalist Papers is a name given to a series of essays written in 1787 by Alexander Hamilton, James Madison, and John Jay. The purpose of the essays was to win support for the new Constitution. This is an excerpt from the first essay, written by Hamilton.

Vocabulary Before you read the selection, find the meanings of these words in a dictionary: **unequivocal, inefficiency, subsisting, propriety.**

Main Idea Hamilton argues that the future of democratic government in the world depends on the success of the Constitution.

After an unequivocal experience of the inefficiency of the subsisting federal government, you are called upon to deliberate on a new Constitution for the United States of America. The subject speaks its own importance; comprehending in its consequences nothing less than the existence of the UNION, the safety and welfare of the parts of which it is composed, the fate of an empire in many respects the most interesting in the world. It has been frequently remarked that it seems to have been reserved to the people of this country, by their conduct and example, to decide the important question whether societies of men are really capable or not of establishing good government from reflection and choice, or whether they are forever destined to depend for their political constitutions on accident and force. If there be any truth in the remark, the crisis at which we are arrived may with propriety be regarded as the era in which that decision is to be made; and a wrong election of the part we shall act may, in this view, deserve to be considered as the general misfortune of mankind. . . .

It may perhaps be thought superfluous to offer arguments to prove the utility of the UNION . . . But the fact is that we already hear it whispered in the private circles of those who oppose the new Constitution, that the thirteen States are of too great extent for any general system, and that we must of necessity resort to separate confederacies . . .

Alexander Hamilton

Analyzing Primary Sources

1. According to Hamilton, Americans must prove to the world that
   A a colony can leave its parent country
   B the United States is superior to other nations
   C people can create their own government
   D the Articles of Confederation can work

2. What does Hamilton fear will happen if the Constitution fails?
   A The states will separate.
   B Britain will regain control.
   C The government will become inefficient.
   D A new Constitution will have to be written.

3. **Critical Thinking and Writing Supporting a Point of View** Do you agree that the American experiment with democratic government was important to the entire world? Explain.

Three State Constitutions

Each of the 50 states has its own constitution. The following are brief excerpts from the constitutions of New York, Texas, and California.

Vocabulary Before you read the selection, find the meanings of these words in a dictionary: **discrimination, rendered, incompetent, diffusion, conservation.**

Main Idea Some topics are common to all state constitutions, while others reflect the concerns of that particular state.

New York Bill of Rights

Sec. 3. The free exercise and enjoyment of religious profession and worship, without discrimination or preference, shall forever be allowed in this state to all mankind; and no person shall be rendered incompetent to be a witness on account of his opinions on matters of religious belief . . .

Sec. 5. Excessive bail shall not be required nor excessive fines imposed, nor shall cruel and unusual punishments be inflicted, nor shall witnesses be unreasonably detained.

Texas Article 7 (Education)

Sec. 1. A general diffusion of knowledge being essential to the preservation of the liberties and rights of the people, it shall be the duty of the Legislature of the State to establish and make suitable provision for the support and maintenance of an efficient system of public free schools.

Sec. 7. (a) One-fourth of the revenue derived from the State occupation taxes shall be set apart annually for the benefit of the public free schools. . . .

California Article 10 (Water)

Sec. 2. It is hereby declared that because of the conditions prevailing in this State the general welfare requires that the water resources of the State be put to beneficial use to the fullest extent of which they are capable, and that the waste or unreasonable use or unreasonable method of use of water be prevented, and that the conservation of such waters is to be exercised with a view to the reasonable and beneficial use thereof in the interest of the people and for the public welfare. . . .

State flags of New York, Texas, and California

Analyzing Primary Sources

1. Section 3 of the New York Bill of Rights is related to which amendment to the United States Constitution?

  A The First Amendment

  B The Second Amendment

  C The Fifth Amendment

  D The Thirteenth Amendment

2. The "conditions" referred to in the California constitution are most likely related to the state's

  A geography

  B history

  C population

  D government

3. Critical Thinking and Writing **Solving Problems** **(a)** What general goal is described in the above excerpt from the Texas constitution? **(b)** Describe one specific way in which the Texas constitution tries to meet that goal.

Literature

Twelve Angry Men
Reginald Rose

Twelve Angry Men takes place inside a jury room at a murder trial. A unanimous vote is needed to convict. Here, Juror #8—the only person to vote "not guilty"—has promised to go along with the others if they still want to vote "guilty." One juror then changes his vote.

Main Idea This play examines the attitudes of different jurors toward serving on a jury.

#11: Please. I would like to say something here. I have always thought that a man was entitled to have unpopular opinions in this country. This is the reason I came here. In my own country, I am ashamed to say . . .

#10: What do we have to listen to now, the whole history of your country?

#7: Yeah, let's stick to the subject. [*He turns to #5.*] Now I'm talking facts. What made you change your vote?

#9: There's nothing for him to tell you. He didn't change his vote. I did.

#7: No, I wouldn't like you to tell me why.

#9: Well, I'd like to make it clear anyway . . .

#10: Do we have to listen to this?

Foreman: The man wants to talk.

#9: . . . [Juror #8] has been standing alone against us. He doesn't say the boy is not guilty. He just isn't sure. Well it's not easy to stand alone against the ridicule of others, even when there's a worthy cause. So he gambled for support, and I gave it to him. I respect his motives. The boy on trial is probably guilty. But I want to hear more. Right now the vote is ten to two.

#11: Pardon. This fighting. This is not why we are here, to fight. We have a responsibility. This, I have always thought, is a remarkable thing about democracy. That we are, uh, what is the word? Notified. That we are notified by mail to come down to this place and decide on the guilt or innocence of a man we have never heard of before. We have nothing to gain or lose by our verdict. This is one of the reasons why we are strong. We should not make it a personal thing. . . . Thank you.

A lawyer and judge meet

Analyzing Literature

1. Which juror is a naturalized citizen?
 A Juror #7
 B Juror #9
 C Juror #10
 D Juror #11

2. Juror #9 changes his vote because he
 A believes the defendant is guilty
 B believes the defendant is not guilty
 C is not sure whether the defendant is guilty
 D is afraid to stand alone against the others

3. Critical Thinking and Writing **Analyzing Information** **(a)** What features of the American jury system does Juror #11 praise? **(b)** Why do you think he feels this way?

Historical Document

Farewell Address

George Washington

After serving two terms as President, George Washington wrote his famous Farewell Address in 1796. In it, he announced that he would not seek a third term. As he retired from public service, the outgoing President gave his views on the best policies for the young republic to follow.

Vocabulary Before you read the selection, find the meanings of these words in a dictionary: **discriminations, distract, ill-founded, primary, detached.**

Main Idea On leaving office, Washington urges the nation to reject political parties and keep out of Europe's affairs.

[On Political Parties]

I have already [told] you the danger of Parties in the State, with particular reference to the founding of them on Geographical discriminations. Let me now take a more [general] view, & warn you in the most solemn manner against the [harmful] effects of the Spirit of Party, generally.

. . . the common & continual mischiefs of the spirit of the Party are sufficient to make it the interest and the duty of a wise People to discourage and restrain it.

It serves always to distract the Public Councils and [weaken] the Public Administration. It [stirs up] the Community with ill-founded Jealousies and false alarms, kindles the [hatred] of one part against another . . .

[On Europe]

Europe has a set of primary interests, which to us have none, or a very remote relation. Hence she must be engaged in frequent controversies, the causes of which are essentially foreign to our concerns. . . .

Our detached & distant situation invites and enables us to pursue a different course. If we remain one People, under an efficient government, the period is not far off, when we may defy material injury. . . .

George Washington

Analyzing Primary Sources

1. What is Washington's view of political parties?

    A They cost too much money.

    B They cause dangerous divisions.

    C They result in the rise of monarchs.

    D They weaken the system of checks and balances.

2. What is Washington's advice on foreign policy?

    A Cancel treaties with European countries.

    B Avoid all links except trade with European countries.

    C Make alliances only with European democracies.

    D Join all foreign alliances.

3. **Critical Thinking and Writing** **Evaluating Information** Washington himself belonged to no political party. Did that increase or decrease the effectiveness of what he had to say? Explain.

Historical Document

A Letter to John Adams, 1796
Thomas Jefferson

Although they were political opponents, Thomas Jefferson and John Adams maintained a deep respect for one another. After their retirements, Jefferson lived in Virginia and Adams in Massachusetts. They corresponded for the rest of their lives—almost until the day when they both died, July 4, 1826.

Vocabulary Before you read the selection, find the meanings of these words in a dictionary: **magistracy, disinterestedness, esteem, contrived.**

Main Idea Jefferson congratulates Adams on winning the presidential election of 1796, even though Jefferson himself became Vice President.

DEAR SIR—The public and the public papers have been much occupied lately in placing us in a point of opposition to each other. I trust with confidence that less of it has been felt by ourselves personally. . . . I knew it impossible you should lose a vote North of the Delaware [River], and even if that of Pennsylvania should be against you in the mass, yet that you would get enough South of that to place your succession out of danger.

. . . No one then will congratulate you with purer disinterestedness than myself. The share indeed which I may have had in the late vote, I shall still value highly, as an evidence of the share I have in the esteem of my fellow citizens. . . . I have no ambition to govern men. It is a painful and thankless office. . . . I devoutly wish you may be able to shun for us this war by which our agriculture, commerce and credit will be destroyed. If you are, the glory will be all your own; and that your administration may be filled with glory and happiness to yourself . . . is the sincere wish of one who tho', in the course of our voyage thro' life, various little incidents have happened or been contrived to separate us, retains still for you the solid esteem of the moments when we were working for our independence, and sentiments of respect and affectionate attachment.

Thomas Jefferson

Analyzing Primary Sources

1. What was Jefferson's attitude toward Adams's election as President?

  A Congratulations from a supporter

  B Congratulations from an opponent, but admirer

  C Anger that the people of the United States had rejected him for President

  D Anger because the election was dishonest

2. Jefferson expected Adams to win the election because

  A he knew Adams to be strong in the North

  B he expected Adams to sweep the region south of the Delaware River

  C Jefferson had campaigned for him

  D Adams was a very good campaigner

3. Critical Thinking and Writing **Summarizing** In three sentences, summarize the ideas expressed by Jefferson in the final paragraph of the letter.

Historical Document

Marbury v. Madison

John Marshall

When William Marbury was denied an appointment as a federal judge in Thomas Jefferson's administration, he decided to sue James Madison. As Secretary of State, Madison had the power to allow the appointment to proceed.

Vocabulary Before you read the selection, find the meanings of these words in a dictionary: **province, opposition, conformably, paramount, void, obligatory, omnipotence.**

Main Idea Chief Justice Marshall's ruling in *Marbury* v. *Madison* expands the power of the Supreme Court and establishes judicial review.

It is, emphatically, the province and duty of the Judicial Department to say what the law is. . . . if a law be in opposition to the Constitution, if both the law and the Constitution apply to a particular case, so that the court must either decide that case conformably to the law, disregarding the Constitution, or conformably to the Constitution, disregarding the law, the court must determine which of these conflicting rules governs the case. This is of the very essence of judicial duty. If, then, the courts are to regard the Constitution, and the Constitution is superior to any ordinary act of the legislature, the Constitution, and not such ordinary act, must govern the case to which they both apply.

Those, then, who [argue] the principle that the Constitution is to be considered in court as a paramount law are reduced to the necessity of maintaining that courts must close their eyes on the Constitution and only see the law.

This doctrine would subvert the very foundation of all written constitutions. It would declare that an act which, according to the principles and theory of our government, is entirely void, is yet, in practice, completely obligatory. . . . It would be giving to the legislature a practical and real omnipotence, with the same breath which professes to restrict their powers within narrow limits. . . .

Bronze doors leading into the Supreme Court in Washington, D.C.

Analyzing Primary Sources

1. Which branch(es) of government are referred to in this decision?

A Executive and judicial

B Legislative and judicial

C Executive and legislative

D Judicial only

2. According to this decision, what can the Supreme Court do?

A Decide what laws the states can propose

B Write new laws

C Decide if a law is constitutional

D Propose new amendments

3. Critical Thinking and Writing **Applying Information** The idea of judicial review enables the Supreme Court to declare a law unconstitutional. How did this ruling change the balance of power among the branches of government?

Literature

"The Star-Spangled Banner"

Francis Scott Key

Francis Scott Key, a young lawyer, watched from the deck of the ship *Tonnant* as the Americans and the British fought at Fort McHenry in 1814. In the morning, Key could see that the American flag was still waving over Fort McHenry. Hastily, Key began to write a poem on the back of a letter he had in his pocket. The poem was later set to music and became the verses of "The Star-Spangled Banner."

Vocabulary Before you read the selection, find the meanings of these words in a dictionary: **perilous, ramparts, haughty, reposes.**

Main Idea Francis Scott Key describes his feelings when he sees the American flag at Fort McHenry.

Oh, say, can you see, by the dawn's early light,
What so proudly we hailed at the twilight's last gleaming,
Whose broad stripes and bright stars through the perilous fight,
O'er the ramparts we watched were so gallantly streaming?
And the rocket's red glare, the bombs bursting in air,
Gave proof through the night that our flag was still there.
Oh, say, does that star-spangled banner yet wave
O'er the land of the free, and the home of the brave?

On the shore, dimly seen through the mists of the deep,
Where the foe's haughty host in dread silence reposes,
What is that which the breeze, o'er the towering steep,
As it fitfully blows, half conceals, half discloses?
Now it catches the gleam of the morning's first beam,
In full glory reflected, now shines on the stream.
'Tis the star-spangled banner; oh, long may it wave
O'er the land of the free, and the home of the brave!

The United States Flag

Analyzing Literature

1. Francis Scott Key uses the word "flag" only once in the anthem. What phrase does he use to describe the flag?

   A Through the mists of the deep

   B Star-spangled banner

   C The gleam of the morning's first beam

   D The breeze o'er the towering steep

2. What seems to be most important to Key about the Americans winning this battle?

   A That the American flag remain at other forts

   B That the Americans gain British land

   C That Americans be able to conquer other nations

   D That Americans protect their freedom

3. **Critical Thinking and Writing** **Evaluating Information** What description in "The Star-Spangled Banner" most impresses you? Explain.

Literature

Life on the Mississippi
Mark Twain

Mark Twain's *Life on the Mississippi* combines a true account of his experiences as a river pilot with an account of his visit to the Mississippi made nearly 20 years after he left the Midwest to live in the East. In this selection, Twain describes a steamboat trip down the Mississippi as a young man. At the time, Twain wanted to be a steamboat pilot. His admiration for the skill and confidence of the pilot, Mr. Bixby, is clear.

Vocabulary Before you read the selection, find the meanings of these words in a dictionary: **imminent, intent, apex.**

Main Idea With coolness under pressure and years of experience, Mr. Bixby manages to guide his steamboat over some very treacherous shallows on the Mississippi.

Mark Twain

. . . Now the engines were stopped altogether, and we drifted with the current. Not that I could see the boat drift, for I could not, the stars being all gone by this time. This drifting was the dismalest work; it held one's heart still. Presently I discovered a blacker gloom than that which surrounded us. It was the head of the island. We were closing right down upon it. We entered its deeper shadow, and so imminent seemed the peril that I was likely to suffocate; and I had the strongest impulse to do SOMETHING, anything, to save the vessel. But still Mr. Bixby stood by his wheel, silent, intent as a cat, and all the pilots stood shoulder to shoulder at his back. . . .

The water grew shallower and shallower, by the leadsman's cries, till it was down to- "Eight-and-a-half! . . . E-i-g-h-t feet! . . . E-i-g-h-t feet! . . . Seven-and— . . ."

We touched bottom! Instantly Mr. Bixby set a lot of bells ringing, shouted through the tube, "NOW, let her have it—every ounce you've got!" . . . The boat rasped and ground her way through the sand, hung upon the apex of disaster a single tremendous instant, and then over she went! And such a shout went up at Mr. Bixby's back never loosened the roof of a pilot-house before!

Analyzing Literature

1. In the dark night, Twain "discovered a blacker gloom than that which surrounded us." What had he discovered?
   A Another steamboat drifting in the night
   B A large log floating down river
   C A large island right in their path
   D A person who had fallen overboard

2. What was the job of the leadsman?
   A Call out the depth of the water
   B Watch out for floating objects
   C Maintain discipline on board the boat
   D Provide leadership for the deckhands

3. Critical Thinking and Writing Comparing Compare Mr. Bixby's skill and calm with an impressive deed you have personally witnessed or read about.

The Monroe Doctrine

James Monroe

As the nations of Latin America gained their independence in the 1820s, the United States became concerned that Spain or other European nations would attempt to establish colonies in the region. In 1823, President James Monroe issued a warning to European powers not to colonize in the Western Hemisphere. The doctrine has helped shape American foreign policy to this day.

Vocabulary Before you read the selection, find the meanings of these words in a dictionary: **henceforth, colonization, candor, amicable, dependencies, interposition, manifestation, disposition.**

Main Idea President James Monroe warns European nations not to attempt to set up any new colonies in the Western Hemisphere.

[T]he occasion has been judged proper for asserting, as a principle in which the rights and interests of the United States are involved, that the American continents, by the free and independent condition which they have assumed and maintain, are henceforth not to be considered as subjects for future colonization by any European powers. . . .

We owe it, therefore, to candor and to the amicable relations existing between the United States and those [European] powers to declare that we should consider any attempt on their part to extend their system to any portion of this hemisphere as dangerous to our peace and safety. With the existing colonies or dependencies of any European power we have not interfered and shall not interfere. But with the Governments who have declared their independence and maintain it, and whose independence we have, on great consideration and on just principles, acknowledged, we could not view any interposition for the purpose of oppressing them, or controlling in any other manner their destiny, by any European power in any other light than as the manifestation of an unfriendly disposition toward the United States. . . .

James Monroe

Analyzing Primary Sources

1. What is the main point of the Monroe Doctrine?

   A It recognizes nations in Latin America.

   B It warns Europe against further colonization in the Americas.

   C It permits Russia to settle in the Northwest.

   D It warns Spain against invading Portugal.

2. How does this doctrine continue the policy suggested by George Washington?

   A Both advise European alliances.

   B Both suggest trade with Spain.

   C Both advise no alliances.

   D Both suggest alliances with Great Britain.

3. **Critical Thinking and Writing Linking Past and Present** Does the Monroe Doctrine have any value today? Give two reasons to support your point of view.

The Inauguration of Andrew Jackson

Mrs. Samuel Harrison Smith

With the inauguration of Andrew Jackson in 1829, a democratic spirit swept through the nation. Thousands of his supporters traveled to Washington, D.C., to celebrate his arrival at the White House. Mrs. Samuel Harrison Smith, an important member of Washington society, attended the celebration.

Vocabulary Before you read the selection, find the meanings of these words in a dictionary: **immense, lodgings, hogshead.**

Main Idea Mrs. Samuel Harrison Smith gives her account of the Jackson inauguration in a letter to a friend.

Andrew Jackson

. . . [I] will give you an account of the inauguration in mere detail. The whole of the preceding day, immense crowds were coming into the city from all parts, lodgings could not be obtained, and the newcomers had to go to Georgetown which soon overflowed . . .

The President, after having been *literally* nearly pressed to death and almost suffocated and torn to pieces by the people in their eagerness to shake hands with Old Hickory, had retreated through the back way, or south front, and had escaped to his lodgings at Gadsby's. Cut glass and china to the amount of several thousand dollars had been broken in the struggle to get the refreshments. Punch and other articles had been carried out in tubs and buckets, but had it been in hogsheads it would have been insufficient; ice creams and cake and lemonade made for 20,000 people, for it is said that number were there, though I think the estimate exaggerated. Ladies fainted, men were seen with bloody noses, and such a scene of confusion took place as is impossible to describe: . . .

. . . Ladies and gentlemen only had been expected at this levee, not the people *en masse*. But it was the people's day, and the people's President, and the people would rule. God grant that one day or other the people do not put down all rule and rulers.

Analyzing an Eyewitness Account

1. Which statement describes the situation the day before the inauguration?

A People slept at the White House.

B Many people had no place to stay.

C Only wealthy people had lodgings in the city.

D People brought food to the celebration.

2. How do you know that the attendance at the inauguration was more than expected?

A The reception was very long; people were tired.

B There was a long line of people to shake hands with the President.

C There was not enough food.

D Some people brought extra dishes.

3. **Critical Thinking and Writing** **Identifying Points of View** How do you think Mrs. Harrison felt about what happened at the inauguration? Explain.

Historical Document

The Second Reply to Hayne

Daniel Webster

States' rights was a critical issue during the mid-1800s. The crisis of the Tariff of 1828 led to a major debate in the Senate, between Robert Hayne of South Carolina and Daniel Webster of Massachusetts, about the right of a state to declare a federal law unconstitutional.

Vocabulary Before you read the selection, find the meanings of these words in a dictionary: **sovereign, behold, dissevered, discordant, belligerent, rent, fraternal, ensign, lustre, delusion, folly, sentiment.**

Main Idea Daniel Webster argues that the states cannot act independently of the federal government.

Daniel Webster

The people of the United States have declared that the Constitution shall be the supreme law. We must either admit the proposition, or dispute their authority. The States are . . . not affected by this supreme law. But the State legislatures . . . are . . . not sovereign over the people. So far as the people have given the power to the general government . . . and the government holds of the people, and not of the State governments. . . .

While the Union lasts, we have high, exciting, gratifying prospects spread out before us and our children. Beyond that I seek not to penetrate the veil. God grant that in my day, at least, that curtain may not rise! . . . When my eyes shall be turned to behold for the last time the sun in heaven, may I not see him shining on the broken and dishonored fragments of a once glorious Union; on States dissevered . . . on a land rent with civil feuds, or drenched . . . in fraternal blood! Let their last feeble and lingering glance rather behold the gorgeous ensign of the republic . . . not a stripe erased or polluted, not a single star obscured, bearing for its motto, no such miserable interrogatory as "What is all this worth?" nor those other words of delusion and folly, "Liberty first and Union afterwards"; but everywhere, spread all over in characters of living light . . . as they float over the sea and over the land, and in every wind under the whole heavens, that other sentiment, dear to every true American heart, Liberty *and* Union, now and for ever, one and inseparable!

Analyzing Primary Sources

1. According to the first paragraph, what does Webster see as the limit of state governments?
   A The state can act without the consent of the people.
   B The state can ignore federal laws.
   C The states must follow the people's will.
   D The state governments can declare laws unconstitutional.

2. What does Webster hope never to see?
   A Liberties taken from some states
   B The Union dissolved
   C The states denying people liberties
   D The states with more power than the federal government

3. **Critical Thinking and Writing** **Drawing Inferences** Webster rejects the idea of "Liberty first and Union afterwards." What does he believe instead? Explain.

Historical Document

Factory Rules From the Handbook to Lowell, 1848

Established in 1813, the textile factory in Lowell, Massachusetts, became the most famous center of textile manufacturing in the country. Employing mostly young women from New England farm families, Lowell represented a model work community. The female workers, or "mill girls," were closely supervised. They were also required to follow the factory rules.

Main Idea — All employees at the Lowell factory must follow company rules.

All persons in the employ of the Hamilton Manufacturing Company, are to observe the regulations of the room where they are employed. They are not to be absent from their work without the consent of the overseer, except in cases of sickness, and then they are to send him word of the cause of their absence. They are to board in one of the houses of the company and give information at the counting room, where they board, when they begin, or, whenever they change their boarding place; and are to observe the regulations of their boarding-house.

Those intending to leave the employment of the company, are to give at least two weeks' notice thereof to their overseer.

All persons entering into the employment of the company, are considered as engaged for twelve months, and those who leave sooner, or do not comply with all these regulations, will not be entitled to a regular discharge.

The company will not employ any one who is habitually absent from public worship on the Sabbath, or known to be guilty of immorality.

A physician will attend once in every month at the counting-room, to vaccinate all who may need it, free of expense.

Any one who shall take from the mills or the yard, any yarn, cloth or other article belonging to the company, will be considered guilty of stealing and be liable for prosecution. . . .

Workers at a textile mill

Analyzing Primary Sources

1. Where must the employees live?
   A In apartments near the factory
   B With friends in the area
   C In housing provided by the company
   D In housing chosen by the employee

2. Which statement best describes the rules listed here?
   A Only women are hired.
   B Most of the rules protect the company from loss of property on workers' time.
   C Injured workers are paid.
   D The worker must complete 18 months of service.

3. Critical Thinking and Writing **Applying Information** How would you describe the relationship between the employer and the employee at the Lowell factory in 1848? Explain.

Eyewitness Account

Life and Times of Frederick Douglass

Frederick Douglass

Born into slavery, Frederick Douglass was in his twenties before he escaped to freedom in Bedford, Massachusetts. A self-educated man, he became a well-known abolitionist and orator. He gave lectures about the evils of slavery in the United States, London, and the West Indies. *Life and Times of Frederick Douglass* is one of his three autobiographies.

Vocabulary Before you read the selection, find the meanings of these words in a dictionary: **lodged, ample.**

Main Idea Frederick Douglass describes his childhood experience as a slave.

As before intimated, I received no severe treatment from the hands of my master, but the insufficiency of both food and clothing was a serious trial to me. . . . In hottest summer and coldest winter, I was kept almost in a state of nudity. My only clothing—a little coarse sackcloth or tow-linen sort of shirt, scarcely reaching to my knees, was worn night and day and changed once a week. In the daytime I could protect myself by keeping on the sunny side of the house, or in stormy weather, in the corner of the kitchen chimney. But the great difficulty was to keep warm during the night. The pigs in the pen had leaves, and the horses in the stable had straw, but the children had no beds. They lodged anywhere in the ample kitchen. I slept generally in a little closet, without even a blanket to cover me. In very cold weather I sometimes got down the bag in which corn was carried to the mill, and crawled into that. . . . Our cornmeal mush, which was our only regular if not all-sufficing diet, . . . was placed in a large tray or trough. This was set down on the floor of the kitchen, or out of doors on the ground, and the children were called like so many pigs, and . . . would come, some with oyster-shells, some with pieces of shingle, but none with spoons. . . . He who could eat the fastest got most, and he that was strongest got the best place, but few left the trough really satisfied.

Frederick Douglass

Analyzing an Eyewitness Account

1. According to Douglass, what was his main discomfort as a slave?
   A His sleeping area was too warm.
   B His sackcloth was not changed often enough.
   C He was repeatedly beaten.
   D He was usually cold and hungry.

2. Aside from insufficient food, why were mealtimes difficult for the slave children?
   A The children had to compete with the farm animals for food.
   B The weakest children suffered most.
   C The mush was served to the oldest children first.
   D The strongest children received less.

3. **Critical Thinking and Writing** **Analyzing Information** What qualities did Douglass need in order to survive his life in slavery?

Declaration of Sentiments

Elizabeth Cady Stanton and Lucretia Mott

When Elizabeth Cady Stanton and Lucretia Mott attended the World Anti-Slavery Convention in 1840, they had to sit and listen from a curtained gallery because women were not allowed on the main convention floor. Outraged, both women vowed to hold a convention for women's rights. Eight years later, Stanton and Mott organized a convention at Seneca Falls, New York.

Vocabulary Before you read the selection, find the meanings of these words in a dictionary: **endowed, inalienable, usurpations, candid, franchise.**

Main Idea Stanton and Mott presented their case for women's rights in the Declaration of Sentiments.

We hold these truths to be self-evident: that all men and women are created equal; that they are endowed by their Creator with certain inalienable rights; that among these are life, liberty, and the pursuit of happiness; that to secure these rights governments are instituted, deriving their just powers from the consent of the governed. . . .

The history of mankind is a history of repeated injuries and usurpations on the part of man toward woman, having in direct object the establishment of an absolute tyranny over her. To prove this, let facts be submitted to a candid world.

He has never permitted her to exercise her inalienable right to the elective franchise.

He has compelled her to submit to laws, in the formation of which she had no voice.

He has withheld from her rights which are given to the most ignorant and degraded men—both natives and foreigners.

Having deprived her of this first right of a citizen, the elective franchise, thereby leaving her without representation in the halls of legislation, he has oppressed her on all sides.

He has made her, if married, in the eye of the law, civilly dead.

He has taken from her all right in property, even to the wages she earns. . . .

Lucretia Mott and
Elizabeth Cady Stanton

Analyzing Primary Sources

1. What truth is obvious according to the Declaration of Sentiments?
   A Women have natural rights.
   B Men and women have natural rights.
   C Women have a right to protest.
   D None of the above

2. According to the Declaration, of which of the following rights do women feel they have been deprived?
   A The right to property
   B The right to submit to laws in which they had a voice
   C The right to money they have earned
   D All of the above

3. **Critical Thinking and Writing** **Analyzing Information** Why do you think the Declaration of Sentiments is based on the Declaration of Independence?

Moby-Dick

Herman Melville

In 1820, a whale hunting ship, the *Essex*, sank after being attacked by a giant whale. Only eight crew members survived. Herman Melville knew of the story, and ten years later it would become part of his best-known seafaring novel, *Moby-Dick*.

Vocabulary Before you read the selection, find the meanings of these words in a dictionary: **dismasted, razeed, imprecations, perdition, splice.**

Main Idea Ahab is the captain of the whale ship *Pequod*. In this scene, Ahab has offered gold to the first sailor who sees the white whale, Moby-Dick.

"It's a white whale, I say," resumed Ahab, as he threw down the [hammer]: "a white whale. Skin your eyes for him, men; look sharp for white water; if ye see but a bubble, sing out." . . .

"Captain Ahab," said Starbuck . . . "Captain Ahab, I have heard of Moby-Dick—but it was not Moby-Dick that took off thy leg?"

"Who told thee that?" cried Ahab; then pausing, "Aye, Starbuck; aye, my hearties all round; it was Moby-Dick that dismasted me; Moby-Dick that brought me to this dead stump I stand on now. Aye, aye," he shouted with a terrific, loud, animal sob, like that of a heart-stricken moose; "Aye, aye! It was that accursed white whale that razeed me; made a poor pegging lubber of me for ever and a day!" Then tossing both arms, with measureless imprecations he shouted out: "Aye, aye! and I'll chase him round Good Hope, and round the Horn, and round the Norway Maelstrom, and round perdition's flames before I give him up. And this is what ye have shipped for, men! to chase that white whale on both sides of land, and over all sides of earth, till he spouts black blood and rolls fin out. What say ye, men, will ye splice hands on it, now? I think ye do look brave."

"Aye, aye!" shouted the harpooneers and seamen, running closer to the excited old man: "A sharp eye for the white whale; a sharp lance for Moby-Dick!"

A painting of the whale, Moby-Dick

Analyzing Literature

1. What does the excerpt explain about Ahab and Moby-Dick?
   - **A** Ahab believes Moby-Dick is a gentle whale.
   - **B** Ahab believes the white whale is harmless.
   - **C** Ahab has never seen the white whale.
   - **D** Moby-Dick previously attacked Ahab.

2. How do the sailors react to Ahab's offer?
   - **A** They decide Ahab is not serious.
   - **B** They join in Ahab's enthusiasm.
   - **C** They do not believe there is a white whale.
   - **D** They try to persuade Ahab to give up the idea.

3. **Critical Thinking and Writing** **Drawing Inferences** Why do you think Ahab is determined to find Moby-Dick? What does this tell you about the kind of man Ahab is?

A Slave Escapes

Levi Coffin

Levi Coffin was an abolitionist who spent a lifetime helping slaves escape on the Underground Railroad. In his *Reminiscences of Levi Coffin* (1876), he describes how he helped an escaped African American man named Louis avoid being returned to slavery. Louis had been recaptured and faced a hearing under the Fugitive Slave Law.

Vocabulary Before you read the selection, find the meanings of these words in a dictionary: **intently, sexton, secreted.**

Main Idea Aided by abolitionists, a slave named Louis makes his escape to freedom.

When the time set for the decision arrived, the court-room was crowded with interested listeners, white and black. . . . Louis . . . to gain more room, slipped his chair back a little way. Neither his master nor the marshal noticed the movement, as they were intently listening to the judge, and he slipped his chair again, until he was back of them. . . . Next he rose quietly to his feet and took a step backward. Some abolitionist friendly to his cause gave him an encouraging touch on the foot, and he stepped farther back. Then . . . he quietly and cautiously made his way around the south end of the room . . .

He was well acquainted with the different streets, and made his way quickly, . . . to Avondale, where he knew the sexton of the colored burying ground. . . .

[*Coffin and other abolitionists now attempt to smuggle Louis, disguised in woman's dress, into a church.*]

I passed on to Vine Street and joined the throng of people going to evening service. Louis followed, at a short distance, and was conducted to the church previously mentioned. I passed in at a side gate and went into the basement of the church. Louis followed me and was soon safely secreted in one of the committee rooms, where he remained for several weeks. The officers of the law made vigorous efforts to find him, but gained no clue to his hiding place. . . .

Fugitive slaves

Analyzing an Eyewitness Account

1. Louis escaped from the courtroom by
  A getting up from his chair and quietly walking out
  B jumping out of a window
  C disguising himself as a policeman
  D taking a hostage

2. Abolitionists helped Louis by doing which of the following?
  A Providing a wagon to take him to Avondale
  B Hiding him in a church
  C Disguising him as a minister
  D Assisting him to the train station

3. Critical Thinking and Writing **Drawing Conclusions** Based on these excerpts, what qualities of character did Louis possess?

★ Reference Section

Historical Document

Dred Scott v. Sandford (1857)

Dred Scott v. *Sandford* was a landmark Supreme Court case which did much to pave the way for the Civil War. In its decision, the Court ruled that African Americans were not United States citizens. The Court also determined that an important part of the Missouri Compromise of 1820 was unconstitutional. The ruling raised anger between the North and the South to the point where it exploded into fighting in 1861.

Vocabulary Before you read the selection, find the meanings of these words in a dictionary: **express, prohibition, dominion.**

Main Idea According to the Dred Scott decision, any act that deprived a citizen of the United States of his slaves was unconstitutional because it violated the Fifth Amendment to the Constitution.

Dred Scott

. . . The rights of property are united with the rights of person, and placed on the same ground by the 5th amendment to the Constitution, which provides that no person shall be deprived of life, liberty, and property, without due process of law. And an act of Congress which deprives a citizen of the United States of his liberty or property, merely because he came himself or brought his property into a particular Territory of the United States, and who had committed no offence against the laws, could hardly be dignified with the name of due process of law. . . .

The powers over person and property of which we speak are not only not granted to Congress, but are in express terms denied, and they are forbidden to exercise them. And this prohibition is not confined to the States, but the words are general, and extend to the whole territory over which the Constitution gives it power to legislate, including those portions of it remaining under Territorial Government, as well as that covered by States. It is a total absence of power everywhere within the dominion of the United States, and places the citizens of a Territory, so far as these rights are concerned, on the same footing with citizens of the States. . . . And if Congress itself cannot do this—if it is beyond the powers conferred on the Federal Government—it will be admitted, we presume, that it could not authorize a Territorial Government to exercise them.

Analyzing Primary Sources

1. What portion of the Constitution provides that no person shall be deprived of life, liberty, and property without due process of law?

  A The First Amendment

  B The Third Amendment

  C The Fifth Amendment

  D The Seventh Amendment

2. According to the ruling, the power to take away a person's property just because he moves to a Territory of the United States

  A belongs to the President

  B is granted to Congress

  C is denied to Congress

  D belongs to the Court

3. **Critical Thinking and Writing** **Summarizing** Using your own words, write three sentences to summarize the ideas expressed in the Dred Scott decision.

The Red Badge of Courage

Stephen Crane

Born six years after the Civil War ended, Stephen Crane never fought in a war. Yet, his portrayal of Henry Fleming as a young Union soldier who manages to overcome his fear during the war is realistic and convincing.

Vocabulary Before you read the selection, find the meanings of these words in a dictionary: **urchin, menacing, regiment, welded.**

Main Idea After spending time in camp, participating in military drills, Henry Fleming is finally thrust into the heat of a real battle.

The captain of the company had been pacing excitedly to and fro in the rear. He coaxed in schoolmistress fashion, as to a congregation of boys with primers. His talk was an endless repetition. "Reserve your ire, boys—don't shoot till I tell you—save your fire—wait till they get close up—don't be damned fools—"

Perspiration streamed down the youth's face, which was soiled like that of a weeping urchin. He frequently, with a nervous movement, wiped his eyes with his coat sleeve. His mouth was still a little ways open.

He got the one glance at the foe-swarming field in front of him, and instantly ceased to debate the question of his piece being loaded. Before he was ready to begin—before he had announced to himself that he was about to fight—he threw the obedient, well-balanced rifle into position and fired a first wild shot. Directly he was working at his weapon like an automatic affair.

He suddenly lost concern for himself, and forgot to look at a menacing fate. He became not a man but a member. He felt that something of which he was a part—a regiment, an army, a cause, or a country—was in a crisis. He was welded into a common personality which was dominated by a single desire. For some moments he could not flee no more than a little finger can commit a revolution from a hand.

Stephen Crane

Analyzing Literature

1. How does Henry feel as he begins to take part in the battle?

  A He is excited and ready.

  B He is sweating, but confident.

  C He is nervous and fearful.

  D He is unable to act.

2. What happens as Henry prepares to shoot his rifle?

  A He loses control and continues to fire wildly.

  B He chooses a target and takes aim.

  C He fires aimlessly once, and then begins to control his shots.

  D He cannot load the rifle.

3. **Critical Thinking and Writing** **Analyzing Information** What does Henry learn about himself during the battle?

Historical Document

The Gettysburg Address

Abraham Lincoln

On November 19, 1863, President Abraham Lincoln gave a brief speech at the dedication of a battlefield at Gettysburg. Lincoln's "Gettysburg Address" is today considered one of the most important and moving statements of American ideals.

Vocabulary Before you read the selection, find the meanings of these words in a dictionary: **score, proposition, consecrate, hallow, detract.**

Main Idea Lincoln argues that the best way to honor the Union dead is to keep alive the principles of democracy.

Four score and seven years ago our fathers brought forth on this continent, a new nation, conceived in liberty, and dedicated to the proposition that all men are created equal. Now we are engaged in a great civil war, testing whether that nation, or any nation so conceived and so dedicated, can long endure. We met on a great battlefield of that war. We have come to dedicate a portion of that field, as a final resting place for those who here gave their lives that that nation might live. It is altogether fitting and proper that we should do this. But, in a larger sense, we can not dedicate, we can not consecrate, we can not hallow, this ground. The brave men, living and dead. who struggled here, have consecrated it, far above our poor power to add or detract. The world will little note, nor long remember what we say here, but it can never forget what they did here. It is for us the living, rather, to be dedicated here to the unfinished work which they who fought here have thus far so nobly advanced. It is rather for us to be here dedicated to the great task remaining before us, that from these honored dead we take increased devotion to that cause for which they gave the last full measure of devotion, that we here highly resolve that these dead shall not have died in vain, that this nation, under God, shall have a new birth of freedom, and that government of the people, by the people, for the people, shall not perish from the earth.

Statue of Abraham Lincoln

Analyzing Primary Sources

1. From what document does Lincoln quote in his opening sentence?

   A   The Declaration of Independence

   B   The Bill of Rights

   C   The "Star-Spangled Banner"

   D   The Emancipation Proclamation

2. Lincoln argues that "we cannot consecrate . . . this ground" because

   A   it is not fitting and proper to do so

   B   the world will little note nor long remember Gettysburg

   C   those who fought at Gettysburg have already consecrated it

   D   the soldiers at Gettysburg died in vain

3. **Critical Thinking and Writing Analyzing Ideas** Give three examples of how Lincoln uses this speech to try to remind people of the ideals upon which the United States was founded.

Ten Years on a Georgia Plantation Since the War

Frances Butler Leigh

Frances Butler Leigh was the daughter of a Georgia planter. In this account, she recalls journeying from the North back to her home in 1866.

Main Idea   Leigh's account describes both the physical and emotional impact that the Civil War had on the South.

The Southern railroads were many of them destroyed for miles, not having been rebuilt since the war, and it was very questionable how we were to get as far as Savannah, a matter we did accomplish however, in a week's time, after the following adventures, of which I find an account in my letters written at the time. We stopped one day in Washington, and went all over the new Capitol, which had been finished since I was there five years ago.

On Saturday we left, reaching Richmond at four o'clock on Sunday morning. I notice that it is a peculiarity of Southern railroads that they always either arrive, or start, at four o'clock in the morning. That day we spent quietly there, and sad enough it was, for besides all the associations with the place which crowded thick and fast upon one's memory, half the town was a heap of burnt ruins, showing how heavily the desolation of war had fallen upon it. And in the afternoon I went out to the cemetery, and after some search found the grave I was looking for. There he lay, with hundreds of others who had sacrificed their lives in vain, their resting place marked merely by small wooden headboards, bearing their names, regiments, and the battles in which they fell. The grief and excitement made me quite ill, so that I was glad to leave the town before daylight the next morning, and I hope I may never be there again.

Richmond, Virginia, after the Civil War

Analyzing an Eyewitness Account

1. Upon what evidence does Leigh base her account?

   A   Her memory only

   B   Letters she wrote at the time

   C   Official records

   D   Newspaper accounts

2. This passage describes all of the following effects of the Civil War on the South EXCEPT the

   A   destruction of railroads

   B   destruction of cities

   C   destruction of plantations

   D   heavy casualties

3. **Critical Thinking and Writing** **Drawing Conclusions** **(a)** What emotions does Leigh feel as she visits Richmond? **(b)** Do you think her reaction was typical of many southerners at the time? Explain.

★ Reference Section

Historical Document

Plessy v. Ferguson
Henry B. Brown and John M. Harlan

In 1892, Homer Plessy boarded a streetcar in Louisiana. He had a first-class ticket. When asked to leave the car because he was African American, Plessy refused. He was arrested. Eventually, the case went to the Supreme Court. Plessy argued that his rights under the Fourteenth Amendment were violated.

Main Idea Justice Brown and Justice Harlan were two of seven judges on the Supreme Court who heard the case. Justice Brown delivers the opinion that establishes segregation in the South for over 50 years. Justice Harlan is the only judge to disagree.

Judge Henry B. Brown

The object of the [Fourteenth Amendment] was undoubtedly to enforce the absolute equality of the two races before the law, but in the nature of things it could not have been intended to abolish distinctions based upon color, or to enforce social . . . equality. . . . Laws permitting, and even requiring, separation [of races] in places . . . do not necessarily imply the inferiority of either race to the other, and have been generally, if not universally, recognized as within the competency of the state legislatures in the exercise of their police powers.

Judge John M. Harlan

The Thirteenth Amendment . . . decreed universal civil freedom in this country. But that amendment having been found inadequate . . . was followed by the Fourteenth Amendment . . .

These notable additions to the fundamental law were welcomed by the friends of liberty throughout the world. This Court has further said, "that the law in the states shall be the same for the black as for the white . . . and, in regard to the colored race, for whose protection the amendment was primarily designed, that no discrimination shall be made against them by law because of their color."

Justice John M. Harlan

Analyzing Primary Sources

1. According to Justice Brown, what is not guaranteed under the Fourteenth Amendment?

  A Voting rights

  B Social equality of all races

  C The power of state legislatures

  D The civil rights of African Americans

2. According to Justice Harlan, why was the Fourteenth Amendment passed?

  A It further protected the rights of formerly enslaved African Americans.

  B It ended slavery.

  C The Thirteenth Amendment was unconstitutional.

  D It gave the states additional rights.

3. **Critical Thinking and Writing** **Summarizing** Using your own words, summarize the arguments of Justice Brown and Justice Harlan in four or five sentences. How were African Americans affected?

How the Other Half Lives

Jacob Riis

After years of drifting from one low-paying job to another, Jacob Riis became a police reporter for *The New York Times*. Most of his stories were about events in poor neighborhoods. Dissatisfied with writing about the events, Riis decided to tell his stories through photography.

Vocabulary Before you read the selection, find the meanings of these words in a dictionary: **notorious, cosmopolitan, successor, scavenger, monopolizes, bootblacking, hod, alderman.**

Main Idea In "How the Other Half Lives," published in 1890, Riis shows the lives of immigrants through pictures and words. In the following passage, he describes the diversity of immigrants in the city.

Immigrants arriving in the United States

When once I asked the agent of a notorious Fourth Ward alley how many people might be living in it I was told: One hundred and forty families, one hundred Irish, thirty-eight Italian, and two that spoke the German tongue. Barring the agent herself, there was not a native-born individual in the court. The answer was characteristic of the cosmopolitan character of lower New York. . . . One may find for the asking an Italian, a German, a French, African, Spanish, Bohemian, Russian, Scandinavian, Jewish, and Chinese colony. . . .

The German ragpicker of thirty years ago, quite as low in the scale as his Italian successor, is the thrifty tradesman or prosperous farmer of today.

The Italian scavenger of our time is fast graduating into exclusive control of the corner fruit stands, while his black-eyed boy monopolizes the bootblacking industry, in which a few years ago he was an intruder. The Irish hod carrier in the second generation has become a brick layer, if not the alderman of his ward; while the Chinese [peasant] is in almost exclusive possession of the laundry business. The poorest immigrant comes here with the ambition to better himself, and, given half a chance, might be reasonably expected to make the most of it.

Analyzing an Eyewitness Account

1. How had lower New York changed by 1890?

A Only native-born people were there.

B There were nearly all immigrants living there.

C Most of the people living there were Russian and Chinese.

D Half of the population was native-born.

2. What happened as generations of immigrants remained in the city?

A All family members worked in factories.

B Most wanted to return home.

C No important change took place; each generation lived the same way.

D Each group made economic improvements.

3. Critical Thinking and Writing Comparing (a) How were the immigrants who came to America different? **(b)** How were they the same?

Historical Document

I Have a Dream
Martin Luther King, Jr.

To celebrate the one hundredth anniversary of the Emancipation Proclamation, civil rights leaders planned a march to Washington, D.C. On August 28, 1963, nearly 200,000 marchers arrived in Washington. The keynote speaker was the well-known civil rights leader, Dr. Martin Luther King, Jr.

Vocabulary Before you read the selection, find the meanings of these words in a dictionary: **creed, prodigious, hamlet.**

Main Idea In his speech, Dr. King describes his dream for racial harmony.

I have a dream that one day this nation will rise up and live out the true meaning of its creed: "We hold these truths to be self-evident: that all men are created equal."

I have a dream that one day on the red hills of Georgia the sons of former slaves and the sons of former slaveowners will be able to sit down together at the table of brotherhood. . . .

I have a dream that my four children will one day live in a nation where they will not be judged by the color of their skin but by the content of their character.

I have a dream today. . . .

So let freedom ring from the prodigious hilltops of New Hampshire. . . .

But not only that; let freedom ring from Stone Mountain of Georgia!

Let freedom ring from Lookout Mountain of Tennessee!

Let freedom ring from every hill and every molehill of Mississippi. From every mountainside, let freedom ring.

When we let freedom ring, when we let it ring from every village and every hamlet, from every state and every city, we will be able to speed up that day when all of God's children, black men and white men, Jews and Gentiles, Protestants and Catholics, will be able to join hands and sing in the words of the old Negro spiritual, "Free at last! free at last! thank God Almighty, we are free at last!"

Dr. Martin Luther King, Jr.

Analyzing Primary Sources

1. Why does Dr. King believe the United States is not living out the meaning of its creed?
   - **A** African American men are denied freedom.
   - **B** White women are denied civil liberties.
   - **C** Only men are treated fairly.
   - **D** Not all Americans are treated equally.

2. What is King's hope for his children?
   - **A** They should be judged as individuals, not by their race.
   - **B** They should be judged racially and by character.
   - **C** They should be judged as King's children.
   - **D** All of the above

3. **Critical Thinking and Writing** **Evaluating Information** Describe the way in which Dr. King uses words and rhythms to make his point.

Presidents of the United States

1 George Washington (1732–1799)

Years in office:
1789–1797
Party:
none
Elected from:
Virginia
Vice President:
John Adams

2 John Adams (1735–1826)

Years in office:
1797–1801
Party:
Federalist
Elected from:
Massachusetts
Vice President:
Thomas Jefferson

3 Thomas Jefferson (1743–1826)

Years in office:
1801–1809
Party:
Democratic Republican
Elected from:
Virginia
Vice President:
1) Aaron Burr,
2) George Clinton

4 James Madison (1751–1836)

Years in office:
1809–1817
Party:
Democratic Republican
Elected from:
Virginia
Vice President:
1) George Clinton,
2) Elbridge Gerry

5 James Monroe (1758–1831)

Years in office:
1817–1825
Party:
Democratic Republican
Elected from:
Virginia
Vice President:
Daniel Tompkins

6 John Quincy Adams (1767–1848)

Years in office:
1825–1829
Party:
National Republican
Elected from:
Massachusetts
Vice President:
John Calhoun

7 Andrew Jackson (1767–1845)

Years in office:
1829–1837
Party:
Democratic
Elected from:
Tennessee
Vice President:
1) John Calhoun,
2) Martin Van Buren

8 Martin Van Buren (1782–1862)

Years in office:
1837–1841
Party:
Democratic
Elected from:
New York
Vice President:
Richard Johnson

9 William Henry Harrison* (1773–1841)

Years in office:
1841
Party:
Whig
Elected from:
Ohio
Vice President:
John Tyler

10 John Tyler (1790–1862)

Years in office:
1841–1845
Party:
Whig
Elected from:
Virginia
Vice President:
none

11 James K. Polk (1795–1849)

Years in office:
1845–1849
Party:
Democratic
Elected from:
Tennessee
Vice President:
George Dallas

12 Zachary Taylor* (1784–1850)

Years in office:
1849–1850
Party:
Whig
Elected from:
Louisiana
Vice President:
Millard Fillmore

*Died in office

13 Millard Fillmore (1800–1874)

Years in office:
1850–1853
Party:
Whig
Elected from:
New York
Vice President:
none

14 Franklin Pierce (1804–1869)

Years in office:
1853–1857
Party:
Democratic
Elected from:
New Hampshire
Vice President:
William King

15 James Buchanan (1791–1868)

Years in office:
1857–1861
Party:
Democratic
Elected from:
Pennsylvania
Vice President:
John Breckinridge

16 Abraham Lincoln** (1809–1865)

Years in office:
1861–1865
Party:
Republican
Elected from:
Illinois
Vice President:
1) Hannibal
    Hamlin,
2) Andrew
    Johnson

17 Andrew Johnson (1808–1875)

Years in office:
1865–1869
Party:
Republican
Elected from:
Tennessee
Vice President:
none

18 Ulysses S. Grant (1822–1885)

Years in office:
1869–1877
Party:
Republican
Elected from:
Illinois
Vice President:
1) Schuyler
    Colfax,
2) Henry Wilson

19 Rutherford B. Hayes (1822–1893)

Years in office:
1877–1881
Party:
Republican
Elected from:
Ohio
Vice President:
William Wheeler

20 James A. Garfield** (1831–1881)

Years in office:
1881
Party:
Republican
Elected from:
Ohio
Vice President:
Chester A. Arthur

21 Chester A. Arthur (1829–1886)

Years in office:
1881–1885
Party:
Republican
Elected from:
New York
Vice President:
none

22 Grover Cleveland (1837–1908)

Years in office:
1885–1889
Party:
Democratic
Elected from:
New York
Vice President:
Thomas
    Hendricks

23 Benjamin Harrison (1833–1901)

Years in office:
1889–1893
Party:
Republican
Elected from:
Indiana
Vice President:
Levi Morton

24 Grover Cleveland (1837–1908)

Years in office:
1893–1897
Party:
Democratic
Elected from:
New York
Vice President:
Adlai Stevenson

**Assassinated

Presidents of the United States

Presidents of the United States ★ 611

25 William McKinley** (1843–1901)

Years in office:
1897–1901
Party:
Republican
Elected from:
Ohio
Vice President:
1) Garret Hobart,
2) Theodore Roosevelt

26 Theodore Roosevelt (1858–1919)

Years in office:
1901–1909
Party:
Republican
Elected from:
New York
Vice President:
Charles Fairbanks

27 William Howard Taft (1857–1930)

Years in office:
1909–1913
Party:
Republican
Elected from:
Ohio
Vice President:
James Sherman

28 Woodrow Wilson (1856–1924)

Years in office:
1913–1921
Party:
Democratic
Elected from:
New Jersey
Vice President:
Thomas Marshall

29 Warren G. Harding* (1865–1923)

Years in office:
1921–1923
Party:
Republican
Elected from:
Ohio
Vice President:
Calvin Coolidge

30 Calvin Coolidge (1872–1933)

Years in office:
1923–1929
Party:
Republican
Elected from:
Massachusetts
Vice President:
Charles Dawes

31 Herbert C. Hoover (1874–1964)

Years in office:
1929–1933
Party:
Republican
Elected from:
California
Vice President:
Charles Curtis

32 Franklin D. Roosevelt* (1882–1945)

Years in office:
1933–1945
Party:
Democratic
Elected from:
New York
Vice President:
1) John Garner,
2) Henry Wallace,
3) Harry S Truman

33 Harry S Truman (1884–1972)

Years in office:
1945–1953
Party:
Democratic
Elected from:
Missouri
Vice President:
Alben Barkley

34 Dwight D. Eisenhower (1890–1969)

Years in office:
1953–1961
Party:
Republican
Elected from:
New York
Vice President:
Richard M. Nixon

35 John F. Kennedy** (1917–1963)

Years in office:
1961–1963
Party:
Democratic
Elected from:
Massachusetts
Vice President:
Lyndon B. Johnson

36 Lyndon B. Johnson (1908–1973)

Years in office:
1963–1969
Party:
Democratic
Elected from:
Texas
Vice President:
Hubert Humphrey

*Died in office
**Assassinated

37 **Richard M. Nixon***** (1913–1994)

Years in office:
1969–1974
Party:
Republican
Elected from:
New York
Vice President:
1) Spiro Agnew,
2) Gerald R. Ford

38 **Gerald R. Ford** (b. 1913)

Years in office:
1974–1977
Party:
Republican
Appointed from:
Michigan
Vice President:
Nelson
    Rockefeller

39 **Jimmy Carter** (b. 1924)

Years in office:
1977–1981
Party:
Democratic
Elected from:
Georgia
Vice President:
Walter Mondale

40 **Ronald W. Reagan** (b. 1911)

Years in office:
1981–1989
Party:
Republican
Elected from:
California
Vice President:
George H.W.
    Bush

41 **George H.W. Bush** (b. 1924)

Years in office:
1989–1993
Party:
Republican
Elected from:
Texas
Vice President:
J. Danforth
    Quayle

42 **William J. Clinton** (b. 1946)

Years in office:
1993–2001
Party:
Democratic
Elected from:
Arkansas
Vice President:
Albert Gore, Jr.

43 **George W. Bush** (b. 1946)

Years in office:
2001–
Party:
Republican
Elected from:
Texas
Vice President:
Richard Cheney

***Resigned

The American Flag

The Flag That Inspired Our National Anthem

During the War of 1812, Mary Young Pickersgill was hired to make a new flag for Fort McHenry in Baltimore harbor. She was told to make a huge flag. Pickersgill and her 13-year-old daughter, Caroline, spent several weeks in the hot summer of 1813 sewing and stitching. When it came time to assemble the flag, Pickersgill realized that she did not have enough space in her workshop. She arranged to finish the sewing in a nearby brewery. Every evening after the brewery had closed for the day, Pickersgill and her daughter worked by candlelight on the flag.

When Pickersgill's flag was hung at Fort McHenry, it could be seen far and wide. In fact, Francis Scott Key could see the flag from eight miles away during the bombardment of the fort by British warships. Its "broad stripes and bright stars" inspired him to write the poem, "The Star-Spangled Banner." Key later suggested that the poem be sung to a popular British tune. A Baltimore music store owner published the poem together with the music, and by 1861, "The Star-Spangled Banner" could be heard at most patriotic events. It was not until 1931, however, that Congress passed a law making "The Star-Spangled Banner" the national anthem of the United States.

"By the dawn's early light," it flew over Fort McHenry. Today, the Star-Spangled Banner hangs at the Smithsonian Institution in Washington, D.C.

Ten Rules for Respecting the American Flag

The American flag should be treated with respect and great care at all times. Following the rules in the Flag Code honors our citizens and our traditions.

1. The flag should be treated courteously, as if it were a person.
2. The flag of the United States of America should be at the center and at the highest point of the group when a number of flags of states or localities are displayed.
3. The flag is usually displayed in the open from sunrise to sunset.
4. The flag should never be displayed upside down except as a signal of distress when there is extreme danger to life or property.
5. When a flag is displayed at half-staff, the flag should first be hoisted briskly to the peak of the staff and then lowered slowly.
6. The flag should never be used as wearing apparel, bedding, or drapery.
7. The flag should never be displayed, used, or stored in such a way that would permit it to be easily torn, soiled, or damaged.
8. The flag should never be used as a covering for a ceiling.
9. The flag should never be used for advertising purposes. It should not be embroidered on such articles as cushions or handkerchiefs.
10. When a flag is no longer in good enough condition to be displayed, it should be destroyed in a dignified way, preferably by burning.

—Adapted from the Federal Flag Code

The Pledge of Allegiance

The Pledge of Allegiance should be said standing at attention, facing the flag, with the right hand over the heart. I pledge allegiance to the Flag of the United States of America, and to the Republic for which it stands, one nation under God, indivisible, with liberty and justice for all.

The High School Student Who Changed Our Flag

Our present 50-star flag was designed by a 17-year-old high school student. In 1958, Robert Heft was a shy high school junior in Lancaster, Ohio. At the time, the United States had 48 states. However, talk of Alaska and Hawaii becoming states led him to design a 50-star flag as a school project. He arranged the 50 stars in alternating rows of six stars and five stars. His teacher was not impressed. He gave Robert a B-minus grade for the project but said he would improve the grade if Heft could get Congress to accept the design. Heft took on the challenge. He sent the flag to his representative in Congress. In 1960, President Dwight D. Eisenhower phoned Heft to tell him that his design had been selected to be the nation's new flag. And Heft's grade? True to his promise, the teacher changed the grade to an A!

The Fifty States

State	Date of Entry to Union (Order of Entry)	Land Area in Square Miles	Population (In Thousands)	Number of Representatives in House*	Capital	Largest City
Alabama	1819 (22)	50,750	4,447	7	Montgomery	Birmingham
Alaska	1959 (49)	570,374	627	1	Juneau	Anchorage
Arizona	1912 (48)	113,642	5,131	8	Phoenix	Phoenix
Arkansas	1836 (25)	52,075	2,673	4	Little Rock	Little Rock
California	1850 (31)	155,973	33,872	53	Sacramento	Los Angeles
Colorado	1876 (38)	103,730	4,301	7	Denver	Denver
Connecticut	1788 (5)	4,845	3,406	5	Hartford	Bridgeport
Delaware	1787 (1)	1,955	784	1	Dover	Wilmington
Florida	1845 (27)	53,997	15,982	25	Tallahassee	Jacksonville
Georgia	1788 (4)	57,919	8,186	13	Atlanta	Atlanta
Hawaii	1959 (50)	6,423	1,212	2	Honolulu	Honolulu
Idaho	1890 (43)	82,751	1,294	2	Boise	Boise
Illinois	1818 (21)	55,593	12,419	19	Springfield	Chicago
Indiana	1816 (19)	35,870	6,080	9	Indianapolis	Indianapolis
Iowa	1846 (29)	55,875	2,926	5	Des Moines	Des Moines
Kansas	1861 (34)	81,823	2,688	4	Topeka	Wichita
Kentucky	1792 (15)	39,732	4,042	6	Frankfort	Louisville
Louisiana	1812 (18)	43,566	4,469	7	Baton Rouge	New Orleans
Maine	1820 (23)	30,865	1,275	2	Augusta	Portland
Maryland	1788 (7)	9,775	5,296	8	Annapolis	Baltimore
Massachusetts	1788 (6)	7,838	6,349	10	Boston	Boston
Michigan	1837 (26)	56,809	9,938	15	Lansing	Detroit
Minnesota	1858 (32)	79,617	4,919	8	St. Paul	Minneapolis
Mississippi	1817 (20)	46,914	2,845	4	Jackson	Jackson
Missouri	1821 (24)	68,898	5,595	9	Jefferson City	Kansas City
Montana	1889 (41)	145,556	902	1	Helena	Billings
Nebraska	1867 (37)	76,878	1,711	3	Lincoln	Omaha
Nevada	1864 (36)	109,806	1,998	3	Carson City	Las Vegas
New Hampshire	1788 (9)	8,969	1,236	2	Concord	Manchester
New Jersey	1787 (3)	7,419	8,414	13	Trenton	Newark
New Mexico	1912 (47)	121,365	1,819	3	Santa Fe	Albuquerque
New York	1788 (11)	47,224	18,976	29	Albany	New York
North Carolina	1789 (12)	48,718	8,049	13	Raleigh	Charlotte
North Dakota	1889 (39)	68,994	642	1	Bismarck	Fargo
Ohio	1803 (17)	40,953	11,353	18	Columbus	Columbus
Oklahoma	1907 (46)	68,679	3,451	5	Oklahoma City	Oklahoma City
Oregon	1859 (33)	96,003	3,421	5	Salem	Portland
Pennsylvania	1787 (2)	44,820	12,281	19	Harrisburg	Philadelphia
Rhode Island	1790 (13)	1,045	1,048	2	Providence	Providence
South Carolina	1788 (8)	30,111	4,012	6	Columbia	Columbia
South Dakota	1889 (40)	75,898	755	1	Pierre	Sioux Falls
Tennessee	1796 (16)	41,220	5,689	9	Nashville	Memphis
Texas	1845 (28)	261,914	20,852	32	Austin	Houston
Utah	1896 (45)	82,168	2,233	3	Salt Lake City	Salt Lake City
Vermont	1791 (14)	9,249	609	1	Montpelier	Burlington
Virginia	1788 (10)	39,598	7,079	11	Richmond	Virginia Beach
Washington	1889 (42)	66,582	5,894	9	Olympia	Seattle
West Virginia	1863 (35)	24,087	1,808	3	Charleston	Charleston
Wisconsin	1848 (30)	54,314	5,364	8	Madison	Milwaukee
Wyoming	1890 (44)	97,105	494	1	Cheyenne	Cheyenne
District of Columbia		61	572	1 (nonvoting)		

Self-Governing Areas, Possessions, and Dependencies	Land Area in Square Miles	Population (In Thousands)	Capital
Puerto Rico	3,515	809	San Juan
Guam	209	155	Agana
U.S. Virgin Islands	132	121	Charlotte Amalie
American Samoa	77	65	Pago Pago

Sources: Department of Commerce, Bureau of the Census

*As of 108th Congress.

The Fifty States

State Flags

 Alabama
 Alaska
 Arizona
 Arkansas
 California

 Colorado
 Connecticut
 Delaware
 Florida
 Georgia

 Hawaii
 Idaho
 Illinois
 Indiana
 Iowa

 Kansas
 Kentucky
 Louisiana
 Maine
 Maryland

 Massachusetts
 Michigan
 Minnesota
 Mississippi
 Missouri

 Montana
 Nebraska
 Nevada
 New Hampshire
 New Jersey

 New Mexico
 New York
 North Carolina
 North Dakota
 Ohio

 Oklahoma
 Oregon
 Pennsylvania
 Rhode Island
 South Carolina

 South Dakota
 Tennessee
 Texas
 Utah
 Vermont

 Virginia
 Washington
 West Virginia
 Wisconsin
 Wyoming

The Fifty States

Geographic Atlas

ARCTIC OCEAN

Greenland (Den.)

80°N

160°W 140°W 120°W 100°W 80°W 60°W

Yukon R.

Alaska (U.S.)

60°N

Aleutian Is. (U.S.)

Mackenzie R.

CANADA

NORTH AMERICA

Ottawa Montréal

Chicago

New York

40°N

San Francisco

Colorado R.

Mississippi R. Ohio R.

Washington, DC

UNITED STATES

Bermuda (U.K.)

Los Angeles

Houston

ATLANTIC OCEAN

Midway Is. (U.S.)

New Orleans

20°N

MEXICO

Hawaii (U.S.)

Mexico City

See inset map

Caracas

GUYANA

VENEZUELA

Bogotá

Georgetown

Paramaribo

French Guiana (Fr.)

COLOMBIA

SURINAME

0° Equator

Galápagos Is. (Ecuador)

ECUADOR

Quito

Negro R.

Amazon R.

SOUTH AMERICA

SAMOA

PERU

Madeira R.

São Francisco R.

American Samoa (U.S.)

French Polynesia (Fr.)

Lima

BRAZIL

BOLIVIA

La Paz

Brasília

TONGA

Cook Is. (N.Z.)

20°S

Sucre

PACIFIC OCEAN

Pitcairn I. (U.K.)

PARAGUAY

Rio de Janeiro

São Paulo

Asunción

Paraná R.

CHILE

Uruguay R.

Easter I. (Chile)

URUGUAY

40°S

Santiago

Buenos Aires

Montevideo

ARGENTINA

60°S

Falkland Is. (U.K.)

S. Georgia (U.K.)

ANTARCTICA

Caribbean

Azimuthal Projection

0 150 300 Miles

0 150 300 Kilometers

UNITED STATES

Gulf of Mexico

Miami

Nassau

B A H A M A S

Havana

CUBA

Turks and Caicos Is. (U.K.)

Br. Virgin Is. (U.K.)

MEXICO

Cayman Islands (U.K.)

Kingston

Port-au-Prince

HAITI

DOMINICAN REPUBLIC

Puerto Rico (U.S.)

ANTIGUA AND BARBUDA

Belmopan

Santo Domingo

Virgin Islands (U.S.)

Guadeloupe (Fr.)

BELIZE

JAMAICA

ST. KITTS AND NEVIS

DOMINICA

GUATEMALA

Guatemala

HONDURAS

Tegucigalpa

Caribbean Sea

Martinique (Fr.)

ST. LUCIA

San Salvador

Neth. Antilles (Neth.)

BARBADOS

NICARAGUA

Aruba (Neth.)

ST. VINCENT AND THE GRENADINES

EL SALVADOR

Managua

GRENADA

ATLANTIC OCEAN

COSTA RICA

San José

TRINIDAD AND TOBAGO

Panamá

Caracas

Port of Spain

PANAMA

COLOMBIA

VENEZUELA

GUYANA

40°W 20°W 0° 20°E 40°E 60°E 80°E 100°E 120°E 140°E 160°E

Svalbard (Nor.)

Reykjavik
ICELAND

Volga R.

Ob R.   RUSSIA   Lena R.

Novosibirsk

Moscow

Astana

EUROPE

Azores (Port.)

KAZAKHSTAN   ASIA   MONGOLIA   Ulanbaatar

GEORGIA   ARMENIA   UZBEKISTAN   Bishkek   KYRGYZSTAN
Istanbul   TURKEY   TURK.   Tashkent   TAJIKISTAN
Ankara   AZERBAIJAN   Ashgabat   Dushanbe
CYPRUS   SYRIA   AFGHANISTAN   Kabul   CHINA
LEBANON   Baghdad   IRAQ   Tehran   Islamabad   PAKISTAN
ISRAEL   JORDAN   KUWAIT   New   NEPAL   BHUTAN

Canary Is. (Spain)   MOROCCO
Tripoli   Tripoli   EGYPT

Western Sahara (Mor.)
ALGERIA   LIBYA

CAPE VERDE   See inset map
NIGER   CHAD   Khartoum   ERITREA
N'Djamena   SUDAN
Bangui   CENTRAL   Addis   ETHIOPIA
CAMEROON   AFRICAN REP.   Ababa
AFRICA

Beijing
N. KOREA
Pyongyang
Tianjin   Seoul   JAPAN
S. KOREA   Tokyo
Chongqing   Shanghai
Hanoi   Taipei
Hong Kong   TAIWAN

PACIFIC OCEAN

BAHRAIN   QATAR
Riyadh   Abu Dhabi   Muscat
SAUDI   U.A.E.   OMAN
ARABIA   Sanaa   YEMEN
DJIBOUTI   SOMALIA

Mumbai   INDIA   BANGLADESH
Yangon   MYANMAR   LAOS   VIETNAM
THAILAND   Bangkok   CAMBODIA
Phnom   Penh
Colombo   SRI   LANKA
MALDIVES   Kuala Lumpur   MALAYSIA   BRUNEI

Northern Mariana Is. (U.S.)   Wake I. (U.S.)
Manila   PHILIPPINES
Guam (U.S.)   MARSHALL IS.
PALAU   FEDERATED STATES OF MICRONESIA
NAURU   KIRIBATI

EQ. GUINEA
SAO TOMÉ & PRÍNCIPE   GABON   CONGO   DEM. REP. OF THE CONGO
Libreville   Yaundé   Nairobi   KENYA
Brazzaville   RWANDA   BURUNDI
Kinshasa   Dodoma   TANZANIA
Cabinda (Angola)   Luanda   Dar es Salaam   COMOROS

UGANDA   Kampala
SEYCHELLES

INDONESIA

SINGAPORE   Jakarta

PAPUA NEW GUINEA   SOLOMON IS.
Port Moresby

TUVALU
VANUATU

ANGOLA   ZAMBIA   MALAWI
Lusaka   Lilongwe   Harare
NAMIBIA   ZIMBABWE   Réunion (Fr.)
Windhoek   BOTSWANA   Antananarivo   MAURITIUS
Gaborone   MADAGASCAR
Pretoria   Maputo
SOUTH   SWAZILAND
AFRICA   LESOTHO
Cape Town

FIJI
New Caledonia (Fr.)

AUSTRALIA

INDIAN OCEAN

Perth

Adelaide   Sydney
Melbourne   Canberra   NEW ZEALAND
Wellington

N   W   E   S

Key

⊛ Capital

• Other city

Robinson Projection
0   1000   2000 Miles
0   1000   2000 Kilometers

Europe   Azimuthal Projection
0   250   500 Miles
0   250   500 Kilometers

FINLAND
Helsinki
NORWAY   Stockholm   ESTONIA   Tallinn   RUSSIA
Oslo   SWEDEN   Riga   LATVIA
N. Ireland (U.K.)   DENMARK   LITHUANIA
Dublin   UNITED   Copenhagen   RUSSIA   Vilnius   Minsk
IRELAND   KINGDOM*   NETHERLANDS   BELARUS
London   Amsterdam   Berlin   Warsaw
ATLANTIC   Brussels   GERMANY   POLAND   Kiev
OCEAN   BELGIUM   LUX.   Prague   CZECH   UKRAINE
Paris   FRANCE   Bern   Vienna   REP.   SLOVAKIA   MOLDOVA
SWITZ.   LIECH.   Bratislava   Chisinau
Ljubljana   AUSTRIA   HUNGARY   ROMANIA
SLOVENIA   Zagreb   Budapest
SAN   CROATIA   Bucharest
MARINO   BOSNIA-   Belgrade   BULGARIA
PORTUGAL   ANDORRA   MONACO   ITALY   HERZ.   Sarajevo   YUGO.   Sofia
Lisbon   Madrid   Rome   Tirana   MACE.
SPAIN   ALBANIA   TURKEY
Mediterranean   Tunis   GREECE
Rabat   Algiers   Sea   MALTA   Athens
MOROCCO   ALGERIA   TUNISIA

Mercator Projection
0   250   500 Miles
0   250   500 Kilometers

Nouakchott
MAURITANIA
Dakar   SENEGAL   MALI   Niamey   NIGER
GAMBIA   Bamako   Niger R.   BURKINA   FASO
Banjul   GUINEA-   Ouagadougou   NIGERIA
Bissau   BISSAU   GUINEA   BENIN   Abuja
Conakry   SIERRA   CÔTE   GHANA   Porto-
Freetown   LEONE   D'IVOIRE   Lomé   Novo   Lagos
Monrovia   Yamoussoukro   Accra   TOGO
LIBERIA

Africa

* The United Kingdom, the official name of the country, is more often referred to as Great Britain.

United States: Political

CANADA

Pacific Time Zone

Mountain Time Zone

Central Time Zone

Seattle •
• Spokane
★ Olympia
Washington (1889)

• Portland
★ Salem
• Eugene
Oregon (1859)

Great Falls •
Helena ★
Montana (1889)

• Billings

Minot •
• Grand Forks
North Dakota (1889)
• Bismarck

South Dakota (1889)
• Pierre
• Rapid City

★ Boise
Idaho (1890)
• Pocatello

Wyoming (1890)
• Casper

• Ogden
Great Salt Lake
★ Salt Lake City

Cheyenne ★

Nebraska (1867)
• Sioux Falls
• Sioux City
• Omaha
Lincoln ★

• Reno
★ Carson City
Nevada (1864)

San Francisco •
★ Sacramento
• Oakland
• San Jose

Utah (1896)

★ Denver
Colorado (1876)
• Colorado Springs

Kansas (1861)
Topeka ★
• Wichita

California (1850)
Las Vegas •

Los Angeles •
Long Beach •
Salton Sea
• San Diego

Arizona (1912)
★ Phoenix
Tucson •

★ Santa Fe
• Albuquerque
New Mexico (1912)
Las Cruces •
• El Paso

Oklahoma (1907)
• Tulsa
Oklahoma City •

• Dallas
Fort Worth •

Texas (1845)
★ Austin

• San Antonio

PACIFIC OCEAN

MEXICO

Geographic Atlas

Hawaii–Aleutian Time Zone
Hawaii (1959)
Honolulu ★
PACIFIC OCEAN
Mercator Projection
0   50   100 Miles
0 50 100 Kilometers

Hawaii–Aleutian Time Zone
PACIFIC OCEAN

RUSSIA

Alaska Time Zone
Alaska (1959)
Fairbanks •
• Anchorage
Bering Sea
Gulf of Alaska
• Juneau
CANADA

Pacific Time Zone
Mountain Time Zone

Albers Conic Equal-Area Projection
0   200   400 Miles
0 200 400 Kilometers

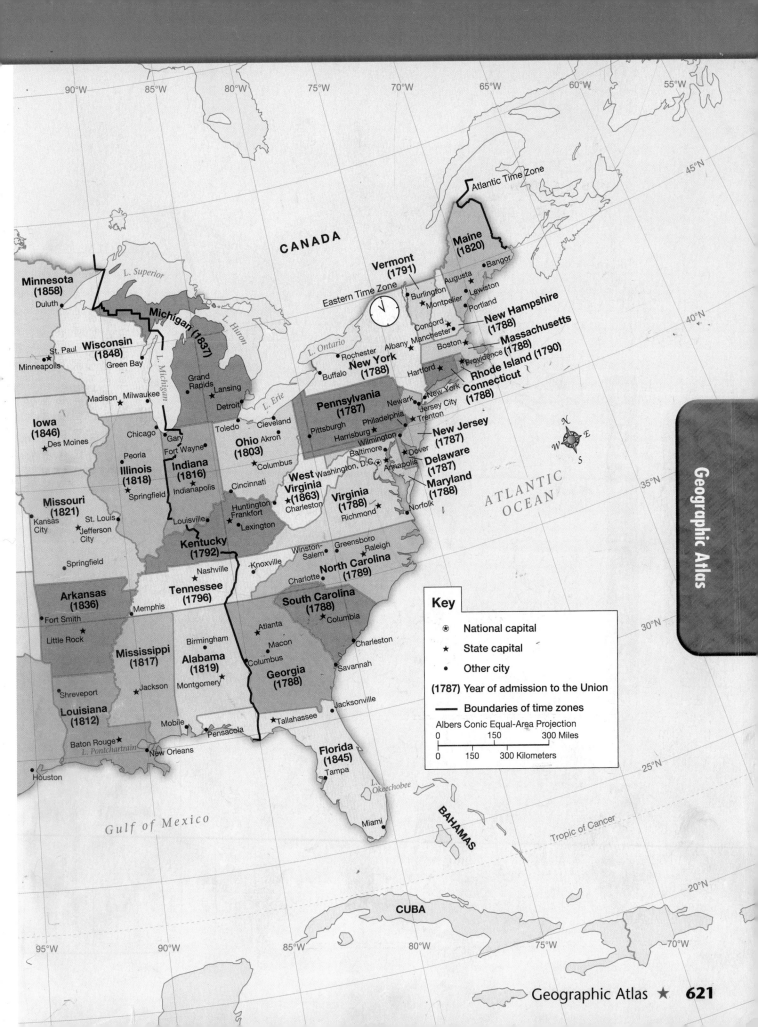

CANADA

Minnesota (1858)
Duluth
St. Paul ★
Minneapolis ●

L. Superior

Michigan (1837)

Wisconsin (1848)
Green Bay ●
Madison ● Milwaukee ●

L. Huron
L. Michigan

Grand Rapids ●
Lansing ★
Detroit ●

Iowa (1846)
Des Moines ●

Chicago ●
Peoria ●
Illinois (1818)
Springfield ★

Gary ●
Fort Wayne ●
Indiana (1816)
Indianapolis ★

Toledo ●
Ohio (1803)
Columbus ●
Cincinnati ●

Cleveland ●
Akron ●

L. Erie

Missouri (1821)
Kansas City ●
St. Louis ●
Jefferson City ★
Springfield ●

Louisville ●
Frankfort ★
Lexington ●
Huntington ●

Kentucky (1792)
Knoxville ●
Nashville ★

West Virginia (1863)
Charleston ★

Virginia (1788)
Richmond ★

Arkansas (1836)
Fort Smith ●
Little Rock ★

Memphis ●

Tennessee (1796)

Winston-Salem ●
Greensboro ●
Raleigh ★

Charlotte ●
North Carolina (1789)

Birmingham ●
Atlanta ★
Macon ●

South Carolina (1788)
Columbia ★
Charleston ●

Mississippi (1817)
Jackson ★

Alabama (1819)
Montgomery ★
Columbus ●

Georgia (1788)
Savannah ●

Louisiana (1812)
Shreveport ●
Baton Rouge ★
L. Pontchartrain
New Orleans ●

Mobile ●
Pensacola ●
Tallahassee ★

Jacksonville ●

Florida (1845)
Tampa ●
L. Okeechobee
Miami ●

Houston ●

Gulf of Mexico

Eastern Time Zone

Vermont (1791)
Burlington ●
Montpelier ●

Maine (1820)
Bangor ●
Augusta ●
Lewiston ●
Portland ●

Atlantic Time Zone

New Hampshire (1788)
Concord ★
Manchester ●

L. Ontario

Rochester ●
Albany ★
Buffalo ●

New York (1788)

Boston ★
Massachusetts (1788)
Providence ★
Rhode Island (1790)
Hartford ★
Connecticut (1788)

Pennsylvania (1787)
Pittsburgh ●
Harrisburg ★
Philadelphia ●

Newark ●
New York ●
Jersey City ●
Trenton ★
New Jersey (1787)

Wilmington ●
Dover ★
Delaware (1787)
Baltimore ●
Washington, D.C. ⊛
Annapolis ★
Maryland (1788)

Norfolk ●

ATLANTIC OCEAN

N
W   E
S

BAHAMAS

Tropic of Cancer

CUBA

Key

- ⊛ National capital
- ★ State capital
- ● Other city
- (1787) Year of admission to the Union
- ▬▬ Boundaries of time zones

Albers Conic Equal-Area Projection

| 0 | 150 | 300 Miles |

| 0 | 150 | 300 Kilometers |

90°W   85°W   80°W   75°W   70°W   65°W   60°W   55°W

95°W   90°W   85°W   80°W   75°W   70°W

45°N   40°N   35°N   30°N   25°N   20°N

Geographic Atlas

Geographic Atlas

United States: Physical Features

Key

Elevations

Above 10,000 feet (3,000 meters)
7,000–10,000 feet (2,000–3,000 meters)
3,000–7,000 feet (1,000–2,000 meters)
700–3,000 feet (200–1,000 meters)
0–700 feet (0–200 meters)
Below sea level

ATLANTIC OCEAN

Cape Cod

Long Island

Chesapeake Bay

Cape Hatteras

APPALACHIAN MOUNTAINS

ATLANTIC COASTAL PLAIN

L. Ontario

L. Erie

L. Huron

L. Michigan

L. Superior

Tennessee R.

Alabama R.

Ohio R.

Mississippi R.

GULF COASTAL PLAIN

Gulf of Mexico

Tropic of Cancer

L. Okeechobee

INTERIOR PLAINS

OZARK PLATEAU

OUACHITA MTS.

Mississippi R.

Missouri R.

Red R.

GREAT PLAINS

BLACK HILLS

Platte R.

Arkansas R.

Pikes Peak

Mt. Elbert

LLANO ESTACADO

Rio Grande

ROCKY MOUNTAINS

Missouri R.

Snake R.

Great Salt Lake

Colorado R.

GRAND CANYON

GREAT BASIN

Columbia R.

CASCADE RANGE

Mt. Rainier

SIERRA NEVADA

Mt. Whitney

PACIFIC OCEAN

Albers Conic Equal-Area Projection
0   150   300 Miles
0   150   300 Kilometers

BROOKS RANGE

Arctic Circle

Yukon R.

Mt. McKinley

Albers Conic Equal-Area Projection
0   250   500 Miles
0   250   500 Kilometers

Kauai
Oahu
Molokai
Maui
Mauna Kea
Hawaii

Mercator Projection
0   100 Miles
0   100 Kilometers

United States: Natural Resources

Key

Bauxite	◄	Gold	■	Mercury	○	Silver	●
Coal	(shaded)	Iron ore	◄	Molybdenum	△	Sulfur	○
Cobalt	◆	Lead	○	Natural Gas	◄	Uranium	◆
Copper	●	Manganese	●	Oil	+	Zinc	+

Albers Equal-Area Projection

0   150   300 Miles
0   150   300 Kilometers

Alaska

Albers Conic Equal-Area Projection

0   250   500 Miles
0   250   500 Kilometers

Hawaii

Mercator Projection

0   100 Miles
0   100 Kilometers

Geographic Atlas

Geographic Atlas

United States: Land Use

Key
- Manufacturing and trade
- Ranching or grazing
- Crops and livestock
- Forest products
- Little or no commercial activity

Albers Conic Equal-Area Projection

| 0 | 150 | 300 Miles |
| 0 | 150 | 300 Kilometers |

ATLANTIC OCEAN

Tropic of Cancer

Gulf of Mexico

PACIFIC OCEAN

Maine
VT
NH
MA
CT
RI
New York
Boston
Pennsylvania
Philadelphia
New York
NJ
Pittsburgh
MD DE
Baltimore
Washington, D.C.
Richmond
Virginia
WV
Ohio
Indianapolis
Kentucky
North Carolina
South Carolina
Georgia
Atlanta
Florida
Miami

Michigan
Detroit
Lake Erie
Lake Huron
Lake Ontario
Lake Superior
Lake Michigan
Chicago
Illinois
Indiana
Tennessee
Memphis
Tennessee R.
Alabama
Alabama R.
MS
Louisiana
New Orleans

Wisconsin
Minnesota
Minneapolis
Iowa
Missouri
St. Louis
Mississippi R.
Arkansas
Arkansas R.
Ohio R.
Kansas City

North Dakota
South Dakota
Nebraska
Platte R.
Missouri R.
Kansas
Oklahoma
Red R.
Texas
Dallas
Houston

Montana
Wyoming
Colorado
Denver
New Mexico
Rio Grande

Washington
Seattle
Columbia R.
Oregon
Idaho
Snake R.
Salt Lake City
Utah
Colorado R.
Nevada
Las Vegas
California
San Francisco
Los Angeles
Arizona
Phoenix

N
W E
S

Alaska
Yukon R.
Anchorage
Arctic Circle
60°N

Albers Conic Equal-Area Projection
| 0 | 250 | 500 Miles |
| 0 | 250 | 500 Kilometers |

Hawaii
Honolulu
Mercator Projection
| 0 | 100 Miles |
| 0 | 100 Kilometers |
22°N
20°N

United States: Population Density

Key

Per sq. mile
- 0–2
- 2–25
- 25–65
- 65–130
- 130–250
- Over 250

Per sq. km
- 0–1
- 1–10
- 10–25
- 25–50
- 50–100
- Over 100

ATLANTIC OCEAN

Gulf of Mexico

PACIFIC OCEAN

Albers Conic Equal-Area Projection

Maine
NH
VT
MA
CT
RI
New York
Boston
Philadelphia
NJ
Baltimore
DE
MD
Washington, D.C.
Pennsylvania
Pittsburgh
Virginia
West Virginia WV
North Carolina
South Carolina
Georgia
Atlanta
Florida
Miami
New York
Lake Ontario
Lake Erie
Lake Huron
Lake Superior
Lake Michigan
Michigan
Detroit
Cleveland
Ohio
Cincinnati
Indiana
Kentucky
Tennessee
Memphis
Alabama
MS
Chicago
Milwaukee
Illinois
St. Louis
Missouri
Wisconsin
Minnesota
Minneapolis
Iowa
Kansas City
Kansas
Missouri R.
Mississippi R.
Arkansas
Louisiana
New Orleans
Houston
Dallas
Texas
San Antonio
Oklahoma
Nebraska
South Dakota
North Dakota
Montana
Wyoming
Colorado
Denver
New Mexico
Rio Grande
Arizona
Phoenix
Utah
Salt Lake City
Nevada
Las Vegas
Idaho
Oregon
Portland
Washington
Seattle
California
San Francisco
Los Angeles
San Diego

Alaska
Anchorage
Arctic Circle
70°N
60°N

Hawaii
Honolulu
22°N
20°N

Mercator Projection
0   100 Miles
0   100 Kilometers

Albers Conic Equal-Area Projection
0   250   500 Miles
0   250   500 Kilometers

0   150   300 Miles
0   150   300 Kilometers

Gazetteer of American History

This gazetteer, or geographic dictionary, lists places that are important in American history. The approximate latitude and longitude are given for cities, towns, and other specific locations. See text page 4 for information about latitude and longitude. In the Gazetteer, after the description of each place, there are usually two numbers in parentheses. The first number refers to the text page where you can find out more about the place. The second appears in slanted, or *italic*, type and refers to a map (*m*) where the place is shown.

A

Africa Second largest continent in the world. (p. 52, *m51*)

Alabama 22nd state. Nicknamed the Heart of Dixie or the Cotton State. (p. 616, *m620–621*)

Alamo (29°N/99°W) Former mission in San Antonio, Texas, where 255 rebels died during the Texas war for independence. (p. 387, *m386*)

Alaska 49th state. Unofficially nicknamed the Last Frontier. Purchased from Russia in 1867. (p. 616, *m620–621*)

Albany (43°N/74°W) Capital of New York. (p. 143, *m142*)

Andes Rugged mountain chain in South America. (p. 39)

Appalachian Mountains Mountain chain that stretches from Georgia to Canada. (p. 13, *m12*)

Appomattox Court House (37°N/79°W) Town in Virginia where Lee surrendered to Grant. (p. 509, *m507*)

Arctic Ocean World's fourth-largest ocean. (p. 11, *m12*)

Argentina Country in South America. (p. 349, *m349*)

Arizona 48th state. Nicknamed the Grand Canyon State. (p. 616, *m620–621*)

Arkansas 25th state. Nicknamed the Land of Opportunity. (p. 616, *m620–621*)

Asia Largest of the world's continents. (p. 50, *m618–619*)

Atlanta (34°N/84°W) Capital and largest city of Georgia. Burned by Sherman during the Civil War. (p. 508, *m470*)

Atlantic Ocean World's second largest ocean. (p. 11, *m618–619*)

Atlantic Plain Low-lying area that stretches along the eastern coast of the United States. (p. 13, *m12*)

B

Baltimore (39°N/77°W) Port city in Maryland. (p. 323, *m323*)

Bering Sea Narrow sea between Asia and North America. Scientists think a land bridge was here during the last ice age. (p. 69, *m37*)

Boston (42°N/71°W) Seaport and industrial city in Massachusetts. (p. 102, *m103*)

Brazil Largest country in South America. (p. 350, *m349*)

Breed's Hill (42°N/71°W) Overlooks Boston harbor. Site of fighting during the Battle of Bunker Hill. (p. 170)

Buena Vista (26°N/101°W) City in Mexico. Site of an American victory in the Mexican War. (p. 396, *m395*)

Buffalo (43°N/79°W) City in New York State on Lake Erie. (p. 341, *m340*)

Bunker Hill (42°N/71°W) Overlooks Boston harbor. Site of first major battle of the Revolution. (p. 170)

C

Cahokia (39°N/90°W) British fort captured by George Rogers Clark during the American Revolution. (p. 189, *m187*)

California 31st state. Nicknamed the Golden State. Ceded to the United States by Mexico in 1848. (p. 616, *m620–621*)

Canada Northern neighbor of the United States. Second largest nation in the world. (p. 145, *m618–619*)

Canadian Shield Lowland region that lies mostly in eastern Canada. (p. 13, *m12*)

Caribbean Sea Tropical sea in the Western Hemisphere. (p. 69, *m76*)

Central America The part of Latin America made up of Guatemala, Honduras, El Salvador, Nicaragua, Costa Rica, Panama, and Belize. (p. 40, *m349*)

Central Plains Large region of the United States located between the Rocky Mountains in the west and the Appalachian Mountains in the east. (p. 13, *m12*)

Chancellorsville (38°N/78°W) Site in Virginia of a Confederate victory in 1863. (p. 493, *m491*)

Charleston (33°N/80°W) City in South Carolina. Site of battles in both the American Revolution and the Civil War. (p. 115, *m115*)

Chesapeake Bay Large inlet of the Atlantic Ocean in Virginia and Maryland. (p. 114, *m115*)

Chicago (42°N/88°W) City in Illinois on Lake Michigan. (p. 410, *m620–621*)

China Country in East Asia. (p. 53, *m618–619*)

Cincinnati (39°N/84°W) City in southern Ohio on the Ohio River. (p. 410, *m620–621*)

Coastal Plains Region consisting of the Atlantic Plain and the Gulf Plain along the Gulf of Mexico. (p. 13, *m12*)

Colorado 38th state. Nicknamed the Centennial State. (p. 616, *m620–621*)

Colorado River River that begins in the Rocky Mountains and flows into Gulf of California. (p. 15, *m12*)

Columbia River Chief river of the Pacific Northwest. (p. 309, *m308*)

Concord (43°N/71°W) Village in Massachusetts where battle occurred between the British and Americans at the start of the American Revolution. (p. 159, *m170*)

Connecticut One of the original 13 states. Nicknamed the Constitution State or the Nutmeg State. (p. 616, *m620–621*)

Cowpens (35°N/82°W) In South Carolina, site of an American victory in the Revolutionary War. (p. 192, *m192*)

Cumberland Gap (37°N/84°W) Pass in the Appalachian Mountains near the borders of Virginia, Kentucky, and Tennessee. (p. 148, *m329*)

Cuzco (14°S/72°W) Capital of the Incan empire. (p. 39, *m35*)

D

Dallas (33°N/97°W) Major city in north central Texas. (p. 7, *m620–621*)

Delaware One of the original 13 states. Nicknamed the First State or the Diamond State. (p. 616, *m620–621*)

Delaware River Flows into the Atlantic Ocean through Delaware Bay. (p. 85, *m90*)

Detroit (42°N/83°W) Largest city in Michigan. (p. 321, *m323*)

District of Columbia Located on the Potomac River. Seat of the federal government of the United States. (p. 281, *m620–621*)

E

England Part of Great Britain. (p. 81, *m82*)

Equator Line of latitude labeled 0° on maps. Separates the Northern and Southern hemispheres. (p. 4, *m618–619*)

Erie Canal Linked the Hudson and Mohawk rivers with Buffalo and Lake Erie in New York State. Built between 1817 and 1825. (p. 340, *m340*)

Europe World's second smallest continent. (p. 68, *m618–619*)

F

Florida 27th state. Nicknamed the Sunshine State. (p. 616, *m620–621*)

Fort Donelson (37°N/88°W) Located in Tennessee. Captured by Grant in 1862. (p. 494, *m503*)

Fort Henry (37°N/88°W) Located in Tennessee. Captured by Grant in 1862. (p. 494, *m503*)

Fort McHenry (39°N/77°W) Located in Baltimore harbor. British bombardment there in 1814 inspired Francis Scott Key to write "The Star-Spangled Banner." (p. 323)

Fort Necessity (40°N/79°W) British fort during the French and Indian War. (p. 143, *m142*)

Fort Pitt (40°N/80°W) British fort in the 1700s on the site of present-day Pittsburgh. (p. 144, *m187*)

Fort Sumter (33°N/80°W) Guarded Charleston harbor in South Carolina. First shots of the Civil War fired there in 1861. (p. 481, *m503*)

Fort Ticonderoga (44°N/74°W) Fort at the south end of Lake Champlain. Captured from the British by Ethan Allen in 1775. (p. 144, *m142*)

France Country in Western Europe. (p. 83, *m618–619*)

Fredericksburg (38°N/78°W) Located in eastern Virginia. Site of a Confederate victory in 1862. (p. 493, *m491*)

G

Gadsden Purchase Land purchased from Mexico in 1853. Now part of Arizona and New Mexico. (p. 397, *m379*)

Georgia One of the original 13 states. Nicknamed the Peach State or the Empire State of the South. (p. 616, *m620–621*)

Germany Country in central Europe (p. 415, *m618–619*)

Gettysburg (40°N/77°W) Town in southern Pennsylvania. Site of a Union victory in 1863 and Lincoln's Gettysburg Address. (p. 506, *m491*)

Goliad (29°N/97°W) Texas town where Mexicans killed several hundred Texans during the Texas war for independence. (p. 388, *m386*)

Gonzales (29°N/97°W) City in Texas near San Antonio. Site of the first Texan victory over Mexico in 1835. (p. 386, *m386*)

Great Britain Island nation of Western Europe. Includes England, Scotland, Wales, and Northern Ireland. (p. 142, *m618–619*)

Great Colombia Country that existed from 1822 to 1830, made up of present-day Ecuador, Venezuela, Panama, and Colombia. (p. 349, *m349*)

Great Lakes Chain of five lakes in central North America. Lakes Superior, Michigan, Huron, Ontario, and Erie. (p. 15, *m12*)

Great Plains Western part of the Interior Plains. (p. 13, *m12*)

Great Salt Lake (41°N/113°W) Lake in northern Utah with highly saline water. (p. 399, *m400*)

Great Wagon Road Early pioneer route across the Appalachians. (p. 112, *m115*)

Gulf of Mexico Body of water along the southern coast of the United States. (p. 14, *m12*)

Gulf Plain Low-lying area stretching along the coast of the Gulf of Mexico. (p. 13, *m12*)

H

Haiti Country in the West Indies. The nation won independence from France in the early 1800s. (p. 307, *m618–619*)

Harpers Ferry (39°N/78°W) Town in West Virginia. John Brown raided the arsenal there in 1859. (p. 475, *m491*)

Hawaii Newest of the 50 states. Nicknamed the Aloha State. (p. 616, *m620–621*)

Hawaiian Islands Region in the Pacific Ocean composed of a group of eight large islands and many small islands. (p. 14, *m12*)

Houston (29°N/95°W) Inland port and largest city in Texas. (p. 7, *m395*)

Hudson River Largest river in New York State. (p. 82, *m90*)

I

Idaho 43rd state. Nicknamed the Gem State. Acquired as part of the Oregon Territory. (p. 616, *m620–621*)

Illinois 21st state. Nicknamed the Inland Empire. Settled as part of the Northwest Territory. (p. 616, *m620–621*)

Indiana 19th state. Nicknamed the Hoosier State. Settled as part of the Northwest Territory. (p. 616, *m620–621*)

Interior Plains Region of the central United States that stretches from the Rockies to the Appalachians. (p. 13, *m12*)

Intermountain Region Rugged region from the Rocky Mountains to the Sierra Nevada and coastal mountains of the western United States. (p. 12, *m12*)

Iowa 29th state. Nicknamed the Hawkeye State. Acquired as part of the Louisiana Purchase. (p. 616, *m620–621*)

Ireland Country in northern Europe occupying part of an island west of Great Britain. (p. 415, *m618–619*)

Italy Country in southern Europe. (p. 545, *m618–619*)

J

Jamestown (37°N/77°W) First successful English colony in North America. (p. 87, *m90*)

K

Kansas 34th state. Nicknamed the Sunflower State. Acquired as part of the Louisiana Purchase. (p. 616, *m620–621*)

Kaskaskia (38°N/90°W) British fort on the Mississippi River captured by George Rogers Clark during the American Revolution. (p. 189, *m187*)

Kentucky 15th state. Nicknamed the Bluegrass State. (p. 616, *m620–621*)

Kilwa (8°S/39°E) East African trading state in the 1400s. (p. 52, *m51*)

King's Mountain (35°N/81°W) In South Carolina, site of an American victory in the Revolutionary War. (p. 191, *m192*)

L

Lancaster Turnpike Road built in the 1790s linking Philadelphia and Lancaster, Pennsylvania. (p. 339, *m329*)

Latin America Name for those parts of the Western Hemisphere where Latin languages such as Spanish, French, and Portuguese are spoken. Includes Mexico, Central America, South America, and the islands of the Caribbean. (p. 348, *m349*)

Lexington (42°N/71°W) Village in Massachusetts. Site of the first clash between minutemen and British troops in 1775. (p. 160, *m170*)

...eria Country in West Africa. Set up in 1822 as a colony for free African Americans. (p. 440, *m618–619*)

London (51°N/0°) Capital of United Kingdom. (*m618–619*)

Long Island Located in New York. Site of a British victory in the Revolution. (p. 181, *m182*)

Los Angeles (34°N/118°W) City in southern California. First settled by Spanish missionaries. (p. 7, *m76*)

Louisbourg (46°N/60°W) Fort in eastern Canada that played a major role in the French and Indian War. (p. 144, *m142*)

Louisiana 18th state. Nicknamed the Pelican State. First state created out of the Louisiana Purchase. (p. 616, *m620–621*)

Lowell (43°N/83°W) City in Massachusetts. Important site of Industrial Revolution. (p. 333)

Maine 23rd state. Nicknamed the Pine Tree State. Originally part of Massachusetts. (p. 616, *m620–621*)

Mali Kingdom in West Africa. Reached its peak between 1200 and 1400. (p. 52)

Maryland One of the original 13 states. Nicknamed the Old Line State or the Free State. (p. 616, *m620–621*)

Mason-Dixon Line Boundary between Pennsylvania and Maryland surveyed and marked in the 1760s. (p. 113)

Massachusetts One of the original 13 states. Nicknamed the Bay State or the Old Colony. (p. 616, *m620–621*)

Memphis (35°N/90°W) City in Tennessee on the Mississippi River. Captured by Union forces in 1862. (p. 494, *m503*)

Mexican Cession Lands acquired by the United States from Mexico under the Treaty of Guadalupe Hidalgo in 1848. (p. 396, *m379*)

Mexico Southern neighbor of the United States. Gained independence from Spain in 1821. (p. 348, *m618–619*)

Mexico City (19°N/99°W) Capital of Mexico. (p. 396, *m77*)

Michigan 26th state. Nicknamed the Great Lake State or the Wolverine State. Settled as part of the Northwest Territory. (p. 616, *m620–621*)

Minnesota 32nd state. Nicknamed the Gopher State. Most of it was acquired as part of the Louisiana Purchase from France. (p. 616, *m620–621*)

Mississippi 20th state. Nicknamed the Magnolia State. (p. 616, *m620–621*)

Mississippi River Longest river in the United States. Links the Great Lakes with the Gulf of Mexico. (p. 14, *m12*)

Missouri 24th state. Nicknamed the Show Me State. Acquired as part of the Louisiana Purchase. (p. 616, *m620–621*)

Missouri River Second longest river in the United States. Rises in the northern Rocky Mountains and joins the Mississippi River near St. Louis, Missouri (p. 14, *m12*)

Montana 41st state. Nicknamed the Treasure State. Acquired in part through the Louisiana Purchase. (p. 616, *m620–621*)

Montreal (46°N/74°W) Major city in Canada. Located in the province of Quebec. (p. 319, *m323*)

National Road Early road to the West that began in Cumberland, Maryland, and eventually reached Illinois. (p. 339, *m329*)

Nauvoo (41°N/91°W) Town founded by the Mormons in Illinois in the 1840s. (p. 398, *m400*)

Nebraska 37th state. Nicknamed the Cornhusker State. Acquired as part of the Louisiana Purchase. (p. 616, *m620–621*)

Nevada 36th state. Nicknamed the Sagebrush State or the Battle Born State. Acquired at the end of the Mexican War. (p. 616, *m620–621*)

New Amsterdam (41°N/74°W) Town established by Dutch settlers on Manhattan Island in the early 1600s. Renamed New York by the British. (p. 85)

New England Region of northeastern United States, including the states of Maine, New Hampshire, Vermont, Massachusetts, Rhode Island, and Connecticut. (p. 93, *m101*)

New France Colony established by France in North America. (p. 83, *m82*)

New Hampshire One of the original 13 states. Nicknamed the Granite State. (p. 616, *m620–621*)

New Jersey One of the original 13 states. Nicknamed the Garden State. (p. 616, *m620–621*)

New Mexico 47th state. Nicknamed the Land of Enchantment. Acquired at the end of the Mexican War. (p. 616, *m620–621*)

New Netherland Dutch colony on the Hudson River. Seized by the English and renamed New York in 1664. (p. 85)

New Orleans (30°N/90°W) Port city in Louisiana near the mouth of the Mississippi River. Settled by the French in the 1600s. (p. 84, *m76*)

New Spain Area in the Americas ruled by Spain for some 300 years. Included much of present-day western United States. (p. 77, *m77*)

New York One of the original 13 states. Nicknamed the Empire State.

(p. 616, *m620–621*)

New York City (41°N/74°W) Port city at the mouth of the Hudson River. (p. 109, *m111*)

Norfolk (37°N/76°W) City and port in southeastern Virginia. (p. 492, *m620–621*)

North America World's third largest continent. (p. 11, *m618–619*)

North Carolina One of the original 13 states. Nicknamed the Tar Heel State or the Old North State. (p. 616, *m620–621*)

North Dakota 39th state. Nicknamed the Sioux State or the Flickertail State. Acquired as part of the Louisiana Purchase. (p. 616, *m620–621*)

Northwest Territory Name for lands north of the Ohio River. Acquired by the Treaty of Paris in 1783. (p. 203, *m203*)

Nueces River Claimed by Mexico in the Mexican War as the southern border of Texas. (p. 395, *m395*)

Ohio 17th state. Nicknamed the Buckeye State. Settled as part of the Northwest Territory. (p. 616, *m620–621*)

Ohio River Important transportation route. Begins at Pittsburgh and flows to the Mississippi River. (p. 141, *m142*)

Oklahoma 46th State. Nicknamed the Sooner State. Acquired as part of the Louisiana Purchase. (p. 616, *m620–621*)

Oregon 33rd state. Nicknamed the Beaver State. Acquired as part of the Oregon Territory. (p. 616, *m620–621*)

Oregon Trail Overland route from Independence, Missouri, to the Columbia River valley. (p. 383, *m400*)

Pacific Coast Highest and most rugged region of the United States. Includes the Cascades and the Sierra Nevada. (p. 12, *m12*)

Pacific Ocean World's largest ocean. (p. 11, *m618–619*)

Panama Country on the isthmus separating North and South America. Gained independence from Colombia in 1903. (p. 550, *m618–619*)

Panama Canal Canal dug through the Isthmus of Panama to link the Atlantic and Pacific oceans. (p. 550)

Paris (49°N/2°E) Capital of France. (p. 183, *m618–619*)

Pennsylvania One of the original 13 states. Nicknamed the Keystone State. (p. 616, *m620–621*)

Petersburg (37°N/78°W) City in Virginia. Union forces kept the city under siege for nine months during the Civil War. (p. 509, *m507*)

Gazetteer

Philadelphia (40°N/75°W) Major port and chief city in Pennsylvania. (p. 110, *m111*)

Philippine Islands Group of islands in the Pacific Ocean. Acquired by the United States in 1898. Gained independence in 1946. (p. 550, *m618–619*)

Pikes Peak (39°N/105°W) Mountain located in the Rocky Mountains of central Colorado. (p. 310, *m308*)

Plymouth (42°N/71°W) New England colony founded in 1620 by Pilgrims. (p. 94, *m90*)

Portugal Country in Western Europe. (p. 60, *m59*)

Potomac River Forms part of the Maryland-Virginia border. Flows through Washington, D.C., and into Chesapeake Bay. (p. 492, *m491*)

Prime Meridian Line of longitude labeled 0° on maps. (p. 5)

Princeton (40°N/75°W) City in New Jersey. Site of an American victory during the Revolution. (p. 182, *m182*)

Puerto Rico (18°N/67°W) Island in the Caribbean Sea. A self-governing commonwealth of the United States. (p. 550, *m618–619*)

Q

Quebec (47°N/71°W) City in eastern Canada. (p. 83, *m82*)

R

Rhode Island One of the original 13 states. Nicknamed Little Rhody or the Ocean State. (p. 616, *m620–621*)

Richmond (38°N/78°W) Capital of Virginia. Capital of the Confederate States of America during the Civil War. (p. 490, *m491*)

Rio Grande River that forms the border between the United States and Mexico. (p. 15, *m12*)

Roanoke Island (36°N/76°W) Island off North Carolina. Site of English "lost colony" founded in 1587. (p. 87, *m90*)

Rocky Mountains Mountains extending through the western United States and Canada. (p. 13, *m12*)

Russia Largest country in the world, spanning Europe and Asia. (p. 545, *m618–619*)

S

Sacramento (39°N/122°W) Capital of California. Developed as a gold rush boomtown. (p. 400, *m400*)

St. Augustine (30°N/81°W) City in Florida. Founded by Spain in 1565. Oldest European settlement in the United States. (p. 77, *m77*)

St. Lawrence River Waterway from the Great Lakes to the Atlantic Ocean. Forms part of the border between the United States and Canada. (p. 15, *m82*)

St. Louis (38°N/90°W) City in Missouri on the Mississippi River. Lewis and Clark began their expedition there. (p. 309, *m308*)

Salt Lake City (41°N/112°W) Largest city in Utah. Founded in 1847 by Mormons. (p. 399, *m400*)

San Antonio (29°N/99°W) City in southern Texas. Site of the Alamo. (p. 386, *m386*)

San Diego (33°N/117°W) City in southern California. Founded as the first Spanish mission in California. (p. 392, *m400*)

San Francisco (38°N/122°W) City in northern California. Boomtown of the California gold rush. (p. 393, *m400*)

Santa Fe (35°N/106°W) Capital of New Mexico. First settled by the Spanish. (p. 77, *m76*)

Santa Fe Trail Overland trail from Independence to Santa Fe. Opened in 1821. (p. 392, *m400*)

Saratoga (43°N/75°W) City in eastern New York. The American victory there in 1777 was a turning point in the Revolution. (p. 183, *m182*)

Savannah (32°N/81°W) Oldest city in Georgia, founded in 1733. (p. 116, *m115*)

Sierra Nevada Mountain range mostly in California. (p. 12, *m12*)

Songhai West African kingdom in the 1400s. (p. 53, *m35*)

South America World's fourth largest continent. (p. 11, *m67*)

South Carolina One of the original 13 states. Nicknamed the Palmetto State. (p. 616, *m620–621*)

South Dakota 40th state. Nicknamed the Coyote State or the Sunshine State. Acquired as part of the Louisiana Purchase. (p. 616, *m620–621*)

Spain Country in southwestern Europe. (p. 60, *m82*)

Spanish Florida Part of New Spain. Purchased by the United States in 1821. (p. 350, *m363*)

T

Tennessee 16th state. Nicknamed the Volunteer State. Gained statehood after North Carolina ceded its western lands to the United States. (p. 616, *m620–621*)

Tenochtitlán (19°N/99°W) Capital of the Aztec empire. Now part of Mexico City. (p. 38, *m35*)

Texas 28th state. Nicknamed the Lone Star State. Proclaimed independence from Mexico in 1836. Was a separate republic until 1845. (p. 616, *m620–621*)

Timbuktu (17°N/3°W) City on the Niger River in Africa. (p. 53, *m51*)

Trenton (41°N/74°W) Capital of New Jersey. Site of an American victory in the Revolution. (p. 182, *m182*)

U

United Kingdom See Great Britain. (*m618–619*)

Utah 45th state. Nicknamed the Beehive State. Settled by Mormons. (p. 616, *m620–621*)

V

Valley Forge (40°N/76°W) Winter headquarters for the Continental Army in 1777–1778. Located near Philadelphia. (p. 185, *m182*)

Veracruz (19°N/96°W) Port city in Mexico on the Gulf of Mexico. (p. 396, *m395*)

Vermont 14th state. Nicknamed the Green Mountain State. (p. 616, *m620–621*)

Vicksburg (42°N/86°W) City in Mississippi. Site of a Union victory in 1863. (p. 505, *m503*)

Vietnam Country in Southeast Asia. Site of a war involving the United States during the Cold War. (p. 562, *m618–619*)

Vincennes (39°N/88°W) City in Indiana. British fort there was captured by George Rogers Clark in 1779. (p. 189, *m187*)

Virginia One of the original 13 states. Nicknamed the Old Dominion. (p. 616, *m620–621*)

W

Washington 42nd state. Nicknamed the Evergreen State. Acquired as part of Oregon Territory. (p. 616, *m620–621*)

Washington, D.C. (39°N/77°W) Capital of the United States since 1800. (p. 281, *m323*)

West Indies Islands in the Caribbean Sea. Explored by Columbus. (p. 69, *m77*)

West Virginia 35th state. Nicknamed the Mountain State. Separated from Virginia early in the Civil War. (p. 616, *m620–621*)

Wisconsin 30th state. Nicknamed the Badger State. Settled as part of the Northwest Territory. (p. 616, *m620–621*)

Wyoming 44th state. Nicknamed the Equality State. (p. 616, *m620–621*)

Y

Yorktown (37°N/76°W) Town in Virginia. Site of the British surrender in 1781. (p. 193, *m192*)

Gazetteer

Glossary

This glossary defines all vocabulary words and many important historical terms and phrases. These words and terms appear in blue type the first time that they are used in the text. The page number(s) after each definition refers to the page(s) on which the word or phrase is defined in the text. For other references, see the index.

Pronunciation Key

When difficult names or terms first appear in the text, they are respelled to help you with pronunciation. A syllable printed in small capital letters receives the greatest stress. The pronunciation key below lists the letters and symbols that will help you pronounce the word. It also includes examples of words using each of the sounds and shows how each word would be pronounced.

Symbol	Example	Respelling
a	hat	(hat)
ay	pay, late	(pay), (layt)
ah	star, hot	(stahr), (haht)
ai	air, dare	(air), (dair)
aw	law, all	(law), (awl)
eh	met	(meht)
ee	bee, eat	(bee), (eet)
er	learn, sir, fur	(lern), (ser), (fer)
ih	fit	(fiht)
i	mile	(mīl)
ir	ear	(ir)
oh	no	(noh)
oi	soil, boy	(soil), (boi)
oo	root, rule	(root), (rool)
or	born, door	(born), (dor)
ow	plow, out	(plow), (owt)

Symbol	Example	Respelling
u	put, book	(put), (buk)
uh	fun	(fuhn)
yoo	few, use	(fyoo), (yooz)
ch	chill, reach	(chihl), (reech)
g	go, dig	(goh), (dihg)
j	jet, gently bridge	(jeht), (JEHNT lee), (brihj)
k	kite, cup	(kīt), (kuhp)
ks	mix	(mihks)
kw	quick	(kwihk)
ng	bring	(brihng)
s	say, cent	(say), (sehnt)
sh	she, crash	(shee), (krash)
th	three	(three)
y	yet, onion	(yeht), (UHN yuhn)
z	zip, always	(zihp), (AWL wayz)
zh	treasure	(TREH zher)

A

abolitionist person who wanted to end slavery completely in the United States (p. 440)

Act of Toleration a 1649 law passed by the Maryland assembly that provided religious freedom for all Christians (p. 114)

Adams-Onís Treaty an 1821 treaty between Spain and the United States in which Spain agreed to give Florida to the United States in exchange for $5 million (p. 350)

adobe sun-dried brick (p. 41)

Alamo old Spanish mission in Texas where Mexican forces under Santa Anna besieged American rebels, who were fighting to make Texas independent of Mexico in 1836 (p. 387)

Albany Plan of Union proposal by Benjamin Franklin to create one government for the 13 colonies (p. 143)

Alien and Sedition acts in 1798, Federalist-supported laws that permitted the President to expel foreigners, made it harder for immigrants to become citizens, and allowed for citizens to be fined or jailed if they criticized the government or its officials (p. 293)

alliance agreement between nations to aid and protect one another (p. 85)

ally nation that works with another nation for a common purpose (p. 183)

altitude height above sea level (p. 15)

amend change (p. 218)

American Colonization Society organization in the early 1800s that proposed to end slavery by helping African Americans move to Africa (p. 440)

American Federation of Labor organization of trade unions (p. 545)

American System program for economic growth promoted by Henry Clay in the early 1800s; called for high tariffs on imports and federal funds to improve transportation (p. 345)

amnesty government pardon (p. 517)

annex to add on (p. 389)

anthropology the study of how people and cultures develop (p. 30)

Antifederalists people who opposed

the Constitution and a strong national government (p. 215)

appeal to ask that a decision be reviewed by a higher court (p. 256)

Appomattox Court House Virginia town that was the site of the Confederate surrender in 1865 (p. 509)

apprentice person who learns a trade or craft from a master (p. 128)

archaeology the study of evidence left by early peoples in order to find out about their way of life (p. 22)

arsenal place where guns are stored (p. 476)

Articles the main body of the Constitution, divided into seven sections, which establishes the framework for the United States government (p. 249)

Articles of Confederation first American constitution, passed in 1777, which created a loose alliance of 13 independent states (p. 201)

artifact object made by humans (p. 22)

artisan skilled worker (p. 413)

astrolabe navigational instrument used to determine latitude while at sea (p. 59)

authenticity the quality or condition of being genuine (p. 21)

B

Bacon's Rebellion a 1676 raid led by Nathaniel Bacon against the governor and Native Americans in Virginia (p. 114)

Bank of the United States bank set up in 1791 to hold government deposits, to issue paper money to pay government bills, and to make loans to farmers and businesses (p. 281)

Battle of Antietam an 1862 Civil War battle in Maryland; in the day-long battle, more than 23,000 soldiers were killed or wounded (p. 493)

Battle of Bull Run first major battle of the Civil War; fought in Virginia in 1861 (p. 491)

Battle of Bunker Hill in 1775, first major battle of the Revolution (p. 170)

Battle of Chancellorsville an 1863 Civil War battle in Virginia; important victory for the Confederacy (p. 493)

Battle of Cowpens a 1781 battle in South Carolina, where Americans won an important victory over the British (p. 192)

Battle of Fredericksburg an 1862 Civil War battle in Virginia; one of the Union's worst defeats (p. 493)

Battle of Gettysburg an 1863 Civil War battle in Pennsylvania that left more

than 50,000 soldiers dead or wounded; the Confederates never invaded the North again (p. 506)

Battle of Lake Erie In the War of 1812, an American victory led by Oliver Perry against the British (p. 322)

Battle of Long Island a 1776 battle in New York in which more than 1,400 Americans were killed, wounded, or captured (p. 181)

Battle of New Orleans At the end of the War of 1812, a battle between British and American forces that ended in an American victory (p. 324)

Battle of San Jacinto an 1836 battle between Texans and Mexicans during the Texas war for independence from Mexico (p. 388)

Battle of Saratoga in 1777, the first major American victory in the Revolution, which ended the British threat to New England (p. 183)

Battle of Shiloh an 1862 Civil War battle in Tennessee that ended in a Union victory; one of the bloodiest encounters of the Civil War (p. 494)

Battle of Tippecanoe In 1811, battle over white settlement in the Indiana Territory (p. 318)

Battle of Trenton a 1776 battle in New Jersey in which George Washington's troops captured a Hessian encampment in a surprise attack (p. 182)

Battle of Yorktown final battle in the Revolution; this 1781 American victory in Virginia forced the British to surrender (p. 193)

battles of Lexington and Concord in 1775, conflicts between Massachusetts colonists and British soldiers that started the Revolutionary War (p. 160)

Bear Flag Republic nickname for California after it declared independence from Mexico in 1846 (p. 396)

Bessemer process method developed in the 1850s for making stronger steel at a lower cost (p. 544)

bias a leaning toward or against a certain person, group, or idea (p. 22)

bill proposed law (p. 253)

bill of rights written list of freedoms that a government promises to protect (pp. 123, 200)

Bill of Rights first 10 amendments to the United States Constitution (p. 218)

black codes laws passed by southern states that severely limited the rights of African Americans after the Civil War (p. 521)

blockade the shutting of a port to keep people or supplies from moving in or out (p. 171)

bond certificate that promises to repay money loaned, plus interest, on a certain date (p. 280)

Border Ruffians proslavery bands from Missouri who often rode across the border into Kansas to battle the antislavery forces there (p. 470)

border state slave state that remained in the Union during the Civil War (p. 487)

Boston Massacre a 1770 conflict between colonists and British troops in which five colonists were killed (p. 152)

Boston Tea Party a 1773 protest in which colonists dressed as Indians dumped British tea into Boston harbor (p. 157)

boycott refusal to buy certain goods and services (p. 150)

Brown v. Board of Education 1954 Supreme Court case that brought about the end of legal segregation in public schools (p. 560)

burgess representative to the colonial Virginia government (p. 90)

C

Cabinet group of officials who head government departments and advise the President (p. 279)

capital money raised for a business venture (pp. 331, 544)

capitalist person who invests in a business in order to make a profit (p. 331)

caravan group of people who travel together for safety (p. 52)

carpetbagger uncomplimentary nickname for a northerner who went to the South after the Civil War (p. 527)

cartographer person who makes maps (p. 8)

cash crop crop sold for money at market (p. 111)

cash economy economy in which people exchange money for goods and services (p. 27)

caucus private meeting; often a political meeting (p. 364)

causeway raised road made of packed earth (p. 38)

cavalry troops on horseback (p. 184)

cede to give up (pp. 202, 396)

Chapultepec fort outside of Mexico City that was the site of an 1847 battle between the United States and Mexico during the Mexican War (p. 396)

charter legal document giving certain rights to a person or company (p. 88)

checks and balances a principle of the United States Constitution that

Glossary

safeguards against abuse of power by giving each branch of government the power to check the other branches (p. 251)

chronology sequence of events over time (p. 25)

circumnavigate travel all the way around the Earth (p. 71)

citizen person who owes loyalty to a particular nation and is entitled to all its rights and protections (p. 265)

city-state large town that has its own government and controls the surrounding countryside (p. 52)

civic virtue the willingness to work for the good of the nation or community even at great sacrifice (p. 266)

civics the study of the rights and responsibilities of citizens (p. 29)

civil relating to lawsuits involving the private rights of individuals, as opposed to criminal lawsuits (p. 261)

civil disobedience idea that people have a right to disobey laws they consider to be unjust if their consciences demand it (p. 451)

civil rights movement the efforts of African Americans to win equal rights (p. 560)

civil service system of government employment that awards federal jobs on the basis of examination scores, not political influence (p. 548)

civil war war between people of the same country (p. 465)

Civil War amendments the Thirteenth, Fourteenth, and Fifteenth amendments to the United States Constitution, which abolished slavery, guaranteed citizenship to former slaves, and gave African American men the right to vote (p. 261)

civilian nonmilitary (p. 249)

clan group of two or more related families (p. 48)

Clermont steamboat built in 1807 by Robert Fulton; first steamboat to be commercially successful in American waters (p. 339)

climate average weather of a place over a period of 20 to 30 years (p. 15)

clipper ship fast-sailing ship of the mid-1800s (p. 410)

Cold War long period of intense rivalry after World War II between the Soviet Union and the United States (p. 558)

colony group of people who settle in a distant land but are still ruled by the government of their native land (p. 70)

Columbian Exchange the global exchange of goods and ideas resulting from the encounter between the peoples of the Eastern and the Western hemispheres (p. 71)

committee of correspondence letter-writing campaign that became a major tool of protest in the colonies (p. 153)

Common Sense published in 1776, an essay by Thomas Paine that urged the colonies to declare independence (p. 173)

compromise settlement in which each side gives up some of its demands in order to reach an agreement (p. 208)

Compromise of 1850 agreement over slavery by which California joined the Union as a free state and a strict fugitive slave law was passed (p. 465)

confederation league of independent states or nations (p. 317)

conquistador name for the Spanish explorers who claimed lands in the Americas for Spain (p. 74)

Conservatives during Reconstruction, white southerners who resisted change (p. 527)

constitution document that sets out the laws, principles, organization, and processes of a government (p. 200)

Constitutional Convention gathering of state representatives on May 25, 1787, to revise the Articles of Confederation (p. 206)

constitutional initiative process by which citizens can petition for amendments to their state constitution (p. 263)

consumer user of goods and services (p. 27)

Continental Army army established by the Second Continental Congress to fight the British (p. 169)

continental divide mountain ridge that separates river systems flowing toward opposite sides of a continent (p. 309)

Copperhead northerner who opposed using force to keep the southern states in the Union (p. 501)

corduroy road road made of logs (p. 339)

corporation business owned by investors (p. 544)

"cottonocracy" name for the wealthy planters who made their money from cotton in the mid-1800s (p. 422)

coureur de bois French colonists who lived and worked in the woods as fur trappers (p. 83)

creole person born in Spain's American colonies to Spanish parents (pp. 78, 348)

Crusades between 1095 and 1300, series of wars fought by Christians to control the Holy Land (p. 58)

Cuban missile crisis major Cold War confrontation between the United States and the Soviet Union in 1962 when the United States blocked a Soviet attempt to install missiles in Cuba (p. 560)

culture entire way of life developed by a people (pp. 22, 40)

culture area region in which people share a similar way of life (p. 42)

currency money (p. 202)

D

D-Day the invasion of western Europe on June 6, 1944, when American, British, and other allied troops landed on the coast of Normandy, France, and pressed eastward toward Germany (p. 557)

dame school private school run by a woman, usually in her own home (p. 128)

debtor person who cannot pay money he or she owes (pp. 116, 436)

Declaration of Independence a 1776 document stating that the 13 English colonies were a free and independent nation (p. 175)

deficit spending government practice of spending more money than it takes in from taxes (p. 555)

democratic ensuring that all people have the same rights (p. 302)

Democratic Republican supporter of Thomas Jefferson, who favored a decentralized government (p. 289)

Democrats supporters of Andrew Jackson; included frontier farmers and factory workers (p. 364)

depression period when business activity slows, prices and wages fall, and unemployment rises (pp. 204, 373)

détente President Nixon's policy, continued under Presidents Ford and Carter, to reduce tensions between the superpowers (p. 564)

dictator ruler with absolute power and authority (p. 386)

dictatorship government in which one person or a small group holds complete authority (p. 212)

direct democracy form of government in which ordinary citizens have the power to govern (p. 57)

discrimination policy or attitude that denies equal rights to certain groups of people (p. 417)

domestic tranquillity peace and order at home; one of the six goals defined in the Preamble to the United States Constitution (p. 249)

draft law requiring certain people to serve in the military (p. 502)

Dred Scott v. Sandford an 1857 Supreme Court case in which a slave,

Dred Scott, sued for his freedom and lost; case brought into question the federal power over slavery in the territories (p. 471)

E

economics the study of how people manage limited resources to satisfy their wants and needs (p. 26)

electoral college group of electors from every state who meet every four years to vote for the President and Vice President of the United States (p. 255)

elevation height above sea level (p. 13)

emancipate to set free (p. 497)

Emancipation Proclamation President Lincoln's 1863 declaration freeing slaves in the Confederacy (p. 497)

embargo ban on trade (p. 314)

Embargo Act an 1807 law that imposed a total ban on foreign trade (p. 314)

encomienda land grant given by the Spanish government to Spanish settlers that included the right to demand labor or taxes from Native Americans (p. 78)

English Bill of Rights a 1689 document that guaranteed the rights of English citizens (pp. 123, 213)

Enlightenment movement in Europe in the 1600s and 1700s that emphasized the use of reason (p. 129)

environmentalist person who works to reduce pollution and protect the environment (p. 566)

Era of Good Feelings the eight years of James Monroe's presidency, from 1817 to 1825, when the Democratic Republicans dominated the nation's politics (p. 343)

Erie Canal artificial waterway opened in 1825 linking Lake Erie to the Hudson River (p. 340)

erosion gradual wearing away (p. 13)

established church chosen religion of a state (p. 94)

execute carry out (p. 201)

executive branch branch of government that carries out laws (p. 208)

expedition long voyage of exploration (p. 308)

export trade product sent to markets outside a country (p. 120)

extended family family group that includes grandparents, parents, children, aunts, uncles, and cousins (pp. 53, 425)

F

faction opposing group within a party (p. 287)

factory system method of producing goods that brought workers and machinery together in one place (p. 331)

famine severe food shortage (p. 415)

Farewell Address final official speech of Presidents as they leave office (p. 286)

federalism a principle of the United States Constitution that establishes the division of power between the federal government and the states (p. 251)

Federalist supporter of the Constitution, who favored a strong federal, or national, government (pp. 215, 289)

The Federalist Papers series of essays by Federalists James Madison, Alexander Hamilton, and John Jay in support of ratifying the Constitution (p. 216)

feudalism system of rule by lords who ruled their own lands but owed loyalty and military service to a monarch (p. 58)

Fifteenth Amendment an 1869 amendment to the United States Constitution that forbids any state to deny African Americans the right to vote because of race (p. 524)

54th Massachusetts Regiment African American unit in the Union Army (p. 499)

First Amendment amendment to the United States Constitution that safeguards basic individual liberties including freedom of religion, speech, and the press (p. 260)

First Continental Congress in 1774, meeting in Philadelphia of delegates from 12 colonies (p. 158)

first global age era at the beginning of the 1400s, when long-distance trade and travel increased dramatically, linking far-off parts of the world (p. 50)

flatboat boat with a flat bottom used for transporting heavy loads on inland waterways (p. 337)

foreign policy actions that a nation takes in relation to other nations (p. 285)

Fort Wagner fort in South Carolina that was the site of an attack by the African American 54th Massachusetts Regiment in 1863 (p. 499)

forty-niner one of the more than 80,000 people who joined the gold rush to California in 1849 (p. 400)

Founding Fathers James Madison, Thomas Jefferson, and other leaders who laid the groundwork for the United States (p. 211)

Fourteenth Amendment an 1868 amendment to the United States Constitution that gives citizenship to all persons born in the United States and guarantees equal protection of the laws (p. 522)

free enterprise system in which the government plays a limited role in the economy (p. 28)

free market economy economic system in which individuals, rather than the government, decide what and how much to produce and sell (pp. 303, 564)

Free-Soil party bipartisan, antislavery party founded in the United States in 1848 to keep slavery out of the western territories (p. 462)

freedmen men and women who had been slaves (p. 517)

Freedmen's Bureau United States government agency founded during Reconstruction to help former slaves (p. 517)

French and Indian War a war that took place from 1754 to 1763 between England and France, both aided by Native American allies, that led to the end of French power in North America (p. 142)

French Revolution a 1789 rebellion in France that ended the French monarchy for a time (p. 284)

frigate fast-sailing ship with many guns (p. 292)

fugitive runaway (p. 464)

Fugitive Slave Act law passed in 1850 that required all citizens to aid in the capture of runaway slaves (p. 465)

Fundamental Orders of Connecticut a 1639 plan of government in the Puritan colony in Connecticut; expanded the idea of representative government in the English colonies (p. 104)

G

Gadsden Purchase strip of land in present-day Arizona and New Mexico for which the United States paid Mexico $10 million in 1853 (p. 397)

General Court elected representative assembly in the Massachusetts Bay Colony (p. 103)

general welfare well-being of all the citizens of a nation; one of the six goals defined in the Preamble to the United States Constitution (p. 249)

gentry highest social class in the 13 English colonies (p. 126)

geography the study of people, their environments, and their resources (p. 4)

Gettysburg Address speech made by President Lincoln in 1863 after the Battle of Gettysburg (p. 507)

Glossary

Gibbons v. Ogden an 1824 case in which the Supreme Court upheld the power of the federal government to regulate interstate commerce (p. 346)

glacier thick sheet of ice (p. 36)

Glorious Revolution in 1688, movement that brought William and Mary to the throne of England and strengthened the rights of English citizens (p. 123)

grandfather clause law that excused a voter from a literacy test if his father or grandfather had been eligible to vote on January 1, 1867; protected the voting rights of southern whites, but not those of southern blacks (p. 532)

Great Awakening religious movement in the English colonies in the early 1700s (p. 127)

Great Compromise plan at the Constitutional Convention that settled the differences between large and small states (p. 208)

Great Depression worst period of economic decline in United States history, beginning in 1929 and lasting until the start of World War II (p. 554)

Green Mountain Boys Vermont colonial militia led by Ethan Allen, which made a surprise attack on Fort Ticonderoga, giving Americans control of the key route into Canada (p. 169)

guerrilla soldier who uses hit-and-run tactics (p. 192)

guerrilla warfare the use of hit-and-run military tactics (p. 470)

Gullah combination of English and West African languages spoken by African Americans in the South Carolina colony (p. 126)

H

habeas corpus the right that no person can be held in prison without first being charged with a specific crime (pp. 213, 502)

Hartford Convention gathering of New England delegates during the War of 1812 to protest the war by threatening to secede from the Union (p. 325)

Holocaust murder of millions of Jews and others by the government of Nazi Germany and its allies during World War II (p. 556)

Homestead Act an 1862 law that gave land to settlers to be developed as farms (p. 543)

House of Burgesses representative assembly in colonial Virginia (p. 90)

House of Representatives the larger of the two bodies that make up the legislative branch of the United States government; representation is based on population (p. 252)

Hudson River School group of American artists who painted landscapes of New York's Hudson River Valley in the mid-1800s (p. 448)

I

immigrant person who enters another country in order to settle there (p. 266)

impeach to bring charges of serious wrongdoing against a public official (pp. 257, 523)

imperialism policy of powerful countries seeking to control the political and economic affairs of weaker countries or regions (p. 549)

import trade product brought into a country (p. 120)

impressment practice of forcing people into military service (p. 313)

inauguration ceremony in which the President officially takes the oath of office (p. 278)

income tax a tax on people's earnings (p. 502)

incriminate to give evidence against (p. 260)

indentured servant person who agreed to work without wages for a period of time in exchange for passage to the colonies (p. 126)

Indian Removal Act law passed in 1830 that forced many Native Americans to move west of the Mississippi River (p. 372)

indigo plant used to make a valuable blue dye (p. 115)

individualism concept that stresses the importance of each individual (p. 451)

Industrial Revolution gradual process by which machines replaced hand tools, and steam and other new sources of power replaced human and animal power (p. 330)

inflation a rise in prices and a decrease in the value of money (p. 503)

infrastructure system of roads, bridges, and tunnels (p. 263)

interchangeable parts identical, machine-made parts for a tool or instrument (p. 332)

internal improvements improvements to roads, bridges, and canals (p. 346)

interstate commerce trade between different states (p. 346)

intervention direct involvement (p. 351)

Intolerable Acts series of laws passed in 1774 to punish Boston for the Tea Party (p. 157)

irrigation bringing water to dry lands (p. 6)

Islam monotheistic religion founded by the prophet Muhammad in the early A.D. 600s (p. 50)

isolationism policy of limiting involvement in the political affairs of foreign nations (p. 549)

isthmus narrow strip of land (p. 11)

J

Jay's Treaty a 1795 agreement between Britain and the United States that called for Britain to pay damages for seized American ships and to give up forts it still held in the West. In exchange, the United States would repay debts owed to British merchants (p. 286)

jazz original American music style that blends West African rhythms, European harmonies, and African American work songs and spirituals (p. 554)

Jim Crow laws laws that separated people of different races in public places in the South (p. 532)

judicial branch branch of government that decides if laws are carried out fairly (p. 208)

judicial review power of the Supreme Court to decide whether acts of a President or laws passed by Congress are constitutional (p. 305)

Judiciary Act a 1789 law that created the structure of the Supreme Court and set up a system of district courts and circuit courts for the nation (p. 279)

jury duty the responsibility of every citizen to serve on a jury when called (p. 268)

K

kachina masked dancer at religious ceremonies of the Southwest Indians (p. 47)

Kansas-Nebraska Act an 1854 law that established the territories of Nebraska and Kansas, giving the settlers the right of popular sovereignty to decide on the issue of slavery (p. 468)

Kentucky and Virginia resolutions declarations passed in 1798 and 1799 that claimed that each state has the right to decide whether a federal law is constitutional and to nullify laws deemed unconstitutional within a state's borders (p. 293)

kinship sharing a common ancestor (p. 53)

"kitchen cabinet" group of unofficial advisers to Andrew Jackson who met

Glossary

with him in the White House kitchen (p. 367)

Know-Nothing party political party of the 1850s that was anti-Catholic and anti-immigrant (p. 416)

Korean War conflict that lasted from 1950 to 1953 between North Korea, aided by China, and South Korea, aided by United Nations forces consisting primarily of United States troops (p. 559)

Ku Klux Klan secret society organized in the South after the Civil War to reassert white supremacy by means of violence (p. 527)

L

laissez faire idea that government should play as small a role as possible in economic affairs (p. 303)

Lancaster Turnpike road built in the 1790s by a private company, linking Philadelphia and Lancaster, Pennsylvania (p. 339)

Land Ordinance of 1785 law setting up a system for settling the Northwest Territory (p. 203)

latitude distance north or south from the equator (p. 4)

lawsuit legal case brought to settle a dispute between a person or group (p. 471)

League of the Iroquois alliance of the five Iroquois nations (p. 48)

legislative branch branch of government that passes laws (p. 208)

legislature group of people who have the power to make laws (p. 122)

libel act of publishing a statement that may unjustly damage a person's reputation (p. 130)

The Liberator most influential antislavery newspaper; begun by William Lloyd Garrison in 1831 (p. 440)

liberty freedom (p. 249)

limited government a principle of the United States Constitution that states that government has only the powers that the Constitution gives it (p. 250)

literacy test examination to see if a person can read and write; used in the past to restrict voting rights (p. 532)

local government government on the county, parish, city, town, village, or district level (p. 263)

locomotive engine that pulls a railroad train (p. 409)

Lone Star Republic nickname for Texas after it won independence from Mexico in 1836 (p. 389)

longitude distance east or west from the Prime Meridian (p. 4)

Louisiana Purchase vast territory between the Mississippi River and Rocky Mountains, purchased from France in 1803 (p. 308)

Lowell girl young woman who worked in the Lowell Mills in Massachusetts during the Industrial Revolution (p. 333)

Loyalist colonist who remained loyal to Britain (p. 170)

lynch to hang without a legal trial (p. 401)

M

Magna Carta signed in 1215, a British document that contains two basic ideas: Monarchs themselves have to obey the laws, and citizens have basic rights (pp. 90, 213)

majority more than half (p. 362)

Manifest Destiny belief held in the 1800s that Americans had the right and the duty to spread across the continent all the way to the Pacific Ocean (p. 393)

manor district ruled by a lord, including the lord's castle and the lands around it (p. 58)

map projection way of drawing Earth on a flat surface (p. 8)

Marbury v. Madison an 1803 court case in which the Supreme Court ruled that it had the power to decide whether laws passed by Congress were constitutional and to reject laws that it considered unconstitutional (p. 305)

margin buying practice by which investors buy stock for a small downpayment and borrow the rest from their brokers, hoping to sell for a profit when the price of the stock rises (p. 554)

Marshall Plan American plan to help European nations rebuild their economies after World War II (p. 559)

martial law rule by the army instead of the elected government (p. 487)

martyr person who dies for his or her beliefs (p. 476)

Mason-Dixon Line boundary between Pennsylvania and Maryland that divided the Middle Colonies from the Southern Colonies (p. 113)

Mayflower Compact a 1620 agreement for ruling the Plymouth Colony, signed by Pilgrims before they landed at Plymouth (p. 95)

McCulloch v. Maryland an 1819 case in which the Supreme Court ruled that states had no right to interfere with federal institutions within their borders (p. 346)

mercantilism theory that a nation's economic strength came from protecting and increasing its home economy by

keeping strict control over its colonial trade (p. 120)

mercenary soldier who fights merely for pay, often for a foreign country (p. 171)

mestizo in Spain's American colonies, person of mixed Spanish and Indian background (p. 78)

Mexican Cession Mexican territory of California and New Mexico given to the United States in 1848 (p. 396)

middle class in the 13 English colonies, a class that included skilled craftsworkers, farmers, and some tradespeople (p. 126)

militia army of citizens who serve as soldiers during an emergency (p. 158)

minuteman colonial militia volunteer who was prepared to fight at a minute's notice (p. 159)

mission religious settlement run by Catholic priests and friars (p. 78)

missionary person who tries to spread certain religious beliefs among a group of people (pp. 56, 84)

Missouri Compromise agreement, proposed in 1819 by Henry Clay, to keep the number of slave and free states equal (p. 460)

Monitor ironclad Union warship (p. 492)

monopoly a single company that controls or dominates an entire industry (p. 544)

Monroe Doctrine President Monroe's foreign policy statement warning European nations not to interfere in Latin America (p. 351)

Mormons members of the Church of Jesus Christ of Latter-Day Saints founded by Joseph Smith in 1830 (p. 398)

Mound Builders the name for various North American cultures that built large earth mounds beginning about 3,000 years ago (p. 41)

mountain man trapper who explored and hunted in Oregon in the early 1800s (p. 381)

muckraker journalist who exposed corruption and other problems of the late 1800s and early 1900s in the United States (p. 547)

mudslinging the use of insults to attack an opponent's reputation (p. 374)

N

national debt total amount of money that a government owes to others (p. 280)

National Road first federally funded national road project, begun in 1811 (p. 339)

Glossary

nationalism devotion to one's country (p. 318)

nativist person who wanted to limit immigration and preserve the United States for native-born, white citizens (p. 416)

natural resources materials that humans can take from the environment to survive and satisfy their needs (p. 5)

natural rights rights that belong to all people from birth (p. 175)

naturalize to complete the official process for becoming a citizen (p. 265)

Nauvoo Mormon community built on the banks of the Mississippi River in Illinois in the 1840s (p. 398)

Navigation Acts series of laws passed by the English Parliament in the 1650s that regulated trade between England and its colonies (p. 121)

Negro Fort settlement of escaped African American slaves in the Spanish colony of Florida (p. 350)

neutral not taking sides in a conflict (p. 285)

Neutrality Proclamation a 1793 statement by President Washington that the United States would not support or aid either France or Britain in their European conflict (p. 285)

New Deal program of President Franklin D. Roosevelt to end the Great Depression (p. 554)

New Jersey Plan plan at the Constitutional Convention, favored by smaller states, that called for three branches of government with a single-chamber legislature (p. 208)

New Mexico Territory huge region in the Southwest owned by Mexico in the 1800s (p. 391)

"New South" term to describe the South in the late 1800s when efforts were made to expand the economy by building up industry (p. 533)

Nineteenth Amendment a 1920 amendment to the United States Constitution that guarantees women's right to vote (pp. 261, 548)

nominating convention meeting at which a political party chooses a candidate (p. 364)

Nonintercourse Act an 1809 law that allowed Americans to carry on trade with all nations except Britain and France (p. 314)

North American Free Trade Agreement (NAFTA) treaty among the United States, Canada, and Mexico to gradually remove tariffs and other trade barriers (p. 566)

Northwest Ordinance a 1787 article that set up a government for the Northwest Territory, guaranteed basic rights to settlers, and outlawed slavery there (p. 203)

northwest passage a natural waterway through or around North America (p. 81)

nullification idea that a state has the right to nullify, or cancel, a federal law that the state leaders consider to be unconstitutional (p. 371)

Nullification Act act passed by South Carolina that declared the 1832 tariff illegal (p. 371)

nullify to cancel (p. 293)

O

Olive Branch Petition peace petition sent to King George by colonial delegates after the battles of Lexington and Concord, declaring their loyalty to the king and asking him to repeal the Intolerable Acts (p. 168)

Oregon Country term used in the early 1800s for the region west of the Rocky Mountains, including present-day Oregon, Washington, Idaho, and parts of Wyoming, Montana, and Canada (p. 380)

Oregon Trail route to Oregon used by wagon trains in the 1800s (p. 383)

override to overrule, as when Congress overrules a presidential veto (p. 257)

P

Parliament representative assembly in England (p. 90)

Patriot colonist who favored war against Britain (p. 169)

patriotism feeling of love and devotion toward one's country (p. 266)

patroon owner of a huge estate in a Dutch colony (p. 109)

peninsulare person from Spain who held a position of power in a Spanish colony (p. 78)

Pennsylvania Dutch German-speaking Protestants who settled in Pennsylvania (p. 110)

persecution mistreatment or punishment of a group of people because of their beliefs (p. 94)

Persian Gulf War war fought in 1991 between Iraq and a coalition of countries led by the United States to free oil-rich Kuwait from occupying Iraqi forces (p. 564)

petition formal written request to someone in authority, signed by a group of people (p. 149)

Pickett's Charge failed Confederate charge at the Battle of Gettysburg (p. 506)

Pilgrims in the 1600s, English settlers who sought religious freedom in the Americas (p. 93)

Pinckney Treaty a 1795 agreement with Spain that let Americans ship their goods down the Mississippi River and store them in New Orleans (p. 306)

pit house house in the Arctic region dug into the ground and covered with wood and skins (p. 43)

Plains of Abraham a field near Quebec; site of a major British victory over the French in the French and Indian War (p. 144)

plantation large estate farmed by many workers (p. 80)

Plessy v. Ferguson an 1896 court case in which the Supreme Court ruled that segregation in public facilities was legal as long as the facilities were equal (p. 532)

political science the study of government (p. 29)

poll tax tax required before a person can vote (p. 532)

Pontiac's War a 1763 conflict between Native Americans and the British over settlement of Indian lands in the Great Lakes area (p. 147)

popular sovereignty a principle of the United States Constitution that states that the people have the right to create, alter, and abolish their government; in the mid-1800s, a term referring to the idea that each territory could decide for itself whether or not to allow slavery (pp. 250, 462)

potlatch ceremonial dinner held by some Native Americans of the Northwest Coast to show off their wealth (p. 44)

preamble introduction to a declaration, constitution, or other official document (pp. 175, 248)

precedent an act or decision that sets the example for others to follow (pp. 96, 278)

precipitation water that falls in the form of rain, sleet, hail, or snow (p. 15)

predestination Protestant idea that God decided in advance which people would attain salvation after death (p. 435)

presidio fort where soldiers lived in the Spanish colonies (p. 77)

primary source firsthand information about people or events (p. 20)

Proclamation of 1763 law forbidding English colonists to settle west of the Appalachian Mountains (p. 147)

profiteer person who takes advantage of a crisis to make money (p. 503)

Progressives reformers who wanted to improve American life in the late

Glossary

1800s and early 1900s (p. 547)

proprietary colony English colony in which the king gave land to proprietors in exchange for a yearly payment (p. 109)

Protestant Reformation movement to reform the Roman Catholic Church in the 1500s; led to the creation of many different Christian churches (p. 83)

psychology the study of how people think and behave (p. 30)

public school school supported by taxes (p. 128)

pueblo a town in the Spanish colonies; Anasazi village (pp. 41, 77)

Puritans group of English Protestants who settled the Massachusetts Bay Colony (p. 102)

Q

Quakers Protestant reformers who believe in the equality of all people (p. 110)

Quebec Act law that set up a government for Canada and protected the rights of French Catholics (p. 158)

quipu device made of cord or string with knots that stood for quantities; used by the Incas to keep accounts and records (p. 40)

Quran sacred book of Islam (p. 51)

R

racism belief that one race is superior to another (p. 119)

radical person who wants to make drastic changes in society (p. 173)

Radical Reconstruction period beginning in 1867 when the Republicans, who had control in both houses of Congress, took charge of Reconstruction (p. 523)

Radical Republican member of Congress during Reconstruction who wanted to break the power of wealthy planters in the South and ensure that freedmen received the right to vote (p. 522)

ratify to approve (p. 194)

Reaganomics President Reagan's economic policy that cut taxes, slowed down spending on social programs, and eliminated many regulations on business (p. 563)

Reconstruction rebuilding of the South after the Civil War (p. 517)

Reconstruction Act an 1867 law that threw out the southern state governments that had refused to ratify the Fourteenth Amendment and required that former Confederate states allow African Americans to vote (p. 523)

refuge a place where one is safe from persecution (p. 399)

religious tolerance willingness to let others practice their own beliefs (p. 104)

Renaissance French word meaning rebirth; burst of learning in Europe from the late 1300s to about 1600 (p. 59)

rendezvous French word meaning "get-together"; yearly meeting where mountain men traded furs (p. 382)

repeal cancel (p. 150)

representative government political system in which voters elect representatives to make laws for them (p. 90)

republic system of government in which citizens choose representatives to govern them (pp. 57, 211)

Republic of Great Colombia independent state composed of the present-day nations of Venezuela, Colombia, Ecuador, and Panama; established in 1819 after the territory declared independence from Spain (p. 349)

Republican party political party established in the United States in 1854 with the goal of keeping slavery out of the western territories (p. 473)

resident alien noncitizen living in the country (p. 266)

revival huge outdoor religious meeting (p. 435)

Roosevelt Corollary policy established by President Theodore Roosevelt that extended the Monroe Doctrine by stating that the United States had the right to intervene in Latin American affairs (p. 550)

royal colony colony under the direct control of the English crown (p. 109)

rugged individualist person who follows his or her own independent course in life (p. 381)

S

Sabbath holy day of rest (p. 106)

sachem member of the tribal chief council in the League of the Iroquois (p. 48)

salvation everlasting life (p. 56)

Santa Fe Trail route to Santa Fe, New Mexico, that was used by traders in the 1800s (p. 392)

savanna region of grasslands (p. 52)

scalawag white southerner who supported the Republicans during Reconstruction (p. 526)

secede to withdraw from membership in a group (p. 463)

Second Amendment amendment to the United States Constitution related to the right to bear arms (p. 260)

Second Great Awakening widespread religious movement in the United States in the early 1800s (p. 435)

secondary source account provided after the fact by people who did not directly witness or participate in the event (p. 21)

sectionalism loyalty to a state or section rather than to the whole country (p. 345)

sedition stirring up rebellion against a government (p. 293)

segregation legal separation of races (p. 532)

self-sufficient able to produce enough for one's own needs (p. 392)

Seminole War conflict that began in Florida in 1817 between the Seminole Indians and the United States Army when the Seminoles resisted removal (p. 373)

Senate the smaller of the two bodies that make up the legislative branch of the United States government; based on equal representation, with two senators for each state (p. 253)

Seneca Falls Convention an 1848 meeting at which leaders of the women's rights movement called for equal rights for women (p. 445)

separation of powers principle by which the powers of government are divided among separate branches (p. 214)

sharecropper person who rents a plot of land from another person and farms it in exchange for a share of the crop (p. 529)

Shays' Rebellion a 1786 revolt in Massachusetts led by farmers in reaction to high taxes (p. 204)

siege military blockade or bombardment of an enemy town or position in order to force it to surrender (pp. 193, 387, 506)

Silk Road overland trade routes linking China to the Middle East (p. 52)

slave code laws that controlled the lives of enslaved African Americans and denied them basic rights (pp. 119)

smuggling importing or exporting goods in violation of trade laws

social reform an organized to improve what is unjust in society (p. 434)

social sciences studies human society and so (p. 29)

Social Security fe begun in the 1930 the elderly and gram was late

sociology behave in

Spanish-American War an 1898 war between the United States and Spain over American expansion; enabled the United States to gain control of Cuba, Puerto Rico, Guam, and the Philippines (p. 550)

speculator someone who invests in a risky venture in the hope of making a large profit (p. 280)

spinning jenny machine developed in 1764 that could spin several threads at once (p. 331)

spoils system practice of rewarding supporters with government jobs (p. 366)

Stamp Act a 1765 law that placed new duties on legal documents and taxed newspapers, almanacs, playing cards, and dice (p. 149)

states' rights the right of states to limit the power of the federal government (pp. 293, 370)

strike refusal by workers to do their jobs until their demands are met (p. 414)

suffrage the right to vote (p. 361)

Supreme Court highest court in the United States established by the Constitution (p. 256)

surplus extra (p. 37)

Sutter's Mill location where gold was discovered in California in 1848, setting off the gold rush (p. 400)

Swahili language that blends Arab words and local African languages spoken widely in East Africa (p. 52)

T

tariff tax on foreign goods brought into a country (p. 281)

Tariff of Abominations tariff passed by Congress in 1828 that favored manufacturing in the North but hurt the farmers in the South (p. 370)

Tea Act a 1773 law that let the British [Ea]st India Company bypass tea mer-[cha]nts and sell directly to colonists [(p. 1]56)

[Tejano] person of Mexican descent [...] [Te]xas (p. 386)

[telegraph] communications device that [sends electri]cal signals along a wire

[temperance m]ovement campaign [against alcohol co]nsumption (p. 436)

[Ten Percent Plan] President Lincoln's [plan for Reconstruct]ion that allowed a [state to form a new govern-]ment [when 10 percent o]f its voters swore [loyalty to th]e United States

[...] [cut into a]

terrorism deliberate use of random violence, especially against civilians, to achieve political goals (p. 564)

Thanksgiving day at the end of the harvest season set aside by the Pilgrims to give thanks to God (p. 97)

thematic map map that deals with a specific topic, such as population, natural resources, or elections (p. 9)

Thirteenth Amendment an 1865 amendment to the United States Constitution that bans slavery throughout the nation (p. 519)

Three-Fifths Compromise agreement at the Constitutional Convention that three fifths of the slaves in any state be counted in its population (p. 209)

total war all-out war that affects civilians at home as well as soldiers in combat (p. 508)

totalitarian state country where a single party controls the government and every aspect of people's lives (p. 556)

town meeting meeting in colonial New England where colonists discussed and voted on issues (p. 107)

Townshend Acts laws passed in 1767 that taxed goods such as glass, paper, paint, lead, and tea (p. 150)

trade union association of trade workers formed to gain higher wages and better working conditions (p. 414)

Trail of Tears forced journey of the Cherokee Indians from Georgia to a region west of the Mississippi during which thousands of Cherokees died (p. 372)

traitor person who betrays his or her country (p. 175)

transcendentalist member of the small, influential group of New England writers and thinkers who believed that the most important truths in life transcended, or went beyond, human reason (p. 450)

transcontinental railroad railroad that stretches across a continent (p. 543)

treason actions against one's country (p. 476)

Treaty of Ghent peace treaty signed by Britain and the United States at the end of the War of 1812 (p. 325)

Treaty of Greenville treaty signed by some Native Americans in 1795, giving up land that would later become part of Ohio in exchange for $20,000 and a promise of more money if they kept the peace (p. 317)

Treaty of Guadalupe-Hidalgo an 1848 treaty in which Mexico gave up California and New Mexico to the United States for $15 million (p. 396)

Treaty of Paris a 1763 agreement between Britain and France that ended the French and Indian War, and marked the end of French power in North America (p. 145); peace treaty between the United States and Britain, ratified in 1783, that recognized the United States as an independent nation (p. 194)

triangular trade colonial trade route between New England, the West Indies, and Africa (p. 121)

tribe community of people that share common customs, language, and rituals (p. 42)

tributary stream or smaller river that flows into a larger one (p. 15)

tribute bribe (p. 313)

turning point moment in history that marks a decisive change (p. 70)

turnpike road built by a private company that charges a toll to use it (p. 339)

tutor private teacher (p. 128)

Twenty-sixth Amendment amendment to the United States Constitution that lowered the minimum voting age from 21 to 18 (p. 261)

U

Uncle Tom's Cabin an 1852 novel by Harriet Beecher Stowe written to show the evils of slavery and the injustice of the Fugitive Slave Act (p. 466)

unconstitutional not allowed under the Constitution (pp. 257, 288)

Underground Railroad network of black and white abolitionists who secretly helped slaves escape to freedom in the North or Canada (p. 441)

United Provinces of Central America federation of the present-day nations of Guatemala, El Salvador, Honduras, Nicaragua, and Costa Rica; established in 1823 after these states declared independence from Spain (p. 349)

urbanization process of a population's shifting from farms to cities (pp. 335, 546)

V

Valley Forge Pennsylvania site of Washington's Continental Army encampment during the winter of 1777–1778 (p. 185)

vaquero Indian or Mexican cowhand (p. 392)

veto reject, as when the President rejects a law passed by Congress (p. 257)

Vietnam War military conflict between the communist forces of North Vietnam, supported by China and the Soviet Union, and the noncommunist forces of South Vietnam, supported by the United States; American involvement lasted from 1961 to 1973 (p. 561)

vigilante self-appointed enforcer of the law (p. 401)

Virginia ironclad warship used by the Confederates to break the Union blockade (p. 492)

Virginia Plan plan at the Constitutional Convention, favored by larger states, that called for a strong national government with three branches and a two-chamber legislature (p. 208)

W

Wade-Davis Bill an 1864 plan for Reconstruction that required a majority of white men in each southern state to swear loyalty to the Union and denied the right to vote or hold office to anyone who had volunteered to fight for the Confederacy (p. 517)

War Hawks members of Congress from the South and the West who called for war with Britain prior to the War of 1812 (p. 318)

Watergate affair series of scandals involving the administration of President Richard Nixon, including the burglarizing of the Democratic headquarters in the Watergate office building in Washington, D.C., in 1972; led to Nixon's resignation in 1974 (p. 563)

weather condition of Earth's atmosphere at a given time and place (p. 15)

Whigs members of John Quincy Adams's former National Republican party; included many business people, southern planters, and former Federalists (p. 363)

Whiskey Rebellion a 1794 protest over a tax on all liquor made and sold in the United States (p. 282)

Wilmot Proviso law passed in 1846 that banned slavery in any territories won by the United States from Mexico (p. 461)

women's rights movement organized campaign to win property, education, and other rights for women (p. 446)

World War I war fought from 1914 to 1918, in which Great Britain, France, Russia, Belgium, Italy, Japan, the United States, and other allies defeated Germany, Austria-Hungary, the Ottoman Empire, and Bulgaria (p. 550)

World War II war fought from 1939 to 1945, in which Great Britain, France, the Soviet Union, the United States, China, and other allies defeated Germany, Italy, Japan, and their allies (p. 556)

writ of assistance legal document that allowed British customs officials to inspect a ship's cargo without giving a reason (p. 150)

X

XYZ Affair a 1797 French attempt to bribe the United States by demanding payment before talks could begin on the issue of French seizure of neutral American ships (p. 292)

Y

Yankee nickname for New England merchants who dominated colonial trade (p. 121)

Glossary

Spanish Glossary

A

abolitionist/abolicionista persona que quería acabar completamente la esclavitud en los Estados Unidos (pág. 440)

Act of Toleration/Acta de Tolerancia ley aprobada por la asamblea de Maryland en 1649 que aseguraba la libertad religiosa para todos los cristianos (pág. 114)

Adams-Onís Treaty/Tratado de Adams-Onís tratado de 1821 entre España y los Estados Unidos según el cual España se comprometía a entregar Florida a los Estados Unidos a cambio de 5 millones de dólares (pág. 350)

adobe/adobe ladrillo secado al sol (pág. 41)

Alamo/Álamo vieja misión española situada en Texas donde las fuerzas mexicanas bajo las órdenes de Santa Anna asediaron a los rebeldes estadounidenses que luchaban en 1836 para que Texas se independizara de México (pág. 387)

Albany Plan of Union/Plan de Unión de Albany propuesta de Benjamin Franklin que consistía en crear un solo gobierno para las 13 colonias (pág. 143)

Alien and Sedition acts/Actas de Extranjería y de Sedición leyes apoyadas por los federalistas que permitían que el presidente expulsara a extranjeros, dificultara la obtención de la ciudadanía a los extranjeros, y multara o encarcelara a ciudadanos por criticar al gobierno o a sus funcionarios (pág. 293)

alliance/alianza acuerdo entre naciones para ayudarse y protegerse mutuamente (pág. 85)

ally/aliado (a) nación que trabaja con otra nación hacia una meta común (pág. 183)

altitude/altura elevación sobre el nivel del mar (pág. 15)

amend/reformar cambiar (pág. 218)

American Colonization Society/Sociedad de Colonización Americana organización de principios del 1800 que proponía acabar con la esclavitud ayudando a los afroamericanos a que se mudaran al Africa (pág. 440)

American Federation of Labor/ Federación Americana del Trabajo organización de gremios (pág. 545)

American System/sistema estadounidense programa para fomentar el crecimiento económico, promovido por Henry Clay a principios del siglo XIX; proponía imponer altas tasas a las importaciones y usar fondos federales para mejorar el sistema de transportes (pág. 345)

amnesty/amnistía perdón del gobierno (pág. 517)

annex/anexar agregar (pág. 389)

anthropology/antropología estudio de cómo se desarrollan las personas y las culturas (pág. 30)

Antifederalists/antifederalistas personas que se oponían a la constitución y a un gobierno nacional fuerte (pág. 215)

appeal/apelar pedir a una corte de mayor autoridad que reconsidere una decisión (pág. 256)

Appomattox Court House/Appomattox Court House Ciudad de Virginia en donde la Confederación se rindió (pág. 509)

apprentice/aprendiz persona que aprende un oficio o artesanía de un maestro (pág.128)

archaeology/arqueología estudio de las evidencias dejadas por culturas antiguas con el objeto de conocer su forma de vida (pág. 22)

arsenal/arsenal depósito de armas (pág. 476)

Articles/artículos parte principal de la Constitución, que está dividida en siete secciones y establece la estructura del gobierno de los Estados Unidos (pág. 249)

Articles of Confederation/Artículos de la Confederación primera constitución americana, aprobada en 1777, que creó una alianza vaga entre los 13 estados independientes (pág. 201)

artifact/artefacto objeto hecho por seres humanos (pág. 22)

artisan/artesano trabajador manual calificado (pág. 413)

astrolabe/astrolabio instrumento de navegación que se usa para determinar la latitud en alta mar (pág. 59)

authenticity/autenticidad cualidad o condición de ser genuino (pág. 21)

B

Bacon's Rebellion/rebelión de Bacon revuelta liderada en 1676 por Nathaniel Bacon en contra del gobernador y de los americanos nativos de Virginia (pág. 114)

Bank of the United States/Banco de los Estados Unidos banco establecido en 1791 para retener los depósitos del gobierno, emitir papel moneda para el pago de las cuentas del gobierno y otorgar préstamos a granjeros y gentes de negocios (pág. 281)

Battle of Antietam/batalla de Antietam batalla librada en Maryland en 1862 durante la Guerra Civil; duró un día y murieron o resultaron heridos más de 23,000 soldados (pág. 493)

Battle of Bull Run/batalla de Bull Run primera gran batalla de la Guerra Civil, librada en Virginia en 1861 (pág. 491)

Battle of Bunker Hill/batalla de Bunker Hill batalla de 1775 que fue la primera gran batalla de la Revolución (pág. 170)

Battle of Chancellorsville/batalla de Chancellorsville batalla librada en Virginia en 1863 durante la Guerra Civil; fue una victoria importante para la Confederación (pág. 493)

Battle of Cowpens/batalla de Cowpens batalla de 1781 que tuvo lugar en Carolina del Norte y por la cual los colonos obtuvieron una victoria importante sobre los británicos (pág. 192)

Battle of Fredericksburg/batalla de Fredericksburg batalla librada en Virginia en 1862 durante la Guerra Civil; fue una de las peores derrotas de la Unión (pág. 493)

Battle of Gettysburg/batalla de Gettysburg batalla librada en Pennsylvania en 1863 durante la Guerra Civil que dejó más de 50,000 soldados muertos o heridos. Los Confederados nunca volvieron a invadir el Norte (pág. 506)

Battle of Lake Erie/batalla del lago Erie batalla de la guerra de 1812 contra los británicos, que terminó con la victoria de las fuerzas de los Estados Unidos lideradas por Oliver Perry (pág. 322)

Battle of Long Island/batalla de Long Island batalla de 1776 en Nueva York, en la que más de 1,400 colonos murieron, resultaron heridos o fueron capturados (pág. 181)

Battle of New Orleans/batalla de Nueva Orleáns batalla entre los británicos y los estadounidenses que terminó con la victoria de las fuerzas de los Estados Unidos, al final de la guerra de 1812 (pág. 324)

Battle of San Jacinto/batalla de San Jacinto una batalla de 1836 entre texanos y mexicanos que se produjo durante la guerra que llevó a cabo Texas para independizarse de México (pág. 388)

Battle of Saratoga/batalla de Saratoga primera victoria importante de la Revolución en la batalla de 1777, que acabó con la amenaza de los ingleses en Nueva Inglaterra (pág. 183)

Battle of Shiloh/batalla de Shiloh batalla librada en 1862 en Tennessee, que terminó con la victoria de la Unión; fue uno de los encuentros más sangrientos de la Guerra Civil (pág. 494)

Battle of Tippecanoe/batalla de Tippecanoe batalla de 1811 a propósito de las colonizaciones blancas en el territorio de Indiana (pág. 318)

Battle of Trenton/batalla de Trenton batalla de 1776 que tuvo lugar en Nueva Jersey, en la que las tropas de George Washington en un ataque sorpresa capturaron un campamento de Hessian (pág. 182)

Battle of Yorktown/batalla de Yorktown última batalla de la Revolución en 1781; esta victoria de los colonos en Virginia obligó a los ingleses a rendirse (pág. 193)

battles of Lexington and Concord/batallas de Lexington y Concord conflictos de 1775 entre colonos de Massachusetts y soldados británicos que dieron origen a la Revolución Americana (pág. 160)

Bear Flag Republic/República de la Bandera del Oso sobrenombre de California después de declararse independiente de México en 1846 (pág. 396)

Bessemer process/proceso de Bessemer método desarrollado en la década de 1850 para fabricar acero más resistente a un precio más bajo (pág. 544)

bias/prejuicio inclinación a favor o en contra de cierta persona, grupo o idea (pág. 22)

bill/proyecto de ley ley que se propone para su aprobación (pág. 253)

bill of rights/declaración de derechos lista escrita de las libertades que el gobierno promete proteger (págs. 123, 200)

Bill of Rights/Declaración de Derechos las primeras 10 enmiendas de la Constitución de Estados Unidos (pág. 218)

black codes/códigos de negros leyes aprobadas por los estados del Sur después de la Guerra Civil que limitaban con severidad los derechos de los afroamericanos (pág. 521)

blockade/bloqueo cierre de un puerto para que ni las personas ni las provisiones puedan entrar o salir (pág. 171)

bond/bono certificado que promete el pago de dinero que se ha prestado, más el interés, en una determinada fecha (pág. 280)

Border Ruffians/rufianes de frontera bandas proesclavistas de Missouri

que a menudo cruzaban la frontera con Kansas para combatir contra las fuerzas antiesclavistas de ese estado (pág. 470)

border state/estado de frontera estado esclavista que permaneció en la Unión durante la Guerra Civil (pág. 487)

Boston Massacre/masacre de Boston conflicto de 1770 entre colonos y tropas británicas en el que se dio muerte a cinco colonos (pág. 152)

Boston Tea Party/Fiesta del Té de Boston protesta de 1773 en la que los colonos se vistieron de indios y lanzaron el té de los británicos a la bahía de Boston (pág. 157)

boycott/boicot negarse a comprar ciertos bienes y servicios (pág. 150)

Brown v. Board of Education/Brown versus el Consejo de Educación caso de 1954 que llegó a la Corte Suprema, acabando con la segregación legal en las escuelas públicas (pág. 560)

burgess/burgués representante del gobierno colonial de Virginia (pág. 90)

C

Cabinet/gabinete grupo de funcionarios que dirigen departamentos gubernamentales y aconsejan al presidente (pág. 279)

capital/capital dinero con el que se inicia un negocio (págs. 331, 544)

capitalist/capitalista persona que invierte en un negocio con el fin de obtener beneficios (pág. 331)

caravan/caravana grupo de personas que viajaban juntas por razones de seguridad (pág. 52)

carpetbagger/*carpetbagger* sobrenombre despreciativo dado a los norteños que se mudaron al Sur después de la Guerra Civil (pág. 527)

cartographer/cartógrafo persona que hace mapas (pág. 8)

cash crop/cosecha de contado cosecha vendida por dinero en el mercado (pág. 111)

cash economy/cultivo comercial economía en la cual las personas intercambian dinero por mercancías y servicios (pág. 27)

caucus/reunión encuentro privado, a menudo de carácter político (pág. 364)

causeway/paso elevado camino elevado hecho con tierra comprimida (pág. 38)

cavalry/caballería tropas a caballo (pág. 184)

cede/ceder entregar (págs. 202, 396)

Chapultepec/Chapultepec fuerte en las afueras de Ciudad de México donde ocurrió una batalla entre los Estados Unidos y México durante la Guerra Mexicana en 1847 (pág. 396)

charter/carta legal documento que da ciertos derechos a una persona o compañía (pág. 88)

checks and balances/controlar y equilibrar principio de la Constitución de los Estados Unidos que ofrece protección contra los abusos de poder al dar a cada rama del gobierno la atribución de vigilar las otras (pág. 251)

chronology/cronología secuencia de sucesos o eventos a través del tiempo (pág. 25)

circumnavigate/circunnavegar viajar alrededor de la Tierra (pág. 71)

citizen/ciudadano persona que debe lealtad a una nación particular y se beneficia de la protección y de todos los derechos de dicha nación (pág. 265)

city-state/ciudad estado ciudad grande que tiene su propio gobierno y controla la zona de campo que la rodea (pág. 52)

civic virtue/virtud cívica deseo de trabajar por el bien de una nación o comunidad incluso a costa de grandes sacrificios (pág. 266)

civics/educación cívica estudio de los derechos y responsabilidades de los ciudadanos (pág. 29)

civil/civil se refiere a los juicios sobre derechos privados de los individuos, y no a los juicios criminales (pág. 261)

civil disobedience/desobediencia civil idea de que las personas tienen derecho a desobedecer las leyes que consideren injustas, si su conciencia lo exige (pág. 451)

civil rights movement/movimiento por los derechos civiles esfuerzo organizado de los afroamericanos para obtener derechos igualitarios (pág. 560)

civil service/servicio civil sistema de empleo gubernamental que otorga empleos federales con base en exámenes, en vez de influencia política (pág. 548)

civil war/guerra civil guerra entre personas del mismo país (pág. 465)

Civil War amendments/enmiendas de la Guerra Civil enmiendas número Trece, Catorce y Quince de la Constitución de los Estados Unidos que abolían la esclavitud, garantizaban la ciudadanía a los ex esclavos y daban el derecho al voto a los afroamericanos de sexo masculino (pág. 261)

civilian/civil no militar (pág. 249)

clan/clan grupo de dos o más familias emparentadas (pág. 48)

Clermont/Clermont barco a vapor construido en 1807 por Robert Fulton; fue el primer barco a vapor que obtuvo éxito comercial en aguas de los Estados Unidos (pág. 339)

Spanish Glossary

climate/clima promedio del tiempo de un lugar durante un período de entre 20 y 30 años (pág. 15)

clipper ship/clíper barco de mediados de los años 1800 que navegaba velozmente (pág. 410)

Cold War/Guerra Fría largo período caracterizado por intensa rivalidad entre los Estados Unidos y la Unión Soviética posterior a la Segunda Guerra Mundial (pág. 558)

colony/colonia grupo de personas que se establece en una tierra distante pero sigue bajo la dirección del gobierno de su tierra natal (pág. 70)

Columbian Exchange/intercambio colombino intercambio global de bienes e ideas que resulta del encuentro entre los pueblos de los hemisferios occidental y oriental (pág. 71)

committee of correspondence/ comité de correspondencia campaña que consistió en escribir cartas y se convirtió en un importante instrumento de protesta en la colonia (pág. 153)

Common Sense*/*Sentido común ensayo de Thomas Paine publicado en 1776 que instaba a las colonias a declarar la independencia (pág. 173)

compromise/compromiso documento en el que cada lado cede en algunas de sus posiciones para poder llegar a un acuerdo (pág. 208)

Compromise of 1850/Compromiso de 1850 acuerdo con respecto a la esclavitud según el cual California se sumó a la Unión como estado libre, y se aprobó una estricta ley sobre esclavos fugitivos (pág. 465)

confederation/confederación liga de estados o naciones independientes (pág. 317)

conquistador/conquistador término que se refiere a los exploradores españoles que ocuparon tierras en América y las declararon propiedad de España (pág. 74)

Conservatives/conservadores durante la Reconstrucción, los blancos del Sur que se resistían al cambio (pág. 527)

constitution/constitución documento que establece las leyes, principios, organización y sistema de un gobierno (pág. 200)

Constitutional Convention/ Convención Constitucional reunión de los representantes de los estados realizada el 25 de mayo de 1787 para revisar los Artículos de la Confederación (pág. 206)

constitutional initiative/iniciativa constitucional proceso para que los ciudadanos puedan pedir enmiendas a la constitución de su estado (pág. 263)

consumer/consumidor el que usa bienes y servicios (pág. 27)

Continental Army/Ejército Continental ejército establecido por el Segundo Congreso Continental para luchar contra los británicos (pág. 169)

continental divide/divisoria continental cadena de montañas que separa sistemas fluviales que corren en direcciones opuestas en un continente (pág. 309)

Copperhead/Copperhead norteño que oponía el uso de la fuerza para mantener los estados del Sur dentro de la Unión (pág. 501)

corduroy road/camino de troncos camino hecho con troncos de árbol (pág. 339)

corporation/corporación negocio cuyos dueños son los inversionistas (pág. 544)

"cottonocracy"/"algodocracia" sobrenombre de los planteros ricos que hicieron su dinero con el algodón a mediados de los años 1800 (pág. 422)

coureur de bois*/*coureur de bois colonos franceses que vivían en los bosques y cazaban animales por sus pieles (pág. 83)

creole/criollo persona de padres españoles nacida en las colonias españolas de América (págs. 78, 348)

Crusades/Cruzadas series de guerras en las que los cristianos lucharon por el control de la Tierra Santa entre 1100 y 1300 (pág. 58)

Cuban missile crisis/crisis cubana de los misiles importante confrontación de 1962 entre los Estados Unidos y la Unión Soviética durante la Guerra Fría; los Estados Unidos bloquearon un intento soviético de instalar misiles en Cuba (pág. 560)

culture/cultura forma de vida desarrollada por un pueblo (págs. 22, 40)

culture area/área cultural región en la que las personas comparten una forma de vida similar (pág. 42)

currency/moneda dinero circulante (pág. 202)

D

D-Day/Día D invasión de Europa Occidental el 6 de junio de 1944 en la cual tropas de los Estados Unidos, Inglaterra y otros aliados desembarcaron en la costa de Normandía, Francia, y avanzaron en dirección este hacia Alemania (pág. 557)

dame school/escuela de damas escuela privada dirigida por una mujer, generalmente en su propia casa (pág. 128)

debtor/deudor persona que no puede pagar el dinero que debe (págs. 116, 436)

Declaration of Independence/ Declaración de Independencia documento de 1776 que declaraba que las 13 colonias formaban una nación libre e independiente (pág. 175)

deficit spending/gasto deficitario práctica gubernamental de gastar más dinero del que se recauda por impuestos (pág. 555)

democratic/democrático que asegura que todas las personas tengan los mismos derechos (pág. 302)

Democratic Republican/republicano demócrata partidario de Thomas Jefferson, quien apoyaba un gobierno descentralizado (pág. 289)

Democrats/demócratas quienes apoyaban a Andrew Jackson, incluyendo granjeros de frontera y trabajadores de fábrica (pág. 364)

depression/depresión período en que la actividad comercial decrece, los precios y los salarios disminuyen, y aumenta el desempleo (págs. 204, 373)

détente/détente política del presidente Nixon continuada por los presidentes Ford y Carter, que procuraba reducir las tensiones entre los superpoderes (pág. 564)

dictator/dictador gobernante que tiene poder y autoridad absolutos (pág. 386)

dictatorship/dictadura gobierno en el cual una persona o pequeño grupo retiene toda la autoridad (pág. 212)

direct democracy/democracia directa forma de gobierno según la cual los ciudadanos comunes tienen el poder de gobernar (pág. 57)

discrimination/discriminación política o actitud que niega derechos igualitarios a ciertos grupos de personas (pág. 417)

domestic tranquility/tranquilidad interna orden y paz interna de una nación, uno de los seis objetivos definidos en el preámbulo de la Constitución de los Estados Unidos (pág. 249)

draft/leva ley que requiere que ciertas personas hagan el servicio militar (pág. 502)

Dred Scott* v. *Sandford*/*Dred Scott* versus *Sandford un caso que llegó a la Corte Suprema en 1857 en el cual un esclavo, Dred Scott, hizo un juicio para obtener su libertad y perdió; este caso puso en duda el poder federal con respecto a la esclavitud en los territorios (pág. 471)

E

economics/economía el estudio de cómo las personas manejan recursos limitados para satisfacer sus deseos y necesidades (pág. 26)

electoral college/colegio electoral grupo de electores de cada estado que cada cuatro años vota para elegir al presidente y vicepresidente de los Estados Unidos (pág. 255)

elevation/elevación altura por encima del nivel del mar (pág. 13)

emancipate/emancipar liberar (pág. 497)

Emancipation Proclamation/ Proclama de Emancipación declaración de 1863 del Presidente Lincoln que liberaba a los esclavos de la Confederación (pág. 497)

embargo/embargo prohibición de comerciar (pág. 314)

Embargo Act/Acta de Embargo ley de 1807 que impuso la prohibición total al comercio exterior (pág. 314)

encomienda/encomienda cesión de tierra otorgada por el gobierno español a los colonos españoles, que incluía el derecho a exigir trabajo o impuestos a los indígenas americanos (pág. 78)

English Bill of Rights/Declaración de Derechos Inglesa documento de 1689 que garantizaba los derechos de los ciudadanos ingleses (págs. 123, 213)

Enlightenment/Ilustración movimiento europeo de los siglos XVII y XVIII que enfatizaba el uso de la razón (pág. 129)

environmentalist/ambientalista persona que trabaja para reducir la polución y proteger el medio ambiente (pág. 566)

Era of Good Feelings/era de los buenos sentimientos los ocho años de la presidencia de James Monroe, desde 1817 a 1825, cuando los Demócratas Republicanos dominaban la política nacional (pág. 343)

Erie Canal/canal de Erie canal artificial construido en 1825 que conectaba el lago Erie con el río Hudson (pág. 340)

erosion/erosión desgaste gradual (pág. 13)

established church/iglesia oficial religión elegida por un estado (pág. 94)

execute/ejecutar llevar a cabo (pág. 201)

executive branch/rama ejecutiva rama del gobierno que hace cumplir las leyes (pág. 208)

expedition/expedición largo viaje de exploración (pág. 308)

export/producto de exportación artículo comercial que se envía a mercados extranjeros (pág. 120)

extended family/familia extendida grupo familiar que incluye abuelos, padres, hijos, tías, tíos y primos (págs. 53, 425)

F

faction/facción grupo de oposición dentro de un partido (pág. 287)

factory system/sistema de fábricas método de producción que reunió en un mismo lugar trabajadores y maquinaria (pág. 331)

famine/hambruna severa escasez de alimentos (pág. 415)

Farewell Address/discurso de despedida el último discurso de los presidentes al expirar sus mandatos (pág. 286)

federalism/federalismo principio de la Constitución de los Estados Unidos que establece la división de poderes entre el gobierno federal y los estados (pág. 251)

Federalist/federalista partidario de la Constitución quien estaba a favor de un gobierno federal o nacional fuerte (págs. 215, 289)

The Federalist Papers/Los Ensayos Federalistas series de ensayos escritos por los Federalistas James Madison, Alexander Hamilton y John Jay que apoyaban la ratificación de la Constitución (pág. 216)

feudalism/feudalismo sistema de gobierno en el que los señores o nobles regían sus propias tierras pero debían lealtad y servicio militar a un monarca (pág. 58)

54th Massachusetts Regiment/ regimiento 54° de Massachusetts unidad afroamericana del ejército de la Unión (pág. 499)

Fifteenth Amendment/Enmienda Decimoquinta enmienda a la Constitución de los Estados Unidos aprobada en 1869 que prohibe a los estados negar a los afroamericanos el derecho al voto por causa de su raza (pág. 524)

First Amendment/Primera Enmienda enmienda a la Constitución de los Estados Unidos que protege las libertades individuales básicas, incluyendo la libertad religiosa, la libertad de expresión y la libertad de prensa (pág. 260)

First Continental Congress/Primer Congreso Continental reunión de delegados de 12 colonias en Filadelfia en 1774 (pág. 158)

first global age/primera era global época a comienzos del siglo XV en la que el comercio y los viajes aumentaron notablemente, conectando partes remotas del mundo (pág. 50)

flatboat/carguero de poco fondo embarcación que se usa para transportar carga pesada en rutas acuáticas de tierra adentro (pág. 337)

foreign policy/política exterior acciones de una nación en relación con otras naciones (pág. 285)

Fort Wagner/fuerte Wagner fuerte de Carolina del Sur objeto de un ataque en 1863 por parte del Regimiento 54° de Massachusetts (pág. 499)

forty-niner/persona del cuarenta y nueve una de los más de 80,000 personas que en 1849 se unieron a la fiebre del oro (pág. 400)

Founding Fathers/padres de la patria James Madison, Thomas Jefferson, y otros líderes que dieron los primeros pasos para la formación de los Estados Unidos (pág. 211)

Fourteenth Amendment/Enmienda Decimocuarta enmienda a la Constitución de los Estados Unidos aprobada en 1968 que otorga la ciudadanía a todas las personas nacidas en los Estados Unidos y les garantiza la protección igualitaria de las leyes (pág. 522)

free enterprise/libre empresa sistema en el cual el gobierno juega un rol limitado en la economía (pág. 28)

free market economy/economía de mercado libre sistema económico en el cual los individuos, en vez del gobierno, deciden qué y cuánto producir y vender (págs. 303, 564)

Free-Soil party/partido del territorio libre partido antiesclavista fundado en 1848 en los Estados Unidos, para mantener la esclavitud fuera de los territorios del oeste que incluía miembros de ambos partidos (pág. 462)

freedmen/libertos hombres y mujeres que habían sido esclavos (pág. 517)

Freedmen's Bureau/Oficina de Libertos agencia del gobierno de los Estados Unidos fundada durante la Reconstrucción para ayudar a los ex esclavos (pág. 517)

French and Indian War/Guerra Franco-Indígena guerra entre Inglaterra y Francia de 1754 a 1763 en la que ambos países tuvieron indios americanos como aliados y que acabó con el poder francés en América del Norte (pág.142)

French Revolution/Revolución Francesa rebelión que tuvo lugar en Francia en 1789 y que acabó con la monarquía (pág. 284)

frigate/fragata barco armado con muchos cañones que navega rápidamente (pág. 292)

fugitive/fugitivo persona que huye (pág. 464)

Fugitive Slave Act/Acta de los Esclavos Fugitivos ley de 1850 que exigía a todos los ciudadanos colaborar en la captura de esclavos fugitivos (pág. 465)

Fundamental Orders of Connecticut/Órdenes Fundamentales de Connecticut plan de gobierno de la Colonia puritana de Connecticut en 1639 que expandía la idea del gobierno representativo en las colonias inglesas (pág. 104)

G

Gadsden Purchase/Compra de Gadsden banda de tierra entre lo que es hoy Arizona y Nuevo México, por la cual los Estados Unidos pagó a México $10 millones en 1853 (pág. 397)

General Court/Corte General asamblea representativa electa de la Colonia de la bahía de Massachusetts (pág. 103)

general welfare/bienestar general bienestar de todos los ciudadanos de una nación, uno de los seis objetivos definidos en el preámbulo de la Constitución de Estados Unidos (pág. 249)

gentry/alta burguesía la clase social más alta en las 13 colonias inglesas (pág. 126)

geography/geografía el estudio de las personas, su medio ambiente y sus recursos (pág. 4)

Gettysburg Address/discurso de Gettysburg discurso pronunciado en 1863 por el Presidente Lincoln después de la Batalla de Gettysburg (pág. 507)

Gibbons v. Ogden/Gibbons versus Ogden caso judicial de 1814 en el que la Corte Suprema confirmó el poder del gobierno federal para regular el comercio (pág. 346)

glacier/glaciar capa gruesa de hielo (pág. 36)

Glorious Revolution/Revolución Gloriosa movimiento de 1688 que llevó a William y a Mary al trono de Inglaterra y reforzó los derechos de los ciudadanos ingleses (pág. 123)

grandfather clause/cláusula del abuelo ley que eximía a un votante de la prueba de alfabetización si su padre o su abuelo había sido elegible para votar el 1º de enero de 1867; la ley protegía el derecho a votar de los blancos pero no el de los negros del Sur (pág. 532)

Great Awakening/Gran Despertar movimiento religioso que tuvo lugar a principios del siglo XVIII en las colonias inglesas (pág. 127)

Great Compromise/Gran Compromiso plan de la Convención Constitucional que resolvió los conflictos entre los estados grandes y los pequeños (pág. 208)

Great Depression/gran depresión el peor período de decadencia económica en la historia de los Estados Unidos; comenzó en 1929 y duró hasta el comienzo de la Segunda Guerra Mundial (pág. 554)

Green Mountain Boys/los muchachos de *Green Mountains* milicia colonial de Vermont liderada por Ethan Allen que llevó a cabo un ataque sorpresa al Fuerte Ticonderoga, obteniendo para los colonos el control de la ruta clave hacia Canadá (pág. 169)

guerilla/guerrillero soldado que usa la táctica de atacar y retirarse (pág. 192)

guerrilla warfare/guerra de guerrillas el uso de tácticas militares basadas en atacar y retirarse rápidamente (pág. 470)

Gullah/*Gullah* combinación del idioma inglés y de lenguas de África Occidental que hablaban los afroamericanos en la colonia de Carolina de Sur (pág. 126)

H

habeas corpus/*habeas corpus* derecho por el cual no puede encarcelarse a ninguna persona por un crimen específico sin haber sido antes condenada (págs. 213, 502)

Hartford Convention/Convención de Hartford reunión de delegados de Nueva Inglaterra durante la guerra de 1812 que amenazó con separarse de la Unión como protesta contra la guerra (pág. 325)

Holocaust/holocausto asesinato de millones de judíos y otras personas por parte del gobierno de la Alemania nazi y sus aliados durante la Segunda Guerra Mundial (pág. 556)

Homestead Act/Acta de Posesión de Tierras ley de 1862 que dio tierras a los colonos para que las convirtieran en granjas (pág. 543)

House of Burgesses/Casa de los Burgueses asamblea de representantes de la Virginia colonial (pág. 90)

House of Representatives/Cámara de Representantes el mayor de los dos cuerpos que forman la rama legislativa del gobierno de los Estados Unidos; la representación se basa en el número de habitantes (pág. 252)

Hudson River School/escuela del río Hudson grupo de artistas de los Estados Unidos que pintaban paisajes del valle del río Hudson en Nueva York, a mediados de los años 1800 (pág. 448)

I

immigrant/inmigrante persona que se establece en otro país (pág. 266)

impeach/juicio político acusar formalmente de faltas serias a un funcionario del gobierno (págs. 257, 523)

imperialism/imperialismo política de los países poderosos para tratar de controlar los asuntos políticos y económicos de países o regiones más débiles (pág. 549)

import/producto de importación artículo comercial que se ha introducido a un país (pág. 120)

impressment/leva práctica de forzar a las personas a que hagan el servicio militar (pág. 313)

inauguration/toma de mando ceremonia en la cual el presidente jura su cargo (pág. 278)

income tax/impuesto a los ingresos un impuesto al dinero que las personas ganan (pág. 502)

incriminate/incriminar presentar evidencias en contra de alguien (pág. 260)

indentured servant/sirviente por contrato persona que aceptaba trabajar sin pago por un período de tiempo a cambio de un pasaje a las colonias (pág. 126)

Indian Removal Act/Acta de Reubicación de los Indios ley aprobada en 1830 que forzaba a muchos americanos nativos a mudarse hacia el oeste del río Mississippi (pág. 372)

indigo/índigo planta usada para hacer una valiosa tintura azul (pág. 115)

individualism/individualismo concepto que destaca la importancia de cada individuo (pág. 451)

Industrial Revolution/Revolución Industrial proceso gradual en el que las máquinas reemplazaron a las herramientas manuales, y el vapor y otras fuentes de energía reemplazaron a las personas y a los animales de carga (pág. 330)

inflation/inflación incremento de los precios y desvalorización del dinero (pág. 503)

infrastructure/infraestructura sistema de caminos, puentes y túneles (pág. 263)

interchangeable parts/partes intercambiables partes o repuestos idénticos para herramientas o instrumentos hechos a máquina (pág. 332)

internal improvements/mejoras internas mejoras hechas a caminos, puentes y canales (pág. 346)

Spanish Glossary

interstate commerce/comercio interestatal comercio entre diferentes estados (pág. 346)

intervention/intervención participación directa (pág. 351)

Intolerable Acts/Actas Intolerables series de leyes aprobadas en 1774 para castigar a Boston por la Fiesta del té (pág. 157)

irrigation/irrigación riego de tierras áridas (pág. 6)

Islam/islam religión monoteísta fundada por el profeta Mahoma a principios del siglo VII (pág. 50)

isolationism/aislamiento política de limitar la ingerencia en los asuntos políticos de naciones extranjeras (pág. 549)

isthmus/istmo estrecha lengua de tierra (pág. 11)

J

Jay's Treaty/Tratado de Jay acuerdo de 1795 entre Gran Bretaña y los Estados Unidos que requería que Gran Bretaña pagara por los daños ocasionados por la captura de barcos estadounidenses, y devolviera los fuertes que aún ocupaba en el Oeste. Por su parte, los Estados Unidos pagaría las deudas contraídas con los comerciantes británicos (pág. 286)

jazz/jazz estilo musical original de los Estados Unidos que une ritmos del África Occidental, harmonías europeas, y canciones laborales y religiosas de los afroamericanos (pág. 554)

Jim Crow laws/leyes de Jim Crow leyes que separaban en los lugares públicos del Sur a las personas de diferentes razas (pág. 532)

judicial branch/rama judicial rama del gobierno que decide si las leyes se practican de manera justa (pág. 208)

judicial review/revisión judicial poder de la Corte Suprema para decidir si los actos de un presidente o las leyes aprobadas por el Congreso son constitucionales (pág. 305)

Judiciary Act/Acta judicial ley de 1789 que creó la estructura de la Corte Suprema y estableció un sistema de cortes de distrito y cortes de circuito a nivel nacional (pág. 279)

jury duty/el deber de ser jurado obligación de todo ciudadano de servir como jurado cuando se le llama (pág. 268)

K

kachina/kachina bailarín enmascarado que participaba en ceremonias religiosas de los indios americanos del Sudoeste (pág. 47)

Kansas-Nebraska Act/Acta de Kansas-Nebraska ley de 1854 que estableció los territorios de Kansas y Nebraska, dando a los colonos el derecho de soberanía popular para decidir con respecto a la esclavitud (pág. 468)

Kentucky and Virginia resolutions/ Acuerdos de Kentucky y Virginia declaraciones aprobadas en 1798 y 1799 que reivindicaban para los estados el derecho de decidir si una ley federal era constitucional y de declararla nula dentro de los límites del estado si se decidía que era inconstitucional (pág. 293)

kinship/parentesco compartir antepasados (pág. 53)

"kitchen cabinet"/"gabinete de cocina" grupo de consejeros extra oficiales de Andrew Jackson que se reunía con él en la cocina de la Casa Blanca (pág. 367)

Know-Nothing Party/Know-Nothing Party partido político de la década de 1850 que estaba en contra del catolicismo y de la inmigración (pág. 416)

Korean War/Guerra de Corea conflicto que duró entre 1950 y 1953 entre Corea del Norte, apoyada por China, y Corea del Sur, apoyada por fuerzas de las Naciones Unidas que consistían principalmente en tropas de los Estados Unidos (pág. 559)

Ku Klux Klan/Ku Klux Klan sociedad secreta organizada en el Sur después de la Guerra Civil para afirmar la supremacía blanca por medio de la violencia (pág. 527)

L

laissez faire/laissez faire idea de que el gobierno debería jugar un rol tan mínimo como fuera posible en los asuntos económicos (pág. 303)

Lancaster Turnpike/carretera de peaje a Lancaster camino de peaje construido en la década de 1790 por una compañía privada, que conectaba Filadelfia con Lancaster, Pennsylvania (pág. 339)

Land Ordinance of 1785/ Ordenanza de Tierras de 1785 ley que establecía un sistema para colonizar el Territorio del Noroeste (pág. 203)

latitude/latitud distancia hacia el norte o el sur del ecuador (pág. 4)

lawsuit/demanda caso legal iniciado para dirimir una disputa entre personas o grupos (pág. 471)

League of the Iroquois/Liga de los Iroquois alianza de las cinco naciones de los Iroquois (pág. 48)

legislative branch/rama legislativa rama del gobierno que aprueba las leyes (pág. 208)

legislature/legislatura grupo de personas que tiene el poder de hacer leyes (pág. 122)

libel/libelo acto de publicar afirmaciones que pueden dañar injustamente la reputación de una persona (pág. 130)

The Liberator/The Liberator el periódico antiesclavista más influyente, fundado por William Lloyd Garrison en 1831 (pág. 440)

liberty/libertad derecho de actuar de una manera u otra (pág. 249)

limited government/gobierno limitado principio de la Constitución de los Estados Unidos que establece que el gobierno sólo tiene los poderes que la constitución le otorga (pág. 250)

literacy test/prueba de alfabetización examen para ver si una persona puede leer y escribir; se usaba en el pasado para restringir el derecho al voto (pág. 532)

local government/gobierno local gobierno del condado, distrito de condado, ciudad, pueblo, villa o distrito (pág. 263)

locomotive/locomotora máquina que arrastra un tren (pág. 409)

Lone Star Republic/República de la Estrella Solitaria sobrenombre de Texas después que obtuvo su independencia de México en 1836 (pág. 389)

longitude/longitud distancia hacia el este o el oeste del primer meridiano (pág. 4)

Louisiana Purchase/Compra de Louisiana vasto territorio entre el río Mississippi y las Montañas Rocosas que se le compró a Francia en 1803 (pág. 308)

Lowell girl/chica Lowell mujer joven que trabajaba para Lowell Mills en Massachusetts durante la revolución industrial (pág. 333)

Loyalist/loyalist colono que permaneció leal a Gran Bretaña (pág. 170)

lynch/linchar colgar a alguien sin un juicio legal (pág. 401)

M

Magna Carta/Carta Magna documento británico de 1215 cuyas dos ideas básicas sostienen que incluso los monarcas tienen que obedecer la ley y que los ciudadanos tienen derechos básicos (págs. 90, 213)

majority/mayoría más de la mitad (pág. 362)

Manifest Destiny/destino manifiesto creencia que se diseminó en los años 1800 de que los estadounidenses tenían el derecho y la obligación de extenderse a través del continente hasta el Océano Pacífico (pág. 393)

manor/señorío distrito regido por un Señor que incluía su castillo y las tierras que lo rodeaban (pág. 58)

map projection/proyección cartográfica manera de dibujar la Tierra sobre una superficie plana (pág. 8)

Marbury v. Madison/Marbury versus Madison caso judicial de 1803 en el cual la Corte Suprema dictaminó que tenía el poder de decidir si las leyes aprobadas por el Congreso eran constitucionales y de rechazar las leyes que considerara inconstitucionales (pág. 305)

margin buying/comprar a crédito práctica según la cual los inversionistas compran acciones con un pequeño adelanto, y obtienen el resto en préstamo de un corredor de bolsa, con la esperanza de vender con una ganancia cuando suban los precios (pág. 554)

Marshall Plan/Plan Marshall plan de los Estados Unidos para ayudar a las naciones europeas a reconstruir sus economías después de la Segunda Guerra Mundial (pág. 559)

martial law/ley marcial gobierno por parte de los militares en vez de un gobierno electo (pág. 487)

martyr/mártir persona que muere por sus creencias (pág. 476)

Mason-Dixon Line/línea de Mason-Dixon límite entre Pennsylvania y Maryland que dividía las Colonias Centrales de las Colonias del Sur (pág. 113)

Mayflower Compact/acuerdo Mayflower acuerdo de 1620 para gobernar la colonia de Plymouth, firmado por los peregrinos antes de desembarcar en Plymouth (pág. 95)

McCulloch v. Maryland/McCullock versus Maryland caso judicial de 1819 en el que la Corte Suprema dictaminó que los estados no tenían derecho a interferir en las instituciones federales aunque estuvieran dentro de sus límites (pág. 346)

mercantilism/mercantilismo teoría de que el poder económico de una nación provenía de proteger y aumentar la economía local manteniendo un estricto control sobre el comercio de sus colonias (pág. 120)

mercenary/mercenario soldado que lucha exclusivamente por dinero, a menudo para un país extranjero (pág. 171)

mestizo/mestizo en las colonias españolas de América, la persona que tiene mezcla de antepasados indios y españoles (pág. 78)

Mexican Cession/cesión mexicana territorio mexicano de California y Nuevo México que se entregó a los Estados Unidos en 1848 (pág. 396)

middle class/clase media en las 13 colonias inglesas, la clase social que incluía artesanos cualificados, granjeros y algunos comerciantes (pág. 126)

militia/milicia ejército de ciudadanos que sirven como soldados en una emergencia (pág. 158)

minuteman/miliciano de la Guerra de Independencia voluntario de una milicia colonial que estaba en todo momento preparado para luchar (pág. 159)

mission/misión colonia religiosa administrada por frailes y monjas católicas (pág. 78)

missionary/misionero persona que intenta transmitir ciertas creencias religiosas a un grupo de gente (págs. 56, 84)

Missouri Compromise/compromiso de Missouri acuerdo, propuesto en 1819 por Henry Clay, para mantener igual el número de estados que aceptaban o rechazaban la esclavitud (pág. 460)

Monitor/Monitor buque de guerra blindado de la Unión (pág. 492)

monopoly/monopolio una compañía que controla o domina toda una industria (pág. 544)

Monroe Doctrine/Doctrina Monroe declaración de política exterior del Presidente Monroe que prevenía a las naciones europeas para que no intervinieran en América Latina (pág. 351)

Mormons/mormones miembros de la Iglesia de Jesús Cristo de los Santos de los Últimos Días fundada en 1830 por Joseph Smith (pág. 398)

Mound Builders/constructores de montículos nombre de varias culturas de América del Norte que construyeron grandes montículos de tierra, comenzando hace unos 3,000 años (pág. 41)

mountain man/hombre de montaña cazador que exploraba Oregón a principios de los años 1800 (pág. 381)

muckraker/*muckraker* periodista que escribía sobre la corrupción y otros problemas de los Estados Unidos a fines de los años 1800 y principios de los años 1900 (pág. 547)

mudslinging/detractar uso de insultos para atacar la reputación de un oponente (pág. 374)

N

national debt/deuda nacional cantidad total de dinero que un gobierno debe a otros (pág. 280)

National Road/Caminos Nacionales primer proyecto nacional de caminos financiado federalmente, que se inició en 1811 (pág. 339)

nationalism/nacionalismo devoción hacia el propio país (pág. 318)

nativist/nativista persona que quería limitar la inmigración y reservar los Estados Unidos para los ciudadanos nativos blancos (pág. 416)

natural resources/recursos naturales materiales que los seres humanos pueden tomar del medio ambiente para sobrevivir y satisfacer sus necesidades (pág. 5)

natural rights/derechos naturales derechos que corresponden a todas las personas desde su nacimiento (pág. 175)

naturalize/naturalizarse completar el proceso oficial de convertirse en ciudadano (pág. 265)

Nauvoo/Nauvoo comunidad mormona formada en la década de 1840 en los bancos del río Mississippi en Illinois (pág. 398)

Navigation Acts/Actas de Navegación series de leyes aprobadas por el parlamento inglés a finales del siglo XVII que regulaban el comercio entre Inglaterra y sus colonias (pág. 121)

Negro Fort/Fuerte de los Negros asentamiento de esclavos afroamericanos fugitivos en la colonia española de Florida (pág. 350)

neutral/neutral que no toma partido en un conflicto (pág. 285)

Neutrality Proclamation/Declaración de neutralidad declaración de 1793 hecha por el presidente Washington que estipulaba que los Estados Unidos no apoyarían ni ayudarían a Francia ni a Gran Bretaña en su conflicto europeo (pág. 285)

New Deal/Nuevo Acuerdo programa del Presidente Franklin D. Roosevelt para acabar con la Gran Depresión (pág. 554)

New Jersey Plan/Plan de Nueva Jersey plan de la Convención Constitucional apoyado por los estados pequeños que requería tres ramas del gobierno con una legislatura de cámara única (pág. 208)

New Mexico Territory/territorio de Nuevo México extensa región del suroeste que pertenecía a México en los años 1800 (pág. 391)

"New South"/"Nuevo Sur" término de fines de los años 1800 que describía el Sur en un momento en que se esforzaba por expandir la economía a través de la industria (pág. 533)

Nineteenth Amendment/Enmienda Decimonovena enmienda de 1920 a la Constitución de los Estados Unidos que garantiza el derecho de votar a la mujer (págs. 261, 548)

Spanish Glossary

nominating convention/convención de postulaciones reunión en la cual un partido político elige sus candidatos (pág. 364)

Nonintercourse Act/Acta de No Intercambio ley de 1809 que permitía a los estadounidenses comerciar con todas las naciones excepto Francia y Gran Bretaña (pág. 314)

North American Free Trade Agreement (NAFTA)/Tratado de Libre Comercio de América del Norte (TLC) tratado entre los Estados Unidos, Canadá y México para reducir gradualmente las tasas y otras barreras al comercio (pág. 566)

Northwest Ordinance/Ordenanza del Noroeste artículo de 1787 que establecía un gobierno para el Territorio del Noroeste, garantizaba derechos básicos a los colonos y declaraba que la esclavitud era allí ilegal (pág. 203)

northwest passage/pasaje noroeste pasaje de agua a través o alrededor de América del Norte (pág. 81)

nullification/anulación idea de que un estado tiene el derecho de anular o cancelar una ley federal que los líderes del estado consideran inconstitucional (pág. 371)

Nullification Act/Acta de Anulación acta aprobada por Carolina del Sur que declaraba ilegal la tasa de 1832 (pág. 371)

nullify/anular declarar nulo (pág. 293)

O

Olive Branch Petition/Petición de la Rama de Olivo petición de paz enviada al rey George por los delegados coloniales después de las batallas de Lexington y Concord, declarando su lealtad a la corona y pidiéndole que cancelara las Actas Intolerables (pág. 168)

Oregon Country/condado de Oregón término usado a principios de 1800 para designar a la extensa región situada al oeste de las Montañas Rocosas, incluyendo lo que es hoy Oregón, Washington, Idaho y partes de Wyoming, Montana y Canadá (pág. 380)

Oregon Trail/camino de Oregón ruta que llevaba a Oregón, usada por los trenes de carga en los años 1800 (pág. 383)

override/invalidar no admitir, como cuando el Congreso decide no admitir el veto presidencial (pág. 257)

P

Parliament/Parlamento en Inglaterra, asamblea representativa (pág. 90)

Patriot/patriota colono que estaba a favor de la guerra contra Gran Bretaña (pág. 169)

patriotism/patriotismo sentimiento de amor y devoción hacia el propio país (pág. 266)

patroon/patrón dueño de una gran propiedad en una colonia holandesa (pág. 109)

peninsulare/peninsular término que se refiere a un español que tenía una posición de poder en una colonia española (pág. 78)

Pennsylvania Dutch/holandeses de Pennsylvania protestantes de habla germana que se establecieron en Pennsylvania (pág. 110)

persecution/persecución maltrato o castigo a un grupo de personas a causa de sus creencias (pág. 94)

Persian Gulf War/Guerra del Golfo Persa guerra librada en 1991 entre Iraq y una alianza de países dirigida por los Estados Unidos para liberar Kuwait, un territorio rico en petróleo, de las fuerzas de ocupación iraquíes (pág. 564)

petition/petición solicitud formal firmada por un grupo de personas dirigida a alguien de mayor autoridad (pág. 149)

Pickett's Charge/Carga de Pickett ataque de la Confederación como parte de la Batalla de Gettysburg que fracasó (pág. 506)

Pilgrims/peregrinos colonos ingleses que, en el siglo XVII, procuraron libertad religiosa en las Américas (pág. 93)

Pinckney Treaty/Tratado de Pinckney acuerdo de 1795 con España que permitió a los Estados Unidos transportar sus mercancías por el río Mississippi y almacenarlas en Nueva Orleáns (pág. 306)

pit house/casa subterránea casa de la región Ártica cavada en la tierra y cubierta con madera y pieles (pág. 43)

Plains of Abraham/Planicies de Abraham campo cerca de Quebec donde en la Guerra Franco-Indígena tuvo lugar una importante victoria de los británicos frente a los franceses (pág. 144)

plantation/plantación gran propiedad cultivada por muchos trabajadores (pág. 80)

Plessy v. Ferguson/Plessy* versus *Ferguson un caso legal de 1896 en el cual la Corte Suprema dictaminó que la segregación en las instalaciones públicas era legal si las instalaciones eran iguales (pág. 532)

political science/ciencias políticas el estudio del gobierno (pág. 29)

poll tax/impuesto al voto impuesto que se requería antes de que las personas pudieran votar (pág. 532)

Pontiac's War/guerra de Pontiac conflicto de 1763 entre los indígenas americanos y los británicos sobre la colonización de tierras indias en el área de los Grandes Lagos (pág. 147)

popular sovereignty/soberanía popular principio de la Constitución de los Estados Unidos que establece que el pueblo tiene el derecho de crear, alterar o abolir su gobierno; a mediados de los años 1800, el término se refería a la idea de que cada territorio podía decidir por sí mismo si permitir o no la esclavitud (págs. 250, 462)

potlatch/*potlatch* cena ceremonial realizada por algunos americanos nativos de la costa noroeste para mostrar su riqueza (pág. 44)

preamble/preámbulo introducción a una declaración, constitución u otro documento oficial (págs. 175, 248)

precedent/precedente acta o decisión que sirve de ejemplo a las que siguen (págs. 96, 278)

precipitation/precipitación agua que cae en forma de lluvia, cellisca, granizo o nieve (pág. 15)

predestination/predestinación idea protestante según la cual Dios decidía de antemano quiénes, después de muertos, se salvarían (pág. 435)

presidio/presidio fuerte de las colonias españolas donde vivían los soldados (pág. 77)

primary source/fuente original información directa acerca de personas o eventos (pág. 20)

Proclamation of 1763/Proclama de 1763 ley que prohibía a los colonos ingleses establecerse al oeste de las montañas Apalaches (pág. 147)

profiteer/aprovechador persona que aprovecha una crisis para hacer dinero (pág. 503)

Progressives/progresistas reformadores que querían mejorar la vida en los Estados Unidos a fines de los años 1800 y principios de los años 1900 (pág. 547)

proprietary colony/colonia de propietarios colonia inglesa en la cual el rey daba tierras a propietarios a cambio de un pago anual (pág. 109)

Protestant Reformation/reforma protestante movimiento ocurrido en el siglo XVI para reformar la iglesia

Spanish Glossary

católica romana y que llevó a la creación de muchas iglesias cristianas diferentes (pág. 83)

psychology/sicología el estudio del modo de pensar y comportarse de los seres humanos (pág. 30)

public school/escuela pública escuela financiada por los impuestos (pág. 128)

pueblo/pueblo ciudad de las colonias españolas; aldea de los anasazi (págs. 41, 77)

Puritans/puritanos grupo de protestantes ingleses que se establecieron en la Colonia de la bahía de Massachusetts (pág. 102)

Q

Quakers/cuáqueros reformistas protestantes que creen en la igualdad de todas las personas (pág. 110)

Quebec Act/Acta de Quebec ley que establecía un gobierno para Canadá y protegía los derechos de los católicos franceses (pág. 158)

quipu/quipu artefacto hecho de cuerda o tiras con nudos que representaban cantidades, usado por los incas para sus registros y contabilidad (pág. 40)

Quran/Corán libro sagrado del islam (pág. 51)

R

racism/racismo creencia en la superioridad de una raza con respecto a otra (pág. 119)

radical/radical persona que quiere realizar cambios drásticos en la sociedad (pág. 173)

Radical Reconstruction/reconstrucción radical período que comenzó en 1867 cuando los Republicanos, que tenían el control de ambas cámaras, se hicieron cargo de la Reconstrucción (pág. 523)

Radical Republican/republicano radical en la época de la Reconstrucción, miembro del Congreso que quería quebrar el poder de los plantadores ricos del Sur y asegurarse de que los libertos recibieran el derecho a votar (pág. 522)

ratify/ratificar aprobar (pág. 194)

Reaganomics/reaganomics política económica del presidente Reagan que redujo los impuestos, limitó los gastos en programas sociales, y eliminó muchas reglas que se aplicaban a los negocios (pág. 563)

Reconstruction/reconstrucción reconstrucción del Sur después de la Guerra Civil (pág. 517)

Reconstruction Act/Acta de la Reconstrucción ley de 1867 que anuló los gobiernos de los estados del Sur que se habían negado a ratificar la Enmienda Decimocuarta y requirió que los ex-estados Confederados permitieran votar a los afroamericanos (pág. 523)

refuge/refugio lugar donde se está libre de persecuciones (pág. 399)

religious tolerance/tolerancia religiosa deseo de permitir que otros practiquen sus propias creencias (pág. 104)

Renaissance/Renacimiento explosión europea de aprendizaje que tuvo lugar desde finales del siglo XIV hasta el siglo XVI (pág. 59)

rendezvous/rendezvous palabra francesa que significa reunión; encuentro anual en el cual los hombres de montaña intercambiaban pieles (pág. 382)

repeal/revocar cancelar (pág. 150)

representative government/gobierno representativo sistema político según el cual los votantes eligen a los representantes que dictarán las leyes (pág. 90)

republic/república sistema de gobierno en el cual los ciudadanos eligen representantes para que los gobiernen (págs. 57, 211)

Republic of Great Colombia/República de la Gran Colombia estado independiente compuesto por lo que hoy son Venezuela, Colombia, Ecuador y Panamá; se fundó después de obtener la independencia de España en 1819 (pág. 349)

Republican party/partido republicano partido político establecido en 1854 en los Estados Unidos, con el fin de mantener la esclavitud fuera de los territorios del oeste (pág. 473)

resident alien/extranjero residente persona que vive en el país sin ser ciudadano (pág. 266)

revival/reunión evangelista gran encuentro religioso al aire libre (pág. 435)

Roosevelt Corollary/corolario de Roosevelt política establecida por el presidente Theodore Roosevelt que extendía la Doctrina Monroe afirmando que los Estados Unidos tenían el derecho a intervenir en los asuntos Latinoamericanos (pág. 550)

royal colony/colonia real colonia bajo el control directo de la corona inglesa (pág. 109)

rugged individualist/individualista recalcitrante persona que sigue en la vida su propio camino independiente (pág. 381)

S

Sabbath/sabbat día de descanso religioso (pág. 106)

sachem/sachem miembro del consejo tribal de jefes de la liga de los iroquois (pág. 48)

salvation/salvación vida eterna (pág. 56)

Santa Fe Trail/camino de Santa Fe ruta a Santa Fe, Nuevo México, que usaban los comerciantes en los años 1800 (pág. 392)

savanna/sabana región de pastos (pág. 52)

scalawag/scalawag blanco sureño que apoyaba a los Republicanos durante la Reconstrucción (pág. 526)

secede/separarse retirarse como miembro de un grupo (pág. 463)

Second Amendment/Segunda Enmienda enmienda a la Constitución de los Estados Unidos que se refiere al derecho a tener armas (pág. 260)

Second Great Awakening/Segundo Gran Despertar extenso movimiento religioso en los Estados Unidos a principios de los años 1800 (pág. 435)

secondary source/fuente secundaria relato de los hechos proporcionado por personas que no participaron directamente o presenciaron los hechos ocurridos (pág. 21)

sectionalism/seccionalismo lealtad a un estado o sección antes que a todo el país (pág. 345)

sedition/sedición rebelión en contra de un gobierno (pág. 293)

segregation/segregación separación legal de las razas (pág. 532)

self-sufficient/autosuficiente capaz de producir lo suficiente para satisfacer las necesidades propias (pág. 392)

Seminole War/guerra de los Seminoles conflicto que se inició en Florida entre los indios seminoles y el ejército de los Estados Unidos cuando los indios se resistieron a mudarse (pág. 373)

Senate/Senado el menor de los dos cuerpos que constituyen la rama legislativa del gobierno de los Estados Unidos; basada en la representación igualitaria de dos senadores por cada estado (pág. 253)

Seneca Falls Convention/convención de Seneca Falls un encuentro de 1848 en el cual líderes del movimiento por los derechos femeninos reclamaron derechos igualitarios para la mujer (pág. 445)

separation of powers/separación de poderes principio según el cual los poderes del gobierno se dividen en ramas separadas (pág. 214)

Spanish Glossary

sharecropper/aparcero persona que alquila un terreno de otra persona y lo trabaja a cambio de parte de la cosecha (pág. 529)

Shays' Rebellion/rebelión de Shays revuelta de Massachussetts liderada por granjeros en 1786 en reacción a los altos impuestos (pág. 204)

siege/sitio cerco por parte del ejército de una ciudad o posición enemiga, seguido de bloqueo o bombardeo para obligarla a que se rinda (págs. 193, 387, 506)

Silk Road/Ruta de la Seda rutas terrestres que conectaban China con el Medio Oriente (pág. 52)

slave codes/códigos de la esclavitud leyes que controlaban la vida de los esclavos afroamericanos y les negaban los derechos básicos (págs. 119, 424)

smuggling/contrabando importar o exportar mercancías violando las leyes de comercio (pág. 314)

social reform/reforma social intento organizado de mejorar lo que es injusto o imperfecto en la sociedad (pág. 434)

social sciences/ciencias sociales estudios que se refieren a la sociedad y a la conducta social (pág. 29)

Social Security/seguridad social programa federal iniciado en la década de 1930 para proveeer ayuda a las personas mayores o sin empleo; el programa se expandió más adelante (pág. 554)

sociology/sociología estudio del comportamiento de las personas en grupos (pág. 30)

Spanish-American War/Guerra entre España y los Estados Unidos guerra de 1898 entre ambas naciones a causa del expansionismo de los Estados Unidos; permitió que los Estados Unidos obtuviera el control de Cuba, Puerto Rico, Guam y las Filipinas (pág. 550)

speculator/especulador alguien que invierte dinero en un negocio arriesgado con la esperanza de obtener grandes ganancias (pág. 280)

spinning jenny/hiladora de varios husos máquina inventada en 1764 que podía hilar varios hilos al mismo tiempo (pág. 331)

spoils system/sistema de sinecuras práctica que recompensaba a los partidarios de un gobierno otorgándoles empleos en dicho gobierno (pág. 366)

Stamp Act/Acta de los Sellos ley de 1765 que imponía nuevas obligaciones a los documentos legales y gravaba con impuestos los periódicos, almanaques, las cartas de jugar y los dados (pág. 149)

states' rights/derechos de los estados el derecho de los estados a limitar el poder del gobierno federal (págs. 293, 370)

strike/huelga acción, por parte de los trabajadores, de negarse a hacer su trabajo hasta que se acepten sus condiciones (pág. 414)

suffrage/sufragio derecho a votar (pág. 361)

Supreme Court/Corte Suprema corte de máxima autoridad de los Estados Unidos, establecida por la Constitución (pág. 256)

surplus/superávit excedente (pág. 37)

Sutter's Mill/Sutter's Mill lugar donde se descubrió oro en 1848, lo cual inició la fiebre del oro (pág. 400)

Swahili/swahili idioma que mezcla palabras árabes con las lenguas africanas locales, hablado en gran parte de África Oriental (pág. 52)

T

tariff/tasa de importación impuesto que afecta a bienes extranjeros que se importan a un país (pág. 281)

Tariff of Abomination/Tasa de Abominaciones tasa aprobada por el Congreso en 1828 que favorecía a la industria del Norte pero perjudicaba a los granjeros del Sur (pág. 370)

Tea Act/Acta del Té ley de 1773 que permitía a la Compañía Británica de las Indias Orientales prescindir de los comerciantes de té y vender sus productos directamente a los colonos (pág. 156)

Tejano/tejano persona nacida en Texas de origen mexicano (pág. 386)

telegraph/telégrafo mecanismo para comunicarse que envía señales eléctricas por un cable (pág. 409)

temperance movement/movimiento por la temperancia campaña en contra del consumo de alcohol (pág. 436)

Ten Percent Plan/Plan del Diez Por Ciento plan del presidente Lincoln para la Reconstrucción que permitía que un estado del Sur formara un nuevo gobierno después de que el 10 por ciento de sus votantes juraran lealtad a los Estados Unidos (pág. 517)

terrace/terraza amplio escalón de tierra que se cava en la ladera de una colina (pág. 40)

terrorism/terrorismo uso deliberado de violencia indiscriminada, especialmente contra civiles, para conseguir objetivos políticos

Thanksgiving/Día de Acción de Gracias día al final de la temporada de cosecha que los peregrinos reservaban para dar gracias a Dios (pág. 97)

thematic map/mapa temático mapa que trata de un tema específico, como población, recursos naturales o elecciones (pág. 9)

Thirteenth Amendment/Enmienda Decimotercera enmienda de 1865 a la Constitución de los Estados Unidos que prohíbe la esclavitud en toda la nación (pág. 519)

Three-Fifths Compromise/Compromiso de los Tres Quintos acuerdo al cual se llegó en la Convención Constitutional, según el cual las tres quintas partes de los esclavos de cada estado se contarían como parte de la población (pág. 209)

total war/guerra total guerra absoluta que afecta tanto a los civiles en sus casas como a los soldados en combate (pág. 508)

totalitarian state/estado totalitario país en el cual un solo partido controla el gobierno y todos los aspectos de la vida del pueblo (pág. 556)

town meeting/cabildo abierto reunión en Nueva Inglaterra durante la colonia donde los colonos discutían y votaban (pág. 107)

Townshend Acts/Actas de Townshend leyes aprobadas en 1767 que gravaban con impuestos bienes como vidrio, papel, pintura, plomo y té (pág. 150)

trade union/gremio asociación de trabajadores de un mismo oficio que se formaba para acceder a una paga mayor y a mejores condiciones de trabajo (pág. 414)

Trail of Tears/Ruta de Lágrimas viaje forzado de los indios cheroquíes desde Georgia hasta la región al oeste del Mississippi en el cual muchos indios murieron (pág. 372)

traitor/traidor persona que traiciona a su país (pág. 175)

transcendentalist/trascendentalista miembro del pequeño e influyente grupo de escritores de Nueva Inglaterra que creían que las verdades más importantes de la vida trascendían, o estaban más allá, de la razón humana (pág. 450)

transcontinental railroad/ferrocarril transcontinental ferrocarril que cruza un continente (pág. 543)

treason/traición acciones contra el propio país (pág. 476)

Treaty of Ghent/Tratado de Gante tratado de paz firmado por Gran Bretaña y los Estados Unidos a fines de la guerra de 1812 (pág. 325)

Treaty of Greenville/Tratado de Greenville tratado firmado por algunos indígenas americanos en 1795, por el cual entregaron tierra que más tarde formaría parte de Ohio a cambio de $20,000 y la promesa de más dinero si mantenían la paz (pág. 317)

Spanish Glossary

Treaty of Guadalupe-Hidalgo/ Tratado de Guadalupe-Hidalgo tratado de 1848 por el cual México entregó California y Nuevo México a los Estados Unidos a cambio de $15 millones (pág. 396)

Treaty of Paris/Tratado de París acuerdo de 1763 entre Francia y Gran Bretaña que puso fin a la Guerra Franco-Indígena, y marcó el fin del poder de Francia en América del Norte (pág. 145); tratado de paz entre los Estados Unidos y Gran Bretaña ratificado en 1783, que reconoció a los Estados Unidos como una nación independiente (pág. 194)

triangular trade/comercio triangular ruta de comercio colonial entre Nueva Inglaterra, las Indias Occidentales y África (pág. 121)

tribe/tribu comunidad de personas que comparten costumbres, lenguaje y rituales (pág. 42)

tributary/tributario arroyo o río pequeño que desemboca en un río mayor (pág. 15)

tribute/tributo contribución de dinero (pág. 313)

turning point/momento decisivo momento histórico que indica un cambio fundamental (pág. 70)

turnpike/camino de peaje camino construido por una compañía privada que cobra un peaje por su uso (pág. 339)

tutor/tutor maestro privado (pág. 128)

Twenty-sixth Amendment/ Enmienda Vigesimosexta enmienda a la Constitución de los Estados Unidos que redujo de 21 a 18 años la edad mínima requerida para votar (pág. 261)

U

Uncle Tom's Cabin/La Cabaña del Tío Tom novela de Harriet Beecher Stowe escrita en 1852 que mostraba los horrores de la esclavitud y la injusticia del Acta de Esclavos Fugitivos (pág. 466)

unconstitutional/inconstitucional que no está permitido por la Constitución (págs. 257, 288)

Underground Railroad/Ruta Clandestina grupo de abolicionistas negros y blancos que trabajaban en secreto para ayudar a los esclavos a huir hacia la libertad en el norte de los Estados Unidos o Canadá (pág. 441)

United Provinces of Central America/Provincias Unidas de América Central federación que comprendía las actuales Guatemala, El Salvador, Honduras, Nicaragua y Costa Rica; fundada después de obtener la independencia de España en 1823 (pág. 349)

urbanization/urbanización proceso por el cual la población pasa de las granjas a las ciudades (págs. 335, 546)

V

Valley Forge/Valley Forge lugar de Pennsylvania donde estaba el campamento del Ejército Continental comandado por Washington durante el invierno de 1777 y 1778 (pág. 185)

vaquero/vaquero peón indio o mexicano que se ocupaba del ganado (pág. 392)

veto/veto rechazar, como cuando el presidente rechaza una ley que ha sido aprobada por el Congreso (pág. 257)

Vietnam War/Guerra de Vietnam conflicto militar entre las fuerzas comunistas de Vietnam del Norte, apoyadas por China y la Unión Soviética, y las fuerzas no comunistas de Vietnam del Sur, apoyadas por los Estados Unidos; los Estados Unidos participó en el conflicto entre 1961 y 1973 (pág. 561)

vigilante/vigilante alguien que se designa a sí mismo para hacer cumplir la ley (pág. 401)

Virginia/Virginia buque de guerra blindado que usaron los Confederados para quebrar el bloqueo de la Unión (pág. 492)

Virginia Plan/Plan de Virginia plan de la Convención Constitucional apoyado por los estados más grandes que recomendaba un gobierno nacional fuerte con tres ramas y una legislatura de dos cámaras (pág. 208)

W

Wade-Davis Bill/Proyecto de Wade-Davis plan de 1864 para la Reconstrucción, que requería que una mayoría de los hombres blancos de cada estado del Sur jurara lealtad a la Unión, y negaba el derecho al voto o el acceso a la función pública a quienes se habían ofrecido a luchar por la Confederación (pág. 517)

War Hawks/halcones de guerra miembros del Congreso que representaban al Oeste y al Sur y que instaban a la guerra contra Gran Bretaña antes de la guerra de 1812 (pág. 318)

Watergate affair/escándalo de Watergate serie de escándalos en los cuales estaba involucrada la administración del presidente Richard Nixon, incluyendo el robo a las oficinas centrales demócratas, situadas en el edificio Watergate en Washington, D.C., en 1972; llevó a la renuncia de Nixon en 1974 (pág. 563)

weather/tiempo condición de la atmósfera terrestre en un lugar y momento determinado (pág. 15)

Whigs/*Whigs* miembros del viejo Partido Republicano Nacional, liderado por John Quincy Adams, que incluía muchas personas de negocios, plantadores sureños y ex-federalistas (pág. 363)

Whiskey Rebellion/rebelión del whisky protesta de 1794 con respecto a un impuesto aplicado a todas las bebidas alcohólicas producidas y vendidas en los Estados Unidos (pág. 282)

Wilmot Proviso/cláusula de Wilmot ley aprobada en 1846 que proscribía la esclavitud en todos los territorios ganados a México por los Estados Unidos (pág. 461)

women's rights movement/ movimiento de los derechos de la mujer campaña organizada para obtener el derecho a la propiedad, la educación, y otros derechos para la mujer (pág. 446)

World War I/Primera Guerra Mundial guerra librada entre 1914 y 1918 en la cual Gran Bretaña, Francia, Rusia, Bélgica, Italia, Japón, los Estados Unidos y otros aliados vencieron a Alemania, el imperio Austrio-Húngaro, el imperio Otomano y Bulgaria (pág. 550)

World War II/Segunda Guerra Mundial guerra librada entre 1939 y 1945 en la cual Inglaterra, Francia, la Unión Soviética, los Estados Unidos y otros aliados derrotaron a Alemania, Italia, Japón y otros aliados (pág. 556)

writ of assistance/mandato de asistencia documento legal que permitía a los funcionarios de la aduana inglesa realizar la inspección de la carga de un barco sin tener que alegar razón alguna (pág. 150)

X

XYZ Affair/*Affair XYZ* intento francés de 1797 de sobornar a los Estados Unidos exigiendo pagos antes de que comenzaran las conversaciones sobre la captura por parte de los franceses de barcos estadounidenses neutrales (pág. 292)

Y

Yankee/yanki sobrenombre de los comerciantes de Nueva Inglaterra que dominaban el comercio colonial (pág. 121)

Spanish Glossary

Index

Page numbers that are italicized refer to illustrations or quotations. An *m, p, c, g,* or *go* after a page number refers to a map *(m)*, picture *(p)*, chart *(c)*, graph *(g)*, or graphic organizer *(go)* on that page. A *q* refers to a quote within the text. A *ps* refers to a primary source feature.

Index

Index

Index

Index

Credits

Staff Credits

The people who made up *The American Nation* team—representing design services, editorial, editorial services, electronic publishing technology, manufacturing and inventory planning, market research, marketing services, online services and multimedia development, planning and budgeting, product planning, production services, project office, publishing processes, and rights and permissions—are listed below. Bold type denotes the core team members.

Ernest Albanese, Robert Aleman, Diane Alimena, **Margaret Antonini**, Rachel Avenia-Prol, Penelope Baker, Renée Beach, Rhett Conklin, Martha Conway, **Lisa DelGatto**, Marlies Dwyer, Libby Forsyth, Doreen Galbraith, Catalina Gavilanes, **Nancy Gilbert**, Evan Holstrom, **John Kingston**, Vicki Lamb, Mary Sue Langan, Carol Lavis, **Marian Manners**, Vickie Menanteaux, LaShonda Morris, Carrie O'Connor, James O'Neill, **Steven Palmé**, **Robert Prol**, **Maureen Raymond**, Bruce Rolff, Gerry Schrenk, Mildred Schulte, Melissa Shustyk, Annette Simmons, Robin Sullivan, Frank Tangredi.

Additional Credits

Greg Abrom, Susan Andariese, Rui Camarinha, John A. Carle, Orquidea Cepin, Lisa Ferrari, Jacki Hasko, Beth Hyslip, Helen Issackedes, Raegan Keida, Elizabeth Kiszonas, Steve Lewin, Kathleen Mercandetti, Art Mkrtchyan, Kenneth Myett, Jeremy Naidus, Xavier W. Niz, Tamara Pellek, Andrew Roney, Robert Siek, Elaine Soares, Linda Westerhoff, Jeff Zoda.

Text Credits

Grateful acknowledgment is made to the following for copyrighted material

The Mother of Nations Excerpt from *The Mother of Nations* by Joseph Bruchac. Copyright © 1989 by Joseph Bruchac. Published by The Crossing Press, 1989. Reprinted by permission.

I Have A Dream "I Have A Dream" by Dr. Martin Luther King, Jr. Copyright © 1963 by Martin Luther King, Jr. Copyright renewed 1991 by Coretta Scott King. Reprinted by arrangement with The Heirs to the Estate of Martin Luther King, Jr., c/o Writer's House, Inc. as agent for the proprietor.

Note: Every effort has been made to locate the copyright owner of material used in this textbook. Omissions brought to our attention will be corrected in subsequent editions.

Map and Art Credits

Maps: Mapping Specialists Limited; **Art: 18–19** John Edwards & Associates; **Charts and Graphs:** Kathleen Mercandetti.

Photo Credits

Photo Research: Omni-Photo Communications, Inc.

Cover and Title Page: Richard Walker/Pearson Education/PH School. Drum: Collections of the Fort Ticonderoga Museum; **ii** *m.* Collections of the Fort Ticonderoga Museum; *t.* Richard Walker/Pearson Education/PH School; **iv** Richard Walker/Pearson Education/PH School; **vi** *t.* North American kachina doll, Hopi tribe. Horniman Museum. ©Michael Holford; *b.* The Granger Collection, New York; **vii** *t.* Christy, Howard Chandler, *Scene at the Signing of the Constitution*, April 1940. Architect of the Capitol; *b.* Courtesy of The Bostonian Society, Old State House; **viii** *t.* ©Copyright 2003 PhotoDisc, Inc.; *b.* George Washington Banner: watercolor, graphite and pen ink on paper. .733 x .534 m. (28¾ in. x 21¹/₁₆ in.). Index of American Design, ©1993 National Gallery of Art. Photograph ©Board of Trustees, National Gallery of Art, Washington DC; **ix** *t.* National Museum of American History, Department of Social History, Political History Collection, Smithsonian Institution; *b.* ©1993 North Wind Picture Archives; **x** *t. Attack at Battery Wagner* © 1993 Tom Lovell © 1993 The Greenwich Workshop, Inc. Courtesy of The Greenwich Workshop, Inc., Shelton CT; **xi** *b.* The Granger Collection, New York; **xx** ©Copyright 2003 PhotoDisc, Inc. **xl–1** Leigh, William Robinson. *Grand Canyon*, 1911. Oil on canvas, 66" x 99". Collection of The Newark Museum, Gift of Henry Washington Wack, 1930. Inv.: 30.203. The Newark Museum, Newark, New Jersey, USA. Art Resource, NY; **2** *l.* Jacques Le Moyne, *Chief Athore and Rene de Laudonniere*. Gouache and metallic pigments on vellum, with traces of black chalk outlines, 27 June 1564. Print Collection, Miriam and Ira D. Wallach Division of Art, Prints and Photographs, The New York Public Library, Astor, Lenox and Tilden Foundations; *r.* ©Hulton Getty/Archive Photos; **3** *l.* The Granger Collection, New York; *r.* Stone; **4** ©Bettmann/CORBIS; **6** ©H. De Lespinasse/The Image Bank; **11** ©1988 Addison Geary/Stock Boston; **13** ©UPI-Bettmann/CORBIS; **14** *t.* ©Adam Jones/Photo Researchers, Inc.; *m.* ©Ansel Adams Publishing Rights Trust/CORBIS; **20** Courtesy of Simon & Schuster; **21** ©Punch-Bill Tidy/Rothco; **23** *m.l.* Courtesy of the Massachusetts Historical Commission, Office of the Secretary of the Commonwealth, City Square Archaeological District, Boston; *m.r.* Courtesy of the Massachusetts Historical Commission, Office of the Secretary of the Commonwealth, American Glass Company site, South Boston; *b.* ©Cary Wolinsky/Stock Boston; **26** Stone; **27** *t.r.* ©2000 The Stock Market/Roger Ball; *t.* ©1997 The Stock Market/Bill Stormont; **28** Denise DeLuise/First Image West, Inc.; **31** *t.l.* ©Roman Soumar/CORBIS; Junior Achievement; *t.l.* Hulton Getty/Liaison

Agency, Inc.; *t.r.* From the Walker Collection of A'Lelia Bundles; *t.r.* From the Walker Collection of A'Lelia Bundles; **34** The Granger Collection, New York; **35** *l.* © Dorling Kindersley. Courtesy of St. Bride Printing; *r.* Diego Rivera, *The Great City of Tenochtitlan*, 1945. Detail of mural, 4.92 x 9.71 m. Patio Corridor, National Palace, Mexico City, D.F., Mexico. Schalkwijk/Art Resource, NY; **36** ©Lowell Georgia/CORBIS; **40** ©North Wind Picture Archives; **41** ©Craig Aurness/CORBIS; **42** ©Denver Art Museum. Accession #1968.330A; **43** *t.r.* ©British Museum; *t.r.* ©British Museum; **45** *t.l.* Inuit polar bears, 14th–15th century. University of British Columbia/The Bridgeman Art Library, London/New York; *t.l.* Two Basket Hats .7464: Twined: hazel shoots, willow root, conifer root, bear grass, maidenhair, fern stems/ .7515: Twined: conifer root and bear grass wefts. The Brooklyn Museum 05.588.7464 + 05.588.7515 Museum Expedition 1905, Museum Collection Fund. ©Justin Kerr/The Brooklyn Museum; *t.l.* North American kachina doll, Hopi tribe. Horniman Museum. ©Michael Holford; *t.l.* The University Museum, University of Pennsylvania (Neg. T4-303); *t.r.* ©2003 British Museum; *t.r.* Werner Forman Archive, Smithsonian Institution, Washington, DC/Art Resource, NY; *t.r.* ©Canadian Museum of Civilization, Photo S93-9725; **46** Knife River Indian Villages National Historic Site, National Park Service Photo by Fred Armstrong; **47** Neg./Trans. no. K 10302. Courtesy Department of Library Services, American Museum of Natural History; **50** The Granger Collection, New York; **52** ©Aldona Sabalis/Photo Researchers, Inc.; **53** *b.r.* The Granger Collection, New York; *b.* ©ChinaStock Photo Library. All rights reserved; **55** The Granger Collection, New York; **57** Art Resource, NY; **58** Limbourg Brothers. The Month of October. Sowing. Detail. Chateau du Louvre. Tres Riches Heures du Duc de Berry. Musee Conde, Chantilly, France. Giraudon/Art Resource, NY; **60** Ivory salt cellar, Benin, 16th century. Nationalmuseet, Copenhagen, Denmark/Bridgeman Art Library, London/New York; **61** ©Copyright 2003 PhotoDisc, Inc.; **63** Florentine Codex, (16th century). Ms Palat. 218–220 Book IX Montezuma II (1466–1520) receiving tributes, from an account of the Aztecs written and illustrated by Bernardino de Sahagun, Spanish, mid 16th century. Biblioteca Medicea-Laurenziana, Florence, Italy/Bridgeman Art Library, London/New York; **64** Prentice Hall; **65** Courtesy Haudenosaunee Onondaga Nation and the New York State Museum; **66** *l.* Sebastiano del Piombo (ca. 1485–1547), *Christopher Columbus*. All rights reserved. Copyright © by the Metropolitan Museum of Art, NY; *r.* ©Wolfgang Kaehler/CORBIS; **67** Equity Management Inc.; **68** Werner Forman Archive/Statens Historiska Museum, Stockholm/ Art Resource, NY; **69** *b.r.* Rare Books Division, New York Public Library; *b.l.* Museum fur Kunst und Gewerbe, Hamburg;

74 Photograph courtesy Florida Division of Historical Resources, Bureau of Archaeological Research; **75** *Hernando Cortes (1485–1547, Spanish conquistador) meeting Indians of Tlaxcala region, Mexico, folio 207R of 1579 manuscript* Historia de las Indias by Diego Duran. ©The Art Archive/Biblioteca Nacional Madrid/Dagli Orti; **81** Image Select/Art Resource, NY; **83** *m.* ©Fotopic/Omni-Photo Communications, Inc.; *b.r.* ©North Wind Picture Archives; **85** The Granger Collection, New York; **86** ©Esbin/Anderson/Omni-Photo Communications, Inc.; **87** Courtesy of The Association for the Preservation of Virginia Antiquities; **88** *t.* ©Richard T. Nowitz/CORBIS; *t.l. Captain John Smith, 1st Governor of Virginia,* c. 1616 (oil on canvas) by English School (17th century). The Berger Collection at the Denver Art Museum, USA/The Bridgeman Art Library, London/New York; **89** *Pocahontas 1616* (detail), National Portrait Gallery, Smithsonian Institution/Art Resource, NY; **92** *b.* Jack Clifton, *First Legislature in the New World.* Oil on canvas. State Capitol, Commonwealth of Virginia. Courtesy The Library of Virginia; Courtesy Cassell & Co.; From "The Chronicle of Western Fashion" by John Peacock, published by Harry N. Abrams, Inc., New York. Used by permission of Thames & Hudson; **93** Courtesy of the Pilgrim Society, Plymouth, Massachusetts; **95** ©Bettmann/CORBIS; **96** ©Ted Curtin/ Stock Boston; **100** *l.* The Granger Collection, New York; *r.* The Historical Society of Pennsylvania (HSP), *Silver Gorget* by Joseph Richardson [S-8-120]; **101** *l.* Peale, Charles Wilson (1741–1827), *Jonathan Edwards.* Engraved by J. D. Gross. Peale Museum; *r.* Courtesy of the Library of Congress; **102** John Lewis Stage; **104** ©Bettmann/CORBIS **105** The Granger Collection, New York; **106** ©Stone; **108** Chippendale mahogany side chair, Philadelphia, 1765–1770. From the collection of May and Howard Joynt/Christie's Images; **109** The Granger Collection, New York; **113** The Granger Collection, New York; **117** Photographer: Ron Blunt. Courtesy of Drayton Hall, Charleston, South Carolina. A property of the National Trust for Historic Preservation. All Rights Reserved; **118** Courtesy, American Antiquarian Society; **120** Culver Pictures, Inc.; **121** *Moses Marcy,* unknown artist. Oil on wood overmantel panel from the Moses Marcy House, Southbridge, MA, mid-18th century (no longer standing). Old Sturbridge Village, Southbridge, MA. [20.19.1] Photo by Henry E. Peach; **124** The Granger Collection, New York; **125** Brady/Prentice Hall, Inc.; **127** The Granger Collection, New York; **129** *t.l.* The Granger Collection, New York; *t.r.* ©Aaron Haupt/Photo Researchers, Inc.; **131** *t.* Chamberlin Mason (English, died 1787), *Portrait of Benjamin Franklin,* 1762 (detail). Oil on canvas, 50⅜" x 40¾". [56-88-1] Philadelphia Museum of Art: Gift of Mr. and Mrs. Wharton Sinkler; *b.l.* Courtesy of the Historical and Interpretive Collections of The Franklin Institute, Philadelphia, PA. Photo by Charles F. Penniman, Jr.; *b.r.* Courtesy of the Historical and Interpretive Collections of The Franklin Institute, Philadelphia, PA. Photo by Charles F. Penniman, Jr.; *m.t.* Musee de l'Amitie Franco-Americaine, Bierancourt, France. ©Photograph by Erich Lessing/Art Resource, NY; *m.b.* Musee de l'Amitie Franco-Americaine, Bierancourt, France. ©Photograph by Erich Lessing/Art Resource, NY; **138** The Granger Collection, New York; **139** *l.* The Granger Collection, New York; *r.* The Granger Collection, New York; **140** The Granger Collection, New York; **141** The Granger Collection, New York; **146** Courtesy of the Library of Congress; **147** *b.l.* The Granger Collection, New York; *b.r.* The Granger Collection, New York; **149** Colonial Williamsburg Foundation; **151** *t.l.* Dawe, Phillip (c. 1750–c.1785). *The Bostonians Paying the Excise-Man or Tarring & Feathering.* London, 1774. Colored Engraving. The Gilder Lehman Collection on deposit at the Pierpont Morgan Library. GL 4961.01. Photography: Joseph Zehavi. The Pierpont Morgan Library. Art Resource, NY; *t.r.* AP Photo/Tony Dejak; **152** The Granger Collection, New York; **154** The Granger Collection, New York; **155** Courtesy, American Antiquarian Society; **156** Samuel Adams (1722–1803) American Revolutionary politician, chief agitator of the Boston Tea Party by Anonymous. Museum of Fine Arts, Boston, MA, USA/The Bridgeman Art Library, London/New York; **157** *t.* The Granger Collection, New York; *m.r.* Courtesy of The Bostonian Society, Old State House; **159** Lisa Poole/AP/Wide World Photos; **164** AP/Wide World Photos; **165** The Granger Collection, New York; **166** *l.* The Granger Collection, New York; *r.* Courtesy of The Bostonian Society, Old State House; **167** *l. Marquis de Lafayette* by Francesco-Guiseppe Casanova, ca. 1781–85, oil on canvas, 18.5 x 16.5 in., accession 1939.9. Collection of The New-York Historical Society; *r.* Gallery of the Republic; **168** West Point Museum Collections, United States Military Academy, West Point, New York. Presented by F. Donald Campbell, No 18,947. Photograph by Paul Warchol, New York; **169** The Granger Collection, New York; **172** The Granger Collection, New York; **173** *m.r.* Independence National Historical Park Collection; *m.r.* The Granger Collection, New York; **177** Letraset Phototone; **176–177** The Granger Collection, New York; **181** The Granger Collection, New York; **186** Unknown artist, *Black Privateer,* panel 4, panel reverse F, oil, ca. 1780. Courtesy of Alexander A. McBurney, M.D.; **187** Valentine Museum, Richmond, Virginia; **189** © Bettmann/CORBIS; **190** *t.l.* The Granger Collection, New York; *t.r.* ©1996 North Wind Picture Archives; *b.* The Granger Collection, New York; **191** Courtesy of Ted Speigel; **194** ©Christine Pemberton/Omni-Photo Communications, Inc.; **197** Courtesy of the Library of Congress; **198** *l.* The Granger Collection, New York; *r.* The Granger Collection, New York; *m.* National Museum of American History, Department of Social History, Political History Collection, Smithsonian Institution; **199** Bas-relief sculpture depicting the signing of the United States Constitution at the South entrance of the Nebraska State Capitol, Lincoln, Nebraska. Image provided by Nebraska Capitol Collections; **200** *Thomas Jefferson.* Unknown artist. Oil on fragment of white marble. Photography by Jeff Goldman, 1986. Maryland Historical Society, Baltimore, Maryland; **202** ©Bettmann/ CORBIS; **205** *m.r.* ©North Wind Picture Archives; *b.* ©North Wind Picture Archives; **206** ©Leif Skoogfors/Woodfin Camp & Associates; **207** ©Grace Davies/Omni-Photo Communications, Inc.; **208** Peale, Charles Wilson, *James Madison,* 1783. Courtesy of the Library of Congress; **209** Christy, Howard Chandler, *Scene at the Signing of the Constitution,* April 1940. Architect of the Capitol; **211** The Granger Collection, New York; **212** *t.* ©Nathan Beck/Omni-Photo Communications, Inc.; *t.l.* Jean-Antoine Houdon (1741–1828), *Benjamin Franklin* (ca. 1778). Plaster bust, 84.2 x 66.6 x 41.1 cm. Gift of the estate of George Francis Parkman, 1908. Boston Athenaeum; **215** National Museum of American History, Smithsonian Institution; **221** Courtesy of the American Antiquarian Society; **246** *l.* ©Joseph Sohm, Chromosohm Inc./CORBIS; *r.* The Granger Collection, New York; **247** *l.* National Museum of American History, Smithsonian Institution; *r.* ©Paul Conklin/ PhotoEdit; **248** Cover, *Time Magazine,* Nov. 20, 2000, Vol. 156, No. 21.TimePix, Inc.; **249** *l.* ©Copyright 2001 PhotoDisc, Inc.; *r.* ©1997 Corbis Stock Market/Ed Wheeler; **252** The Granger Collection, New York; **255** ©Spencer Grant/Stock Boston; **257** ©Arthur Grace/Stock Boston; **259** ©Stock Boston; **262** ©Stephen Varone/Omni-Photo Communications, Inc.; **263** ©Michael Mancuso/Omni-Photo Communications, Inc.; **265** *People Weekly* ©1997 Andrew Kaufman; **266** Art Resource, NY; **267** ©The New Yorker Collection 2003, Barney Tobey, from cartoonbank.com. All Rights Reserved; **269** George Jones III/Photo Researchers, Inc. **274–275** John Hill, *Junction of the Erie and Northern (Champlain) Canals.* Aquatint, Number 34684. Courtesy of The New-York Historical Society; **276** *l. George Washington Banner:* watercolor, graphite and pen ink on paper. .733 x .534 m. (28¾ in. x 21¹/₁₆ in.). Index of American Design, ©1993 National Gallery of Art. Photograph ©Board of Trustees, National Gallery of Art, Washington DC; *r.* Courtesy of the Library of Congress; *c.* Courtesy of the Library of Congress; **277** Copyright © By the Metropolitan Museum of Art, NY **278** ©2000 North Wind Picture Archives; **279** ©Chromosohm/Sohm MCMXCII/Photo Researchers, Inc.; **280** The Granger Collection, New York; **283** *l.* Isaac Fowle (1818–1853), *Lady with a Scarf Figurehead.* Courtesy of The Bostonian Society/Old State House; *t.r. Swordsman Whirligig,* c. 1870. Carved, polychromed wood, 44.5 x 12.7 x 9.5 (excluding base) (17½ x 5 x 3¾). ©Shelburne Museum, Shelburne, Vermont (27.FW-43). Photograph by Ken Burris; *m.* The Granger Collection, New York; *b.r. Gabriel,* c. 1800. Sawn, polychromed wood with iron reinforcements. 33 x 85.1 x 1.3 (13 x 33½ x ½). Found in Ridgefield, Connecticut. ©Shelburne Museum, Shelburne, Vermont (27.FW-2). Photograph by Ken Burris; **284** ©Jorn Fabricius; **285** ©Gianni Dagli

York; **483** The Granger Collection, New York; **484** ©1997 North Wind Picture Archives; **485** *l.* Courtesy of the Library of Congress; *r.* Culver Pictures, Inc.; **486** West Point Museum Collections, United States Military Academy, West Point, New York; **489** ©Omni-Photo Communications, Inc.; **490** Smithsonian Institute; **494** Photograph by Matthew Brady. ©CORBIS; **495** ©2001 North Wind Picture Archives; **496** *Unidentified African-American Civil War soldier.* Tintype, unknown photographer, no date. Chicago Historical Society, ICHi-08068; **498** *Attack at Battery Wagner* © 1993 Tom Lovell © 1993 The Greenwich Workshop, Inc. Courtesy of The Greenwich Workshop, Inc., Shelton CT; **500** *Home Coming, 1865,* watercolor by William L. Sheppard. The Museum of the Confederacy, Richmond, Virginia. Copy Photography by Katherine Wetzel; *l.* Massachusetts Commandery, Military Order of the Loyal Legion and the U.S. Army Military History Institute; *t.l.* U.S. Army Military History Institute; *m.l.* U.S. Army Military History Institute; **501** *r.* ©Eric Kroll/Omni-Photo Communications, Inc.; **505** ©CORBIS; **506** The Granger Collection, New York; **511** Courtesy of the Library of Congress; **513** Photograph by Matthew Brady. Culver Pictures, Inc.; **514** *l.* Culver Pictures, Inc.; *r.* Culver Pictures, Inc.; *m.* Upholstered walnut parlor rocking chair. Used by President Abraham Lincoln at Ford's Theatre, Washington, DC, April 14, 1865. H: 10.00 x 106.68 cm., W: 36.625 in., L: 34.5 in. (29.1451.1). From the Collections of Henry Ford Museum and Greenfield Village, No. 11-A-35(A); **515** *l.* The Granger Collection, New York; *r.* The Granger Collection, New York; **516** ©Bern Keating; **517** The Granger Collection, New York; **518** Courtesy of Ford's Theatre, Washington, DC. Photo by Andrew Lautman; **521** AP Photo/Lou Krasky; **523** The Granger Collection, New York; **525** *t.* ©Copyright 2001 PhotoDisc, Inc.; *b.* ©Bettmann/COR-BIS; **526** ©1994 North Wind Picture Archives; **527** The Granger Collection, New York; **528** The Granger Collection, New York; **530** SuperStock; **532** ©1998 North Wind Picture Archives; **536** The National Portrait Gallery, Smithsonian Institution; **537** ©Copyright 2003 PhotoDisc, Inc.; **540** *l.* Culver Pictures, Inc.; *r.* Courtesy of the Library of Congress; **541** *l.* ©Robert Mills/Bettmann/CORBIS; *r.,* staff photographer Thomas E. Franklin/©2001 *The Record* (Bergen County, NJ)/CORBIS/SABA; **542** *m.l.* ©1996 North Wind Picture Archives; **544** *m.l.* The Granger Collection, New York; **545** *t.* ©Bettmann/CORBIS; *m.r.* East-Asiatic Company, Limited, Baltic America Line inspection card for immigration and steerage passengers. SS *Estonia.* Port of departure, Danzig, Poland. Date of departure, 20 November 1925. Stamped "Sent to Hospital, Dec. 4, 1925." National Park Service, Statue of Liberty National Monument; **547** *m.r.* Photo by R. Y. Young. Courtesy of the Library of Congress; **548** The Granger Collection, New York; **550** *t.l.* Equity Management Inc.; **552** *t.r.* ©Jack Kurtz/Impact Visuals; *inset* Courtesy of the Veterans of Foreign Wars of the United States; *b.* ©CORBIS; **553** *Vauxhall 30/98*

Wensum, 1925 by Griffin, 1966. Private Collection./The Bridgeman Art Library, London/New York; **555** ©CORBIS; **556** *t.l.* ©H. K. Owen/Black Star; **558** *t.l.* Flag Research Center; *b.l.* The Granger Collection, New York; **560** Steve Schapiro/Black Star; **562** National Museum of American History, Department of Social History, Political History Collection, Smithsonian Institution; **564** ©Ron Edmonds/AP/Wide World Photos; **570** The Granger Collection, New York; **571** ©Copyright 2003 PhotoDisc, Inc.; **572** ©Ansel Adams Publishing Rights Trust/CORBIS; ©Copyright 2003 PhotoDisc, Inc.; **573** The Granger Collection, New York; ©Copyright 2003 PhotoDisc, Inc.; **574** Courtesy Haudenosaunee Onondaga Nation and the New York State Museum; ©Copyright 2003 PhotoDisc, Inc.; **575** © Dorling Kindersley. Courtesy of St. Bride Printing; ©Copyright 2003 PhotoDisc, Inc; **576** Photograph courtesy Florida Division of Historical Resources, Bureau of Archaeological Research; ©Copyright 2003 PhotoDisc, Inc.; **577** *Captain John Smith, 1st Governor of Virginia,* c. 1616 (oil on canvas) by English School (17th century). The Berger Collection at the Denver Art Museum, USA/The Bridgeman Art Library, London/New York; ©Copyright 2003 PhotoDisc, Inc.; **578** The Granger Collection, New York; ©Copyright 2003 PhotoDisc, Inc.; **579** Chamberlin Mason (English, died 1787), *Portrait of Benjamin Franklin,* 1762 (detail). Oil on canvas, 50³/₈" x 40³/₄". [56-88-1] Philadelphia Museum of Art: Gift of Mr. and Mrs. Wharton Sinkler; ©Copyright 2003 PhotoDisc, Inc.; **580** The Granger Collection, New York; ©Copyright 2003 PhotoDisc, Inc.; **581** Colonial Williamsburg Foundation; ©Copyright 2003 PhotoDisc, Inc.; **582** Independence National Historical Park Collection; ©Copyright 2003 PhotoDisc, Inc.; **583** Culver Pictures, Inc.; ©Copyright 2003 PhotoDisc, Inc.; **584** ©Leif Skoogfors/Woodfin Camp & Associates; ©Copyright 2003 PhotoDisc, Inc.; **585** Culver Pictures, Inc.; ©Copyright 2003 PhotoDisc, Inc.; **586** *b.l.* Corel Professional Photos CD-ROM™; ©Copyright 2003 PhotoDisc, Inc.; **587** ©1997 Corbis Stock Market/Ed Wheeler; ©Copyright 2003 PhotoDisc, Inc.; **588** Art Resource, NY; ©Copyright 2003 PhotoDisc, Inc.; **589** *Thomas Jefferson.* Unknown artist. Oil on fragment of white marble. Maryland Historical Society, Baltimore, Maryland; ©Copyright 2003 PhotoDisc, Inc.; **590** Photograph ©1995 Fred J. Maroon; ©Copyright 2003 PhotoDisc, Inc.; **591** *t.* Donovan Reese/Stone; *b.* ©Copyright 2003 PhotoDisc, Inc.; **592** The Granger Collection, New York; ©Copyright 2003 PhotoDisc, Inc.; **593** The Granger Collection, New York; ©Copyright 2003 PhotoDisc, Inc.; **594** Index Stock Imagery, Inc.; ©Copyright 2003 PhotoDisc, Inc.; **595** Courtesy of the Library of Congress; ©Copyright 2003 PhotoDisc, Inc.; **596** ©2000 North Wind Picture Archives; ©Copyright 2003 PhotoDisc, Inc.; **597** Seaver Center for Western History Research, Natural History Museum of Los Angeles County. Museum Collection Number 277; ©Copyright 2003 PhotoDisc, Inc.; **598** The Granger Collection, New York; ©Copyright

2003 PhotoDisc, Inc.; **599** ©1998 North Wind Picture Archives; ©Copyright 2003 PhotoDisc, Inc.; **600** *r.* Culver Pictures, Inc.; ©Copyright 2003 PhotoDisc, Inc.; **601** The Granger Collection, New York; ©Copyright 2003 PhotoDisc, Inc.; **602** Eastman Johnson, *A Ride for Liberty—the Fugitive Slaves.* (detail) The Brooklyn Museum; ©Copyright 2003 PhotoDisc, Inc.; **603** The Granger Collection, New York; **604** The Granger Collection, New York; **605** National Portrait Gallery, Smithsonian Institution; **606** The Granger Collection, New York; **607** Culver Pictures, Inc.; *l.* ©CORBIS; **608** ©Bettmann/CORBIS; **609** ©Robert Mills/Bettmann/ CORBIS; **610** *l.* National Portrait Gallery, Smithsonian Institution/Art Resource, NY; *m.l.* National Portrait Gallery, Smithsonian Institution/Art Resource, NY; *m.l.* White House Collection, copyright White House Historical Association; *m.t.* National Portrait Gallery, Smithsonian Institution/Art Resource, NY; *b.l.* National Portrait Gallery, Smithsonian Institution/Art Resource, NY; *t.r.* White House Collection, copyright White House Historical Association; *m.m.* National Portrait Gallery, Smithsonian Institution/ Art Resource, NY; *m.r.* National Portrait Gallery, Smithsonian Institution/Art Resource, NY; *m.m.* White House Collection, copyright White House Historical Association; *m.r.* National Portrait Gallery, Smithsonian Institution/Art Resource, NY; *m.b.* White House Collection, copyright White House Historical Association; *b.r.* National Portrait Gallery, Smithsonian Institution/ Art Resource, NY; **611** *t.l.* White House Collection, copyright White House Historical Association; *m.l.* White House Collection, copyright White House Historical Association; *m.l.* White House Collection, copyright White House Historical Association; *m.t.* National Portrait Gallery, Smithsonian Institution/Art Resource, NY; *t.r.* National Portrait Gallery, Smithsonian Institution/Art Resource, NY; *m.m.* White House Collection, copyright White House Historical Association; *m.r.* National Portrait Gallery, Smithsonian Institution/Art Resource, NY; *m.m.* National Portrait Gallery, Smithsonian Institution/Art Resource, NY; *m.r.* National Portrait Gallery, Smithsonian Institution/Art Resource, NY; *b.r.* White House Collection, copyright White House Historical Association; *m.b.* White House Collection, copyright White House Historical Association; *b.r.* White House Collection, copyright White House Historical Association; **612** *t.l.* National Portrait Gallery, Smithsonian Institution/Art Resource, NY; *m.l.* White House Collection, copyright White House Historical Association; *m.l.* White House Collection, copyright White House Historical Association; *b.l.* White House Collection, copyright White House Historical Association; *m.t.* National Portrait Gallery, Smithsonian Institution/Art Resource, NY; *t.r.* National Portrait Gallery, Smithsonian Institution/Art Resource, NY; *m.m.* White House Collection, copyright White House Historical Association; *m.r.* White House Collection, copyright White House Historical Association; *m.r.* White House Collection, copyright White House Historical Association; *m.m.* White House Collection,

Credits

Useful Questions

How's it going? Nǐ zěnme yàng? *(nee dzummuh yahng)*

Do you speak English? Nǐ huì shuō Yīngyǔ ma? *(nee hway shwaw eeng yew mah)*

Can you help me? Néng bùnéng bāngmáng? *(nung boo nung bahng mahng)*

What is your name? Nǐ jiào shénme míngzi? *(nee jyaow shummah meeng dzuh)*

What time is it? Xiànzài jǐ diǎn zhōng? *(shyan dzye jee dyan joong)*

What's the weather like? Tiānqi zěnme yàng? *(tyan chee dzummuh yahng)*

How much is this? Zhèige duōshǎo qián? *(jay guh dwaw shaow chyan)*

Where do I find . . . ? Zài nǎr zhǎo . . . ? *(dzye nar jaow . . .)*

Where is the bathroom? Cèsuǒ zài nǎr? *(tsuh swaw dzye nar)*

What time do you open/close? Nín jǐ diǎn zhōng kāi/guān mén? *(neen jee dyan joong kye/gwahn mun)*

Could you please talk more slowly? Qǐng nǐ shuō màn yìdiǎr. *(cheeng nee shwaw mahn ee dyar)*

Could you repeat that please? Qǐng nǐ zài shuō yícì. (cheeng nee dzye shwaw ee tsuh)

Useful Expressions

Hello. Nǐ hǎo. *(nee how)*

Good morning. Zǎo. *(dzaow)*

Good night. Wǎn ān. *(wahn ahn)*

Please. Qǐng. *(cheeng)*

Thank you. Xièxiè. *(shyeh shyeh)*

Excuse me. Duìbùqǐ. *(dway boo chee)*

I'm so sorry. Hěn bàoqiàn. *(hun baow chyan)*

I don't understand. Wǒ bùdǒng. *(waw boo doong)*

Phrases for Emergencies

Help! Jiù mìng! *(jyo meeng)*

Stop, thief! Zhuā zéi! *(jwah dzay)*

Fire! Zháohuǒ! *(jaow hwaw)*

Call an ambulance! Jiào jiùhùchē! *(jyaow jyo hoo chuh)*

Call the police! Jiào jǐngchá! *(jyaow jeeng chah)*

I am sick. Wǒ bìng le. *(waw beeng luh)*

Get a doctor. Kuài qù zhǎo yīshēng. *(kwye chyew jaow ee shung)*

I'm lost. Wǒ mílù le. *(waw mee loo luh)*

The Chinese Calendar

Days

Monday Xīngqīyī *(sheeng chee ee)*

Tuesday Xīngqī'èr *(sheeng chee are)*

Wednesday Xīngqīsān *(sheeng chee sahn)*

Thursday Xīngqīsì *(sheeng chee suh)*

Friday Xīngqīwǔ *(sheeng chee woo)*

Saturday Xīngqīliù *(sheeng chee lyo)*

Sunday Xīngqītiān *(sheeng chee tyan)*

Months

January Yīyuè *(ee yweh)*

February Èryuè *(are yweh)*

March Sānyuè *(sahn yweh)*

April Sìyuè *(suh yweh)*

May Wǔyuè *(woo yweh)*

June Liùyuè *(lyo yweh)*

July Qīyuè *(chee yweh)*

August Bāyuè *(bah yweh)*

September Jiǔyuè *(jyo yweh)*

October Shíyuè *(shir yweh)*

November Shíyīyuè *(shir ee yweh)*

December Shí'èryuè *(shir are yweh)*

Numbers

0 líng *(leeng)*	15 shíwǔ *(shir woo)*	30 sānshí *(sahn shir)*
1 yī *(ee)*	16 shíliù *(shir lyo)*	40 sìshí *(suh shir)*
2 èr *(are)*	17 shíqī *(shir chee)*	50 wǔshí *(woo shir)*
3 sān *(sahn)*	18 shíbā *(shir bah)*	60 liùshí *(lyo shir)*
4 sì *(suh)*	19 shíjiǔ *(shir jyoe)*	70 qīshí *(chee shir)*
5 wǔ *(woo)*	20 èrshí *(are shir)*	80 bāshí *(bah shir)*
6 liù *(lyo)*	21 èrshíyī *(are shir ee)*	90 jiǔshí *(jyoe shir)*
7 qī *(chee)*	22 èrshí'èr *(are shir are)*	100 yì bǎi *(ee bye)*
8 bā *(bah)*	23 èrshísān *(are shir sahn)*	1,000 yì qiān *(ee chyan)*
9 jiǔ *(jyoe)*	24 èrshísì *(are shir ssuh)*	10,000 yí wàn *(ee wahn)*
10 shí *(shir)*	25 èrshíwǔ *(are shir woo)*	100,000 shí wàn *(shir wahn)*
11 shíyī *(shir ee)*	26 èrshíliù *(are shir lyo)*	1,000,000 yì bǎi wàn *(ee bye wahn)*
12 shí'èr *(shir are)*	27 èrshíqī *(are shir chee)*	100,000,000 yí yì *(ee ee)*
13 shísān *(shir sahn)*	28 èrshíbā *(are shir bah)*	
14 shísì *(shir suh)*	29 èrshíjiǔ *(are shir jyoe)*	

For Dummies: Bestselling Book Series for Beginners

Chinese

FOR

DUMMIES®

REVISED EDITION

Right up there with Woo Fong Restaurant was *The Inn of the Sixth Happiness*— that 1958 classic that had Ingrid Bergman, the missionary, saving all those orphans in northern China during the Sino-Japanese War. Acknowledgments to those who played a part in my early childhood exposure to all things Chinese can't be made until that film's name has been solemnly uttered. In addition to clinching my passion for China, it made me want to adopt a hundred orphans from Xi'an, and it began my great love affair with the movies.

First in line for childhood recognition is my beloved aunt, Carol Rothenstein, who regularly schlepped a gaggle of us cousins down to New York City's Chinatown and plied us with all manner of colorful Chinese knick-knacks to take home.

To my childhood friend, Cynthia Sargent, who went with me on jaunts to visit our elementary school buddy Wanda Chin at her family's Laundry (Chin's) on Springfield Boulevard, where the back room doubled as home for the family of four. I can still smell the freshly starched shirts and see the swirls of steam wafting up from the ironing boards as we passed by on our way to the back.

From my days at Hunter College, where I distinguished myself by being the only Jewish kid to try to join the Chinese Students Association, I'm proud to have hung out with the likes of Jon Ho, Winnie Chin, Mon Lan Jee, Nora Lee, Karen Lee, and our classmate Conmay, whose untimely death while we were all undergrads bonded us for one brief but memorable moment. Jon and Winnie in particular have remained good, loyal friends, and I'm grateful for their fun (Jon) and calming (Winnie) presence this past year. Mention of Hunter College in the '70s wouldn't be complete if it didn't also include a serious note of thanks to my very first Chinese language teacher, professor Yu-shih Chen, whom we all loved.

From my Georgetown days, I would like to especially thank my best friend of nearly three decades now, Pei Dalin, for being his wonderful self. Thanks also to his wife, Mian, and my little talented Godchildren, Julia and Christopher. Dalin also helped immensely with the "cultural" editing of this book; he was on call at all hours as emergency questions popped up.

To my dear friend Wen Yang, for all his help as technical editor of this project and for our great years at Georgetown together. Some things really do come full circle.

I would also like to mention places of particular importance in my study of the Chinese language. To Middlebury College, for an incredible summer intensive language program, and to National Chengchi University in Taiwan, for giving me the once-in-a-lifetime opportunity to study oracle bones from the Shang dynasty for one whole glorious year. And especially to my former language teacher from Nankai University in Tianjin, Professor Pang Bingjun—poet-laureate and scholar-gentleman—who spent countless hours helping me transcribe my taped oral histories of the Chinese Jewish descendants of Kaifeng.

To all the Chinese Jewish descendants of Kaifeng, whose lives have so deeply touched my own and whose regional dialect I can never hope to master.

At Stanford, I'd like to thank Carl Bielefeldt, Director of the Stanford Center for Buddhist Studies, for his compassion, patience, and understanding these last few months and, as always, for his signature Zen sense of humor. To Rabbi Dov Greenberg of Stanford Chabad, for his amazing ability to listen for the spoken as well as the unspoken, for his wise counsel and keen intellect, and most of all for his humorous common sense. To Carol Zimbelman, for her dedication and innate decency. And to all my new friends in Palo Alto, who keep showing me why not to give up just five minutes before the miracle happens.

For entrusting me with this project in the first place, immediate and heartfelt thanks go to my literary agent for this book, Carol Susan Roth. Immense thanks are also due to Project Editor Tim Gallan for his patient prodding and gentle suggestions while making sure this book went to print, to Acquisitions Editor Stacy Kennedy for keeping tabs on the whole process, and to the incredible trio of Copy Editors, Josh Dials, Kristin DeMint, and Tina Sims, who made the book come alive.

Finally, words can't quite express my deep gratitude to Christine Huo, Kristina Smith, and F. Marland Chancellor III for ensuring that this book would be only the first of many to come.

About the Author

Wendy Abraham is the Associate Director of the Stanford Center for Buddhist Studies and the Asian Religions & Cultures Initiative. She has taught courses on Chinese language, Chinese literature, and Asian cultures at Hunter College, Georgetown University, New York University, and Stanford University, where she's currently pursuing her second doctorate in modern Chinese literature. She spent a year researching Shang Dynasty oracle bones in Taiwan, which sparked her deep interest in the development of China's written language. Wendy has directed Chinese language programs for American students in Beijing and Shanghai and has interpreted for high-level arts delegations from China. Her first doctoral dissertation from Teachers College (Columbia University) was on the Chinese Jews of Kaifeng, a subject about which she has written widely and continues to lecture frequently throughout the United States. She also created Jewish Historical Tours of China, bringing people to visit Shanghai and Kaifeng on educational trips. Her interest in all things Chinese continues unabated.

Introduction

Globalization has made familiarity with other people, cultures, and languages not only preferable in the 21st century, but also essential. With the help of the Internet, reaching out and touching someone on the other side of the earth has become as easy as the click of a mouse. And yet, nothing quite beats the excitement of a face-to-face encounter with someone who hails from the other side of the globe in his or her own language. Communication in cyberspace doesn't even come close.

Whether you're an inveterate traveler, going overseas for business, about to study overseas, interested in frequenting Chinatown, befriending a Chinese-speaking classmate or coworker, or just plain curious about China, *Chinese For Dummies* can help you get acquainted with enough Chinese to carry on a decent conversation on any number of topics. You won't become fluent instantly, of course, but this book helps you greet a stranger, buy a plane ticket, and order some food. This book also gives you some invaluable cultural tips so that you can not only rattle off those newly acquired words and phrases, but also back them up with the right behavior at the right time.

I designed this book to help guide you toward the successful use of one of the most difficult languages on earth. Chinese should also just be plain fun to learn.

About This Book

The good news is that you can use *Chinese For Dummies* anytime, anywhere. No mandatory class sessions, no exams, and no homework assignments to dread. Need to get to a new city for a business meeting? Just turn to the chapter on travel to find out how to haggle for a plane ticket, determine the price, and get to the airport on time. Have to make a sudden trip to the doctor? Turn to the chapter on your health and figure out in advance how to tell your caregivers exactly what ails you.

The beauty of this book is that it can be all things to all people. You don't have to memorize Chapter 5 before moving on to Chapter 6, if what Chapter 6 deals with is what you really need. Each chapter provides you with different bits of information about the Chinese language and highlights different parts of Chinese grammar. Read as much or as little as you want, as quickly or as slowly as you like. Whatever interests you is what you should focus on. And remember: You're discovering a language that simultaneously represents one of the world's oldest civilizations and one of its fastest growing economies in the 21st century.

Conventions Used in This Book

Pay attention to a couple of conventions that can help you navigate this book's contents:

- ✔ Chinese terms are set in **boldface** to make them stand out.
- ✔ Pronunciations and meanings appear in parentheses immediately after the Chinese terms. The pronunciations are in *italics*.

This book uses the *pīnyīn* (*literally:* spelling the way it sounds) romanization system of Chinese words. What does that mean? Well, if you go to China, you see signs in Chinese characters all around, but if you look for something in English, you may be hard pressed to find it. Whatever signs you see in roman letters will be of *pīnyīn*, the romanization system developed by the Communists in the 1950s, so seeing pīnyīn in this book is good practice for you.

Another thing you should keep in mind as you begin to understand Chinese is that many of the English translations you see in this book aren't exactly literal. It's more important to know the gist of what you hear or see instead of what individual words in any given phrase mean. For example, if you translate "horse horse tiger tiger" literally into Chinese, you have the phrase meaning "so so." You're not actually talking about animals. Whenever I give a literal translation, I preface it with *"literally"* in italics.

The following elements you find in *Chinese For Dummies* help to reinforce the new terms and phrases you're studying:

- ✔ **Talkin' the Talk dialogues:** Nothing beats seeing and hearing an actual conversation to learn Chinese, so I intersperse dialogues throughout this book. They come under the heading "Talkin' the Talk." They show you the Chinese words, the pronunciations, and the English translations, and I often put cultural dos and don'ts into context, which should come in handy.

Dialogues with a CD icon beside them appear on the CD that comes with this book so you can practice the sentences after you hear how they should sound. With the tonal nature of the Chinese language, this feature is indispensable as you learn Chinese.

✔ **Words to Know blackboards:** Memorizing key words and phrases is very useful in language learning. The words and phrases on the blackboard-like boxes are the ones I think are most important in the preceding section or sections, so they appear on a chalkboard with the heading "Words to Know."

✔ **Fun & Games activities:** Working through word games can be a fun way to review the words and phrases you encounter in each chapter. This element of *Chinese For Dummies* is a great way to gauge your progress and tease your brain at the same time. Look for these activities at the end of each chapter.

Foolish Assumptions

Some of the foolish assumptions I made about you while writing *Chinese For Dummies* are:

✔ You don't know any Chinese, except for maybe a couple of words you picked up from a good kung-fu movie or the word "tofu," which you picked up while grocery shopping.

✔ Your goal in life isn't to become an interpreter of Chinese at the U.N.; you just want to pick up some useful words, phrases, and sentence constructions to make yourself understood in a Chinese-speaking environment.

✔ You have no intention of spending hours and hours memorizing Chinese vocabulary and grammar patterns.

✔ You basically want to have fun while speaking a little Chinese.

How This Book Is Organized

This book is divided by topic into parts, chapters, and appendixes. Each part focuses on one aspect of the Chinese language, and the chapters cover different useful topics, such as how to dine at a restaurant, how to handle emergencies, or how to plan a vacation. The following sections tell you what types of information you can expect to find in each part.

Part 1: Getting Started

This part familiarizes you with some basics of Chinese: how to pronounce words, how to create the proper pitch (also known as tone) for each word, and so on. Because Chinese is a tonal language, if you pronounce a word with an incorrect tone, you may say a whole different word. Sometimes the only way to know whether you've said something you didn't intend is by the look on the listener's face, so you should pay particular attention to the tones as you speak.

Part 11: Chinese in Action

In this part, you really begin to use Chinese. Instead of focusing strictly on grammar, this part helps guide you through everyday situations that you encounter while meeting people, eating at restaurants, going shopping, or yakking on the phone.

Part 111: Chinese on the Go

This part of the book gives you the tools you need to use Chinese in any number of practical settings. You find out how to change money, how to ask for and give directions, how to book a room at a hotel, and how to tell a doctor what ails you. It covers all aspects of travel into Chinese-speaking parts of the world. Whether your travels take you all the way to Shanghai or just to your cubicle at work is up to you.

Part 1V: The Part of Tens

Ever wish you could distill the Chinese culture into 10 simple rules of what to do and what not to do? Well, Part IV is a collection of simple phrases you can use, popular Chinese expressions, and reminders of what not to do in a Chinese setting that you should always keep in the back of your mind as you interact with the Chinese. You not only sound more like a native Chinese speaker when you open your mouth, but you also start internalizing some of the cardinal cultural rules and taboos for social settings that the average student of the Chinese language may never discover.

Part V: Appendixes

This part contains helpful references that you may want to refer to occasionally as you snoop through the rest of the chapters. Appendix A contains a useful verb table, which can help in any setting. Appendix B is a handy mini-dictionary of both Chinese to English and English to Chinese. Feel free to check this section when you encounter unfamiliar words on a need-to-know basis. Appendix C contains the answers to the Fun & Games exercises at the end of each chapter. Finally, Appendix D provides a list of the tracks that appear on the audio CD. This appendix comes in handy when you're ready to hear a selection of the Talkin' the Talk dialogues from the book.

Icons Used in This Book

Cute little icons appear in the left-hand margins, next to sidebars, and adjacent some of the introductions to the Talkin' the Talk sections throughout this book. These beacons shed light on what kind of information you're looking at and can help you locate certain types of information in a hurry. The six icons used in this book are:

The bull's-eye appears wherever I've highlighted a great idea to help make your study of Chinese easier.

This icon, appropriately showing a string around a finger, should serve as a reminder about particularly important information concerning Chinese.

The bomb should act as a stop sign in your mind. It warns you about things to avoid saying or doing so that you don't make a fool of yourself overseas or with a new Chinese-speaking acquaintance.

This icon clues you in on fascinating bits of information about China and Chinese culture. Knowledge of a culture goes hand in hand with knowledge of a foreign language, so these icons help light the way as you embark on your journey.

This icon highlights various rules of grammar that may be out of the norm. Even though this book doesn't focus primarily on grammar, your successful execution of the language can only be enhanced by paying attention to little grammatical rules as they pop up.

The audio CD that comes with this book gives you the chance to hear native Chinese speakers so you can better understand the way Chinese really sounds. This proves especially helpful because of all the tones you have to keep in mind. This icon indicates the basic sounds and Talkin' the Talk dialogues you can find on the CD.

Where to Go from Here

Chinese is often considered one of the toughest languages in the world to master. Don't worry. The good news is that you're not trying to master it. All you want to do is be understandable when you open your mouth so that you don't ask for the mens' room when you really want the ladies' room. All you have to do now is keep listening to and repeating the words and phrases you find in this book. Turn to whichever chapter piques your curiosity, listen to the accompanying audio CD at home or in your car, and keep practicing your favorite Chinese phrases when you're with your family and friends in Chinatown.

Part I
Getting Started

The 5th Wave   By Rich Tennant

"You mean, 'wo', 'ta', 'baba', and 'mama' are all words in the Mandarin dialect? My gosh, Alice, our baby's been speaking Chinese the last few weeks!"

In this part . . .

Part I warmly welcomes you to the Chinese language. I give you the lowdown on all the essentials of Chinese: how to pronounce Chinese sounds (and tones) like a native, how to string Chinese words together so that they make sense, how to count in Chinese, and how to communicate in Chinese with all the cultural trimmings. **Wǒmen kāishǐ ba!** (*waw mun kye shir bah;* Let's begin!)

Chapter 1

Getting to Know a Little Chinese

Time to get your feet wet with the basics of Chinese. This chapter gives you guidelines that help you pronounce words in standard Mandarin (the official language of both the People's Republic of China and Taiwan) like a native speaker and helps you get a handle on the four tones that distinguish Mandarin Chinese. After you have the basics down, I show you how to construct basic Chinese phrases.

But before you dive in, here's a bit of advice: Don't be intimidated by all the tones! The best thing you can do when learning a foreign language is to not worry about making mistakes the minute you open your mouth. Practice speaking Chinese first to your dog or cat, and then work your way up to a couple of goldfish or a niece or nephew under the age of 10. When you finally get the nerve to rattle off a few phrases to your local Chinatown grocer, you'll know you've made it. And when you visit China for the first time, you discover how incredibly appreciative the Chinese are of anyone who even remotely attempts to speak their language. All the hours you spent yakking away with the family pet start to pay off, and you'll be rewarded greatly. Still have doubts? You'll be amazed at how much you can say after snooping through *Chinese For Dummies*.

Encountering the Chinese culture is just as important as exploring the Chinese language. In fact, you can't quite master the language without absorbing a little of the culture by osmosis. Just making the effort to speak Chinese is an act of positive diplomacy. Don't worry about how you sound when you open your mouth — you're contributing to international friendship no matter what comes out.

Grasping Chinese Dialects

Give yourself a big pat on the back right now. Yup, right now — before you even begin to utter one iota of Chinese. If you don't do it now, you may be too shocked later on when it sinks in that you've taken on a language that has hundreds (yes, hundreds) of dialects — each one mutually incomprehensible to speakers of the other ones. Practically every major town, and certainly every province, in China has its own regional dialect that folks grow up learning (see Table 1-1). Of the seven major dialects, Shanghainese, Taiwanese, and Cantonese are the ones you may have heard of before.

And then there's Mandarin, dialect of the masses. Mandarin Chinese is spoken by more people on earth than any other language today. Pretty much a quarter of humanity uses it, given China's immense population. So just why was this particular dialect chosen to become the official dialect taught in all schools throughout China, regardless of whatever additional dialects people speak at home or in their communities?

With only four tones, **Guānhuà** (*gwan hwah;* Mandarin; *literally:* the language of the officials, who were also known as Mandarins) has served as the hybrid language of China since the 15th century, because it was based on the educated speech of the region around Beijing. Instead of referring to it as **Guānhuà**, mainlanders in China now call it **Pǔtōnghuà** (*poo toong hwah;* the common language). People in Taiwan, Hong Kong, and in overseas Chinese communities call it **Guóyǔ** (*gwaw yew;* the national language). You may also hear it referred to as **Zhōngwén** (*joong one;* the language of the Chinese people) and **Hànyǔ** (*hahn yew;* the language of the Han people), because the Chinese have often referred to themselves as descendants of the Han dynasty (206 BCE to 220 CE), one of the golden eras of Chinese history. Because Chinese is the language of ethnic Chinese and China's minority groups, the more all-encompassing term **Zhōngwén** is preferred.

Table 1-1	Major Chinese Dialects	
Dialect	*Pronunciation*	*Region Where Spoken*
Pǔtōnghuà / Guóyǔ (Mandarin)	poo toong hwah / gwaw yew	North of the Yangzi River, but taught in schools everywhere; official language of the People's Republic of China and spoken all over Taiwan
Wú	woo	Shanghai, southeastern Anhui, and much of Zhejiang
Xiāng	shyahng	Hunan
Gàn	gahn	Jiangxi, southern Anhui, and southeastern Hubei
Kèjiā (Hakka)	kuh jyah	Scattered parts of eastern and southwestern Guangxi and in northern Guangdong (Canton)
Yuè (Cantonese)	yweh	Southeastern Guangxi, Guangdong (Canton), and Hong Kong
Mǐn	meen	Fujian, southern Zhejiang, northeastern Guangdong, Hainan, and Taiwan

The term **Pǔtōnghuà** (*literally:* the common language) is used to refer to Mandarin in the People's Republic of China, and the term **Guóyǔ** (*literally:* the national language) is the term used for Mandarin in Taiwan. If you simply say **Hànyǔ** (the language of the Han people), however, you can use it anywhere.

The Written Word: Yikes! No Alphabet!

I bet you're beginning to wonder just how the Chinese have managed to communicate with each other for the better part of five millennia if their spoken language comes in so many distinct forms and dialects. The answer lies in (drum roll) . . . the written word.

CULTURAL WISDOM

Early bare-bones Chinese writing

The earliest specimens of Chinese writing appeared on oracle bones, dating from China's first archaeologically proven dynasty, the Shang (circa 1766 to 1122 BCE). Written on ox scapulae or tortoise shells, the writing was used for divination purposes by shamans who asked questions on behalf of the king. Only about a thousand or so characters have been identified on oracle bones, but the findings show that the written language had already attained a solid foundation in China by the second millennium, BCE.

Say you see two Chinese people sitting next to each other on a train traveling from Canton to Shanghai. If the Cantonese speaker reads the newspaper out loud, the guy from Shanghai won't have a clue what he's saying. But if they both read the same newspaper article to themselves, they could understand what's going on in the world. That's because Chinese characters are uniform all across the country.

Chinese words are written in beautiful, often symbolic configurations called *characters*. Each character is a word in and of itself, and sometimes it's a part of a compound word. It makes no difference if you write the characters from right to left, left to right, or top to bottom, because you can read and understand them in any order. If you see a Chinese movie in Chinatown, you can often choose between two types of subtitles: English, which you read from left to right, and Chinese characters on another line, which you read from right to left. (They can also go from left to right, so be careful.) You may go cross-eyed for a while trying to follow them both.

During the Han dynasty, a lexicographer named Xu Shen identified six ways in which Chinese characters reflected meanings and sounds. Of these, four were the most common:

- **Pictographs:** These characters are formed according to the shape of the objects themselves, such as the sun and the moon. They show the meaning of the character rather than the sound.

- **Ideographs:** These characters represent more abstract concepts. The characters for "above" and "below," for example, each have a horizontal line representing the horizon and another stroke leading out above or below the horizon.

- **Complex ideographs:** Combinations of simpler characters.

- **Phonetic compounds:** Also called logographs, these compound characters are formed by two graphic elements — one hinting at the meaning of the word and the other providing a clue to the sound. Phonetic compounds account for over 80 percent of all Chinese characters.

No matter which type of characters you see, you won't find any letters stringing them together like you see in English. So how in the world do Chinese people consult a Chinese dictionary? (How did you know I could read your mind?) In several different ways.

Because Chinese characters are composed of several (often many) strokes of the writing brush, one way to look up a character is by counting the number of strokes and then looking up the character under the portion of the dictionary that notes characters by strokes. But to do so, you have to know which radical to check under first. Chinese characters have 214 *radicals* — parts of the character that can help identify what the character may signify, such as three dots on the left hand side of the character representing water. Each radical is itself composed of a certain number of strokes, so you have to first look up the radical by the number of strokes it takes to write it, and after you locate that radical, you start looking once more under the number of strokes left in the character *after* that radical to locate the character you wanted to look up in the first place.

You can always just check under the pronunciation of the character (if you already know how to pronounce it), but you have to sift through every single character with the same pronunciation. You also have to look further under the various tones to see which one of all the words pronounced the same way comes with the first, second, third, or fourth tone you want to locate. And because there are so many homonyms in Chinese, this task isn't as easy as it may sound (no pun intended).

I bet you feel really relieved that you're only focusing on spoken Chinese and not the written language.

Pinyin Spelling: Beijing, Not Peking

To spell the way it sounds . . . that's the literal meaning of **pīnyīn**. For decades, Chinese had been transliterated in any number of ways. Finally, in 1979, the People's Republic of China officially adopted **pīnyīn** as its official romanization system. After the adoption, U.S. libraries and government agencies diligently changed all their prior records from other romanization systems into **pīnyīn**.

You should keep in mind the following quick facts about some of the initial sounds in Mandarin when you see them written in the relatively new **pīnyīn** system:

- **J:** Sounds like the "g" in "gee whiz." An "i" often follows a "j." "**Jǐ kuài qián**?" *(jee kwye chyan)* means "How much money?"

- **Q:** Sounds like the "ch" in "cheek." You never see it followed by a "u" like in English, but an "i" always follows it in Chinese, possibly before another vowel or a consonant. **Qīngdǎo** *(cheeng daow)* beer used to be spelled "ch'ing tao" or "Tsingtao."

- ✔ **X:** The third letter that's often followed by an "i." It sounds like the "sh" in "she." One famous Chinese leader, **Dèng Xiǎopíng** *(dung shyaow peeng),* boasted this letter in his name.

- ✔ **Zh:** Unlike "j," which often precedes a vowel to make it sound like you're opening your mouth, "zh" is followed by vowels, which make it sound like your mouth is a bit more closed. Take **Zhōu Ēnlái** *(joe un lye),* for example, the great statesman of 20th-century China. When you say his name, it should sound like Joe En-lye.

- ✔ **Z:** Sounds like a "dz." You see it in the name of the PRC's first leader, **Máo Zédōng** *(maow dzuh doong),* which used to be spelled Mao Tse-tung.

- ✔ **C:** Pronounced like "ts" in such words as **cài** *(tsye;* food) or **cèsuǒ** *(tsuh swaw;* bathroom).

- ✔ **B, D, and G:** In the past, the sounds made by these three letters were represented by P, T, and K, respectively. In the past, if the corresponding initial sounds were *aspirated* (had air coming out of the speaker, like in the words "pie," "tie," and "kite"), they would've been written as "p'," "t'," and "k'." Today, the letters "P," "T," and "K" represent the aspirated sounds.

Sounding Off: Basic Chinese Sounds

Don't worry about sounding like a native speaker the first time you utter a Chinese syllable — after all, who does? But the longer you procrastinate becoming familiar with the basic elements of Chinese words, the greater your fear of this unique language may become. After you begin to practice the sounds (and eventually the tones) out loud, you may wonder if you'll ever come close to sounding like Bruce Lee in a kung-fu movie or even your local Chinatown grocer. Hearing Chinese spoken at a normal speed is definitely intimidating at the beginning, so you should enjoy taking plenty of baby steps and reveling in the praise from waiters who appreciate all your effort the next time you frequent a Chinese restaurant.

The main thing to remember about the Chinese language is that each *morpheme* (the smallest unit of meaning in a language) is represented by one syllable, which in turn consists of an initial sound and a final sound, topped off by a tone. This applies to each and every syllable. Without any one of these three components, your words may be incomprehensible to the average Chinese person. For example, the syllable "**mā**" is comprised of the initial "m" and the final "a," and you pronounce it with what's called a first tone. Together, the parts mean "mother." If you substitute the first tone for a third tone, which is written as "**mǎ**," you say the word "horse." So be careful not to call your mother a horse when you practice the initials, finals, and tones. The following sections break up the three parts and give each their due.

Before you can participate in sports or play games, you must become familiar with all the rules. The same goes for practicing a new language. Do your best to understand the basic rules of pronunciation, and keep practicing over and over to begin feeling comfortable speaking the language.

Starting off with initials

In Chinese, initials always consist of consonants. Table 1-2 lists the initials you encounter in the Chinese language.

 Listen to these sounds on the CD as you practice pronouncing initials.

Table 1-2	Chinese Initials	
Chinese Letter	*Sound*	*English Example*
b	baw	bore
p	paw	paw
m	maw	more
f	faw	four
d	duh	done
t	tuh	ton
n	nuh	null
l	luh	lull
g	guh	gull
k	kuh	come
h	huh	hunt
j	gee	gee
q	chee	cheat
x	she	she
z	dzuh	"ds" in suds
c	tsuh	"ts" in huts
s	suh	sun

(continued)

Table 1-2 (continued)

Chinese Letter	Sound	English Example
zh	jir	germ
ch	chir	churn
sh	shir	shirt
r	ir	"er" in bigger
w	wuh	won
y	yuh	yup

The initials **–n** and **-r** in Table 1-2 can also appear as finals, so don't be surprised if you see them there.

Ending with finals

Chinese boasts many more consonants than vowels. In fact, the language has only six vowels all together: **a, o, e, i, u,** and **ü.** If you pronounce the vowels in sequence, your mouth starts off very wide and your tongue starts off very low. Eventually, when you get to **ü,** your mouth becomes much more closed and your tongue ends pretty high. You can also combine the vowels in various ways to form compound vowels. Table 1-3 lists the vowels and some possible combinations.

Table 1-3		Chinese Vowels
Chinese Vowel	Sound	English Example
a	ah	hot
ai	i	eye
ao	ow	chow
an	ahn	on
ang	ahng	thong
o	aw	straw
ong	oong	too + ng
ou	oh	oh

Chinese Vowel	Sound	English Example
e	uh	bush
ei	ay	way
en	un	fun
eng	ung	tongue
er	ar	are
i	ee	tea
ia	ya	gotcha
iao	yaow	meow
ie	yeh	yet
iu	yo	leo
ian	yan	cheyenne
iang	yahng	y + angst
in	een	seen
ing	eeng	going
iong	yoong	you + ng
u	oo	too
ua	wa	suave
uo	waw	war
ui	way	way
uai	why	why
uan	wan	want
un	one	one
uang	wahng	wan + ng
ueng	wung	one + ng
ü	yew	ewe
üe	yweh	you + eh
üan	ywan	you + wan
ün	yewn	you + n

Tone marks in **pīnyīn** always appear above the vowel, but if you see a couple of vowels in a row, the tone mark appears above the first vowel in that sequence. One exception is when you see the vowels **iu** and **ui** together. In that case, the tone mark falls on the second vowel.

Sometimes vowels appear without initial consonant accompaniment, but they still mean something. The word **ǎi**, meaning "short" (of stature), is one example.

Perfect pitch: Presenting . . . the four tones

Mee meeeee (cough cough)! Pardon me. I'm getting carried away with warming up before I get into the four tones. Just think of the tones this way: They can be your best friends when it comes to being understood in Chinese, and they're the hip part of this ancient language.

If you combine all the possible initial sounds of Chinese with all the possible permutations of the final sounds, you come up with only about 400 sound combinations — not nearly enough to express all the ideas in your head. If you add the four basic tones of Mandarin to the mix, the number of possible permutations increases fourfold. Tones are also a great way to reduce the number of homophones in Chinese. Even so, any given syllable with a specific tone can often have more than one meaning. Sometimes the only way to decipher the intended meaning is to see the written word.

Mandarin has only four tones. The best way to imagine what each of the four tones sounds like is to visualize these short descriptions:

- ✔ **First tone:** High level. The first tone is supposed to be as high as your individual pitch range can be, without wavering. It appears like this above the letter a: **ā**.

- ✔ **Second tone:** Rising. The second tone sounds like you're asking a question. It goes from the middle level of your voice to the top. It doesn't automatically indicate that you're asking a question, however — it just sounds like you are. It appears like this above the letter a: **á**.

- ✔ **Third tone:** Falling and then rising. The third tone starts in the middle level of your voice range and then falls deeply before slightly rising at the end. It looks like this above the letter a: **ǎ**.

- ✔ **Fourth tone:** Falling. The fourth tone sounds like you're giving someone an order (unlike the more plaintive-sounding second tone). It falls from the high pitch level it starts at. Here's how it looks above the letter a: **à**.

One third tone after another

Here's something interesting about tones: When you have to say one third tone followed by another third tone out loud in consecutive fashion, the first one actually becomes a second tone. If you hear someone say "**Tā hěn hǎo**" (*tah hun how;* she's very well), you may not realize that both "**hěn**" and "**hǎo**" individually are third tone syllables. It sounds like "**hén**" is a second tone and "**hǎo**" is a full third tone.

Half-third tones

Whenever a third tone is followed by any of the other tones — first, second, fourth, or even a neutral tone — it becomes a *half-third tone.* You only pronounce the first half of the tone — the falling half — before you pronounce the other syllables with the other tones. In fact, a half-third tone barely falls at all. It sounds more like a level, low tone (kind of the opposite of the high level first tone). Get it?

Neutral tones

A fifth tone exists that you can't exactly count amongst the four basic tones, because it's actually toneless, or neutral. You never see a tone mark over a fifth tone, and you say it only when you attach it to grammatical particles or the second character of repetitive syllables, such as **bàba** (*bah bah;* father) or **māma** (*mah mah;* mother).

Tonal changes in yī and bù

Just when you think you're getting a handle on all the possible tones and tone changes in Chinese, I have one more aspect to report: The words **yī** (*ee;* one) and **bù** (*boo;* not or no) are truly unusual in Chinese, in that their tones may change automatically depending on what comes after them. You pronounce **yī** by itself with the first tone. However, when a first, second, or third tone follows it, **yī** instantly turns into a fourth tone, such as in **yìzhāng zhǐ** (*ee jahng jir;* a piece of paper). If a fourth tone follows **yī**, however, it automatically becomes a second tone, such as in the word **yíyàng** (*ee yahng;* the same). I know this all sounds very complicated, but when you get the hang of tones, pronunciation becomes second nature. Just keep listening to the accompanying CD. These concepts will sink in quicker than you expect.

Adding Idioms and Popular Expressions to Your Repertoire

Even though Chinese seems like it has absolutely nothing in common with English when you listen to it, especially in terms of pronunciation and tones, it uses distinctive *idioms* (groups of words whose collective meanings differ from their individual parts) to express specific ideas or situations, just like in English. If you try to translate these idioms word for word, however, you won't get very far.

For example, if you suddenly announced to your Chinese college roommate **"Wǒ huì lā yíge quán yègē"** (*waw hway lah ee guh chwan yeh guh; literally:* I'm going to pull an all-nighter), he would be clueless and would begin to question what he was thinking when he agreed to room with a foreigner. Similarly, you'd be just as confused if he broke out with **"Wǒ huì kāi yè chē."** (*waw hway kye yeh chuh; literally:* I'm going to ride the night train.) Both of you mean the same thing, of course, but he'd start imagining just how heavy something called an all-nighter is to actually pull, and you'd worry about which city he's going to end up in the next morning. You may even be tempted to join him instead of studying for your exam.

The Chinese language has thousands of idiomatic expressions known as **chéngyǔ** (*chung yew*). Most of these **chéngyǔ** originated in anecdotes, fables, fairy tales, or ancient literary works, and some of the expressions are thousands of years old. The vast majority consist of four characters, succinctly expressing morals behind very long, ancient stories. Others are more than four characters. Either way, the Chinese pepper these pithy expressions throughout any given conversation.

Here are a few **chéngyǔ** you frequently hear in Chinese:

- **Mò míng qí miào.** (*maw meeng chee meow; literally:* No one can explain the wonder and mystery of it all.) This saying describes anything that's tough to figure out, including unusual behavior.

- **Yǐ shēn zuò zé.** (*ee shun dzwaw dzuh;* To set a good example.)

- **Yì mó yí yàng.** (*ee maw ee yahng;* exactly alike)

- **Quán xīn quán yì.** (*chwan sheen chwan ee; literally:* entire heart, entire mind)

- **Àn bù jiù bān.** (*ahn boo jyoe bahn;* To take one step at a time.)

- **Hú shuō bā dào.** (*hoo shwaw bah daow; literally:* To talk nonsense in eight directions.) To talk nonsense.

- **Huǒ shàng jiā yóu.** (*hwaw shahng jyah yo;* To add fuel to the fire; to aggravate the problem.)

- **Yì zhēn jiàn xiě.** (*ee jun jyan shyeh;* To hit the nail on the head.)

- **Yì jǔ liǎng dé.** (*ee jyew lyahng duh;* To kill two birds with one stone.)

- **Rù xiāng suí sú.** (*roo shyahng sway soo;* When in Rome, do as the Romans do.)

Another fact you quickly become aware of when you start speaking with **chéngyǔ** is that the expressions are sometimes full of references to animals. Here are some of those:

✔ **gǒu zhàng rén shì** (*go jahng run shir; literally:* the dog acts fierce when his master is present; to take advantage of one's connections with powerful people)

✔ **guà yáng tóu mài gǒu ròu** (*gwah yahng toe my go roe; literally:* to display a lamb's head but sell dog meat; to cheat others with false claims)

✔ **dǎ cǎo jǐng shé** (*dah tsaow jeeng shuh; literally:* to beat the grass to frighten the snake; to give a warning)

✔ **duì niú tán qín** (*dway nyo tahn cheen; literally:* to play music to a cow; to cast pearls before swine)

✔ **xuán yá lè mǎ** (*shywan yah luh mah; literally:* to rein in the horse before it goes over the edge; to halt)

✔ **huà shé tiān zú** (*hwah shuh tyan dzoo; literally:* to pain a snake and add legs; to gild the lily; to do something superfluous)

✔ **hǔ tóu shé wěi** (*hoo toe shuh way; literally:* with the head of a tiger but the tail of a snake; to start strong but end poorly)

✔ **chē shuǐ mǎ lóng** (*chuh shway mah loong; literally:* cars flowing like water and horses creating a solid line looking like a dragon; heavy traffic)

Mastering Basic Phrases

If you make it a habit to use the following short Chinese phrases whenever you get the chance, you can master them in no time. You'll also shock everyone around you — especially if they don't speak Chinese. It doesn't matter. You know what you're saying, at least. So the next time you meet up with a Chinese waiter or take your clothes to a Chinese laundry down the block, you can impress the heck out of everyone. Try these phrases:

✔ **Nǐ hǎo!** (*nee how;* Hi; How are you?)

✔ **Xièxiè.** (*shyeh shyeh;* Thank you.)

✔ **Bú kèqì.** (*boo kuh chee;* You're welcome; Don't mention it.)

✔ **Méi shì.** (*may shir;* It's nothing; Don't mention it.)

✔ **Hǎo jíle.** (*how jee luh;* Great; Fantastic.)

✔ **Duì le.** (*dway luh;* That's right.)

✔ **Gōngxǐ gōngxǐ!** (*goong she goong she;* Congratulations!)

✔ **Duìbuqǐ.** (*dway boo chee;* Excuse me.)

✔ **Suàn le.** (*swan luh;* Forget it; Nevermind.)

✔ **Méiyǒu guānxi.** (*mayo gwan she;* It doesn't matter.)

✔ **Děng yíxià.** (*dung ee shyah;* Wait a minute.)

Talkin' the Talk

David and Rachel talk about practicing some Chinese expressions while they wait for a bus in Taipei.

David: **Rachel! Wǒ yǐjīng huì shuō Zhōngwén le.**
           Rachel! Waw ee jeeng hway shwaw joong one lah.
           Rachel! I already know how to speak Chinese.

Rachel: **Děng yíxià. Nǐ yídìng hú shuō bā dào. Nǐ zěnme huì Zhōngwén ne?**
           Dung ee shyah. Nee ee deeng who shwaw bah daow. Nee dzummuh hway joong one nuh?
           Wait a minute. You're definitely talking nonsense. How could you possibly speak Chinese?

David: **Duì le. Wǒ měige xīngqī chī Zhōngguó fàn de shíhòu, yìbiān chīfàn, yìbiān gēn fúwùyuán xuéxí Zhōngwén. Yǐjīng huì shuō hěn duō chéngyǔ le. Yì jǔ liǎng dé.**
           Dway luh. Waw may guh sheeng chee chir joong gwaw fahn duh shir ho, ee byan chir fahn, ee byan gun foo woo ywan shyweh she joong one. Ee jeeng hway shwaw hun dwaw chung yew luh. Ee jyew lyahng duh.
           That's right. Every week when I eat Chinese food, on the one hand I eat, and on the other hand I study Chinese with the waiters. I already know lots of idioms. I kill two birds with one stone.

Rachel: **Nà, nǐ yǐ shēn zuò zé. Wǒ xiàge xīngqī gēn nǐ yìqǐ qù chīfàn, hǎo bù hǎo?**
           Nah, nee ee shun dzwaw zuh. Waw shyah guh sheeng chee gun nee ee chee chyew chir fahn, how boo how?
           Well, in that case you're setting a good example. Next week I'll go with you to eat, okay?

David: **Hǎo jíle.**
           How jee luh.
           Great.

CULTURAL WISDOM

Communicating with body language

Ever think you know what certain couples are saying or thinking just by observing their gestures and body language? Well, people can make the same observations in China. Although the gestures are different, they contain important clues as to social status between people, their emotions, and so on. Observe Chinese people wherever you can to see if you notice any of the following gestures:

- ✔ **Pointing to one's own nose:** You may find this hard to believe, but Chinese people often point to their own noses, often touching them, when they refer to themselves by saying the word "**wǒ**" (*waw;* I). The Chinese are probably just as curious as to why Westerners point to their hearts.

- ✔ **Nodding and bowing slightly:** When greeting older people, professors, or others in

positions of power or prestige, people lower their heads slightly to acknowledge them and show respect. Unlike the Japanese, who bow deeply, the Chinese basically bow with their heads in a slight fashion.

- ✔ **Shaking hands:** People of vastly different status generally don't give each other a handshake, but it's common among friends and business colleagues.

- ✔ **Bowing with hands clasped:** If you see hand clasping and bowing going on at the same time, you know the participants have something to celebrate. It indicates conveying congratulations or greeting others during special festival occasions. Their hands are held at chest level and their heads are slightly bowed (and they often have big smiles on their faces).

Fun & Games

Listen to the accompanying CD to see if you can imitate the following words, which are only distinguished by their tones. (Be on the lookout: Any given sound with the same accompanying tone may have several other meanings, distinguishable only by context or by seeing the appropriate written character.) Good luck!

- ✔ **mā**; mother
- ✔ **má**; hemp
- ✔ **mǎ**; horse
- ✔ **mà**; to scold
- ✔ **fēi**; to fly
- ✔ **féi**; fat
- ✔ **fěi**; bandit
- ✔ **fèi**; lungs
- ✔ **qīng**; clear
- ✔ **qíng**; affection
- ✔ **qǐng**; please
- ✔ **qìng**; celebrate
- ✔ **zhū**; pig (or pearl)
- ✔ **zhú**; bamboo
- ✔ **zhǔ**; master
- ✔ **zhù**; to reside

Chapter 2

The Nitty Gritty: Basic Chinese Grammar and Numbers

Maybe you're one of those people who cringe at the mere mention of the word *grammar*. Just the thought of all those rules on how to construct sentences can put you into a cold sweat.

Hey, don't sweat it! This chapter could just as easily be called "Chinese without Tears." It gives you some quick and easy shortcuts on how to combine the basic building blocks of Chinese (which, by the way, are the same components that make up English) — nouns to name things, adjectives to qualify the nouns, verbs to show action or passive states of being, and adverbs to describe the verbs, adjectives, or other adverbs. After you know how to combine these parts of any given sentence, you'll be able to express your ideas and interests spanning the past, present, and future.

When you speak English, I bet you don't sit and analyze the word order before opening your mouth to say something. Well, the same can hold true when you begin speaking Chinese. You probably didn't even know the word for grammar before someone taught you that it was the framework for analyzing the structure of a language. Instead of overwhelming you, this chapter makes understanding Chinese grammar as easy as punch.

If you be patient with yourself, have fun following the dialogues illustrating basic sentences, and listen to them on the accompanying CD, you'll do just fine.

The Basics of Chinese Parts of Speech

Admit it. Most of us took the better part of our first two years of life to master the basics when it came to forming English sentences. With this book, you can whittle this same skill in Chinese down to just a few minutes. Just keep reading this chapter. I promise it will save you a lot of time in the long run.

The basic word order of Chinese is exactly the same as in English. Hard to imagine? Just think of it this way: When you say "I love spinach," you're using the subject (I), verb (love), object (spinach) sentence order. It's the same in Chinese. Only in Beijing, it sounds more like **Wǒ xǐhuān bōcài** *(waw she hwahn baw tsye)*.

And if that isn't enough to endear you to Chinese already, maybe these tidbits of information will:

- ✔ You don't need to conjugate verbs.

- ✔ You don't need to master verb tenses. (Don't you just love it already?)

- ✔ You don't need to distinguish between singular and plural nouns.

- ✔ There's no such thing as gender-specific nouns.

- ✔ The same word can be both the subject and the object.

How could such news not warm the hearts of all those who've had grammar-phobia since grade school? The way you can tell how one part of a Chinese sentence relates to another is generally by the use of particles and what form the word order takes. (Particles, for those of you presently scratching your heads, can be found at the beginning or end of sentences and serve mainly to distinguish different types of emphatic statements but can't be translated in and of themselves.)

Some interesting characteristics of the Chinese language include the fact that there's no such thing as first, second, or third person (for example, "I eat" versus "he eats"); no such thing as active or passive voices (for example, "hear" versus "be heard"); and no such thing as past or present ("I like him" versus "I liked him"). In addition, Chinese language has only two aspects — complete and continuous — whereas English has all sorts of different aspects: indefinite, continuous, perfect, perfect continuous, and so on. (Examples include ways of distinguishing between "I eat," "I ate," "I will eat," "I said I would eat," "I am eating," and so on.) *Aspects* are what characterize the Chinese language in place of tenses. They refer to how a speaker views an event or state of being.

Nouns

Chinese is just chock-full of nouns:

- Common nouns that represent tangible things, such as **háizi** (*hi dzuh;* child) or **yè** (*yeh;* leaf)

- Proper nouns for such things as names of countries or people, like **Fǎguó** (*fah gwaw;* France) and **Zhāng Xiānshēng** (*jahng shyan shung;* Mr. Zhang)

- Material nouns for such nondiscrete things as **kāfēi** (*kah fay;* coffee) or **jīn** (*jin;* gold)

- Abstract nouns for such things as **zhèngzhì** (*juhng jir;* politics) or **wénhuà** (*one hwah;* culture)

Pronouns

Pronouns are easy to make plural in Chinese. Here's what you need to know: Just add the plural suffix -**men** to the three basic pronouns:

- **Wǒ** (*waw;* I/me) becomes **wǒmen** (*waw mun;* we/us).

- **Nǐ** (*nee;* you) becomes **nǐmen** (*nee mun;* you [plural]).

- **Tā** (*tah;* he/him, she/her, it) becomes **tāmen** (*tah mun;* they/them).

Sometimes instead of the term **wǒmen** for "us," you hear the term **zánmen** (*dzah mun*). This word is used in very familiar settings when the speaker wants to include the listener in an action, like when you say **Zánmen zǒu ba** (*dzah mun dzoe bah;* let's go).

When speaking to an elder or someone you don't know too well and the person is someone to whom you should show respect, you need to use the pronoun **nín** (*neen*) instead of the more informal **nǐ** (*nee*). On the other hand, if you're speaking to several people who fit that description, the plural remains **nǐmen** (*nee men*).

Classifiers

Classifiers are sometimes called measure words, even though they don't really measure anything. They actually help classify particular nouns. For example, the classifier **běn** (*bun*) can refer to books, magazines, dictionaries, and just about anything else that's printed and bound like a book. You might hear **Wǒ yào yìběn shū** (*waw yaow ee bun shoo;* I want a book) just as easily as you hear **Wǒ yào kàn yìběn zázhì** (*waw yaow kahn ee bun dzah jir;* I want to read a magazine).

Classifiers are found in between a number (or a demonstrative pronoun such as "this" or "that") and a noun. They're similar to English words such as "herd" (of elephants) or "school" (of fish). Although English doesn't use classifiers too often, in Chinese you find them wherever a number is followed by a noun, or at least an implied noun (such as "I'll have another one," referring to a cup of coffee, for example).

Because you have so many potential classifiers to choose from in Chinese, the general rule of thumb is: When in doubt, use **ge** *(guh)*. It's the all-purpose classifier and the one used the most in the Chinese language. You usually can't go wrong by using **ge.** If you're tempted to leave a classifier out altogether because you're not sure which one is the right one, don't give in to the temptation! You may not be understood at all.

Chinese has lots of different classifiers because they're each used to refer to different types of things. For example, Table 2-1 lists classifiers for natural objects. Here are some other examples:

- ✔ **gēn** *(gun)*: Used for anything looking like a stick, such as a string or even a blade of grass

- ✔ **zhāng** *(jahng)*: Used for anything with a flat surface, such as a newspaper, table, or bed

- ✔ **kē** *(kuh)*: Used for anything round and tiny, such as a pearl

Table 2-1	Some Typical Classifiers for Natural Objects	
Classifier	*Pronunciation*	*Use*
duǒ	dwaw	flowers
kē	kuh	trees
lì	lee	grain (of rice, sand, and so on)
zhī	jir	animals, insects, birds
zuò	dzwaw	hills, mountains

Whenever you have a pair of anything, you can use the classifier **shuāng** *(shwahng)*. That goes for **yì shuāng kuàizi** *(ee shwahng kwye dzuh;* a pair of chopsticks) as well as for **yì shuāng shǒu** *(ee shwahng show;* a pair of hands). Sometimes a pair is indicated by the classifier **duì** *(dway)*, as in **yí duì ěrhuán** *(ee dway are hwahn;* a pair of earrings).

Singular and plural: It's a nonissue

Chinese makes no distinction between singular and plural. If you say the word **shū** *(shoo),* it could mean "book" just as easily as "books." The only way you know whether it's singular or plural is if a number followed by a classifier precedes the word **shū**, as in **Wǒ yǒu sān běn shū** *(waw yo sahn bun shoo;* I have three books).

One way to indicate plurality after personal pronouns **wǒ** *(waw;* I), **nǐ** *(nee;* you), and **tā** *(tah;* he, she, or it) and human nouns such as **háizi** *(hi dzuh;* child) or **xuéshēng** *(shweh shuhng;* student) is by adding the suffix **-men** at the end. It acts as the equivalent of adding an "s" to nouns in English.

Talkin' the Talk

Susan and Michael are looking at a beautiful field.

Susan: **Zhèr de fēngjǐng zhēn piàoliàng!**
         Jar duh fung jeeng juhn pyaow lyahng.
         This scenery is really beautiful!

Michael: **Nǐ kàn! Nà zuò shān yǒu nàmme duō shù, nàmme
         duō huā.**
         *Nee kahn! Nah dzwaw shahn yo nummuh dwaw
         shoo, nummuh dwaw hwah.*
         Look! That mountain has so many trees and flowers.

Susan: **Duì le. Nèi kē shù tèbié piàoliàng. Zhè duǒ huā yě
         hěn yǒu tèsè.**
         *Dway luh. Nay kuh shoo tuh byeh pyaow lyahng. Jay
         dwaw hwah yeah hun yo tuh suh.*
         You're right. That tree is particularly beautiful. And
         this flower is also really unique.

Michael: **Nà kē shù shàng yě yǒu sān zhī niǎo.**
         Nah kuh shoe shahng lee yeah yo sahn jir nyaow.
         That tree also has three birds in it.

If a number and a measure word already appear in front of a pronoun or human noun, such as **sān ge háizi** *(sahn guh hi dzuh;* three children), don't add the suffix **–men** after **háizi** because plurality is already understood.

Never attach the suffix **-men** to anything not human. People will think you're nuts if you start referring to your two pet cats as **wǒde xiǎo māomen** (*waw duh shyaow maow mun*). Just say **Wǒde xiǎo māo hěn hǎo, xiè xiè** (*waw duh shyaow maow hun how, shyeh shyeh;* My cats are fine, thank you), and that should do the trick.

Definite versus indefinite articles

If you're looking for those little words in Chinese you can't seem to do without in English, such as "a," "an," and "the" — articles, as grammarians call them — you'll find they simply don't exist in Chinese. The only way you can tell if something is being referred to specifically (hence, considered definite) or just generally (and therefore, indefinite) is by the word order. Nouns that refer specifically to something are usually found at the beginning of the sentence, before the verb:

- **Shū zài nàr.** (*shoo dzye nar;* The book(s) are there.)
- **Háizimen xǐhuān tā.** (*hi dzuh mun she hwahn tah;* The children like her.)
- **Pánzi zài zhuōzishàng.** (*pahn dzuh dzye jwaw dzuh shahng;* There's a plate on the table.)

Nouns that refer to something more general (and are therefore "indefinite") can more often be found at the end of the sentence, after the verb:

- **Nǎr yǒu huā?** (*nar yo hwah;* Where are some flowers; Where is there a flower?)
- **Nàr yǒu huā.** (*nar yo hwah;* There are some flowers over there; There's a flower over there.)
- **Zhèige yǒu wèntí.** (*jay guh yo one tee;* There's a problem with this; There are some problems with this.)

There are some exceptions to these rules: If you find a noun at the beginning of a sentence, it may actually refer to something indefinite if the sentence makes a general comment (instead of telling a whole story), like when you see the verb **shì** (*shir;* to be) as part of the comment:

Xióngmāo shì dòngwù. (*shyoong maow shir doong woo;* Pandas are animals.)

Same thing goes if an adjective comes after the noun, such as

Pútáo hěn tián. (*poo taow hun tyan;* Grapes are very sweet.)

Or if there's an auxiliary verb:

Xiǎo māo huì zhuā lǎoshǔ. (*shyaow maow hway jwah laow shoo;* Kittens can catch mice.)

Or a verb indicating that the action occurs habitually:

Niú chī cǎo. (*nyo chir tsaow;* Cows eat grass.)

Nouns that are preceded by a numeral and a classifier, especially when the word **dōu** (*doe;* all) exists in the same breath, are also considered definite:

Sìge xuéshēng dōu hěn cōngmíng. (*suh guh shweh shung doe hun tsoong meeng;* The four students are all very smart.)

If the word **yǒu** (*yo;* to exist) comes before the noun and is then followed by a verb, it can also mean the reference is indefinite:

Yǒu shū zài zhuōzishàng. (*yo shoo dzye jwaw dzuh shahng;* There are books on top of the table.)

If you see the word **zhè** (*juh;* this) or **nà** (*nah;* that), plus a classifier used when a noun comes after the verb, it indicates a definite reference:

Wǒ yào mǎi nà zhāng huà. (*waw yaow my nah jahng hwah;* I want to buy that painting.)

Adjectives

As you learned in grade school (you were paying close attention, weren't you?), adjectives describe nouns. The question is where to put them. The general rule of thumb in Chinese is, if the adjective is pronounced with only one syllable, it appears immediately in front of the noun it qualifies:

- **lǜ chá** (*lyew chah;* green tea)
- **cháng zhītiáo** (*chahng jir tyaow;* long stick)

If the adjective has two syllables, though, the possessive particle **de** (*duh*) comes between it and whatever it qualifies:

- **gānjìng de yīfu** (*gahn jeeng duh ee foo;* clean clothes)
- **cāozá de wǎnhuì** (*tsaow dzah duh wahn hway;* noisy party)

And if a numeral is followed by a classifier, those should both go in front of the adjective and what it qualifies:

- **yí jiàn xīn yīfu** (*ee jyan shin ee foo;* a [piece of] new clothing)
- **sān běn yǒuyìsī de shū** (*sahn bun yo ee suh duh shoo;* three interesting books)

One unique thing about Chinese is that when an adjective is also the predicate, appearing at the end of a sentence, it follows the subject or the topic without needing the verb **shì** (*shir;* to be):

- **Tā de fángzi hěn gānjìng.** (*tah duh fahng dzuh hun gahn jeeng;* His house [is] very clean.)
- **Nà jiàn yīfu tài jiù.** (*nah jyan ee foo tye jyoe;* That piece of clothing [is] too old.)

Verbs

Good news! You never have to worry about conjugating a Chinese verb in your entire life! If you hear someone say **Tāmen chī Yìdàlì fàn** (*tah men chir ee dah lee fahn*), it could mean "They eat Italian food" just as easily as it could mean "They are eating Italian food." Table 2-2 lists some common verbs.

Table 2-2	Common Chinese Verbs	
Chinese	*Pronunciation*	*Translation*
chī	chir	to eat
kàn	kahn	to see
mǎi	my	to buy
mài	my	to sell
rènshi	run shir	to know (a person)
shì	shir	to be
yào	yaow	to want/to need
yǒu	yo	to have
zhīdào	jir daow	to know (a fact)
zǒu lù	dzoe loo	to walk
zuò fàn	dzwaw fahn	to cook

To be or not to be: The verb shì

Does the Chinese verb **shì** *(shir)* really mean "to be"? Or is it not to be? It is indeed similar to English in usage because it's often followed by a noun that defines the topic, such as **Tā shì wǒde lǎobǎn** *(tah shir waw duh laow bahn;* He's my boss) or **Nà shì yīge huài huà** *(nah shir ee guh hwye hwah;* That's a bad word).

Be careful not to put the verb **shì** in front of an adjective unless you really mean to make an emphatic statement. In the course of normal conversation, you might say **Nà zhǐ bǐ tài guì** *(nah jir bee tye gway;* That pen [is] too expensive). You wouldn't say **Nà zhǐ bǐ shì tài guì** *(nah jir bee shir tye gway)* unless you really want to say "That pen IS too expensive!" in which case you'd emphasize the word **shì** when saying it.

To negate the verb **shì**, put the negative prefix **bù** in front of it. **"Shì bú shì?"** *(shir boo shir;* Is it or isn't it?) **"Zhè bú shì táng cù yú"** *(jay boo shir tahng tsoo yew;* This isn't sweet and sour fish).

Feeling tense? Le, guò, and other aspect markers

Okay, you can relax now. There's nothing to get tense about with Chinese because verbs don't indicate tenses all by themselves. That's the job of *aspect markers.* Those are little syllables that indicate whether an action has been completed, is continuing, has just begun, and just about everything in between.

Take the syllable **le** *(luh),* for example. It can indicate an action has been completed if it's used as a suffix to a verb:

- ✔ **Nǐ mǎi le hěn duō shū.** *(nee my luh hun dwaw shoo;* You bought many books.)
- ✔ **Tā dài le tāde yǔsǎn.** *(tah dye luh tah duh yew sahn;* He brought his umbrella.)

And if you want to turn it into a question, just add **méiyǒu** at the end. It automatically negates the action completed by **le:**

- ✔ **Nǐ mǎi le hěn duō shū méiyǒu?** *(nee my luh hun dwaw shoo mayo;* Have you bought many books; Did you buy many books?)
- ✔ **Tā dài le tāde yǔsǎn méiyǒu?** *(tah dye luh tah duh yew sahn mayo;* Did he bring his umbrella?)

There's also **guò** *(gwaw).* It basically means that something has been done at one point or another even though it's not happening right now:

- ✔ **Tā qù guò Měiguó.** *(ta chyew gwaw may gwaw;* He has been to America.)
- ✔ **Wǒmen chī guò Fǎguó cài.** *(waw mun chir gwaw fah gwaw tsye;* We have eaten French food before.)

If an action is happening just as you speak, you use the aspect marker **zài** *(dzye)*:

> ✔ **Wŏmen zài chīfàn.** *(waw mun dzye chir fahn;* We are eating.*)*
>
> ✔ **Nĭ māma zài zuòfàn.** *(nee mah mah dzye dzwaw fahn;* Your mother is cooking.*)*

When using the aspect marker **zài**, you can also add the word **zhèng** *(juhng)* in front of it to add emphasis. It can be translated as "to be right in the middle of" doing something.

If something is or was happening continually and resulted from something else you did, just add the syllable **zhe** *(juh)* to the end of the verb to say things like

> ✔ **Tā dài zhe yíge huáng màozi.** *(tah dye juh ee guh hwahng maow dzuh;* He's wearing a yellow hat.*)*
>
> ✔ **Nĭ chuān zhè yí jiàn piàoliàng de chènshān.** *(nee chwan juh ee jyan pyaow lyahng duh ee foo;* You're wearing a pretty shirt.*)*

Another way you can use **zhe** is when you want to indicate two actions occurring at the same time:

> **Tā zuò zhe chīfàn.** *(tah dzwaw juh chir fahn;* She is/was sitting there eating.*)*

Talkin' the Talk

 Carol and Joe have fun people-watching on the streets of Shanghai.

Carol:	**Nĭ kàn! Nàge xiǎo háizi dài zhe yíge hěn qíguài de màozi, shì bú shì?** *Nee kahn! Nah guh shyaow hi dzuh dye juh ee guh hun chee gwye duh maow dzuh, shir boo shir?* Look! That little kid is wearing a really strange hat, isn't she?
Joe:	**Duì le. Tā hái yìbiān zǒu, yìbiān chàng gē.** *Dway luh. Tah hi ee byan dzoe, ee byan chahng guh.* Yeah. She's also singing while she walks.
Carol:	**Wǒ méiyǒu kàn guò nàmme kě'ài de xiǎo háizi.** *Waw mayo kahn gwaw nummuh kuh eye duh shyaow hi dzuh.* I've never seen such a cute child.

Joe: **Zài Zhōngguó nǐ yǐjīng kàn le tài duō kě'ài de xiǎo háizi.**
Dzye joong gwaw nee ee jeeng kahn luh tye dwaw kuh eye duh shyaow hi dzuh.
You've already seen too many adorable little kids in China.

Words to Know

kě'ài	kuh eye	cute; adorable
shì bú shì?	shir boo shir	Isn't that so?
qíguài	chee gwye	strange
chàng gē	chahng guh	to sing

The special verb: Yǒu (to have)

Do you **yǒu** *(yo)* a computer? No?! Too bad. Everyone else seems to have one these days. How about a Ferrari? Do you **yǒu** one of those? If not, welcome to the club. People who have lots of things use the word **yǒu** pretty often. It means "to have":

✔ **Wǒ yǒu yí wàn kuài qián.** (*waw yo ee wahn kwye chyan;* I have $10,000.)

✔ **Wǒ yǒu sānge fángzi — yíge zài Ōuzhōu, yíge zài Yàzhōu, yíge zài Měiguó.** (*waw yo sahn guh fahng dzuh — ee guh dzye oh joe, ee guh dzye yah joe, ee guh dzye may gwaw;* I have three homes — one in Europe, one in Asia, and one in America.)

Another way **yǒu** can be translated is "there is" or "there are":

✔ **Yǒu hěn duō háizi** (*yo hun dwaw hi dzuh;* There are many children), as opposed to **Wǒ yǒu hěn duō háizi.** (*waw yo hun dwaw hi dzuh;* I have many children.)

✔ **Shūzhuōshàng yǒu wǔ zhāng zhǐ.** (*shoo jwaw shahng yo woo jahng jir;* There are five pieces of paper on the desk.)

To negate the verb **yǒu,** you can't use the usual negative prefix **bù.** Instead, you must use another term indicating negation, **méi:**

- **Méiyǒu hěn duō háizi.** (*mayo hun dwaw hi dzuh;* There aren't many children.)

- **Shūzhuōshàng méiyǒu wǔ zhāng zhǐ.** (*shoe jwaw shahng may yo woo jahng jir;* There aren't five pieces of paper on the desk.)

Talkin' the Talk

Ramona and Linda talk about each other's families.

Ramona: **Nǐ yǒu méiyǒu xiōngdì jiěmèi?**
Nee yo mayo shyoong dee jyeh may?
Do you have any brothers or sisters?

Linda: **Wǒ yǒu liǎngge mèimei. Méiyǒu dìdi yě méiyǒu gēge. Nǐ ne?**
Waw yo lyahng guh may may. Mayo dee dee yeah mayo guh guh. Nee nuh?
I have two younger sisters. I don't have any younger or older brothers. How about you?

Ramona: **Wǒ méiyǒu mèimei. Zhǐ yǒu yíge dìdi.**
Waw mayo may may. Jir yo ee guh dee dee.
I don't have any younger sisters. Just one younger brother.

Linda: **Yǒu háizi ma?**
Yo hi dzuh mah?
Are there any children? (Do you have any children?)

Ramona: **Yǒu. Yǒu sānge háizi.**
Yo. Yo sahn guh hi dzuh.
Yes. I have three children.

Words to Know

wǒ yǒu	waw yo	I have
nǐ méiyǒu	nee mayo	you don't have
xiōngdì jiěmèi	shyoong dee jyeh may	brothers and/or sisters
háizi	hi dzuh	child/children

Asking for what you want: The verb yào

Ever since the 7-foot-6-inch basketball superstar from China, Yao Ming, came on the scene, the verb **yào** has gotten some great advance publicity in the United States. The character for his name isn't written quite the same as the verb **"yào,"** but at least everyone knows how to pronounce it already: *yow!*

Yào is one of the coolest verbs in Chinese. When you say it, you usually get what you want. In fact, the mere mention of the word **yào** means that you want something:

✔ **Wǒ yào yí bēi kāfēi.** (*waw yaow ee bay kah fay;* I want a cup of coffee.)

✔ **Wǒ yào gēn nǐ yìqǐ qù kàn diànyǐng.** (*waw yaow gun nee ee chee chyew kahn dyan yeeng;* I want to go to the movies with you.)

You can also give someone an order with the verb **yào,** but only if it's used with a second-person pronoun:

✔ **Nǐ yào xiǎoxīn!** (*nee yaow shyaow sheen;* You should be careful!)

✔ **Nǐ yào xǐ shǒu.** (*nee yaow she show;* You need to wash your hands.)

Adverbs

Adverbs serve to modify verbs or adjectives and always appear in front of them. The most common ones you find in Chinese are **hěn** (*hun;* very) and **yě** (*yeah;* also).

If you want to say that something is not just **hǎo** (*how;* good), but that it's *very* good, you say it's **hěn hǎo** (*hun how;* very good). If your friend wants to put his two cents in and say that something else is also really good, he says **"Zhèige yě hěn hǎo"** (*jay guh yeah hun how;* This is also very good) because **yě** always comes before **hěn**.

The adverb **yě** always comes not only before the adverb **hěn** but also before the negative prefix **bù**.

Bù and méiyǒu: Total negation

Boo! Scare you? Don't worry. I'm just being negative in Chinese. That's right, the word **bù** is pronounced the same way a ghost might say it *(boo)* and is often spoken with the same intensity.

Bù can negate something you've done in the past or the present (or at least indicate you don't generally do it these days), and it can also help negate something in the future:

- ✔ **Tā xiǎo de shíhòu bù xǐhuān chī shūcài.** (*tah shyaow duh shir ho boo she hwahn chir shoo tsye;* When he was young he didn't like to eat vegetables.)
- ✔ **Wǒ búyào chàng gē.** (*waw boo yaow chahng guh;* I don't want to sing.)
- ✔ **Wǒ bú huà huàr.** (*waw boo hwah hwar;* I don't paint.)
- ✔ **Diànyǐngyuàn xīngqīliù bù kāimén.** (*dyan yeeng ywan sheeng chee lyo boo kye mun;* The movie theatre won't be open on Saturday.)

The negative prefix **bù** is usually spoken with a fourth (falling) tone. However, when it precedes a syllable with another fourth tone, it becomes a second (rising) tone instead, as in such words as **búqù** (won't/didn't/doesn't go) and **búyào** (don't/didn't/won't want). (For more about tones, see Chapter 1.)

Méiyǒu is another negative prefix that also goes before a verb. It refers only to the past, though, and means either something didn't happen or at least didn't happen on a particular occasion:

- ✔ **Wǒ méiyǒu kàn nèi bù diànyǐng.** (*waw mayo kahn nay boo dyan yeeng;* I didn't see that movie.)
- ✔ **Zuótiān méiyǒu xiàyǔ.** (*dzwaw tyan mayo shyah yew;* It didn't rain yesterday.)

If the aspect marker **guò** is at the end of the verb **méiyǒu**, it means it never happened (up until now) in the past. By the way, you'll sometimes find that **méiyǒu** is shortened just to **méi**:

✔ **Wǒ méi qù guò Fǎguó.** (*waw may chyew gwaw fah gwaw;* I've never been to France.)

✔ **Wǒ méi chī guò Yìndù cài.** (*wo may chir gwaw een doo tsye;* I've never eaten Indian food.)

Talkin' the Talk

 Harvey, Stella, and Laurie discuss where to go for dinner.

Harvey: **Nǐmen jīntiān wǎnshàng yào búyào qù fànguǎn chīfàn?**
Nee mun jin tyan wahn shahng yaow boo yaow chyew fahn gwahn chir fahn?
Do you both want to go to a restaurant tonight?

Stella: **Nà tài hǎole. Dāngrán yào.**
Nah tye how luh. Dahng rahn yaow.
That's a great idea. Of course I'd like to go.

Laurie: **Wǒ búyào. Wǒ méiyǒu qián.**
Waw boo yaow. Waw mayo chyan.
I don't want to. I have no money.

Harvey: **Wǒ yě méiyǒu qián, dànshì méiyǒu guānxi. Wǒ zhīdào yíge hěn hǎo, hěn piányì de Zhōngguó fànguǎn.**
Waw yeah mayo chyan, dahn shir mayo gwahn she. Waw jir daow ee guh hun how, hun pyan yee duh joong gwaw fahn gwan.
I don't have any money either, but it doesn't matter. I know a great but very inexpensive Chinese restaurant.

Laurie: **Hǎo ba. Zánmen zǒu ba.**
How bah. Dzah men dzoe bah.
Okay. Let's go.

Words to Know

jīntiān wǎnshàng	jin tyan wahn shahng	tonight
tài hǎole	tye how luh	that's great
dāngrán	dahng rahn	of course
dànshì	dahn shir	but; however
zǒu ba	dzoe bah	let's go

Getting possessive with the particle de

The particle **de** is ubiquitous in Chinese. Wherever you turn, there it is. **Wǒde tiān!** (*waw duh tyan;* My goodness!) Oops . . . there it is again. It's easy to use. All you have to do is attach it to the end of the pronoun, such as **nǐde chē** (*nee duh chuh;* your car), or other modifier, such as **tā gōngsī de jīnglǐ** (*tah goong suh duh jeeng lee;* his company's manager), and — *voilà* — it indicates possession.

The particle **de** acts as an apostrophe "s" ('s) in English when it's not attached to a pronoun. It also makes the process of modification exactly the opposite of the French possessive "de" or the English "of," with which you may be tempted to compare it.

Talkin' the Talk

Lorna asks Ali about her computer.

Lorna: **Nǐde diànnǎo yǒu méiyǒu yīntèwǎng?**
Nee duh dyan now yo mayo een tuh wahng?
Does your computer have Internet?

Ali: **Kěxi méiyǒu. Nǐde ne?**
Kuh she mayo. Nee duh nuh?
Unfortunately not. How about yours?

Lorna:	**Dāngrán yǒu.**
	Dahng rahn yo.
	Definitely.

Ali:	**Nǐ yǒu méiyǒu yíge shǒutíshì?**
	Nee yo mayo ee guh show tee shir?
	Do you have a laptop?

Lorna:	**Táishì, shǒutíshì, liǎngge dōu yǒu.**
	Tye shir, show tee shir, lyahng guh doe yo.
	I have both a desktop and a laptop.

Words to Know

wǒ méiyǒu	waw mayo	I don't have
kěxi	kuh she	too bad; unfortunately
yīntèwǎng	een tuh wahng	Internet
táishì	tye shir	desktop
shǒutíshì	show tee shir	laptop

Asking Questions

There are a couple of easy ways to ask questions in Chinese. Hopefully you're so curious about the world around you these days that you're itching to ask lots of questions once you know how.

The question particle "ma"

By far the easiest way to ask a question is simply to end any given statement with a **"ma."** That automatically makes it into a question. For example, **Tā chīfàn** (*tah chir fahn*; He's eating/he eats) becomes **Tā chīfàn ma?** (*tah chir fahn mah*; Is he/does he eat?) **Nǐ shuō Zhōngwén** (*nee shwaw joong one*; You speak Chinese) becomes **Nǐ shuō Zhōngwén ma?** (*nee shwaw joong one mah*; Do you speak Chinese?)

Alternate choice questions using bù in between repeating verbs

The second way you can ask a question is to repeat the verb in its negative form. The English equivalent is to say something like "Do you eat, not eat?" This format can be used for only a yes or no question, though. For example:

- ✔ **Nǐ shì búshì Zhōngguórén?** (*nee shir boo shir joong gwaw run;* Are you Chinese?)

- ✔ **Tā yào búyào háizi?** (*tah yaow boo yaow hi dzuh;* Does he want children?)

- ✔ **Tāmen xǐhuān bùxǐhuān chī Zhōngguó cài?** (*tah men she hwahn boo she hwahn chir joong gwaw tsye;* Do they like to eat Chinese food?)

Interrogative pronouns

The last way to ask questions in Chinese is to use interrogative pronouns. The following are pronouns that act as questions in Chinese:

- ✔ **shéi** (*shay;* who/whom)

- ✔ **shéi de** (*shay duh;* whose)

- ✔ **shénme** (*shummuh;* what)

- ✔ **nǎ** (*nah* + classifier; which)

- ✔ **nǎr** (*nar;* where)

- ✔ **shénme dìfāng** (*shummah dee fahng;* where)

Don't confuse **nǎ** with **nǎr**. That one extra letter makes the difference between saying "which" (**nǎ**) and "where" (**nǎr**).

Figuring out where such interrogative pronouns should go in any given sentence is easy. Just put them wherever the answer would be found. For example:

- ✔ Question: **Nǐ shì shéi?** (*nee shir shay;* Who are you?)

- ✔ Answer: **Nǐ shì wǒ péngyǒu.** (*nee shir waw puhng yo;* You are my friend.)

- ✔ Question: **Tāde nǚpéngyǒu zài nǎr?** (*tah duh nyew puhng yo dzye nar;* Where is his girlfriend?)

- ✔ Answer: **Tāde nǚpéngyǒu zài jiālǐ.** (*tah duh nyew puhng yo dzye jyah lee;* His girlfriend is at home.)

This also goes for the verb-bù-verb pattern. All you have to do to answer that type of question is omit either the positive verb or the negative prefix and the verb following it:

✔ Question: **Nǐ hǎo bù hǎo?** (*nee how boo how;* How are you? *Literally:* Are you good or not good?)

✔ Answer: **Wǒ hǎo** (*waw how;* I'm okay) or **Wǒ bùhǎo** (*waw boo how;* I'm not okay).

A way of asking "who" or "which person" without sounding rude or too familiar is to use the term **něi wèi:** *literally,* "which person." For example, **Nǐ yéye shì něi wèi?** (*nee yeh yeh shir nay way;* Which one is your grandfather?)

You'll often find interrogative pronouns at the beginning of sentences if they're followed by the verb **yǒu** (*yo;* to exist), such as **Shéi yǒu wǒde bǐ?** (*shay yo waw duh bee;* Who has my pen?)

Talkin' the Talk

Ruth asks Seymour what he thinks of her new car.

Ruth: **Nǐ xǐhuān bùxǐhuān wǒde xīn qìchē?**
Nee she hwahn boo she hwahn waw duh shin chee chuh?
Do you like my new car?

Seymour: **Shéi bùxǐhuān zhè liàng chē? Tā hěn piàoliàng!**
Shay boo she hwahn jay lyahng chuh? Tah hun pyaow lyahng!
Who wouldn't like this car? It's really beautiful!

Ruth: **Kěnéng yǒu yìxiē péngyǒu yǐwéi tài guì.**
Kuh nung yo ee shyeh puhng yo ee way tye gway.
Maybe some friends would think it's too expensive.

Seymour: **Nà yǒu shénme guānxi?**
Nah yo shummuh gwahn she?
What difference does that make? (Who cares?)

Ruth: **Duì le. Nǎr yǒu gèng hǎo de qìchē?**
Dway luh. Nar yo guhng how duh chee chuh?
You're right. Where could you find a better car?

Seymour: **Méiyǒu gèng hǎo de qìchē. Nǐde yùnqì búcuò!**
Mayo guhng how duh chee chuh. Nee duh yewn chee boo tswaw!
There isn't a better car around. You're really lucky!

Words to Know

xǐhuān	she hwahn	to like
qìchē	chee chuh	car
búcuò	boo tswaw	not bad; really good
yǒu shénme guānxi	yo shummuh gwahn she	What difference does it make?

Counting in Chinese

Figuring out things like how to specify the number of pounds of meat you want to buy at the market, how much money you want to change at the airport, or how much that cab ride from your hotel is really going to cost can be quite an ordeal if you don't know the basic words for numbers.

Numbers from 1 to 10

Learning to count from 1 to 10 in Chinese is as easy as **yī** (*ee;* one), **èr** (*are;* two), **sān** (*sahn;* three). Table 2-3 lists numbers from 1 to 10.

Table 2-3	Numbers from 1 to 10	
Chinese	**Pronunciation**	**Translation**
líng	leeng	0
yī	ee	1
èr	are	2
sān	sahn	3
sì	suh	4
wǔ	woo	5
liù	lyo	6

Chinese	Pronunciation	Translation
qī	chee	7
bā	bah	8
jiǔ	jyoe	9
shí	shir	10

If the number two comes before a classifier (see the section "Classifiers" earlier in this chapter), use the word **liǎng** rather than **èr.** So you would say that you have **liǎng běn shū** (_lyahng bun shoo;_ two books) rather than **èr běn shū** (_are bun shoo_).

Practice saying these numbers by listening to the accompanying CD at bedtime, and you'll be counting sheep in Chinese in no time.

Numbers from 11 to 99

After the number 10, numbers are created by saying the word 10 followed by the single digit that, when added to it, will combine to create numbers 11 through 19. It's real easy. For example, 11 is **shíyī** (_shir ee_) — literally, 10 plus 1. Same thing goes for 12, and so on through 19. Table 2-4 lists numbers from 11 to 19.

Table 2-4	Numbers from 11 to 19	
Chinese	**Pronunciation**	**Translation**
shíyī	shir ee	11 (literally 10 + 1)
shí'èr	shir are	12 (literally 10 + 2)
shísān	shir sahn	13
shísì	shir suh	14
shíwǔ	shir woo	15
shíliù	shir lyo	16
shíqī	shir chee	17
shíbā	shir bah	18
shíjiǔ	shir jyoe	19

When you get to 20, you have to literally think "two 10s" — plus whatever single digit you want to add to that up until 9 for 21 through 29, as shown in Table 2-5.

Table 2-5	Numbers from 20 to 29	
Chinese	*Pronunciation*	*Translation*
èrshí	are shir	20 (literally two 10s)
èrshíyī	are shir ee	21 (two 10s + 1)
èrshí'èr	are shir are	22
èrshísān	are shir sahn	23
èrshísì	are shir suh	24
èrshíwǔ	are shir woo	25
èrshíliù	are shir lyo	26
èrshíqī	are shir chee	27
èrshíbā	are shir bah	28
èrshíjiǔ	are shir jyoe	29

The same basic idea goes for **sānshí** (*sahn shir;* 30; *literally:* three 10s), **sìshí** (*suh shir;* 40), **wǔshí** (*woo shir;* 50), **liùshí** (*lyo shir;* 60), **qīshí** (*chee shir;* 70), **bāshí** (*bah shir;* 80), and **jiǔshí** (*jyoe shir;* 90). What could be easier?

Numbers from 100 to 9,999

After the number 99, you can no longer count by tens.

- ✔ 100 is **yì bǎi** (*ee bye*).
- ✔ 1,000 is **yì qiān** (*ee chyan*).

Chinese people count all the way up to **wàn** (*wahn;* ten thousand) and then repeat up to **yì** (*ee;* a hundred million), unlike in English, where counting goes up to a thousand before being repeated all the way to a million.

Numbers are represented with the higher units of value first. So the number 387 is **sān bǎi bā shí qī** (*sahn bye bah shir chee*). The number 15,492 is **yí wàn wǔ qiān sì bǎi jiǔ shí èr** (*ee wahn woo chyan suh bye jyoe shir are*).

The number one (**yī**) changes its tone from the first (high) to the fourth (falling) tone when followed by a first (high) tone, as in **yì qiān** (*ee chyan;* 1,000), by a second (rising) tone, as in **yì nián** (*ee nyan;* one year), and by a third (low dipping) tone, as in **yì bǎi** (*ee bye;* 100). And it changes to the second (rising) tone when followed by a fourth (falling) tone, as in **yí wàn** (*ee wahn;* 10,000). It remains its original first tone mark only when people count numbers: one, two, three, and so on.

Numbers from 10,000 to 100,000 and beyond

Here are the big numbers:

- 10,000 is **yí wàn** (*ee wahn; literally:* one unit of ten thousand).
- 100,000 is **shí wàn** (*shir wahn; literally:* ten units of ten thousand).
- 1,000,000 is **yì bǎi wàn** (*ee bye wahn: literally:* one hundred units of ten thousand).
- 100,000,000 is **yí yì** (*ee ee;* one hundred million).

Numbers play an interesting role in everyday speech in China. Sometimes you'll hear someone say emphatically **Nǐ qiānwàn búyào xìn tāde huà** (*nee chyan wahn boo yaow sheen tah duh hwah;* No matter what, you're not to believe what he says!) **Qiān** means one thousand, and **wàn** means ten thousand, but when you put those two words together in front of the negative prefix **bù,** you emphasize a point even more. Another phrase that has been heard often in the Chinese past is the partial phrase **wàn suì!** (*wahn sway;* long live). After that phrase, the person may add the name of someone in power, so you hear something like **Máo zhǔxí wàn suì!** (*maow joo she wahn sway;* Long live Chairman Mao!) These days if you use this expression, you're kind of parodying a phrase taken extremely seriously just a few short decades ago.

How 'bout those halves?

So what happens if you want to add a half to anything? You might be asking yourself this about now. Well, the word for half is **bàn** *(bahn),* and it can either come at the beginning, such as in **bàn bēi kělè** (*bahn bay kuh luh;* a half a glass of cola), or after a number and classifier but before the object to mean "and a half," such as in **yí ge bàn xīngqī** (*ee guh bahn sheeng chee;* a week and a half).

Ordinal numbers

If you want to indicate the order of something, add the word **dì** *(dee)* before the numeral:

Chinese	Pronunciation	Translation
dì yī	dee ee	first
dì èr	dee are	second
dì sān	dee sahn	third
dì sì	dee suh	fourth
dì wǔ	dee woo	fifth
dì liù	dee lyo	sixth
dì qī	dee chee	seventh
dì bā	dee bah	eighth
dì jiǔ	dee jyoe	ninth
dì shí	dee shir	tenth

If a noun follows the ordinal number, a classifier needs to go in between them, such as **dì bā ge xuésheng** *(dee bah guh shweh shuhng;* the eighth student) or **dì yī ge háizi** *(dee ee guy hi dzuh;* the first child).

Asking how many or how much

There are two ways to ask how much something is or how many of something there are. You can either use the question word **duōshǎo** *(dwaw shaow),* when referring to something for which the answer is probably more than 10, or **jǐ (ge)** *(jee guh),* when referring to something for which the answer is probably going to be less than 10:

- **Nàge qìchē duōshǎo qián?** *(nah guh chee chuh dwaw shaow chyan;* How much is that car?)

- **Nǐ xiǎo nǚ'ér jīnnián jǐ suì?** *(nee shyaow nyew are jin nyan jee sway;* How old is your little girl this year?)

Fun & Games

Count to 10 and then to 100 in multiples of 10 by filling in the blanks with the correct numbers. Turn to Appendix C for the answers.

yī

èr

sān

sì

_____

liù

_____

bā

jiǔ

_____

èrshí

_____

sìshí

wǔshí

_____

qīshí

bāshí

_____

yìbǎi

Chapter 3

Introductions and Greetings: Nǐ Hǎo!

· ·

In This Chapter

▶ Introducing yourself and others

▶ Greeting and chatting with family, friends, and colleagues

· ·

Nǐ hǎo! (*nee how;* Hello!; How are you?) Those are probably the two most important words you need to know to start a conversation with your Chinese neighbors, with your Chinese in-laws coming into town, with a Chinese classmate, or with airport personnel upon your arrival in China. When you say them, you take the first step in making new friends and establishing contact with just about anybody.

In this chapter, I show you how to start your new connection off with just the right words. The only other thing you have to do is smile. That's something all people understand, no matter what country they're from.

Making Introductions

Nothing beats making new friends at a **wǎnhuì** (*wahn hway;* party), a **xīn gōngzuò** (*sheen goong dzwaw;* new job), on the **dìtiě** (*dee tyeh;* subway), or just **zài lùshàng** (*dzye loo shahng;* on the street). You may meet someone right after reading this chapter who becomes a good friend for life. This section gives you a head start in making a good first impression. Go ahead and practice these greetings to get ready for anything.

Acquainting yourself

When you make Chinese acquaintances or travel abroad, you soon discover that a little knowledge of even a few key expressions in their native language goes a long way in creating good will between your two cultures. Chinese people in particular are very appreciative of anyone who takes the time to learn their intricate and difficult language, so your efforts will be rewarded many times over.

You have options other than **nǐ hǎo** (*nee how;* hi; how are you) when you first meet someone, such as **Hěn gāoxìng jiàndào nǐ** (*hun gaow sheeng jyan daow nee;* Glad to meet you) or **Wǒ hěn róngxìng** (*waw hun roong sheeng;* I'm honored to meet you). Go ahead and tell the person your **míngzi** (*meeng dzuh;* name) and take the conversation from there.

Don't know what to say after the first **nǐ hǎo?** Here are a few examples of common opening lines to get you started:

- ✔ **Qǐng ràng wǒ jièshào wǒ zìjǐ.** (*cheeng rahng waw jyeh shaow waw dzuh jee;* Please let me introduce myself.)

- ✔ **Wǒ jiào _____. Nǐ ne?** (*waw jyaow ____. nee nuh;* My name is _____. What's yours?)

- ✔ **Nǐ jiào shénme míngzi?** (*nee jyaow shummuh meeng dzuh;* What's your name?)

- ✔ **Wǒ shì Měiguórén.** (*waw shir may gwaw run;* I'm an American.)

Introducing your friends and family

You can help your friends make even more friends if you start introducing them to each other. All you have to do is say **Qǐng ràng wǒ jièshào wǒde péngyǒu, Carl.** (*cheeng rahng waw jyeh shaow waw duh puhng yo, Carl;* Let me introduce my friend, Carl.) In addition to introducing your **péngyǒu** (*puhng yo;* friend), you can also introduce these important people:

- ✔ **māma** (*mah mah;* mother)
- ✔ **bàba** (*bah bah;* father)
- ✔ **tàitai** (*tye tye;* wife)
- ✔ **zhàngfu** (*jahng foo;* husband)
- ✔ **lǎoshī** (*laow shir;* teacher)

✔ **tóngwū** (*toong woo;* roommate)

✔ **tóngxué** (*toong shweh;* classmate)

✔ **wǒde péngyǒu** (*waw duh puhng yo;* my friend)

✔ **nán péngyǒu** (*nahn puhng yo;* boyfriend)

✔ **nǚ péngyǒu** (*nyew pung yo;* girlfriend)

✔ **tóngshì** (*toong shir;* colleague)

✔ **lǎobǎn** (*laow bahn;* boss)

When introducing two people to each other, always introduce the one with the lower social status and/or age to the person with the higher social status. The Chinese consider it polite.

Asking people for their names

Many situations call for informal greetings like **Wǒ jiào Sarah. Nǐ ne?** (*waw jyaow Sarah. nee nuh;* My name is Sarah. And yours?) or **Nǐ jiào shénme míngzi?** (*nee jyaow shummuh meeng dzuh;* What's your name?), but you can show a greater level of politeness and respect by asking **Nín guì xìng?** (*neeng gway sheeng; literally:* What's your honorable surname?) But if you're asking this of someone who's younger than you or lower in social status, you can easily just say **Nǐ jiào shénme míngzi?** (*nee jyaow shummah meeng dzuh;* What's your name?) Even though **míngzi** usually means "given name," when you ask this question, it may elicit an answer of first and last name. Keep practicing these different opening lines to ask who people are and you're bound to make friends quickly (or you're bound to get to know a lot of Chinese names at least).

If someone asks **Nín guì xìng**, don't use the honorific **guì** when you answer, referring to yourself. Your new acquaintance would consider you too boastful. Such a response is like saying "My esteemed family name is Smith." The best way to answer is to say **Wǒ xìng Smith.** (*waw sheeng Smith;* My family name is Smith.)

If a guy tells you his name in Chinese, you can be sure the first syllable he utters will be his surname, not his given name. So if he says his name is **Lǐ Shìmín,** for example, his family name is **Lǐ** and his given name is **Shìmín.** You should keep referring to him as **Lǐ Shìmín** (rather than just **Shìmín**) until you become really good friends. If you want to address him as **Xiānshēng** (*shyan shuhng;* Mr.), or if you're addressing a female as **Xiǎojiě** (*shyaow jyeh;* Miss), you put that title after his or her last name and say **Lǐ Xiānshēng** or **Lǐ Xiǎojiě.** Even though the Chinese language has words for Mr., Miss, and Mrs. (**Tàitài;** *tye tye*), it has no equivalent term for "Ms." At least not yet.

Talkin' the Talk

 Sylvia introduces her friends, Irene and Mel, to each other.

Sylvia: **Irene, qǐng ràng wǒ jièshào wǒde péngyǒu Mel.**
Irene, cheeng rahng waw jyeh shaow waw duh puhng yo Mel.
Irene, allow me to introduce my friend Mel.

Irene: **Nǐ hǎo. Hěn gāoxìng jiàndào nǐ.**
Nee how. Hun gaow sheeng jyan daow nee.
Hi. Nice to meet you.

Mel: **Hěn gāoxìng jiàndào nǐ. Wǒ shì Sylvia de tóngxué.**
Hun gaow sheeng jyan daow nee. Waw shir Sylvia duh toong shweh.
Good to meet you. I'm Sylvia's classmate.

Irene: **Hěn gāoxìng jiàndào nǐ.**
Hun gaow sheeng jyan daow nee.
Nice to meet you.

Mel: **Nǐmen zénme rènshì?**
Nee mun dzummuh run shir?
How do you happen to know each other?

Irene: **Wǒmen shì tóngshì.**
Waw mun shir toong shir.
We're co-workers.

Greeting and Chatting

When you **dǎ zhāohu** (*dah jaow who;* extend greetings), you're sure to maintain and possibly even improve your connections with others. This goes for starting the day right with your **àirén** (*eye run;* spouse), showing respect for your **lǎoshī** (*laow shir;* teacher), keeping on the good side of your **lǎobǎn** (*laow bahn;* boss), or paving the way for that deal with your new **shēngyì huǒbàn** (*shuhng yee hwaw bahn;* business partner).

After the opening greeting, stick around to chat for a bit so you can get to know each other better. You can make new friends and find out more about each other through small conversations. This section gives you the important phrases to know.

Addressing new friends and strangers

In your hometown or home country, you may have plenty of **lǎo péngyǒu** (*laow puhng yo;* old friends), but in any other city or country, you need to get off on the right foot by addressing people the way they're used to being addressed. You can get chummier as time goes by, but try to avoid sounding too friendly or presumptuous too soon.

It's always safe to greet people in professional settings by announcing their last name followed by their title, such as **Wáng Xiàozhǎng** (*wahng shyaow jahng;* President [of an educational institution] Wang) or **Jīn Zhǔrèn** (*jeen joo run;* Director Jin). Here are some other examples of occupational titles:

- **bùzhǎng** (*boo jahng;* department head or minister)
- **fùzhǔrèn** (*foo joo run;* assistant director)
- **jiàoshòu** (*jyaow show;* professor)
- **jīnglǐ** (*jeeng lee;* manager)
- **lǎoshī** (*laow shir;* teacher)

If you don't know someone's title, you can safely address the person by saying his or her family name and then either **Xiānshēng** (*shyan shuhng;* Mr.) or **Xiǎojiě** (*shyaow jyeh;* Miss).

One of the perks of getting to know someone's family in China is that the person often instructs his or her young children to address an older person as **shúshu** (*shoo shoo;* uncle) or **āyí** (*ah yee;* aunt). It makes you feel like you're part of the family in a new country.

Sometimes people add the terms **lǎo** (*laow;* old) or **xiǎo** (*shyaow;* young) in front of the last name and omit the first name completely. It indicates a comfortable degree of familiarity and friendliness that can only develop over time. But make sure you know which one to use — **lǎo** is for someone who's older than you, and **xiǎo** is for someone who's younger than you. Sometimes these names can sound kind of funny to non-Chinese. If someone's surname is pronounced **Yáng** (*yahng*), which sounds like the word for goat, you may end up sounding like you're calling the person an old goat when you become good friends.

Conversing around the clock

You can always say **nǐ hǎo** (*nee how;* hi; how are you) when you meet someone, but at certain times of the day, you can use specific ways to express your greetings.

A word about culturally acceptable behavior

The Chinese are very friendly people and sometimes don't hesitate to come up to a foreigner on the street in order to practice their English. This can be a great chance to practice your Chinese as well. You have all sorts of cultural differences to get used to, however, so don't be surprised if a person you meet for the first time starts asking you about your salary or the cost of that cute sweater you're wearing. Subjects that are taboo as conversation pieces in the United States aren't off limits in China. (***Note:*** Try not to inquire about a person's political views or love life unless you know the person really well, or you may hit a brick wall.)

In general, Chinese people are loath to show negative emotions in public. Anger and disappointment or disapproval are major no-nos. Try to do the same when you're in a Chinese setting, because you may run the risk of insulting someone unintentionally. To do so means that you make them lose face — a cardinal sin if you want to get along in China. The last thing you want to do is insult, yell at, or otherwise embarrass anyone publicly, so keep a lid on any negative reactions you may have. You earn respect by controlling your emotions.

You may be surprised that many Chinese have no compunction about performing certain bodily functions in public. The Chinese don't consider it rude, for example, to belch, spit, or even pass gas in front of others. And because there's no such thing as a nonsmoking area, most smokers don't even think to ask if you mind them lighting up near you. In addition to all these things that tend to offend foreigners, you may find people pointing or even staring at you — especially in smaller towns and villages, which rarely get foreign visitors. These behaviors are considered perfectly acceptable, so don't let them get your dander up. Just go with the flow and offer a polite smile in return.

The Chinese have a different idea about keeping a certain polite physical distance when speaking to someone. It isn't uncommon to find someone standing or sitting pretty close to you, no matter how much you keep trying to inch away. And if you find two friends of the same sex walking arm in arm or holding hands, don't jump to any conclusions. It just means that they're friends.

Note: Avoid slaps on the back to Chinese people you don't know well, no matter how excited you are to meet them. And when dealing with members of the opposite sex, any physical contact with folks you don't know too well will be misinterpreted, so try to avoid it.

In the morning when you meet family, friends, co-workers, or fellow students in class, you can say **zǎo** (*dzaow;* good morning) or **zǎo ān** (*dzaow ahn;* good morning; *literally:* early peace).

In the evening or before you go to sleep, you can say **wǎn ān** (*wahn ahn;* good night). Just as **zǎo** means *early,* **wǎn** means *late.* So if someone says **Nǐ lái de tài wǎn** (*nee lye duh tye wahn*) or **Nǐ lái de tài zǎo** (*nee lye duh tye dzaow),* he means "You came too late" or "You came too early."

Talkin' the Talk

 Ricky and Norman are good friends who meet in front of school one morning. Norman introduces Ricky to a new student named Lǐ.

Norman: **Zǎo. Nǐ zěnme yàng?**
Dzaow. Nee dzummuh yahng?
Good morning. How's it going?

Ricky: **Hěn hǎo, xièxiè. Nǐ ne?**
Hun how, shyeh shyeh. Nee nuh?
Very well, thanks. And you?

Norman: **Wǒ yě hěn hǎo. Zhè wèi shì wǒmen de xīn tóngxué.**
Waw yeah hun how. Jay way shir waw mun duh sheen toong shweh.
I'm good, too. This is our new classmate.

Ricky: **Nǐ hǎo. Qǐng wèn, nǐ xìng shénme?**
Nee how. Cheeng one, nee sheeng shummuh?
Hi. What's your (sur)name?

Lily: **Wǒ xìng Lǐ. Nǐ jiào shénme míngzi?**
Waw sheeng Lǐ. Nee jyaow shummuh meeng dzuh?
My last name is Lǐ. What's your (first) name?

Ricky: **Wǒ jiào Ricky. Nǐ xué shénme?**
Waw jyaow Ricky. Nee shweh shummuh?
My name is Ricky. What do you study?

Lily: **Wǒ xué lìshǐ. Nǐ ne?**
Waw shweh lee shir. Nee nuh?
I study history. How about you?

Ricky: **Wǒ xué kuàijì.**
Waw shweh kwye jee.
I study accounting.

Words to Know

míngzi	meeng dzuh	first name
xìng	sheeng	last name
tóngxué	toong shweh	classmate
xué	shweh	to study
yǔyīnxué	yew een shweh	linguistics
lìshǐ	lee shir	history
gōngchéng	goong chuhng	engineering
kuàijì	kwye jee	accounting

Talking about the weather

Talking about the **tiānqì** (*tyan chee;* weather) is always a safe topic in any conversation. In fact, it's kind of the universal ice breaker. If the skies are blue and all seems right with the world, you can start by saying **"Jīntiān de tiānqì zhēn hǎo, duì bú duì?"** (*jin tyan duh tyan chee juhn how, dway boo dway;* The weather today is sure nice, isn't it?) Here are some adjectives to describe temperature and humidity:

- ✔ **lěng** (*lung;* cold)
- ✔ **liángkuài** (*lyahng kwye;* cool)
- ✔ **mēnrè** (*mun ruh;* muggy)
- ✔ **nuǎnhuó** (*nwan hwaw;* warm)
- ✔ **rè** (*ruh;* hot)

If the weather is hot, you can use the word **rè** to describe it. But if your food is spicy, which you sometimes refer to as "hot" in English, you can't use **rè** to describe it. You have to say it's **là** *(lah)* instead. And if your food is too hot (in terms of temperature) to even put into your mouth, you say it's **tàng** *(tahng).*

The **sìjì** (*suh jee;* four seasons) — **dōngtiān** (*doong tyan;* winter), **chūntiān** (*chwun tyan;* spring), **xiàtiān** (*shyah tyan;* summer), and **qiūtiān** (*chyo tyan;* fall) — all have their charms. They also all have their distinctive characteristics when it comes to the weather, which you can express with the following words in any conversation:

- **bàofēngxuě** (*baow fuhng shweh;* blizzard)
- **dàfēng** (*dah fuhng;* gusty winds)
- **duōyún** (*dwaw yewn;* cloudy)
- **fēng hěn dà** (*fuhng hun dah;* windy)
- **léiyǔ** (*lay yew;* thunderstorm)
- **qínglǎng** (*cheeng lahng;* sunny)
- **qíngtiān** (*cheeng tyan;* clear)
- **xià máomáoyǔ** (*shyah maow maow yew;* drizzle)
- **xiàwù** (*shyah woo;* fog)
- **xiàxuě** (*shyah shweh;* snow)
- **xiàyǔ** (*shyah yew;* rainy)
- **yīntiān** (*yeen tyan;* overcast)

Talkin' the Talk

Jean and Bill discuss the weather in Harbin, one of the coldest places in northern China.

Jean: **Hā'ěrbīn dōngtiān hěn lěng. Chángcháng xiàxuě.**
Hah are been doong tyan hun lung. Chahng chahng shyah shweh.
Harbin is very cold in the winter. It snows often.

Bill: **Zhēnde ma?**
Jun duh mah?
Really?

Jean: **Zhēnde. Yě yǒu bàofēngxuě. Xiàtiān hái hǎo. Bǐjiào nuǎnhuó.**
Jun duh. Yeh yo baow fuhng shweh. Shyah tyan hi how. Bee jyaow nwan hwaw.
Really. There are also blizzards. Summertime is okay, though. It's relatively warm.

Bill:	**Lěng tiān kéyǐ qù huáxuě, hái kéyǐ qù liūbīng. Nèmme Hā'ěrbīn dōngtiān de shíhòu hěn hǎo wán.**
	Lung tyan kuh yee chyew hwah shweh, hi kuh yee chyew lyo beeng. Nummah hah are been doong tyan duh shir ho hun how wahn.
	In cold weather, you can go skiing or ice skating. So Harbin during the winter is a lot of fun.

Finding out where people are from

It's natural to wonder where people are from when you first meet them. Maybe they hail from your hometown. Maybe your new friend's mother and your father went to the same high school way back when. Either way, whatever motivates you to pose the question, you ask it by saying **"Nǐ shì nǎr de rén?"** (*nee shir nar duh run;* Where are you from?)

To answer this question, you replace the word **nǐ** (*nee;* you) with **wǒ** (*waw;* I) and put the name of wherever you're from where the word **nǎr** is.

People in Taiwan say **nálǐ** (*nah lee*) rather than **nǎr** (*nar*) for the word "where." **Nǎr** indicates a northern accent and is used primarily by people from mainland China.

Here' a list of countries that may come up in conversation:

- ✔ **Fǎguó** (*fah gwaw;* France)
- ✔ **Měiguó** (*may gwaw;* America)
- ✔ **Rìběn** (*ir bun;* Japan)
- ✔ **Ruìdiǎn** (*rway dyan;* Sweden)
- ✔ **Ruìshì** (*rway shir;* Switzerland)
- ✔ **Yìdàlì** (*ee dah lee;* Italy)
- ✔ **Yuènán** (*yweh nahn;* Vietnam)
- ✔ **Zhōngguó** (*joong gwaw;* China)

Talkin' the Talk

Cynthia has just introduced herself to Adrienne at their mutual friend's house. Cynthia asks Adrienne where she is from.

Cynthia: **Adrienne, nǐ shì nǎr de rén?**
Adrienne, nee shir nar duh run?
Adrienne, where are you from?

Adrienne: **Wǒ shì Jiāzhōu rén. Nǐ ne?**
Waw shir jyah joe run. Nee nuh?
I'm from California. How about you?

Cynthia: **Wǒ búshì Měiguórén. Wǒ shì Yīngguó Lúndūn láide.**
Waw boo shir may gwaw run. Waw shir eeng gwaw lwun dun run.
I'm not American. I'm from London, England.

Adrienne: **Nà tài hǎole.**
Nah tye how luh.
That's great.

Words to Know

Jiāzhōu	jyah joe	California
Měiguórén	may gwaw run	American
Yīngguó	eeng gwaw	England
Nà tài hǎole	nah tye how luh	That's great

Taking (a.k.a. rejecting) compliments

Chinese people are always impressed whenever they meet a foreigner who has taken the time to learn their language. So when you speak **Zhōngwén** (*joong one;* Chinese) to a **Zhōngguórén** (*joong gwaw run;* Chinese person), he may very well say **Nǐde Zhōngwén tài hǎole.** (*nee duh joong one tye how luh;* Your Chinese is fantastic.) Instead of patting yourself on the back, however, you should be slightly self-deprecating in your response (see Chapter 18 for more things you should never do). Don't give in to the temptation to accept the compliment easily and say **xiè xiè** (*shyeh shyeh;* thanks), because that implies that you agree wholeheartedly with the complimentary assessment. Instead, try one of the following replies. Each of them can be roughly translated as "It's nothing" or the equivalent of "No, no, I don't deserve any praise":

✔ **guò jiǎng guò jiǎng** (*gwaw jyahng gwaw jyahng*)

✔ **nálǐ nálǐ** (*nah lee nah lee*)

✔ **nǎr de huà** (*nar duh hwah*)

Saying goodbye

When it comes time to say goodbye, you can always say **zài jiàn** (*dzye jyan;* goodbye). If you're just leaving for a little while and plan to be back soon, you can say **yīhuǐr jiàn** (*ee hwahr jyan;* see you in a bit). And if you won't see someone until the next day, you can say **míngtiān jiàn** (*meeng tyan jyan;* see you tomorrow). For a quick "see you later," you can say **huítóu jiàn** (*hway toe jyan*). Here's a list of other phrases you can use to say goodbye:

✔ **huítóu jiàn** (*hway toe jyan;* see you later)

✔ **míngnián jiàn** (*meeng nyan jyan;* see you next year)

✔ **míngtiān jiàn** (*meeng tyan jyan;* see you tomorrow)

✔ **xiàge lǐbài jiàn** (*shyah guh lee bye jyan;* see you next week)

✔ **xīngqī'èr jiàn** (*sheeng chee are jyan;* see you on Tuesday)

✔ **yīhuǐr jiàn** (*ee hwahr jyan;* see you soon)

✔ **yílù píng'ān** (*ee loo peeng ahn;* have a good trip)

✔ **zài jiàn** (*dzye jyan;* goodbye)

The importance of the common good

In China, the collective always comes before the individual. The Chinese are certainly not as self-centered as Westerners and generally subordinate their individual desires in favor of the greatest common good, whether the "common good" refers to the good of the family, the class at school, or co-workers. You even see this mentality in the way envelopes are addressed — the country first, followed by the province, the city, the street address, and then, on the last line, the person's name to whom it is addressed. And even on that last line, the person's name is written with the family name first and the given name last. The same holds true for the way people refer to where they're from — the larger unit always comes before the smaller. That's why a person would say, for example, that he's from **Yīngguó Lúndūn** (*eeng gwaw lwun dun;* England, London) rather than London, England, as you say in English.

Talkin' the Talk

Christopher runs into his history professor in the morning after the conclusion of class.

Christopher: **Lǎoshī zǎo.**
Laow shir dzaow.
Good morning, Professor.

Professor: **Zǎo. Nǐ hǎo.**
Dzaow. Nee how.
Good morning. Hello.

Christopher: **Jīntiān de tiānqì hěn hǎo, duì búduì?**
Jin tyan duh tyan chee hun how, dway boo dway?
The weather today is great, isn't it?

Professor: **Duì le. Hěn hǎo.**
Dway luh. Hun how.
Yes, it is. It's very nice.

Christopher: **Nèmme, míngtiān shàngkè de shíhòu zài jiàn.**
Nummuh, meeng tyan shahng kuh duh shir ho dzye jyan.
So, I'll see you again in class tomorrow.

Professor: **Hǎo. Míngtiān jiàn.**
How. Meeng tyan jyan.
Okay. See you tomorrow.

Fun & Games

Here's a list of words that got loose. See if you can put them back where they belong in the following text and dialogue.

míngzi, bàofēngxuě, jiàn, Déguórén, hǎo

Zǎo. Nǐ _____. Wǒde _____ jiào John. Wǒ shì _____. Jīntiān de tiānqì hěn hǎo. Méiyǒu _____. Huítóu _____.

The answers are in Appendix C.

Match the situation with the appropriate expression. You can find the answers in Appendix C.

1. You see someone again after a long time.

2. You see your friend in the evening.

3. You see your teacher in the morning.

4. Someone compliments you on your new hair style.

5. Someone introduces you to his brother.

6. Your best friend is about to board a plane for France.

a. Hěn gāoxìng jiàndào nǐ.

b. Yílù píng'ān.

c. Hǎo jiǔ méi jiàn.

d. Wǎn ān.

e. Zǎo.

f. Nǎr de huà.

Part II
Chinese in Action

The 5th Wave

By Rich Tennant

"I'll be screaming in Chinese throughout the ride. It helps me affect the proper inflections."

In this part . . .

This part helps you jump right in to everyday activities: shooting the breeze with friends, eating, drinking, shopping 'til you drop, working at the office, hanging out at home, and just plain ol' enjoying your spare time. I cover it all so that you can do it in Chinese. Choose your favorite topic and start putting your Chinese into action!

Chapter 4

Getting to Know You: Making Small Talk

Small talk can really break the ice when you're interacting with someone you've just met or barely know. It's how you get to know someone, have a brief chat with the man on the plane sitting next to you, or get acquainted with the folks you'll be working with. This chapter helps you master a few key phrases and questions you can use to establish a relationship.

Xiánliáo *(shyan lyaow)* means "small talk" in Chinese. **Xiántán** *(shyan tahn)* is "to chat" . . . either term does the trick.

Establishing a Connection

A surefire way of initiating a conversation is to ask someone a question. Here are some basic question words to keep in mind as you approach the moment of acquaintance:

- ✔ **Shéi** *(shay;* Who?)

- ✔ **Shénme?** *(shummuh;* What?)

- ✔ **Zài nǎr?** *(dzye nar;* Where?)

- ✔ **Shénme shíhòu?** *(shummuh shir ho;* When?)

- ✔ **Wèishénme?** *(way shummuh;* Why?)

- ✔ **Zěnme?** *(dzummuh;* How?)

- ✔ **Duō jiǔ?** *(dwaw jyoe;* For how long?)

Here are a few examples of how to use these question words in simple sentences — sometimes you can also use some of them on their own, just as in English:

- ✔ **Tā shì shéi?** (*tah shir shay;* Who is he/she?)

- ✔ **Nǐ yào shénme?** (*nee yaow shummuh;* What would you like?)

- ✔ **Jǐ diǎn zhōng?** (*jee dyan joong;* What time is it?)

- ✔ **Cèsuǒ zài nǎr?** (*tsuh swaw dzye nar;* Where's the bathroom?)

- ✔ **Nǐ shénme shíhòu chīfàn?** (*nee shummuh shir ho chir fahn;* When do you eat?)

- ✔ **Nǐ wèishénme yào qù Zhōngguó?** (*nee way shummuh yaow chyew joong gwaw;* Why do you want to go to China?)

- ✔ **Nǐ zěnme yàng?** (*nee zummuh yahng;* How's it going?)

- ✔ **Nǐ yǐjǐng zài zhèr duō jiǔ le?** (*nee ee jeeng dzye jar dwaw jyoe luh;* How long have you been here already?)

- ✔ **Xiànzài jǐ diǎn zhōng?** (*shyan dzye jee dyan joong;* What time is it now?)

You can also use the following responses to the questions in the preceding list if someone happens to approach you. These statements are the basics of small talk and really come in handy when you're learning a foreign language:

- ✔ **Wǒ bùdǒng.** (*waw boo doong;* I don't understand.)

- ✔ **Wǒ bùzhīdào.** (*waw boo jir daow;* I don't know.)

- ✔ **Wǒ búrènshi tā.** (*waw boo run shir tah;* I don't know him/her.)

- ✔ **Duìbùqǐ.** (*dway boo chee;* Excuse me.)

- ✔ **Hěn bàoqiàn.** (*hun baow chyan;* I'm so sorry.)

Talkin' the Talk

Molly doesn't have a watch and wants to know what time it is. She asks a man on the street.

Molly: **Duìbùqǐ. Qǐngwèn, xiànzài jǐdiǎn zhōng?**
Dway boo chee. Cheeng one, shyan dzye jee dyan joong?
Excuse me. May I ask, what time is it?

Man: **Xiànzài yīdiǎn bàn.**
Shyan dzye ee dyan bahn.
It's 1:30.

Molly: **Hǎo. Xièxiè nǐ.**
How. Shyeh shyeh nee.
Great. Thank you.

Man: **Bú kèqì.**
Boo kuh chee.
You're welcome.

Molly: **Máfán nǐ, sì lù chēzhàn zài nǎr?**
Mah fahn nee, suh loo chuh jahn dzye nar?
Sorry to trouble you again, but where's the #4 bus stop?

Man: **Chēzhàn jiù zài nàr.**
Chuh jahn jyoe dzye nar.
The bus stop is just over there.

Molly: **Hǎo. Xièxiè.**
How. Shyeh shyeh.
Okay. Thanks.

Man: **Méi wèntí.**
May one tee.
No problem.

Words to Know

Xiànzài jǐ diǎn zhōng?	shyan dzye jee dyan joong	What time is it?
chēzhàn	chuh jahn	bus stop
méi wèntí	may one tee	no problem

Posing simple introductory questions

The following is a list of simple questions you can use when you meet people. (To find out how to respond, or to talk about yourself, flip back to Chapter 3.)

✔ **Nǐ jiào shénme míngzi?** (*nee jyaow shummuh meeng dzuh;* What's your name?)

✔ **Nǐ niánjì duō dà?** (*nee nyan jee dwaw dah;* How old are you?)

✔ **Nǐ zhù zài nǎr?** (*nee joo dzye nar;* Where do you live?)

✔ **Nǐ jiéhūn le méiyǒu?** (*nee jyeh hwun luh mayo;* Are you married?)

✔ **Nǐ yǒu háizi ma?** (*nee yo hi dzuh mah;* Do you have children?)

✔ **Nǐ zuò shénme gōngzuò?** (*nee dzwaw shummuh goong dzwaw;* What kind of work do you do?)

✔ **Nǐ huì jiǎng Zhōngwén ma?** (*nee hway jiahng joong one mah;* Do you speak Chinese?)

✔ **Nǐ xǐhuān kàn diànyǐng ma?** (*nee she hwahn kahn dyan yeeng mah;* Do you like to see movies?)

✔ **Nǐ shénme shíhòu zǒu?** (*nee shummuh shir ho dzoe;* When are you leaving?)

✔ **Jīntiān de tiānqì zěnme yàng?** (*jeen tyan duh tyan chee zummuh yahng;* How's the weather today?)

Chatting about family

If you want to talk about your family when answering questions or making small talk, you need to know these common words:

✔ **àirén** (*eye run;* spouse — used mostly in mainland China [as opposed to Taiwan])

✔ **tàitài** (*tye tye;* wife — used mostly in Taiwan)

✔ **qīzi** (*chee dzuh;* wife)

✔ **zhàngfu** (*jahng foo;* husband)

✔ **fùmǔ** (*foo moo;* parents)

✔ **xiōngdì jiěmèi** (*shyoong dee jyeh may;* brothers and sisters)

✔ **mǔqīn** (*moo cheen;* mother)

✔ **fùqīn** (*foo cheen;* father)

✔ **háizi** (*hi dzuh;* children)

✔ **érzi** (*are dzuh;* son)

✔ **nǚ'ér** (*nyew are;* daughter)

✔ **zǔfù** (*dzoo foo;* grandfather)

✔ **zǔmǔ** (*dzoo moo;* grandmother)

✔ **sūnzi** (*swun dzuh;* grandson)

✔ **sūnnǚ** (*swun nyew;* granddaughter)

Talkin' the Talk

Lǐ Huá meets her daughter's classmate, Beverly, and she asks about Beverly's family.

Lǐ Huá:	**Beverly, nǐ yǒu méiyǒu xiōngdì jiěmèi?** *Beverly, nee yo mayo shyoong dee jyeh may?* Beverly, do you have any brothers or sisters?
Beverly:	**Wǒ yǒu yíge jiějie. Tā shíwǔ suì. Bǐ wǒ dà liǎngsuì.** *Waw yo ee guh jyeh jyeh. Tah shir woo sway. Bee waw dah lyahng sway.* I have an older sister. She's 15. She's two years older than me.
Lǐ Huá:	**Tā yě huì jiǎng Zhōngwén ma?** *Tah yeah hway jyahng joong one mah?* Can she also speak Chinese?
Beverly:	**Búhuì. Tā zhǐ huì Yīngyǔ.** *Boo hway. Tah jir hway eeng yew.* No. She only speaks English.
Lǐ Huá:	**Nǐde fùmǔ zhù zài nǎr?** *Nee duh foo moo joo dzye nar?* Where do your parents live?
Beverly:	**Wǒmen dōu zhù zài Běijīng. Wǒ bàba shì wàijiāoguān.** *Waw mun doe joo dzye bay jeeng. Waw bah bah shir why jyaow gwan.* We all live in Beijing. My father is a diplomat.
Lǐ Huá:	**Nà tài hǎo le.** *Nah tye how luh.* That's great.

Words to Know

jiǎng	jyahng	to talk
zhù	joo	to live
wàijiāoguān	why jyaow gwahn	diplomat
Yīngyǔ	eeng yew	English
Zhōngwén	joong one	Chinese

Making Small Talk on the Job

The kind of job you have can say plenty about you. It can also be a great topic of conversation or spice up an otherwise dull exchange. To ask someone about his or her **gōngzuò** (*goong dzwaw;* work), you can say, **"Nǐ zuò shénme gōngzuò?"** (*nee dzwaw shummuh goong dzwaw;* What kind of work do you do?) You may even try to guess and say, for example, **"Nǐ shì lǎoshī ma?"** (*nee shir laow shir mah;* Are you a teacher?)

The following are some occupations you or the person you're talking with may hold:

- **lǎoshī** (*laow shir;* teacher)
- **jiàoshòu** (*jyaow show;* professor)
- **lǜshī** (*lyew shir;* lawyer)
- **yīshēng** (*ee shung;* doctor)
- **hùshì** (*who shir;* nurse)
- **biānjí** (*byan jee;* editor)
- **kuàijì** (*kwye jee;* accountant)
- **shuǐnuǎngōng** (*shway nwan goong;* plumber)
- **diàngōng** (*dyan goong;* electrician)
- **yǎnyuán** (*yan ywan;* actor)
- **zhǔguǎn** (*joo gwan;* CEO)

✔ **fēixíngyuán** (*fay sheeng ywan;* pilot)

✔ **chéngwùyuán** (*chuhng woo ywan;* flight attendant)

✔ **hǎiguān guānyuán** (*hi gwan gwan ywan;* customs agent)

✔ **lièchēyuán** (*lyeh chuh ywan;* train conductor)

✔ **jiēxiànyuán** (*jyeh shyan ywan;* telephone operator)

✔ **qiántái fúwùyuán** (*chyan tye foo woo ywan;* receptionist)

✔ **kèfáng fúwùyuán** (*kuh fahng foo woo ywan;* housekeeper)

✔ **chūnàyuán** (*choo nah ywan;* bank teller)

✔ **yóudìyuán** (*yo dee ywan;* mail carrier)

✔ **cáifeng** (*tsye fung;* tailor)

The following are some useful job terms and job-related expressions:

✔ **bàn rì gōngzuò** (*bahn ir goong dzwaw;* part-time work)

✔ **quán rì gōngzuò** (*chwan ir goong dzwaw;* full-time work)

✔ **shīyè** (*shir yeh;* unemployed)

✔ **miànshì** (*myan shir;* interview)

✔ **jīnglǐ** (*jeeng lee;* manager)

✔ **gùyuán** (*goo ywan;* employee)

✔ **gùzhǔ** (*goo joo;* employer)

In China, your **dānwèi** (*dahn way;* work unit) is an important part of your life. (This term refers to your place of work, which can be anywhere in the country. Your **dānwèi** is the group that's responsible for both taking care of you and being responsible for any missteps you happen to make.) In fact, when people ask you to identify yourself over the phone, they often say **"Nǐ nǎr?"** (*nee nar; literally:* Where are you from?) to find out what **dānwèi** you belong to. Under Chairman Mao Zedong (the leader of the Chinese Communist Party, who founded the People's Republic of China in 1949), people were assigned jobs right out of high school and didn't even think of marrying until they knew the location of their assignment. They could've been given a job in the northern hinterlands of China, and their fiancées could've been sent south — only to see each other once a year during the Chinese New Year. The **dānwèi** continues to provide housing for its employees and also enforces government policies, such as the one-child-per-family policy. You need the unit's permission to get married, have a child, or receive any government benefits.

Talkin' the Talk

 Yáng and Xiǎo Liú discuss their respective professions, which are quite different from each other. Xiǎo Liú is a nurse in a city located in Henan Province, not far from the famed Shaolin Temple.

Xiǎo Liú: **Yáng, nǐ zuò shénme gōngzuò?**
Yahng, nee dzwaw shummuh goong dzwaw?
Yang, what kind of work do you do?

Yáng: **Wǒ shì lánqiú duìyuán.**
Waw shir lahn chyo dway ywan.
I'm a basketball player.

Xiǎo Liú: **Nà hěn yǒuyìsi.**
Nah hun yo ee suh.
That's very interesting.

Yáng: **Nǐ ne?**
Nee nuh?
How about you?

Xiǎo Liú: **Wǒ shì hùshì. Wǒ zài Kāifēng dìyī yīyuàn gōngzuò.**
Waw shir hoo shir. Waw dzye Kye fung dee ee ee ywan goong dzwaw.
I'm a nurse. I work at Kaifeng's No. 1 Hospital.

Yáng: **Nán bùnán?**
Nahn boo nahn?
Is it difficult?

Xiǎo Liú: **Bùnán. Wǒ hěn xǐhuān wǒde zhíyè.**
Boo nahn. Waw hun she hwahn waw duh jir yeh.
It's not difficult. I really like my profession.

Words to Know

zhīyè	jir yeh	profession
nán	nahn	difficult
xǐhuān	she hwahn	to like; to enjoy
yīyuàn	ee ywan	hospital
gōngzuò	goong dzwaw	to work
hùshī	hoo shir	nurse

Talking About Where You Live

After folks get to know each other through small talk, they may exchange addresses and phone numbers to keep in touch. That introductory question covered earlier in this chapter, **"Nǐ zhù zài nǎr?"** (*nee joo dzye nar;* Where do you live?), may pop up. You may also want to ask a few of these questions:

- **Nǐde dìzhǐ shì shénme?** (*nee duh dee jir shir shummuh;* What's your address?)
- **Nǐde diànhuà hàomǎ duōshǎo?** (*nee duh dyan hwah how mah dwaw shaow;* What's your phone number?)
- **Nǐ shénme shíhòu zài jiā?** (*nee shummuh shir ho dzye jyah;* When will you be at home?/When are you home?)

You may also talk about your home from time to time. These words and phrases can come in handy:

- **Wǒmen zhù de shì fángzi.** (*waw mun joo duh shir fahng dzuh;* We live in a house.)
- **Tā zhù de shì gōngyù.** (*tah joo duh shir goong yew;* She lives in an apartment.)
- **Tāmen yǒu yíge yuànzi.** (*tah mun yo ee guh ywan dzuh;* They have a yard.)
- **Nǐ yǒu yíge huāyuán.** (*nee yo ee guh hwah ywan;* You have a garden.)

✔ **Wǒ zhù zài chénglǐ.** (*waw joo dzye chuhng lee;* I live in the city.)

✔ **Wǒ zhù zài jiāowài.** (*waw joo dzye jyaow why;* I live in the suburbs.)

✔ **Wǒ zhù zài nóngcūn.** (*waw joo dzye noong tswun;* I live in the country.)

In addition to your **diànhuà hàomǎ** (*dyan hwah how mah;* phone number) and your **dìzhǐ** (*dee jir;* address), most people also want to know your **diànzǐ yóuxiāng dìzhǐ** (*dyan dzuh yo shyahng dee jir;* e-mail address). And if you find yourself in a more formal situation, it may be appropriate to give someone your **míngpiàn** (*meeng pyan;* business card). (To find out how to pronounce numbers, see Chapter 2.)

Talkin' the Talk

Beverly meets Alison at a conference in Wuhan and thinks she would be a great partner for her electronics project.

Beverly: **Zhè shì wǒde míngpiàn. Yǒu dìzhǐ, diànhuà hàomǎ, hé diànzǐ yóuxiāng dìzhǐ.**
Jay shir waw duh meeng pyan. Yo dee jir, dyan hwah how mah, huh dyan dzuh yo shyahng dee jir.
Here's my business card. It has my street address, phone number, and e-mail address.

Alison: **Xièxiè.**
Shyeh shyeh.
Thanks.

Beverly: **Kěshì wǒde diànhuà hàomǎ biàn le. Xiànzài shì (650) 721-0000.**
Kuh shir waw duh dyan hwah how mah byan luh. Shyan dzye shir lyo woo leeng, chee are ee, leeng leeng leeng leeng.
But my telephone number has changed. It's now (650) 721-0000.

Alison: **Hǎo. Xièxiè.**
How. Shyeh shyeh.
Okay. Thanks.

Beverly: **Yǒu kōng, qǐng gěi wǒ dǎ diànhuà.**
Yo koong, cheeng gay waw dah dyan hwah.
When you have a chance, please give me a call.

Alison: **Yídìng huì.**
Ee deeng hway.
I certainly will.

Words to Know

dǎ diànhuà	dah dyan hwah	to make a phone call
diànhuà hàomǎ	dyan hwah how mah	telephone number
gǎibiàn	gye byan	to change
míngpiàn	meeng pyan	business card
diànzǐ yóuxiāng dìzhǐ	dyan dzuh yo shyahng dee jir	e-mail address

Fun & Games

Match these people with the words that identify their professions. Check out Appendix C for the answers.

yīshēng   soccer player

lǎoshī   doctor

fēixíngyuán   pilot

zúqiú duìyuán   teacher

Chapter 5

Eating and Drinking: Gānbēi!

In This Chapter
▶ Eating, Chinese style
▶ Ordering and conversing in restaurants
▶ Paying for your meal
▶ Shopping for groceries

You may think you already know what Chinese food is all about, but if you suddenly find yourself a guest in a Chinese friend's home or the guest of honor at a banquet for your company's new branch in Shanghai, you may want to keep reading. This chapter not only helps you communicate when you're hungry or thirsty, go grocery shopping, and order food in a restaurant, but also gives you some useful tips on how to be both a wonderful guest and a gracious host when you have only one shot at making a good impression.

Feeling hungry yet? Allow me to whet your appetite by inviting you to take a closer look at world-renowned Chinese cuisine. No doubt you're already familiar with a great many Chinese dishes, from chow mein and chop suey, to sweet and sour pork, to that delicious favorite of all Chinese fare, dim sum.

Exploring Chinese food and Chinese eating etiquette is a great way to discover Chinese culture. You can also use what you discover in this chapter to impress your date by ordering in Chinese the next time you eat out.

All About Meals

If you feel hungry when beginning this section, you should stop to **chī** (*chir;* eat) **fàn** (*fahn;* food). In fact, **fàn** always comes up when you talk about meals in China. Different meals throughout the day, for example, are called

- **zǎofàn** (*dzaow fahn;* breakfast)
- **wǔfàn** (*woo fahn;* lunch)
- **wǎnfàn** (*wahn fahn;* dinner)

For centuries, Chinese people greeted each other not by saying **"Nǐ hǎo ma?"** (*nee how ma;* How are you?), but by saying **"Nǐ chīfàn le méiyǒu?"** (*nee chir fahn luh mayo;* literally: "Have you eaten?")

In China, **fàn** actually means some kind of grain or starch-based staple. You can have **mǐfàn** (*mee fahn;* rice), which can be **chǎo fàn** (*chaow fahn;* fried white rice) or **bái mǐfàn** (*bye mee fahn;* boiled white rice); **miàntiáo** (*myan tyaow;* noodles); **màntóu** (*mahn toe;* steamed bread); **bāozi** (*baow dzuh;* steamed buns); or **jiǎozi** (*jyaow dzuh;* dumplings). As you can see, you have many types of **fàn** to choose from.

Satisfying your hunger

If you're hungry, you can say **wǒ hěn è** (*waw hun uh;* I'm very hungry) and wait for a friend to invite you for a bite to eat. If you're thirsty, just say **wǒde kǒu hěn kě** (*waw duh ko hun kuh;* literally: my mouth is very dry) to hear offers for all sorts of drinks. You may not get a chance to even utter these words, however, because Chinese rules of hospitality dictate offering food and drink to guests right off the bat.

You have a couple of subtle ways to get across the idea that you're hungry so you don't appear too forward. You can say

- ✔ **Nǐ è ma?** (*nee uh mah;* Are you hungry?)
- ✔ **Nǐ è bú è?** (*nee uh boo uh;* Are you hungry?)
- ✔ **Nǐ hái méi chī wǎnfàn ba.** (*nee hi may chir wahn fahn bah;* I bet you haven't had dinner yet.)

By checking to see if the other person is hungry first, you display the prized Chinese sensibility of consideration for others, and you give yourself a chance to gracefully get out of announcing that you, in fact, are really the one who's dying for some Chinese food. If you want, you can always come right out and say that you're the one who's hungry by substituting **wǒ** (*waw;* I) for **nǐ** (*nee;* you).

If you hear the sound **ba** (*bah*) at the end of a sentence, you can probably interpret it as "I bet," as in **Nǐ hái méi chī wǎnfàn ba** (*nee hi may chir wahn fahn bah;* I bet you haven't had dinner yet), or as "let's," as in **Wǒmen qù chīfàn ba** (*waw men chyew chir fahn bah;* Let's go have dinner). One little utterance serves to soften the sound of making a request (or a command).

You can say something like **Nǐ xiān hē jiǔ** (*nee shyan huh jyoe;* Drink wine first), but you sound nicer and friendlier if you say **Nǐ xiān hē jiǔ ba** (*nee shyan huh jyoe bah;* Better drink some wine first; Why not have some wine first?)?

When an acquaintance invities you for dinner, he may ask, **Nǐ yào chī fàn háishì yào chī miàn?** (*nee yaow chir fahn hi shir yaow chir myan;* Do you want to eat rice or noodles?) Naturally, your host doesn't just serve you a bowl of rice or noodles, because he wants to know what basic staple to prepare before he adds the actual **cài** (*tsye;* the various dishes that go with the rice or noodles).

The many varieties of **cài** have made China the envy of the culinary world. Centuries of subsistence-level existence have taught the Chinese not to waste one morsel of an animal, mineral, or vegetable when they can use the morsel as food. Chronic shortages of food at various points in Chinese history have lent credence to the saying "Necessity is the mother of invention." The Chinese say it another way, however: They eat "anything with legs that's not a table and anything with wings that's not an airplane." Either way, you get the idea.

Sitting down to eat

Once you've chosen what you'd like to order and it's actually been served and sits staring you in the face on the table, you'll probably want to know what utensils to use in order to eat the meal. Don't be shy about asking for a good old fork and knife, even if you're in a Chinese restaurant. It's a myth that Chinese people all eat with chopsticks anyway. Table 5-1 presents a handy list of utensils you'll want to know how to say at one point or another.

Table 5-1	Utensils and Eating Accoutrements	
Chinese Word	*Pronunciation*	*English Word*
yáqiān	yah chyan	toothpick
chāzi	chah dzuh	fork
dāozi	daow dzuh	knife
tiáogēng	tyaow gung	spoon
bēizi	bay dzuh	cup
pánzi	pahn dzuh	plate
wǎn	wahn	bowl
cānjīnzhǐ	tsahn jeen jir	napkin

Do you prefer meat háishì (*hi shir;* or) fish?

When you can choose between more than one item on a Chinese menu, you can use the alternative question structure for interrogative expressions by placing the word **háishì** (*hi shir;* or) between the two choices. If you use the term "or" in affirmative sentences, however — such as when you say she's arriving either today or tomorrow — you should use the word **huò** (*hwaw*) or **huò zhe** (*hwaw juh*) instead.

Even though Chinese food is so varied and great you could have it three meals a day forever, once in a while you might really find yourself hankering for a good old American hamburger or a stack of French fries. In fact, you may be surprised to find places like McDonald's and Kentucky Fried Chicken in Asia when you least expect to. Table 5-2 lists some items you can order when you're in need of some old fashioned comfort food, and Table 5-3 lists common beverages.

Table 5-2	Western Food	
Chinese Word(s)	*Pronunciation*	*English Word(s)*
hànbǎobāo	hahn baow baow	hamburger
règǒu	ruh go	hot dog
zhá shǔtiáo	jah shoo tyaow	French fries
zhá jī	jah jee	fried chicken
zhá yángcōng quān	jah yahng tsoong chwan	onion rings
bǐsā bǐng	bee sah beeng	pizza
káo tǔdòu	cow too doe	baked potato
tǔdòuní	too doe nee	mashed potatoes
yìdàlì shì miàntiáo	ee dah lee shir myan tyaow	spaghetti
yáng pái	yahng pye	lamb chops
zhū pái	joo pye	pork chops
sānmíngzhì	sahn meeng jir	sandwich
shālā zìzhùguì	shah lah dzuh joo gway	salad bar
shālā jiàng	shah lah jyahng	salad dressing

Table 5-3	Beverages	
Chinese Word(s)	*Pronunciation*	*English Word(s)*
jiǔdān	jyoe dahn	wine list
píjiǔ	pee jyoe	beer
gān hóng pūtáojiǔ	gahn hoong poo taow jyoe	dry red wine
kuāngquánshuǐ	kwahng chwan shway	mineral water
guǒzhī	gwaw jir	fruit juice
niúnǎi	nyoe nye	milk
kāfēi	kah fay	coffee
chá	chah	tea
níngmén qìshuǐ	neeng muhng chee shway	lemonade
kělè	kuh luh	soda

Talkin' the Talk

Marilyn and Ramona have a hankering for some Western food during a trip to Beijing. They discuss what to eat among the types of food they've been missing while on their tour of China.

Marilyn: **Ramona, wǒmen zhōngyú qù chī Xīcān la!**
Ramona, waw mun joong yew chyew chir she tsahn lah!
Ramona, let's go have some Western food finally!

Ramona: **Nà shì yīge hǎo zhùyì.**
Nah shir ee guh how joo ee.
That's a great idea.

Marilyn: **Yǐjīng yīge duō xīngqī wǒ méiyǒu chī yīge hànbǎobāo le. Wǒ hěn xiǎng Xīcān.**
Ee jeeng ee guh dwaw sheeng chee waw mayo chir ee guh hahn baow baow lah. Waw hun shyahng she tsahn.
It's already been over a week since I've had a hamburger. I really miss Western food.

Ramona:	**Nǐ xiǎng chī shénme cài? Fǎguó cài, Yìdàlì cài, Mòxīgē cài háishì Yìndù cài? Zhè zhǒng fànguǎn wǒmen de lǚguǎn dōu yǒu.**

Nee shyahng chir shummuh tsye? Fah gwaw tsye, ee dah lee tsye, maw she guh tsye hi shir een doo tsye? Jay joong fahn gwahn waw mun duh lyew gwahn doe yo.

What kind of food do you want to eat? French food, Italian food, Mexican food, or Indian food? Our hotel has all these kinds of restaurants.

Marilyn:	**Nǐ shuō duìle. Zhè zhǒng cài dōu bǐ chī yíge hànbǎobāo hǎo. Wǒmen qù chī Yìndù cài ba. Kěshì wǒ búyào chī làde.**

Nee shwaw dway luh. Jay joong tsye doe bee chir ee guh hahn baow baow how. Waw men chew chir een doo tsye bah. Kuh shir waw boo yaow chir lah duh.

You're right. All these kinds of food beat eating a hamburger. Let's go have Indian food then. But I don't want to eat anything spicy.

Ramona:	**Hǎo. Wǒ tóngyì, wǒ yě búyào chī làde cài. Zǒu ba, yǐjīng kuài liù diǎn le.**

How. Waw toong ee, waw yeah boo yaow chir lah duh tsye. Dzoe bah, ee jeeng kwye lyoe dyan lah.

Fine. I agree, I also don't like to eat spicy food. Let's go, it's already 6 o'clock.

The word **xiǎng** (*shyahng*) in Chinese can mean "to think" and "to miss." So you may hear someone say, **Wǒ xiǎng wǒ hěn xiǎng jiā.** (*waw shyahng waw hun shyahng jya;* I think I really miss home.)

Practicing proper table manners

When you receive an invitation to someone's home, always remember to bring a small gift and to toast others before you take a drink yourself during the meal (see Chapter 18 for a list of things never to do). The Chinese have no problem slurping their soup or belching during or after a meal, by the way, so don't be surprised if you witness both at a perfectly formal gathering. And to remain polite and in good graces, you should always make an attempt to serve someone else before yourself when dining with others; otherwise, you run the risk of appearing rude and self-centered.

Don't be hesitant to use some of these phrases at the table:

- **Màn chī** or **màn màn chī!** (*mahn chir* or *mahn mahn chir;* Bon appetite!) This phrase literally means "Eat slowly," but it's loosely translated as "Take your time and enjoy your food."

- **Zìjǐ lái.** (*dzuh jee lye;* I'll help myself.)

- **Gānbēi!** (*gahn bay;* Bottoms up!)

- **Duō chī yìdiǎr ba!** (*dwaw chir ee dyar bah;* Have some more!)

- **Wǒ chībǎo le.** (*waw chir baow luh;* I'm full.)

Whenever a dining partner begins to serve you food, as is the custom, you must always feign protest with a few mentions of **zìjǐ lái** (*dzuh jee lye;* I'll help myself) so you don't appear to assume that someone *should* be serving you. In the end, you should permit the person to follow proper etiquette by serving you portions from each dish if you're the guest.

And whatever you do, don't use a **yáqiān** (*yah chyan;* toothpick) without covering your mouth. One of the ultimate dining faux pas is to make your teeth visible during toothpick use.

Getting to Know Chinese Cuisines

You may have already discovered that different regions of China specialize in different types of cuisine. Each province has its own specialties, cooking style, and favorite ingredients. Some corner the market on spicy food, and others showcase rather bland food. But no matter where you go, you're sure to discover a new taste bud or two along the way.

Northern Chinese food, found in places like Beijing, is famous for all sorts of meat dishes. You find plenty of beef, lamb, and duck (remember Peking Duck?). To garnish the meat, garlic and scallions are added for good measure. Northern cooking is bland because of the lack of excessive condiments, so don't expect anything overtly salty, sweet, or spicy.

Shanghai dining, as well as that of the neighboring Jiangsu and Zhejiang provinces, represents Eastern cuisine. Because these places are close to the sea and boast many lakes, you can find an infinite variety of seafood in this part of China. Fresh vegetables, different kinds of bamboo, and plenty of soy sauce and sugar are also hallmarks of this region's cuisine.

Food from Sichuan and Hunan provinces is considered Western Chinese cuisine. Western food is common in Chinese restaurants in the United States.

Because this part of China is hot and humid, hot peppers and salt are commonly found here. Not only is the food considered fiery, but also some famous revolutionaries who've hailed from this part of China, such as Mao Zedong.

Southern Chinese cuisine hails from Guangdong (formerly known as Canton) province, as well as from Fujian and Taiwan. Like Shanghai cuisine, it offers plentiful amounts of seafood, fresh fruits, and vegetables. One of the most famous types of food from Guangdong that you've no doubt heard of is **dim sum** *(deem sum)*, which in standard Mandarin is pronounced **diǎn xīn** *(dyan sheen)*.

Dining Out

Whether you eat in a friend's home or in a fancy Chinese restaurant, you need to know how to ask for some basic utensils and how to refer to items already on the table.

You ask for something politely by saying **Qǐng nǐ gěi wǒ . . .** *(cheeng nee gay waw;* Would you mind please getting me a . . .)

You can also say **Máfan nǐ gěi wǒ . . .** *(mah fahn nee gay waw;* May I trouble you to please get me a . . .)

Here are some items you commonly encounter or need to ask for when dining out:

- ✔ **yíge wǎn** *(ee guh wahn;* a bowl)
- ✔ **yíge pánzi** *(ee guh pahn dzuh;* a plate)
- ✔ **yíge bēizi** *(ee guh bay dzuh;* a glass)
- ✔ **yíge tiáogēng** *(ee guh tyaow guhng;* a spoon)
- ✔ **yíge dāozi** *(ee guh daow dzuh;* a knife)
- ✔ **yíge chāzi** *(ee guh chah dzuh;* a fork)
- ✔ **yì zhāng cānjīn** *(ee jahng tsahn jeen;* a napkin)
- ✔ **yì gēn yáqiān** *(ee gun yah chyan;* a toothpick)
- ✔ **yíge shī máojīn** *(ee guh shir maow jeen;* a wet towel)
- ✔ **yíge rè máojīn** *(ee guh ruh maow jeen;* a hot towel)
- ✔ **yì shuāng kuàizi** *(ee shwahng kwye dzuh;* a pair of chopsticks)

When in doubt, use the measure word **ge** *(guh)* in front of the noun you want to modify by a numeral or a specifier, such as "this" (**zhè;** *jay*) or "that" (**nà;** *nah*). As you can see from the previous list, the word for "a" always begins with **yī** *(ee),* meaning the number 1 in Chinese. In between **yī** and the noun is the measure word. For chopsticks, it's **shuāng** *(shwahng),* meaning pair; for napkin, it's **zhāng** *(jahng),* used for anything with a flat surface (such as paper, a map, or even a bed); and a toothpick's measuring word is **gēn** *(gun),* referring to anything resembling a stick, such as rope, a thread, or a blade of grass. Chinese has many different measure words, but **ge** *(guh)* is by far the most common.

Talkin' the Talk

Livia and Charlotte meet after work in New York and decide where to eat.

Livia: **Charlotte, nǐ hǎo!**
Charlotte, nee how!
Charlotte, hi!

Charlotte: **Nǐ hǎo. Hǎo jiǔ méi jiàn.**
Nee how. How jyoe may jyan.
Hi there. Long time no see.

Livia: **Nǐ è bú è?**
Nee uh boo uh?
Are you hungry?

Charlotte: **Wǒ hěn è. Nǐ ne?**
Waw hun uh. Nee nuh?
Yes, very hungry. How about you?

Livia: **Wǒ yě hěn è.**
Waw yeah hun uh.
I'm also pretty hungry.

Charlotte: **Wǒmen qù Zhōngguóchéng chī Zhōngguó cài, hǎo bù hǎo?**
Waw men chyew joong gwaw chuhng chir joong gwaw tsye, how boo how?
Let's go to Chinatown and have Chinese food, okay?

Livia:	**Hǎo. Nǐ zhīdào Zhōngguóchéng nǎ jiā cānguǎn hǎo ma?**
	How. Nee jir daow joong gwaw chuhng nah jya tsahn gwahn how ma?
	Okay. Do you know which restaurant in Chinatown is good?
Charlotte:	**Běijīng kǎo yā diàn hǎoxiàng bú cuò.**
	Bay jeeng cow ya dyan how shyang boo tswaw.
	The Peking Duck place seems very good.
Livia:	**Hǎo jíle. Wǒmen zǒu ba.**
	How jee luh. Waw men dzoe bah.
	Great. Let's go.

Words to Know

Nǐ è bú è?	nee uh boo uh	Are you hungry?
Zhōngguó cài	joong gwaw tsye	Chinese food
cānguǎn	tsahng gwahn	restaurant

Nǐ hǎo *(nee how)*, which appears in the preceding Talkin' the Talk dialogue, can be translated as either "hi," "hello," or "how are you?"

Understanding what's on the menu

Are you a vegetarian? If so, you'll want to order **sùcài** (*sue tsye;* vegetable dishes). If you're a died-in-the-wool carnivor, however, you should definitely keep your eye on the kind of **hūncài** (*hwun tsye;* meat or fish dishes) listed on the **càidān** (*tsye dahn;* menu). Unlike the **fàn** (*fahn;* rice) or **miàn** (*myan;* noodles) you may order, which come in individual bowls for everyone at the table, the **cài** (*tsye;* dishes) you order arrive on large plates, which you're expected to share with others.

You should become familiar with the basic types of food on the menu in case you have only Chinese characters and pīnyīn romanization to go on. Having the knowledge allows you to immediately know which section to focus on (or, likewise, to avoid).

Take meat, for example. In English, the words for "pork," "beef," and "mutton" have no hints of the words for the animals themselves, such as **zhū** (*joo;* pig), **niú** (*nyoe;* cow), or **yáng** (*yahng;* lamb). Chinese is much simpler. Just combine the word for the animal and the word **ròu** (*row),* meaning "meat," after it, such as **zhū ròu** (*joo row;* pork), **niú ròu** (*nyoe row;* beef), or **yáng ròu** (*yahng row;* mutton). Voilà! You have the dish.

Table 5-4 shows the typical elements of a **càidān** (*tsye dahn;* Chinese menu).

Table 5-4	Typical Sections of a Chinese Menu	
Chinese Word(s)	*Pronunciation*	*English Word(s)*
kāiwèicài	kye way tsye	appetizer
ròu lèi	row lay	meat dishes
jī lèi	jee lay	poultry dishes
hǎixiān	hi shyan	seafood dishes
sùcài	soo tsye	vegetarian dishes
tāng	tahng	soup
diǎnxīn	dyan sheen	dessert
yǐnliào	een lyaow	drinks

Talkin' the Talk

 Gerry, Jean, and Leslie meet at a restaurant in Shanghai after work, and a host greets them on the way in.

Host: **Jī wèi?**
        Jee way?
        How many are in your party?

Leslie: **Sān wèi.**
        Sahn way.
        There are three of us.

The host shows them to their table. The three must now decide what to order for their meals.

Host: **Qǐng zuò zhèr. Zhè shì càidān.**
               Cheeng dzwaw jar. Jay shir tsye dahn.
               Please sit here. Here's the menu.

Leslie: **Nǐ yào chī fàn háishì yào chī miàn?**
               Nee yaow chir fahn hi shir yaow chir myan?
               Do you want to eat rice or noodles?

Gerry: **Liǎngge dōu kěyǐ.**
               Lyahng guh doe kuh yee.
               Either one is fine.

Jean: **Wǒ hěn xǐhuān yāoguǒ jīdīng. Nǐmen ne?**
               *Waw hun she hwan yaow gwaw jee deeng. Nee men
               nuh?*
               I love diced chicken with cashew nuts. How about you
               guys?

Gerry: **Duìbùqǐ, wǒ chī sù. Wǒmen néng bù néng diǎn yìdiǎr
               dòufu?**
               *Dway boo chee, waw chir soo. Waw mun nung boo
               nung dyan ee dyar doe foo?*
               Sorry, I'm a vegetarian. Can we order some tofu?

Jean: **Dāngrán kěyǐ.**
               Dahng rahn kuh yee.
               Of course we can.

Leslie: **Bù guǎn zěnme yàng, wǒmen lái sān píng jiǔ, hǎo bù
               hǎo?**
               *Boo gwahn dzummuh yahng, waw mun lye san
               peeng jyoe, how boo how?*
               No matter what, let's get three bottles of beer, okay?

Gerry: **Hěn hǎo!**
               Hun how!
               Very good!

Words to Know

bù guǎn zěnme yàng	boo gwahn dzummah yahng	no matter what
fànguǎn	fahn gwahn	restaurant
gāojí jiǔlóu	gaow jee jyoe low	fancy restaurant
xiǎochīdiàn	shyaow chir dyan	snack shop
Zhōngcān	joong tsahn	Chinese food
Xīcān	she tsahn	Western food
kuàicān	kwye tsahn	fast food
kāfēitīng	kah fay teeng	café
píjiǔ	pee jyoe	beer

Vegetarian's delight

If you're a vegetarian, you may feel lost when looking at a menu filled with mostly pork (the staple meat of China), beef, and fish dishes. Not to worry. As long as you memorize a couple of the terms shown in Table 5-5, you won't go hungry.

Table 5-5	Vegetables Commonly Found in Chinese Dishes	
Chinese Word(s)	*Pronunciation*	*English Word(s)*
biǎndòu	byan doe	string bean
bōcài	baw tsye	spinach
dòufu	doe foo	bean curd
fānqié	fahn chyeh	tomato
gāilán	gye lahn	Chinese broccoli
mógū	maw goo	mushroom

(continued)

Table 5-5 *(continued)*

Chinese Word(s)	Pronunciation	English Word(s)
qiézi	chyeh dzuh	eggplant
qīngjiāo	cheeng jyaow	green pepper
tǔdòu	too doe	potato
xīlánhuā	she lahn hwah	broccoli
yáng báicài	yahng bye tsye	cabbage
yùmǐ	yew me	corn
zhúsǔn	joo swoon	bamboo shoot

When you have a good understanding of the vegetables that go into Chinese dishes, you, oh proud vegetarian, can start to order specialized vegetarian dishes at all your favorite restaurants. Table 5-6 shows some vegetarian dishes good for a night on the town or for preparing dinner for friends.

Table 5-6   Vegetarian Dishes

Chinese Words	Pronunciation	English Words
dànhuā tāng	dahn hwah tahng	egg drop soup
gānbiān sìjìdòu	gahn byan suh jee doe	sautéed string beans
hóngshāo dòufu	hoong shaow doe foo	braised bean curd in soy sauce
suān là tāng	swan lah tahng	hot-and-sour soup
yúxiāng qiézi	yew shyang chyeh dzuh	spicy eggplant with garlic

Some favorite Chinese dishes

You may be familiar with many of the following dishes if you've ever been in a Chinese restaurant:

- **Běijīng kǎo yā** (*bay jeeng cow yah;* Peking roast duck)
- **chūnjuǎn** (*chwun jwan;* spring roll)
- **dànhuā tāng** (*dahn hwah tahng;* egg drop soup)
- **dòufu gān** (*doe foo gahn;* dried beancurd)

- ✔ **gàilán niúròu** (*guy lahn nyoe row;* beef with broccoli)

- ✔ **gōngbǎo jīdīng** (*goong baow jee deeng;* diced chicken with hot peppers)

- ✔ **háoyóu niúròu** (*how yo nyoe row;* beef with oyster sauce)

- ✔ **hóngshāo dòufu** (*hoong shaow doe foo;* braised beancurd in soy sauce)

- ✔ **húntūn tāng** (*hwun dwun tahng;* wonton soup)

- ✔ **shuàn yángròu** (*shwahn yahng row;* Mongolian hot pot)

- ✔ **suān là tāng** (*swan lah tahng;* hot-and-sour soup)

- ✔ **tángcù yú** (*tahng tsoo yew;* sweet-and-sour fish)

- ✔ **yān huángguā** (*yan hwahng gwah;* pickled cucumber)

Sauces and seasonings

The Chinese use all kinds of seasonings and sauces to make their dishes so tasty. Check out *Chinese Cooking For Dummies* by Martin Yan for much more info. Here are just a few of the basics:

- ✔ **jiāng** (*jyahng;* ginger)

- ✔ **làyóu** (*lah yo;* hot sauce)

- ✔ **yán** (*yan;* salt)

- ✔ **máyóu** (*mah yo;* sesame oil)

- ✔ **jiàngyóu** (*jyahng yo;* soy sauce)

- ✔ **cù** (*tsoo;* vinegar)

CULTURAL WISDOM

Chowing down on the Chinese New Year

On the eve of the Chinese lunar New Year, known as **chú xī** *(choo she),* the Chinese eat a big **niányèfàn** (*nyan yeh fahn;* New Year's Eve dinner). The dinner almost always includes a whole cooked **yú** (*yew;* fish), because the word for fish rhymes with the word for abundance **(yú),** even though the written characters for the words look quite different. In some of the poorer parts of northern China, people often eat **jiǎozi** (*jyaow dzuh;* dumplings) rather than fish because their shape resembles traditional **yuánbāo** (*ywan baow;* gold ingots) used in pre-modern times by people of means. These people hope that the prosperity and abundance of such wealthy families will also come into their lives through the eating of the **jiǎozi** *(jyaow dzuh).* Southerners often eat **fā cài** (*fah tsye;* a kind of stringy black vegetable), which rhymes with **fā cái** *(fah tsye),* although you pronounce the words in different tones. **Fā cái** means to get wealthy and prosper; in fact, the most common greeting on New Year's day is **gōngxǐ fā cái!** (*goong she fah tsye;* Congratulations and may you prosper!)

Placing an order and chatting with the wait staff

I bet you're used to everyone ordering one dish for themselves, right? Well, in China, diners almost always share dishes by putting them on common platters smack in the middle of the table where everyone can pick and choose. You get used to ordering with the whole group in mind, not just yourself — just one more example of how the collective is always considered before the individual in Chinese culture.

Chinese table etiquette dictates that everyone decides together what to order. The two main categories you must decide upon are the **cài** (*tsye;* food dishes) and the **tāng** (*tahng;* soup). Feel free to be the first one to ask **Wŏmen yīnggāi jiào jīge cài jīge tāng?** (*waw men eeng gye jyaow jee guh tsye jee guh tahng;* How many dishes and how many soups should we order?) Ideally, one of each of the five major tastes should appear in the dishes you choose for your meal to be a "true" Chinese meal: **suān** (*swan;* sour), **tián** (*tyan;* sweet), **kŭ** (*koo;* bitter), **là** (*lah;* spicy), and **xián** (*shyan;* salty).

I know it can be hard to choose what to eat from all the fantastic choices staring back at you from most any Chinese menu; after all, the Chinese perfected the art of cooking long before the French and Italians appeared on the scene. But when you finally hit on something you like, you have to figure out how to tell the waiter what you want to **chī** (*chir;* eat), whether you like **là** (*lah;* spicy) food or not, if you want to avoid **wèijīng** (*way jeeng;* MSG), what kind of **píjiŭ** (*pee jyoe;* beer) you want to **hē** (*huh;* drink), and that you want to know what kind of **náshŏu cài** (*nah show tsye;* house specialty) the restaurant has going today.

Here are some questions your waiter or waitress is likely to ask you:

- ✔ **Nĭmen yào shénme cài?** (*nee men yaow shummuh tsye;* What would you like to order; *literally:* What kind of food would you like?)

- ✔ **Nĭmen yào hē diăr shénme?** (*nee men yaow huh dyar shummuh;* What would you like to drink?)

- ✔ **Yào jĭ píng píjiŭ?** (*yaow jee peeng pee jyoe;* How many bottles of beer do you want?)

And here are some phrases that come in handy when you need to give an answer:

- ✔ **Wŏmen yào yíge suān là tāng.** (*waw men yaow ee guh swan lah tahng;* We'd like a hot-and-sour soup.)

✔ **Wǒ bù chī là de.** (*waw boo chir lah duh;* I don't eat spicy food.)

✔ **Qǐng bié fàng wèijǐng, wǒ guòmǐn.** (*cheeng byeh fahng way jeeng, waw gwaw meen;* Please don't use any MSG, I'm allergic.)

When addressing a waiter or waitress, you can call them by the same name: **fúwùyuán** (*foo woo ywan;* service personnel). In fact, "he," "she," and "it" all share the same Chinese word, too: **tā** (*tah*). Isn't that easy to remember?

✔ **Qǐng gěi wǒ càidān.** (*cheeng gay waw tsye dahn;* Please give me the menu.)

✔ **Nǐ gěi wǒmen jièshào cài hǎo ma?** (*nee gay waw men jyeh shaow tsye how ma;* Can you recommend some dishes?)

✔ **Dà shīfu náshǒu cài shì shénme?** (*dah shir foo nah show tsye shir shummuh;* What's the chef's specialty?)

✔ **Yú xīnxiān ma?** (*yew shin shyan mah;* Is the fish fresh?)

✔ **Wǒ bú yuànyì chī hǎishēn.** (*waw boo ywan yee chir hi shun;* I don't want to try sea slugs.)

✔ **Nǐmen yǒu kuàngquán shuǐ ma?** (*nee men yo kwahng chwan shway mah;* Do you have any mineral water?)

✔ **Wǒ bú yào là de cài.** (*waw boo yaow lah duh tsye;* I don't want anything spicy.)

✔ **Wǒ bù néng chī yǒu táng de cài.** (*waw boo nuhng chir yo tahng duh tsye;* I can't eat anything made with sugar.)

✔ **Wǒ bù chī zhūròu.** (*waw boo chir joo row;* I don't eat pork.)

✔ **Qǐng cā zhuōzi.** (*cheeng tsah jwaw dzuh;* Please wipe off the table.)

✔ **Qǐng bǎ yǐnliào sòng lái.** (*cheeng bah yin lyaow soong lye;* Please bring our drinks.)

✔ **Wǒ méi jiào zhèige.** (*waw may jyaow jay guh;* I didn't order this.)

Regular nouns in Chinese make no distinction between singular and plural. Whether you want to talk about one **píngguǒ** (*peeng gwaw;* apple), two **júzi** (*jyew dzuh;* oranges), or both **píngguǒ hé júzi** (*peeng gwaw huh jyew dzuh;* apples and oranges), the fruits always sound the same in Chinese. On the other hand, if you want to refer to human beings, you can always add the suffix **men** (*mun*). The word for "I" or "me" is **wǒ** (*waw*), but "we" becomes **wǒmen** (*waw mun*). The same goes for **nǐ** (*nee;* you) and **tā** (*tah;* he, she, and it). "They" becomes **nǐmen** (*nee mun*) or **tāmen** (*tah mun*). If you want to refer to a specific number of apples, however, you don't use **"men"** as a suffix. You can either say **píngguǒ** (*peeng gwaw*) for apple (or apples) or **liǎngge píngguǒ** (*lyahng guh peeng gwaw*), meaning two apples. Got it?

Talkin' the Talk

Tom and Wendy go to a Chinese restaurant that specializes in Hunan and Sichuan cuisine — the two spiciest cuisines of China. They hail the waiter to ask for a menu.

Tom: **Wǒmen néng bùnéng kànkàn càidān?**
Waw mun nung boo nung kahn kahn tsye dahn?
May we see the menu?

Waiter: **Dāngrán kěyǐ.**
Dahng rahn kuh yee.
Of course you may.

A few minutes later, the two diners still can't decide what to order, so they call over the waiter once again.

Waiter: **Nǐmen xiǎng diǎn shénme cài?**
Nee men shyang dyan shummah tsye?
What dishes would you like to order?

Tom: **Qǐng wèn, nǐmen de náshǒu cài shì shénme?**
Cheeng one, nee mun duh nah show tsye shir shummuh?
Excuse me, may I ask what your house specialty is?

Waiter: **Mápō dòufu hé Chángshā jī dōu yǒumíng.**
Mah paw doe foo huh chahng shah jee doe yo meeng.
Sichuan beancurd and Changsha chicken are both very famous.

Wendy: **Tīngshuō mápō dòufu hěn là. Duìbùqǐ, kěshì wǒ bùchī là de. Yǒu méiyǒu biéde cài?**
Teeng shwaw mah paw doe foo hun lah. Dway boo chee, kuh shir waw boo chir lah duh. Yo mayo byeh duh tsye?
I've heard the Sichuan beancurd is very spicy. I'm sorry, but I don't like spicy food. Do you have any other kinds of dishes?

Waiter: **Dāngrán yǒu. Jièlán jī hé xiā lóng hú dōu bú là. Hǎo bùhǎo?**
Dahng rahn yo. Jyeh lahn jee huh shyah loong hoo doe boo lah. How boo how?
Of course we do. Chicken with broccoli and shrimp with lobster sauce are both relatively mild. How about those?

Wendy: **Hěn hǎo. Xièxiè.**
Hun how. Shyeh shyeh.
Very good. Thank you.

Tom: **Qǐng lìngwài gěi wǒmen làjiāo jiàng. Wǒ hěn xǐhuān chī làde.**
              Cheeng leeng wye gay waw men lah jyaow jyahng.
              Waw hun she hwan chir lah duh.
              Please also bring us some hot pepper sauce. I love spicy food.

Waiter: **Hái yào biéde ma?**
              Hi yaow byeh duh ma?
              Would you like anything else?

Tom: **Qǐng lìngwài lái yíge chǎo qīngcài.**
              Cheeng leeng wye lye ee guh chaow cheeng tsye.
              Please also bring a sautéed green vegetable.

Waiter: **Hǎo. Xièxiè.**
              How. Shyeh shyeh.
              Very good. Thank you.

Words to Know

Wǒ hěn è	waw hun uh	I'm very hungry
Wǒde kǒu hěn kě	waw duh ko hun kuh	I'm thirsty
náshǒu cài	nah show tsye	house specialty
tuījiàn	tway jyan	recommend
yán	yan	salty
suān	swan	sour
là	lah	spicy
tián	tyan	sweet
yóu	yo	greasy
wèijīng	way jeeng	MSG
guòmǐn	gwaw meen	allergic
kuàizi	kwye dzuh	chopsticks

Dipping into some dim sum

Dim sum is probably the most popular food of Chinese in the United States and of people in Guangdong Province and all over Hong Kong, where you can find it served for breakfast, lunch, and sometimes dinner. Vendors even sell dim sum snacks in subway stations.

The dish's main claim to fame is that it takes the shape of mini portions, and it's often served with tea to help cut through the oil and grease afterwards. You have to signal the waiters when you want a dish of whatever is on the dim sum cart they push in the restaurant, however, or they just pass on by. Dim sum restaurants are typically crowded and noisy, which only adds to the fun.

Part of the allure of dim sum is that you get to sample a whole range of different tastes while you catch up with old friends. Dim sum meals can last for hours, which is why most Chinese people choose the weekends to have dim sum. No problem lingering on a Saturday or Sunday.

Because dim sum portions are so small, your waiter often tallys the total by the number of plates left on your table. You can tell the waiter you want a specific kind of dim sum by saying: **Qǐng lái yì dié** _____. (*cheeng lye ee dyeh* _____; please give me a plate of _____). Fill in the blank with one of the tasty choices I list in Table 5-7.

Table 5-7	Common Dim Sum Dishes	
Chinese Word(s)	*Pronunciation*	*English Word(s)*
guō tiē	gwaw tyeh	fried pork dumplings
xiǎolóng bāo	shyaow loong baow	steamed pork buns
xiā jiǎo	shyah jyaow	shrimp dumplings
xiā wán	shyah wahn	shrimp balls
niúròu wán	nyoe row wahn	beef balls
yùjiǎo	yew jyaow	deep fried taro root
dàntǎ	dahn tah	egg tarts
luóbō gāo	law baw gaow	turnip cake

Chinese Word(s)	Pronunciation	English Word(s)
niàng qīngjiāo	nyahng cheeng jyaow	stuffed peppers
chūnjuǎn	chwun jwan	spring rolls
dòushā bāo	doe shah baow	sweet bean buns

Finding the restrooms

After you have a bite to eat, you may be in need of a restroom. The need may be dire if you're smack in the middle of a 12-course banquet in Beijing and already have a couple of glasses of **máotái** *(maow tye)*, the stiffest of all Chinese drinks, under your belt.

Now all you have to do is garner the energy to ask **"Cèsuǒ zài nǎr?"** *(tsuh swaw dzye nar;* Where's the restroom?) if you're in mainland China or **"Cèsuǒ zài nǎlǐ"** *(tsuh swaw dzye nah lee)* if you're in Taiwan. You can also ask **"Nǎlǐ kěyǐ xǐ shǒu?"** *(nah lee kuh yee she show;* Where can I wash my hands?)

No matter what way you ask for directions to the restroom, don't forget to take some toilet paper with you before you leave the hotel if you're in mainland China, because many public restrooms don't supply it there. In most cases, the pictures on the bathroom doors are self-explanatory, but you may also see the pīnyīn for male (**nán;** *nahn*) and female (**nǚ;** *nyew*) before the word **cèsuǒ.** Those are the words you want to pay attention to above all else.

You can also find the word **cèsuǒ** in the term for graffiti: **cèsuǒ wénxué** *(tsuh swaw one shweh; literally:* bathroom literature). How apropos.

Finishing your meal and paying the bill

Once you're through sampling all possible permutations of Chinese cuisine (or French or Italian, for that matter), you won't be able to just slink away unnoticed out the front door and on into the sunset. Time to pay the bill, my friend. Hopefully it was worth the expense. Here are some phrases you should know when the time comes:

- ✔ **jiézhàng** *(jyeh jahng;* to pay the bill)
- ✔ **fēnkāi suàn** *(fun kye swahn;* to go Dutch)
- ✔ **Wǒ qǐng kè.** *(waw cheeng kuh;* It's on me.)

✔ **Qǐng jiézhàng.** (*cheeng jyeh jahng;* The check, please.)

✔ **Zhàngdān yǒu cuò.** (*jahng dahn yo tswaw;* The bill is incorrect.)

✔ **Bāokuò fúwùfèi.** (*baow kwaw foo woo fay;* The tip is included.)

✔ **Qǐng kāi shōujù.** (*cheeng kye show jyew;* Please give me the receipt.)

✔ **Wǒ kěyǐ yòng xìnyòng kǎ ma?** (*waw kuh yee yoong sheen yoong kah mah;* May I use a credit card?)

All the Tea in China

You encounter about as many different kinds of tea as you do Chinese dialects. Hundreds, in fact. To make ordering or buying this beverage easier, however, you really need to know only the most common kinds of tea:

✔ **Lǜ chá.** (*lyew chah;* Green tea) Green tea is the oldest of all the teas in China, with many unfermented subvarieties. The most famous kind of Green tea is called **lóngjǐng chá** (*loong jeeng chah*), meaning Dragon Well tea. You can find it near the famous West Lake region in Hangzhou, but people in the south generally prefer this kind of tea.

✔ **Hóng chá.** (*hoong chah;* Black tea) Even though **hóng** means red in Chinese, you translate this phrase as Black tea instead. Unlike Green tea, Black teas are fermented and enjoyed primarily by people in the Fujian Province.

✔ **Wūlóng chá.** (*oo loong;* Black Dragon tea) This kind of tea is semi-fermented. It's a favorite in the Guangdong and Fujian provinces and in Taiwan.

✔ **Mòlì huā chá.** (*maw lee hwah chah;* Jasmine) This kind of tea is made up of a combination of Black, Green, and Wūlóng teas, in addition to some fragrant flowers like jasmine or magnolia thrown in for good measure. Most northerners are partial to Jasmine tea, probably because the north is cold and this type of tea raises the body's temperature.

Tea is always offered to guests the minute they enter a Chinese home. The hosts aren't just being polite; the offering of tea shows respect to the guest and presents a way to share something that all parties can enjoy together. It may be considered rude not to at least take a sip. Chinese custom says that a host only fills the teacup to 70 percent of its capacity. The other 30 percent is supposed to contain friendship and affection. Isn't that a nice concept?

You often use the adjective **hǎo** (*how;* good) with a verb to create an adjective that means "good to." Here are a couple of examples:

✔ **hǎohē** (*how huh;* tasty; *literally:* good to drink)

✔ **hǎochī** (*how chir;* tasty; *literally:* good to eat)

✔ **hǎowán** (*how wahn;* fun, interesting; *literally:* good to play)

✔ **hǎokàn** (*how kahn;* pretty, interesting; *literally:* good to look at or watch. This can apply to people or even movies.)

You may be tempted to **chī** (*chir;* eat) your soup in a Chinese restaurant, but you should actually **hē** (*huh;* drink) it instead. If it tastes really good, you can say the soup is **hěn hǎohē** (*hun how huh;* very tasty), just like anything else you may have ordered to drink.

Talkin' the Talk

George, Susan, and Rhoda are all eating dim sum during their trip to Hong Kong, a place famous for dim sum restaurants.

George: **Nǐ chī guò dim sum ma?**
Nee chir gwaw deem sum mah?
Have you ever had dim sum before?

Rhoda: **Méiyǒu. Zhè shì dì yī cì.**
Mayo. Jay shir dee yee tsuh.
No. This is the first time.

Susan: **Wèidào zěnme yàng?**
Way daow dzummuh yahng?
How does it taste?

Rhoda: **Hǎo jíle.**
How jee luh.
It's great.

George: **Nǐ xǐ bùxǐhuān chī dim sum?**
Nee she boo she hwahn chir deem sum?
Do you like dim sum?

Susan: **Yídìng. Hěn xǐhuān.**
Ee deeng. Hun she hwahn.
Absolutely. I like it very much.

Rhoda: **Nǐ zuì xǐhuān chī de dim sum shì shénme?**
Nee dzway she hwahn chir duh deem sum shir shummuh?
What's your favorite dim sum dish?

Susan: **Nà hěn nán shuō. Bú shì guōtiē jiù shì xiā jiǎo ba. Dim sum wǒ dōu xǐhuān chī.**
Nah hun nahn shwaw. Boo shir gwaw tyeh jyoe shir shyah jyaow bah. Deem sum waw doe she hwahn chir.
It's difficult to say. If not pork dumplings then definitely shrimp dumplings. I love all dim sum dishes.

If you want to ask if someone has ever done something, use the word **guò** *(gwaw)* directly after the verb to get your point across. **Nǐ qù guò Měiguó méiyǒu?** *(nee chew gwaw may gwaw mayo;* Have you ever been to America?) **Nǐ chī guò Yìdàlì fàn ma?** *(nee chir gwaw ee dah lee fahn ma;* Have you ever eaten Italian food?) So, have you ever used the particle **guò?**

Some verbs in Chinese have two syllables. **Yào** *(yaow;* to want) is not one of them. **Xǐhuān** *(she hwan;* to like or to want), on the other **shǒu** *(show;* hand), is an example. When Chinese people speak quickly, they may leave out the second syllable in a few bisyllabic verbs and even a few auxiliary verbs the first time they come up in the "verb-**bù**-verb" pattern (**"bù"** between two verbs automatically creates a question). So instead of saying **"Tā xǐhuān bùxǐhuān hē jiǔ?"** *(tah she hwan boo she hwan huh jyo;* Does he or she like to drink wine?), you may hear someone say **"Tā xǐ bùxǐhuān hē jiǔ?"** *(tah she boo she hwan huh jyoe)*

Taking Your Chinese to Go

Restaurants are great, but once in a while you may want to mingle with the masses as people go about buying food for a home-cooked family dinner. Outdoor food markets abound in China and are great places to see how the locals shop and what they buy. And what better way to try out your Chinese? You can always point to what you want and discover the correct term for it from the vendor.

In addition to clothes, books, and kitchen utensils, outdoor markets may offer all sorts of food items:

- ✔ **Ròu** *(row;* meat): **niúròu** *(nyoe row;* beef), **yángròu** *(yahng row;* lamb), or **jīròu** *(jee row;* chicken)

- ✔ **Yú** *(yew;* fish): **xiā** *(shyah;* shrimp), **pángxiè** *(pahng shyeh;* crab), **lóngxiā** *(loong shyah;* lobster), or **yóuyú** *(yo yew;* squid)

- ✔ **Shuǐguǒ** *(shway gwaw;* fruit): **píngguǒ** *(peeng gwaw;* apples) or **júzi** *(jyew dzuh;* oranges)

Chinese people generally don't eat any raw food. The idea of a raw salad bar is truly foreign to them. In fact, **shēngcài** (*shung tsye;* lettuce) literally translates as raw food, and the Chinese generally consider it fit only for farm animals.

Sizing up weights and measures

The metric system is standard in both mainland China and Taiwan. The basic unit of weight is the **gōngkè** (*goong kuh;* gram), so you usually buy fruits and vegetables in multiples of that measure. The standard liquid measurement is the **shēng** (*shung;* liter). One liter equals about 1.06 quarts. Table 5-8 gives you a list of weights and measures.

Table 5-8	Weights and Measures	
Chinese Word	*Pronunciation*	*English Word*
pǐntuō	peen twaw	pint
bàng	bahng	pound
kuātuō	kwah twaw	quart
àngsi	ahng suh	ounce
jiālún	jyah lwun	gallon
gōngkè	goong kuh	gram
jīn; gōngjīn	jeen; goong jeen	kilogram
háokè	how kuh	milligram
shēng	shung	liter
límǐ	lee mee	centimeter
gōnglǐ	goong lee	kilometer
mǐ	mee	meter
yīnglǐ	eeng lee	mile
mǎ	mah	yard
yīngcùn	eeng tswun	inch
yīngchǐ	eeng chir	foot

Although the Chinese use the metric system, more often than not you encounter traditional measurement terms that predate the metric system, such as the words **cún** *(tswun)* for "inch" and **chǐ** *(chir)* for "foot."

Making comparisons

When you want to compare people or objects, you generally put the word **bǐ** *(bee;* compared to) between two nouns, followed by an adjective: A **bǐ** B (Adjective). This means A is more ____ than B.

Here are a few examples:

- ✔ **Píngguǒ bǐ júzi hǎochī.** *(peeng gwaw bee jyew dzuh how chir;* Apples are tastier than oranges.)
- ✔ **Zhèige fànguǎr bǐ nèige fànguǎr guì.** *(jay guh fahn gwar bee nay guh fahng gwar gway;* This restaurant is more expensive than that one.)
- ✔ **Tā bǐ nǐ niánqīng.** *(tah bee nee nyan cheeng;* She's younger than you.)

How much is that thousand-year-old egg?

When you're ready to buy some merchandise after making all the necessary comparisons, here are two simple ways to ask how much the products cost:

- ✔ **Duōshǎo qián?** *(dwaw shaow chyan;* How much money is it?)
- ✔ **Jǐkuài qián?** *(jee kwye chyan; literally:* How many dollars does it cost?)

The only difference between the two questions is the implied amount of the cost. If you use the question word **"duōshǎo"** *(dwaw shaow),* you want to inquire about something that's most likely greater than $10.00. If you use **"jǐ"** in front of **kuài** *(kwye;* the term for dollars), you assume the product costs less than $10.00.

You can also use **jǐ** in front of **suì** *(sway;* years) when you want to know how old a child under 10 is. You say, **"Tā jǐ suì?"** *(tah jee sway;* How old is he [or she]?)

Talkin' the Talk

 At the local open-air market in Kaifeng, Lindsey and Adam eye some vegetables and discuss the price with the older man selling them in his stall. **Shīfu** *(shir foo)* is a term used to indicate someone providing a service, and indicates more respect due to age than the term **fúwùyuán** *(foo woo ywan)*, meaning any kind of attendant.

Lindsey: **Shīfu, qǐng wèn, nǐ yǒu méiyǒu bōcài?**
            Shir foo, cheeng one, nee yo mayo baw tsye?
            Sir, may I ask, do you have any spinach?

Shīfu: **Dāngrán. Yào jǐjīn?**
            Dahng rahn. Yaow jee jeen?
            Of course. How many kilograms would you like?

Adam: **Wǒmen mǎi sānjīn, hǎo bùhǎo?**
            Waw men my sahn jeen, how boo how?
            Let's get three jin, okay?

Lindsey: **Hǎo. Sānjīn ba.**
            How. Sahn jeen bah.
            Okay. It'll be three jin then.

Shīfu: **Méi wèntǐ. Yìjīn sān kuài qián. Nèmme, yíigòng jiǔ
            kuài.**
            *May one tee. Ee jeen sahn kwye chyan. Nummuh, ee
            goong jyoe kwye.*
            No problem. It's $3 a jin. So, that will be $9 altogether.

Adam: **Děng yíxià. Bōcài bǐ gàilán guì duōle. Wǒmen mǎi
            gàilán ba.**
            *Dung ee shyah. Baw tsye bee guy lahn gway. Waw
            mun my guy lahn bah.*
            Wait a minute. Spinach is more expensive than
            Chinese broccoli. Let's buy Chinese broccoli then.

Shīfu: **Hǎo. Gàilán liǎngkuài yìjīn. Hái yào sānjīn ma?**
            *How. Guy lahn lyahng kwye ee jeen. Hi yaow sahn
            jeen mah?*
            Okay. Chinese broccoli is $2 a jin. Do you still want
            three jin?

Lindsey: **Shì de.**
             Shir duh.
             Yes.

Shīfu: **Nà, sānjīn yígòng liù kuài.**
             Nah, sahn jeen ee goong lyo kwye.
             In that case, three jin will be $6.00.

Adam: **Hǎo. Zhè shì liù kuài.**
             How. Juh shir lyoe kwye.
             Okay. Here's $6.00.

Shīfu: **Xièxiè.**
             Shyeh shyeh.
             Thank you.

Adam: **Xièxiè. Zàijiàn.**
             Shyeh shyeh. Dzye jyan.
             Thanks. Good bye.

Shīfu: **Zàijiàn.**
             Dzye jyan.
             Good bye.

Words to Know

chāojí shìchǎng	chow jee shir chahng	supermarket
shìchǎng	shir chahng	market
shòuhuòtān	show hwaw tahn	stall
cánshāzhě	tsahn shah juh	butcher
záhuòshāng	dzah hwaw shahng	grocer
shìpǐn záhuò	shir peen dzah hwaw	groceries
zhǐ dài	jir dye	a paper bag

Fun & Games

Identify these fruits and vegetables and write their Chinese names below. Check out Appendix C for the answers.

A.   B.   C.   D.

E.   F.   G.

A. _____

B. _____

C. _____

D. _____

E. _____

F. _____

G. _____

Chapter 6

Shopping Made Easy

. . . .

In This Chapter

▶ Checking out the stores

▶ Looking for clothes and other items

▶ Bargaining for a better price

. . . .

*E*ver dreamed of shopping till you dropped in a foreign country where the rate of exchange is really great? Or in faraway lands where lively outdoor night markets abound? This chapter helps you navigate both small shops and fancy department stores; get a handle on prices, colors, and merchandise; and in general negotiate the best deal wherever possible.

To **mǎi dōngxi** (*my doong she;* buy things) is one of the most enjoyable pastimes for people the world over. Whether you're just going **guàngshāngdiàn** (*gwahng shahng dyan;* window shopping) or actually about to **mǎi dōngxi** doesn't matter. You can still enjoy looking at all the **shāngpǐn** (*shahng peen;* merchandise), fantasizing about buying that **zuànshí jièzhi** (*dzwan shir jye jir;* diamond ring), and haggling over the **jiàgé** (*jyah guh;* price).

Going to Stores

If you don't have a clue how to begin shopping in China, much less what you want to buy, you might want to start off at one of the many **bǎihuò shāngdiàn** (*bye hwaw shahng dyan;* department stores) that have sprouted up throughout China in the last decade. Here you can get almost anything you're looking for, from **zhūbǎo** (*joo baow;* jewelry) and **huāpíng** (*hwah peeng;* vases) to **yīfu** (*ee foo;* clothing) and **yuèqì** (*yweh chee;* musical instruments).

Department stores aren't the only places you can shop, but they're certainly the easiest because everything is right there within walking distance and you can browse without fighting off vendors trying to push their wares. Or you might be someone who actually enjoys all the haggling that goes on at street fairs and prefers to experience a lively outdoor **cài shìchǎng** (*tsye shir chahng;* food market).

Even though traditional alley markets and shop fronts still exist in China, Western-style shopping malls are quickly putting their imprint on places like Beijing and Shanghai. You can still get the best prices, though, at the many open-air markets and street vendors, which sell traditional arts and crafts and other specialties. Beijing's #1 shopping area is not far from **Tiān'ānmén Square** *(tyan ahn mun)* **Square** on **Wángfǔjǐng** *(wahng foo jeeng)* and **Dōngdān** *(doong dahn)* streets. Or on **Jiànguóménwài Dàjiē** *(jyan gwaw mun why dah jyeh)*.

Here are some types of stores and the things you can find in them:

- ✔ **Zài yíge shūdiàn nǐ kéyǐ mǎi shū, zázhì hé bàozhǐ.** *(dzye ee guh shoo dyan nee kuh yee my shoo, dzah jir huh baow jir;* In a bookstore, you can buy books, magazines, and newspapers.)

- ✔ **Zài yíge wǔjǐn diàn nǐ kéyǐ mǎi zhuǎnjiē qì, chātóu hé yānwù bàojǐng qì.** *(dzye ee guh woo jeen dyan nee kuh yee my jwan jyeh chee, chah toe huh yan woo baow jeeng chee;* In a hardware store, you can buy adaptors, plugs, and smoke detectors.)

- ✔ **Zài yíge yāncǎo diàn nǐ kéyǐ mǎi xuějiāyān, xiāngyān, yāndǒu hé gèzhǒng gèyàng de yāncǎo.** *(dzye ee guh yan tsaow dyan nee kuh yee my shyweh jyah yan, shyahng yan, yan doe huh guh joong guh yahng duh yan tsaow;* In a tobacco shop, you can buy cigars, cigarettes, pipes, and all kinds of tobacco.)

- ✔ **Zài yíge zhūbǎo diàn nǐ kéyǐ mǎi shǒuzhuó, ěrhuán, xiàngliàn, xiōngzhēn hé jièzhi.** *(dzye ee guh joo baow dyan nee kuh yee my show jwaw, are hwahn, shyahng lyan, shyoong juhn huh jyeh jir;* In a jewelry store, you can buy bracelets, earrings, necklaces, pins, and rings.)

When you finally make up your mind about what to shop for, you may want to call ahead to check out the store's hours. Here are some questions that can be of help:

- ✔ **Nín jǐ diǎn zhōng kāi/guān mén?** *(neen jee dyan joong kye/gwahn mun;* What time do you open/close?)

- ✔ **Nǐmen wǔdiǎn zhōng yǐhòu hái kāi ma?** *(nee men woo dyan joong ee hoe hi kye mah;* Are you open after 5 p.m.?)

- ✔ **Nǐmen xīngqītiān kāi bùkāi?** *(nee mun sheeng chee tyan kye boo kye;* Are you open on Sundays?)

Most stores in China are open quite early, around 8 a.m., and don't close until 8 p.m. or even later. If you want a less harried shopping experience, avoid shopping on the weekends, when seemingly a quarter of humanity is out doing the same thing.

Talkin' the Talk

Muriel and Helayne discuss going shopping for the day. Here's how they start out.

Muriel: **Wǒ jīntiān xiǎng qù mǎi dōngxi.**
Waw jin tyan shyahng chyew my doong she.
I want to go shopping today.

Helayne: **Nǐ qù nǎr mǎi dōngxi?**
Nee chyew nar my doong she?
Where will you go to shop?

Muriel: **Wǒ yào qù bǎihuògōngsī mǎi yīfu.**
Waw yaow chyew bye hwaw goong suh my ee foo.
I want to go to the department store to buy some clothes.

Helayne: **Tīngshuō zài zhèige chénglǐ dōngxi dōu hěn guì.**
Teeng shwaw dzye jay guh chuhng lee doong she doe hun gway.
I've heard that everything's very expensive in this city.

Muriel: **Nà bùyídìng. Kàn shì shénme diàn. Yǒude hěn guì, yǒude yìdiǎn dōu búguì.**
Nah boo ee deeng. Kahn shir shummuh dyan. Yo duh hun gway, yo duh ee dyan doe boo gway.
Not necessarily. It depends on the store. Some are really expensive and some aren't expensive at all.

Helayne: **Hǎo ba. Wǒmen zǒu ba. Wǒmen qù mǎi yīfu.**
How bah. Waw mun dzoe bah. Waw mun chyew my ee foo.
Great. Let's go. Let's buy some clothes.

Whenever you see the words "**yìdiǎn dōu bú___**" (*ee dyan doe boo ___*) before an adjective, it means *not at all (adjective)*. It's a great way to emphasize something. You can say something like **Wǒ yìdiǎn dōu búlèi** (*waw ee dyan doe boo lay;* I'm not tired in the least.) or **Tā yìdiǎn dōu búpiàoliàng** (*Tah ee dyan doe boo pyaow lyahng;* She's not at all pretty.) to get your point across.

Words to Know

bǎihuò shāngdiàn	bye hwaw shahng dyan	department store
cài shìchǎng	tsye shir chahng	food market
chàngpiàn diàn	chahng pyan dyan	record store
chāojí shìchǎng	chow jee shir chahng	supermarket
fúzhuāng diàn	foo jwahng dyan	clothing store
lǐpǐn diàn	lee peen dyan	gift shop
shūdiàn	shoo dyan	bookstore
wánjù diàn	wahn jyew dyan	toy store
wǔjīn diàn	woo jeen dyan	hardware store
xiédiàn	shyeh dyan	shoe store
yàofáng	yaow fahng	drugstore
zhūbǎo diàn	joo baow dyan	jewelry store

Just browsing

You may want to call ahead of time to see when the biggest department store in town opens before you decide to stroll on over. It's a nice day outside, you're in a mellow mood, all's right with the world, and all you want to do is just window shop —inside the store. You start out on the **yī céng** (*ee tsuhng;* first floor), take the **zìdòng lóutī** (*dzuh doong low tee;* escalator) all the way up to the **sān céng** (*sahn tsuhng;* third floor), and enjoy checking out tons of **shāngpǐn** (*shahng peen;* merchandise) quietly by yourself, when all of a sudden a **shòuhuòyuán** (*show hwaw ywan;* salesperson) sneaks up behind you and says **Nǐ xiǎng mǎi shénme?** (*nee shyahng my shummuh;* What would you like to buy?)

At this point, you really just want to be left alone, so you say **Wǒ zhǐ shì kànkàn. Xièxiè.** (*waw jir shir kahn kahn. shyeh shyeh;* I'm just looking. Thanks.)

Asking for help

But what if you really do want help? First, you'd better look around for that salesperson you just told to go away. You may not find too many others nearby when you finally need them. If your luck holds, though, here are some questions you may want to ask:

- **Néng bùnéng bāngmáng?** (*nung boo nung bahng mahng;* Can you help me?)

- **Wǒ zhǎo yì běn yǒu guān Zhōngguó lìshǐ de shū.** (*waw jaow ee bun yo gwan joong gwaw lee shir duh shoo;* I'm looking for a book about Chinese history.)

- **Nǐ yǒu méiyǒu Yīngwén de shū?** (*nee yo mayo eeng one duh shoo;* Do you have any books in English?)

- **Nǎr yǒu wàitào?** (*Nar yo why taow;* Where are the jackets?)

- **Qǐng nǐ gěi wǒ kànkàn nǐde xǐzhuāng.** (*cheeng nee gay waw kahn kahn nee duh she jwahng;* Please show me your [Western] suits.)

- **Nǐmen mài búmài guāngpán?** (*nee mun my boo my gwahng pahn;* Do you sell CDs?)

- **Nǎr yǒu ruǎnjiàn?** (*nar yo rwahn jyan;* Where is the software?)

Talkin' the Talk

Barbara and Kate are in a clothing store. The try to get a **fúwùyuán** (foo woo ywan; attendant) to help them locate dresses in their sizes.

Barbara: **Xiǎojiě! Nǐ néng bāng wǒmen ma?**
Shyaow jyeh! Nee nung bahng waw men mah?
Miss! Can you help us?

Fúwùyuán: **Kéyǐ. Qǐng děng yíxià.**
Kuh yee. Cheeng dung ee shyah.
Yes. Just a moment.

After the store attendant puts some boxes away, she returns to help Barbara and Kate.

Fúwùyuán:	**Hǎo. Nǐmen yào mǎi shénme?** *How. Nee men yow my shummuh?* Okay. What did you want to buy?
Barbara:	**Nǎr yǒu qúnzi?** *Nar yo chwun dzuh?* Where are the skirts?
Fúwùyuán:	**Qúnzi jiù zài nàr.** *Chwun dzuh jyo dzye nar.* The skirts are just over there.

Barbara and Kate walk over to the skirt section.

Kate:	**Zhè tiáo hóng qúnzi duōshǎo qián?** *Jay tyaow hoong chwun dzuh dwaw shaow chyan?* How much is this red skirt?
Fúwùyuán:	**Nà tiáo qúnzi èrshíwǔ kuài qián.** *Nah tyaow chwun dzuh are shir woo kwye chyan.* That skirt is $25.
Barbara:	**Nà tài guìle! Nǐ néng bùnéng dǎ zhé?** *Nah tye gway luh! Nee nung boo nung dah juh?* That's too expensive! Can you give me a discount?
Fúwùyuán:	**Kěnéng.** *Kuh nung.* Perhaps.
Barbara:	**Nǐ néng gěi wǒ duōdà de zhékòu?** *Nee nung gay waw dwaw dah duh juh ko?* How much of a discount can you give me?
Fúwùyuán:	**Bǎi fēn zhī shí, hǎo bùhǎo?** *Bye fun jir shir, how boo how?* How's 10 percent?
Barbara:	**Nà tài hǎo le. Xièxiè.** *Nah tye how luh. Shyeh shyeh.* That's great. Thanks.

Words to Know

bǎi fēn zhī shí	bye fun jir shir	10 percent
bǎi fēn zhī shíwǔ	bye fun jir shir woo	15 percent
dǎ zhé	dah juh	to give a discount
Duōshǎo qián?	dwaw shaow chyan	How much is it?
fúwùyuán	foo woo ywan	attendant
shīfu	shir foo	Sir
xiáojiě	shyaow jyeh	Miss

GRAMMATICALLY SPEAKING

You can use two classifiers when it comes to clothing: **jiàn** and **tiáo.** Classifiers are the words used in between a number or the words *this* or *that* and the clothing you're talking about. **Jiàn** is used when you're talking about clothing worn on the upper part of the body, and **tiáo** is used for clothes worn on the lower part. So you'd say **yíjiàn chènshān** (*ee jyan chun shahn;* one shirt) or **sāntiáo kùzi** (*sahn tyaow koo dzuh;* three pairs of pants).

Shopping for Clothes

Going shopping for clothes is an art — one requiring lots of patience and fortitude, not to mention lots of new vocabulary if you're going to do it in Chinese. You need to know how to ask for your own size, how to see whether something is available in a different color or fabric, and in general how to compare apples and oranges (or at least skirts and shirts).

What's your size?

If you ask for clothing in the **dàxiǎo** (*dah shyaow;* size) you're used to quoting in the United States when you're in Taiwan or mainland China, you'll be in for a surprise. The numbers you generally throw out when talking to salespeople in the United States are vastly different from the ones you'll have to get used to using when dealing with Chinese sizes.

Here are some useful phrases you might want to know:

- **Nín chuān duō dà hào?** (*neen chwan dwaw dah how;* What size are you?*)

- **Dàxiǎo búduì.** (*dah shyaow boo dway;* It's the wrong size.*)

- **Hěn héshēn.** (*hun huh shun;* It fits really well.*)

- **Zài Měiguó wǒde chǐcùn shì wǔ hào.** (*dzye may gwaw waw duh chir tswun shir woo how;* In America I wear a size 5.*)

Instead of using the word **dàxiǎo** (*dah shyaow;* size), you can say things like

- **Wǒ chuān sānshíqī hào.** (*waw chwahn sahn shir chee how;* I wear a size 37.*)

- **Nín chuān jǐ hào de chènshān?** (*neen chwahn jee how duh chun shahn;* What size shirt do you wear?*)

- **Wǒ chuān xiǎohào.** (*waw chwahn shyaow how;* I wear a size small.*)

Of course, you can always guess your approximate size just by indicating you'd like to see something in one of the following categories:

- **xiǎo** (*shyaow;* small)

- **zhōng** (*joong;* medium)

- **dà** (*dah;* large)

Talkin' the Talk

Julia approaches a salesperson at the Friendship Store in Beijing. She's unsure of what size to ask for because the measurement systems are different in China than they are in the United States.

Julia:	**Xiǎojiě!** *Shyaow jyeh!* Miss!
Fúwùyuán:	**Nǐ hǎo. Xiǎng mǎi shénme?** *Nee how. Shyahng my shummuh?* Hello. What would you like to buy?
Julia:	**Wǒ xiǎng mǎi yíjiàn jiákè.** *Waw shyahng my ee jyan jyah kuh.* I'm looking for a jacket.
Fúwùyuán:	**Hǎo ba. Nǐ chuān jǐ hào?** *How bah. Nee chwahn jee how?* Very well. What size are you?

Julia: **Wǒ bùzhīdào. Měiguó de hàomǎ hé Zhōngguó de hàomǎ hěn bùyíyàng.**
             Waw boo jir daow. May gwaw duh how ma huh joong gwaw duh how ma hun boo ee yahng.
             I don't know. American sizes are quite different from Chinese sizes.

Fúwùyuán: **Wǒ gūjì nǐ chuān xiǎohào.**
             Waw goo jee nee chwahn shyaow how.
             I would estimate you wear a size small.

Julia: **Hǎo ba. Nà, máfán nǐ gěi wǒ kànkàn xiǎohào de jiákè. Xièxiè.**
             How bah. Nah, mah fahn nee gay waw kahn kahn shyaow how duh jyah kuh. Shyeh shyeh.
             That sounds about right. Would you mind showing me the small size jackets, then? Thank you.

Words to Know

chǐcùn	chir tswun	measurement
dàhào	dah how	large
jiādàhào	jyah dah how	extra-large
kuān	kwan	wide
sōng	soong	loose
wǒ bùzhīdào	waw boo jir daow	I don't know
xiǎohào	shyaow how	small
zhǎi	jye	narrow
zhōnghào	joong how	medium

Comparing quality: Good, better, best

When you want to let loose with a superlative in order to say something is absolutely the best — or, for that matter, the worst —always keep this one little word in mind: **zuì** *(dzway)* which means the most (it's the equivalent of the suffix *-est*).

Zuì is a word just waiting for something to follow it; otherwise it won't have much meaning. Here are some superlatives you may need to use from time to time:

- ✔ **zuì lèi** *(dzway lay;* the most tired)
- ✔ **zuì màn** *(dzway mahn;* the slowest)
- ✔ **zuì máng** *(dzway mahng;* the busiest)
- ✔ **zuì qíguài** *(dzway chee gwye;* the strangest)
- ✔ **zuì yǒumíng** *(dzway yo meeng;* the most famous)
- ✔ **zuì yǒuqián** *(dzway yo chyan;* the richest)

If you just want to say that something is better than something else, or "more" something, rather than the best necessarily, you use the word **gèng** *(guhng)* before an adjective. You can consider these the equivalent of the suffix *-er.* Another word that has the meaning of *more* or *-er* is **yìdiǎn** *(ee dyan;* or ee dyan). While the term **gèng** comes before an adjective, the term **yìdiǎn** must appear after it. Instead of saying **gèng kuài** *(gung kwye;* faster), for example, you'd say **kuài yìdiǎn** *(kwye ee dyan)* to mean *faster.*

Here are some examples:

- ✔ **gèng cōngmíng** *(guhng tsoong meeng;* smarter)
- ✔ **gèng guì** *(guhng gway;* more expensive)
- ✔ **piányǐ yìdiǎn** *(pyan yee ee dyan;* cheaper)
- ✔ **gèng kuài** *(guhng kwye;* faster)
- ✔ **gèng màn** *(guhng mahn;* slower)
- ✔ **hǎo** *(how;* good)
- ✔ **gèng hǎo** *(guhng how;* better)
- ✔ **zuì hǎo** *(dzway how;* best)
- ✔ **duǎn yìdiǎn** *(dwahn ee dyan;* shorter)
- ✔ **cháng yìdiǎn** *(chahng ee dyan;* longer)

- **xiǎo yìdiǎn** (*shyaow ee dyan;* smaller)
- **dà yìdiǎn** (*dah ee dyan;* larger)
- **gèng piányì** (*gung pyan yee;* cheaper)

Comparing two items

The simplest way to compare two items is by using the coverb (the part of speech akin to a preposition) **bǐ** (*bee;* compared with) in between the two things you're comparing, followed by an adjective. If you say A **bǐ** B **hǎo** (*A bee B how*) you're saying *A is better than B.*

Here are some ways to make comparisons with **bǐ:**

- **Tā bǐ wǒ lǎo.** (*tah bee waw laow;* She's older than me.)
- **Zhèige wūzi bǐ nèige dà.** (*jay guh woo dzuh bee nay guh dah;* This room is bigger than that one.)
- **Hóngde bǐ huángde hǎo.** (*hoong duh bee hwahng duh how;* The red one is better than the yellow one.)

One way to convey similarity between two things is to use the coverbs **gēn** (*gun)* or **hé** *(huh)* in between the two things being compared, followed by the word **yíyàng** (*ee yahng;* the same) and then the adjective. So if you say A **gēn** B **yíyàng dà** *(A gun B ee yahng dah),* you're saying that A and B are equally large or as big as each other. You can also just say A **gēn** B **yíyàng**, meaning A and B are the same. Here are some other things you can say with this sentence pattern:

- **Gēge hé dìdi yíyàng gāo.** (*guh guh huh dee dee ee yahng gaow;* My older brother is as tall as my younger brother.)
- **Māo gēn gǒu yíyàng tiáopí.** (*maow gun go ee yahng tyaow pee;* Cats are just as naughty as dogs.)
- **Wǒ gēn nǐ yíyàng dà.** (*waw gun nee ee yahng dah;* You and I are the same age.)

So what if you want to make a negative comparison, such as *I'm not as tall as him?* For that you'd have to use the following sentence pattern:

A **méiyǒu** B **nèmme** adjective

The means "A is not as (adjective) as B." You can see this pattern in action in the following sentences:

✔ **Shāyú méiyǒu jīnyú nèmme kě'ài.** (*shah yew mayo jeen yew nummuh kuh eye;* Sharks are not as cute as goldfish.)

✔ **Yīngwén méiyǒu Zhōngwén nèmme nán.** (*eeng one mayo joong one nummuh nahn;* English is not as difficult as Chinese.)

✔ **Māo de wěiba méiyǒu tùzi de wěiba nèmme cū.** (*maow duh way bah mayo too dzuh duh way bah nummuh tsoo;* Cats' tails aren't as thick as the tails of rabbits.)

Talkin' the Talk

Olivia and Lěiléi go shopping and check out some traditional Chinese women's dresses known as **qípáo** *(chee paow).* Those are the ankle-length dresses with high necks, and a high slit up the side of one leg.

Olivia: **Zhèi jiàn qípáo zěnmeyàng?**
Jay jyan chee paow dzummuh yahng?
What do you think of this traditional Chinese dress?

Lěiléi: **Wǒ juéde hěn hǎo.**
Waw jweh duh hun how.
I think it looks great.

Olivia: **Zhēnde ma?**
Jun duh mah?
Really?

Lěiléi: **Zhēnde. Kěshì jīnsède méiyǒu hóngde nèmme piàoliàng.**
Jun duh. Kuh shir jeen suh duh mayo hoong duh nummuh pyaow lyahng.
Reallly. But the gold one isn't as pretty as the red one.

Olivia: **Jīnsède hé hóngde yíyàng guì ma?**
Jeen suh duh huh hoong duh ee yahng gway mah?
Are the gold one and the red one the same price?

Lěiléi: **Méiyǒu. Jīnsède bǐ hóngde piányi.**
Mayo. Jeen suh duh bee hoong duh pyan yee.
No. The gold one is less expensive than the red one.

Olivia: **Nà, wǒ jiù mǎi jīnsède.**
Nah, waw jyoe my jeen suh duh.
In that case I'll buy the gold one.

What are you wearing? Chuān versus dài

Dài *(dye)* and **chuān** *(chwan)* both mean *to wear,* but they're used for different types of things you put on your body. In English, you can say you're "wearing" everything from hats to socks to skirts or even a necklace. In Chinese, though, you can only **dài** things like **màozi** *(maow dzuh;* hats), **yǎnjìng** *(yan jeeng;* glasses), and **xiézi** *(shyeh dzuh;* shoes) — in other words, articles more akin to accessories rather than actual clothing, but you **chuān** things like **qúnzi** *(chewn dzuh;* skirts) and **dàyī** *(dah ee;* coats).

Here are some things you can **chuān**:

- **bèixīn** *(bay sheen;* vest)
- **chángkù** *(chahng koo;* pants; also referred to simply as **kùzi**)
- **chángxiù** *(chahng shyow;* long sleeve)
- **chènshān** *(chun shahn;* blouse)
- **dàyī** *(dah ee;* coat)
- **duǎnkù** *(dwan koo;* shorts)
- **duǎnxiù** *(dwahn shyow;* short sleeve)
- **jiákè** *(jyah kuh;* jacket)
- **kùzi** *(koo dzuh;* pants)
- **nèiyī** *(nay ee;* underwear)
- **niúzǎikù** *(nyo dzye koo;* blue jeans)
- **qúnzi** *(chewn dzuh;* skirt)
- **tuōxié** *(twaw shyeh;* slippers)
- **wàzi** *(wah dzuh;* socks)
- **yǔyī** *(yew ee;* raincoat)
- **gāogēnxié** *(gaow gun shyeh;* high heels)

Here are some things you can't **chuān** but you can **dài**:

- **lǐngdài** *(leen dye;* necktie)
- **shǒubiǎo** *(show byaow;* wristwatch)
- **shǒutào** *(show taow;* gloves)
- **zhūbǎo** *(joo bao;* jewelry)

Asking about the color

When you go shopping for **yīfu** (*ee foo;* clothes), you have a chance to compare all the different **yánsè** (*yan suh;* colors) they come in and choose the one that looks the best on you. Do you generally prefer **dānsè** (*dahn suh;* solid colors) or **huā** (*hwah;* patterned) shirts? How about **hēi** (*hey;* black) hats or **fěnhóng** (*fun hoong;* pink) skirts? Whatever your clothing preferences are, after you know how to express your heart's desire with the correct word, you can be sure to ask for what you like.

The following is a list of handy words the next time you go shopping either for clothes or for material to create your own. **Shénme yánsè** (*shummuh yan suh;* what color) is your favorite from the list below? Don't be shy to speak up about your preferences. If someone wants you to wear pink with purple polka dots to a wedding, you can always politely just say, "**Yánsè búduì**" (*yan suh boo dway;* the color is wrong) and leave it at that.

- **bái** (*bye;* white)
- **fěnhóng** (*fun hoong;* pink)
- **hēi** (*hey;* black)
- **hóng** (*hoong;* red)
- **huáng** (*hwahng;* yellow)
- **júhóng** (*jyew hoong;* orange)
- **lán** (*lahn;* blue)
- **zǐ** (*dzuh;* purple)
- **dānsè** (*dahn suh;* solid color)
- **dàn yìdiǎn** (*dahn ee dyan;* lighter)
- **duànzi** (*dwahn dzuh;* satin)
- **huā** (*hwah;* patterned)
- **kāishìmǐ** (*kye shir mee;* cashmere)
- **liàozi** (*lyaow dzuh;* fabric)
- **shēn yìdiǎn** (*shun ee dyan;* darker)
- **sīchóu** (*suh cho;* silk)
- **yángmáo** (*yahng maow;* wool)

Talkin' the Talk

Laurel goes shopping for sweaters with her husband John and asks him to weigh in on which color looks best on her.

Laurel: **Zhèi jiàn máoyī nǐ juéde zěnmeyàng?**
Jay jyan maow ee nee jweh duh dzummuh yahng?
What do you think of this sweater?

John: **Neì jiàn máoyī tài xiǎo. Yánsè yě búpiàoliàng.**
Nay jyan mow ee tye shyaow. Yan suh yeh boo pyaow lyahng.
That sweater is too small. The color doesn't look good either.

Laurel: **Nǐ xǐhuān shénme yánsè?**
Nee she hwahn shummuh yan suh?
What color do you like?

John: **Wǒ xǐhuān hóngde. Búyào nèige hēide.**
Waw she hwahn hoong duh. Boo yaow nay guh hey duh.
I like the red one. You shouldn't get the black one.

Laurel: **Hǎole. Nà, wǒ jiù mǎi hóngde ba.**
How luh. Nah, waw jyo my hoong duh bah.
Okay. In that case I'll buy the red one.

When the possessive particle **de** is attached to an adjective and there's no noun following it, it can be translated as *the one which is (adjective),* as in **hóngde** (*hoong duh;* the red one), **dà de** (*dah duh;* the big one), **tián de** (*tyan duh;* the sweet one), and so on.

Shopping for Other Items

Of course clothes aren't the only things in the world to shop for (although I know some would beg to differ with me). How about some antiques or hi tech toys? The possibilities are endless in this consumer-oriented world of ours.

Hunting for antiques

One of the best places in the world to go searching for **gǔdǒng** (*goo doong;* antiques) is — you guessed it — China. **Gǔdǒng diàn** (*goo doong dyan;* antique shops) abound in major cities near large stores and in small alley-ways. You can buy everything from 200-year-old **diāokè pǐn** (*dyaow kuh peen;* carved objects) to 100-year-old **bí yān hú** (*bee yan who;* snuff bottles). You can find all sorts of rare things.

After you find the perfect antique item, though, you need to deal with all the possible export restrictions, like for porcelain that is older than 200 years or some types of rare wood products. You have to have a red wax seal put on the item in order to legally take it out of China. The cultural artifacts bureau of the city in which you buy the item must apply the seal.

Slightly southwest of **Tiān'ānmén Square** in **Beijing** lies **Liúlìchǎng** *(lyoe lee chahng),* an area considered the best in the city for antiques and other tradi-tional arts and crafts. In **Shanghai,** the **Dōngtái** *(doong tye)* antiques market is the one to look for, not far from **Huáihǎi Lù** *(hwye hi loo).* There's even a Ghost Market in the Old Town Bazaar where folks go for weekend antique shopping. The Ghost Market is so named because of the ungodly hour the vendors begin setting up shop — a time before sunrise when only ghosts can check out what's on sale. If you purchase antiques in China, you need to have a red wax seal applied by the local cultural artifacts bureau before you can legally take it out of the country. Even though you're dealing with antiques, you're still allowed to haggle over the price, so don't be shy trying to get the best deal possible.

Here are some words and phrases that should come in handy when hunting for antiques:

- ✔ **Zhèi shì něige cháodài de?** (*jay shir nay guh chaow dye duh;* Which dynasty is this from?)

- ✔ **Néng dài chūguó ma?** (*nung dye choo gwaw mah;* Can it be taken out of China?)

- ✔ **Nǐde gǔdǒng dìtǎn zài nǎr?** (*nee duh goo doong dee tahn dzye nar;* Where are your antique carpets?)

- ✔ **Kéyǐ bùkéyǐ jiā zhúnxǔ chūguó de huǒqī yìn?** (*kuh yee boo kuh yee jyah jwun shyew choo gwaw duh hwaw chee yeen;* Can you put the export seal on it?)

- ✔ **Zhèige duōshǎo nián?** (*jay guh dwaw shaow nyan;* How old is this?)

- ✔ **Něige cháodài de?** (*nay guh chaow dye duh?* Which dynasty is it from?)

- **bí yān hú** (*bee yan who;* snuff bottles)
- **dēnglóng** (*dung loong;* lantern)
- **diāokè pǐn** (*dyaow kuh peen;* carved objects)
- **fóxiàng** (*faw shyahng;* Buddhas)
- **gǔdǒng diàn** (*goo doong dyan;* antique shop)
- **gǔdǒng jiājù** (*goo doong jyah jyew;* antique furniture)
- **guìzi** (*gway dzuh;* chest)
- **jìbài yòng de zhuōzi** (*jee bye yoong duh jwaw dzuh;* altar table)
- **jǐngtàilán** (*jeeng tye lahn;* cloisonné)
- **píngfēng** (*peeng fung;* screen)
- **shénxiàng** (*shun shyahng;* idol)
- **shūfǎ** (*shoo fah;* calligraphy)
- **xiōngzhēn** (*shyoong juhn;* brooch)
- **xiùhuā zhìpǐn** (*shyow hwah jir peen;* embroidery)
- **yù** (*yew;* jade)

Buying high-tech and electronic things

New electronic gadgets appear on the market every two minutes these days, or so it seems. Just when you think you've gotten the latest model of something, another one comes out with great fanfare. Below is a list of the most commonly used (and most commonly bought) items you might be in need of — even while reading *Chinese For Dummies*. Now you'll know how to ask for what you want when you walk in that store.

- **chuánzhēn jī** (*chwahn juhn jee;* fax machine)
- **dǎyìnjī** (*dah yeen jee;* printer)
- **diànnǎo shèbèi** (*dyan now shuh bay;* computer equipment)
- **diànshì jī** (*dyan shir jee;* TV)
- **gèrén diànnǎo** (*guh run dyan now;* PC)
- **guāngpán** (*gwahng pahn;* CD)
- **shǔbiāo** (*shoo byaow;* mouse)
- **jiànpán** (*jyan pahn;* keyboard)

- ✔ **jìsuàn jī** (*jee swan jee;* computer)
- ✔ **kǎlāōukèi jī** (*kah lah okay jee;* karaoke machine)
- ✔ **ruǎnjiàn** (*rwahn jyan;* software)
- ✔ **sǎomiáoyí** (*saow myaow ee;* scanner)
- ✔ **shèxiàng jī** (*shuh shyahng jee;* camcorder)
- ✔ **shǒutíshì** (*show tee shir;* laptop)
- ✔ **xiǎnshìqì** (*shyan shir chee;* monitor)
- ✔ **yìngjiàn** (*eeng jyan;* computer hardware)
- ✔ **zǔhé yīnxiǎng** (*dzoo huh yeen shyahng;* stereo system)

Getting a Good Price and Paying

Folks the world over want to get good deals on their purchases. At least they should. This section helps you discover the joys (and pitfalls) of haggling in Chinese.

Negotiating prices at the night market

Among the more fun things to do in Taiwan and mainland China is visit one of the many lively night markets that abound. There, you can find anything from clothing and jewelry to antiques and food. Because the Chinese love to **mǎi dōngxi** (*my doong she;* shop) and **tǎojià huánjià** (*taow jyah hwahn jyah;* haggle), you'll have plenty of company on your sojourns.

You should always assume that prices are negotiable in an open air market. You can always ask one of the following and see what happens:

- ✔ **Néng bùnéng piányì yìdiǎr?** (*nung boo nung pyan yee ee dyar;* Can you sell it more cheaply?)
- ✔ **Néng bùnéng shǎo yìdiǎr?** (*nung boo nung shaow ee dyar;* Can you lower the price?)

Or you can always play hardball and say something like **Zěnme zhèmma guì ah?** (*dzuh muh juh muh gway ah;* Why is this so expensive?) in an exasperated voice, start walking away and see what happens. (Bet they come back with a lower price.)

These haggling-related phrases are also worth knowing:

- **Nǐmen shōu bù shōu Měiyuán?** (*nee men show boo show may ywan;* Do you accept U.S. dollars?)

- **Zhèige duōshǎo qián?** (*jay guh dwaw shaow chyan;* How much is this?)

- **Dǎ zhé, hǎo bùhǎo?** (*dah juh, how boo how;* How about giving me a discount?)

- **Kéyǐ jiǎng jià ma?** (*kuh yee jyahng jyah mah;* Can we negotiate the price?)

CULTURAL WISDOM

If you see something called a **Yǒuyí Shāngdiàn** (*yo ee shahng dyan;* Friendship Store) be aware that it is one of the ubiquitous state-run stores in China, so prices are generally fixed. However, bargaining is the norm everywhere else. Beware of goods with no prices marked on them! If you ask about them, you'll probably be quoted a price far different than that charged to the locals. Often you'll be able to have 5 to 10 percent taken off any price quoted verbally, so try to practice bargaining before you set foot in a street market.

Paying for your purchase (or demanding a refund)

When you finish checking out all the merchandise, haggling (or not) over the price, and deciding on just what to **mǎi** (*my;* buy), you'll probably start reaching for your **qiánbāo** (*chyan baow;* wallet) to see whether you should take out your **xìnyòng kǎ** (*sheen yoong kah;* credit card) or some **xiànqián** (*shyan chyan;* cash) or, if you got a really good deal, just some **língqián** (*leeng chyan;* small change). When you **fùqián** (*foo chyan;* pay), you might also want to get a **shōujù** (*show jyew;* receipt).

If you end up being **bùyúkuài** (*boo yew kwye;* unhappy) about your purchase, one of these phrases may come in handy when you try to **tuì** (*tway;* return) your **huò** (*hwaw;* merchandise):

- **Wǒ yāoqiú tuìkuǎn.** (*waw yaow chyo tway kwahn;* I want a refund.)

- **Wǒ yào tuì huò.** (*waw yaow tway hwaw;* I would like to return this.)

- **Qǐng nǐ bǎ qián jìrù wǒde xìnyòng kǎ.** (*cheeng nee bah chyan jee roo waw duh sheen yoong kah;* Please refund my credit card.)

- **Wǒ néng bùnéng jiàn zǒngjīnglǐ?** (*waw nung boo nung jyan dzoong jeeng lee;* May I see the manager?)

- **Qǐng nǐ bāo qǐlái.** (*cheeng nee baow chee lye;* Please wrap these/this.)

- **Duì wǒ bù héshēn.** (*dway waw boo huh shun;* It doesn't fit me.)

Fun & Games

Take a look at the illustrations below. In what type of store would you find these items? The answers are in Appendix C.

    a. Zhūbǎo diàn _____

    b. Cài shìchǎng _____

    c. Huādiàn _____

    d. Yàofáng _____

    e. Wánjù diàn _____

Chapter 7

Exploring the Town

....

In This Chapter

▶ Counting down days and time

▶ Dropping in on a show

▶ Checking out museums and historical sites

▶ Taking in a movie or concert

▶ Hanging out in bars and clubs

....

Don't even think of staying around your **lǚguǎn** (*lyew gwahn;* hotel) or house on a beautiful sunny day — especially if you're about to explore a new **chéngshì** (*chuhng shir;* city) in China. You have so much to see and do. You may want to check out a performance of **Jīngjù** (*jeeng jyew;* Peking Opera) or head over to the nearest **bówùguǎn** (*baw woo gwahn;* museum) to take in the latest **yìshù zhǎnlǎn** (*ee shoo jahn lahn;* art exhibit). If you don't know where you're going, you need to know how to ask for **fāngxiàng** (*fahng shyahng;* directions); how to read a **dìtú** (*dee too;* map); and how to get from here to there via **gōnggòngqìchē** (*goong goong chee chuh;* bus), **dìtiě** (*dee tyeh;* subway), or **chūzūchē** (*choo dzoo chuh;* taxi). If you want to look at a train or bus **shíjiānbiǎo** (*shir jyan byaow;* schedule), you may ask yourself what day it is **jīntiān** (*jin tyan;* today) and what time it is **xiànzài** (*shyan dzye;* now).

Knowing the Time and Day

So what day is it today? Could it be **xīngqīliù** (*sheeng chee lyo;* Saturday), when you can sleep late and go see a **diànyǐng** (*dyan yeeng;* movie) in the evening with friends? Or is it **xīngqīyī** (*sheeng chee ee;* Monday), when you have to be at work by **jiǔ diǎn zhōng** (*jyo dyan joong;* 9:00) in the morning to prepare for a 10 a.m. **kāi huì** (*kye hway;* meeting)? Or maybe it's **xīngqīwǔ** (*sheeng chee woo;* Friday) and you already have **liǎng zhāng piào** (*lyahng jahng pyaow;* two tickets) for the **jiāoxiǎng yuè** (*jyow shyahng yweh;* symphony) that begins at **wǎnshàng bā diǎn** (*wahn shahng bah dyan;* 8 p.m.).

Talking about days, weeks, months, and more

You may not be a big fan of going to work from **xīngqīyī** (*sheeng chee ee;* Monday) to **xīngqīwǔ** (*sheeng chee woo;* Friday), but when the **zhōumò** (*joe maw;* weekend) comes, you have two days of freedom and fun. Before you know it, though, **xīngqīyī** comes again.

The days of the week

Although Chinese people recognize seven days in the week just as Americans do, the Chinese week begins on **xīngqīyī** (*sheeng chee ee;* Monday) and ends on **xīngqītiān** (*sheeng chee tyan;* Sunday). If you're talking about **zhèige xīngqī** (*jay guh sheeng chee;* this week) in Chinese, you're talking about any time between this past Monday through this coming Sunday. Anything earlier is considered **shàngge xīngqī** (*shahng guh sheeng chee;* last week). Any day after this coming Sunday is automatically part of **xiàge xīngqī** (*shyah guh sheeng chee;* next week). See Table 7-1 for a list of days of the week.

Table 7-1	Days of the Week	
Chinese Word	*Pronunciation*	*English Word*
xīngqīyī	sheeng chee ee	Monday
xīngqī'èr	sheeng chee are	Tuesday
xīngqīsān	sheeng chee sahn	Wednesday
xīngqīsì	sheeng chee suh	Thursday
xīngqīwǔ	sheeng chee woo	Friday
xīngqīliù	sheeng chee lyo	Saturday
xīngqītiān	sheeng chee tyan	Sunday

So, **jīntiān xīngqījǐ?** (*jin tyan sheeng chee jee;* What day is it today?) Where does today fit in your weekly routine?

- **Jīntiān xīngqī'èr.** (*jin tyan sheeng chee are;* Today is Tuesday.)

- **Wǒ xīngqīyī dào xīngqīwǔ gōngzuò.** (*waw sheeng chee ee daow sheeng chee woo goong dzwaw;* I work from Monday to Friday.)

- **Wǒmen měige xīngqīyī kāihuì.** (*waw men may guh sheeng chee ee kye hway;* We have meetings every Monday.)

- **Xiàge xīngqīsān shì wǒde shēngrì.** (*shyah guh sheeng chee sahn shir waw duh shung ir;* Next Wednesday is my birthday.)

Talkin' the Talk

Michael and Virginia discover that the weekend is coming up and begin to make plans.

Michael: **Jīntiān xīngqī jǐ?**
Jin tyan sheeng chee jee?
What day is today?

Virginia: **Jīntiān xīngqīwǔ.**
Jin tyan sheeng chee woo.
Today is Friday.

Michael: **Hǎojíle. Míngtiān bùgōngzuò.**
How jee luh. Meeng tyan boo goong dzwaw.
Great. No work tomorrow.

Virginia: **Duìle. Hòutiān qù jiàotáng.**
Dway luh. Ho tyan chyew jyaow tahng.
That's right. The day after tomorrow I'll go to church.

Michael: **Hǎo. Wǒ gēn nǐ yìqǐ qù.**
How. Waw gun nee ee chee chyew.
Okay. I'll go with you.

Words to Know

zhèige xīngqī	jay guh sheeng chee	this week
shàngge xīngqī	shahng guh sheeng chee	last week
xiàge xīngqī	shyah guh sheeng chee	next week
zuótiān	dzwaw tyan	yesterday
jīntiān	jin tyan	today
míngtiān	meeng tyan	tomorrow
hòutiān	ho tyan	the day after tomorrow
qiántiān	chyan tyan	the day before yesterday

The months and seasons

Days don't exist in a vacuum — or even just in a week — and weeks exist within months. So if you don't just want to say today is Monday, but rather Monday, June 1st, you have to say the **yuè** (*yweh;* month) before the day and end with the day of the week:

- ✔ **liùyuè yī hào, xīngqīyī** (*lyo yweh ee how, sheeng chee ee;* Monday, June 1st)

- ✔ **sìyuè èr hào, xīngqītiān** (*suh yweh are how, sheeng chee tyan;* Sunday, April 2nd)

The larger unit of the month always comes before the smaller unit of the date in Chinese:

- ✔ **yīyuè èr hào** (*ee yweh are how;* January 2nd)

- ✔ **sānyuè sì hào** (*sahn yweh suh how;* March 4th)

- ✔ **shí'èryuè sānshí hào** (*shir are yweh sahn shir how;* December 30th)

To ask what today's date is, you simply say **jīntiān jǐyuè jǐhào?** (*jin tyan jee yweh jee how; literally:* Today is what month and what day?)

Even though you say each month by adding the number of the month in front of the word **yuè** (which means "month"), if you add the classifier **ge** (*guh*) in between the number and the word **yuè,** you say "one month," "two months," and so on. For example, **bā yuè** (*bah yweh*) means August (which is the 8th month), but **bā ge yuè** (*bah guh yweh*) means eight months.

The same basic idea goes for saying the days of the week. All you have to do is add the number of the day of the week (Monday: Day #1), preceded by the word **lǐbài** (*lee bye*) or **xīngqī** (*sheeng chee*), meaning "week," to say the day you mean. The only exception is Sunday, when you have to add the word **tiān** (*tyan;* heaven, or day) in place of a number. **Wǒde tiān!** (*waw duh tyan;* My heavens!) Isn't this easy?

I list the months of the year in Table 7-2 and the seasons in Table 7-3.

Table 7-2	Months of the Year and Other Pertinent Terms	
Chinese Word or Phrase	*Pronunciation*	*English Word or Phrase*
Yīyuè	ee yweh	January
Èryuè	are yweh	February
Sānyuè	sahn yweh	March
Sìyuè	suh yweh	April

Chinese Word or Phrase	Pronunciation	English Word or Phrase
Wǔyuè	woo yweh	May
Liùyuè	lyo yweh	June
Qīyuè	chee yweh	July
Bāyuè	bah yweh	August
Jiǔyuè	jyo yweh	September
Shíyuè	shir yweh	October
Shíyīyuè	shir ee yweh	November
Shí'èryuè	shir are yweh	December
zhèige yuè	jay guh yweh	this month
shàngge yuè	shahng guh yweh	last month
xiàge yuè	shyah guh yweh	next month
shēngrì	shung ir	Birthday

Table 7-3	Seasonal Terms	
Chinese Word or Phrase	Pronunciation	English Word or Phrase
sì jì	suh jee	The four seasons
dōngjì	doong jee	Winter
chūnjì	chwun jee	Spring
xiàjì	shyah jee	Summer
qiūjì	chyo jee	Fall

Talkin' the Talk

Steve asks Xiǎo Lán about her birthday.

Steve: **Xiǎo Lán, nǐde shēngrì shì jǐyuè jǐhào?**
Shyaow lahn nee duh shung ir shir jee yweh jee how?
Xiǎo Lán, when's your birthday?

Xiǎo Lán: **Wǒde shēngrì shì liùyuè èr hào. Nǐde ne?**
Waw duh shung ir shir lyo yweh are how. Nee duh nuh?
My birthday is June 2nd. How about yours?

Steve: **Wǒde shēngrì shì wǔyuè qī hào.**
Waw duh shung ir shir woo yweh chee how.
My birthday is May 7th.

Xiǎo Lán: **Nèmme, xiàge xīngqīsān jiù shì nǐde shēngrì! Zhù nǐ chàjǐtiān shēngrì kuàilè!**
Nummuh, shyah guh sheeng chee sahn jyo shir nee duh shung ir! Joo nee chah jee tyan shung ir kwye luh!
In that case, next Wednesday is your birthday! Happy almost birthday!

Words to Know

Zhù nǐ shēngrì kuàilè!	joo nee shung ir kwye luh	Happy Birthday!
jīnnián	jin nyan	this year
qùnián	chyew nyan	last year
míngnián	meeng nyan	next year
měinián	may nyan	every year
hòunián	ho nyan	the year after next
qiánnián	chyan nyan	the year before last
xiàge xīngqīyī	shyah guh sheeng chee ee	next Monday
shàngge xīngqīsì	shahng guh sheeng chee suh	last Thursday

Telling time in Chinese

All you have to do to find out the **shíjiān** (*shir jyan;* time) is take a peek at your **shǒubiǎo** (*show byaow;* watch) or look at the **zhōng** (*joong;* clock) on the wall. These days, even your **jìsuànjī** (*jee swan jee;* computer) or **shǒujī** (*show jee;* cell phone) show the time. And you can always revert to that beloved **luòdìshì dà bǎizhōng** (*lwaw dee shir dah bye joong;* grandfather clock) in your parents' living room. You no longer have any excuse to **chídào** (*chir daow;* be late), especially if you own a **nào zhōng** (*now joong;* alarm clock)!

You can express time in Chinese by using the words **diǎn** (*dyan;* hour) and **fēn** (*fun;* minute). Isn't using **fēn** fun? You can even talk about time in **miǎo** (*meow;* seconds) if you like and sound like a cat. Table 7-4 shows you how to prounounce all the hours on the clock.

You can indicate the hour by saying **3-diǎn** or **3-diǎn zhōng**. **Diǎn** (*dyan*) means "hour," but it's also a classifier, and **zhōng** (*joong*) means "clock." Feel free to use either to say what time it is.

Table 7-4	Telling Time in Chinese	
Chinese Phrase	*Pronunciation*	*English Phrase*
1-diǎn zhōng	ee dyan joong	1 o'clock
2-diǎn zhōng	lyahng dyan joong	2 o'clock
3-diǎn zhōng	sahn dyan joong	3 o'clock
4-diǎn zhōng	suh dyan joong	4 o'clock
5-diǎn zhōng	woo dyan joong	5 o'clock
6-diǎn zhōng	lyo dyan joong	6 o'clock
7-diǎn zhōng	chee dyan joong	7 o'clock
8-diǎn zhōng	bah dyan joong	8 o'clock
9-diǎn zhōng	jyo dyan joong	9 o'clock
10-diǎn zhōng	shir dyan joong	10 o'clock
11-diǎn zhōng	shir ee dyan joong	11 o'clock
12-diǎn zhōng	shir are dyan joong	12 o'clock

When mentioning 12 o'clock, be careful! The way to say noon is simply **zhōngwǔ** *(joong woo)*, and the way to say midnight is **bànyè** *(bahn yeh)*.

The Chinese are very precise when they tell time. You can't just say **3-diǎn zhōng** *(sahn dyan joong)* when you want to say 3 o'clock. Do you mean to say **qīngzǎo sān diǎn zhōng** *(cheeng dzaow sahn dyan joong;* 3 a.m.) or **xiàwǔ sāndiǎn zhōng** *(shyah woo sahn dyan joong;* 3 p.m.)?

The segment of the day that you refer to needs to come before the actual time itself in Chinese. Here's a list of the major segments of the day:

- **qīngzǎo** *(cheeng dzaow;* midnight to dawn)
- **zǎoshàng** *(dzaow shahng;* 6 a.m. to noon)
- **xiàwǔ** *(shyah woo;* noon to 6 p.m.)
- **wǎnshàng** *(wahn shahng;* 6 p.m. to midnight)

Here are some samples of combining the segment of the day with the time of day:

- **wǎnshàng qī diǎn zhōng** *(wahn shahng chee dyan joong;* 7 p.m.)
- **xiàwǔ sān diǎn bàn** *(shyah woo sahn dyan bahn;* 3:30 p.m.)
- **qīngzǎo yì diǎn yí kè** *(cheeng dzaow ee dyan ee kuh;* 1:15 a.m.)
- **zǎoshàng bā diǎn èrshíwǔ fēn** *(dzaow shahng bah dyan are shir woo fun;* 8:25 a.m.)

If you want to indicate half an hour, just add **bàn** *(bahn;* half) after the hour:

- **3-diǎn bàn** *(sahn dyan bahn;* 3:30)
- **4-diǎn bàn** *(suh dyan bahn;* 4:30)
- **11-diǎn bàn** *(shir ee dyan bahn;* 11:30)

Do you want to indicate a quarter of an hour or three quarters of an hour? Just use the phrases **yí kè** *(ee kuh)* and **sān kè** *(sahn kuh)* after the hour:

- **2-diǎn yí kè** *(lyahng dyan ee kuh;* 2:15)
- **4-diǎn yí kè** *(suh dyan ee kuh;* 4:15)
- **5-diǎn sān kè** *(woo dyan sahn kuh;* 5:45)
- **7-diǎn sān kè** *(chee dyan sahn kuh;* 7:45)

Of course, you have other ways to indicate time in Chinese. On the hour, half hour, and quarter of an hour aren't the only parts of time which exist, after all. For example, instead of saying **qī diǎn wǔshí fēn** (*chee dyan woo shir fun;* 7:50), you can say **bā diǎn chà shí fēn** (*bah dyan chah shir fun;* 10 to 8; *literally:* 8 o'clock minus 10 minutes). **"Chà"** (*chah*) means "to lack." Unlike **fēn** (*fun;* minute), **kè** (*kuh;* quarter of an hour), and **bàn** (*bahn;* half), you can use **chà** either before or after **diǎn** (*dyan;* hour).

Here are some other examples of alternative ways to indicate the time:

- ✔ **chà shí fēn wǔ diǎn** (*chah shir fun woo dyan;* 10 to 5)
- ✔ **wǔ diǎn chà shí fēn** (*woo dyan chah shir fun;* 10 to 5)
- ✔ **sì diǎn wǔshí fēn** (*suh dyan woo shir fun;* 4:50)
- ✔ **chà yí kè qī diǎn** (*chah ee kuh chee dyan;* a quarter to 7)
- ✔ **qī diǎn chà yí kè** (*chee dyan chah ee kuh;* a quarter to 7)
- ✔ **liù diǎn sān kè** (*lyo dyan sahn kuh;* 6:45)
- ✔ **liù diǎn sìshíwǔ fēn** (*lyo dyan suh shir woo fun;* 6:45)

When talking about time, you may prefer to say before or after a certain hour. To do so, you use either **yǐqián** (*ee chyan;* before) or **yǐhòu** (*ee ho;* after) along with the time, day, month, or anything else. Here are some examples:

- ✔ **xiàwǔ 3-diǎn zhōng yǐqián** (*shyah woo sahn dyan joong ee chyan;* before 3:00 p.m.)
- ✔ **qīngzǎo 4-diǎn bàn yǐhòu** (*cheeng dzaow suh dyan bahn ee ho;* after 4:30 a.m.)
- ✔ **sìyuè yǐqián** (*suh yweh ee chyan;* before April)
- ✔ **xiàge xīngqī yǐhòu** (*shyah guh sheeng chee ee ho;* after next week)
- ✔ **wǔyuè sān hào yǐqián** (*woo yweh sahn how ee chyan;* before May 3rd)

Talkin' the Talk

Xiǎo Huá and Chén Míng discuss their plans to see a movie.

Xiǎo Huá: **Wǒmen jīntiān wǎnshàng qù kàn diànyǐng hǎo bùhǎo?**
Waw men jin tyan wahn shahng chyew kahn dyan yeeng how boo how?
Let's go see a movie tonight, okay?

Chén Míng:	**Bùxíng. Wǒde fùmǔ jīntiān wǎnshàng yídìng yào wǒ gēn tāmen yìqǐ chī wǎnfàn.**

Boo sheeng. Waw duh foo moo jin tyan wahn shahng ee deeng yaow waw gun tah men ee chee chir wahn fahn.

No can do. My parents are adamant that I have dinner with them tonight.

Xiǎo Huá:	**Nǐmen jǐdiǎn zhōng chīfàn?**

Nee men jee dyan joong chir fahn?

What time do you eat?

Chén Míng:	**Píngcháng wǒmen liùdiǎn dào qīdiǎn zhōng chīfàn.**

Peeng chahng waw men lyo dyan daow chee dyan joong chir fahn.

We usually eat from 6 to 7.

Xiǎo Huá:	**Hǎo ba. Nǐ chīfàn yǐhòu wǒmen qù kàn yíbù jiǔdiǎn zhōng yǐqián de piānzi, hǎo bùhǎo?**

How bah. Nee chir fahn ee ho waw men chyew kahn ee boo jyo dyan joong ee chyan duh pyan dzuh, how boo how?

Okay. How about we see a movie that starts before 9 after you're finished eating?

Chén Míng:	**Hěn hǎo. Yìhuǐr jiàn.**

Hun how. Ee hwar jyan.

Okay. See you later.

Attending a Performance

Plan on taking in a few **yǎnchū** (*yan choo;* shows) in the near future? You have so much to choose from nowadays. You can check out some **gējù** (*guh jyew;* operas), or, if you prefer, a **bāléi** (*bah lay;* ballet) or a **yǐnyuèhuì** (*yin yweh hway;* music concert).

Shanghai in particular is pretty famous for its **zájì tuán** (*dzah jee twahn;* acrobatics troupes).

Take a peek at Peking Opera

Have you ever been to **Jīngjù** (*jeeng jyew;* Peking Opera)? This Chinese opera is one of the most beloved art forms in China, with a history of over 200 years. The opera is a great spectacle of music, song, and acrobatics, telling and retelling great works of Chinese history and literature. Performances abound, especially during the traditional festivals when everyone is off of work.

Even though its title is Peking (Beijing) Opera, it actually originated in the Anhui and Hubei provinces. Originally staged for the royal family, it came to Beijing in 1790 and later became familiar to the general public. Thousands of local branches of Chinese Opera exist, each with a unique dialect. Opera is the one art form in a country of over a billion people that appeals to every strata of society.

Before you can attend any performances, however, or even try to catch a **diànyǐng** (*dyan yeeng;* movie), you have to buy a **piào** (*pyaow;* ticket) or two. The following phrases should help you get what you want, or at least understand what you're being told:

✔ **Zài nǎr kéyǐ mǎidào piào?** (*dzye nar kuh yee my daow pyaow;* Where can I buy tickets?)

✔ **Yǒu méiyǒu jīntiān wǎnshàng yǎnchū de piào?** (*yo mayo jin tyan wahn shahng yan choo duh pyaow;* Are there any tickets to tonight's performance?)

✔ **Duìbùqǐ, jīntiān wǎnshàng de piào dōu màiwán le.** (*dway boo chee, jin tyan wahn shahng duh pyaow doe my wahn luh;* I'm sorry, tickets for tonight are all sold out.)

✔ **Wǒ yào mǎi yì zhāng dàrén piào, liǎng zhāng értóng piào.** (*waw yaow my ee jahng dah run pyaow, lyahng jahng are toong pyaow;* I'd like to buy one adult ticket and two kid's tickets.)

If you want to ask a person if he or she has ever done anything, just add the particle **–guò** (*gwaw*) to the verb and use the question word **ma** (*mah*) or **méiyǒu** (*mayo*) at the end. Here are some examples:

✔ **Nǐ kànguò Jīngjù ma?** (*nee kahn gwaw jeeng jyew mah;* Have you ever seen Peking Opera?)

✔ **Nǐ chīguò xiā méiyǒu?** (*nee chir gwaw shyah mayo;* Have you ever eaten shrimp?)

✔ **Nǐ qùguò Měiguó ma?** (*nee chyew gwaw may gwaw mah;* Have you ever been to America?)

To answer any these questions, you can repeat the verb plus **guò** if the answer is yes, or simply say **méiyǒu**, meaning "No, I haven't." You can also say **méiyǒu** — *verb* — **guò** if you like.

If you happen to do something **chángcháng** (*chahng chahng;* often) or just **yǒude shíhòu** (*yo duh shir ho;* sometimes), don't be shy about saying so. You can use these adverbs in both the questions and the answers.

Talkin' the Talk

Maria, Catherine, and Elizabeth discuss what kind of performance they want to see this evening.

Maria: **Nǐmen jīntiān wǎnshàng xiǎng kàn shénme? Kàn huàjù ma?**
Nee men jin tyan wahn shahng shyahng kahn shummuh? Kahn hwah jyew mah?
What do you guys want to see tonight? A play?

Catherine: **Wǒ hěn xiǎng qù kàn wǔshù biǎoyǎn. Zájì biǎoyǎn yě kéyǐ.**
Waw hun shyahng chyew kahn woo shoo byaow yan. Dzah jee byaow yan yeah kuh yee.
I'd really like to see a martial arts performance. Acrobatics would be okay, too.

Elizabeth: **Wǒ xiǎng kàn huàjù.**
Waw shyahng kahn hwah jyew.
I want to see a play.

Maria: **Nǐmen kànguò Jīngjù ma?**
Nee men kahn gwaw jeeng jyew mah?
Have you ever seen Peking Opera?

Catherine: **Méiyǒu.**
Mayo.
No.

Maria: **Nà, wǒmen qù kàn Jīngjù ba! Jīngjù shénme dōu yǒu. Yǒu huàjù, yǒu wǔshù, lián zájì yě yǒu.**
Nah, waw men chyew kahn jeeng jyew bah! Jeeng jyew shummuh doe yo. Hwah jyew yo, woo shoo yo, lyan dzah jee yeah yo.
In that case, let's go to see Peking Opera! It has everything. It has a play, it has martial arts, it even has acrobatics.

Elizabeth: **Tài hǎo le!**
              Tye how luh!
              That's great!

Maria goes to the theater box office to buy tickets for tonight's Peking Opera performance and speaks with the clerk.

Maria: **Nǐ hǎo. Wǒ xiǎng mǎi sānzhāng jīntiān wǎnshàng de piào.**
              Nee how. Waw shyahng my sahn jahng jin tyan wahn shahng duh pyaow.
              Hello. I'd like to buy three tickets to tonight's performance.

Clerk: **Hǎo ba. Jīntiān wǎnshàng de piào chàbùduō dōu màiwán le. Zhǐ yǒu èr lóu de zuòwèi.**
              How bah. Jin tyan wahn shahng duh pyaow chah boo dwaw doe my wahn luh. Jir yo are lo duh dzwaw way.
              Sure. Tickets for tonight are almost all sold out. We only have second floor seats left.

Maria: **Èr lóu méiyǒu wèntí. Qián pái zuòwèi de piào yǒu méiyǒu?**
              Are lo mayo one tee. Chyan pye dzwaw way duh pyaow yo mayo?
              Second floor is no problem. Do you have any front row seats, though?

Clerk: **Yǒu. Yígòng sānshí kuài qián.**
              Yo. Ee goong sahn shir kwye chyan.
              Yes. That will be $30 all together.

Maria gives the clerk $30, and the clerk gives her the tickets.

Maria: **Xièxiè.**
              Shyeh shyeh.
              Thank you.

Words to Know

Shénme shíhòu kāiyǎn?	shummuh shir ho kye yan	What time does the show begin?
Shénme shíhòu yǎn wán?	shummuh shir ho yan wahn	What time does the show end?
lóuxià de wèizi	lo shyah duh way dzuh	orchestra seats
lóushàng de wèizi	lo shahng duh way dzuh	balcony seats
piào	pyaow	tickets
yīnyuè tīng	yin yweh teeng	concert hall
jùchǎng	jyew chahng	theatre
lǐtáng	lee tahng	auditorium
mùjiān xiūxi	moo jyan shyo she	intermission
zájì biáoyǎn	dzah jee byaow yan	acrobatic performance
wǔshù biáoyǎn	woo shoo byaow yan	martial arts performance
bāléi wǔ	bah lay woo	ballet
gēwǔ	guh woo	song and dance
Yuèjù	yweh jyew	Cantonese opera
Jīngjù	jeeng jyew	Peking opera
dìfāng xì	dee fahng she	local folk opera

From sex to art: Interesting Chinese museums

The Museum of Ancient Chinese Sex Culture, which opened in Shanghai in 1999, displays the private collection of a Shanhghai University professor. The collection contains all sorts of sexual artifacts ranging from ancient tomb paintings and erotic devices, exhibits dealing with that old Chinese fetish footbinding, and even furniture for lovemaking.

The Shanghai Museum, which opened at People's Plaza in 1996, is a world-class museum.

Considered China's top museum, it consists of four stories of 11 galleries with audiophones and explanatory signs in English as well as Chinese — a rare feature in any other Chinese museum. Arranged by themes rather than dynasties, it houses everything from ancient bronzes, to Tang and Ming ceramics, to paintings and calligraphy. It has an impressive jade gallery as well.

Exploring Museums and Galleries

Theatre shows and live musical performances aren't the only forms of entertainment you can see to get your fill of **wénhuà** (*one hwah;* culture). One of the nicest, calmest activities to do at your own pace is to visit a **bówùguǎn** (*baw woo gwahn;* museum) or **huàláng** (*hwah lahng;* gallery). You can check out anything from **gǔdàide yìshù pǐn** (*goo dye duh ee shoo peen;* ancient artifacts), to **shānshuǐ huà** (*shahn shway hwah;* landscape painting), to **xiàndài yìshù** (*shyan dye ee shoo;* modern art). Sometimes the best reason to go to a **bówùguǎn** is to buy some **lǐwù** (*lee woo;* gifts) and some cool **zhāotiē** (*jaow tyeh;* posters) for yourself.

Here are some questions you may want to ask in a museum or gallery:

✔ **Bówùguǎn jǐdiǎn zhōng kāimén?** (*baw woo gwahn jee dyan joong kye mun;* What time does the museum open?)

✔ **Lǐpǐn shāngdiàn shénme shíhòu guānmén?** (*lee peeng shahng dyan shummuh shir ho gwahn mun;* What time does the gift shop close?)

✔ **Nǐmen mài búmài zhāotiē?** (*nee mun my boo my jaow tyeh;* Do you sell posters?)

Talkin' the Talk

 John arrives at the local art museum pretty late in the day, so he approaches the clerk to ask some questions.

John: **Qǐng wèn, nǐmen jǐdiǎn zhōng guānmén?**
        Cheeng one, nee mun jee dyan joong gwhan mun?
        Excuse me, what time do you close?

Clerk:	**Zhèige bówùguǎn wǎnshàng liù diǎn zhōng guānmén.**
	Jay guh baw woo gwahn wahn shahng lyo dyan joong gwahn mun.
	This museum closes at 6:00 p.m.
John:	**Xiànzài yǐjīng wǔdiǎn duō le. Wǒ néng bùnéng miǎnfèi jìnqù?**
	Shyan dzye ee jeeng woo dyan dwaw luh. Waw nung boo nung myan fay jeen chyew?
	It's now already after 5. May I enter for free?
Clerk:	**Bùxíng. Hái yào fùqián. Shí kuài yì zhāng.**
	Boo sheeng. Hi yaow foo chyan. Shir kwye ee jahng.
	No. You still have to pay. It's 10 dollars a ticket.
John:	**Nà, wǒ míngtiān zài lái, duō huā yìdiǎr shíjiān zài zhèr. Xièxiè.**
	Nah, waw meeng tyan dzye lye, dwaw hwah ee dyar shir jyan dzye jar. Shyeh shyeh.
	In that case, I'll come back tomorrow to spend a little more time here. Thanks.

Words to Know

bówùguǎn	baw woo gwahn	museum
huàláng	hwah lahng	gallery
yìshù	ee shoo	art
shǒuyìrén	show ee run	artisan
yìshùjiā	ee shoo jyah	artist
jiézuò	jyeh dzwaw	masterpiece

Visiting Historical Sites

You shouldn't pass up at least one well-coordinated trip to a historical site if you visit China, even if you have only a week for business. Take the **Cháng Chéng** (*chahng chung;* Great Wall), for example. Just north of Beijing, the wall is one of the greatest man-made objects on earth.

And while you're on your way to the Great Wall, you may want to stop off at the **Míng shísān líng** (*meeng shir sahn leeng;* Ming Tombs), which contain the mausoleums of thirteen Ming dynasty (1368-1644) emperors guarded by stone animals and warrior statues.

By far the easiest way to see the major historical sites in China is to join a tour. Here are some phrases that may come in handy:

- **Lǚxíngshè zài nǎr?** (*lyew sheeng shuh dzye nar;* Where's the travel agency?)

- **Yǒu méiyǒu shuō Yīngwén de dǎoyóu?** (*yo mayo shwaw eeng one duh daow yo;* Are there any English speaking guides?)

- **Bàn tiān duōshǎo qián?** (*bahn tyan dwaw shaow chyan;* How much for half a day?)

- **Nǐ yǒu méiyǒu lǚyóu shǒucè?** (*nee yo mayo lyew yo show tsuh;* Do you have a guidebook?)

Some of China's most-visited historical sites include the Great Wall, the Forbidden City in Beijing, and the terra-cotta warriors of Xi'an, where an army of over 6,000 carved warriors and horses stands guard over the tomb of China's first Emperor, Qin Shihuang *(chin shir hwahng),* who dates back to the third century BCE.

Talkin' the Talk

Phil hires a taxi and takes his two children to the Jade Buddha Temple in Shanghai, where he tries to get entrance tickets from the clerk. He's eager to show his children the temple's Song dynasty (960-1279) architecture.

Phil: **Qǐngwèn, zài nǎr kéyǐ mǎi piào?**
Cheeng one, dzye nar kuh yee my pyaow?
Excuse me, where can I buy tickets for admission?

Clerk: **Jiù zài zhèr.**
Jyo dzye jar.
You can buy them here.

Phil:	**Hǎojíle. Piàojià duōshǎo?**
	How jee luh. Pyaow jyah dwaw shaow?
	Great. How much is the ticket price?
Clerk:	**Yìzhāng shí kuài.**
	Ee jahng shir kwye.
	Tickets are $10 each.
Phil:	**Xiǎo háizi miǎnfèi ma?**
	Shyaow hi dzuh myan fay mah?
	Do children get in free?
Clerk:	**Bù miǎnfèi, kěshì xiǎo háizi bànpiào.**
	Boo myan fay, kuh shir shyaow hi dzuh bahn pyaow.
	No, but they're half price.
Phil:	**Wǒmen kě bù kěyǐ zhàoxiàng?**
	Waw mun kuh boo kuh yee jaow shyahng?
	May we take pictures?
Clerk:	**Dāngrán kěyǐ. Méiyǒu wèntí.**
	Dahng rahn kuh yee. Mayo one tee.
	Of course you can. No problem.

Going to the Movies

After a full day of sightseeing, you may want to relax, kick back, and take in a movie. At the movies you can sit and watch what's on the **yínmù** (*yeen moo;* screen) without walking or talking. But what to do when the lights dim and you suddenly realize the film is completely in **Zhōngwén** (*joong one;* Chinese), without any **Yīngwén zìmù** (*eeng one dzuh moo;* English subtitles) whatsoever? You read this book, of course!

What kind of movie do you want to see? Table 7-5 gives you a few genres to choose from:

Table 7-5	Movie Genres	
Chinese Word(s)	*Pronunciation*	*English Word(s)*
xǐjù piān	she jyew pyan	comedy
gùshi piān	goo shir pyan	drama

Chinese Word(s)	Pronunciation	English Word(s)
àiqíng piān	eye cheeng pyan	romance
dòngzuò piān	doong dzwaw pyan	action
jìlù piān	jee loo pyan	documentary
dònghuà piān	doong hwah pyan	cartoon
kǒngbù piān	koong boo pyan	horror
wǔxiá piān	woo shyah pyan	kung-fu

Talkin' the Talk

Wendy and Tom decide to go to the movies tonight.

Wendy: **Wǒmen jīntiān wǎnshàng qù kàn yíbù diànyǐng ba.**
Waw men jin tyan wahn shahng chyew kahn ee boo dyan yeeng bah.
Let's go see a movie tonight.

Tom: **Jīntiān yǎn shénme?**
Jin tyan yan shummuh?
What's playing today?

Wendy: **Yíge Zhāng Yìmóu dǎoyǎn de piānzi. Wǒ wàngle nèige míngzi.**
Ee guh jahng ee moe daow yan duh pyan dzuh. Waw wahng luh nay guh meeng dzuh.
A film directed by Zhang Yimou. I forget the name.

Tom: **Shì shuō Yīngwén de ma?**
Shir shwaw eeng one duh mah?
Is it in English?

Wendy: **Búshì, kěshì yǒu Yīngwén zìmù.**
Boo shir, kuh shir yo eeng one dzuh moo.
No, but there are English subtitles.

Words to Know

nán yǎnyuán	nahn yan ywan	actor
nǚ yǎnyuán	nyew yan ywan	actress
dǎoyǎn	daow yan	director
Yīngwén zìmù	eeng one dzuh moo	English subtitles
diànyǐng yuàn	dyan yeeng ywan	movie theater
wàiguópiān	wye gwaw pyan	foreign film
Diànyǐng yuàn zài nǎr?	dyan yeeng ywan dzye nar	Where's the movie theater?

Listening to a Concert

You often hear that the language of music crosses international boundaries. If you're feeling a bit exhausted after practicing Chinese, you can head to a concert in the evening where you can relax. Let the music transport you to another mental space.

At the end of a concert in China, you don't hear anyone yelling "Encore!" What you do hear, however, is **"Zài lái yíge, zài lái yíge!"** (*dzye lye ee guh, dzye lye ee guh;* Bring on one more!)

Talkin' the Talk

Susan and George discuss what kind of concert to attend this weekend.

George: **Wǒmen zhèige zhōumò qù yīnyuè tīng tīng Zhōngguó gǔdiǎn yīnyuè.**
Waw men jay guh joe maw chyew een yweh teeng teeng joong gwaw goo dyan een yweh.
This weekend we're going to the concert hall to hear a classical Chinese music concert.

Susan: **Wǒ bùxǐhuān Zhōngguó gǔdiǎn yīnyuè. Wǒ gèng xǐhuān juéshì yīnyuè.**

Waw boo she hwahn joong gwaw goo dyan yeen yweh. Waw gung she hwahn jyweh shir een yweh.
I don't like classical Chinese music. I prefer jazz.

George: **Juéshì yīnyuè tài qíguài. Yáogǔn yuè yě bùxǐhuān.**
Jyweh shir een yweh tye chee gwye. Yaow gun yweh yeh boo she hwahn.
Jazz is too strange. I also don't like rock 'n roll.

Susan: **Nǐ dàgài zhǐ xǐhuān jiāoxiǎng yuè nèi lèi de yīnyuè ba.**
Nee dah gye jir she hwahn jyaow shyahng yweh nay lay duh een yweh bah.
You probably only like symphonic music and that sort of thing.

George: **Duì le.**
Dway luh.
Yup.

Words to Know

yīnyuè huì	een yweh hway	concert
dàiwèiyuán	dye way ywan	usher
jiémùdān	jyeh moo dahn	program
Zhōngguó gǔdiǎnyīnyuè	joong gwaw goo dyan yeen yweh	classical Chinese music
gē chàng huì	guh chahng hway	choral recital
shìnèi yuè	shir nay yweh	chamber music
gǔdiǎn yīnyuè	goo dyan een yweh	classical music
míngē	meen guh	folk song
qì yuè	chee yweh	instrumental music
juéshì yīnyuè	jyweh shir een yweh	jazz music
yáogǔn yuè	yaow gun yweh	rock 'n roll
jiāoxiǎng yuè	jyaow shyahng yweh	symphonic music

Hopping Around Bars and Clubs

Are you a night owl who, after a full day of sightseeing and even an evening concert, still has the energy to go bar hopping and carousing around fun clubs? If so, you need to know some common barspeak, especially when you're on vacation in a toddlin' town like Shanghai — or Chicago, for that matter. After all, not everyone you meet or go out with may be fluent in English.

Before the Communist takeover of the mainland in 1949, Shanghai was known as the Paris of the Orient. It has always been the most delightfully decadent city in China and continues to live up to its reputation. Bars, clubs, and all sorts of nightlife abound.

The following phrases may come in handy when you're out exploring the local pubs and dance halls:

- **Qǐng lái yìpíng píjiǔ.** (*cheeng lye ee peeng pee jyoe;* Please bring me a bottle of beer.)

- **Nǐ xiǎng gēn wǒ tiàowǔ ma?** (*nee shyahng gun waw tyaow woo mah;* Would you like to dance?)

- **Wǒ néng bùnéng qǐng nǐ hē jiǔ?** (*waw nung boo nung cheeng nee huh jyoe;* May I get you a drink?)

- **Wǒmen dào nǎr qù tiàowǔ?** (*waw men daow nar chyew tyaow woo;* Where can we go to dance?)

- **Yǒu méiyǒu rùchǎng fèi?** (*yo mayo roo chahng fay;* Is there a cover charge?)

When you go to a bar with friends, you may ask for some **bīngzhèn de píjiǔ** (*beeng juhn duh pee jyoe;* cold beer) or maybe some **hóng** (*hoong;* red) or **bái** (*bye;* white) **pútáo jiǔ** (*poo taow jyoe;* wine). And don't forget to ask for some **huāshēngmǐ** (*hwah shung mee;* peanuts) or **tǔdòupiàn** (*too doe pyan;* potato chips) so you don't get too sloshed with all that **píjiǔ.**

Fun & Games

Matching: Draw a line between the matching pairs.

9:15 a.m.	bànyè
Next month	xiàwǔ sì diǎn bàn
Midnight	xiàge yuè
Two weeks ago	zǎoshàng jiǔ diǎn yíkè
4:30 p.m.	liǎngge xīngqī yǐqián

Chapter 8

Enjoying Yourself: Recreation and Sports

. . . .

In This Chapter

▶ Talking about your hobbies

▶ Appreciating Mother Nature

▶ Pretending to be Picasso

▶ Creating your own tunes

▶ Exercising as an athlete

. . . .

After a hard day at work, most people are ready to kick back and relax. But where to begin? Do you feel so consumed by your **gōngzuò** (*goong dzwaw;* work) that you can't seem to switch gears? Get a life! Better yet, get a **yèyú àihào** (*yeh yew eye how;* hobby). Play some **yīnyuè** (*yeen yweh;* music) on your **xiǎotíqín** (*shyaow tee cheen;* violin). Paint a **huà** (*hwah;* picture). Kick a **zúqiú** (*dzoo chyo;* football) around. Do whatever it takes to make you relax and have some fun. Your outside interests will make you more interesting to be around, and you'll make new friends at the same time — especially if you join a **duì** (*dway;* team). And if you're into **lánqiú** (*lahn chyo;* basketball), just utter the name **Yao Ming** (*yaow meeng*) and you'll instantly discover hordes of potential language exchange partners from among the many fans of this Shanghai native who made it big as a Houston Rockets superstar.

Yao Ming, the 7-foot 6-inch former Shanghai Mavericks basketball player, earned fame and fortune as an NBA player with the Houston Rockets. With the 2008 Olympics set to take place in Beijing, basketball is sure to be of keen interest to the local spectators. If you find yourself in that city, check out the Sports Bar at the Gloria International Hotel, where basketball takes center stage.

Naming Your Hobbies

Are you someone who likes to collect **yóupiào** (*yo pyaow;* stamps) from different **guójiā** (*gwaw jyah;* countries)? Or do you prefer to play **guójì xiàngqí** (*gwaw jee shyahng chee;* chess) in your spare time? How about watching some **niǎo** (*nyaow;* birds) through a pair of **wàngyuǎnjìng** (*wahng ywan jeeng;* binoculars) in **Zhōngyāng Gōngyuán** (*joong yahng goong ywan;* Central Park)? Whatever you enjoy doing, your hobbies are always a good conversation piece. Having at least one **yèyú àihào** (*yeh yew eye how;* hobby) is always a good thing. How about getting involved in some of the following?

- ✔ **kàn shū** (*kahn shoo;* reading)
- ✔ **diàoyú** (*dyaow yew;* fishing)
- ✔ **yuányì** (*ywan ee;* gardening)
- ✔ **pēngtiáo** (*pung tyaow;* cooking)

Some of the things you can **dǎ** (*dah;* do or play with), which literally means to strike, hit, or beat, are **qiú** (*chyo;* balls), **tàijíquán** (*tye jee chwan;* commonly referred to just as *Tai Ji,* a slow form of martial arts), and **pú kè** (poo kuh; cards). But you can also **wán** (*wahn;* play) ball games as well — including games with little **qiú**, such as **pīngpāngqiú** (*peeng pahng chyo;* ping pong). Here are some quick questions using the verb **dǎ** that will help get a conversation started:

- ✔ **Nǐ huì búhuì dǎ tài jí quán?** (*nee hway boo hway dah tiye jee chwahn;* Do you know how to do Tai Ji?)
- ✔ **Nǐ dǎ bùdǎ pīngpāngqiú?** (*nee dah boo dah peeng pahng chyo;* Do you play ping pong?)
- ✔ **Nǐ dǎ májiàng ma?** (*nee dah mah jyahng mah;* Do you play mah-jong?)

Both **tàijíquán** and **májiàng** are quintessential Chinese pastimes. In addition to **tàijíquán**, everyone is familiar with other forms of **wǔshù** (woo shoo; martial arts), including kung fu — a martial art practiced since the Tang (tahng) dynasty back in the eighth century. In fact, you can still see kung fu masters practicing at the Shaolin Temple in Zhengzhou, Henan Province — one great reason for making a trip off the beaten path if you ever visit China.

Tàijíquán is considered an internal martial art and is the most widely practiced form throughout the world. The term **tài jí** ("the Great Ultimate") refers to the interplay between opposing yet complementary forces in the universe — yin and yang — as the basis of creation. **Quán** means "fist," emphasizing that this art is a kind of unarmed combat. Very early every morning in China, tons of people flock to local parks to practice this slow-motion form of exercise together.

Talkin' the Talk

Donald and Helga discuss their knowledge of Taijiquan with each other.

Donald:	**Nǐ huì búhuì dǎ tàijíquán?** *Nee hway boo hway dah tye jee chwan?* Do you know how to do Tai Ji?
Helga:	**Búhuì. Kěshì wǒ zhīdào tàijíquán shì yì zhǒng hěn liúxíng de jiànshēn yùndòng.** *Boo hway. Kuh shir waw jir daow tye jee chwan shir ee joong hun lyo sheeng duh jyan shun yoon doong.* No, but I know that Tai Ji is a very popular kind of workout.
Donald:	**Duìle. Měitiān zǎoshàng hěn zǎo hěn duō rén yìqǐ dǎ tàijíquán.** *Dway luh. May tyan dzaow shahng hun dzaow hun dwaw run ee chee dah tye jee chwan.* That's right. Very early every morning, lots of people practice Tai Ji together.
Helga:	**Tàijíquán de dòngzuò kànqǐlái hěn màn.** *Tye jee chwan duh doong dzwaw kahn chee lye hun mahn.* Tai Ji movements look very slow.
Donald:	**Yòu shuō duìle! Shēntǐ zǒngshì yào wěndìng. Dòngzuò zǒngshì yào xiétiáo.** *Yo shwaw dway luh! Shun tee dzoong shir yaow one deeng. Doong dzwaw dzoong shir yaow shyeh tyaow.* Right again! The body is always stable, and the movements are always well coordinated.

Words to Know

tàijíquán	tye jee chwan	Tai Ji
shǒuxíng	show sheeng	hand form
quán	chwan	fist
zhǎng	jahng	palm
dòngzuò	doong dzwaw	movement
yùndòng	yoon doong	exercise
hòutuì	ho tway	step backward
shíbù	shir boo	weighted step
xūbù	shyew boo	unweighted step
hūxī	hoo she	breathe
yídòng	ee doong	shift
liúxíng	lyo sheeng	popular

Exploring Nature

If you're working overseas in China and want to get really far from the madding crowds, or even just far enough away from your **bàngōngshì** (*bahn goong shir;* office) to feel refreshed, try going to one of the seven sacred **shān** (*shahn;* mountains) or a beautiful **hǎitān** (*hi tahn;* beach) to take in the **shānshuǐ** (*shahn shway;* scenery), which is sure to include **niǎo** (*nyaow;* birds), **shù** (*shoo;* trees), **yún** (*yewn;* clouds), and the **hǎi** (*hi;* ocean). You may want to **qù lùyíng** (*chyew lyew eeng;* go camping) or set up camp on the beach and have a **yěcān** (*yeh tsahn;* picnic) before you **pá shān** (*pah shahn;* climb a mountain).

Here are some things you would see along the way if you were to travel through the Chinese countryside:

- ✔ **bǎotǎ** (*baow tah;* pagoda)

- ✔ **miào** (*meow;* temple)

- ✔ **fómiào** (*faw meow;* Buddhist temple)

- ✔ **dàomiào** (*daow meow;* Daoist temple)

- ✔ **kǒngmiào** (*koong meow;* Confucian temple)

- ✔ **dàotián** (*daow tyan;* rice paddies)

- ✔ **nóngmín** (*noong meen;* farmers)

If you're ever exploring **dàzìrán** (*dah dzuh rahn;* nature) with a friend who speaks Chinese, a few of these words may come in handy:

- ✔ **hé** (*huh;* river)

- ✔ **hú** (*hoo;* lake)

- ✔ **chítáng** (*chir tahng;* pond)

- ✔ **shāndòng** (*shahn doong;* cave)

- ✔ **hǎitān** (*hi tahn;* beach)

- ✔ **àn** (*ahn;* shore)

- ✔ **shāmò** (*shah maw;* desert)

- ✔ **shān** (*shahn;* mountains)

- ✔ **xiǎo shān** (*shyaow shahn;* hills)

- ✔ **hǎi** (*hi;* ocean)

China's sacred mountains

Both Buddhists and Daoists have traditionally built monasteries high on quiet mountaintops or deep inside lush forests to meditate. Nine of China's mountains — five Daoist and four Buddhist — are still considered sacred today, all which remain sites of pilgrimage. **Huáng** **Shān** (*hwahng shahn;* Yellow Mountain) is perhaps China's most famous sacred mountain, distinguished by rare pine trees, unusual rock formations, and hot springs, and surrounded by lakes and waterfalls.

Talkin' the Talk

 Jack and Nell discover the beauty of the seaside resort of **Běidàihé** (bay dye huh) in northern China.

Jack: **Nǐ kàn! Zhèr de fēngjǐng duōme piàoliàng!**
Nee kahn! Jar duh fung jeeng dwaw muh pyaow lyahng!
Look! How gorgeous the scenery here is!

Nell: **Nǐ shuō duìle. Zhēn piàoliàng.**
Nee shwaw dway luh. Jun pyaow lyahng.
You're right. It's truly beautiful.

Jack: **Shénme dōu yǒu. Shān, shēn lán de hǎi, lán tiān.**
Shummuh doe yo. Shahn, shun lahn duh hi, lahn, cheeng tyan.
It has everything. Mountains, deep blue ocean and clear sky.

Nell: **Nǐ shuō duìle. Xiàng tiāntáng yíyàng.**
Nee shwaw dway luh. Shyahng tyan tahng ee yahng.
You're right. It's like paradise.

Words to Know

piàoliàng	pyaow lyahng	beautiful
fēngjǐng	fung jeeng	scenery
tiāntáng	tyan tahng	paradise

 To indicate a similarity between two ideas or objects, as in the last line of the "Talking the Talk" involving Jack and Nell, use the phrase **xiàng . . . yíyàng.** Here are some examples:

- **xiàng nǐ dìdì yíyàng** (*shyahng nee dee dee ee yahng;* like your younger brother)

- **xiàng qīngwā yíyàng** (*shyahng cheeng wah ee yahng;* like a frog)

- **xiàng fēngzi yíyàng** (*shyahng fungdzuh ee yahng;* like a crazy person)

CULTURAL WISDOM

The Shanghai Children's Palace

If you ever visit Shanghai, make time for a visit to the **Shàoniángōng** (*shaow nyan goong;* the Children's Palace), where gifted children take part in an assortment of extracurricular activities in areas such as music, art, dance, and science. Founded in 1953 by Song Qingling, the wife of the Republic of China's founder, Dr. Sun Yat-sen, the Children's Palace is in a grand old building originally known as Marble Hall. It was built by the Baghdadi Jewish tycoon Elly Kadoorie in 1924 and still boasts grand marble hallways, winding staircases, ornate fireplaces, chandeliers, and French windows.

Tapping into Your Artistic Side

You may pride yourself on having been the biggest jock who ever played varsity football, but I bet you still get teary-eyed when you see a beautiful painting or listen to Beethoven. It's okay, just admit it. You're a regular Renaissance man and you can't help it. No more apologies.

Okay, now you're ready to tap into your more sensitive, artistic side in Chinese. Don't be afraid of expressing your **gǎnqíng** (*gahn cheeng;* emotions). The Chinese will appreciate your sensitivity to their Song (*soong*) dynasty **shānshuǐ huà** (*shahn shway hwah;* landscape painting) or the beauty of a Ming (*meeng*) dynasty **cíqì** (*tsuh chee;* porcelain).

I bet you have tons of **chuàngzàoxìng** (*chwahng dzaow sheeng;* creativity). If so, try your hand at one of these fine arts:

- ✔ **huà** (*hwah;* painting)
- ✔ **sùmiáohuà** (*soo meow hwah;* drawing)
- ✔ **diāokè** (*dyaow kuh;* sculpting)
- ✔ **shuǐcǎihuà** (*shway tsye hwah;* watercolor)
- ✔ **táoqì** (*taow chee;* pottery)
- ✔ **shūfǎ** (*shoo fah;* calligraphy)

Striking Up the Band

Like kids all over the world, lots of Chinese children take **xiǎo tíqín** (*shyaow tee cheen;* violin) and **gāngqín** (*gahng cheen;* piano) classes — often under duress. They appreciate the forced lessons when they get older, though, and have their own kids.

Traditional Chinese Instruments

If you've heard any traditional Chinese music at a concert or on a CD, you've probably heard one of these Chinese **yuè qì** (*yweh chee;* musical instruments) at one point or another:

✔ **pípa** (*pee pah;* a plucked string instrument with a fretted fingerboard that sits on your lap)

✔ **gǔzhēng** (*goo juhng;* a long, plucked string instrument that rests on a large stand in front of you)

✔ **èrhú** (*are hoo;* a two-stringed bowed instrument)

Do you play a **yuè qì** (*yweh chee;* musical instrument)? It's never too late to learn, you know. You don't have to become a professional **yīnyuèjiā** (*een yweh jyah;* musician) to enjoy playing an instrument. How about trying your hand (or mouth) at one of these?

✔ **xiǎo tíqín** (*shyaow tee cheen;* violin)

✔ **zhōng tíqín** (*joong tee cheen;* viola)

✔ **dà tíqín** (*dah tee cheen;* cello)

✔ **gāngqín** (*gahng cheen;* piano)

✔ **sākèsīguǎn** (*sah kuh suh gwahn;* saxophone)

✔ **chángdí** (*chahng dee;* flute)

✔ **nán dǐyǐn** (*nahn dee een;* double bass)

✔ **lǎba** (*lah bah;* trumpet)

✔ **chánghào** (*chahng how;* trombone)

✔ **dà hào** (*dah how;* tuba)

✔ **dānhuángguǎn** (*dahn hwahng gwan;* clarinet)

✔ **shuānghuángguǎn** (*shwahng hwahng gwan;* oboe)

✔ **gǔ** (*goo;* drums)

✔ **shùqín** (*shoo cheen;* harp)

✔ **liùxiánqín** (*lyo shyan cheen;* guitar)

The Chinese language has a couple of different verbs that you can use to indicate the practice of various instruments. Those who play stringed instruments should use the verb **lā** (*lah;* to draw, as in draw a bow) before the name of the instrument. For example, you can say that you **lā zhōng tíqín** (*lah joong tee cheen;* play the viola), but you can only **tán** (*tahn;* play) a **gāngqín** (*gahng cheen;* piano). For wind instruments, you have to **chuī** (*chway;* blow) them.

Playing on a Team

No matter where you go in the world, you'll find a national pastime. In America, it's **bàngqiú** (*bahng chyo;* baseball). In most of Europe, it's **zúqiú** (*dzoo chyo;* soccer). And in China, it's **pīngpāngqiú** (*peeng pahng chyo;* ping pong), although now that Yao Ming is on the scene, **lánqiú** (*lahn chyo;* basketball) is getting some attention as well. Here's a list of these and many other popular sports.

- **yǔmáoqiú** (*yew maow chyo;* badminton)
- **bàngqiú** (*bahng chyo;* baseball)
- **lánqiú** (*lahn chyo;* basketball)
- **shǒuqiú** (*show chyo;* handball)
- **bǐngqiú** (*beeng chyo;* hockey)
- **pīngpāngqiú** (*peeng pahng chyo;* ping pong)
- **zúqiú** (*dzoo chyo;* football)
- **yīngshì zúqiú** (*eeng shir dzoo chyo;* soccer (literally, English-style football)
- **lěiqiú** (*lay chyo;* softball)
- **yóuyǒng** (*yo yoong;* swimming)
- **wǎngqiú** (*wahng chyo;* tennis)
- **páiqiú** (*pye chyo;* volleyball)

The Olympics is the best known conglomeration of all sorts of sports. **Tǐcāo** (*tee tsaow;* gymnastics), such as **zìyóu tǐcāo** (*dzih yo tee tsaow;* floor exercises), the **dān gàng** (*dahn gahng;* horizontal bar), the **shuāng gàng** (*shwahng gahng;* parallel bars), the **gāo dǐ gàng** (*gaow dee gahng;* uneven parallel bars) and the **ān mǎ** (*ahn mah;* pommelled horse), are all familiar to viewing audiences around the world.

Yóuyǒng (*yo yoong;* swimming) is also quite popular. Whether you do the **dié yǒng** (*dyeh yoong;* butterfly stroke), the **yǎng yǒng** (*yahng yoong;* backstroke), the **cè yǒng** (*tsuh yoong;* side stroke), prefer to swim **wā yǒng** (*wah yoong;* frog-style or breast stroke) or **zìyóu yǒng** (*dzuh yo yoong;* freestyle swimming), don't forget to keep breathing. (And don't forget to wear your **yóuyǒng mào** (*yo yoong maow;* swimming cap). And if you're a **tiàoshuǐ yùndòngyuán** (*tyaow shway yewn doong ywan;* diver), you'd better not **pà gāo** (*pah gaow;* be scared of heights).

Some games require the use of **pīngpāngqiú pāi** (*peeng pahng chyo pye;* ping-pong paddles); others require **wǎngqiú pāi** (*wahng chyo pye;* tennis rackets) or **lánqiú** (*lahn chyo;* basketballs). All games, however, require a sense of **gōngpíng jìngzhēng** (*goong peeng jeeng jung;* fair play).

Soccer season in Beijing is from May to October, but in southern China it goes year-round. As in Europe, soccer is the spectator sport of preference throughout the country. And just as in Europe, passionate fans sometimes boil over into brawling hordes. If you ever find yourself in Shanghai, check out the game at the Hong Kou Stadium. In Beijing, try the Workers' Stadium near the City Hotel.

Here are some useful phrases to know, whether you're an amateur or a professional athlete. At one time or another, you've certainly heard (or said) them all.

- ✔ **Wǒ xiǎng qù kàn qiúsài.** (*waw shyahng chyew kahn chyo sye;* I want to see a ballgame.)

- ✔ **Bǐfēn duōshǎo?** (*bee fun dwaw shaow;* What's the score?)

- ✔ **Něixie duì cānjiā bǐsài?** (*nay shyeh dway tsahn jya bee sye;* Which teams are playing?)

- ✔ **Wǒ yíngle.** (*waw yeeng luh;* I won.)

- ✔ **Nǐ shūle.** (*nee shoo luh;* You lost.)

- ✔ **Wǒ zhēn xūyào liànxí.** (*waw jun shyew yaow lyan she;* I really need to practice.)

- ✔ **Wǒ dǎ de bútài hǎo.** (*waw dah duh boo tye how;* I don't play very well.)

Here's a list of things that happen at sports events. You'll need to know these terms if you want to follow the action:

- ✔ **chuī shàozi** (*chway shaow dzuh;* to blow a whistle)

- ✔ **dǎngzhù qiú** (*dahng joo chyo;* to block the ball)

- ✔ **dé yì fēn** (*duh ee fun;* to score a point)

- ✔ **tíjìn yì qiú** (*tee jeen ee chyo;* to make a goal)

- ✔ **fā qiú** (*fah chyo;* to serve the ball)

- ✔ **méi tóuzhòng** (*may toe joong;* to miss the shot)

Today you can find such sports as hot-air ballooning and gliding in Anyang. Kind of amazing when you discover Anyang was the capital of China's very first dynasty, almost two millennia before the Common Era. You can even hook up with a hot-air balloon tour of the Great Wall and the Silk Road. These sports certainly present a good way to cover such great distances without requiring you to have been a Hun on horseback. Speaking of which, if camel treks are your thing, Chinese travel agencies can now even arrange for you to ride with the Mongols, those horsemen who've perfected the art of riding over the centuries.

Talkin' the Talk

 Tim and Lacie go to a basketball game together.

Tim: **Bǐsài shénme shíhòu kāishǐ?**
Bee sye shummuh shir ho kye shir?
When does the game begin?

Lacie: **Kuài yào kāishǐ le.**
Kwye yaow kye shir luh.
It's going to start soon.

A few minutes later the game finally begins.

Tim: **Wà! Tā méi tóuzhòng!!**
Wah! Tah may toe joong!
Wow! He missed the shot!

Lacie: **Méi guānxi. Lìngwài nèige duìyuán gāng gāng kòulán défēn.**
May gwahn she. Leeng why nay guh dway ywan gahng gahng ko lahn duh fun.
It doesn't matter. That other player just gained a point with a slam dunk.

Words to Know

tǐyù chǎng	tee yew chahng	stadium
cáipànyuán	tsye pahn ywan	referee
duìfāng	dway fahng	the opposing team
zúqiú chǎng	dzoo chyo chahng	soccer field
píngjú	peeng jyew	tied
fēnshù	fun shoo	the score
jìfēnbǎn	jee fun bahn	scoreboard
fànguī	fahn gway	foul
shàngbànchǎng	shahng bahn chahng	first half of a game
xiàbànchǎng	shyah bahn chahng	second half of a game

Fun & Games

. . . .

What are the people in the pictures doing? Use the correct verb in your response.
(See Appendix C for the answers.)

A. _____

B. _____

C. _____

D. _____

E. _____

Chapter 9

Talking on the Phone

Although e-mail may be the preferred method of communication these days, you can't duplicate hearing your loved one's **shēngyīn** (*shung yeen;* voice) on the other end of the line or reaching just the right person you need to begin discussing a merger over the computer. All the more reason to know how to use the telephone in addition to surfing the Net.

The art of making a phone call in another language, and even in another country, is just that — an art. To master it, you have to feel comfortable with such basics as using the **diànhuà** (*dyan hwah;* telephone) in the first place. Be sure to check out a few things beforehand, like what **dìqū hàomǎ** (*dee chyew how mah;* area code) to **bō** (*baw;* dial) first. What do you actually say when someone picks up on the other end? This chapter helps you navigate the communication terrain, whether you're in Idaho or China.

Using a Telephone

Before even going near a **diànhuà** (*dyan hwah;* telephone), you may want to become familiar with some common Chinese words and phrases connected to using one. In fact, you see so many different kinds of phones nowadays, you shouldn't have a problem finding out which one best suits your needs:

- **shǒujī** (*show jee;* cell phone)
- **wúxiàn diànhuà** (*woo shyan dyan hwah;* cordless phone)
- **gōngyòng diànhuà** (*goong yoong dyan hwah;* public telephone)

Sometimes you need the help of a **jiēxiànyuán** (*jyeh shyan ywan;* operator) for things like **guójì diànhuà** (*gwaw jee dyan hwah;* international phone calls) or to help you look up a **diànhuà hàomǎ** (*dyan hwah how mah;* telephone number). Of course, you don't need a **jiēxiànyuán** to help you make a **běnshì diànhuà** (*bun shir dyan hwah;* local call) or even a **chángtú diànhuà** (*chahng too dyan hwah;* long-distance call). By and large, you can take care of most anything else on your own. Except, perhaps, a **duìfāng fùfèi diànhuà** (*dway fahng foo fay dyan hwah;* collect call).

Here are some other communication tools you may want to use:

- **dǎ diànhuà** (*dah dyan hwah;* to make a phone call)

- **chá diànhuà hàomǎbù** (*chah dyan hwah how mah boo;* look a number up in a phone book)

- **diànhuà hàomǎ** (*dyan hwah how mah;* telephone number)

- **diànhuàkǎ** (*dyan hwah kah;* phone card)

If you're like me, you need to ask plenty of basic questions before you figure out what you're doing with a telephone overseas. Here are a couple questions that may come in handy:

- **Zěnme dǎ diànhuà?** (*dzummuh dah dyan hwah;* How can I place a phone call?)

- **Zài nǎr kéyǐ dǎ diànhuà?** (*dzye nar kuh yee dah dyan hwah;* Where can I make a call?)

- **Běnshì diànhuà shōufèi duōshǎo qián?** (*bun shir dyan hwah show fay dwaw shaow chyan;* How much is a local phone call?)

Going Mobile with a Cell Phone

The majority of folks in the world don't have telephones in their homes. Can you imagine? That goes for mainland China as well, where a quarter of humanity resides. You can find them everywhere in Taiwan, however, as well as in Singapore and Hong Kong. In big cities across the globe you're apt to see a million people (sometimes literally in places like Shanghai) on the street with their **shǒujī** (*show jee;* cell phone) in tow . . . or, rather, in hand, right next to their **zuǐbā** (*dzway bah;* mouth), yakking away. It's the preferred mode of communication these days.

Although the more well-known cell phone brands have tried to make their mark on the vast Chinese market of cell phone users, home grown brands such as TCL and Ningbo Bird corner the market on their home turf nowadays.

Here are some words that may come in handy now that everyone's using a cell phone or beeper:

- **hū** (*who;* beep)
- **hūjī** (*who jee;* beeper)
- **hūjī hàomǎ** (*who jee how mah;* beeper number)
- **shǒujī** (*show jee;* cell phone)
- **shǒujī hàomǎ** (*show jee how mah;* cell phone number)

Cell phones have become so wildly popular that even as recently as 1998, over 10,000 phones were confiscated in northern China after officials discovered that members of high government used them as bribes or gifts for friends and family. They even became the subject of a government anti-corruption campaign.

So now that you have the lowdown on how crucial cell phones appear to be in contemporary China, you're probably itching to make a phone call. On to the basics. . . .

Making a Phone Call

"**Wéi?**" (*way;* hello). You hear this word spoken in the second (or rising) tone a lot on the other end of the line when you make a phone call. It's kind of like testing the waters to see if someone is there. You can reply with the same word in the fourth (or falling) tone so it sounds like you're making a statement, or you can just get right to asking if the person you want to speak with is in at the moment. (For more about the four tones, see Chapter 1.)

A phrase you may hear on the other end of the line in mainland China is "**Nǐ nǎr?**" (*nee nar; literally:* where are you?) It asks what **dānwèi** (*dahn way;* work unit) you're attached to. After these first little questions, you may finally be ready to ask for the person you intended to call in the first place.

For decades after the Communist rule took over mainland China in 1949, all Chinese people were assigned a **dānwèi,** which pretty much regulated every aspect of one's life — from where one lived, when one married, and even when one had children. Asking about one's **dānwèi** is still pretty common when answering the phone.

Here are some things you can do before, during, or after your call:

- **náqǐ diànhuà** (*nah chee dyan hwah;* pick up the phone)
- **dǎ diànhuà** (*dah dyan hwah;* make a phone call)
- **shōudào diànhuà** (*show daow dyan hwah;* receive a phone call)
- **jiē diànhuà** (*jyeh dyan hwah;* answer a phone call)
- **huí diànhuà** (*hway dyan hwah;* return a phone call)
- **liú yíge huà** (*lyo ee guh hwah;* leave a message)
- **guà diànhuà** (*gwah dyan hwah;* hang up)

Calling your friends

Feel like getting in touch with a **péngyǒu** (*puhng yo;* friend) or **tóngshì** (*toong shir;* co-worker) to **liáotiān** (*lyaow tyan;* chat) after class or work? Want to confer with your **tóngxué** (*toong shweh;* classmate) about tomorrow's **kǎoshì** (*cow shir;* exam)? Maybe you two are planning a **wǎnhuì** (*wahn hway;* party) over the **zhōumò** (*joe maw;* weekend) and you need to confer about the details. To get the party started, you have to pick up that phone and start talking.

Talkin' the Talk

Margaret calls to see if her friend Luò Chéng is at home and speaks with his father.

Mr. Chéng:	**Wéi?** *Way?* Hello?
Margaret:	**Qǐngwèn, Luò Chéng zài ma?** *Cheeng won, law chung dzye mah?* May I please speak to Luo Cheng?
Mr. Chéng:	**Qǐngwèn, nín shì nǎ yí wèi?** *Cheeng won, neen shir nah ee way?* May I ask who's calling?
Margaret:	**Wǒ shì tāde tóngxué, Margaret.** *Waw shir tah duh toong shweh, Margaret.* I'm his classmate, Margaret.
Mr. Chéng:	**Hǎo. Shāoděng. Wǒ qù jiào tā.** *How. Shaow dung. Waw chyew jyao tah.* Okay. Just a moment. I'll go get him.

Words to Know

Wéi?	way	Hello?
Wèi.	way	Hello.
Qǐngwèn, nín shì nǎ yí wèi?	cheeng won, neen shir nah ee way	May I ask who's calling?
shāoděng	shaow dung	Just a moment.

Ringing hotels and places of business

Calling places of business may be a bit different than the more informal call to a friend or co-worker. When you call a **lǚguǎn** (*lyew gwahn;* hotel), **shāngdiàn** (*shahng dyan;* store), or a particular **gōngsī** (*goong suh;* company), you may be asked what **fēnjī hàomǎ** (*fun jee how mah;* extension) you want. If you don't know, you can ask for the same:

> **Qǐngwèn, fēnjī hàomǎ shì duōshǎo?** (*cheeng one, fun jee how mah shir dwaw shaow;* May I ask what the extension number is?)

After you figure out the extension, the **jiēxiànshēng** (*jyeh shyan shung;* operator) will hopefully say:

> **Wǒ xiànzài jiù gěi nǐ jiē hào.** (*waw shyan dzye jyo gay nee jyeh how;* I'll transfer you now.)

Even after all your work thus far, you may find that you **jiē bù tōng** (*jyeh boo toong;* can't connect) or that **méiyǒu rén jiē** (*mayo run jyeh;* no one answers). Maybe the **diànhuàxiàn duànle** (*dyan hwah shyan dwahn luh;* the line has been disconnected). That's really **máfan** (*mah fahn;* annoying), isn't it? Here are some other **máfan** problems you may encounter while trying to make a phone call:

- **méiyǒu bōhàoyīn** (*mayo baw how yeen;* no dial tone)
- **nǐ bōcuò hàomǎle** (*nee baw tswaw how mah luh;* you dialed the wrong number)
- **záyīn** (*dzah yeen;* static)
- **méi rén jiē diànhuà** (*may run jyeh dyan hwah;* no one answers)

✔ **diànhuà huàile** (*dyan hwah hwye luh;* the phone is broken)

✔ **zhànxiàn** (*jahn shyan;* the line is busy)

✔ **děnghòu** (*dung ho;* be on hold)

If you finally do get through to an employee's office only to discover the person isn't there, you can always leave a **yǒu shēng yóujiàn** (*yo shung yo jyan;* voicemail). When dealing with voicemail, you may have to deal with the following kinds of instructions on a recorded message:

✔ **Nín rúguǒ shǐyòng ànjiàn shì diànhuàjī, qǐng àn 3.** (*neen roo gwaw shir yoong ahn jyan shir dyan hwah jee, cheeng ahn sahn;* If you have a touch-tone phone, please press 3 now.)

✔ **Nín rúguǒ shǐyòng xuánzhuǎn bōhào jī, qǐng bíe guà.** (*neen roo gwaw shir yoong shwan jwan baw how jee, cheeng byeh gwah;* If you have a rotary phone, please stay on the line.)

✔ **Yào huí dào zhǔ mùlù qǐng àn jǐngzìhào.** (*yaow hway daow joo moo loo cheeng ahn jeeng dzuh how;* If you want to return to the main menu, please press # (pound) now.)

Phoning a client

If you want to reach your **kèhù** (*kuh hoo;* client) or your **shēng yì huǒ bàn** (*shuhng yee haw ban;* business partner) in today's business world, you just have to pick up that phone. Personally connecting with a phone call is a good way to maintain good **guānxi** (*gwan she;* relationships; connections). It's the next best thing to being there.

Sometimes you need a little help from the **mìshū** (mee shoo; secretary) to connect to the person you want to reach.

Talkin' the Talk

Jacob enlists the help of Liú Xiǎojiě (Miss Liu), his trusty secretary in Taipei, to help him make a call.

Jacob: **Liú Xiǎojiě, zěnme jiē wàixiàn?**
Lyo shyaow jyeh, dzummuh jyeh why shyan?
Miss Liu, how can I get an outside line?

Liú Xiǎojiě: **Méi wèntí. Wǒ bāng nǐ dǎ zhèige hàomǎ.**
May one tee. Waw bahng nee dah jay guh how mah.
Don't worry. I'll help you dial the number.

Jacob: **Xièxiè.**
Shyeh shyeh.
Thanks.

Miss Liu gets through and speaks to Mr. Wang's secretary.

Liú Xiǎojiě: **Wéi? Zhè shì Wáng Xiānshēng de bàngōngshì ma?**
Way? Jay shir wahng shyan shung duh bahn goong shir ma?
Hello? Do I have the office of Mr. Wang?

Secretary: **Duì le. Jiù shì.**
Dway luh. Jyo shir.
Yes it is.

Liú Xiǎojiě: **Kéyǐ gěi wǒ jiē tā ma?**
Kuh yee gay waw jyeh tah mah?
Can you connect me with him please?

Secretary: **Duìbùqǐ, tā xiànzài kāihuì. Nǐ yào liúyán ma?**
Dway boo chee, tah shyan dzye kye hway. Nee yaow lyo yan mah?
I'm sorry, he's in a meeting at the moment. Would you like to leave a message?

Liú Xiǎojiě: **Máfan nǐ gàosù tā ABC gōngsī de jīnglǐ Jacob Smith gěi ta dǎ diànhuà le?**
Mah fahn nee gaow soo tah ABC goong suh duh jeeng lee Jacob Smith gay tah dah dyan hwah lah?
May I trouble you to tell him that Jacob Smith, the Manager of ABC Company, called him?

Words to Know

wàixiàn	why shyan	outside line
jīnglǐ	jeeng lee	manager
zǒngcái	dzoong tsye	president
fù zǒngcái	foo dzoong tsye	vice president
zhǔrèn	joo run	director

Using a calling card

Sometimes you may find yourself on the road without a cell phone or **yìngbì** (*yeeng bee;* coins) to make a phone call directly from the nearest **gōngyòng diànhuàtíng** (*goong yoong dyan hwah teeng;* public telephone booth). However, you have a **diànhuàkǎ** (*dyan hwah kah;* phone card) in your pocket, so you decide to try it out.

Sorry, I'm Not Home Right Now . . .

Because people lead such busy lives, more often than not you don't find them in when you try to **gěi tāmen dǎ diànhuà** (*gay tah mun dah dyan hwah;* give them a call). You have no choice but to **liúhuà** (*lyo hwah;* leave a message) on the **lùyīn diànhuà** (*loo yeen dyan hwah;* answering machine). You can always try to **liúhuà** with a real **rén** (*run;* person), too. Sometimes you have to press the **jīngzìjiàn** (*jeen dzuh jyan;* pound key) before leaving a **xìnxi** (*sheen she;* message). In that case, you have to recognize the **jīngzìhào** (*jeeng dzuh how;* pound sign).

Listening to messages that people leave you

If you return home from a long, hard day at work to discover that many callers have **liúle huà** (*lyo luh hwah;* left messages) for you, you may be tempted to **tīng** (*teeng;* listen to) them right away rather than **bùlǐ** (*boo lee;* ignore) them. Relax. Take a hot bath. Have a glass of wine while you cook dinner. After a break you'll be ready to tackle all the messages on that ol' answering machine.

Here's what a typical message sounds like:

> **Wéi? Jeremy, zhè shì Jason. Zhèige zhōumò wǒmen yìqǐ qù nèige wǎnhuì, hǎo bùhǎo? Yīnggāi hěn bàng. Yǒu kòng gěi wǒ dǎ diànhuà. Wǒde shǒujī hàomǎ shì (212) 939-9991. Xièxiè.**

> *Way? Jeremy, jay shir Jason. Jay guh joe maw waw men ee chee chyew nay guh wahn hway, how boo how? Eeng guy hun bahng. Yo koong gay waw dah dyan hwah. Waw duh show jee how mah shir are ee are, jyo sahn jyo, jyo jyo jyo ee. Shyeh shyeh.*

> Hello? Jeremy, this is Jason. Want to go to that party together this weekend? It should be awesome. When you get a chance give me a call. My cell number is (212) 939-9991. Thanks.

Understanding other people's greeting messages

Here are some common greetings you may hear if you reach an answering machine:

- **Zhè shì Barry Jones.** (*jay shir Barry Jones;* You have reached Barry Jones.)

- **Wǒ xiànzài búzài.** (*waw shyan dzye boo dzye;* I'm not in at the moment/I'm away from my desk.)

- **Sān yuè sì hào zhǐqián wǒ zài dùjià.** (*sahn yweh suh how jir chyan waw dzye doo jyah;* I'm on vacation until March 4th.)

- **Nín rúguǒ xiǎng gēn wǒde zhùshǒu tōnghuà, qǐng bō fēnjī 108.** (*neen roo gwaw shyahng gun waw duh joo show toong hwah, cheeng baw fun jee yaow leeng bah;* If you'd like to speak with my assistant, please dial extension 108.)

- **Qǐng liú xià nínde míngzi, diànhuà hàomǎ hé jiǎnduǎn de liúyán. Wǒ huì gěi nín huí diànhuà.** (*cheeng lyo shyah neen duh meeng dzuh, dyan hwah how mah huh jyan dwahn duh lyo yan. Waw hway gay neen hway dyan hwah;* Please leave your name, number, and a brief message. I'll get back to you.)

Leaving messages

When you leave a message on an answering machine, be sure to leave clear instructions about what you want the person to do:

- **Wǒ zài gěi nǐ dǎ diànhuà** (*waw dzye gay nee dah dyan hwah;* I'll call you again.)

- **Nǐ huí jiā zhǐhòu qǐng gěi wǒ dǎ diànhuà.** (*nee hway jyah jir ho cheeng gay waw dah dyan hwah;* After you get home, please give me a call.)

- **Bié wàngle huí wǒde diànhuà.** (*byeh wahng luh hway waw duh dyan hwah;* Don't forget to return my call.)

If a live person answers and you have to leave a message, be sure to be polite. Here are some good phrases to keep in mind:

- **Qǐng gàosù tā wǒ gěi tā dǎ diànhuà le.** (*cheeng gaow soo tah waw gay tah dah dyan hwah luh;* Please tell her I called.)

- **Máfan nǐ qǐng tā huí wǒde diànhuà?** (*mah fahn nee cheeng tah hway waw duh dyan hwah;* May I trouble you to please have him return my call?)

▶ **Qǐng gàosù tā wǒ huì wǎn yìdiǎr lái.** (*cheeng gaow soo tah waw hway wahn ee dyar lye;* Please let him know I'll be a little late.)

▶ **Qǐng gěi wǒ zhuǎn tāde liúyánjī?** (*cheeng gay waw jwan tah duh lyo yan jee;* Could you please transfer me to his voicemail?)

Answering machines are still something of an oddity in China, so many Chinese don't know quite what to do when they hear your recorded voice on the other end of the line. Be clear in your message that the caller should leave a name and phone number after the **hū** (who; beep).

Talkin' the Talk

Ruby calls Betty and discovers she's not home. She has to leave a message with her mother.

Mom: **Wéi?**
Way?
Hello?

Ruby: **Qǐngwèn, Betty zài ma?**
Cheeng one, Betty dzye mah?
Hello, is Betty there?

Mom: **Tā búzài. Tā qù yóujú le. Qǐngwèn, nín shì nǎ yí wèi?**
Tah boo dzye. Tah chyew yo jyew luh. Cheeng one, neen shir nah ee way?
She's not home. She went to the post office. May I ask who this is?

Ruby: **Wǒ shì Ruby, tāde tóngbān tóngxué. Máfan nǐ qǐng gàosù tā wǒ gěi tā dǎ diànhuà le.**
Waw shir Ruby, tah duh toong bahn toong shweh. Mah fahn nee cheeng gaow soo tah waw gay tah dah dyan hwah luh.
I'm Ruby, her classmate. May I trouble you to please tell her I called?

Mom: **Yídìng huì.**
Ee deeng hway.
Certainly.

Words to Know

Máfan nǐ?	mah fahn nee	May I trouble you?
Yídìng huì	ee deeng hway	I certainly will.
Qǐngwèn, nín shì nǎ yí wèi?	Cheeng one neen shir nah ee way?	May I ask who this is?

Fun & Games

Match each of the Chinese phrases to the correct English phrase. Turn to Appendix C for the answers.

English Phrases:

Just a moment.

Is she at home?

Hello.

Sorry, you dialed the wrong number.

Please leave a message.

Chinese Phrases:

Wéi?

Duìbùqǐ, nǐ bōcuò hàomǎle.

Shāoděng

Qǐng nǐ liú yíge huà.

Tā zài ma?

Chapter 10

At the Office and Around the House

Time to get down to **shēng yì** (*shuhng yee;* business). Your **shēng yi,** that is. Want to know how to manage that job in Jiangsu or how to deal with the head honcho? This chapter will help you do business in Chinese — everything from making a business appointment to conducting a meeting to checking your e-mail on the fly. It also tells you how to look for a new apartment and search for furniture so that you can finally come home and relax after all that work.

Because China has the fastest growing economy in the world, it's no wonder you gravitated to this chapter. Think of it. China is the fastest-growing source of international profits for U.S. companies, with over a billion potential customers. The United States is China's second largest trading partner (after Japan), and has hundreds of satellite offices everywhere from Shanghai to Shenzhen. With hundreds of billions (that's right, billions) of dollars in exports throughout the world, China is most decidedly making its mark.

Your Office Digs

Whether you're a **mìshū** (*mee shoo;* secretary) or the **zhǔxí** (*joo she;* chairman) of the Board, the atmosphere and physical environment of your **bàngōngshì** (*bahn goong shir;* office) is pretty important. It can even help get you through an otherwise tough day. Might as well make it as **shūfu** (*shoo* *foo;* comfortable) as possible. Why not put a **zhàopiàn** (*jaow pyan;* photo) of the family **gǒu** (*go;* dog) on your **bàngōngzhuō** (*bahn goong jwaw;* desk) for starters? That should put a smile on your face as you start the day.

You don't even have to get up out of your **yǐzi** (*ee dzuh;* chair) to notice all the techie stuff around you. These days, just about any office you work in or visit has the following basic things:

- ✔ **diànhuà** (*dyan hwah;* telephone)
- ✔ **fùyìnjī** (*foo een jee;* copier)
- ✔ **diànnǎo** (*dyan now;* computer)
- ✔ **chuánzhēn** (*chwan jun;* fax)
- ✔ **dǎyìnjī** (*dah een jee;* printer)

Of course, the first thing you might look around for when you get to work in the morning is the **kāfēijī** (*kah fay jee;* coffee machine). In fact, the one part of the day you may look forward to the most is the **xiūxi** (*shyo she;* coffee break).

As you look around your **xiǎogéjiān** (*shyaow guh jyan;* cubicle), I bet you can find all these things:

- ✔ **gāngbǐ** (*gahng bee;* pen)
- ✔ **qiānbǐ** (*chyan bee;* pencil)
- ✔ **dǎng'àn** (*dahng ahn;* file)
- ✔ **huíwénzhēn** (*hway one jun;* paper clip)
- ✔ **dìngshūjī** (*deeng shoo jee;* stapler)
- ✔ **xiàngpíjīn** (*shyahng pee jeen;* rubberband)
- ✔ **bǐjìběn** (*bee jee bun;* notebook)
- ✔ **jiāo dài** (*jyaow dye;* scotch tape)

If you can't find some indispensable item just when you need it, you can always ask someone in the next **xiǎogéjiān** (*shyaow guh jyan;* cubicle). The simplest way to ask is by using the phrase "**Nǐ yǒu méiyǒu ____?**" (*nee yo mayo _____;* Do you have any ____?) Use that phrase as often as you like. Just make sure you can reciprocate whenever your **tóngshì** (*toong shir;* co-worker) needs something as well.

- ✔ **Nǐ yǒu méiyǒu gāngbǐ?** (*nee yo mayo gahng bee;* Do you have a pen?)
- ✔ **Nǐ yǒu méiyǒu dìngshūjī?** (*nee yo mayo deeng shoo jee;* Do you have a stapler?)

Talkin' the Talk

Mínglěi and Shirley are co-workers in Xi'an. Shirley is about to go into a meeting but can't find her notebook. She quickly checks with her good friend Mínglěi in the next cubicle.

Shirley: **Mínglěi! Wǒ jíde yào mìng! Kuài yào kāihuì le, kěshì zhǎobúdào wǒde bǐjìběn.**
Meeng lay! Waw jee duh yaow meeng! Kwye yaow kye hway luh, kuh shir jaow boo daow waw duh bee jee bun.
Minglei! I'm in such a hurry! We're about to have a meeting, and I can't find my notebook.

Mínglěi: **Wǒ yǒu bǐjìběn. Jiè gěi nǐ.**
Waw yo bee jee bun. Jyeh gay nee.
I have a notebook. I'll loan it to you.

Shirley: **Tài hǎo le! Xièxiè.**
Tye how luh! Shyeh shyeh.
That's great. Thanks.

Whenever you add **"-de yào mìng"** (*duh yaow meeng*) right after a verb, you add a touch of drama and emphasize whatever the verb is. For example, if you say you're **lèi** (*lay*), that means you're tired. But if you say you're **lèi de yào mìng** (*lay duh yaow meeng*), that means you're absolutely exhausted. If you're not just **máng** (*mahng;* busy), but **máng de yào mìng** (*mahng duh yaow meeng*), you're extremely busy, running around like a chicken without a head. Here are some useful phrases to compare:

- **Wǒ lěng.** (*waw lung;* I'm cold.)

- **Wǒ lěng de yào mìng.** (*waw lung duh yaow meeng;* I'm freezing.)

- **Jīntiān hěn rè.** (*jeen tyan hun ruh;* It's very hot today.)

- **Jīntiān rè de yào mìng.** (*jeen tyan ruh duh yaow meeng;* It's a real scorcher today.)

If you're going to emphasize a verb by adding **-de yào mìng** after it, you can't also use **hěn** (*hun;* very) in the same breath. It makes your statement redundant.

Words to Know

jiè	jyeh	to borrow; also to loan
jíde yào mìng	jee duh yaow meeng	in an extreme hurry
bǐjìběn	bee jee bun	notebook
hěn	hun	very

Conducting a Meeting

Congratulations! You've finally set up shop in your new office in Beijing or welcomed your business partners from China and are all set to have your first business meeting. But just what is the **mùdì** (*moo dee;* purpose) of your **huìyì** (*hway ee;* meeting)? Is it to **yǎnshì** (*yan shir;* give a presentation) about a new **chǎnpǐn** (*chahn peen;* product)? Is it to **tánpàn** (*tahn pahn;* negotiate) a **hétóng** (*huh toong;* contract)? How about for the purpose of **shòuxùn** (*show shwun;* training) — either you or your Chinese colleagues? Do you have a specific **yìchéng** (*ee chung;* agenda) in mind already? I hope so. You definitely don't want to look unprepared.

Scheduling and planning a meeting

You might be one of those people who needs to **ānpái huìyì yìchéng** (*ahn pye hway ee ee chung;* schedule a meeting) just to prepare for another meeting. Here are some things you may want to do at such a preliminary meeting:

- **zhìdìng huìyì yìchéng** (*jir deeng hway ee ee chung;* set an agenda)
- **tǎolùn wèntí** (*taow lwun one tee;* discuss problems)
- **jiějué wèntí** (*jyeh jweh one tee;* solve problems)
- **tuánduì jiànshè** (*twan dway jyan shuh;* team building)

What will your role be at these meetings? Will you be the one to **zhǔchí huìyì** (*joo chir hway ee;* lead the meeting) or just **cānjiā huìyì** (*tsahn jya hway ee;* participate in the meeting)? Will you be the **xiétiáorén** (*shyeh tyaow run;* facilitator) of the meeting, trying to elicit as much **fǎnkuì** (*fahn kway;* feedback) as possible? Or do you always have the unenviable task of contacting everyone in order to **qǔxiāo huìyì** (*chyew shyaow hway ee;* cancel the meeting)?

Suppose you're the one who's **zhǔchí huìyì** (*joo chir hway ee;* leading the meeting) and you want to make sure everyone has a say in matters. Here are some phrases you can use to try and include everyone in the process:

✔ **Jack, nǐ hái yǒu shénme xūyào bǔchōng ma?** (*Jack, nee hi yo shummuh shyew yaow boo choong mah;* Jack, do you have anything else to add?)

✔ **Wǒmen xūyào duì zhèige xiàngmù biǎojué ma?** (*waw men shyew yaow dway jay guh shyahng moo byaow jweh mah;* Do we need to vote on this item?)

✔ **Shéi hái yǒu shénme yìjiàn huòzhě wèntí?** (*shay hi yo shummuh ee jyan hwaw juh one tee;* Who still has any comments or questions?)

Making the initial greeting

Suppose you've already had some contacts with your business counterparts on the phone or via e-mail but have never actually met them until now. A mere "nice to meet you" may not suffice, especially if you want to emphasize how very glad you are to finally be speaking face to face. Here are a couple of phrases you can use:

✔ **Zǒngsuàn jiàn dào nín le, shízài ràng wǒ hěn gāoxìng.** (*dzoong swan jyan daow neen luh, shir dzye rahng waw hun gaow sheeng;* It's a pleasure to finally meet you.)

✔ **Hěn gāoxìng jiàn dào nín běnrén.** (*hun gaow sheeng jyan daow neen bun run;* I'm glad to meet you in person.)

Always greet the person who holds the highest rank first before saying hello to others. Hierarchy is important to the Chinese, so try to always be conscious of this or you may unintentionally cause someone to "lose face" by not acknowledging his or her importance in the overall scheme of things. This goes for your side of the equation as well. The leader of your team should enter the room first and then wait to be seated by the host of the meeting.

And one more thing: Try to get a list of the names of your Chinese counterparts in advance so you can practice pronouncing them correctly. That's sure to win a few brownie points right there.

The people you meet with may have one of the following titles:

✔ **zhǔxí** (*joo she;* chairman)

✔ **zhǔrèn** (*joo run;* director of a department)

✔ **dǒngshì** (*doong shir;* director of the board)

✔ **jīnglǐ** (*jeeng lee;* manager)

✔ **zǒngcái** (*dzoong tsye;* president)

✔ **fù zǒngcái** (*foo dzoong tsye;* vice president)

✔ **shǒuxí kuàijì** (*show she kwye jee;* chief financial officer)

✔ **chǎngzhǎng** (*chahng jahng;* factory director)

✔ **zǔzhǎng** (*dzoo jahng;* team leader)

In Chinese, last names always come first. When addressing someone with a title, always say the last name first, followed by the title. So if you know someone's name is Li Peijie (Li being the surname), and he's the Director of the company, you address him as **Lǐ Zhǔrèn** (*lee joo run;* Director Li).

Be sure you have business cards ready to give out when you go to China. It is most appreciated if they are in Chinese as well as English. You should always hand and receive each business card with two hands. Feel free to lay out the name cards in the exact same order as those seated so you'll remember who is who.

If you are the guest of honor at a dinner banquet, you're seated facing the entrance to the room. Don't worry if you get confused figuring out where to sit when facing a round table. Your host will make sure to show you to your seat. (See Chapter 5 for more eating tips.)

Starting the meeting

Here are some things to say when you're ready to get the business meeting started:

✔ **Zǎoshàng hǎo.** (*dzaow shahng how;* Good morning.)

✔ **Huānyíng nín dào wǒmen de bàngōngshì.** (*hwahn eeng neen daow waw mun duh bahn goong shir;* Welcome to our office.)

✔ **Zài kāihuì yǐqián, ràng wǒmen zuò yíge zìwǒ jièshào.** (*dzye kye hway ee chyan, rahng waw men dzwaw yee guh dzuh waw jyeh shaow;* Before the meeting begins, let's introduce ourselves.)

✔ **Wǒ xiǎng jièshào yíxià huìyì de cānjiāzhě.** (*waw shyahng jyeh shaow ee shyah hway ee duh tsahn jya juh;* I'd like to introduce the conference participants.)

✔ **Zánmen kāishǐ ba.** (*dzah mun kye shir bah;* Let's begin.)

Making a presentation

When it's time to give a presentation during the meeting, here are some words that you may want to use:

- **bǎnzi** (*bahn dzuh;* board) and **fěnbǐ** (*fun bee;* chalk)
- **huàbǎn** (*hwah bahn;* easel) and **cǎibǐ** (*tsye bee;* marker)
- **caí liào** (*tsye lyaow;* handouts)
- **chātú** (*chah too;* illustrations)
- **biǎogé** (*byaow guh;* charts)
- **túbiāo** (*too byaow;* diagrams)

Planning to go hi-tech instead? In that case, you may want one of these:

- **PowerPoint yǎnshì** (*PowerPoint yan shir;* PowerPoint presentation)
- **huángdēngjī** (*hwahn dung jee;* slide projector) and **píngmù** (*peeng moo;* screen)
- **tóu yǐng piàn** (*toe yeeng pyan;* transparency)

If you plan on videotaping your presentation, you need a **lùxiàngjī** (*loo shyahng jee;* video recorder), and if the room is pretty big, you may also want to use a **màikèfēng** (*my kuh fung;* microphone).

Ending the meeting

Here are some phrases that may come in handy at the conclusion of the meeting:

- **Gǎnxiè dàjiā jīntiān chūxí huìyì.** (*gahn shyeh dah jyah jeen tyan choo she hway ee;* Thank you everyone for participating in today's meeting.)
- **Wǒmen xūyào zài kāihuì tǎolùn zhè jiàn shìqíng ma?** (*waw men shyew yaow dzye kye hway taow lwun jay jyan shir cheeng mah;* Do we need another meeting to continue the discussion?)
- **Zài líkāi zhīqián, wǒmen bǎ xià cì huìyì de rìqī dìng xiàlái ba.** (*dzye lee kye jir chyan, waw mun bah shyah tsuh hway ee duh ir chee deeng shyah lye bah;* Before we leave, let's confirm a date for the next meeting.)

Talkin' the Talk

Catherine and Joseph have introduced themselves to their Chinese counterparts at the ABC Company in Shenzhen. They plan to give a presentation on their new software product a little later on.

Catherine: **Dàjiā hǎo. Zhè cì huìyì de mùdì shì gěi nǐmen jièshào ABC gōngsī de xīn chǎnpǐn — yīzhǒng bào biǎo de ruǎnjiàn.**
Dah jyah how. Jay tsuh hway ee duh moo dee shir gay nee men jyeh shaow ABC goong suh duh sheen chahn peen — ee joong baow byaow duh rwahn jyan.
Hello everyone. The purpose of this meeting is to introduce you all to ABC Company's new product — a type of spreadsheet software.

Joseph: **Měi gè rén dōu yǒu huìyì yìchéng ma?**
May guh run doe yo hway ee ee chung mah?
Does everyone have a copy of the agenda?

Catherine: **Xièxiè, Joseph. Duì le. Dàjiā dōu yǐjīng nádào zīliào le ma?**
Shyeh shyeh Joseph. Dway luh. Dah jyah doe ee jeeng nah daow dzuh lyaow luh mah?
Thank you, Joseph. Yes, has everyone already received the materials?

Words to Know

zīliào	dzuh lyaow	material
huìyì	hway ee	meeting; conference
huìyì yìchéng	hway ee ee chung	conference agenda
mùdì	moo dee	purpose
bào biǎo	baow byaow	spreadsheet
ruǎnjiàn	rwahn jyan	software

Discussing Business and Industry

Because China has opened up to the world so quickly since the death of Mao Zedong in 1976 (the United States established diplomatic relations with the People's Republic in 1979), U.S. businesses in many areas have set up shop in many parts of the country. Whether your company has an office in mainland China, Taiwan, or Hong Kong, you're sure to find one or more of the industries listed in Table 10-1 represented in those places.

Table 10-1	Foreign Industries with Representation in China, Taiwan, and Hong Kong	
Chinese	*Pronunciation*	*English*
guǎnggào hé gōngguān	gwahng gaow huh goong gwan	advertising and public relations
qìchē	chee chuh	automotive
yínháng yǔ cáiwù	yeen hahng yew tsye woo	banking and finance
diànnǎo	dyan now	computers
jiànzào	jyan dzaow	construction
gōngchéng	goong chung	engineering
yúlè	yew luh	entertainment
shízhuāng	shir jwahng	fashion
bǎoxiǎn	baow shyan	insurance
xīnwén	sheen one	journalism
guǎnlǐ zīxún	gwahn lee dzuh shwun	management consulting
cǎikuǎng yú shíyóu	tsye kwahng yew shir yo	mining and petroleum
zhìyào	jir yaow	pharmaceuticals
chūbǎn	choo bahn	publishing
fángdìchǎn	fahng dee chahn	real estate
yùn shū	yewn shoo	shipping

Regardless of what industry you're in, here are some things that you can do to help you decide how to advertise your company and its products or services or to determine how it's going:

- ✔ **xiāofèizhě yánjiū** (*shyaow fay juh yan jyo;* consumer research)

- ✔ **shìchǎng yánjiū** (*shir chahng yan jyo;* market research)

- ✔ **guǎnggào xuānchuán** (*gwahng gaow shwan chwan;* ad campaign)

- ✔ **pǐnpái tuīguǎng** (*peen pye tway gwahng;* brand-name promotion)

- ✔ **zhíxiāo yùndòng** (*jir shyaow yoon doong;* direct marketing campaign)

- ✔ **diàn tái yú diànshì guǎnggào** (*dyan tie yew dyan shir gwahng gaow;* radio and television ads)

- ✔ **xìnxī guǎnggào** (*sheen she gwahng gaow;* infomercial)

- ✔ **dīngdāng** (*deeng dahng;* jingle)

And here are some things you should have on hand in meetings or at that **màoyì zhǎnxiāohuì** (*maow ee jahn shyaow hway;* trade show):

- ✔ **xiǎocèzǐ** (*shyaow tsuh dzuh;* brochure)

- ✔ **chǎnpǐn mù lù** (*chahn peen moo loo;* catalogue)

- ✔ **túbiāo** (*too byaow;* logo)

Of course, if your product is so good it virtually sells itself, your greatest source of business is undoubtedly going to come from good ol' **kǒuchuán guǎnggào** (*ko chwan gwahng gaow;* word-of-mouth advertising).

Talkin' the Talk

Joel and Peter, two salesmen, visit Guangdong to see if the Flying Peacock Company wants to buy their product. They're in a meeting with the Flying Peacock Company president. They have already gone through the preliminary introductions and small talk.

Joel: **Zhè shì yǒu guān wǒmen chǎnpǐn de xiǎocèzǐ.**
Jay shir yo gwan waw mun chahn peen duh shyaow tsuh dzuh.
Here's a brochure on our product.

Peter: **Wǒmen de chǎnpǐn shì yóu wǒmen zìjǐ de zhuānjiā shèjì de érqiě zhèngmíng shì mǎn chénggōng de.**
Waw men duh chahn peen shir yo waw men dzuh jee duh jwan jyah shuh jee duh are chyeh jung meeng shir mahn chung goong duh.
Our product was designed by our own experts and has proven to be quite successful.

Joel:	**Duì le, kěshì wǒmen yě kéyǐ gēnjù nǐde guīgé lái shèjì chǎnpǐn.**
	Dway luh, kuh shir waw men yeah kuh yee gun jyew nee duh gway guh lye shuh jee chahn peen.
	That's correct, but we can also tailor the product to meet your specifications.
Peter:	**Wǒmen de jiàgé yě hěn yǒu jìngzhēnglì.**
	Waw mun duh jyah guh yeah hun yo jeeng juhng lee.
	Our prices are also quite competitive.

Words to Know

jiàgé	jyah guh	price
hěn yǒu jìngzhēnglì	hun yo jeeng juhng lee	very competitive
gēnjù nǐde guīgé	gun jyew nee duh gway guh	according to your specifications
chǎnpǐn	chahn peen	product
mǎn chénggōng de	mahn chung goong duh	very successful

Using the Internet

These days you can reach your business partner in Beijing in a matter of seconds through **diànzǐ kōngjiān** (*dyan dzuh koong jyan;* cyberspace). With **shǒutí shì** (*show tee shir;* portable) computers and multiple **jiǎnsuǒ yǐnqín** (*jyan swaw yeen cheen;* search engines), it's possible to **jiǎnsuǒ guójì wǎngluò** (*jyan swaw gwaw jee wahng lwaw;* search the Internet) and find just about anything you're looking for. Not sure what you're doing with computers? Forget your **mìmǎ** (*mee mah;* password)? **Jìshù fúwù** (*jee shoo foo woo;* technical support) is only a phone call away. Here are some things you can do nowadays with computers and through the Internet

- ✔ **dǎkāi diànnǎo** (*dah kye dyan now;* turn on the computer)
- ✔ **guāndiào diànnǎo** (*gwahn dyaow dyan now;* turn off the computer)
- ✔ **jìn rù** (*gin roo;* log on)

- **tuì chū** (*tway choo;* log off)

- **jiànlì yíge zhànghù** (*jyan lee ee guh jahng hoo;* set up an account)

- **xiàzài wénjiàn** (*shyah dzye one jyan;* download a file)

- **chóngxīn kāijī** (*choong sheen kye jee;* reboot)

- **xuǎnzé yìjiā wǎngshàng fúwù tígōng shāng** (*shwan dzuh ee jya wahng shahng foo woo tee goong shahng;* choose an Internet service provider)

- **ānzhuāng tiáozhì jiětiáoqì** (*ahn jwahng tyaow jir jyeh tyaow chee;* install a modem)

By the beginning of the 21st century, there were over 10 million PCs and 26 million Internet users in China, even though the government strictly controls its use. Individuals are charged by the minute if they use their own home computers, so folks may not be that keen on checking their e-mail too frequently. If something's really important, you might want to resort to a phone call so you know they'll pick up on the other end of the line.

Talkin' the Talk

Eugene and Sarah discuss the wonders of the Internet.

Eugene: **Yīntèwǎng dàodǐ shì shénme dōngxi?**
Een tuh wahng daow dee shir shummuh doong she?
Just what exactly is the Internet?

Sarah: **Yīntèwǎng shì yìzhǒng diànnǎo de guójì hùlián wǎng. Tā tígòng xìnxī fúwù.**
Een tuh wahng shir ee joong dyan now duh gwaw jee hoo lyan wahng. Tah tee goong sheen she foo woo.
The Internet is a kind of interconnected international network that provides information.

Eugene: **Tīngshuō wànwéiwǎng shénme dōu yǒu.**
Teeng shwaw wahn way wahng shummuh doe yo.
I've heard that the World Wide Web has everything.

Sarah: **Duì le. Nǐ yí shàngwǎng jiù kěyǐ liúlǎn hěn duō bùtóng de wǎngzhàn.**
Dway luh. Nee ee shahng wahng jyo kuh yee lyo lahn hun dwaw boo toong duh wahng jahng.
That's correct. The minute you go online you can browse all sorts of different Web sites.

Words to Know

dàodǐ	daow dee	in the end; after all
yīntèwǎng	een tuh wahng	the Internet
guójì	gwaw jee	international
wànwéiwǎng	wahn way wahng	World Wide Web
shàngwǎng	shahng wahng	to go online
liúlǎn	lyo lahn	browse
liúlǎnqì	lyo lahn chee	browser
fúwùqì	foo woo chee	server
wǎngzhàn	wahng jahn	Web site
wǎngyè	wahng yeh	Web page
wǎngzhǐ	wahng jir	URL
yònghù xìngmíng	yoong hoo sheeng meeng	user name
léishè guāngdié	lay shuh gwahng dyeh	CD-ROM

Checking Your E-Mail

These days your **diànzǐ yóuxiāng dìzhǐ** (*dyan dzuh yo shyahng dee jir;* e-mail address) is as important as your **míngzi** (*meeng dzuh;* name) and your **diànhuà hàomǎ** (*dyan hwah how mah;* phone number) when it comes to keeping in touch. It's almost indispensable if you want to do business. Just check your **shōuxìnxiāng** (*show sheen shyahng;* inbox) and you'll probably have received a few more **diànzǐ yóujiàn** (*dyan dzuh yo jyan;* e-mails) while reading this section alone.

Here are some things you can do with e-mail when you have your own account:

✔ **fā diànzǐ yóujiàn** (*fah dyan dzuh yo jyan;* send an e-mail)

✔ **sòng wénjiàn** (*soong one jyan;* send a file)

✔ **zhuǎnfā xìnxī** (*jwan fah sheen she;* forward a message)

✔ **bǎ wénjiàn fùjiā zài diànzǐ yóujiàn** (*bah one jyan foo jyah dzye dyan dzuh yo jyan;* attach a file to an e-mail)

Talkin' the Talk

Lonnie and Terry discuss how to e-mail each other.

Lonnie: **Zěnme fā yíge diànzǐ yóujiàn ne?**
Dzummuh fah ee guh dyan dzuh yo jyan nuh?
So how do you send an e-mail?

Terry: **Shǒuxiān nǐ děi dǎkāi "xīn yóujiàn."**
Show shyan nee day dah kye "sheen yo jyan."
First you have to open up to "new mail."

Lonnie: **Ránhòu ne?**
Rahn ho nuh?
And then?

Terry: **Ránhòu tiánhǎo shōujiànrén de diànzǐ yóuxiāng dìzhǐ hé yóujiàn de tímù. Xiěhǎo xìn, jiù kěyǐ fā le.**
Rahn ho tyan how show jyan run duh dyan dzuh yo shyahng dee jir huh yo jyan duh tee moo. Shyeh how sheen, jyo kuh yee fah luh.
After that, you have to fill in the recipient's e-mail address and type in the subject. After you're finished writing the message, you can finally send it.

Hunting for an Apartment

Are you one of the hundreds of people considering making a long-term move to China for business purposes? Starting to think about purchasing some **fángdìchǎn** (*fahng dee chahn;* real estate) in the form of a **gōngyùfáng** (*goong yew fahng;* condominium) or a **hézuò gōngyù** (*huh dzwaw goong yew;* co-op) in Beijing or Shanghai? Just a few decades ago, contemplating such a purchase of **cáichǎn** (*tsye chahn;* property) was unthinkable. These days, though, with the enormous influx of foreign investment and joint-venture companies, countless foreigners are beginning to take advantage of the many reputable **fángdìchǎn jīngjìrén** (*fahng dee chahn jeeng jee run;* realtors) to help them do just that. And if you've already purchased some **cáichǎn** and now want to **chūzū** (*choo dzoo;* rent) or **zhuǎnzū** (*jwan dzoo;* sublet) a **kòng gōngyù fángjiān** (*koong goong yew fahng jyan;* vacant apartment) to someone else, there are services that help you, the **wùzhǔ** (*woo joo;* owner), find a trust-worthy **chéngzūrén** (*chung dzoo run;* tenant). Here are some terms you might want to know when thinking of buying a place in China:

- **dàilǐ** (*dye lee;* agent)

- **píngjià** (*peeng jya;* appraisal)

- **tóubiāo** (*toe byaow;* bid)

- **jīngjìrén** (*jeeng jee run;* broker)

- **jiànzhù guīzé** (*jyan joo gway dzuh;* building code)

- **ànjiēfèi** (*ahn jyeh fay;* closing costs)

- **hétóng** (*huh toong;* contract)

- **xìnyòng bàogào** (*sheen yoong baow gaow;* credit report)

- **tóukuǎn** (*toe kwahn;* down payment)

- **gǔběn** (*goo bun;* equity)

- **lìxī** (*lee she;* interest)

- **dǐyājīn** (*dee yah jeen;* mortgage)

Talkin' the Talk

 Iris contacts a realtor about buying a condo in Shanghai.

Iris: **Nǐ hǎo. Wǒ xiǎng zài Shànghǎi mǎi yíge gōngyùfáng.**
Nee how. Waw shyahng dzye Shahng hi my ee guh goong yew fahng.
Hi. I'm thinking of buying a condo in Shanghai.

Realtor: **Méiyǒu wèntǐ. Wǒ jiù shì yíge fángdìchǎn jīngjìrén. Hěn yuànyì bāngmáng.**
Mayo one tee. Waw jyo shir ee guh fahng dee chahn jeeng jee run. Hun ywan yee bahng mahng.
No problem. I'm a real estate broker. I'd be more than happy to help you.

Iris: **Nà tài hǎole. Zài něige dìqū mǎi fángzi zuì hǎo?**
Nah tye haow luh. Dzye nay guh dee chyew my fahng dzuh dzway how?
That's great. Which area do you consider to be the best to buy some property?

Realtor:	**Shànghǎi yǒu hěn duō hěn hǎo de fángdìchǎn. Kěnéng zuì qiǎngshǒu de shì Hóngqiáo hé Jīnqiáo. Hěn duō wàiguó bàngōngshì xiànzài zài Pǔdōng.**
	Shahng hi yo hun dwaw hun how duh fahng dee chahn. Kuh nung dzway chyahng show duh shir hoong chyaow huh jeen chyaow. Hun dwaw why gwaw bahn goong shir shyan dzye dzye poo doong.
	Shanghai has many excellent properties. Perhaps the most popular locations are Hongqiao and Jinqiao. Many foreign offices are now in Pudong.

Words to Know

fángdìchǎn jīngjìrén	fahng dee chahn jeeng jee run	realtor
cáichǎn	tsye chahn	property
mǎi yíge gōngyùfáng	my ee guh goong yew fahng	to buy a condo
mài yíge gōngyùfáng	my ee guh goong yew fahng	to sell a condo
hézuò gōngyù	huh dzwaw goong yew	co-op
qiǎngshǒu	chyahng show	popular
dìqū	dee chyew	area; location
línjìn dìqū	leen jeen dee chyew	neighborhood

Be real sure you're using the correct tone when you pronounce the letters "m-a-i" (pronounced *my*) in Chinese. If you say it with a third (dipping) tone, **mǎi**, it means to buy. If you say it with a fourth (falling) tone, however, **mài**, it means to sell. If you're not careful, you may end up selling something you had hoped to live in yourself.

The growth of Pudong

Pudong ("Pu" is short for the Huangpu River and "dong" means East) is the stretch of land east of the Huangpu River in the city of Shanghai. Just a decade ago, this piece of land was indistinguishable from many other backwater Chinese villages. Today it is a city within a city, boasting a population of over 1.5 million on a piece of real estate larger than the entire country of Singapore. Foreign investment in this part of Shanghai is enormous. In addition to its claim to fame as the fastest growing business area in China, it also boasts Asia's largest department store, its highest TV tower, and, needless to say, the Shanghai Stock Exchange.

The Chinese language is fascinating and incredibly logical. Although **măi** (spoken with a third tone) means to buy and **mài** (spoken with a fourth tone) means to sell, if you put them together and add the word **zuò** (*dzwaw;* to do) in front of them, to say **zuò măimài** (*dzwaw my my*), it means to do business. (To buy and to sell . . . get it?)

Furnishing Your New Digs

Whether you've bought a **gōngyùfáng** (*goong yew fahng;* condo) or a **hézuò gōngyù** (*huh dzwaw goong yew;* co-op), have rented a **gōngyù fángjiān** (*goong yew fahng jyan;* apartment) or are spending a semester in Xi'an and live in a **sùshè** (*soo shuh;* dormitory), you'll probably want to start buying some **jiājù** (*jyah jyew;* furniture) or otherwise **zhuāngshì** (*jwahng shir;* decorate) your new digs and put your individual stamp on the place.

How many of the following **fángjiān** (*fahng jyan;* rooms) does your new place have?

- ✔ **yùshì** (*yew shir;* bathroom)
- ✔ **wòshì** (*waw shir;* bedroom)
- ✔ **fàntīng** (*fahn teeng;* dining room)
- ✔ **xiūxishì** (*shyo she shir;* den)
- ✔ **chúfáng** (*choo fahng;* kitchen)
- ✔ **kètīng** (*kuh teeng;* living room)
- ✔ **shūfáng** (*shoo fahng;* study)
- ✔ **kòngfáng** (*koong fahng;* spare room)

Does your new place have a **yuānzi** (*ywan dzuh;* backyard) with a pretty **huāyuán** (*hwah ywan;* garden), perhaps? How about a **yángtái** (*yahng tye;* balcony) or a more romantic little **tōngdào** (*toong daow;* veranda)? You can put some really nice **zhíwù** (*jir woo;* plants) out there, or even some **huā** (*hwah;* flowers), like **júhuā** (*jyew hwah;* chrysanthemums) or **lánhuā** (*lahn hwah;* orchids) or even some **méihuā** (*may hwah;* plum blossoms). Wouldn't that be nice?

Is there a **lóushàng** (*low shahng;* upstairs) as well as a **lóuxià** (*low shyah;* downstairs)? Is there a grand **ménkǒu** (*mun koe;* entrance) or at least a **diàntī** (*dyan tee;* elevator) if you're on the top floor? Are there lots of floor-to-ceiling **chuānghu** (*chwahng hoo;* windows) with great views, or do they look straight into an air shaft, forcing you to cover them with **chuānglián** (*chwahng lyan;* curtains) the first chance you get? No matter. At least you finally have a place you can call your own.

After you finally move in and discover how much empty space there really is, you probably want to go out and buy at least the bare bones basics as far as **jiājù** (*jyah jyew;* furniture) is concerned. How about some of these?

- **chuáng** (*chwahng;* bed)
- **chuángdiàn** (*chwahng dyan;* mattress)
- **zhuōzi** (*jwaw dzuh;* table)
- **yǐzi** (*ee dzuh;* chair)
- **chájī** (*chah jee;* coffee table)
- **shūzhuō** (*shoo jwaw;* desk)
- **yīguì** (*ee gway;* chest of drawers)
- **shāfā** (*shah fah;* sofa)

And once you have your bed, you'll probably want to buy some of the following items to put on it. (The list just never ends. Try to make sure you don't run up too much of a **xìnyòng kǎ** [*sheen yoong kah;* credit card] bill too quickly or you may regret having made that move from Poughkeepsie to Pudong in the first place.)

- **chuángzhào** (*chwahng jaow;* bedspread)
- **tǎnzi** (*tahn dzuh;* blanket)
- **chuángdān** (*chwahng dahn;* sheets)
- **zhěntóu** (*juhn toe;* pillow)
- **bèizi** (*bay dzuh;* quilt)

The good news, of course, is that after you've purchased all the above items, you can actually sleep on your own new bed in China. The bad news, though, is that now you have no excuse not to **pūchuáng** (*poo chwahng;* make the bed) every morning.

Okay, there's one last thing I almost forgot to remind you to get before you settle in for the night. Trust me, it will make all the difference in the world when it comes to your ability to relax and enjoy your new digs. It's something that you don't want to realize you've forgotten to stock up on before turning in for the night. Here's a hint: It belongs in the **yùshì** (*yew shir;* bathroom). Give up? It's **weìshēngzhǐ** (*way shung jir;* toilet paper), silly. (Don't say I didn't warn you.)

Fun & Games

For the following household items, match the English word to the Chinese word. Check Appendix C for the answers.

Chinese Phrases	English Phrases
yùshì	dining room
wòshì	balcony
fàntīng	sofa
tǎnzi	desk
yángtái	quilt
zhěntóu	bedroom
bèizi	bathroom
shūzhuō	blanket
shāfā	pillow

Part III
Chinese on the Go

The 5th Wave   By Rich Tennant

©RICHTENNANT

"This is why you shouldn't use the Chinese you picked up in oriental restaurants when making a reservation. We've got a room with a view and a queen size eggroll."

In this part . . .

Ah, to travel the world! These chapters help you with every aspect of your travel, from getting a visa and making hotel reservations to deciphering foreign currency, asking for directions, and getting to your destination. I even include a chapter on handling emergencies, although I hope you never have to use it. **Yí lù píng'ān!** (*ee loo peeng ahn; Bon Voyage!*)

Chapter 11

Money, Money, Money

. . . .

In This Chapter

▶ Understanding Chinese currencies

▶ Knowing how (and where) to change money

▶ Cashing checks and charging to plastic

▶ Exchanging money at banks and ATMs

▶ Leaving proper tips

. . . .

Qián (*chyan;* money) makes the world go around. Of course, family and friends are priceless, but you can't very well support yourself or help those you love, much less donate to a charity of your choice, unless you have something to give. And that's what life is really all about. (Unless, of course, your main goal in life is to buy a Ferrari, acquire rare works of art, and live in the south of France . . . in which case you need a LOT of **qián.** All the more reason to read this chapter.)

In this chapter, I share with you important words and phrases for acquiring and spending money — things you can easily do nowadays all over the world. I give you some banking terms to help you deal with everything from live tellers to inanimate objects like ATM machines. I even give you tips on tipping.

Staying Current with Chinese Currency

Depending on where in Asia (or any place where Chinese is spoken) you live, work, or visit, you have to get used to dealing with different types of **huòbì** (*hwaw bee;* currency), each with its own **duìhuànlǜ** (*dway hwahn lyew;* rate of exchange). See Table 11-1 for the Chinese versions of international currency and the following sections for the main forms of Chinese **huòbì.**

Table 11-1	International Currencies	
Chinese Words	*Pronunciation*	*English Words*
Měiyuán	may ywan	U.S. dollar
Rénmínbì	run meen bee	Mainland Chinese dollar
Xīn tái bì	shin tye bee	Taiwan dollar
Gǎng bì	gahng bee	Hong Kong dollar
Xīng bì	sheeng bee	Singapore dollar
Rì yuán	ir ywan	Japanese dollar
Ōu yuán	oh ywan	Euro

Rénmínbì (RMB) in the PRC

In the People's Republic of China, the equivalent of the **Měiyuán** (*may ywan;* U.S. dollar) is the **yuán** (*ywan*). The **yuán** is also known as **rénmínbì** (*run meen bee; literally:* the people's money). As of early 2005, 1 U.S. dollar is equivalent to about 8.25 (mainland) Chinese dollars. Here's how you say that in Chinese:

> **Yì měiyuán huàn bā diǎn èr wǔ yuán rénmínbì.** (*ee may ywan hwahn bah dyan are woo ywan run meen bee;* One U.S. dollar is 8.25 (mainland) Chinese dollars.)

The Chinese **yuán**, which is a paper bill, comes in denominations of 1, 2, 5, 10, 20, 50, and 100. You also see coins worth 1, 2, or 5 **yuán**. In addition to saying you have **yì yuán,** you can say you have **yí kuài qián** (*ee kwye chyan*), which means the exact same thing — one Chinese dollar. Over a billion people around the globe currently use this currency.

Want to know how much money I have right now in my pocket, Nosy? Why not just ask me?

✔ **Nǐ yǒu jǐ kuài qián?** (*nee yo jee kwye chyan;* How much money do you have?)

Use this phrase if you assume the amount is less than $10.00.

✔ **Nǐ yǒu duōshǎo qián?** (*nee yo dwaw shaow chyan;* How much money do you have?)

Use this phrase if you assume the amount is greater than $10.00.

One **yuán** is the equivalent of 10 **máo** *(maow),* which may also be referred to as **jiǎo** *(jyaow)* — the equivalent of 10 cents. Each **máo** or **jiǎo** is the equivalent of 100 **fēn** *(fun),* which compare to American pennies. Paper bills, in addition to the **yuán,** also come in denominations of 2 and 5 **jiǎo.** Coins come in denominations of 1, 2, and 5 **fēn;** 1, 2, and 5 **jiǎo;** and 1, 2, and 5 **yuán.**

The difference between **yuán** and **kuài,** and between **jiǎo** and **máo,** is that **yuán** and **jiǎo** are formal, written ways of saying those denominations and **kuài** and **máo** are the more colloquial forms.

Xīn Táibì in the ROC

In Taiwan, also known as the Republic of China, or ROC, 1 U.S. dollar equals about 31.80 **xīn táibì** *(shin tye bee;* New Taiwan dollars).

Here's how you say that in Chinese:

> **Yì měiyuán huàn sānshíyī diǎn bā yuán xīn táibì.** *(ee may ywan hwahn sahn shir ee dyan bah ywan shin tye bee;* One U.S. dollar is 31.80 New Taiwan dollars.)

You see bills in denominations of 50, 100, 500, and 1,000 and coins in denominations of 1, 5, 10, and 50 cents. Coins, or **língqián** *(leeng chyan;* small change), in Taiwan are particularly beautiful — they have all sorts of flowers etched into them — so you may want to save a few to bring back to the States or to show friends. Just make sure you keep enough on hand for all the great items you can buy cheaply at the wonderful night markets.

Here's how you ask for change:

> **Nǐ yǒu méiyǒu yí kuài qián de língqián?** *(nee yo mayo ee kwye chyan duh leeng chyan;* Do you have change for a dollar?)

Hong Kong dollars

Xiāng gǎng *(shyahng gahng;* Hong Kong; *literally:* fragrant harbour), the long-time financial dynamo of Asia, uses the Hong Kong dollar, or the **gǎngbì** *(gahng bee).* Currently, 1 U.S. dollar is equivalent to 7.65 Hong Kong dollars. Here's how you say that in Chinese:

> **Yì měiyuán huàn qī diǎn liù wǔ yuán gǎngbì.** *(ee may ywan hwahn chee dyan lyo woo ywan gahng bee;* One U.S. dollar is 7.65 Hong Kong dollars.)

Singapore dollars

Singapore is a Mandarin-speaking country in Asia. Its dollars are called **xīng bì** (*sheeng bee*) and come in denominations of 2, 5, 10, 50, and 100. You can find coins in denominations of 1 cent, 5 cents, 10 cents, 20 cents, 50 cents, and 1 dollar.

In Singapore, if you want to say $1.25, you don't use the number **wǔ** (*woo;* five) to refer to the final 5 cents in the amount. You use the term **bàn** (*bahn*), which means half: **yí kuài liǎng máo bàn** (*ee kwye lyahng maow bahn*) rather than **yí kuài liǎng máo wǔ** (*ee kwye lyahng maow woo*). You can definitely use the number **wǔ** in Taiwan, Hong Kong, or mainland China, however.

Making and Exchanging Money

People make their money in all sorts of ways. Most ways are legitimate. (If you've attained yours through nefarious means, I'm not sure I want to know, so don't tell me!) You may be one of those lucky people who win the **cǎi juàn** (*tsye jywahn;* lottery) or receive a large **yí chǎn** (*yee chahn;* inheritance) you use to traipse to the other side of the world. Or perhaps you have a modest amount saved up from working hard and paying your bills on time, and you hope to make it go a long way. However you get your money, you find out how to change it (and then spend it) with the help of this chapter.

You can always **huàn qián** (*hwahn chyan;* exchange money) the minute you arrive at the **fēijī chǎng** (*fay jee chahng;* airport) at the many **duìhuànchù** (*dway hwahn choo;* exchange bureaus), or you can wait until you get to a major **yínháng** (*een hahng;* bank) or check in at your **lǚguǎn** (*lyew gwahn;* hotel). Of course, you can't make it to a bank or hotel if you don't have enough money to hail a **chūzū chē** (*choo dzoo chuh;* taxi) to reach the **yínháng** or **lǚguǎn**, and you don't want to find yourself in **jiānyù** (*jyan yew;* jail) — where you won't be able to make **bǎoshìjīn** (*baow shir jeen;* bail) — because you still don't have any local **huòbì** (*hwaw bee;* currency).

The following phrases come in handy when you're ready to **huàn qián:**

- ✔ **Qǐng wèn, zài nǎr kěyǐ huàn qián?** (*cheeng one, dzye nar kuh yee hwahn chyan;* Excuse me, where can I change money?)

- ✔ **Qǐng wèn, yínháng zài nǎr?** (*cheeng one, eeng hahng dzye nar;* Excuse me, where is the bank?)

- ✔ **Jīntiān de duìhuàn lǜ shì shénme?** (*jin tyan duh dway hwahn lyew shir shummuh;* What's today's exchange rate?)

✔ **Qǐng nǐ gěi wǒ sì zhāng wǔshí yuán de.** (*cheeng nee gay waw suh jahng woo shir ywan duh;* Please give me four 50-yuan bills.)

✔ **Wǒ yào huàn yì bǎi měiyuán.** (*waw yaow hwahn ee bye may ywan;* I'd like to change $100.)

✔ **Nǐmen shōu duōshǎo qián shǒuxùfèi?** (*nee men show dwaw shaow chyan show shyew fay;* How much commission do you charge?)

No matter where you get money or how much money you plan to convert into local currency, you may have to show your **hùzhào** (*hoo jaow;* passport), so always have that ready to whip out.

Talkin' the Talk

Jane arrives at the airport in Beijing and needs to change some money. She asks a **xínglǐyuán** (*sheeng lee ywan;* porter) where she can find a place to exchange money.

Jane: **Qǐng wèn, zài nǎr kěyǐ huàn qián?**
               Cheeng one, dzye nar kuh yee hwahn chyan?
               Excuse me, where can I change money?

Xíngliyuán: **Duìhuànchù jiù zài nàr.**
               Dway hwahn choo jyoe dzye nar.
               The exchange bureau is just over there.

Jane: **Xièxiè.**
               Shyeh shyeh.
               Thank you.

Jane goes to the money exchange counter to change some U.S. dollars into Chinese **yuán** with the help of the **chūnàyuán** (*choo nah ywan;* cashier).

Jane: **Nǐ hǎo. Wǒ yào huàn yì bǎi měiyuán de rénmínbì.**
               Nee how. Waw yaow hwahn ee bye may ywan duh run meen bee.
               Hello. I'd like to change USD $100 into RMB.

Chūnàyuán: **Méiyǒu wèntí.**
               Mayo one tee.
               No problem.

Jane: **Jīntiān de duìhuàn lǜ shì duōshǎo?**
               Jin tyan duh dway hwahn lyew shir dwaw shaow?
               What's today's exchange rate?

Chūnàyuán: **Yì měiyuán huàn bā diǎn èr wǔ yuán rénmínbì.**
Ee may ywan hwahn bah dyan are woo ywan run meen bee.
One U.S. dollar is 8.25 (mainland) Chinese dollars.

Jane: **Hǎo. Qǐng gěi wǒ liǎng zhāng wǔshí yuán de.**
How. Cheeng gay waw lyahng jahng woo shir ywan duh.
Great. Please give me two 50 yuán bills.

Chūnàyuán: **Méiyǒu wèntí. Qǐng gěi wǒ kànkàn nǐde hùzhào.**
Mayo one tee. Cheeng gay waw kahn kahn nee duh hoo jaow.
No problem. Please show me your passport.

Words to Know

měiyuán	may ywan	U.S. dollars
yī měiyuán	ee may ywan	one U.S. dollar
rénmínbì	run meen bee	Chinese dollar (mainland)
xīn táibì	shin tye bee	New Taiwan dollars
huàn	hwahn	to exchange
duìhuàn lǜ	dway hwahn lyew	exchange rate
duìhuànchù	dway hwahn choo	exchange counter
chūnàyuán	choo nah ywan	cashier
huàn qián	hwahn chyan	to exchange money
wàibì	why bee	foreign currency
shǒuxùfèi	show shyew fay	commission
Qǐng gěi wǒ kànkàn nǐde hùzhào.	cheeng gay waw kahn kahn nee duh hoo jaow	Please show me your passport.

Spending Money

I don't think I'll have trouble selling you on (no pun intended) the thought of spending money. Whenever you see something you want, whether in a **shāngdiàn** (*shahng dyan;* store), on the **jiēshàng** (*jyeh shahng;* street), or at a **yè shì** (*yeh shir;* night market), you may as well give in to temptation and buy it, as long as you have enough **qián**. It's as easy as that. Have money, will travel. Or, rather, have money, will spend.

When you're ready to buy something, you can do it with **xiànjīn** (*shyan jeen;* cash), **zhīpiào** (*jir pyaow;* check), or **xìnyòng kǎ** (*sheen yoong kah;* credit card). And when traveling overseas, you often use **lǚxíng zhīpiào** (*lyew sheeng jir pyaow;* traveler's checks).

If you end up buying so many items that you can barely hold them all with both hands, here's one adverb you should remember. It comes in handy when you start adding up the cost of everything before you fork over all your money: I'm speaking of **yígòng** *(ee goong),* which means "altogether," as in "How much are these 20 toys and 80 sweaters altogether?"

You may overhear the following conversation in a store:

> **Zhèige hé nèige yígòng duōshǎo qián?** (*jay guh huh nay guh ee goong dwaw shaow chyan;* How much are this and that altogether?)

> **Zhèige sān kuài liǎng máo wǔ, nèige yí kuài liǎng máo, suǒyǐ yígòng sì kuài sì máo wǔ.** (*jay guh sahn kwye lyahng maow woo, nay guh ee kwye lyahng maow, swaw yee ee goong suh kwye suh maow woo;* This is $3.25, and that is $1.20, so altogether that will be $4.45.)

Before you decide to **mǎi dōngxi** (*my doong she;* buy things), be sure you have enough money **yígòng** to buy everything you want so you don't feel disappointed after spending many hours in your favorite store.

The term **dōngxi** (*doong she;* things) is literally a combination of "east" **(dōng)** and "west" **(xī)**. The Chinese language often combines two such opposite words to come up with various concepts. **Dōngxi** always refers to physical objects.

Cashing checks and checking your cash

I don't care what anybody tries to tell you, **xiànjīn** (*shyan jin;* cash) in local currency is always useful, no matter where you are and what time of day it is. Sometimes you can buy things and go places with **xiànjīn** that you can't swing with a **xìnyòngkǎ** (*sheen yoong kah;* credit card). For example, if your kid hears the ice cream truck coming down the street, you can't just whip out your **xìnyòngkǎ** to buy him an ice cream cone when the truck stops in front of your house. You can't even try to convince the guy to take a **zhīpiào** (*jir pyaow;* check). For times like these, my friend, you need cold, hard **xiànjīn**. You can use it to buy everything from **bīngqílín** (*beeng chee leen;* ice cream) on the street to a **diànyǐng piào** (*dyan yeeng pyaow;* movie ticket) at the theater. Just make sure you put your **qián** (*chyan;* money) in a sturdy **qiánbāo** (*chyan baow;* wallet or purse) and keep it in your front **kǒudài** (*ko dye;* pocket) so a **zéi** (*dzay;* thief) can't easily steal it.

When you talk about how much something costs, you put the numerical value before the word for bill or coin. For example, you can call a dollar **yí kuài** (*ee kwye;* one dollar) or **sān kuài** (*sahn kwye;* three dollars). You translate 10 cents, literally, as one 10-cent coin — **yì máo** *(ee maow)* — or 30 cents as, literally, three 10-cent coins — **sān máo** *(sahn maow).*

Here's how you speak of increasing amounts of money. You mention the larger units before the smaller units, just like in English:

- ✔ **sān kuài** (*sahn kwye;* $3.00)
- ✔ **sān kuài yì máo** (*sahn kwye ee maow;* $3.10)
- ✔ **sān kuài yì máo wǔ** (*sahn kwye ee maow woo;* $3.15)

As useful and convenient as **xiànjīn** is, you really have to pay with **zhīpiào** for some things. Take your **zūjīn** (*dzoo jeen;* rent) and electricity bills, for example. Can't use cash for these expenses, that's for sure. And when you travel overseas, everyone knows the safest way to carry money is in the form of **lǚxíng zhīpiào** (*lyew sheeng jir pyaow;* traveler's checks) so you can replace them if they get lost or stolen.

The basic elements of all Chinese currency are the **yuán** (colloquially referred to as a **kuài**), which you can think of as a dollar, the **jiǎo** (colloquially referred to as the **máo**), which is the equivalent of a dime, and the **fēn** *(fun),* which is equivalent to the penny.

Talkin' the Talk

Jacqueline goes shopping in Taipei and finds something she likes. She asks the clerk how much it is.

Jacqueline: **Qǐng wèn, zhè jiàn yīfu duōshǎo qián?**
Cheeng one, jay jyan ee foo dwaw shaow chyan?
Excuse me, how much is this piece of clothing?

Clerk:	**Èrshíwǔ kuài.**
	Are shir woo kwye.
	It's $25.00.

Jacqueline:	**Nǐmen shōu bù shōu zhīpiào?**
	Nee men show boo show jir pyaow?
	Do you take checks?

Clerk:	**Lǔxíng zhīpiào kěyǐ. Xìnyòng kǎ yě kěyǐ.**
	Lyew sheeng jir pyaow kuh yee. Sheen yoong kah yeah kuh yee.
	Traveler's checks are okay. Credit cards are also okay.

Words to Know

qiánbāo	chyan baow	wallet; purse
kǒudài	ko dye	pocket
zhīpiào	jir pyaow	checks
zhīpiào bù	jir pyaow boo	checkbook
lǔxíng zhīpiào	lyew sheeng jir pyaow	traveler's checks
fù zhàng	foo jahng	to pay a bill
língqián	leeng chyan	small change
dà piàozi	dah pyaow dzuh	large bills
huàn kāi	hwahn kye	to break (a large bill)

Paying with plastic

The **xìnyòng kǎ** (*sheen yoong kah;* credit card) may be the greatest invention of the 20th century — for credit card **gōngsī** (*goong suh;* companies), that is. The rest of us are often stuck paying all kinds of potentially exorbitant **lìlǜ** (*lee lyew;* interest rates) if we're not careful. Still, credit cards do make paying for things much more convenient, don't you agree?

To find out if a store accepts credit cards, all you have to say is:

Nǐmen shōu bù shōu xìnyòng kǎ? (*nee men show boo show sheen yoong kah;* Do you accept credit cards?*)

Overseas, many places accept **Měiguó yùntòng kǎ** (*may gwaw yewn toong kah;* American Express). Closer to America, businesses may only **shōu** (*show;* accept) MasterCard or Visa. In some out-of-the-way parts of China, you can't use plastic at all, so have plenty of **xiànjīn** (*shyan jeen;* cash) or **lǚxíng zhīpiào** (*lyew sheeng jir pyaow;* traveler's checks) on hand, just in case.

Whether the **jiàgé** (*jyah guh;* price) of the items you want to buy is **guì** (*gway;* expensive) or **piányì** (*pyan yee;* cheap), the **xìnyòng kǎ** comes in handy.

Read on for a list of credit-card-related terms:

✔ **xìnyòng** (*sheen yoong;* credit)

✔ **xìnyòng kǎ** (*sheen yoong kah;* credit card)

✔ **xìnyòng xiàn'é** (*sheen yoong shyan uh;* credit limit)

✔ **shēzhàng de zuì gāo é** (*shuh jahng duh dzway gaow uh;* credit line)

Doing Your Banking

If you plan on staying in Asia for an extended time or you want to continue doing business with a Chinese company, you may want to open a **huóqī zhànghù** (*hwaw chee jahng hoo;* checking account) where you can both **cún qián** (*tswun chyan;* deposit money) and **qǔ qián** (*chyew chyan;* withdraw money). If you stay long enough, you should open a **dìngqī cúnkuǎn hùtóu** (*deeng chee tswun kwan hoo toe;* savings account) so you can start earning some **lìxí** (*lee she;* interest). Sure beats stuffing **dà piàozi** (*dah pyaow dzuh;* large bills) under your **chuáng diàn** (*chwahng dyan;* mattress) for years.

How about trying to make your money work for you by investing in one of the following:

✔ **gǔpiào** (*goo pyaow;* stock)

✔ **zhàiquàn** (*jye chwan;* bond)

✔ **tàotóu jījīn** (*taow toe jee jeen;* hedge fund)

✔ **hùzhù jījīn** (*hoo joo jee jeen;* mutual fund)

✔ **chǔxù cúnkuǎn** (*choo shyew tswun kwan;* Certificate of Deposit; CD)

✔ **guókù quàn** (*gwaw koo chwan;* treasury bond)

Talkin' the Talk

 Dan decides to open a savings account in Hong Kong. He enters a bank and approaches the teller.

Dan: **Nín hǎo. Wǒ xiǎng kāi yíge dìngqī cúnkuǎn hùtóu.**
Neen how. Waw shyahng kye ee guh deeng chee tswun kwan hoo toe.
Hello. I'd like to open a savings account.

Teller: **Méiyǒu wèntí. Nín yào xiān cún duōshǎo qián?**
Mayo one tee. Neen yaow shyan tswun dwaw shaow chyan?
No problem. How much would you like to deposit initially?

Dan: **Wǒ yào cún yìbǎi kuài qián.**
Waw yaow tswun ee bye kwye chyan.
I'd like to deposit $100.

Teller: **Hǎo. Qǐng tián zhèige biǎo. Wǒ yě xūyào kànkàn nínde hùzhào.**
How. Cheeng tyan jay guh byaow. Waw yeah shyew yaow kahn kahn neen duh hoo jaow.
Fine. Please fill out this form. I will also need to see your passport.

Words to Know

yínháng	een hahng	bank
xiànjīn	shyan jeen	cash
chūnà chuāngkǒu	choo nah chwahng ko	cashier's window
cúnkuǎn	tswun kwan	savings
chūnàyuán	choo nah ywan	bank teller
kāi yíge cúnkuǎn hùtóu	kye ee guh tswun kwan hoo toe	to open a savings account
cún qián	tswun chyan	to deposit money
qǔ qián	chyew chyan	to withdraw money

Banks in the PRC are generally open at 8:30 a.m. from Monday through Saturday. They close for two hours from 12-2 p.m. and then reopen from 2-5:30 p.m. Many branches of the Bank of China are open on Sunday mornings, but some close on Wednesday afternoons. In Taiwan, banks close at 3:30 p.m., and in Hong Kong they're usually open from 9 a.m. to 4:30 p.m. during the week and from 9 a.m. to 12 p.m. on Saturdays.

Making withdrawals and deposits

Whether you need to **cún qián** (*tswun chyan;* deposit money) or **qǔ qián** (*chyew chyan;* withdraw money), you need to make sure you have enough **qián** in the first place to do so. One way to ensure you don't overextend is to make sure you know what your **jiéyú** (*jyeh yew;* account balance) is at any given moment. Sometimes you can check your available balance if you **shàngwǎng** (*shahng wahng;* go online) to see which **zhīpiào** (*jir pyaow;* checks) may have already cleared. If someone gives you an **yínháng běnpiào** (*een hahng bun pyaow;* cashier's check), however, it cashes immediately. Lucky you!

If you plan to cash some checks along with your deposits, here are a couple of useful phrases to know:

✔ **Wǒ yào duìxiàn zhèi zhāng zhīpiào.** (*waw yaow dway shyan jay jahng jir pyow;* I'd like to cash this check.)

✔ **Bèimiàn qiān zì xiě zài nǎr?** (*bay myan chyan dzuh shyeh dzye nar;* Where shall I endorse it?)

One of the most convenient ways to access some quick cash is to go to the nearest **zìdòng tíkuǎnjī** (*dzuh doong tee kwan jee;* ATM machine).

Accessing an ATM machine

Zìdòng tíkuǎnjī (*dzuh doong tee kwan jee;* ATM machines) are truly ubiquitous these days. Wherever you turn, there they are, on every other street corner. Sometimes I wonder how we ever survived without them. (Same goes for the personal computer . . . but I digress.)

In order to use a **zìdòng tíkuǎnjī,** you need a **zìdòng tíkuǎn kǎ** (*dzuh doong tee kwan kah;* ATM card) to find out your **jiéyú** (*jyeh yew;* account balance) or to **cún qián** (*tswun chyan;* deposit money) or **qǔ qián** (*chyew chyan;* withdraw money). And you definitely need to know your **mìmǎ** (*mee mah;* PIN number); otherwise, the **zìdòng tíkuǎnjī** is useless.

And one more thing: Make sure you don't let anyone else know your **mìmǎ.** It's a **mìmì** (*mee mee;* secret).

Tips on Tipping

Píngcháng (*peeng chahng;* usually) in the United States, a 15 percent tip is customary at restaurants, and you often give a 10 percent tip to taxi drivers. Giving **xiǎo fèi** (*shyaow fay;* tips) is expected everywhere from here to Timbuktu. In some instances, you should even give **xiǎo fèi** to people setting up towels in the public **xǐshǒu jiān** (*she show jyan;* bathroom). Better to know in advance of your trip how much (or how little) is expected of you so you don't embarrass yourself (and by extension, your countrymen).

In Taiwan, **xiǎo fèi** are generally included in restaurant bills. If not, 10 percent is standard. You can **gěi** (*gay;* give) bellboys and porters a dollar (USD) per bag.

In Hong Kong, most restaurants automatically include a 10 percent tip, but feel free to give an additional 5 percent if the **fúwù** (*foo woo;* service) is good. Small tips are also okay for taxi drivers, bellboys, and washroom attendants.

Tipping in mainland China used to be rare, but the idea is finally catching on, especially now that service with a scowl rather than a smile is fast becoming a thing of the past. (For the longest time, workers simply had no incentive to work harder or with a more pleasant demeanor after the Cultural Revolution. Can you blame workers for having no reason to perform their duties with the idea of customer service in mind?) A 3 percent tip is standard in restaurants (still low compared to Taiwan and Hong Kong). Bellboys and room service attendants typically expect a dollar or two (USD). Tipping in **Měijīn** (*may jeen;* U.S. currency) is still very much appreciated, because it's worth about eight times as much as the Chinese dollar.

If you get a bill and can't make heads or tails of it, you can always ask the following question to find out if the tip is included:

> **Zhàngdān bāokuò fúwùfèi ma?** (*jahng dahn baow kwaw foo woo fay mah;* Does the bill include a service charge/tip?)

In English, when you say "15 percent," you mean 15 percent out of a total of 100. The way to express **bǎifēnbǐ** (*bye fun bee;* percentages) in Chinese is to start with the larger denomination of **bǎi** (*bye;* 100) first and then work your way backwards with the percentage of that amount. Here are some examples:

- **bǎifēn zhī bǎi** (*bye fun jir bye;* 100 percent; *literally:* 100 out of 100 parts)

- **bǎifēn zhī bāshíwǔ** (*bye fun jir bah shir woo;* 85 percent; *literally:* 85 out of 100 parts)

- **bǎifēn zhī shíwǔ** (*bye fun jir shir woo;* 15 percent; *literally:* 15 out of 100 parts)

   ✔ **bǎi fēn zhǐ sān** (*bye fun jir sahn;* 3 percent; *literally:* 3 out of 100 parts)

   ✔ **bǎi fēn zhǐ líng diǎn sān** (*bye fun jir leeng dyan sahn;* 0.3 percent; *literally:* 0.3 out of 100 parts)

For more information on numbers, see Chapter 2.

Talkin' the Talk

Rebecca and Rachel are in a restaurant. They get their bill and discuss how much of a tip to leave.

Rebecca: **Wǒmen de zhàngdān yígòng sānshí kuài qián. Xiǎo fèi yīnggāi duōshǎo?**
Waw men duh jahng dahn ee goong sahn shir kwye chyan. Shyaow fay eeng guy dwaw shaow?
Our bill comes to $30.00 altogether. How much should the tip be?

Rachel: **Yīnwèi fúwù hěn hǎo, suǒyǐ xiǎo fèi kěyǐ bǎi fēn zhǐ èr shí. Nǐ tóngyì ma?**
Een way foo woo hun how, swaw yee shyaow fay kuh yee bai fun jir are shir. Nee toong ee mah?
Because the service was really good, I think we can leave a 20 percent tip. Do you agree?

Rebecca: **Tóngyì.**
Toong ee.
I agree.

Words to Know

zhàngdān	jahng dahn	the bill
yígòng	ee goong	altogether
yīnggāi	eeng guy	should
yīnwèi . . . suǒyǐ	een way . . . swaw yee	because . . . therefore
tóngyì	toong ee	to agree

Fun & Games

Identify what the following illustrations depict in Chinese. See Appendix C for the correct answers.

A.

B.

C.

D.

E.

F.

A. _____

B. _____

C. _____

D. _____

E. _____

F. _____

Chapter 12

Taking the Road Less Traveled: Asking for (and Giving) Directions

*E*veryone (yes, even you) has to ask for **fāngxiàng** (*fahng shyahng;* directions) at some time or another. Even if you just need to find the **cèsuǒ** (*tsuh swaw;* bathroom) — when you've got to go, you'd better know.

You may find yourself baffled by the boulevards in Beihai or dumbfounded by directions in Dalian. This chapter helps you figure out exactly how to ask for directions before you ever **mílù** (*mee loo;* get lost). Whether you lose your bearings in Beijing or wander off the path in Luoyang, this chapter gives you helpful tips that make it easier to find your way back home. Or at least back to your hotel.

You definitely need to know how to ask where certain places are in mainland China, where most people don't speak English. You have a greater likelihood of hailing an English-speaking cabbie in Taipei or Kowloon to take you where you need to go but not in one of the cities or towns in mainland China.

Avoiding 20 Questions: Just Ask "Where"

Okay, so you're searching for the closest **yóujú** (*yo jyew;* post office) to mail a package home before your mother's birthday next week. A passerby tells you to go right down the **jiēdào** (*jyeh daow;* street), but for the life of you, all you see are a couple of **shūdiàn** (*shoo dyan;* bookstores) and an occasional **dìtiě zhàn** (*dee tyeh jahn;* subway station). Time to ask for directions. But how?

The easiest way to ask where something is in Chinese is to use the question word **nǎr** (*nar*). It means "where." But you can't just say **nǎr**, or folks still won't know what you're talking about. You have to use the coverb **zài** (*dzye*) in front of **nǎr (zài nǎr)**, which can be translated as "in" or "at." Just put the name of whatever you're looking for before the word **zài** to create a complete question:

- **Yóujú zài nǎr?** (*yo jyew dzye nar;* Where's the post office?)
- **Shūdiàn zài nǎr?** (*shoo dyan dzye nar;* Where's the bookstore?)
- **Nǐ zài nǎr?** (*nee dzye nar;* Where are you?)

Here are some more places you may be looking for when you lose your way:

- **cèsuǒ** (*tsuh swaw;* bathroom)
- **Měiguó dàshǐguǎn** (*may gwaw dah shir gwahn;* American Embassy)
- **xuéxiào** (*shweh shyaow;* school)
- **yínháng** (*een hahng;* bank)
- **fànguǎn** (*fahn gwahn;* restaurant)
- **gōnggòngqìchēzhàn** (*goong goong chee chuh jahn;* bus stop)
- **huǒchēzhàn** (*hwaw chuh jahn;* train station)
- **dìtiězhàn** (*dee tyeh jahn;* subway station)
- **chūzū qìchēzhàn** (*choo dzoo chee chuh jahn;* taxi stand)
- **jízhěnshì** (*jee juhn shir;* emergency room)
- **piàofáng** (*pyaow fahng;* ticket office)

When you travel in unknown areas, you may need to determine whether you can walk or if you need to take a **gōnggòng qìchē** (*goong goong chee chuh;* bus) or **chūzū qìchē** (*choo dzoo chee chuh;* taxi) to reach your destination:

| ✔ **Hĕn jìn ma?** (*hun jeen mah;* Is it near?)

| ✔ **Hĕn yuǎn ma?** (*hun ywan mah;* Is it far?)

Different strokes for different folks: năr versus nălĭ

Chinese people immediately know where you're from, where you've studied, or at least where your Chinese language teacher is from by the way you say the word "where." If you say **năr** (*nahr*) with an "r" sound at the end of the word, you represent a northern Chinese accent commonly found in Beijing. If you say it with a "lee" sound at the end rather than an "r" sound, as in **nălĭ** (*nah lee*), it indicates you've probably lived or studied in Taiwan.

When someone gives you a compliment, proper Chinese etiquette dictates that your response should be a swift and decisive **"nălĭ, nălĭ,"** which literally means "Where? Where?" but translates more loosely into "No, no, you're too kind." When a Chinese person says something nice about you, your clothes, your car, or your kids, never accept a compliment the way you do in English, which is with a gracious and accepting "Why, thank you." Instead, you should insist that the compliment is undeserved and vociferously disagree with a quick **nălĭ, nălĭ.** In mainland China, the equivalent expression is **"năr de huà."** (*nar duh hwah; literally:* where are such words coming from?) Humility about your attributes, even if you have to feign it, is always well respected in Chinese culture.

The word **năr** spoken with a third (low falling and then rising) tone means "where," but the same word said with a fourth (falling) tone, **nàr,** means "there," so be particularly careful which tone you use when you ask for directions. The person you ask may think you're making a statement, not asking a question.

Talkin' the Talk

Helayne is about to leave her hotel in Beijing to head for the American Embassy to renew her passport. She's not sure where to find it, so she asks a hotel attendant how to get there.

Helayne: **Qĭng wèn, Mĕiguó dàshĭguǎn zài năr?**
Cheeng one, may gwaw dah shir gwahn dzye nar?
Excuse me, where's the American Embassy?

Attendant: **Mĕiguó dàshĭguǎn zài Xiù Shuĭ Bĕi Jiē.**
May gwaw dah shir gwahn dzye shyow shway bay jyeh.
The American Embassy is on Xiu Shui Bei Street.

Helayne: **Hěn yuǎn ma?**
Hun ywan mah?
Is it far?

Attendant: **Hěn yuǎn. Nǐ zuì hǎo zuò chūzū qìchē qù.**
Hun ywan. Nee dzway how zwaw choo dzoo chee chuh chyew.
Yes, it's quite far. You'd best take a taxi.

Helayne: **Xièxiè.**
Shyeh shyeh.
Thanks.

As Helayne starts to leave, the attendant comments on the skirt she's wearing.

Attendant: **Xiǎojiě, nǐde qúnzi hěn piàoliàng.**
Shyaow jyeh, nee duh chwun dzuh hun pyaow lyahng.
Miss, your skirt is very pretty.

Helayne: **Nǎr de huà!**
Nar duh hwah!
No, it's not really!

Words to Know

fāngxiàng	fahng shyahng	directions
dìtú	dee too	map
shíjiānbiǎo	shir jyan byaow	timetable
dìzhǐ	dee jir	address
zuò chūzū qìchē	dzwaw choo dzoo chee chuh	to take a taxi
zuò gōnggòng qìchē	dzwaw goong goong chee chuh	to take the bus
zuò fēijī	dzwaw fay jee	to take an airplane

Getting direction about directions

Knowing how to ask where you can find a particular place is the first step, but you also need to know how to get there. (Otherwise, why would you ask where it is in the first place, right?) Here's the simplest way to find out:

> **Qù_____zěnme zǒu?** (*chyew_____dzummuh dzoe;* How do I get to_____?)

Here are some examples of how to use this question pattern:

- **Qù fēijīchǎng zěnme zǒu?** (*chyew fay jee chahng dzummuh dzoe;* How do I get to the airport?)

- **Qù túshūguǎn zěnme zǒu?** (*chyew too shoo gwahn dzummuh dzoe;* How do I get to the library?)

- **Qù xuéxiào zěnme zǒu?** (*chyew shweh shyaow dzummuh dzoe;* How do I get to the school?)

Answering "where" questions

Short of using international sign language with a pantomime act, you may want to get a handle on some basic terms that indicate direction and location. Read on for a quick list:

- **yòu** (*yo;* right)
- **zuǒ** (*dzwaw;* left)
- **qián** (*chyan;* front)
- **hòu** (*ho;* back)
- **lǐ** (*lee;* inside)
- **wài** (*why;* outside)
- **shàng** (*shahng;* above)
- **xià** (*shyah;* below)
- **duìmiàn** (*dway myan;* opposite)
- **kàojìn** (*kaow jeen;* next to)

If you plan to indicate that something is inside, outside, above, below, in front of, or behind something else, you can use three different, completely interchangeable word endings with any of the location words:

✔ **biān** (*byan*)

✔ **miān** (*myan*)

✔ **tóu** (*toe*)

So, for example, if you want to say that the dog is outside, you can say it in any of the following ways:

✔ **Gǒu zài wàimiàn.** (*go dzye why myan;* The dog is outside.)

✔ **Gǒu zài wàibiān.** (*go dzye why byan;* The dog is outside.)

✔ **Gǒu zài wàitóu.** (*go dzye why toe;* The dog is outside.)

Sometimes you may have the need to use a more complex location expression, such as when you don't want to simply note where something is. Perhaps you want to tell someone where a certain action should take place. For example, if you want to say "Wait in front of the school," here's what you say:

> **Qǐng nǐ zài xuéxiào qiánmiàn děng.** (*cheeng nee dzye shweh shyaow chyan myan dung;* Please wait in front of the school.)

In such cases, the verb **děng** (*dung;* to wait) comes after the specified location (**xuéxiào qiánmiàn**). Here are some other examples:

✔ **Zài xuéxiào hòumiàn děng.** (*dzye shweh shyaow ho myan dung;* Wait in back of the school.)

✔ **Zài wūzi lǐ chīfàn.** (*dzye woo dzuh lee chir fahn;* Eat in the room.)

✔ **Zài túshūguǎn kànshū.** (*dzye too shoo gwahn kahn shoo;* Read in the library.)

Talkin' the Talk

 Corey asks Casey for directions in Tainan. He wants to get to the post office.

Corey: **Qǐng wèn, Casey, yóujú zài nǎr?**
           Cheeng one, Casey, yo jyew dzye nar?
           Excuse me, Casey, where's the post office?

Casey: **Yóujú jiù zài yínháng duìmiàn. Guò liǎng tiáo lù jiù shì.**
Yo jyew jyo dzye een hahng dway myan. Gwaw lyahng tyaow loo jyo shir.
The post office is right opposite the bank. If you go two more blocks it's right there.

Corey: **Xièxiè. Qù yóujú zěnme zǒu?**
Shyeh shyeh. Chyew yo jyew dzummuh dzoe?
Thank you. How should I walk to the post office?

Casey: **Wàng nán zǒu. Yìzhí zǒu jiù dào le.**
Wahng nahn dzoe. Ee jir dzoe jyoe daow luh.
Walk south. Go straight and you'll see it.

Words to Know

wàng	wahng	toward
duì miàn	dway myan	opposite
zài yínháng duìmiàn	dzye een hahng dway myan	opposite the bank
zǒu (zǒu lù)	dzoe (dzoe loo)	to walk
kāi chē	kye chuh	to drive
zuò huǒchē	zwaw hwaw chuh	to take the train
shàng	shahng	to get on
xià	shyah	to get off

Giving Directions

Are you the kind of know-it-all who thinks you're pretty familiar with a foreign city by virtue of having pored over a couple of **dìtú** (*dee too;* maps) before arrival? If so, you may want to be the one giving directions on occasion rather than just asking for them. Knowing your stuff comes in handy when you think the taxi driver is about to take you for a ride (figuratively, that is) because he figures you don't know your way around town.

If you want to **jiào** (*jyaow;* hail) a cab, say this to your hotel door attendant:

> **Wǒ yào jiào jìchéngchē.** (*waw yaow jyaow jee chung chuh;* I would like a taxi.)

You can also say:

> **Wǒ yào jiāo chūzūchē.** (*waw yaow jyaow choo dzoo chuh;* I would like a taxi.)

The two methods are interchangeable, just like saying "taxi" or "cab."

If you really do know your way around the city, you can instruct the taxi driver as to which **gāosùgōnglù** (*gaow soo goong loo;* freeway), **gōnglù** (*goong loo;* highway), **qiáo** (*chyaow;* bridge), or **lù** (*loo;* road) to take; where to turn the **guǎijiǎo** (*gwye jyaow;* corner); or which **xiàngzi** (*shyahng dzuh;* alley or lane) to travel down. Or perhaps you want to avoid going over a particular **tiānqiáo** (*tyan chyaow;* overpass) or under a particular **dìxiàdào** (*dee shyah daow;* underpass).

Wherever you want to go, you need to know a few key verbs to instruct the cab driver:

- **guò** (*gwaw;* to pass)
- **shàng** (*shahng;* to go up)
- **xià** (*shyah;* to go down)
- **yòu zhuǎn** (*yo jwan;* turn right)
- **zuǒ zhuǎn** (*dzwaw jwan;* turn left)
- **zhí zǒu** (*jir dzoe;* go straight ahead)
- **zhuǎn wān** (*jwan wahn;* turn around)

If you don't know an exact location, you can also convey less specific details:

- **fùjìn** (*foo jeen;* near)
- **sìzhōu** (*suh joe;* around)

Talkin' the Talk

Jon and Minnie discuss where they want to meet later today in Taiwan.

Minnie: **Wǒmen jīntiān xiàwǔ liǎng diǎn zhōng jiàn, hǎo bù hǎo?**
Waw men jin tyan shyah woo lyahng dyan joong jyan, how boo how?
Let's meet this afternoon at 2:00, okay?

Jon: **Hǎo. Nǐ yào zài nǎr jiàn?**
How. Nee yaow dzye nar jyan?
Okay. Where would you like to meet?

Minnie: **Wǒmen zài gùgōng bówùguǎn qiánmiàn jiàn.**
Waw men dzye goo goong baw woo gwahn chyan myan jyan.
Let's meet each other in front of the National Palace Museum.

Jon: **Hǎo, yīhuǐr jiàn.**
How, ee hwar jyan.
Okay, see you later.

At around 1:30, Minnie leaves her hotel in downtown Taipei and asks for help hailing a cab.

Minnie: **Máfan nǐ bāng wǒ jiào jìchéngchē?**
Mah fahn nee bahng waw jyaow jee chung chuh?
May I trouble you to help me hail a cab?

After she enters the cab, Minnie asks the taxi driver what route he plans to take to get to the National Palace Museum.

Minnie: **Nǐ hǎo. Wǒ yào dào gùgōng bówùguǎn qù. Cóng zhèr dào nàr zěnme zǒu?**
Nee how. Waw yaow daow goo goong baw woo gwahn chyew. Tsoong jar daow nar dzummuh dzoe?
Hello. I'd like to go to the National Palace Museum. How do you get there from here?

Taxi Driver: **Cóng zhèr wǒmen guò mǎlù, wàng yòu guǎi, zhí zǒu jiù dàole.**
Tsoong jar waw men gwaw mah loo, wahng yo gwye, jir dzoe jyo daow luh.
From here we cross the avenue, make a right, and then go straight and we're there.

Words to Know

cóng . . . dào	tsoong . . . daow	from . . . to
guò mǎlù	gwah mah loo	cross the avenue
máfan nǐ	mah fahn nee	excuse me
yīhuǐr jiàn	ee hwahr jyan	see you later

Expressing Distances (Time and Space) with Lí

Even though you can use the **cóng . . . dào** pattern to literally say "from here to there" (**cóng zhèr dào nàr;** *tsoong jar daow nar*) when you want to indicate the distance from one place to another, you need to use the "distance from" coverb "**lí**" *(lee)*. The general sentence pattern looks something like this:

Place word + **lí** + place word + description of the distance

For example:

- ✔ **Gōngyuán lí túshūguǎn hěn jìn.** (*goong ywan lee too shoo gwan hun jeen;* The park is very close to the library.)

- ✔ **Wǒ jiā lí nǐ jiā tǐng yuǎn.** (*waw jyah lee nee jyah teeng ywan;* My home is really far from your home.)

If you want to specify exactly how far one place is from another, you use the number of **lǐ** (*lee;* the Chinese equivalent of a kilometer) followed by the word **lǐ** and then the word **lù** (*loo; literally:* road). Whether you say **sì lǐ lù** (*suh lee loo;* 4 kilometers), **bā lǐ lù** (*bah lee loo;* 8 kilometers), or **èrshísān lǐ lù** (*are shir sahn lee loo;* 23 kilometers), people know the exact distance when you use this pattern. You also have to use the word **yǒu** (*yo;* to have) before the number of kilometers. If the answer includes an adjectival verb such as **yuǎn** (*ywan;* far) or **jìn** (*jin;* close) rather than a numerical distance, however, you don't need to specify the number of kilometers or use the word **yǒu**.

Check out the following sample questions and answers that use these new patterns:

- **Gōngyuán lí túshūguǎn duōme yuǎn?** (*goong ywan lee too shoo gwahn dwaw muh ywan;* How far is the park from the library?)

- **Gōngyuán lí túshūguǎn yǒu bā lǐ lù.** (*goong ywan lee too shoo gwahn yo bah lee loo;* The park is 8 kilometers from the library.)

- **Yínháng lí nǐ jiā duōme jìn?** (*eeng hahng lee nee jyah dwaw muh jin;* How close is the bank from your home?)

- **Hěn jìn. Zhǐ yǐ lǐ lù.** (*hun jin. jir ee lee loo;* Very close. Just 1 kilometer.)

You may have some other questions when you inquire about locations and distances:

- **Yào duō cháng shíjiān?** (*yaow dwaw chahng shir jyan;* How long will it take?)

- **Zǒu de dào ma?** (*dzoe duh daow mah;* Can I walk there?)

- **Zǒu de dào, zǒu bú dào?** (*dzoe duh daow, dzoe boo daow;* Can one walk there?)

To indicate whether something is likely to happen or unlikely to be attained, the pattern you use includes *potential complements.* You do this by putting the words **de** *(duh)* and **bù** *(boo)* between the verb and the complement to indicate whether a positive or negative potential is involved.

If you say **"Nǐ kànjiàn,"** you mean "you see." If instead you say **"Nǐ kàn de jiàn ma?"** you mean "Can you see?" And if you use the negative **"bù"** rather than the positive implication that goes with **de** to ask **"Nǐ kàn bú jiàn ma?"** you mean "You can't see?" Finally, if you use both positive and negative potential forms in the same breath by asking **"Nǐ kàn de jiàn, kàn bú jiàn?"** you mean "Can you see (or not)?"

Here are some other examples of this pattern:

- **zuò wán** (*dzwaw wahn;* to finish [doing something])

- **zuò de wán** (*dzwaw duh wahn;* can finish)

- **zuò bù wán** (*dzwaw boo wahn;* can't finish)

- **zuò de wán; zuò bù wán?** (*dzwaw duh wahn; dzwaw boo wahn;* can you finish it; can it be finished?)

- **xǐ gānjìng** (*she gahn jeeng;* to wash [and make clean])

> ✔ **xǐ de gānjìng** (*she duh gahn jeeng;* can be washed)
>
> ✔ **xǐ bù gānjìng** (*she boo gahn jeeng;* can't be washed)
>
> ✔ **xǐ de gānjìng; xǐ bù gānjìng?** (*she duh gahn jeeng; she boo gahn jeeng;* can you wash it; can it be washed?)

When you ask for directions, the following questions may come in handy:

> ✔ **Wǒmen zǒu de dào, zǒu bú dào?** (*waw mun dzoe duh daow, dzoe boo daow;* Can we walk [to get there]?)
>
> ✔ **Wǒmen lái de jí, lái bù jí?** (*waw mun lye duh jee, lye boo jee;* Will we make it on time?)

Discovering Ordinal Numbers

Ever tell someone to make a right at the second **jiāotōng dēng** (*jyaow toong dung;* traffic light) or that your house is the third one on the left?

You can't simply use the numeral plus a classifier in Chinese, such as when you say **sān ge** (*sahn guh;* three) of something. If you say **sān ge jiāotōng dēng** (*sahn guh jyaow toong dung*), the person hears "three traffic lights." If you want to say "the third traffic light," you have to add the word "**dì**" (*dee*) before the numeral to create **dì sān ge jiāotōng dēng,** which indicates the third traffic light.

If you use an ordinal number followed by a noun, you must always have a classifier between them. You can't combine **dì sān** (*dee sahn;* the third) with **qìchē** (*chee chuh;* car). You have to put the classifier **"ge"** in between the number and the noun to say **dì sān ge qìchē** (*dee sahn guh chee chuh*), meaning "the third car."

Creating ordinal numbers (numbers that indicate the order of things) in Chinese is quite easy. Just put **dì** in front of the numeral:

> ✔ **dì yī** (*dee ee;* first)
>
> ✔ **dì èr** (*dee are;* second)
>
> ✔ **dì sān** (*dee sahn;* third)
>
> ✔ **dì sì** (*dee suh;* fourth)
>
> ✔ **dì wǔ** (*dee woo;* fifth)
>
> ✔ **dì liù** (*dee lyoe;* sixth)

- **dì qī** (*dee chee;* seventh)
- **dì bā** (*dee bah;* eighth)
- **dì jiǔ** (*dee jyoe;* ninth)
- **dì shí** (*dee shir;* tenth)

You may need to use these examples to give directions:

- **dì yī tiáo lù** (*dee ee tyaow loo;* the first street)
- **dì èr ge fángzi** (*dee are guh fahng dzuh;* the second house)
- **zuǒ biān dì bā ge fángzi** (*dzwaw byan dee bah guh fahng dzuh;* the eighth house on the left)

Specifying Cardinal Points with Directional Coverbs

You can tell someone to go **yòu** (*yo;* right) or **zuǒ** (*dzwaw;* left) until you're blue in the face, but sometimes the best way to give people directions is to point them the right way with the cardinal points: north, south, east, or west.

In Chinese, however, you say them in this order:

- **dōng** (*doong;* east)
- **nán** (*nahn;* south)
- **xī** (*she;* west)
- **běi** (*bay;* north)

To give more precise directions, you may have to use the following:

- **dōng běi** (*doong bay;* northeast)
- **xī běi** (*she bay;* northwest)
- **dōng nán** (*doong nahn;* southeast)
- **xī nán** (*she nahn;* southwest)

When it comes to indicating north, south, east, west, left, or right, you can use either **-biān** (*byan*) or **-miàn** (*myan*) as a word ending, but not **–tóu** (*to*), which you can use with other position words such as front, back, inside, and outside.

Giving directions often entails multiple instructions. You can't always say "make a right and you're there" or "go straight and you'll see it right in front of you." Sometimes you have to use a common Chinese pattern for giving multiple directions. That pattern is:

> **xiān** + Verb #1, **zài** + Verb #2

This translates into "first you do X, and then you do Y." Here are some examples:

- ✔ **Xiān wàng dōng zǒu, zài wàng yòu zhuǎn.** (*shyan wahng doong dzoe, dzye wahng yo jwan;* First walk east, and then turn right.)

- ✔ **Xiān zhí zǒu, zài wàng xī zǒu.** (*shyan jir dzoe, dzye wahng she dzoe;* First go straight, and then turn west.)

Talkin' the Talk

George is walking around Shanghai looking for the Shanghai Museum. He begins to wonder if he's going in the right direction, so he decides to ask a stranger how to get there.

George:
Qǐng wèn, Shànghǎi bówùguǎn lí zhèr hěn yuǎn ma?
Cheeng one, shahng hi baw woo gwahn lee jar hun ywan mah?
Excuse me, is the Shanghai Museum very far from here?

Stranger:
Bù yuǎn. Shànghǎi bówùguǎn jiù zài rénmín dà dào.
Boo ywan. Shahng hi baw woo gwahn jyo dzye run meen dah daow.
It's not far at all. The Shanghai Museum is on the Avenue of the People.

George:
Rénmín dà dào lí zhèr duōme yuǎn?
Run meen dah daow lee jar dwaw muh ywan?
How far is the Avenue of the People from here?

Stranger:
Rénmín dà dào lí zhèr zhǐ yǒu yì lǐ lù zuǒyòu.
Run meen dah daow lee jar jir yo ee lee loo dzwaw yo.
The Avenue of the People is only about 1 kilometer from here.

George:
Cóng zhèr zǒu de dào, zǒu bú dào?
Tsoong jar dzoe duh daow, dzoe boo daow?
Can I walk there from here?

Stranger:	**Kěndìng zǒu de dào. Nǐ xiān wàng nán zǒu, zài dì èr tiáo lù wàng xī zhuǎn. Dì yī ge lóu jiù shì.**

Kun deeng dzoe duh daow. Nee shyan wahng nahn dzoe, dzye dee are tyaow loo wahng she jwan. Dee ee guh low jyoe shir.

It's certainly walkable. Walk north first, and then turn west at the second street. It'll be the first building you see.

George:	**Fēicháng gǎnxiè nǐ.**

Fay chahng gahn shyeh nee.

I'm extremely grateful (for your help).

Stranger:	**Méi shì.**

May shir.

It's nothing.

Words to Know

xiān . . . zài . . .	shyan . . . dzye . . .	first . . . then . . .
fēicháng gǎnxiè	fay chahng gahn shyeh	many thanks
méi shì	may shir	it's nothing
kěndìng	kun deeng	definitely
zuǒyòu	dzwaw yo	approximately
bówùguǎn	baw woo gwahn	museum

If you get lost in any city in mainland China, you can often get back on track by asking where **"Zhōngshān Lù"** *(joong shahn loo)* or **"Jiěfàng Lù"** *(jyeh fahng loo)* is. **"Zhōngshān,"** literally meaning the middle mountain, refers to the birthplace of Dr. Sun Yat-sen, founder of the modern Chinese Republic in 1911. **"Jiěfàng,"** on the other hand, means "liberation," referring to the "liberation" of the mainland by the Communists in 1949. **"Lù"** just means "road." Generally, these streets are located in the middle of town. They serve as the Chinese equivalent of "Main Street" in "Anytown, U.S.A." Always a safe bet.

Fun & Games

According to the illustration below, say in Chinese which cardinal direction these buildings are located in. (See Appendix C for the answers.)

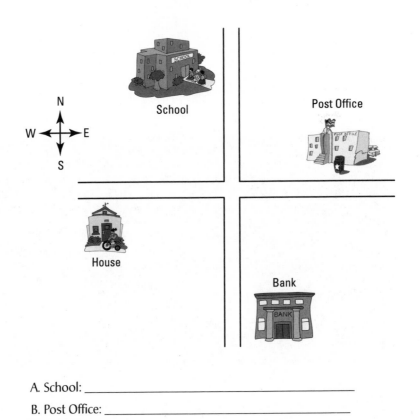

A. School: _____

B. Post Office: _____

C. Bank: _____

D. House: _____

Chapter 13

Staying at a Hotel

In This Chapter

▶ Booking your room reservation

▶ Checking in upon arrival

▶ Requesting hotel service

▶ Packing your bags and paying your bill

The right **lǚguǎn** (*lyew gwahn;* hotel) can make or break a vacation. Whether you stay in a capital city or a little backwater town with only one **lǚguǎn** to its name, you still need to know how to check in, check out, and ask for anything you need in between (including the check). This chapter runs you through the gamut of booking your hotel, checking in at the front desk, checking out at the designated time, and dealing with all sorts of issues that may come up in between.

First, however, I have an astounding fact for you: You have not one, not two, but as many as five ways to say the word "hotel" in Chinese:

✔ **lǚguǎn** (*lyew gwahn;* hotel)

✔ **fàndiàn** (*fahn dyan; literally:* a place for meals)

✔ **jiǔdiàn** (*jyo dyan; literally:* a place for wine)

✔ **zhāodàisuǒ** (*jaow dye swaw; literally:* a place to receive people)

✔ **bīnuǎn** (*been gwahn; literally:* a place for guests)

Making a Room Reservation

Thinking of **yùdìng** (*yew deeng;* reserving) a hotel **fángjiān** (*fahng jyan;* room)? What kind do you want? A **dānrén fángjiān** (*dahn run fahng jyan;* single room) all for yourself? A **shuāngrén fángjiān** (*shwahng run fahng jyan;* double room) for you and your special someone? Or perhaps a penthouse **tàojiān** (*taow jyan;* suite) for a special occasion like your 50th wedding **zhōunián** (*joe nyan;* anniversary)?

Whatever the occasion and whatever kind of room you want, you need to know how to make a reservation. Just make sure you know your **yùsuàn** (*yew swan;* budget) in advance (and stick to it). You're sure to find a decent hotel no matter the price range if you spend some time checking out the competition. Oh, and when you do finally pick up your phone to reserve a room, make sure you have your **xìnyòng kǎ** (*sheen yoong kah;* credit card) in front of you (see Chapter 11 for more money talk).

Here are some questions you may want to ask over the phone as you begin the search for your **lǐxiǎng** (*lee shyahng;* ideal) hotel:

- **Nǐmen hái yǒu fángjiān ma?** (*nee mun hi yo fahng jyan mah;* Do you have any rooms available?)
- **Nǐmen fángjiān de jiàgé shì duōshǎo?** (*nee mun fahng jyan duh jyah guh shir dwaw shaow;* How much are your rooms?)
- **Wǒ yào yíge fángjiān zhù liǎng ge wǎnshàng.** (*waw yaow ee guh fahng jyan joo lyahng guh wahn shahng;* I'd like a room for two nights.)
- **Nǐmen shōu bù shōu xìnyòng kǎ?** (*nee men show boo show sheen yoong kah;* Do you accept credit cards?)
- **Yǒu méiyǒu shāngwù zhōngxīn?** (*yo mayo shahng woo joong sheen;* Is there a business center?)
- **Nǐmen de fángjiān yǒu méiyǒu wǎngluò liánjié?** (*nee men duh fahng jyan yo mayo wahng lwaw lyan jyeh;* Do your rooms have Internet access?)

You have many kinds of rooms to choose from, depending on your budget and your unique needs:

- **yíge ānjìng de fángjiān** (*ee guh ahn jeeng duh fahng jyan;* a quiet room)
- **yíge guāngxiàn hǎo de fángjiān** (*ee guh gwahng shyan how duh fahng jyan;* a bright room)
- **yíge cháo hǎi de fángjiān** (*ee guh chaow hi duh fahng jyan;* a room with an ocean view)
- **yíge cháo yuànzi de fángjiān** (*ee guh chaow ywan dzuh duh fahng jyan;* a room facing the courtyard)
- **yíge yǒu kōngtiáo de fángjiān** (*ee guh yo koong tyaow duh fahng jyan;* a room with air conditioning)
- **yíge dài yángtái de fángjiān** (*ee guh dye yahng tye duh fahng jyan;* a room with a balcony)
- **yíge bù xīyān de fángjiān** (*ee guh boo she yan duh fahng jyan;* a non-smoking room)
- **yíge fāngbiàn cánjí rén de fángjiān** (*ee guh fahng byan tsahn jee run duh fahng jyan;* a room equipped for handicapped people)

Talkin' the Talk

Elly calls a well-known hotel chain in Hong Kong to make a three-day reservation for his whole family. The hotel clerk quickly answers his call.

Elly: **Qǐng wèn, nǐmen fángjiān de jiàgé shì duōshǎo?**
          Cheeng one, nee men fahng jyan duh jyah guh shir dwaw shaow?
          May I ask, how much are your rooms?

Hotel Clerk: **Wǒmen de fángjiān yì tiān wǎnshàng yì bǎi wǔ shí kuài měi yuán.**
          Waw men duh fahng jyan ee tyan wahn shahng ee bye woo shir kwye may ywan.
          Our rooms are $150 U.S. dollars a night.

Elly: **Nà shì dānrén fángjiān hái shì shuāngrén fángjiān de jiàgé?**
          Nah shir dahn run fahng jyan hi shir shwahng run fahng jyan duh jyah guh?
          Is that the price of a single room or a double?

Hotel Clerk: **Dānrén fángjiān hé shuāngrén fángjiān de jiàgé dōu yíyàng.**
          Dahn run fahng jyan huh shwahng run fahng jyan duh jyah guh doe ee yahng.
          The price of our single and double rooms is the same.

Elly: **Hǎo jíle. Wǒ yào liǎngge dānrén fángjiān yíge shuāngrén fángjiān.**
          How jee luh. Waw yaow lyahng guh dahn run fahng jyan ee guh shwahng run fahng jyan.
          Great. I'd like two single rooms and one double.

Hotel Clerk: **Méiyǒu wèntí. Nǐmen yào dāi jǐ ge wǎnshàng?**
          Mayo one tee. Nee men yaow dye jee guh wahn shahng?
          No problem. How many nights will you be staying?

Elly: **Yígòng sān ge wǎnshàng.**
          Ee goong sahn guh wahn shahng.
          Altogether three nights.

Hotel Clerk: **Hǎo. Nà yígòng jiǔ bǎi kuài.**
          How. Nah ee goong jyo bye kwye.
          Very well. That will be $900 altogether.

Words to Know

dānrén fángjiān	dahn run fahng jyan	single room
shuāngrén fángjiān	shwahng run fahng jyan	double room
tàojiān	taow jyan	suite
yígòng	ee goong	altogether
yíyàng	ee yahng	the same
jiàgé	jyah guh	price
hé	huh	and
dōu	doe	both; all
dōu yíyàng	doe ee yahng	they're both the same
dāi	dye	to stay

The coverb **hé** (*huh;* and), along with the noun that always follows it, precedes the main verb or adjective of a sentence. Some synonyms of **hé** are **gēn** (*gun*), **yǔ** (*yew*), and **tóng** (*toong*), although **tóng** translates more closely as "with."

CULTURAL WISDOM

Hotel or apartment?

China's booming economy has become a magnet for foreign businesses, and scores of foreign business people have begun taking up residence there. Because living in mainland China can be quite expensive and nice apartments that don't come with long waiting lists are hard to come by, many foreigners opt to stay in a permanent hotel room or a serviced apartment connected to a foreign-run hotel. A friend of mine in Shanghai rents out his nice-sized apartment for $2,000 U.S. dollars a month, comparable to the rent of major U.S. cities like New York or Chicago. And you can expect the hotels to run $150 per night, just like in metropolitan U.S. cities.

Checking In Before You Hit the Pool

Aaahhh, **Yàzhōu** (*yah joe;* Asia)! Its allure often begins as soon as you pull up to the front entrance and walk through the hotel door. You may even find yourself mysteriously lingering a bit in the **dàtīng** (*dah teeng;* lobby), visually casing the joint long enough to take in all sorts of amenities. The luxuries at your disposal may include the following:

- **yóuyǒngchí** (*yo yoong chir;* swimming pool)
- **diànshì** (*dyan shir;* television)
- **gānxǐ fúwù** (*gahn she foo woo;* dry cleaning service)
- **huíyā ànmōchí** (*hway yah ahn maw chir;* jacuzzi)
- **tǐyùguǎn** (*tee yew gwahn;* gym)
- **shāngwù zhōngxīn** (*shahng woo joong sheen;* business center)
- **lǚguǎn fàndiàn** (*lyew gwahn fahn dyan;* hotel restaurant)

Before you can take advantage of these conveniences, however, you have to officially **bànlǐ rùzhù shǒuxù** (*bahn lee roo joo show shyew;* check in). You don't want to be caught red handed running in the **tǐyùguǎn** or relaxing in the **huíyā ànmōchí** unless you're a bona fide guest, right? (Don't answer that.)

When you walk up to the **fàndiàn qiántái** (*fahn dyan chyan tye;* reception desk), you'll invariably find yourself needing to say one of the following sentences:

- **Wǒ yǐjīng yùdìng le fángjiān.** (*waw ee jeeng yew deeng luh fahng jyan;* I already made a reservation.)
- **Wǒ méiyǒu yùdìng fángjiān.** (*waw mayo yew deeng fahng jyan;* I don't have a reservation.)
- **Nǐmen hái yǒu fángjiān ma?** (*nee men hi yo fahng jyan mah;* Do you have any rooms available?)

If you're in luck, the hotel will have at least one **kōng** (*koong;* empty, vacant) **fángjiān** (*fahng jyan;* room). If the hotel has no available space, you'll hear "**Duìbùqǐ, wǒmen kèmǎn le.**" (*dway boo chee, waw men kuh mahn luh;* Sorry, there are no vacancies/we're full.)

The **qiántái fúwùyuán** (*chyan tye foo woo ywan;* front desk clerk) will ask you to **tián** (*tyan;* fill out) a couple of **biǎo** (*byaow;* forms) to book your room, so have a **gāngbǐ** (*gahng bee;* pen) and some form of **zhèngjiàn** (*juhng jyan;* ID) ready — especially your **hùzhào** (*hoo jaow;* passport). Voilà! You're officially a hotel **kèrén** (*kuh run;* guest).

After you successfully manage to check in, a **xíngliyuán** (*sheeng lee ywan;* porter/bell boy) immediately appears to help take your **xíngli** (*sheeng lee;* luggage) to your **fángjiān**. After he lets you in, he'll give you the **yàoshi** (*yaow shir;* key) if you didn't get it from the **qiántái fúwùyuán** downstairs.

Now you can finally **xiūxi** (*shyo she;* take a rest) and maybe even fall asleep. Before you do, however, you may want to put in for a wake-up call. All you have to say is

> **Qǐng nǐ jiào wǒ qǐchuáng.** (*cheeng nee jyaow waw chee chwahng; literally:* Please call me to get out of bed.)

Talkin' the Talk

Beverly arrives in Taiwan and wants to check into a hotel in downtown Taipei, but the clerk informs her that the hotel has no vacancy.

Beverly: **Nǐ hǎo. Qǐng wèn, nǐmen hái yǒu fángjiān ma?**
Nee how. Cheeng one, nee men hi yo fahng jyan mah?
Hello. May I ask, do you have any rooms available?

Clerk: **Duìbùqǐ, wǒmen jīntiān kèmǎn le. Méiyǒu kōng fángjiān le.**
Dway boo chee, waw men jin tyan kuh mahn luh. Mayo koong fahng jyan luh.
I'm sorry, but we're full today. There aren't any vacant rooms.

Beverly: **Zāogāo! Nǐ néng bù néng tuījiàn biéde lǚguǎn?**
Dzaow gaow! Nee nung boo nung tway jyan byeh duh lyew gwahn?
Rats! Could you perhaps recommend another hotel then?

Clerk: **Kéyǐ. Gébì de lǚguǎn yǒu kōng fángjiān. Nǐ zuì hǎo zǒu guò qù shì shì kàn.**
Kuh yee. Guh bee duh lyew gwahn yo koong fahng jyan. Nee dzway how dzoe gwaw chyew shir shir kahn.
Yes. The hotel next door has vacancies. You may as well walk over there and have a look.

Beverly: **Xièxiè.**
Shyeh shyeh.
Thank you.

Words to Know

duìbùqǐ	dway boo chee	I'm sorry
zāogāo	dzaow gaow	rats!/what a shame
tuījiàn	tway jyan	recommend
biéde	byeh duh	other
lǚguǎn	lyew gwahn	hotel
gébì	guh bee	next door

Taking Advantage of Hotel Service

Uh oh . . . you're finally ensconced in your big, beautiful hotel room when you discover that the **mén suǒ bú shàng** (*mun swaw boo shahng;* door doesn't lock) and the **kōngtiáo huài le** (*koong tyaow hwye luh;* air conditioning doesn't work). To make matters worse, your **chuānghu dǎ bù kāi** (*chwahng hoo dah boo kye;* window won't open). Heat wave! It may be hard to believe, but in addition to all that, your **mǎtǒng dǔzhùle** (*mah toong doo joo luh;* toilet is clogged). Time to call the nearest **kèfáng fúwùyuán** (*kuh fahng foo woo ywan;* hotel housekeeper) and yell for help.

You may want the **kèfáng fúwùyuán** to **sòng** (*soong;* send) the following items right over:

- **chuīfēngjī** (*chway fung jee;* hair dryer)
- **máotǎn** (*maow tahn;* blanket)
- **zhěntóu** (*jun toe;* pillow)
- **máojīn** (*maow jeen;* towel)
- **wèishēngzhǐ** (*way shung jir;* toilet paper)

Call quick if the following pieces of equipment are **huàile** (*hwye luh;* broken) and need immediate fixing:

- **nuǎnqì** (*nwan chee;* heater)
- **kōngtiáo** (*koong tyaow;* air conditioner)

- ✔ **mǎtǒng** (*mah toong;* toilet)
- ✔ **kāiguān** (*kye gwahn;* light switch)
- ✔ **chāzuò** (*chah dzwaw;* electric outlet)
- ✔ **yáokòng qì** (*yaow koong chee;* remote control)

Maybe you just need someone to **dǎsǎo fángjiān** (*dah saow fahng jyan;* clean the room). Oh well. Even the best hotels need some tweaking every now and then.

You interact with many different employees on any given hotel stay:

- ✔ **fúwùtái jīnglǐ** (*foo woo tye jeeng lee;* concierge)
- ✔ **zǒngjīnglǐ** (*dzoong jeeng lee;* general manager)
- ✔ **zhùlǐ jīnglǐ** (*joo lee jeeng lee;* assistant manager)
- ✔ **fúwùyuán lǐngbān** (*foo woo ywan leeng bahn;* bell captain)
- ✔ **fúwùyuán** (*foo woo ywan;* attendant)

Hey! I almost forgot one of the best kinds of service you can take advantage of on occasion . . . room service! Before you decide to order room service for food, however, just remember that it's often **guì liǎng bèi** (*gway lyahng bay;* twice as expensive) as dining in the **lǚguǎn fàndiàn** (*lyew gwahn fahn dyan;* hotel restaurant), because the service is more **fāngbiàn** (*fahng byan;* convenient).

To make a comparison by saying that something is a number of times more expensive than something else, you first use the word **guì** (*gway;* expensive), followed by the number of times you think it's more expensive and the word **bèi** (*bay;* roughly translated as "times"). You can compare the relative cost of two products or services by using the word **bǐ** (*bee;* compared to) in the following pattern:

> X **bǐ** Y **guì** # **bèi**

Here are some examples:

- ✔ **Zuò chūzūchē bǐ zuò gōnggòng qìchē guì wǔ bèi.** (*zwaw choo dzoo chuh bee dzwaw goong goong chee chuh gway woo bay;* Taking a cab is five times more expensive than taking the bus.)
- ✔ **Zhèitiáo qúnzi bǐ nèige guì shí bèi.** (*jay tyaow chwun dzuh bee nay guh gway shir bay;* This skirt is 10 times more expensive than that one.)

Every hotel room in China has a large flask of boiling water that you can use to make tea or for drinking water. Never drink directly from the tap. You can brush your teeth with tap water, because you just spit it out. Local Chinese don't dare drink the tap water either, so you're in good company.

Talkin' the Talk

David enters his hotel room after he checks in, only to discover the bathroom faucet is broken. He calls for housekeeping and a few minutes later hears a knock on his door.

Housekeeper: **Kèfáng fúwùyuán!**
Kuh fahng foo woo ywan!
Housekeeping!

David: **Qǐng jìn!**
Cheeng jin!
Come on in!

Housekeeper: **Yǒu shénme wèntí?**
Yo shummuh one tee?
What seems to be the trouble?

David: **Zhèige shuǐlóngtóu huàile. Yě méiyǒu rèshuǐ.**
Jay guh shway loong toe hwye luh. Yeah mayo ruh shway.
This faucet is broken. There's also no hot water.

Housekeeper: **Hěn duìbùqǐ. Mǎshàng sòng shuǐnuǎngōng guòlái kànkàn.**
Hun dway boo chee. Mah shahng soong shway nwan goong gwaw lye kahn kahn.
I'm so sorry. We'll send a plumber right away to have a look.

David: **Xièxiè.**
Shyeh shyeh.
Thank you.

As the housekeeper starts to leave, David suddenly remembers some other things that the housekeeper may be able to take care of as long as she's there.

David: **Xiǎojiě, nǐmen yǒu méiyǒu xǐyī fúwù?**
Shyaow jyeh, nee men yo mayo she ee foo woo?
Miss, do you have any laundry service?

Housekeeper: **Yǒu.**
Yo.
Yes we do.

David: **Hǎo jíle. Jīntiān kěyǐ bǎ zhè xiē yīfú xǐ hǎo ma?**
              How jee luh. Jin tyan kuh yee bah jay shyeh ee foo she how mah?
              Great. Can I have these clothes cleaned today?

Housekeeper: **Kěyǐ.**
              Kuh yee.
              Yes.

David: **Yóuqíshì zhèige wūdiǎn. Néng bùnéng qùdiào?**
              Yo chee shir jay guh woo dyan. Nung boo nung chyew dyaow?
              Especially this stain. Can it be removed?

Housekeeper: **Méiyǒu wèntí.**
              Mayo one tee.
              No problem.

David: **Hǎo. Xièxiè.**
              How. Shyeh shyeh.
              Great. Thanks.

Words to Know

qǐng jìn	cheeng jin	come in, please
xǐ	she	to wash
yóuqíshì	yo chee shir	especially
wūdiǎn	woo dyan	stain
qùdiào	chyew dyaow	erase; remove
méiyǒu wèntí	mayo one tee	no problem
xǐyī fúwù	she ee foo woo	laundry service
mǎshàng	mah shahng	immediately
shuǐnuǎngōng	shway nwan goong	plumber

As you can see in the previous Talkin' the Talk section, the coverb **bǎ** often appears right after the subject of the sentence, separating it from the direct object, which is always something concrete rather than an abstract idea. It separates the indirect and direct objects.

Instead of having the following sentence pattern:

> Subject + Verb + Complement (+ Indirect Object) + Object

You have:

> Subject + **bǎ** + Object + Verb + Complement (+ Indirect Object)

Here are some examples:

- ✔ **Wǒ bǎ shū jiè gěi nǐ.** (*waw bah shoo jyeh gay nee;* I'll loan you the book.)
- ✔ **Qǐng nǐ bǎ běnzi ná gěi lǎoshī.** (*cheeng nee bah bun dzuh nah gay laow shir;* Please give the notebook to the teacher.)

Checking Out Before Heading Out

That oh-so-depressing time has come again. Time to say **zàijiàn** (*dzye jyan;* goodbye). Time to **téngchū** (*tuhng choo;* vacate) your hotel **fángjiān** (*fahng jyan;* room) and **tuìfáng** (*tway fahng;* check out).

You may need to say some of the following as you begin the end of your stay:

- ✔ **Wǒ yào fù zhàng.** (*waw yaow foo jahng;* I'd like to pay the bill.)
- ✔ **Nǐmen jiēshòu shénme xìnyòng kǎ?** (*nee men jyeh show shummuh sheen yoong kah;* Which credit cards do you accept?)
- ✔ **Zhè búshì wǒde zhāngdàn.** (*jay boo shir waw duh jahng dahn;* This isn't my bill.)
- ✔ **Wǒ bù yīnggāi fù zhè xiàng.** (*waw boo eeng gye foo jay shyahng;* I shouldn't be charged for this.)
- ✔ **Jiézhàng yǐhòu wǒ néng bùnéng bǎ bāoguǒ liú zài qiántái?** (*jyeh jahng ee ho waw nung boo nung bah baow gwaw lyo dzye chyan tye;* After checking out, may I leave my bags at the front desk?)
- ✔ **Yǒu méiyǒu qù fēijīchǎng de bānchē?** (*yo mayo chyew fay jee chahng duh ban chuh;* Is there a shuttle to the airport?)

Talkin' the Talk

Sandy is ready to check out after his three-day stay at a five-star hotel in Shanghai. He approaches the reception clerk to check out.

Sandy: **Nǐ hǎo. Wǒ jīntiān yào tuìfáng, suǒyǐ yào fù zhàng.**
Nee how. Waw jin tyan yaow tway fahng, swaw yee yaow foo jahng.
Hello. I'd like to check out today, so I'd like to pay the bill.

Clerk: **Qǐng wèn, nín de fángjiān hàomǎ shì duōshǎo?**
Cheeng one, neen duh fahng jyan how mah shir dwaw shaow?
May I ask, what's your room number?

Sandy: **Wǔlíngliù hào fángjiān.**
Woo leeng lyo how fahng jyan.
Room # 506.

Clerk: **Hǎo. Zhè shì nínde zhàngdān. Yígòng yìqiān wǔbǎi kuài.**
How. Jay shir neen duh jahng dahn. Ee goong ee chyan woo bye kwye.
Okay. This is your bill. It's altogether $1,500.

Sandy pays the bill with his credit card.

Sandy: **Zhè shì wǒmen fángjiān de yàoshi.**
Jay shir waw mun fahng jyan duh yaow shir.
This is my room key.

Clerk: **Xièxiè.**
Shyeh shyeh.
Thank you.

Sandy: **Jiézhàng yǐhòu wǒ néng bùnéng bǎ bāoguǒ liú zài qiántái?**
Jyeh jahng ee ho waw nung boo nung bah baow gwaw lyo dzye chyan tye?
After checking out, may I leave my bags at the front desk?

Clerk: **Kěyǐ. Méiyǒu wèntí.**
Kuh yee. Mayo one tee.
Yes. No problem.

Words to Know

tuìfáng	tway fahng	check out
zhàngdān	jahng dahn	bill
jié zhàng	jyeh jahng	figure out the bill
fángjià	fahng jya	room charge
suǒyǐ	swaw yee	so; therefore
yàoshi	yaow shir	key

Fun & Games

Fill in the blanks, using the following words: **tuìfáng, zhàngdān, fángjiān, kèmǎn, qǐchuáng.** See the answer key in Appendix C.

1. **Nǐmen de _____ yǒu méiyǒu wǎngluò liánjié?**

   Do your rooms have Internet access?

2. **Duìbùqǐ, wǒmen _____ le.**

   I'm sorry, we have no vacancies.

3. **Qǐng nǐ jiào wǒ _____.**

   Please give me a wake up call.

4. **Zhè búshì wǒde _____.**

   This isn't my bill.

5. **Wǒ jīntiān yào _____.**

   I'd like to check out today.

Chapter 14

Transportation

In This Chapter

▶ Traveling by plane

▶ Surviving customs

▶ Getting around town

Traveling halfway around the world to **Zhōngguó** (*joong gwaw;* China) can be a long haul. Knowing the magic traveling words and phrases in Chinese can make your journey as efficient and **shūfu** (*shoo foo;* comfortable) as possible. This chapter helps you make your way around the **fēijīchǎng** (*fay jee chahng;* airport) and the **fēijī** (*fay jee;* airplane), survive the **hǎiguān** (*hi gwahn;* customs) experience, and board different types of **jiāotōng** (*jyaow toong;* transportation) after you reach your destination.

Flying Around the Airport

Consider yourself a veteran traveler just because you've been all through **Ōuzhōu** (*oh joe;* Europe) and the Americas? Well, my friend, you're in for a rude awakening. When it comes to finding your way around China, English, or any other Western language, does you little good. You spend a lot of unproductive time trying to interpret the signs to get some sense of which line to stand in and where to go next at the airport. You need to at least know the **Pīnyīn** (*pin yin;* literally: spelled the way it sounds) romanization system, if not Chinese characters themselves. If you don't, you'll be up a creek without a paddle. You may end up following the guy next to you, even if it takes you to the bathroom rather than baggage claims. (See Chapter 1 for more about the pīnyīn system of spelling Chinese words.)

Good move to get a head start by reading *Chinese For Dummies* in advance of your trip. You can bone up on some essential words and phrases before the whole airport experience makes you want to get right back on the next plane bound for home.

Making it past the check-in counter

Ready to **bànlǐ dēngjī shǒuxù** (*bahn lee duhng jee show shyew;* check in)? After lugging your bags up to this point, you finally get to **tuōyùn** (*twaw yewn;* check) your **xíngli** (*sheeng lee;* luggage). You receive a **dēngjīpái** (*duhng jee pye;* boarding pass) at the check-in counter, at which point you're ready to make your way to the appropriate **chūkǒu** (*choo ko;* gate), taking only your **shǒutí xíngli** (*show tee sheeng lee;* carry-on luggage).

All sorts of questions may be running through your mind about now. Here are some basic phrases that may come in handy during check in:

- ✔ **Wǒ xiǎng yào kào guòdào de wèizi.** (*waw shyahng yaow cow gwaw daow duh way dzuh;* I'd like an aisle seat.)

- ✔ **Wǒ xiǎng yào kào chuāng de wèizi.** (*waw shyahng yaow cow chwahng duh way dzuh;* I'd like a window seat.)

- ✔ **Wǒ xiǎng tuōyùn xíngli.** (*waw shyahng twaw yewn sheeng lee;* I'd like to check my luggage.)

- ✔ **Fēijī jǐ diǎn qǐfēi?** (*fay jee jee dyan chee fay;* What time does it depart?)

- ✔ **Wǒde hángbān hàomǎ shì duōshǎo?** (*waw duh hahng bahn how mah shir dwaw shaow;* What's my flight number?)

- ✔ **Zài jǐ hào mén hòujī?** (*dzye jee how mun ho jee;* Which gate do we leave from?)

After you check in, you may encounter all sorts of unpleasant surprises. Perhaps the plane can't **zhèngdiǎn qǐfēi** (*juhng dyan chee fay;* depart on time) after all and the airline must **tuīchí** (*tway chir;* postpone) your departure or **qǔxiāo** (*chyew shyaow;* cancel) it altogether. Maybe the **tiānqì** (*tyan chee;* weather) is causing the problems. Better that than a **kǒngbù fènzǐ** (*koong boo fun dzuh;* terrorist) scare in this day and age, right?

Talkin' the Talk

 Gordon is checking in at the airport in New York for a business trip to Beijing. He shows his ticket and passport to the **zhíyuán** (*jir ywan;* agent) and checks his luggage.

Zhíyuán: **Nín hǎo. Qǐng chūshì nínde jīpiào.**
Neen how. Cheeng choo shir neen duh jee pyaow.
Hello. Your ticket, please.

Gordon: **Jiù zài zhèr.**
Jyo dzye jar.
Here it is.

Zhíyuán: **Nín shì bú shì qù Běijīng? Néng kànkàn nínde hùzhào ma?**
Neen shir boo shir chyew bay jeeng? Nuhng kahn kahn neen duh hoo jaow mah?
Are you going to Beijing? May I see your passport?

Gordon: **Kěyǐ.**
Kuh yee.
Here you are.

Zhíyuán: **Yǒu jǐ jiàn xíngli?**
Yo jee jyan sheeng lee?
How many suitcases do you have?

Gordon: **Wǒ yǒu sānge xiāngzi.**
Waw yo sahn guh shyahng dzuh.
I have three suitcases.

Zhíyuán: **Yǒu méiyǒu shǒutí xíngli?**
Yo mayo show tee sheeng lee?
Do you have any carry-on luggage?

Gordon: **Wǒ zhǐ yǒu yíge gōngwénbāo.**
Waw jir yo ee guh goong one baow.
I have only one briefcase.

Zhíyuán: **Hǎo. Nín yào kào guòdào de wèizi háishì yào kào chuāng de wèizi?**
How. Neen yow cow gwaw daow duh way dzuh hi shir yaow cow chwahng duh way dzuh?
Alright. Would you like an aisle or a window seat?

Gordon: **Wǒ xiǎng yào kào guòdào de wèizi.**
Waw shyahng yaow cow gwaw daow duh way dzuh.
I'd like an aisle seat.

Zhíyuán: **Hǎo. Zhèi shì nínde dēngjīpái. Qù Běijīng de 108 cì bānjī, 19 pái, B zuò.**
How. Jay shir neen duh duhng jee pye. Chyew bay jeeng duh ee bye leeng bah tsuh bahn jee, shir jyo pye, B dzwaw.
Fine. Here's your boarding pass. Flight #108 to Beijing, Row 19, Seat B.

Gordon: **Xièxiè.**
Shyeh shyeh.
Thanks.

Zhíyuán: **Zhè shì nínde xíngli lǐngqǔdān. Dàole Běijīng yǐhòu kěyǐ lǐngqǔ nínde xíngli.**
Jay shir neen duh sheeng lee leeng chyew dahn. Dow luh bay jeeng ee ho kuh yee leeng chyew neen duh sheeng lee.
Here are your luggage claim tags. After you arrive in Beijing, you can claim your luggage.

Gordon: **Xièxiè.**
Shyeh shyeh.
Thanks.

Zhíyuán: **Zhù nín yí lù píng ān.**
Joo neen ee loo peeng ahn.
Have a nice trip.

Words to Know

guónèi	gwaw nay	domestic
guójì	gwaw jee	international
piào	pyaow	ticket
hùzhào	hoo jaow	passport
qiānzhèng	chyan juhng	visa
dàodá	dow dah	arrivals
qǐfēi	chee fay	departures
mén or chūkǒu	mun or choo ko	gate
shǒutí xíngli	show tee sheeng lee	carry-on luggage
gōngwénbāo	goong one baow	briefcase
lǐngqǔdān	leeng chyew dahn	luggage claim tag
fàngjìn zuòwèi dǐxià	fahng jeen dzwaw way dee shyah	fit under the seat
tóudǐng shàngfāng de xínglicāng	toe deeng shahng fahng duh sheeng lee tsahng	overhead compartment
yí lù píng ān	ee loo peeng ahn	have a good trip

Boarding your flight

Okay! You're all set to board the plane. Are you lucky enough to sit in the **tóudĕngcāng** (*toe duhng tsahng;* first class) section, or do you have to sit in **jīngjìcāng** (*jeeng jee tsahng;* economy class) the whole time? Either way, international flights no longer have a **chōuyān qū** (*cho yan chyew;* smoking area), so if you indulge in that sort of thing, you'll have to white-knuckle it for the next 10 hours or so.

In the meantime, here are some people you see get on the plane before you (at least I hope you do):

- **jiàshǐyuán** (*jyah shih ywan;* pilot)
- **jīzǔ** (*jee dzoo;* crew)
- **chéngwùyuán** (*chung woo ywan;* flight attendants)

And if you're like me, you get worried about some things as the plane begins to taxi down the runway:

- **qǐfēi** (*chee fay;* take off)
- **qìliú** (*chee lyo;* turbulence)
- **zhuólù** (*jwaw loo;* landing)

Aaah! I get nervous just thinking about them. It's okay, though. The **chéng-wùyuán** are on to people like you and me. That's why they make sure to tell you before takeoff where the **jiùshēngyī** (*jyo shung ee;* life vests) and **jǐnjí chūkǒu** (*jin jee choo ko;* emergency exits) are located. You may also hear them bark out the following instructions, if you haven't already managed to tune everything out:

- **Jìjǐn nǐde ānquándài.** (*jee jin nee duh ahn chwan dye;* Fasten your seat belt.)
- **Bù zhǔn chōuyān.** (*boo jwun cho yan;* No smoking permitted.)
- **Bǎ zuòyǐ kàobèi fàngzhí.** (*bah dzwaw ee cow bay fahng jir;* Put your seat back to the upright position.)
- **Bǎ tuōpán cānzhuō shōu qǐlái.** (*bah twaw pahn tsahn jwaw show chee lye;* Put your tray table back.)
- **Rúguǒ kōngqì yālì yǒu biànhuà, yǎngqìzhào huì zìdòng luòxià.** (*roo gwaw koong chee yah lee yo byan hwah, yahng chee jaow hway dzuh doong lwaw shyah;* If there's any change in air pressure, the oxygen mask will automatically drop down.)

If you're not a nervous flyer, you'll probably spend all your time listening to **yīnyuè** (*een yweh;* music) through the **ěrjī** (*are jee;* headset), flipping **píndào** (*peen daow;* dials) on the radio or **diànshì tái** (*dyan shir tye;* channels) on the television, or trying to **shuìjiào** (*shway jyaow;* sleep). Hopefully the flight is showing a good **diànyǐng** (*dyan yeeng;* movie) on such a long trip. But if the show is boring, at least it may help you **shuìjiào**.

You use the coverb **bǎ** *(bah)* when you want to put the object right up front before you state the verb that tells what you did or will do with the object. (See Chapter 13 for more on this unique coverb.)

Talkin' the Talk

Carl asks an agent in the boarding area if his flight will be on time.

Carl: **Qǐng wèn, wǒmen de fēijī huì búhuì zhèngdiǎn qǐfēi?**
Cheeng one, waw mun duh fay jee hway boo hway juhng dyan chee fay?
Excuse me, but will our plane be departing on time?

Agent: **Hěn duìbùqǐ. Fēijī yào tuīchí chàbùduō bànge xiǎoshí.**
Hun dway boo chee. Fay jee yaow tway chir chah boo dwaw bahn guh shyaow shir.
I'm very sorry. Takeoff has been postponed for about a half an hour.

Carl: **Zāogāo!**
Dzaow gaow!
That's awful!

Words to Know

zhèngdiǎn	juhng dyan	on time
chàbùduō	chah boo dwaw	about; almost (approximately)
zuǒyòu	dzwaw yo	approximately
zāogāo	dzow gow	that's awful!

Going through customs

If you survive all the **tuānliú** (*twan lyo;* turbulence) and the boring **diànyǐng** (*dyan yeeng;* movie) on your long flight without having a breakdown, good for you! The next test you have to survive is the **hǎiguān** (*hi gwahn;* customs) experience. After you get to customs, you see many **hǎiguān guānyuán** (*hi gwahn gwahn ywan;* customs officers), none of whom may **dǒng Yīngyǔ** (*doong eeng yew;* understand English). Table 14-1 lists the items you need to have ready at customs. The following phrases should come in handy, too:

- ✔ **Nǐ dǒng Yīngyǔ ma?** (*nee doong eeng yew mah;* Do you understand English?)
- ✔ **Wǒ shì Měiguó rén.** (*waw shir may gwaw run;* I'm American.)
- ✔ **Wǒ shì Yīngguó rén.** (*waw shir eeng gwaw run;* I'm British.)
- ✔ **Wǒ shì Jiānádà rén.** (*waw shir jyah nah dah run;* I'm Canadian.)
- ✔ **Xǐshǒujiān zài nǎr?** (*she show jyan dzye nar;* Where are the restrooms?)

Table 14-1	Items to Have Ready at Customs	
Chinese Word(s)	*Pronunciation*	*English Word(s)*
rùjìng dēngjì kǎ	roo jeeng duhng jee kah	arrival card
chūjìng dēngjì kǎ	choo jeeng duhng jee kah	departure card
jiànkāng zhèng	jyan kahng jung	health certificate
shēnbào de wùpǐn	shun baow duh woo peen	articles to declare
xiāngyān	shyahng yan	cigarettes
jiǔ	jyo	alcohol
bāo	baow	bag
xiāngzi	shyahng dzuh	suitcase
xíngli	sheeng lee	luggage

The **hǎiguān guānyuán** may ask you a couple of these important questions:

- ✔ **Nǐ yǒu méiyǒu yào shēnbào de wùpǐn?** (*nee yo mayo yaow shun baow duh woo peen;* Do you have anything you want to declare?)
- ✔ **Qǐng gěi wǒ kànkàn nǐde hùzhào.** (*cheeng gay waw kahn kahn nee duh hoo jaow;* Please show me your passport.)

✔ **Qǐng gěi wǒ kànkàn nǐde hǎiguān shēnbàodān.** (*cheeng gay waw kahn kahn nee duh hi gwan shun baow dahn;* Please show me your customs declaration form.)

✔ **Nǐ dǎsuàn zài zhèr dāi duōjiǔ?** (*nee dah swan dzye jar dye dwaw jyo;* How long do you plan on staying?)

✔ **Nǐ lái zhèr shì bàn gōngwù háishì lǚyóu?** (*nee lye jar shir bahn goong woo hi shir lyew yo;* Are you here on business or as a tourist?)

Customs agents aren't the only people with questions to ask. You may have some questions you want to try out yourself:

✔ **Xíngli yào dǎkāi ma?** (*sheeng lee yaow dah kye mah;* Should I open my luggage?)

✔ **Xíngli kéyǐ shōu qǐlái ma?** (*sheeng lee kuh yee show chee lye mah;* May I close my suitcases now?)

✔ **X guāng huì sǔnhuài wǒde jiāojuǎn ma?** (*X gwahng hway swuhn hwye waw duh jyaow jwan mah;* Will the X-ray damage my film?)

✔ **Wǒ yào fù shuì ma?** (*waw yaow foo shway mah;* Must I pay duty?)

Talkin' the Talk

Cynthia gets off her plane in Shanghai and begins the customs process by approaching an agent.

Agent: **Qǐng gěi wǒ kànkàn nǐde hùzhào.**
Cheeng gay waw kahn kahn nee duh hoo jaow.
Please show me your passport.

Cynthia shows him her passport, and the agent asks her some important questions.

Agent: **Měiguórén. Nǐ yǒu méiyǒu yào shēnbào de wùpǐn?**
May gwaw run. Nee yo mayo yaow shun baow duh woo peen?
American. Do you have anything you'd like to declare?

Cynthia: **Méiyǒu. Wǒ zhǐ yǒu yìtiáo xiāngyān.**
Mayo. Waw jir yo ee tyaow shyahng yan.
No. I have only a carton of cigarettes.

Agent: **Nǐ lái zhèr shìbàn gōngwù háishì lǚyóu?**
Nee lye jar shirbahn goong woo hi shir lyew yo?
Are you here on business or as a tourist?

Cynthia:	**Wǒ lái zuò shēngyì.**
	Waw lye dzwaw shung ee.
	I've come on business.
Agent:	**Nǐ kéyǐ zǒu le.**
	Nee kuh yee dzoe luh.
	You may go.

Words to Know

qǔ xíngli chù	chyew sheeng lee choo	baggage-claim area
gōngwù	goong woo	to be on business
lǚyóu	lyew yo	tour
lùguò	loo gwaw	passing through
jiāo shuì	jyaow shway	pay duty
yìtiáo xiāngyān	ee tyaow shyahng yan	a carton of cigarettes

Navigating Around Town

It's virtually impossible to rent a car in China. Cars just aren't available. And even if you can find a rental, you may not want to, given the bureaucracy and driving conditions. Signs aren't printed in English, which is probably the main reason you shouldn't even attempt it. Just think of the upside. You don't have to suddenly learn how to use a **shǒupáidǎng** (*show pye dahng;* stick shift) or purchase any extra car **bǎoxiǎn** (*baow shyan;* insurance). Take a taxi and relax. Let the driver worry about how to get you from point A to point B.

No matter what form of transportation you end up taking from the airport, and later on around town, here are a few crucial words and phrases to know:

- **fāngxiàng** (*fahng shyahng;* directions)
- **dìtú** (*dee too;* map)
- **Wǒ mílù le.** (*waw mee loo luh;* I'm lost.)

Hailing a cab

It's Friday night, and you just had a pretty successful day doing business with your Chinese counterparts. You've finally mustered the courage to venture out of your hotel room for a night on the town. You decide to check out a popular **wǔtīng** (*woo teeng;* dance hall), and you begin to determine what mode of transport can best get you there.

Although **zìxíngchē** (*dzuh sheeng chuh;* bicycles), **mótuōchē** (*maw twaw chuh;* motorcycles), **mǎchē** (*mah chuh;* horse-drawn carts), and even **niú** (*nyo;* cows) are still the main forms of transportation for the average individual in some parts of mainland China, most foreigners take taxis wherever they go. You can easily find taxis around hotels, and cabs are certainly more **shūfu** (*shoo foo;* comfortable) and **fāngbiàn** (*fahng byan;* convenient) than having to deal with nonexistent rules of the road, breathing in **kōngqì wūrǎn** (*koong chee woo rahn;* air pollution) while bicycling, finding your way through a maze of old alleyways, or, depending on the time of year, leaving yourself to the mercy of the natural elements.

Here's what you say to the hotel door attendant if you want help hailing a cab:

> **Wǒ yào jiào jìchéngchē.** (*waw yaow jyaow jee chung chuh;* I would like a taxi.)

After you're safely ensconced in the cab, you need to know how to say the following phrases:

- **Qǐng dài wǒ dào zhèige dìzhǐ.** (*cheeng dye waw daow jay guh dee jir;* Please take me to this address.)
- **Qǐng dǎ biǎo.** (*cheeng dah byaow;* Please turn on the meter.)
- **Qǐng kāi màn yìdiǎr.** (*cheeng kye mahn ee dyar;* Please drive a little slower.)
- **Qǐng kāi kuài yìdiǎr.** (*cheeng kye kwye ee dyar;* Please drive a little faster.)
- **Wǒ děi gǎn shíjiān.** (*waw day gahn shir jyan;* I'm in a hurry.)
- **Qǐng zǒu fēngjǐng hǎo de lù.** (*cheeng dzoe fung jeeng how duh loo;* Please take a scenic route.)
- **Zài zhèr guǎi wār.** (*dzye jar gwye wahr;* Turn here.)
- **Nǐ kéyǐ děng jǐ fēn zhōng ma?** (*nee kuh yee duhng jee fun joong mah;* Can you wait a few minutes?)

Oh, and one more thing. As you **chūfā** (*choo fah;* set off) with your taxi **sījī** (*suh jee;* driver), make sure you put on your **ānquándài** (*ahn chwan dye;* seat belt).

Finally, before you get out of the cab, these phrases may come in handy for price negotiations:

- **Wǒ gāi gěi nǐ duōshǎo qián?** (*waw guy gay nee dwaw shaow chyan;* How much do I owe you?)

- **Wǒ huì àn biǎo fù kuǎn.** (*waw hway ahn byaow foo kwahn;* I'll pay what the meter says.)

- **Bié qīpiàn wǒ.** (*byeh chee pyan waw;* Don't cheat me.)

- **Kāi wán xiào! Wǒ jùjué fù zhèmme duō qián.** (*kye wahn shyaow! waw jyew jweh foo juhmmuh dwaw chyan;* You've got to be kidding! I refuse to pay so much.)

- **Bú yòng zhǎo le.** (*boo yoong jaow luh;* Keep the change.)

- **Qǐng gěi wǒ shōujù.** (*cheeng gay waw show jyew;* Please give me a receipt.)

Because most people in China don't speak English, always remember to take a hotel card when you leave your hotel. Your card has the name and address in English and Chinese. You can always show the card to a taxi driver when you want to get back. If you're walking around town, you may want to take a **dìtú** (*dee too;* map) that shows local landmarks such as pagodas or train stations near your hotel.

Talkin' the Talk

Herby ventures out for a night on the town and needs a cab. He enlists the help of his hotel doorman.

Herby: **Wǒ yào jiào jìchéngchē.**
Waw yaow jyaow jee chung chuh.
I would like a taxi.

Doorman: **Hǎo.**
How.
Certainly.

The doorman hails a cab and then opens the cab door. Herby gives him a ridiculously large tip of USD$5.

Herby: **Bú yòng zhǎo le.**
Boo yoong jaow luh.
Keep the change.

Doorman: **Xièxiè!**
             Shyeh shyeh!
             Thank you!

Herby enters the cab and shows the driver a card with the name and address of a local nightclub.

Herby: **Qǐng dài wǒ dào zhèige yèzǒnghuì.**
             Cheeng dye waw daow jay guh yeh dzoong hway.
             Please take me to this nightclub.

Driver: **Méiyǒu wèntí.**
             Mayo one tee.
             No problem.

Herby: **Wǒ bùjí. Qǐng kāi màn yìdiǎr.**
             Waw boo jee. Cheeng kye mahn ee dyar.
             I'm not in a hurry. Please drive a little slower.

Herby finally reaches the nightclub after his scenic cab drive.

Herby: **Wǒ gāi gěi nǐ duōshǎo qián?**
             Waw guy gay nee dwaw shaow chyan?
             How much do I owe you?

Driver: **Shí kuài liǎng máo wǔ.**
             Shir kwye lyahng maow woo.
             That will be $10.25.

Herby hands the driver USD $15.

Herby: **Qǐng gěi wǒ shōujù. Bú yòng zhǎo le.**
             Cheeng gay waw show jyew. Boo yoong jaow luh.
             Please give me a receipt. Keep the change.

Driver: **Hǎo. Xièxiè.**
             How. Shyeh shyeh.
             Okay. Thanks.

Words to Know

chē	chuh	car
chūzūchē	choo dzoo chuh	taxi
sījī	suh jee	driver
kāi chē	kye chuh	to drive a car
jìchéngbiǎo	jee chuhng byaow	meter
xiǎofèi	shyaow fay	tip
chéngkè	chuhng kuh	passenger
wènlù	one loo	to ask for directions
gāofēngqī	gaow fung chee	rush hour
dǔchē	doo chuh	traffic jam

Hopping on the bus

Gōnggòng qìchē (*goong goong chee chuh;* buses) are almost as common as bicycles in China. They also cost much less than **chūzūchē** (*choo dzoo chuh;* taxis). But here's the catch: Bus drivers usually don't speak a word of English, signs are only in Chinese, and the buses are always super crowded. Still, if you're game for a unique travel experience, and you don't mind killing time waiting for the bus, put these phrases in your carry-on bag:

- **Yīnggāi zuò jǐ lù chē?** (*eeng guy dzwaw jee loo chuh;* Which (number) bus should I take?)

- **Chē piào duōshǎo qián?** (*chuh pyaow dwaw shaow chyan;* How much is the fare?)

- **Gōnggòng qìchē zhàn zài nǎr?** (*goong goong chee chuh jahn dzye nar;* Where's the bus station?)

- **Duōjiǔ lái yítàng?** (*dwaw jyo lye ee tahng;* How often does it come?)

- **Qǐng gàosù wǒ zài nǎr xià chē.** (*cheeng gaow soo waw dzye nar shyah chuh;* Please let me know where to get off.)

Talkin' the Talk

Alina is walking along the street, trying to find a bus that can take her to the famous Shilin night market in Taiwan. She sees her old friend Gretchen, and after saying hello, she asks her for help.

Alina:	**Qù Shílín yīnggāi zuò jǐ lù gōnggòng qìchē?** *Chyew shir leen eeng guy dzwaw jee loo goong goong chee chuh?* Which bus should I take to go to Shilin?
Gretchen:	**Yīnggāi zuò sān lù chē. Nèige gōnggòng qìchē zhàn jiù zài zhèr.** *Eeng guy dzwaw sahn loo chuh. Nay guh goong goong chee chuh jahn jyo dzye jar.* You should take the number 3 bus. That bus stop is right here.
Alina:	**Tài hǎo le. Duōjiǔ lái yítàng?** *Tye how luh. Dwaw jyo lye ee tahng?* That's great. How often does it come?
Gretchen:	**Měi sānshí fēn zhōng. Hái hǎo.** *May sahn shir fun joong. Hi how.* Every 30 minutes. That's not too bad.
Alina:	**Xièxiè nǐ.** *Shyeh shyeh nee.* Thank you.

Words to Know

gōnggòng qìchē	goong goong chee chuh	bus
gōnggòng qìchē zhàn	goong goong chee chuh jahn	bus station
Jǐ lù?	jee loo	Which route?
Jǐ lù chē?	jee loo chuh	Which number bus?
yuè piào	yweh pyaow	monthly pass
hái hǎo	hi how	it's okay; not too bad

Riding the rails

If you want to get where you need to go really quickly, especially in Hong Kong or New York, the fastest way to get there may take you below the ground — to the **dìtiě** (*dee tyeh;* subway). Most **dìtiě zhàn** (*dee tyeh jahn;* subway stations) are pretty easy to navigate.

Unlike in Hong Kong, the subway system in mainland China is relatively new, and you find stations in less than a handful of cities. Above-ground **huǒchē** (*hwaw chuh;* train) travel, however, is tried and true — especially because China is such a huge place and distances between cities are so great. Unlike the number of subway stations, you can find plenty of **huǒchēzhàn** (*hwaw chuh jahn;* train stations) in China. They even come equipped with **hòuchēshì** (*ho chuh shir;* waiting rooms).

February is a particularly risky month to attempt long-distance train travel, because the shortest month features the Chinese New Year, and you're bound to meet what seems like the entire country traveling from one part of China to another. Make sure you consult a **shíkèbiǎo** (*shir kuh byaow;* time schedule) in advance and note the correct **dàodá shíjiān** (*daow dah shir jyan;* arrival time) and **kāichē shíjiān** (*key chuh shir jyan;* departure time) of your train.

If you plan to travel a long distance, be sure to book a **ruǎnwò** (*rwan waw;* soft sleeper) for such occasions — or at least ask for a **ruǎnzuò** (*rwan dzwaw;* soft seat) — because they're the more comfortable accommodations and not as jam-packed as other parts of the train. Trust me. Soft sleepers are worth the extra cost. For more on the types of seats in trains, see Table 14-2.

Table 14-2	Seating Accommodations on Trains	
Chinese Word	*Pronunciation*	*English Words*
yìngzuò	eeng dzwaw	hard seat
ruǎnzuò	rwan dzwaw	soft seat
yìngwò	eeng waw	hard sleeper
ruǎnwò	rwahn waw	soft sleeper
xiàpù	shyah poo	lower berth
shàngpù	shahng poo	upper berth

Taking the subway around China

Hong Kong constantly upgrades and extends its subway system, making it quite reliable. Taipei also has an excellent and efficient subway system. In Shanghai, China's major commercial center of Pudong is expected to soon have a subway that connects the east and west sides of the Huangpu River. And with the 2008 Olympics coming up, Beijing's Metro system is undergoing expansion in preparation for the hordes that will descend in a few short years.

Before you **shàngchē** (*shahng chuh;* board the train) to enjoy your comfy, soft seat, you need to go to the **shòupiàochù** (*show pyaow choo;* ticket office) to buy your **piào** (*pyaow;* ticket). You use the following words and phrases to get the job done:

- **piào** (*pyaow;* ticket)
- **piàojià** (*pyaow jyah;* fare)
- **dānchéngpiào** (*dahn chuhng pyaow;* one-way ticket)
- **láihuípiào** (*lye hway pyaow;* round-trip ticket)
- **shòupiàochù** (*show pyaow choo;* ticket office)
- **tèkuài** (*tuh kwye;* express train)
- **mànchē** (*mahn chuh;* local train)

The following may come in handy at the train station:

- **Piàofáng zài nǎr?** (*pyaow fahng dzye nar;* Where's the ticket office?)

  Notice the different way of saying ticket office in this question. Options abound in the Chinese language.

- **Wǒ yào yìzhāng yìngwò piào.** (*waw yow ee jahng eeng waw pyaow;* I'd like a hard-sleeper ticket.)

- **Huǒchē cóng něige zhàntái kāi?** (*hwaw chuh tsoong nay guh jahn tye kye;* Which gate does the train leave from?)

And when you finally hear the **lièchēyuán** (*lyeh chuh ywan;* conductor) say **"Shàng chē le!"** (*shahng chuh luh;* All aboard!), you can board and ask the following questions:

- **Zhèige zuòwèi yǒu rén ma?** (*jay guh dzwaw way yo run mah;* Is this seat taken?)

- **Cānchē zài nǎr?** (*tsahn chuh dzye nar;* Where's the dining car?)

Talkin' the Talk

Lorna is at the Beijing train station to buy a round-trip ticket to Shanghai for tomorrow. She approaches a ticket agent to purchase her ticket.

Lorna: **Qǐng wèn, yǒu méiyǒu míngtiān qù Shànghǎi de huǒchē piào?**
Cheeng one, yo mayo meeng tyan chyew shahng hi duh hwaw chuh pyaow?
Excuse me, do you have any train tickets to Shanghai for tomorrow?

Ticket Agent: **Yǒu. Yào jǐ zhāng?**
Yo. Yaow jee jahng?
Yes. How many would you like?

Lorna: **Zhǐ yì zhāng lái huí piào. Xiàge lǐbàiyī yào huí lái.**
Jir ee jahng lye hway pyaow. Shyah guh lee bye ee yaow hway lye.
Just one round-trip ticket. I'd like to return next Monday.

Ticket Agent: **Hǎo. Yào yìngwò, ruǎnwò, háishì ruǎnzuò?**
How. Yaow eeng waw, rwahn waw, hi shir rwahn dzwaw?
Okay. Would you like a hard sleeper, a soft sleeper, or a soft seat?

Lorna: **Wǒ yào yì zhāng ruǎn wò. Xièxiè.**
Waw yaow ee jahng rwahn waw. Shyeh shyeh.
I'd like a soft sleeper. Thanks.

Words to Know

lái huí piào	lye hway pyaow	round-trip ticket
huí lái	hway lye	to return
huànchē	hwahn chuh	change trains
chápiào	chah pyaow	check the ticket
cānchē	tsahn chuh	dining car
zhàntái	jahn tye	platform

Fun & Games

How do you say these types of transportation in Chinese? (See Appendix C for the answers.)

A. _____

B. _____

C. _____

D. _____

E. _____

Chapter 15

Traveling Abroad

- -

In This Chapter

▶ Checking your calendar for open dates

▶ Choosing a travel destination

▶ Filling your luggage

▶ Dealing with travel agents

- -

Careful planning is the key to a successful vacation or business trip. You have to keep in mind not only where you want to go, but also the best time to travel. This chapter tells you how to prepare for a trip abroad and how to choose the exact day, date, and year you want to travel. When it comes to making sure your **hùzhào** (*hoo jaow;* passport) is still valid and your **qiānzhèng** (*chyan juhng;* visa) is in order, however, you're on your own. **Yí lù píng ān!** (*ee loo peeng ahn;* Have a good trip!)

When Do You Want to Travel?

The time of year you choose to travel can make all the difference in the world for a great (or lousy) vacation. Should you plan it for **dōngtiān** (*doong tyan;* winter), **chūntiān** (*chwun tyan;* spring), **xiàtiān** (*shyah tyan;* summer), or **qiūtiān** (*chyo tyan;* fall)? A trip to Beijing during **sān yuè** (*sahn yweh;* March), just when the dust storms are blowing in from the Gobi Desert, for example, is quite different than a trip during **wǔ yuè** (*woo yweh;* May) or **shí yuè** (*shir yweh;* October), when pollution is at a minimum and sunny skies are at a maximum. Of course, **wǔ yuè** and **shí yuè** are peak seasons to travel to China for exactly these reasons, which means hotel prices are also at their peak. Paris in the **chūntiān** is just as great (and just as expensive) for the same reason. Can't do much to help you there. For more on dates, weeks, months, and years, head to Chapter 7.

Want to find out when friends plan to leave on their vacation? Just ask them one of these basic questions:

✔ **Nǐ jǐ yuè jǐ hào zǒu?** (*nee jee yweh jee how dzoe;* When are you leaving; *literally:* What month and day are you leaving?)

✔ **Nǐ jǐ yuè jǐ hào qù Zhōngguó?** (*nee jee yweh jee how chyew joong gwaw;* When will you be going to China; *literally:* What month and day will you be going to China?)

If you have to answer the preceding questions, just fill in the month and the number of the day you plan on leaving and put those words in place of **yuè** and **hào.** Here are some examples:

✔ **Nǐ jǐ yuè jǐ hào zǒu?** (*nee jee yweh jee how dzoe;* When are you leaving?)

✔ **Wǒ wǔ yuè sānshí hào zǒu.** (*waw woo yweh sahn shir how dzoe;* I'm leaving on May 30th.)

✔ **Nǐ jǐ yuè jǐ hào qù Měiguó?** (*nee jee yweh jee how chyew may gwaw;* When will you be going to America?)

✔ **Wǒ sān yuè yī hào qù Měiguó.** (*waw sahn yweh ee how chyew may gwaw;* I'm going to America on March 1st.)

Bet you can't wait to start making those travel plans now. Which brings me to my next point . . .

Celebrating the Chinese Holidays

You may want to time your trip to mainland China, Taiwan, or Hong Kong to coincide with certain holidays — or, just as important, to avoid certain days and weeks.

First you celebrate **xīnnián** (*shin nyan;* New Year's Day; also known as **yuándàn;** *ywan dahn*) on **yī yuè yī hào** (*ee yweh ee how;* January 1st), in addition to a three-day celebration coinciding with the lunar New Year known as **chūn jié** (*chwun jyeh;* Spring Festival, or Chinese New Year). Every year the dates for **chūn jié** change because — you guessed it — it follows the **yīnlì** (*yeen lee;* lunar calendar) rather than the **yánglì** (*yahng lee;* solar calendar). **Chūn jié** always occurs sometime in January or February.

If you travel to China **jīn nián** (*jin nyan;* this year) during 2005, you arrive during **jǐ nián** (*jee nyan;* the Year of the Rooster). Want to travel in the coming years instead?

✔ 2006: **gǒu nián** (*go nyan*), Year of the Dog

✔ 2007: **zhū nián** (*joo nyan*), Year of the Pig

✔ 2008: **shǔ nián** (*shoo nyan*), Year of the Rat

The Year of the Rat is actually the beginning of a whole new 12-year cycle of animals. Table 15-1 shows all the animals of the Chinese zodiac. Just as in Western astrology, each of the Chinese animals represents a different personality type.

Table 15-1	Animals of the Chinese Zodiac	
Chinese Word	*Pronunciation*	*English Word*
shǔ	shoo	Rat
niú	nyo	Ox
hǔ	hoo	Tiger
tù	too	Rabbit
lóng	loong	Dragon
shé	shuh	Snake
mǎ	mah	Horse
yáng	yahng	Goat
hóu	ho	Monkey
jī	jee	Rooster
gǒu	go	Dog
zhū	joo	Pig

In mainland China, **Láodòng jié** (*laow doong jyeh;* Labor Day) is celebrated on **wǔ yuè yī hào** (*woo yweh ee how;* May 1st), and **Guó qìng jié** (*gwaw cheeng jyeh;* National Day) is celebrated on **shí yuè yī hào** (*shir yweh ee how;* October 1st) in commemoration of the day Mao Zedong and the Chinese Communist Party declared the founding of **Zhōnghuá rénmín gònghé guó** (*joong hwah run meen goong huh gwaw;* the People's Republic of China) in 1949. In Taiwan, **Guó qìng jié** is celebrated on **shí yuè shí hào** (*shir yweh shir how;* October 10th) to commemorate the day in 1911 when China's long dynastic history ended and a new era of **Zhōnghuá mín guó** (*joong hwah meen gwaw;* the Republic of China) began, under the leadership of Dr. Sun Yat-sen.

National Day in Taiwan is often referred to as **shuāng shí jié** (*shwahng shir jyeh; literally:* double 10 day), because it occurs on the 10th day of the 10th month.

In Taiwan, you often see years written out that seem to be 11 years short of what you think is correct. That's because the founding of the Republic of China in 1911 is considered the base line for all future years. So 1921 is listed as **mín guó shí nián** (*meen gwaw shir nyan;* "meen gwaw" is the abbreviation for **Zhōnghuá mín guó** [*joong hwah meen gwaw*], or the Republic of China, and "shir nyan," meaning 10 years, refers to 10 years following the founding of the Republic of China). The year 2005 is noted as **mín guó jiǔshí sì nián** (*meen gwaw jyo shir suh nyan;* 94 years after the establishment of the Republic of China).

In addition to the major public holidays worthy of closing down businesses, you may want to experience some of the other fun and interesting Chinese holidays first-hand:

- **Yuánxiāo jié** (*ywan shyaow jyeh;* The Lantern Festival) is celebrated on the 15th day of the lunar New Year. It marks the end of **chūn jié** (*chwun jyeh;* Spring Festival). Folks display colorful and creative lanterns on the street and eat boiled dumplings with glutinous rice and red bean paste.

- **Qīngmíng jié** (*cheeng meeng jyeh;* The Clear and Bright Festival) takes place in April to honor one's ancestors by sweeping their graves and burning incense and paper money for their use in the next world. This holiday is primarily celebrated in Taiwan, where you can still see entire families having veritable picnics on the graves of their ancestors, which are often located along the sides of hills and mountains.

- **Duānwǔ jié** (*dwan woo jyeh;* The Dragon Boat Festival) occurs on the fifth day of the fifth lunar month and always features a real dragon boat race (well, as real as a dragon can be on a boat, that is). It commemorates the life and, more specifically, the death of China's first great poet, Qu Yuan, who lived during the Warring States (475–221 BCE) period. He drowned himself in the Milo River in Hunan Province while exiled after failing to persuade the king to adequately defend the country. On **Duānwǔ jié,** people eat sticky rice wrapped in grape leaves known as **zòngzi** (*dzoong dzuh*).

- **Zhōngqiū jié** (*joong chyo jyeh;* The Mid-autumn Festival) is celebrated on the 15th day of the 8th lunar month as a kind of harvest festival, when families get together and everyone eats **yuèbǐng** (*yweh beeng;* moon cakes) — round pastries with lotus seeds. Everyone takes a moment to really look at the moon on this evening — the subject of much Chinese classical poetry.

All sorts of folk festivals take place in villages throughout mainland China and Taiwan when you least expect them, so if you suddenly find yourself surrounded by a throng of jovial, clapping, and singing people, just follow the crowd and see where the action takes you. You won't be disappointed. Even funeral processions can be the most fascinating and musical of events, with mourners dressed in white sackcloth playing all manner of wind and percussion instruments.

Where Do You Want to Travel?

So, now that you know the time you plan to **lǚyóu** (*lyew yo;* travel), I can't wait to finally ask you: **Nǐ xiǎng dào nǎr qù?** (*nee shyahng daow nar chyew;* Where do you want to go?) Planning a trip to **Yàzhōu** (*yah joe;* Asia), **Fēizhōu** (*fay joe;* Africa), **Ōuzhōu** (*oh joe;* Europe), or **Měizhōu** (*may joe;* the Americas)? Will your voyage be **zài guó nèi** (*dzye gwaw nay;* within the country; domestic) or **zài guó wài** (*dzye gwaw why;* outside the country)? Table 15-2 shows some countries you may **xuǎnzé** (*shwan dzuh;* choose) to visit.

Table 15-2	Places to Visit Around the Globe	
Chinese Word	*Pronunciation*	*English Word*
Jiānádà	jyah nah dah	Canada
Zhōngguó dàlù	joong gwaw dah loo	Mainland China
Fǎguó	fah gwaw	France
Déguó	duh gwaw	Germany
Xiānggǎng	shyahng gahng	Hong Kong
Xiōngyálì	shyoong yah lee	Hungary
Àiěrlán	eye are lahn	Ireland
Yǐsèliè	ee suh lyeh	Israel
Rìběn	ir bun	Japan
Mòxīgē	maw she guh	Mexico
Éguó	uh gwaw	Russia
Nánfēi	nahn fay	South Africa
Ruìshì	rway shir	Switzerland
Ruìdiǎn	rway dyan	Sweden
Táiwān	tye wahn	Taiwan
Tǎnsāngníyà	tahn sahng nee yah	Tanzania
Yuènán	yweh nahn	Vietnam
Zāyǐěr	zah ee are	Zaire

Depending on the type of activities you enjoy doing while on vacation, you may want to consider traveling to a place that has plenty of the following features (or at least one special one to make it well worth the trip):

- **hǎitān** (*hi tahn;* beach)
- **shān** (*shahn;* mountain)
- **shāmò** (*shah maw;* desert)
- **zhíwùyuán** (*jir woo ywan;* botanical gardens)
- **xióngmāo** (*shyoong maow;* pandas)
- **yóuliè** (*yo lyeh;* safari)
- **tǎ** (*tah;* pagoda)
- **fó miào** (*faw myaow;* Buddhist temple)
- **mótiāndàlóu** (*maw tyan dah lo;* skyscraper)
- **gǔdǒngdiàn** (*goo doong dyan;* antique shop)
- **měishùguǎn** (*may shoo gwahn;* art gallery)
- **xìyuàn** (*she ywan;* theatre)

Unless you're the type who thrives on danger and excitement (or works for a relief agency), try to avoid places where the following natural phenomena occur:

- **táifēng** (*tye fung;* typhoon)
- **hànzāi** (*hahn dzye;* drought)
- **dìzhèn** (*dee juhn;* earthquake)
- **huǒzāi** (*hwaw dzye;* fire)
- **shuǐzāi** (*shway dzye;* flood)
- **yǔjì** (*yew jee;* rainy season)

Planning to travel **cóng** (*tsoong;* from) **Xiōngyálì** (*shyoong yah lee;* Hungary) **dào** (*daow;* to) **Xiānggǎng** (*shyahng gahng;* Hong Kong) anytime soon? How about **cóng Rìběn** (*tsoong ir bun;* from Japan) **dào Mòxīgē** (*daow maw she guh;* to Mexico) instead? Wherever you travel, you always go **cóng** one place **dào** another. Here are some good phrases to know when you tell people about your upcoming travel plans, using the **cóng . . . dào** pattern:

- **Wǒ cóng Niǔyuē dào Jiāzhōu qù.** (*waw tsoong nyo yweh daow jyah joe chyew;* I'm going from New York to California.)
- **Tā míngtiān cóng Yǐsèliè dào Ruìdiǎn qù.** (*tah meeng tyan tsoong ee suh lyeh daow rway dyan chyew;* She's going from Israel to Sweden tomorrow.)

✔ **Nĭmen shénme shíhòu cóng Zhōngguó dào zhèr lái?** (*nee mun shum-muh shir ho tsoong joong gwaw daow jar lye;* When are you all coming here from China?)

✔ **Cóng Nánfēi dào Zāyĭĕr duō cháng shíjiān?** (*tsoong nahn fay daow zah ee are dwaw chahng shir jyan;* How long does it take to get from South Africa to Zaire?)

Talkin' the Talk

Páng Lăoshī (*pahng laow shir;* Professor Pang) asks his American student, Kristina, where she plans to go during the upcoming winter vacation, because she has already been in Tianjin studying Chinese for four months.

Páng Lăoshī: **Kristina, nĭ hán jià de shíhòu xiăng qù năr?**
Kristina, nee hahn jyah duh shir ho shyahng chyew nar?
Kristina, where do you plan on going during the winter vacation?

Kristina: **Yīnwèi wŏ yĭjīng zài Tiānjīn sì ge yuè le, suŏyĭ wŏ xiăng zuì zhōng qù Fēizhōu kànkàn.**
Een way waw ee jeeng dzye tyan jeen suh guh yweh luh, swaw yee waw shyahng dzway joong chyew fay joe kahn kahn.
Because I've already been in Tianjin for four months, I'd finally like to go to Africa to have a look.

Páng Lăoshī: **Fēizhōu! Nèmme yuán. Wèishénme yào qù nàr?**
Fay joe! Nummuh ywan. Way shummuh yaow chyew nar?
Africa! So far away. Why do you want to go there?

Kristina: **Yīnwèi dōngtiān de shíhòu Tiānjīn tài lĕng. Érqiĕ zài Fēizhōu kĕyĭ cānjiā yóuliè!**
Een way doong tyan duh shir ho tyan jeen tye lung. Are chyeh dzye fay joe kuh yee tsahn jyah yo lyeh!
Because winters in Beijing are too cold. What's more, in Africa I can take part in a safari!

Páng Lăoshī: **Cóng Yàzhōu dào Fēizhōu zuò fēijī jĭge xiăoshí?**
Tsoong yah joe daow fay joe dzwaw fay jee jee guh shyaow shir?
How many hours is it from Asia to Africa by plane?

Kristina:	**Cóng Tiānjīn dào Tǎnsāngníyà yào chàbùduō shísān ge xiǎoshí.**
	Tsoong tyan jeen daow tahn sahng nee yah yaow chah boo dwaw shir sahn guh shyaow shir.
	From Tianjin to Tanzania it takes about 13 hours.
Páng Lǎoshī:	**Qǐng dài huí lái hěn duō xiàngpiàn gěi wǒ kànkàn.**
	Cheeng dye hway lye hun dwaw shyahng pyan gay waw kahn kahn.
	Please bring back lots of pictures to show me.
Kristina:	**Yídìng huì.**
	Ee deeng hway.
	I certainly will.

Words to Know

hán jià	hahn jyah	winter vacation
shǔ jià	shoo jyah	summer vacation
fàng jià	fahng jyah	to take a vacation
yóulǎn	yo lahn	to sightsee
zhōngyú	joong yew	finally
érqiě	are chyeh	moreover

Passports and visas: Don't leave home without 'em

Surprise! Actually, it should come as no surprise that you need a valid **hùzhào** (*hoo jaow;* passport) and a **qiānzhèng** (*chyan juhng;* visa) if you want to enter mainland China or Taiwan. (For more on passports, visas, and navigating your way around airports, see Chapter 14.) And if you plan on visiting a couple of different countries in the region for any length of time, you may need a couple of different **qiānzhèng** to go with each destination. Check to see what regulations apply before you board your **fēijī** (*fay jee;* airplane), or you may have the shortest vacation experience of your life.

Check out Chapter 13 for hotel tips after you get where you're going.

Packing for Your Trip

Are you the type who likes to **zhuāngrù** (*jwahng roo;* pack) everything under the **tàiyáng** (*tye yahng;* sun) in three different pieces of oversized **xíngli** (*sheeng lee;* luggage) before a trip? Or are you more the **bēibāo** (*bay baow;* backpack) type, content to take only the bare essentials? Either way, you have to prepare your bags in advance if you want to qualify them as **shǒutí xíngli** (*show tee sheeng lee;* carry-on luggage) or **tuōyùn xíngli** (*twaw yewn sheeng lee;* checked luggage).

What should you pack for a trip to the **hǎitān** (*hi tahn;* beach)? Maybe some of the following items:

- **yóuyǒngyī** (*yo yoong ee;* bathing suit)
- **tàiyáng yǎnjìng** (*tye yahng yan jeeng;* sunglasses)
- **duǎn kù** (*dwahn koo;* shorts)
- **liángxié** (*lyahng shyeh;* sandals)

No matter where you plan to go, you should pack some of these items:

- **yáshuā** (*yah shwah;* toothbrush)
- **yágāo** (*yah gaow;* toothpaste)
- **huàzhuāng pǐn** (*hwah jwahng peen;* makeup)
- **chúchòu jì** (*choo cho jee;* deodorant)
- **shuāzi** (*shwah dzuh;* brush)
- **shùkǒu shuǐ** (*shoo ko shway;* mouthwash)
- **nào zhōng** (*naow joong;* alarm clock)
- **guāhú dāo** (*gwah hoo daow;* razor)
- **wèi shēng jīn** (*way shung geen;* sanitary napkins)
- **yuèjīng yòng miánsāi** (*yweh jeeng yoong myan sye;* tampons)
- **féizào** (*fay dzaow;* soap)
- **zhàoxiàng jī** (*jaow shyahng jee;* camera)
- **zhuǎnjiē qì** (*jwahn jyeh chee;* adaptor)
- **yùndǒu** (*yewn doe;* iron)
- **yǔsǎn** (*yew sahn;* umbrella)

Talkin' the Talk

Chén Xiānshēng (*chun shyan shung;* Mr. Chen) and **Chén Tàitài** (*chun tye tye;* Mrs. Chen) are deciding what to pack for a trip to Hong Kong in October.

Chén Xiānshēng:
Wǒmen yīng bùyīnggāi bǎ yǔsǎn zhuāngrù xǐngli?
Waw men eeng boo eeng guy bah yew sahn jwahng roo sheeng lee?
Should we pack an umbrella (in the suitcase)?

Chén Tàitài:
Búyòng le. Xiānggǎng de tiānqì shíyuè fèn hěn hǎo.
Boo yoong luh. Shyahng gahng duh tyan chee shir yweh fun hun how.
There's no need to. The weather in Hong Kong in October is real nice.

Chén Xiānshēng:
Duǎn kù ne?
Dwahn koo nuh?
How about shorts then?

Chén Tàitài:
Duǎn kù dàgài yě búyào. Shíyuè fèn de tiānqì yǒu yīdiǎn lěng.
Dwahn koo dah gye yeah boo yaow. Shir yweh fun duh tyan chee yo ee dyan luhng.
You probably don't need to pack shorts. The weather in October is a little cool.

Chén Xiānshēng:
Nà, wǒmen dàodǐ yào zhuāng shénme dōngxi?
Nah, waw men daow dee yaow jwahng shum-muh doong she?
Well, then, what in the world should we pack?

Chén Tàitài:
Wǒmen jiù bǎ yáshuā hé zhàoxiàng jī zhuāngrù xǐnglǐ jiù wǎn le.
Waw men jyo bah yah shwah huh jaow shyahng jee jwahng roo sheeng lee jyo wahn luh.
Just a toothbrush and a camera, that's it.

Chén Xiānshēng:
Nǐ yídìng kāi wán xiào ba!
Nee ee deeng kye wahn shyaow bah!
You've got to be kidding!

Words to Know

kāi wán xiào	kye wahn shyaow	just kidding
jiù wán le	jyo wahn luh	that's all
dàodǐ	daow dee	in the end; after all
dàgài	dah gye	probably
búyòng le	boo yoong luh	it's not necessary

 The sentence structure for the verb **zhuāng** (*jwahng;* to pack) is: **bǎ *A* zhuāngrù *B*,** which translates into "pack *A* into *B*," even though the word for "pack" comes in between what you're packing (*A*) and what you pack it into (*B*).

Enlisting the Help of a Travel Agency

Think you can handle traipsing around the world without an advance plan or hotel reservations? Think again. China, for example, is one country you should travel to as part of a **guānguāng tuán** (*gwahn gwahng twahn;* tour group). If you don't like the idea of group travel, you should at least make advance reservations for hotels and domestic travel and even for your own private **dǎoyóu** (*daow yo;* tour guide) through a **lǚxíngshè** (*lyew sheeng shuh;* travel agency). Remember, you generally hear no **Yīngyǔ** (*eeng yew;* English) spoken anywhere in China.

Talkin' the Talk

 Daisy and Michael discuss their travel plans with a local travel agent, Miss Lǐ, in Hong Kong.

Miss Lǐ: **Nǐmen hǎo. Wǒ néng bāng shénme máng?**
Nee men how. Waw nung bahng shummuh mahng?
Hello. How may I be of help?

Daisy: **Wǒmen hěn xiǎng qù Zhōngguó dàlù. Néng bùnéng yùdìng yíge lǚguǎn?**
Waw men hun shyahng chyew joong gwaw dah loo. Nung boo nung yew deeng ee guh lyew gwahn?

We're very interested in traveling to mainland China. Would you be able to reserve hotels for us in advance?

Miss Lǐ: **Méiyǒu wèntǐ. Nǐmen shénme shíhòu yào zǒu?**
Mayo one tee. Nee mun shummuh shir ho yaow dzoe?
No problem. When would you like to go?

Michael: **Tīngshuō wǔ yuè fèn de tiānqì zuì hǎo.**
Teeng shwaw woo yweh fun duh tyan chee dzway how.
I've heard the weather in May is the best.

Miss Lǐ: **Duì le. Wǒ yě jiànyì nǐmen gēn yíge guānguāng tuán yíkuàr qù.**
Dway luh. Waw yeah jyan ee nee mun gun ee guh gwahn gwahng twan ee kwar chyew.
That's correct. I also suggest you go with a tour group.

Daisy: **Wèishénme?**
Way shummuh?
Why?

Miss Lǐ: **Guānguāng tuán yǒu shuō Yīngyǔ de dǎoyóu hé yóulǎnchē. Nà zuì fāngbiàn.**
Gwahn gwahng twahn yo shwaw eeng yew duh daow yo huh yo lahn chuh. Nah dzway fahng byan.
Tour groups have an English-speaking tour guide and a sightseeing bus. That's the most convenient way to go.

Michael: **Hǎo. Juédìng le.**
How. Jweh deeng luh.
Okay. It's decided.

Words to Know

guānguāng tuán	gwahn gwahng twahn	tour group
dǎoyóu	daow yo	tour guide
lǚxíng	lyew sheeng	travel
lǚxíng dàilǐrén	lyew sheeng dye lee run	travel agent
lǚxíngshè	lyew sheeng shuh	travel agency
yùdìng	yew deeng	to make a reservation
yóulǎnchē	yo lahn chuh	sightseeing bus
qǔxiāo fèi	chyew shyaow fay	cancellation fee
juédìng le	jweh deeng luh	it's decided
fāngbiàn	fahng byan	convenient
jiànyì	jyan ee	to suggest

Fun & Games

Fill in the missing words with one of the three possible answers under each sentence. See Appendix C for the answers.

1. **Wǒmen jīnnián qù** _____. (This year we're going to Ireland.)

   a. Àiěrlán

   b. Éguó

   c. Nánfēi

2. **Tāmen** _____ **zǒu.** (They're leaving on June 8th.)

   a. sì yuè wǔ hào

   b. wǔ yuè jiǔ hào

   c. liù yuè bā hào

3. **Wǒmen yídìng yào kàn** _____. (We definitely want to see Buddhist Temples.)

   a. xióngmāo

   b. fó miào

   c. yóuliè

4. **Bié wàngle zhuāngrù** _____. (Don't forget to pack a toothbrush.)

   a. yáshuā

   b. yágāo

   c. huàzhuāng pǐn

5. **Méiyǒu wèntǐ.** _____. (No problem. Just kidding.)

   a. Juédìng le

   b. Kāi wǎn xiào

   c. Jiù wǎn le

Chapter 16

Handling Emergencies

. . . .

In This Chapter

▶ Yelling for help

▶ Visiting your doctor

▶ Going to the authorities

▶ Looking for legal advice

. . . .

*Y*ou can easily plan the fun and exciting things you want to experience while you travel or go out with friends, but you can't predict needing to call the police to report a theft or rushing to an emergency room with appendicitis on your trip to the Great Wall. Such things can and do happen, and this chapter gives you the language tools you need to communicate your problems during your times of need.

Calling for Help in Times of Need

When you're faced with an emergency, the last way you want to spend your time is searching for an oversized Chinese-English dictionary to figure out how to quickly call for help. Try memorizing these phrases before a situation arises:

✔ **Jiù mìng!** (*jyo meeng;* Help; Save me!)

✔ **Zhuā zéi!** (*jwah dzay;* Stop, thief!)

✔ **Zháohuǒ lā!** (*jaow hwaw lah;* Fire!)

✔ **Jiào jiùhùchē!** (*jyaow jyo hoo chuh;* Call an ambulance!)

✔ **Jiào jǐngchá!** (*jyaow jeeng chah;* Call the police!)

Be careful when you say the words **jiào** (*jyow;* to call) and **jiù** (*jyo;* to save) in the phrases above. You don't want to mistakenly ask someone to save the police when you want him to call the police.

Sometimes you have to ask for someone who speaks English. Here are some phrases you can quickly blurt out during emergencies:

- **Nǐ shuō Yǐngwén ma?** (*nee shwaw eeng one mah;* Do you speak English?)

- **Wǒ xūyào yíge jiǎng Yǐngwén de lùshǐ.** (*waw shyew yaow ee guh jyahng eeng one duh lyew shir;* I need a lawyer who speaks English.)

- **Yǒu méiyǒu jiǎng Yǐngwén de dàifu?** (*yo mayo jyahng eeng one duh dye foo;* Are there any English-speaking doctors?)

When you finally get someone on the line who can help you, you need to know what to say to get immediate help:

- **Wǒ bèi rén qiǎng le.** (*waw bay run chyahng luh;* I've been robbed.)

- **Yǒu rén shòu shāng le.** (*yo run show shahng luh;* People are injured.)

- **Wǒ yào huì bào yíge chē huò.** (*waw yaow hway baow yee guh chuh hwaw;* I'd like to report a car accident.)

Word to the wise: Chinese people don't have O-negative blood, so Chinese hospitals don't store it. If you have a medical emergency in China that requires O-negative blood, you should check directly with your country's nearest Embassy or Consulate for help. You may need to be airlifted out to get the appropriate care. You may also want to take your own hypodermic needles in case you need an injection, because you can't guarantee that the needles you may come across are sterilized. Better safe than sorry away from home.

Receiving Medical Care

It's everyone's greatest nightmare — getting sick and not knowing why or how to make it better. If you suddenly find yourself in the **yīyuàn** (*ee ywan;* hospital) or otherwise visiting an **yīshēng** (*ee shung;* doctor), you need to explain what ails you — often in a hurry. This may be easier said than done, especially if you have to explain yourself in Chinese (or help a Chinese-speaking victim who's having trouble communicating). You may not have the energy to remember both the pronunciation *and* the proper tone for the word you mean to use. You may want to say you're feeling kind of **tóuyūn** (*toe yewn;* dizzy), but if it comes out sounding like **tuōyùn** (*twaw yewn*) instead, you alert your caregiver that you're sending your luggage on ahead of you. You don't want your doctor to move on to the next patient. Use Table 16-1 to figure out how to say the basic body parts.

Table 16-1	Basic Body Parts	
Chinese Word	*Pronunciation*	*English Word*
shēntǐ	shun tee	Body
gēbo	guh baw	Arm
jiānbǎng	jyan bahng	Shoulder
shǒu	show	Hand
shǒuzhǐ	show jir	Finger
tuǐ	tway	Leg
jiǎo	jyaow	Foot
tóu	toe	Head
bózi	baw dzuh	Neck
xiōng	shyoong	Chest
bèi	bay	Back
liǎn	lyan	Face
yǎnjīng	yan jeeng	Eye
ěrduō	are dwaw	Ear
bízi	bee dzuh	Nose
hóulóng	ho loong	Throat
gǔtóu	goo toe	Bone
jīròu	jee row	Muscles
shénjīng	shun jeeng	Nerves
fèi	fay	Lungs
gān	gahn	Liver
shèn	shun	Kidney
xīn	shin	Heart
dùzi	doo dzuh	Stomach

When you travel, don't forget to bring your prescription medicines. Carry them in a separate carry-on bag or in your purse. You don't want to pack them in a piece of check-in luggage, never to be seen again if the luggage gets lost.

Unless you're in a big city like Beijing or Shanghai, if you get seriously ill while staying in mainland China, your best bet is to fly to Hong Kong or back home for medical care. Don't forget to check into evacuation insurance before you go.

Finding a doctor

If your **yùnqì** (*yewn chee;* luck) is good, you'll never need to use any of the phrases I present in this chapter. If you end up running **dǎoméi** (*daow may;* out of luck), however, keep reading. Even if you've never **chōuyān** (*cho yan;* smoked) a day in your life, you can still develop **késòu** (*kuh so;* a cough) or even **qìguǎnyán** (*chee gwahn yan;* bronchitis). Time to see a **yīshēng** (*ee shung;* doctor).

Talkin' the Talk

Dàlín and his wife, Miǎn, are on their first trip back to China in 20 years. Miǎn becomes concerned about a sudden onset of dizziness. The two discuss her symptoms.

Dàlín: **Nǐ zěnme bùshūfu?**
Nee dzummuh boo shoo foo?
What's wrong?

Miǎn: **Wǒ gǎnjué bùshūfu kěshì bù zhīdào wǒ déle shénme bìng.**
Waw gahn jweh boo shoo foo kuh shir boo jir daow waw duh luh shummuh beeng.
I don't feel well, but I don't know what I have.

Dàlín: **Nǐ fā shāo ma?**
Nee fah shaow mah?
Are you running a fever?

Miǎn: **Méiyǒu, dànshì wǒ tóuyūn. Yěxǔ wǒ xūyào kàn nèikē yīshēng.**
Mayo, dahn shir waw toe yewn. Yeh shyew waw shyew yaow kahn nay kuh ee shung.
No, but I feel dizzy. Perhaps I need to see an internist.

Dàlín calls the nearest medical clinic to make an appointment and then returns to Miǎn.

Dàlín:	**Wǒ jīntiān xiàwǔ sān diǎn zhōng yuē le yíge shíjiān. Nǐ zuì hǎo zànshí zuò xiàlái.**
	Waw jin tyan shyah woo sahn dyan joong yweh luh ee guh shir jyan. Nee dzway how dzahn shir dzwaw shyah lye.
	I've made an appointment for 3 p.m. this afternoon. In the meantime, you'd better sit down for a while.

Words to Know

kànbìng	kahn beeng	to see a doctor
yīshēng	ee shung	doctor
yáyī	yah ee	dentist
hùshì	hoo shir	nurse
bìngrén	beeng run	patient

Although verbs don't express tense in Chinese, you often connect them to things called *aspect markers,* which come directly after the verb and indicate the degree of completion of an action. The aspect markers **"xiàlái"** *(shyah lye)* and **"xiàqù"***(shyah chyew)* are two such examples. **Xiàlái** refers to an action that slowly turns into a non-action or a calmer state, such as **"zuò** *(dzwaw)* **xiàlái"** (meaning to sit down and rest) in the previous Talkin' the Talk section. **Xiàqù** refers to continuing action.

Describing what ails you

Did your doctor say those magic words: **Méi shénme** *(may shummuh;* It's nothing)? Yeah, neither did mine. Too bad. Maybe you're just now checking your old **wēndùjì** *(one doo jee;* thermometer) and finding out, **"Wǒ fā shāo le!"** *(waw fah shaow luh;* I have a fever!) **Āiya!** *(eye yah;* Oh my goodness!) Time to figure out what the problem is. Whether you make a sudden trip to the **jízhěnshì** *(jee jun shir;* emergency room) or take a normal visit to a private doctor's office, you'll probably field the same basic questions about insurance and your symptoms. Table 16-2 lists some symptoms you may have.

Table 16-2	Common Medical Symptoms	
Chinese Phrase	*Pronunciation*	*English Phrase*
pàngle	pahng luh	Put on weight
shòule	show luh	Lose weight
fāshāo	fah shaow	To have a fever
lādùzi	lah doo dzuh	Diarrhea
biànmì	byan mee	Constipation
ěxīn	uh sheen	Nauseous
hóulóng téng	ho loong tung	Sore throat
tóuténg	toe tung	Headache
wèi tòng	way toong	Stomachache
bèi tòng	bay toong	Backache
ěr tòng	are toong	Earache
yá tòng	yah toong	Toothache
xiàntǐ zhǒngle	shyan tee joong luh	Swollen glands

Your doctor has a laundry list of inspections she must perform when you hit the check-up table:

- ✔ **Qǐng juǎnqǐ nǐde xiùzi.** (*cheeng jwan chee nee duh shyo dzuh;* Please roll up your sleeve.)

- ✔ **Wǒ yòng tīngzhěnqì tīng yíxià nǐde xīnzàng.** (*waw yoong teeng jun chee teeng ee shyah nee duh shin dzahng;* I'm going to use a stethoscope to listen to your heart.)

- ✔ **Shēn hūxī.** (*shun hoo she;* Take a deep breath.)

- ✔ **Bǎ zuǐ zhāngkāi.** (*bah dzway jahng kye;* Open your mouth.)

- ✔ **Bǎ shétóu shēn chūlái.** (*bah shuh toe shun choo lye;* Stick out your tongue.)

- ✔ **Wǒmen huàyàn yíxià xiǎobiàn.** (*waw men hwah yan ee shyah shyaow byan;* Let's have your urine tested.)

Fighting off air pollution in China

Air pollution is a serious problem in mainland China, so if you have respiratory conditions such as asthma and chronic bronchitis, you should wear a facemask in big cities and dusty back roads. Although immunizations aren't required for travel to China, make sure your tetanus shots are up to date, and check with your doctor about a Hepatitis B vaccine if you plan an extended stay.

Talkin' the Talk

Kristina shows up for her appointment to see Huò Dàifu (Dr. Huo). Because this is her first visit to Dr. Huo, the **jiēdàiyuán** (*jyeh dye ywan;* receptionist) needs her to fill out some forms before she sees the doctor to discuss her symptoms.

Jiēdàiyuán: **Nǐ shì lái kànbìng de ma?**
Nee shir lye kahn beeng duh mah?
Have you come to see a doctor?

Kristina: **Shì de.**
Shir duh.
Yes.

Jiēdàiyuán: **Yǒu méiyǒu yīliáo bǎoxiǎn?**
Yo mayo ee lyaow baow shyan?
Do you have any medical insurance?

Kristina: **Yǒu.**
Yo.
Yes, I do.

Jiēdàiyuán: **Hǎo. Qǐng tián yíxià zhèi zhāng biǎo.**
How. Cheeng tyan ee shyah jay jahng byaow.
Alright. Please fill out this form.

A short while later, the receptionist introduces Kristina to a **hùshì** (*hoo shir;* nurse) who plans to take her blood pressure.

Jiēdàiyuán: **Hùshì huì xiān liáng yíxià xuèyā.**
Hoo shir hway shyan lyahng ee shyah shweh yah.
The nurse will first take your blood pressure.

Hùshì: **Qǐng juǎnqǐ nǐde xiùzi.**
Cheeng jwan chee nee duh shyo dzuh.
Please roll up your sleeve.

Hùshì: **Hǎo. Huò Dàifu xiànzài gěi nǐ kànbìng.**
How. Hwaw dye foo shyan dzye gay nee kahn beeng.
Alright. Dr. Huo will see you now.

Kristina enters Dr. Huo's office, and after a few basic introductory
questions, Dr. Huo asks her what brings her to his office.

Huò Dàifu: **Yǒu shénme zhèngzhuàng?**
Yo shummuh juhng jwahng?
What sorts of symptoms do you have?

Kristina: **Wǒde hóulóng cóng zuótiān jiù tòngle.**
Waw duh ho loong tsoong dzwaw tyan jyo toong luh.
I've had this pain in my throat since yesterday.

Huò Dàifu: **Hǎo. Wǒ xiān yòng tīngzhěnqì tīng yíxià nǐde
xīnzàng.**
*How. Waw shyan yoong teng jun chee teeng ee
shyah nee duh shin dzahng.*
Alright. I'm first going to use a stethoscope to listen
to your heart.

Dr. Huo puts the stethoscope to Kristina's chest.

Huò Dàifu: **Shēn hūxī.**
Shun hoo she.
Take a deep breath.

Dr. Huo finishes listening with the stethoscope and takes out a
tongue depressor.

Huò Dàifu: **Qǐng bǎ zuǐ zhāngkāi, bǎ shétóu shēn chūlái . . . duì
le. Nǐde hóulóng hǎoxiàng yǒu yìdiǎn fāyán.**
*Cheeng bah dzway jahng kye, bah shuh to shun choo
lye . . . dway luh. Nee duh ho loong how shyahng yo
ee dyan fah yan.*
Please open your mouth and stick out your
tongue . . . yes. Your throat seems to be inflamed.

Words to Know

jiǎnchá	jyan chah	to examine
wǒ bùshūfu	waw boo shoo foo	I don't feel well
bìngle	beeng luh	to be sick
bìngrén	beeng run	patient
zháoliáng	jaow lyahng	to catch a cold
gǎnmào	gahn maow	to have a cold
shòushāng	show shahng	be injured
liúgǎn	lyo gahn	the flu
fāyán le	fah yan luh	it's inflamed
gāo xuěyā	gaow shweh yah	high blood pressure
bìng lì	beeng lee	medical history

Discussing your medical history

When you see a doctor for the first time, he or she will want to find out about your **bìng lì** (*beeng lee;* medical history). You'll hear the following query:

Nǐ jiā yǒu méiyǒu ____ de bìnglì? (*nee jyah yo mayo ___ duh beeng lee;* Does your family have any history of ___?)

Table 16-3 lists some of the more serious illnesses that hopefully neither you nor your family members have ever had.

Table 16-3	Serious Illnesses	
Chinese Word(s)	*Pronunciation*	*English Word(s)*
áizhèng	eye juhng	Cancer
fèi'ái	fay eye	Lung cancer

(continued)

Table 16-3 *(continued)*

Chinese Word(s)	Pronunciation	English Word(s)
qìchuǎnbìng	chee chwan beeng	Asthma
xīnzàng yǒu máobìng	shin dzahng yo maow beeng	Heart trouble
tángniàobìng	tahng nyaow beeng	Diabetes
àizībìng	eye dzuh beeng	AIDS
lìjí	lee jee	Dysentery
shuǐdòu	shway doe	Chicken pox
huòluàn	hwaw lwan	Cholera
jiǎxíng gānyán	jya sheeng gahn yan	Hepatitis A
yǐxíng gānyán	ee sheeng gahn yan	Hepatitis B
bǐngxíng gānyán	beeng sheeng gahn yan	Hepatitis C
fèi jiéhé	fay jyeh huh	Tuberculosis

Making a diagnosis

I bet you've heard stories about how doctors who use traditional medical techniques from ancient cultures can just take one look at a person and immediately know what ails them. The truth is, aside from simple colds and the flu, most doctors still need to take all kinds of tests to give a proper diagnosis. They may even need to perform the following tasks:

✔ **huà yàn** (*hwah yan;* lab tests)

✔ **xīndiàntú** (*shin dyan too;* electrocardiogram)

✔ **huàyàn yíxià xiǎobiàn** (*hwah yan ee shyah shyaow byan;* have your urine tested)

Talkin' the Talk

 Marland takes his daughter, Katherine, to the **yīshēng** (*ee shung;* doctor) after he notices her bad cough. The doctor takes her temperature and discusses what she may have with the family.

Yīshēng: **Katherine, hǎo xiāoxi! Nǐde tǐwēn zhèngcháng.**
Katherine, how shyaow she! Nee duh tee one juhng chahng.
Katherine, good news! Your temperature is normal.

Katherine: **Hǎo jí le.**
How jee luh.
Great.

Yīshēng: **Kěnéng zhǐ shì gǎnmào.**
Kuh nung jir shir gahn maow.
Perhaps it's just a little cold.

Marland: **Huì chuánrǎn ma?**
Hway chwahn rahn mah?
Is it contagious?

Yīshēng: **Bú huì.**
Boo hway.
No.

Katherine: **Yánzhòng ma?**
Yan joong mah?
Is it serious?

Yīshēng: **Bù yánzhòng. Nǐ zuì hǎo xiūxi jǐ tiān hē hěn duō shuǐ, jiù hǎo le.**
Boo yan joong. Nee dzway how shyow she jee tyan huh hun dwaw shway, jyo how luh.
No. You should rest for a few days and drink lots of liquids, and it should get better.

Marland: **Tā děi zài chuángshàng tǎng duōjiǔ?**
Tah day dzye chwahng shahng tahng dwaw jyo?
How long must she rest in bed?

Yīshēng: **Zuì hǎo liǎng sān tiān.**
Dzway how lyahng sahn tyan.
Ideally for two or three days.

In Chinese, you generally put a negative prefix, such as **bù** *(boo)*, in front of the verb you're negating. It sounds redundant in English to literally translate a response as "not serious" when someone asks about the seriousness of a situation. It's more colloquial and appropriate to translate it as "no," as you see in the previous Talkin' the Talk section when Katherine asks the doctor if her ailment is serious.

When you give approximate numbers or amounts, you don't need to use the word "or" (**huò zhe**), as in "three or four days." Just say the numbers right after each other to automatically imply the "or." For example, **wǔ liù ge rén** *(woo lyo guh run)* means "five or six people," and **sì wǔ tiān** *(suh woo tyan)* means "four or five days."

Words to Know

xiě/xuè	shyeh/shweh	blood
chōu xiě	cho shyeh	to draw blood
xuèyā	shweh yah	blood pressure
xiǎobiàn	shyaow byan	to urinate
dàbiàn	dah byan	to have a bowel movement
wēndù jì	one doo jee	thermometer
liáng tǐwēn	lyahng tee one	take one's temperature
màibó	my baw	pulse

Treating yourself to better health

Not everything can be cured with a bowl of **jī tāng** *(jee tahng;* chicken soup), despite what my grandmother told me. If your grandmother cooks as well as mine did, however, the soup couldn't hurt . . .

Your doctor may prescribe some **yào** *(yaow;* medicine) to make you feel better. After you **lǐn** *(leen;* fill) your **yàofāng** *(yaow fahng;* prescription), you may find the following instructions on the bottle:

❧ **Měi sìge xiǎoshí chī yícì.** (*may suh guh shyaow shir chir ee tsuh;* Take one tablet every four hours.)

❧ **Měi tiān chī liǎng cì, měi cì sān piàn.** (*may tyan chir lyahng tsuh, may tsuh sahn pyan;* Take three tablets, twice a day.)

❧ **Fàn hòu chī.** (*fahn ho chir;* Take after eating.)

Talkin' the Talk

Maxine talks to the **yàojìshī** (*yaow jee shir;* pharmacist) about her prescription and about curing a lingering cough of hers.

Maxine:	**Nín néng bùnéng gěi wǒ pèi hǎo zhèige yào?** *Neen nung boo nung gay waw pay how jay guh yaow?* Can you fill this prescription for me?
Yàojìshī:	**Kěyǐ.** *Kuh yee.* Yes, I can.
Maxine:	**Wǒ hái yào zhì késòu de yào.** *Waw hye yaow jir kuh so duh yaow.* I'd also like something for a cough.
Yàojìshī:	**Nǐ zuì hǎo chī késòu tángjiāng. Késòu yào yě kěyǐ.** *Nee dzway how chir kuh so tahng jyahng. Kuh so yaow yeah kuh yee.* Your best bet is to have some cough syrup. You can also have some cough drops.

Maxine looks at another medicine on the shelf and asks the pharmacist about it.

Maxine:	**Zhèige zěnme yàng?** *Jay guh dzummuh yahng?* How about this?
Yàojìshī:	(Laughing) **Bùxíng! Nà shì xièyào. Chúfēi nǐ yǒu biànmì, nà méiyòng!** *Boo sheeng! Nah shir shyeh yaow. Choo fay nee you byan mee, nah may yoong!* Definitely not! That's a laxative. Unless you're constipated, that won't be of any use!
Maxine:	**Bùhǎoyìsi!** *Boo how ee suh!* How embarrassing!

Words to Know

nà méiyòng	nah may yoong	that's useless
bùhǎoyìsi	boo how ee suh	how embarrassing
jiùhùchē	jyo hoo chuh	ambulance
zhēnjiǔ	juhn jyo	acupuncture
yào	yaow	medicine
Zhōng yào	joong yaow	Chinese medicine
Xī yào	she yaow	Western medicine
chī yào	chir yaow	to take medicine
yàofáng	yaow fahng	pharmacy
yàowán	yaow wahn	pill
kàngshēngsù	kahng shung soo	antibiotics
dǎ zhēn	dah juhn	injection
wàikē	why kuh	surgery
dòng shǒushù	doong show shoo	to undergo an operation
sǐ	suh	to die
zhěnliáosuǒ	juhn lyaow swaw	clinic
yīyuàn	ee ywan	hospital
dānjià	dahn jya	stretcher
jiùhùchē	jyo hoo chuh	ambulance
jízhěnshì	jee juhn shir	emergency room
kàngsuānyào	kahng swan yaow	antacid
āsīpǐlín	ah suh pee leen	aspirin
wéitāmìng	way tah meeng	vitamin
Wǒ duì qīngméisù guòmǐn	waw dway cheeng may soo gwaw meen	I'm allergic to penicillin

CULTURAL WISDOM

Sticking to acupuncture and herbal remedies

Chinese acupuncture and herbal medicine are gaining currency in places outside of China. Little wonder, because these remedies have proven their efficacy in China for over a thousand years. Herbal medicine remedies from the jungles and rain forests of rural China have helped every ailment from rheumatism to cancer, and healers often use them in conjunction with Western medicine these days. As for acupuncture, proper placement of needles in certain key points of the body has proven so useful in alleviating pain and in numbing patients that you can undergo major surgery without Western anesthesia.

Calling the Police

Ever have your pocketbook **tōu le** (*toe luh;* stolen)? Being a victim is an awful feeling, as I can tell you from experience. You feel **shēngqì** (*shung chee;* angry) at such a **kěpà** (*kuh pah;* scary) experience, especially if it happens in another country and the **zéi** (*dzay;* thief) **táopǎo** (*taow paow;* escapes) quickly.

I hope you're never the victim of a crime like theft (or something worse). Still, you should always be prepared with some key words you can use when the **jǐngchá** (*jeeng chah;* police) finally pull up in the **jǐngchē** (*jeeng chuh;* police car) and take you back to the **jǐngchájú** (*jeeng chah jyew;* police station) to identify a potential **zéi**. Hopefully the culprit will be **zhuā le** (*jwah luh;* arrested).

You may also find yourself in an emergency that doesn't involve you. If you ever witness an accident, here are some phrases you can relay to the police, emergency workers, or victims:

- **Tā bèi qìchē yàzháo le.** (*tah bay chee chuh yah jaw luh;* He was run over by a car.)
- **Tā zài liúxiě.** (*tah dzye lyo shyeh;* He's bleeding.)
- **Bié kū. Jǐngchá hé jiùhùchē láile.** (*byeh koo. jeeng chah huh jyo hoo chuh lye luh;* Don't cry. The police and the ambulance have arrived.)

Don't sweat the Chinese justice

Justice is meted out quickly in the People's Republic of China, often without recourse to appeals. Many times the crime ends in a death sentence carried out quickly, for everything from murder and rape to white collar type crimes and corruption. The flip side of the coin is that as far as tourism is concerned, foreigners rarely experience crime. China is considered an extremely safe place for tourists and business people alike. Policemen are always willing to help a lost foreigner in any city.

Acquiring Legal Help

Nine out of ten foreigners never need to look for a lawyer during a stay in China, which isn't as litigious a society as the United States, to be sure. If you do need a **lǜshī** (*lyew shir;* lawyer), however, your best bet is to check with your country's **dàshǐguǎn** (*dah shir gwahn;* Embassy) or **língshìguǎn** (*leeng shir gwahn;* Consulate) for advice.

It can be very **máf an** (*mah fun;* annoying) and stressful to have to deal with **lǜshī,** no matter what country you're in, but you have to admit — they do know the **fǎlǜ** (*fah lyew;* law). And if you have to go to **fǎyuàn** (*fah ywan;* court) for any serious **shìjiàn** (*shir jyan;* incident), you want the judge to **pànjué** (*pahn jweh;* make a decision) in your favor. Moral of the story: Good **lǜshī** are worth their weight in **jīn** (*gin;* gold), even if you still consider them **shāyú** (*shah yew;* sharks) in the end.

Identify the following body parts in Chinese. Check Appendix C for the answers.

1. Arm: _____

2. Shoulder: _____

3. Finger: _____

4. Leg: _____

5. Neck: _____

6. Chest: _____

7. Eye: _____

8. Ear: _____

9. Nose: _____

Part IV
The Part of Tens

The 5th Wave   By Rich Tennant

"Here's a recipe for Chinese Thousand Year Old Eggs. Thank *goodness* for microwave ovens."

In this part . . .

This part is short and sweet. It's also essential if you don't want to make all sorts of cultural faux pas when you start using your Chinese. I give you practical tips to keep in mind and Chinese expressions and phrases that make you sound like a native. Equally important, I give you 10 things to avoid doing when you're in China or with Chinese acquaintances. Dive right in. These chapters are fun!

Chapter 17

Ten Ways to Pick Up Chinese Quickly

This chapter contains ten good activities that can help speed up your Chinese learning curve. Having useful, easy-to-access, and easy-to-follow learning tools makes a big difference in your progress. And besides, you can have fun with them, too.

Listen to Chinese-Language Tapes, CDs, and CD-ROMs

Just imagine trying to figure out what Chinese tones sound like without actually hearing them spoken out loud. Kind of like imagining what Beethoven's Fifth sounds like based on a written description. Even if you read this book cover to cover, you'll be hard pressed to figure out just what the first, second, third, and fourth tones actually sound like unless you listen to the accompanying CD. Be creative with your discovery of the language (and your language listening) by picking up all the language tapes, CDs, and CD-ROMS you can find out there. Keep mimicking what you hear over and over again so that your pronunciation and intonation become better with each go-round. Pretty soon you'll be able to tell a native Mandarin speaker from a native Cantonese speaker.

Attend a Peking Opera Performance

Okay, I admit that the first time I attended a performance of Peking Opera, I wished I had brought a pair of ear plugs. The opera is an acquired taste to be sure. Kind of like caviar. But I recommend spending time cultivating an appreciation for it. Peking Opera originated in the late 1700s, when opera troupes originally staged performances for the royal family. Only later did it become such a public art, and now it's all the rage for any person who claims to appreciate Chinese culture. The makeup, costumes, cacophonous music, and stylized movements are predictable and much treasured by the Chinese people. Listening to Peking Opera not only helps you develop an appreciation for a great Chinese art form, but also fine-tunes your recognition of the pronunciation of standard Mandarin. You can even learn a few tunes at the same time. A win-win situation all around.

Cook with a Wok

You may be surprised what cooking with a wok can do for your Chinese. Not only do you start eating healthier, but because you're forced to visit some Asian food markets to gather the ingredients you need to cook with, you also soak in Chinese words by osmosis. Ever hear of **dòufu** *(doe foo)?* That means soy bean curd in Mandarin. How about bok choi? Okay, so that's Cantonese, but the Mandarin is **bái cài** *(bye tsye;* Chinese cabbage). The best traditional Chinese cooking, all done with a wok, puts you in the proper frame of mind to want to soak up some more Chinese language. Try following some recipes from a Chinese cookbook and repeat the names of the ingredients over and over, a sure fire way to speak more Chinese. And if you're not a great cook, get into the habit of eating at Chinese restaurants and mastering the names of at least ten dishes before the end of the meal.

Shop for Food in Chinatown

Mingle with the Mandarin-speaking masses while you attune your ear to the sounds and tones of Chinese. This is only one of the fun things to do in Chinatown, of course, but one worth doing often. Not only do you cultivate a good ear for Chinese, but you also become privy to the gestures that often go along with the sounds. (And you thought the Italians had cornered the market on hand gestures.)

Surf the Net

Tons of information on Chinese language and culture is only a mouse click away. Now that you're in the information age, take advantage of it. Everything from how to write Chinese characters to discovering Peking Opera is out there. Whatever motivated you to start speaking Chinese in the first place, the World Wide Web keeps you involved. Just do a quick search for places like Shanghai, Beijing, or Taipei or cultural keywords like wok or pagoda. You'll be amazed at what you can come up with.

Watch Kung-Fu Flicks

Bruce Lee is only the tip of the iceberg. Go to your local public library and ask to see the list of kung-fu movies. Everything from Hong Kong action films to mainland martial arts flicks — you should find them all there. Pick whatever interests you. Directors like Zhang Yimou and Chen Kaige have become famous around the world. (Okay, so they didn't direct kung-fu movies . . . but they're still worth checking out.)

The best way to grasp Chinese is to watch them over and over to see how many words and phrases you can pick up in one sitting. You soon become adept at anticipating which gestures go with which words, and you develop a great ear for all those tones.

Exchange Language Lessons

Finding a language partner has to be one of the best ways to pick up Chinese. Not only do you get to learn the language, but you also develop a friendship along the way. Tons of students come to the States every year from China. Whether you're in school at the moment or just live near one, you should have no problem putting up a sign offering a language exchange. And don't forget to ask your language partner to compare notes about Chinese and American culture. That's when the real fun begins.

Make Chinese Friends

Possibilities for meeting Chinese-speaking people are endless. Check out the cubicle next to you at your office or the desk ahead of you in class. Or how about the mother of the kid who's in your son's karate class? Wherever you go, you have a chance to make a new friend who not only knows Chinese, but who also can teach you a little about the culture. You may even find a new friend to see that kung-fu movie with or to help you navigate grocery shopping in Chinatown (not to mention how to use a wok after you buy all your food).

Study Chinese Calligraphy

Chinese calligraphy is one of the most beautiful art forms in the world. Why not pick up a brush and create those beautiful strokes yourself on rice paper? The whole ritual of preparing the ink and paper is an exercise in patience and meditation, and you get to appreciate the difficulty Chinese school children have in learning to write Chinese. You can discover how to write your name in Chinese (have your English name transliterated, because there's no alphabet in Chinese) and then practice writing those characters over and over until you can sign your name to a Chinese News Year's card and mail it to a friend.

Be Curious and Creative

If you look for opportunities to practice Chinese, I guarantee you can find them. Be imaginative. And stop worrying about failing. In fact, make as many mistakes as it takes so that you can make a mental note of what you should do or say differently the next time around. Give yourself a pat on the back every time you discover something new in Chinese or figure out a novel way to discover more about the Chinese language and people. Keep yakking away with the new words and phrases you find in *Chinese For Dummies* and enjoy watching the reactions on people's faces when you open your mouth.

Chapter 18

Ten Things Never to Do in China

In This Chapter

▶ Understanding Chinese etiquette

▶ Being gracious and humble in social situations

*T*his chapter may save you from certain embarrassment and possibly even outright humiliation one day. It gives you ten important tips on what not to do if you really want to win friends and make a good impression with your Chinese acquaintances. Take my tips to heart.

Never Accept a Compliment Graciously

You may find yourself at a loss for words when you compliment a Chinese host on a wonderful meal, and you get in response, "No, no, the food was really horrible." You hear the same thing when you tell a Chinese parent how smart or handsome his son is — he meets the compliment with a rebuff of "No, he's really stupid" or "He's not good looking at all." These people aren't being nasty . . . just humble and polite. Moral of the story here: Feign humility, even if it kills you! A little less boasting and fewer self-congratulatory remarks go a long way towards scoring cultural sensitivity points with the Chinese.

Never Make Someone Lose Face

The worst thing you can possibly do to Chinese acquaintances is publicly humiliate or otherwise embarrass them. Doing so makes them lose face. Don't point out a mistake in front of others or yell at someone.

The good news is that you can actually help someone gain face by complimenting them and giving credit where credit is due. Do this whenever the opportunity arises. Your graciousness is much appreciated.

Never Get Angry in Public

Public displays of anger are frowned upon by the Chinese and are most uncomfortable for them to deal with — especially if the people getting angry are foreign tourists, for example. This goes right along with making someone (usually the Chinese host) lose face, which you should avoid at all costs. The Chinese place a premium on group harmony, so foreigners should try to swallow hard, be polite, and cope privately.

Never Address People by Their First Names First

Chinese people have first and last names like everyone else. However, in China, the last name always comes first. The family (and the collective in general) always takes precedence over the individual. Joe Smith in Minnesota is known as Smith Joe (or the equivalent) in Shanghai. If a man is introduced to you as Lǐ Míng, you can safely refer to him as Mr. Lǐ (not Mr. Míng).

Unlike people in the West, the Chinese don't feel very comfortable calling each other by their first names. Only family members and a few close friends ever refer to the man above, for example, as simply "Míng." They may, however, add the prefix **lǎo** (*laow;* old) or **xiǎo** (*shyaow;* young) before the family name to show familiarity and closeness. **Lǎo Lǐ** (Old Lǐ) may refer to his younger friend as **Xiǎo Chén** (Young Chén).

Never Take Food with the Wrong End of Your Chopsticks

The next time you gather around a dinner table with a Chinese host, you may discover that serving spoons for the many communal dishes are non-existent. This is because everyone serves themselves (or others) by turning their chopsticks upside down to take food from the main dishes before putting the food on the individual plates.

Never Drink Alcohol Without First Offering a Toast

Chinese banquets include eight to ten courses of food and plenty of alcohol. Sometimes you drink rice wine, and sometimes you drink industrial strength Máo Tái, known to put a foreigner or two under the table in no time. One way to slow the drinking is to observe Chinese etiquette by always offering a toast to the host or someone else at the table before taking a sip yourself. This not only prevents you from drinking too much too quickly, but also shows your gratitude toward the host and your regard for the other guests. If someone toasts you with a **"gān bēi,"** *(gahn bay)* however, watch out.

Gān bēi means "bottoms up," and you may be expected to drink the whole drink rather quickly. Don't worry. You can always say **"shuí yì"** *(shway ee; as you wish)* in return and take just a little sip instead.

Never Let Someone Else Pay the Bill Without Fighting for It

Most Westerners are stunned the first time they witness the many fairly chaotic, noisy scenes at the end of a Chinese restaurant meal. The time to pay the bill has come and everyone is simply doing what they're expected to do — fight to be the one to pay it. The Chinese consider it good manners to vociferously and strenuously attempt to wrest the bill out of the very hands of whoever happens to have it. This may go on, back and forth, for a good few minutes, until someone "wins" and pays the bill. The gesture of being eager and willing to pay is always appreciated.

Never Show Up Empty Handed

Gifts are exchanged frequently between the Chinese, and not just on special occasions. If you have dinner in someone's house to meet a prospective business partner or for any other pre-arranged meeting, both parties commonly exchange gifts as small tokens of friendship and good will. Westerners are often surprised at the number of gifts the Chinese hosts give. The general rule of thumb is to bring many little (gender non-specific) gifts when you travel to China. You never know when you'll meet someone who wants to present you with a special memento, so you should arrive with your own as well.

Never Accept Food, Drinks, or Gifts Without First Refusing a Few Times

No self-respecting guests immediately accept whatever may be offered to them in someone's home. No matter how much they may be eager to accept the food, drink, or gift, proper Chinese etiquette prevents them from doing anything that makes them appear greedy or eager to receive it, so be sure to politely refuse a couple of times.

Never Take the First "No, Thank You" Literally

Chinese people automatically refuse food or drinks several times — even if they really feel hungry or thirsty. Never take the first "No, thank you" literally. Even if they say it once or twice, offer it again. A good guest is supposed to refuse at least once, but a good host is also supposed to make the offer at least twice.

Chapter 19

Ten Favorite Chinese Expressions

In This Chapter

▶ Sounding like a native

▶ Getting to know the lingo of daily life

Some English words and phrases are common expressions you hear repeatedly during the course of a day. The Chinese language is no different. It accommodates this tendency with tons of colorful expressions. Some expressions are known as **chéngyǔ** *(chung yew)* — four-character sayings — which help describe any given situation or put sentiments into words in a nutshell. Mastering these popular Chinese expressions and knowing when to use them helps you put a welcoming smile on the face of the native speaker when appropriate situations arise.

This chapter offers some idiomatic expressions that make you sound like a native. You hear these expressions all the time in typical daily situations.

Gōngxǐ Gōngxǐ

> *goong-she goong-she;* Congratulations!

You say **gōngxǐ gōngxǐ** for happy occasions when congratulations are in order.

"My wife just had a baby!" your friend says. "Wow! I didn't even know she was pregnant," you say. "**Gōngxǐ gōngxǐ!**"

Your brother finally passes the Bar Exam (on the third try). **Gōngxǐ gōngxǐ!**

Hey! You just turned 21. Now you can finally go to a bar. **Gōngxǐ gōngxǐ!** Let's go!

On the Chinese New Year, you hear not only **"gōngxǐ gōngxǐ,"** but also **"gōngxǐ fācái"** (goong she fah-tsye), which means "Congratulations and may you prosper."

Yí Lù Píng'ān

ee loo peeng ahn; Bon Voyage! Have a good trip.

This is a great phrase to use when a friend or acquaintance is about to embark on a long journey. When you see someone off at the airport, you hear many people say this. You may want to teach your family and friends **yí lù píng'ān** before you board the plane!

Yì Yán Nán Jìn

ee yan nahn jeen; It's a long story.

Maybe someone wants to know how you got that black eye. Maybe you don't really want to go into the details. Just say **yì yán nán jìn** to save the blow-by-blow description for when you're ready.

Mǎmǎ Hūhū

mah mah hoo hoo; So-so.

The phrase mǎmǎ hūhū literally means "horse horse tiger tiger." You use this expression when you want to indicate a situation is just okay or mediocre.

Just barely pass that test? You did **mǎmǎ hūhū.** Slightly under the weather today? You're feeling **mǎmǎ hūhū.** Food at that new restaurant not so great? It's just **mǎmǎ hūhū.**

Kāi Wán Xiào

kye (rhymes with pie) *wahn shyaow;* Just kidding, or You've got to be kidding!

You say **kāi wán xiào** when you can't believe your ears. Suppose your co-worker just told you she's been fired, even though she was promoted only a month ago. That definitely calls for a **kāi wán xiào** in response. When she finally tells you it's not true, she adds **kāi wán xiào** at the end. She was just kidding. (Now you're really angry.)

Máfan Nǐ

mah fahn nee; Sorry to trouble you.

You say **máfan nǐ** when, although you don't want to put anyone out, you politely accept an extended offer to do something for you. If you can't reach the salt at the other end of the dinner table and someone offers to pass it to you, you say **máfan nǐ.** It means, "So sorry to trouble you, but would you mind?"

You can also say something (or someone) is a real pain in the neck by proclaiming, **"Tā hěn máfan."** (He's really a pain, or it's really an inconvenient annoyance.)

Zěnme Yàng?

dzummuh yahng; How's it going, or what's up?

A great catch-all expression when you run into old friends and want to find out how they've been or what they're up to these days. You just say: Hey! **Zěnme yàng?**

You don't say it to a stranger or someone you've just met in a more formal situation, but it's a great expression to use between friends.

Another way you can use **zěnme** is by adding **"le"** in place of **"yàng"** at the end. **(Nǐ zěnme le?)** If you do, you say, "Hey, what's wrong with you?" Kind of like, "What could you possibly have been thinking when you did such a stupid thing?"

Qǐng Wèn

cheeng one; Please, may I ask; excuse me, but . . .

Before you ask a question, be polite and preface it with **qǐng wèn.** You're asking if you can even ask about something. You can use it when you go shopping and need to address a store clerk:

Qǐng wèn (Please, may I ask), how much is that thousand-year-old egg?

You can also use it when you need directions and have to approach a total stranger:

Qǐng wèn (Excuse me), which bus can take me to the Temple of Heaven?

Zìjǐ Lái

dzuh jee lye; I'll help myself, thanks.

The rules of Chinese eating etiquette dictate that you should never start to fill up your plate before at least attempting to serve someone else first. **Zìjǐ lái** is a polite expression you use to indicate that you can help yourself as soon as someone starts to serve you. A host always starts to serve the guests sitting closest, but the guests should always say **zìjǐ lái** (and then relent and let the person serve them anyway) for each and every course. After the host has started a dish, however, you may indeed begin to serve yourself.

And just as you should never serve yourself first, you should also never take even a sip of alcohol without at least toasting someone else first (see Chapter 18 for more things you should never do). For that, you can say **gānbēi!** (*gahn bay;* bottoms up!)

Āiyà!

eye yah; Oh my!

Āiyàs can be heard all over China whenever people feel frustrated, shocked, or even just plain old annoyed. You hear it when you show up to your parents' home for dinner with a friend who looks like he's in a punk rock band. You may even say it yourself when you realize you left your briefcase in the taxi, which is now halfway across town. And you definitely have an **āiyá** moment when you wonder how to look anything up in a Chinese dictionary after finding out that there's no alphabet.

Chapter 20

Ten Phrases That Make You Sound Chinese

In This Chapter

▶ Saying the right things in social situations

▶ Maintaining your humility and graciousness

This chapter gives you phrases that help your conversation for many social occasions. Knowing these phrases provides you with an authentic flavor of Chinese culture and hospitality. Use them liberally to fit right in with any crowd.

As you read this chapter, you may notice that the Chinese often repeat phrases. Repeating words happens often in spoken Chinese.

Huānyíng Huānyíng!

hwan yeeng hwan yeeng; Welcome!

You use this phrase when guests arrive at your home or in your country to make them feel right at home. And if you say **huānyíng zài lái** (*hwan yeeng dzye lye*) before they leave, it means you welcome them to come again. A bit of Chinese hospitality in action.

Bǐcǐ Bǐcǐ

bee tsuh bee tsuh; Same to you; You too.

This little phrase comes in handy when someone wishes you well or gives you a compliment that merits return so you don't appear vain. What's that you say? Great looking dress I have on? **Bǐcǐ bǐcǐ.** (Yours looks great, too.) May you have a long and happy retirement. **Bǐcǐ bǐcǐ.** (Same to you.)

Jiŭyăng Jiŭyăng

jyoe yahng jyoe yahng; Pleased to meet you; *literally:* I have admired you for a long time.

Saying **Jiŭyăng jiŭyăng** when you first meet someone you've heard something about is a polite gesture.

Màn Màn Chī!

mahn mahn chir; Bon Appetit!

Be sure to say **màn màn chī** to the others at your table before you take your first bite. You'll win hearts all around. It actually means "eat real slowly"; saying the phrase lets everyone know you hope they take their time and enjoy the meal.

Wŏ Qĭng Kè

waw cheeng kuh; It's on me; My treat.

You hear this phrase day in and day out all over China. Everyone wants to be the one to pay the bill (see Chapter 18), so folks make a big deal out of being the first person to go to the hip when the check comes. Even if you don't mean it, ask for the bill at least once or twice while others protest. Whoever keeps insisting gets to pay the bill.

Friends often make a joke by adding **"nĭ fù qián"** (*nee foo chyan*) at the end of this phrase. If you hear someone say **"wŏ qĭng kè, nĭ fù qián,"** it means "I'll take the bill, but you'll be the one to pay it." Only say this when you dine with a good friend who can take a joke, however, or you'll be sunk just when you were starting to impress people with your newly acquired Chinese.

Yŏu Kōng Lái Wán

yo koong lye wahn; Please come again.

Just before guests leave your home, you should always say **"Yŏu kōng lái wán."** (*Literally:* When you have time, come back and play.) Sometimes you also hear people say **"màn zŏu,"** (*mahn dzoe*) which literally means "walk slowly" and is loosely translated as "careful going home." A good host doesn't forget to wish his or her guests well as they depart. The saying implies they'll be back again anyway. Chinese hospitality at its best.

When you're in mainland China, you may hear the last word pronounced as "*wahr*" rather than "*wahn,*" which is the way the Taiwanese pronounce it. In fact, any time you hear a word end in "r," it indicates the person is speaking a northern dialect, like Mandarin spoken in Beijing. People in Taiwan speak in one of the southern dialects, so they invariably pronounce certain words with an "n" sound at the end rather than an "r" sound.

Láojià Láojià

laow jyah laow jyah; Excuse me; Pardon me.

Ever wonder what to say when you need to pass a person who's standing in your way? Especially if you find yourself in busy Shanghai where it often feels like you're in a sea of humanity, **láojià láojià** is exactly the phrase you want to remember for crowded moments. It offers you a nice way of getting someone's attention without being rude.

Zhù Nǐ Zǎo Rì Kāng Fú

joo nee dzaow ir kahng foo; Get well soon.

Hopefully you won't have to use this expression too often, but if you do, at least the folks hearing it will know your colloquial Chinese is good. You'll fit right in with the rest of the well-wishers, and your Chinese friends are sure to appreciate your good wishes.

Búkèqi

boo kuh chee; You're welcome; No problem; Don't mention it.

You say **búkèqi** as the bookend to **xièxiè** (*shyeh shyeh;* thanks). You can't say one without expecting to hear the other. **Búkèqi** represents more than just a response to "thank you," however. It's part and parcel of a larger group of words that express a humble spirit, which the Chinese always treasure in friends and acquaintances. If someone thanks you profusely for something you do, whether big or small, never accept the thanks as something you agree you deserve. Giving yourself a pat on the back is the opposite of what you want to convey. Always make it sound like your deed is no big deal, something you prefer to downplay. Doing so puts you in the correct frame of mind for the kind of public humility prized by the Chinese. (See Chapter 18 for more tips on Chinese faux pas.)

Hǎo Jiǔ Méi Jiàn

how jyoe may jyan; Long time no see.

You can use this phrase in all seriousness or in jest if you've just seen someone an hour before. Either way, it puts people in a good mood to know that you care about being in their presence again. You can even say it to your *Chinese For Dummies* book if it stays on your bookshelf for too long.

Part V

Appendixes

In this part . . .

The appendixes in this part give you easy-to-access Chinese reference sources. I include a simple list of verbs in Chinese, because Chinese has no equivalent of English verb conjugation. I provide a mini-dictionary with some of the words you use most often. Next, you get the answers to the Fun & Games exercises that appear at the ends of the chapters. Finally, I list the tracks of the audio CD included with this book so you can read along as you listen and then practice speaking Chinese with the correct tones.

Appendix A

Chinese Verbs

• •

*H*ere's a handy list of useful Chinese verbs. For a general description of how verbs work in Chinese, see Chapter 2.

àn/*ahn*/to press

ānpái/*ahn pye*/to arrange; to schedule

ānzhuāng/*ahn jwahng*/to install

bāngmáng/*bahng mahng*/to help

bō/*baw*/to dial

cānjiā/*tsahn jyah*/to participate

chàng/*chahng*/to sing

chī/*chir*/to eat

chídào/*chir daow*/to be late

chóngxīn kāijī/*choong sheen kye jee*/to reboot

chuān/*chwan*/to wear

chuī/*chway*/to blow

cún qián/*tswun chyan*/to deposit money

dǎ/*dah*/to hit; to strike; to play

dài/*dye*/to bring; to carry; to wear (accessories)

děng/*duhng*/to wait

diǎn/*dyan*/to order (food)

dǒng/*doong*/to understand

è/*uh*/to be hungry

fēi/*fay*/to fly

fù zhàng/*foo jahng*/to pay a bill

gǎibiàn/*gye byan*/to change

gǎnjué/*gahn jweh*/to feel

gǎnxiè/*gahn shyeh*/to thank

gàosù/*gaow soo*/to tell

gāoxìng/*gaow sheeng*/to be happy

gěi/*gay*/to give

gōngzuò/*goong dzwaw*/to work

guà/*gwah*/to hang up

guān/*gwan*/to close

gūjì/*goo jee*/to estimate

guò/*gwaw*/to pass

hē/*huh*/to drink

hézuò/*huh dzwaw*/to cooperate

huà/*hwah*/to paint

huàn/*hwahn*/to exchange

huānyíng/*hwahn eeng*/to welcome

huí/*hway*/to return

huì/*hway*/to know how to do something

hūxī/*hoo she*/to breathe

jiàn/*jyan*/to see

jiǎng/*jyahng*/to speak

jiànlì/*jyan lee*/to set up

jiànyì/*jyan ee*/to suggest

jiào/*jyaow*/to call

jiē/*jyeh*/to answer (a phone call)

jiè/*jyeh*/to loan; to borrow

jiěfàng/*jyeh fahng*/to liberate

jiéhūn/*jyeh hwun*/to marry

jiějué/*jyeh jweh* /to solve

jièshào/*jyeh shaow*/to introduce

jiézhàng/*jyeh jahng*/to pay the bill

jiù/*jyoe*/to save (a life)

juédìng/*jyweh deeng*/to decide

kāi/*kye*/to open

kāi chē/*kye chuh*/to drive

kāihuì/*kye hway*/to have or be in a meeting

kàn/*kahn*/to read; to look; to see

kě/*kuh*/to be thirsty

lái/*lye*/to come

liànxí/*lyan she*/to practice

líkāi/*lee kye*/to leave

liú/*lyoe*/to leave (an object; a message)

mà/*mah*/to scold

mǎi/*my*/to buy

mài/*my*/to sell

máng/*mahng*/to be busy

mílù/*mee loo*/to get lost

ná/*nah*/to pick up; to take

néng/*nuhng*/to be able to

pànjué/*pahn jweh*/to make a legal decision

qiān rù/*chyan roo*/to log on

qiān chū/*chyan choo*/to log off

qǐng/*cheeng*/to invite

qù/*chyew*/to go

qǔ qián/*chyew chyan*/to withdraw money

qǔxiāo/*chyew shyaow*/to cancel

ràng/*rahng*/to permit

rènshi/*run shir*/to know (a person); to recognize

shàng/*shahng*/to get on

shàngwǎng/*shahng wahng*/to go online

shì/*shir*/to be

shōu/*show*/to receive

shòu/*show*/to accept (money, tickets, etc.)

shū/*shoo*/to lose

shuō/*shwaw*/to speak

sòng/*soong*/to send

tánpàn/*tahn pahn*/to negotiate

tǎolùn/*taow lwun*/to discuss

tián/*tyan*/to fill out (a form)

tīng/*teeng*/to hear; to listen to

tóngyì/*toong ee*/to agree

tuìfáng/*tway fahng*/to check out (of hotel room)

tuìhuí/*tway hway*/to return (merchandise)

tuōyùn/*twaw yewn*/to check in luggage

wán/*wahn*/to play

wàng/*wahng*/to forget

wèn/*one*/to ask

xǐ/*she*/to wash

xià/*shyah*/to get off

xiǎng/*shyahng*/to think; to miss

xiàzài/*shyah dzye*/to download

xǐhuān/*she hwan*/to like; to enjoy

xìn/*sheen*/to believe

xuǎnzé/*shwan dzuh*/to choose

xuéxí/*shweh she*/to study

yǎnshì/*yan shir*/to give a presentation

yào/*yaow*/to want

yíng/*eeng*/to win

yòng/*yoong*/to use

yǒu/*yo*/to have; there are

yóulǎn/*yo lahn*/to sightsee

yóuyǒng/*yo yoong*/to swim

yuànyì/*ywan yee*/to be willing to

yùsuàn/*yew swan*/to budget

zhǎo/*jaow*/to look for

zhàoxiàng/*jaow shyahng*/to take pictures

zhīdào/*jir daow*/to know (a fact)

zhù/*joo*/to reside; to extend wishes

zhuā/*jwah*/to catch

zhuǎn/*jwan*/to transfer; to turn

zhuāngrù/*jwahng roo*/to pack

zhuǎnzū/*jwan dzoo*/to sublet

zhǔchí/*joo chir*/to lead

zǒu (lù)/*dzoe (loo)*/to walk

zū/*dzoo*/to rent

zuò/*dzwaw*/to do; to make; to sit

zuò fàn/*dzwaw fahn*/to cook

Chinese-English Mini-Dictionary

A

ǎi/*eye*/short

àirén/*eye run*/spouse (used only in the PRC)

āiyà/*eye yah*/oh my goodness!

ānjìng/*ahn jeeng*/quiet

ānpái/*ahn pye*/to arrange

ānquándài/*ahn chwan dye*/seat belt

B

bàba/*bah bah*/father

bǎifēnbǐ/*bye fun bee*/percentage

bàn/*bahn*/half

bāngmáng/*bahng mahng*/to help

bàngōngshì/*bahn goong shir*/office

bàngōngzhuō/*bahn goong jwaw*/desk

bànyè/*bahn yeh*/midnight

bàoqiàn/*baow chyan*/I'm sorry

bàozhǐ/*baow jir*/newspaper

biéde/*byeh duh*/other

bìng/*beeng*/to be sick

bīnguǎn/*been gwahn*/hotel

bō/*baw*/to dial

bówùguǎn/*baw woo gwahn*/museum

bù/*boo*/not; no

bú kèqì/*boo kuh chee*/you're welcome

bǔchōng/*boo choong*/to add

búcuò/*boo tswaw*/not bad; really good

bùzhǎng/*boo jahng*/department head; minister

C

cā/*tsah*/to sweep

cài/*tsye*/food

càidān/*tsye dahn*/menu

cānguǎn/*tsahn gwahn*/restaurant

cānjīnzhǐ/*tsahn jeen jir*/napkin

cèsuǒ/*tsuh swaw*/toilet

chá/*chah*/tea; to look something up

chángcháng/*chahng chahng*/often

chángtú diànhuà/*chahng too dyan hwah*/long-distance phone call

chāojí shìchǎng/*chaow jee shir chahng*/supermarket

chātóu/*chah toe*/adaptor

chāzi/*chah dzuh*/fork

chéngshì/*chung shir*/city

chī yào/*chir yaow*/to take medicine

chīfàn/*chir fahn*/to eat

chuān/*chwahn*/to wear

chuáng/*chwahng*/bed

chuánzhēn jī/*chwan juhn jee*/fax machine

chūfā/*choo fah*/to leave the house; to set off

chūzū/*choo dzoo*/to rent

chūzū chē/*choo dzoo chuh*/taxi

cóng/*tsoong*/from

cōngmíng/*tsoong meeng*/intelligent

cuò/*tswaw*/incorrect; mistake

D

dà/*dah*/big

dǎ/*dah*/to do, play, or hit

dàlù/*dah loo*/mainland (China)

dānchéngpiào/*dahn chuhng pyaow*/one-way ticket

dāngrán/*dahng rahn*/of course

dànshì/*dahn shir*/but; however

dàshǐguǎn/*dah shir gwahn*/embassy

dàtīng/*dah teeng*/lobby

děng/*duhng*/to wait

dēngjīpái/*duhng jee pye*/boarding pass

diǎn/*dyan*/to order (food)

diànhuà/*dyan hwah*/telephone

diànhuà hàomǎ/*dyan hwah how mah*/telephone number

diànhuà hàomǎbù/*dyan hwah how mah boo*/telephone book

diànnǎo/*dyan now*/computer

diànshì/*dyan shir*/television

diàntī/*dyan tee*/elevator

diànyǐng/*dyan yeeng*/movie

diànzǐ yóujiàn/*dyan dzuh yo jyan*/e-mail

diànzǐ yóuxiāng dìzhǐ/*dyan dzuh yo shyahng dee jir*/e-mail address

dìfāng/*dee fahng*/place

dìng wèi/*deeng way*/to make a reservation

dìqū/*dee chyew*/area; location

dìtiě/*dee tyeh*/subway

dìtú/*dee too*/map

dìzhǐ/*dee jir*/address

dōngxi/*doong she*/thing

dōu/*doe*/both; all

duìbùqǐ/*dway boo chee*/excuse me; I'm sorry

duìfāng fùfèi diànhuà/*dway fahng foo fay dyan hwah*/collect call

duìhuàn lǜ/*dway hwahn lyew*/exchange rate

duìhuànchù/*dway hwahn choo*/exchange bureaus

duìmiàn/*dway myan*/opposite

dùjià/*doo jyah*/on vacation

duō/*dwaw*/many

duō jiǔ?/*dwaw jyoe*/how long?

duōshǎo?/*dwaw shaow*/how much?

E

è/*uh*/hungry

érzi/*are dzuh*/son

F

fǎlǜ/*fah lyew*/law

fàn/*fahn*/food

fàndiàn/*fahn dyan*/restaurant

fàndiàn qiántái/*fahn dyan chyan tye*/reception desk

fáng jià/*fahng jyah*/to take a vacation

fángjiān/*fahng jyan*/room

fànguǎn/*fahn gwahn*/hotel

fángzi/*fahng dzuh*/house

fàntīng/*fahn teeng*/dining room

fēijī/*fay jee*/airplane

fēijīchǎng/*fay jee chahng*/airport

féizào/*fay dzaow*/soap

fēn/*fun*/minute; one cent

fùjìn/*foo jeen*/area; vicinity

fùmǔ/*foo moo*/parents

fùqián/*foo chyan*/to pay

fùqīn/*foo cheen*/father

fúwùqì/*foo woo chee*/server

fúwùtái jīnglǐ/*foo woo tye jeeng lee*/concierge

fúwùyuán/*foo woo ywan*/attendant

G

gǎibiàn/*guy byan*/to change (attitude; behavior)

Gǎng bì/*gahng bee*/Hong Kong dollar

gāngbǐ/*gahng bee*/pen

gānjìng/*gahn jeeng*/clean
gǎnxiè/*gahn shyeh*/many thanks
gāofēngqí/*gaow fung chee*/rush hour
gàosù/*gaow soo*/to tell
gāosùgōnglù/*gaow soo goong loo*/freeway
gāoxìng/*gaow sheeng*/happy
gěi/*gay*/to give
gèng/*guhng*/more
gèrén diànnǎo/*guh run dyan now*/PC (personal computer)
gōnggòng qìchē/*goong goong chee chuh*/public bus
gōnggòng qìchē zhàn/*goong goong chee chuh jahn*/bus stop
gōnglù/*goong loo*/highway
gōngsī/*goong suh*/company
gōngwénbāo/*goong one baow*/briefcase
gōngxǐ/*goong she*/congratulations
gōngyòng diànhuà/*goong yoong dyan hwah*/public telephone
gōngzuò/*goong dzwaw*/to work; job
guà/*gwah*/to hang up
guǎn/*gwan*/to care about
guānguāng tuán/*gwahn gwahng twahn*/tour group
guāngpán/*gwahng pahn*/CD (music)
gǔdài/*goo dye*/ancient; antique
guì/*gway*/expensive
guójì diànhuà/*gwaw jee dyan hwah*/international phone call
guójì wǎngluò/*gwaw jee wahng lwaw*/the Internet
guójiā/*gwaw jyah*/country
guóyǔ/*gwaw yew*/Mandarin (term used in Taiwan)

H

hǎiguān/*hi gwahn*/customs
háizi/*hi dzuh*/child
Hànyǔ/*hahn yew*/Chinese (language)
hǎo/*how*/good

hǎokàn/*how kahn*/pretty
hàomǎ/*how mah*/number
hē/*huh*/to drink
hétóng/*huh toong*/contract
huài/*hwye*/broken; bad
huàn/*hwahn*/to change (trains, money, and so on)
huándēngjī/*hwahn duhng jee*/slide projector
huándēngpiàn/*hwahn duhng pyan*/slides
huānyíng/*hwahn yeeng*/welcome
huí/*hway*/to answer; return
huì/*hway*/to know (how to do something)
huí lái/*hway lye*/to return (come back)
huìyì/*hway ee*/meeting
huò zhe/*hwaw juh*/or
huòbì/*hwaw bee*/currency
huǒchē zhàn/*hwaw chuh jahn*/train station
hùshì/*hoo shir*/nurse
hùtóu/*hoo toe*/bank account
hùzhào/*hoo jaow*/passport

J

jǐ/*jee*/several; how many
jiā/*jyah*/family; home
jiàgé/*jyah guh*/price
jiàn/*jyan*/to see; a classifier
jiǎnchá/*jyan chah*/to examine
jiǎng/*jyahng*/to talk
jiànshēn yùndòng/*jyan shun yewn doong*/to work out
jiǎnsuǒ/*jyan swaw*/to search
jiànyì/*jyan ee*/to suggest; suggestion
jiào/*jyaow*/to be called
jiāo/*jyaow*/to teach
jiàoshòu/*jyaow show*/professor
jiāotōng/*jyaow toong*/transportation
jiàrì/*jyah ir*/vacation day
jí/*jee*/hurry

jiè/*jyeh*/to borrow; also to loan

jiē/*jyeh*/to answer the phone; street

jiéhūn/*jyeh hwun*/to marry

jiějué/*jyeh jweh*/to resolve; to solve

jiérì/*jyeh ir*/holiday

jièshào/*jyeh shaow*/to introduce

jiéyú/*jyeh yew*/account balance

jìn/*jin*/close

jǐngchá/*jeeng chah*/police

jǐngchájú/*jeeng chah jyew*/police station

jīngjìcāng/*jeeng jee tsahng*/economy class

jīngjìrén/*jeeng jee run*/broker

jīnglǐ/*jeeng lee*/manager

jǐnjí chūkǒu/*jin jee choo koe*/emergency exits

jīntiān/*jin tyan*/today

jiǔ/*jyoe*/wine; alcohol

jiùhùchē/*jyoe hoo chuh*/ambulance

jiùshēngyī/*jyoe shung ee*/life vests

jízhěnshì/*jee juhn shir*/emergency room

K

kāfēi/*kah fay*/coffee

kāfēitīng/*kah fay teeng*/café

kāi/*kye*/to open

kāi chē/*kye chuh*/to drive

kāihuì/*kye hway*/to have a meeting

kāimén/*kye mun*/to open the door

kāishǐ/*kye shir*/to start

kàn/*kahn*/to read; to see

kànbìng/*kahn beeng*/to see a doctor

kàojìn/*cow jeen*/next to

kè/*kuh*/class (academic)

kě/*kuh*/thirsty

kè hu/*kuh hoo*/client

kěndìng/*kuhn deeng*/definitely

kěnéng/*kuh nung*/perhaps

kěpà/*kuh pah*/scary

kèrén/*kuh run*/guest

kěxi/*kuh she*/too bad; unfortunately

kěyǐ/*kuh yee*/can; to be able to

kōngtiáo/*koong tyaow*/air conditioning

kòngwèi/*koong way*/vacant

kuài/*kwye*/fast; dollar

kuàijì/*kwye jee*/accounting

kuàizi/*kwye dzuh*/chopsticks

L

lái/*lye*/to come

lái huí piào/*lye hway pyaow*/round-trip ticket

lǎo/*laow*/old; overdone

lǎobǎn/*laow bahn*/a boss

lǎoshī/*laow shir*/teacher

lèi/*lay*/tired

léishè guāngdié/*lay shuh gwahng dyeh*/CD-ROM

lěng/*luhng*/cold

lǐ/*lee*/inside; Chinese equivalent of a kilometer

liáotiān/*lyaow tyan*/to chat

lǐbài/*lee bye*/to pray; week

líkāi/*lee kye*/to leave

lǐngqǔdān/*leeng chyew dahn*/luggage claim tag

lǐngshìguǎn/*leeng shir gwahn*/consulate

lǐtáng/*lee tahng*/auditorium

liúhuà/*lyoe hwah*/to leave a message

liúlǎn/*lyoe lahn*/to browse

liúxíng/*lyoe sheeng*/popular

lǐwù/*lee woo*/gifts

lóushàng/*low shahng*/upstairs

lóuxià/*low shyah*/downstairs

lù/*loo*/road

lǚguǎn/*lyew gwahn*/hotel

lǜshī/*lyew shir*/lawyer

lùxiàngjī/*loo shyahng jee*/video recorder

lǚxíng/*lyew sheeng*/to travel

lǚxíng dàilǐrén/*lyew sheeng dye lee run*/travel agent

lǚxíng zhīpiào/*lyew sheeng jir pyaow*/traveler's checks

lǚxíngshè/*lyew sheeng shuh*/travel agency

lùyīn diànhuà/*loo een dyan hwah*/answering machine

lǚyóu/*lyew yoe*/tour

lǚyóu shǒucè/*lyew yoe show tsuh*/guidebook

M

máfan/*mah fahn*/annoying

mài/*my*/to sell

mǎi/*my*/to buy

māma/*mah mah*/mother

màn/*mahn*/slow

mànchē/*mahn chuh*/local train

máng/*mahng*/busy

máojīn/*maow jeen*/towel

máotǎn/*maow tahn*/blanket

màoyì zhǎnxiāohuì/*maow ee jahn shyaow hway*/trade show

měige/*may guh*/each

Měiguó/*may gwaw*/America

Měiguóren/*may gwaw run*/American

méiyǒu/*mayo*/don't have

Měiyuán/*may ywan*/U.S. dollar

mén/*mun*/door

ménkǒu/*mun ko*/entrance

miàn/*myan*/face

miǎnfèi/*myan fay*/free

miàntiáo/*myan tyaow*/noodles

mǐfàn/*mee fahn*/rice

mílù/*mee loo*/to get lost

mìmǎ/*mee mah*/personal identification number; password

míngnián/*meeng nyan*/next year

míngpiàn/*meeng pyan*/business card

míngtiān/*meeng tyan*/tomorrow

mìshū/*mee shoo*/secretary

mǔqīn/*moo cheen*/mother

N

ná/*nah*/to pick up

nà/*nah*/that

nǎ/*nah*/which

nán péngyǒu/*nahn pung yo*/boyfriend

nào zhōng/*now joong*/alarm clock

nǎr/*nar*/where

nǐ/*nee*/you

niánjì/*nyan jee*/age

niánqīng/*nyan cheeng*/young

nǐmen/*nee mun*/you (plural)

nín/*neen*/you (polite)

nuǎnhuó/*nwan hwaw*/warm

nǚpéngyǒu/*nyew puhng yo*/girlfriend

O

Ōu yuán/*oh ywan*/Euro

Ōuzhōu/*oh joe*/Europe

P

pànjué/*pahn jweh*/to make a legal decision

pēngtiáo yìshù/*puhng tyaow ee shoo*/cooking

péngyǒu/*puhng yo*/friend

piányì/*pyan yee*/cheap

piānzi/*pyan dzuh*/movie

piào/*pyaow*/ticket

piàoliàng/*pyaow lyahng*/pretty

píngcháng/*peeng chahng*/usually; often

pǐntuō/*peen twaw*/pint

pīnyīn/*peen yeen*/Chinese romanization system

Pǔtōnghuà/*poo toong hwah*/Mandarin (term used in mainland China)

Q

qián/*chyan*/front; money

qiān chū/*chyan choo*/to log off

qiánbāo/*chyan baow*/wallet

qiānbǐ/*chyan bee*/pencil

qiántái fúwùyuán/*chyan tye foo woo ywan*/receptionist

qiānzhèng/*chyan juhng*/visa

qiáo/*chyaow*/bridge

qìchē/*chee chuh*/car

qǐfēi/*chee fay*/to take off (airplane)

qíguài/*chee gwye*/strange

qiān rù/*chyan roo*/to log on

qíng/*cheeng*/affection

qìng/*cheeng*/to celebrate

qǐng/*cheeng*/please

qīng/*cheeng*/clear

qīngzǎo/*cheeng dzaow*/time (midnight to dawn)

qítā/*chee tah*/other; anything else

qīzi/*chee dzuh*/wife

qù/*chyew*/to go

qǔ qián/*chyew chyan*/to withdraw money

quánbù/*chwan boo*/entire; the whole thing

qùdiào/*chyew dyaow*/erase; remove

qùnián/*chyew nyan*/last year

qúnzi/*chwun dzuh*/skirt

qǔxiāo/*chyew shyaow*/to cancel

R

ràng/*rahng*/to let; to allow

rè/*ruh*/hot

rén/*run*/person

rénmínbì/*run meen bee*/PRC dollar

rènshi/*run shir*/to know (someone)

Rì yuán/*ir ywan*/Japanese dollar

Rìběn/*ir bun*/Japan

rìlì/*ir lee*/calendar

rìqī/*ir chee*/date

róngxìng/*roong sheeng*/to be honored

róngyì/*roong ee*/easy

ròu/*row*/meat

ruǎnjiàn/*rwahn jyan*/software

S

shàng/*shahng*/above; on top

shàng/*shahng*/to go up; get on; above

shāngdiàn/*shahng dyan*/store

shàngge xīngqī/*shahng guh sheeng chee*/last week

shàngge yuè/*shahng guh yweh*/last month

shàngwǎng/*shahng wahng*/to go online

shāngwù zhōngxīn/*shahng woo joong sheen*/business center

shāngyè/*shahng yeh*/business

shéi/*shay*/who; whom

shēn/*shun*/dark; deep

shēngqì/*shung chee*/angry

shēngrì/*shung ir*/birthday

shēng yì huǒ bàn/*shuhng yee hwaw bahn*/business partner

shēngyīn/*shung een*/voice

shénme/*shummuh*/what

shēntǐ/*shun tee*/body

shì/*shir*/yes; is

shīfu/*shir foo*/master; cook

shíhòu/*shir ho*/time

shíjiānbiǎo/*shir jyan byaow*/schedule

shìpǐn záhuò/*shir peen dzah hwaw*/groceries

shuǐzāi/*shway dzye*/flood

shōudào/*show daow*/to receive

shǒujī/*show jee*/cell phone

shǒujī hàomǎ/*show jee how mah*/cell-phone number

shōujù/*show jyew*/receipt

shòushāng/*show shahng*/to be injured

shǒutí xíngli/*show tee sheeng lee*/carry on luggage

shǒutíshì/*show tee shir*/laptop

shū/*shoo*/to lose; book

shuāng/*shwahng*/a pair

shuāngrén fángjiān/*shwahng run fahng jyan*/double room
shūfu/*shoo foo*/comfortable
shuǐguǒ/*shway gwaw*/fruit
shuìjiào/*shway jyaow*/sleep
shuō/*shwaw*/to speak
sījī/*suh jee*/driver
sìzhōu/*suh joe*/around
sòng/*soong*/to send
sōng/*soong*/loose
sùcài/*soo tsye*/vegetarian dishes
suì/*sway*/age
suǒ/*swaw*/to lock
sùshè/*soo shuh*/dormitory

T

tā/*tah*/he; him
tāde/*tah duh*/his
tài/*tye*/too much
táishì/*tye shir*/desktop
tàitài/*tye tye*/wife (used mostly in Taiwan)
Táiwān/*tye wahn*/Taiwan
tàiyáng yǎnjìng/*tye yahng yan jeeng*/sunglasses
tāmen/*tah mun*/they; them
tāng/*tahng*/soup
tánpàn/*tahn pahn*/negotiate
tǎnzi/*tahn dzuh*/blanket
tàojiān/*taow jyan*/suite
tǎolùn/*taow loon*/to discuss
tèsè/*tuh suh*/special
tián/*tyan*/fill out (a form)
tiānqì/*tyan chee*/weather
tiàowǔ/*tiaow woo*/to dance
tīng/*teeng*/to listen to
tóngshì/*toong shir*/colleague
tóngwū/*toong woo*/roommate
tóngyì/*toong ee*/to agree
tóudēngcāng/*toe dung tsahng*/first class
tóuténg/*toe tung*/headache

tuīchí/*tway chir*/postponed
tuìfáng/*tway fahng*/to check out of a room
tuìhuí/*tway hway*/to return (merchandise)
tuìkuǎn/*tway kwahn*/refund
tuōyùn/*twaw yewn*/to check in luggage

W

wài/*wye*/outside
wàibì/*wye bee*/foreign currency
wàijiāoguān/*wye jyaow gwahn*/diplomat
wǎnfàn/*wahn fahn*/dinner
wǎngluò liánjié/*wahng lwaw lyan jyeh*/Internet access
wǎngshàng fúwù tígōng shāng/*wahng shahng foo woo tee goong shahng*/Internet service provider
wǎngzhàn/*wahng jahn*/Web site
wǎnhuì/*wahn hway*/party
wǎnshàng/*wahn shahng*/evening (6 p.m. to midnight)
wéi/*way*/hello (on phone only)
wèishēngzhǐ/*way shung jir*/toilet paper
wèishénme/*way shummuh*/why
wénjiàn/*one jyan*/a file
wènlù/*one loo*/to ask for directions
wèntí/*one tee*/problem
wǒ/*waw*/I; me
wǒde/*waw duh*/mine
wǒmen/*waw mun*/we; us
wòshì/*waw shir*/bedroom
wǔfàn/*woo fahn*/lunch
wǔyuè/*woo yweh*/May

X

xǐ/*she*/to wash
xià/*shyah*/below; go down; get off; next
xiàge/*shyah guh*/next
xiàge xīngqī/*shyah guh sheeng chee*/next week

xiàge yuè/*shyah guh yweh*/next month
xiǎng/*shyahng*/to think
Xiānggǎng/*shyahng gahng*/Hong Kong
xiàngmù/*shyahng moo*/item
xiāngzi/*shyahng dzuh*/suitcase
xiànjīn/*shyan jeen*/cash
xiánliáo/*shyan lyaow*/small talk
xiántán/*shyan tahn*/to chat
xiànzài/*shyan dzye*/now
xiǎo/*shyaow*/small
xiǎofèi/*shyaow fay*/tip
xiǎogéjiān/*shyaow guh jyan*/cubicle
xiǎoxīn/*shyaow sheen*/be careful
xiàwǔ/*shyah woo*/afternoon (12 – 6 p.m.)
xiàzài/*shyah dzye*/to download
xīcān/*she tsahn*/Western food
xièxiè/*shyeh shyeh*/thanks
xiézi/*shyeh dzuh*/shoes
xǐhuān/*she hwahn*/to like
xīn/*shin*/new
Xīng bì/*sheeng bee*/Singapore dollar
xíngli/*sheeng lee*/luggage
xīngqī'èr/*sheeng chee are*/Tuesday
xīngqīliù/*sheeng chee lyo*/Saturday
xīngqīsān/*sheeng chee sahn*/Wednesday
xīngqīsì/*sheeng chee suh*/Thursday
xīngqītiān/*sheeng chee tyan*/Sunday
xīngqīwǔ/*sheeng chee woo*/Friday
xīngqīyī/*sheeng chee ee*/Monday
xìnxi/*sheen she*/a message
xìnyòng kǎ/*sheen yoong kah*/credit card
xǐshǒu jiān/*she show jyan*/bathroom
xiūxi/*shyo she*/to rest
xǐyī fúwù/*she ee foo woo*/laundry service
xuǎnzé/*shwan dzuh*/to choose
xuéshēng/*shweh shung*/student
xuéxí/*shweh she*/to study
xuéxiào/*shweh shyaow*/school
xūyào/*shyew yaow*/to need

Y

yǎnjìng/*yan jeeng*/glasses
yǎnjīng/*yan jeeng*/eye
yǎnshì/*yan shir*/a presentation
yào/*yaow*/to want; medicine
yàofáng/*yaow fahng*/pharmacy
yáokòng qì/*yaow koong chee*/
    remote control
yàoshi/*yaow shir*/key
yàowán/*yaow wahn*/pill
yáshuā/*yah shwah*/toothbrush
yáyī/*yah ee*/dentist
Yàzhōu/*yah joe*/Asia
yě/*yeah*/also
yī/*ee*/one
yìchéng/*ee chung*/agenda
yīfu/*ee foo*/clothing
yǐhòu/*ee ho*/after
yìhuǎr jiàn/*ee hwar jyan*/see you later
yìhuǎr/*ee hwar*/in a little while
yìjiàn/*ee jyan*/opinion
yíng/*eeng*/to win
yìngbì/*eeng bee*/coins
yīnggāi/*eeng guy*/should
yínháng/*een hahng*/bank
Yīngwén; Yīngyǔ/*eeng one; eeng
    yew*/English (language)
yǐnliào/*een lyaow*/drinks
yīnwèi/*een way*/because
yīnyuè/*een yweh*/music
yìqǐ/*ee chee*/together
yīshēng/*ee shung*/doctor
yǐwéi/*ee way*/to consider
yìxie/*ee shyeh*/a few
yíyàng/*ee yahng*/the same
yīyuàn/*ee ywan*/hospital
yǐzi/*ee dzuh*/chair
yòng/*yoong*/to use
yònghù xìngmíng/*yoong hoo sheeng
    meeng*/user name

yòu/*yo*/right
yǒu/*yo*/to have
yǒu shēng yóujiàn/*yo shung yo jyan*/voicemail
yóujú/*yo jyew*/post office
yóulǎn/*yo lahn*/to sightsee
yǔ/*yew*/rain
yuán/*ywan*/Chinese dollar
yuǎn/*ywan*/far
yùdìng/*yew deeng*/to make a reservation
Yuènán/*yweh nahn*/Vietnam
yùndòng/*yewn doong*/exercise
yùnqì/*yewn chee*/luck
yǔsǎn/*yew sahn*/umbrella
yùsuàn/*yew swan*/budget
yǔyī/*yew ee*/raincoat

Z

zàijiàn/*dzye jyan*/goodbye
zánmen/*dzahn mun*/we; us (informal)
zǎofàn/*dzaow fahn*/breakfast
zāogāo/*dzaow gaow*/rats!; what a shame
zǎoshàng/*dzaow shahng*/morning (6 a.m. to noon)
zázhì/*dzah jir*/magazine
zéi/*dzay*/thief
zěnme/*dzummah*/how
zhàngdān/*jahng dahn*/bill
zhàngfu/*jahng foo*/husband
zhàntái/*jahn tye*/platform
zhǎo/*jaow*/to look for
zhāohu/*jaow hoo*/greeting
zhàopiàn/*jaow pyan*/photo
zhàoxiàng/*jaow shyahng*/to take pictures
zhàoxiàng jī/*jaow shyahng jee*/camera
zhēn/*juhn*/really; truly
zhèngdiǎn/*juhng dyan*/on time
zhèngjiàn/*juhng jyan*/ID

zhí/*jir*/straight
zhǐ/*jir*/only
zhīdào/*jir daow*/to know (information)
zhìliàng/*jir lyahng*/quality
zhīpiào/*jir pyaow*/check (money)
zhīpiào bù/*jir pyaow boo*/checkbook
zhōng/*joong*/time; size medium
Zhōngguó/*joong gwaw*/China
Zhōngguórén/*joong gwaw run*/Chinese person
Zhōngwén/*joong one*/Chinese language
zhōngwǔ/*joong woo*/afternoon
zhōngyú/*joong yew*/finally
zhōumò/*joe maw*/weekend
zhù/*joo*/to reside
zhuǎn/*jwan*/to transfer; to turn
zhūbǎo/*joo baow*/jewelry
zhǔguǎn/*joo gwan*/CEO
zhuólù/*jwaw loo*/landing
zhuōzi/*jwaw dzuh*/table
zìdòng lóutī/*dzuh doong low tee*/escalator
zìdòng tíkuǎn kǎ/*dzuh doong tee kwan kah*/ATM card
zìdòng tíkuǎnjī/*dzuh doong tee kwan jee*/ATM
zìjǐ/*dzuh jee*/self
zǒngcái/*dzoong tsye*/president (of company)
zǒngshì/*dzoong shir*/always
zǒngsuàn/*dzoong swahn*/finally
zǒu/*dzoe*/to walk
zūfèi/*dzoo fay*/rent
zǔfù/*dzoo foo*/grandfather
zuì/*dzway*/the most
zuǒ/*dzwaw*/left
zuótiān/*dzwaw tyan*/yesterday

English-Chinese Mini-Dictionary

A

above; on top/**shàng**/*shahng*
account balance/**jiéyú**/*jyeh yew*
accounting/**kuàijì**/*kwye jee*
adaptor/**chātóu**/*chah toe*
add/**bǔchōng**/*boo choong*
address/**dìzhǐ**/*dee jir*
affection/**qíng**/*cheeng*
after/**yǐhòu**/*ee ho*
afternoon/**zhōngwǔ**/*joong woo*
afternoon (12 – 6 p.m.)/**xiàwǔ**/*shyah woo*
age/**niánjì; suì**/*nyan jee; sway*
agenda/**yìchéng**/*ee chung*
agree/**tóngyì**/*toong ee*
air conditioning/**kōngtiáo**/*koong tyaow*
airplane/**fēijī**/*fay jee*
airport/**fēijīchǎng**/*fay jee chahng*
alarm clock/**nào zhōng**/*naow joong*
also/**yě**/*yeh*
always/**zǒngshì**/*dzoong shir*
ambulance/**jiùhùchē**/*jyoe hoo chuh*
America/**Měiguó**/*may gwaw*
American/**Měiguóren**/*may gwaw run*
ancient; antique/**gǔdài**/*goo dye*
angry/**shēngqì**/*shung chee*
annoying/**máfan**/*mah fahn*
answer the phone/**jiē**/*jyeh*
answer; return/**huí**/*hway*
answering machine/**lùyǐn diànhuà**/*loo een dyan hwah*
area; location/**dìqū**/*dee chyew*

area; vicinity; neighborhood/**fùjìn**/*foo jeen*
around/**sìzhōu**/*suh joe*
arrange/**ānpái**/*ahn pye*
Asia/**Yàzhōu**/*yah joe*
ask for directions/**wènlù**/*one loo*
ATM card/**zìdòng tíkuǎn kǎ**/*dzuh doong tee kwan kah*
ATM/**zìdòng tíkuǎnjī**/*dzuh doong tee kwan jee*
attendant/**fúwùyuán**/*foo woo ywan*
auditorium/**lǐtáng**/*lee tahng*

B

bank/**yínháng**/*een hahng*
bank account/**hùtóu**/*hoo toe*
bathroom/**xǐshǒu jiān**/*she show jyan*
be called/**jiào**/*jyaow*
be careful/**xiǎoxīn**/*shyaow sheen*
be honored/**róngxìng**/*roong sheeng*
be injured/**shòushāng**/*show shahng*
be sick/**bìng**/*beeng*
because/**yīnwèi**/*een way*
bed/**chuáng**/*chwahng*
bedroom/**wòshì**/*waw shir*
below/**xià**/*shyah*
big/**dà**/*dah*
bill/**zhàngdān**/*jahng dahn*
birthday/**shēngrì**/*shung ir*
blanket/**máotǎn; tǎnzi**/*maow tahn; tahn dzuh*
boarding pass/**dēngjīpái**/*dung jee pye*

body/**shēntǐ**/*shun tee*
book/**shū**/*shoo*
borrow; loan/**jiè**/*jyeh*
boss/**lǎobǎn**/*laow bahn*
both; all/**dōu**/*doe*
boyfriend/**nán péngyǒu**/*nahn pung yo*
breakfast/**zǎofàn**/*dzaow fahn*
bridge/**qiáo**/*chyaow*
briefcase/**gōngwénbāo**/*goong one baow*
broken; bad/**huài**/*hwye*
broker/**jīngjìrén**/*jeeng jee run*
browse/**liúlǎn**/*lyo lahn*
budget/**yùsuàn**/*yew swan*
bus stop/**gōnggòng qìchē zhàn**/*goong goong chee chuh jahn*
business/**shēngyi**/*shung yee*
business card/**míngpiàn**/*meeng pyan*
business center/**shāngwù zhōngxīn**/*shahng woo joong sheen*
business partner/**shēng yì huǒ bàn**/*shung yee hwaw bahn*
busy/**máng**/*mahng*
but; however/**dànshì**/*dahn shir*
buy/**mǎi**/*my*

C

café/**kāfēitīng**/*kah fay teeng*
calendar/**rìlì**/*ir lee*
camera/**zhàoxiàng jī**/*jaow shyahng jee*
can; to be able to/**kěyǐ**/*kuh yee*
cancel/**qǔxiāo**/*chyew shyaow*
car/**qìchē**/*chee chuh*
care about/**guǎn**/*gwan*
carry-on luggage/**shǒutí xíngli**/*show tee sheeng lee*
cash/**xiànjīn**/*shyan jeen*
CD (music)/**guāngpán**/*gwahng pahn*
CD-ROM/**léishè guāngdié**/*lay shuh gwahng dyeh*
celebrate/**qìng**/*cheeng*
cell phone/**shǒujī**/*show jee*

cell-phone number/**shǒujī hàomǎ**/*show jee how mah*
CEO/**zhǔguǎn**/*joo gwan*
chair/**yǐzi**/*ee dzuh*
change (attitude; behavior)/**gǎibiàn**/*guy byan*
change (trains, money, and so on)/ **huàn**/*hwahn chuh*
chat/**liáotiān; xiántán**/*lyaow tyan; shyan tahn*
cheap/**piányì**/*pyan yee*
check (money)/**zhīpiào**/*jir pyaow*
check in luggage/**tuōyùn**/*twaw yewn*
check out of a room/**tuìfáng**/*tway fahng*
checkbook/**zhīpiào bù**/*jir pyaow boo*
child/**háizi**/*hi dzuh*
China/**Zhōngguó**/*joong gwaw*
Chinese (language)/**Hànyǔ**/*hahn yew;* **Zhōngwén**/*joong one*
Chinese dollar/**yuán**/*ywan*
Chinese person/**Zhōngguórén**/*joong gwaw run*
Chinese romanization system/**pīnyīn**/*peen yeen*
choose/**xuǎnzé**/*shwan dzuh*
chopsticks/**kuàizi**/*kwye dzuh*
city/**chéngshì**/*chung shir*
class (academic)/**kè**/*kuh*
clean/**gānjìng**/*gahn jeeng*
clear/**qīng**/*cheeng*
client/**kè hù**/*kuh hoo*
close/**jìn**/*jeen*
clothing/**yīfu**/*ee foo*
coffee/**kāfēi**/*kah fay*
coins/**yìngbì**/*eeng bee*
cold/**lěng**/*luhng*
colleague/**tóngshì**/*toong shir*
collect call/**duìfāng fùfèi diànhuà**/*dway fahng foo fay dyan hwah*
come/**lái**/*lye*
comfortable/**shūfu**/*shoo foo*
company/**gōngsī**/*goong suh*

computer/**diànnǎo**/*dyan now*

concierge/**fúwùtái jīnglǐ**/*foo woo tye jeeng lee*

congratulations/**gōngxǐ**/*goong she*

consider/**yǐwéi**/*ee way*

consulate/**lǐnshìguǎn**/*leeng shir gwahn*

contract/**hétóng**/*huh toong*

cooking/**pēngtiáo yìshù**/*puhng tyaow ee shoo*

country/**guójiā**/*gwaw jyah*

credit card/**xìnyòng kǎ**/*sheen yoong kah*

cubicle/**xiǎogéjiān**/*shyaow guh jyan*

currency/**huòbì**/*hwaw bee*

customs/**hǎiguān**/*hi gwahn*

D

dance/**tiàowǔ**/*tiaow woo*

dark; deep/**shēn**/*shun*

date/**rìqī**/*ir chee*

definitely/**kěndìng**/*kuhn deeng*

dentist/**yáyī**/*yah ee*

department head; minister/**bùzhǎng**/*boo jahng*

desk/**bàngōngzhuō**/*bahn goong jwaw*

desktop/**táishì**/*tye shir*

dial/**bō**/*baw*

dining room/**fàntīng**/*fahn teeng*

dinner/**wǎnfàn**/*wahn fahn*

diplomat/**wàijiāoguān**/*wye jyaow gwahn*

discuss/**tǎolùn**/*taow loon*

do, play, or hit/**dǎ**/*dah*

doctor/**yīshēng**/*ee shung*

don't have/**méiyǒu**/*mayo*

door/**mén**/*mun*

dormitory/**sùshè**/*soo shuh*

double room/**shuāngrén fángjiān**/*shwahng run fahng jyan*

download/**xiàzài**/*shyah dzye*

downstairs/**lóuxià**/*low shyah*

drink/**hē**/*huh*

drinks/**yǐnliào**/*een lyaow*

drive/**kāi chē**/*kye chuh*

driver/**sījī**/*suh jee*

E

each/**měige**/*may guh*

easy/**róngyì**/*roong ee*

eat/**chīfàn**/*chir fahn*

economy class/**jīngjìcāng**/*jeeng jee tsahng*

elevator/**diàntī**/*dyan tee*

e-mail/**diànzǐ yóujiàn**/*dyan dzuh yo jyan*

e-mail address/**diànzǐ yóuxiāng dìzhǐ**/*dyan dzuh yo shyahng dee jir*

embassy/**dàshǐguǎn**/*dah shir gwahn*

emergency exits/**jǐnjí chūkǒu**/*jeen jee choo ko*

emergency room/**jízhěnshì**/*jee jun shir*

English (language)/**Yīngwén; Yīngyǔ**/*eeng one; eeng yew*

entire; the whole thing/**quánbù**/*chwan boo*

entrance/**ménkǒu**/*mun ko*

erase; remove/**qùdiào**/*chyew dyaow*

escalator/**zìdòng lóutī**/*dzuh doong low tee*

Euro/**Ōu yuán**/*oh ywan*

Europe/**Ōuzhōu**/*oh joe*

evening (6 p.m. to midnight)/**wǎnshàng**/*wahn shahng*

examine/**jiǎnchá**/*jyan chah*

exchange bureaus/**duìhuànchù**/*dway hwahn choo*

exchange rate/**duìhuàn lǜ**/*dway hwahn lyew*

excuse me; I'm sorry/**duìbùqǐ**/*dway boo chee*

exercise/**yùndòng**/*yewn doong*

expensive/**guì**/*gway*

eye/**yǎnjīng**/*yan jeeng*

F

face/**miàn**/*myan*

family; home/**jiā**/*jyah*

far/**yuǎn**/*ywan*

fast; dollar/**kuài**/*kwye*

father/**bàba; fùqīn**/*bah bah; foo cheen*

fax machine/**chuánzhēn jī**/*chwahn juhn jee*

few/**yīxiē**/*ee shyeh*

file/**wénjiàn**/*one jyan*

fill out (a form)/**tián**/*tyan*

finally/**zhōngyú**/*joong yew*

first class/**tóudēngcāng**/*toe dung tsahng*

flood/**shuǐzāi**/*shway dzye*

food/**cài; fàn**/*tsye; fahn*

foreign currency/**wàibì**/*wye bee*

fork/**chāzi**/*chah dzuh*

free/**miǎnfèi**/*myan fay*

freeway/**gāosùgōnglù**/*gaow soo goong loo*

Friday/**xīngqīwǔ**/*sheeng chee woo*

friend/**péngyǒu**/*puhng yo*

from/**cóng**/*tsoong*

front; money/**qián**/*chyan*

fruit/**shuǐguǒ**/*shway gwaw*

G

get lost/**mílù**/*mee loo*

gifts/**lǐwù**/*lee woo*

girlfriend/**nǚpéngyǒu**/*nyew puhng yoe*

give/**gěi**/*gay*

glasses/**yǎnjìng**/*yan jeeng*

go/**qù**/*chyew*

go down; get off; next/**xià**/*shyah*

go online/**shàngwǎng**/*shahng wahng*

go up; get on/**shàng**/*shahng*

good/**hǎo**/*how*

goodbye/**zàijiàn**/*dzye jyan*

grandfather/**zǔfù**/*dzoo foo*

greeting/**zhāohu**/*jaow hoo*

groceries/**shípǐn záhuò**/*shir peen dzah hwaw*

guest/**kèrén**/*kuh run*

guidebook/**lǚyóu shǒucè**/*lyew yo show tsuh*

H

half/**bàn**/*bahn*

hang up/**guà**/*guah*

happy/**gāoxìng**/*gaow sheeng*

have/**yǒu**/*yo*

have a meeting/**kāihuì**/*kye hway*

he; him/**tā**/*tah*

headache/**tóuténg**/*toe tuhng*

hello (on phone only)/**wéi**/*way*

help/**bāngmáng**/*bahng mahng*

highway/**gōnglù**/*goong loo*

his/**tāde**/*tah duh*

holiday/**jiérì**/*jyeh ir*

Hong Kong/**Xiānggǎng**/*shyahng gahng*

Hong Kong dollar/**Gǎng bì**/*gahng bee*

hospital/**yīyuàn**/*ee ywan*

hot/**rè**/*ruh*

hotel/**bīnuǎn**/*been gwahn*

hotel/**fànguǎn**/*fahn gwahn*

hotel/**lǚguǎn**/*lyew gwahn*

house/**fángzi**/*fahng dzuh*

how/**zěnme**/*dzummuh*

how long?/**duō jiǔ?**/*dwaw jyoe*

how much?/**duōshǎo?**/*dwaw shaow*

hungry/**è**/*uh*

hurry/**jí**/*jee*

husband/**zhàngfu**/*jahng foo*

I

I; me/**wǒ**/*waw*

I'm sorry/**bàoqiàn**/*baow chyan*

ID/**zhèngjiàn**/*juhng jyan*

in a little while/**yīhuǐr**/*ee hwar*

incorrect; mistake/**cuò**/*tswaw*

inside; Chinese equivalent of a kilometer/**lǐ**/*lee*

intelligent/**cōngmíng**/*tsoong meeng*

international phone call/**guójì diànhuà**/*gwaw jee dyan hwah*

Internet/**guójì wǎngluò**/*gwaw jee wahng lwaw*

Internet access/**wǎngluò liánjié**/*wahng lwaw lyan jyeh*

Internet service provider/**wǎngshàng fúwù tígōng shāng**/*wahng shahng foo woo tee goong shahng*

introduce/**jièshào**/*jyeh shaow*

item/**xiàngmù**/*shyahng moo*

J

Japan/**Rìběn**/*ir bun*

Japanese dollar/**Rì yuán**/*ir ywan*

jewelry/**zhūbǎo**/*joo baow*

K

key/**yàoshi**/*yaow shir*

know (how to do something)/**huì**/*hway*

know (information)/**zhīdào**/*jir daow*

know (someone)/**rènshi**/*run shir*

kilometer (Chinese equivalent)/**lǐ**/*lee*

L

landing/**zhuólù**/*jwaw loo*

laptop/**shǒutíshì**/*show tee shir*

last month/**shàngge yuè**/*shahng guh yweh*

last week/**shàngge xīngqī**/*shahng guh sheeng chee*

last year/**qùnián**/*chyew nyan*

laundry service/**xǐyī fúwù**/*she ee foo woo*

law/**fǎlǜ**/*fah lyew*

lawyer/**lǜshī**/*lyew shir*

leave/**líkāi**/*lee kye*

leave a message/**liúhuà**/*lyoe hwah*

leave the house; to set off/**chūfā**/*choo fah*

left/**zuǒ**/*dzwaw*

let; to allow/**ràng**/*rahng*

life vests/**jiùshēngyī**/*jyoe shung ee*

like/**xǐhuān**/*she hwahn*

listen to/**tīng**/*teeng*

lobby/**dàtīng**/*dah teeng*

local train/**mànchē**/*mahn chuh*

lock/**suǒ**/*swaw*

log off/**qiān chū**/*chyan choo*

log on/**qiān rù**/*chyan roo*

long-distance phone call/**chángtú diànhuà**/*chahng too dyan hwah*

look for/**zhǎo**/*jaow*

look something up/**chá**/*chah*

loose/**sōng**/*soong*

lose; book/**shū**/*shoo*

luck/**yùnqì**/*yewn chee*

luggage/**xíngli**/*sheeng lee*

luggage claim tag/**lǐngqǔdān**/*leeng chyew dahn*

lunch/**wǔfàn**/*woo fahn*

M

magazine/**zázhì**/*dzah jir*

mainland (China)/**dàlù**/*dah loo*

make a legal decision/**pànjué**/*pahn jweh*

make a reservation (seats)/**dìng wèi**/*deeng way*

make a reservation (room, tickets, and so on)/**yùdìng**/*yew deeng*

manager/**jīnglǐ**/*jeeng lee*

Mandarin/**guóyǔ; pǔtōnghuà**/*gwaw yew (term used in Taiwan); poo toong hwah (term used in mainland China)*

many/**duō**/*dwaw*

many thanks/**gǎnxiè**/*gahn shyeh*

map/**dìtú**/*dee too*

marry/**jiéhūn**/*jyeh hwun*

master; cook/**shīfu**/*shir foo*

May/**wǔyuè**/*woo yweh*

meat/**ròu**/*row*

meeting/**huìyì**/*hway ee*

menu/**càidān**/*tsye dahn*

message/**xìnxi**/*sheen she*

midnight/**bànyè**/*bahn yeh*

mine; my/**wǒde**/*waw duh*

minute; one cent/**fēn**/*fun*

Monday/**xīngqīyī**/*sheeng chee ee*

more/**gèng**/*guhng*

morning (6 a.m. to noon)/**zǎoshàng**/*dzaow shahng*

most/**zuì**/*dzway*

mother/**māma; mǔqīn**/*mah mah; moo cheen*

movie/**diànyǐng; piānzi**/*dyan yeeng; pyan dzuh*

museum/**bówùguǎn**/*baw woo gwahn*

music/**yīnyuè**/*een yweh*

N

napkin/**cānjīnzhǐ**/*tsahn jeen jir*

need/**xūyào**/*shyew yaow*

negotiate/**tánpàn**/*tahn pahn*

new/**xīn**/*shin*

newspaper/**bàozhǐ**/*baow jir*

next/**xiàge**/*shyah guh*

next month/**xiàge yuè**/*shyah guh yweh*

next to/**kàojìn**/*cow jeen*

next week/**xiàge xīngqī**/*shyah guh sheeng chee*

next year/**míngnián**/*meeng nyan*

noodles/**miàntiáo**/*myan tyaow*

not bad; really good/**búcuò**/*boo tswaw*

not; no/**bù**/*boo*

now/**xiànzài**/*shyan dzye*

number/**hàomǎ**/*how mah*

nurse/**hùshì**/*hoo shir*

O

of course/**dāngrán**/*dahng rahn*

office/**bàngōngshì**/*bahn goong shir*

often/**chángcháng**/*chahng chahng*

oh my goodness!/**āiyà**/*eye yah*

old; overdone/**lǎo**/*laow*

on time/**zhèngdiǎn**/*juhng dyan*

on vacation/**dùjià**/*doo jyah*

one/**yī**/*ee*

one-way ticket/**dānchéngpiào**/*dahn chuhng pyaow*

only/**zhǐ**/*jir*

open/**kāi**/*kye*

open the door/**kāimén**/*kye mun*

opinion/**yìjiàn**/*ee jyan*

opposite/**duìmiàn**/*dway myan*

or/**huò zhe**/*hwaw juh*

order (food)/**diǎn**/*dyan*

other/**biéde**/*byeh duh*

other; anything else/**qítā**/*chee tah*

outside/**wài**/*wye*

P

pair/**shuāng**/*shwahng*

parents/**fùmǔ**/*foo moo*

party/**wǎnhuì**/*wahn hway*

passport/**hùzhào**/*hoo jaow*

password/**mìmǎ**/*mee mah*

pay/**fùqián**/*foo chyan*

PC (personal computer)/**gèrén diànnǎo**/*guh run dyan now*

pen/**gāngbǐ**/*gahng bee*

pencil/**qiānbǐ**/*chyan bee*

percentage/**bǎifēnbǐ**/*bye fun bee*

perhaps/**kěnéng**/*kuh nuhng*

person/**rén**/*run*

pharmacy/**yàofáng**/*yaow fahng*

photo/**zhàopiàn**/*jaow pyan*

pick up/**ná**/*nah*

pill/**yàowán**/*yaow wahn*

PIN/**mìmǎ**/*mee mah*

pint/**pǐntuō**/*peen twaw*

place/**dìfāng**/*dee fahng*

platform/**zhàntái**/*jahn tye*

please/**qǐng**/*cheeng*

police/**jǐngchá**/*jeeng chah*

police station/**jǐngchájú**/*jeeng chah jyew*

popular/**liúxíng**/*lyo sheeng*

post office/**yóujú**/*yo jyew*

postponed/**tuīchí**/*tway chir*

pray; week/**lǐbài**/*lee bye*

PRC dollar/**rénmínbì**/*run meen bee*

presentation/**yǎnshì**/*yan shir*

president (of company)/**zǒngcái**/*dzoong tsye*

pretty/**hǎokàn**/*how kahn*

pretty/**piàoliàng**/*pyaow lyahng*

price/**jiàgé**/*jyah guh*

problem/**wèntí**/*one tee*

professor/**jiàoshòu**/*jyaow show*

public bus/**gōnggòng qìchē**/*goong goong chee chuh*

public telephone/**gōngyòng diànhuà**/*goong yoong dyan hwah*

Q

quality/**zhìliàng**/*jir lyahng*

quiet/**ānjìng**/*ahn jeeng*

R

rain/**yǔ**/*yew*

raincoat/**yǔyī**/*yew ee*

rats!; what a shame/**zāogāo**/*dzaow gaow*

read; to see/**kàn**/*kahn*

really; truly/**zhēn**/*juhn*

receipt/**shōujù**/*show jyew*

receive/**shōudào**/*show daow*

reception desk/**fàndiàn qiántái**/*fahn dyan chyan tye*

receptionist/**qiántái fúwùyuán**/*chyan tye foo woo ywan*

refund/**tuìkuǎn**/*tway kwahn*

remote control/**yáokòng qì**/*yaow koong chee*

rent/**zūfèi**/*dzoo fay*

rent/**chūzū**/*choo dzoo*

reside/**zhù**/*joo*

resolve; solve/**jiějué**/*jyeh jweh*

rest/**xiūxi**/*shyo she*

restaurant/**cānguǎn**/*tsahn gwahn*

restaurant/**fàndiàn**/*fahn dyan*

return (come back)/**huílái**/*hway lye*

return (merchandise)/**tuìhuí**/*tway hway*

rice/**mǐfàn**/*mee fahn*

right/**yòu**/*yo*

road/**lù**/*loo*

room/**fángjiān**/*fahng jyan*

roommate/**tóngwū**/*toong woo*

round-trip ticket/**lái huí piào**/*lye hway pyaow*

rush hour/**gāofēngqī**/*gaow fuhng chee*

S

same/**yíyàng**/*ee yahng*

Saturday/**xīngqīliù**/*sheeng chee lyo*

scary/**kěpà**/*kuh pah*

schedule/**shíjiānbiǎo**/*shir jyan byaow*

school/**xuéxiào**/*shweh shyaow*

search/**jiǎnsuǒ**/*jyan swaw*

seat belt/**ānquándài**/*ahn chwan dye*

secretary/**mìshū**/*mee shoo*

see a doctor/**kànbìng**/*kahn beeng*

see you later/**yíhuǐr jiàn**/*ee hwar jyan*

see; a classifier/**jiàn**/*jyan*

self/**zìjǐ**/*dzuh jee*

sell/**mài**/*my*

send/**sòng**/*soong*

server/**fúwùqì**/*foo woo chee*

several; how many/**jǐ**/*jee*

shoes/**xiézi**/*shyeh dzuh*

short/**ǎi**/*eye*

should/**yīnggāi**/*eeng guy*

sightsee/**yóulǎn**/*yo lahn*

Singapore dollar/**Xīng bì**/*sheeng bee*

skirt/**qúnzi**/*chwun dzuh*

sleep/**shuìjiào**/*shway jyaow*

slide projector/**huàndēngjī**/*hwahn duhng jee*

slow/**màn**/*mahn*

small/**xiǎo**/*shyaow*

small talk/**xiánliáo**/*shyan lyaow*

soap/**féizào**/*fay dzaow*

software/**ruǎnjiàn**/*rwahn jyan*

son/**érzi**/*are dzuh*

soup/**tāng**/*tahng*

speak/**shuō**/*shwaw*

special/**tèsè**/*tuh suh*

spouse (used only in the PRC)/**àirén**/*eye run*

start/**kāishǐ**/*kye shir*

store/**shāngdiàn**/*shahng dyan*

straight/**zhí**/*jir*

strange/**qíguài**/*chee gwye*

street/**jiē**/*jyeh*

student/**xuéshēng**/*shweh shung*

study/**xuéxí**/*shweh she*

subway/**dìtiě**/*dee tyeh*

suggest; suggestion/**jiànyì**/*jyan ee*

suitcase/**xiāngzi**/*shyahng dzuh*

suite/**tàojiān**/*taow jyan*

Sunday/**xīngqītiān**/*sheeng chee tyan*

sunglasses/**tàiyáng yǎnjìng**/*tye yahng yan jeeng*

supermarket/**chāojí shìchǎng**/*chaow jee shir chahng*

sweep/**cá**/*tsah*

T

table/**zhuōzi**/*jwaw dzuh*

Taiwan/**Táiwān**/*tye wahn*

take a vacation/**fàng jià**/*fahng jyah*

take medicine/**chī yào**/*chir yaow*

take off (airplane)/**qǐfēi**/*chee fay*

take pictures/**zhàoxiàng**/*jaow shyahng*

talk/**jiǎng**/*jyahng*

taxi/**chūzū chē**/*choo dzoo chuh*

tea/**chá**/*chah*

teach/**jiāo**/*jyaow*

teacher/**lǎoshī**/*laow shir*

telephone/**diànhuà**/*dyan hwah*

telephone book/**diànhuà hàomǎbù**/*dyan hwah how mah boo*

telephone number/**diànhuà hàomǎ**/*dyan hwah how mah*

tell/**gàosù**/*gaow soo*

thanks/**xièxiè**/*shyeh shyeh*

that/**nà**/*nah*

that's awful!/**zāogāo**/*dzaow gaow*

they; them/**tāmen**/*tah mun*

thief/**zéi**/*dzay*

thing/**dōngxi**/*doong she*

think/**xiǎng**/*shyahng*

thirsty/**kě**/*kuh*

Thursday/**xīngqīsì**/*sheeng chee suh*

ticket/**piào**/*pyaow*

time/**shíhòu**/*shir ho*

time (midnight to dawn)/**qīngzǎo**/*cheeng dzaow*

time; size medium/**zhōng**/*joong*

tip/**xiǎofèi**/*shyaow fay*

tired/**lèi**/*lay*

today/**jīntiān**/*jin tyan*

together/**yìqǐ**/*ee chee*

toilet/**cèsuǒ**/*tsuh swaw*

toilet paper/**wèishēngzhǐ**/*way shung jir*

tomorrow/**míngtiān**/*meeng tyan*

too bad; unfortunately/**kěxī**/*kuh she*

too much/**tài**/*tye*

toothbrush/**yáshuā**/*yah shwah*

tour/**lǚyóu**/*lyew yo*

tour group/**guānguāng tuán**/*gwahng gwahng twahn*

towel/**máojīn**/*maow jeen*

trade show/**màoyì zhǎnxiāohuì**/*maow ee jahn shyaow hway*

train station/**huǒchē zhàn**/*hwaw chuh jahn*

transfer/**zhuǎn**/*jwan*

transparency/**tóuyǐngpiàn**/*toe eeng pyan*

transportation/**jiāotōng**/*jyaow toong*

travel/**lǚxíng**/*lyew sheeng*

travel agency/**lǚxíngshè**/*lyew sheeng shuh*

travel agent/**lǚxíng dàilǐrén**/*lyew sheeng dye lee run*

traveler's checks/**lǚxíng zhipiào**/*lyew sheeng jir pyaow*

Tuesday/**xīngqī'èr**/*sheeng chee are*

turn/**zhuǎn**/*jwan*

TV/**diànshì**/*dyan shir*

U

U.S. dollar/**Měiyuán**/*may ywan*

umbrella/**yǔsǎn**/*yew sahn*

upstairs/**lóushàng**/*low shahng*

use/**yòng**/*yoong*

user name/**yònghù xìngmíng**/*yoong hoo sheeng meeng*

usually; often/**píngcháng**/*peeng chahng*

V

vacant/**kòngwèi**/*koong way*

vacation day/**jiàrì**/*jyah ir*

vegetarian dishes/**sùcài**/*soo tsye*

video recorder/**lùxiàngjī**/*loo shyahng jee*

Vietnam/**Yuènán**/*yweh nahn*

visa/**qiānzhèng**/*chyan juhng*

voice/**shēngyīn**/*shung een*

voicemail/**yǒu shēng yóujiàn**/*yo shung yo jyan*

W

wait/**děng**/*duhng*

walk/**zǒu**/*dzoe*

wallet/**qiánbāo**/*chyan baow*

want; medicine/**yào**/*yaow*

warm/**nuǎnhuó**/*nwan hwaw*

wash/**xǐ**/*she*

we; us (informal)/**zánmen**/*dzahn mun*

we; us/**wǒmen**/*waw mun*

wear/**chuān**/*chwahn*

weather/**tiānqì**/*tyan chee*

Web site/**wǎngzhàn**/*wahng jahn*

Wednesday/**xīngqīsān**/*sheeng chee sahn*

weekend/**zhōumò**/*joe maw*

welcome/**huānyíng**/*hwahn yeeng*

Western food/**xīcān**/*she tsahn*

what/**shénme**/*shummuh*

where/**nǎr**/*nar*

which/**nǎ**/*nah*

who; whom/**shéi**/*shay*

why/**wèishénme**/*way shummuh*

wife/**qīzi**/*chee dzuh*

wife (used mostly in Taiwan)/**tàitài**/*tye tye*

win/**yíng**/*eeng*

wine; alcohol/**jiǔ**/*jyoe*

withdraw money/**qǔ qián**/*chyew chyan*

work; job/**gōngzuò**/*goong dzwaw*

work out/**jiànshēn yùndòng**/*jyan shun yewn doong*

Y

yes; is/**shì**/*shir*

yesterday/**zuótiān**/*dzwaw tyan*

you/**nǐ**/*nee*

you (plural)/**nǐmen**/*nee mun*

you (polite)/**nín**/*neen*

you're welcome/**bú kèqì**/*boo kuh chee*

young/**niánqīng**/*nyan cheeng*

Appendix C

Answer Key

The following are all of the answers to the Fun & Games quizzes.

Chapter 2

wǔ, qī, shí, sānshí, liùshí, jiǔshí

Chapter 3

hǎo, míngzi, Déguórén, bàofēngxuě, jiàn

1. Hǎo jiǔ méi jiàn.
2. Wǎn ān.
3. Zǎo.
4. Nǎr de huà.
5. Hěn gāoxìng jiàndào nǐ.
6. Yílù píng'ān.

Chapter 4

yīshēng: doctor

lǎoshī: teacher

fēixíngyuán: pilot

zúqiú duìyuán: soccer player

Chapter 5

A. píngguǒ (apple)
B. júzi (orange)
C. shēngcài (lettuce)
D. fānqié (tomato)

E. hú luóbo (carrot)

F. yángcōng (onion)

G. xǐlánhuā (broccoli)

Chapter 6

A. Zhūbǎo diàn: jewelry store

B. Cài shìchǎng: food market

B. Huādiàn: flower shop

D. Yàofáng: drugstore

E. Wánjù diàn: toy store

Chapter 7

9:15 a.m.: zǎoshàng jiǔ diǎn yíkè

next month: xiàge yuè

midnight: bànyè

two weeks ago: liǎngge xīngqī yǐqián

4:30 p.m.: xiàwǔ sì diǎn bàn

Chapter 8

A. dǎ pīngpōngqiú

B. tán gāngqín

C. dǎ tàijíquán

D. chuī chángdí

E. pá shān

Chapter 9

Just a moment.: Shāoděng

Is she at home?: Tā zài ma?

Hello.: Wéi?

Sorry, you dialed the wrong number.: Duìbùqǐ, nǐ bōcuòle hàomǎ.

Please leave a message.: Qǐng nǐ liú yǐge huà.

Chapter 10

1. yùshì: bathroom

2. wòshì: bedroom

3. fàntīng: dining room

4. tǎnzi: blanket

5. yángtái: balcony

6. zhěntóu: pillow

7. bèizi: quilt

8. shūzhuō: desk

9. shāfā: sofa

Chapter 11

A. zìdòng tíkuǎnjī (ATM machine)

B. chūnàyuán (bank teller)

C. yíngháng (bank)

D. hùzhào (passport)

E. xìnyòng kǎ (credit card)

F. qiánbāo (wallet)

Chapter 12

Xuéxiào zài běibiān (or běimiàn). The school is to the north.

Yóujú zài dōngbiān (or dōngmiàn). The post office is to the east.

Yíngháng zài nánbiān (or nánmiàn). The bank is to the south.

Fángzi zài xībiān (or xīmiàn). The house is to the west.

Chapter 13

1. fángjiān

2. kèmǎn

3. qǐchuáng

4. zhāngdàn

5. tuìfáng

Chapter 14

A. fēijǐ

B. huǒchē

C. dìtiě

D. gōnggòng qìchē

E. chūzū chē

Chapter 15

1. šiěrlán

2. liù yuè bā hào

3. fó miào

4. yáshuā

5. Kāi wǎn xiào.

Chapter 16

1. gēbō: arm

2. jiānbǎng: shoulder

3. shǒuzhǐ: finger

4. tuǐ: leg

5. bózi: neck

6. xiōngqiāng: chest

7. yǎnjǐng: eye

8. ěrduō: ear

9. bízi: nose

Appendix D

About the CD

The following is a list of tracks that appear on the book's audio CD.

Chapter 1

Track 1: Practicing Chinese initials

Track 2: Practicing Chinese tones

Chapter 2

Track 3: People watching

Track 4: Deciding where to go to dinner

Chapter 3

Track 5: Introducing friends

Track 6: Meeting someone new

Chapter 4

Track 7: Finding out what time it is

Track 8: Discussing professions

Chapter 5

Track 9: Meeting at a restaurant

Track 10: Shopping at the food market

Chapter 6

Track 11: Shopping for the right clothing size

Track 12: Deciding on the right color

Chapter 7

Track 13: Planning to see a movie

Track 14: Visiting the museum

Index

Notes

BUSINESS, CAREERS & PERSONAL FINANCE

0-7645-5307-0

0-7645-5331-3 *†

Also available:

- Accounting For Dummies †
  0-7645-5314-3
- Business Plans Kit For Dummies †
  0-7645-5365-8
- Cover Letters For Dummies
  0-7645-5224-4
- Frugal Living For Dummies
  0-7645-5403-4
- Leadership For Dummies
  0-7645-5176-0
- Managing For Dummies
  0-7645-1771-6

- Marketing For Dummies
  0-7645-5600-2
- Personal Finance For Dummies *
  0-7645-2590-5
- Project Management For Dummies
  0-7645-5283-X
- Resumes For Dummies †
  0-7645-5471-9
- Selling For Dummies
  0-7645-5363-1
- Small Business Kit For Dummies *†
  0-7645-5093-4

HOME & BUSINESS COMPUTER BASICS

0-7645-4074-2

0-7645-3758-X

Also available:

- ACT! 6 For Dummies
  0-7645-2645-6
- iLife '04 All-in-One Desk Reference
  For Dummies
  0-7645-7347-0
- iPAQ For Dummies
  0-7645-6769-1
- Mac OS X Panther Timesaving
  Techniques For Dummies
  0-7645-5812-9
- Macs For Dummies
  0-7645-5656-8

- Microsoft Money 2004 For Dummies
  0-7645-4195-1
- Office 2003 All-in-One Desk Reference
  For Dummies
  0-7645-3883-7
- Outlook 2003 For Dummies
  0-7645-3759-8
- PCs For Dummies
  0-7645-4074-2
- TiVo For Dummies
  0-7645-6923-6
- Upgrading and Fixing PCs For Dummies
  0-7645-1665-5
- Windows XP Timesaving Techniques
  For Dummies
  0-7645-3748-2

FOOD, HOME, GARDEN, HOBBIES, MUSIC & PETS

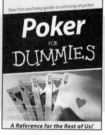

0-7645-5295-3

0-7645-5232-5

Also available:

- Bass Guitar For Dummies
  0-7645-2487-9
- Diabetes Cookbook For Dummies
  0-7645-5230-9
- Gardening For Dummies *
  0-7645-5130-2
- Guitar For Dummies
  0-7645-5106-X
- Holiday Decorating For Dummies
  0-7645-2570-0
- Home Improvement All-in-One
  For Dummies
  0-7645-5680-0

- Knitting For Dummies
  0-7645-5395-X
- Piano For Dummies
  0-7645-5105-1
- Puppies For Dummies
  0-7645-5255-4
- Scrapbooking For Dummies
  0-7645-7208-3
- Senior Dogs For Dummies
  0-7645-5818-8
- Singing For Dummies
  0-7645-2475-5
- 30-Minute Meals For Dummies
  0-7645-2589-1

INTERNET & DIGITAL MEDIA

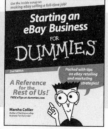

0-7645-1664-7

0-7645-6924-4

Also available:

- 2005 Online Shopping Directory
  For Dummies
  0-7645-7495-7
- CD & DVD Recording For Dummies
  0-7645-5956-7
- eBay For Dummies
  0-7645-5654-1
- Fighting Spam For Dummies
  0-7645-5965-6
- Genealogy Online For Dummies
  0-7645-5964-8
- Google For Dummies
  0-7645-4420-9

- Home Recording For Musicians
  For Dummies
  0-7645-1634-5
- The Internet For Dummies
  0-7645-4173-0
- iPod & iTunes For Dummies
  0-7645-7772-7
- Preventing Identity Theft For Dummies
  0-7645-7336-5
- Pro Tools All-in-One Desk Reference
  For Dummies
  0-7645-5714-9
- Roxio Easy Media Creator For Dummies
  0-7645-7131-1

SPORTS, FITNESS, PARENTING, RELIGION & SPIRITUALITY

0-7645-5146-9

0-7645-5418-2

Also available:

- Adoption For Dummies
  0-7645-5488-3
- Basketball For Dummies
  0-7645-5248-1
- The Bible For Dummies
  0-7645-5296-1
- Buddhism For Dummies
  0-7645-5359-3
- Catholicism For Dummies
  0-7645-5391-7
- Hockey For Dummies
  0-7645-5228-7

- Judaism For Dummies
  0-7645-5299-6
- Martial Arts For Dummies
  0-7645-5358-5
- Pilates For Dummies
  0-7645-5397-6
- Religion For Dummies
  0-7645-5264-3
- Teaching Kids to Read For Dummies
  0-7645-4043-2
- Weight Training For Dummies
  0-7645-5168-X
- Yoga For Dummies
  0-7645-5117-5

TRAVEL

0-7645-5438-7

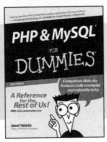

0-7645-5453-0

Also available:

- Alaska For Dummies
  0-7645-1761-9
- Arizona For Dummies
  0-7645-6938-4
- Cancún and the Yucatán For Dummies
  0-7645-2437-2
- Cruise Vacations For Dummies
  0-7645-6941-4
- Europe For Dummies
  0-7645-5456-5
- Ireland For Dummies
  0-7645-5455-7

- Las Vegas For Dummies
  0-7645-5448-4
- London For Dummies
  0-7645-4277-X
- New York City For Dummies
  0-7645-6945-7
- Paris For Dummies
  0-7645-5494-8
- RV Vacations For Dummies
  0-7645-5443-3
- Walt Disney World & Orlando For Dummies
  0-7645-6943-0

GRAPHICS, DESIGN & WEB DEVELOPMENT

0-7645-4345-8

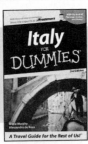

0-7645-5589-8

Also available:

- Adobe Acrobat 6 PDF For Dummies
  0-7645-3760-1
- Building a Web Site For Dummies
  0-7645-7144-3
- Dreamweaver MX 2004 For Dummies
  0-7645-4342-3
- FrontPage 2003 For Dummies
  0-7645-3882-9
- HTML 4 For Dummies
  0-7645-1995-6
- Illustrator cs For Dummies
  0-7645-4084-X

- Macromedia Flash MX 2004 For Dummies
  0-7645-4358-X
- Photoshop 7 All-in-One Desk Reference For Dummies
  0-7645-1667-1
- Photoshop cs Timesaving Techniques For Dummies
  0-7645-6782-9
- PHP 5 For Dummies
  0-7645-4166-8
- PowerPoint 2003 For Dummies
  0-7645-3908-6
- QuarkXPress 6 For Dummies
  0-7645-2593-X

NETWORKING, SECURITY, PROGRAMMING & DATABASES

0-7645-6852-3

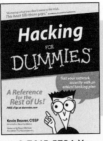

0-7645-5784-X

Also available:

- A+ Certification For Dummies
  0-7645-4187-0
- Access 2003 All-in-One Desk Reference For Dummies
  0-7645-3988-4
- Beginning Programming For Dummies
  0-7645-4997-9
- C For Dummies
  0-7645-7068-4
- Firewalls For Dummies
  0-7645-4048-3
- Home Networking For Dummies
  0-7645-42796

- Network Security For Dummies
  0-7645-1679-5
- Networking For Dummies
  0-7645-1677-9
- TCP/IP For Dummies
  0-7645-1760-0
- VBA For Dummies
  0-7645-3989-2
- Wireless All In-One Desk Reference For Dummies
  0-7645-7496-5
- Wireless Home Networking For Dummies
  0-7645-3910-8

HEALTH & SELF-HELP

0-7645-6820-5 *†

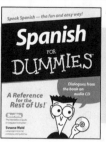

0-7645-2566-2

Also available:

Alzheimer's For Dummies
0-7645-3899-3

Asthma For Dummies
0-7645-4233-8

Controlling Cholesterol For Dummies
0-7645-5440-9

Depression For Dummies
0-7645-3900-0

Dieting For Dummies
0-7645-4149-8

Fertility For Dummies
0-7645-2549-2

Fibromyalgia For Dummies
0-7645-5441-7

Improving Your Memory For Dummies
0-7645-5435-2

Pregnancy For Dummies †
0-7645-4483-7

Quitting Smoking For Dummies
0-7645-2629-4

Relationships For Dummies
0-7645-5384-4

Thyroid For Dummies
0-7645-5385-2

EDUCATION, HISTORY, REFERENCE & TEST PREPARATION

0-7645-5194-9

0-7645-4186-2

Also available:

Algebra For Dummies
0-7645-5325-9

British History For Dummies
0-7645-7021-8

Calculus For Dummies
0-7645-2498-4

English Grammar For Dummies
0-7645-5322-4

Forensics For Dummies
0-7645-5580-4

The GMAT For Dummies
0-7645-5251-1

Inglés Para Dummies
0-7645-5427-1

Italian For Dummies
0-7645-5196-5

Latin For Dummies
0-7645-5431-X

Lewis & Clark For Dummies
0-7645-2545-X

Research Papers For Dummies
0-7645-5426-3

The SAT I For Dummies
0-7645-7193-1

Science Fair Projects For Dummies
0-7645-5460-3

U.S. History For Dummies
0-7645-5249-X

Get smart @ dummies.com®

- **Find a full list of Dummies titles**
- **Look into loads of FREE on-site articles**
- **Sign up for FREE eTips e-mailed to you weekly**
- **See what other products carry the Dummies name**
- **Shop directly from the Dummies bookstore**
- **Enter to win new prizes every month!**

* Separate Canadian edition also available
† Separate U.K. edition also available

Available wherever books are sold. For more information or to order direct: U.S. customers visit www.dummies.com or call 1-877-762-2974.
U.K. customers visit www.wileyeurope.com or call 0800 243407. Canadian customers visit www.wiley.ca or call 1-800-567-4797.